College Student's Guide to Merit and Other No-Need Funding 2008-2010

RSP FINANCIAL AID DIRECTORIES OF INTEREST TO COLLEGE STUDENTS

College Student's Guide to Merit and Other No-Need Funding, 2008-2010
More than 1,300 funding opportunities for currently-enrolled or returning college students are described in this award-winning directory. 498 pages. ISBN 1-58841-0102-8. $32.50, plus $6 shipping.

Directory of Financial Aids for Women, 2007-2009
More than 1,500 funding programs set aside for women are described in this biennial directory, which *School Library Journal* calls "the cream of the crop." 560 pages. ISBN 1-58841-167-2. $45, plus $6 shipping.

Financial Aid for African Americans, 2008-2010
More than 1,300 scholarships, fellowships, grants, and internships open to African Americans are described in this award-winning directory. 538 pages. ISBN 1-58841-177-X. $40, plus $6 shipping.

Financial Aid for Asian Americans, 2008-2010
This is the source to use if you are looking for financial aid for Asian Americans; nearly 1,000 funding opportunities are described. 356 pages. ISBN 1-58841-178-8. $37.50, plus $6 shipping.

Financial Aid for Hispanic Americans, 2008-2010
Nearly 1,300 funding programs open to Americans of Mexican, Puerto Rican, Central American, or other Latin American heritage are described here. 492 pages. ISBN 1-58841-179-6. $40, plus $6 shipping.

Financial Aid for Native Americans, 2008-2010
Detailed information is provided on 1,300 funding opportunities open to American Indians, Native Alaskans, and Native Pacific Islanders. 526 pages. ISBN 1-58841-180-X. $42.50, plus $6 shipping.

Financial Aid for Study and Training Abroad, 2008-2010
This directory, which *Children's Bookwatch* calls "invaluable," describes nearly 1,000 financial aid opportunities available to support study abroad. 354 pages. ISBN 1-58841-189-3. $40, plus $6 shipping.

Financial Aid for the Disabled and Their Families, 2008-2010
Named one of the "Best Reference Books of the Year" by *Library Journal,* this directory describes in detail more than 1,200 funding opportunities. 502 pages. ISBN 1-58841-183-4. $40, plus $6 shipping.

Financial Aid for Veterans, Military Personnel, and Their Dependents, 2008-2010
According to *Reference Book Review,* this directory (with its 1,100 entries) is "the most comprehensive guide available on the subject." 443 pages. ISBN 1-58841-182-6. $40, plus $6 shipping.

How to Pay for Your Degree in Business & Related Fields, 2007-2009
Use this directory to identify more than 800 scholarships, fellowships, grants, and awards available to support undergraduate and graduate students working on a degree in business or a related field. 298 pages. ISBN 1-58841-145-1. $30, plus $6 shipping.

How to Pay for Your Degree in Education & Related Fields, 2008-2010
Here's hundreds of funding opportunities to support undergraduate and graduate students preparing for a career in teaching, guidance, etc. 290 pages. ISBN 1-58841-190-7. $30, plus $6 shipping.

How to Pay for Your Degree in Engineering, 2008-2010
Previously issued as *RSP Funding for Engineering Students,* this directory identifies the 900+ biggest and best scholarships, fellowships, awards, grants and other funding opportunities available to support undergraduate or graduate studies in all types of engineering. 260 pages. ISBN 1-58841-191-5. $30, plus $6 shipping.

Money for Christian College Students, 2007-2009
This is the only directory to describe nearly 800 funding opportunities available to support Christian students working on an undergraduate or graduate degree (secular or religious). 238 pages. ISBN 1-58841-169-9. $30, plus $6 shipping.

RSP Funding for Nursing Students, 2008-2010
You'll find 900 scholarships, fellowships, loans, grants, and awards here that can be used for study, research, professional, or other nursing activities. 290 pages. ISBN 1-58841-192-3. $30, plus $6 shipping.

College Student's Guide to Merit and Other No-Need Funding 2008-2010

Gail Ann Schlachter
R. David Weber

A List of 1,323 Merit Scholarships and Other No-Need Funding Programs Set Aside Specifically for College Students and a Set of Six Indexes: Program Title, Sponsor, Residency, Tenability, Subject, and Deadline Date

Reference Service Press
2008

©2008 Gail Ann Schlachter

All rights reserved. No part of this publication may be reproduced, stored in a retrieval system, or transmitted, in any form or by any means, electronic, mechanical, photocopying, recording, or otherwise, except for the inclusion of brief quotations in a review, without the prior permission in writing from the publisher. Reference Service Press vigorously defends its copyright protection.

ISBN 10: 1588411664
ISBN 13: 9781588411662

10 9 8 7 6 5 4 3 2 1

Reference Service Press (RSP) began in 1977 with a single financial aid publication *(Directory of Financial Aids for Women)* and now specializes in the development of financial aid resources in multiple formats, including books, large print books, disks, CD-ROMs, print-on-demand reports, eBooks, and online sources. Long recognized as a leader in the field, RSP has been called, by the *Simba Report on Directory Publishing,* "a true success in the world of independent directory publishers." Both Kaplan Educational Centers and Military.com have hailed RSP as "the leading authority on scholarships."

Reference Service Press
El Dorado Hills Business Park
5000 Windplay Drive, Suite 4
El Dorado Hills, CA 95762-9600
    (916) 939-9620
    Fax: (916) 939-9626
    E-mail: info@rspfunding.com
Visit our web site: www.rspfunding.com

Manufactured in the United States of America

Price: $32.50, plus $6 shipping

ACADEMIC INSTITUTIONS, LIBRARIES, ORGANIZATIONS, AND OTHER QUANTITY BUYERS:
Discounts on this book are available for bulk purchases. Write or call for information on our discount program.

Contents

Introduction 5

    Why another financial aid directory 5
    What's included 5
    What's excluded 6
    Sample entry 8
    What's updated 8
    How the directory is organized 8
    How to use the directory 10
    Plans to update the directory 11
    Other related publications 11
    Acknowledgements 11

About the Authors 12

Merit and Other No-Need Funding for College Students 13

    Sciences 15
    Social Sciences 173
    Humanities 247
    Any Subject Area 321

Indexes 415

    Program Title 417
    Sponsoring Organization 457
    Residency 469
    Tenability 473
    Subject 479
    Calendar 489

Introduction

WHY ANOTHER FINANCIAL AID DIRECTORY?

Getting a college degree is definitely a smart move. According to the U.S. Census Bureau, college graduates on the average make $25,000 a year more than high school graduates. Going to college, however, is expensive. It can cost over $100,000 just to complete a bachelor's degree. That's more than most students can afford to pay on their own. Where can they turn for help?

If the students come from low-income families, there are thousands of well-publicized federal, state, and private funding programs available to support them. But, what about the students caught in the middle—who have too much family income to meet financial need requirements but not enough to be able to pay for college without help?

Traditional financial aid directories don't offer much assistance. Most of the programs listed in such standard guides as *Scholarships, Fellowships, and Loans* (published by Thomson Gale) and *Chronicle Financial Aid Guide* (published by Chronicle Guidance) are need based and open primarily to lower-income students. Only a few publications have focused on no-need programs, and those have been very limited in scope. For example, *Winning Money for College* (published by Peterson's Guides) describes fewer than 200 national contests and has not been updated since 1997.

As a result, many college students (along with the counselors and librarians trying to serve them) have believed the myth that only the neediest can qualify for financial aid. That's just not true. In fact, there are more than 1,300 funding programs available to currently-enrolled and returning college students that never look at income level. But, since they are generally not covered or separately identified in the existing financial aid directories, it used to be impossible to identify those opportunities easily. Now, with the ongoing publication of the **College Student's Guide to Merit and Other No-Need Funding,** all that has changed. Here, in one place, you can find out about the wide array of no-need funding programs set aside just for currently-enrolled and returning college students.

Called a "unique directory" by *Scholarship Watch,* the *College Student's Guide* has been highly praised by the reviewers. According to *American Reference Books Annual,* this is "an excellent resource for both prospective college students and those who will most likely be paying for this college education, their parents." In recognition of that fact, the *College Student's Guide* was named the "best of the best" by *Choice* and selected as one of the "Outstanding Academic Titles" of the year.

WHAT'S INCLUDED?

The *College Student's Guide* is unlike any other financial aid listing. First of all, the directory only covers programs open to currently-enrolled or returning college students. Most other directories mix together programs for a number of groups—high school students, college students, and even graduate students or postdoctorates. Now, you won't have to spend your time sifting through programs that aren't aimed at you.

Second, only merit and other no-need funding is included. If a program requires financial need, it's not listed. Here's your chance to find out about programs that award money solely on the basis of:

- career plans
- creative activities
- academic record
- writing ability
- research skills
- religious or ethnic background
- military or organizational activities
- athletic success
- or just pure luck in random drawings

And, none of these programs consider income in the selection process.

Third, many of the programs listed here are not covered in the other general financial aid directories. So, even students who can qualify for need-based programs will want to look at the *College Student's Guide* for additional leads.

Fourth, only the biggest and best funding programs are described in this book. To be included here, the no-need funding program has to offer at least $1,000 per year. The majority of the listings go way beyond that, paying up to $20,000 or more annually, or covering the full cost of college attendance.

Further, only free money is identified. If an award must be paid back, it's not listed. Here's your chance to find out about more than $1 billion in aid, knowing that not one dollar of that will ever need to be repaid.

Sixth, unlike other funding directories, which tend to follow a straight alphabetical arrangement, this one groups entries by discipline: sciences, social sciences, humanities, and any subject area (unrestricted by discipline). This arrangement will facilitate your search for appropriate funding opportunities. The same convenience is offered in the indexes, where program title, sponsoring organization, residency, tenability, subject, and deadline date entries are each subdivided by field of study.

In addition, you can take the money awarded by these scholarships to any number of schools. Unlike other financial aid directories that often list large numbers of scholarships available only to students enrolled at one specific school, all of the entries in this book are "portable."

Finally, the directory has been designed to make your search as easy as possible. You can identify programs by discipline, specific subject, sponsoring organization, program title, where you live, where your school of choice is located, and even deadline date. Plus, you'll find all the information you need to decide if a program is right for you: purpose, eligibility requirements, financial data, duration, special features, limitations, number awarded, and application date. You even get fax numbers, toll-free numbers, e-mail addresses, and web site locations (when available), along with complete contact information.

WHAT'S EXCLUDED?

The focus of the *College Student's Guide* is on "portable" merit and no-need funding that currently-enrolled and returning students can use to support their studies at practically any college or university in the United States. Excluded from this listing are:

- *Programs that consider income level in the selection process:* If a program requires applicants to demonstrate need as part of the primary selection process, it is not listed here.

- *Programs not aimed at currently-enrolled or returning college students:* Even if a program is no-need, it's not listed if it is open only to a different category of student (e.g., high school students) or if it is not specifically for college students (e.g., a photographic competition open to adults of any age).

INTRODUCTION

SAMPLE ENTRY

(1) **[1186]**

(2) **NACA REGIONAL COUNCIL STUDENT LEADER SCHOLARSHIPS**

(3) National Association for Campus Activities
Attn: NACA Foundation
13 Harbison Way
Columbia, SC 29212-3401
(803) 732-6222   Fax: (803) 749-1047
E-mail: scholarships@naca.org
Web: www.naca.org

(4) **Purpose** To provide financial assistance to outstanding college student leaders.

(5) **Eligibility** Eligible for this program are full-time undergraduate students who have made significant contributions to their campus communities, have played leadership roles in campus activities, and have demonstrated leadership skills and abilities. Financial need is not considered in the selection process.

(6) **Financial data** The amounts of the awards vary each year; scholarships are to be used for educational expenses, including tuition, books, fees, or other related expenses.

(7) **Duration** 1 year.

(8) **Additional information** This program was established in 1996.

(9) **Number awarded** 7 each year: 1 in each of the association's regions.

(10) **Deadline** April of each year.

DEFINITION

(1) **Entry number:** Consecutive number assigned to the references and used to index the entry.

(2) **Program title:** Title of scholarship, grant, award, or other no-need funding opportunity.

(3) **Sponsoring organization:** Name, address, telephone number, toll-free number, fax number, e-mail address, and web site location (when information was supplied) for organization sponsoring the program.

(4) **Purpose:** Basic program requirements; read the rest of the entry for additional detail.

(5) **Eligibility:** Qualifications required of applicants and factors considered in the selection process.

(6) **Financial data:** Financial details of the program, including fixed sum, average amount, or range of funds offered, expenses for which funds may and may not be applied, and cash-related benefits supplied (e.g., room and board).

(7) **Duration:** Time period for which support is provided; renewal prospects.

(8) **Additional information:** Any unusual (generally nonmonetary) benefits, features, restrictions or requirement associated with the program.

(9) **Number of awards:** Total number of recipients each year or other specified period.

(10) **Deadline:** The month by which applications must be submitted.

- *School-based programs:* The directory identifies "portable" programs—ones that can be used at any number of schools. Financial aid administered by individual schools solely for the benefit of their own students is not covered. Write directly to the schools you are considering to get information on their offerings.

- *Money for study outside the United States:* Since there are comprehensive and up-to-date directories that describe all available funding for study and research abroad (see the list of Reference Service Press titles opposite the directory's title page), only programs that support study in the United States are covered here.

- *Very restrictive programs:* In general, programs are excluded if they are open only to a limited geographic area (less than statewide), are available to a very limited membership group (e.g., a local union or a tightly targeted organization), or offer limited financial support (under $1,000).

- *Programs that did not respond to our research inquiries:* Programs are included in the *College Student's Guide* only if the sponsors responded to our requests for up-to-date information or posted that information on their web site (we never write program descriptions from secondary sources).

WHAT'S UPDATED?

The preparation of each new edition of the *College Student's Guide* involves extensive updating and revision. To make sure that the information included here is both reliable and current, the editors at Reference Service Press 1) review and update all relevant programs currently in our funding database and 2) search exhaustively for new program leads in a variety of sources, including directories, news reports, newsletters, annual reports, and sites on the Internet. We only include program descriptions in the *Guide* that are written directly from information supplied by the sponsoring organization on their web site or in response to our inquiries (up to four data collection letters followed by up to three telephone inquiries, if necessary). Despite our best efforts, we were not able to get information from some sponsoring organizations and, as a result, their programs are not included in this edition of the guide.

The 2008-2010 edition of the *College Student's Guide* completely revises and updates the previous (fifth) edition. Programs that have ceased operations or now offer awards less than $1,000 have been dropped. Similarly, programs that have broadened their focus to include need-based applicants have also been removed from the listing. Profiles of continuing programs have been rewritten to reflect current requirements; nearly 80 percent of the continuing programs reported substantive changes in their locations, deadlines, or benefits since 2002. In addition, more than 425 new entries have been added. The result is a listing of 1,323 scholarships, grants, awards, and other funding opportunities set aside for continuing or returning college students.

HOW THE DIRECTORY IS ORGANIZED

The directory is divided into two sections: a detailed list of merit and other no-need funding programs for college students; and a set of indexes to help you pinpoint appropriate funding programs.

Merit and Other No-Need Funding. The first section of the directory describes more than 1,300 scholarships, grants, awards, prizes, contests, competitions, and other funding opportunities for college students that do not consider income in the primary selection process. The programs listed are sponsored by federal and state government agencies, professional organizations, foundations, educational associations, and military/veterans organizations. All areas of the sciences, social sciences, and humanities are covered.

To help you tailor your search, the entries in this section are grouped into four main categories:

INTRODUCTION

- **Sciences.** Described here are 527 merit and other no-need funding programs that 1) reward outstanding speeches, essays, organizational involvement, and other activities in the sciences or 2) support college studies in a number of scientific fields, including agricultural sciences, chemistry, computer science, engineering, environmental sciences, food science, horticulture, mathematics, marine sciences, nursing, nutrition, pharmacology, and technology.

- **Social Sciences.** Described here are 246 merit and other no-need funding programs that 1) reward outstanding speeches, essays, organizational involvement, and other activities in the social sciences or 2) support college studies in various social science fields, including accounting, business administration, criminology, economics, education, geography, home economics, international relations, labor relations, political science, sales and marketing, sociology, social services, sports and recreation, and tourism.

- **Humanities,** Described here are 241 merit and other no-need funding programs that 1) reward outstanding artistic and creative work or 2) support college studies in the humanities, including architecture, art, creative writing, design, history, journalism, languages, literature, music, and religion.

- **Any Subject Area.** In addition, there is a listing of 309 funding sources that can be used to support study in any subject area (although the programs may be restricted in other ways).

Each program entry in the first section of the guide has been prepared to give you a concise but clear picture of the available funding. Information (when available) is provided on organization address and telephone numbers (including fax and toll-free numbers), e-mail address and web site location, purpose, eligibility, money awarded, duration, special features, limitations, number of awards, and application deadline. The sample entry on page 8 illustrates and explains the program entry structure.

The information provided for each of the programs covered in this section was supplied by sponsoring organizations in response to questionnaires we sent through the end of 2007. While the *College Student's Guide* is intended to cover as comprehensively as possible the no-need funding available to this group, some sponsoring organizations did not respond to our research inquiries and, consequently, are not included in this edition of the directory.

Indexes. To help you find the aid you need, we have included six indexes; these will let you access the listings by program title, sponsoring organization, residency (where you live), tenability (where you plan to go to school), subject, and deadline. These indexes use a word-by-word alphabetical arrangement. Note: numbers in the index refer to entry numbers, not to page numbers in the book.

Program Title Index. If you know the name of a particular funding program and want to find out where it is covered in the directory, use the Program Title Index. Here, program titles are arranged alphabetically, word by word. To assist you in your search, every program is listed by all its known names or abbreviations. In addition, we use a code to help you determine if the program falls within your general subject interest (sciences, social sciences, humanities, or any subject area).

Sponsoring Organization Index. This index makes it easy to identify agencies that offer merit and other no-need college funding. More than 1,000 sponsoring organizations are listed alphabetically, word by word. In addition, we've used a code to help you identify which programs sponsored by these organizations fall within your general area of interest (sciences, social sciences, humanities, or any subject area).

Residency Index. Some programs listed in this book are restricted to residents of a state or region. Others are open to students wherever they live. This index helps you identify programs available only to residents in your area as well as programs that have no residency restrictions.

Tenability Index. Some programs in this book can be used only in specific cities, counties, states, or regions. Others may be used anywhere in the United States (or even abroad). Use this index to find out what programs are available to support your studies in a particular geographic area.

Subject Index. Use this index when you want to identify merit/no-need funding programs by specific subject (more than 200 are included in this index). To help you pinpoint your search, we've also included numerous "see" and "see also" references.

Calendar Index. Since most financial aid programs have specific deadline dates, some may have closed by the time you begin to look for funding. You can use the Calendar Index to identify which programs are still open. This index is arranged by broad discipline and divided by month during which the deadline falls. Filing dates can and quite often do vary from year to year; consequently, the dates in this index should be viewed only as approximations after 2010.

HOW TO USE THE DIRECTORY

Here are some tips to help you get the most out of the financial listings in the *College Student's Guide:*

To Locate Financial Aid by Discipline. If you want to get an overall picture of what kind of funding is available in the sciences, social sciences, or humanities, turn to the appropriate category in the first section of the guide and browse through the listings there. Also, be sure to take a look at the fourth chapter, "Any Subject Area." You'll find hundreds of general programs described there that are available to support study in any area (although they may be restricted in other ways).

To Find Information on a Particular Financial Aid Program. If you know the name and disciplinary focus of a particular financial aid program, you can go directly to the appropriate category in the first section of the directory, where you'll find program profiles grouped by discipline and arranged alphabetically by title. If you are looking for a specific program and do not find it in the chapter you have checked, be sure to refer to the Program Title Index, to see if it is covered elsewhere in the directory. To save time, always check the Program Title Index first if you know the name of a specific award but are not sure under which subsection it would be placed. Since we index each program by all its known names or abbreviations, you'll also be able to track down a program there when you only know its popular rather than official name.

To Locate Financial Aid Programs Sponsored by a Particular Organization. The Sponsoring Organization Index makes it easy to determine which groups are providing no-need funding (more than 1,000 are listed here) and to identify specific financial aid programs offered by a particular sponsor. Each entry number in the index is coded to indicate broad subject coverage, to help you target appropriate entries.

To Browse Quickly Through the Listings. Turn to the section that interests you (sciences, social sciences, humanities, or any subject area) and read the "Purpose" field in each entry. In seconds, you'll know if this is an opportunity that might apply to you. If it is, be sure to read the rest of the information in the entry, to determine if you meet all of the program requirements before writing for an application form. Remember: don't apply if you don't qualify!

To Locate Financial Aid Based on Residency or Where You Want to Study. Use the Residency Index to identify funding that has been set aside to support applicants from your area. If you are looking for funding to support studies in a particular city, county, state, or region, turn to the Tenability Index. Both of these indexes are subdivided by broad subject area, to help you identify the funding that's right for you. When using these indexes, always check the listings under the term "United States," since the programs indexed there have no geographic restrictions and can be used in any area.

To Locate Financial Aid for Studies in a Particular Subject Area. Turn to the subject index first if you are interested in identifying available funding in a specific subject area (more than 200 different subject areas are indexed there). As part of your search, be sure to check the listings in the index under the heading "General Programs;" those programs support studies in any subject area (although they may be restricted in other ways).

To Locate Financial Aid by Deadline Date. If you are working with specific time constraints and want to weed out financial aid programs whose filing dates you won't be able to meet, turn first to the

INTRODUCTION

Calendar Index and check the program references listed under the appropriate area and month. Note: not all sponsoring organizations supplied deadline information, so not all programs are covered in this index. To identify every relevant financial aid program, regardless of filing dates, read through all the entries in the category that represents your interest (sciences, social sciences, or humanities). Don't forget to look at the listings in the Any Subject Area category, as well.

PLANS TO UPDATE THE DIRECTORY

This volume, covering 2008-2010, is the sixth edition of the *College Student's Guide to Merit and Other No-Need Funding.* The next biennial edition will cover the years 2010-2012 and will be released early in 2007.

OTHER RELATED PUBLICATIONS

In addition to the *College Student's Guide to Merit and Other No-Need Funding,* Reference Service Press publishes several other titles dealing with fundseeking, including the companion volume, *High School Senior's Guide to Merit and Other No-Need Funding.* For more information on this and other related publications, you can 1) write to Reference Service Press's marketing department at 5000 Windplay Drive, Suite 4, El Dorado Hills, CA 95762-9319; 2) call us at (916) 939-9620; 3) fax us at (916) 939-9626; 4) send us an e-mail message at info@rspfunding.com; or 5) visit us at our Internet site: http://www.rspfunding.com.

ACKNOWLEDGEMENTS

A debt of gratitude is owed all the organizations that contributed information to this edition of the *College Student's Guide to Merit and Other No-Need Funding.* Their generous cooperation has helped to make the sixth edition of this award-winning publication a current and comprehensive survey of no-need awards.

ABOUT THE AUTHORS

Dr. Gail Schlachter has worked for more than three decades as a library manager, a library educator, and an administrator of library-related publishing companies. Among the reference books to her credit are the biennially-issued *Directory of Financial Aids for Women* and two award-winning bibliographic guides: *Minorities and Women: A Guide to Reference Literature in the Social Sciences* (which was chosen as an "Outstanding Reference Title of the Year" by *Choice*) and *Reference Sources in Library and Information Services* (which won the first Knowledge Industry Publications "Award for Library Literature"). She is the former editor of *Reference and User Services Quarterly,* was the reference book review editor for *RQ* (now *Reference and User Services Quarterly)* for 10 years, is a past president of the American Library Association's Reference and User Services Association, and recently was elected to her fourth term on the American Library Association's governing council. In recognition of her outstanding contributions to reference service, Dr. Schlachter has been awarded both the Isadore Gilbert Mudge Citation and the Louis Shores-Oryx Press Award and was named the "Outstanding Alumna" by the University of Wisconsin's School of Library and Information Studies.

Dr. R. David Weber has been teaching economics and history at Los Angeles Harbor College (Wilmington, California), since 1975. He is the author of a number of critically-acclaimed reference works, including *Dissertations in Urban History* and the three-volume *Energy Information Guide.* With Gail Schlachter, he is the author of Reference Service Press's award-winning *Financial Aid for the Disabled and Their Families* and a number of other financial aid titles, including *Money for Graduate Students in the Social Sciences* and *Financial Aid for African Americans.*

Merit and Other No-Need Funding Programs for College Students

- *Sciences*
- *Social Sciences*
- *Humanities*
- *Any Subject Area*

Sciences

Described here are 527 merit and other no-need funding programs that 1) reward outstanding speeches, essays, organizational involvement, and other activities in the sciences or 2) support college studies in a number of scientific fields, including agricultural sciences, chemistry, computer science, engineering, environmental sciences, food science, horticulture, mathematics, marine sciences, nursing, nutrition, pharmacology, and technology. These programs are available to currently-enrolled and returning college students to fund studies on the undergraduate level in the United States. If you are looking for a particular program and don't find it here, be sure to check the Program Title Index to see if it is covered elsewhere in the directory.

SCIENCES

[1]
AACC INTERNATIONAL FOUNDATION UNDERGRADUATE SCHOLARSHIP PROGRAM

AACC International
Attn: AACC International Foundation
3340 Pilot Knob Road
St. Paul, MN 55121-2097
(651) 454-7250   Fax: (651) 454-0766
E-mail: aacc@scisoc.org
Web: www.aaccnet.org

Purpose To provide financial assistance for college to members of AACC International.

Eligibility This program is open to AACC International student members who are entering their junior or senior year of college with a GPA of 3.0 or higher both cumulatively and in science and mathematics courses. Applicants must demonstrate an interest in and intent to prepare for a career in grain-based food science and technology or in a related area in industry, academia, or government. They must be working on a degree from an institution that conducts fundamental investigations for the advancement of cereal science and technology, including oilseeds. Selection is based on scholarships previously or currently held; awards and honors received in high school and/or college; extracurricular activities and hobbies; work experience, internships, and related to projects; 3 letters of recommendation; transcripts of college or university undergraduate work; and a letter that describes career plans and their relationship to pertinent courses taken or planned, especially courses related to cereal science or technology, including oilseeds. Age, sex, race, financial need, and previous receipt or nonreceipt of this scholarship are not considered.

Financial data Stipends are $2,000, $1,500, or $1,000 per year.

Duration 1 year; may be renewed.

Additional information The sponsoring organization was formerly the American Association of Cereal Chemists.

Number awarded Up to 15 each year.

Deadline February of each year.

[2]
AACE INTERNATIONAL COMPETITIVE SCHOLARSHIPS

Association for the Advancement of Cost Engineering
209 Prairie Avenue, Suite 100
Morgantown, WV 26505
(304) 296-8444   Toll-free: (800) 858-COST
Fax: (304) 291-5728   E-mail: info@aacei.org
Web: www.aacei.org

Purpose To provide financial assistance to undergraduate and graduate students in the United States or Canada working on a degree related to total cost management (the effective application of professional and technical expertise to plan and control resources, costs, profitability, and risk).

Eligibility Applicants may be undergraduate students (second year standing or higher) or graduate students. They must be enrolled full time in a degree program in the United States or Canada that is related to the field of cost management/cost engineering, including agricultural engineering, architectural engineering, building construction, business administration, chemical engineering, civil engineering, computer science, electrical engineering, industrial engineering, manufacturing engineering, mechanical engineering, mining engineering, and quantity surveying. Selection is based on academic performance (35%), extracurricular activities (35%), and an essay (30%) on the value of study in cost engineering or total cost management and why it is important to their academic objectives and career goals.

Financial data Stipends range from $1,000 to $4,000 per year.

Duration 1 year.

Additional information AACE International was formerly the Association for the Advancement of Cost Engineering.

Number awarded Varies each year; recently, 28 of these scholarships were awarded.

Deadline October of each year.

[3]
AAPA VETERAN'S CAUCUS SCHOLARSHIPS

American Academy of Physician Assistants-Veterans Caucus
Attn: Veterans Caucus
950 North Washington Street
Alexandria, VA 22314-1552
(703) 836-2272   Fax: (703) 684-1924
E-mail: aapa@aapa.org
Web: www.veteranscaucus.org

Purpose To provide financial assistance to veterans and Reserve component personnel who are studying to become physician assistants.

Eligibility This program is open to U.S. citizens who are currently enrolled in a physician assistant program. The program must be approved by the Commission on Accreditation of Allied Health Education. Applicants must be honorably discharged members of a uniformed service of the United States or an active member of the Guard or Reserve of a uniformed service of the United States. Selection is based on military honors and awards received, civic and college honors and awards received, professional memberships and activities, and GPA. An electronic copy of the applicant's DD Form 214 must accompany the application.

Financial data Stipends are $2,000, $1,500, or $1,250.

Duration 1 year.

Additional information This program includes the following named scholarships: the Donna Jones Moritsugu Memorial Awards, the SSGT Craig Ivory Memorial Scholarships, the Order of St. Lazarus/Green Cross Project Award, the Andrea Long Memorial Scholarships, the Society of Air Force Physician Assistants Scholarship, the Society of Army Physician Assistants Scholarship, the Naval Association of Physician Assistants Scholarship, the Major Jessie and Sharon Edwards Scholarship (established in 2004), the John M. Dwyer Memorial Scholarship (established in 2004), and the Vicki Moritsugu Memorial Scholarship (established in 2004). Information is also available from Sharon Hanley, P.O. Box 362, Danville, PA 17821-0362, (570) 271-6692, (800) 271-6692, Fax: (570) 271-5850, E-mail: skhanley@ptd.net.

Number awarded Varies each year. Recently, 15 of these scholarships were awarded: 1 at $2,000, 2 at $1,500, and 12 at $1,250.

Deadline February of each year.

[4]
AATCC MATERIALS DESIGN COMPETITION
American Association of Textile Chemists and Colorists
Attn: Technical Center
1 Davis Drive
P.O. Box 12215
Research Triangle Park, NC 27709-2215
(919) 549-8141   Fax: (919) 549-8933
E-mail: holmes@aatcc.org
Web: www.aatcc.org

Purpose To recognize and reward undergraduate and graduate students who submit outstanding materials designs in a national competition.

Eligibility This competition is open to undergraduate and graduate students who work as individual or in teams of up to 4 members. Applicants are invited to submit materials designs in 3 areas: 1) industrial and technical, covering structures and materials for technical and engineering applications including nano-technologies, composites, and high performance structures and materials; 2) protective, medical, and biomedical, covering structures external to the body intended for use in hazardous or medical environments to protect the wearer from such threats as fire, chemical agents, projectiles, and biological agents, as well as artificial internal body implants; and 3) smart/electronic, covering structures that incorporate computing, sensing, monitoring, imaging, and or broadcasting electronics directly into the material to attain particular end uses. The preliminary design proposal must contain a single paragraph description of the intended material product or device design. The final design must include 1) a full text proposal, including up to 10 pages of text, supporting documentation in appendices, a material list for producing the product, proposed manufacturing process schematic/flow diagram, and reference bibliography; and 2) an electronic/digital post board of their proposal to be submitted digitally in files less than 50 megabytes with resolution no less than 300 dpi. Selection is based on concept originality, design element integration, technical feasibility, clarity of supporting documentation, technical and materials rationales, efficacy of the proposed commercialization of the idea, and viability of economic cost analysis.

Financial data For each area, first prize is $1,000 and second prize is $500. Winners also receive complimentary student registration for the international conference and exhibition of the American Association of Textile Chemists and Colorists (AATCC).

Duration The competition is held annually.

Number awarded 6 each year: 1 first prize and 1 second prize in each of the 3 areas.

Deadline Preliminary proposals must be submitted by February of each year. Final designs are due in April.

[5]
ACADEMY OF NEONATAL NURSING SCHOLARSHIP AWARD
Academy of Neonatal Nursing
2270 Northpoint Parkway
Santa Rosa, CA 95407-7398
(707) 568-2168   Fax: (707) 569-0786
Web: www.academyonline.org

Purpose To provide financial assistance to members of the Academy of Neonatal Nursing (ANN) who are working on an undergraduate or graduate degree in neonatal nursing or a related nursing major.

Eligibility This program is open to ANN members who have been in good standing for at least 2 years. Applicants must have at least 2 years of neonatal practice experience with at least 1 of those years completed in the past 18 months. They must be enrolled in a nursing academic degree program or a neonatal graduate program in which they have completed at least 2 degree-required courses with a GPA of 3.0 or higher. Only professionally-active neonatal nurses are eligible, i.e., currently engaged in a clinical, research, or educational role that contributes directly to the health care of neonates or to the nursing profession and maintaining professional education in neonatal nursing by obtaining 15 contact hours of continuing education a year. Along with their application, they must submit a 200-word essay on why they are pursuing their education and how attainment of this degree will benefit them in their professional role. Financial need is not considered in the selection process.

Financial data The stipend is $1,000. Funds are paid directly to the recipient and the educational program.

Duration 1 year; recipients are not eligible for another scholarship for 5 years.

Number awarded 1 or more each year.

Deadline April of each year.

[6]
ACCESS INTELLIGENCE SCHOLARSHIP
Society of Satellite Professionals International
Attn: Scholarship Program
New York Information Technology Center
55 Broad Street, 14th Floor
New York, NY 10004
(212) 809-5199   Fax: (212) 825-0075
E-mail: sspi@sspi.org
Web: www.sspi.org

Purpose To provide financial assistance to student members of the Society of Satellite Professionals International (SSPI) who are interested in working on an undergraduate or graduate degree in the satellite field.

Eligibility This program is open to SSPI members who are high school seniors, college undergraduates, or graduate students interested in preparing for a career in satellite technologies, policies, or applications. Applicants must be interested in majoring in a satellite-related field that emphasizes the commercial and/or humanitarian aspects of new technologies and services. They may be from any country. The scholarships is presented to the applicant who best analyzes the entrepreneurial possibilities of new satellite services, technologies, or applications from a profit-driven or public service-oriented perspective. Financial need is not considered.

Financial data The stipend ranges from $2,000 to $5,000.
Duration 1 year.
Number awarded 1 each year.
Deadline Preliminary applications must be submitted by February of each year.

[7]
ACSM FELLOWS SCHOLARSHIP

American Congress on Surveying and Mapping
Attn: Scholarships
6 Montgomery Village Avenue, Suite 403
Gaithersburg, MD 20879
(240) 632-9716, ext. 113   Fax: (240) 632-1321
E-mail: pat.canfield@acsm.net
Web: www.acsm.net/scholar.html

Purpose To provide financial assistance for the undergraduate study of surveying to members of the American Congress on Surveying and Mapping (ACSM).
Eligibility This program is open to ACSM members who are enrolled at a 4-year college or university as juniors or higher. Applicants must be majoring in surveying or a closely-related program (e.g., geomatics, surveying engineering). Along with their application, they must submit a statement describing their educational program, future plans for study or research, and why the award is merited. Selection is based on that statement (30%), academic record (30%), letters of recommendation (20%), and professional activities (20%).
Financial data The stipend is $2,000.
Duration 1 year.
Number awarded 1 each year.
Deadline October of each year.

[8]
ADC COMMUNICATIONS AND FOUNDATION SCHOLARSHIP

Society of Women Engineers
230 East Ohio Street, Suite 400
Chicago, IL 60611-3265
(312) 596-5223   Toll-free: (877) SWE-INFO
Fax: (312) 644-8557
E-mail: scholarshipapplication@swe.org
Web: www.swe.org/scholarships

Purpose To provide financial assistance to upper-division women who are members of the Society of Women Engineers and majoring in engineering.
Eligibility This program is open to women who are entering their junior or senior year at an ABET-accredited college or university. Applicants must be studying computer science or electrical or computer engineering with a GPA of 3.0 or higher. They must be U.S. citizens and members of the society. Along with their application, they must submit a 1-page essay on why they want to be an engineer or computer scientist, how they believe they will make a difference as an engineer or computer scientist, and what influenced them to study engineering or computer science. Selection is based on merit.
Financial data The stipend is $2,250.
Duration 1 year.
Additional information This program is sponsored by the ADC Foundation.
Number awarded 4 each year.
Deadline January of each year.

[9]
ADOBE SYSTEMS COMPUTER SCIENCE SCHOLARSHIPS

Society of Women Engineers
230 East Ohio Street, Suite 400
Chicago, IL 60611-3265
(312) 596-5223   Toll-free: (877) SWE-INFO
Fax: (312) 644-8557
E-mail: scholarshipapplication@swe.org
Web: www.swe.org/scholarships

Purpose To provide financial assistance to upper-division women majoring in computer science.
Eligibility This program is open to women entering their junior or senior year at an ABET-accredited college or university. Applicants must be majoring in computer science and have a GPA of 3.0 or higher. Along with their application, they must submit a 1-page essay on why they want to be a computer scientist, how they believe they will make a difference as a computer scientist, and what influenced them to study computer science. Preference is given to students attending selected schools; for a list, contact the sponsor. Selection is based on merit.
Financial data Stipends are $2,000 or $1,500.
Duration 1 year.
Additional information This program, established in 2000, is sponsored by Adobe Systems Incorporated.
Number awarded 2 each year: 1 at $2,000 and 1 at $1,500.
Deadline January of each year.

[10]
AESF UNDERGRADUATE SCHOLARSHIP PROGRAM

American Electroplaters and Surface Finishers Society
Attn: Scholarship Committee
1155 15th Street, N.W., Suite 500
Washington, DC 20005
(202) 457-8401   Fax: (202) 530-0659
E-mail: janice@aesf.org
Web: www.aesf.org/programs/scholar.html

Purpose To provide financial assistance to undergraduate students who are interested in majoring in subjects related to plating and surface finishing technologies.
Eligibility This program is open to juniors and seniors in college who are majoring in chemistry, chemical engineering, environmental engineering, metallurgy, materials science, or metallurgical engineering. Applicants must submit a 2-page statement describing their career objectives, intended plans for study in plating and surface finishing technologies, and long-range goals. Selection is based on academic history, extracurricular activities, and employment history. Financial need is not considered.
Financial data The stipend is at least $1,500 per year. Funds are sent directly to the recipient's college or univer-

sity. Schools are requested not to reduce federal, state, or institutional support for students who receive this scholarship.

Duration 1 year; recipients may reapply for 1 additional year.

Additional information Recipients are encouraged to submit a report or paper at the conclusion of the award period. They must be in school full time during the academic year the scholarship is received.

Number awarded At least 1 each year.

Deadline April of each year.

[11]
AFCEA DISTANCE-LEARNING/ON-LINE SCHOLARSHIPS

Armed Forces Communications and Electronics Association
Attn: AFCEA Educational Foundation
4400 Fair Lakes Court
Fairfax, VA 22033-3899
(703) 631-6149   Toll-free: (800) 336-4583, ext. 6149
Fax: (703) 631-4693   E-mail: scholarship@afcea.org
Web: www.afcea.org

Purpose To provide financial assistance to undergraduate students who are working full time on a degree in selected scientific fields using distance-learning or online programs.

Eligibility This program is open to U.S. citizens working full time on a bachelor's degree by means of a distance-learning or online program affiliated with a major accredited 4-year college or university in the United States. Applicants must have completed at least 1 year of course work based on a 30-semester hour equivalent; classes in progress at the time of application cannot be used towards the 1-year minimum completion requirement. Completed courses must include at least 2 semesters of calculus (not pre-calculus). Majors are limited to the fields of engineering (chemical, computer, electrical, or systems), mathematics, physics, or computer science. Selection is based primarily on academic excellence.

Financial data The stipend is $1,000.

Duration 1 year.

Number awarded 1 each year.

Deadline July of each year.

[12]
AFRICAN AMERICAN HEALTH SOLUTIONS SCHOLARS PROGRAM

PacifiCare
Attn: African American Health Solutions Scholars
5995 Plaza Drive, CY20-182
Cypress, CA 90630
Toll-free: (800) 967-4347   E-mail: AAHS@phs.com
Web: www.pacificare.com

Purpose To provide financial assistance to African American students from designated states interested in preparing for a career in the health industry.

Eligibility This program is open to African Americans from California, Georgia, Maryland, and Texas who are graduating high school seniors or already enrolled full time at a community college, university, or accredited technical school. Applicants must be majoring or planning to major in an approved health care program, including (but not limited to) gerontology, health claims examiner, health information technology program, medical research, nursing (R.N., L.V.N.), pharmacy technician, pre-medical, psychology, or public health. They must have a GPA of 3.0 or higher and be able to demonstrate a commitment to a career in the health care field. Along with their application, they must submit a 2-page essay that includes personal and academic accomplishments, community involvement, volunteer and leadership activities, and the reasons for wanting to prepare for a career in the health industry.

Financial data The stipend is $2,000. Funds are paid directly to the community college, university, or technical school the student is attending.

Duration 1 year.

Additional information Awards are distributed through the African American Health Solutions Pacific Region Scholars Program, the Tavis Smiley Foundation, Historically Black Colleges and Universities, and the Tom Joyner Foundation.

Number awarded 30 each year.

Deadline July of each year.

[13]
AGCO STUDENT DESIGN COMPETITION

American Society of Agricultural and Biological Engineers
Attn: Awards Coordinator
2950 Niles Road
St. Joseph, MI 49085-9659
(269) 429-0300   Fax: (269) 429-3852
E-mail: hq@asabe.org
Web: www.asabe.org

Purpose To recognize and reward student members of the American Society of Agricultural and Biological Engineers (ASABE) who participate in the basic design of an engineering product useful to agriculture.

Eligibility This program is open to biological and agricultural engineering students who are student members of the society. Applicants, operating as teams or individuals, submit an engineering design that involves devising a machine, component, system, or process to meet a desired need related to agricultural, food, or biological engineering. The project description they submit is judged on: establishment of need and benefit to agriculture (5 points); approach and originality (6 points); definition of design objectives and criteria (5 points); extent of analysis and synthesis of alternatives (10 points); evidence of sound evaluation and adherence to good engineering design and safety considerations (10 points); adequacy of drawings and specifications (7 points); appropriateness of tests and/or performance data (7 points); and achievement of objectives (10 points). They must also include a written report that is judged on: organization, clarity, and ease of reading (10 points); effective use of graphics, illustrations, video, etc. (5 points); and neatness, accuracy, and style (5 points). Based on the project description and written report, the top 3 entrants are invited to the society's annual meeting for an oral presentation; those are judged on: general effectiveness and audience appeal (8 points); organization and information flow (5

points); quality and adequacy of visuals (5 points); and compliance with 15-minute limit (2 points). The 3 finalists are then ranked on the basis of their total scores.
Financial data First prize is $1,250, second $1,000, and third $750. Teams decide among themselves how to divide the money. The academic department of the first-place entry receives a $300 scholarship and a wall plaque.
Duration The competition is held annually.
Number awarded 3 each year.
Deadline May of each year.

[14]
AGLIFE FOR AMERICA SCHOLARSHIPS
Scholarship Administrative Services, Inc.
Attn: ALfA Program
2000 Rock Street, Suite 3
Mountain View, CA 94043

Purpose To provide financial assistance to entering or continuing undergraduate and graduate students working on a degree in a field related to agriculture.
Eligibility This program is open to full-time students working on or planning to work on an undergraduate or graduate degree in an agriculture-related field. Applicants must have a GPA of 3.0 or higher and be able to demonstrate a record of involvement in extracurricular and work activities related to agriculture. Along with their application, they must submit a 1,000-word essay on their educational and career goals, why they believe agriculture is essential to America, and why they have decided to prepare for a career in agriculture. Financial need is not considered in the selection process.
Financial data The stipend is $5,000 per year.
Duration 1 year; may be renewed 1 additional year if the recipient maintains full-time enrollment and a GPA of 3.0 or higher.
Additional information This program is sponsored by AgLife for America (ALfA) and administered by Scholarship Administrative Services, Inc. ALfA was established in 2003 to encourage more American students to consider remaining on the farm. Requests for applications should be accompanied by a self-addressed stamped envelope, the student's e-mail address, and the source where they found the scholarship information.
Number awarded Up to 20 each year.
Deadline April of each year.

[15]
AGRISCIENCE STUDENT PROGRAM
National FFA Organization
Attn: Agriscience Program
6060 FFA Drive
P.O. Box 68960
Indianapolis, IN 46268-0960
(317) 802-4402   Fax: (317) 802-5402
E-mail: agriscience@ffa.org
Web: www.ffa.org/programs/ag_sci/index.html

Purpose To recognize and reward, with college scholarships, members of FFA who submit the most outstanding reports on agriscience projects.
Eligibility This program is open to current members who are 1) juniors or seniors in high school enrolled in agriculture, agriscience, or agribusiness, or 2) college freshmen who are immediate high school graduates majoring in a field related to agriculture. Applicants should be planning a career in agricultural sciences that requires postsecondary training. They must have completed a research project related to agriscience while still enrolled in high school. The project may include personal, school, university, public, or private sector research (based on local school curriculum and implemented under the overall direction of the agriculture teacher). Based on applications and state competitions, 8 national finalists are invited to present their results at the National Agricultural Career Show as a part of the national FFA convention. Winners are selected from among those finalists.
Financial data Each state winner receives a scholarship and each national finalist receives an additional scholarship and a plaque. The national winner receives an additional $3,500 scholarship and the national runner-up receives an additional $1,500 scholarship.
Duration The competition is held annually.
Number awarded 2 each year: 1 winner and 1 runner-up.
Deadline July of each year.

[16]
AIAA FOUNDATION UNDERGRADUATE DESIGN COMPETITIONS
American Institute of Aeronautics and Astronautics
Attn: Student Programs Director
1801 Alexander Bell Drive, Suite 500
Reston, VA 20191-4344
(703) 264-7536   Toll-free: (800) 639-AIAA, ext. 536
Fax: (703) 264-7657   E-mail: stephenb@aiaa.org
Web: www.aiaa.org/content.cfm?pageid=210

Purpose To recognize and reward outstanding designs prepared by undergraduate student members of the American Institute of Aeronautics and Astronautics (AIAA).
Eligibility This program is open to undergraduate students who are AIAA branch or at-large student members. Individuals may enter the aircraft design competition. Teams of 3 to 10 students may enter in 4 competitions: the engine design competition, the aircraft design competition, the space design competition, and the space transportation design competition. Design projects that are used as part of an organized classroom requirement are eligible and encouraged. Designs that are submitted must be the work of the students, but a faculty advisor may provide guidance. Selection is based on technical content (35 points), organization and presentation (20 points), originality (20 points), and practical application and feasibility (25 points).
Financial data For each of the 5 competitions, first place is $2,500, second place is $1,500, and third place is $1,000.
Duration The competitions are held annually.
Number awarded 3 cash awards are presented in each of the 5 competitions.
Deadline Letters of intent must be submitted by March of each year; completed entries are due by the end of May.

[17]
AIAA FOUNDATION UNDERGRADUATE SCHOLARSHIP PROGRAM

American Institute of Aeronautics and Astronautics
Attn: Student Programs Director
1801 Alexander Bell Drive, Suite 500
Reston, VA 20191-4344
(703) 264-7536   Toll-free: (800) 639-AIAA, ext. 536
Fax: (703) 264-7657   E-mail: stephenb@aiaa.org
Web: www.aiaa.org/content.cfm?pageid=226

Purpose To provide financial assistance to undergraduate student members of the American Institute of Aeronautics and Astronautics (AIAA).

Eligibility This program is open to college students who have completed at least 1 semester or quarter of full-time college work in engineering or science fields that relate to aerospace or aeronautics. Applicants must have a GPA of 3.3 or higher, be student members or willing to become student members of the sponsoring organization, and be interested in a career in the aerospace field. They may be of any nationality. Along with their application, they must submit an essay of 500 to 1,000 words on their career objectives and the academic program required to achieve those objectives. Selection is based on that essay, GPA, letters of recommendation, and extracurricular activities.

Financial data The stipend ranges from $2,000 to $2,500.

Duration 1 year; recipients may reapply if they have a GPA of 3.3 or higher.

Additional information This program, established in 1977, includes 5 scholarships named for the first 5 presidents of the AIAA Foundation and awarded to the top senior applicants: the A. Thomas Young Scholarship, the L.S. "Skip" Fletcher Scholarship, the Sam F. Iacobellis Scholarship, the Robert L. Crippen Scholarship, and the E.C. "Pete" Aldridge Scholarship. Other scholarships are named after noteworthy donors to the program; those include the Liquid Propulsion Technical Committee Scholarship, the Space Transportation Technical Committee Scholarship, the Digital Avionics Technical Committee Scholarships, and the Next Century of Flight Scholarships.

Number awarded 30 each year.

Deadline January of each year.

[18]
AIR FORCE ROTC BIOMEDICAL SCIENCES CORPS

U.S. Air Force
Attn: Headquarters AFROTC/RRUC
551 East Maxwell Boulevard
Maxwell AFB, AL 36112-5917
(334) 953-2091   Toll-free: (866) 423-7682
Fax: (334) 953-6167
Web: www.afrotc.com

Purpose To provide financial assistance to students who are interested in joining Air Force ROTC in college and preparing for a career as a physical therapist, optometrist, or pharmacist.

Eligibility This program is open to U.S. citizens who are freshmen or sophomores in college and interested in a career as a physical therapist, optometrist, or pharmacist. Applicants must have a GPA of 2.0 or higher and meet all other academic and physical requirements for participation in AFROTC. At the time of their Air Force commissioning, they may be no more than 31 years of age. They must agree to serve for at least 4 years as nonline active-duty Air Force officers following graduation from college.

Financial data Awards are type 2 AFROTC scholarships that provide for payment of tuition and fees, to a maximum of $15,000 per year, plus an annual book allowance of $600. All recipients are also awarded a tax-free subsistence allowance for 10 months of each year that is $300 per month during their sophomore year, $350 during their junior year, and $400 during their senior year.

Duration 2 or 3 years, provided the recipient maintains a GPA of 2.0 or higher.

Additional information Recipients must also complete 4 years of aerospace studies courses at 1 of the 144 colleges and universities that have an Air Force ROTC unit on campus or 1 of the approximately 900 colleges that have cross-enrollment agreements with those institutions. They must also attend a 4-week summer training camp at an Air Force base, usually between their sophomore and junior years. Following completion of their bachelor's degree, scholarship recipients earn a commission as a second lieutenant in the Air Force and serve at least 4 years.

Deadline June of each year.

[19]
AIR FORCE ROTC EXPRESS SCHOLARSHIPS

U.S. Air Force
Attn: Headquarters AFROTC/RRUC
551 East Maxwell Boulevard
Maxwell AFB, AL 36112-5917
(334) 953-2091   Toll-free: (866) 423-7682
Fax: (334) 953-6167
Web: www.afrotc.com

Purpose To provide financial assistance to students who are interested in joining Air Force ROTC and majoring in critical Air Force officer fields in college.

Eligibility This program is open to U.S. citizens who are completing at least their first year of college and are working on a degree in fields that may change annually but are of critical interest to the Air Force. Applicants must have a GPA of 2.5 or higher and meet all other academic and physical requirements for participation in AFROTC. At the time of their Air Force commissioning, they may be no more than 31 years of age. They must be able to pass the Air Force Officer Qualifying Test (AFOQT) and the Air Force ROTC Physical Fitness Test. years as active-duty Air Force officers following graduation from college.

Financial data Awards are type 2 AFROTC scholarships that provide for payment of tuition and fees, to a maximum of $15,000 per year, plus an annual book allowance of $600. All recipients are also awarded a tax-free monthly subsistence allowance that is $250 for freshmen, $300 for sophomores, $350 for juniors, and $400 for seniors.

Duration 3 and a half years, until completion of a bachelor's degree.

Additional information Recently, freshmen were eligible if they were majoring in computer, electrical, or environmental engineering. Sophomores and juniors were eligible if they were majoring in those fields, meteorology and atmospheric sciences, or in the following engineering disciplines: aeronautical, aerospace, astronautical, civil, or mechanical. Recipients must also complete 4 years of aerospace studies courses at 1 of the 144 colleges and universities that have an Air Force ROTC unit on campus or 1 of the approximately 900 colleges that have cross-enrollment agreements with those institutions. They must also attend a 4-week summer training camp at an Air Force base, usually between their sophomore and junior years. Following completion of their bachelor's degree, scholarship recipients earn a commission as a second lieutenant in the Air Force and serve at least 4 years.

[20]
AIR FORCE ROTC IN-COLLEGE SCHOLARSHIP PROGRAM
U.S. Air Force
Attn: Headquarters AFROTC/RRUC
551 East Maxwell Boulevard
Maxwell AFB, AL 36112-5917
(334) 953-2091   Toll-free: (866) 423-7682
Fax: (334) 953-6167
Web: www.afrotc.com

Purpose To provide financial assistance to undergraduate students who are willing to join Air Force ROTC in college and serve as Air Force officers following completion of their bachelor's degree.

Eligibility This program is open to U.S. citizens enrolled as freshmen or sophomores at 1 of the 144 colleges and universities that have an Air Force ROTC unit on campus. Applicants must have a cumulative GPA of 2.5 or higher and be able to pass the Air Force Officer Qualifying Test and the Air Force ROTC Physical Fitness Test. At the time of commissioning, they may be no more than 31 years of age. They must agree to serve for at least 4 years as active-duty Air Force officers following graduation from college. Phase 1 is open to students enrolled in the Air Force ROTC program who do not currently have a scholarship but now wish to apply. Phase 2 is open to Phase 1 nonselects and students not enrolled in Air Force ROTC. Phase 3 is open only to Phase 2 nonselects. Recently, the program gave preference to students majoring in the science and technical fields of architecture, chemistry, computer science, engineering (aeronautical, aerospace, astronautical, architectural, civil, computer, electrical, environmental, or mechanical), mathematics, meteorology and atmospheric sciences, operations research, or physics.

Financial data Cadets selected in Phase 1 are awarded type 2 AFROTC scholarships that provide for payment of tuition and fees, to a maximum of $15,000 per year. A limited number of cadets selected in Phase 2 are also awarded type 2 AFROTC scholarships, but most are awarded type 3 AFROTC scholarships with tuition capped at $9,000 per year. Cadets selected in Phase 3 are awarded type 6 AFROTC scholarships with tuition capped at $3,000 per year. All recipients are also awarded a book allowance of $600 and a tax-free subsistence allowance for 10 months of each year that is $300 per month during the sophomore year, $350 during the junior year, and $400 during the senior year.

Duration 3 years for students selected as freshmen or 2 years for students selected as sophomores.

Additional information While scholarship recipients can major in any subject, they must complete 4 years of aerospace studies courses at 1 of the 144 colleges or universities that have an Air Force ROTC unit on campus. Recipients must also attend a 4-week summer training camp at an Air Force base, usually between their sophomore and junior years; 2-year scholarship awardees attend in the summer after their junior year. Current military personnel are eligible for early release from active duty in order to enter the Air Force ROTC program. Following completion of their bachelor's degree, scholarship recipients earn a commission as a second lieutenant in the Air Force and serve at least 4 years.

Number awarded Varies each year.
Deadline January of each year.

[21]
AIR FORCE ROTC NURSING SCHOLARSHIPS
U.S. Air Force
Attn: Headquarters AFROTC/RRUC
551 East Maxwell Boulevard
Maxwell AFB, AL 36112-5917
(334) 953-2091   Toll-free: (866) 423-7682
Fax: (334) 953-6167
Web: www.afrotc.com

Purpose To provide financial assistance to college students who are interested in a career as a nurse, are interested in joining Air Force ROTC, and are willing to serve as Air Force officers following completion of their bachelor's degree.

Eligibility This program is open to U.S. citizens who are freshmen or sophomores in college and interested in a career as a nurse. Applicants must have a cumulative GPA of 2.5 or higher at the end of their freshman year and meet all other academic and physical requirements for participation in AFROTC. They must be interested in working on a nursing degree from an accredited program. At the time of Air Force commissioning, they may be no more than 31 years of age. They must be able to pass the Air Force Officer Qualifying Test (AFOQT) and the Air Force ROTC Physical Fitness Test.

Financial data Awards are type 2 AFROTC scholarships that provide for payment of tuition and fees, to a maximum of $15,000 per year, plus an annual book allowance of $600. All recipients are also awarded a tax-free subsistence allowance for 10 months of each year that is $300 per month during their sophomore year, $350 during their junior year, and $400 during their senior year.

Duration 2 or 3 years, provided the recipient maintains a GPA of 2.5 or higher.

Additional information Recipients must also complete 4 years of aerospace studies courses at 1 of the 144 colleges and universities that have an Air Force ROTC unit on campus or 1 of the approximately 900 colleges that have cross-enrollment agreements with those institutions. They must also attend a 4-week summer training camp at an Air Force base, usually between their sophomore and junior years. Following completion of their bachelor's degree, scholarship recipients earn a commission as a second lieutenant in the Air Force and serve at least 4 years.

Deadline June of each year.

[22]
AISES IBM SCHOLARSHIP
American Indian Science and Engineering Society
Attn: Scholarship Coordinator
2305 Renard, S.E., Suite 200
P.O. Box 9828
Albuquerque, NM 87119-9828
(505) 765-1052, ext. 106   Fax: (505) 765-5608
E-mail: shirley@aises.org
Web: www.aises.org/highered/scholarships

Purpose To provide financial assistance to members of the American Indian Science and Engineering Society (AISES) who are working on an undergraduate or graduate degree in engineering or a related field.

Eligibility This program is open to AISES members who are full-time undergraduate or graduate students at a 4-year college or university or a full-time student at a 2-year college enrolled in a program leading to a 4-year degree. Applicants must be majoring in computer science, mathematics, management information systems, material science, computer information systems, or 1 of the following engineering disciplines: chemical, computer, electrical, industrial, or mechanical. They must have a GPA of 3.2 or higher and be members of an American Indian tribe or Alaskan Native group. Along with their application, they must submit a 500-word essay on their educational and/or career goals, interest in and motivation to continue higher education, understanding of the importance of college and commitment to completion, commitment to learning, and giving back to the community. Financial need is not considered in the selection process. U.S. citizenship is required.

Financial data The stipend is $1,000 per year for undergraduates with a GPA of 3.2 or higher, $1,500 per year for undergraduates or graduate students with a GPA of 3.5 or higher, or $3,000 for undergraduates or graduate students with a GPA of 3.7 or higher.

Duration 1 year; nonrenewable.

Additional information This program, established in 2006, is funded by the IBM Corporation.

Number awarded 28 each year: 12 for undergraduates at $1,000, 7 for undergraduates at $1,500, 3 for graduate students at $1,500, 3 for undergraduates at $3,000, and 3 for graduate students at $3,000.

Deadline July of each year.

[23]
ALBUQUERQUE VETERINARY ASSOCIATION SCHOLARSHIPS
Albuquerque Veterinary Association, Inc.
c/o Teri Wheeler, Scholarship Committee Chair
1921 Carlisle Boulevard, N.E.
Albuquerque, NM 87110

Purpose To provide financial assistance to college students in New Mexico who are interested in preparing for a career in veterinary science.

Eligibility This program is open to residents of New Mexico who are currently enrolled in college, in a pre-veterinary program. Selection is based on academic achievement, letters of recommendation, and professional activities. Financial need is not considered in the selection process.

Financial data A stipend is awarded (amount not specified).

Duration 1 year.

Number awarded 1 or more each year.

Deadline April of each year.

[24]
ALCOA FOUNDATION ACADEMIC SCHOLARSHIP
American Association of Occupational Health Nurses, Inc.
Attn: AAOHN Foundation
2920 Brandywine Road, Suite 100
Atlanta, GA 30341-4146
(770) 455-7757   Fax: (770) 455-7271
E-mail: foundation@aaohn.org
Web: www.aaohn.org

Purpose To provide financial assistance to registered nurses who are working on a bachelor's or graduate degree to prepare for a career in occupational and environmental health.

Eligibility This program is open to registered nurses who are enrolled in a baccalaureate or graduate degree program. Applicants must demonstrate an interest in, and commitment to, occupational and environmental health. Along with their application, they must submit a 500-word narrative on their professional goals as they relate to the academic activity and the field of occupational and environmental health. Selection is based on that essay (50%), impact of education on applicant's career (20%), and 2 letters of recommendation (30%).

Financial data The stipend is $3,000.

Duration 1 year; may be renewed up to 2 additional years.

Additional information Funding for this program is provided by the Alcoa Foundation.

Number awarded 2 each year.

Deadline November of each year.

[25]
ALFRED STEELE ENGINEERING SCHOLARSHIP
American Society of Plumbing Engineers
Attn: Scholarship Selection Committee
8614 West Catalpa Avenue, Suite 1007
Chicago, IL 60656-1116
(773) 693-ASPE   Fax: (773) 695-9007
E-mail: info@aspe.org
Web: www.aspe.org

Purpose To provide financial assistance for the study of engineering to members of the American Society of Plumbing Engineers (ASPE) and their families.

Eligibility This program is open to members of the society, their spouses, and children. Applicants who are already in college must be full-time students in a school or program of engineering and have a GPA of 3.0 or higher. Seniors in high school who will graduate in June of the application year are also eligible if they have a GPA of 3.0 or higher and have been accepted into a college, university, or technical school where they plan to enroll in a school or program of engineering as a full-time student. Selection is based on

GPA (1 to 5 points), letters of recommendation (10 to 15 points), personal activities and community involvement (10 to 15 points), a statement of personal achievement (15 to 30 points), and an essay on interest in engineering that demonstrates the imaginative and creative nature of the applicant (20 to 35 points).

Financial data The stipend is $1,000 per year. Funds are paid directly to the recipient's tuition account at a college, university, or technical school.

Duration 1 year.

Number awarded Up to 5 each year.

Deadline August of each year.

[26]
ALICE T. SCHAFER MATHEMATICS PRIZE

Association for Women in Mathematics
11240 Waples Mill Road, Suite 200
Fairfax, VA 22030
(703) 934-0163   Fax: (703) 359-7562
E-mail: awm@math.umd.edu
Web: www.awm-math.org/schaferprize.html

Purpose To recognize and reward undergraduate women who have demonstrated excellence in mathematics.

Eligibility Women may not apply for this award; they must be nominated by a member of the mathematical community. The nominee may be at any level in her undergraduate career. Selection is based on the quality of the student's performance in advanced mathematics courses and special programs, evidence of a real interest in mathematics, an ability to work independently, and performance in local and national mathematics competitions.

Financial data The prize is $1,000.

Duration The prize is presented annually.

Additional information This prize was first presented in 1990.

Number awarded 1 each year.

Deadline Nominations must be submitted by September of each year.

[27]
ALLEN W. PLUMB SCHOLARSHIP

New Hampshire Land Surveyors Foundation
Attn: Scholarship Committee
77 Main Street
P.O. Box 689
Raymond, NH 03077-0689
(603) 895-4822   Toll-free: (800) 698-5447
Fax: (603) 895-0157   E-mail: info@nhlsa.org
Web: www.nhlsa.org/scholarship.htm

Purpose To provide financial assistance to residents of New Hampshire who are studying forestry in college as preparation for a career in land surveying.

Eligibility This program is open to New Hampshire residents enrolled in the second, third, or fourth year of a 2-year or 4-year college program in forestry. Applicants must have shown serious interest, capability, and outstanding accomplishments in surveying courses. They must be preparing for a career in land surveying. Along with their application, they must submit an essay about their professional aspirations, their goals in college and afterwards, and factors that make them particularly deserving of support. Financial need is not required.

Financial data The stipend is $2,000.

Duration 1 year.

Number awarded 1 each year.

Deadline October of each year.

[28]
ALPHA GAMMA RHO EXCELLENCE SCHOLARSHIPS

Alpha Gamma Rho Fraternity
Attn: Educational Foundation of AGR
10101 North Ambassador Drive
Kansas City, MO 64153-1395
(816) 891-9200   Fax: (816) 891-9401
E-mail: agr@AlphaGammaRho.org
Web: www.agrs.org

Purpose To provide financial assistance to undergraduate males who belong to Alpha Gamma Rho Fraternity, a national agricultural fraternity.

Eligibility This program is open to undergraduate members of the fraternity. Selection is based on scholarship, leadership, citizenship, activities, and fraternal involvement. Brothers living in the chapter house (where applicable) are given priority in the selection process.

Financial data The stipend is $1,000.

Duration 1 year.

Number awarded Up to 4 each year.

Deadline April of each year.

[29]
AMERICAN ASSOCIATION OF OCCUPATIONAL HEALTH NURSES FOUNDATION ACADEMIC SCHOLARSHIP

American Association of Occupational Health Nurses, Inc.
Attn: AAOHN Foundation
2920 Brandywine Road, Suite 100
Atlanta, GA 30341-4146
(770) 455-7757   Fax: (770) 455-7271
E-mail: foundation@aaohn.org
Web: www.aaohn.org

Purpose To provide financial assistance to registered nurses who are working on a bachelor's or graduate degree to prepare for a career in occupational and environmental health.

Eligibility This program is open to registered nurses who are enrolled in a baccalaureate or graduate degree program. Applicants must demonstrate an interest in, and commitment to, occupational and environmental health. Along with their application, they must submit a 500-word narrative on their professional goals as they relate to the academic activity and the field of occupational and environmental health. Selection is based on that essay (50%), impact of education on applicant's career (20%), and 2 letters of recommendation (30%).

Financial data The stipend is $3,000.

Duration 1 year; may be renewed up to 2 additional years.

Number awarded 1 each year.
Deadline November of each year.

[30]
AMERICAN COUNCIL OF ENGINEERING COMPANIES SCHOLARSHIP PROGRAM
American Council of Engineering Companies
Attn: Awards Programs Director
1015 15th Street, N.W., Eighth Floor
Washington, DC 20005-2605
(202) 347-7474   Fax: (202) 898-0068
E-mail: acec@acec.org
Web: www.acec.org/awards/scholarships.cfm

Purpose To provide financial assistance to students currently working on a bachelor's degree in engineering.
Eligibility This program is open to students working on a bachelor's degree in an ABET-approved engineering program. Applicants must be U.S. citizens entering their junior, senior, or fifth year. They must have received a scholarship from a participating state Member Organization (MO) of the American Council of Engineering Companies (ACEC). Along with their application, they must submit a 500-word essay on "What is the role or responsibility of the consulting engineer or land surveyor to shaping and protecting the natural environment?" Selection is based on the essay (25 points), cumulative GPA (28 points), work experience (20 points), a letter of recommendation (17 points), and extracurricular college activities (10 points).
Financial data Stipends are $5,000 or $3,000.
Duration 1 year.
Number awarded 2 each year: the Scholar of the Year at $5,000 and the College of Fellows award at $3,000.
Deadline Participating MOs must forward applications by December of each year.

[31]
AMERICAN HELICOPTER SOCIETY STUDENT DESIGN COMPETITION
American Helicopter Society
Attn: Deputy Director
217 North Washington Street
Alexandria, VA 22314-2538
(703) 684-6777   Fax: (703) 739-9279
E-mail: Staff@vtol.org
Web: www.vtol.org/awards/sdcomp.html

Purpose To recognize and reward undergraduate and graduate students who submit outstanding designs for a helicopter.
Eligibility This competition is open to undergraduate and graduate students who may enter as individuals or as teams up to 10 members. Undergraduates and graduate students compete in separate categories. A third category is limited to new entrants from schools (graduate or undergraduate) that have not participated in at least 2 of the prior 3 competitions. Applicants must submit a completed design for a helicopter that meets annual competition specifications; recently, the program called for a mountain rescue helicopter. Selection is based on technical content (40 points), application and feasibility (25 points), originality (20 points), and organization and presentation (15 points).
Financial data Awards in the graduate category are $1,300 for first place and $650 for second. In the undergraduate category, first place is $750 and second $350. The best new entrant receives $500. The sponsor also reimburses up to $1,000 in travel expenses for the team member who presents a technical summary of the design at the international forum.
Duration The competition is held annually.
Additional information This competition was first held in 1984. The competition is sponsored by various corporations on a rotating basis: 2008, Eurocopter; 2009, Agusta Corporation; 2010, Sikorsky Aircraft Corporation.
Number awarded 5 awards are presented each year: 2 to undergraduates, 2 to graduate students, and 1 to a new entry.
Deadline Letters of intent must be submitted by February of each year.

[32]
AMERICAN METEOROLOGICAL SOCIETY UNDERGRADUATE SCHOLARSHIPS
American Meteorological Society
Attn: Fellowship/Scholarship Program
45 Beacon Street
Boston, MA 02108-3693
(617) 227-2426, ext. 246   Fax: (617) 742-8718
E-mail: scholar@ametsoc.org
Web: www.ametsoc.org

Purpose To provide financial assistance to undergraduates majoring in meteorology or an aspect of atmospheric sciences.
Eligibility This program is open to full-time students entering their final year of undergraduate study and majoring in meteorology or an aspect of the atmospheric or related oceanic and hydrologic sciences. Applicants must intend to make atmospheric or related sciences their career. They must be U.S. citizens or permanent residents enrolled at a U.S. institution and have a cumulative GPA of 3.25 or higher. Along with their application, they must submit 200-word essays on 1) their most important achievements that qualify them for this scholarship, and 2) their career goals in the atmospheric or related oceanic or hydrologic fields. Selection is based on academic excellence and achievement; financial need is not considered. The sponsor specifically encourages applications from women, minorities, and students with disabilities who are traditionally underrepresented in the atmospheric and related oceanic sciences.
Financial data Stipends range from $700 to $5,000 per year.
Duration 1 year.
Additional information This program includes the following named scholarships: the Howard H. Hanks, Jr. Scholarship in Meteorology ($700), the AMS 75th Anniversary Endowed Scholarship ($2,000), the Om and Saraswati (Sara) Bahethi Scholarship ($2,000), the Howard T. Orville Endowed Scholarship in Meteorology ($5,000), the George S. Benton Scholarship ($3,500), the Carl W. Kreitzberg Endowed Scholarship ($2,000), the Dr. Pedro Grau Undergraduate Scholarship ($2,500), the Guillermo Salazar Rodriguez Scholarship ($2,500), the John R. Hope Endowed Scholarship in Atmospheric Science ($2,500), the Richard

SCIENCES

and Helen Hagemeyer Scholarship ($3,000), the Paros-Digiquartz Scholarship ($2,500) and the Werner A. Baum Endowed Scholarship ($5,000). Requests for an application must be accompanied by a self-addressed stamped envelope.

Number awarded Varies each year; recently, 15 of these scholarships were awarded.

Deadline February of each year.

[33]
AMERICAN SOCIETY FOR ENOLOGY AND VITICULTURE SCHOLARSHIPS

American Society for Enology and Viticulture
1784 Picasso Avenue, Suite D
P.O. Box 1855
Davis, CA 95617-1855
(530) 753-3142   Fax: (530) 753-3318
E-mail: society@asev.org
Web: www.asev.org/scholarship-program

Purpose To provide financial assistance to graduate and undergraduate students interested in working on a degree in enology, viticulture, or another area related to the wine and grape industry.

Eligibility This program is open to upper-division and graduate students working on a degree in enology, viticulture, or another field emphasizing a science basic to the wine and grade industry. Applicants must be enrolled or accepted full time at a 4-year accredited college or university. They must reside in North America (including Canada and Mexico) and have earned a GPA of 3.0 or higher for undergraduates or 3.2 for graduate students. Along with their application, they must supply a written statement of intent to prepare for a career in the wine or grape industry. Financial need is not considered in the selection process.

Financial data The awards are not in predetermined amounts and may vary from year to year.

Duration Students receive quarter or semester stipends. Recipients are eligible to reapply each year in open competition with new applicants.

Number awarded Varies each year.

Deadline February of each year.

[34]
AMERICAN SOCIETY OF FARM MANAGERS AND RURAL APPRAISERS AGRICULTURAL SCHOLARSHIP

California 4-H Foundation
Attn: Youth Development Program
University of California
Agriculture and Natural Resources
One Hopkins Road
Davis, CA 95616-8575
(530) 754-8518   Fax: (530) 757-8739
E-mail: fourhstateofc@ucdavis.edu
Web: www.ca4h.org/4hresource/ir

Purpose To provide financial assistance to students in California and Nevada who have belonged to 4-H and are interested in majoring in a field related to agribusiness or education at a college in California.

Eligibility This program is open to residents of California or Nevada who are or were (at the time of their high school graduation) enrolled in the California or Nevada 4-H Youth Development Program. Applicants must have a GPA of 3.0 or higher and be high school seniors, high school graduates, or currently-enrolled college students between 16 and 25 years of age. If they are already in college, they must be enrolled full time. They must be attending or planning to attend a California 4-year university or 2-year community college to work on a degree and prepare for a career in the field of rural appraising, agricultural education, agricultural management, or agricultural financial services. Selection is based on leadership and citizenship experiences, agriculture-related 4-H project work, and future plans in agriculture.

Financial data The stipend is $1,000 for students at 4-year universities or $250 for students at 2-year community colleges. Funds are sent directly to the recipient's school.

Duration 1 year.

Additional information These scholarships, first awarded in 2006, are supported by the California chapter of the American Society of Farm Managers and Rural Appraisers (ASFMRA).

Number awarded 3 each year: 2 at $1,000 for 4-year university students and 1 at $250 for community college students.

Deadline April of each year.

[35]
AMERICAN STANDARD SCHOLARSHIPS

Plumbing-Heating-Cooling Contractors-National Association
Attn: PHCC Educational Foundation
180 South Washington Street
P.O. Box 6808
Falls Church, VA 22040
(703) 237-8100, ext. 221   Toll-free: (800) 533-7694
Fax: (703) 237-7442
E-mail: scholarships@naphcc.org
Web: www.foundation.phccweb.org

Purpose To provide financial assistance to entering or continuing undergraduate students interested in the plumbing, heating, and cooling industry.

Eligibility This program is open to 1) full-time undergraduate students (entering or continuing) who are majoring in a field related to plumbing, heating, and cooling (e.g., business management, construction management with a specialization in mechanical construction, mechanical engineering) at a 4-year college or university, and 2) students enrolled in an approved apprenticeship program or a full-time certificate or degree program at a 2-year technical college, community college, or trade school in business management, mechanical CAD design, construction management with a specialty in mechanical construction, or plumbing or HVACR installation, service, and repair. Students enrolled in an approved plumbing or HVAC apprenticeship program must be working full time for a licensed plumbing or HVAC contractor who is a member of the Plumbing-Heating-Cooling Contractors-National Association (PHCC). Applicants must submit a letter of recommendation from a member with 2 years' good standing in the PHCC; a copy of school transcripts; and a letter of recommendation from a school principal, counselor, or dean. U.S. or Canadian citizenship is required. Financial need is not considered in the selection process.

Financial data The stipend is $2,500 per year.

Duration 1 year; nonrenewable.

Additional information This program is sponsored by American Standard Companies.

Number awarded 4 each year.

Deadline May of each year.

[36] AMERICAN STAR FARMER AWARD

National FFA Organization
Attn: Star Award Program
6060 FFA Drive
P.O. Box 68960
Indianapolis, IN 46268-0960
(317) 802-4255   Fax: (317) 802-5255
E-mail: star@ffa.org
Web: www.ffa.org

Purpose To recognize and reward members of FFA who participate in a Supervised Agricultural Experience (SAE) in production agriculture.

Eligibility This program is open to current members who have been working on an SAE and have completed the degree level of Greenhand, Chapter FFA Degree, and State FFA Degree. Applicants for the American FFA Degree must have been an active member for the past 3 years, have a record of satisfactory participation in chapter and state activities, have completed the equivalent of at least 3 years of secondary school instruction in an agricultural education program or have completed the program of agricultural education offered in the secondary school last attended, have graduated from high school at least 12 months prior to the national convention at which the award is to be granted with a GPA of 2.0 or better, and have operated and maintained an SAE in production agriculture in which they have earned and productively invested at least $7,500 or at least $1,150 in combination with at least 2,250 hours of work beyond class time. The outstanding recipients of the American FFA degree are considered for these awards.

Financial data The first-place winner receives $2,000, a plaque, and a medal. Each runner-up receives $1,000 and a plaque.

Duration The competition is held annually.

Additional information Recently, approximately 1,900 members received the American FFA Degree and qualified for these awards. This program is sponsored by the National FFA Foundation, Pioneer Hi-Bred International, Inc. of Des Moines, Iowa, Case IH of Lake Forest, Illinois, and the Farm Credit System of Washington, D.C. Similar awards are offered for agricultural placement and agriscience.

Number awarded 4 each year: 1 winner and 3 runners-up.

Deadline June of each year.

[37] AMGEN BACHELOR'S SCHOLARSHIPS

Oncology Nursing Society
Attn: ONS Foundation
125 Enterprise Drive
Pittsburgh, PA 15275-1214
(412) 859-6100, ext. 8503   Toll-free: (866) 257-4ONS
Fax: (412) 859-6160   E-mail: foundation@ons.org
Web: www.ons.org

Purpose To provide financial assistance to registered nurses who are interested in working on a bachelor's degree in oncology nursing.

Eligibility This program is open to registered nurses with a demonstrated interest in and commitment to oncology nursing. Applicants must be currently enrolled in an undergraduate degree program at an NLN- or CCNE-accredited school of nursing. They may not have previously received a bachelor's level scholarship from this sponsor. Applicants must submit an essay of 250 words or less on their role in caring for persons with cancer and a statement of their professional goals and their relationship to the advancement of oncology nursing. Financial need is not considered in the selection process.

Financial data The stipend is $2,000.

Duration 1 year.

Additional information This program, supported by Amgen, Inc., began in 2005. At the end of each year of scholarship participation, recipients must submit a summary describing their educational activities. Applications must be accompanied by a $5 fee.

Number awarded 2 each year.

Deadline January of each year.

[38] ANAC STUDENT DIVERSITY MENTORSHIP SCHOLARSHIP

Association of Nurses in AIDS Care
3538 Ridgewood Road
Akron, OH 44333
(330) 670-0101   Toll-free: (800) 260-6780
Fax: (330) 670-0109   E-mail: anac@anacnet.org
Web: www.anacnet.org/programs_pubs-awards.php

Purpose To provide financial assistance to student nurses from minority groups who are interested in HIV/AIDS nursing and in attending the national conference of the Association of Nurses in AIDS Care (ANAC).

Eligibility This program is open to student nurses from a diverse racial or ethnic background, defined to include African Americans, Hispanics/Latinos, Asians/Pacific Islanders, and American Indians/Alaskan Natives. Candidates must have a genuine interest in HIV/AIDS nursing, be interested in attending the ANAC national conference, and desire to develop a mentorship relationship with a member of the ANAC Diversity Specialty Committee. They must be currently enrolled in an accredited nursing program at any level (e.g., L.P.N., A.D.N., diploma, B.S.N., or graduate nursing). Nominees may be recommended by themselves, nursing faculty, or an ANAC member, but their nomination must be supported by an ANAC member. Along with their nomination form, they must submit a 500-word personal statement describing their interest or experience in HIV/AIDS care and why they want to attend the ANAC conference.

Financial data Recipients are awarded a $1,000 scholarship (paid directly to the school), up to $599 in reimbursement of travel expenses to attend the ANAC annual conference, free conference registration, an award plaque, a free ticket to the awards ceremony at the conference, and a 1-year ANAC membership.

Duration 1 year.

Additional information The mentor will be assigned at the conference and will maintain contact during the period of study.

Number awarded 1 each year.

Deadline May of each year.

[39]
ANGUS FOUNDATION SCHOLARSHIPS

National Junior Angus Association
Attn: Director Junior Activities
3201 Frederick Avenue
St. Joseph, MO 64506
(816) 383-5100   Fax: (816) 233-9703
E-mail: info@njaa.info
Web: www.angusfoundation.org

Purpose To provide financial assistance to students who have been members of the National Junior Angus Association (NJAA) and are enrolled or planning to enroll in any field in college.

Eligibility Applicants must have been a member of the NJAA in the past and presently must be a junior, regular, or life member of the American Angus Association. They must be either a high school senior or already enrolled in college working full time on an undergraduate degree with a GPA of 2.0 or higher and younger than 25 years of age. All fields of study are eligible. Selection is based on involvement in Angus associations, other agriculture-related associations, school organizations, and church, civic, and community groups.

Financial data The stipends are $5,000, $3,000, or $1,000.

Duration 1 year. The $3,000 and $1,000 awards are renewable, but the $5,000 awards are for 1 year only and recipients may not reapply.

Additional information This program, established in 1997, is sponsored by the Angus Foundation. the $5,000 awards are designated as the Richard "Dick" Spader Scholarships.

Number awarded 52 each year: 2 at $5,000, 20 at $3,000, and 30 at $1,000.

Deadline April of each year.

[40]
ANITA BORG SCHOLARSHIPS

Google Inc.
Attn: Scholarships
1600 Amphitheatre Parkway
Mountain View, CA 94043-8303
(650) 623-4000   Fax: (650) 618-1499
E-mail: anitaborgscholars@google.com
Web: www.google.com/anitaborg

Purpose To provide financial assistance to women working on a bachelor's or graduate degree in a computer-related field.

Eligibility This program is open to women who are entering their senior year of undergraduate study or are enrolled in a graduate program in computer science, computer engineering, or a related field. Applicants must be full-time students at a university in the United States with a GPA of 3.5 or higher. They must submit essays of 400 to 600 words on 1) a significant technical project on which they have worked; 2) examples of their leadership abilities; 3) what they would do if someone gave them the funding and resources for a 3- to 12-month project to investigate a technical topic of their choice; and 4) what they would do if someone gave them $1,000 to plan an event or project to benefit women in technical fields. Selection is based on academic background and demonstrated leadership.

Financial data The stipend is $10,000.

Duration 1 year.

Additional information These scholarships were first offered in 2004.

Number awarded Varies each year. Recently, 4 of these scholarships were awarded: 1 to an undergraduate, 2 to master's degree candidates, and 1 to a doctoral candidate.

Deadline January of each year.

[41]
ANNE MAUREEN WHITNEY BARROW MEMORIAL SCHOLARSHIP

Society of Women Engineers
230 East Ohio Street, Suite 400
Chicago, IL 60611-3265
(312) 596-5223   Toll-free: (877) SWE-INFO
Fax: (312) 644-8557
E-mail: scholarshipapplication@swe.org
Web: www.swe.org/scholarships

Purpose To provide financial assistance to women interested in studying engineering or engineering technology in college.

Eligibility This program is open to women who are enrolled or planning to enroll full time at an ABET-accredited 4-year college or university. Applicants must have a GPA of 3.0 or higher and be planning to major in engineering or engineering technology. Along with their application, they must submit a 1-page essay on why they want to be an engineer, how they believe they will make a difference as an engineer, and what influenced them to study engineering. Selection is based on merit.

Financial data The stipend is $5,000.

Duration 1 year; may be renewed for 3 additional years.

Additional information This program was established in 1992.

Number awarded 1 every 4 years.
Deadline May of the years in which it is offered.

[42]
ANNIE'S ENVIRONMENTAL STUDIES SCHOLARSHIPS

Annie's Homegrown, Inc.
Attn: Consumer Relations
564 Gateway Drive
Napa, CA 94558
Toll-free: (800) 288-1089   E-mail: cfc@annies.com
Web: www.annies.com

Purpose To provide financial assistance to entering or continuing undergraduate and graduate students working on a degree in environmental studies.
Eligibility This program is open to students beginning or returning to an accredited 2-year or 4-year technical or college program and majoring in the environmental studies field. Graduate students are also eligible. Applicants must include a personal statement in which they answer 1 of 3 assigned questions that change annually. Selection is based on that statement, a transcript, 2 letters of recommendation, and a brief telephone interview. Financial need is not considered.
Financial data The stipend is $1,000.
Duration 1 year.
Number awarded Varies each year; recently, 13 undergraduates and 10 graduate students received these scholarships.
Deadline August of each year.

[43]
ANS UNDERGRADUATE SCHOLARSHIPS

American Nuclear Society
Attn: Scholarship Coordinator
555 North Kensington Avenue
La Grange Park, IL 60526-5592
(708) 352-6611   Fax: (708) 352-0499
E-mail: outreach@ans.org
Web: www.ans.org/honors/scholarships

Purpose To provide financial assistance to undergraduate students who are interested in preparing for a career in nuclear science or nuclear engineering.
Eligibility Eligible to apply are undergraduate students enrolled in nuclear science, nuclear engineering, or a nuclear-related field at an accredited institution in the United States. There are separate competitions for 1) students who have completed at least 1 academic year and who will be sophomores, and 2) students who have completed 2 or more years and will be entering as juniors or seniors. All applicants must be U.S. citizens or permanent residents and be able to demonstrate academic achievement.
Financial data The stipend is $2,000.
Duration 1 year; nonrenewable.
Additional information This program includes the following named scholarships: the Angelo S. Bisesti Memorial Scholarship, the Joseph R. Dietrich Memorial Scholarship, the Raymond DiSalvo Memorial Scholarship, the Robert G. Lacy Memorial Scholarship, the John R. Lamarsh Memorial Scholarship, and the Robert T. Liner Memorial Scholarship.

Number awarded 31 each year: 4 for students entering their sophomore year and 27 (including the 6 named scholarships plus 21 others) for students entering their junior or senior year.
Deadline January of each year.

[44]
A.O. SMITH WATER HEATERS SCHOLARSHIP

Plumbing-Heating-Cooling Contractors-National Association
Attn: PHCC Educational Foundation
180 South Washington Street
P.O. Box 6808
Falls Church, VA 22040
(703) 237-8100, ext. 221   Toll-free: (800) 533-7694
Fax: (703) 237-7442
E-mail: scholarships@naphcc.org
Web: www.foundation.phccweb.org

Purpose To provide financial assistance to entering or continuing undergraduate students interested in the plumbing, heating, and cooling industry.
Eligibility This program is open to 1) full-time undergraduate students (entering or continuing) who are majoring in a field related to plumbing, heating, and cooling (e.g., business management, construction management with a specialization in mechanical construction, mechanical engineering) at a 4-year college or university, and 2) students enrolled in an approved apprenticeship program or a full-time certificate or degree program at a 2-year technical college, community college, or trade school in business management, mechanical CAD design, construction management with a specialty in mechanical construction, or plumbing or HVACR installation, service, and repair. Students enrolled in an approved plumbing or HVAC apprenticeship program must be working full time for a licensed plumbing or HVAC contractor who is a member of the Plumbing-Heating-Cooling Contractors-National Association (PHCC). Applicants must submit a letter of recommendation from a member with 2 years' good standing in the PHCC; a copy of school transcripts; and a letter of recommendation from a school principal, counselor, or dean. U.S. or Canadian citizenship is required. Financial need is not considered in the selection process.
Financial data The stipend is $2,500 per year.
Duration 1 year; nonrenewable.
Additional information This program is sponsored by A.O. Smith Water Heaters.
Number awarded 1 each year.
Deadline May of each year.

[45]
APS SCHOLARSHIPS FOR MINORITY UNDERGRADUATE STUDENTS WHO MAJOR IN PHYSICS

American Physical Society
Attn: Committee on Minorities
One Physics Ellipse
College Park, MD 20740-3844
(301) 209-3232   Fax: (301) 209-0865
Web: www.aps.org

Purpose To provide financial assistance to underrepresented minority students interested in studying physics on the undergraduate level.

Eligibility Any African American, Hispanic American, or Native American who plans to major in physics and who is a high school senior or college freshman or sophomore may apply. U.S. citizenship or permanent resident status is required. The selection committee especially encourages applications from students who are attending or planning to attend institutions with historically or predominantly Black, Hispanic, or Native American enrollment. Selection is based on commitment to the study of physics and plans to work on a physics baccalaureate degree.

Financial data Stipends are $2,000 per year in the first year or $3,000 in the second year; funds must be used for tuition, room, and board. In addition, $500 is awarded to the host department.

Duration 1 year; renewable for 1 additional year with the approval of the APS selection committee.

Additional information APS conducts this program, which began in 1980 as the Corporate-Sponsored Scholarships for Minority Undergraduate Students Who Major in Physics, in conjunction with the Corporate Associates of the American Institute of Physics. Each scholarship is sponsored by a corporation, which is normally designated as the sponsor. A corporation generally sponsors from 1 to 10 scholarships, depending upon its size and utilization of physics in the business.

Number awarded Varies each year; recently, 26 of these scholarships were awarded.

Deadline January of each year.

[46]
AQUATROLS ESSAY CONTEST

Aquatrols Corporation
1273 Imperial Way
Paulsboro, NJ 08066
(856) 537-6003   Toll-free: (800) 257-7797
Fax: (856) 537-6018
E-mail: essay.contest@aquatrols.com
Web: www.aquatrols.com

Purpose To recognize and reward, with college scholarships, students whose parents are employed in a turf or landscape management capacity and who submit outstanding essays on a related subject.

Eligibility This competition is open to children of employees in a turf or landscape management capacity. Applicants must be enrolled or planning to enroll in an undergraduate program. They must submit an original essay of 1,500 to 2,000 words on a topic that changes annually; recently, students were invited to write on "The role of surfactants in enhancing water use and/or irrigation efficiency." Essays should be original, compelling, well-organized, readable, persuasive, and creative. Technical accuracy, composition skills, and adherence to contest rules are also considered.

Financial data First prize is a $2,000 scholarship and second prize is a $1,000 scholarship.

Duration The contest is held annually.

Number awarded 2 each year.

Deadline February of each year.

[47]
ARC OF WASHINGTON TRUST FUND STIPEND AWARD PROGRAM

ARC of Washington Trust Fund
c/o Neal Lessenger, Secretary
P.O. Box 27028
Seattle, WA 98125-1428
(206) 363-2206   E-mail: arcwatrust@charter.net
Web: www.arcwa.org/student_grants.htm

Purpose To provide financial assistance to undergraduate and graduate students in northwestern states who have a career interest in work relating to mental retardation.

Eligibility This program is open to upper-division and graduate students in schools in Washington, Oregon, Alaska, and Idaho who have a demonstrated interest in the field of mental retardation or other developmental or intellectual disabilities. Applicants must submit a statement of interest in the field of mental retardation or closely-related field, academic and other qualifications, achievements, immediate and long-term goals, and letters of endorsement from at least 2 faculty sponsors. Financial need is not considered in the selection process.

Financial data The stipend is $5,000 per year, paid in 4 equal installments. Funds are sent to the recipient's school and must be used for tuition, books, and general living expenses.

Duration 1 year.

Number awarded Several each year.

Deadline February of each year.

[48]
ARC WELDING AWARDS—DIVISION II

James F. Lincoln Arc Welding Foundation
Attn: Secretary
22801 Saint Clair Avenue
P.O. Box 17188
Cleveland, OH 44117-1199
(216) 481-8100   Fax: (216) 486-1751
E-mail: innovate@lincolnelectric.com
Web: www.jflf.org/awards/division2.asp

Purpose To recognize and reward students older than 18 years of age who submit outstanding arc welding problems.

Eligibility This program is open to students older than 18 years of age other than college students studying for a bachelor's or master's degree. Applicants may be enrolled in evening adult classes, high schools, vocational schools, private trade schools, in-plant training classes, technical institutes, apprenticeship programs, junior colleges, community colleges, or other 2-year college courses. They must submit a problem concerned with the use and knowledge of arc welding. It may involve the use of a welding technique, process or material, joint design, testing, welding procedure, tooling, or fixturing. Entries must be submitted as a 3- to 25-page written description of the problem; drawings, photographs, and sketches are encouraged, but models or specimens may not be submitted. Written entries must have been completed during the previous 12-month period. Selection is based on the practicality or usefulness of the problem, how well the use or knowledge of arc welding was applied, the skill and ability with which the problem was completed, how clearly the problem is described, and how well the entry conforms to requirements.

Financial data The gold award is $1,000, the silver award is $500, the bronze award is $250, and merit awards are $50. A special award of an additional $1,000 is presented to the winner, regardless of region, that has a shop-related welding project.

Duration The competition is held annually.

Number awarded 1 gold award, 2 silver awards, 3 bronze awards, 40 merit awards, and 1 special award are presented each year.

Deadline May of each year.

[49]
ARC WELDING AWARDS—DIVISION IV
James F. Lincoln Arc Welding Foundation
Attn: Secretary
22801 Saint Clair Avenue
P.O. Box 17188
Cleveland, OH 44117-1199
(216) 481-8100   Fax: (216) 486-1751
E-mail: innovate@lincolnelectric.com
Web: www.jflf.org/awards/division4.asp

Purpose To recognize and reward engineering and technology undergraduate and graduate students who submit outstanding papers involving the knowledge or application of arc welding.

Eligibility This competition is open to undergraduate and graduate students enrolled in a 4-year engineering or technology program at an accredited college or university in the United States. Participants must submit papers representing their work on design, engineering, or fabrication problems relating to 1) any type of building, bridge, or other generally stationary structure; 2) any type of machine, project, or mechanical apparatus; or 3) arc welding research, testing, procedure, or process development. Applicants may participate as individuals or in groups of up to 10 students. Reports prepared for course work, projects, or theses are eligible. Any number of entries may be submitted from 1 school, but no student may participate in more than 1 entry. Selection is based on originality or ingenuity, feasibility, results achieved or expected, engineering competence, and clarity of the presentation.

Financial data The most outstanding entry receives the Chairman's Award of $1,000.

Duration The competition is held annually.

Additional information This program began in 1936.

Number awarded 1 each year.

Deadline June of each year.

[50]
AREMA EDUCATIONAL FOUNDATION UNDERGRADUATE SCHOLARSHIPS
American Railway Engineering and Maintenance of Way Association
Attn: AREMA Educational Foundation Scholarship Committee
10003 Derekwood Lane, Suite 210
Lanham, MD 20706
(301) 459-3200, ext. 706   Fax: (301) 459-8077
E-mail: selder@arema.org
Web: www.arema.org

Purpose To provide financial assistance to undergraduate students who are interested in preparing for a career in railway engineering.

Eligibility This program is open to full-time undergraduate students at ABET-accredited 4-year or 5-year programs (or comparably accredited programs in Canada or Mexico) leading to a bachelor's degree in engineering or engineering technology. Applicants must have completed at least 1 quarter or semester and have a GPA of 2.0 or higher. They must be interested in a career in railway engineering. Along with their application, they must submit a resume, official transcript, 2 letters of recommendation, and a 350-word cover letter explaining why they believe they are deserving of this scholarship. Financial need is not considered in the selection process.

Financial data Stipends range from $1,000 to $6,000.

Duration 1 year.

Additional information This program receives support from the Burlington Northern Santa Fe Foundation.

Number awarded Varies each year. Recently, 11 of these scholarships were awarded: 1 at $6,000, 1 at $3,000, 1 at $1,500, and 8 at $1,000.

Deadline March of each year.

[51]
ARKANSAS GAME AND FISH SCHOLARSHIP
Arkansas Game and Fish Commission
Attn: Human Resources Division
Two Natural Resources Drive
Little Rock, AR 72205
(501) 223-6317   Toll-free: (800) 364-4263
Web: www.agfc.com

Purpose To provide financial assistance to high school seniors, undergraduates, and graduate students from Arkansas interested in preparing for a career in fish and wildlife management.

Eligibility Applicants must be Arkansas high school seniors or Arkansas college undergraduates or graduate students interested in preparing for a career in the field of natural resource conservation and/or wildlife law enforcement, including fishery management, wildlife management, public relations, environmental education and interpretation, and related fields. They must be Arkansas residents, have at least a 2.5 GPA, and intend to attend school on a full-time basis. Along with their application, they must submit essays of 150 words on how their field of study relates to natural resource conservation and their choice as a possible career; of 200 words on their accomplishments in leadership roles; of 100 words on their outdoor-related work or volunteer experience; of 300 words on their philosophy of fish and wildlife conservation as it relates to environmental stewardship; and of 200 words on their career goals. Selection is based solely on merit. Full-time employees of the Arkansas Game and Fish Commission, their spouses, and their children are not eligible for these scholarships.

Financial data The stipend is $2,000 per year for freshmen and sophomores or $3,000 per year for juniors, seniors, and graduate students. Funds are to be used for tuition, books, fees, and lodging.

Duration 1 year; may be renewed for up to 4 additional years.

Additional information Applicants may not have received a full scholarship from another source. They must attend or be accepted for admission at an accredited 4-year college or university in the state.

Number awarded 25 each year.

Deadline June of each year.

[52]
ARNOLD SADLER MEMORIAL SCHOLARSHIP

American Council of the Blind
Attn: Coordinator, Scholarship Program
1155 15th Street, N.W., Suite 1004
Washington, DC 20005
(202) 467-5081   Toll-free: (800) 424-8666
Fax: (202) 467-5085   E-mail: info@acb.org
Web: www.acb.org

Purpose To provide financial assistance to undergraduate or graduate students who are blind and are interested in studying in a field of service to persons with disabilities.

Eligibility This program is open to students in rehabilitation, education, law, or other fields of service to persons with disabilities. Applicants must be legally blind and U.S. citizens. In addition to letters of recommendation and copies of academic transcripts, applications must include an autobiographical sketch. A cumulative GPA of 3.3 or higher is generally required. Selection is based on demonstrated academic record, involvement in extracurricular and civic activities, and academic objectives. The severity of the applicant's visual impairment and his/her study methods are also taken into account.

Financial data The stipend is $2,000. In addition, the winner receives a Kurzweil-1000 Reading System.

Duration 1 year.

Additional information This scholarship is funded by the Arnold Sadler Memorial Scholarship Fund. Scholarship winners are expected to be present at the council's annual conference; the council will cover all reasonable expenses connected with convention attendance.

Number awarded 1 each year.

Deadline February of each year.

[53]
ARTHUR T. SCHRAMM MEMORIAL SCHOLARSHIP

Institute of Food Technologists
Attn: Scholarship Department
525 West Van Buren, Suite 1000
Chicago, IL 60607
(312) 782-8424   Fax: (312) 782-8348
E-mail: info@ift.org
Web: www.ift.org

Purpose To provide financial assistance to undergraduates interested in studying food science or food technology.

Eligibility This program is open to sophomores, juniors, and seniors in a food science or food technology program at an educational institution in the United States or Canada. Applicants must have an outstanding scholastic record and a well-rounded personality. Along with their application, they must submit an essay on their career aspirations; a list of awards, honors, and scholarships they have received; a list of extracurricular activities and/or hobbies; and a summary of their work experience. Financial need is not considered in the selection process.

Financial data The stipend is $2,250.

Duration 1 year; recipients may reapply if they are members of the Institute of Food Technologists (IFT).

Additional information Correspondence and completed applications must be submitted to the department head of the educational institution the applicant is attending.

Number awarded 1 each year.

Deadline January of each year.

[54]
ARTHUR W. PENSE SCHOLARSHIP

NYSARC, Inc.
393 Delaware Avenue
Delmar, NY 12054
(518) 439-8311   Fax: (518) 439-1893
E-mail: info@nysarc.org
Web: www.nysarc.org

Purpose To provide financial assistance to currently-enrolled college students in New York majoring in occupational or physical therapy.

Eligibility Nominations for this funding are to be submitted through the departments of physical or occupational therapy at the various colleges and universities in New York. Nominees must be working on a 4- or 5-year degree program leading to a career in physical or occupational therapy. They must be at least at the sophomore level. Financial need is not considered in the selection process.

Financial data The stipend is $1,500 per year.

Duration 2 years.

Additional information NYSARC, Inc. was formerly the New York State Association for Retarded Children.

Number awarded 1 each year.

Deadline Nominations must be submitted by November of each year.

[55]
ASCE/AISC STUDENT STEEL BRIDGE COMPETITION

American Institute of Steel Construction
Attn: Director of University Relations
1 East Wacker Drive, Suite 700
Chicago, IL 60601-1802
(312) 670-5408   Fax: (312) 670-5403
E-mail: rosenberg@aisc.com
Web: www.aisc.org

Purpose To recognize and reward outstanding student entries in a national steel bridge competition.

Eligibility This competition is open to teams of undergraduate and graduate student members of the American Society of Civil Engineers (ASCE). Applicants are required to design, fabricate, and construct a steel bridge, based on specified site conditions, spans, member sizes, weight limitations, and design loads representative of a real bridge. Winning teams and first runners-up from each region are invited to compete at the national level (invitations are extended only to the winner if the region has only 2 to 4 participating universities, and to the top 3 teams if the region has 11 or more participating universities).

Financial data Each university entering a steel bridge in any regional competition receives $175 from the sponsor. The regional host university receives $500, to assist with expenses incurred in organizing the regional Student Steel Bridge Competition. On the national level, the first-place team from each region receives $1,000 and the second-place team from each region receives $500.

Duration The competition is held annually.

Additional information This competition, first held in 1992, is sponsored by the American Institute of Steel Construction (AISC) with support from the ASCE, American Iron and Steel Institute, National Steel Bridge Alliance, James F. Lincoln Arc Welding Foundation, and Nucor Corporation. There is a $65 registration fee.

Number awarded On the national level: 2 winning teams from each region are selected each year.

Deadline April of each year.

[56]
ASCLS-PA MEMORIAL UNDERGRADUATE SCHOLARSHIP

American Society for Clinical Laboratory Science-
  Pennsylvania
P.O. Box 284
Camp Hill, Pa 17001
Toll-free: (800) 484-1002, ext. 4767
E-mail: bsnyderman@msn.com
Web: ascls-pa.org/scholarships.htm

Purpose To provide financial assistance to student members of the American Society for Clinical Laboratory Science (ASCLS) in Pennsylvania.

Eligibility This program is open to ASCLS-PA student members who are enrolled in a laboratory technologist/technician program approved by the National Accrediting Agency for Clinical Laboratory Sciences. Applicants must submit a current official college transcript, a short essay (up to 500 words) on why they deserve the award (including their academic performance, extracurricular activities, and community and professional interests), and 2 letters of recommendation.

Financial data A stipend is awarded (amount not specified). Funds are paid directly to the recipient.

Duration 1 year.

Additional information This program is dedicated to former ASCLS-PA presidents Mercedes T. Cole and Sandra L. Keener. The sponsor was formerly the Pennsylvania Society for Clinical Laboratory Science. Information is also available from Nellie Bering, 4000 Gypsy Lane, Unit 342, Philadelphia, PA 19129-5424.

Number awarded 1 each year.

Deadline January of each year.

[57]
ASEI UNDERGRADUATE SCHOLARSHIPS

American Society of Engineers of Indian Origin
c/o Ramu Ramamurthy, Scholarship Committee Chair
47790 Pavillon Road
Canton, MI 48188
(248) 226-6895   Fax: (248) 226-7166
E-mail: awards@aseimichigan.org.
Web: www.aseisocal.org/scholarships.html

Purpose To provide financial assistance to undergraduate students of Indian origin (from India) who are majoring in architecture, engineering, or related areas.

Eligibility This program is open to undergraduate students of Indian origin (by birth, ancestry, or relation). They must be enrolled full time at an accredited college or university in the United States and majoring in engineering, architecture, computer science, or allied science with a GPA of 3.2 or higher. They must be members of the American Society of Engineers of Indian Origin (ASEI) Selection is based on demonstrated ability, academic achievement (including GPA, honors, and awards), career objectives, faculty recommendations, involvement in science fair and campus activities, and industrial exposure (including part-time work and internships).

Financial data Stipends range from $500 to $1,000.

Duration 1 year.

Number awarded Several each year.

Deadline July of each year.

[58]
ASHRAE STUDENT DESIGN PROJECT COMPETITION

American Society of Heating, Refrigerating and Air-
  Conditioning Engineers, Inc.
Attn: Manager of Student Activities
1791 Tullie Circle, N.E.
Atlanta, GA 30329-2305
(404) 539-1212   Fax: (404) 321-5478
E-mail: apruett@ashrae.org
Web: www.ashrae.org

Purpose To recognize and reward outstanding student designs in a competition involving heating, ventilating, and air conditioning (HVAC) engineering.

Eligibility Undergraduate architecture and engineering students are invited to submit entries in 3 categories: architectural system design, HVAC system selection, and HVAC system design. Judging criteria are, for architectural system design: design objectives (40%), project requirements (10%), project goals (40%), and communication of results (10%); for HVAC system selection: performance matrix evaluation criteria (10%), life cycle (10%), environmental impact (10%), comfort and health (10%), synergy with architecture (10%), creativity (10%), and communication of results (40%); for HVAC system design: life cycle cost (20%), environmental impact (20%), creativity (30%), and communication of results (30%). Students entering the architectural competition use site plans and criteria provided by the American Society of Heating, Refrigerating and Air-Conditioning Engineers (ASHRAE) to generate their building designs. Both the HVAC system selection groups and the HVAC system design groups must prepare their designs using CADD-generated architectural plans provided by ASHRAE.

Financial data In each of the 3 categories, the first-place team receives $1,500 and 1 of its representatives receives free transportation, 2 nights' lodging, and up to $100 in expenses to attend the ASHRAE winter meeting where the award is presented. The second-place and third-place team in each category also are entitled to send a representative to that meeting, with ASHRAE providing transportation, 2 nights' lodging, and up to $100 in expenses.

Duration The competition is held annually.

Number awarded 3 teams (1 in each category) receive cash prizes; 9 individual team members (3 in each category) receive funds to attend the meeting.

Deadline May of each year.

[59]
ASHRAE UNDERGRADUATE SENIOR PROJECT GRANTS

American Society of Heating, Refrigerating and Air-
  Conditioning Engineers, Inc.
Attn: Manager of Student Activities
1791 Tullie Circle, N.E.
Atlanta, GA 30329-2305
(404) 539-1212   Fax: (404) 321-5478
E-mail: apruett@ashrae.org
Web: www.ashrae.org

Purpose To provide funding to architecture and engineering students interested in working on a senior project on a topic of interest to the American Society of Heating, Refrigerating and Air-Conditioning Engineers (ASHRAE).

Eligibility This program is open to architecture, engineering, and engineering technology students in the final year of an undergraduate or 2-year technical school program who wish to work on a senior project on an ASHRAE-related topic. Students may participate as individuals or groups, but their application must be submitted by a faculty member responsible for a project the students plan to complete. Projects involving the building of working models, test equipment, experimental teaching aids, and laboratory experiments are encouraged. Projects involving only data collection, computer modeling, or computer programming receive lower priority. Selection is based on relevance of topic to ASHRAE (20%), adherence to guidelines (20%), quality of the student experience (20%), number of students participating (20%), and appropriateness of funding request (20%).

Financial data The maximum grant is $5,000. Funds may be used only for materials and supplies. University overhead and faculty or student salaries are not supported.

Duration 1 academic term to 1 year.

Number awarded Varies each year; recently, 22 of these grants were awarded.

Deadline November of each year.

[60]
ASHS SCHOLARS AWARD

American Society for Horticultural Science
113 South West Street, Suite 200
Alexandria, VA 22314-2851
(703) 836-4606   Fax: (703) 836-2024
E-mail: ashs@ashs.org
Web: www.ashs.org/awards/student.html

Purpose To provide financial assistance to undergraduate students majoring in horticulture.

Eligibility This program is open to full-time undergraduate students of any class standing who are actively working on a degree in horticulture at a 4-year college or university. Applicants must be nominated by the chair of the department in which they are majoring; each department may nominate only 1 student. They must submit transcripts, 3 letters of reference, a complete resume and/or vitae, and an essay of 250 to 500 words on their reasons for interest in horticulture and for selecting their intended field of work after graduation. Selection is based on academic excellence in the major and supporting areas of science; participation in extracurricular, leadership, and research activities relating to horticulture; participation in university and community service; demonstrated commitment to the horticultural science profession and related career fields; and related horticultural experiences. Financial need is not considered.

Financial data The stipend is $1,500.

Duration 1 year.

Additional information This program was established in 2001.

Number awarded 2 each year.

Deadline February of each year.

[61]
ASME FOUNDATION SCHOLARSHIPS

ASME International
Attn: Coordinator, Educational Operations
Three Park Avenue
New York, NY 10016-5990
(212) 591-8131   Toll-free: (800) THE-ASME
Fax: (212) 591-7143   E-mail: OluwanifiseK@asme.org
Web: www.asme.org

Purpose To provide financial assistance to undergraduate students who are members of the American Society of Mechanical Engineers (ASME).

Eligibility This program is open to student members in good standing who are enrolled in an ABET-accredited mechanical engineering program, mechanical engineering technology program, or related program. They must be entering their sophomore, junior, or senior year of study. Applicants should submit a nomination from their department head, a recommendation from a faculty member, and an official transcript. Only 1 nomination may be submitted per department. There are no geographic or citizenship limitations. Selection is based on scholastic ability and potential contribution to the mechanical engineering profession.

Financial data The stipend is $1,500.

Duration 1 year.

Additional information This program was established in 1999.

Number awarded 16 each year.

Deadline March of each year.

[62]
ASME STUDENT DESIGN CONTEST

ASME International
Attn: Student Center
Three Park Avenue
New York, NY 10016-5990
(212) 591-8131   Toll-free: (800) THE-ASME
Fax: (212) 591-7143   E-mail: OluwanifiseK@asme.org
Web: www.asme.org

Purpose To recognize and reward outstanding designs by student members of the American Society of Mechanical Engineers (ASME).

Eligibility This competition is open to student members of the society who have not yet received their first engineering degree. They may enter as individuals, but teams of 2 to 4 members are encouraged. Regional winners compete on the national level. Each year, a problem statement for a mechanical design is presented and students complete a design that meets the specifications of the problem. A recent problem involved a human-powered potable water still.

Financial data Within each region, the first-place winner receives $200, a trophy, and up to $1,000 travel allowance to participate in the finals; the second-place winner receives $100 and a plaque; and the third-place winner receives $50 and a plaque. The national first-place winner receives $3,000 and $1,000 for the student section at their institution; the second-place winner receives $1,000 and $500 for the student section at their institution; the third-place winner receives $500 and $250 for the student section at their institution.

Duration The competition is held annually.

Additional information Applications are submitted to the 12 regional student conferences; students in Region XIII (all the world except for the United States, Canada, and Mexico) submit applications to ASME International. Major funding is provided by the Boeing Company.

Number awarded 3 winners in the national finals and 3 in each regional student conference.

Deadline Each region sets its own deadline; for Region XIII, the deadline is in June of each year.

[63]
ASSOCIATION FOR IRON & STEEL TECHNOLOGY SCHOLARSHIPS

Association for Iron & Steel Technology
Attn: AIST Foundation
186 Thorn Hill Road
Warrendale, PA 15086-7528
(724) 776-6040, ext. 621   Fax: (724) 776-1880
E-mail: lwharrey@aist.org
Web: www.aist.org/foundation/scholarships.htm

Purpose To provide financial assistance for college to students interested in preparing for a career in the iron and steel or steel-related industries.

Eligibility This program is open to full-time students majoring in metallurgy, materials science, or engineering at accredited universities in North America. Applicants must have a GPA of 3.0 or higher and a demonstrated interest in the iron and steel industry. Along with their application, they must submit 3 letters of recommendation; a resume with work experience and extracurricular activities, noting any leadership positions; a current academic transcript; and a 2-page essay on their professional goals, explaining why they are interested in a career in the steel industry and how their skills could be applied to enhance the industry. Financial need is not considered in the selection process.

Financial data The stipend is $2,000.

Duration 1 year; recipients may reapply.

Additional information The AIST was formed in 2004 by the merger of the Iron and Steel Society (ISS) and the Association of Iron and Steel Engineers (AISE).

Number awarded 7 each year, including 3 Willy Korf Memorial Fund Scholarships, 2 Ronald E. Lincoln Memorial Scholarship, and 2 Benjamin F. Fairless Scholarships.

Deadline April of each year.

[64]
ASSOCIATION FOR WOMEN GEOSCIENTISTS MINORITY SCHOLARSHIP

Association for Women Geoscientists
Attn: AWG Foundation
P.O. Box 30645
Lincoln, NE 68503-0645
E-mail: minorityscholarship@awg.org
Web: www.awg.org/eas/minority.html

Purpose To provide financial assistance to minority women who are interested in working on an undergraduate degree in the geosciences.

Eligibility This program is open to women who are African American, Hispanic, or Native American (including Eskimo, Hawaiian, Samoan, or American Indian). Applicants must be full-time students working on, or planning to work on, an undergraduate degree in the geosciences (including geology, geophysics, geochemistry, hydrology, meteorology, physical oceanography, planetary geology, or earth science education). They must submit a 500-word essay on why they have chosen to major in the geosciences and their career goals, 2 letters of recommendation, high school and/or college transcripts, and SAT or ACT scores. Financial need is not considered in the selection process.

Financial data A total of $5,000 is available for this program each year.

Duration 1 year; may be renewed.
Additional information This program, first offered in 2004, is supported by ExxonMobil Foundation.
Number awarded 1 or more each year.
Deadline May of each year.

[65]
ASSOCIATION OF CUBAN ENGINEERS SCHOLARSHIPS

Association of Cuban Engineers
Attn: Selection Committee
P.O. Box 557575
Miami, FL 33255-7575
(305) 649-7429
Web: www.a-i-c.org

Purpose To provide financial assistance to undergraduate and graduate students of Cuban American heritage who are interested in preparing for a career in engineering.
Eligibility This program is open to U.S. citizens and legal residents who have completed at least 30 units of college work in the United States and are majoring or planning to major in some aspect of engineering. Applicants must be attending an ABET-accredited college or university within the United States or Puerto Rico as a full-time student with a GPA of 3.0 or higher. They must be of Cuban or other Hispanic heritage (at least 1 grandparent Cuban or other Hispanic nationality). Along with their application, they must submit brief essays on their family history, professional goals, extracurricular activities, work experience, and how they will help other Cuban and Hispanic engineering students in the future. Financial need is not considered in the selection process.
Financial data Stipends range from $500 to $1,000.
Duration 1 year.
Additional information This program includes the Luciano Goicochea Award (for the top-rated Cuban American student at the University of Miami) and the Noel Betancourt Award (for the top-rated Cuban American student at Florida International University).
Number awarded Up to 20 each year.
Deadline November of each year.

[66]
ASSOCIATION OF REHABILITATION NURSES BSN SCHOLARSHIP

Association of Rehabilitation Nurses
Attn: Scholarship Program
4700 West Lake Avenue
Glenview, IL 60025-1485
(847) 375-4710   Toll-free: (800) 229-7530
Fax: (888) 458-0456   E-mail: info@rehabnurse.org
Web: www.rehabnurse.org/awards/allscholar.html

Purpose To provide financial assistance to members of the Association of Rehabilitation Nurses (ARN) who are working on a bachelor's degree in nursing.
Eligibility This program is open to ARN members who are currently practicing rehabilitation nursing and have at least 2 years of experience in the field. Applicants must be enrolled in a B.S.N. degree program and have successfully completed at least 1 course. Along with their application, they must submit a 1- to 3-page summary of their professional and educational goals that includes 1) involvement in ARN at the national and local levels; 2) continuing education participation in the past 3 to 5 years; 3) professional publications or presentations; 4) community involvement, particularly relating to advocating for individuals with disabilities; and 5) efforts they have made to improve their rehabilitation nursing practice and the delivery of care in their work setting. Financial need is not considered in the selection process.
Financial data The stipend is $1,000.
Duration 1 year.
Number awarded 1 or more each year.
Deadline May of each year.

[67]
ASSOCIATION OF UNITED NURSES SCHOLARSHIPS

Scholarship Administrative Services, Inc.
Attn: AUN Program
2000 Rock Street, Suite 3
Mountain View, CA 94043

Purpose To provide financial assistance to undergraduate and graduate students working on a degree in nursing.
Eligibility This program is open to full-time students working on or planning to work on an undergraduate or graduate degree in nursing. Applicants must have a GPA of 3.0 or higher and be able to demonstrate a record of involvement in extracurricular and work activities related to nursing. Along with their application, they must submit a 1,000-word essay on their educational and career goals, why they believe nursing is essential to America, and why they have decided to prepare for a career in nursing. Financial need is not considered in the selection process.
Financial data The stipend is $5,000 per year.
Duration 1 year; may be renewed 1 additional year if the recipient maintains full-time enrollment and a GPA of 3.0 or higher.
Additional information This program is sponsored by the Association of United Nurses (AUN) and administered by Scholarship Administrative Services, Inc. AUN was established in 2005 to encourage more American students to consider a career as a nurse. Requests for applications should be accompanied by a self-addressed stamped envelope, the student's e-mail address, and the source where they found the scholarship information.
Number awarded Up to 20 each year.
Deadline April of each year.

[68]
A.T. ANDERSON MEMORIAL SCHOLARSHIP PROGRAM
American Indian Science and Engineering Society
Attn: Scholarship Coordinator
2305 Renard, S.E., Suite 200
P.O. Box 9828
Albuquerque, NM 87119-9828
(505) 765-1052, ext. 106   Fax: (505) 765-5608
E-mail: shirley@aises.org
Web: www.aises.org/highered/scholarships

Purpose To provide financial assistance to members of the American Indian Science and Engineering Society who are majoring in designated fields as undergraduate or graduate students.

Eligibility This program is open to members of the society who can furnish proof of tribal enrollment or Certificate of Degree of Indian Blood. Applicants must be full-time students at the undergraduate or graduate level attending an accredited 4-year college or university or a 2-year college leading to an academic degree in engineering, mathematics, medicine, natural resources, physical science, or the sciences. They must submit a 500-word essay that demonstrates their interest in and motivation to continue higher education, an understanding of the importance of college and a commitment to completion, their educational and/or career goals, and a commitment to learning and giving back to the community. Selection is based on the essay, academic achievement (GPA of 2.7 or higher), leadership potential, and commitment to helping other American Indians. Financial need is not considered.

Financial data The annual stipend is $1,000 for undergraduates or $2,000 for graduate students.

Duration 1 year; nonrenewable.

Additional information This program was launched in 1983 in memory of A.T. Anderson, a Mohawk and a chemical engineer who worked with Albert Einstein. Anderson was 1 of the society's founders and was the society's first executive director. The program includes the following named awards: the Al Qöyawayma Award for an applicant who is majoring in science or engineering and also has a strong interest in the arts, the Norbert S. Hill, Jr. Leadership Award, the Polingaysi Qöyawayma Award for an applicant who is working on a teaching degree in order to teach mathematics or science in a Native community or an advanced degree for personal improvement or teaching at the college level, and the Robert W. Brocksbank Scholarship.

Number awarded Varies; generally, 200 or more each year, depending upon the availability of funds from corporate and other sponsors.

Deadline June of each year.

[69]
AUCTION SCHOLARSHIP
Minnesota Livestock Breeders' Association
Attn: Secretary
18950 Langly Avenue North
Marine, MN 55047
(651) 288-4314   Fax: (651) 642-2456
E-mail: steve.pooch@mnstatefair.org

Purpose To provide financial assistance to students in Minnesota working on an undergraduate degree in agriculture.

Eligibility This program is open to Minnesota residents who are attending college and preparing for an education and career that will support agriculture in the future. Applicants must have been a 4-H or FFA member for at least 3 years. Along with their application, they must submit essays on why they are interested in getting a college education, their plans after graduation from college, the 4-H or FFA livestock projects in which they participated, and their other community activities.

Financial data The stipend is $1,000.

Duration 1 year nonrenewable.

Number awarded At least 10 each year.

Deadline July of each year.

[70]
BARBARA MCBRIDE SCHOLARSHIP
Society of Exploration Geophysicists
Attn: SEG Foundation
8801 South Yale, Suite 500
P.O. Box 702740
Tulsa, OK 74170-2740
(918) 497-5513   Fax: (918) 497-5557
E-mail: scholarships@seg.org
Web: seg.org

Purpose To provide financial assistance to women who are interested in studying applied geophysics on the undergraduate or graduate school level.

Eligibility This program is open to women who are 1) high school students planning to enter college in the fall, or 2) undergraduate or graduate students whose grades are above average. Applicants must intend to work on a degree directed toward a career in applied geophysics or a closely-related field. Along with their application, they must submit a 150-word essay on how they plan to use geophysics in their future. Financial need is not considered in the selection process.

Financial data The stipend ranges from $1,000 to $3,000 per year.

Duration 1 academic year; may be renewable, based on scholastic standing, availability of funds, and continuance of a course of study leading to a career in applied geophysics.

Number awarded 1 each year.

Deadline January of each year.

SCIENCES

[71]
BARRY AND JULIA SMITH FAMILY NURSE SCHOLARSHIP PROGRAM

Scholarship America
Attn: Scholarship Management Services
One Scholarship Way
P.O. Box 297
St. Peter, MN 56082
(507) 931-1682   Toll-free: (866) 243-4644
Fax: (507) 931-9168
Web: www.hospicenurse.scholarshipamerica.org

Purpose To provide financial assistance to nursing students interested in a career in hospice or end of life care nursing.

Eligibility This program is open to college juniors enrolled in a full-time undergraduate course of study in nursing at an eligible 4-year college or university. Applicants must be at least 25 years of age and interested in a career in hospice or end of life care nursing. They must submit a personal essay describing their interest or plans to practice nursing involving hospice or end of life care. Selection is based on the essay, academic record, demonstrated leadership and participation in school and community activities, honors, work experience, a statement of goals and aspirations, unusual personal or family circumstances, and an outside appraisal. Financial need is not considered.

Financial data The stipend is $1,000.

Duration 1 year. Awards are not renewable, but recipients may reapply.

Additional information This program, established in 2003, is supported by the VistaCare Hospice Foundation of Scottsdale, Arizona.

Number awarded Varies each year; no more than 2 awards are granted to students attending the same school.

Deadline April of each year.

[72]
BARRY M. GOLDWATER SCHOLARSHIPS

Barry M. Goldwater Scholarship and Excellence in
   Education Foundation
Springfield Corporate Center
6225 Brandon Avenue, Suite 315
Springfield, VA 22150-2519
(703) 756-6012   Fax: (703) 756-6015
E-mail: goldh2o@vacoxmail.com
Web: www.act.org/goldwater

Purpose To provide financial assistance to outstanding college students planning careers in mathematics, engineering, or the natural sciences.

Eligibility Eligible to be nominated are full-time students enrolled as sophomores or juniors who are in the top quarter of their class and majoring in the natural sciences, mathematics, or engineering with a GPA of at least 3.0. Students intending to enter medical school are eligible if they plan a career in research rather than private practice. Status as a U.S. citizen, national, or resident alien is also required. Students must be nominated by their institutions; 4-year colleges and universities may nominate up to 4 current sophomores or juniors and 2-year colleges may nominate up to 2 sophomores. Applicants must submit a 2-page essay on a significant issue or problem in their field of study that is of particular interest to them. Selection is based on academic performance and demonstrated potential for and commitment to a career in mathematics, engineering, or the natural sciences.

Financial data Scholarships cover the cost of tuition, fees, books, and room and board up to a maximum of $7,500 per year.

Duration Students who receive scholarships as juniors are eligible for 2 years of support or until they complete their baccalaureate degree; students who receive scholarships as seniors are eligible for 1 year of support or until they complete their baccalaureate degree.

Additional information This program was authorized by the U.S. Congress in 1986. Information is also available from the Goldwater Scholarship Review Committee, 2201 North Dodge Street, P.O. Box 4030, Iowa City, IA 52243-4030.

Number awarded Up to 300 each year.

Deadline Institutions set their own deadlines; they must submit nominations to the foundation by January of each year.

[73]
BECAUSE GREEN MATTERS SCHOLARSHIP PROGRAM

Project EverGreen
Attn: Executive Director
120 West Main Street
P.O. Box 156
New Prague, MN 56071
(952) 758-6340   Toll-free: (877) 758-4835
E-mail: dengardner@projectevergreen.com
Web: www.projectevergreen.com

Purpose To provide financial assistance to undergraduates preparing for a career in the green industry.

Eligibility This program is open to undergraduates majoring or minoring in a green industry-related field such as horticulture, plant sciences, botany, agronomy, plant pathology, or water management. Applicants must be attending a 2- or 4-year college or university that offers a turf, landscape, and golf management program. They must have a GPA of 2.5 or higher. Along with their application, they must submit a 500-word essay on how they became interested in the green industry, their experience, what they bring to the field, and their professional goals.

Financial data The stipend is $2,500. Funds are disbursed to the bursar's office at the recipient's college or university.

Duration 1 year.

Number awarded 2 each year.

Deadline May of each year.

[74]
BECHTEL FOUNDATION SCHOLARSHIP
Society of Women Engineers
230 East Ohio Street, Suite 400
Chicago, IL 60611-3265
(312) 596-5223   Toll-free: (877) SWE-INFO
Fax: (312) 644-8557
E-mail: scholarshipapplication@swe.org
Web: www.swe.org/scholarships

Purpose To provide financial assistance to undergraduate women who are members of the Society of Women Engineers and majoring in engineering.

Eligibility This program is open to women who are entering their sophomore, junior, or senior year at an ABET-accredited college or university. Applicants must be studying computer science or architectural, civil, electrical, environmental, or mechanical engineering with a GPA of 3.0 or higher. Along with their application, they must submit a 1-page essay on why they want to be an engineer, how they believe they will make a difference as an engineer, and what influenced them to study engineering. Only members of the society are considered for this award. Selection is based on merit.

Financial data The stipend is $1,400.

Duration 1 year.

Additional information This program, established in 2000, is sponsored by Bechtel Foundation.

Number awarded 2 each year.

Deadline January of each year.

[75]
BEN MEADOWS NATURAL RESOURCE SCHOLARSHIPS
Society of American Foresters
Attn: Ben Meadows Natural Resource Scholarships
5400 Grosvenor Lane
Bethesda, MD 20814-2198
(301) 897-8720   Toll-free: (866) 897-8720
Fax: (301) 897-3690   E-mail: safweb@safnet.org
Web: www.benmeadows.com/scholarships

Purpose To provide financial assistance to upper-division students working on a degree in a field related to natural resources.

Eligibility This program is open to students entering their junior or senior year at an accredited college or university. They must be working on a bachelor's degree in agro forestry, urban forestry, environmental studies, natural resource management, natural resource recreation, wildlife management, wood science, fisheries management, or a related field. Applicants for the academic achievement scholarship must have a GPA of 3.2 or higher; they must submit a summary or list of accomplishments relating to their field of study and a 300-word essay on how those achievements have helped them grow individually and expand their interest in their field of study. Applicants for the leadership scholarship must have a GPA of 2.5 or higher; they must submit a summary of involvement and projects within leadership roles relating to their field of study and a 300-word essay on how those leadership roles have helped them grow individually and expand their interest in their field of study.

Financial data The stipend is $2,500.

Duration 1 year.

Additional information This program is sponsored by the Ben Meadows Company, P.O. Box 5277, Janesville, WI 53547-5277, (608) 743-8801, (800) 241-6401, Fax: (800) 628-2068, E-mail: mail@benmeadows.com.

Number awarded 2 each year: 1 for academic achievement and 1 for leadership.

Deadline June of each year.

[76]
BEN W. FORTSON, JR. SCHOLARSHIP
Surveying and Mapping Society of Georgia
Attn: Executive Director
P.O. Box 778
Douglasville, GA 30133-1272
(770) 489-1440   Fax: (770) 489-1425
E-mail: fhagin@aol.com
Web: www.samsog.org/displaycommon.cfm?an=24

Purpose To provide financial assistance for college to Georgia residents interested in preparing for a career in land surveying.

Eligibility This program is open to residents of Georgia working on a degree in land surveying at an accredited college or university. Applicants must have completed at least 20% of their degree requirements with a GPA of 2.4 or higher overall and 2.75 or higher in surveying courses. Preference is given to full-time students working on a bachelor's degree, although part-time students and associate degree students are also eligible. Along with their application, they must submit a brief essay on what prompted them to prepare for a career in the surveying (or cartographic or geodetic) profession. Financial need is not considered in the selection process.

Financial data A stipend is awarded (amount not specified).

Duration 1 year.

Additional information This program was established in 1980. Information is also available from Al Vedder, 1648 Juliette Road, Forsyth, GA 31029, (404) 506-3428.

Number awarded 1 or more each year.

[77]
BENJAMIN C. BLACKBURN SCHOLARSHIP
Friends of the Frelinghuysen Arboretum
Attn: Scholarship Committee
53 East Hanover Avenue
P.O. Box 1295
Morristown, NJ 07962-1295
(973) 326-7603   Fax: (973) 644-9627
TDD: (800) 852-7899
Web: www.arboretumfriends.org/blackburn.html

Purpose To provide financial assistance to residents of New Jersey who are working on an undergraduate or graduate degree in horticulture, landscape architecture, or related fields.

Eligibility This program is open to New Jersey residents who are working on an undergraduate or graduate degree in 1 of the following: horticulture, botany, landscape architecture, or a related field. Undergraduates must have com-

pleted at least 24 college credits with a GPA of 3.0 or higher. Applicants must submit brief essays on their short-term goals, work experience related to their career goals, involvement in community activities, and long-term career goals. Selection is based on those essays, college transcripts, 2 letters of recommendation from professors, and 2 letters of recommendation from people in their community. Financial need is not considered in the selection process.
Financial data The stipend is $5,000. Funds are sent directly to the recipient's institution.
Duration 1 year.
Number awarded 1 each year.
Deadline April of each year.

[78]
BERNTSEN INTERNATIONAL SCHOLARSHIP IN SURVEYING
American Congress on Surveying and Mapping
Attn: Scholarships
6 Montgomery Village Avenue, Suite 403
Gaithersburg, MD 20879
(240) 632-9716, ext. 113   Fax: (240) 632-1321
E-mail: pat.canfield@acsm.net
Web: www.acsm.net/scholar.html

Purpose To provide financial assistance for the undergraduate study of surveying to members of the American Congress on Surveying and Mapping.
Eligibility This program is open to ACSM members who are enrolled at a 4-year college or university. Applicants must be majoring in surveying or a closely-related program (e.g., geomatics, surveying engineering). Along with their application, they must submit a statement describing their educational program, future plans for study or research, and why the award is merited. Selection is based on that statement (30%), academic record (30%), letters of recommendation (20%), and professional activities (20%).
Financial data The stipend is $1,500.
Duration 1 year.
Additional information This award is made possible by Berntsen International, Inc., of Madison, Wisconsin.
Number awarded 1 each year.
Deadline October of each year.

[79]
BILL KANE UNDERGRADUATE SCHOLARSHIP
American Association for Health Education
Attn: Scholarship Committee
1900 Association Drive
Reston, VA 20191-1599
(703) 476-3437   Toll-free: (800) 213-7193, ext. 437
Fax: (703) 476-6638   E-mail: aahe@aahperd.org
Web: www.aahperd.org/aahe/heawards/AAHE.html

Purpose To provide financial assistance to undergraduates who are currently enrolled in a health education program.
Eligibility This program is open to undergraduate students who are enrolled full time in a health education program at a 4-year college or university. Applicants must have a GPA of 3.25 or higher as a sophomore, junior, or senior. Along with their application, they must submit an essay of 400 to 500 words on what they hope to accomplish as a health educator (during training and in the future) and the attributes and aspirations they bring to the field of health education. Selection is based on evidence of leadership potential, academic talent, and activity in health education profession-related activities or organizations at the college, university, and/or community level.
Financial data The stipend is $1,000 plus a 1-year complimentary student membership in the association.
Duration 1 year; nonrenewable.
Additional information This program was formerly known as the American Association for Health Education Undergraduate Scholarship.
Number awarded 1 each year.
Deadline November of each year.

[80]
B.K. KRENZER REENTRY SCHOLARSHIP
Society of Women Engineers
230 East Ohio Street, Suite 400
Chicago, IL 60611-3265
(312) 596-5223   Toll-free: (877) SWE-INFO
Fax: (312) 644-8557
E-mail: scholarshipapplication@swe.org
Web: www.swe.org/scholarships

Purpose To provide financial assistance to women interested in returning to college or graduate school to study engineering or computer science.
Eligibility This program is open to women who are planning to enroll at an ABET-accredited 4-year college or university. Applicants must have been out of the engineering workforce and school for at least 2 years and must be planning to return as an undergraduate or graduate student to major in computer science or engineering. Along with their application, they must submit a 1-page essay on why they want to be an engineer or computer scientist, how they believe they will make a difference as an engineer or computer scientist, and what influenced them to study engineering or computer science. Selection is based on merit. Preference is given to engineers who already have a degree and are planning to reenter the engineering workforce after a period of temporary retirement.
Financial data The stipend is $2,000.
Duration 1 year.
Additional information This program was established in 1996.
Number awarded 1 each year.
Deadline January of each year.

[81]
BP EXPLORATION AND PRODUCTION PROCESS TECHNOLOGY SCHOLARSHIP

Center for the Advancement of Process Technology
Attn: CAPT Scholarships
1200 Amburn Road
Texas City, TX 77591
(409) 938-1211, ext. 103   Fax: (409) 938-1285
E-mail: info@cpatech.org
Web: www.captech/org/careers/scholarship.htm

Purpose To provide financial assistance to students interested in a college degree in process technology.

Eligibility This program is open to students currently enrolled or planning to enroll in a process technology (or instrumentation technology) 2-year degree program. Preference is given to students from programs approved by the Gulf Coast Process Technology Alliance. Applicants must submit a 1-page essay on why they should be considered for this scholarship and selected over other qualified, worthy applicants. They must have a GPA of 2.5 or higher. Preference is also given to students in programs that offer oil and gas exploration related curricula. Selection is based on scholastic performance; financial need is not considered.

Financial data Stipends are $500 per semester for full-time students or $300 per semester for part-time students. Eligible expenses are limited to tuition, books, fees, and educational supplies.

Duration Recipients have up to 3 years to complete the 2-year process technology degree program. The maximum amount of support they may receive is $2,000.

Additional information This program is supported by BP Exploration and Production, Inc.

Number awarded 1 or more each year.

Deadline March of each year.

[82]
BRADFORD WHITE SCHOLARSHIPS

Plumbing-Heating-Cooling Contractors-National Association
Attn: PHCC Educational Foundation
180 South Washington Street
P.O. Box 6808
Falls Church, VA 22040
(703) 237-8100, ext. 221   Toll-free: (800) 533-7694
Fax: (703) 237-7442
E-mail: scholarships@naphcc.org
Web: www.foundation.phccweb.org

Purpose To provide financial assistance to entering or continuing undergraduate students interested in the plumbing, heating, and cooling industry.

Eligibility This program is open to students enrolled in an approved apprenticeship program or a full-time certificate or degree program at a 2-year technical college, community college, or trade school in business management, mechanical CAD design, construction management with a specialty in mechanical construction, or plumbing or HVACR installation, service, and repair. Students enrolled in an approved plumbing or HVAC apprenticeship program must be working full time for a licensed plumbing or HVAC contractor who is a member of the Plumbing-Heating-Cooling Contractors-National Association (PHCC). Applicants must submit a letter of recommendation from a member with 2 years' good standing in the PHCC; a copy of school transcripts; and a letter of recommendation from a school principal, counselor, or dean. U.S. or Canadian citizenship is required. Financial need is not considered in the selection process.

Financial data The stipend is $2,500 per year.

Duration 1 year; nonrenewable.

Additional information This program is sponsored by Bradford White Corporation.

Number awarded 3 each year.

Deadline May of each year.

[83]
BRIAN JENNEMAN MEMORIAL SCHOLARSHIP

Community Foundation of Louisville
Attn: Director of Grants
Waterfront Plaza, Suite 1110
325 West Main Street
Louisville, KY 40202-4251
(502) 585-4649, ext. 1005   Fax: (502) 587-7484
E-mail: info@cflouisville.org
Web: www.cflouisville.org

Purpose To provide financial assistance to students enrolled in a certified paramedic training program.

Eligibility This program is open to residents of any state who are 18 years of age or older and enrolled in a certified paramedic training program offered by an educational institution, fire department, city, county, or other municipality. Applicants must submit essays on how they became interested in being a paramedic, where they plan to serve when they complete their training program, and why they are deserving of this scholarship. Financial need is not considered in the selection process.

Financial data The stipend is $1,500. Funds are paid directly to the training institution.

Duration 1 year.

Additional information This program was established in 2001.

Number awarded 4 each year.

Deadline July of each year.

[84]
BUD GLOVER MEMORIAL SCHOLARSHIP

Aircraft Electronics Association
Attn: AEA Educational Foundation
4217 South Hocker Drive
Independence, MO 64055-4723
(816) 373-6565   Fax: (816) 478-3100
E-mail: info@aea.net
Web: www.aea.net

Purpose To provide financial assistance to students interested in preparing for a career in avionics or aircraft repair.

Eligibility This program is open to high school seniors and currently-enrolled college students who are attending (or planning to attend) an accredited postsecondary institution in an avionics or aircraft repair program. Applicants must submit an official transcript (cumulative GPA of 2.5 or higher), a statement about their career plans, a description of their involvement in school and community activities, and a 300-word essay on how the job requirements of aviation technicians will change with advancements in technology. Selection is based on merit.

Financial data The stipend is $1,000.
Duration 1 year.
Number awarded 1 each year.
Deadline February of each year.

[85]
CA-ASA SCHOLARSHIPS

American Society of Agronomy-California Chapter
c/o Casey Walsh Cady, Scholarship Committee
California Department of Food and Agriculture
Office of Agriculture and Environmental Stewardship
1220 N Street, Room 444
Sacramento, CA 95814
(916) 651-9447   Fax: (916) 657-5017
E-mail: ccady@cdfa.ca.gov
Web: calasa.ucdavis.edu

Purpose To provide financial assistance to California residents enrolled in a program in plant or soil management at designated universities in the state.

Eligibility This program is open to California residents enrolled full time as sophomores or higher at the following schools: California State University at Chico or Fresno, California State Polytechnic University at Pomona, California Polytechnic State University at San Luis Obispo, or the University of California at Berkeley, Davis, Riverside, or Santa Cruz. Applicants must be working on a degree in plant or soil management with a GPA of 2.5 or higher. Along with their application, they must submit a 300-word essay on a topic that changes annually; recently, students were asked to write on the role of biofuels in the future of California agriculture. Selection is based on the essay (50%), leadership and extracurricular activities (20%), letters of recommendation (20%), and work or business experience in agriculture (10%).

Financial data The stipend is $1,000.
Duration 1 year.
Number awarded 1 or more each year.
Deadline December of each year.

[86]
CAB/NJAA SCHOLARSHIP

National Junior Angus Association
Attn: Director Junior Activities
3201 Frederick Avenue
St. Joseph, MO 64506
(816) 383-5100   Fax: (816) 233-9703
E-mail: info@njaa.info
Web: www.angusfoundation.org

Purpose To provide financial assistance to students who have been members of the National Junior Angus Association (NJAA) and are interested in taking courses in selected beef-related topics in college.

Eligibility Applicants must have been a member of the NJAA in the past and must presently be a junior, regular, or life member of the American Angus Association. They must be entering their sophomore, junior, or senior year of college. The primary course work/declared major must be in animal science, meat science, food science, agricultural communications, or a related field. Selection is based on involvement in Angus associations, professional organizations, other agriculture-related groups, school organizations, and church and civic groups; experience in livestock production, marketing, and judging; experience in meats evaluation and processing; a statement of ambitions and goals; and transcripts.

Financial data The stipend is $1,000.
Duration 1 year; recipients may reapply.
Additional information This program, established in 1990, is sponsored by the Certified Angus Beef (CAB) Program and the NJAA.
Number awarded 1 each year.
Deadline April of each year.

[87]
CADY MCDONNELL MEMORIAL SCHOLARSHIP

American Congress on Surveying and Mapping
Attn: Scholarships
6 Montgomery Village Avenue, Suite 403
Gaithersburg, MD 20879
(240) 632-9716, ext. 113   Fax: (240) 632-1321
E-mail: pat.canfield@acsm.net
Web: www.acsm.net/scholar.html

Purpose To provide financial assistance for undergraduate study in surveying to women members of the American Congress on Surveying and Mapping (ACSM) from designated western states.

Eligibility This program is open to women ACSM members who are enrolled at a 2-year or 4-year college or university. Applicants must be residents of Alaska, Arizona, California, Colorado, Hawaii, Idaho, Montana, Nevada, New Mexico, Oregon, Utah, Washington, or Wyoming. They must be majoring in surveying or a closely-related program (e.g., geomatics, surveying engineering). Along with their application, they must submit a statement describing their educational program, future plans for study or research, and why the award is merited. Selection is based on that statement (30%), academic record (30%), letters of recommendation (20%), and professional activities (20%).

Financial data The stipend is $1,000.
Duration 1 year.
Number awarded 1 each year.
Deadline October of each year.

[88]
CALIFORNIA AGRICULTURAL IRRIGATION ASSOCIATION SCHOLARSHIP PROGRAM

California Agricultural Irrigation Association
c/o A&E Associates
P.O. Box 365
Maxwell, CA 95955
(530) 438-2026   Fax: (530) 438-2940
E-mail: caia@caia-irrigation.org
Web: www.caia-irrigation.org

Purpose To provide financial assistance to college students in California who can demonstrate an interest in irrigation and/or the irrigation industry.

Eligibility This program is open to residents of California who are returning students at an accredited college or university in the state. Applicants must demonstrate an interest in irrigation, the irrigation industry, and/or a related field. They must have a GPA of 2.7 or higher. Along with their application, they must provide information on their leadership activities; school, community, and church activities; work and business experience in agriculture; and a 300-word narrative on the effect the advances in irrigation technology will have on the future of agriculture in California. Financial need is not considered in the selection process. U.S. citizenship is required.

Financial data The stipend is $1,000.
Duration 1 year.
Additional information Recipients must attend an annual meeting of the association.
Number awarded 1 or more each year.
Deadline April of each year.

[89]
CALIFORNIA FARM BUREAU SCHOLARSHIPS

California Farm Bureau Scholarship Foundation
Attn: Scholarship Coordinator
2300 River Plaza Drive
Sacramento, CA 95833
(916) 561-5520   Toll-free: (800) 698-FARM (within CA)
Fax: (916) 561-5699   E-mail: dlicciardo@cfbf.com
Web: www.cfbf.com/programs/scholar/index.cfm

Purpose To provide financial assistance for college to residents of California who are interested in preparing for a career in agriculture.
Eligibility This program is open to students entering or attending a 4-year accredited college or university in California who are majoring or planning to major in an agriculture-related field. Students entering a junior college are not eligible. Applicants must submit an essay on the most important educational or personal experience that has led them to pursue a university education. Selection is based on academic achievement, career goals, extracurricular activities, leadership skills, determination, and commitment to study agriculture.
Financial data The stipend ranges from $2,000 to $2,750 per year.
Duration 1 year; recipients may reapply.
Number awarded Varies; generally, 30 or more each year.
Deadline February of each year.

[90]
CALIFORNIA MARINE SCIENCES SCHOLARSHIP

Central California Council of Diving Clubs
c/o James L. Kaller, Scholarship Director
155 Montgomery Street, Suite 1004
San Francisco, CA 94104
(415) 362-9134, ext. 12   Fax: (415) 434-1880
E-mail: jameskaller@batnet.com
Web: www.cencal.org/scholarship.html

Purpose To provide financial assistance to college students in California engaged in the study of underwater habitats.
Eligibility Eligible to apply are California residents who are enrolled full time in a California academic institute, are at least 18 years of age, are a certified diver holding current national certification, and have at least a 3.0 GPA. Applicants must be engaged in the study of underwater habitats. Aquatic-related programs in the disciplines of biology, physical sciences, marine education, maritime archaeology, historical and social aspects of marine resources, and the science of diving are considered relevant for this program. Selection is based on college grades, letters of recommendation, honors earned, and professional goals. Financial need is not considered in the selection process.

Financial data The stipend is $1,000.
Duration 1 year.
Additional information This award, offered since 1989, was previously named the Seaviews/Cen Cal Marine Science Scholarship. The sponsoring organization, Central California Council of Diving Clubs, is commonly known as Cen Cal.
Number awarded 1 each year.
Deadline April of each year.

[91]
CALIFORNIA STATE FAIR UNIVERSITY SCHOLARSHIPS IN AGRICULTURE

California State Fair
Attn: Friends of the Fair Scholarship Program
1600 Exposition Boulevard
P.O. Box 15649
Sacramento, CA 95852
(916) 274-5969   E-mail: entryoffice@calexpo.com
Web: www.bigfun.org

Purpose To provide financial assistance to undergraduate and graduate students in California who are studying agriculture.
Eligibility This program is open to undergraduate and graduate students currently enrolled at 4-year colleges and universities in California. Applicants must have completed at least 12 units of course work in agricultural classes. They must have a GPA of 3.0 or higher. Along with their application, they must submit a 2-page essay on why they are pursuing their desired career and life goals. Selection is based on personal commitment, goals established for their chosen field, leadership potential, and civic accomplishments.
Financial data Stipends are $1,000 or $500.
Duration 1 year.
Additional information The Friends of the Fair Scholarship Program was established in 1993.
Number awarded 2 each year: 1 at $1,000 and 1 at $500.
Deadline March of each year.

SCIENCES

[92]
CALIFORNIA STATE FAIR VITICULTURE/ENOLOGY SCHOLARSHIPS
California State Fair
Attn: Friends of the Fair Scholarship Program
1600 Exposition Boulevard
P.O. Box 15649
Sacramento, CA 95852
(916) 274-5969   E-mail: entryoffice@calexpo.com
Web: www.bigfun.org

Purpose To provide financial assistance to residents of California who are working on an undergraduate or graduate degree in viticulture or enology.

Eligibility This program is open to residents of California currently working on an undergraduate or graduate degree at a college or university in the state. Applicants must be studying or majoring in viticulture or enology. They must have a GPA of 3.0 or higher. Along with their application, they must submit a 2-page essay on why they are pursuing their desired career and life goals. Selection is based on personal commitment, goals established for their chosen field, leadership potential, and civic accomplishments.

Financial data Stipends are $1,000 or $500.

Duration 1 year.

Additional information The Friends of the Fair Scholarship Program was established in 1993.

Number awarded 2 each year: 1 at $1,000 and 1 at $500.

Deadline March of each year.

[93]
CANERS COLLEGE SCHOLARSHIPS
California Association of Nurseries and Garden Centers
Attn: CANERS
3947 Lennane Drive, Suite 150
Sacramento, CA 95834-1973
(916) 928-3900   Toll-free: (800) 748-6214
Fax: (916) 567-0505   E-mail: association@cangc.org
Web: www.cangc.org

Purpose To provide financial assistance to college students in California who are majoring in ornamental horticulture or related fields.

Eligibility This program is open to residents of California at 2-year and 4-year colleges and universities in the state who are currently enrolled in at least 6 credits and are majoring or planning to major in a field related to horticulture (e.g., agribusiness, viticulture, pomology). Applicants, must submit essays on their educational objectives and their occupational goals as they relate to the nursery industry or horticulture. Selection is based on those essays, transcripts, high school and college activities related to horticulture, work experience, community activities related to horticulture, and 2 letters of reference. Financial need is not considered.

Financial data Stipends range from $100 to $5,000.

Duration 1 year.

Additional information This program is offered by the California Association of Nurserymen Endowment for Research and Scholarship (CANERS).

Number awarded 1 or more each year.

Deadline March of each year.

[94]
CARMEN E. TURNER SCHOLARSHIPS
Conference of Minority Transportation Officials
Attn: National Scholarship Program
818 18th Street, N.W., Suite 850
Washington, DC 20006
(202) 530-0551   Fax: (202) 530-0617
Web: www.comto.org/scholarship.htm

Purpose To provide financial assistance for college or graduate school to members of the Conference of Minority Transportation Officials (COMTO).

Eligibility This program is open to undergraduate and graduate students who have been members of COMTO for at least 1 year. Applicants must be working on a degree in a field related to transportation with a GPA of 2.5 or higher. Along with their application, they must submit a cover letter with a 500-word statement of career goals. Financial need is not considered in the selection process. U.S. citizenship is required.

Financial data The stipend is $3,500. Funds are paid directly to the recipient's college or university.

Duration 1 year.

Additional information COMTO was established in 1971 to promote, strengthen, and expand the roles of minorities in all aspects of transportation. Recipients are expected to attend the COMTO National Scholarship Luncheon.

Number awarded 2 each year.

Deadline April of each year.

[95]
CAROL A. RATZA MEMORIAL SCHOLARSHIP
Great Lakes Commission
Attn: Program Manager, Communications and Internet Technology
2805 South Industrial Highway, Suite 100
Ann Arbor, MI 48104-6791
(734) 971-9135   Fax: (734) 971-9150
E-mail: manninen@glc.org
Web: www.glc.org/about/scholarships

Purpose To recognize and reward outstanding student writings and web sites on a current Great Lakes issue.

Eligibility This program is open to high school seniors and currently-enrolled full-time college students located in the Great Lakes region: Illinois, Indiana, Michigan, Minnesota, New York, Ohio, Pennsylvania, Wisconsin, or the Canadian provinces of Ontario or Québec. Applicants must be able to demonstrate a career interest in electronic communications technologies and their application to Great Lakes protection and restoration. Along with their application, they must submit a 500-word essay or an original web page (designed and populated by the applicant) on creative new ideas for the Great Lakes Information Network web site. Selection is based on demonstrated interest in the environmental or economic applications of electronic communications technology, academic excellence, and appreciation for the Great Lakes and their protection.

Financial data The stipend is $1,000.

Duration 1 year; nonrenewable.

Additional information This scholarship was first awarded in 1998.

Number awarded 1 each year.

Deadline March of each year.

[96]
CAROLYN S. RICHARDSON MEMORIAL SCHOLARSHIP
California Farm Bureau Scholarship Foundation
Attn: Scholarship Coordinator
2300 River Plaza Drive
Sacramento, CA 95833
(916) 561-5520   Toll-free: (800) 698-FARM (within CA)
Fax: (916) 561-5699   E-mail: dlicciardo@cfbf.com
Web: www.cfbf.com/programs/scholar/index.cfm

Purpose To provide financial assistance for college to residents of California who are interested in preparing for a career in agriculture.

Eligibility This program is open to students entering or attending a 4-year accredited college or university in California who are majoring or planning to major in an agriculture-related field. Students entering a junior college are not eligible. Applicants must be planning to specialize in agricultural resource issues. They must submit an essay on the most important educational or personal experience that has led them to pursue a university education. Selection is based on academic achievement, career goals, extracurricular activities, leadership skills, determination, and commitment to study agriculture.

Financial data The stipend is $2,250 per year.

Duration 1 year; recipients may reapply.

Number awarded 1 each year.

Deadline February of each year.

[97]
CARTOGRAPHY AND GEOGRAPHIC INFORMATION SOCIETY SCHOLARSHIP AWARD
American Congress on Surveying and Mapping
Attn: Scholarships
6 Montgomery Village Avenue, Suite 403
Gaithersburg, MD 20879
(240) 632-9716, ext. 113   Fax: (240) 632-1321
E-mail: pat.canfield@acsm.net
Web: www.acsm.net/scholar.html

Purpose To provide financial assistance for undergraduate or graduate study in cartography or geographic information science to members of the American Congress on Surveying and Mapping (ACSM).

Eligibility This program is open to ACSM members who are enrolled full time in a 4-year or graduate degree program in cartography, GIS, or other mapping sciences. Applicants must submit a statement describing their educational program, future plans for study or research, and why the award is merited. Selection is based on that statement (30%), academic record (30%), letters of recommendation (20%), and professional activities (20%).

Financial data The stipend is $1,000.

Duration 1 year.

Additional information This award is funded by the Cartography and Geographic Information Society (CaGIS) and administered by ACSM.

Number awarded 1 each year.

Deadline January of each year.

[98]
CATERPILLAR SCHOLARS AWARD
Society of Manufacturing Engineers
Attn: SME Education Foundation
One SME Drive
P.O. Box 930
Dearborn, MI 48121-0930
(313) 425-3300   Toll-free: (800) 733-4763, ext. 3300
Fax: (313) 425-3411   E-mail: foundation@sme.org
Web: www.sme.org

Purpose To provide financial assistance to undergraduates enrolled in a degree program in manufacturing engineering or manufacturing engineering technology.

Eligibility Applicants must be full-time students attending a degree-granting institution in North America and preparing for a career in manufacturing engineering. They must have completed at least 30 units in a manufacturing engineering or manufacturing engineering technology curriculum with a minimum GPA of 3.0. Minority applicants may apply as incoming freshmen. Along with their application, they must submit a 300-word essay that covers their career and educational objectives, how this scholarship will help them attain those objectives, and why they want to enter this field. Financial need is not considered in the selection process.

Financial data The stipend is $2,000.

Duration 1 year; may be renewed.

Additional information This program is sponsored by Caterpillar, Inc.

Number awarded Varies each year; recently, 10 of these scholarships were awarded.

Deadline January of each year.

[99]
CEDARCREST FARMS SCHOLARSHIP
American Jersey Cattle Association
Attn: Dr. Cherie L. Bayer
6486 East Main Street
Reynoldsburg, OH 43068-2362
(614) 861-3636   Fax: (614) 861-8040
E-mail: cbayer@usjersey.com
Web: www.usjersey.com

Purpose To provide financial assistance to undergraduate and graduate students working on a degree related to the dairy industry.

Eligibility This program is open to undergraduate and graduate students who are working on a degree in large animal veterinary practice, dairy production, dairy manufacturing, or dairy product marketing. Applicants must be members of the American Jersey Cattle Association with significant and extensive experience in breeding, managing, and showing Jersey cattle. They must demonstrate significant progress toward their intended degree and an intention to prepare for a career in agriculture. A GPA of 2.5 or higher is required. Financial need is not considered in the selection process.

Financial data The stipend is approximately $1,000.

Duration 1 year.

Number awarded 1 each year.

Deadline June of each year.

SCIENCES

[100]
CESSNA/RAYTHEON STUDENT DESIGN/BUILD/FLY COMPETITION

American Institute of Aeronautics and Astronautics
Attn: Student Programs Director
1801 Alexander Bell Drive, Suite 500
Reston, VA 20191-4344
(703) 264-7536   Toll-free: (800) 639-AIAA, ext. 536
Fax: (703) 264-7657   E-mail: stephenb@aiaa.org
Web: www.aiaa.org/content.cfm?pageid=210

Purpose To recognize and reward outstanding aircraft that are designed, built, and flown by undergraduate and graduate student members of the American Institute of Aeronautics and Astronautics (AIAA).

Eligibility This program is open to undergraduate and graduate students who are AIAA branch or at-large student members. Teams of 3 to 10 students (at least one third of whom must be freshmen, sophomores, or juniors) may enter this competition to design, build, and fly an unmanned, radio-controlled, propeller-driven, electric-powered aircraft. The design must comply with precise specifications; once those specifications are met, the aircraft must be able to take off, circle the field, and land within designated areas. Design projects that are used as part of an organized classroom requirement are eligible and encouraged. Designs that are submitted must be the work of the students, but a faculty advisor may provide guidance. The pilot is not required to be a student, but must be a member of the Academy of Model Aeronautics (AMA). Flight scores are based on the demonstrated mission performance in the best 3 flights obtained during the contest.

Financial data First place is $2,500, second place is $1,500, and third place is $1,000.

Duration The competition is held annually.

Additional information This competition, which began in 1996, is sponsored by Cessna Aircraft Company and Raytheon Missile Systems. Information is also available from Kelly Laflin, Cessna Aircraft Company, Department 363 P, 5800 East Pawnee, Wichita, KS 67218, (316) 831-2247.

Number awarded 3 cash awards are presented each year.

Deadline Letters of intent must be submitted by October of each year; the competition takes place in April.

[101]
CHAN-PADGETT SPECIAL FORCES MEMORIAL SCHOLARSHIP

American Academy of Physician Assistants-Veterans Caucus
Attn: Veterans Caucus
950 North Washington Street
Alexandria, VA 22314-1552
(703) 836-2272   Fax: (703) 684-1924
E-mail: aapa@aapa.org
Web: www.veteranscaucus.org

Purpose To provide financial assistance to children of veterans of the Army Special Forces who are studying to become physician assistants.

Eligibility This program is open to U.S. citizens who are currently enrolled in a physician assistant program. The program must be approved by the Commission on Accreditation of Allied Health Education. Applicants must be children of honorably discharged members of the Army Special Forces. Selection is based on military honors and awards received, civic and college honors and awards received, professional memberships and activities, and GPA. An electronic copy of the sponsor's DD Form 214 must accompany the application.

Financial data The stipend is $1,250.

Duration 1 year.

Additional information This program was established in 2002. Information is also available from Sharon Hanley, P.O. Box 362, Danville, PA 17821-0362, (570) 271-6692, (800) 271-6692, Fax: (570) 271-5850, E-mail: skhanley@ptd.net.

Number awarded 1 each year.

Deadline February of each year.

[102]
CHARLES R. MORRIS STUDENT RESEARCH AWARD

American Academy of Oral and Maxillofacial Radiology
Attn: Executive Director
P.O. Box 1010
Evans, GA 30809-1010
(706) 721-2607   E-mail: mshrout@mail.mcq.edu
Web: www.aaomr.org/crm_info1.htm

Purpose To recognize and reward outstanding student papers on oral and maxillofacial radiology.

Eligibility This award is open to candidates from accredited dental and dental hygiene programs who, at the time the research was conducted, were full-time predoctoral or undergraduate students. The manuscript must be accompanied by a nomination from the institution in which the research was conducted. Applicants are judged on the following: clarity of conceptual definition, adequacy of literature review, originality, soundness of methodology, significance of contribution to the science of oral and maxillofacial radiology, and manuscript format and style. Students are encouraged to secure faculty guidance in designing the research project, in determining the extent of the literature review, and in composing the manuscript. All manuscripts must represent original research not submitted for publication elsewhere.

Financial data The awardee receives a certificate, a check for $1,000, free conference registration, an invitation to present the research paper at the annual meeting, and free membership in the academy.

Duration The prize is awarded annually.

Additional information Information is also available from Dr. J. Sean Hubar, Louisiana State University, School of Dentistry, 1100 Florida Avenue, New Orleans, LA 70119, (504) 619-8623.

Number awarded At least 1 each year.

Deadline June of each year.

[103]
CHARLES (TOMMY) THOMAS MEMORIAL SCHOLARSHIP
American Nuclear Society
Attn: Scholarship Coordinator
555 North Kensington Avenue
La Grange Park, IL 60526-5592
(708) 352-6611   Fax: (708) 352-0499
E-mail: outreach@ans.org
Web: www.ans.org/honors/scholarships

Purpose To provide financial assistance to upper-division students who are interested in preparing for a career dealing with the environmental aspects of nuclear science or nuclear engineering.

Eligibility This program is open to students entering their junior or senior year in nuclear science, nuclear engineering, or a nuclear-related field at an accredited institution in the United States. Applicants must be interested in preparing for a career dealing with the environmental aspects of nuclear science or nuclear engineering. They must be U.S. citizens or permanent residents and able to demonstrate academic achievement.

Financial data The stipend is $2,000.

Duration 1 year; nonrenewable.

Additional information This program is offered by the Environmental Sciences Division of the ANS. It was formerly known as the Environmental Sciences Division Scholarship.

Number awarded 1 each year.

Deadline January of each year.

[104]
CHARLINE HAMILTON POWELL SCHOLARSHIP
Tennessee 4-H Club Foundation, Inc.
205 Morgan Hall
2621 Morgan Circle
Knoxville, TN 37996-4510
(865) 974-7436   Fax: (865) 974-1628
E-mail: mgateley@utk.edu
Web: www.utextension.utk.edu

Purpose To provide financial assistance for college to members of 4-H in Tennessee who have participated in the sheep project.

Eligibility This program is open to 4-H members in Tennessee who have participated in the sheep project. Applicants must be entering freshmen or sophomores at a college, university, or technical school. They may be majoring in any field. Selection is based on participation in the 4-H sheep project (40%); other 4-H experiences, including leadership and citizenship (30%); participation in school, community, and church activities (10%); and scholarship (20%).

Financial data The stipend is $1,000.

Duration 1 year.

Number awarded 1 or more each year.

Deadline April of each year.

[105]
CHEM-E-CAR COMPETITION
American Institute of Chemical Engineers
Attn: Awards Administrator
Three Park Avenue
New York, NY 10016-5991
(212) 591-7107   Fax: (212) 591-8890
E-mail: awards@aiche.org
Web: www.aiche.org

Purpose To recognize and reward student members of the American Institute of Chemical Engineers (AIChE) who design a chemically powered vehicle.

Eligibility This program is open to AIChE student members who design and construct a chemically powered vehicle within certain size constraints that is designed to carry a specified cargo a given distance and stop. Entries must be submitted by teams of undergraduate students that have at least 5 participants, including students from at least 2 chemical engineering classes. The percentage of students from each class must not be greater than 80% of the total number of students on the team. Faculty and graduate students may only act as sounding boards for team members and may not be idea generators for the project. Teams are told at the time of the competition the distance that the car must travel and the cargo it will carry. Winners are determined by a combined score, for traveling the correct distance, and for creativity. Competitions are first held at the regional level, from which top entries proceed to the national competition.

Financial data At the regional level, first prize is $200 and second prize is $100. At the national level, first prize is $2,000, second prize is $1,000, and third prize is $500.

Duration The competition is held annually.

Additional information This competition, first held in 1999, is sponsored by AIChE and General Mills, Inc.

Number awarded 3 national winners are selected each year.

Deadline Regional competitions are held in spring of each year. Eligible winners must submit applications to participate in the national competition, held in November, by June of each year.

[106]
CHEVRON CORPORATION SCHOLARSHIPS
Society of Women Engineers
230 East Ohio Street, Suite 400
Chicago, IL 60611-3265
(312) 596-5223   Toll-free: (877) SWE-INFO
Fax: (312) 644-8557
E-mail: scholarshipapplication@swe.org
Web: www.swe.org/scholarships

Purpose To provide financial assistance to undergraduate women who are members of the Society of Women Engineers (SWE) and majoring in designated engineering specialties.

Eligibility This program is open to women who are entering their sophomore or junior year at an ABET-accredited 4-year college or university. Applicants must be majoring in computer science or chemical, civil, computer, mechanical, or petroleum engineering and have a GPA of 3.0 or higher. Along with their application, they must submit a 1-page essay on why they want to be an engineer or computer scientist, how they believe they will make a difference as an engineer or computer scientist, and what influenced them to study engineering or computer science. Selection is based on merit. Only members of the society are considered for this award.

Financial data The stipend is $2,000. The award includes a travel grant for the recipient to attend the SWE national conference.

Duration 1 year.

Additional information This program, established in 1991, is sponsored by Chevron Corporation.

Number awarded 8 each year.

Deadline January of each year.

[107]
CHICAGO MERCANTILE EXCHANGE BEEF INDUSTRY SCHOLARSHIP PROGRAM

National Cattlemen's Beef Association
Attn: National Cattlemen's Foundation
9110 East Nichols Avenue, Suite 300
Centennial, CO 80112
(303) 694-0305   Fax: (303) 694-7372
E-mail: ncf@beef.org
Web: www.nationalcattlemensfoundation.org

Purpose To provide financial assistance to students who are interested in preparing for a career in the beef industry.

Eligibility This program is open to graduating high school seniors and full-time undergraduate students enrolled at a 2-year or 4-year academic institution. Applicants must have demonstrated a commitment to a career in an area of the beef industry, through classes, internships, or life experiences. They must write a brief letter, indicating what role they see themselves playing in the beef industry after graduation; write an essay (up to 750 words) on an issue confronting the beef industry and offering their solution; and submit 2 letters of recommendation. A career in the beef industry may include: education, communications, production, research, or other related areas. Essays are judged on the basis of clarity of expression, persuasiveness, originality, accuracy, relevance, and solutions offered.

Financial data The stipend is $1,500.

Duration 1 year.

Additional information This program, which began in 1989, is cosponsored by the Chicago Mercantile Exchange (CME) and the National Cattlemen's Foundation.

Number awarded 20 each year.

Deadline October of each year.

[108]
CHUCK PEACOCK MEMORIAL SCHOLARSHIP

Aircraft Electronics Association
Attn: AEA Educational Foundation
4217 South Hocker Drive
Independence, MO 64055-4723
(816) 373-6565   Fax: (816) 478-3100
E-mail: info@aea.net
Web: www.aea.net

Purpose To provide financial assistance to students interested in preparing for a career in aviation management.

Eligibility This program is open to high school seniors and currently-enrolled college students who are attending (or planning to attend) an accredited postsecondary institution in an aviation management program. Applicants must submit an official transcript (cumulative GPA of 2.5 or higher), a statement about their career plans, a description of their involvement in school and community activities, and a 300-word essay on how the job requirements of aviation technicians will change with advancements in technology. Selection is based on merit.

Financial data The stipend is $1,000.

Duration 1 year.

Number awarded 1 each year.

Deadline February of each year.

[109]
CHUNGHI HONG PARK SCHOLARSHIP

Korean-American Scientists and Engineers Association
1952 Gallows Drive, Suite 300
Vienna, VA 22182
(703) 748-1221   Fax: (703) 748-1331
E-mail: sejong@ksea.org
Web: ksea.org/KSEA/indexe.asp?p=3

Purpose To provide financial assistance to women who are undergraduate or graduate student members of the Korean-American Scientists and Engineers Association (KSEA).

Eligibility This program is open to women who are Korean American undergraduate or graduate students, graduated from a high school in the United States, are KSEA members, and are majoring in science, engineering, or a related field. Along with their application, they must submit a 500-word essay on either of the following topics: 1) their career goals and intended contributions to society, or 2) the meaning of Korean heritage in their life. Selection is based on the essay (20%), work experience and extracurricular activities (20%), recommendation letters (30%), and academic performance (30%).

Financial data The stipend is $1,000.

Duration 1 year.

Number awarded 2 each year.

Deadline February of each year.

[110]
CIVIL ENGINEERS OF AMERICA SCHOLARSHIPS

Scholarship Administrative Services, Inc.
Attn: CEA Program
2000 Rock Street, Suite 3
Mountain View, CA 94043

Purpose To provide financial assistance to students interested in working on an undergraduate or graduate degree in civil engineering.

Eligibility This program is open to full-time students working on or planning to work on an undergraduate or graduate degree in civil engineering. Applicants must have a GPA of 3.0 or higher and be able to demonstrate a record of involvement in extracurricular and work activities related to civil engineering. Along with their application, they must submit a 1,000-word essay on their educational and career goals, how they became interested in civil engineering as a career, and what contributions they believe they can make to the civil engineering profession. Financial need is not considered in the selection process.

Financial data The stipend is $5,000 per year.

Duration 1 year; may be renewed 1 additional year if the recipient maintains full-time enrollment and a GPA of 3.0 or higher.

Additional information This program is sponsored by Civil Engineers of America (CEA) and administered by Scholarship Administrative Services, Inc. CEA was established in 2002 to encourage more American students to consider civil engineering as a career. Requests for applications should be accompanied by a self-addressed stamped envelope, the student's e-mail address, and the source where they found the scholarship information.

Number awarded Up to 20 each year.

Deadline April of each year.

[111]
CNF PROFESSIONAL GROWTH SCHOLARSHIPS

School Nutrition Association
Attn: Child Nutrition Foundation Scholarship Committee
700 South Washington Street, Suite 300
Alexandria, VA 22314-4287
(703) 739-3900   Toll-free: (800) 877-8822
Fax: (703) 739-3915   E-mail: cnf@schoolnutrition.org
Web: www.schoolnutrition.org/Index.aspx?ID=1043

Purpose To provide financial assistance to members of the School Nutrition Association (SNA) who are interested in additional undergraduate or graduate study.

Eligibility This program is open to active SNA members who meet all 4 of the following criteria: 1) plan to work on an undergraduate or graduate degree at a college or vocational/technical institution that has a program designed to improve school food service (e.g., nutrition, food service management, business administration); 2) have a history of employment in school food service and at least 1 year's SNA membership; 3) have a satisfactory academic record; and 4) express a desire to make school food service a career. Applicants must submit a 1-page personal essay (up to 500 words) stating their reason for selecting school food service as a profession; what they expect to gain from continuing their education; and their long-term professional goals/plans. Selection is based on the essay (35 points), letters of recommendation (20 points), SNA state and local chapter activity participation (15 points), organization and neatness (10 points), program of study (15 points), and GPA (5 points).

Financial data Stipends up to $1,000 are available.

Duration 1 year; may be renewed up to 3 additional years.

Additional information The SNA was formerly the American School Food Service Administration.

Number awarded Varies each year; recently, 21 of these scholarships were awarded.

Deadline April of each year.

[112]
COATING AND GRAPHIC ARTS DIVISION SCHOLARSHIPS

Technical Association of the Pulp and Paper Industry
Attn: TAPPI Foundation
15 Technology Parkway South
Norcross, GA 30092
(770) 209-7536   Toll-free: (800) 332-8686
Fax: (770) 446-6947   E-mail: vedmondson@tappi.org
Web: www.tappi.org

Purpose To provide financial assistance to student members of the Technical Association of the Pulp and Paper Industry (TAPPI) who are interested in preparing for a career in the paper industry, with a focus on coating and graphic arts.

Eligibility This program is open to TAPPI student members who are enrolled full time in a program related to the coated paper and paperboard or the graphic arts industries. Applicants must be juniors or higher with a GPA of 3.0 or higher; graduate students are also eligible if they have not advanced to doctoral candidacy. Selection is based on demonstrated interest in a career in the coating and graphic arts industry; financial need is not considered.

Financial data The stipend is $1,000.

Duration 1 year.

Additional information This program includes the Robert W. Hagemeyer Scholarship.

Number awarded Up to 4 each year.

Deadline January of each year.

[113]
COLLEGIATE DISCUSSION MEET AWARDS

Texas Farm Bureau
Attn: Organization Programs Director
7420 Fish Pond Road
P.O. Box 2689
Waco, TX 76702-2689
(254) 399-5037   Fax: (254) 751-8723
E-mail: cdavis@txfb.org
Web: www.txfb.org/youth.asp

Purpose To recognize and reward college students in Texas who participate in a group discussion on topics related to agriculture.

Eligibility This competition is open to Texas college students who are 18 to 35 years of age and currently working on a degree in agriculture or studying an agricultural program. Participants meet at the office of the Texas Farm Bureau in groups of 6 and engage in a 25-minute discussion on a topic related to agriculture; recently, those included how American agriculture can increase the opportunities for new uses of traditional agricultural products, how we can influence policy that affects agriculture, the effects of animal ID on U.S. agriculture, and how current land prices and profitability affect production agriculture. Each student must participate in at least 2 rounds of discussions. They are judged on the basis of cooperative attitude (200 points), problem solving and implementation (100 points), delivery (100 points), analysis of topic or problem (100 points), opening statement (100 points), and closing statement (100 points). After several preliminary rounds, the 4 competitors with the highest scores participate in a 30-minute final discussion.

Financial data The winner receives a $1,000 cash award and the other finalists receive $200 cash awards. All finalists receive travel expenses to attend the Texas Farm Bureau annual meeting, and the winner receives travel expenses to compete in the National American Farm Bureau Collegiate Discussion Meet contest. The university of the winner receives a $500 cash award.

Duration The competition is held annually.

Additional information This competition was first held in 2003.

Number awarded 4 finalists receive cash awards each year.

Deadline March each year.

[114]
COLLEGIATE INVENTORS COMPETITION

National Inventors Hall of Fame
Attn: Collegiate Inventors Competition
221 South Broadway Street
Akron, OH 44308-1595
(330) 849-6887   E-mail: collegiate@invent.org
Web: www.invent.org/collegiate

Purpose To recognize and reward outstanding inventions by college or university students in the fields of science, engineering, and technology.

Eligibility This competition is open to undergraduate and graduate students who are (or have been) enrolled full time at least part of the 12-month period prior to entry in a college or university in the United States. Entries may also be submitted by teams, up to 4 members, of whom at least 1 must meet the full-time requirement and all others must have been enrolled at least half time sometime during the preceding 24-month period. Applicants must submit a description of their invention, including a patent search and summary of current literature that describes the state of the art and identifies the originality of the invention; test data demonstrating that the idea, invention, or design is workable; the societal, economic, and environmental benefits of the invention; and supplemental material that may include photos, slides, disks, videotapes, and even samples. Entries must be original ideas and the work of a student or team and a university advisor; the invention should be reproducible and may not have been 1) made available to the public as a commercial product or process, or 2) patented or published more than 1 year prior to the date of submission for this competition. Entries are first reviewed by a committee of judges that selects the finalists. The committee is comprised of mathematicians, engineers, biologists, chemists, environmentalists, physicists, computer specialists, members of the medical and veterinary profession, and specialists in invention and development of technology. Entries are judged on the basis of originality, inventiveness, potential value to society (socially, environmentally, and economically), and range or scope of use.

Financial data Finalists receive an all-expense paid trip to Washington, D.C. to participate in a final round of judging and in the awards dinner and presentation. The Grand Prize winner or team receives $25,000. Other prizes are $10,000 for an undergraduate winner or team and $15,000 for a graduate winner or team. Academic advisors of the winning entries each receive a $3,000 cash prize. Awards are unrestricted cash gifts, not scholarships or grants.

Duration The competition is held annually.

Additional information This program is co-sponsored by Abbott Laboratories and the United States Patent and Trademark Office. It was established in 1990 as the BFGoodrich Collegiate Inventors Program.

Number awarded 15 semifinalists are selected each year; of those, 3 individuals or teams win prizes.

Deadline May of each year.

[115]
COLORADO YOUNG FARMERS SCHOLARSHIPS

Colorado Young Farmers Educational Association
c/o Northeastern Junior College
100 College Drive
Sterling, CO 80751
(970) 521-6690   Fax: (970) 521-6801
E-mail: info@coloradoyoungfarmer.com
Web: www.coloradoyoungfarmer.com

Purpose To provide financial assistance to entering or continuing undergraduate students in Colorado interested in preparing for a career teaching agricultural education.

Eligibility This program is open to Colorado residents who are 1) freshmen and sophomores majoring in agriculture, and 2) juniors and seniors majoring in agricultural education and working toward teacher certification. Applicants must be enrolled full time at a community college, university, or college in Colorado. Selection is based on scholarship, activities, and interest in agriculture and teaching agricultural education.

Financial data Stipends are $500 for freshmen and sophomores, $750 for juniors, or $1,250 for seniors.

Duration 1 year.

Additional information This program, which began in 1992, is supported by Case IH.

Number awarded 5 each year: 2 to entering freshmen and 1 each to a sophomore, junior, and senior.

Deadline March of each year.

[116]
COMMITTEE 12-RAIL TRANSIT UNDERGRADUATE SCHOLARSHIP

American Railway Engineering and Maintenance of Way Association
Attn: AREMA Educational Foundation Scholarship Committee
10003 Derekwood Lane, Suite 210
Lanham, MD 20706
(301) 459-3200, ext. 706   Fax: (301) 459-8077
E-mail: selder@arema.org
Web: www.arema.org

Purpose To provide financial assistance to undergraduate students and current railway employees who are interested in preparing for a career in railway engineering.

Eligibility This program is open to 1) full-time undergraduate students, and 2) part-time students who are working full time in the railway industry. Applicants must have completed at least 1 quarter or semester at an ABET-accredited 4-year or 5-year program (or a comparably accredited program in Canada or Mexico) leading to a bachelor's degree in engineering or engineering technology with a GPA of 2.0 or higher. They must be interested in a career in railway engineering. Along with their application, they must submit a resume, official transcript, 2 letters of recommendation, and 350-word cover letter explaining why they believe they are deserving of this scholarship, the areas of railroading in which they are particularly interested, and (for current railway employees) describing their position. Financial need is not considered in the selection process.

Financial data The stipend is $1,000.
Duration 1 year.
Number awarded 1 each year.
Deadline March of each year.

[117]
COMPUTER SOCIETY INTERNATIONAL DESIGN COMPETITION

IEEE Computer Society
Attn: Student Awards
1730 Massachusetts Avenue, N.W.
Washington, DC 20036-1992
(202) 371-1013   Fax: (202) 778-0884
E-mail: csidc@computer.org
Web: www.computer.org/csidc

Purpose To recognize and reward undergraduate students who design and implement computer-based solutions to real-world problems.

Eligibility The competition is open to teams of undergraduate students in computer science, computer engineering, and related fields. Each team consists of 4 undergraduates plus a faculty mentor. Teams must design and implement a computer-based project on a topic that changes annually; a recent topic was "Preserving, Protecting, and Enhancing the Environment." They must submit a report that includes an abstract, a system overview (with a statement of what the system hardware and software are meant to accomplish, a statement of the performance requirements it is intended to meet, a summary of the design methodology used and why it was chosen, and a statement of what is unique or innovative about this project and any novel ideas that the design includes), a description of implementation and engineering considerations (with a detailed description of the system and the algorithms involved, the trade-offs considered and used, any tools that were developed in the context of the project, and verification and testing), and a summary. Based on those reports, finalists are chosen and invited to present their projects to the judging panel. Selection of winners is based on originality of the project, its relevance to the theme of being beneficial to society, the substance of the project, taking a systems approach, teamwork, quality and presentation of reports, creativity in design, plan for the project period, and practicality and feasibility of the project. The Microsoft Award for Software Engineering is awarded to the team that makes the best use of appropriate software engineering techniques in the planning, design, construction, testing, and documentation of their software. The Microsoft Multimedia Award is awarded to the team that makes best use of multimedia techniques in their formal presentation at the finals.

Financial data Prizes are $20,000 for first, $12,000 for second, $8,000 for third, and $4,000 for honorable mentions. Students determine how the prize money is distributed among the team members. The 2 special Microsoft Prizes are each $2,000.

Duration The competition is held annually.

Additional information This competition was first held in 2000. The 2 special Microsoft Prizes were first awarded in 2003.

Number awarded The competition is limited to 300 teams. If more teams apply, team selection is made at random. Of the entrants, 10 teams are selected as finalists and to receive prizes (including 7 honorable mentions).

Deadline Applications must be submitted by November of each year. Project reports are due in April, and the world finals are held at the end of June.

[118]
COMTO NJ SCHOLARSHIPS

Conference of Minority Transportation Officials-New Jersey Chapter
Attn: Scholarship Committee
P.O. Box 22968
Newark, NJ 07101
E-mail: comtonj@mail.comtonj.org
Web: www.comtonj.org/scholarshipInfo.asp

Purpose To provide financial assistance to entering or enrolled college students from New Jersey interested in working on a degree in a field related to transportation.

Eligibility This program is open to students entering or attending colleges and universities in New Jersey to major in a field related to transportation (e.g., environmental disciplines, public service, safety, transportation, urban planning). Applicants must have a GPA of 3.0 or higher. Along with their application, they must submit a 500-word essay on why they chose a career in transportation. Selection is based on the essay, academic achievement, extracurricular and community activities, and letters of recommendation.

Financial data Stipends are $1,000 or $500.

Duration 1 year.

Additional information The sponsor is the New Jersey chapter of the Conference of Minority Transportation Officials (COMTO). The national organization was founded in 1971 to promote, strengthen, and expand the roles of minorities in all aspects of transportation. This program includes the Lewis R. Rosser Scholarship, the Paul Smith Scholarship, and the Garrett Morgan Scholarship. Recipients must attend the COMTO NJ Scholarship Gala to accept the award.

Number awarded 4 each year: 1 at $1,000 and 3 at $500.

Deadline April of each year.

SCIENCES

[119]
CONNECTICUT CHAPTER SCHOLARSHIP

Air & Waste Management Association-Connecticut Chapter
Attn: Ray Yarmac, Secretary
Sci-Tech, Inc.
185 Silas Deane Highway
Wethersfield, CT 06109
(860) 257-0767, ext. 215
E-mail: ryarmac@sce-techinc.com
Web: www.awma-nes.org/connecticut_chapter.htm

Purpose To provide financial assistance to residents of Connecticut who are interested in studying fields related to air and waste management in college.

Eligibility This program is open to 1) seniors graduating from high schools in Connecticut who plan to enroll full time in college, and 2) Connecticut residents already enrolled full time in college. Applicants must be interested in working on a degree in science or engineering leading to careers in the environmental field, especially air pollution control or waste management. Selection is based on their proposed plan of study, transcripts, work experience, and volunteer and extracurricular activities; financial need is not considered.

Financial data The stipend is $1,000.

Duration 1 year; recipients may reapply.

Number awarded 1 each year.

Deadline April of each year.

[120]
CONSTRUCTMYFUTURE.COM SCHOLARSHIPS

ConstructMyFuture.com
111 East Wisconsin Avenue, Suite 1000
Milwaukee, WI 53202
(414) 272-0943   Toll-free: (866) AEM-0442
Fax: (414) 272-1170   E-mail: nhallada@aem.org
Web: www.constructmyfuture.com

Purpose To provide financial assistance for college to students who are interested in preparing for a career in the construction industry.

Eligibility This program is open to 1) graduating high school seniors; 2) students currently enrolled in a postsecondary educational institution; and 3) workers currently employed in the construction industry. Applicants must be interested in 1) entering or continuing in a college program to prepare for a career in the construction industry; or 2) purchasing tools for use in a construction industry job. Along with their application, they must submit a 1,000-word essay on their interest in the construction industry, their educational goals, and any other information such as specialized hobbies, skills, rewards, or achievements they wish to share. Selection is based on current and past involvement in the construction field; financial need is not considered.

Financial data The stipend is $1,000.

Duration 1 year; nonrenewable.

Number awarded 3 each year.

Deadline February of each year.

[121]
CRA UNDERGRADUATE AWARDS

Computing Research Association
1100 17th Street, N.W., Suite 507
Washington, DC 20036-4632
(202) 234-2111   Fax: (202) 667-1066
E-mail: awards@cra.org
Web: www.cra.org

Purpose To recognize and reward undergraduate students who show exceptional promise in an area of importance to computing research.

Eligibility Eligible to be nominated by their department chairs for this award are undergraduate students in the United States or Canada who are majoring in computer science, computer engineering, or an equivalent program. A department may nominate more than 1 candidate. The nomination package must include a completed nomination form, the nominee's resume (up to 2 pages), the nominee's transcript, a verification statement signed by the department chair, 2 letters of support, and a 1-page description of the student's research or other achievements. Out of the pool of candidates, the most outstanding woman and the most outstanding man are selected on the basis of academic record and computing research contributions.

Financial data The award is $1,000.

Duration The competition is held annually.

Additional information This award is sponsored by Microsoft Corporation (in odd-numbered years) and Mitsubishi Electric Research Labs (in even-numbered years). The 2 first-prize winners also receive financial assistance to attend a major computing research conference, where the prizes are awarded.

Number awarded 2 cash prizes (1 to a woman and 1 to a man) and a number of certificates of honorable mention.

Deadline October of each year.

[122]
CRSI FOUNDATION UNDERGRADUATE SCHOLARSHIP PROGRAM

Concrete Reinforcing Steel Institute
Attn: CRSI Foundation
933 North Plum Grove Road
Schaumburg, IL 60173-4758
(847) 517-1200, ext. 14   Fax: (847) 517-1206
E-mail: lkelly@crsi.org
Web: www.crsi.org

Purpose To provide financial assistance to undergraduate students in civil or architectural engineering who are interested in preparing for a career in site-cast reinforced concrete construction.

Eligibility This program is open to U.S. citizens who are entering their senior year as a full-time student in an ABET-accredited program in civil or architectural engineering. Applicants must demonstrate a career goal of employment in the site-cast reinforced concrete construction industry. Preference is given to students who have shown an interest, either through their educational program or by work experience, in a phase of that industry. Students having "hands-on" experience from full-time, part-time, or co-op work in the industry are especially encouraged to apply. Financial need is not considered in the selection process.

Financial data The stipend is $2,500.
Duration 1 year.
Number awarded Varies each year; recently, 8 of these scholarships were awarded.
Deadline June of each year.

[123]
CSHEMA SCHOLARSHIP AWARD PROGRAM
National Safety Council
Attn: CSHEMA
1121 Spring Lake Drive
Itasca, IL 60143-3201
(630) 775-2227   Fax: (630) 285-1613
E-mail: postmaster@cshema.org
Web: www.cshema.org/awards/scholarship.htm

Purpose To provide financial assistance to undergraduate and graduate students working on a degree in a field related to the concerns of the Campus Safety Health and Environmental Management Association (CSHEMA).
Eligibility This program is open to full-time undergraduate and graduate students who are majoring in any field but are interested in the study of environmental and occupational health, safety, or related disciplines. Applicants must have at least 1 year of study remaining in their degree program. Along with their application, they must submit a 1-page essay in which they describe a health, safety, or environmental issue relevant to their university or college and examine and discuss what actions and/or programs are needed to solve this issue. Financial need is not considered.
Financial data The stipend is $2,000.
Duration 1 year.
Additional information This program was established in 1977.
Number awarded 1 each year.
Deadline March of each year.

[124]
DAEDALIAN ACADEMIC MATCHING SCHOLARSHIP PROGRAM
Daedalian Foundation
Attn: Scholarship Committee
55 Main Circle (Building 676)
P.O. Box 249
Randolph AFB, TX 78148-0249
(210) 945-2113   Fax: (210) 945-2112
E-mail: daedalus@daedalians.org
Web: www.daedalians.org

Purpose To provide financial assistance to ROTC and other college students who wish to become military pilots.
Eligibility Eligible are students who are attending or have been accepted at an accredited 4-year college or university and have demonstrated the desire and potential to become a commissioned military pilot. Usually, students in ROTC units of all services apply to local chapters (Flights) of Daedalian; if the Flight awards a scholarship, the application is forwarded to the Daedalian Foundation for 1 of these matching scholarships. College students not part of a ROTC program are eligible if their undergraduate goals and performance are consistent with Daedalian criteria. Selection is based on intention to pursue a career as a military pilot, demonstrated moral character and patriotism, scholastic and military standing and aptitude, and physical condition and aptitude for flight. Additional eligibility criteria may be set by a Flight Scholarship Selection Board.
Financial data The amount awarded varies but is intended to serve as matching funds for the Flight scholarship. Generally, the maximum awarded is $2,000.
Number awarded Up to 99 each year.
Deadline Applications may be submitted at any time.

[125]
DAEDALIAN FOUNDATION DESCENDANTS' SCHOLARSHIP PROGRAM
Daedalian Foundation
Attn: Scholarship Committee
55 Main Circle (Building 676)
P.O. Box 249
Randolph AFB, TX 78148-0249
(210) 945-2113   Fax: (210) 945-2112
E-mail: daedalus@daedalians.org
Web: www.daedalians.org

Purpose To provide financial assistance to descendants of members of the Order of Daedalians who wish to prepare for a career in military aviation or space.
Eligibility This program is open to descendants of members of the order who are working on or planning to work on a baccalaureate or higher degree. Applicants must be interested in and willing to commit to a career as a commissioned military pilot, flight crew member, astronaut, or a commissioned officer in 1 of the armed forces of the United States in a discipline directly supporting aeronautics or astronautics. They must be physically and mentally qualified for flight and/or space; if they intend to pursue a non-flying career as a commissioned officer in a scientific or engineering discipline supporting aviation or space, they must pass a physical examination qualifying for active commissioned duty in the U.S. armed forces. Nominations must be submitted by a local chapter (Flight) of Daedalian. Selection is based on academic achievement and recognition, extracurricular activities, honors, and employment experience. Financial need may also be considered, but only if all other factors are equal.
Financial data The stipend is $2,000.
Additional information The Order of Daedalians was founded in 1934 as an organization of the nearly 14,000 aviators who served as military pilots during World War I and are still listed and designated as Founder Members. In the 1950s, the organization expanded eligibility to include 1) on a sponsorship basis, current and former commissioned military pilots from all services, and 2) on a hereditary basis, descendants of Founder Members.
Number awarded Up to 3 each year.
Deadline June of each year.

SCIENCES

[126]
DAIMLERCHRYSLER CORPORATION FUND SCHOLARSHIP

Society of Women Engineers
230 East Ohio Street, Suite 400
Chicago, IL 60611-3265
(312) 596-5223   Toll-free: (877) SWE-INFO
Fax: (312) 644-8557
E-mail: scholarshipapplication@swe.org
Web: www.swe.org/scholarships

Purpose To provide financial assistance to undergraduate women majoring in designated engineering specialties.

Eligibility This program is open to women who are entering their sophomore year at an ABET-accredited 4-year college or university. Applicants must be majoring in electrical or mechanical engineering and have a GPA of 3.0 or higher. Along with their application, they must submit a 1-page essay on why they want to be an engineer, how they believe they will make a difference as an engineer, and what influenced them to study engineering. Selection is based on merit.

Financial data The stipend is $2,000.

Duration 1 year; may be renewed for up to 2 additional years.

Additional information This program, established in 1997, is sponsored by DaimlerChrysler Corporation.

Number awarded 1 each year.

Deadline January of each year.

[127]
DAN L. MEISINGER, SR. MEMORIAL LEARN TO FLY SCHOLARSHIP

National Air Transportation Foundation
Attn: Manager, Education and Training
4226 King Street
Alexandria, VA 22302
(703) 845-9000, ext. 125   Toll-free: (800) 808-6282
Fax: (703) 845-8176   E-mail: dhighsmith@nata.aero
Web: www.nata.aero/about/sch_meisinger.jsp

Purpose To provide financial assistance for flight training to college students.

Eligibility This program is open to college students currently enrolled in an aviation program with a GPA of 3.0 or higher. Preference is given to residents of Kansas, Missouri, and Illinois. Along with their application, they must submit a statement of their plans as they relate to their educational, flight training, and career objectives; future goals; and contributions and commitment to general aviation. Selection is based on academic record, potential to succeed, leadership and participation in school and community activities, and relevant work experience.

Financial data The stipend is $2,500. Funds may be used only for initial or primary flight training. Scholarship checks are made payable jointly to the recipient and the participating flight school.

Duration 1 year.

Additional information A $5 application fee is required.

Number awarded 1 each year.

Deadline November of each year.

[128]
DAVID ARVER MEMORIAL SCHOLARSHIP

Aircraft Electronics Association
Attn: AEA Educational Foundation
4217 South Hocker Drive
Independence, MO 64055-4723
(816) 373-6565   Fax: (816) 478-3100
E-mail: info@aea.net
Web: www.aea.net

Purpose To provide financial assistance to students in selected states who are interested in studying avionics or aircraft repair at a midwestern college.

Eligibility This program is open to high school seniors and college students who plan to attend an accredited vocational or technical school in the Aircraft Electronics Association Region III; this includes the states of Illinois, Indiana, Iowa, Kansas, Michigan, Minnesota, Missouri, Nebraska, North Dakota, South Dakota, and Wisconsin. Applicants must be planning to enroll in an avionics or aircraft repair program. They must submit an official transcript (cumulative GPA of 2.5 or higher), a statement about their career plans, a description of their involvement in school and community activities, and a 300-word essay on how the job requirements of aviation technicians will change with advancements in technology. Selection is based on merit.

Financial data The stipend is $1,000.

Duration 1 year.

Number awarded 1 each year.

Deadline February of each year.

[129]
DAVID J. FITZMAURICE SCHOLARSHIP

International Union of Electronic, Electrical, Salaried, Machine, and Furniture Workers
Attn: IUE-CWA International Scholarship Program
501 Third Street, N.W., Suite 975
Washington, DC 20001
(202) 434-1417   Fax: (202) 434-1250
E-mail: bgray@iue-cwa.org
Web: www.iue-cwa.org/skills.html

Purpose To provide financial assistance children and grandchildren of members of the International Union of Electronic, Electrical, Salaried, Machine, and Furniture Workers (IUE)-Communications Workers of America (CWA) who are interested in majoring in engineering.

Eligibility This program is open to children and grandchildren of IUE-CWA members (including retired or deceased members). Applicants must be accepted for admission or already enrolled as full-time students at an accredited college, university, or technical school in an engineering program. Along with their application, they must submit an academic transcript (including rank in class, GPA, and SAT/ACT scores); a short statement of interests and civic activities; and an essay (300 to 500 words) describing their career goals and aspirations, highlighting their relationship with the union and the labor movement, and explaining why they are deserving of a union scholarship. They must also have demonstrated a commitment to equality of opportunity for all, a concern for improving the quality of life for all people, an interest in service to the community, good character, leadership ability, and a desire to improve and move ahead.

Financial data The stipend is $2,000 per year.
Duration 1 year.
Number awarded 1 each year.
Deadline March of each year.

[130]
DAVID MANN SCHOLARSHIP

American Mensa Education and Research Foundation
1229 Corporate Drive West
Arlington, TX 76006-6103
(817) 607-0060   Toll-free: (800) 66-MENSA
Fax: (817) 649-5232
E-mail: info@mensafoundation.org
Web: www.mensafoundation.org

Purpose To provide financial assistance for undergraduate or graduate study in aeronautical engineering or an aerospace field.
Eligibility This program is open to students who are enrolled or planning to enroll in a degree program at an accredited American institution of postsecondary education with a major or career plans in aeronautical engineering or an aerospace field. Membership in Mensa is not required, but applicants must be U.S. citizens or permanent residents. There are no restrictions as to age, race, gender, level of postsecondary education, GPA, or financial need. Selection is based on a 550-word essay that describes the applicant's career, vocational, or academic goals.
Financial data The stipend is $1,000.
Duration 1 year; nonrenewable.
Additional information Applications are only available through the advertising efforts of participating Mensa local groups.
Number awarded 1 each year.
Deadline January of each year.

[131]
DEAN MEMORIAL LEGACY SCHOLARSHIPS

California 4-H Foundation
Attn: Youth Development Program
University of California
Agriculture and Natural Resources
One Hopkins Road
Davis, CA 95616-8575
(530) 754-8518   Fax: (530) 757-8739
E-mail: fourhstateofc@ucdavis.edu
Web: www.ca4h.org/4hresource/ir

Purpose To provide financial assistance for college to students in California who have belonged to 4-H.
Eligibility Applicants must be residents of California who are or were (at the time of their high school graduation) enrolled in the 4-H Youth Development Program. They may be high school seniors or high school graduates between 16 and 25 years of age enrolled or planning to enroll at a college or university. Selection is based on leadership and citizenship experiences, how 4-H has shaped their future goals, and demonstrated level of skill and knowledge in a project area.
Financial data The stipend is $1,000. Funds are sent directly to the recipient's school.
Duration 1 year.

Additional information This scholarship was first awarded in 2006. Recipients may major in any subject field, but they must attend school in the United States.
Number awarded 3 each year.
Deadline April of each year.

[132]
DECOMMISSIONING, DECONTAMINATION AND REUTILIZATION SCHOLARSHIP

American Nuclear Society
Attn: Scholarship Coordinator
555 North Kensington Avenue
La Grange Park, IL 60526-5592
(708) 352-6611   Fax: (708) 352-0499
E-mail: outreach@ans.org
Web: www.ans.org/honors/scholarships

Purpose To provide financial assistance to undergraduate students who are working on a degree in engineering or science that is associated with decommissioning, decontamination, or environmental restoration aspects of nuclear power.
Eligibility This program is open to students entering their junior or senior year in an engineering or science program at an accredited institution in the United States. The program must be associated with 1) decommissioning or decontamination of nuclear facilities; 2) management or characterization of nuclear waste; or 3) restoration of the environment. Applicants must be U.S. citizens and able to demonstrate academic achievement. Along with their application, they must submit a brief essay discussing the importance of an aspect of decommissioning, decontamination, and reutilization to the future of the nuclear field.
Financial data The stipend is $2,000.
Duration 1 year; nonrenewable.
Additional information This program is offered by the Decommissioning, Decontamination and Reutilization (DD&R) Division of the ANS. Recipients must agree to join the ANS and designate the DD&R Division as 1 of their professional divisions. They must commit to participating in DD&R Division activities by attending the annual and winter meetings of the ANS and serving as a student representative at the DD&R executive committee meetings at both ANS meetings.
Number awarded 1 each year.
Deadline January of each year.

[133]
DEED TECHNICAL DESIGN PROJECT

American Public Power Association
Attn: DEED Administrator
2301 M Street, N.W.
Washington, DC 20037-1484
(202) 467-2960   Fax: (202) 467-2910
E-mail: deed@appanet.org
Web: www.appanet.org

Purpose To recognize and reward undergraduate and graduate students who develop and demonstrate outstanding projects related to energy innovation.
Eligibility Eligible are undergraduate and graduate students in energy-related disciplines at accredited colleges

SCIENCES

and universities in the United States and Canada. Applicants must complete a technical design project and submit a final report on the project, describing activities, cost, sources used, achievements, problems, results, and recommendations. The project must relate to energy innovation, improving efficiencies, and lowering the cost of providing energy services to the customers of publicly owned electric utilities. Selection is based on the applicability of benefits to public power systems, the applicant's major in an academic field related to the electric power or energy service industries, academic performance, generalizable methodologies, and promotion of energy efficiency.

Financial data The grant is $5,000. An additional $3,000 is available to pay for travel expenses to attend the engineering and operations technical conference of the American Public Power Association (APPA) and present their project. If more than 1 student is involved in a project, the award funds are split among all participants.

Duration This competition is held annually.

Additional information The APPA is the national trade organization representing approximately 2,000 publicly-owned electric utilities. Its research project, the Demonstration of Energy-Efficient Developments (DEED), was established in 1980.

Number awarded 1 each year.

Deadline October of each year.

[134]
DELTA FAUCET COMPANY SCHOLARSHIPS

Plumbing-Heating-Cooling Contractors-National
  Association
Attn: PHCC Educational Foundation
180 South Washington Street
P.O. Box 6808
Falls Church, VA 22040
(703) 237-8100, ext. 221   Toll-free: (800) 533-7694
Fax: (703) 237-7442
E-mail: scholarships@naphcc.org
Web: www.foundation.phccweb.org

Purpose To provide financial assistance to entering or continuing undergraduate students interested in the plumbing, heating, and cooling industry.

Eligibility This program is open to 1) full-time undergraduate students (entering or continuing) who are majoring in a field related to plumbing, heating, and cooling (e.g., business management, construction management with a specialization in mechanical construction, mechanical engineering) at a 4-year college or university, and 2) students enrolled in an approved apprenticeship program or a full-time certificate or degree program at a 2-year technical college, community college, or trade school in business management, mechanical CAD design, construction management with a specialty in mechanical construction, or plumbing or HVACR installation, service, and repair. Students enrolled in an approved plumbing or HVAC apprenticeship program must be working full time for a licensed plumbing or HVAC contractor who is a member of the Plumbing-Heating-Cooling Contractors-National Association (PHCC). Applicants must submit a letter of recommendation from a member with 2 years' good standing in the PHCC; a copy of school transcripts; and a letter of recommendation from a school principal, counselor, or dean. U.S. or Canadian citizenship is required. Financial need is not considered in the selection process.

Financial data The stipend is $2,500 per year.

Duration 1 year; nonrenewable.

Additional information This program is sponsored by the Delta Faucet Company.

Number awarded 6 each year: 4 to students at 4-year institutions and 2 to students at 2-year institutions.

Deadline May of each year.

[135]
DEVELOPMENT DISABILITIES SCHOLASTIC EXCELLENCE AWARD FOR LUTHERAN STUDENTS IN COLLEGE

Bethesda Lutheran Homes and Services, Inc.
Attn: National Christian Resource Center
600 Hoffmann Drive
Watertown, WI 53094
(920) 261-3050   Toll-free: (800) 369-4636, ext. 3418
Fax: (920) 262-6513   E-mail: ncrc@blhs.org
Web: www.blhs.org/youth/scholarships

Purpose To provide financial assistance to undergraduates who are Lutherans and interested in preparing for a career in any area of service to people with developmental disabilities.

Eligibility Applicants must be active communicant members of a Lutheran congregation; be classified as a sophomore or junior; have an overall GPA of 3.0 or higher; and be interested in preparing for a career in the field of developmental disabilities. Along with their application, they must submit 1) an essay of 1 to 2 pages on the career they are planning in the field of developmental disabilities, why they chose that particular career goal, and how they are preparing for that career; 2) 4 letters of recommendation; 3) an official college transcript; 4) a 1-page autobiographical narrative, detailing their academic and community honors, awards, and activities; and 5) documentation that they have completed at least 100 hours of volunteer and/or paid work to benefit people who are developmentally disabled. Financial need is not considered in the selection process.

Financial data The stipend is $1,500.

Duration 1 year.

Number awarded Up to 3 each year.

Deadline March of each year.

[136]
DOLORES E. FISHER AWARD

Mel Fisher Maritime Heritage Society and Museum
Attn: Curator, Department of Education
200 Greene Street
Key West, FL 33040
(305) 294-2633   Fax: (305) 294-5671
Web: www.melfisher.org/deoaward.htm

Purpose To recognize and reward, with funding for college or graduate school, women who submit outstanding essays on the oceans.

Eligibility This competition is open to women between 16 and 30 years of age. Candidates must submit a 1,000-word essay on how they hope to make a difference in the world through their passion for the oceans, their career goals, and how this award will help them achieve those goals. They must also include 3 letters of recommendation and a brief statement on the personality characteristic they value most in themselves and why. If they are currently enrolled in school, they must identify their program, but school enrollment is not required.

Financial data The award is $1,000.

Duration The award is presented annually.

Number awarded 1 each year.

Deadline March of each year.

[137]
DONALD F. & MILDRED TOPP OTHMER NATIONAL SCHOLARSHIP AWARDS

American Institute of Chemical Engineers
Attn: Awards Administrator
Three Park Avenue
New York, NY 10016-5991
(212) 591-7107   Fax: (212) 591-8890
E-mail: awards@aiche.org
Web: www.aiche.org/Students/Awards/index.aspx

Purpose To provide financial assistance to student members of the American Institute of Chemical Engineers (AIChE).

Eligibility This program is open to AIChE student members who are undergraduates in chemical engineering. Each student chapter advisor may nominate 1 student member. Nominees must have completed approximately half of their degree requirements at the start of the academic year (i.e., junior standing in a 4-year program or equivalent for a 5-year co-op program). They must submit a 300-word statement outlining their career plans and objectives in chemical engineering. Selection is based on that statement, academic record, support of the nominee by the student chapter advisor, and involvement in student chapter and other professional activities.

Financial data The stipend is $1,000.

Duration 1 year.

Additional information This program is sponsored by the Donald F. & Mildred Topp Othmer Foundation. Information is also available from Walter P. Walawender, Kansas State University, Chemical Engineering Department, Durland Hall, Manhattan, KS 66506-5102, (785) 532-4318, Fax; (785) 532-7372, E-mail: walawen@earth.cheme.ksu.edu.

Number awarded 15 each year.

Deadline May of each year.

[138]
DONALD G. WILLEMS SCHOLARSHIP

American Water Works Association-Montana Section
Attn: Executive Secretary
1029 Washington Avenue
Havre, MT 59501
(406) 265-9753   Fax: (406) 265-2277
E-mail: bcoffman@3riversdbs.net
Web: www.montana-awwa.org/scholarship.htm

Purpose To provide financial assistance to students at colleges and universities in Montana who are working on undergraduate or graduate degrees in water-related fields.

Eligibility This program is open to students currently enrolled at colleges and universities in Montana who have completed at least 1 academic year with a GPA of 2.0 or higher. Applicants must be working on an associate, bachelor's, or graduate degree in a field that will lead to employment in the water and wastewater fields, including water treatment and distribution, wastewater treatment and collection, water resources, watershed protection, groundwater remediation, and related subdisciplines. Along with their application, they must submit 3 references, a resume, and a 750-word statement of their professional goals. Financial need is not considered.

Financial data The stipend is $1,000.

Duration 1 year.

Additional information This program is jointly sponsored by the Montana Section of the American Water Works Association (AWWA) and the Montana Water Environment Association (MWEA), the Montana affiliate of the Water Environment Federation. The scholarship winners also receive a 1-year student membership of their choice in AWWA or MWEA.

Number awarded 1 or 2 each year.

Deadline February of each year.

[139]
DONNIE ARTHUR MEMORIAL TURFGRASS SCHOLARSHIP

Alabama Golf Course Superintendents Association
Attn: Scholarship Committee
P.O. Box 661214
Birmingham, AL 35266-1214
(205) 967-0397   Fax: (205) 967-1466
E-mail: agcsa@charter.net
Web: www.agcsa.org/scholarshipprogram.htm

Purpose To provide financial assistance to students from Alabama who are majoring in turfgrass management in college.

Eligibility This program is open to residents of Alabama who are currently enrolled full time in an agricultural program emphasizing turfgrass management. Applicants must have a GPA of 2.0 or higher. Along with their application, they must submit a description of themselves that covers their academic ability, dependability, work habits, potential for leadership, and thoughts on what a superintendent needs in the 21st century to be successful.

Financial data The stipend is $1,000. Funds are paid directly to the recipient.

Duration 1 year.

Number awarded 2 each year.

Deadline October of each year.

SCIENCES

[140]
DOROTHY LEMKE HOWARTH SCHOLARSHIPS
Society of Women Engineers
230 East Ohio Street, Suite 400
Chicago, IL 60611-3265
(312) 596-5223   Toll-free: (877) SWE-INFO
Fax: (312) 644-8557
E-mail: scholarshipapplication@swe.org
Web: www.swe.org/scholarships

Purpose To provide financial assistance to lower-division women majoring in computer science or engineering.

Eligibility This program is open to women who are entering their sophomore year at a 4-year ABET-accredited college or university. Applicants must be U.S. citizens majoring in computer science or engineering who have a GPA of 3.0 or higher. Along with their application, they must submit a 1-page essay on why they want to be an engineer or computer scientist, how they believe they will make a difference as an engineer or computer scientist, and what influenced them to study engineering or computer science. Selection is based on merit.

Financial data The stipend is $2,000.

Duration 1 year.

Additional information This program was established in 1991.

Number awarded 5 each year.

Deadline January of each year.

[141]
DOROTHY P. MORRIS SCHOLARSHIP
Society of Women Engineers
230 East Ohio Street, Suite 400
Chicago, IL 60611-3265
(312) 596-5223   Toll-free: (877) SWE-INFO
Fax: (312) 644-8557
E-mail: scholarshipapplication@swe.org
Web: www.swe.org/scholarships

Purpose To provide financial assistance to undergraduate women majoring in computer science or engineering.

Eligibility This program is open to women who are entering their sophomore, junior, or senior year at a 4-year ABET-accredited college or university. Applicants must be U.S. citizens majoring in computer science or engineering and have a GPA of 3.0 or higher. Along with their application, they must submit a 1-page essay on why they want to be an engineer or computer scientist, how they believe they will make a difference as an engineer or computer scientist, and what influenced them to study engineering or computer science. Selection is based on merit.

Financial data The stipend is $1,000.

Duration 1 year.

Number awarded 1 each year.

Deadline January of each year.

[142]
DR. AND MRS. H.H. NININGER METEORITE AWARD
Arizona State University
Attn: Center for Meteorite Studies
P.O. Box 871404
Tempe, AZ 85287-1404
(602) 965-6511   E-mail: meteorites@asu.edu
Web: meteorites.asu.edu/nininger

Purpose To recognize and reward outstanding student papers dealing with aspects of meteoritic investigation.

Eligibility This competition is open to both undergraduate and graduate students. They are invited to submit a paper (under 10,000 words) reflecting an aspect of meteoritic investigation. Research topics may include (but are not limited to) physical and chemical properties of meteorites, origin of meteoritic material, and cratering. Observational, experimental, statistical, and theoretical investigations are allowed. Students must be the first author of the paper, but they do not have to be the sole author. Papers must have been written, submitted, or published during the first 10 and a half months of the calendar year. They must cover original research conducted by the student.

Financial data The prize is $2,500.

Duration The competition is held annually.

Additional information Entries not awarded the prize may be resubmitted in the original or a revised form as long as the author is a student at an American college or university.

Number awarded 1 each year.

Deadline November of each year.

[143]
DR. AUREL ZAJTA SCHOLARSHIP
Electronic Document Systems Foundation
Attn: EDSF Scholarship Awards
608 Silver Spur Road, Suite 280
Rolling Hills Estates, CA 90274-3616
(310) 265-5510   Fax: (310) 265-5588
E-mail: jmowlds@edsf.org
Web: www.edsf.org/scholarships.cfm

Purpose To provide financial assistance to undergraduate and graduate students working on a degree in mathematics-based studies related to the graphic arts.

Eligibility This program is open to undergraduate and graduate students who are working on a degree in mathematics-based studies related to the graphic arts, font, print, or Internet-related studies. Applicants must be enrolled full time at a technical school, trade school, community college, university, college, or graduate school in the United States with a GPA of 3.0 or higher. Along with their application, they must submit a statement of their career goals in the field of document communications, an essay on a topic related to their view of the future of the document management and production industry, a list of current professional and college extracurricular activities and achievements, college transcripts, samples of their creative work, and 2 letters of recommendation. Financial need is not considered.

Financial data The stipend is $1,000.

Duration 1 year.

MERIT/NO-NEED FUNDING

Additional information This program is sponsored by COPI/OutputLinks.
Number awarded 1 each year.
Deadline May of each year.

[144]
DR. HAROLD S. WOOD AWARD FOR EXCELLENCE
General Aviation Manufacturers Association
Attn: Director of Administration
1400 K Street, N.W., Suite 801
Washington, DC 20005-2485
(202) 393-1500 Fax: (202) 842-4063
E-mail: bbailey@GAMA.aero
Web: www.gama.aero

Purpose To provide financial assistance to students at schools belonging to the National Intercollegiate Flying Association (NIFA).
Eligibility Nominations are solicited from NIFA-member schools in each of the 11 NIFA regions. There is no limit to the number of applications submitted by each school. Eligible to be nominated by these schools are currently-enrolled students who have at least a 3.0 GPA. Each NIFA region chooses 1 winning finalist from the entries. A national winner is then chosen from the 11 finalists. Selection, on both levels, is based on academic record (30%), aviation-related extracurricular activities (50%), and service and contributions to school and community (20%).
Financial data The national winner is presented with an engraved propeller trophy and a $1,000 cash award.
Duration 1 year; nonrenewable.
Number awarded 11 district winners and 1 national winner.
Deadline Nominations must be submitted in February of each year.

[145]
DR. LEWIS C. HOFFMAN SCHOLARSHIP
American Ceramic Society
Attn: Electronics Division
735 Ceramic Place, Suite 100
Westerville, OH 43081
(614) 890-4700 Fax: (614) 899-6109
E-mail: info@ceramics.org
Web: www.ceramics.org

Purpose To provide financial assistance to undergraduate students in a field related to ceramic science.
Eligibility This program is open to juniors enrolled in a program related to ceramics/materials science and engineering. Applicants must submit a 500-word essay on a topic that changes annually; recently, the topic was "Electronic Ceramics in Clean Energy Technologies." Selection is based on the essay, extracurricular activities, a letter of recommendation from a faculty advisor, PSAT/SAT/ACT scores, and GPA (cumulative and in science courses).
Financial data The stipend is $2,000.
Duration 1 year.
Additional information Further information is also available from the Chair of the Awards and Scholarships Committee, Amit Goyal, Oak Ridge National Laboratory, Metals and Ceramics Division, Superconducting Materials Research, Oak Ridge, TN 37831-6116, (865) 574-1587, Fax: (865) 574-7659, E-mail: goyala@ornl.gov.
Number awarded 1 each year.
Deadline March of each year.

[146]
DR. RAYMOND K.J. LUOMANEN FUND
Finlandia Foundation-New York Metropolitan Chapter
Attn: Scholarships
P.O. Box 165, Bowling Green Station
New York, NY 10274-0165
E-mail: scholarships@finlandiafoundationny.org
Web: www.finlandiafoundationny.org

Purpose To provide financial assistance to students interested in studying or conducting research on medicine and health care in Finland or the United States.
Eligibility This program is open to students at colleges and universities in the United States who are interested in studying or conducting research on medicine or health care in Finland or the United States. Applicants must submit information on their language proficiency, work experience, memberships (academic, professional, and social), fellowships and scholarships, awards, publications, exhibitions, performances, and future goals and ambitions. Financial need is not considered in the selection process.
Financial data Stipends range from $500 to $5,000 per year.
Duration 1 year.
Additional information Information is also available from Leena Toivonen, (718) 680-1716, E-mail: leenat@hotmail.com.
Number awarded 1 or more each year.
Deadline February of each year.

[147]
DR. ROBERT W. SIMS MEMORIAL SCHOLARSHIP
Florida Association of Educational Data Systems
c/o Marsha Cole, Scholarship Chair
Duval County Public Schools
4037 Boulevard Center Drive, Building B, Second Floor
Jacksonville, FL 32207
(904) 348-5167 Fax: (904) 348-5737
E-mail: colem@educationcentral.org
Web: www.faeds.org/Scholarships.htm

Purpose To provide financial assistance to students attending a Florida college or university and majoring in computer science or information technology.
Eligibility Any currently-enrolled college student who has at least a 2.5 GPA and is attending a Florida private or public college or university is eligible. Applicants must be enrolled full time and be majoring or planning to major in computer science or information technology. Along with their application, they must submit a 2-page essay indicating their interest in computer science and/or information technology and 3 letters of recommendation. Financial need is not considered in the selection process.
Financial data The stipend is $2,000.
Duration 1 year.

SCIENCES

Additional information This scholarship was established in 1969.
Number awarded Up to 3 each year.
Deadline February of each year.

[148]
DR. S. BRADLEY BURSON MEMORIAL SCHOLARSHIP

American Council of the Blind
Attn: Coordinator, Scholarship Program
1155 15th Street, N.W., Suite 1004
Washington, DC 20005
(202) 467-5081 Toll-free: (800) 424-8666
Fax: (202) 467-5085 E-mail: info@acb.org
Web: www.acb.org

Purpose To provide financial assistance to blind students who are working on an undergraduate or graduate degree in science at an accredited college or university.
Eligibility This program is open to legally blind undergraduate or graduate students majoring in the "hard" sciences (i.e., biology, chemistry, physics, and engineering, but not computer science) in college. They must be U.S. citizens. In addition to letters of recommendation and copies of academic transcripts, applications must include an autobiographical sketch. A cumulative GPA of 3.3 or higher is generally required. Selection is based on demonstrated academic record, involvement in extracurricular and civic activities, and academic objectives. The severity of the applicant's visual impairment and his/her study methods are also taken into account.
Financial data The stipend is $1,000. In addition, the winner receives a Kurzweil-1000 Reading System.
Duration 1 year.
Additional information Scholarship winners are expected to be present at the council's annual conference; the council will cover all reasonable expenses connected with convention attendance.
Number awarded 1 each year.
Deadline February of each year.

[149]
DR. WILLIAM S. BOYD SCHOLARSHIP

Chiropractic Association of Louisiana
c/o Scholarship Committee
10636 Timberlake Drive
Baton Rouge, LA 70810
(225) 769-5560
Web: www.cal-online.org

Purpose To provide financial assistance to residents of Louisiana enrolled in chiropractic colleges.
Eligibility This program is open to Louisiana residents who are currently enrolled (as a junior or senior) in a CCE-accredited chiropractic college. Applicants must have earned at least a 2.75 GPA, be recommended by an active member of the Chiropractic Association of Louisiana, and intend to practice in Louisiana upon graduation. Also required are 3 letters of recommendation. Financial need is not considered in the selection process.
Financial data A stipend is awarded (amount not specified). Funds are sent directly to the recipient.
Duration 1 year.
Additional information This program was established in 1995. Winners are invited to attend the association's annual convention; lodging and registration are paid by the association.
Number awarded 1 or more each year.
Deadline June of each year.

[150]
DUTCH AND GINGER ARVER SCHOLARSHIP

Aircraft Electronics Association
Attn: AEA Educational Foundation
4217 South Hocker Drive
Independence, MO 64055-4723
(816) 373-6565 Fax: (816) 478-3100
E-mail: info@aea.net
Web: www.aea.net

Purpose To provide financial assistance to students preparing for a career in avionics.
Eligibility This program is open to high school seniors and currently-enrolled college students who are attending (or planning to attend) an accredited postsecondary institution in an avionics program. Applicants must submit an official transcript (cumulative GPA of 2.5 or higher), a statement about their career plans, a description of their involvement in school and community activities, and a 300-word essay on how the job requirements of aviation technicians will change with advancements in technology. Selection is based on merit.
Financial data The stipend is $1,000.
Duration 1 year.
Number awarded 1 each year.
Deadline February of each year.

[151]
E. TED SIMS, JR. MEMORIAL SCHOLARSHIP

American Society for Horticultural Science
113 South West Street, Suite 200
Alexandria, VA 22314-2851
(703) 836-4606 Fax: (703) 836-2024
E-mail: ashs@ashs.org
Web: www.ashs.org/awards/student.html

Purpose To provide financial assistance to upper-division students majoring in horticulture.
Eligibility This program is open to full-time juniors and seniors majoring in horticulture at a 4-year institution of higher education. Applicants must be able to demonstrate excellent academic performance in their major, participation in extracurricular activities related to horticulture, and commitment to the horticulture profession. They must be nominated by the chair or head of their department; only 1 applicant may be nominated per department. Nominees must complete an application form, write an essay of 250 to 500 words on their reasons for interest in horticulture and for selecting their intended field of work after graduating from college, and provide 3 letters of reference. Financial need is not considered in the selection process.
Financial data The stipend is $1,000.
Duration 1 year.

Additional information This scholarship was established in 1991.
Number awarded 1 each year.
Deadline February of each year.

[152]
E. WAYNE KAY CO-OP SCHOLARSHIP

Society of Manufacturing Engineers
Attn: SME Education Foundation
One SME Drive
P.O. Box 930
Dearborn, MI 48121-0930
(313) 425-3300   Toll-free: (800) 733-4763, ext. 3300
Fax: (313) 425-3411   E-mail: foundation@sme.org
Web: www.sme.org

Purpose To provide financial assistance to undergraduate students enrolled in a co-op degree program in manufacturing engineering or manufacturing engineering technology.
Eligibility This program is open to full-time undergraduate students enrolled in a manufacturing engineering or technology degree program in North America and working in a co-op program in a manufacturing-related environment. Applicants must have completed at least 30 units in a manufacturing engineering or manufacturing engineering technology curriculum with a GPA of 3.0 or higher. Along with their application, they must submit a 300-word essay that covers their career and educational objectives, how this scholarship will help them attain those objectives, and why they want to enter this field. Financial need is not considered in the selection process.
Financial data The stipend is $2,500.
Duration 1 year; may be renewed.
Number awarded 2 each year.
Deadline January of each year.

[153]
E. WAYNE KAY COMMUNITY COLLEGE SCHOLARSHIPS

Society of Manufacturing Engineers
Attn: SME Education Foundation
One SME Drive
P.O. Box 930
Dearborn, MI 48121-0930
(313) 425-3300   Toll-free: (800) 733-4763, ext. 3300
Fax: (313) 425-3411   E-mail: foundation@sme.org
Web: www.sme.org

Purpose To provide financial assistance to students enrolled or planning to enroll in a community college program in manufacturing engineering or manufacturing engineering technology.
Eligibility This program is open to entering freshmen and sophomores with less than 60 college credit hours at a community college, trade school, or other 2-year degree-granting institution in the United States or Canada. Applicants must be full-time students interested in preparing for a career in manufacturing engineering or technology and have a GPA of 3.0 or higher. Along with their application, they must submit a 300-word essay that covers their career and educational objectives, how this scholarship will help them attain those objectives, and why they want to enter this field. Financial need is not considered in the selection process.
Financial data The stipend is $1,000.
Duration 1 year.
Number awarded 2 each year.
Deadline January of each year.

[154]
E. WAYNE KAY SCHOLARSHIPS

Society of Manufacturing Engineers
Attn: SME Education Foundation
One SME Drive
P.O. Box 930
Dearborn, MI 48121-0930
(313) 425-3300   Toll-free: (800) 733-4763, ext. 3300
Fax: (313) 425-3411   E-mail: foundation@sme.org
Web: www.sme.org

Purpose To provide financial assistance to undergraduate students enrolled in a degree program in manufacturing engineering or manufacturing engineering technology.
Eligibility This program is open to full-time undergraduate students enrolled in a manufacturing engineering or technology degree program at a college or university in North America. Applicants must have completed at least 30 units in a manufacturing engineering or manufacturing engineering technology curriculum with a GPA of 3.0 or higher. Along with their application, they must submit a 300-word essay that covers their career and educational objectives, how this scholarship will help them attain those objectives, and why they want to enter this field. Financial need is not considered in the selection process.
Financial data The stipend is $2,500.
Duration 1 year; may be renewed.
Number awarded 10 each year.
Deadline January of each year.

[155]
E.B. MILLER MEMORIAL SCHOLARSHIP

Ohio Forestry Association, Inc.
4080 South High Street
Columbus, OH 43207
(614) 497-9580   Fax: (614) 497-9581
E-mail: info@ohioforest.org
Web: www.ohioforest.org

Purpose To provide financial assistance to residents of Ohio who are interested in working on an undergraduate degree in forest resources.
Eligibility This program is open to high school seniors and current undergraduate students who are residents of Ohio. Applicants must be interested in preparing for a career in forest resource management. Along with their application, they must submit brief essays on their goals and plans for a career, the challenges facing the forest resources profession, and additional information relevant to their consideration for this scholarship. U.S. citizenship is required. Financial need is not considered in the selection process.
Financial data Stipends range from $500 to $1,000 per year.

Duration 1 year.
Number awarded Varies each year; recently, 4 of these scholarships were awarded.
Deadline April of each year.

[156]
EDDIE G. COLE MEMORIAL SCHOLARSHIPS
California State Fair
Attn: Friends of the Fair Scholarship Program
1600 Exposition Boulevard
P.O. Box 15649
Sacramento, CA 95852
(916) 274-5969   E-mail: entryoffice@calexpo.com
Web: www.bigfun.org

Purpose To provide financial assistance for college to residents of California who are interested in majoring in designated fields or preparing for a career in the Fair industry.
Eligibility This program is open to residents of California currently working on an undergraduate degree at a college or university in the state. Applicants must be 1) majoring in physical education, agriculture, or equine studies; or 2) preparing for a career in the Fair industry. They must have a GPA of 3.0 or higher. Along with their application, they must submit a 2-page essay on why they are pursuing their desired career and life goals. Selection is based on personal commitment, goals established for their chosen field, leadership potential, and civic accomplishments.
Financial data Stipends are $1,000 or $250.
Duration 1 year.
Additional information The Friends of the Fair Scholarship Program was established in 1993.
Number awarded 2 each year: 1 at $1,000 and 1 at $250.
Deadline March of each year.

[157]
EDUCATIONAL PARTNERSHIP PROGRAM UNDERGRADUATE SCHOLARSHIPS
National Oceanic and Atmospheric Administration
Attn: Office of Education
1315 East-West Highway
SSMC3, Room 10703
Silver Spring, MD 20910
(301) 713-9437, ext. 125   Fax: (301) 713-9465
E-mail: StudentScholarshipPrograms@noaa.gov
Web: epp.noaa.gov/undergrad_scholar/welcome.html

Purpose To provide financial assistance and summer research experience to upper-division students at minority serving institutions who are working on a degree in a field of interest to the National Oceanic and Atmospheric Administration (NOAA).
Eligibility This program is open to full-time students entering their junior or senior year at minority serving institutions (MSIs), including Hispanic Serving Institutions (HSIs), Historically Black Colleges and Universities (HBCUs), Tribal Colleges and Universities (TCUs), and Alaska Native or Native Hawaiian Serving Institutions. Applicants must be majoring in atmospheric science, biology, cartography, chemistry, computer science, engineering, environmental science, geodesy, geography, marine science, mathematics, meteorology, photogrammetry, physical science, physics, or remote sensing. They must have a GPA of 3.0 or higher. Along with their application, they must submit a 2-page description of their academic and career plans and how those plans support NOAA's mission. As part of their program, they must be interested in participating in summer research and development activities at a NOAA office or site. U.S. citizenship is required. Selection is based on background and experience, accomplishments, academic records, the statement of career interests and goals, recommendations, and compatibility of the applicant's background with the interests of NOAA.
Financial data This program provides a stipend of $4,000 per academic year and $650 per week during the internship, a housing subsidy and limited travel reimbursement for round-trip transportation to the internship site, and travel expenses to the scholarship program conference at the completion of the internship.
Duration 2 academic years plus 2 summer internships of 10 weeks each.
Number awarded Varies each year; recently, 28 of these scholarships were awarded.
Deadline February of each year.

[158]
ELECTRONICS FOR IMAGING SCHOLARSHIPS
Society of Women Engineers
230 East Ohio Street, Suite 400
Chicago, IL 60611-3265
(312) 596-5223   Toll-free: (877) SWE-INFO
Fax: (312) 644-8557
E-mail: scholarshipapplication@swe.org
Web: www.swe.org/scholarships

Purpose To provide financial assistance to women working on an undergraduate or graduate degree in engineering or computer science.
Eligibility This program is open to women who will be sophomores, juniors, seniors, or graduate students at ABET-accredited colleges and universities. Applicants must be majoring in computer science or engineering and have a GPA of 3.0 or higher. Along with their application, they must submit a 1-page essay on why they want to be an engineer or computer scientist, how they believe they will make a difference as an engineer or computer scientist, and what influenced them to study engineering or computer science. Selection is based on merit. Preference is given to students at designated colleges and universities; for a list, contact the sponsor.
Financial data The stipend is $4,000.
Duration 1 year.
Additional information This program, established in 2001, is sponsored by Electronics for Imaging, Inc.
Number awarded 4 each year.
Deadline January of each year.

[159]
ELIZABETH LOWELL PUTNAM PRIZE

Mathematical Association of America
1529 18th Street, N.W.
Washington, DC 20036-1358
(202) 387-5200 Toll-free: (800) 741-9415
Fax: (202) 265-2384 E-mail: maahq@maa.org
Web: www.maa.org/Awards/putnam.html

Purpose To recognize and reward outstanding women participants in a mathematics competition.

Eligibility This program is open to women at colleges and universities in Canada and the United States. Entrants participate in an examination containing mathematics problems designed to test originality as well as technical competence. The woman with the highest score receives this prize.

Financial data The prize is $1,000.

Duration The competition is held annually.

Additional information This program was established in 1992.

Number awarded 1 each year.

[160]
ELIZABETH MCLEAN MEMORIAL SCHOLARSHIP

Society of Women Engineers
230 East Ohio Street, Suite 400
Chicago, IL 60611-3265
(312) 596-5223 Toll-free: (877) SWE-INFO
Fax: (312) 644-8557
E-mail: scholarshipapplication@swe.org
Web: www.swe.org/scholarships

Purpose To provide financial assistance to undergraduate women majoring in civil engineering.

Eligibility This program is open to women who are entering their sophomore year at an ABET-accredited 4-year college or university. Applicants must be majoring in civil engineering and have a GPA of 3.0 or higher. Along with their application, they must submit a 1-page essay on why they want to be an engineer, how they believe they will make a difference as an engineer, and what influenced them to study engineering. Selection is based on merit.

Financial data The stipend is $1,000.

Duration 1 year.

Number awarded 1 each year.

Deadline January of each year.

[161]
ELMER S. IMES SCHOLARSHIP IN PHYSICS

National Society of Black Physicists
Attn: Scholarship Committee Chair
6704G Lee Highway
Arlington, VA 22205
(703) 536-4207 Fax: (703) 536-4203
E-mail: scholarship@nsbp.org
Web: www.nsbp.org

Purpose To provide financial assistance to African American students majoring in astronomy in college.

Eligibility This program is open to African American students who are entering their junior or senior year of college and majoring in physics. Applicants must submit an essay on their academic and career objectives, information on their participation in extracurricular activities, a description of any awards and honors they have received, and 3 letters of recommendation. Financial need is not considered.

Financial data A stipend is awarded (amount not specified).

Duration 1 year; nonrenewable.

Number awarded 1 each year.

Deadline November of each year.

[162]
EMPIRE STATE CHAPTER SCHOLARSHIP

Soil and Water Conservation Society-Empire State Chapter
c/o Josh Hornesky, Scholarship Committee
USDA-NRCS
903 Hanshaw Road
Ithaca, NY 14850
(607) 257-2737, ext. 3
Web: www.swcsnewyork.org

Purpose To provide financial assistance to college students in New York who are majoring in conservation and related fields.

Eligibility This program is open to students in their sophomore, junior, or senior year at a college or university in New York. Applicants must be majoring in agriculture, environmental sciences, natural resources, conservation, or related fields of study. They must submit a college transcript and a short essay on their interest in a career in the conservation of natural resources and previous volunteer or work experience in the conservation of natural resources. Students with demonstrated accomplishments and/or interests in the field of soil and water conservation are encouraged to apply. Selection is based on the essay and academic accomplishment. Preference is given to members of the Soil and Water Conservation Society.

Financial data The stipend is $1,000.

Duration 1 year.

Additional information Recipients are also given a 1-year student membership in the Soil and Water Conservation Society, a subscription to *The Journal of Soil and Water Conservation,* and a certificate awarded at the annual meeting of the sponsoring organization.

Number awarded 2 each year.

Deadline October of each year.

[163]
ENGINEERING DIVISION SCHOLARSHIPS

Technical Association of the Pulp and Paper Industry
Attn: TAPPI Foundation
15 Technology Parkway South
Norcross, GA 30092
(770) 209-7536 Toll-free: (800) 332-8686
Fax: (770) 446-6947 E-mail: vedmondson@tappi.org
Web: www.tappi.org

Purpose To provide financial assistance to student members of the Technical Association of the Pulp and Paper Industry (TAPPI) who are studying engineering or science to prepare for a career in the paper industry.

Eligibility This program is open to TAPPI student members who are entering their junior or senior year of college as full-time students with a GPA of 3.0 or higher. Applicants must be able to demonstrate a significant interest in the pulp and paper industry. They must be majoring in science or engineering with a focus on the application of engineering principles to the design, construction, operation, and maintenance of facilities for the manufacture of pulp, paper, and related products. Selection is based on potential career contributions to engineering in the pulp and paper industry; financial need is not considered.
Financial data The stipend is $1,500.
Duration 1 year.
Additional information In addition to the financial award, scholarship recipients are encouraged to take summer employment in the pulp and paper industry. The scholarship committee will contact companies related to the pulp and paper industry on behalf of the scholarship recipients, to help them find summer employment with appropriate companies.
Number awarded Up to 2 each year: 1 to a rising junior and 1 to a rising senior.
Deadline January of each year.

[164]
ENGINEERING IN MEDICINE AND BIOLOGY SOCIETY STUDENT DESIGN COMPETITION AWARDS

Institute of Electrical and Electronics Engineers
Engineering in Medicine and Biology Society
Attn: Executive Office
445 Hoes Lane
P.O. Box 1331
Piscataway, NJ 08855-1331
(732) 981-3433   Fax: (732) 465-6435
E-mail: emb-exec@ieee.org
Web: embs.gsbme.unsw.edu.au/students.html

Purpose To recognize and reward outstanding devices or products in biomedical engineering designed by student members of the Engineering in Medicine and Biology Society (EMBS) of the Institute of Electrical and Electronics Engineers (IEEE).
Eligibility This competition is open to teams of up to 5 undergraduate and graduate student members of the society. Applicants must design and build an original device or product not currently offered on the market that applies engineering principles and technology to problems in medicine and biology. Other acceptable designs include a modification of an existing product, which may consist of hardware, software, or a combination of both. Selection is based on technical merit, structure (abstract, introduction, methods, analysis, results, conclusion, and references), clarity of composition, and originality. Based on the papers describing the designs, 3 finalists are selected to describe their work at the international conference either as an oral or poster presentation.
Financial data First place is $1,000, second $500, and third $250. In addition, each finalist receives complimentary registration at the society's annual international conference, a social function ticket, and up to $250 per person for reimbursement of travel expenses, hotel accommodations, and meals.
Duration The competition is held annually.
Additional information This competition, established in 1995, is funded by the IEEE-EMBS Foundation.
Number awarded 3 cash prizes are awarded each year.
Deadline April of each year.

[165]
ENVIRONMENTAL EDUCATIONAL SCHOLARSHIP PROGRAM

Missouri Department of Natural Resources
Attn: Human Resources Program
P.O. Box 176
Jefferson City, MO 65102-0176
(573) 526-8411   Toll-free: (800) 361-4827
E-mail: daspec@dnr.mo.gov
Web: www.dnr.mo.gov/hr/scholarship/htm

Purpose To provide financial assistance to underrepresented and minority students from Missouri who are or will be working on a bachelor's or master's degree in an environmental field.
Eligibility This program is open to minority and underrepresented residents of Missouri who are high school seniors or current undergraduate or graduate students. Applicants must be enrolled or planning to enroll full time at a college or university in Missouri to work on a bachelor's or master's degree in 1) engineering (civil, chemical, environmental, mechanical, or agricultural); 2) environmental studies (geology, biology, wildlife management, planning, natural resources, or a closely-related course of study); 3) chemistry; or 4) environmental law enforcement. Graduating high school seniors must have a GPA of 3.0 or higher; students currently enrolled in college or graduate school must have a GPA of 2.5 or higher. Along with their application, they must submit a 1-page essay on why they desire this scholarship, 3 letters of recommendation, a list of school and community activities, a record of SAT or ACT scores, and transcripts. Financial need is not considered in the selection process.
Financial data The stipend is $2,000 per year.
Duration 1 year; may be renewed if the recipient maintains a GPA of 2.5 or higher and full-time enrollment.
Number awarded Varies each year.
Deadline May of each year.

[166]
EPOC SCHOLARSHIP FUND

Environmental Professionals' Organization of Connecticut
Attn: Executive Director
P.O. Box 176
Amston, CT 06231-0176
(860) 228-2492   Fax: (860) 228-4902
E-mail: sjm@epoc.org
Web: www.epoc.org

Purpose To provide financial assistance to upper-division and graduate students from Connecticut interested in preparing for a career as an environmental professional.

Eligibility This program is open to Connecticut residents who are preparing for a career as an environmental professional in the state. Applicants must be enrolled as juniors, seniors, or graduate students, but their college or university may be in any state. They must be majoring in a relevant field, including biology, chemistry, earth science, ecology, engineering (agricultural, chemical, civil, environmental, mechanical), environmental science, environmental studies, geology, hydrogeology, hydrology, natural resource management, soil sciences, toxicology, water resources, or wetland science. Along with their application, they must submit an essay of 400 to 500 words on their reasons for choosing their major, what they expect from a career in that field of study, and why this scholarship is important to them. Financial need is not considered in the selection process.

Financial data A stipend is awarded (amount not specified).

Duration 1 year.

Additional information This program was established in 1998. Information is also available from John Figurelli, Scholarship Fund Committee Chair, (860) 513-1473.

Number awarded Varies each year; recently, 2 of these scholarships were awarded.

Deadline April of each year.

[167]
ERNEST F. HOLLINGS UNDERGRADUATE SCHOLARSHIP PROGRAM

National Oceanic and Atmospheric Administration
Attn: Office of Education
1315 East-West Highway
SSMC3, Room 10703
Silver Spring, MD 20910
(301) 713-9437   Fax: (301) 713-9465
E-mail: StudentScholarshipPrograms@noaa.gov
Web: www.oesd.noaa.gov/Hollings_info.html

Purpose To provide financial assistance and summer research experience to upper-division students who are working on a degree in a field of interest to the National Oceanic and Atmospheric Administration (NOAA).

Eligibility This program is open to full-time students entering their junior year at an accredited college or university in the United States or its territories. Applicants must be majoring in a discipline related to oceanic and atmospheric science, research, technology, and education, and supportive of the purposes of NOAA's programs and mission, including, but not limited to biological, life, and agricultural sciences; computer and information sciences; mathematics; engineering; physical sciences; behavioral and social sciences; or teacher education. They must have a GPA of 3.0 or higher. As part of their program, they must be interested in participating in summer research and development activities at NOAA headquarters (Silver Spring, Maryland) or field centers. U.S. citizenship is required.

Financial data This program provides a stipend of $8,000 per academic year and $650 per week during the internship, a housing subsidy and limited travel reimbursement for round-trip transportation to the internship site, and travel expenses to the scholarship program conference at the completion of the internship.

Duration 2 academic years plus 10 weeks during the intervening summer.

Additional information This program was established in 2005.

Number awarded Approximately 100 each year.

Deadline February of each year.

[168]
ERNIE AYER AVIATION SCHOLARSHIP

Ernie Ayer Aviation Education Foundation
5 Rogers Court
Midland Park, NJ 07432
(201) 447-4164   E-mail: TAyer73352@aol.com

Purpose To provide financial assistance to students enrolled or planning to enroll in an aviation program.

Eligibility This program is open to students who have been accepted to a professional aviation training program, aviation institution of higher learning, or aviation technical school. Students accepted to a college or technical program must submit transcripts and proof of enrollment and attendance at classes. Students in a recognized flight school receive the award in installments following the achievement of certain goals (i.e., after the first solo, after the first solo cross country flight, after the written FAA examination is passed, and after the pilot certificate is received). For students seeking advanced ratings, selection is based on records, experience, potential, and demonstrated commitment to aviation. Applicants for all types of training must submit essays on 2 topics: 1) their goals in aviation and how receiving a scholarship would help them to realize those goals, and 2) a significant person or event in their life that has been a major influence in their decision to prepare for a career in aviation. Financial need is not considered in the selection process.

Financial data The stipend is $1,000.

Duration 1 year.

Additional information This program was established in 1999.

Number awarded 2 each year.

Deadline April of each year.

[169]
ESTHER MAYO SHERARD SCHOLARSHIP

American Health Information Management Association
Attn: Foundation of Research and Education
233 North Michigan Avenue, Suite 2150
Chicago, IL 60601-5806
(312) 233-1131   Fax: (312) 233-1431
E-mail: fore@ahima.org
Web: www.ahima.org/fore/student/programs.asp

Purpose To provide financial assistance to African American members of the American Health Information Management Association (AHIMA) who are interested in working on an undergraduate or graduate degree in health information administration or technology.

Eligibility This program is open to AHIMA members who are African Americans enrolled in a health information administration or health information technology program accredited by the Commission on Accreditation of Allied Health Education Programs. Applicants must be working on an undergraduate or graduate degree on at least a half-time basis and have a GPA of 3.0 or higher. U.S. citizenship is required. Selection is based (in order of importance) on GPA and academic achievement, volunteer and work experience, commitment to the health information management profession, suitability to the health information management profession, quality and suitability of references provided, and clarity of application.

Financial data The stipend ranges from $1,000 to $5,000.
Duration 1 year; nonrenewable.
Additional information This program was established in 2000 by the Esther Mayo Sherard Foundation.
Number awarded 1 each year.
Deadline April of each year.

[170]
ETHAN AND ALLAN MURPHY ENDOWED MEMORIAL SCHOLARSHIP

American Meteorological Society
Attn: Fellowship/Scholarship Program
45 Beacon Street
Boston, MA 02108-3693
(617) 227-2426, ext. 246   Fax: (617) 742-8718
E-mail: scholar@ametsoc.org
Web: www.ametsoc.org

Purpose To provide financial assistance to undergraduates majoring in meteorology or an aspect of atmospheric sciences with an interest in weather forecasting.
Eligibility This program is open to full-time students entering their final year of undergraduate study and majoring in meteorology or an aspect of the atmospheric or related oceanic and hydrologic sciences. Applicants must intend to make atmospheric or related sciences their career and be able to demonstrate, through curricular or extracurricular activities, an interest in weather forecasting or in the value and utilization of forecasts. They must be U.S. citizens or permanent residents enrolled at a U.S. institution and have a cumulative GPA of 3.25 or higher. Along with their application, they must submit 200-word essays on 1) their most important achievements that qualify them for this scholarship, and 2) their career goals in the atmospheric or related oceanic or hydrologic fields. Selection is based on academic excellence and achievement; financial need is not considered. The sponsor specifically encourages applications from women, minorities, and students with disabilities who are traditionally underrepresented in the atmospheric and related oceanic sciences.
Financial data The stipend is $2,000 per year.
Duration 1 year.
Additional information Requests for an application must be accompanied by a self-addressed stamped envelope.
Number awarded 1 each year.
Deadline February of each year.

[171]
EVERT CLARK/SETH PAYNE AWARD FOR YOUNG SCIENCE JOURNALISTS

National Press Foundation
1211 Connecticut Avenue, N.W., Suite 310
Washington, DC 20036
(202) 663-7280   Fax: (202) 530-2855
E-mail: npf@nationalpress.org
Web: www.nationalpress.org

Purpose To recognize and reward young science writers and reporters.
Eligibility The award is limited to non-technical print journalism only. Articles published in newspapers (including college newspapers), magazines, and newsletters are eligible. Both freelancers and staff writers may enter. Books, as well as articles in technical journals and trade association publications, are not considered. Since the prize is managed by *Business Week* staffers, stories in that magazine will not be accepted. Science writing is broadly defined. It includes, but is not limited to, writing in the biological, physical, environmental, computer, and space sciences, along with technology, mathematics, medicine, health, and science policy. Entries are judged on the basis of accuracy, clarity, insightfulness, fairness, resourcefulness, and timeliness. Applicants must be 30 years of age or younger. They may submit a single article or series, up to 4 individual pieces. Applications may be submitted by the author or on the author's behalf.
Financial data The winner receives $1,000 and expenses to attend the annual meeting of the American Association for the Advancement of Science.
Duration The award is presented annually.
Additional information This award was first presented in 1989. It is given by the Evert Clark Fund and the National Association of Science Writers, in conjunction with the National Press Foundation, which administers the endowment.
Number awarded 1 each year.
Deadline December of each year.

[172]
EXCEL GEOPHYSICS SCHOLARSHIP

Society of Exploration Geophysicists
Attn: SEG Foundation
8801 South Yale, Suite 500
P.O. Box 702740
Tulsa, OK 74170-2740
(918) 497-5513   Fax: (918) 497-5557
E-mail: scholarships@seg.org
Web: seg.org

Purpose To provide financial assistance to entering or continuing undergraduate and graduate students at universities in the United States and Canada who are interested in studying applied geophysics.
Eligibility This program is open to 1) high school students planning to enter college in the fall, and 2) undergraduate or graduate students whose grades are above average. Applicants must intend to work on a degree directed toward a career in applied geophysics or a closely-related field at a university in the United States or Canada. Along with their application, they must submit a 150-word essay on how

they plan to use geophysics in their future. Financial need is not considered in the selection process.

Financial data Stipends range from $1,000 to $3,000 per year.

Duration 1 academic year; may be renewable, based on scholastic standing, availability of funds, and continuance of a course of study leading to a career in applied geophysics.

Additional information This program is sponsored by Excel Geophysics.

Number awarded 1 each year.

Deadline January of each year.

[173]
EXCELLENCE IN SONOGRAPHY AWARD

Society of Diagnostic Medical Sonography
Attn: SDMS Educational Foundation
2745 North Dallas Parkway, Suite 350
Plano, TX 75093-8730
(214) 473-8057   Toll-free: (800) 229-9506
Fax: (214) 473-8563   E-mail: foundation@sdms.org
Web: www.sdms.org/foundation/gems.asp

Purpose To recognize and reward members of the Society of Diagnostic Medical Sonography (SDMS) who make outstanding contributions to research in sonography.

Eligibility This award is available to SDMS members, including undergraduate and graduate student members, who have conducted research that advances the goals of promoting the art and science of diagnostic ultrasound to the sonography and medical communities. Selection is based on the significance and quality of the achievement, innovation, impact on diagnostic medical sonography, and impact on enhancing patient care.

Financial data The award is $1,000.

Duration The award is presented annually.

Additional information This award is sponsored by GE Healthcare. The society also sponsors a number of other awards recognizing outstanding contributions to specific aspects of sonography, including ultrasound imaging and medical imaging.

Number awarded 1 each year.

Deadline May of each year.

[174]
F. MAYNARD LIPE SCHOLARSHIP AWARD

American College of Chiropractic Orthopedists
c/o Bill Fisher, Scholarship Committee Chair
P.O. Box 424
Delmont, PA 15626
(724) 523-5505   Fax: (724) 523-6875
Web: www.accoweb.org

Purpose To provide financial assistance to students enrolled in their fifth term or later of chiropractic college.

Eligibility This program is open to students who have completed at least 4 terms in an approved college of chiropractic. Applicants must have a GPA of 3.0 or higher and a career objective to specialize in chiropractic orthopedics. Along with their application, they must submit an article from 1,000 to 2,500 words in length on a subject related to chiropractic orthopedics. Selection is based on the excellence of the article.

Financial data The award is $1,000. Funds are sent to the recipient's school and may be used to pay for tuition (not for books, lab fees, or other ancillary expenses).

Duration The award is granted annually.

Additional information When possible, the student is a guest at the association's convention.

Number awarded 1 each year.

Deadline January of each year.

[175]
FABRICATORS AND MANUFACTURERS ASSOCIATION FOUNDATION COLLEGE SCHOLARSHIPS

Fabricators and Manufacturers Association
Attn: FMA Foundation
833 Featherstone Road
Rockford, IL 61107-6302
(815) 381-1338   Fax: (815) 484-7767
E-mail: foundation@fmanet.org
Web: www.fma-foundation.org/Scholarships.cfm

Purpose To provide financial assistance for college to students connected in some way to the Fabricators and Manufacturers Association, International (FMA) or the Tube and Pipe Association, International (TPA).

Eligibility This program is open to personal members of the FMA and TPA, children and dependents of personal members of the FMA and TPA, student members of the FMA and TPA, and employees of member companies of the FMA and TPA. Applicants must be planning to attend a college or university to major in an engineering or related program that may lead to a career in manufacturing. They must have a GPA of 3.0 or higher and be enrolled or planning to enroll full time. Along with their application, they must submit information on their educational and career objectives, employment experience, extracurricular activities, and the experience that has influenced or confirmed their decision to prepare for a career in manufacturing. Financial need is not considered in the selection process.

Financial data Stipends are $3,000 per year for freshmen or $2,000 per year for sophomores, juniors, and seniors.

Duration 1 year; may be renewed.

Additional information Recipients are also offered a 3-day internship, worth $1,500, to the FMA exposition and conference. The internship includes travel, hotel, meals, technical educational sessions, and free admission.

Number awarded Varies each year. Recently, 13 of these scholarships were awarded: 5 to freshmen and 8 to advanced undergraduates.

Deadline April of each year.

[176]
FAR WEST ATHLETIC TRAINERS' ASSOCIATION UNDERGRADUATE SCHOLARSHIPS

Far West Athletic Trainers' Association
c/o Jason Bennett, Scholarship Chair
Chapman University
1 University Drive
Orange, CA 92866
(714) 997-6567 E-mail: jbennett@chapman.edu
Web: www.fwata.org/com_scholarships.html

Purpose To provide financial assistance to members of the National Athletic Trainers Association (NATA) who are working on a bachelor's degree in its District 8.

Eligibility This program is open to students enrolled as undergraduates at colleges and universities in California, Guam, Hawaii, or Nevada who are preparing for a career as an athletic trainer. Applicants must be student members of NATA and a District 8 member of NATA working full time on a bachelor's degree in athletic training. They must have a GPA of 3.0 or higher and a record of distinction in their athletic training program, academic major, institution, intercollegiate athletics, and higher education. Along with their application, they must submit a statement on their athletic training background, experience, philosophy, and goals. Financial need is not considered in the selection process.

Financial data The stipend is $1,000.

Duration 1 year.

Additional information FWATA serves as District 8 of NATA. This program includes the following scholarships: the NEV-ATA/Alert Scholarship, the Gary Millay Memorial Scholarship, the Jerry Lloyd Memorial Scholarship, and the Gail Wegdon Memorial Scholarship.

Number awarded 4 each year.

Deadline February of each year.

[177]
FCRV SCHOLARSHIPS

Family Campers and RVers
c/o Herb and Marie Petersen
76 Gaymore Road
Port Jefferson Station, NY 11776
E-mail: petersen76@aol.com
Web: www.fcrv.org/programs/scholarship.php

Purpose To provide financial assistance for college to members of the Family Campers and RVers (FCRV) and their dependent children.

Eligibility Applicants must have been members of FCRV for at least 1 year or be their dependent children and have been accepted in a 2-year or 4-year accredited institution of higher learning. Applications are accepted from the United States and Canada, but those from other countries will be considered within the educational framework of that country. Students currently enrolled in college are given equal consideration with incoming freshmen; high school students or recent graduates should be in the upper 40% of their graduating class and students already in college should have a GPA of 2.7 or higher. Special consideration is given to students majoring in fields related to conservation, ecology, or outdoor activities, although applicants with any major are considered. Awards are based on maturity, leadership, related activities, and goals of the applicant as related to the objectives of FCRV.

Financial data Scholarships range from $500 to $2,000 per year.

Duration 1 year; may be renewed upon reapplication.

Additional information Family Campers and RVers was founded as the National Campers and Hikers Association, and these scholarships are awarded by the National Campers and Hikers Association Scholarship, Inc. (NCHA).

Deadline April of each year.

[178]
FEDERAL LAND BANK ASSOCIATION OF HAWAII SCHOLARSHIP

Farm Credit Services of Hawaii, ACA
Attn: Branch Manager
2850 Pa'a Street, Suite 100
P.O. Box 31306
Honolulu, HI 96820
(808) 836-8009
Toll-free: (800) 894-4996, ext. 22 (within HI)
Fax: (808) 836-8610
Web: www.farmcreditservicesofhi.org

Purpose To provide financial assistance to high school seniors and graduates in Hawaii who are interested in majoring in agriculture in college.

Eligibility This program is open to graduating seniors and recent graduates of high schools in Hawaii. Applicants must be able to supply proof of acceptance or enrollment at an accredited college, university, or trade school and intend to major in a field related to agriculture. Along with their application, they must submit 2 letters of recommendation, a transcript, a short essay (up to 500 words) on "What future does Tropical Agriculture have for the young," and a list of agriculturally-related activities (e.g., 4-H, FFA) in which they have been involved. Selection is based on recommendations, academics, the essay, and agricultural activities.

Financial data The stipend is $1,000.

Duration 1 year; nonrenewable.

Additional information Recipients may attend college in any state.

Number awarded 2 each year.

Deadline April of each year.

[179]
FERROUS METALLURGY EDUCATION TODAY (FEMET) SCHOLARSHIPS

Association for Iron & Steel Technology
Attn: AIST Foundation
186 Thorn Hill Road
Warrendale, PA 15086-7528
(724) 776-6040, ext. 621 Fax: (724) 776-1880
E-mail: lwharrey@aist.org
Web: www.aist.org/femet/femet_scholarship.htm

Purpose To provide financial assistance and work experience to college juniors working on a degree in metallurgy or materials sciences.

Eligibility This program is open to full-time students entering their junior year in a metallurgy or materials science program at a college or university in North America (Canada, Mexico, and the United States). Applicants must have a GPA of 3.0 or higher and a demonstrated interest in the iron and steel industry. They must be available for employment at a steel company during the summer after their junior year; students unable to accept an internship will not be considered. Along with their application, they must submit a 2-page essay on their professional goals, why they are interested in a career in the steel industry, and how their skills could be applied to enhance the industry. Selection is based on the essay; a resume with work experience and extracurricular activities, noting any leadership positions; letters of recommendation; a current academic transcript; and a list of the source and amount of other grants and scholarships.

Financial data The program provides a stipend of $5,000 for the junior year, a paid internship during the following summer, and a stipend of $5,000 for the senior year.

Duration 2 years.

Additional information The AIST was formed in 2004 by the merger of the Iron and Steel Society (ISS) and the Association of Iron and Steel Engineers (AISE). This program was established in 2005 by the AIST Foundation and the American Iron and Steel Institute, (202) 452-7143, E-mail: blakshmi@steel.org.

Number awarded 10 each year.

Deadline April of each year.

[180]
FESTIVAL OF TREES SCHOLARSHIP FUND
New Hampshire Charitable Foundation
37 Pleasant Street
Concord, NH 03301-4005
(603) 225-6641   Toll-free: (800) 464-6641
Fax: (603) 225-1700   E-mail: info@nhcf.org
Web: www.nhcf.org/page16960.cfm

Purpose To provide financial assistance to students, preferably those from New Hampshire, working on a degree in natural resources or horticulture.

Eligibility This program is open to students working on a degree in natural resources or horticulture. Preference is given to residents of the seacoast region of New Hampshire and students enrolled at a college or university in that state. Applicants must have a GPA of 3.0 or higher, be able to demonstrate involvement in school and community activities, and have some work experience that supports their career goals and aspirations in life. Financial need is not considered in the selection process.

Financial data The stipend is generally $1,000.

Duration 1 year.

Additional information This program was established in 1983 with support from the Portsmouth Garden Club and the New Hampshire Department of Resources and Economic Development.

Number awarded 1 or more each year.

Deadline April of each year.

[181]
FLEXIBLE PACKAGING INDUSTRY SCHOLARSHIP/INTERNSHIP PROGRAM
Flexible Packaging Association
Attn: Scholarship/Internship Program
971 Corporate Boulevard, Suite 403
Linthicum, MD 21090
(410) 694-0800   Fax: (410) 694-0900
E-mail: fpa@flexpack.org
Web: www.flexpack.org

Purpose To provide financial assistance and work experience to students interested in preparing for a career in the flexible packaging industry.

Eligibility This program is open to students working on an associate, bachelor's, or master's degree to prepare for a career in the packaging converting industry. Applicants must have completed at least 24 credit hours (including at least 9 credits in packaging-related course work) with a GPA of 2.7 or higher. They must have been accepted as an intern for a participating flexible packaging manufacturer. Along with their application, they must submit a 500-word essay on how they expect to apply what they have learned in their course work to an internship with a flexible packaging converter. Financial need is not considered in the selection process.

Financial data The scholarship stipend is $3,000. For the internship, participants receive a competitive salary.

Duration The scholarship is for 1 year; the internship is for 1 summer.

Additional information This program was established in 2005.

Number awarded 10 each year.

Deadline February of each year.

[182]
FLINT GROUP TECHNICAL WRITING AWARDS
Gravure Association of America
Attn: Gravure Education Foundation
1200-A Scottsville Road
Rochester, NY 14624
(315) 589-8879   Fax: (585) 436-7689
E-mail: lwshatch@gaa.org
Web: www.gaa.org

Purpose To recognize and reward undergraduate and graduate students who submit outstanding technical research papers on gravure technology.

Eligibility This competition is open to full-time undergraduate and graduate students who submit technical research papers, approximately 10 pages in length, that address an aspect of gravure technology. Selection is based on the relevancy of the topic to gravure, the depth and comprehensiveness of the research, the organization of material, and the clarity of presentation.

Financial data Prizes are $1,500 for the graduate student winner, $1,000 for the undergraduate first-place winner, and $500 for the undergraduate second-place winner.

Duration The competition is held annually.

Additional information This program is supported by Flint Ink.

Number awarded 3 each year.

SCIENCES

Deadline February of each year.

[183]
FOOD ENGINEERING SCHOLARSHIPS PROGRAM

Food Processing Suppliers Association
Attn: FPSA Foundation
1451 Dolley Madison Boulevard, Suite 200
McLean, VA 22101-3850
(703) 761-2600 Fax: (703) 761-4334
E-mail: info@fpsa.org
Web: www.fpsa.org

Purpose To provide financial assistance to upper-division engineering students preparing for a career in the food industry.

Eligibility This program is open to engineering students entering their junior or senior year at educational institutions in the United States and Canada who are preparing for a career in the food industry. Applicants should be able to demonstrate academic excellence, a well-rounded personality, and an intent to prepare for a career in the food industry. Along with their application, they must submit a 250-word statement on their rationale for choosing the food industry as a career. Age, sex, race, and financial need are not considered in the selection process.

Financial data The stipend is $2,500. Each winner also receives a $500 travel grant to attend the next Expo of the sponsoring organization.

Duration 1 year.

Additional information This program was established in 1983 when the sponsor's name was the International Association of Food Industry Suppliers.

Number awarded 2 each year.

Deadline March of each year.

[184]
FORD MOTOR COMPANY ENGINEERING AND LEADERSHIP SCHOLARSHIP

Golden Key International Honour Society
621 North Avenue N.E., Suite C-100
Atlanta, GA 30308
(404) 377-2400 Toll-free: (800) 377-2401
Fax: (678) 420-6757
E-mail: scholarships@goldenkey.org
Web: www.goldenkey.org

Purpose To provide financial assistance to members of the Golden Key International Honour Society who are working on an undergraduate or graduate degree in engineering.

Eligibility This program is open to members of the society who are either undergraduates or recent graduates (within the past 3 years) in engineering. Applicants must submit 1) a personal resume that includes a list of extracurricular activities, involvement in Golden Key, work history, and special circumstances; 2) a 1,000-word essay that states why they are applying for the scholarship, how they have demonstrated leadership on their campus, and how the society's commitment to academic excellence will be furthered by their studies; 3) academic transcripts; 4) at least 3 letters of recommendation; and 5) either a paper they have prepared or some other piece of work related to the field of engineering. Selection is based on academic achievement, leadership achievement, involvement in their local chapter, and extracurricular activities.

Financial data The stipend is $10,000.

Duration 1 year; nonrenewable.

Additional information This program is sponsored by Ford Motor Company.

Number awarded 1 each year.

Deadline February of each year.

[185]
FORD MOTOR COMPANY SWE SCHOLARSHIPS

Society of Women Engineers
230 East Ohio Street, Suite 400
Chicago, IL 60611-3265
(312) 596-5223 Toll-free: (877) SWE-INFO
Fax: (312) 644-8557
E-mail: scholarshipapplication@swe.org
Web: www.swe.org/scholarships

Purpose To provide financial assistance to lower-division women majoring in designated engineering specialties.

Eligibility This program is open to women who are entering their sophomore or junior year at a 4-year ABET-accredited college or university. Applicants must be majoring in automotive, electrical, industrial, manufacturing, or mechanical engineering and have a GPA of 3.5 or higher. Along with their application, they must submit a 1-page essay on why they want to be an engineer, how they believe they will make a difference as an engineer, and what influenced them to study engineering. Selection is based on merit and leadership potential.

Financial data The stipend is $1,000.

Duration 1 year.

Additional information This program, established in 2002, is sponsored by the Ford Motor Company.

Number awarded 2 each year: 1 for a sophomore and 1 for a junior.

Deadline January of each year.

[186]
FORE UNDERGRADUATE MERIT SCHOLARSHIPS

American Health Information Management Association
Attn: Foundation of Research and Education
233 North Michigan Avenue, Suite 2150
Chicago, IL 60601-5806
(312) 233-1131 Fax: (312) 233-1431
E-mail: fore@ahima.org
Web: www.ahima.org/fore/student/programs.asp

Purpose To provide financial assistance to members of the American Health Information Management Association (AHIMA) who are interested in working on an undergraduate degree in health information administration or technology.

Eligibility This program is open to AHIMA members who are enrolled in a health information administration or health information technology program accredited by the Commission on Accreditation of Allied Health Education Programs. Applicants must be working on a degree on at least a half-time basis and have a GPA of 3.0 or higher. U.S. citizenship is required. Selection is based (in order of importance) on GPA and academic achievement, volunteer and work experience, commitment to the health information management profession, suitability to the health information management profession, quality and suitability of references provided, and clarity of application.

Financial data Stipends range from $1,000 to $5,000.

Duration 1 year; nonrenewable.

Additional information This program includes the following named scholarships (not all of which may be offered each year): the David A. Cohen Scholarship (established in 2004), the Jimmy Gamble Memorial Scholarship (established in 2001 and sponsored by 3M Health Information Systems), the Sanfra L. Key Memorial Scholarship (established in 2003 and sponsored by Healthcare Contract Resources), the Lucretia Spears Scholarship (established in 1998), the Julia LeBlond Memorial Undergraduate Scholarships (sponsored by Ingenix Companies), the Rita Finnegan Memorial Scholarship (established in 2001 and sponsored by MC Strategies, Inc.), the Annie Blaylock Memorial Scholarship (established in 2002), the Connie Marshall Memorial Scholarship (established in 2004 and sponsored by MedQuist Inc.), the Bright Future Scholarship (sponsored by previous Merit Scholarship recipients).

Number awarded Varies each year; recently, 65 of these scholarships were awarded.

Deadline April of each year.

[187]
FORMULA SAE COMPETITION AWARDS

Society of Automotive Engineers
Attn: Customer Service
400 Commonwealth Drive
Warrendale, PA 15096-0001
(724) 776-4790   Toll-free: (877) 606-7323
Fax: (724) 776-0790
E-mail: CustomerService@sae.org
Web: students.sae.org/competitions/formulaseries

Purpose To recognize and reward student members of the Society of Automotive Engineers (SAE) who design outstanding small formula-style racing cars.

Eligibility This competition is open to teams of student members of the society who design and build a prototype car for evaluation as a production item by a fictitious manufacturing firm. The intended sales market is the nonprofessional weekend autocross racer. Teams are judged on how well they meet specified criteria in static and dynamic events. There are 3 separate competitions: the United States, the United Kingdom, and Australia. All competitions accept student teams representing universities from any country. All team members must be 1) enrolled as degree-seeking undergraduate or graduate students (team members who have graduated during the 7-month period prior to the competition remain eligible to participate) and 2) SAE members. The car must be conceived, designed, and fabricated by the students without direct involvement from professional engineers, automotive engineers, racers, machinists, or related professionals. Awards are presented for overall excellence and in many specified categories that vary each year (e.g., highest score from acceleration and fuel economy scores, best engineering design, best vehicle performance regarding ease of manufacturing and overall cost, innovation and excellence in powertrain engineering, best powertrain cooling systems).

Financial data The Spirit of Excellence Awards for overall excellence are $3,000 for first place, $2,000 for second, $1,000 for third, $600 for fourth, $500 for fifth, $400 for sixth, $300 for seventh, $250 for eighth, $250 for ninth, and $250 for tenth. Other recent awards included the Robert Bosch Corporation Engine Management System Awards for excellence in the design and performance of the engine management system ($750 for first place, $500 for second, and $250 for third); the Society of Plastic Engineers' Composites Division Awards for the most effective use of polymer-matrix composites ($1,000 for first place, $750 for second, and $300 for third); the ArvinMeritor Suspension System Awards for the best suspension system design and development ($1,000 for first place, $500 for second, and $250 for third); the Polaris Intake Systems Design Award for the team that displays the most innovation in their air intake and fuel delivery systems ($1,000); the Yazaki North America Cost Award for the team that receives the best score in cost ($500); the Yazaki North American Presentation Award for the team that receives the best score in presentation ($500); and the Bruel and Kjaer Quiet Car Cup for the car that measures the lowest dBA reading on the first try during the noise event ($250).

Duration The competition is held annually.

Additional information Prizes are sponsored by many corporate sponsors (that change each year). This competition began in 1982. The registration fee is $600. Registration is limited to the first 140 teams.

Number awarded Varies each year, depending on the support provided by corporate sponsors.

Deadline January of each year.

[188]
FORREST BASSFORD STUDENT AWARD

Livestock Publications Council
910 Currie Street
Fort Worth, TX 76107
(817) 336-1130   Fax: (817) 232-4820
E-mail: dianej@flash.net
Web: www.livestockpublications.com/awards.htm

Purpose To provide financial assistance to students majoring in agricultural communications or related fields.

Eligibility This program is open to college juniors and seniors majoring in agricultural journalism, agricultural communications, or agricultural public relations. Applicants must have at least 1 semester of school remaining at the time they receive the award. Along with their application, they must submit a 200-word essay on the future of agricultural communications and how they fit in that career. Selection is based on that essay, a transcript of college work completed and a list of courses in progress, scholarships and awards received, club and other organization memberships, extracurricular activities, employment record, a 1-page press release announcing that they have won this award, and 3 samples of communications work.

Financial data The winner receives a $1,500 scholarship, plus a $500 travel scholarship (to attend the council's annual meeting). The runners-up receive $500 travel scholarships to attend the meeting.

Duration 1 year.

Additional information The funds for this program are provided by the Livestock Publications Council and the Chicago Mercantile Exchange. Information is also available from Angie Stump Denton, *Hereford World,* 1039 Vista Road, Blue Rapids, KS 66411, (785) 363-7263.

Number awarded 1 winner and 3 runners-up are selected each year.

Deadline February of each year.

[189]
FOUNDATION FOR NEONATAL RESEARCH AND EDUCATION SCHOLARSHIPS

Academy of Neonatal Nursing
Attn: Foundation for Neonatal Research and Education
200 East Holly Avenue
P.O. Box 56
Pitman, NJ 08071-0056
(856) 256-2343   Fax: (856) 589-7463
E-mail: FNRE@ajj.com
Web: www.inurse.com/fnre/scholarship.htm

Purpose To provide financial assistance to neonatal nurses interested in working on a degree.

Eligibility Applicants must be professionally active neonatal nurses, engaged in a service, research, or educational role that contributes directly to the health care of neonates or to the neonatal nursing profession. They must be an active member of a professional association dedicated to enhancing neonatal nursing and the care of neonates. Participation in ongoing professional education in neonatal nursing must be demonstrated by at least 10 contact hours in neonatal content over the past 24 months. Qualified nurses must have been admitted to a college or school of higher education to work on 1 of the following: bachelor of science in nursing, master of science in nursing for advanced practice in neonatal nursing, doctoral degree in nursing, or master's or postmaster's degree in nursing administration or business management. They must have a GPA of 3.0 or higher. Along with their application, they must submit a 250-word statement on how they plan to make a significant difference in neonatal nursing practice. Financial need is not considered in the selection process.

Financial data The stipends are $1,500 or $1,000.

Duration 1 year.

Additional information The Foundation for Neonatal Research and Education was established in 1992 by the National Association of Neonatal Nurses (NANN), 2270 Northpoint Parkway, Santa Rosa, CA 95407, (707) 568-2168. Originally housed at the NANN office, it moved to its current location in 1998. This program includes the Matthew Hester Memorial Scholarship, sponsored by Anthony J. Jannetti, Inc.

Number awarded The Matthew Hester Scholarship of $1,500 and several scholarships at $1,000 (the exact number depending on the availability of funds) are awarded each year.

Deadline April of each year.

[190]
FOUNDATION OR RESEARCH AND EDUCATION DIVERSITY SCHOLARSHIPS

American Health Information Management Association
Attn: Foundation of Research and Education
233 North Michigan Avenue, Suite 2150
Chicago, IL 60601-5806
(312) 233-1131   Fax: (312) 233-1431
E-mail: fore@ahima.org
Web: www.ahima.org/fore/student/programs.asp

Purpose To provide financial assistance to minority members of the American Health Information Management Association (AHIMA) who are interested in working on an undergraduate or graduate degree in health information administration or technology.

Eligibility This program is open to AHIMA members who are enrolled in a health information administration or health information technology program accredited by the Commission on Accreditation of Allied Health Education Programs. Applicants must be minorities, be working on an undergraduate or graduate degree on at least a half-time basis, and have a GPA of 3.0 or higher. U.S. citizenship is required. Selection is based (in order of importance) on GPA and academic achievement, volunteer and work experience, commitment to the health information management profession, suitability to the health information management profession, quality and suitability of references provided, and clarity of application.

Financial data Stipends range from $1,000 to $5,000.

Duration 1 year; nonrenewable.

Number awarded Varies each year. Recently, 9 of these scholarships were awarded.

Deadline April of each year.

[191]
FRANCES A. MAYS SCHOLARSHIP AWARD

Virginia Association for Health, Physical Education, Recreation, and Dance
c/o Jack Schiltz, Executive Director
817 West Franklin Street
P.O. Box 842020
Richmond, VA 23284-2020
(804) 828-1948   Toll-free: (800) 918-9899
Fax: (804) 828-1946   E-mail: info@vahperd.org
Web: www.vahperd.org

Purpose To provide financial assistance to college seniors majoring in health, physical education, recreation, or dance in Virginia.

Eligibility This program is open to students who have been working full time for 3 years on a degree in health, physical education, recreation, or dance at a college or university in Virginia. Candidates must be nominated by their school and be members of the Virginia Association of Health, Physical Education, Recreation, and Dance (VAHPERD) and the American Association for Health, Physical Education, Recreation, and Dance (AAHPERD). Selection is based on academic achievement, leadership in campus life activities, service to college or university, awards and honors, and service to the community.

Financial data A stipend is awarded (amount not specified).

Duration 1 year.
Number awarded 1 each year.
Deadline September of each year.

[192]
FRANK AND BRENNIE MORGAN PRIZE

Mathematical Association of America
1529 18th Street, N.W.
Washington, DC 20036-1358
(202) 387-5200   Toll-free: (800) 741-9415
Fax: (202) 265-2384   E-mail: maahq@maa.org
Web: www.maa.org/Awards/morgan.html

Purpose To recognize and reward outstanding mathematical research papers by undergraduate students.

Eligibility This program is open to students at colleges and universities in Canada, Mexico, and the United States. Either the student or a professor may submit a nomination that consists of a single research paper or several papers. The paper or papers must be submitted while the student is an undergraduate, not after the student's graduation. Publication of the research is not required. Selection is based on the quality of completed research projects in mathematics.

Financial data The prize is $1,000.
Duration The prize is awarded annually.
Additional information This prize, first awarded in 1995, is jointly sponsored by the American Mathematical Society, the Mathematical Association of America, and the Society for Industrial and Applied Mathematics. Information is also available from the American Mathematical Society, Morgan Prize Committee, c/o Herbert Medina, Loyola Marymount University, Department of Mathematics, 1 LMU Drive, Suite 2700, Los Angeles, CA 90045-2659, (310) 338-5113, Fax: (310) 338-3768, E-mail: hmedina@lmu.edu.
Number awarded 1 each year.
Deadline Nominations must be submitted by June of each year.

[193]
FRANK AND DOROTHY MILLER ASME AUXILIARY SCHOLARSHIPS

ASME International
Attn: Coordinator, Educational Operations
Three Park Avenue
New York, NY 10016-5990
(212) 591-8131   Toll-free: (800) THE-ASME
Fax: (212) 591-7143   E-mail: OluwanifiseK@asme.org
Web: www.asme.org

Purpose To provide financial assistance to undergraduate students who are members of the American Society of Mechanical Engineers (ASME).

Eligibility This program is open to student members in good standing who are enrolled in an ABET-accredited mechanical engineering, mechanical engineering technology, or related baccalaureate program. Applicants must be U.S. citizens entering their sophomore, junior, or senior year. Along with their application, they must submit a nomination from their department head, a recommendation from a faculty member, and an official transcript. Only 1 nomination may be submitted per department. Selection is based on character, integrity, leadership, scholastic ability, and potential contribution to the mechanical engineering profession.

Financial data The stipend is $1,500.
Duration 1 year.
Additional information This program was established in 1993.
Number awarded 2 each year.
Deadline March of each year.

[194]
FREDERICK J. HERINGER HONORARY AWARD

California Farm Bureau Scholarship Foundation
Attn: Scholarship Coordinator
2300 River Plaza Drive
Sacramento, CA 95833
(916) 561-5520 Toll-free: (800) 698-FARM (within CA)
Fax: (916) 561-5699   E-mail: dlicciardo@cfbf.com
Web: www.cfbf.com/programs/scholar/index.cfm

Purpose To provide financial assistance for college to residents of California who come from a farm family and are interested in preparing for a career in agriculture.

Eligibility This program is open to students entering or attending a 4-year accredited college or university in California who are majoring or planning to major in an agriculture-related field. Students entering a junior college are not eligible. Applicants must come from a farm family (or have substantial farming experience). They must submit an essay on the most important educational or personal experience that has led them to pursue a university education. Selection is based on academic achievement, career goals, extracurricular activities, leadership skills, determination, and commitment to study agriculture.

Financial data The stipend is $2,500 per year.
Duration 1 year; recipients may reapply.
Number awarded 1 each year.
Deadline February of each year.

[195]
FTE UNDERGRADUATE MAJOR IN TECHNOLOGY EDUCATION SCHOLARSHIP

International Technology Education Association
Attn: Foundation for Technology Education
1914 Association Drive, Suite 201
Reston, VA 20191-1539
(703) 860-2100   Fax: (703) 860-0353
E-mail: itea@iteaconnect.org
Web: www.iteaconnect.org/l3d.html

Purpose To provide financial support to undergraduate members of the International Technology Education Association (ITEA) who are majoring in technology education teacher preparation.

Eligibility Applicants must be members of the association (membership may be enclosed with the scholarship application), in college but not yet seniors, majoring in technology education teacher preparation with a GPA of 2.5 or higher, and enrolled full time. Selection is based on interest in teaching, academic ability, and faculty recommendations.

Financial data The stipend is $1,000. Funds are provided directly to the recipient.
Duration 1 year.
Number awarded 1 each year.
Deadline November of each year.

[196]
FUELS AND COMBUSTION TECHNOLOGIES DIVISION BEST STUDENT PAPER AWARD

ASME International
Attn: Fuels and Combustion Technologies Division
Three Park Avenue
New York, NY 10016-5990
(212) 591-7055   Toll-free: (800) THE-ASME
Fax: (212) 591-7671   E-mail: bendoj@asme.org
Web: divisions.asme.org/fact/awards/index.htm

Purpose To recognize and reward outstanding student papers on fuel technology.
Eligibility This competition is open to both undergraduate and graduate students; graduate students may not have completed their thesis. Applicants must prepare a paper on an aspect of fuel, combustion, and combustion technology. Examples of acceptable topics include, but are not limited to, furnaces, combustors, pollution control, experimental research, mathematical modeling, combustion of fuels, waste and/or alternative fuels, and development of new diagnostics for conducting fuel and combustion experiments. Review and survey papers and papers in the area of internal combustion engines are not acceptable. Applicants first submit a 200-word abstract; based on those abstracts, finalists are invited to submit full papers. Selection of the best paper is based on originality of the technical work described, significance of the technical work and paper, thoroughness of approach and presentation, organization of the paper, logic of approach, clarity of expression, and other pertinent factors.
Financial data The author of the best paper receives a $1,000 honorarium, a certificate of merit, and a 1-year membership in ASME International.
Duration The competition is held annually.
Additional information This competition began in 1995.
Number awarded 1 each year.
Deadline Abstracts must be submitted by mid-October of each year. Full papers are due in early January.

[197]
FUELS AND COMBUSTION TECHNOLOGIES DIVISION SCHOLARSHIPS

ASME International
Attn: Fuels and Combustion Technologies Division
Three Park Avenue
New York, NY 10016-5990
(212) 591-7055   Toll-free: (800) THE-ASME
Fax: (212) 591-7671   E-mail: bendoj@asme.org
Web: divisions.asme.org

Purpose To provide financial assistance to undergraduate engineering students working on a degree in an area of interest to the Fuels and Combustion Technologies (FACT) division of ASME International (the professional society of mechanical engineers).

Eligibility This program is open to undergraduate students in engineering disciplines (e.g., mechanical, aerospace, chemical) relevant to FACT division area interests. Preference is given to juniors and seniors. Selection is based on student GPA and academic merit, leadership activities, energy and power-related courses taken, institutional geographical location, course offerings and research activities for undergraduates at the student's university, and a letter of recommendation.
Financial data Stipends are $1,500 or $1,000.
Duration 1 year.
Additional information Further information is also available from Ashwani K. Gupta, University of Maryland, Department of Mechanical Engineering, College Park, MD 20742, (301) 405-5276, Fax: (301) 314-9477.
Number awarded 4 each year: 2 at $1,500 and 2 at $1,000.
Deadline February of each year.

[198]
FULFILLING THE LEGACY SCHOLARSHIPS

National Society of Black Engineers
Attn: Programs Department
1454 Duke Street
Alexandria, VA 22314
(703) 549-2207, ext. 305   Fax: (703) 683-5312
E-mail: scholarships@nsbe.org
Web: www.nsbe.org/programs/schol_legacy.php

Purpose To provide financial assistance to members of the National Society of Black Engineers (NSBE) who are working on an undergraduate or graduate degree in engineering.
Eligibility This program is open to members of the society who are undergraduate or graduate engineering students. Selection is based on an essay; academic achievement; service to the society at the chapter, regional, and/or national level; and other professional, campus, and community activities.
Financial data The stipend depends on the availability of funds.
Duration 1 year; may be renewed.
Number awarded Varies each year, depending on the availability of funds. Recently, 20 of these scholarships were awarded.
Deadline January of each year.

[199]
FUTURE LEADERS OF MANUFACTURING SCHOLARSHIP

Society of Manufacturing Engineers
Attn: SME Education Foundation
One SME Drive
P.O. Box 930
Dearborn, MI 48121-0930
(313) 425-3300   Toll-free: (800) 733-4763, ext. 3300
Fax: (313) 425-3411   E-mail: foundation@sme.org
Web: www.sme.org

Purpose To provide financial assistance to student members of the Society of Manufacturing Engineers (SME) who are working on an undergraduate or graduate degree in manufacturing engineering or a related field.

Eligibility This program is open to undergraduate and graduate student members of SME who are working full time on a degree in manufacturing engineering, industrial technology, engineering technology, or a related field. They must be nominated by their SME faculty advisor; each advisor may nominate only 1 student. Letters of nomination must explain why the student should be selected, including participation in the student chapter, accomplishments, awards and honors, work experience, reasons for choosing a career in manufacturing, and how the scholarship will increase the student's leadership skills and career. Financial need is not considered.

Financial data The stipend is $1,000 per year.

Duration 1 year.

Number awarded Varies each year. Recently, 6 of these scholarships were awarded: 4 to undergraduates and 2 to graduate students.

Deadline January of each year.

[200]
GARMIN INTERNATIONAL SCHOLARSHIP

Aircraft Electronics Association
Attn: AEA Educational Foundation
4217 South Hocker Drive
Independence, MO 64055-4723
(816) 373-6565   Fax: (816) 478-3100
E-mail: info@aea.net
Web: www.aea.net

Purpose To provide financial assistance to students preparing for a career in avionics or aircraft repair.

Eligibility This program is open to high school seniors and currently-enrolled college students who are attending (or planning to attend) an accredited postsecondary institution in an avionics or aircraft repair program. Applicants must submit an official transcript (cumulative GPA of 2.5 or higher), a statement about their career plans, a description of their involvement in school and community activities, and a 300-word essay on how the job requirements of aviation technicians will change with advancements in technology. Selection is based on merit.

Financial data The stipend is $2,000.

Duration 1 year.

Number awarded 1 each year.

Deadline February of each year.

[201]
GARY B. MULTANEN/CM MAGAZINE SCHOLARSHIP

American Composites Manufacturers Association
Attn: Scholarship Office
1010 North Glebe Road, Suite 450
Arlington, VA 22201
(703) 525-0511   Fax: (703) 525-0743
E-mail: info@acmanet.org
Web: www.acmanet.org/cm/scholarship.cfm

Purpose To recognize and reward, with college scholarships, students who submit outstanding reports on research related to composites.

Eligibility This competition is open to undergraduate and graduate students who submit reports of research they have conducted in the field of composites, including industrial technology and plastics engineering. Entrants must be working on a degree in engineering, research, or other composites-based program. Art students working with composite materials in restoration or sculpture are also encouraged to apply.

Financial data Winners receive a $1,000 scholarship and a trip to the American Composites Manufacturers Association conference where they present their research.

Duration The competition is held annually.

Additional information This competition is sponsored by *Composites Manufacturing Magazine,* the official magazine of the American Composites Manufacturers Association.

Number awarded 1 each year.

Deadline June of each year.

[202]
G.B. GUNLOGSON STUDENT ENVIRONMENTAL DESIGN COMPETITION

American Society of Agricultural and Biological
  Engineers
Attn: Awards Coordinator
2950 Niles Road
St. Joseph, MI 49085-9659
(269) 429-0300   Fax: (269) 429-3852
E-mail: hq@asabe.org
Web: www.asabe.org

Purpose To recognize and reward student members of the American Society of Agricultural and Biological Engineers (ASABE) who participate in the basic design of an environmental or biological application in engineering.

Eligibility This program is open to biological and agricultural engineering students who are student members of the society. Applicant teams must submit an engineering design that involves an environmental or biological application. Designs should reflect a wide spectrum of approaches, including management practices development, equipment design, or bioreactor or ecological system design. Sociological, economic, aesthetic, legal, and ethical considerations can (and often must) be included as part of the design process. The report must include drawings and/or specifications that describe the design, as well as extensive or substantial test or performance data obtained from a 1) prototype or physical model of the machine or critical component, or 2) computer simulated test of the system or process.

Financial data First prize is $1,000, second $700, and third $300. Teams decide among themselves how to divide the money. The academic department of the first-place entry receives a wall plaque.

Duration The competition is held annually.

Number awarded 3 each year.

Deadline May of each year.

SCIENCES

[203]
GCA ZONE VI FELLOWSHIP IN URBAN FORESTRY

Garden Club of America
Attn: Scholarship Committee
14 East 60th Street
New York, NY 10022-1006
(212) 753-8287   Fax: (212) 753-0134
E-mail: scholarship@gcamerica.org
Web: www.gcamerica.org

Purpose To provide financial assistance to upper-division and graduate students interested in working on a degree in a field related to urban forestry.

Eligibility This program is open to advanced undergraduates and graduate students working on a degree in urban forestry, environmental studies, horticulture, forestry, or related courses of study with a special interest in the urban forest. Applicants must be enrolled at a 4-year college or university in the United States. Along with their application, they must submit brief statements on their career goals and how this fellowship will benefit them and help to further their academic and career goals. Financial need is not considered in the selection process.

Financial data The stipend is $4,000.

Duration 1 year; may be renewed 1 additional year.

Additional information This program was established in 2005 in cooperation with the Virginia Polytechnic Institute and State University's Department of Forestry, 228 Cheatham Hall, Blacksburg, VA 24061, (540) 231-7264.

Number awarded 1 each year.

Deadline January of each year.

[204]
GCSAA SCHOLARS COMPETITION

Golf Course Superintendents Association of America
Attn: Environmental Institute for Golf
1421 Research Park Drive
Lawrence, KS 66049-3859
(785) 832-4424   Toll-free: (800) 472-7878, ext. 4424
Fax: (785) 832-3673   E-mail: ahoward@gcsaa.org
Web: www.gcsaa.org

Purpose To provide financial assistance to undergraduate student members of the Golf Course Superintendents Association of America (GCSAA) who are preparing for a career in golf course management.

Eligibility Eligible to apply for this program are members of the association who are planning careers as golf course superintendents. Applicants must have completed at least 1 year of full-time study in a recognized undergraduate program with a major related to golf/turf management. Selection is based on academic skill, potential to become a leading professional, employment history, extracurricular activities, and letters of recommendation. Financial need is not considered. The highest ranked applicant receives the Chet Mendenhall Award and the second-highest ranked applicant receives the Allan MacCurrach Scholarship.

Financial data Stipends range from $500 to $6,000.

Duration 1 year.

Number awarded Varies each year. Recently, 22 of these scholarships were awarded; including 1 Chet Mendenhall Award (at $6,000), 1 Allan MacCurrach Scholarship (at $5,000), 3 at $2,000, 8 at $1,750, and 9 at $500.

Deadline May of each year.

[205]
GEF CORPORATE LEADERSHIP SCHOLARSHIPS

Gravure Association of America
Attn: Gravure Education Foundation
1200-A Scottsville Road
Rochester, NY 14624
(315) 589-8879   Fax: (585) 436-7689
E-mail: lwshatch@gaa.org
Web: www.gaa.org/GEF/scholarships.htm

Purpose To provide financial assistance to undergraduate and graduate students who are interested in a career in printing.

Eligibility This program is open to sophomores, juniors, seniors, and graduate students who are enrolled full time with a major in printing, graphic arts, or graphic communications. Applicants must be attending a designated learning resource center or an educational partner program supported by the Gravure Education Foundation (GEF) of the Gravure Association of America. They must have a GPA of 3.0 or higher. Along with their application, they must submit a 300-word essay on "How I Can Contribute My Leadership Skills to the Print Communications Industry." Selection is based on the essay, academic success, and leadership development efforts through clubs or associations, sports, community participation, or volunteer activity. Financial need is not considered.

Financial data The stipend is $1,500.

Duration 1 year.

Additional information GEF learning resource centers are located at the following universities: Rochester Institute of Technology, Western Michigan University, California Polytechnic State University at San Luis Obispo, Arizona State University, Clemson University, Murray State University, and the University of Wisconsin at Stout. GEF educational partner programs are at Central Missouri State University and Pittsburg State University of Kansas. This program is supported by the following corporate sponsors: The Cerutti Group, Johnson Polymer, Resinall Corporation, Shamrock Technologies, Stora Enso North America, and IMC America.

Number awarded 6 each year.

Deadline May of each year.

[206]
GENE SWACKHAMER AG ECONOMICS/AG BUSINESS GRANT

Alpha Gamma Rho Fraternity
Attn: Educational Foundation of AGR
10101 North Ambassador Drive
Kansas City, MO 64153-1395
(816) 891-9200   Fax: (816) 891-9401
E-mail: agr@AlphaGammaRho.org
Web: www.agrs.org

Purpose To provide financial assistance to members of Alpha Gamma Rho Fraternity (a national agricultural fraternity) who are majoring in agribusiness in college.

Eligibility This program is open to undergraduate members of the fraternity who are majoring in agricultural economics, agribusiness, resource management, or a closely-related field of study. Applicants must submit 3 essays on their involvement in the fraternity. Brothers living in the chapter house (where applicable) are given priority in the selection process. Financial need is not considered.
Financial data The stipend is $1,000.
Duration 1 year.
Number awarded 1 each year.
Deadline April of each year.

[207]
GENERAL ELECTRIC FUND/LEAGUE OF UNITED LATIN AMERICAN CITIZENS SCHOLARSHIPS

League of United Latin American Citizens
Attn: LULAC National Education Service Centers
2000 L Street, N.W., Suite 610
Washington, DC 20036
(202) 835-9646 Fax: (202) 835-9685
E-mail: scholarships@lnesc.org
Web: www.lnesc.org

Purpose To provide financial assistance to minority students who are studying engineering or business in college.
Eligibility Eligible to apply are minority students who will be enrolled as college sophomores pursuing full-time studies in a program leading to a baccalaureate degree in engineering or business at colleges or universities in the United States approved by the League of United Latin American Citizens (LULAC) and General Electric. They must have a GPA of 3.25 or higher and be U.S. citizens or legal residents. Selection is based on academic performance, likelihood of preparing for a career in business or engineering, performance in business or engineering subjects, writing ability, extracurricular activities, and community involvement.
Financial data The stipends are $5,000 per year. The funds are to be used to pay for tuition, required fees, room and board, and required educational materials and books. The funds are sent directly to the college or university and deposited in the scholarship recipient's name.
Duration 1 year; may be renewed if the recipient maintains a GPA of 3.0 or higher.
Additional information Funding for this program is provided by the General Electric Fund. All requests for applications or information must include a self-addressed stamped envelope.
Number awarded Varies each year; recently, 6 of these scholarships were awarded.
Deadline July of each year.

[208]
GENERAL ELECTRIC WOMEN'S NETWORK SCHOLARSHIPS

Society of Women Engineers
230 East Ohio Street, Suite 400
Chicago, IL 60611-3265
(312) 596-5223 Toll-free: (877) SWE-INFO
Fax: (312) 644-8557
E-mail: scholarshipapplication@swe.org
Web: www.swe.org/scholarships

Purpose To provide financial assistance to undergraduate women majoring in computer science or engineering.
Eligibility This program is open to women who are entering their sophomore, junior, or senior year at a 4-year ABET-accredited college or university. Applicants must be U.S. citizens majoring in computer science or engineering and have a GPA of 3.0 or higher. Along with their application, they must submit a 1-page essay on why they want to be an engineer or computer scientist, how they believe they will make a difference as an engineer or computer scientist, and what influenced them to study engineering or computer science. Selection is based on merit. Preference is given to students attending selected schools; for a list, contact the sponsor.
Financial data The stipend is $2,425.
Duration 1 year.
Additional information This program, established in 2002, is sponsored by the General Electric Women's Network of the General Electric Company.
Number awarded 13 each year.
Deadline January of each year.

[209]
GENERAL MOTORS FOUNDATION UNDERGRADUATE SCHOLARSHIPS

Society of Women Engineers
230 East Ohio Street, Suite 400
Chicago, IL 60611-3265
(312) 596-5223 Toll-free: (877) SWE-INFO
Fax: (312) 644-8557
E-mail: scholarshipapplication@swe.org
Web: www.swe.org/scholarships

Purpose To provide financial assistance to upper-division women majoring in designated engineering specialties.
Eligibility This program is open to women who are entering their junior year at a designated ABET-accredited college or university. Applicants must be majoring in automotive, chemical, electrical, industrial, manufacturing, materials, or mechanical engineering and have a GPA of 3.5 or higher. Along with their application, they must submit a 1-page essay on why they want to be an engineer, how they believe they will make a difference as an engineer, and what influenced them to study engineering. Selection is based on merit.
Financial data The stipend is $1,225 per year. Also provided is a $500 travel grant for the recipient to attend the society's national convention and student conference.
Duration 1 year; may be renewed for 1 additional year.
Additional information This program, established in 1991, is sponsored by the General Motors Foundation.

Recipients must attend a designated college or university. For a list, contact the sponsor.
Number awarded 2 each year.
Deadline January of each year.

[210]
GENERAL MOTORS MINORITY ENGINEERING AND SCIENCE SCHOLARSHIP PROGRAM
General Motors Corporation
Attn: GM Scholarship Administration Center
700 West Fifth Avenue
Naperville, IL 60563
Toll-free: (888) 377-5233   Fax: (630) 428-2695
E-mail: scholarshipinfo@gmsac.com
Web: www.gm.com

Purpose To provide financial assistance to underrepresented minority college students interested in majoring in an engineering or science program of interest to General Motors.
Eligibility This program is open to minority (African American, Hispanic, or Native American) students currently enrolled or planning to enroll full time at a 4-year college or university with sufficient credits to be classified as a sophomore or junior. Applicants must have a GPA of 3.0 or higher and plans to enroll in engineering or science; preference is given to students in chemical, electrical, industrial, manufacturing, or mechanical engineering or other closely-related fields of science or engineering. They must be U.S. citizens or have eligibility to work permanently in the United States. Along with their application, they must include a letter of recommendation from a college instructor or other representative, official transcripts from their college, and a personal statement (500 to 750 words) about how their college experiences (academics, extracurricular activities, outside activities, work experience) are shaping their educational and career goals. Selection is based on that statement, academic performance, proficiencies, and demonstrated skills in areas of interest to General Motors. Financial need is not considered.
Financial data The stipend is $5,000 per year.
Duration 1 year.
Additional information Summer internships at a General Motors facility may also be available to recipients.
Number awarded A limited number are awarded each year.
Deadline May of each year.

[211]
GENERAL MOTORS/LEAGUE OF UNITED LATIN AMERICAN CITIZENS SCHOLARSHIPS
League of United Latin American Citizens
Attn: LULAC National Education Service Centers
2000 L Street, N.W., Suite 610
Washington, DC 20036
(202) 835-9646   Fax: (202) 835-9685
E-mail: scholarships@lnesc.org
Web: www.lnesc.org

Purpose To provide financial assistance to Latino students interested in working on a degree in engineering in college.
Eligibility Eligible to apply are Latino students who are enrolled or planning to enroll as full-time students in a program leading to a baccalaureate degree in engineering at colleges or universities in the United States approved by the League of United Latin American Citizens (LULAC) and General Motors. Continuing college students must have a GPA of 3.2 or better; entering college freshmen must have a high school GPA of 3.5 or higher and either an ACT composite score of at least 23 or an SAT combined score of at least 970. Selection is based on academic performance; likelihood of preparing for a career in engineering; performance in science, mathematics, and engineering subjects; writing ability; extracurricular activities; and community involvement.
Financial data The stipends are $2,000 per year. The funds are to be used to pay for tuition, required fees, room and board, and required educational materials and books. The funds are sent directly to the college or university and deposited in the scholarship recipient's name.
Duration 1 year.
Additional information All requests for applications or information must include a self-addressed stamped envelope.
Number awarded Varies each year; recently, 26 of these scholarships were awarded.
Deadline July of each year.

[212]
GENEVIEVE CHRISTEN DISTINGUISHED UNDERGRADUATE STUDENT AWARD
American Dairy Science Association
Attn: Awards Coordinator
1111 North Dunlap Avenue
Savoy, IL 61874
(217) 356-5146   Fax: (217) 398-4119
E-mail: adsa@assochq.org
Web: www.adsa.org/awards/christen.html

Purpose To recognize and reward undergraduate students who have participated in dairy science activities.
Eligibility This program is open to undergraduate students nominated by a faculty member at their institution; only 1 student may be nominated by a college or university each year. The nominator must be a member of the American Dairy Science Association (ADSA). Nominees must be residents of Canada, Mexico, or the United States. Selection is based on demonstrated leadership ability (25 points), academic standing (15 points), interest and experience in the dairy industry (20 points), participation in ADSA Student Affiliate Division and local club activities (30 points), and a statement of their plans for the future (10 points).
Financial data The award consists of a plaque and a $1,000 honorarium.
Duration The award is presented annually.
Number awarded 1 each year.
Deadline Nominations must be submitted by December of each year.

[213]
GEORGE D. MILLER SCHOLARSHIP
National Fire Protection Association
Attn: Fire Safety Educational Memorial Fund Committee
1 Batterymarch Park
Quincy, MA 02169-7471
(617) 984-7244 Fax: (617) 984-7222
E-mail: cellis@nfpa.org
Web: www.nfpa.org

Purpose To provide financial assistance to undergraduate and graduate students enrolled in fire service or public administration programs.

Eligibility Colleges and universities in the United States and Canada are invited to nominate up to 2 undergraduate or graduate students enrolled in a fire service or public administration program. Nominees must exhibit scholastic achievement, leadership qualities, concern for others (volunteerism), and intent to prepare for a career in fire service or public administration.

Financial data The stipend is at least $5,000.

Duration 1 year.

Additional information This fund was established in 2001.

Number awarded 1 each year.

Deadline March of each year.

[214]
GEORGIA SPACE GRANT CONSORTIUM FELLOWSHIPS
Georgia Space Grant Consortium
c/o Georgia Institute of Technology
Aerospace Engineering
Paul Weber Space Science and Technology Building, Room 210
Atlanta, GA 30332-0150
(404) 894-0521 Fax: (404) 894-9313
E-mail: wanda.pierson@aerospace.gatech.edu
Web: www.ae.gatech.edu

Purpose To provide financial assistance for undergraduate and graduate study of space-related fields to students at member institutions of the Georgia Space Grant Consortium (GSGC).

Eligibility This program is open to U.S. citizens who are undergraduate and graduate students at member institutions of the GSGC. Applicants must be working on a degree in mathematics, science, engineering, computer science, or a technical discipline related to space. Selection is based on transcripts, 3 letters of reference, and an essay of 100 to 500 words on the applicant's professional interests and objectives and their relationship to the field of aerospace. Awards are provided as part of the Space Grant program of the U.S. National Aeronautics and Space Administration (NASA), which encourages participation by women, minorities, and people with disabilities.

Financial data A stipend is awarded (amount not specified).

Additional information Institutions that are members of the GSGC include Albany State University, Clark Atlanta University, Columbus State University, Fort Valley State University, Georgia Institute of Technology, Georgia State University, Kennesaw State University, Mercer University, Morehouse College, Spelman College, State University of West Georgia, and the University of Georgia. This program is funded by NASA.

Number awarded 1 each year.

[215]
GERALDINE COLBY ZEILER AWARDS
American Society of Cytopathology
400 West Ninth Street, Suite 201
Wilmington, DE 19801
(302) 429-8802 Fax: (302) 429-8807
E-mail: asc@cytopathology.org
Web: www.cytopathology.org

Purpose To recognize and reward, with scholarships, students enrolled in a program of cytology.

Eligibility This program is open to students enrolled in a program of cytopathology approved by the American Society of Cytopathology. Applicants must have completed the first 6 months of the 12-month training program and must intend to complete the program. Selection is based on academic performance and microscopic diagnostic skills as demonstrated within the program, leadership ability, initiative, acceptance of responsibility, dedication, and relationship to colleagues.

Financial data The award is $1,000.

Duration The awards are presented annually.

Additional information These awards were first presented in 1994.

Number awarded 5 each year.

Deadline Applications must be submitted within 1 month after completing the first 6 months of the training.

[216]
GIVAUDAN FLAVOR CORPORATION SCHOLARSHIP
Institute of Food Technologists
Attn: Scholarship Department
525 West Van Buren, Suite 1000
Chicago, IL 60607
(312) 782-8424 Fax: (312) 782-8348
E-mail: info@ift.org
Web: www.ift.org

Purpose To provide financial assistance to undergraduates interested in studying food science or food technology.

Eligibility This program is open to sophomores, juniors, and seniors in a food science or food technology program at an educational institution in the United States or Canada. Applicants must have an outstanding scholastic record and a well-rounded personality. Along with their application, they must submit an essay on their career aspirations; a list of awards, honors, and scholarships they have received; a list of extracurricular activities and/or hobbies; and a summary of their work experience. Financial need is not considered in the selection process.

Financial data The stipend is $1,000.

Duration 1 year; recipients may reapply if they are members of the Institute of Food Technologists.

Additional information Funding for this scholarship is provided by Givaudan Flavor Corporation. Correspondence and completed applications must be submitted to the

department head of the educational institution the applicant is attending.
Number awarded 3 each year.
Deadline January of each year.

[217]
GOLDEN KEY ENGINEERING/TECHNOLOGY ACHIEVEMENT AWARDS

Golden Key International Honour Society
621 North Avenue N.E., Suite C-100
Atlanta, GA 30308
(404) 377-2400 Toll-free: (800) 377-2401
Fax: (678) 420-6757
E-mail: scholarships@goldenkey.org
Web: www.goldenkey.org

Purpose To recognize and reward undergraduate and graduate members of the Golden Key International Honour Society who submit outstanding papers on topics related to the field of engineering or technology.
Eligibility This program is open to undergraduate, graduate, and postgraduate members of the society who submit a paper or report, up to 10 pages in length, on a topic related to engineering or technology. Applicants must also submit 1) an essay, up to 2 pages in length, describing the assignment for writing the paper, the greatest challenge in writing the paper, the lessons learned from completing the assignment, and what they would change if they could redo the paper; 2) a letter of recommendation; and 3) academic transcripts. Selection of the winners is based on academic achievement and the quality of the paper.
Financial data The winner receives a $1,000 scholarship, second place a $750 scholarship, and third place a $500 scholarship.
Duration These awards are presented annually.
Additional information This program began in 2001.
Number awarded 3 each year.
Deadline February of each year.

[218]
GOLDMAN, SACHS SCHOLARSHIPS

Society of Women Engineers
230 East Ohio Street, Suite 400
Chicago, IL 60611-3265
(312) 596-5223 Toll-free: (877) SWE-INFO
Fax: (312) 644-8557
E-mail: scholarshipapplication@swe.org
Web: www.swe.org/scholarships

Purpose To provide financial assistance to upper-division women who are members of the Society of Women Engineers and majoring in designated engineering specialties.
Eligibility This program is open to women who are entering their junior or senior year at an ABET-accredited 4-year college or university. Applicants must be studying computer science or electrical or computer engineering with a GPA of 3.2 or higher. Along with their application, they must submit a 1-page essay on why they want to be an engineer or computer scientist, how they believe they will make a difference as an engineer or computer scientist, and what influenced them to study engineering or computer science. Selection is based on merit.

Financial data The stipend is $2,000.
Duration 1 year.
Additional information This program is sponsored by Goldman, Sachs & Company.
Number awarded 4 each year.
Deadline January of each year.

[219]
GOLF COURSE SUPERINTENDENTS ASSOCIATION OF AMERICA STUDENT ESSAY CONTEST

Golf Course Superintendents Association of America
Attn: Environmental Institute for Golf
1421 Research Park Drive
Lawrence, KS 66049-3859
(785) 832-4424 Toll-free: (800) 472-7878, ext. 4424
Fax: (785) 832-3673 E-mail: ahoward@gcsaa.org
Web: www.gcsaa.org

Purpose To recognize and reward outstanding undergraduate and graduate essays written on golf course management by members of the Golf Course Superintendents Association of America (GCSAA).
Eligibility This contest is open to undergraduate and graduate students working on a degree in turfgrass science, agronomy, or another field related to golf course management. The essay should focus on golf course management and be from 7 to 12 pages in length. References and/or a bibliography must be included. Essays should be original, compelling, well organized, readable, persuasive, and creative. Technical accuracy, composition skills (spelling, grammar, etc.), and the student's adherence to the contest rules are considered in the selection process.
Financial data First prize is $2,000, second prize is $1,500, and third prize is $1,000.
Duration The competition is held annually.
Additional information Winning entries may be published or excerpted in 1 of the magazines published by the sponsoring organization.
Number awarded 3 each year.
Deadline March of each year.

[220]
GOVERNOR'S BLUE RIBBON LIVESTOCK AUCTION SCHOLARSHIP

Wisconsin State Fair
Attn: Agriculture Department
640 South 84th Street
P.O. Box 14990
West Allis, WI 53214-0990
(414) 266-7050 Fax: (414) 266-7007
E-mail: wsfp@sfp.state.wi.us
Web: www.wistatefair.com

Purpose To provide financial assistance for college to current and past livestock exhibitors at the Wisconsin State Fair.
Eligibility This program is open to individuals between 17 and 19 years of age who have exhibited beef, sheep, and/or swine at the Wisconsin State Fair. Applicants must be enrolled or planning to enroll at a university, vocation-

al/technical school, or university short course. Along with their application, they must submit a 1-page summary of their involvement and experiences while exhibiting at the Wisconsin State Fair. Finalists are interviewed. Selection is based on State Fair participation (35%), leadership activities (30%), the interview (20%), scholastic achievement (10%), and career plans (5%).

Financial data Stipends are $1,500, $1,000, or $500.
Duration 1 year; nonrenewable.
Number awarded 15 each year: 5 at $1,500, 5 at $1,000, and 5 at $500.
Deadline June of each year.

[221]
GRAVURE CATALOG AND INSERT COUNCIL SCHOLARSHIP

Gravure Association of America
Attn: Gravure Education Foundation
1200-A Scottsville Road
Rochester, NY 14624
(315) 589-8879   Fax: (585) 436-7689
E-mail: lwshatch@gaa.org
Web: www.gaa.org/GEF/scholarships.htm

Purpose To provide financial assistance to upper-division students interested in a career in printing.

Eligibility This program is open to juniors or seniors who are enrolled full time in a field related to printing at a designated learning resource center supported by the Gravure Education Foundation (GEF) of the Gravure Association of America. Applicants must have a GPA of 3.0 or higher. Along with their application, they must submit a 300-word essay that demonstrates their interest in gravure technology and the print communications industry. Financial need is not considered in the selection process.

Financial data The stipend is $1,000.
Duration 1 year.
Additional information GEF learning resource centers are located at the following universities: Rochester Institute of Technology, Western Michigan University, California Polytechnic State University at San Luis Obispo, Arizona State University, Clemson University, Murray State University, and the University of Wisconsin at Stout. The Gravure Catalog and Insert Council is an organization headed by end-users of gravure printing.
Number awarded 1 each year.
Deadline May of each year.

[222]
GUIDANT FOUNDATION SCHOLARSHIPS

Society of Women Engineers
230 East Ohio Street, Suite 400
Chicago, IL 60611-3265
(312) 596-5223   Toll-free: (877) SWE-INFO
Fax: (312) 644-8557
E-mail: scholarshipapplication@swe.org
Web: www.swe.org/scholarships

Purpose To provide financial assistance to upper-division women majoring in computer science or designated engineering specialties.

Eligibility This program is open to women who are entering their senior year at a designated ABET-accredited college or university. Applicants must be majoring in computer science or chemical, computer, electrical, industrial, manufacturing, materials, or mechanical engineering and have a GPA of 3.5 or higher. Along with their application, they must submit a 1-page essay on why they want to be an engineer or computer scientist, how they believe they will make a difference as an engineer or computer scientist, and what influenced them to study engineering or computer science. Selection is based on merit.

Financial data The stipend is $5,000.
Duration 1 year.
Additional information This program, established in 2004, is supported by Guidant Foundation. For a list of the designated colleges and universities, contact the sponsor.
Number awarded 2 each year.
Deadline January of each year.

[223]
GUILIANO MAZZETTI SCHOLARSHIPS

Society of Manufacturing Engineers
Attn: SME Education Foundation
One SME Drive
P.O. Box 930
Dearborn, MI 48121-0930
(313) 425-3300   Toll-free: (800) 733-4763, ext. 3300
Fax: (313) 425-3411   E-mail: foundation@sme.org
Web: www.sme.org

Purpose To provide financial assistance to undergraduate students enrolled in a degree program in manufacturing engineering or manufacturing engineering technology.

Eligibility This program is open to full-time undergraduate students enrolled in a manufacturing engineering or technology degree program at a college or university in North America. Applicants must have completed a minimum of 30 units in a manufacturing engineering or manufacturing engineering technology curriculum with a GPA of 3.0 or higher. Along with their application, they must submit a 300-word essay that covers their career and educational objectives, how this scholarship will help them attain those objectives, and why they want to enter this field. Financial need is not considered in the selection process.

Financial data The stipend is $2,000.
Duration 1 year.
Number awarded 2 each year.
Deadline January of each year.

[224]
G.W. HOHMANN SCHOLARSHIPS

Society of Exploration Geophysicists
Attn: SEG Foundation
8801 South Yale, Suite 500
P.O. Box 702740
Tulsa, OK 74170-2740
(918) 497-5513   Fax: (918) 497-5557
E-mail: scholarships@seg.org
Web: seg.org

Purpose To provide financial assistance to high school seniors, undergraduates, and graduate students who are interested in the field of applied geophysics related to mining or electrical methods.

Eligibility This program is open to 1) high school students planning to enter college in the fall, and 2) undergraduate or graduate students whose grades are above average. Applicants must intend to work on a degree directed toward a career in applied geophysics with an emphasis on mining or electrical methods. Along with their application, they must submit a 150-word essay on how they plan to use geophysics in their future. Financial need is not considered in the selection process.

Financial data The stipend is $3,000 per year for graduate students or $1,000 per year for undergraduates.

Duration 1 academic year; may be renewable, based on scholastic standing, availability of funds, and continuance of a course of study leading to a career in applied geophysics.

Number awarded 2 each year: 1 for an undergraduate and 1 for a graduate student.

Deadline January of each year.

[225] HAROLD E. ENNES SCHOLARSHIP

Society of Broadcast Engineers
Attn: Scholarship Committee
9102 North Meridian Street, Suite 150
Indianapolis, IN 46260
(317) 846-9000   Fax: (317) 846-9120
Web: www.sbe.org/edu_ennes_scholarships.php

Purpose To provide financial assistance for college to students interested in the technical aspects of broadcasting.

Eligibility Applicants must have a career interest in the technical aspects of broadcasting and must be recommended by 2 members of the Society of Broadcast Engineers (SBE). They must submit 1) a brief autobiography that includes their interest and goals in broadcasting, and 2) a summary of the technical changes they anticipate in broadcasting within the next 5 years. Preference is given to members of the SBE and to students currently employed at least part time in broadcast engineering. Both new students just entering college and students already enrolled in college may apply. Financial need is not considered in the selection process.

Financial data The stipend ranges from $1,000 to $3,000, depending on the availability of funds. Awards may be used for 1) tuition, room, board, or textbook costs at postsecondary educational institutions, or 2) other technical training programs approved by the sponsor.

Duration 1 year.

Additional information This scholarship fund was established in 1980.

Number awarded 1 each year.

Deadline June of each year.

[226] HARTLEY LORD SCHOLARSHIP

Senior Center at Lower Village
Attn: Scholarship Committee
175 Port Road
Kennebunk, ME 04043
(207) 967-8514
Web: www.seniorcenterkennebunk.org

Purpose To provide financial assistance to college students preparing for a career in service to the elderly.

Eligibility This program is open to students working on a degree or certificate in a field that focuses on the well-being and needs of the senior members of society. Those fields include, but are not limited to, community service, eldercare, nursing, or medicine. Applicants must submit essays on why their career choice is consistent with the requirements of the scholarship, extracurricular or community activities in which they have participated, and any awards or other recognition they have received for excellence in scholarship, athletics, or community activities. Selection is based on academic standing, future promise, recommendations, and academic major.

Financial data The stipend is $1,000. Funds are paid directly to the institution.

Duration 1 year.

Number awarded 1 each year.

Deadline April of each year.

[227] HARVEY WASHINGTON BANKS SCHOLARSHIP IN ASTRONOMY

National Society of Black Physicists
Attn: Scholarship Committee Chair
6704G Lee Highway
Arlington, VA 22205
(703) 536-4207   Fax: (703) 536-4203
E-mail: scholarship@nsbp.org
Web: www.nsbp.org

Purpose To provide financial assistance to African American students majoring in astronomy in college.

Eligibility This program is open to African American students who are entering their junior or senior year of college and majoring in astronomy. Applicants must submit an essay on their academic and career objectives, information on their participation in extracurricular activities, a description of any awards and honors they have received, and 3 letters of recommendation. Financial need is not considered.

Financial data The stipend is $1,000.

Duration 1 year; nonrenewable.

Additional information This program is offered in partnership with the American Astronomical Society.

Number awarded 1 each year.

Deadline November of each year.

[228]
HAWAII CHAPTER AFCEA SCHOLARSHIPS
Armed Forces Communications and Electronics
  Association-Hawaii Chapter
Attn: Scholarship Committee
P.O. Box 31156
Honolulu, HI 96820
(808) 864-5098   E-mail: MurphyJrJ@saic.com
Web: www.afceahi.org/subpage.asp?section=22

Purpose To provide financial assistance to high school seniors and undergraduate students from Hawaii interested in studying engineering, computer science, or information technology in college.

Eligibility This program is open to residents of Hawaii who are either graduating high school seniors or students already enrolled as undergraduates. Applicants must be majoring or planning to major in computer science, engineering, information technology, or related fields at a 4-year college or university in the United States. Selection is based on academic standing, community involvement and volunteerism, demonstrated leadership, extracurricular activities, and athletic achievement. Financial need is not considered.

Financial data The stipend is $2,000.

Duration 1 year.

Additional information This program includes the following named scholarships: the COL Bill Haney, USA (Ret) Award for Leadership, the CAPT Ken Wiedking, USN (Ret) Award for Community Service, the CAPT Jim Hickerson, USN (Ret) Award for Academic Achievement, the Maj Gen Rockly Triantafellu, USAF (Ret) Award for Academic Achievement, the Eugene C. Renzi Award for Academic Achievement, and the LTG Thomas M. Rienzi, USA (Ret) Award for Academic Achievement.

Number awarded Varies each year; recently, 12 high school seniors and 5 college students received these scholarships.

Deadline July of each year.

[229]
HAWAIIAN HOMES COMMISSION CAREER AND TECHNICAL EDUCATION SCHOLARSHIP
Hawai'i Community Foundation
Attn: Scholarship Department
1164 Bishop Street, Suite 800
Honolulu, HI 96813
(808) 566-5570   Toll-free: (888) 731-3863
Fax: (808) 521-6286
E-mail: scholarships@hcf-hawaii.org
Web: www.hawaiicommunityfoundation.org

Purpose To provide financial assistance to residents of Hawaii who are interested in enrolling in a vocational training program in the state.

Eligibility This program is open to residents of Hawaii who are native Hawaiian (50% or more Hawaiian ancestry) or a homestead lessee (at least 25% Hawaiian ancestry). Applicants must be attending or planning to attend a vocational college or institution that is part of the University of Hawaii community college system. Programs include culinary arts, auto repair, diesel mechanics, cosmetology, computer graphics, and assistive medical technology. Applicants must submit a personal statement explaining their personal background and interests, the vocational program they plan to pursue, their career goals, and anything else that demonstrates their worthiness to receive this scholarship. Financial need is not considered in the selection process.

Financial data The stipend is $500 per semester. Funds are mailed directly to the financial aid office at the recipient's institution.

Duration 1 semester; may be renewed for up to 3 additional semesters.

Additional information This program, which began in 2006, is sponsored by the state Department of Hawaiian Home Lands.

Number awarded Varies each year.

Deadline June of each year for fall and spring semester scholarships; September of each year for spring semester scholarships.

[230]
HEALTHCARE INFORMATION MANAGEMENT SYSTEMS SCHOLARSHIPS
Healthcare Information and Management Systems
  Society
Attn: HIMSS Foundation Scholarship Program
  Coordinator
230 East Ohio Street, Suite 500
Chicago, IL 60611-3270
(312) 664-HIMSS   Fax: (312) 664-6143
E-mail: foundation@himss.org
Web: www.himss.org/ASP/scholarship_hims.asp

Purpose To provide financial assistance to upper-division and graduate student members of the Healthcare Information and Management Systems Society (HIMSS) who are interested in the field of health care information and management systems.

Eligibility This program is open to student members of the society, although an application for membership, including dues, may accompany the scholarship application. Applicants must be upper-division or graduate students enrolled in an accredited program designed to prepare them for a career in health care information or management systems, which may include industrial engineering, health care informatics, operations research, computer science and information systems, mathematics, and quantitative programs in business administration and hospital administration. Selection is based on academic achievement and demonstration of leadership potential, including communication skills and participation in society activity.

Financial data The stipend is $5,000. The award also includes an all-expense paid trip to the annual HIMSS conference and exhibition.

Duration 1 year.

Additional information This program was established in 1986 for undergraduate and master's degree students. The first Ph.D. scholarship was awarded in 2002.

Number awarded 3 each year: 1 to an undergraduate student, 1 to a master's degree student, and 1 to a Ph.D. candidate.

Deadline October of each year.

SCIENCES

[231]
HEART OF AMERICA GOLF COURSE SUPERINTENDENTS ASSOCIATION SCHOLARSHIPS

Heart of America Golf Course Superintendents Association
Attn: Scholarship and Research Committee
638 West 39th Street
P.O. Box 419264
Kansas City, MO 64141-6264
(816) 561-5323   Fax: (816) 561-1991
E-mail: kswank@swassn.com
Web: www.hagcsa.org/scholarships.htm

Purpose To provide financial assistance to undergraduate and graduate students working on a degree in turfgrass management in Missouri or Kansas.

Eligibility This program is open to undergraduate and graduate students working on a degree in turfgrass management at colleges and universities in Kansas and Missouri. Applicants must submit brief essays on what stimulated their initial interest in golf and the turf profession, why they believe the sponsor should grant them a scholarship, their goals upon graduation, and their professional goals with their degree as a golf course superintendent or other management position. Financial need is not considered in the selection process.

Financial data Stipends are $2,500, $1,500 or $1,000.

Duration 1 year.

Additional information This program includes the Chester Mendenhall Scholarship and the Dave Fearis Scholarship.

Number awarded 3 each year.

Deadline December of each year.

[232]
HELP DESK SCHOLARSHIP CONTEST

Thomson Course Technology
c/o Suelaine Frongello
25 Thomson Place
Boston, MA 02210
(617) 757-7900
E-mail: Suelaine.Frongello@course.com
Web: www.course.com/helpdesk/scholarship.cfm

Purpose To recognize and reward, with scholarships, college students who submit outstanding essays related to help desk courses.

Eligibility This competition is open to U.S. citizens who are enrolled in a public or private college, university, or career school. Applicants must be enrolled in a help desk course at the time of entry. They must submit an essay on 1 of the following topics: 1) describe a help desk internship that you've recently held and how it will help you land a job in the help desk industry; or 2) identify the ways in which you can contribute to the help desk field. Selection is based on the thoughtfulness of the essay.

Financial data The award is $1,000, paid directly to the college or university as a credit toward tuition.

Duration The competition is held annually.

Additional information This competition was first held in 2001.

Number awarded 1 each year.

Deadline May of each year.

[233]
HOME BUILDERS ASSOCIATION OF ILLINOIS STUDENT OF THE YEAR SCHOLARSHIPS

Home Builders Association of Illinois
112 West Edwards Street
Springfield, IL 62704
(217) 753-3963   TDD: (800) 255-6047
Fax: (217) 753-3811
Web: www.hbai.org/Student/index.asp

Purpose To recognize and reward, with funds for continuing education, students in Illinois who are preparing for a career in the building industry.

Eligibility This program is open to students enrolled in a building trades or architecture program at a high school, university, community college, or technical school in Illinois. Students must be nominated by a local affiliate of the Home Builders Association of Illinois. They must have a "C+" average or higher. Selection is based on academics, involvement with the building industry, leadership and extracurricular activities, community involvement, and awards and honors.

Financial data Awards are $2,000 for first place, $1,500 for second place, and $1,000 for third place. Funds are paid to the student's school to be used for continuing education. If the recipients do not remain in school, they may use the award for certified graduate builder or remodeler courses offered through the home builders association.

Duration Awards are offered annually.

Number awarded 3 each year.

[234]
HONEYWELL AVIONICS SCHOLARSHIP

Aircraft Electronics Association
Attn: AEA Educational Foundation
4217 South Hocker Drive
Independence, MO 64055-4723
(816) 373-6565   Fax: (816) 478-3100
E-mail: info@aea.net
Web: www.aea.net

Purpose To provide financial assistance for college to students who are interested in preparing for a career in avionics or aircraft repair.

Eligibility This program is open to high school seniors and college students who are attending (or planning to attend) an accredited school in an avionics or aircraft repair program. Applicants must submit an official transcript (cumulative GPA of 2.5 or higher), a statement about their career plans, a description of their involvement in school and community activities, and a 300-word essay on how the job requirements of aviation technicians will change with advancements in technology. Selection is based on merit.

Financial data The stipend is $1,000.

Duration 1 year.

Number awarded 1 each year.

Deadline February of each year.

[235]
HOOSIER HAMPSHIRE SWINE BREEDERS ASSOCIATION JUNIOR SCHOLARSHIPS
Hoosier Hampshire Swine Breeders Association
c/o Sherry Hazelett, Committee Chair
781 East CR 700 North
Frankfort, IN 46041
Web: www.bccn.boone.in.us

Purpose To provide financial assistance for college to residents of Indiana who have been involved in raising Hampshire pigs.

Eligibility This program is open to Indiana residents who are high school seniors or students in their freshman, sophomore, or junior year at a college, junior college, or trade school. Applicants must have shown a Hampshire pig at least 5 years at the Indiana State Fair during their 4-H or FFA career. They do not have to be majoring in agriculture, but preference is given to applicants pursuing higher education in an agricultural field. Preference is also given to children of the National and Hoosier Hampshire Swine Breeders Association. Selection is based on activity in the Hoosier Hampshire Swine Breeders Association, involvement in junior swine activities through 4-H and FFA, community activities and involvement, and future plans. A personal interview may also be required. Financial need is not considered.

Financial data The stipend is $1,000 per year.

Duration 1 year; nonrenewable.

Number awarded Up to 5 each year.

Deadline June of each year.

[236]
HOWARD E. ADKINS MEMORIAL SCHOLARSHIP
American Welding Society
Attn: AWS Foundation, Inc.
550 N.W. LeJeune Road
Miami, FL 33126
(305) 445-6628   Toll-free: (800) 443-9353, ext. 461
Fax: (305) 443-7559   E-mail: found@aws.org
Web: www.aws.org

Purpose To provide financial assistance to upper-division students interested in preparing for a career related to welding.

Eligibility This program is open to full-time college juniors and seniors who are working on a 4-year bachelor's degree in welding engineering or welding engineering technology; preference is given to students in welding engineering. Applicants must have a GPA of 3.2 or higher in engineering, science, and technical subjects and 2.8 overall. Priority is given to applicants residing or attending school in Wisconsin or Kentucky. U.S. citizenship is required. Financial need is not considered in the selection process.

Financial data The stipend is $2,500.

Duration 1 year; recipients may reapply.

Additional information This program was established in 1994.

Number awarded 1 each year.

Deadline January of each year.

[237]
HOWARD P. WACKMAN II MEMORIAL AWARD
California Farm Bureau Scholarship Foundation
Attn: Scholarship Coordinator
2300 River Plaza Drive
Sacramento, CA 95833
(916) 561-5520   Toll-free: (800) 698-FARM (within CA)
Fax: (916) 561-5699   E-mail: dlicciardo@cfbf.com
Web: www.cfbf.com/programs/scholar/index.cfm

Purpose To provide financial assistance for college to residents of California who are interested in preparing for a career in agriculture.

Eligibility This program is open to students entering or attending a 4-year accredited college or university in California who are majoring or planning to major in an agriculture-related field. Students entering a junior college are not eligible. Applicants must have a GPA of 3.0 or higher in high school or college. They must submit an essay on the most important educational or personal experience that has led them to pursue a university education. Selection is based on academic achievement, career goals, extracurricular activities, leadership skills, determination, and commitment to study agriculture.

Financial data The stipend is $2,750 per year.

Duration 1 year; recipients may reapply.

Number awarded 1 each year.

Deadline February of each year.

[238]
HVTO STEWARDSHIP AWARD
Electronic Document Systems Foundation
Attn: EDSF Scholarship Awards
608 Silver Spur Road, Suite 280
Rolling Hills Estates, CA 90274-3616
(310) 265-5510   Fax: (310) 265-5588
E-mail: jmowlds@edsf.org
Web: www.edsf.org/scholarships.cfm

Purpose To provide financial assistance to students working on an undergraduate or graduate degree in a field related to the high volume transaction output (HVTO) industry.

Eligibility This program is open to undergraduate and graduate students who are working on a degree in field related to the HVTO industry, including information technology, graphic arts, or business. Applicants must be enrolled full time at a technical school, trade school, community college, university, college, or graduate school in the United States with a GPA of 3.0 or higher. They must be able to demonstrate leadership and contribution to volunteer and community activities. Along with their application, they must submit a statement of their career goals in the field of document communications, an essay on a topic related to their view of the future of the document management and production industry, a list of current professional and college extracurricular activities and achievements, college transcripts, samples of their creative work, and 2 letters of recommendation. Financial need is not considered.

Financial data The stipend is $1,000.

Duration 1 year.

Additional information This program is sponsored by COPI/OutputLinks.

Number awarded 1 each year.
Deadline May of each year.

[239]
IADR/UNILEVER HATTON AWARDS COMPETITION

International Association for Dental Research
Attn: Awards, Grants and Fellowships Administrator
1619 Duke Street
Alexandria, VA 22314-3406
(703) 299-8094   Fax: (703) 548-1883
E-mail: sherren@iadr.com
Web: www.iadr.com/awards/hattoniadr.html

Purpose To recognize and reward outstanding dental research papers.

Eligibility This competition is open to investigators worldwide who exhibit potential for a productive career in dental research. Junior candidates must be currently enrolled in a bachelor's or dental degree program and have carried out their research as an undergraduate science student, a dental student, or while working on an intercalated science degree as a dental student. Senior candidates may be enrolled in a post-dental, postgraduate, Ph.D., or post-doctoral program and have carried out research as part of master's, Ph.D., or M.D. program with previous laboratory experience, as part of specialty training, or within 3 years of completion of a Ph.D. The senior category is divided into 2 sections: 1) clinical or preclinical research involving human subjects and/or epidemiological studies, and 2) basic science research involving laboratory or animal research. Students are selected to compete by winning an award in a division of the International Association for Dental Research. They are then invited to submit abstracts of entries to be presented at posters at the IADR annual meeting. Selection is based on a 10-minute verbal presentation (50%) and a 5-minute question and answer period (50%). The factors considered are originality and design of the investigation, quality of the data produced, suitability of the methods of analysis used, scientific value of the work, quality of the poster presentation, and demonstrated mastery of the subject.

Financial data Each first-place winner receives $1,000 and each second-place winner receives $500.

Duration The competition is held annually.

Additional information This competition is sponsored by Unilever Corporation. In the United States, the appropriate division is the American Association for Dental Research (AADR).

Number awarded 6 entrants (a first-place and second-place winner for the junior category, for the clinical senior category, and for the basic science senior category) receive prizes.

Deadline Divisions must submit the names of their winners by September of each year.

[240]
IAGER DAIRY SCHOLARSHIP

National Dairy Shrine
Attn: Office of Executive Director
1224 Alton Darby Creek Road
Columbus, OH 43228-9792
(614) 878-5333   Fax: (614) 870-2622
E-mail: shrine@cobaselect.com
Web: www.dairyshrine.org/students.asp

Purpose To provide financial assistance to 2-year college students majoring in dairy science.

Eligibility This program is open to students completing their first year at a 2-year agricultural school and preparing for a career in the dairy industry. Applicants must have a GPA of 2.5 or higher. Along with their application, they must submit a 500-word essay on why they are interested in the dairy industry and their plans for the future. Selection is based on that essay, academic standing, leadership ability, and interest in the dairy industry.

Financial data The stipend is $1,000.

Duration 1 year.

Additional information This scholarship, first awarded in 2004, is sponsored by Maple Lawn Farms, Inc. of Fulton, Maryland.

Number awarded 1 each year.

Deadline June of each year.

[241]
IAHPERD SCHOLARSHIPS

Illinois Association for Health, Physical Education, Recreation and Dance
Attn: Executive Secretary
1713 South West Street
Jacksonville, IL 62650
(217) 245-6413   Fax: (217) 245-5261
E-mail: iahperd@iahperd.org
Web: www.iahperd.org

Purpose To provide financial assistance to upper-division students in Illinois who are majoring in health, physical education, recreation, or dance.

Eligibility This program is open to juniors and seniors at colleges and universities in Illinois who are majoring in health, physical education, recreation, or dance. Applicants must submit a personal letter explaining why they chose to go into their field and where they see themselves professionally in 5 years. Selection is based on that letter, involvement in professional organizations, involvement in extracurricular activities, involvement in community organizations, transcripts, and 2 letters of recommendation.

Financial data Stipends are $1,000 or $750.

Duration 1 year.

Number awarded 6 each year: 1 at $1,000 and 5 at $750.

Deadline April of each year.

[242]
IBM CORPORATION SWE SCHOLARSHIPS
Society of Women Engineers
230 East Ohio Street, Suite 400
Chicago, IL 60611-3265
(312) 596-5223 Toll-free: (877) SWE-INFO
Fax: (312) 644-8557
E-mail: scholarshipapplication@swe.org
Web: www.swe.org/scholarships

Purpose To provide financial assistance to lower-division women majoring in designated engineering specialties.

Eligibility This program is open to women who are entering their sophomore or junior year at a 4-year ABET-accredited college or university. Applicants must be majoring in computer science or electrical or computer engineering and have a GPA of 3.4 or higher. They must be U.S. citizens or authorized to work in the United States. Along with their application, they must submit a 1-page essay on why they want to be an engineer or computer scientist, how they believe they will make a difference as an engineer or computer scientist, and what influenced them to study engineering or computer science. Selection is based on merit.

Financial data The stipend is $1,000.

Duration 1 year.

Additional information This program is sponsored by the IBM Corporation.

Number awarded 4 each year.

Deadline January of each year.

[243]
IDDBA SCHOLARSHIP
International Dairy-Deli-Bakery Association
Attn: Scholarship Committee
636 Science Drive
P.O. Box 5528
Madison, WI 53705-0528
(608) 310-5000 Fax: (608) 238-6330
E-mail: iddba@iddba.org
Web: www.iddba.org/scholars.htm

Purpose To provide financial assistance to high school seniors, undergraduates, or graduate students employed in a supermarket dairy, deli, or bakery department who are interested in majoring in a food-related field.

Eligibility This program is open to high school seniors, college students, vocational/technical students, and graduate students. Applicants must be currently employed in a supermarket dairy, deli, or bakery department or be employed by a company that services those departments (e.g., food manufacturers, brokers, or wholesalers). They must be majoring in a food-related field, e.g., culinary arts, baking/pastry arts, food science, business, or marketing. Their employer must be a member of the International Dairy-Deli-Bakery Association (IDDBA). While a GPA of 2.5 or higher is required, this may be waived for first-time applicants. Selection is based on academic achievement, work experience, and a statement of career goals and/or how their degree will be beneficial to their job. Financial need is not considered.

Financial data Stipends range from $250 to $1,000. Funds are paid jointly to the recipient and the recipient's school. If the award exceeds tuition fees, the excess may be used for other educational expenses.

Duration 1 year; recipients may reapply.

Number awarded Varies each year; a total of $75,000 is available for this program annually.

Deadline Applications must be submitted prior to the end of March, June, September, or December of each year.

[244]
ILLINOIS CHAPTER ASHRAE SCHOLARSHIP
American Society of Heating, Refrigerating and Air-Conditioning Engineers, Inc.-Illinois Chapter
P.O. Box 428020
Evergreen Park, IL 60805-8020
(708) 636-5819 Fax: (708) 636-5847
E-mail: dkdoherty@chicagosite.org
Web: www.illinoisashrae.org

Purpose To provide financial assistance to high school seniors and current undergraduates in Illinois who are working on or planning to work on a degree in engineering, science, or mathematics as preparation for a career in the heating, ventilating, refrigeration, and air conditioning field.

Eligibility This program is open to students entering or attending a college or university in Illinois. Applicants must be interested in preparing for a career in the heating, ventilating, refrigeration, and air conditioning field by majoring in a relevant field of engineering, science, or mathematics. Along with their application, they must submit an essay of 100 to 200 words on their goals as they relate to their education, career, and future plans. Financial need is not considered in the selection process.

Financial data A stipend is awarded (amount not specified).

Duration 1 year.

Number awarded Varies each year; recently, 4 of these scholarships were awarded.

Deadline December of each year.

[245]
ILLINOIS PORK DONOR-ADVISED FUND SCHOLARSHIPS
Illinois Pork Producers Association
6411 South Sixth Street Road
Springfield, IL 62712-6817
(217) 529-3100 Fax: (217) 529-1771
E-mail: info@ilpork.com
Web: www.ilpork.com/youth_page/scholarships.html

Purpose To provide financial assistance for college to Illinois residents who have been involved in the pork industry, especially those who are active in the Illinois Pork Producers Association (IPPA).

Eligibility This program is open to Illinois residents who are enrolled or planning to enroll as an undergraduate student. Applicants must submit an essay (up to 3 pages) on a specific topic identifying the greatest challenge facing the Illinois pork industry. Selection is based on the essay (35 points), participation in the IPPA Ambassador Program (10 points), IPPA membership (15 points), activities (20 points), and grades (20 points).

Financial data Stipends are $1,250, $750, or $500.

Duration 1 year.

Additional information This program was formerly limited to members of the IPPA and their families and called the IPPA Scholarships. Previous winners are only eligible to receive a scholarship of greater value.

Number awarded 9 each year: 3 at each monetary level.

Deadline May of each year.

[246]
INCE STUDENT PAPER PRIZE COMPETITION

Institute of Noise Control Engineering
c/o Iowa State University
College of Engineering
210 Marston Hall
Ames, IA 50011-2153
(515) 294-6142   Fax: (515) 294-3528
E-mail: ibo@inceusa.org
Web: www.inceusa.org

Purpose To recognize and reward outstanding papers written by student members of the Institute of Noise Control Engineering (INCE).

Eligibility This competition is open to associates or members of the institute who are registered as students at a U.S. college or university. Applicants must submit an original paper (8 pages in length) that deals with a practical aspect of noise control; it does not have to relate to thesis research. Literature reviews are discouraged. Selection is based on the difficulty of the problem addressed, the practical value of the work to noise control engineering, the technical quality of the investigation, the quality of the technical communication, and the quality of the oral presentation.

Financial data Winners receive a cash award of $500 plus an additional $500 if they attend the awards ceremony and another $500 if the paper is expanded and accepted for publication in *Noise Control Engineering Journal*.

Duration The competition is held annually.

Number awarded Up to 5 each year.

Deadline Abstracts must be submitted by April of each year.

[247]
INSTITUTE OF FOOD TECHNOLOGISTS COLLEGE SCHOLARSHIPS

Institute of Food Technologists
Attn: Scholarship Department
525 West Van Buren, Suite 1000
Chicago, IL 60607
(312) 782-8424   Fax: (312) 782-8348
E-mail: info@ift.org
Web: www.ift.org

Purpose To provide financial assistance to undergraduates interested in studying food science or food technology.

Eligibility This program is open to sophomores, juniors, and seniors in a food science or food technology program at an educational institution in the United States or Canada. Applicants must have an outstanding scholastic record and a well-rounded personality. Along with their application, they must submit an essay on their career aspirations; a list of awards, honors, and scholarships they have received; a list of extracurricular activities and/or hobbies; and a summary of their work experience. Financial need is not considered in the selection process.

Financial data Stipends are $2,000, $1,500, or $1,000.

Duration 1 year; recipients may reapply if they are members of the Institute of Food Technologists.

Additional information Correspondence and completed applications must be submitted to the department head at the educational institution the applicant is attending.

Number awarded Varies each year; recently, 48 of these scholarships were awarded: 5 at $2,000. 2 at $1,500, and 41 at $1,000.

Deadline January of each year.

[248]
INTERNATIONAL COMMUNICATIONS INDUSTRIES FOUNDATION AV SCHOLARSHIPS

InfoComm International
International Communications Industries Foundation
11242 Waples Mill Road, Suite 200
Fairfax, VA 22030
(703) 273-7200   Toll-free: (800) 659-7469
Fax: (703) 278-8082 E-mail: dwilbert@infocomm.org
Web: www.infocomm.org/Foundation/Scholarships

Purpose To provide financial assistance to high school seniors and college students who are interested in preparing for a career in the audiovisual (AV) industry.

Eligibility This program is open to high school seniors and students already enrolled in college. Applicants must have a GPA of 2.75 or higher and be majoring or planning to major in audiovisual subjects, including audio, visual, electronics, telecommunications, technical aspects of the theater, data networking, software development, or information technology. Students in other programs, such as journalism, may be eligible if they can demonstrate a relationship to career goals in the AV industry. Along with their application, they must submit essays on why they are applying for this scholarship, why they are interested in the audiovisual industry, and their professional plans following graduation. Minority and women candidates are especially encouraged to apply. Selection is based on the essays, presentation of the application, GPA, work experience, and letters of recommendation.

Financial data The stipend is $1,200.

Duration 1 year.

Additional information InfoComm International, formerly the International Communications Industries Association, established the International Communications Industries Foundation (ICIF) to manage its charitable and educational activities.

Number awarded Varies each year; recently, 29 of these scholarships were awarded.

Deadline April of each year.

[249]
INTERNATIONAL CONGRESS ON INSECT NEUROCHEMISTRY AND NEUROPHYSIOLOGY STUDENT RECOGNITION AWARD IN INSECT PHYSIOLOGY, BIOCHEMISTRY, TOXICOLOGY, AND MOLECULAR BIOLOGY

Entomological Society of America
Attn: Entomological Foundation
9332 Annapolis Road, Suite 210
Lanham, MD 20706-3150
(301) 459-9082   Fax: (301) 459-9084
E-mail: April@entfdn.org
Web: www.entsoc.org/awards/student/icinn.htm

Purpose To recognize and reward student members of the Entomological Society of America (ESA) who have conducted innovative research.

Eligibility This program is open to undergraduate and graduate students who are ESA members. Applicants must have conducted innovative research in the areas of insect physiology, biochemistry, toxicology, and molecular biology in the broad sense. Areas of research may include development, genetics, defense mechanisms, and other offshoots of physiology, biochemistry, and toxicology.

Financial data A cash award is presented (amount not specified).

Duration The award is presented annually.

Additional information This award, first presented in 2004, is sponsored by the International Congress on Insect Neurochemistry and Neurophysiology.

Number awarded 1 each year.

Deadline June of each year.

[250]
INTERNATIONAL FUTURE ENERGY CHALLENGE STUDENT COMPETITION

Institute of Electrical and Electronics Engineers
Industry Applications Society
Attn: Administrative Secretary
799 North Beverly Glen
Los Angeles, CA 90077
(310) 446-8360   Fax: (310) 446-8390
E-mail: bob.myers@ieee.org
Web: www.energychallenge.org

Purpose To recognize and reward undergraduate engineering students who design and build prototype equipment to support fuel cell power systems.

Eligibility This program is open to teams of undergraduate students enrolled in an engineering program at a college or university that is ABET-accredited or equivalent. Applicants must have a faculty advisor and the support of the school's administration to design and build a prototype of a low-cost, manufacturable piece of equipment that would accelerate deployment of distributed generation systems. They may submit an entry for 1 of the following topics: a single-phase adjustable speed motor drive, or a utility interactive inverter system for small distributed generation. Selection is based on cost effectiveness, performance, quality of the prototype and other results, engineering reports, adherence to rules and deadlines, innovation, future, and other criteria related to the specific topic.

Financial data Prizes vary each year, depending on the funding available from sponsors. Recently, they ranged up to $10,000.

Duration The competition is held biennially, extending from mid-May of each even-numbered year to mid-August of the following odd-numbered year.

Additional information This program was established for 2001 by the U.S. Department of Energy (DOE), the U.S. Department of Defense, the National Association of State Energy Officials, and the following components of the Institute of Electrical and Electronics Engineers (IEEE): the Industry Applications Society, the Power Electronics Society, the Industrial Electronics Society, and the Power Engineering Society. Recent sponsors included the IEEE components, the DOE's National Renewable Energy Laboratory, and the European Power Electronics Association. The 2001 competition was limited to students at North American colleges and universities, but subsequent events have been open to students at any college or university.

Number awarded Varies; recently, prizes for the motor topic included first place at $10,000, outstanding design innovation at $6,500, outstanding educational impact at $2,000, outstanding presentation at $2,000, and outstanding technical report at $2,500. For the inverter topic, prizes included first place at $10,000, second place at $8,000, third place at $5,000, outstanding presentation at $2,000, outstanding technical report at $2,000, outstanding educational impact at $1,500, innovative design at $1,500, innovative packaging at $1,000, and outstanding teamwork at $1,000.

Deadline Initial proposals must be submitted by April of each even-numbered year.

[251]
ITS WASHINGTON/WTS SCHOLARSHIP

Women's Transportation Seminar-Puget Sound Chapter
c/o Kristin Overleese, Scholarship Chair
City of Shoreline, Capital Projects Manager
17544 Midvale Avenue North
Shoreline, WA 98133-4821
(206) 546-1700   Fax: (206) 546-2200
TDD: (206) 546-0457
Web: www.wtsinternational.org/puget_sound

Purpose To provide financial assistance to undergraduate and graduate students from Washington working on a degree related to intelligent transportation systems (ITS).

Eligibility This program is open to students who are residents of Washington, studying at a college in the state, or working as an intern in the state. Applicants must be currently enrolled in an undergraduate or graduate degree program related to the design, implementation, operation, and maintenance of ITS technologies. They must be majoring in transportation or a related field, including transportation engineering, systems engineering, electrical engineering, planning, finance, or logistics, and be taking courses in such ITS-related fields of study as computer science, electronics, and digital communications. In addition, they must have a GPA of 3.0 or higher and plans to prepare for a career in a transportation-related field. Minority candidates are encouraged to apply. Along with their application, they must submit a 500-word statement about their career goals after graduation, how those relate to ITS, and why they think they should receive this scholarship award. Selection is

based on that statement, academic record, and transportation-related activities or job skills. Financial need is not considered.
Financial data The stipend is $1,500.
Duration 1 year.
Additional information This program is co-sponsored by ITS Washington.
Number awarded 1 each year.
Deadline October of each year.

[252]
ITW WELDING COMPANIES SCHOLARSHIP
American Welding Society
Attn: AWS Foundation, Inc.
550 N.W. LeJeune Road
Miami, FL 33126
(305) 445-6628   Toll-free: (800) 443-9353, ext. 461
Fax: (305) 443-7559   E-mail: found@aws.org
Web: www.aws.org/foundation/scholarships/itw.html

Purpose To provide financial assistance to college seniors majoring in welding engineering.
Eligibility This program is open to entering college seniors who are working full time on a 4-year bachelor's degree in welding engineering or welding engineering technology; preference is given to welding engineering technology students. Applicants must have an overall GPA of 3.0 or higher. Financial need is not required. Priority is given to applicants who exhibit a strong interest in welding equipment and have prior work experience in the welding equipment field. U.S. citizenship is required.
Financial data The stipend is $3,000.
Duration 1 year; nonrenewable.
Additional information This program is sponsored by Illinois Tool Works (ITW) Welding Companies.
Number awarded 2 each year.
Deadline January of each year.

[253]
J. FIELDING REED SCHOLARSHIP
American Society of Agronomy
Attn: Scholarship Committee
677 South Segoe Road
Madison, WI 53711
(608) 273-8008   Fax: (608) 273-2021
E-mail: awards@agronomy.org
Web: www.agronomy.org/awards/award/detail/?a=6

Purpose To provide financial assistance to undergraduate students preparing for a career in soil or plant sciences.
Eligibility This program is open to undergraduates who are preparing for a career in the plant or soil sciences. Applicants must have a GPA of 3.0 or higher and be able to document a history of community and campus leadership activities, particularly in agriculture.
Financial data The stipend is $1,000.
Duration 1 year.
Additional information Funds for this program, initiated in 1998, are administered by the Agronomic Science Foundation; the selection process is administered by the American Society of Agronomy.

Number awarded 1 each year.
Deadline March of each year.

[254]
JAMES F. REVILLE SCHOLARSHIP
NYSARC, Inc.
393 Delaware Avenue
Delmar, NY 12054
(518) 439-8311   Fax: (518) 439-1893
E-mail: info@nysarc.org
Web: www.nysarc.org

Purpose To provide financial assistance to currently-enrolled college students in New York majoring in a field related to mental retardation.
Eligibility This program is open to high school graduates enrolled full time in any year of college training in a field related to mental retardation or developmental disabilities. Applications are available through local chapters of NYSARC. Applicants must submit an essay on their career plans and how they relate to mental retardation or developmental disabilities. Financial need is not considered in the selection process.
Financial data The stipend is $1,500 per year.
Duration 2 years.
Additional information NYSARC, Inc. was formerly the New York State Association for Retarded Children.
Number awarded 2 each year.
Deadline January of each year.

[255]
JAMES L. ALLHANDS ESSAY COMPETITION
Associated General Contractors of America
Attn: AGC Education and Research Foundation
2300 Wilson Boulevard, Suite 400
Arlington, VA 22201
(703) 837-5342   Fax: (703) 837-5402
E-mail: foundation@agc.org
Web: www.agcfoundation.org

Purpose To recognize and reward outstanding student essays on a topic related to construction or civil engineering.
Eligibility Eligible to apply are college seniors who are enrolled in a 4-year ABET- or ACCE-accredited construction or construction-related engineering degree program. Applicants must submit an essay, up to 10 pages in length, on a topic that changes annually; recently, it was "The Effective Use of Building Information Modeling (BIM) as it Applies to Construction Firms." Selection is based on clear expression of thought, completeness of subject matter, use of specific examples to support opinions, grammar, neatness, creativity, originality and uniqueness of ideas, and adherence to competition guidelines for essay length.
Financial data The first-prize winner receives $1,000 and a trip to the annual convention of the Associated General Contractors (AGC) of America; the second-prize winner receives $500; the third-prize winner receives $300. In addition, the faculty sponsor of the first-prize winner receives $500 and a trip to the AGC convention.
Duration The competition is held annually.
Deadline October of each year.

[256]
JAMES R. VOGT RADIOCHEMISTRY SCHOLARSHIP

American Nuclear Society
Attn: Scholarship Coordinator
555 North Kensington Avenue
La Grange Park, IL 60526-5592
(708) 352-6611   Fax: (708) 352-0499
E-mail: outreach@ans.org
Web: www.ans.org/honors/scholarships

Purpose To provide financial assistance to undergraduate and graduate students who are interested in preparing for a career in nuclear science.

Eligibility This program is open to juniors, seniors, and first-year graduate students who are enrolled in or proposing to undertake research in radio-analytical chemistry, analytical chemistry, or analytical applications of nuclear science. Applicants must be U.S. citizens or permanent residents and able to demonstrate academic achievement.

Financial data The stipend is $2,000 for undergraduate students or $3,000 for graduate students.

Duration 1 year; nonrenewable.

Number awarded 1 each year.

Deadline January of each year.

[257]
JAY WOODWARD SCHOLARSHIPS

Cactus and Pine Golf Course Superintendents Association
Attn: Scholarship Committee
10685 North 69th Street
Scottsdale, AZ 85254
(480) 609-6778   Fax: (480) 348-5976
E-mail: carmella@cactusandpine.com
Web: www.cactusandpine.com

Purpose To provide financial assistance to undergraduate or graduate students from Arizona who are preparing for a career in turfgrass management.

Eligibility Applicants must have been residents of Arizona for at least 1 year and either attending school or working on a golf course in the state. They must have completed the first year of a 2-year, 4-year, or certificate program in a field related to golf course management or be a graduate student planning a career as a golf course superintendent. Their GPA must be 3.0 or higher. Along with their application, they must submit 100-word essays on why they want to become a golf course superintendent, what they have done to prepare themselves to become a golf course superintendent, and what they expect from a career as a golf course superintendent. They must also identify any academic distinctions and honors they have received, school or college activities in which they have participated (e.g., athletics, clubs, school paper, fines arts), activities outside of school or college, employment experience, and the ways in which they have contributed toward their financial support or some else's support while in high school or college. Selection is based on academic excellence, career preparation, and potential to make an outstanding professional contribution.

Financial data For students attending a school within Arizona, the stipend is $1,000 in a 4-year degree program, $750 in a 2-year degree program, or $500 in a certificate program. For students attending a school outside Arizona, the stipend is $750 in a 4-year degree program or $500 in a 2-year degree program.

Duration 1 year.

Number awarded 1 or more each year.

Deadline June of each year.

[258]
J.C. AND RHEBA COBB MEMORIAL SCHOLARSHIP

National Community Pharmacists Association
Attn: NCPA Foundation
100 Daingerfield Road
Alexandria, VA 22314-2888
(703) 683-8200   Toll-free: (800) 544-7447
Fax: (703) 683-3619   E-mail: info@ncpanet.org
Web: www.ncpanet.org.org

Purpose To provide financial assistance for full-time education in pharmacy to student members of the National Community Pharmacists Association (NCPA).

Eligibility All pharmacy students who are student members of the association and enrolled in an accredited U.S. school or college of pharmacy on a full-time basis are eligible. Applicants must submit a copy of the most recent transcript of their college grades, 2 letters of recommendation, a resume or curriculum vitae, and a statement outlining their scholastic achievement, leadership activities, objectives for the future, and interest in civic and government affairs. Selection is based on leadership qualities, demonstrated interest in civic and government affairs, and academic achievement.

Financial data The stipend is $2,000, paid directly to the recipient's school or college of pharmacy.

Duration 1 year; nonrenewable.

Additional information Until October 1996, the NCPA, the national association representing independent retail pharmacy, was known as NARD (the National Association of Retail Druggists).

Number awarded 1 each year.

Deadline February of each year.

[259]
JERRY RHEA/ATLANTA FALCONS UNDERGRADUATE SCHOLARSHIP AWARD

Southeast Athletic Trainers Association
c/o Janet Passman, Scholarship Committee Chair
Louisiana College
1140 College Drive
Pineville, LA 71359
(318) 487-7290   Fax: (318) 487-7174
E-mail: passman@lacollege.edu
Web: www.seata.org/Scholarshipdetails.htm

Purpose To provide financial assistance to undergraduate student members of the Southeast Athletic Trainers Association (SEATA).

Eligibility This program is open to undergraduates at colleges and universities in Alabama, Florida, Georgia, Kentucky, Louisiana, Mississippi, and Tennessee who are members of SEATA and the National Association of Athletic

Trainers (NATA). Applicants must be in at least their junior year in a degree program as an athletic trainer with a GPA of 3.0 or higher. They must be sponsored by a certified athletic trainer who is a current member of SEATA and NATA. Along with their application, they must submit a brief biographical sketch that includes their reasons for wanting the scholarship, why they merit this award, high school and college awards and honors, athletic teams with which they have worked, and jobs they have held. Selection is based on academic achievement, character, and athletic training abilities and experiences.

Financial data The stipend is $1,000.

Duration 1 year; nonrenewable.

Additional information SEATA serves as District 9 of NATA.

Number awarded 1 each year.

Deadline December of each year.

[260]
JILL S. TIETJEN SCHOLARSHIP

Society of Women Engineers
230 East Ohio Street, Suite 400
Chicago, IL 60611-3265
(312) 596-5223   Toll-free: (877) SWE-INFO
Fax: (312) 644-8557
E-mail: scholarshipapplication@swe.org
Web: www.swe.org/scholarships

Purpose To provide financial assistance to women working on an undergraduate or graduate degree in engineering or computer science.

Eligibility This program is open to women who will be sophomores, juniors, seniors, or graduate students at ABET-accredited colleges and universities. Applicants must be U.S. citizens majoring in computer science or engineering and have a GPA of 3.0 or higher. Along with their application, they must submit a 1-page essay on why they want to be an engineer or computer scientist, how they believe they will make a difference as an engineer or computer scientist, and what influenced them to study engineering or computer science. Selection is based on merit.

Financial data The stipend is $1,000.

Duration 1 year.

Number awarded 1 each year.

Deadline January of each year.

[261]
JIMMY A. YOUNG MEMORIAL EDUCATION RECOGNITION AWARD

American Association for Respiratory Care
Attn: American Respiratory Care Foundation
9425 North MacArthur Boulevard, Suite 100
Irving, TX 75063-4706
(972) 243-2272   Fax: (972) 484-2720
E-mail: info@arcfoundation.org
Web: www.arcfoundation.org

Purpose To provide financial assistance to college students, especially minorities, interested in becoming respiratory therapists.

Eligibility Candidates must be enrolled in an accredited respiratory therapy program, have completed at least 1 semester/quarter of the program, and have a GPA of 3.0 or higher. Preference is given to nominees of minority origin. Applications must include 6 copies of an original referenced paper on some aspect of respiratory care and letters of recommendation. The foundation prefers that the candidates be nominated by a school or program, but any student may initiate a request for sponsorship by a school (in order that a deserving candidate is not denied the opportunity to compete simply because the school does not initiate the application).

Financial data The stipend is $1,000. The award also provides airfare, 1 night's lodging, and registration for the association's international congress.

Duration 1 year.

Number awarded 1 each year.

Deadline June of each year.

[262]
JOHANNA DREW CLUNEY FUND

Hawai'i Community Foundation
Attn: Scholarship Department
1164 Bishop Street, Suite 800
Honolulu, HI 96813
(808) 566-5570   Toll-free: (888) 731-3863
Fax: (808) 521-6286
E-mail: scholarships@hcf-hawaii.org
Web: www.hawaiicommunityfoundation.org

Purpose To provide financial assistance to residents of Hawaii who are interested in enrolling in a vocational training program in the state.

Eligibility This program is open to residents of Hawaii who are attending or planning to attend a vocational college or institution that is part of the University of Hawaii community college system. Programs include culinary arts, auto repair, diesel mechanics, cosmetology, computer graphics, and assistive medical technology. Applicants must submit a personal statement explaining their personal background and interests, the vocational program they plan to pursue, their career goals, and anything else that demonstrates their worthiness to receive this scholarship. Financial need is not considered in the selection process.

Financial data The stipend is $500 per semester. Funds are mailed directly to the financial aid office at the recipient's institution.

Duration 1 semester; may be renewed for up to 3 additional semesters.

Additional information This program began in 2006.

Number awarded Varies each year.

Deadline June of each year for fall and spring semester scholarships; September of each year for spring semester scholarships.

[263]
JOHN A. LOPIANO SCHOLARSHIP
Electronic Document Systems Foundation
Attn: EDSF Scholarship Awards
608 Silver Spur Road, Suite 280
Rolling Hills Estates, CA 90274-3616
(310) 265-5510　　　　　　　Fax: (310) 265-5588
E-mail: jmowlds@edsf.org
Web: www.edsf.org/scholarships.cfm

Purpose To provide financial assistance to college juniors, seniors, and graduate students interested in working with electronic documents as a career.

Eligibility This program is open to juniors, seniors, and graduate students who are committed to preparing for a career in document management and communications marketplace, including computer science and engineering, graphic and media communications, e-commerce, imaging science, printing, web authoring, electronic publishing, telecommunications, and business (e.g., sales, marketing). Applicants must be enrolled full time at a college, university, or graduate school in the United States with a GPA of 3.0 or higher. Along with their application, they must submit a statement of their career goals in the field of document communications, an essay on a topic related to their view of the future of the document management and production industry, a list of current professional and college extracurricular activities and achievements, college transcripts, samples of their creative work, and 2 letters of recommendation. Priority consideration is given to students who work in or whose family member has worked or currently works in a segment of the high volume transaction output (HVTO) industry. Financial need is not considered.

Financial data The stipend is $2,000.

Duration 1 year.

Additional information This program is sponsored by COPI/OutputLinks.

Number awarded 1 each year.

Deadline May of each year.

[264]
JOHN AND ALICE EGAN MULTI-YEAR MENTORING SCHOLARSHIP PROGRAM
Daedalian Foundation
Attn: Scholarship Committee
55 Main Circle (Building 676)
P.O. Box 249
Randolph AFB, TX 78148-0249
(210) 945-2113　　　　　　　Fax: (210) 945-2112
E-mail: daedalus@daedalians.org
Web: www.daedalians.org

Purpose To provide financial assistance to college students who are participating in a ROTC program and wish to become military pilots.

Eligibility This program is open to students who have completed at least the freshman year at an accredited 4-year college or university and have a GPA of 3.0 or higher. Applicants must be participating in an ROTC program and be medically qualified for flight training. They must plan to apply for and be awarded a military pilot training allocation at the appropriate juncture in their ROTC program. Selection is based on intention to prepare for a career as a military pilot, demonstrated moral character and patriotism, scholastic and military standing and aptitude, and physical condition and aptitude for flight.

Financial data The stipend is $2,500 per year.

Duration 1 year; may be renewed up to 2 or 3 additional years, provided the recipient maintains a GPA of 3.0 or higher and is enrolled in an undergraduate program.

Additional information This program began in 2003. It includes a mentoring component.

Number awarded Up to 11 each year.

Deadline July of each year.

[265]
JOHN C. BAJUS SCHOLARSHIP
Marine Technology Society
Attn: Student Scholarships
5565 Sterrett Place, Suite 108
Columbia, MD 21044
(410) 884-5330　　　　　　　Fax: (410) 884-9060
Web: www.mtsociety.org

Purpose To provide financial assistance to members of the Marine Technology Society (MTS) who are working on an undergraduate or graduate degree.

Eligibility This program is open to MTS members who are working full time on an undergraduate or graduate degree in a marine-related field. Applicants must submit a statement explaining their interest in marine engineering or technology; a biographical sketch, including academic, personal, and professional goals; official school transcript; recommendation from a current teacher or counselor in a marine-related field; and a personal letter of reference. Preference is given to applicants who have shown a commitment to community service and/or volunteer activities. Financial need is not considered in the selection process.

Financial data The stipend is $1,000. Funds are sent directly to the recipient's college bursar's office.

Duration 1 year.

Additional information This scholarship was first awarded in 2006.

Number awarded 1 each year.

Deadline April of each year.

[266]
JOHN CHARLES WILSON SCHOLARSHIPS
International Association of Arson Investigators
Attn: Educational Foundation
12772 Boenker Road
St. Louis, MO 63044
(314) 739-4224　　　　　　　Fax: (314) 739-4219
E-mail: jimwhitaker@firearson.com
Web: www.firearson.com/ef/jwscholar/index.asp

Purpose To provide financial assistance to the members and dependents or nominees of members of the International Association of Arson Investigators (IAAI) who are interested in preparing for a career in fire and arson investigation.

Eligibility This program is open to association members and their immediate families who are enrolled or planning to enroll at an accredited 2- or 4-year college or university that offers course work in fire science, law enforcement, or

fire and arson investigation. Also eligible are nonmembers who are recommended and sponsored by association members in good standing. Applicants must submit transcripts and an essay of 500 words or less providing background information and their future plans in police or fire sciences. Financial need is not considered.
Financial data Stipends are $1,000 or $500.
Duration 1 year.
Additional information These scholarships were first awarded in 1981.
Number awarded Varies each year. Recently, 7 of these scholarships were awarded: 1 at $1,000 and 6 at $500.
Deadline February of each year.

[267]
JOHN H. WIECHMAN MEMORIAL SCHOLARSHIP
California Farm Bureau Scholarship Foundation
Attn: Scholarship Coordinator
2300 River Plaza Drive
Sacramento, CA 95833
(916) 561-5520 Toll-free: (800) 698-FARM (within CA)
Fax: (916) 561-5699   E-mail: dlicciardo@cfbf.com
Web: www.cfbf.com/programs/scholar/index.cfm

Purpose To provide financial assistance for college to residents of California who are interested in preparing for a career in agriculture.
Eligibility This program is open to students entering or attending a 4-year accredited college or university in California who are majoring or planning to major in an agriculture-related field. Students entering a junior college are not eligible. Applicants must submit an essay on the most important educational or personal experience that has led them to pursue a university education. Selection is based on academic achievement, career goals, extracurricular activities, leadership skills, determination, and commitment to study agriculture.
Financial data The stipend is $2,250 per year.
Duration 1 year; recipients may reapply.
Number awarded 1 each year.
Deadline February of each year.

[268]
JOHN J. AND IRENE T. POWERS SCHOLARSHIP
Institute of Food Technologists
Attn: Scholarship Department
525 West Van Buren, Suite 1000
Chicago, IL 60607
(312) 782-8424   Fax: (312) 782-8348
E-mail: info@ift.org
Web: www.ift.org

Purpose To provide financial assistance to undergraduates interested in studying food science or food technology.
Eligibility This program is open to sophomores, juniors, and seniors in a food science or food technology program at an educational institution in the United States or Canada. Applicants must have an outstanding scholastic record and a well-rounded personality. Along with their application, they must submit an essay on their career aspirations; a list of awards, honors, and scholarships they have received; a list of extracurricular activities and/or hobbies; and a summary of their work experience. Financial need is not considered in the selection process.
Financial data The stipend is $1,500.
Duration 1 year; recipients may reapply if they are members of the Institute of Food Technologists (IFT).
Additional information Correspondence and completed applications must be submitted to the department head of the educational institution the applicant is attending.
Number awarded 1 each year.
Deadline January of each year.

[269]
JOHN J. MCKETTA UNDERGRADUATE SCHOLARSHIP
American Institute of Chemical Engineers
Attn: Awards Administrator
Three Park Avenue
New York, NY 10016-5991
(212) 591-7107   Fax: (212) 591-8890
E-mail: awards@aiche.org
Web: www.aiche.org

Purpose To provide financial assistance to upper-division students majoring in chemical engineering.
Eligibility This program is open to students entering their junior or senior year of a 4-year program in chemical engineering (or equivalent for a 5-year co-op program). Applicants must be attending an ABET-accredited school in the United States, Canada, or Mexico and have a GPA of 3.0 or higher. Along with their application, they must submit a 2-page essay outlining their career goals in the chemical engineering process industries. Preference is given to student members of the American Institute of Chemical Engineers (AIChE) and to applicants who can show leadership or activity in either their school's AIChE student chapter or other university-sponsored campus activity. Financial need is not considered in the selection process.
Financial data The stipend is $5,000.
Duration 1 year.
Additional information This program is sponsored by the Dekker Foundation.
Number awarded 1 each year.
Deadline May of each year.

[270]
JOHN L. AND SARAH G. MERRIAM SCHOLARSHIP
American Society of Agricultural and Biological Engineers
Attn: ASABE Foundation
2950 Niles Road
St. Joseph, MI 49085-9659
(269) 429-0300   Fax: (269) 429-3852
E-mail: hq@asabe.org
Web: www.asabe.org/membership/merriam.html

Purpose To provide financial assistance to undergraduate student members of the American Society of Agricultural Engineers (ASAE) interested in soil and water issues.
Eligibility This program is open to undergraduate students who have a declared major in biological or agricultural

engineering (must be accredited by ABET or CEAB), are student members of the society, are in at least the second year of college, have a GPA of 2.5 or higher, have at least 1 year of undergraduate study remaining, and have a special interest in soil and water issues. Interested applicants should submit a personal letter (up to 2 pages long) explaining why they have selected the soil and water discipline as the focus of their degree. Financial need is not considered in the selection process.

Financial data The stipend is $1,000.

Duration 1 year.

Additional information This scholarship was first awarded in 2001.

Number awarded 1 each year.

Deadline March of each year.

[271]
JOHN M. CHAMBERS STATISTICAL SOFTWARE AWARD

American Statistical Association
Attn: Statistical Computing Section
732 North Washington Street
Alexandria, VA 22314-1943
(703) 684-1221   Toll-free: (888) 231-3473
Fax: (703) 684-6456
Web: www.statcomputing.org/awards/jmc/index.html

Purpose To recognize and reward undergraduate and graduate students who have written outstanding statistical software.

Eligibility This award is presented to teams of up to 3 undergraduate or graduate students who have designed and implemented a piece of statistical software. Applicants must have begun the development while students, and must either currently be students or have completed all requirements for their last degree within the past 3 years. They must submit a current curriculum vitae for each team member; a letter from a faculty mentor at their academic institution confirming that the software is their work and discussing its importance to statistical practice; and a brief description of the software, summarizing what it does, how it does it, and why it is an important contribution. They must also provide the award committee members with access to the software for their use on inputs of their choosing.

Financial data The award includes an honorarium of $1,000 (to be divided among members of the team) and a substantial allowance for travel and housing at the JSM (paid to 1 member of the team who will be presented the award).

Duration The award is presented annually.

Additional information This award was established in 1998.

Number awarded 1 each year.

Deadline February of each year.

[272]
JOHNNY DAVIS MEMORIAL SCHOLARSHIP

Aircraft Electronics Association
Attn: AEA Educational Foundation
4217 South Hocker Drive
Independence, MO 64055-4723
(816) 373-6565   Fax: (816) 478-3100
E-mail: info@aea.net
Web: www.aea.net

Purpose To provide financial assistance to students preparing for a career in avionics or aircraft repair.

Eligibility This program is open to high school seniors and currently-enrolled college students who are attending (or planning to attend) an accredited postsecondary institution in an avionics or aircraft repair program. Applicants must submit an official transcript (cumulative GPA of 2.5 or higher), a statement about their career plans, a description of their involvement in school and community activities, and a 300-word essay on how the job requirements of aviation technicians will change with advancements in technology. Selection is based on merit.

Financial data The stipend is $1,000.

Duration 1 year.

Number awarded 1 each year.

Deadline February of each year.

[273]
JOSEPH F. DRACUP SCHOLARSHIP AWARD

American Congress on Surveying and Mapping
Attn: Scholarships
6 Montgomery Village Avenue, Suite 403
Gaithersburg, MD 20879
(240) 632-9716, ext. 113   Fax: (240) 632-1321
E-mail: pat.canfield@acsm.net
Web: www.acsm.net/scholar.html

Purpose To recognize and reward outstanding college students who are members of the American Congress on Surveying and Mapping (ACSM) and interested in preparing for a career in geodetic surveying.

Eligibility This program is open to ACSM members who are enrolled at a 4-year college or university. Applicants must be majoring in surveying or a closely-related program (e.g., geomatics, surveying engineering). Preference is given to students whose program has a significant emphasis on geodetic surveying. Along with their application, they must submit a statement describing their educational program, future plans for study or research, and why the award is merited. Selection is based on that statement (30%), academic record (30%), letters of recommendation (20%), and professional activities (20%); if 2 or more applicants are judged equal based on those criteria, financial need may be considered.

Financial data The stipend is $2,000.

Duration The competition is held annually.

Additional information Funds for this award are provided by the American Association for Geodetic Surveying.

Number awarded 1 each year.

Deadline October of each year.

SCIENCES

[274]
JOSEPH P. AND HELEN T. CRIBBINS SCHOLARSHIP

Association of the United States Army
Attn: National Secretary
2425 Wilson Boulevard
Arlington, VA 22201
(703) 841-4300, ext. 655
Toll-free: (800) 336-4570, ext. 655
E-mail: ausa-info@ausa.org
Web: www.ausa.org

Purpose To provide financial assistance to active-duty and honorably-discharged soldiers interested in studying engineering in college.

Eligibility This program is open to 1) soldiers currently serving in the active Army, Army Reserve, or Army National Guard of any rank; and 2) honorably-discharged soldiers from any component of the total Army. Applicants must have been accepted at an accredited college or university to work on a degree in engineering or a related field. Along with their application, they must submit a 1-page autobiography, 3 letters of recommendation, and a transcript of high school or college grades (depending on which they are currently attending). Selection is based on academic merit and personal achievement. Financial need is not normally a selection criterion, but in some cases of extreme need it may be used as a factor; the lack of financial need, however, is never a cause for non-selection.

Financial data The stipend is $2,000.

Duration 1 year.

Number awarded 1 or more each year.

Deadline June of each year.

[275]
J.R. HAINES MEMORIAL SCHOLARSHIP

Cumberland Valley Volunteer Firemen's Association
Attn: Home Office Manager
11018 Clinton Street
Hagerstown, MD 21740-7701
(301) 582-2345   E-mail: info@respondersafety.com
Web: cvvfa.org/scholarship.html

Purpose To provide financial assistance to residents of designated eastern states who are interested in working on a degree in fire science.

Eligibility This program is open to residents of Delaware, Maryland, New Jersey, New York, North Carolina, Pennsylvania, Virginia, and West Virginia. Applicants must be enrolled or planning to enroll at a 2- or 4-year accredited college or university to work on a degree in fire science, including fire, fire investigation, and related subjects. Along with their application, they must submit a 250-word essay on why they are interested in a fire science-related career.

Financial data The stipend is $1,000 per year.

Duration 1 year.

Number awarded 1 each year.

Deadline February of each year.

[276]
JUDITH RESNIK MEMORIAL SCHOLARSHIP

Society of Women Engineers
230 East Ohio Street, Suite 400
Chicago, IL 60611-3265
(312) 596-5223   Toll-free: (877) SWE-INFO
Fax: (312) 644-8557
E-mail: scholarshipapplication@swe.org
Web: www.swe.org/scholarships

Purpose To provide financial assistance to undergraduate women who are members of the Society of Women Engineers and majoring in designated engineering specialties.

Eligibility This program is open to women who are entering their sophomore, junior, or senior year at an ABET-accredited 4-year college or university. Applicants must be studying aerospace, aeronautical, or astronautical engineering with a GPA of 3.0 or higher. Along with their application, they must submit a 1-page essay on why they want to be an engineer, how they believe they will make a difference as an engineer, and what influenced them to study engineering. Only members of the society are considered for this award. Selection is based on merit.

Financial data The stipend is $2,500.

Duration 1 year.

Additional information This award was established in 1988 to honor society member Judith Resnik, who was killed aboard the Challenger space shuttle.

Number awarded 1 each year.

Deadline January of each year.

[277]
JULIE VANDE VELDE LEADERSHIP SCHOLARSHIP

Institute of Food Technologists
Attn: Scholarship Department
525 West Van Buren, Suite 1000
Chicago, IL 60607
(312) 782-8424   Fax: (312) 782-8348
E-mail: info@ift.org
Web: www.ift.org

Purpose To provide financial assistance to undergraduates interested in studying food science or food technology.

Eligibility This program is open to sophomores, juniors, and seniors in a food science or food technology program at an educational institution in the United States or Canada. Applicants must have an outstanding scholastic record and a well-rounded personality. Along with their application, they must submit an essay on their career aspirations; a list of awards, honors, and scholarships they have received; a list of extracurricular activities and/or hobbies; and a summary of their work experience. Financial need is not considered in the selection process.

Financial data The stipend is $1,000.

Duration 1 year; recipients may reapply if they are members of the Institute of Food Technologists.

Additional information Correspondence and completed applications must be submitted to the department head of the educational institution the applicant is attending.

Number awarded 1 each year.

Deadline January of each year.

[278]
JUNE P. GALLOWAY SCHOLARSHIP
North Carolina Alliance for Athletics, Health, Physical Education, Recreation and Dance
Attn: Executive Director
P.O. Box 27751
Raleigh, NC 27611
Toll-free: (888) 840-6500   Fax: (919) 833-7700
E-mail: ncaahperd@ncaahperd.org
Web: www.ncaahperd.org/awards/scholarships.htm

Purpose To provide financial assistance for college to members of the North Carolina Alliance for Athletics, Health, Physical Education, Recreation and Dance (NCAAHPERD).

Eligibility This program is open to rising seniors majoring in health, physical education, recreation, and/or dance who are members of NCAAHPERD. Applicants must have a GPA of 2.0 or higher for all college work and 3.0 or higher for their major. Selection is based two-thirds on academic achievement and one-third on leadership and contributions to the profession. Financial need is not considered.

Financial data The stipend is $1,000 per year.

Duration 1 year.

Number awarded 1 each year.

Deadline June of each year.

[279]
KATHRYN D. SULLIVAN SCIENCE AND ENGINEERING FELLOWSHIP
South Carolina Space Grant Consortium
c/o College of Charleston
Department of Geology and Environmental Sciences
66 George Street
Charleston, SC 29424
(843) 953-5463   Fax: (843) 953-5446
E-mail: scozzarot@cofc.edu
Web: www.cofc.edu/~scsgrant/scholar/overview.html

Purpose To provide financial assistance to outstanding science students in South Carolina.

Eligibility This program is open to students entering their senior year at a college or university in South Carolina or at the University of the Virgin Islands. Applicants must be studying natural science or engineering. Selection is based on academic qualifications of the applicant; 2 letters of recommendation; a description of past activities, current interests, and future plans concerning natural science-related and engineering-related studies; and faculty sponsorship. U.S. citizenship is required.

Financial data The stipend is $7,000 per year.

Duration 1 year.

Additional information This program is funded by the National Aeronautics and Space Administration (NASA) through its Space Grant program and the National Oceanic and Atmospheric Administration (NOAA) through its Sea Grant program.

Number awarded 1 each year.

Deadline January of each year.

[280]
KELLIE CANNON MEMORIAL SCHOLARSHIP
American Council of the Blind
Attn: Coordinator, Scholarship Program
1155 15th Street, N.W., Suite 1004
Washington, DC 20005
(202) 467-5081   Toll-free: (800) 424-8666
Fax: (202) 467-5085   E-mail: info@acb.org
Web: www.acb.org

Purpose To provide financial assistance to students who are blind and interested in preparing for a career in the computer field.

Eligibility Eligible to apply are high school seniors, high school graduates, and college students who are blind and are interested in majoring in college in computer information systems or data processing. In addition to letters of recommendation and copies of academic transcripts, applications must include an autobiographical sketch. A cumulative GPA of 3.3 or higher is generally required. Selection is based on demonstrated academic record, involvement in extracurricular and civic activities, and academic objectives. The severity of the applicant's visual impairment and his/her study methods are also taken into account.

Financial data The stipend is $2,000. In addition, the winner receives a Kurzweil-1000 Reading System.

Duration 1 year.

Additional information This program is sponsored by Blind Information Technology Specialist (BITS), Inc, a special interest affiliate of the American Council of the Blind. The scholarship winner is expected to be present at the council's annual national convention; the council will cover all reasonable costs connected with convention attendance.

Number awarded 1 each year.

Deadline February of each year.

[281]
KENNETH ANDREW ROE SCHOLARSHIP
ASME International
Attn: Coordinator, Educational Operations
Three Park Avenue
New York, NY 10016-5990
(212) 591-8131   Toll-free: (800) THE-ASME
Fax: (212) 591-7143   E-mail: OluwanifiseK@asme.org
Web: www.asme.org

Purpose To provide financial assistance to upper-division students who are members of the American Society of Mechanical Engineers (ASME).

Eligibility This program is open to student members in good standing who are enrolled in an ABET-accredited mechanical engineering baccalaureate program. Applicants must be U.S. citizens entering their junior or senior year. Along with their application, they must submit a nomination from their department head, a recommendation from a faculty member, and an official transcript. Only 1 nomination may be submitted per department. Selection is based on character, integrity, leadership, scholastic ability, and potential contribution to the mechanical engineering profession.

Financial data The stipend is $10,000.

Duration 1 year.

Additional information This program was established in 1991.
Number awarded 1 each year.
Deadline March of each year.

[282]
KENTUCKY HORSE COUNCIL SCHOLARSHIPS
Kentucky Horse Council
4063 Iron Works Parkway, Building B, Suite 2
Lexington, KY 40511
(859) 367-0509   Toll-free: (800) 459-4677
E-mail: khc_info@kentuckyhorse.org
Web: www.kentuckyhorse.org/scholarships.shtml

Purpose To provide financial assistance to undergraduate and graduate students in Kentucky who are preparing for a career in the equine industry.

Eligibility This program is open to undergraduate and graduate students working on a horse-related degree or certificate at a university, college, or program in Kentucky. Courses of study include, but are not limited to, equine science, equine business management, equine therapy, pre-veterinary, farrier training, professional jockey, or professional horseman. Applicants must submit a 500-word essay on the impact the equine industry has had on their professional, educational, and life goals. Selection is based on academic success, equine industry involvement, and community service.

Financial data The stipend is $1,000.
Duration 1 year.
Number awarded 6 each year: 3 awarded in fall and 3 in spring.
Deadline The fall deadline is September of each year. The spring deadline is April of each year.

[283]
KENTUCKY SPACE GRANT CONSORTIUM UNDERGRADUATE SCHOLARSHIPS
Kentucky Space Grant Consortium
c/o Western Kentucky University
Department of Physics and Astronomy, TCCW 246
1906 College Heights Boulevard 11077
Bowling Green, KY 42101-1077
(270) 745-4156   Fax: (270) 745-4255
E-mail: Richard.Hackney@wku.edu
Web: www.wku.edu/KSGC

Purpose To provide financial assistance to undergraduate students at member institutions of the Kentucky Space Grant Consortium (KSGC) interested in pursuing education and research in space-related fields.

Eligibility This program is open to undergraduate students at member institutions of the KSGC. Applicants must be enrolled in a baccalaureate degree program in a space-related field or teaching specialization. As part of the program, a faculty member must agree to serve as a mentor on a research project. U.S. citizenship is required. Selection is based on academic qualifications of the applicant, quality of the proposed research program and its relevance to space-related science and technology, and applicant's motivation for a space-related career as expressed in an essay on interests and goals. Applications are especially encouraged from women, members of other underrepresented groups (including minorities and people with disabilities), and students involved in projects of the U.S. National Aeronautics and Space Administration (NASA) such as NASA EPSCoR and SHARP.

Financial data The grant is $5,000, including a stipend of $4,500 and an additional $500 to support the student's mentored research project. Matching grants of at least $4,000 are required. Preference is given to applicants from schools that agree to waive tuition for the scholar as part of the program.

Duration 1 year; may be renewed depending on the quality of the student's research and satisfactory performance in the program of study as evidenced by grades, presentation of research results, and evaluation of progress by the mentor.

Additional information This program is funded by NASA. The KSGC member institutions are Bellarmine University, Centre College, Eastern Kentucky University, Kentucky State University, Morehead State University, Murray State University, Northern Kentucky University, Thomas More College, Transylvania University, University of Kentucky, University of Louisville, and Western Kentucky University.

Number awarded Varies each year.
Deadline February of each year.

[284]
KIRSTEN R. LORENTZEN AWARD
Association for Women in Science
Attn: AWIS Educational Foundation
1200 New York Avenue, N.W., Suite 650
Washington, DC 20005
(202) 326-8940   Toll-free: (866) 657-AWIS
Fax: (202) 326-8960   E-mail: awisedfd@awis.org
Web: www.awis.org/careers/edfoundation.html

Purpose To provide financial assistance to women undergraduates majoring in physics or geoscience.

Eligibility This program is open to women who are sophomores or juniors in college and U.S. citizens. Applicants must be studying physics (including space physics and geophysics) or geoscience. They must demonstrate excellence in their studies as well as outdoor activities, service, sports, music or other non-academic pursuits, or a record of overcoming significant obstacles. Along with their application, they must submit a 2- to 3-page essay on 1) their academic interests and plans, including class work and any relevant research, teaching, or outreach activities; 2) their career goals; 3) the non-academic pursuits that are most important to them; and 4) any significant barriers they have faced and how they overcame them. Financial need is not considered.

Financial data The stipend is $1,000.
Duration 1 year.
Additional information This program was established in 2004. Information is also available from Barbara Filner, President, AWIS Educational Foundation, 7008 Richard Drive, Bethesda, MD 20817-4838.
Number awarded 1 each year.
Deadline January of each year.

[285]
KLUSSENDORF ASSOCIATION SCHOLARSHIP
National Dairy Shrine
Attn: Office of Executive Director
1224 Alton Darby Creek Road
Columbus, OH 43228-9792
(614) 878-5333	Fax: (614) 870-2622
E-mail: shrine@cobaselect.com
Web: www.dairyshrine.org/students.asp

Purpose To provide financial assistance to college students majoring in dairy science.

Eligibility This program is open to students who are completing their first, second, or third year at a 2-year or 4-year college or university. Applicants must be majoring in dairy science (or animal science with a dairy emphasis) and planning to enter the dairy cattle field as a breeder, owner, herdsperson, or fitter. They must submit essays on their dairy cattle experiences; their dairy-related participation in 4-H, FFA, judging, breed association, and other activities; and why they want to be part of the U.S. or Canadian dairy industry's future. Financial need is not considered in the selection process.

Financial data The stipend is $1,000.

Duration 1 year.

Additional information This scholarship, first awarded in 2003, is sponsored by the Arthur B. Klussendorf Memorial Association.

Number awarded 1 each year.

Deadline March of each year.

[286]
KSEA SCHOLARSHIPS
Korean-American Scientists and Engineers Association
1952 Gallows Drive, Suite 300
Vienna, VA 22182
(703) 748-1221	Fax: (703) 748-1331
E-mail: sejong@ksea.org
Web: ksea.org/KSEA/indexe.asp?p=3

Purpose To provide financial assistance to undergraduate and graduate student members of the Korean-American Scientists and Engineers Association (KSEA).

Eligibility This program is open to Korean American undergraduate and graduate students who graduated from a high school in the United States, are KSEA members, and are majoring in science, engineering, or a related field. Along with their application, they must submit a 500-word essay on either of the following topics: 1) their career goals and intended contributions to society, or 2) the meaning of Korean heritage in their life. Selection is based on the essay (20%), work experience and extracurricular activities (20%), recommendation letters (30%), and academic performance (30%).

Financial data The stipend is $1,000.

Duration 1 year.

Additional information This program includes the following named scholarships: the Inyong Ham Scholarship, the Yohan and Rumie Cho Scholarship, the Shoon Kyung Kim Scholarship, the Nam Sook and Je Hyun Kim Scholarship, the SeAh-Haiam Scholarship, and the Hyundai Scholarships.

Number awarded Varies each year.

Deadline February of each year.

[287]
L-3 AVIONICS SYSTEMS SCHOLARSHIP
Aircraft Electronics Association
Attn: AEA Educational Foundation
4217 South Hocker Drive
Independence, MO 64055-4723
(816) 373-6565	Fax: (816) 478-3100
E-mail: info@aea.net
Web: www.aea.net

Purpose To provide financial assistance to students who are interested in studying avionics or aircraft repair in college.

Eligibility This program is open to high school seniors and currently-enrolled college students who are attending (or planning to attend) an accredited school in an avionics or aircraft repair program. Applicants must submit an official transcript (cumulative GPA of 2.5 or higher), a statement about their career plans, a description of their involvement in school and community activities, and a 300-word essay on how the job requirements of aviation technicians will change with advancements in technology. Selection is based on merit.

Financial data The stipend is $2,500.

Duration 1 year.

Number awarded 1 each year.

Deadline February of each year.

[288]
LARRY WILSON SCHOLARSHIP FOR ENVIRONMENTAL STUDIES
Arkansas Environmental Federation
Attn: Scholarship Program
1400 West Markham, Suite 250
Little Rock, AR 72201
(501) 374-0263	Fax: (501) 374-8752
E-mail: joliver@environmentark.org
Web: www.environmentark.org/randallmathis.htm

Purpose To provide financial assistance to residents of Arkansas working on an undergraduate or graduate degree in environmental studies at a college or university in the state.

Eligibility This program is open to Arkansas residents who have completed at least 40 credit hours as a full-time undergraduate or graduate student at a college or university in the state. Applicants must be majoring in a field related to environmental studies, including agriculture with an environmental emphasis, chemical engineering with an environmental emphasis, civil engineering with an environmental emphasis, environmental engineering, environmental health science, fisheries and wildlife biology, forestry, geology, or wildlife management. They must have a GPA of 2.8 or higher. Along with their application, they must submit an essay of 1 to 3 pages explaining their professional career goals relating to the fields of environmental health and safety. U.S. citizenship is required. Financial need is not considered in the selection process.

Financial data The stipend is $2,500.

Duration 1 year.

Additional information This program is sponsored by Northstar Engineering Consultants, Inc.
Number awarded 1 each year.
Deadline January of each year.

[289]
LEADING EDGE STUDENT DESIGN COMPETITION
New Buildings Institute
Attn: Program Manager
142 East Jewett Boulevard
P.O. Box 2349
White Salmon, WA 98672
(509) 493-4468, ext. 12   Fax: (509) 493-4078
E-mail: pat@newbuildings.org
Web: www.leadingedgecompetition.org

Purpose To recognize and reward undergraduate and graduate students who submit outstanding energy-efficient entries in a design competition.
Eligibility This competition is open to undergraduate and graduate students enrolled in architecture, engineering, drafting, or environmental design programs at 2-year colleges, 4- or 5-year colleges or programs, graduate programs, and technical schools. The first category is for students in their third, fourth, or fifth year of undergraduate study and all graduate and post-baccalaureate students; the second category is for students in the first or second year of their undergraduate design education. Entries may be submitted by individuals or teams. Participants are invited to submit designs for a problem at an actual site. Complete information is provided on site history, demographics, climate, utilities, site description, and special requirements. Each design must satisfy the sociological and environmental concerns of the community while also addressing advanced energy efficiency and sustainable building design issues.
Financial data In each category, first prize is $3,000 and second prize is $2,000. If winning entries are submitted by teams of students, the prizes must be divided equally among them. The schools of the winning teams receive $1,500 for first prize and $1,000 for second prize.
Duration The competition is held annually.
Additional information This competition was first held in 1992.
Number awarded 4 cash prizes are awarded each year: 2 in each category.
Deadline Registration must be completed by March of each year. Completed entries are due in June.

[290]
LEAF SCHOLARSHIPS
California Landscape Contractors Association
Attn: Landscape Educational Advancement Foundation
1491 River Park Drive, Suite 100
Sacramento, CA 95815
(916) 830-2780   Fax: (916) 830-2788
E-mail: hq@clca.org
Web: www.clca.org/about/leaf.php

Purpose To provide financial assistance to students in California who are majoring in ornamental horticulture.
Eligibility This program is open to undergraduate students attending an accredited California community college or state university and majoring in ornamental horticulture. Applications must submit brief essays on their educational objectives, occupational goals as they relate to the landscape industry, reasons for choosing that field, and reasons for requesting financial assistance. Selection is based on those essays; educational background; awards and honors; high school, college, and community activities related to landscaping; and work experience. Financial need is not considered.
Financial data A stipend is awarded (amount not specified).
Duration 1 year.
Additional information These scholarships were first awarded in 1972.
Number awarded Varies each year; recently, 14 of these scholarships were awarded.
Deadline March of each year.

[291]
LEE TARBOX MEMORIAL SCHOLARSHIP
Aircraft Electronics Association
Attn: AEA Educational Foundation
4217 South Hocker Drive
Independence, MO 64055-4723
(816) 373-6565   Fax: (816) 478-3100
E-mail: info@aea.net
Web: www.aea.net

Purpose To provide financial assistance to students who are interested in studying avionics or aircraft repair in college.
Eligibility This program is open to high school seniors and currently-enrolled college students who are attending (or planning to attend) an accredited school in an avionics or aircraft repair program. Applicants must submit an official transcript (cumulative GPA of 2.5 or higher), a statement about their career plans, a description of their involvement in school and community activities, and a 300-word essay on how the job requirements of aviation technicians will change with advancements in technology. Selection is based on merit.
Financial data The stipend is $2,500.
Duration 1 year.
Additional information Funding for this program is provided by Pacific Southwest Instruments.
Number awarded 1 each year.
Deadline February of each year.

[292]
LEROY APKER AWARD
American Physical Society
Attn: Honors Program
One Physics Ellipse
College Park, MD 20740-3844
(301) 209-3268   Fax: (301) 209-0865
E-mail: honors@aps.org
Web: www.aps.org

Purpose To recognize and reward undergraduate students for outstanding work in physics.

Eligibility This program is open to undergraduate students at colleges and universities in the United States. Nominees should have completed or be completing the requirements for an undergraduate degree with an excellent academic record and should have demonstrated exceptional potential for scientific research by making an original contribution to physics. Each department of physics in the United States may nominate only 1 student. Each nomination packet should include the student's academic transcript, a description of the original contribution written by the student (such as a manuscript or reprint of a research publication or senior thesis), a 1,000-word summary, and 2 letters of recommendation.

Financial data The award consists of a $5,000 honorarium for the student, a certificate citing the work and school of the recipient, and an allowance for travel expenses to the meeting of the American Physical Society (APS) at which the prize is presented. Each of the finalists receives an honorarium of $2,000 and a certificate. Each of the physics departments whose nominees are selected as recipients and finalists receives a certificate and an award; the departmental award is $5,000 for recipients and $1,000 for finalists.

Duration The award is presented annually.

Additional information This award was established in 1978.

Number awarded 2 recipients each year: 1 to a student at a Ph.D. granting institution and 1 at a non-Ph.D. granting institution.

Deadline June of each year.

[293]
LIBERTY LEADERSHIP FUND ACADEMIC SCHOLARSHIP

American Association of Occupational Health Nurses, Inc.
Attn: AAOHN Foundation
2920 Brandywine Road, Suite 100
Atlanta, GA 30341-4146
(770) 455-7757   Fax: (770) 455-7271
E-mail: foundation@aaohn.org
Web: www.aaohn.org

Purpose To provide financial assistance to registered nurses who are working on a bachelor's or graduate degree to prepare for a career in occupational and environmental health.

Eligibility This program is open to registered nurses who are enrolled in a baccalaureate or graduate degree program. Applicants must demonstrate an interest in, and commitment to, occupational and environmental health. Along with their application, they must submit a 500-word narrative on their professional goals as they relate to the academic activity and the field of occupational and environmental health. Selection is based on that essay (50%), impact of education on applicant's career (20%), and 2 letters of recommendation (30%).

Financial data The stipend is $3,500.

Duration 1 year; may be renewed up to 2 additional years.

Additional information Funding for this program is provided by the Liberty Leadership Fund.

Number awarded 1 each year.

Deadline November of each year.

[294]
LILLIAN MOLLER GILBRETH SCHOLARSHIP

Society of Women Engineers
230 East Ohio Street, Suite 400
Chicago, IL 60611-3265
(312) 596-5223   Toll-free: (877) SWE-INFO
Fax: (312) 644-8557
E-mail: scholarshipapplication@swe.org
Web: www.swe.org/scholarships

Purpose To provide financial assistance to upper-division women majoring in computer science or engineering.

Eligibility This program is open to women who are entering their junior or senior year at an ABET-accredited college or university. Applicants must be majoring in computer science or engineering and have a GPA of 3.0 or higher. Along with their application, they must submit a 1-page essay on why they want to be an engineer or computer scientist, how they believe they will make a difference as an engineer or computer scientist, and what influenced them to study engineering or computer science. Selection is based on merit.

Financial data The stipend is $6,000 per year.

Duration 1 year; may be renewed.

Additional information This program was established in 1958.

Number awarded 1 each year.

Deadline January of each year.

[295]
LINDA CRAIG MEMORIAL SCHOLARSHIPS

Pacers Foundation, Inc.
Foundation Coordinator
125 South Pennsylvania Street
Indianapolis, IN 46204
(317) 917-2864   Fax: (317) 917-2599
E-mail: Foundation@pacers.com
Web: www.nba.com

Purpose To provide financial assistance to undergraduates currently majoring in medicine or sports medicine at an Indiana college or university.

Eligibility This program is open to U.S. citizens who are currently enrolled at a 2-year or 4-year college or university in Indiana. Applicants must have completed at least 1 grading period (semester, quarter) and have declared a major in medicine, sports medicine, physical therapy, and/or a related discipline. A GPA of 3.0 or higher is required. Selection criteria include character, integrity, and leadership.

Financial data The stipend is $2,000. Funds are paid directly to the recipient's school.

Duration 1 year; recipients may reapply.

Additional information This program is supported by the St. Vincent Sports Medicine Center.

Number awarded 2 each year.

Deadline February of each year.

SCIENCES

[296]
L.L. WATERS SCHOLARSHIP PROGRAM

American Society of Transportation and Logistics, Inc.
Attn: Scholarship Judging Panel
1700 North Moore Street, Suite 1900
Arlington, VA 22209-1904
(703) 524-5011　　　　　　　Fax: (703) 524-5017
E-mail: astl@nitl.org
Web: www.astl.org/scholar.htm

Purpose To provide financial assistance to advanced undergraduate and graduate students in the field of transportation.

Eligibility This program is open to undergraduate students in their junior year at fully-accredited 4-year colleges or universities who are majoring in transportation, logistics, or physical distribution. Students in graduate school in the same areas are also eligible. Applicants must submit a letter explaining why they have chosen transportation, logistics, or physical distribution as their field of study and describing their professional objectives. Recipients are selected without regard to race, color, religion, sex, or national origin. Selection is based on scholastic performance and potential as well as commitment to a professional career in the field. Financial need is not considered.

Financial data The stipend is $2,000.

Duration 1 year; recipients may apply again but not in consecutive years.

Number awarded 1 or more each year.

Deadline September of each year.

[297]
LOCKHEED MARTIN AERONAUTICS COMPANY SCHOLARSHIPS

Society of Women Engineers
230 East Ohio Street, Suite 400
Chicago, IL 60611-3265
(312) 596-5223　　　　　　　Toll-free: (877) SWE-INFO
Fax: (312) 644-8557
E-mail: scholarshipapplication@swe.org
Web: www.swe.org/scholarships

Purpose To provide financial assistance to upper-division women majoring in designated engineering specialties.

Eligibility This program is open to women who are entering their junior year at an ABET-accredited 4-year college or university. Applicants must be majoring in electrical or mechanical engineering and have a GPA of 3.5 or higher. Along with their application, they must submit a 1-page essay on why they want to be an engineer, how they believe they will make a difference as an engineer, and what influenced them to study engineering. Selection is based on merit.

Financial data The stipend is $1,000.

Duration 1 year.

Additional information This program, established in 1996, is supported by Lockheed Martin Aeronautics Company.

Number awarded 2 each year: 1 to a student in electrical engineering and 1 to a student in mechanical engineering.

Deadline January of each year.

[298]
LOGAN NAINOA FUJIMOTO MEMORIAL SCHOLARSHIP

Hawai'i Community Foundation
Attn: Scholarship Department
1164 Bishop Street, Suite 800
Honolulu, HI 96813
(808) 566-5570　　　　　　　Toll-free: (888) 731-3863
Fax: (808) 521-6286
E-mail: scholarships@hcf-hawaii.org
Web: www.hawaiicommunityfoundation.org

Purpose To provide financial assistance to residents of Hawaii who are interested in enrolling in a vocational training program in automotive technology in the state.

Eligibility This program is open to residents of Hawaii who are attending or planning to attend a vocational college or institution that is part of the University of Hawaii community college system. Applicants must be concentrating in an automotive technology program. Along with their application, they must submit a personal statement explaining their personal background and interests, the vocational program they plan to pursue, their career goals, and anything else that demonstrates their worthiness to receive this scholarship. Financial need is not considered in the selection process. Preference is given to students attending Universal Technical Institute.

Financial data The stipend is $500 per semester. Funds are mailed directly to the financial aid office at the recipient's institution.

Duration 1 semester; may be renewed for up to 3 additional semesters.

Additional information This program began in 2006.

Number awarded Varies each year.

Deadline June of each year for fall and spring semester scholarships; September of each year for spring semester scholarships.

[299]
LOREN W. CROW MEMORIAL SCHOLARSHIP

American Meteorological Society
Attn: Fellowship/Scholarship Program
45 Beacon Street
Boston, MA 02108-3693
(617) 227-2426, ext. 246　　　Fax: (617) 742-8718
E-mail: scholar@ametsoc.org
Web: www.ametsoc.org

Purpose To provide financial assistance to undergraduates majoring in meteorology or an aspect of atmospheric sciences with an interest in applied meteorology.

Eligibility This program is open to full-time students entering their final year of undergraduate study and majoring in meteorology or an aspect of the atmospheric or related oceanic and hydrologic sciences. Applicants must intend to make atmospheric or related sciences their career; preference is given to students who have demonstrated a strong interest in applied meteorology. They must be U.S. citizens or permanent residents enrolled at a U.S. institution and have a cumulative GPA of 3.25 or higher. Along with their application, they must submit 200-word essays on 1) their most important achievements that qualify them for this scholarship, and 2) their career goals in the atmospheric or related oceanic or hydrologic fields. Selection is based on academic excellence and achievement; financial need is not considered. The sponsor specifically encourages applications from women, minorities, and students with disabilities who are traditionally underrepresented in the atmospheric and related oceanic sciences.

Financial data The stipend is $2,000 per year.

Duration 1 year.

Additional information Requests for an application must be accompanied by a self-addressed stamped envelope.

Number awarded 1 each year.

Deadline February of each year.

[300]
LOU WOLF MEMORIAL SCHOLARSHIP

Society of Motion Picture and Television Engineers
Attn: Secretary, Scholarship Committee
3 Barker Avenue
White Plains, NY 10601
(914) 761-1100   Fax: (914) 761-3115
E-mail: smpte@smpte.org
Web: www.smpte.org/students/awards.cfm

Purpose To provide financial assistance to undergraduate and graduate student members of the Society of Motion Picture and Television Engineers (SMPTE) interested in majoring in film or television.

Eligibility This program is open to undergraduate and graduate student members of SMPTE who are currently enrolled full time in an accredited high school, 2-year or 4-year college, or university. Applicants must be majoring or planning to major in film or television, with an emphasis on technology. Along with their application, they must submit personal statements on their 1) work experience and/or interests that are relevant to the application; 2) goals and objectives of study, including the reasons why they wish to pursue studies in motion pictures and television; and 3) proposed use of the funds (tuition, books, supplies, and/or equipment that will further their studies).

Financial data The maximum stipend is $2,000.

Duration 1 year.

Additional information SMPTE is the leading technical society for the motion imaging industry with more than 10,000 members in 85 countries.

Number awarded Varies each year; recently, 3 of these scholarships were awarded.

Deadline May of each year.

[301]
LOUISE MORITZ MOLITORIS LEADERSHIP AWARD

Women's Transportation Seminar
Attn: National Headquarters
1701 K Street, N.W., Suite 800
Washington, DC 20006
(202) 955-5085   Fax: (202) 955-5088
E-mail: wts@wtsinternational.org
Web: www.wtsinternational.org

Purpose To provide financial assistance to undergraduate women interested in a career in transportation.

Eligibility This program is open to women who are working on an undergraduate degree in transportation or a transportation-related field (e.g., transportation engineering, planning, finance, or logistics). Applicants must have a GPA of 3.0 or higher. Along with their application, they must submit a 500-word statement about their career goals after graduation and why they think they should receive the scholarship award; their statement should specifically address the issue of leadership. Applications must be submitted first to a local chapter; the chapters forward selected applications for consideration on the national level. Minority candidates are encouraged to apply. Selection is based on transportation involvement and goals, job skills, academic record, and leadership potential; financial need is not considered.

Financial data The stipend is $3,000.

Duration 1 year.

Additional information Local chapters may also award additional funding to winners for their area.

Number awarded 1 each year.

Deadline Applications must be submitted by November to a local WTS chapter.

[302]
LOUISIANA AGRICULTURAL CONSULTANTS ASSOCIATION SCHOLARSHIPS

Louisiana Agricultural Consultants Association
Attn: Executive Director
P.O. Box 104
Morrow, LA 71356
(318) 346-6728   E-mail: glpblues@bellsouth.net
Web: www.laagcon.org

Purpose To provide financial assistance to undergraduate and graduate students in Louisiana who are working on a degree in an agriculture-related field.

Eligibility This program is open to undergraduate and graduate students at colleges and universities in Louisiana who have completed at least 45 semester hours with a GPA of 2.5 or higher. Applicants must be working on a degree in the following fields: agribusiness, agronomy, biology, botany, entomology, horticulture, microbiology, plant pathology, plant science, vocational agriculture, or weed science.

Financial data The stipend is $1,000.

Duration 1 year.

Additional information Information is also available from Rusty Elston, Scholarship Committee Chair, 152 Loyd Bridge Road, Cheneyville, LA 71325, (318) 201-4220, E-mail: randkelston@juno.com.

Number awarded 2 each year: 1 to an undergraduate and 1 to a graduate student.

Deadline January of each year.

SCIENCES

[303] LOWELL GAYLOR MEMORIAL SCHOLARSHIP

Aircraft Electronics Association
Attn: AEA Educational Foundation
4217 South Hocker Drive
Independence, MO 64055-4723
(816) 373-6565   Fax: (816) 478-3100
E-mail: info@aea.net
Web: www.aea.net

Purpose To provide financial assistance to students who are interested in studying avionics or aircraft repair in college.

Eligibility This program is open to high school seniors and currently-enrolled college students who are attending (or planning to attend) an accredited school in an avionics or aircraft repair program. Applicants must submit an official transcript (cumulative GPA of 2.5 or higher), a statement about their career plans, a description of their involvement in school and community activities, and a 300-word essay on how the job requirements of aviation technicians will change with advancements in technology. Selection is based on merit.

Financial data The stipend is $1,000.

Duration 1 year.

Number awarded 1 each year.

Deadline February of each year.

[304] LUCILE B. KAUFMAN WOMEN'S SCHOLARSHIPS

Society of Manufacturing Engineers
Attn: SME Education Foundation
One SME Drive
P.O. Box 930
Dearborn, MI 48121-0930
(313) 425-3300   Toll-free: (800) 733-4763, ext. 3700
Fax: (313) 425-3411   E-mail: foundation@sme.org
Web: www.sme.org

Purpose To provide financial assistance to undergraduate women enrolled in a degree program in manufacturing engineering or manufacturing engineering technology.

Eligibility Applicants must be female students attending a degree-granting institution in North America on a full-time basis and preparing for a career in manufacturing engineering. They must have completed at least 30 units in a manufacturing engineering or manufacturing engineering technology curriculum with a GPA of 3.0 or higher. Along with their application, they must submit a 300-word essay that covers their career and educational objectives, how this scholarship will help them attain those objectives, and why they want to enter this field. Financial need is not considered in the selection process.

Financial data The stipend is $1,500.

Duration 1 year; may be renewed.

Number awarded 1 or 2 each year.

Deadline January of each year.

[305] LYDIA I. PICKUP MEMORIAL SCHOLARSHIP

Society of Women Engineers
230 East Ohio Street, Suite 400
Chicago, IL 60611-3265
(312) 596-5223   Toll-free: (877) SWE-INFO
Fax: (312) 644-8557
E-mail: scholarshipapplication@swe.org
Web: www.swe.org/scholarships

Purpose To provide financial assistance to women working on an undergraduate or graduate degree in engineering or computer science.

Eligibility This program is open to women who will be sophomores, juniors, seniors, or graduate students at ABET-accredited colleges and universities. Applicants must be majoring in computer science or engineering and have a GPA of 3.0 or higher. Along with their application, they must submit a 1-page essay on why they want to be an engineer or computer scientist, how they believe they will make a difference as an engineer or computer scientist, and what influenced them to study engineering or computer science. Preference is given to graduate student. Selection is based on merit.

Financial data The stipend is $2,000.

Duration 1 year.

Additional information This program was established in 2001.

Number awarded 1 each year.

Deadline January of each year.

[306] M. BLAHA MEDICAL GRANT

Resource Center Scholarship Service
16362 Wilson Boulevard
Masaryktown, FL 34604-7335
(352) 796-0459
E-mail: info@resourcecenterscholarshipinfo.com
Web: www.resourcecenterscholarshipinfo.com

Purpose To provide financial assistance for college to students interested in a medical field.

Eligibility This program is open to students currently enrolled or planning to enroll in college to study a medical field. Along with their application, they must submit a 250-word essay on how they can make a difference. GPA and financial need are not considered in the selection process.

Financial data The stipend is $1,000.

Duration 1 year.

Additional information The processing fee is $5.

Number awarded 2 each year: 1 in spring and 1 in fall.

Deadline June or December of each year.

[307]
MARLIAVE SCHOLAR AWARD

Association of Environmental and Engineering
  Geologists
Attn: AEG Foundation
300 South Jackson Street, Suite 100
P.O. Box 460518
Denver, CO 80246
(303) 757-2926   Fax: (303) 757-2969
E-mail: aeg@aegweb.org
Web: www.aegfoundation.org/index2.php

Purpose To provide financial assistance for college or graduate school to student members of the Association of Environmental and Engineering Geologists.

Eligibility Applicants must be college seniors or graduate students in engineering geology or geological engineering, must be enrolled full time in a college or university offering a degree program directly applicable to engineering geology or geological engineering, and must be a student member of the association. Along with their application, they must submit official transcripts covering all undergraduate and graduate work, 3 letters of reference, copies of pertinent publications and abstracts, and a 2-page statement of career goals. Selection is based on demonstrated ability, academic record, potential for contributions to the profession, character, and activities in student/professional societies. Financial need is not considered.

Financial data The stipend is $1,000.

Duration 1 year.

Additional information This program was established in 1968. Information is also available from Paul M. Santi, Colorado School of Mines, Department of Geology and Geological Engineering, Berthoud Hall, Golden, CO 80401, (303) 273-3108, E-mail: psanti@mines.edu.

Number awarded 1 each year.

Deadline April of each year.

[308]
MARTIN L. STOUT SCHOLARSHIP

Association of Environmental and Engineering
  Geologists
Attn: AEG Foundation
300 South Jackson Street, Suite 100
P.O. Box 460518
Denver, CO 80246
(303) 757-2926   Fax: (303) 757-2969
E-mail: aeg@aegweb.org
Web: www.aegfoundation.org/index2.php

Purpose To provide financial assistance to members of the Association of Environmental and Engineering Geologists (AEG) who are working on an undergraduate degree in geology or a graduate degree with an environmental or engineering geology emphasis.

Eligibility This program is open to student members of the association who are undergraduate geology majors in their sophomore through senior year or graduate students with an environmental or engineering geology emphasis. Applicants must submit a 500-word essay on either of the following questions: 1) how they intend to become a competent professional environmental and/or engineering geologist, or 2) why they need to become a competent field geologist. Selection is based on the essay and letters of recommendation.

Financial data The stipend is $1,000.

Duration 1 year.

Additional information This program was established in 1994 by the Southern California section of the Association of Engineering Geologists and transferred to the AEG Foundation in 2004. Information is also available from Robert A. Larson, 13376 Azores Avenue, Sylmar, CA 91342, (818) 362-0363, E-mail: ralarson@rampageusa.com.

Number awarded 1 each year.

Deadline January of each year.

[309]
MARTIN SMILO UNDERGRADUATE SCHOLARSHIP

California Environmental Health Association
110 South Fairfax, A11-175
Los Angeles, CA 90036
(323) 634-7698   Fax: (323) 571-1889
E-mail: support@ceha.org
Web: www.ceha.org/awards.html

Purpose To provide financial assistance to undergraduates in California interested in preparing for a career in the sciences, especially environmental health.

Eligibility This program is open to California students who have completed at least 48 semester units of undergraduate study, including at least 12 semester units in science, with a GPA of 3.0 or higher. Applicants must be enrolled full time at an accredited 4-year college or university with an intention to work on a degree and prepare for a career in science. Preference is given to students in environmental health. Along with their application, they must submit a 3-page essay on 1 of 3 assigned topics related to public health and the role of professional organizations. Financial need is not considered in the selection process.

Financial data The stipend is $2,500.

Duration 1 year.

Additional information Information is also available from Matt Fore, CEHA Awards Committee, 160 Gibson Drive, Number 17, Hollister, CA 95023, (831) 636-4035, E-mail: matt@sanbenitoco.org.

Number awarded 1 each year.

Deadline February of each year.

[310]
MARY FEINDT SCHOLARSHIP

American Congress on Surveying and Mapping
Attn: Scholarships
6 Montgomery Village Avenue, Suite 403
Gaithersburg, MD 20879
(240) 632-9716, ext. 113   Fax: (240) 632-1321
E-mail: pat.canfield@acsm.net
Web: www.acsm.net/scholar.html

Purpose To provide financial assistance to female members of the American Congress on Surveying and Mapping (ACSM) who are working on an undergraduate degree in surveying.

SCIENCES

Eligibility This program is open to female ACSM members who are enrolled at a 4-year college or university. Applicants must be majoring in a surveying or mapping program. Along with their application, they must submit a statement describing their educational program, future plans for study or research, and why the award is merited. Selection is based on that statement (30%), academic record (30%), letters of recommendation (20%), and professional activities (20%).

Financial data The stipend is $1,000.

Duration 1 year.

Additional information Funding for these scholarships is provided by Forum for Equal Opportunity of the National Society of Professional Surveyors (NSPS).

Number awarded 1 each year.

Deadline October of each year.

[311]
MARY V. MUNGER MEMORIAL SCHOLARSHIP

Society of Women Engineers
230 East Ohio Street, Suite 400
Chicago, IL 60611-3265
(312) 596-5223   Toll-free: (877) SWE-INFO
Fax: (312) 644-8557
E-mail: scholarshipapplication@swe.org
Web: www.swe.org/scholarships

Purpose To provide financial assistance to undergraduate women majoring in computer science or engineering.

Eligibility This program is open to women who are entering their sophomore, junior, or senior year at a 4-year ABET-accredited college or university. Applicants must be majoring in computer science or engineering and have a GPA of 3.0 or higher. Along with their application, they must submit a 1-page essay on why they want to be an engineer or computer scientist, how they believe they will make a difference as an engineer or computer scientist, and what influenced them to study engineering or computer science. Selection is based on merit.

Financial data The stipend is $4,000.

Duration 1 year.

Number awarded 1 each year.

Deadline January of each year.

[312]
MASONIC-RANGE SCIENCE SCHOLARSHIP

Society for Range Management
10030 West 27th Avenue
Wheat Ridge, CO 80215-6601
(303) 986-3309   Fax: (303) 986-3892
E-mail: info@rangelands.org
Web: www.rangelands.org

Purpose To provide financial assistance to students who are interested in majoring in range science in college.

Eligibility This program is open to high school seniors and college freshmen and sophomores. Applicants must be interested in majoring in range science in college. They must be sponsored by a member of the Society for Range Management, the National Association of Conservation Districts, or the Soil and Water Conservation Society. Along with their application, they must submit an essay on why they are interested in a career in range science, including any experiences that have led them to choose a range science major. Selection is based on that essay, letters of reference, academic record, leadership experience, community service, and honors and awards.

Financial data The amount awarded each year varies; recently, the stipend was $8,500.

Duration 1 year; may be renewed provided the recipient maintains a GPA of 2.5 or higher.

Additional information Information is also available from Paul Loeffler, Texas General Land Office, 500 West Avenue H, Box 2, Alpine, TX 79830-6008.

Number awarded 1 each year.

Deadline January of each year.

[313]
MCCORMICK AND COMPANY ENDOWMENT SCHOLARSHIP

Institute of Food Technologists
Attn: Scholarship Department
525 West Van Buren, Suite 1000
Chicago, IL 60607
(312) 782-8424   Fax: (312) 782-8348
E-mail: info@ift.org
Web: www.ift.org

Purpose To provide financial assistance to undergraduates interested in studying food science or food technology.

Eligibility This program is open to sophomores, juniors, and seniors in a food science or food technology program at an educational institution in the United States or Canada. Applicants must have an outstanding scholastic record and a well-rounded personality. Along with their application, they must submit an essay on their career aspirations; a list of awards, honors, and scholarships they have received; a list of extracurricular activities and/or hobbies; and a summary of their work experience. Financial need is not considered in the selection process.

Financial data The stipend is $2,500.

Duration 1 year; recipients may reapply if they are members of the Institute of Food Technologists (IFT).

Additional information Correspondence and completed applications must be submitted to the department head of the educational institution the applicant is attending.

Number awarded 1 each year.

Deadline January of each year.

[314]
MEDTRONIC EMERGENCY RESPONSE SYSTEMS ACADEMIC SCHOLARSHIP

American Association of Occupational Health Nurses, Inc.
Attn: AAOHN Foundation
2920 Brandywine Road, Suite 100
Atlanta, GA 30341-4146
(770) 455-7757   Fax: (770) 455-7271
E-mail: foundation@aaohn.org
Web: www.aaohn.org

Purpose To provide financial assistance to registered nurses who are working on a bachelor's or graduate degree to prepare for a career in occupational and environmental health.

Eligibility This program is open to registered nurses who are enrolled in a baccalaureate or graduate degree program. Applicants must demonstrate an interest in, and commitment to, occupational and environmental health. Along with their application, they must submit a 500-word narrative on their professional goals as they relate to the academic activity and the field of occupational and environmental health. Selection is based on that essay (50%), impact of education on applicant's career (20%), and 2 letters of recommendation (30%).

Financial data The stipend is $3,000.

Duration 1 year; may be renewed up to 2 additional years.

Additional information Funding for this program is provided by Medtronic Physio-Control Corporation.

Number awarded 1 each year.

Deadline November of each year.

[315]
MERIDITH THOMS MEMORIAL SCHOLARSHIPS

Society of Women Engineers
230 East Ohio Street, Suite 400
Chicago, IL 60611-3265
(312) 596-5223   Toll-free: (877) SWE-INFO
Fax: (312) 644-8557
E-mail: scholarshipapplication@swe.org
Web: www.swe.org/scholarships

Purpose To provide financial assistance to undergraduate women majoring in computer science or engineering.

Eligibility This program is open to women who are entering their sophomore, junior, or senior year at a 4-year ABET-accredited college or university. Applicants must be majoring in computer science or engineering and have a GPA of 3.0 or higher. Along with their application, they must submit a 1-page essay on why they want to be an engineer or computer scientist, how they believe they will make a difference as an engineer or computer scientist, and what influenced them to study engineering or computer science. Selection is based on merit.

Financial data The stipend is $2,000.

Duration 1 year.

Additional information This program was established in 2001.

Number awarded 6 each year.

Deadline January of each year.

[316]
MICHAEL AND GINA GARCIA RAIL ENGINEERING SCHOLARSHIP

American Railway Engineering and Maintenance of Way Association
Attn: AREMA Educational Foundation Scholarship Committee
10003 Derekwood Lane, Suite 210
Lanham, MD 20706
(301) 459-3200, ext. 706   Fax: (301) 459-8077
E-mail: selder@arema.org
Web: www.arema.org

Purpose To provide financial assistance to undergraduate students who are interested in preparing for a career in railway engineering.

Eligibility This program is open to undergraduate students who have completed at least 1 quarter or semester at an ABET-accredited 4-year or 5-year program (or a comparably accredited program in Canada or Mexico) leading to a bachelor's degree in engineering or engineering technology with a GPA of 2.0 or higher. They must be interested in a career in railway engineering. Along with their application, they must submit a resume, official transcript, 2 letters of recommendation, and a 350-word cover letter explaining why they believe they are deserving of this scholarship and the areas of railroading in which they are particularly interested. Financial need is not considered in the selection process. First priority is given to students who are married and/or are supporting a family while enrolled in college.

Financial data The stipend is $2,000.

Duration 1 year.

Number awarded 1 each year.

Deadline March of each year.

[317]
MICHAEL KIDGER MEMORIAL SCHOLARSHIP

SPIE-The International Society for Optical Engineering
Attn: Michael Kidger Memorial Scholarship
1000 20th Street
P.O. Box 10
Bellingham, WA 98227-0010
(360) 676-3290   Fax: (360) 647-1445
E-mail: education@spie.org
Web: www.kidger.com/mkms_home.html

Purpose To provide financial assistance to undergraduate and graduate students who are preparing for a career in optical design.

Eligibility This program is open to students of optical design from any country at the undergraduate and graduate level. Applicants must have at least 1 more year, after the award, to complete their current course of study. They must submit 2 letters of recommendation and a 5-page essay explaining how the scholarship will help them contribute to long-term development in the field of optical design. Financial need is not considered in the selection process.

Financial data The stipend is $5,000.

Duration 1 year.

Additional information The International Society for Optical Engineering was founded in 1955 as the Society of Photo-Optical Instrumentation Engineers (SPIE). This schol-

arship was established in 1998 by Kidger Optics Associates of East Sussex, United Kingdom.
Number awarded 1 or more each year.
Deadline March of each year.

[318]
MICHAEL P. ANDERSON SCHOLARSHIP IN SPACE SCIENCE
National Society of Black Physicists
Attn: Scholarship Committee Chair
6704G Lee Highway
Arlington, VA 22205
(703) 536-4207　　　　　　　Fax: (703) 536-4203
E-mail: scholarship@nsbp.org
Web: www.nsbp.org

Purpose To provide financial assistance to African American students majoring in space science in college.

Eligibility This program is open to African American students who are entering their junior or senior year of college and majoring in space science. Applicants must submit an essay on their academic and career objectives, information on their participation in extracurricular activities, a description of any awards and honors they have received, and 3 letters of recommendation. Financial need is not considered.

Financial data The stipend is $1,000.

Duration 1 year; nonrenewable.

Additional information This program is offered in partnership with the American Astronomical Society.

Number awarded 1 each year.

Deadline November of each year.

[319]
MICROSOFT CORPORATION SCHOLARSHIPS
Society of Women Engineers
230 East Ohio Street, Suite 400
Chicago, IL 60611-3265
(312) 596-5223　　　　　　Toll-free: (877) SWE-INFO
Fax: (312) 644-8557
E-mail: scholarshipapplication@swe.org
Web: www.swe.org/scholarships

Purpose To provide financial assistance to women working on an undergraduate or graduate degree in computer engineering or computer science.

Eligibility This program is open to women who will be sophomores, juniors, seniors, or first year master's degree students at ABET-accredited colleges and universities. Applicants must be majoring in computer science or engineering and have a GPA of 3.5 or higher. Along with their application, they must submit a 1-page essay on why they want to be an engineer or computer scientist, how they believe they will make a difference as an engineer or computer scientist, and what influenced them to study engineering or computer science. Selection is based on merit.

Financial data The stipend is $2,500.

Duration 1 year.

Additional information This program, established in 1994, is sponsored by Microsoft Corporation.

Number awarded 2 each year.

Deadline January of each year.

[320]
MICROSOFT NATIONAL SCHOLARSHIPS
Microsoft Corporation
Attn: National Minority Technical Scholarship
One Microsoft Way
Redmond, WA 98052-8303
(425) 882-8080　　　　　　　TTY: (800) 892-9811
E-mail: scholars@microsoft.com
Web: www.microsoft.com/college/ss_overview.mspx

Purpose To provide financial assistance and summer work experience to undergraduate students, especially members of underrepresented groups, interested in preparing for a career in computer science or other related technical fields.

Eligibility This program is open to students who are enrolled full time and making satisfactory progress toward an undergraduate degree in computer science, computer engineering, or a related technical discipline (such as electrical engineering, mathematics, or physics) with a demonstrated interest in computer science. Applicants must be enrolled at a 4-year college or university in the United States, Canada, or Mexico. They must have a GPA of 3.0 or higher. Although all students who meet the eligibility criteria may apply, a large majority of scholarships are awarded to women, underrepresented minorities (African Americans, Hispanics, and Native Americans), and students with disabilities. Along with their application, students must submit an essay that describes the following 4 items: 1) how they demonstrate their passion for technology outside the classroom; 2) the toughest technical problem they have worked on, how they addressed the problem, their role in reaching the outcome if it was team-based, and the final outcome; 3) a situation that demonstrates initiative and their willingness to go above and beyond; and 4) how they are currently funding their college education.

Financial data Scholarships cover 100% of the tuition as posted by the financial aid office of the university or college the recipient designates. Scholarships are made through that school and are not transferable to other academic institutions. Funds may be used for tuition only and may not be used for other costs on the recipient's bursar bill, such as room and board.

Duration 1 year.

Additional information Selected recipients are offered a paid summer internship where they will have a chance to develop Microsoft products.

Number awarded Varies. A total of $540,000 is available for this program each year.

Deadline January of each year.

[321]
MID-CONTINENT INSTRUMENT SCHOLARSHIP
Aircraft Electronics Association
Attn: AEA Educational Foundation
4217 South Hocker Drive
Independence, MO 64055-4723
(816) 373-6565   Fax: (816) 478-3100
E-mail: info@aea.net
Web: www.aea.net

Purpose To provide financial assistance to students who are interested in studying avionics in college.
Eligibility This program is open to high school seniors and currently-enrolled college students who are attending (or planning to attend) an accredited school in an avionics program. Applicants must submit an official transcript (cumulative GPA of 2.5 or higher), a statement about their career plans, a description of their involvement in school and community activities, and a 300-word essay on how the job requirements of aviation technicians will change with advancements in technology. Selection is based on merit.
Financial data The stipend is $1,000.
Duration 1 year.
Number awarded 1 each year.
Deadline February of each year.

[322]
MINERAL AND METALLURGICAL PROCESSING DIVISION SCHOLARSHIP
Society for Mining, Metallurgy, and Exploration, Inc.
Attn: Student Center
8307 Shaffer Parkway
Littleton, CO 80127-4102
(303) 973-9550   Toll-free: (800) 763-3132
Fax: (303) 973-3845   E-mail: sme@smenet.org
Web: www.smenet.org

Purpose To provide financial assistance to student members of the Society for Mining, Metallurgy, and Exploration (SME) who are preparing for a career in minerals processing.
Eligibility This program is open to student members of the society who have completed their sophomore year in college; are enrolled full time in an undergraduate degree program that has required course work in minerals processing, hydrometallurgy, and/or metallurgical engineering; are U.S. citizens; and have a GPA of 2.5 or higher. Only 1 candidate from each eligible department may be nominated each academic year. Applicants must demonstrate an interest in preparing for a career in mineral processing or metallurgical engineering in the mining industry.
Financial data The first-place recipient is given $2,000 (plus travel to the society's annual meeting). The other winners each receive a $1,000 scholarship.
Duration 1 year.
Number awarded Up to 6 each year.
Deadline October of each year.

[323]
MINNESOTA CHAPTER WTS SCHOLARSHIPS
Women's Transportation Seminar-Minnesota Chapter
c/o Jessica Overmohle, Director
URS Corporation
700 Third Street South
Minneapolis, MN 55415-1199
(612) 373-6404   Fax: (612) 370-1378
E-mail: Jessica_Overmohle@URSCorp.com
Web: www.wtsinternational.org

Purpose To provide financial assistance to women working on an undergraduate or graduate degree in a transportation-related field at colleges and universities in Minnesota.
Eligibility This program is open to women currently enrolled in an undergraduate or graduate degree program at a college or university in Minnesota. Applicants must be preparing for a career in transportation or a transportation-related field and be majoring in such fields as transportation engineering, planning, finance, or logistics. They must have a GPA of 3.0 or higher. Along with their application, they must submit a 750-word statement on their career goals after graduation and why they think they should receive this award. Selection is based on transportation goals, academic record, and transportation-related activities or job skills.
Financial data The stipend is $2,000.
Duration 1 year.
Additional information Winners are also nominated for scholarships offered by the national organization of the Women's Transportation Seminar.
Number awarded 2 each year: 1 undergraduate and 1 graduate student.
Deadline November of each year.

[324]
MINORITY AFFAIRS COMMITTEE AWARD FOR OUTSTANDING SCHOLASTIC ACHIEVEMENT
American Institute of Chemical Engineers
Attn: Awards Administrator
Three Park Avenue
New York, NY 10016-5991
(212) 591-7107   Fax: (212) 591-8890
E-mail: awards@aiche.org
Web: www.aiche.org

Purpose To recognize and reward underrepresented minority students majoring in chemical engineering who serve as role models for other minority students.
Eligibility Members of the American Institute of Chemical Engineers (AIChE) may nominate any chemical engineering student who serves as a role model for minority students in that field. Nominees must be members of a minority group that is underrepresented in chemical engineering (i.e., African American, Hispanic, Native American, Alaskan Native). Selection is based on the nominee's academic and scholarship achievements, including a GPA of 3.0 or higher, scholastic awards, research contributions, and technical presentations; the nominee's exemplary outreach activities that directly benefit or encourage minority youth in their academic pursuits; a letter from the nominee describing his or her outreach activities; and extraordinary circumstances,

such as job or family matters, that impose additional responsibility.

Financial data The award consists of a plaque and a $1,500 honorarium.

Duration The award is presented annually.

Additional information This award was first presented in 1996.

Number awarded 1 each year.

Deadline Nominations must be submitted by May of each year.

[325] MINORITY SCHOLARSHIP AWARD IN PHYSICAL THERAPY

American Physical Therapy Association
Attn: Department of Minority/International Affairs
1111 North Fairfax Street
Alexandria, VA 22314-1488
(703) 706-3144 Toll-free: (800) 999-APTA, ext. 3144
Fax: (703) 706-8519 TDD: (703) 683-6748
E-mail: min-intl@apta.org
Web: www.apta.org

Purpose To provide financial assistance to minority students who are interested in becoming a physical therapist or physical therapy assistant.

Eligibility This program is open to U.S. citizens and permanent residents who are members of the following minority groups: African American or Black, Asian, Native Hawaiian or other Pacific Islander, American Indian or Alaska Native, or Hispanic/Latino. Applicants must be in the final year of a professional physical therapy or physical therapy assistant education program. They must submit a personal essay outlining their professional goals and minority service. U.S. citizenship or permanent resident status is required. Selection is based on 1) demonstrated evidence of contributions in the area of minority affairs and services with an emphasis on contributions made while enrolled in a physical therapy program; 2) potential to contribute to the profession of physical therapy; and 3) scholastic achievement.

Financial data The stipend varies; recently, minimum awards were $6,000 for physical therapy students or $3,000 for physical therapy assistant students.

Duration 1 year.

Number awarded Varies each year; recently, 8 of these awards were granted to physical therapy students and 1 to a physical therapy assistant student.

Deadline November of each year.

[326] MISSOURI ANGUS AUXILIARY AMBASSADOR PROGRAM

Missouri Angus Association
Attn: General Manager
795 Highway M
Everton, MO 65646-8107
(417) 535-0044 Fax: (417) 535-0045
E-mail: worthington@missouriangus.org
Web: www.missouriangus.org

Purpose To recognize and reward, with college scholarships, young men in Missouri who are involved in the Angus cattle industry.

Eligibility This program is open to male members of the Missouri Junior Angus Association (MJAA) between 16 and 21 years of age. Applicants must be involved in the production and/or promotion of Angus cattle and be committed to the promotion of the breed. They must be willing to commit to attend several promotional events in Missouri (e.g., state fairs, livestock shows) and serve as a spokesperson for the association. Along with their application, they must submit a list of their school activities, a list of their community and/or service activities, information on their involvement in activities of the MJAA and the National Junior Angus Association (NJAA), an explanation of how their MJAA or NJAA experiences positively impacted them and/or another person, and an explanation of why they wish to be selected for this honor.

Financial data The man chosen as ambassador receives 2 American Angus Association dress shirts, round-trip mileage of 25 cents per mile for each of the required events, and a $50 lodging allowance for each night's stay at each required event. Upon successful completion of all required appearances and submission of a written report on his experience, he receives a $1,000 college scholarship.

Duration An ambassador is selected each year.

Additional information Information is also available from Deb Thummel, RR2, Box 162, Sheridan, MO 64486, (660) 799-3268.

Number awarded 1 each year.

Deadline April of each year.

[327] MISSOURI ANGUS AUXILIARY QUEEN PROGRAM

Missouri Angus Association
Attn: General Manager
795 Highway M
Everton, MO 65646-8107
(417) 535-0044 Fax: (417) 535-0045
E-mail: worthington@missouriangus.org
Web: www.missouriangus.org

Purpose To recognize and reward, with college scholarships, young women in Missouri who are involved in the Angus cattle industry.

Eligibility This program is open to female members of the Missouri Junior Angus Association (MJAA) between 16 and 21 years of age. Applicants must be involved in the production and/or promotion of Angus cattle and be committed to the promotion of the breed. They must be willing to commit to attend several promotional events in Missouri (e.g., state fairs, livestock shows) and serve as a spokesperson for the association. Along with their application, they must submit a list of their school activities, a list of their community and/or service activities, information on their involvement in activities of the MJAA and the National Junior Angus Association (NJAA), an explanation of how their MJAA or NJAA experiences positively impacted them and/or another person, and an explanation of why they wish to be selected for this honor.

Financial data The woman chosen as queen receives a $150 clothing allowance, round-trip mileage of 25 cents per mile for each of the required events, and a $50 lodging allowance for each night's stay at each required event. Upon successful completion of all required appearances and submission of a written report on her experience, she receives a $1,000 college scholarship.

Duration A queen is selected each year.

Additional information Information is also available from Deb Thummel, RR2, Box 162, Sheridan, MO 64486, (660) 799-3268.

Number awarded 1 each year.

Deadline April of each year.

[328]
MISSOURI SOIL AND WATER CONSERVATION SOCIETY SCHOLARSHIPS

Soil and Water Conservation Society-Missouri
 Show-Me Chapter
c/o Natural Resources Conservation Service
Parkade Center, Suite 250
601 Business Loop 70 West
Columbia, MO 65203-2546
(573) 876-0912
Web: swcs.missouri.edu

Purpose To provide financial assistance to entering or continuing undergraduate students at Missouri colleges and universities interested in preparing for a career in natural resources conservation.

Eligibility This program is open to residents of Missouri who are graduating high school seniors or full-time undergraduates at an accredited college or university. Applicants must be majoring or planning to major in a natural resource conservation or resource-related field, including soil science, land use planning, fisheries, forestry, wildlife management, agricultural engineering, hydrology, rural sociology, agronomy, agricultural economics, agricultural education, water management, or a related environmental field. They must submit 2 letters of recommendation; an essay on a topic that changes annually; a list of positions of leadership in such organizations as the Soil and Water Conservation Society, 4-H, FFA, and student groups; publishing and speaking activities in which they participated; and their most recent high school, college, or university transcript. Financial need is not considered in the selection process.

Financial data First place is $2,000 and second place is $1,000. Payment is made directly to the college or university.

Duration 1 year.

Additional information These scholarships were formerly known as the Betty Broemmelsiek Memorial Conservation Scholarships. Information is also available from Beverly Maltsberger, Buchanan County Extension Center, 4125 Mitchell Avenue, P.O. Box 7077, St. Joseph, MO 64507-7077, (816) 279-1691, E-mail: maltsbergerb@missouri.edu.

Number awarded 2 each year.

Deadline November of each year.

[329]
MOBIL DELVAC SCHOLARSHIP

ExxonMobil Corporation
Attn: Automotive Marketing/Agriculture
3225 Gallows Road, 6C-0420
Fairfax, VA 22037
(703) 846-4467
Web: www.mobil.com

Purpose To recognize and reward agriculture students who submit outstanding essays or photographs on the "changing landscape of agriculture."

Eligibility This program is open to students who are working on a college degree at an accredited U.S. agriculture school. Applicants may enter 1 of 3 categories whose requirements change annually. Recently, they were invited to submit 1 of the following: 1) an essay on whether there is a correlation between equipment longevity and farm longevity; 2) an essay on whether equipment maintenance decisions are any more or less critical 80 years ago than they are today; or 3) a photograph or drawing, along with 100 words or less, depicting a result of effective equipment maintenance. Students may enter only 1 of the categories. The maximum length of the essays in the first 2 categories is 1 single-spaced page.

Financial data Winners receive $4,000 scholarships. Funds are paid directly to the institutions where the recipients are enrolled.

Duration The competition is held annually.

Additional information This competition was first held in 2003.

Number awarded 3 each year: 1 in each of the categories.

Deadline June of each year.

[330]
MORRIS K. UDALL SCHOLARSHIPS

Morris K. Udall Foundation
130 South Scott Avenue
Tucson, AZ 85701-1922
(520) 670-5529   Fax: (520) 670-5530
Web: www.udall.gov/scholarship

Purpose To provide financial assistance to 1) college sophomores and juniors who intend to prepare for a career in environmental public policy and 2) Native American and Alaska Native students who intend to prepare for a career in health care or tribal public policy.

Eligibility Each 2-year and 4-year college and university in the United States and its possessions may nominate up to 6 sophomores or juniors for either or both categories of this program: 1) students who intend to prepare for a career in environmental public policy, and 2) Native American and Alaska Native students who intend to prepare for a career in health care or tribal public policy. For the first category, the program seeks future leaders across a wide spectrum of environmental fields, such as policy, engineering, science, education, urban planning and renewal, business, health, justice, and economics. For the second category, the program seeks future Native American and Alaska Native leaders in public and community health care, tribal government, and public policy affecting Native American communities, including land and resource management, economic development, and education. Nominees must be U.S. citizens, nationals, or permanent residents with a GPA of 3.0 or higher. Along with their application, they must submit an 800-word essay discussing a significant public speech, legislative act, or public policy statement by former Congressman Morris K. Udall and its impact on their field of study, interests, and career goals. Selection is based on demonstrated commitment to 1) environmental issues through substantial commitment to and participation in 1 or more of the following: campus activities, research, community service, or public service; or 2) tribal public policy or Native American health through substantial contributions to and participation in 1 or more of the following: campus activities, tribal involvement, community or public service, or research; a course of study and proposed career likely to lead to positions where the nominee can make significant contributions to the shaping of environmental, tribal public policy, or Native American health care issues; and leadership, character, desire to make a difference, and general well-roundedness.

Financial data The maximum stipend for scholarship winners is $5,000 per year. Funds are to be used for tuition, fees, books, and room and board. Honorable mention stipends are $350.

Duration 1 year; recipients nominated as sophomores may be renominated in their junior year.

Number awarded Approximately 80 scholarships and 50 honorable mentions are awarded each year.

Deadline Faculty representatives must submit their nominations by early March of each year.

[331]
MORTON B. DUGGAN, JR. MEMORIAL EDUCATION RECOGNITION AWARD

American Association for Respiratory Care
Attn: American Respiratory Care Foundation
9425 North MacArthur Boulevard, Suite 100
Irving, TX 75063-4706
(972) 243-2272   Fax: (972) 484-2720
E-mail: info@arcfoundation.org
Web: www.arcfoundation.org

Purpose To provide financial assistance to college students interested in becoming respiratory therapists.

Eligibility This program is open to U.S. citizens who are enrolled in an accredited respiratory care program and have a GPA of 3.0 or higher. Candidates must submit an original referenced paper on an aspect of respiratory care, an official transcript, and letters of recommendation. Nominations are accepted from all states, but preference is given to applicants from Georgia and South Carolina. Financial need is not considered in the selection process.

Financial data The stipend is $1,000. The award also provides airfare, 1 night's lodging, and registration for the international congress of the association.

Duration 1 year.

Number awarded 1 each year.

Deadline June of each year.

[332]
MTS STUDENT SCHOLARSHIPS

Marine Technology Society
Attn: Student Scholarships
5565 Sterrett Place, Suite 108
Columbia, MD 21044
(410) 884-5330   Fax: (410) 884-9060
Web: www.mtsociety.org

Purpose To provide financial assistance to entering or continuing undergraduate and graduate students working on a degree in a field related to marine science.

Eligibility This program is open to high school seniors accepted into a full-time undergraduate program and current undergraduate and graduate students. Applicants must be planning to work on a degree in a marine-related field. Along with their application, they must submit a statement explaining their interest in marine engineering or technology; a biographical sketch, including academic, personal, and professional goals; official school transcript; recommendation from a current teacher or counselor in a marine-related field; and a personal letter of reference. Membership in the Marine Technology Society (MTS) is not required. Financial need is not considered in the selection process.

Financial data The stipend is $2,000. Funds are sent directly to the recipient's college bursar's office.

Duration 1 year.

Number awarded Varies each year; recently, 13 of these scholarships were awarded.

Deadline April of each year.

[333]
MUSIC THERAPY SCHOLARSHIP

Sigma Alpha Iota Philanthropies, Inc.
One Tunnel Road
Asheville, NC 28805
(828) 251-0606   Fax: (828) 251-0644
E-mail: philonline@sai-national.org
Web: www.sai-national.org/phil/philsch1.html

Purpose To provide financial assistance to members of Sigma Alpha Iota (an organization of women musicians) who are interested in working on an undergraduate or graduate degree in music therapy.

Eligibility Members of the organization may apply for these scholarships if they wish to study music therapy at the undergraduate or graduate level. Applicants must submit an essay that includes their personal definition of music therapy, their career plans and professional goals as a music therapist, and why they feel they are deserving of this scholarship. Selection is based on music therapy skills, musicianship, fraternity service, community service, leadership, self-reliance, and dedication to the field of music therapy as a career.

Financial data The stipend is $1,000.

Duration 1 year.

Additional information There is a $25 nonrefundable application fee.

Number awarded 1 each year.

Deadline March of each year.

[334]
MYRTLE AND EARL WALKER SCHOLARSHIPS
Society of Manufacturing Engineers
Attn: SME Education Foundation
One SME Drive
P.O. Box 930
Dearborn, MI 48121-0930
(313) 425-3300   Toll-free: (800) 733-4763, ext. 3300
Fax: (313) 425-3411   E-mail: foundation@sme.org
Web: www.sme.org

Purpose To provide financial assistance to undergraduate students enrolled in a degree program in manufacturing engineering or manufacturing engineering technology.

Eligibility Applicants must be full-time students attending a North American degree-granting institution or accredited trade school to prepare for a career in manufacturing engineering. They must have completed at least 15 units in a manufacturing engineering or manufacturing engineering technology curriculum with a GPA of 3.0 or higher. Along with their application, they must submit a 300-word essay that covers their career and educational objectives, how this scholarship will help them attain those objectives, and why they want to enter this field. Financial need is not considered in the selection process.

Financial data The scholarship is $2,000 per year.

Duration 1 year; may be renewed.

Number awarded Varies each year; recently, 25 of these scholarships were awarded.

Deadline January of each year.

[335]
NANCY CURRY SCHOLARSHIP
School Nutrition Association
Attn: Child Nutrition Foundation Scholarship Committee
700 South Washington Street, Suite 300
Alexandria, VA 22314-4287
(703) 739-3900   Toll-free: (800) 877-8822
Fax: (703) 739-3915   E-mail: cnf@schoolnutrition.org
Web: www.schoolnutrition.org/Index.aspx?ID=1043

Purpose To provide assistance to members (or children of members) of the School Nutrition Association (SNA) who are interested in studying school food service management on the undergraduate or graduate school level.

Eligibility This program is open to high school, undergraduate, and graduate students who meet all 4 of the following criteria: 1) plan to attend a college or vocational/technical institution that has a program designed to improve school food service (e.g., nutrition, food service management, business administration); 2) be an active SNA member or the child of an active member with a history of employment in school food service; 3) have a GPA of 3.0 or higher; and 4) express a desire to make school food service a career. Applicants must submit a 1-page personal essay stating their reason for selecting school food service as a profession; what they expect to gain from continuing their education; and their long-term professional goals/plans. Selection is based on the essay (35 points), letters of recommendation (20 points), SNA state and local chapter activity participation (15 points), organization and neatness (10 points), program of study (15 points), and GPA (5 points).

Financial data A stipend is awarded (amount not specified).

Duration 1 year.

Additional information The SNA was formerly the American School Food Service Administration. This program is sponsored by Handgards Inc.

Number awarded 1 each year.

Deadline April of each year.

[336]
NATA UNDERGRADUATE SCHOLARSHIPS
National Athletic Trainers' Association
Attn: Research and Education Foundation
2952 Stemmons Freeway, Suite 200
Dallas, TX 75247-6103
(214) 637-6282   Toll-free: (800) TRY-NATA, ext. 121
Fax: (214) 637-2206   E-mail: barbaran@nata.org
Web: www.natafoundation.org/scholarship.html

Purpose To provide financial aid to undergraduate student members of the National Athletic Trainers' Association (NATA).

Eligibility This program is open to members of the association who are sponsored by an NATA certified athletic trainer, have a GPA of 3.2 or higher, and intend to pursue athletic training as a profession. Applicants must apply during their junior year or immediately prior to their final undergraduate year. They must submit a statement on their athletic training background, experience, philosophy, and goals. Selection is based on that essay; participation in their school's athletic training program, academic major, institution, intercollegiate athletics, and American higher education; and participation in campus activities other than academic and athletic training. Financial need is not considered.

Financial data The stipend is $2,000 per year.

Duration 1 year.

Number awarded Varies each year; recently, 39 of these scholarships were awarded.

Deadline February of each year.

[337]
NATHAN TAYLOR DODSON SCHOLARSHIP
North Carolina Alliance for Athletics, Health, Physical Education, Recreation and Dance
Attn: Executive Director
P.O. Box 27751
Raleigh, NC 27611
Toll-free: (888) 840-6500   Fax: (919) 833-7700
E-mail: ncaahperd@ncaahperd.org
Web: www.ncaahperd.org/awards/scholarships.htm

Purpose To provide financial assistance for college to members of the North Carolina Alliance for Athletics, Health, Physical Education, Recreation and Dance (NCAAHPERD).

Eligibility This program is open to rising seniors majoring in health, physical education, recreation, and/or dance who are members of NCAAHPERD. Applicants must have a GPA of 2.0 or higher for all college work and 3.0 or higher for their major. Selection is based two-thirds on academic achievement and one-third on leadership and contributions to the profession. Financial need is not considered.

Financial data The stipend is $1,000 per year.

Duration 1 year.

Number awarded 1 each year.

Deadline June of each year.

[338]
NATIONAL ACADEMY OF SPORTS MEDICINE SCHOLARSHIP

Southeast Athletic Trainers Association
c/o Janet Passman, Scholarship Committee Chair
Louisiana College
1140 College Drive
Pineville, LA 71359
(318) 487-7290   Fax: (318) 487-7174
E-mail: passman@lacollege.edu
Web: www.seata.org/Scholarshipdetails.htm

Purpose To provide financial assistance to undergraduate student members of the Southeast Athletic Trainers Association (SEATA).

Eligibility This program is open to undergraduates at colleges and universities in Alabama, Florida, Georgia, Kentucky, Louisiana, Mississippi, and Tennessee who are members of SEATA and the National Association of Athletic Trainers (NATA). Applicants must be in at least their junior year in a degree program as an athletic trainer with a GPA of 3.0 or higher. They must be sponsored by a certified athletic trainer who is a current member of SEATA and NATA. Along with their application, they must submit a brief biographical sketch that includes their reasons for wanting the scholarship, why they merit this award, high school and college awards and honors, athletic teams with which they have worked, and jobs they have held. Selection is based on academic achievement, character, and athletic training abilities and experiences.

Financial data The stipend is $1,000.

Duration 1 year; nonrenewable.

Additional information SEATA serves as District 9 of NATA.

Number awarded 1 each year.

Deadline December of each year.

[339]
NATIONAL AVIATION EXPLORER SCHOLARSHIPS

Boy Scouts of America
Attn: Learning for Life Division, S210
1325 West Walnut Hill Lane
P.O. Box 152079
Irving, TX 75015-2079
(972) 580-2418   Fax: (972) 580-2137
Web: www.learning-for-life.org

Purpose To provide financial assistance to Explorer Scouts who are interested in studying aviation in college.

Eligibility This program is open to high school seniors and students at a college, university, or technical school who are currently registered and active in an aviation Explorer post. Applicants may be applying for any of the following categories of activity: 1) a college or university degree leading to an aviation profession; 2) an accredited school in an avionics repair program; 3) flight training for a recreational or private pilot certificate; 4) an accredited school in an aircraft repair program; or 5) an aviation management program (including design, engineering, airport management) at an accredited college or university. Along with their application, they must submit 3 letters of recommendation and a 500-word educational plan for a career in education. Selection is based on the essay, leadership involvement, aviation accomplishments, and achievement.

Financial data The stipend is $10,000 for the college or university professional degree category or $3,000 for the other categories.

Duration 1 year; nonrenewable.

Additional information Sponsors of this program include the Air Line Pilots Association, the Aircraft Electronics Association, the Aircraft Owners and Pilots Association, the Experimental Aviation Association, the General Aviation Manufacturers Association, and Women in Aviation, International.

Number awarded 5 each year: 1 for each category.

Deadline Applications must be submitted to the local council by March of each year.

[340]
NATIONAL BEEF AMBASSADOR PROGRAM

American National CattleWomen, Inc.
Attn: National Beef Ambassador Coordinator
9110 East Nichols Avenue, Suite 302
P.O. Box 3881
Centennial, CO 80112
(303) 694-0313   Fax: (303) 694-2390
E-mail: ancw@beef.org
Web: www.nationalbeefambassador.org

Purpose To recognize and reward young people who can serve as spokespersons for the beef industry.

Eligibility This competition is open to students between 17 and 20 years of age who are able to serve as spokespersons for the beef industry within their schools and their communities. Students first compete on the state level. Each state sends 1 winner to the national competition. At the national competition, students make a 5- to 8-minute oral presentation on beef and/or the beef industry, spend 2 to 3 minutes answering questions about the industry posed by the judges, and then have an interview conducted by a panel of judges. Their speech must be based on facts provided in the information packet from the sponsor. They must have made the presentation at least 7 times prior to the competition. At least 5 of the 7 presentations must have been to non-agricultural groups.

Financial data Awards are $2,500 for first place, $1,200 for second, $800 for third, $250 for fourth, and $250 for fifth. In addition, scholarships of $1,000 are presented to the first-place winner, $750 to the second-place winner, and $500 to the third-place winner.

Duration The competition is held annually.

Additional information This program is sponsored by American National CattleWomen, Inc. in cooperation with the Cattlemen's Beef Board.

Number awarded 5 cash awards and 3 scholarships are presented each year.
Deadline August of each year.

[341]
NATIONAL DAIRY SHRINE/DMI MILK MARKETING SCHOLARSHIPS
National Dairy Shrine
Attn: Office of Executive Director
1224 Alton Darby Creek Road
Columbus, OH 43228-9792
(614) 878-5333 Fax: (614) 870-2622
E-mail: shrine@cobaselect.com
Web: www.dairyshrine.org/students.asp

Purpose To provide financial assistance to college students enrolled in a dairy science program who are preparing for careers in the marketing of dairy products.
Eligibility Applicants must be college sophomores, juniors, or seniors who have a cumulative GPA of 2.5 or higher. They must be majoring in dairy science, animal science, agricultural economics, agricultural communications, agricultural education, general agriculture, or food and nutrition. Selection is based on student organizational activities (15%), other organizational activities (10%), academic standing and course work associated with marketing (25%), honors and awards (10%), marketing experiences (10%), and reasons for interest in dairy product marketing, including plans for the future (30%).
Financial data Stipends are $1,500 or $1,000.
Duration 1 year.
Additional information This program, which began in 1976, is jointly sponsored by the National Dairy Shrine and Dairy Management Inc. (DMI).
Number awarded 7 each year; 1 at $1,500 and 6 at $1,000 each.
Deadline March of each year.

[342]
NATIONAL FFA SCHOLARSHIPS FOR UNDERGRADUATES IN THE SCIENCES
National FFA Organization
Attn: Scholarship Office
6060 FFA Drive
P.O. Box 68960
Indianapolis, IN 46268-0960
(317) 802-4321 Fax: (317) 802-5321
E-mail: scholarships@ffa.org
Web: www.ffa.org/programs/scholarships/index.html

Purpose To provide financial assistance to FFA members who wish to study agriculture and related fields in college.
Eligibility This program is open to current and former members of the organization who are working or planning to work full time on a degree in fields related to agriculture; this includes: agricultural mechanics and engineering, agricultural technology, animal science, conservation, dairy science, equine science, floriculture, food science, horticulture, irrigation, lawn and landscaping, and natural resources. For most of the scholarships, applicants must be high school seniors; others are open to students currently enrolled in college. The program includes a large number of designated scholarships that specify the locations where the members must live, the schools they must attend, the fields of study they must pursue, or other requirements. Some consider family income in the selection process, but most do not. Selection is based on academic achievement (10 points for GPA, 10 points for SAT or ACT score, 10 points for class rank), leadership in FFA activities (30 points), leadership in community activities (10 points), and participation in the Supervised Agricultural Experience (SAE) program (30 points). U.S. citizenship is required.
Financial data Stipends vary, but most are at least $1,000.
Duration 1 year or more.
Additional information Funding for these scholarships is provided by many different corporate sponsors.
Number awarded Varies; generally, a total of approximately 1,000 scholarships are awarded annually by the association.
Deadline February of each year.

[343]
NATIONAL SOCIETY OF BLACK ENGINEERS SCHOLARSHIP PROGRAM
National Society of Black Engineers
Attn: Programs Department
1454 Duke Street
Alexandria, VA 22314
(703) 549-2207, ext. 305 Fax: (703) 683-5312
E-mail: scholarships@nsbe.org
Web: www.nsbe.org/programs/nsbescholarships.php

Purpose To provide financial assistance to members of the National Society of Black Engineers (NSBE) who are working on an undergraduate or graduate degree in engineering or related subjects.
Eligibility These scholarships are available to members of the society who are undergraduate or graduate students of engineering or closely-related subjects. The program includes many designated awards with varying GPA and other requirements. Selection is based on an essay; academic achievement; service to the society at the chapter, regional, and/or national level; and other professional, campus, and community activities. The Mike Shinn Distinguished Member of the Year Awards are presented to the highest-ranked female and male applicants.
Financial data Stipends range up to $7,500.
Duration 1 year.
Additional information This program includes the following named awards: the Adobe Systems Computer Science Corporate Scholarships, the Delta Air Lines NSBE Scholarship, the Eli Lilly and Company Corporate Scholarship, the ExxonMobil Corporation NSBE Scholarships, the Freescale Semiconductor NSBE scholarship, the Fulfilling the Legacy Scholarships, the GE Lloyd Trotter African American Forum Scholarship, the Golden Torch Awards, the Johnson & Johnson NSBE Corporate Scholarship Program, the Lockheed Martin NSBE Corporate Scholarship Program, the Microsoft Corporation NSBE Scholarships, the National Society of Black Engineers Alumni Extension Technical Scholarships, the National Society of Black Engineers Fellows Scholarship Program, the Northrop Grumman NSBE Scholarships, and the Praxair NSBE Partnership Scholar-

ship Program. Corporate sponsors include Adobe Systems Incorporated, Delta Air Lines, Eli Lilly and Company, ExxonMobil Corporation, Freescale Semiconductor, GE Fund, Johnson & Johnson Medical, Inc., Lockheed Martin Corporation, Microsoft Corporation, Northrop Grumman Corporation, and Praxair, Inc.
Number awarded Varies each year.
Deadline January of each year.

[344]
NATIONAL SOCIETY OF BLACK PHYSICISTS UNDERGRADUATE SCHOLARSHIP AWARD

National Society of Black Physicists
Attn: Scholarship Committee Chair
6704G Lee Highway
Arlington, VA 22205
(703) 536-4207   Fax: (703) 536-4203
E-mail: scholarship@nsbp.org
Web: www.nsbp.org

Purpose To provide financial assistance and work experience to African Americans interested in majoring in physics in college.
Eligibility This program is open to African American students who are graduating high school seniors or currently enrolled as an undergraduate in an accredited 4-year institution. Applicants must be majoring or planning to major in physics and have a GPA of 3.0 or higher. Along with their application, they must submit an essay on their academic and career objectives, information on their participation in extracurricular activities, a description of any awards and honors they have received, and 3 letters of recommendation. Financial need is not considered.
Financial data The stipend is $5,000 per year.
Duration Up to 4 years, provided the recipient remains an undergraduate physics major with a GPA of 3.0 or higher.
Additional information This program was initiated in 1992. Information is also available from Ellen Hill, Lawrence Livermore National Laboratory, P.O. Box 808, L-716, Livermore, CA 94550, (925) 422-0894, Fax: (925) 422-9537, E-mail: hill10@llnl.gov. Recipients are required to accept a summer internship at Lawrence Livermore National Laboratory (which sponsors this program) for at least 1 of the 4 summers during their undergraduate education.
Number awarded 1 each year.
Deadline November each year.

[345]
NAVY COLLEGE ASSISTANCE/STUDENT HEADSTART (NAVY-CASH) PROGRAM

U.S. Navy
Attn: Navy Personnel Command
5722 Integrity Drive
Millington, TN 38054-5057
(901) 874-3070   Toll-free: (888) 633-9674
Fax: (901) 874-2651
E-mail: nukeprograms@cnrc.navy.mil
Web: www.cnrc.navy.mil

Purpose To provide financial assistance to high school seniors and current college students interested in attending college for a year and then entering the Navy's nuclear program.
Eligibility Applicants must be able to meet the specific requirements of the Navy's Enlisted Nuclear Field Program. They must be enrolled or accepted for enrollment at an accredited 2-year community or junior college or 4-year college or university.
Financial data While they attend school, participants are paid a regular Navy salary at a pay grade up to E-3 (starting at $1,303.50 per month). They are also eligible for all of the Navy's enlistment incentives, including the Navy College Fund, the Loan Repayment Program, and an enlistment bonus up to $12,000.
Duration 12 months.
Additional information After 1 year of college, participants report for enlisted recruit training in the Navy's nuclear field. Further information on this program is available from a local Navy recruiter.
Number awarded Varies each year.

[346]
NAVY NURSE CANDIDATE PROGRAM

U.S. Navy
Attn: Naval Medical Education and Training Command
Code OH
8901 Wisconsin Avenue
Bethesda, MD 20889-5611
(301) 295-2373   Toll-free: (800) USA-NAVY
Fax: (301) 295-6014 E-mail: OH@nmetc.med.navy.mil
Web: nshs.med.navy.mil/hpsp/Pages/Programs.htm

Purpose To provide financial assistance for nursing education to students interested in serving in the Navy.
Eligibility This program is open to full-time students in a bachelor of science in nursing program. Prior to or during their junior year of college, applicants must enlist in the U.S. Navy Nurse Corps Reserve. Following receipt of their degree, they must be willing to serve as a nurse in the Navy.
Financial data This program pays a $10,000 accession bonus upon enlistment and a stipend of $1,000 per month. Students are responsible for paying all school expenses.
Duration Up to 24 months.
Number awarded Varies each year.

[347]
NCCE SCHOLARSHIPS

National Commission for Cooperative Education
360 Huntington Avenue, 384 CP
Boston, MA 02115-5096
(617) 373-3770   Fax: (617) 373-3463
E-mail: ncce@co-op.edu
Web: www.co-op.edu/scholarships.htm

Purpose To provide financial assistance to students participating or planning to participate in cooperative education projects at designated colleges and universities.
Eligibility This program is open to high school seniors and community college transfer students entering 1 of the 10 partner colleges and universities. Applicants must be planning to participate in college cooperative education. They must have a GPA of 3.5 or higher. Along with their application, they must submit a 1-page essay describing

why they have chosen to enter a college cooperative education program. Applications are especially encouraged from minorities, women, and students interested in science, mathematics, engineering, and technology. Selection is based on merit; financial need is not considered.

Financial data The stipend is $5,000.

Duration 1 year.

Additional information The schools currently participating in this program are Antioch College (Yellow Springs, Ohio), Drexel University (Philadelphia, Pennsylvania), Johnson & Wales University (Providence, Rhode Island; Charleston, South Carolina; Norfolk, Virginia; North Miami, Florida; Denver, Colorado; and Charlotte, North Carolina), Kettering University (Flint, Michigan), C.W. Post Campus of Long Island University (Brookville, New York), Northeastern University (Boston, Massachusetts), Pace University (New York, New York; White Plains, New York; and Pleasantville, New York), Rochester Institute of Technology (Rochester, New York), University of Cincinnati (Cincinnati, Ohio), and University of Toledo (Toledo, Ohio). Applications must be sent directly to the college or university.

Number awarded 113 each year: 5 at Antioch, 15 at Drexel, 15 at Johnson & Wales, 15 at Kettering, 8 at C.W. Post Campus of LIU, 15 at Northeastern, 10 at Pace, 10 at Rochester Tech, 10 at Cincinnati, and 10 at Toledo.

Deadline February of each year for Antioch, Johnson & Wales, C.W. Post Campus of LIU, Northeastern, and Rochester Tech; March of each year for Drexel, Kettering, Pace, Cincinnati, and Toledo.

[348]
NCPA FOUNDATION PRESIDENTIAL SCHOLARSHIPS

National Community Pharmacists Association
Attn: NCPA Foundation
100 Daingerfield Road
Alexandria, VA 22314-2888
(703) 683-8200   Toll-free: (800) 544-7447
Fax: (703) 683-3619   E-mail: info@ncpanet.org
Web: www.ncpanet.org.org

Purpose To provide financial assistance for full-time education in pharmacy to student members of the National Community Pharmacists Association (NCPA).

Eligibility All pharmacy students who are student members of the association and enrolled in an accredited U.S. school or college of pharmacy on a full-time basis are eligible. Applicants must submit a copy of the most recent college transcript, 2 letters of recommendation, a resume or curriculum vitae, and a statement outlining their school and citizenship accomplishments and future career objectives in independent community pharmacy. Selection is based on leadership qualities and academic achievement.

Financial data The stipend is $2,000, paid directly to the recipient's school or college of pharmacy.

Duration 1 year; nonrenewable.

Additional information Until October 1996, the NCPA, the national association representing independent retail pharmacy, was known as NARD (the National Association of Retail Druggists).

Number awarded 15 each year.

Deadline February of each year.

[349]
NDPRB UNDERGRADUATE SCHOLARSHIP PROGRAM

National Dairy Promotion and Research Board
c/o Dairy Management Inc.
10255 West Higgins Road, Suite 900
Rosemont, IL 60018-5616
(847) 803-2000   Fax: (847) 803-2077
E-mail: marykateg@rosedmi.com
Web: www.dairycheckoff.com

Purpose To provide financial assistance to undergraduate students in fields related to the dairy industry.

Eligibility This program is open to sophomores, juniors, and seniors enrolled in college and university programs that emphasize dairy. Eligible majors include agricultural education, business, communications and/or public relations, economics, food science, journalism, marketing, and nutrition. Fields related to production (e.g., animal science) are not eligible. Selection is based on academic performance; interest in a career in dairy; involvement in extracurricular activities, especially those relating to dairy; and evidence of leadership ability, initiative, character, and integrity. The applicant who is judged most outstanding is awarded the James H. Loper Jr. Memorial Scholarship.

Financial data Stipends are $2,500 or $1,500.

Duration 1 year; may be renewed.

Additional information Dairy Management Inc. manages this program on behalf of the National Dairy Promotion and Research Board (NDPRB).

Number awarded 20 each year: the James H. Loper Jr. Memorial Scholarship at $2,500 and 19 other scholarships at $1,500.

Deadline May of each year.

[350]
NDTA ACADEMIC SCHOLARSHIP PROGRAM A

National Defense Transportation Association
Attn: Forum, Education and Professional Development Committee
50 South Pickett Street, Suite 220
Alexandria, VA 22304-7296
(703) 751-5011   Fax: (703) 823-8761
E-mail: info@ndtahq.com
Web: www.ndtahq.com/scholarships.htm

Purpose To provide financial assistance to college students who are members or dependents of members of the National Defense Transportation Association (NDTA) and are majoring in transportation.

Eligibility This program is open to NDTA members and dependents of members who have satisfactorily completed 45 semester hours of work at a regionally accredited college or university. Applicants must be majoring in transportation, physical distribution, logistics, or a combination of those. They must 1) provide college transcripts; 2) attach a listing of academic and other honors and awards received, extracurricular activities, and work experiences; 3) identify the courses in transportation, physical distribution, or logistics that they plan to incorporate into their degree program; and 4) submit a 300- to 500-word statement outlining their career goals and methods of attaining those goals, indicating why they should be awarded the scholarship. Financial need is not considered in the selection process.

Financial data A stipend is awarded (amount not specified).

Duration 1 year; may be renewed.

Number awarded 1 or more each year.

Deadline April of each year.

[351]
NEHA/AAS SCHOLARSHIPS

National Environmental Health Association
Attn: Scholarship Coordinator
720 South Colorado Boulevard, Suite 1000-N
Denver, CO 80246-1926
(303) 756-9090, ext. 343   Fax: (303) 691-9490
E-mail: cdimmitt@neha.org
Web: www.neha.org/scholarship/scholarship.html

Purpose To provide financial assistance to upper-division and graduate students interested in preparing for a career in environmental health.

Eligibility This program is open to undergraduate and graduate students preparing for a career in environmental health. Undergraduates must be entering their junior or senior year in an approved environmental health curriculum at a 4-year college or university accredited by the Environmental Health Accreditation Council (EHAC). Graduate applicants may be enrolled in a college or university with a program of studies in environmental health sciences and/or public health. Selection for both levels is based on academic record and letters of recommendation; at least 1 letter of recommendation must be from an active member of the National Environmental Health Association (NEHA).

Financial data Stipends range from $400 to $1,000.

Duration 1 year; may be renewed.

Additional information The NEHA began this scholarship program in 1984; the American Academy of Sanitarians (AAS) joined it in 1989. Information is also available from the AAS, Executive Secretary/Treasurer, 3815 Stone Briar Court, Duluth, GA 30097-2240, (770) 623-5691.

Number awarded Up to 3 each year.

Deadline January of each year.

[352]
NETTIE DRACUP MEMORIAL SCHOLARSHIP

American Congress on Surveying and Mapping
Attn: Scholarships
6 Montgomery Village Avenue, Suite 403
Gaithersburg, MD 20879
(240) 632-9716, ext. 113   Fax: (240) 632-1321
E-mail: pat.canfield@acsm.net
Web: www.acsm.net/scholar.html

Purpose To provide financial assistance for the undergraduate study of geodetic surveying to members of the American Congress on Surveying and Mapping (ACSM).

Eligibility This program is open to ACSM members who are enrolled at a 4-year college or university. Applicants must be majoring in geodetic surveying. U.S. citizenship is required. Along with their application, they must submit a statement describing their educational program, future plans for study or research, and why the award is merited.

Selection is based on that statement (30%), academic record (30%), letters of recommendation (20%), and professional activities (20%).

Financial data The stipend is $2,000.

Duration 1 year.

Number awarded 1 each year.

Deadline October of each year.

[353]
NEUROSCIENCE NURSING FOUNDATION REGULAR SCHOLARSHIPS

American Association of Neuroscience Nurses
Attn: Neuroscience Nursing Foundation
4700 West Lake Avenue
Glenview, IL 60025-1485
(847) 375-4733   Toll-free: (888) 557-2266
Fax: (877) 734-8677   E-mail: info@aann.org
Web: www.aann.org/nnf/index.htm

Purpose To provide financial assistance to nurses interested in further study in neuroscience nursing.

Eligibility This program is open to nurses who have a diploma or associate degree and are working on a bachelor's degree in neuroscience nursing. Applicants must submit their resume and a personal statement on their anticipated contribution to neuroscience nursing practice, research, and/or education.

Financial data The stipend is $1,500.

Duration 1 year.

Additional information This program was established in 1994.

Number awarded The award is presented when a suitable candidate applies.

Deadline January of each year.

[354]
NEVADA SPACE GRANT CONSORTIUM UNDERGRADUATE SCHOLARSHIP PROGRAM

Nevada Space Grant Consortium
c/o University of Nevada at Reno
Mackay School of Mines Building, Room 308
MS 168
Reno, NV 89557
(775) 784-6261   Fax: (775) 327-2235
E-mail: nvsg@mines.unr.edu
Web: www.unr.edu/spacegrant

Purpose To provide financial assistance for space-related study to undergraduate students at institutions that are members of the University and Community College System of Nevada (UCCSN) and participate in the Nevada Space Grant Consortium (NSGC).

Eligibility This program is open to undergraduate students at UCCSN member institutions. Applicants must be working on a degree in an aerospace-related field, including any science, mathematics, engineering, or technology discipline that is concerned with or likely to improve the understanding, assessment, development, and utilization of space. They must be U.S. citizens and enrolled full time. This program is part of the Space Grant program of the U.S. National Aeronautics and Space Administration (NASA), which encourages participation by members of underrepresented groups (African Americans, Hispanics, American Indians, Pacific Islanders, people with physical disabilities, and women of all races). Selection is based on the academic qualifications of the applicant, the quality of a career goal statement, and an assessment of the applicant's motivation for an aerospace career.

Financial data The stipend is $2,500 per year. Funds may be used for tuition or registration fees. Funds may not be regarded as payment for research work or any other work.

Duration 1 year; may be renewed.

Additional information Funding for this program is provided by NASA.

Number awarded Varies each year; recently, 13 of these awards were granted.

Deadline March of each year.

[355]
NEW HAMPSHIRE GOLF COURSE SUPERINTENDENTS ASSOCIATION SCHOLARSHIP

New Hampshire Golf Course Superintendents Association
80 Nashua Road
C3, Box 15
Londonderry, NH 03053
(603) 623-3075   Fax: (603) 623-3074
E-mail: turfking99@aol.com
Web: nhgcs.memfirstweb.net

Purpose To provide financial assistance for college to relatives of members of the New Hampshire Golf Course Superintendents Association (NHGCSA) and to residents of New Hampshire who are interested in majoring in turfgrass management.

Eligibility This program is open to 1) children, grandchildren, and spouses of NHGCSA members who are currently active and have been members for 3 or more consecutive years; and 2) nonmembers enrolled in fields related to turfgrass management. Applicants must be New Hampshire residents currently enrolled or (if high school seniors) accepted as a full-time student at an accredited institution of higher education. Along with their application, they must submit a 500-word essay on their personal achievements and why they are a deserving candidate for this scholarship. Selection is based on the essay, academic achievement, extracurricular activities, community involvement, leadership, and outside employment. Financial need is not considered.

Financial data Stipends range from $500 to $1,000, depending upon available funds.

Duration 1 year; recipients may reapply.

Number awarded 1 or more each year.

Deadline October of each year.

[356]
NEW MEXICO PROFESSIONAL SURVEYORS SCHOLARSHIPS

New Mexico Professional Surveyors
Attn: NMPS Educational Foundation, Inc.
412 North Dal Paso
Hobbs, NM 88240
(505) 393-1462   Fax: (505) 393-4836
E-mail: info@nmps.org
Web: www.nmps.org/NMPSED.htm

Purpose To provide financial assistance to students working on a degree in surveying at a college or university in New Mexico.

Eligibility This program is open to students enrolled at a college or university in New Mexico in a program that will lead to a technical or professional degree in surveying. Applicants must submit an essay on 1) activities (community, school, surveying) that demonstrate their leadership and/or service abilities; and 2) their educational and career goals. Financial need is not considered in the selection process.

Financial data A stipend is awarded (amount not specified).

Duration 1 year.

Additional information Information is also available from the Educational Foundation, P.O. Box 90504, Albuquerque, NM 87199.

Number awarded 1 or more each year.

[357]
NEW YORK BEEF PRODUCERS' ASSOCIATION SCHOLARSHIP

New York Beef Producers' Association
Attn: Executive Secretary
3 Second Street
Camden, NY 13316
(315) 245-3386   E-mail: nybpa1@twcny.rr.com
Web: www.tjbailey.com/nybpa/youthprograms.htm

Purpose To provide financial assistance to college students from New York who are preparing for a career in the cattle industry.

Eligibility This program is open to residents of New York who are currently enrolled in an accredited 2-year or 4-year agricultural college. Applicants must be majoring in a field of study related to agriculture (e.g., animal and/or crop science, business, economics, communications, agricultural engineering) and planning a career related to the beef industry. Along with their application, they must submit an essay that covers the following: 1) their experience and interest in the beef industry; 2) their involvement in agricultural-related activities, including organizations (community, school, 4-H), events, awards, and leadership positions; 3) their future intentions and career plans as they relate to the beef industry; and 4) how they view the future of the beef industry. Selection is based primarily on involvement in the beef industry and future plans. Financial need is not considered.

Financial data The stipend is $1,000.

Duration 1 year.

Number awarded 1 each year.

Deadline December of each year.

[358]
NEW YORK SECTION SCHOLARSHIPS
Institute of Food Technologists
Attn: Scholarship Department
525 West Van Buren, Suite 1000
Chicago, IL 60607
(312) 782-8424   Fax: (312) 782-8348
E-mail: info@ift.org
Web: www.ift.org

Purpose To provide financial assistance to undergraduates interested in studying food science or food technology.
Eligibility This program is open to sophomores, juniors, and seniors in a food science or food technology program at an educational institution in the United States or Canada. Applicants must have an outstanding scholastic record and a well-rounded personality. Along with their application, they must submit an essay on their career aspirations; a list of awards, honors, and scholarships they have received; a list of extracurricular activities and/or hobbies; and a summary of their work experience. Financial need is not considered in the selection process.
Financial data The stipend is $1,000.
Duration 1 year; recipients may reapply if they are members of the Institute of Food Technologists.
Additional information Correspondence and completed applications must be submitted to the department head of the educational institution the applicant is attending.
Number awarded 2 each year.
Deadline January of each year.

[359]
NMA UNDERGRADUATE SCHOLARSHIPS
National Meat Association
Attn: NMA Scholarship Foundation
1970 Broadway, Suite 825
Oakland, CA 94612
(510) 763-1533   Fax: (510) 763-6186
E-mail: staff@nmaonline.org
Web: www.nmascholars.org

Purpose To provide financial assistance to undergraduates working on a degree in the animal, meat, and food sciences.
Eligibility This program is open to students entering their sophomore, junior, or senior year in an approved program in animal science, meat science, food science, or a related discipline. Applicants must be attending a 4-year college or university and have a GPA of 2.75 or higher. Along with their application, they must submit an essay of 200 to 250 words on their career goals and future endeavors, focusing on how those relate to post harvest and production of meat food products. Financial need, age, gender, race, religion, or national origin are not conditions for eligibility; essays that cite those as reasons for applying are marked down. Selection is based on the essay (25%), work experience (25%), awards and honors (5%), extracurricular activities (5%), a faculty letter of recommendation (10%), official transcript (20%), a list of completed and current courses (5%), and a list of pending courses (5%).
Financial data Stipends are $2,500 or $2,000. Awardees who attend the annual convention of the National Meat Association (NMA) receive a $500 travel award and plaque.
Duration 1 year; nonrenewable.
Additional information This program includes the following named scholarships: the Frank DeBenedetti Memorial Scholarship (at $2,500), the Edie Schmidt NMA Memorial Scholarship (at $2,000), and the Al Piccetti NMA Memorial Scholarship (at $2,000).
Number awarded Varies each year: the 3 named scholarships plus several others at $2,000.
Deadline April of each year.

[360]
NONWOVENS DIVISION SCHOLARSHIP
Technical Association of the Pulp and Paper Industry
Attn: TAPPI Foundation
15 Technology Parkway South
Norcross, GA 30092
(770) 209-7536   Toll-free: (800) 332-8686
Fax: (770) 446-6947   E-mail: vedmondson@tappi.org
Web: www.tappi.org

Purpose To provide financial assistance to undergraduate students who are interested in preparing for a career in the paper industry.
Eligibility This program is open to students who are attending a state-accredited college full time, have earned a GPA of 3.0 or higher, are enrolled in a program preparatory to a career in the nonwovens industry or can demonstrate an interest in the areas covered by the Nonwovens Division of the Technical Association of the Pulp and Paper Industry, and are recommended and endorsed by an instructor or faculty member. Applicants must be interested in preparing for a career in the paper industry with a focus on the materials, equipment, and processes for the manufacture and use of nonwovens. Selection is based on the candidates' potential career contributions to the pulp and paper industry as it relates to nonwovens; financial need is not considered.
Financial data The stipend is $1,000.
Duration 1 year.
Number awarded 1 each year.
Deadline January of each year.

[361]
NORTH CAROLINA SPACE GRANT CONSORTIUM UNDERGRADUATE SCHOLARSHIPS
North Carolina Space Grant Consortium
c/o North Carolina State University
Mechanical and Aerospace Engineering
1009 Capability Drive, Suite 210
Box 7515
Raleigh, NC 27695-7515
(919) 515-4240   Fax: (919) 515-5934
E-mail: scholarships@ncspacegrant.org
Web: www.ncspacegrant.org

Purpose To provide funding to undergraduate students at institutions affiliated with the North Carolina Space Grant Consortium (NCSGC) interested in major in space-related fields.
Eligibility This program is open to full-time undergraduate students at institutions affiliated with the NCSGC who

are freshmen, sophomores, or recent transfers from a community or junior college. Applicants must be working on a degree in a science, technology, engineering, or mathematics (STEM) discipline of interest to the U.S. National Aeronautics and Space Administration (NASA). Selection is based on the student's academic achievement, a letter of recommendation, and exhibited leadership qualities. U.S. citizenship is required. A primary goal of this program is the recruitment and retention of underrepresented minorities, women, and persons with disabilities into space-related fields.

Financial data The stipend is $1,000 per year.

Duration 1 year; may be renewed 1 additional year.

Additional information The affiliated institutions are North Carolina State University, North Carolina A&T State University, Duke University, North Carolina Central University, the University of North Carolina at Charlotte, the University of North Carolina at Chapel Hill, the University of North Carolina at Pembroke, and Winston-Salem State University. This program is funded by NASA.

Number awarded Varies each year.

Deadline March of each year.

[362]
NSPS BOARD OF GOVERNORS SCHOLARSHIP

American Congress on Surveying and Mapping
Attn: Scholarships
6 Montgomery Village Avenue, Suite 403
Gaithersburg, MD 20879
(240) 632-9716, ext. 113   Fax: (240) 632-1321
E-mail: pat.canfield@acsm.net
Web: www.acsm.net/scholar.html

Purpose To provide financial assistance for the undergraduate study of surveying to upper-division members of the American Congress on Surveying and Mapping (ACSM).

Eligibility This program is open to ACSM members who are enrolled at a 4-year college or university as juniors or higher with at least a 3.0 GPA. Applicants must be majoring in surveying or a closely-related program (e.g., geomatics, surveying engineering). Along with their application, they must submit a statement describing their educational program, future plans for study or research, and why the award is merited. Selection is based on that statement (30%), academic record (30%), letters of recommendation (20%), and professional activities (20%).

Financial data The stipend is $1,000.

Duration 1 year.

Additional information Funding for these scholarships is provided by the National Society of Professional Surveyors (NSPS).

Number awarded 1 each year.

Deadline October of each year.

[363]
NSPS SCHOLARSHIPS

American Congress on Surveying and Mapping
Attn: Scholarships
6 Montgomery Village Avenue, Suite 403
Gaithersburg, MD 20879
(240) 632-9716, ext. 113   Fax: (240) 632-1321
E-mail: pat.canfield@acsm.net
Web: www.acsm.net/scholar.html

Purpose To provide financial assistance for full-time undergraduate study of surveying to members of the American Congress on Surveying and Mapping (ACSM).

Eligibility This program is open to ACSM members who are enrolled full time at a 4-year college or university. Applicants must be majoring in surveying or a closely-related program (e.g., geomatics, surveying engineering). Along with their application, they must submit a statement describing their educational program, future plans for study or research, and why the award is merited. Selection is based on that statement (30%), academic record (30%), letters of recommendation (20%), and professional activities (20%).

Financial data The stipend is $1,000.

Duration 1 year.

Additional information Funding for these scholarships is provided by the National Society of Professional Surveyors (NSPS).

Number awarded 2 each year.

Deadline November of each year.

[364]
NUCLEAR PROPULSION OFFICER CANDIDATE (NUPOC) PROGRAM

U.S. Navy
Attn: Navy Personnel Command
5722 Integrity Drive
Millington, TN 38054-5057
(901) 874-3070   Toll-free: (888) 633-9674
Fax: (901) 874-2651
E-mail: nukeprograms@cnrc.navy.mil
Web: www.cnrc.navy.mil

Purpose To provide financial assistance to college juniors and seniors who wish to serve in the Navy's nuclear propulsion training program following graduation.

Eligibility This program is open to U.S. citizens who are entering their junior or senior year of college as a full-time student. Strong technical majors (mathematics, physics, chemistry, or an engineering field) are encouraged but not required. Applicants must have completed at least 1 year of calculus and 1 year of physics and must have earned a grade of "C" or better in all mathematics, science, and technical courses. Normally, they must be 26 years of age or younger at the expected date of commissioning, although applicants for the design and research specialty may be 29 years old.

Financial data Participants become Active Reserve enlisted Navy personnel and receive a salary of up to $2,500 per month; the exact amount depends on the local cost of living and other factors. A bonus of $10,000 is also paid at the time of enlistment and another $2,000 upon completion of nuclear power training.

Duration Up to 30 months, until completion of a bachelor's degree.

Additional information Following graduation, participants attend Officer Candidate School in Pensacola, Florida for 4 months and receive their commissions. They have a service obligation of 8 years (of which at least 5 years must be on active duty), beginning with 6 months at the Navy Nuclear Power Training Command in Charleston, South Carolina and 6 more months of hands-on training at a nuclear reactor facility. Further information on this program is available from a local Navy recruiter or the Navy Recruiting Command, 801 North Randolph Street, Arlington, VA 22203-1991.

Number awarded Varies each year.

[365]
NYWEA SCHOLARSHIPS

New York Water Environment Association
Attn: Executive Director
525 Plum Street, Suite 102
Syracuse, NY 13204
(315) 422-7811   Fax: (315) 422-3851
E-mail: pcr@nywea.org
Web: www.nywea.org/schol

Purpose To provide financial assistance to students who are enrolled or planning to enroll in an environmentally-related program in college.

Eligibility This program is open to 3 categories of students: 1) children of members of the New York Water Environment Association (NYWEA) who are enrolled or planning to enroll full time at a college or university in a program that will prepare them for a professional career in the environmental field; 2) students enrolled full time in a program that will prepare them for a professional career in the environmental field at a college or university that has an NYWEA student chapter; and 3) high school seniors who plan to enroll in an environmentally-related program at a 4-year college or university. All applicants must submit essays, from 200 to 300 words in length, on 1) their interest in the environment and how that interest influences their career goals, and 2) a current environmental issue that impacts their life and their community and how it affects them. Selection is based on career objective, academic potential, other activities, character, and environmental interest.

Financial data The stipend is $1,500.

Duration 1 year.

Number awarded 6 each year: 2 in each of the 3 categories.

Deadline January of each year.

[366]
OHIO ASPHALT SCHOLARSHIP PROGRAM

Flexible Pavements of Ohio
Attn: Ohio Asphalt Scholarship Fund
37 West Broad Street, Suite 460
P.O. Box 16186
Columbus, OH 43216-6186
(614) 221-5402   Toll-free: (888) 4-HOTMIX
Fax: (614) 221-0394
E-mail: info@flexiblepavements.org
Web: www.flexiblepavements.org/scholarship.cfm

Purpose To provide financial assistance to undergraduate and graduate students at colleges and universities in Ohio who are interested in preparing for a career in a field related to asphalt pavement technology.

Eligibility This program is open to students entering their junior, senior, or fifth year of study in a civil engineering, construction management, or construction engineering curriculum at a participating university in Ohio. Preference is given to students who show an interest in the design and construction of Ohio's highways and transportation facilities. The university must offer, and the student must take, at least 1 course on hot mix asphalt technology. Graduate students with their major focus of study related to asphalt and attending an Ohio university or college are also considered. All applicants must be full-time students and U.S. citizens. Selection is based on academic performance and potential, leadership and participation in school and community activities, work experience, level of career and educational aspirations in the transportation industry, goals, and special personal or family circumstances. Although it is not a criterion, applicants should indicate if there is a need for financial assistance.

Financial data The stipend is $1,000 per year.

Duration 1 year; may be renewed for up to 2 years or until graduation, whichever comes first.

Additional information The following universities participate in this program: Bowling Green State University, Ohio Northern University, Ohio State University, Ohio University, University of Cincinnati, University of Dayton, Youngstown State University, University of Toledo, and University of Akron.

Number awarded Varies each year; recently, 26 of these scholarships were awarded.

Deadline January of each year.

[367]
OHIO CATTLEWOMEN SCHOLARSHIPS

Ohio Cattlemen's Association
Attn: Foundation
10600 U.S. Highway 42
Marysville, OH 43040
(614) 873-6736   Fax: (614) 873-6835
E-mail: beef@ohiobeef.org
Web: ohiocattle.org/scholarships.aspx

Purpose To provide financial assistance to upper-division student at colleges and universities in Ohio, especially those who are studying agriculture.

Eligibility This program is open to students entering their junior or senior year at a college or university in Ohio. Applicants may be studying any field, but preference is given to students majoring in agriculture, specifically relating to beef. They must have a GPA of 2.75 or higher. Along with their application, they must submit a brief statement on their involvement in the beef industry, ambitions, goals, and background. Selection is based on academic achievement and extracurricular activities.

Financial data The stipend is $1,000.

Duration 1 year.

Additional information This program is sponsored by Ohio CattleWomen. Information is also available from Patty Spengler, (740) 472-5313.

Number awarded Up to 5 each year.

Deadline December of each year.

[368] OLD GUARD PRIZES

ASME International
Attn: Committee on Honors
Three Park Avenue
New York, NY 10016-5990
(212) 591-7736   Toll-free: (800) THE-ASME
Fax: (212) 591-7739   E-mail: MervynC@asme.org
Web: www.asme.org

Purpose To recognize and reward student members of ASME International (the professional society of mechanical engineers) who deliver outstanding oral presentations on engineering subjects.

Eligibility This program is open to student members who make 15-minute oral presentations, followed by 5-minute question-and-answer sessions, on subjects related to mechanical engineering. Entrants must be dues-paid student members who have not yet received an engineering degree, have been selected by their student sections to participate, and have been certified by their regional office as a student member in good standing. Selection is based on content, organization, delivery, effectiveness, and discussion. Students first compete on the regional level, from which the winners advance to the national competition.

Financial data At the regional level, the first-place winner receives $500 plus reimbursement of expenses to participate in the national competition, second place $150, third place $100, fourth place $50, and fifth place $25. At the national level, first prize is $2,000, second $1,500, third $1,000, and fourth $500.

Duration The prizes are presented annually.

Additional information This program was established in 1956, expanded in 1981 to include second and third prizes, and expanded in 1992 to include fourth prize. The "Old Guard" consists of ASME dues exempt members who are over the age of 65 and have retired.

Number awarded Each year, there are 5 winners in each region and 4 in the national competition.

[369] OLIVE LYNN SALEMBIER SCHOLARSHIP

Society of Women Engineers
230 East Ohio Street, Suite 400
Chicago, IL 60611-3265
(312) 596-5223   Toll-free: (877) SWE-INFO
Fax: (312) 644-8557
E-mail: scholarshipapplication@swe.org
Web: www.swe.org/scholarships

Purpose To provide financial assistance to women interested in returning to college or graduate school to study engineering or computer science.

Eligibility This program is open to women who are planning to enroll at an ABET-accredited 4-year college or university. Applicants must have been out of the engineering workforce and school for at least 2 years and must be planning to return as an undergraduate or graduate student to major in computer science or engineering. Along with their application, they must submit a 1-page essay on why they want to be an engineer or computer scientist, how they believe they will make a difference as an engineer or computer scientist, and what influenced them to study engineering or computer science. Selection is based on merit.

Financial data The award is $2,000.

Duration 1 year.

Additional information This program was established in 1979.

Number awarded 1 each year.

Deadline May of each year.

[370] ONCOLOGY NURSING CERTIFICATION CORPORATION BACHELOR'S SCHOLARSHIPS

Oncology Nursing Society
Attn: ONS Foundation
125 Enterprise Drive
Pittsburgh, PA 15275-1214
(412) 859-6100, ext. 8503   Toll-free: (866) 257-4ONS
Fax: (412) 859-6160   E-mail: foundation@ons.org
Web: www.ons.org

Purpose To provide financial assistance to nurses who are interested in working on a bachelor's degree in oncology nursing.

Eligibility This program is open to registered nurses and licensed practical (vocational) nurses with a demonstrated interest in and commitment to oncology nursing. They must be currently enrolled in an undergraduate degree program at an NLN- or CCNE-accredited school of nursing. They may not have previously received a bachelor's level scholarship from this sponsor. Applicants must submit an essay of 250 words or less on their role in caring for persons with cancer and a statement of their professional goals and their relationship to the advancement of oncology nursing. Financial need is not considered in the selection process.

Financial data The stipend is $2,000.

Duration 1 year.

Additional information This program, supported by the Oncology Nursing Certification Corporation, awarded its first scholarships in 1992. At the end of each year of scholarship participation, recipients must submit a summary

describing their educational activities. Applications must be accompanied by a $5 fee.
Number awarded Varies each year; recently, 10 of these scholarships were awarded.
Deadline January of each year.

[371]
OREGON SPACE GRANT UNDERGRADUATE SCHOLARSHIP PROGRAM
Oregon NASA Space Grant Consortium
c/o Oregon State University
92 Kerr Administration Building
Corvallis, OR 97331-2103
(541) 737-2414   Fax: (541) 737-9946
E-mail: spacegrant@oregonstate.edu
Web: www.oregonspacegrant.orst.edu

Purpose To provide financial assistance for study in space-related fields to undergraduate students at colleges and universities that are members of the Oregon Space Grant Consortium (OSGC).
Eligibility This program is open to U.S. citizens enrolled full time at OSGC member institutions. Applicants must be working on 1) a baccalaureate degree in a science, technology, engineering, or mathematics (STEM) field (including mathematics or science education) related to the mission of the U.S. National Aeronautics and Space Administration (NASA); or 2) an associate degree in applied science and planning to transfer to a 4-year institution to complete a baccalaureate in the same fields. Along with their application, they must submit a letter of intent of 250 to 300 words on their career goals as they relate to NASA and how this scholarship will contribute to those goals. Selection is based on scholastic achievement, aerospace-related career goals, and 2 letters of recommendation. Applications are especially encouraged from members of underrepresented groups (women, minorities, and people with disabilities).
Financial data The stipend is $2,000.
Duration 1 year.
Additional information Institutions that are members of OSG include Oregon State University, Portland State University, the University of Oregon, Southern Oregon University, Eastern Oregon University, Western Oregon University, George Fox University, Lane Community College, Linfield College, Portland Community College, and Oregon Institute of Technology. This program is funded by NASA.
Number awarded Varies each year.
Deadline January of each year.

[372]
PACIFIC NORTHWEST CHAPTER ARPAS SCHOLARSHIP
American Registry of Professional Animal Scientists-
  Pacific Northwest Chapter
c/o Carl Hunt
University of Idaho
Department of Animal and Veterinary Science
Moscow, ID 83844
(208) 885-6932   Fax: (208) 885-6420
E-mail: chunt@uidaho.edu

Purpose To provide financial assistance to upper-division students at colleges and university in the Pacific Northwest who are majoring in animal science or dairy science.
Eligibility This program is open to students entering their junior or senior year at colleges and universities in Idaho, Oregon, and Washington. Applicants must have a GPA of 3.2 or higher and a major in animal science or dairy science with a demonstrated interest in animal nutrition or the livestock feed industry. Along with their application, they must submit a statement of career goals. Proven work experience in nutrition or feeds is highly desirable. Financial need is not considered in the selection process.
Financial data The stipend is $1,000.
Duration 1 year.
Number awarded 1 each year.
Deadline September of each year.

[373]
PAPER AND BOARD DIVISION SCHOLARSHIPS
Technical Association of the Pulp and Paper Industry
Attn: TAPPI Foundation
15 Technology Parkway South
Norcross, GA 30092
(770) 209-7536   Toll-free: (800) 332-8686
Fax: (770) 446-6947   E-mail: vedmondson@tappi.org
Web: www.tappi.org

Purpose To provide financial assistance to student members of the Technical Association of the Pulp and Paper Industry (TAPPI) who are majoring in a scientific or technical discipline related to the manufacture of paper and paperboard.
Eligibility This program is open to students who are members of the association, are attending college full time or participating full time in a cooperative work-study program recognized and supported by their college, are at least sophomores on the undergraduate level, are enrolled in an engineering or science program, and are able to demonstrate a significant interest in the paper industry. Selection is based on the candidates' seriousness of purpose in pursuing a course of study related to the science and technology of the paper industry and an intent to make a career in the industry; financial need is not considered.
Financial data The stipend is $1,000.
Duration 1 year.
Additional information This program was established in 1990.
Number awarded Varies each year; recently, 2 of these scholarships were awarded.
Deadline January of each year.

[374]
PAROS-DIGIQUARTZ SCHOLARSHIP
Marine Technology Society
Attn: Student Scholarships
5565 Sterrett Place, Suite 108
Columbia, MD 21044
(410) 884-5330 Fax: (410) 884-9060
Web: www.mtsociety.org

Purpose To provide financial assistance to entering or continuing undergraduate and graduate students working on a degree in a field related to marine science.

Eligibility This program is open to high school seniors accepted into a full-time undergraduate program and current undergraduate and graduate students. Applicants must be planning to work on a degree in a marine-related field. Along with their application, they must submit a statement explaining their interest in marine engineering or technology; a biographical sketch, including academic, personal, and professional goals; an official school transcript; a recommendation from a current teacher or counselor in a marine-related field; and a personal letter of reference. Special consideration is given to applicants with an interest in marine instrumentation. Membership in the Marine Technology Society (MTS) is not required. Financial need is not considered in the selection process.

Financial data The stipend is $2,000. Funds are sent directly to the recipient's college bursar's office.

Duration 1 year.

Additional information This scholarship was first awarded in 2006.

Number awarded 1 each year.

Deadline April of each year.

[375]
PAST PRESIDENTS SCHOLARSHIP
Institute of Food Technologists
Attn: Scholarship Department
525 West Van Buren, Suite 1000
Chicago, IL 60607
(312) 782-8424 Fax: (312) 782-8348
E-mail: info@ift.org
Web: www.ift.org

Purpose To provide financial assistance to undergraduates interested in studying food science or food technology.

Eligibility This program is open to sophomores, juniors, and seniors in a food science or food technology program at an educational institution in the United States or Canada. Applicants must have an outstanding scholastic record and a well-rounded personality. Along with their application, they must submit an essay on their career aspirations; a list of awards, honors, and scholarships they have received; a list of extracurricular activities and/or hobbies; and a summary of their work experience. Financial need is not considered in the selection process.

Financial data The stipend is $1,000.

Duration 1 year; recipients may reapply if they are members of the Institute of Food Technologists.

Additional information Correspondence and completed applications must be submitted to the department head of the educational institution the applicant is attending.

Number awarded 1 each year.

Deadline January of each year.

[376]
PAT ROBERTS INTELLIGENCE SCHOLARS PROGRAM FOR GLOBAL NETWORK ANALYSTS
National Security Agency
Attn: Office of Recruitment and Staffing (Roberts)
9800 Savage Road, Suite 6779
P.O. Box 1661, Suite 6779
Fort Meade, MD 20755-6779
(410) 854-4725 Toll-free: (866) 672-4473
Web: www.nsa.gov/careers/students_4.cfm

Purpose To provide financial assistance and work experience to college sophomores and juniors interested in preparing for a career with the National Security Agency (NSA) as a global network analyst.

Eligibility This program is open to college sophomores and juniors whose academic program includes 1 of the following areas of emphasis: 1) technical studies (computer science major with a minor in political science or international relations); 2) topical studies (terrorism, proliferation or related sciences, international banking and finance, or telecommunications and information systems networks); or 3) disciplines (technical intelligence analysis, information assurance, networks, and telecommunications). Applicants must be enrolled full time with a GPA of 3.0 or higher. Along with their application, they must submit a 1-page essay describing how the proposed program of study will improve their ability to analyze information and to think and write critically. U.S. citizenship and eligibility to obtain a high-level security clearance are required.

Financial data The stipend is $25,000 per year. During the summer after application, students participate in a Global Network Analysis internship. After graduation, they have an employment obligation to NSA equal to 1.5 times the length of educational support provided.

Duration 1 year; may be renewed 1 additional year. The summer internship program is for 12 weeks.

Additional information After graduation, participants enter NSA's Global Network Analysis Internship Program as a full-time employee.

Number awarded Varies each year.

Deadline October of each year.

[377]
PAT ROBERTS INTELLIGENCE SCHOLARS PROGRAM FOR INTELLIGENCE ANALYSTS
National Security Agency
Attn: Office of Recruitment and Staffing (Roberts)
9800 Savage Road, Suite 6779
P.O. Box 1661, Suite 6779
Fort Meade, MD 20755-6779
(410) 854-4725 Toll-free: (866) 672-4473
Web: www.nsa.gov/careers/students_4.cfm

Purpose To provide financial assistance to college juniors interested in preparing for a career with the National Security Agency (NSA) as an intelligence analyst.

Eligibility This program is open to college juniors whose academic program includes 1 of the following areas of emphasis: 1) regional studies (Middle East or south, east, or central Asia); 2) topical studies (terrorism, proliferation or related sciences, international banking and finance, or telecommunications and information systems networks); or 3) disciplines (intelligence analysis, philosophy, or international relations; familiarity with foreign languages, particularly Arabic, Chinese, Dari, Farsi, Hindi, Korean, Pashto, Urdu, or a central Asian language is desirable; highly qualified applicants studying social network analysis, library science, or geographic information systems may also be considered). Applicants must be enrolled full time with a GPA of 3.0 or higher. Along with their application, they must submit a 1-page essay describing how the proposed program of study will improve their ability to analyze information and to think and write critically. U.S. citizenship and eligibility to obtain a high-level security clearance are required.

Financial data The stipend is $25,000 per year. After graduation, recipients have an employment obligation to NSA equal to 1.5 times the length of educational support provided.

Duration 1 year (the senior year of college).

Additional information After graduation, participants enter NSA's Intelligence Analysis Development Program as a full-time employee.

Number awarded Varies each year.

Deadline October of each year.

[378]
PAUL A. WHELAN AVIATION SCHOLARSHIP

University Aviation Association
3410 Skyway Drive
Auburn, AL 36830-6444
(334) 844-2434   E-mail: uaa@auburn.edu
Web: www.uaa.aero

Purpose To provide financial assistance to students working on an undergraduate or graduate degree in aviation or a space-related field.

Eligibility This program is open to sophomores, juniors, seniors, and graduate students who are currently enrolled at a college, university, or community college affiliated with the University Aviation Association (UAA). Applicants must be majoring in aviation or a space-related field and have a GPA of 2.5 or higher overall and 3.0 in their aviation courses. They must be able to demonstrate a love of aviation, extracurricular and community involvement, and leadership. Preference is given to applicants who have Federal Aviation Administration certification as a pilot or mechanic; former or current military service through active duty, ROTC, Air National Guard, or Reserves while in school; or membership in an aviation-related association or professional group.

Financial data The stipend is $2,000.

Duration 1 year.

Additional information Information is also available from David A. NewMyer, Southern Illinois University at Carbondale, College of Applied Sciences and Arts, 1365 Douglas Drive, Carbondale, IL 62901-6623, (618) 453-8898.

Deadline August of each year.

[379]
PAUL AND ELLEN RUCKES SCHOLARSHIP

American Foundation for the Blind
Attn: Scholarship Committee
11 Penn Plaza, Suite 300
New York, NY 10001
(212) 502-7661   Toll-free: (800) AFB-LINE
Fax: (212) 502-7771   TDD: (212) 502-7662
E-mail: afbinfo@afb.net
Web: www.afb.org/scholarships.asp

Purpose To provide financial assistance to visually impaired students who wish to work on a graduate or undergraduate degree in engineering or computer, physical, or life sciences.

Eligibility This program is open to visually impaired undergraduate or graduate students who are U.S. citizens working on a degree in engineering or the computer, physical, or life sciences. Legal blindness is not required. Along with their application, they must submit an essay that includes the field of study they are pursuing and why they have chosen it; their educational and personal goals; their work experience; any extracurricular activities with which they have been involved, including those in school, religious organizations, and the community; and how they intend to use scholarship monies that may be awarded.

Financial data The stipend is $1,000.

Duration 1 year.

Number awarded 1 each year.

Deadline April of each year.

[380]
PAUL JACKSON MEMORIAL SCHOLARSHIP

American Jersey Cattle Association
Attn: Dr. Cherie L. Bayer
6486 East Main Street
Reynoldsburg, OH 43068-2362
(614) 861-3636   Fax: (614) 861-8040
E-mail: cbayer@usjersey.com
Web: www.usjersey.com

Purpose To provide financial assistance for college to members of the American Jersey Cattle Association (AJCA) who have worked with Jersey cattle.

Eligibility This program is open to AJCA members who have significant and extensive experience in breeding, managing, and showing Jersey cattle. Applicants must have completed at least 1 year of college. Along with their application, they must describe their activities with Jersey cattle; summarize their extracurricular activities during high school and college; and describe their background, ambitions, and goals. They must have a GPA of 2.5 or higher. Financial need is not considered in the selection process.

Financial data The stipend is approximately $1,000.

Duration 1 year.

Number awarded 1 each year.

Deadline June of each year.

[381]
PAUL W. RODGERS SCHOLARSHIP

International Association for Great Lakes Research
Attn: Business Office
2205 Commonwealth Boulevard
Ann Arbor, MI 48105
(734) 665-5303   Fax: (734) 741-2055
E-mail: office@iaglr.org
Web: www.iaglr.org/as/rodgers.php

Purpose To provide financial assistance to college seniors and graduate students interested in pursuing a course of study related to the Great Lakes aquatic ecosystem health and management.

Eligibility This program is open to college seniors, master's degree students, or doctoral students who wish to prepare for a future in research, conservation, education, communication, management, or other knowledge-based activity pertaining to the Great Lakes. Applicants must submit 1) official transcripts, 2) 2 letters of reference, 3) a letter of application that includes a summary of past and prevent involvement with Great Lakes concerns, a brief description of their proposed program or thesis research topic, and relevance of the proposed program of study to Great Lakes concerns; and 4) a statement explaining how further academic training and personal goals will help them to fulfill their personal goals as they relate to the purpose of the scholarship. Selection is based on academic record, letters of support, involvement in activities related to Great Lakes issues, and the candidate's statement. Financial need is not considered.

Financial data The stipend is $2,000.

Duration 1 year; nonrenewable.

Additional information Recipients are also given a 1-year membership in the sponsoring organization and a subscription to the *Journal of Great Lakes Research*. This program was established in 1999. Recipients may not keep the scholarship if they are awarded more than $10,000 from other scholarship sources (excluding graduate assistantships). They must submit a summary of their accomplishments relevant to Great Lakes issues upon completion of their program.

Number awarded 1 each year.

Deadline February of each year.

[382]
PCI ENGINEERING STUDENT DESIGN "BIG BEAM" COMPETITION

Precast/Prestressed Concrete Institute
Attn: Director of Education
209 West Jackson Boulevard
Chicago, IL 60604-9773
(312) 786-0300   Fax: (312) 786-0353
E-mail: pjohal@pci.org
Web: www.pci.org

Purpose To recognize and reward engineering students who submit outstanding entries in a competition for precast concrete beams.

Eligibility This competition is open to students enrolled in a 2-year degree program, a 4- or 5-year bachelor's degree program, or a graduate degree program in any of the following areas: civil engineering (including all sub-disciplines) or technology; construction engineering or technology; architecture, architectural engineering, or technology; or building sciences or technology. Students enter as teams, preferably of 3 or 4 members, although any size is acceptable; graduate and undergraduate students and/or students from different degree programs within a university or college may be on the same team. Each team must work with a producer member of the Precast/Prestressed Concrete Institute (PCI) to build a precast concrete beam, no more than 16 feet long. Points are awarded in 7 categories (design accuracy, lowest cost, lowest weight, largest measured deflection before failure, most accurate prediction of cracking load and deflection at maximum load, report quality, and practicality/innovation). Prizes are awarded to teams with the highest scores. The open division accepts entries that do not conform to the traditional standards but utilize innovative and original designs.

Financial data Up to $25,000 in prizes is awarded each year.

Duration The competition is held annually.

Number awarded Prizes are awarded to individual zone winners and overall winners from 7 zones and to the winners in the open division.

Deadline March of each year.

[383]
PEGGY DIXON TWO-YEAR COLLEGE SCHOLARSHIP

Society of Physics Students
c/o American Institute of Physics
One Physics Ellipse
College Park, MD 20740-3843
(301) 209-3007   Fax: (301) 209-0839
E-mail: sps@aip.org
Web: www.spsnational.org/programs/two_year.htm

Purpose To provide financial assistance to members of the Society of Physics Students (SPS) who are transitioning from a 2-year college into a physics bachelor's degree program.

Eligibility This program is open to students at 2-year colleges who are entering a bachelor's degree program in physics. Applicants must have completed at least 1 semester or quarter of the introductory physics sequence and be currently enrolled in the appropriate subsequent physics courses. They must be members of the society. Selection is based on 1) high scholarship performance both in physics and overall studies, 2) potential for continued scholastic development in physics, and 3) active participation in society programs; those 3 criteria are given equal weight.

Financial data The stipend is $2,000.

Duration 1 year.

Additional information This program is sponsored by the Sigma Pi Sigma Trust Fund and the American Institute of Physics.

Number awarded 1 each year.

Deadline February of each year.

SCIENCES

[384]
PEI SCHOLARSHIP

National Society of Professional Engineers
Attn: Practice Division Manager
1420 King Street
Alexandria, VA 22314-2794
(703) 684-2884   Fax: (703) 836-4875
E-mail: egarcia@nspe.org
Web: www.nspe.org/scholarships/sc1-pei.asp

Purpose To provide financial assistance to engineering students sponsored by a member of the Professional Engineers in Industry (PEI) division of the National Society of Professional Engineers (NSPE).
Eligibility This program is open to undergraduate and graduate students who have completed at least 2 semesters or 3 quarters of undergraduate engineering studies (or are enrolled in a graduate program) with a GPA of 2.5 or higher. Applicants must be sponsored by a PEI member. Their program must be accredited by the Accreditation Board for Engineering and Technology (ABET). Preference is given to the children and grandchildren of PEI members. Students attending a community or junior college must have applied as an undergraduate engineering student at an ABET-accredited program. Along with their application, they must submit a 500-word essay discussing their interest in engineering, the specific field of engineering that is being pursued, and the occupation they propose to follow after graduation. Selection is based on work experience (25 points), professional and technical society membership and activities (25 points), the essay (25 points), and activities and honors (25 points).
Financial data The stipend is $2,500.
Duration 1 year.
Number awarded 1 or more each year.
Deadline March of each year.

[385]
PETER K. NEW STUDENT PRIZE COMPETITION

Society for Applied Anthropology
P.O. Box 2436
Oklahoma City, OK 73101-2436
(405) 843-5113   Fax: (405) 843-8553
E-mail: info@sfaa.net
Web: www.sfaa.net/pknew/pknew.html

Purpose To recognize and reward the best student research papers in applied social, health, or behavioral sciences.
Eligibility This competition is open to currently-enrolled undergraduate and graduate students in the applied social, health, and behavioral sciences. Applicants must not have already earned a doctoral degree (e.g., a person with an M.D. degree who is now registered as a student in a Ph.D. program is not eligible). Eligible students are invited to submit a manuscript that reports on research which, in large measure, has not been previously published. Research should be in the domain of health care or human services (broadly defined). The competition is limited to manuscripts that have a single author; multiple-authored papers are not eligible. The paper should be double spaced and must be less than 45 pages in length, including footnotes, tables, and appendices. Selection is based on originality, research design/method, clarity of analysis and presentation, and contribution to the social or behavioral sciences.
Financial data The winner receives $1,000 plus a $350 travel allowance to partially offset the cost of transportation and lodging at the society's annual meeting.
Duration The competition is held annually.
Additional information The winning paper is published in the society's journal, *Human Organization*. Applicants who transmit their manuscripts by fax must pay a fee for duplication. Manuscripts may not be submitted electronically. The winner must attend the society's annual meeting to present the paper.
Number awarded 2 each year.
Deadline December of each year.

[386]
PETROLEUM DIVISION COLLEGE SCHOLARSHIPS

International Petroleum Technology Institute
Attn: Student Scholarship Program
11757 Katy Freeway, Suite 865
Houston, TX 77079
(281) 493-3491   Fax: (281) 493-3493
E-mail: monesm@asme.org
Web: www.asme-ipti.org

Purpose To provide financial assistance to college students majoring in engineering fields related to the petroleum industry.
Eligibility This program is open to students at an ABET-accredited college or university (or international equivalent) who have completed at least 1 semester in an engineering program but still have at least 1 semester of undergraduate work remaining before graduation. Applicants must be ASME International student members with a GPA of 2.5 or higher. Along with their application, they must submit a 1-page essay that indicates their interest in the petroleum industry, including drilling, completions, facilities, pipelines, rigs, operations, materials, equipment manufacturing, plant design and operation, maintenance, environmental protection, and innovations. Financial need is not considered in the selection process.
Financial data The stipend is $2,000.
Duration 1 year.
Additional information The International Petroleum Technology Institute was formerly the Petroleum Division of ASME International (the professional society of mechanical engineers).
Number awarded 5 each year.
Deadline April of each year.

[387]
PFIZER HATTON AWARDS COMPETITION
American Association for Dental Research
Attn: Awards, Grants and Fellowships Administrator
1619 Duke Street
Alexandria, VA 22314-3406
(703) 299-8094   Fax: (703) 548-1883
E-mail: sherren@iadr.com
Web: www.iadr.com/awards/pfizerhatton.html

Purpose To recognize and reward outstanding dental research papers.

Eligibility This competition is open to 3 categories of investigators who exhibit potential for a productive career in dental research: 1) junior, for candidates who carried out their research as an undergraduate science student, a dental student, or while working on an intercalated science degree in training as a dental student; 2) senior, for candidates who have carried out research as part of master's, Ph.D., or M.D. program with previous laboratory experience or as part of specialty training; and 3) postdoctoral, for candidates whose research was performed within 3 years of completion of a Ph.D. Applicants must be U.S. citizens, permanent residents, or persons of other nationalities whose research is performed in the United States; they may be of any age. They are invited to submit preliminary abstracts of entries to be presented as posters at the annual meeting of the American Association for Dental Research (AADR). Based on those preliminary abstracts, 27 candidates are invited to submit extended abstracts. Selection is based on the extended abstract (20%), 5-minute verbal presentation of the poster (40%), and a 7-minute question and answer period (40%).

Financial data Each first-place winner receives $1,000 and each second-place winner receives $500.

Duration The competition is held annually.

Additional information This competition is sponsored by Pfizer Consumer Healthcare. The most outstanding presentations are invited to compete with other worldwide divisional winners at the annual meeting of the International Association for Dental Research in the IADR/Unilever Hatton Awards Competition.

Number awarded 6 entrants (a first-place and second-place winner in each category) receive prizes. Those 6, plus 3 others, are selected to advance to the IADR competition.

Deadline Preliminary abstracts must be submitted by September of each year.

[388]
PHCC EDUCATIONAL FOUNDATION SCHOLARSHIP PROGRAM
Plumbing-Heating-Cooling Contractors-National Association
Attn: PHCC Educational Foundation
180 South Washington Street
P.O. Box 6808
Falls Church, VA 22040
(703) 237-8100   Toll-free: (800) 533-7694
Fax: (703) 237-7442
E-mail: scholarships@naphcc.org
Web: www.foundation.phccweb.org

Purpose To provide financial assistance to undergraduate students interested in the plumbing, heating, and cooling industry.

Eligibility This program is open to 1) full-time undergraduate students (entering or continuing) who are majoring in a field related to plumbing, heating, and cooling (e.g., business management, construction management with a specialization in mechanical construction, mechanical engineering) at a 4-year college or university, and 2) students enrolled in an approved apprenticeship program or a full-time certificate or degree program at a 2-year technical college, community college, or trade school in business management, mechanical CAD design, construction management with a specialty in mechanical construction, or plumbing or HVACR installation, service, and repair. Students enrolled in an approved plumbing or HVAC apprenticeship program must be working full time for a licensed plumbing or HVAC contractor who is a member of the Plumbing-Heating-Cooling Contractors-National Association (PHCC). Applicants must submit a letter of recommendation from a member with 2 years' good standing in the PHCC; a copy of school transcripts; and a letter of recommendation from a school principal, counselor, or dean. U.S. or Canadian citizenship is required. Financial need is not considered in the selection process.

Financial data The stipend is $3,000 per year for students at a 4-year institution or $1,500 per year for students at a 2-year institution.

Duration Up to 4 years for students at a 4-year college or university or 2 years for students at a 2-year technical college, community college, or trade school.

Number awarded 5 each year: 3 to students at 4-year institutions and 2 to students at 2-year institutions.

Deadline April of each year.

[389]
PHILLIP M. FIELDS SCHOLARSHIP
South Carolina Aquatic Plant Management Society
c/o Steve deKozlowski
South Carolina Department of Natural Resources
P.O. Box 167
Columbia, SC 29201
(803) 734-9100   E-mail: dekozlowskis@dnr.sc.gov
Web: www.scapms.org/scapmsscholarshp.htm

Purpose To provide funding for study or research to undergraduate and graduate students interested in the biology, ecology, or management of aquatic plants in the Southeast.

Eligibility This program is open to full-time undergraduate and graduate students at accredited colleges and universities in the United States. Preference is given to students at southeastern and South Carolina academic institutions. Applicants must be involved in course work or research related to the biology, ecology, or management of aquatic plants in the Southeast. Selection is based on relevant test scores (ACT, SAT, GRE, etc.), high school and/or college grades, quality and relevance of course work or research, a proposed budget, information obtained from references, and other related considerations.

Financial data The grant is $3,000. Funds may be used by the recipient to cover costs associated with education and research expenses.

Duration 1 year.

Additional information The recipient may be requested to present an oral report on research activities at the annual meeting of the sponsoring organization.

Number awarded 1 each year.

Deadline April of each year.

[390]
PHOENIX CHAPTER 67 SCHOLARSHIPS

Society of Manufacturing Engineers
Attn: SME Education Foundation
One SME Drive
P.O. Box 930
Dearborn, MI 48121-0930
(313) 425-3300   Toll-free: (800) 733-4763, ext. 3300
Fax: (313) 425-3411   E-mail: foundation@sme.org
Web: www.sme.org

Purpose To provide financial assistance to students enrolled or planning to enroll in a degree program in manufacturing or industrial technology in Arizona.

Eligibility This program is open to graduating high school seniors and current full-time undergraduate students enrolled or planning to enrolled at an accredited college or university in Arizona. Applicants must be majoring in manufacturing engineering technology, manufacturing technology, industrial technology, or a closely-related field. They must have a GPA of 2.5 or higher. Along with their application, they must submit a 300-word essay that covers their career and educational objectives, how this scholarship will help them attain those objectives, and why they want to enter this field. Financial need is not considered in the selection process.

Financial data The stipend is $2,000.

Duration 1 year; may be renewed if the recipient maintains a GPA of 2.5 or higher.

Additional information This program is supported by Chapter 67 of the Society of Manufacturing Engineers.

Number awarded 2 each year: 1 to a high school senior and 1 to an undergraduate.

Deadline January of each year.

[391]
PIERRE H. GUILLEMETTE SCHOLARSHIP

Rhode Island Society of Professional Land Surveyors
Attn: Scholarship Committee
280 Drybridge Road
North Kingstown, RI 02852-5207
(401) 294-1262   E-mail: info@rispls.org
Web: www.rispls.org

Purpose To provide financial assistance to Rhode Island residents studying surveying.

Eligibility This program is open to residents of Rhode Island who are enrolled in a course of study leading to a certificate program or degree in land surveying offered by a qualified institution of higher learning. Applicants must submit brief essays on 1) any special skills or qualifications they have acquired from employment, previous volunteer work, or through other activities, including hobbies or sports; and 2) their previous surveying experience. Financial need is not considered in the selection process.

Financial data The amount of the award depends on the availability of funds.

Duration 1 year.

Number awarded 1 or more each year.

Deadline October of each year.

[392]
PIONEERS OF FLIGHT SCHOLARSHIP PROGRAM

National Air Transportation Foundation
Attn: Manager, Education and Training
4226 King Street
Alexandria, VA 22302
(703) 845-9000, ext. 125   Toll-free: (800) 808-6282
Fax: (703) 845-8176   E-mail: dhighsmith@nata.aero
Web: www.nata.aero/about/sch_pioneersofflight.jsp

Purpose To provide financial assistance for college to students planning careers in general aviation.

Eligibility This program is open to students intending to enroll full time at an accredited 4-year college or university as juniors or seniors. Applicants must demonstrate an interest in a career in general aviation (not the major commercial airlines) and have a GPA of 3.0 or higher. Along with their application, they must submit a 250-word essay on their goals in general aviation. Selection is based on that essay, academic record, and letter of recommendation.

Financial data The stipend is $1,000.

Duration 1 year; may be renewed 1 additional year if the recipient maintains a 3.0 GPA and full-time enrollment.

Additional information This program, established in 1989, is administered by the University Aviation Association (UAA), which selects the semifinalists. The National Air Transportation Foundation selects the final winners. Further information is available from the UAA, c/o Gregory Schwab, Indiana State University, Department of Aerospace Technology, TC 216, Terre Haute, IN 47809. A $5 application fee is required.

Number awarded 2 each year.

Deadline December of each year.

[393]
PLASTICS PIONEERS ASSOCIATION SCHOLARSHIPS

Plastics Institute of America
c/o University of Massachusetts at Lowell
Attn: Plastics Pioneers Association
333 Aiken Street
Lowell, MA 01854
(978) 934-3130 Fax: (978) 458-4141
E-mail: info@plasticsinstitute.org
Web: www.plasticsinstitute.org/scholarships.php

Purpose To provide financial assistance to college students taking courses related to plastics technology.

Eligibility This program is open to students enrolled in a 2-year, 4-year, or certificate program. Applicants must be studying plastics/polymer science, engineering, technology, and management. They must be U.S. citizens and interested in preparing for a career in the plastics industry. Selection is based on academic record, extracurricular activities, recommendations, and an essay on their interest in a career in plastics.

Financial data The stipend is $1,500 per year.

Duration 1 year; may be renewed for 1 additional year.

Additional information This program is funded by the Education Fund of the Plastics Pioneers Association and administered by the Plastics Institute of America.

Number awarded Varies each year; recently, 15 of these scholarships were awarded.

Deadline March of each year.

[394]
POWDER RIVER BASIN SECTION ANNUAL SCHOLARSHIP AWARDS

Society of Petroleum Engineers-Powder River Basin Section
P.O. Box 3977
Gillette, WY 82717-3977

Purpose To provide financial assistance to Wyoming students interested in preparing for a career in the oil and gas industry.

Eligibility This program is open to Wyoming students preparing for a career in the oil and gas industry. Applicants should be majoring in engineering (especially petroleum engineering and petroleum technology), although some of the scholarships may go to non-engineering students. They must be enrolled full time as entering freshmen, sophomores, juniors, or seniors in a 4-year program or freshmen or sophomores in a 2-year program and have a GPA of 2.75 or higher. Along with their application, they must submit a letter that covers their academic qualifications, primary career interests, extracurricular activities, and names of 2 references. Financial need is not considered in the selection process.

Financial data Stipends range from $250 to $1,000.

Duration 1 year.

Additional information Information is also available from Bob Christofferson, Citation Oil and Gas Corporation, 1016 East Lincoln, Gillette, WY 82716, (307) 682-4853.

Number awarded 5 to 15 each year.

Deadline March of each year.

[395]
POWER ENGINEERING SOCIETY STUDENT PRIZE PAPER AWARD IN HONOR OF T. BURKE HAYES

Institute of Electrical and Electronics Engineers
Attn: Power Engineering Society
445 Hoes Lane
P.O. Box 1331
Piscataway, NJ 08855-1331
(732) 562-3883 Fax: (732) 562-3881
E-mail: pes@ieee.org
Web: www.ieee.org/organizations/society/power

Purpose To recognize and reward outstanding papers on power engineering by student members of the Institute of Electrical and Electronics Engineers (IEEE).

Eligibility This program is open to student members in a program leading to a bachelor's or master's degree in electrical engineering, or the equivalent if the student is from an institution outside the United States. Applicants must submit a paper of approximately 5,000 words on a topic related to the electric power industry. Faculty sponsorship is encouraged, but papers co-authored by faculty are not eligible. Along with the paper, students must submit a supporting letter from their faculty sponsor, a short autobiographical sketch, and a permanent address and telephone number.

Financial data The award is $1,500, a plaque, and a travel subsidy up to $1,000 for the recipient to attend the winter meeting of the Power Engineering Society.

Duration The competition is held annually.

Additional information This award, first presented in 1967, is funded by CH2M Hill. Information is also available from Karen L. Butler-Purry, PES Awards and Recognition Chair, 3204 Liesl Court, College Station, TX 77845, (979) 847-9048, Fax: (979) 845-6259, E-mail: klbutler@ece.tamu.edu.

Number awarded 1 each year.

Deadline September of each year.

[396]
POWER SYSTEMS PROFESSIONAL SCHOLARSHIP

National Strength and Conditioning Association
Attn: Grants and Scholarships
1885 Bob Johnson Drive
Colorado Springs, CO 80906
(719) 632-6722, ext. 105 Toll-free: (800) 815-6826
Fax: (719) 632-6367 E-mail: nsca@nsca-lift.org
Web: www.nsca-lift.org/Foundation

Purpose To provide financial assistance for undergraduate or graduate study in strength training and conditioning to members of the National Strength and Conditioning Association (NSCA).

Eligibility This program is open to undergraduate and graduate students working as a strength and conditioning coach (student assistant, volunteer, or graduate assistant) in their school's athletic department. Applicants must have been members of the association for at least 1 year. They must be nominated by the head strength coach at their school. Along with their application, they must submit an essay of no more than 500 words explaining their career goals and objectives. Selection is based on scholarship (25 points), strength and conditioning experience (15 points), the essay (15 points), recommendations (5 points), honors and awards (10 points), community involvement (10 points), and NSCA involvement (20 points).

Financial data The stipend is $1,000, to be applied toward tuition.

Additional information The NSCA is a nonprofit organization of strength and conditioning professionals, including coaches, athletic trainers, physical therapists, educators, researchers, and physicians. This program is funded in part by Power Systems, Inc.

Number awarded 1 each year.

Deadline March of each year.

[397]
PRAXAIR INTERNATIONAL SCHOLARSHIP

American Welding Society
Attn: AWS Foundation, Inc.
550 N.W. LeJeune Road
Miami, FL 33126
(305) 445-6628   Toll-free: (800) 443-9353, ext. 461
Fax: (305) 443-7559   E-mail: found@aws.org
Web: www.aws.org

Purpose To provide financial assistance to college students majoring in welding engineering.

Eligibility This program is open to undergraduate students who are working on a 4-year bachelor's degree in welding engineering or welding engineering technology; preference is given to welding engineering students. Applicants must be full-time students with an overall GPA of 2.5 or higher. They must be U.S. or Canadian citizens attending an academic institution within the United States or Canada. Selection is based on demonstrated leadership abilities in clubs and organizations, extracurricular and academic activities, and community involvement; financial need is not required.

Financial data The stipend is $2,500.

Duration 1 year; recipients may reapply.

Additional information This program is supported by Praxair, Inc.

Number awarded 1 each year.

Deadline January of each year.

[398]
PRESSMAN SCHOLARSHIP

Society of Women Engineers
230 East Ohio Street, Suite 400
Chicago, IL 60611-3265
(312) 596-5223   Toll-free: (877) SWE-INFO
Fax: (312) 644-8557
E-mail: scholarshipapplication@swe.org
Web: www.swe.org/scholarships

Purpose To provide financial assistance to women working on an undergraduate or graduate degree in engineering or computer science.

Eligibility This program is open to women who will be sophomores, juniors, seniors, or graduate students at ABET-accredited colleges and universities. Applicants must be majoring in computer science or engineering and have a GPA of 3.0 or higher. Along with their application, they must submit a 1-page essay on why they want to be an engineer or computer scientist, how they believe they will make a difference as an engineer or computer scientist, and what influenced them to study engineering or computer science. U.S. citizenship is required. Selection is based on merit.

Financial data The stipend is $5,000.

Duration 1 year.

Number awarded 1 each year.

Deadline January of each year.

[399]
PRESSURE VESSELS AND PIPING DIVISION STUDENT PAPER COMPETITION

ASME International
Attn: Pressure Vessels and Piping Division
Three Park Avenue
New York, NY 10016-5990
(212) 591-7863   Toll-free: (800) THE-ASME
Fax: (212) 591-7671   E-mail: ulvilar@asme.org
Web: divisions.asme.org

Purpose To recognize and reward outstanding student papers on pressure vessels and piping.

Eligibility This competition is open to senior undergraduate and graduate students in an engineering or scientific curriculum. Applicants submit previously unpublished papers that present new knowledge or experience in a field related to pressure vessels and piping. The paper must be technically correct and should be of interest to a reasonable number of people working in the field. It may be theoretical or may present the results of laboratory studies, and it may state or analyze a problem. The paper may also be a review-type paper, but it must be of significant value to the technical field. Applicants first submit abstracts; based on those abstracts, finalists are invited to present papers at the annual Pressure Vessels and Piping Conference, where the winning papers are selected on the basis of written technical content (70%) and presentation effectiveness (30%).

Financial data Each finalist receives $600 and a certificate. The authors of the winning papers receive an additional $500.

Duration The competition is held annually.

Number awarded 10 finalists are selected each year. Of those, 2 (1 undergraduate and 1 graduate student) are chosen as the winners.

Deadline Abstracts must be submitted by the end of October of each year.

[400]
PSSC LEGACY FUND SCHOLARSHIP
Society of Satellite Professionals International
Attn: Scholarship Program
New York Information Technology Center
55 Broad Street, 14th Floor
New York, NY 10004
(212) 809-5199   Fax: (212) 825-0075
E-mail: sspi@sspi.org
Web: www.sspi.org

Purpose To provide financial assistance to student members of the Society of Satellite Professionals International (SSPI) who are interested in working on an undergraduate or graduate degree in international satellite applications and/or distance education.

Eligibility This program is open to SSPI members who are high school seniors, college undergraduates, or graduate students interested in preparing for a career in satellite technologies, policies, or applications. Applicants must be interested in majoring in international satellite applications and/or distance education. They may be from any country. Selection is based on academic and leadership achievement; commitment to pursue educational and career opportunities in the satellite industry or a field making direct use of satellite technology; potential for significant contribution to that industry; and a scientific, engineering, research, business or creative submission. Financial need is not considered.

Financial data The stipend is $2,500.
Duration 1 year.
Number awarded 1 each year.
Deadline Preliminary applications must be submitted by February of each year.

[401]
QUALITY ASSURANCE DIVISION SCHOLARSHIPS
Institute of Food Technologists
Attn: Scholarship Department
525 West Van Buren, Suite 1000
Chicago, IL 60607
(312) 782-8424   Fax: (312) 782-8348
E-mail: info@ift.org
Web: www.ift.org

Purpose To provide financial assistance to undergraduates interested in studying food science or food technology.

Eligibility This program is open to sophomores, juniors, and seniors in a food science or food technology program at an educational institution in the United States or Canada. Applicants must have an outstanding scholastic record and a well-rounded personality. Along with their application, they must submit an essay on their career aspirations; a list of awards, honors, and scholarships they have received; a list of extracurricular activities and/or hobbies; and a summary of their work experience. Preference is given to students who are taking or have taken at least 1 course in quality assurance and who demonstrate a definite interest in the quality assurance area. Financial need is not considered in the selection process.

Financial data The stipend is $2,000.
Duration 1 year; recipients may reapply if they are members of the Institute of Food Technologists (IFT).
Additional information These scholarships are designated as the Abe Mittler Memorial Scholarship and the Louis J. Bianco Memorial Scholarship. Correspondence and completed applications must be submitted to the department head of the educational institution the applicant is attending.
Number awarded 2 each year.
Deadline January of each year.

[402]
RALPH A. KLUCKEN SCHOLARSHIP
Technical Association of the Pulp and Paper Industry
Attn: TAPPI Foundation
15 Technology Parkway South
Norcross, GA 30092
(770) 209-7536   Toll-free: (800) 332-8686
Fax: (770) 446-6947   E-mail: vedmondson@tappi.org
Web: www.tappi.org

Purpose To provide financial assistance for college or graduate school to students who are interested in preparing for a career in the pulp and paper industry.

Eligibility This program is open to high school seniors, undergraduates, and graduate students who are either enrolled full time or working full time and attending night school as a part-time student. Applicants must be able to demonstrate responsibility and maturity through a history of part-time and summer employment; an interest in the technological areas covered by the Polymers, Laminations, Adhesives, Coatings and Extrusions (PLACE) Division of the Technical Association of the Pulp and Paper Industry (TAPPI); and a GPA of 3.0 or higher. Selection is based on the candidates' potential career contributions to the pulp and paper industry; financial need is not considered.

Financial data The stipend is $1,000.
Duration 1 year. A student may apply for the scholarship each year, but the award will not be given to the same person twice consecutively.
Additional information This program, established in 1987, is sponsored by the PLACE Division.
Number awarded 1 each year.
Deadline May of each year.

[403]
RALPH K. HILLQUIST HONORARY SAE SCHOLARSHIP
Society of Automotive Engineers
Attn: Scholarship Administrator
400 Commonwealth Drive
Warrendale, PA 15096-0001
(724) 772-4047   Fax: (724) 776-3049
E-mail: scholarships@sae.org
Web: students.sae.org

Purpose To provide financial assistance to college juniors who are majoring in mechanical or automotive engineering.

Eligibility This program is open to juniors enrolled full time at U.S. universities. Applicants must have a declared major in mechanical engineering or an automotive-related engineering discipline, with preference given to those who have completed studies or courses in the areas of expertise related to noise and vibration (e.g., statics, dynamics, physics, vibration). They must be U.S. citizens with a GPA of 3.0 or higher and significant academic and leadership achievements. along with their application, they must submit a 300-word essay on the single experience that most strongly convinced them or confirmed their decision to prepare for a career in engineering. Financial need is not considered in the selection process.

Financial data The stipend is $1,000.
Duration 1 year; nonrenewable.
Additional information This scholarship, first awarded in 2005, is funded by the Noise & Vibration Conference of the Society of Automotive Engineers (SAE).
Number awarded 1 each odd-numbered year.
Deadline January of each odd-numbered year.

[404]
RALPH W. BAIRD SCHOLARSHIP

Society of Exploration Geophysicists
Attn: SEG Foundation
8801 South Yale, Suite 500
P.O. Box 702740
Tulsa, OK 74170-2740
(918) 497-5513   Fax: (918) 497-5557
E-mail: scholarships@seg.org
Web: seg.org

Purpose To provide financial assistance to upper-division students working on a degree in geophysical engineering.
Eligibility This program is open to juniors and seniors working on a degree in geophysical engineering. Along with their application, they must submit a 150-word essay on how they plan to use geophysics in their future. Financial need is not considered in the selection process.
Financial data Stipends range from $1,000 to $3,000 per year.
Duration 1 academic year.
Number awarded 1 each year.
Deadline January of each year.

[405]
RANDALL MATHIS SCHOLARSHIP FOR ENVIRONMENTAL STUDIES

Arkansas Environmental Federation
Attn: Scholarship Program
1400 West Markham, Suite 250
Little Rock, AR 72201
(501) 374-0263   Fax: (501) 374-8752
E-mail: joliver@environmentark.org
Web: www.environmentark.org/randallmathis.htm

Purpose To provide financial assistance to residents of Arkansas working on an undergraduate or graduate degree in environmental studies at a college or university in the state.
Eligibility This program is open to Arkansas residents who have completed at least 40 credit hours as a full-time undergraduate or graduate student at a college or university in the state. Applicants must be majoring in a field related to environmental studies, including agriculture with an environmental emphasis, chemical engineering with an environmental emphasis, civil engineering with an environmental emphasis, environmental engineering, environmental health science, fisheries and wildlife biology, forestry, geology, or wildlife management. They must have a GPA of 2.8 or higher. Along with their application, they must submit an essay of 1 to 3 pages explaining their professional career goals relating to the fields of environmental health and safety. U.S. citizenship is required. Financial need is not considered in the selection process.

Financial data The stipend is $2,500.
Duration 1 year.
Number awarded 1 each year.
Deadline January of each year.

[406]
REDI-TAG CORPORATION SCHOLARSHIP

American Health Information Management Association
Attn: Foundation of Research and Education
233 North Michigan Avenue, Suite 2150
Chicago, IL 60601-5806
(312) 233-1131   Fax: (312) 233-1431
E-mail: fore@ahima.org
Web: www.ahima.org/fore/student/programs.asp

Purpose To provide financial assistance to members of the American Health Information Management Association (AHIMA) who are single parents interested in working on an undergraduate or graduate degree in health information administration or technology.
Eligibility This program is open to AHIMA members who are single parents enrolled in a health information administration or health information technology program accredited by the Commission on Accreditation of Allied Health Education Programs. Applicants must be working on an undergraduate or graduate degree on at least a half-time basis and have a GPA of 3.0 or higher. U.S. citizenship is required. Selection is based (in order of importance) on GPA and academic achievement, volunteer and work experience, commitment to the health information management profession, suitability to the health information management profession, quality and suitability of references provided, and clarity of application.

Financial data The stipend ranges from $1,000 to $5,000.
Duration 1 year; nonrenewable.
Additional information Funding for this program is provided by the Redi-Tag Corporation.
Number awarded 1 each year.
Deadline April of each year.

[407]
RESISTANCE WELDER MANUFACTURERS' ASSOCIATION SCHOLARSHIP

American Welding Society
Attn: AWS Foundation, Inc.
550 N.W. LeJeune Road
Miami, FL 33126
(305) 445-6628   Toll-free: (800) 443-9353, ext. 461
Fax: (305) 443-7559   E-mail: found@aws.org
Web: www.aws.org

Purpose To provide financial assistance to college juniors majoring in welding engineering.

Eligibility This program is open to juniors who are working on a degree in welding engineering or welding engineering technology. Applicants must show an interest in the resistance welding process. They must have a GPA of 3.0 or higher overall. Along with their application, they must submit a 500-word essay on why they wish to become involved in the resistance welding industry. Financial need is not considered. U.S. or Canadian citizenship is required.

Financial data The stipend is $2,500.

Duration 1 year; nonrenewable.

Additional information This program was established in 2005 upon the dissolution of the Resistance Welder Manufacturers' Association.

Number awarded 1 each year.

Deadline September of each year.

[408]
REUBEN R. COWLES YOUTH AWARD

American Jersey Cattle Association
Attn: Dr. Cherie L. Bayer
6486 East Main Street
Reynoldsburg, OH 43068-2362
(614) 861-3636 Fax: (614) 861-8040
E-mail: cbayer@usjersey.com
Web: www.usjersey.com

Purpose To provide financial assistance for college to residents of selected southeastern states who have worked with Jersey cattle.

Eligibility This program is open to residents of Florida, Georgia, North Carolina, South Carolina, Tennessee, and Virginia who have significant and extensive experience in breeding, managing, and showing Jersey cattle. Applicants must be at least seniors in high school and not older than 36 years of age. Along with their application, they must describe their activities with Jersey cattle; summarize their extracurricular activities during high school and/or college; and describe their background, ambitions, and goals. They must have a GPA of 2.5 or higher. Financial need is not considered in the selection process.

Financial data The stipend is approximately $1,000.

Duration 1 year.

Number awarded 1 each year.

Deadline June of each year.

[409]
RICHARD A. HERBERT MEMORIAL UNDERGRADUATE SCHOLARSHIP

American Water Resources Association
Attn: Scholarship Coordinator
4 West Federal Street
P.O. Box 1626
Middleburg, VA 20118-1626
(540) 687-8390 Fax: (540) 687-8395
E-mail: info@awra.org
Web: www.awra.org/student/herbert.pdf

Purpose To provide financial assistance to undergraduate students enrolled in a program related to water resources.

Eligibility This program is open to full-time undergraduate students enrolled in a program related to water resources. Applicants must submit a 2-page summary of their academic interests and achievements, extracurricular activities, and career goals. Selection is based on that statement, cumulative GPA, relevance of the student's curriculum to water resources, and leadership in extracurricular activities related to water resources.

Financial data The stipend is $2,000.

Duration 1 year.

Additional information This program was established in 1980.

Number awarded 1 each year.

Deadline April of each year.

[410]
RICHARD E. MERWIN STUDENT SCHOLARSHIP

IEEE Computer Society
Attn: Student Awards
1730 Massachusetts Avenue, N.W.
Washington, DC 20036-1992
(202) 371-1013 Fax: (202) 778-0884
E-mail: hqofc@computer.org
Web: www.computer.org/students/schlrshp.htm

Purpose To recognize and reward students who are active leaders in the IEEE Computer Society student branch chapters.

Eligibility Juniors, seniors, and graduate students in electrical engineering, computer engineering, computer science, or a well-defined computer-related field of engineering (e.g., biomedical computer engineering, design automation) are eligible to apply if they are full-time students and active members of the society's student branch chapter at their institution. Applicants must have a cumulative GPA of 2.5 or higher. Selection is based on involvement in chapter activities (40%), academic achievement (30%), other extracurricular activities in college (10%), and a letter of evaluation by the branch chapter advisor (20%).

Financial data The stipend is $4,000, paid in 4 equal installments.

Duration 1 academic year.

Additional information A brief statement outlining accomplishments must be submitted by each recipient at the end of the academic year.

Number awarded Up to 10 each year.

Deadline May of each year.

[411]
RICHARD P. COVERT, PH.D., FHIMSS SCHOLARSHIP

Healthcare Information and Management Systems Society
Attn: HIMSS Foundation Scholarship Program Coordinator
230 East Ohio Street, Suite 500
Chicago, IL 60611-3270
(312) 664-HIMSS Fax: (312) 664-6143
E-mail: foundation@himss.org
Web: www.himss.org/ASP/scholarship_ms.asp

Purpose To provide financial assistance to student members of the Healthcare Information and Management Systems Society (HIMSS) who are working on an undergraduate or graduate degree in management engineering.

Eligibility This program is open to student members of the society, although an application for membership, including dues, may accompany the scholarship application. Applicants must be upper-division or graduate students working on a degree in management engineering. Selection is based on academic achievement and demonstration of leadership potential, including communication skills and participation in society activity.

Financial data The stipend is $5,000. The award includes an all-expense paid trip to the annual HIMSS conference and exhibition.

Duration 1 year.

Additional information This program was established in 2004.

Number awarded 1 each year.

Deadline October of each year.

[412]
RITA LOWE COLLEGE SCHOLARSHIPS

Washington State Mathematics Council
c/o Pat Reistroffer, Scholarship Chair
146 Scenic View Drive
Longview, WA 98632
(360) 636-5125 E-mail: preistrof@aol.com
Web: www.wsmc.net/ritalowe

Purpose To provide financial assistance to students majoring in mathematics education at colleges and universities in Washington.

Eligibility This program is open to students currently attending a college or university in Washington and majoring in mathematics education. Applicants must be preparing for teaching certification in order to become a professional educator teaching mathematics at the elementary or secondary level. They must submit a transcript (from the ninth grade to the date of application), a 300-word statement on their experience with and interest in mathematics, and 2 letters of recommendation. Selection is based on academic achievement, demonstrated intent to become a mathematics educator, character, academic potential, and leadership potential.

Financial data The stipend is $1,000 per year.

Duration 1 year.

Number awarded 2 each year.

Deadline April of each year.

[413]
RMEL FOUNDATION SCHOLARSHIPS

Rocky Mountain Electrical League
Attn: RMEL Foundation
2170 South Parker Road, Suite 225
Denver, CO 80231
(303) 695-0089 Fax: (303) 695-0704
E-mail: edblum@rmel.org
Web: www.rmel.org

Purpose To provide financial assistance to students sponsored by a member of the Rocky Mountain Electrical League (RMEL) who wish to study selected fields in college in order to prepare for a career in the electric energy industry.

Eligibility This program is open to high school seniors, high school graduates, and college undergraduates who have an RMEL-member company as a sponsor. Applicants must be working on or planning to work on 1) an electric industry position certificate or associate degree, or 2) a full-time undergraduate degree. Their field of study must be engineering; business; information systems; plant, line, or distribution technology; line worker; or other program related to a career in the electric energy industry. U.S. citizenship is required. Selection is based on goals and aspirations in the electric energy industry, motivation to succeed, service to community and school, and academic ability.

Financial data The stipend is $1,000.

Duration 1 year.

Additional information The RMEL serves 17 states: Arizona, Colorado, Idaho, Iowa, Kansas, Minnesota, Missouri, Montana, Nebraska, Nevada, New Mexico, North Dakota, Oklahoma, South Dakota, Texas, Utah, and Wyoming.

Number awarded Varies each year; recently, 5 of these scholarships were awarded.

Deadline March of each year.

[414]
RN ADVANCING EDUCATION SCHOLARSHIP

Society of Gastroenterology Nurses and Associates, Inc.
Attn: Awards Committee
401 North Michigan Avenue
Chicago, IL 60611-4267
(312) 321-5165 Toll-free: (800) 245-SGNA
Fax: (312) 527-6658 E-mail: sgna@smithbucklin.com
Web: www.sgna.org/Education/scholarships.cfm

Purpose To provide financial assistance to registered nurses (R.N.s) working in gastroenterology who are interested in enrolling in an advanced degree program.

Eligibility This program is open to R.N.s working in gastroenterology who are members of the Society of Gastroenterology Nurses and Associates (SGNA). Applicants must be enrolled in an accredited advanced degree program working on a B.S.N., M.S.N., or Ph.D. degree with a GPA of 3.0 or higher. Along with their application, they must submit a 500-word essay on a challenging situation they see in the health care environment today and how they, as an R.N., would best address and meet that challenge. Financial need is not considered in the selection process.

Financial data The stipend is $2,500 for full-time students or $1,000 for part-time students. Funds are issued as reimbursement after the recipient has completed the proposed course work with a GPA of 3.0 or higher.

Duration 1 year.

Number awarded 1 or more each year.

Deadline July of each year.

[415]
ROBERT A. ELLIS SCHOLARSHIP IN PHYSICS
National Society of Black Physicists
Attn: Scholarship Committee Chair
6704G Lee Highway
Arlington, VA 22205
(703) 536-4207 Fax: (703) 536-4203
E-mail: scholarship@nsbp.org
Web: www.nsbp.org

Purpose To provide financial assistance to African American students majoring in physics in college.

Eligibility This program is open to African American students who are entering their junior or senior year of college and majoring in physics. Applicants must submit an essay on their academic and career objectives, information on their participation in extracurricular activities, a description of any awards and honors they have received, and 3 letters of recommendation. Financial need is not considered.

Financial data A stipend is awarded (amount not specified).

Duration 1 year; nonrenewable.

Number awarded 1 each year.

Deadline November of each year.

[416]
ROBERT B. OLIVER ASNT SCHOLARSHIPS
American Society for Nondestructive Testing, Inc.
Attn: Executive Assistant
1711 Arlingate Lane
P.O. Box 28518
Columbus, OH 43228-0518
(614) 274-6003 Toll-free: (800) 222-2768, ext. 223
Fax: (614) 274-6899 E-mail: sthomas@asnt.org
Web: www.asnt.org

Purpose To recognize and reward undergraduate students who submit outstanding papers in the field of nondestructive testing.

Eligibility This program is open to students who are enrolled in a program related to nondestructive testing that leads to an undergraduate degree, associate degree, or postsecondary certificate. The award is offered to students submitting the best original manuscript (up to 5,000 words) on the topic. The manuscript should develop an original concept and may be based on practical experience, laboratory work, or library research. Papers may be classroom assignments in courses outside the area of nondestructive testing, such as an English class. Applicants must be currently enrolled in school and should submit 4 copies of their paper, their curriculum, a transcript of grades, and a letter from a school official verifying the student's enrollment. Selection is based on creativity (10 points), content (50 points), format and readability (25 points), and the student's hands-on involvement in the project (15 points).

Financial data The award is $2,500.

Duration The award is presented annually.

Additional information Because the award may be made after the completion of studies, there is no requirement that the recipient use the funds for school expenses. Winning manuscripts may be published in the society's journal, *Materials Evaluation*.

Number awarded Up to 3 each year.

Deadline February of each year.

[417]
ROBERT D. GREENBERG SCHOLARSHIP
Society of Broadcast Engineers
Attn: Scholarship Committee
9102 North Meridian Street, Suite 150
Indianapolis, IN 46260
(317) 846-9000 Fax: (317) 846-9120
Web: www.sbe.org/edu_ennes_scholarships.php

Purpose To provide financial assistance for college to students interested in the technical aspects of broadcasting.

Eligibility Applicants must have a career interest in the technical aspects of broadcasting and must be recommended by 2 members of the Society of Broadcast Engineers (SBE). They must submit 1) a brief autobiography that includes their interest and goals in broadcasting, and 2) a summary of the technical changes they anticipate in broadcasting within the next 5 years. Preference is given to members of the SBE and to students currently employed at least part time in broadcast engineering. Both new students just entering college and students already enrolled in college may apply. Financial need is not considered in the selection process.

Financial data The stipend ranges from $1,000 to $3,000, depending on the availability of funds. Awards may be used for 1) tuition, room, board, or textbook costs at postsecondary educational institutions, or 2) other technical training programs approved by the sponsor.

Duration 1 year.

Number awarded 1 each year.

Deadline June of each year.

[418]
ROBERT E. PEARSON SCHOLARSHIP
American Society of Highway Engineers-Carolina Triangle Section
Attn: Scholarship Committee
801 Jones Franklin Road, Suite 300
Raleigh, NC 27606
(919) 851-6866 E-mail: scott.boyles@stantec.com
Web: www.carolinatriangle.org

Purpose To provide financial assistance to currently-enrolled college students from North Carolina who are majoring in a transportation-related field.

Eligibility This program is open to residents of North Carolina who are U.S. citizens currently enrolled full time in a 4-year college or university in any state (must have completed at least 1 semester) working on a bachelor's degree in a transportation-related field, preferably civil engineering. A copy of the applicant's college transcript is required; high school transcripts, SAT scores, and resumes may also be submitted but are not required. Along with their application, students must submit a paragraph on their career goals, including a description of the value they place on civil engineering or other transportation-related field. Selection is based on that essay (25 points), academic performance (40 points), activities, honors, work experience, leadership, and distinguishing qualifications (25 points), and enrollment in

a civil engineering curriculum (10 points). A personal interview may be requested. Financial need is not considered.
Financial data The stipend is $2,500.
Duration 1 year; nonrenewable.
Number awarded 1 each year.
Deadline March of each year.

[419]
ROBERT F. SAMMATARO PRESSURE VESSEL PIPING DIVISION SCHOLARSHIP

ASME International
Attn: Coordinator, Educational Operations
Three Park Avenue
New York, NY 10016-5990
(212) 591-8131   Toll-free: (800) THE-ASME
Fax: (212) 591-7143   E-mail: OluwanifiseK@asme.org
Web: www.asme.org

Purpose To provide financial assistance to undergraduate students who are members of the American Society of Mechanical Engineers (ASME).
Eligibility This program is open to student members in good standing who are enrolled in an ABET-accredited mechanical engineering, mechanical engineering technology, or related program. Applicants must be entering their sophomore, junior, or senior year. Along with their application, they must submit a nomination from their department head, a recommendation from a faculty member, and an official transcript. Only 1 nomination may be submitted per department. Selection is based on scholastic ability and demonstrated special interest in pressure vessels and piping.
Financial data The stipend is $1,000.
Duration 1 year.
Additional information This program was established in 2001.
Number awarded 1 each year.
Deadline March of each year.

[420]
ROBERT FELIX MEMORIAL SCHOLARSHIP

Tree Research and Education Endowment Fund
Attn: Executive Director
711 East Roosevelt Road
Wheaton, IL 60187
(630) 221-8127   Fax: (630) 690-0702
E-mail: treefund@treefund.org
Web: www.treefund.org/grants/Grants.aspx

Purpose To provide financial assistance to undergraduate and technical school students interested in preparing for a career in commercial arboriculture.
Eligibility This program is open to student members of the International Society of Arboriculture who are entering the second year of a 2-year program or the third or fourth year of a 4-year program. Applicants must be preparing for a career in commercial arboriculture. They must have a GPA of 3.0 or higher. Along with their application, they must submit a 1,000-word essay describing their reasons for pursuing their chosen career, their goals and objectives, and why they should be chosen for this scholarship. Financial need is not considered in the selection process.
Financial data The stipend is $3,000.
Duration 1 year.
Additional information The Tree Research and Education Endowment (TREE) Fund was established in 2002 as the result of a merger of the International Society of Arboriculture Research Trust (established in 1976) and the National Arborist Foundation (established in 1985). Fields of study often considered appropriate for a career in commercial arboriculture include agriculture, entomology, horticulture, landscape architecture, or soils science.
Number awarded 4 each year.
Deadline April of each year.

[421]
ROBERT J. DORAN SCHOLARSHIP

International Association of Arson Investigators
Attn: Educational Foundation
12772 Boenker Road
St. Louis, MO 63044
(314) 739-4224   Fax: (314) 739-4219
E-mail: jimwhitaker@firearson.com
Web: www.firearson.com/ef/jwscholar/index.asp

Purpose To provide financial assistance to the members and dependents or nominees of members of the International Association of Arson Investigators (IAAI) who are interested in preparing for a career in fire and arson investigation.
Eligibility This program is open to association members and their immediate families who are enrolled or planning to enroll at an accredited 2- or 4-year college or university that offers course work in fire science, law enforcement, or fire and arson investigation. Also eligible are nonmembers who are recommended and sponsored by association members in good standing. Applicants must submit transcripts and an essay of 500 words or less providing background information and their future plans in police or fire sciences. Financial need is not considered.
Financial data The stipend is $1,000.
Duration 1 year.
Additional information This scholarship was first awarded in 2006.
Number awarded 1 each year.
Deadline February of each year.

[422]
ROBERT L. PEASLEE-DETROIT BRAZING AND SOLDERING DIVISION SCHOLARSHIP

American Welding Society
Attn: AWS Foundation, Inc.
550 N.W. LeJeune Road
Miami, FL 33126
(305) 445-6628   Toll-free: (800) 443-9353, ext. 461
Fax: (305) 443-7559   E-mail: found@aws.org
Web: www.aws.org

Purpose To provide financial assistance to upper-division and graduate students majoring in welding engineering.
Eligibility This program is open to juniors, seniors, and graduate student who are working on a degree in welding engineering or welding engineering technology. Applicants must show an emphasis on brazing and soldering applica-

tions in their course work. They must have a GPA of 3.0 or higher in engineering courses. Financial need is not required. U.S. or Canadian citizenship is required.
Financial data The stipend is $2,500.
Duration 1 year; nonrenewable.
Additional information This program was established in 2004.
Number awarded 1 each year.
Deadline January of each year.

[423]
ROBERT M. LAWRENCE, MD EDUCATION RECOGNITION AWARD

American Association for Respiratory Care
Attn: American Respiratory Care Foundation
9425 North MacArthur Boulevard, Suite 100
Irving, TX 75063-4706
(972) 243-2272   Fax: (972) 484-2720
E-mail: info@arcfoundation.org
Web: www.arcfoundation.org

Purpose To provide financial assistance to upper-division students interested in becoming respiratory therapists.
Eligibility This program is open to students who have completed at least 2 years in an accredited respiratory care bachelor's degree program. Applicants must be U.S. citizens with a GPA of 3.0 or higher. They must submit an original referenced paper on an aspect of respiratory care and a paper of at least 1,200 words describing how the award will assist them in reaching their objective of a baccalaureate degree and their ultimate goal of leadership in health care. Selection is based on academic performance.
Financial data The stipend is $2,500. The award also provides airfare, 1 night's lodging, and registration for the international congress of the association.
Duration 1 year.
Additional information This program is sponsored by the National Board for Respiratory Care (NBRC) and its wholly owned subsidiary, Applied Measurement Professionals, Inc. (AMP).
Number awarded 1 each year.
Deadline June of each year.

[424]
ROBERTA PIERCE SCOFIELD BACHELOR'S SCHOLARSHIPS

Oncology Nursing Society
Attn: ONS Foundation
125 Enterprise Drive
Pittsburgh, PA 15275-1214
(412) 859-6100, ext. 8503   Toll-free: (866) 257-4ONS
Fax: (412) 859-6160   E-mail: foundation@ons.org
Web: www.ons.org

Purpose To provide financial assistance to registered nurses who are interested in working on a bachelor's degree in oncology nursing.
Eligibility This program is open to registered nurses with a demonstrated interest in and commitment to oncology nursing. Applicants must be currently enrolled in an undergraduate degree program at an NLN- or CCNE-accredited school of nursing. They may not have previously received a bachelor's level scholarship from this sponsor. Applicants must submit an essay of 250 words or less on their role in caring for persons with cancer and a statement of their professional goals and their relationship to the advancement of oncology nursing. Financial need is not considered in the selection process.
Financial data The stipend is $2,000.
Duration 1 year.
Additional information These scholarships were first awarded in 1988. At the end of each year of scholarship participation, recipients must submit a summary describing their educational activities. Applications must be accompanied by a $5 fee.
Number awarded 2 each year.
Deadline January of each year.

[425]
ROCKEFELLER STATE WILDLIFE SCHOLARSHIP

Louisiana Office of Student Financial Assistance
1885 Wooddale Boulevard
P.O. Box 91202
Baton Rouge, LA 70821-9202
(225) 922-3258   Toll-free: (800) 259-LOAN, ext. 1012
Fax: (225) 922-0790 E-mail: custserv@osfa.state.la.us
Web: www.osfa.state.la.us

Purpose To provide financial assistance to high school seniors, college undergraduates, and graduate students in Louisiana who are interested in working on a degree in forestry, wildlife, or marine science.
Eligibility This program is open to U.S. citizens and eligible noncitizens who have been residents of Louisiana for at least 1 year. Applicants must be high school graduates, college undergraduates, or graduate students working or planning to work full time on a degree in forestry, wildlife, or marine science at a Louisiana college or university. They must 1) have graduated from high school with a GPA of 2.5 or higher and have an ACT score of 20 or higher; 2) have completed the 12th grade of an approved home study program and have an ACT score of 22 or higher: 3) have completed at least 24 college credit hours with a GPA of 2.5 or higher; or 4) be a graduate student with a GPA of 3.0 or higher. This is a merit-based award; financial need is not considered.
Financial data The stipend is $1,000 per year.
Duration Support is provided for up to 5 years of undergraduate and 2 years of graduate study, provided the recipient remains enrolled full time with a GPA of 2.5 or higher.
Additional information The recipient must agree to complete a degree in 1 of the 3 eligible fields at a Louisiana public college or university offering these degrees or repay all scholarship funds received plus interest.
Number awarded Varies; generally, 60 students (30 new and 30 continuing) receive awards each year.
Deadline July of each year.

[426]
ROCKWELL AUTOMATION SCHOLARSHIPS
Society of Women Engineers
230 East Ohio Street, Suite 400
Chicago, IL 60611-3265
(312) 596-5223 Toll-free: (877) SWE-INFO
Fax: (312) 644-8557
E-mail: scholarshipapplication@swe.org
Web: www.swe.org/scholarships

Purpose To provide financial assistance to upper-division women majoring in computer science or selected engineering specialties at specified colleges and universities.

Eligibility This program is open to women who are entering their junior year at a designated ABET-accredited college or university. Applicants must be majoring in computer science or computer, electrical, industrial, mechanical, or software engineering and have at GPA of 3.0 or higher. Along with their application, they must submit a 1-page essay on why they want to be an engineer, how they believe they will make a difference as an engineer, and what influenced them to study engineering. Selection is based on merit and leadership potential. Preference is given to members of underrepresented minority groups.

Financial data The stipend is $2,500.

Duration 1 year.

Additional information This program, established in 1991, is supported by Rockwell Automation, Inc. Recipients must attend a designated college or university. For a list, contact the sponsor.

Number awarded 2 each year.

Deadline January of each year.

[427]
ROCKY MOUNTAIN NASA SPACE GRANT CONSORTIUM UNDERGRADUATE SCHOLARSHIPS
Rocky Mountain NASA Space Grant Consortium
c/o Utah State University
EL Building, Room 302
Logan, UT 84322-4140
(435) 797-3666 Fax: (435) 797-3382
E-mail: spacegrant@cc.usu.edu
Web: spacegrant.usu.edu

Purpose To provide financial support to undergraduate students at designated universities in Utah or Colorado who are working on a degree in fields of interest to the National Aeronautics and Space Administration (NASA).

Eligibility This program is open to undergraduate students at member institutions of the Rocky Mountain NASA Space Grant Consortium who are studying engineering, science, medicine, or technology. U.S. citizenship is required. Selection is based on academic performance to date and potential for the future, with emphasis on space-related research interests. This program is part of the NASA Space Grant program, which encourages participation by women, underrepresented minorities, and persons with disabilities.

Financial data The amount of the awards depends on the availability of funds.

Duration 1 year.

Additional information Members of the consortium are Utah State University, the University of Utah, Brigham Young University, Dixie State College, Salt Lake Community College, Shoshone-Bannock School, Snow College, Southern Utah University, the University of Denver, and Weber State University. This program is funded by NASA.

Number awarded Varies each year.

Deadline June of each year.

[428]
ROGERS FAMILY SCHOLARSHIP
Morris Land Conservancy
Attn: Scholarship Program
19 Boonton Avenue
Boonton, NJ 07005
(973) 541-1010 Fax: (973) 541-1131
E-mail: info@morrislandconservancy.org
Web: www.morrislandconservancy.org

Purpose To provide financial assistance to undergraduate and graduate students from New Jersey who are working on a degree in an environmental field.

Eligibility This program is open to New Jersey residents who have completed at least 15 credits at a college or university offering a degree in environmental science, natural resource management, conservation, horticulture, park administration, or a related field. Applicants must have a cumulative GPA of 3.0 or higher. They must be considering a career in New Jersey in an environmental field. Along with their application, they must submit a 500-word essay on their career goals and how those will advance the effort of open space preservation, public education, or public recreation. Financial need is not considered in the selection process.

Financial data The stipend is $5,000.

Duration 1 year.

Additional information This program was established in 2005.

Number awarded 1 each year.

Deadline March of each year.

[429]
ROHM AND HAAS AWARDS
National Organization for the Professional Advancement of Black Chemists and Chemical Engineers
c/o Howard University
P.O. Box 77040
Washington, DC 20013
(202) 667-1699 Toll-free: (800) 776-1419
Fax: (267) 200-0156
Web: www.nobcche.org

Purpose To recognize and reward outstanding research papers written by African American undergraduates in chemistry and chemical engineering.

Eligibility African Americans who are full-time undergraduate students enrolled at a college or university working on a degree in chemistry, materials, polymer science, or chemical engineering may enter this competition. They are invited to prepare papers up to 20 pages in length on the results of their research. The authors of the 6 best papers are invited to present their papers at the annual conference of the National Organization for the Professional Advancement of Black Chemists and Chemical Engineers (NOBCChE). Winners are selected on the basis of the presentations at the NOBCChE convention. Selection is based on 1) the content, presentation, and relevance of the written paper; and 2) effectiveness of the oral presentation.

Financial data Finalists receive transportation, food, and lodging for the NOBCChE convention. Prizes are $1,000 for first, $750 for second, $500 for third, and $250 for honorable mention. All finalists are offered a 12-week, paid summer internship in the research division of Rohm and Haas Company in Philadelphia.

Duration The competition is held annually.

Additional information This program is sponsored by Rohm and Haas, Attn: Dr. Vere O. Archibald, 727 Norristown Road, Spring House, PA 19477, (215) 619-5004, Fax: (215) 619-5001, E-mail: VArchibald@rohmhaas.com.

Number awarded 6 prizes are awarded each year: 1 for first, 1 for second, 1 for third, and 3 for honorable mention.

Deadline December of each year for abstracts and January of the following year for full papers.

[430]
RONALD E. MCNAIR SCHOLARSHIP IN SPACE AND OPTICAL PHYSICS

National Society of Black Physicists
Attn: Scholarship Committee Chair
6704G Lee Highway
Arlington, VA 22205
(703) 536-4207 Fax: (703) 536-4203
E-mail: scholarship@nsbp.org
Web: www.nsbp.org

Purpose To provide financial assistance to African American students majoring in space or optical physics in college.

Eligibility This program is open to African American students who are entering their junior or senior year of college and majoring in space or optical physics. Applicants must submit an essay on their academic and career objectives, information on their participation in extracurricular activities, a description of any awards and honors they have received, and 3 letters of recommendation. Financial need is not considered.

Financial data The stipend is $1,000.

Duration 1 year; nonrenewable.

Additional information This program is offered in partnership with the American Astronomical Society.

Number awarded 1 each year.

Deadline November of each year.

[431]
ROSA L. PARKS SCHOLARSHIPS

Conference of Minority Transportation Officials
Attn: National Scholarship Program
818 18th Street, N.W., Suite 850
Washington, DC 20006
(202) 530-0551 Fax: (202) 530-0617
Web: www.comto.org/scholarship.htm

Purpose To provide financial assistance for college to children of members of the Conference of Minority Transportation Officials (COMTO) and to other students working on a bachelor's or master's degree in transportation.

Eligibility This program is open to 1) college-bound high school seniors whose parent has been a COMTO member for at least 1 year; 2) undergraduates who have completed at least 60 semester credit hours in a transportation discipline; and 3) students working on a master's degree in transportation who have completed at least 15 credits. Applicants must have a GPA of 3.0 or higher. Along with their application, they must submit a cover letter with a 500-word statement of career goals. Financial need is not considered in the selection process. U.S. citizenship is required.

Financial data The stipend is $4,500. Funds are paid directly to the recipient's college or university.

Duration 1 year.

Additional information COMTO was established in 1971 to promote, strengthen, and expand the roles of minorities in all aspects of transportation. Recipients are expected to attend the COMTO National Scholarship Luncheon.

Number awarded 2 each year.

Deadline April of each year.

[432]
ROV SCHOLARSHIPS

Marine Technology Society
Attn: Student Scholarships
5565 Sterrett Place, Suite 108
Columbia, MD 21044
(410) 884-5330 Fax: (410) 884-9060
Web: www.mtsociety.org

Purpose To provide financial assistance to entering or continuing undergraduate and graduate students working on a degree related to remotely-operated vehicles (ROVs) in marine science.

Eligibility This program is open to high school seniors accepted into a full-time undergraduate program and current undergraduate and graduate students who are members of the Marine Technology Society (MTS). Applicants must be interested in ROVs or work that supports ROVs in a marine-related field. Along with their application, they must submit a 1-page essay on their interest in ROVs or underwater work that furthers the use of ROVs; a biographical sketch; an official transcript; a recommendation from a current teacher or counselor in a marine-related field; and 3 personal letters of reference. Financial need is not considered in the selection process.

Financial data The stipend generally ranges from $1,250 to $5,000. Funds are sent directly to the recipient's college bursar's office.

Duration 1 year.

Additional information This program was established in 1994. Information is also available from Chuck Richards, ROV Scholarship Committee Chair, C.A. Richards and Associates Inc., 777 North Eldridge Parkway, Suite 280, Houston, TX 77079.

Number awarded Varies each year. Recently, 6 of these scholarships were awarded: 1 at $5,000, 1 at $3,000, 1 at $2,500, 1 at $2,000, and 2 at $1,250.

Deadline April of each year.

SCIENCES

[433]
RUDOLPH DILLMAN MEMORIAL SCHOLARSHIP
American Foundation for the Blind
Attn: Scholarship Committee
11 Penn Plaza, Suite 300
New York, NY 10001
(212) 502-7661   Toll-free: (800) AFB-LINE
Fax: (212) 502-7771   TDD: (212) 502-7662
E-mail: afbinfo@afb.net
Web: www.afb.org/scholarships.asp

Purpose To provide financial assistance to legally blind undergraduate or graduate students studying in the field of rehabilitation and/or education of visually impaired and blind persons.

Eligibility Applicants must be able to submit evidence of legal blindness, U.S. citizenship, and acceptance in an accredited undergraduate or graduate training program within the broad field of rehabilitation and/or education of blind and visually impaired persons. Along with their application, they must submit an essay that includes the field of study they are pursuing and why they have chosen it; their educational and personal goals; their work experience; any extracurricular activities with which they have been involved, including those in school, religious organizations, and the community; and how they intend to use scholarship monies that may be awarded.

Financial data The stipend is $2,500 per year.

Duration 1 academic year; previous recipients may not reapply.

Number awarded 4 each year: 3 without consideration of financial need and 1 to an applicant who can submit evidence of financial need.

Deadline April of each year.

[434]
RUSSELL W. MYERS SCHOLARSHIP
Morris Land Conservancy
Attn: Scholarship Program
19 Boonton Avenue
Boonton, NJ 07005
(973) 541-1010   Fax: (973) 541-1131
E-mail: info@morrislandconservancy.org
Web: www.morrislandconservancy.org

Purpose To provide financial assistance to undergraduate and graduate students from New Jersey who are working on a degree in an environmental field.

Eligibility This program is open to New Jersey residents who have completed at least 15 credits at a college or university offering a degree in environmental science, natural resource management, conservation, horticulture, park administration, or a related field. Applicants must have a cumulative GPA of 3.0 or higher. They must be considering a career in New Jersey in an environmental field. Along with their application, they must submit a 500-word essay on their career goals and how those will advance the effort of open space preservation, public education, or public recreation. Financial need is not considered in the selection process.

Financial data The stipend is $5,000.

Duration 1 year.

Additional information This program was established in 1983.

Number awarded 1 each year.

Deadline March of each year.

[435]
RUTH ABERNATHY UNDERGRADUATE PRESIDENTIAL SCHOLARSHIP
American Alliance for Health, Physical Education, Recreation and Dance
Attn: Presidential Scholarships
1900 Association Drive
Reston, VA 20191-1598
(703) 476-3400   Toll-free: (800) 213-7193
E-mail: dcallis@aahperd.org
Web: www.aahperd.org

Purpose To provide financial assistance to undergraduate student members of the American Alliance for Health, Physical Education, Recreation and Dance (AAHPERD).

Eligibility This program is open to AAHPERD members who are juniors or seniors at a baccalaureate-granting college or university. Applicants must be majoring in health, physical education, recreation, or dance and have a GPA of 3.5 or higher. They must submit a statement of their professional goals. Selection is based on academic proficiency; evidence of leadership; school, community, and professional activity and service; and character attributes.

Financial data The stipend is $1,000.

Duration 1 year; nonrenewable.

Additional information This program, established in 1995, was formerly designated the National Presidential Undergraduate Scholarships of AAHPERD.

Number awarded 3 each year.

Deadline October of each year.

[436]
SAE LONG TERM MEMBER SPONSORED SCHOLARSHIPS
Society of Automotive Engineers
Attn: Scholarship Administrator
400 Commonwealth Drive
Warrendale, PA 15096-0001
(724) 772-4047   Fax: (724) 776-3049
E-mail: scholarships@sae.org
Web: students.sae.org

Purpose To provide financial support to engineering majors who are student members of the Society of Automotive Engineers (SAE).

Eligibility This program is open to student members entering their senior year between August and February of the academic year following receipt of the award. Candidates must be nominated by their faculty advisor, section chair, or vice chair for student activities. Selection is based on the nominee's involvement in the society, the collegiate chapter, or the local section and its programs. GPA and financial need are not considered.

Financial data The stipend is $1,000.

Duration 1 year; nonrenewable.

Additional information Funding for this program is provided by long-term (25, 35, and 50 year) members of the society, many of whom have chosen to fund this scholarship program in lieu of receiving a Long Term Recognition Award. The program was established in 1994.

Number awarded Varies each year; recently, 6 of these scholarships were awarded.

Deadline March of each year.

[437]
SAFARI CLUB INTERNATIONAL UPPER-LEVEL TWO-YEAR CONSERVATION SCHOLARSHIPS

Safari Club International
SCI Foundation
Attn: Education Department
4800 West Gates Pass Road
Tucson, AZ 85745
(520) 620-1220, ext. 231 Toll-free: (800) 377-5399
Fax: (520) 622-1205
Web: www.safariclubfoundation.org/education

Purpose To provide financial assistance to entering college juniors interested in studying a field related to conservation.

Eligibility This program is open to college students entering their junior year at an accredited 4-year college or university. Preference is given to students working on a degree in a field related to conservation (e.g., natural resource management, forestry, environmental studies, conservation education, outdoor education and recreation, or animal science). Applicants must be recommended by their college or university faculty advisor. They must be able to demonstrate academic ability and a concern for their school and community. Along with their application, they must submit 1) a 500-word essay describing their commitment to a conservation-related field, citing how their past experiences (academic accomplishments, volunteer or paid work, and life experience) support their career goals; and 2) an essay or report (5 pages or longer) that they have submitted for a college course. Financial need is not considered.

Financial data The stipend is $2,200 per year.

Duration 2 years.

Number awarded Up to 4 each year.

Deadline April of each year.

[438]
SAFE FOUNDATION SCHOLARSHIPS

Sports Turf Managers Association
Attn: SAFE Foundation
805 New Hampshire, Suite E
Lawrence, KS 66044
Toll-free: (800) 323-3875 Fax: (800) 366-0391
E-mail: stmainfo@sportsturfmanager.com
Web: www.sportsturfmanager.org

Purpose To provide financial assistance to student members of the Sports Turf Managers Association (STMA) who are interested in preparing for a career in the turf management industry.

Eligibility This program is open to STMA student members who are preparing for a career in the sports turf industry (excluding golf course management). Applicants must submit lists of 1) awards, honors, or scholarships that they have received; 2) activities in which they have participated related to their school, department, or community; and 3) professional associations and university organizations to which they belong. Selection is based on academic preparation, cumulative GPA, experience in sports turf management, and references. Financial need is not considered.

Financial data The stipend is $1,000. Winners also receive $500 for travel or lodging expenses to attend the annual conference of the STMA.

Duration 1 year.

Additional information The SAFE (Safer Athletic Field Environments) Foundation was established in 2000.

Number awarded 1 or more each year.

Deadline September of each year.

[439]
SAGEBRUSH CIRCUIT–LEW AND JOANN EKLUND EDUCATIONAL SCHOLARSHIP

Appaloosa Youth Foundation, Inc.
c/o Appaloosa Horse Club
Attn: Youth Coordinator
2720 West Pullman Road
Moscow, ID 83843-4024
(208) 882-5578, ext. 264 Fax: (208) 882-8150
E-mail: aphc@appaloosa.com
Web: www.appaloosa.com/youth/ycontests.shtm

Purpose To provide financial assistance for undergraduate or graduate study in a field related to the equine industry to members or dependents of members of the Appaloosa Horse Club.

Eligibility This program is open to members and children of members of the Appaloosa Horse Club who are college juniors, seniors, or graduate students. Applicants must be majoring in a field closely related to the equine industry and have a GPA of 3.5 or higher. They must submit an essay on what their experience with horses has meant to them, why they desire to continue their education, their career goals, the personal qualities that qualify them to receive a scholarship, any circumstances regarding financial need, and how receiving this scholarship will enhance their educational experiences. Selection is based on the essay, leadership potential, sportsmanship, involvement in the Appaloosa and equine industries, GPA, extracurricular equine activities, extracurricular school and community activities, career goals, and general knowledge and accomplishments in horsemanship.

Financial data The stipend is $2,000.

Duration 1 year.

Number awarded 1 each year.

Deadline June of each year.

SCIENCES

[440]
SAP AMERICA SCHOLARSHIP PROGRAM

SAP America, Inc.
Attn: Director, University Alliances
3999 West Chester Pike
Newtown Square, PA 19073
(610) 661-1000　　　　Toll-free: (800) 227-1727
E-mail: citizenship.usa@sap.com
Web: www.sap.com

Purpose To provide financial assistance to upper-division students working on a degree in designated fields at selected universities.

Eligibility This program is open to full-time juniors and seniors working on a degree in business, mathematics, computer science, or engineering. Applicants must have a GPA of 3.0 or higher. They must be attending a university that is an active member of the SAT University Alliances program in the United States. Along with their application, they must submit a research paper of 10 to 15 pages on a problem or issue that is current and relevant to their area of interest but also relevant to Enterprise Resource Planning (ERP) or other state-of-the-art technology (i.e., corporate governance, fraud in business, computer security). Selection is based primarily on that paper, but consideration is also given to academic achievement, written communication skills, a resume, intended degree, year in school, school participation in SAP University Alliances program, and demonstrated knowledge or proficiency in their field. Financial need is not considered.

Financial data The stipend is $10,000. Funds are disbursed directly to the university for payment of tuition only. If tuition is less than $10,000, the balance of the funds may be applied to tuition for the following year.

Duration 1 year.

Additional information For a list of participating universities, contact SAP America.

Number awarded 10 each year.

Deadline May of each year.

[441]
SCHOLARSHIPS IN MATHEMATICS EDUCATION

Illinois Council of Teachers of Mathematics
c/o Sue Pippen, ICTM Scholarship
24807 Winterberry Lane
Plainfield, IL 60585
E-mail: bsrich@ilstu.edu
Web: www.ictm.org/scholarship.html

Purpose To provide financial assistance to undergraduate students in Illinois who are interested in preparing for a career as a mathematics teacher.

Eligibility This program is open to juniors and seniors at accredited colleges and universities in Illinois. Applicants must have a GPA of 3.0 or higher and a mathematics education major, a mathematics major with an education minor, or an education major with an official mathematics concentration. Along with their application, they must submit an essay of 200 to 300 words on why they wish to teach mathematics and what they see as their contribution to the profession. Selection is based on the essay, a lesson plan, transcripts from all colleges attended, and letters of recommendation from 2 mathematics teachers (high school or college).

Financial data The stipend is $1,500.

Duration 1 year.

Additional information This program began in 1989. Requests for applications must be accompanied by a self-addressed stamped envelope.

Number awarded 2 to 5 each year.

Deadline March of each year.

[442]
SCHOLARSHIPS IN TECHNICAL COMMUNICATION

Society for Technical Communication
901 North Stuart Street, Suite 904
Arlington, VA 22203-1822
(703) 522-4114　　　　Fax: (703) 522-2075
E-mail: stc@stc.org
Web: www.stc.org/scholarshipInfo01_national.asp

Purpose To provide financial assistance to undergraduate and graduate students who are preparing for a career in some area of technical communications.

Eligibility This program is open to 1) full-time undergraduate students working on a bachelor's degree in technical communications who have completed at least 1 year of college and 2) full-time graduate students working on a master's or doctoral degree in technical communications. Applicants must be studying communication of information about technical subjects; other majors, such as general journalism, electronic communication engineering, computer programming, entertainment, and creative writing are not eligible. Selection is based on academic record, experience with technical communication, and potential for contributing to the profession.

Financial data The stipend is $1,500; funds are paid to the school for the benefit of the recipient.

Duration 1 year.

Number awarded 4 each year: 2 to undergraduate students and 2 to graduate students.

Deadline February of each year.

[443]
SCHONSTEDT SCHOLARSHIP IN SURVEYING

American Congress on Surveying and Mapping
Attn: Scholarships
6 Montgomery Village Avenue, Suite 403
Gaithersburg, MD 20879
(240) 632-9716, ext. 113　　　　Fax: (240) 632-1321
E-mail: pat.canfield@acsm.net
Web: www.acsm.net/scholar.html

Purpose To provide financial assistance for the undergraduate study of surveying to members of the American Congress on Surveying and Mapping (ACSM).

Eligibility This program is open to ACSM members who are enrolled at a 4-year college or university. Preference is given to juniors and seniors. Applicants must be majoring in surveying or a closely-related program (e.g., geomatics, surveying engineering). Along with their application, they must submit a statement describing their educational program, future plans for study or research, and why the award is merited. Selection is based on that statement (30%), academic record (30%), letters of recommendation (20%), and professional activities (20%).

Financial data The stipend is $1,500. In addition, the surveying programs at the recipients' schools are awarded a magnetic locator.

Duration 1 year.

Additional information Funds for this scholarship are provided by the Schonstedt Instrument Company of Kearneysville, West Virginia.

Number awarded 2 each year.

Deadline October of each year.

[444]
SCHWAN'S FOOD SERVICE SCHOLARSHIPS

School Nutrition Association
Attn: Child Nutrition Foundation Scholarship Committee
700 South Washington Street, Suite 300
Alexandria, VA 22314-4287
(703) 739-3900   Toll-free: (800) 877-8822
Fax: (703) 739-3915   E-mail: cnf@schoolnutrition.org
Web: www.schoolnutrition.org/Index.aspx?ID=1043

Purpose To provide assistance to members (or children of members) of the School Nutrition Association (SNA) who are interested in studying school food service management on the undergraduate or graduate school level.

Eligibility This program is open to undergraduate and graduate students who meet all 4 of the following criteria: 1) plan to attend a college or vocational/technical institution that has a program designed to improve school food service (e.g., nutrition, food service management, business administration); 2) be an active SNA member or the child of an active member planning to study in a school food service-related field; 3) have a satisfactory academic record; and 4) express a desire to make school food service a career. Applicants must submit a 1-page personal essay (up to 500 words) stating the reason for selecting school food service as a profession; what they expect to gain from continuing their education; and their long-term professional goals/plans. Selection is based on the essay (35 points), letters of recommendation (20 points), SNA state and local chapter activity participation (15 points), organization and neatness (10 points), program of study (15 points), and GPA (5 points).

Financial data The stipend ranges up to $1,000.

Duration 1 year; may be renewed up to 3 additional years.

Additional information The SNA was formerly the American School Food Service Administration. This program, established in 1983, is sponsored by Schwan's Food Service.

Number awarded Varies each year; recently, 53 of these scholarships were awarded.

Deadline April of each year.

[445]
SCOTT TARBELL SCHOLARSHIPS

Hemophilia Health Services
Attn: Scholarship Committee
6820 Charlotte Pike, Suite 100
Nashville, TN 37209-4234
(615) 850-5175   Toll-free: (800) 800-6606, ext. 5175
Fax: (615) 352-2588
E-mail: Scholarship@HemophiliaHealth.com
Web: www.hemophiliahealth.com

Purpose To provide financial assistance to high school seniors and current college students who have hemophilia and are interested in working on a degree or certification in computer science and/or mathematics.

Eligibility This program is open to high school seniors and college freshmen, sophomores, and juniors who have hemophilia A or B severe. Applicants must be enrolled or planning to enroll at an accredited nonprofit college, university, or vocational/technical school in the United States or Puerto Rico. They must be interested in working on a degree or certification in computer science and/or mathematics. Along with their application, they must submit an essay, up to 250 words, on the following topic: "Upon receiving your education in math and/or computer science, how will you use the new technologies (i.e., computer, internet, etc.) to better mankind and what ethical issues will you need to address?" U.S. citizenship is required. Selection is based on academic achievement in relation to tested ability and dedication to the field of computer science or mathematics. Financial need is not considered.

Financial data The stipend is $1,500. Funds are issued payable to the recipient's school.

Duration 1 year; recipients may reapply.

Additional information This program, which started in 2003, is administered by Scholarship Program Administrators, Inc., 1201 Eighth Avenue South, P.O. Box 23737, Nashville, TN 27202-3737, (615) 320-3149, Fax: (615) 320-3151, E-mail: info@spaprog.com.

Number awarded Varies each year, depending on the availability of funds.

Deadline April of each year.

[446]
SCOTTS COMPANY SCHOLARS PROGRAM

Golf Course Superintendents Association of America
Attn: Environmental Institute for Golf
1421 Research Park Drive
Lawrence, KS 66049-3859
(785) 832-4424   Toll-free: (800) 472-7878, ext. 4424
Fax: (785) 832-3673   E-mail: ahoward@gcsaa.org
Web: www.gcsaa.org

Purpose To provide financial assistance and summer work experience to high school seniors and college students, particularly those from diverse backgrounds, who are preparing for a career in golf management.

Eligibility This program is open to high school seniors and college students (freshmen, sophomores, and juniors) who are interested in preparing for a career in golf management (the "green industry"). Applicants should come from diverse ethnic, cultural, and socioeconomic backgrounds, defined to include women, minorities, and people with disabilities. Selection is based on cultural diversity, academic achievement, extracurricular activities, leadership, employment potential, essay responses, and letters of recommendation. Financial need is not considered. Finalists are selected for summer internships and then compete for scholarships.

Financial data The finalists receive a $500 award to supplement their summer internship income. Scholarship stipends are $2,500.

Duration 1 year.

Additional information The program is funded by a permanent endowment established by Scotts Company. Finalists are responsible for securing their own internships.

Number awarded 5 finalists, of whom 2 receive scholarships, are selected each year.

Deadline February of each year.

[447]
SEATA MEMORIAL UNDERGRADUATE SCHOLARSHIP

Southeast Athletic Trainers Association
c/o Janet Passman, Scholarship Committee Chair
Louisiana College
1140 College Drive
Pineville, LA 71359
(318) 487-7290   Fax: (318) 487-7174
E-mail: passman@lacollege.edu
Web: www.seata.org/Scholarshipdetails.htm

Purpose To provide financial assistance to undergraduate student members of the Southeast Athletic Trainers Association (SEATA).

Eligibility This program is open to undergraduates at colleges and universities in Alabama, Florida, Georgia, Kentucky, Louisiana, Mississippi, and Tennessee who are members of SEATA and the National Association of Athletic Trainers (NATA). Applicants must be in at least their junior year in a degree program as an athletic trainer with a GPA of 3.0 or higher. They must be sponsored by a certified athletic trainer who is a current member of SEATA and NATA. Along with their application, they must submit a brief biographical sketch that includes their reasons for wanting the scholarship, why they merit this award, high school and college awards and honors, athletic teams with which they have worked, and jobs they have held. Selection is based on academic achievement, character, and athletic training abilities and experiences.

Financial data The stipend is $1,000.

Duration 1 year; nonrenewable.

Additional information SEATA serves as District 9 of NATA. This program was established in 1981.

Number awarded 1 each year.

Deadline December of each year.

[448]
SEG SCHOLARSHIP PROGRAM

Society of Exploration Geophysicists
Attn: SEG Foundation
8801 South Yale, Suite 500
P.O. Box 702740
Tulsa, OK 74170-2740
(918) 497-5513   Fax: (918) 497-5557
E-mail: scholarships@seg.org
Web: seg.org

Purpose To provide financial assistance to entering or continuing undergraduate and graduate students who are interested in the field of applied geophysics.

Eligibility This program is open to 1) high school students planning to enter college in the fall, and 2) undergraduate or graduate students whose grades are above average. Applicants must intend to work on a degree directed toward a career in applied geophysics or a closely-related field. Along with their application, they must submit a 150-word essay on how they plan to use geophysics in their future. Financial need is not considered in the selection process. Some of the scholarships are set aside for students at recognized colleges or universities in countries outside of the United States.

Financial data The stipends generally range from $500 to $14,000 per year and average $1,500 per year.

Duration 1 academic year; may be renewable, based on scholastic standing, availability of funds, and continuance of a course of study leading to a career in applied geophysics.

Additional information This program includes a number of named scholarships; among them are the Donald R. Allen Memorial Scholarship, the Ted Born Memorial Scholarship, the Michael Forrest Scholarship, the Jim and Ruth Harrison Scholarship, the Jene and Marvin Hewitt Scholarship, the Fred Hilterman Scholarship, the Landmark Graphics Scholarship, the Permian Basic Geophysical Society Scholarship, the Schlumberger Scholarship, the WesternGeco Scholarship, the WesternGeco/Henry Salvatori Scholarship, and the David Worthington Scholarship.

Number awarded Varies each year; recently, 70 renewals and 66 new scholarships were awarded. The total value of the scholarships was $268,100.

Deadline January of each year.

[449]
SGNA RN GENERAL EDUCATION SCHOLARSHIP

Society of Gastroenterology Nurses and Associates, Inc.
Attn: Awards Committee
401 North Michigan Avenue
Chicago, IL 60611-4267
(312) 321-5165   Toll-free: (800) 245-SGNA
Fax: (312) 527-6658   E-mail: sgna@smithbucklin.com
Web: www.sgna.org/Education/scholarships.cfm

Purpose To provide financial assistance to full-time students working toward licensure as a registered nurse (R.N.).

Eligibility This program is open to students currently enrolled full time in an accredited nursing program with a GPA of 3.0 or higher. Applicants must be studying to become an R.N. Along with their application, they must submit a 2-page essay on a challenging situation they see in the health care environment today and how they, as an R.N., would best address and meet that challenge. Financial need is not considered in the selection process.

Financial data The stipend is $2,500. Funds are issued as reimbursement after the recipient has completed the proposed course work with a GPA of 3.0 or higher.

Duration 1 year.

Number awarded 1 or more each year.

Deadline July of each year.

[450]
SHARON D. BANKS MEMORIAL UNDERGRADUATE SCHOLARSHIP

Women's Transportation Seminar
Attn: National Headquarters
1701 K Street, N.W., Suite 800
Washington, DC 20006
(202) 955-5085   Fax: (202) 955-5088
E-mail: wts@wtsinternational.org
Web: www.wtsinternational.org

Purpose To provide financial assistance to undergraduate women interested in a career in transportation.

Eligibility This program is open to women who are working on an undergraduate degree in transportation or a transportation-related field (e.g., transportation engineering, planning, finance, or logistics). Applicants must have a GPA of 3.0 or higher and be interested in a career in transportation. Along with their application, they must submit a 500-word statement about their career goals after graduation and why they think they should receive the scholarship award. Applications must be submitted first to a local chapter; the chapters forward selected applications for consideration on the national level. Minority candidates are encouraged to apply. Selection is based on transportation involvement and goals, job skills, and academic record; financial need is not considered.

Financial data The stipend is $3,000.

Duration 1 year.

Additional information This program was established in 1992. Local chapters may also award additional funding to winners for their area.

Number awarded 1 each year.

Deadline Applications must be submitted by November to a local WTS chapter.

[451]
SHELL OIL COMPANY PROCESS TECHNOLOGY SCHOLARSHIP

Center for the Advancement of Process Technology
Attn: CAPT Scholarships
1200 Amburn Road
Texas City, TX 77591
(409) 938-1211, ext. 103   Fax: (409) 938-1285
E-mail: info@cpatech.org
Web: www.captech/org/careers/scholarship.htm

Purpose To provide financial assistance to students interested in a college degree in process technology.

Eligibility This program is open to students currently enrolled or planning to enroll in a process technology (or instrumentation technology) 2-year degree program. Preference is given to students from programs approved by the Gulf Coast Process Technology Alliance. Applicants must submit a 1-page essay on why they should be considered for this scholarship and selected over other qualified, worthy applicants. They must have a GPA of 2.5 or higher. Preference is also given to students located near Shell facilities in Alabama, California, Louisiana, Texas, and Washington who are interested in job opportunities in refineries, chemical plants, and oil and gas exploration and production. Selection is based on scholastic performance; financial need is not considered.

Financial data Stipends are $500 per semester for full-time students or $300 per semester for part-time students. Eligible expenses are limited to tuition, books, fees, and educational supplies.

Duration Recipients have up to 3 years to complete the 2-year process technology degree program. The maximum amount of support they may receive is $2,000.

Additional information This program is supported by Shell Oil Company.

Number awarded 1 or more each year.

Deadline March of each year.

[452]
SHELL OIL INTERNATIONAL SCHOLARSHIPS

Society of Exploration Geophysicists
Attn: SEG Foundation
8801 South Yale, Suite 500
P.O. Box 702740
Tulsa, OK 74170-2740
(918) 497-5513   Fax: (918) 497-5557
E-mail: scholarships@seg.org
Web: seg.org

Purpose To provide financial assistance to entering or continuing undergraduate and graduate students who are interested in studying applied geophysics.

Eligibility This program is open to 1) high school students planning to enter college in the fall, and 2) undergraduate or graduate students whose grades are above average. Applicants must intend to work on a degree directed toward a career in applied geophysics or a closely-related field; preference is given to undergraduates. Along with their application, they must submit a 150-word essay on how they plan to use geophysics in their future. Financial need is not considered in the selection process.

Financial data Stipends range from $1,000 to $3,000 per year.

Duration 1 academic year; may be renewable, based on scholastic standing, availability of funds, and continuance of a course of study leading to a career in applied geophysics.

Additional information This program is sponsored by Shell Oil International.

Number awarded 1 or more each year.

Deadline January of each year.

SCIENCES

[453]
SIEGEL SERVICE TECHNOLOGY SCHOLARSHIPS

Society of Automotive Engineers
Attn: Scholarship Administrator
400 Commonwealth Drive
Warrendale, PA 15096-0001
(724) 772-7158   Fax: (724) 776-3049
E-mail: scholarships@sae.org
Web: students.sae.org

Purpose To provide financial assistance to students at designated colleges of technology in Montana who are interested in a career in the mobility community.

Eligibility This program is open to second-year students at designated colleges of technology in Montana. Applicants must be preparing for a career as a service technician in the mobility community. Selection is based on academic achievement and community spirit. Financial need is not considered.

Financial data The stipend is $1,000.

Duration 1 year; nonrenewable.

Additional information The designated schools are Helena College of Technology, Missoula College of Technology, Montana State University at Billings College of Technology, Montana State University at Great Falls College of Technology, Montana State University Northern at Havre College of Technology, and Montana Tech at Butte College of Technology. Funding for this program is provided by the state of Montana Office of Higher Education, the Society of Automotive Engineers, the 6 participating colleges, and the family of Arne Siegel.

Number awarded 6 each year: 1 at each of the participating colleges of technology.

Deadline March of each year.

[454]
SME EDUCATION FOUNDATION FAMILY SCHOLARSHIP

Society of Manufacturing Engineers
Attn: SME Education Foundation
One SME Drive
P.O. Box 930
Dearborn, MI 48121-0930
(313) 425-3300   Toll-free: (800) 733-4763, ext. 3300
Fax: (313) 425-3411   E-mail: foundation@sme.org
Web: www.sme.org

Purpose To provide financial assistance to high school seniors and undergraduate students who are descendants of members of the Society of Manufacturing Engineers (SME) and plan to enroll in a degree program in manufacturing engineering or manufacturing engineering technology.

Eligibility This program is open to graduating high school seniors and undergraduate students with up to 30 credit hours completed who have at least 1 parent or grandparent who has been an SME member in good standing for at least the last 2 years. Applicants must work on a degree in manufacturing engineering, manufacturing engineering technology, or a closely-related engineering field of study at an accredited college or university in 1 of SME's 14 regions in the United States or Canada. They must have a high school GPA of 3.0 or higher and a minimum score of 1000 on the SAT or 21 on the ACT. Along with their application, they must submit 1) a 300-word essay that covers their career and educational objectives, how this scholarship will help them attain those objectives, and why they want to enter this field; and 2) an essay on their favorite manufacturing engineer, including what about this person interests and inspires them. Selection is based on overall academic excellence, communication skills, interpersonal skills, demonstrated interest and aptitude for and potential future success in a manufacturing engineering or manufacturing engineering technology-related field, and extracurricular activities.

Financial data The stipends are $70,000 or $10,000.

Duration 1 year; may be renewed if the recipient maintains a GPA of 3.0 or higher.

Additional information Recipients must enroll as full-time students.

Number awarded 3 each year: 1 at $70,000 and 2 at $10,000.

Deadline January of each year.

[455]
SOCIETY OF FLIGHT TEST ENGINEERS SCHOLARSHIPS

Society of Flight Test Engineers
44814 North Elm Avenue
P.O. Box 4037
Lancaster, CA 93539-4037
(661) 949-2095   Fax: (661) 949-2096
E-mail: sfte@sfte.org
Web: www.sfte.org

Purpose To provide financial assistance for college to student members and children of members of the Society of Flight Test Engineers (SFTE).

Eligibility This program is open to college students who have completed at least their freshman year. Applicants must be a student member of SFTE or the child of a member. They must be working on an undergraduate degree in engineering, computer sciences, mathematics, physics, or another technical discipline. Selection is based primarily on academic achievement; financial need is not considered.

Financial data Stipends range from $200 to $2,000.

Duration 1 year; recipients may reapply.

Number awarded 1 or more each year.

Deadline June of each year.

[456]
SOCIETY OF MANUFACTURING ENGINEERS DIRECTORS' SCHOLARSHIPS

Society of Manufacturing Engineers
Attn: SME Education Foundation
One SME Drive
P.O. Box 930
Dearborn, MI 48121-0930
(313) 425-3300   Toll-free: (800) 733-4763, ext. 3300
Fax: (313) 425-3411   E-mail: foundation@sme.org
Web: www.sme.org

Purpose To provide financial assistance to undergraduate students enrolled in a degree program in manufacturing.

Eligibility This program is open to full-time undergraduate students enrolled in a manufacturing degree program at a college or university in North America. Applicants must have completed at least 30 units with a GPA of 3.5 or higher and be interested in preparing for a career in manufacturing. Preference is given to students who demonstrate leadership skills in a community, academic, or professional environment. Along with their application, they must submit a 300-word essay that covers their career and educational objectives, how this scholarship will help them attain those objectives, and why they want to enter this field. Financial need is not considered in the selection process.

Financial data The stipend is $5,000.
Duration 1 year; may be renewed.
Number awarded 2 each year.
Deadline January of each year.

[457]
SOCIETY OF PHYSICS STUDENTS LEADERSHIP SCHOLARSHIPS

Society of Physics Students
c/o American Institute of Physics
One Physics Ellipse
College Park, MD 20740-3843
(301) 209-3007   Fax: (301) 209-0839
E-mail: sps@aip.org
Web: www.spsnational.org

Purpose To provide financial assistance to members of the Society of Physics Students (SPS) in their final year of undergraduate study.
Eligibility Eligible are full-time college juniors majoring in physics who are active members of the society. Selection is based on 1) high scholarship performance both in physics and overall studies, 2) potential for continued scholastic development in physics, and 3) active participation in society programs; those 3 criteria are given equal weight.
Financial data Stipends are $5,000 or $2,000.
Duration 1 year.
Additional information This program is sponsored by the Sigma Pi Sigma Trust Fund and the American Institute of Physics.
Number awarded Varies each year; recently, 26 of these scholarships were awarded.
Deadline February of each year.

[458]
SOLID WASTE PROGRAM MANAGEMENT UNDERGRADUATE SCHOLARSHIP PROGRAM

ASME International
Attn: Solid Waste Processing Division
Three Park Avenue
New York, NY 10016-5990
(212) 591-7797   Toll-free: (800) THE-ASME
Fax: (212) 591-7674   E-mail: manese@asme.org
Web: divisions.asme.org

Purpose To provide financial assistance to undergraduate students working on a degree in solid waste management.
Eligibility Applicants must be undergraduate students in any branch of engineering who are currently enrolled full time in a solid waste management program. They must attend or plan to attend a college or university in North America (including Alaska, Canada, Hawaii, Mexico, and Puerto Rico). Applications must be submitted jointly by an appropriate faculty member and the student. Required from the faculty member are a description of the school's environmental program and solid waste management courses, an identification of undergraduate and graduate courses offered in the program, an indication of the number of students in the program, future plans for the solid waste management program, and proposed use of the school's portion of the award money. Students must submit a statement of intent to pursue a branch of engineering as a career, a statement of interest in solid waste management, their perception of the importance of good solid waste management to protection of the environment, information on any prior experience in the solid waste management field, copies of any papers written on solid waste management, information on proposed studies, a list of current courses, transcripts for previous college years, and a letter of recommendation from the faculty advisor or department head. Financial need is not considered.

Financial data The award is $2,000 per year. One half is given to the student and the other half is given to the recipient's school for support of its solid waste management program.
Duration 1 year.
Number awarded 1 each year.
Deadline June of each year.

[459]
SOPHOMORE SCHOLARSHIPS

Institute of Food Technologists
Attn: Scholarship Department
525 West Van Buren, Suite 1000
Chicago, IL 60607
(312) 782-8424   Fax: (312) 782-8348
E-mail: info@ift.org
Web: www.ift.org

Purpose To provide financial assistance to lower-division students interested in majoring in food science or food technology.
Eligibility This program is open to college freshmen entering their sophomore year in a food science or food technology program at an educational institution in the United States or Canada. Applicants must have an outstanding scholastic record (GPA of 2.5 or higher) and a well-rounded personality. Food science majors must submit an essay on why they want to continue in food technology; other majors and transfer students must submit a brief biographical sketch and an essay on why they would like to become a food technologist. Financial need is not considered in the selection process.
Financial data The stipend is $1,000.
Duration 1 year; recipients may reapply if they are members of the Institute of Food Technologists.
Additional information Correspondence and completed applications must be submitted to the department head at the educational institution the applicant is attending.
Number awarded Varies each year; recently, 22 of these scholarships were awarded.

Deadline February of each year.

[460]
SOUTH DAKOTA SPACE GRANT CONSORTIUM GRADUATE FELLOWSHIPS AND UNDERGRADUATE SCHOLARSHIPS

South Dakota Space Grant Consortium
Attn: Deputy Director and Outreach Coordinator
South Dakota School of Mines and Technology
Mineral Industries Building, Room 228
501 East St. Joseph Street
Rapid City, SD 57701-3995
(605) 394-1975 Fax: (605) 394-5360
E-mail: Thomas.Durkin@sdsmt.edu
Web: www.sdsmt.edu/space

Purpose To provide funding to undergraduate and graduate students for space-related activities in South Dakota.

Eligibility This program is open to undergraduate and graduate students at member and affiliated institutions of the South Dakota Space Grant Consortium. Applicants must be interested in 1) earth- and space-science related educational and research projects in fields relevant to the goals of the U.S. National Aeronautics and Space Administration (NASA); or 2) eventual employment with NASA or in a NASA-related career field in science, technology, engineering, and mathematics (STEM) education. Activities may include student research and educational efforts in remote sensing, GIS, global and regional geoscience, environmental science, and K-12 educational outreach; exposure to NASA-relevant projects; and internship experiences at various NASA centers and the Earth Resources Observation and Science (EROS) Center in Sioux Falls. U.S. citizenship is required. Women, members of underrepresented groups (African Americans, Hispanics, Pacific Islanders, Asian Americans, Native Americans, and persons with disabilities), and Tribal College students are specifically encouraged to apply. Selection is based on academic qualifications of the application (preference is given to students with a GPA of 3.0 or higher), quality of the application and its career goal statement, and assessment of the applicant's motivation toward an earth science, aerospace, or engineering career or research.

Financial data Stipends range from $1,000 to $7,500.
Duration 1 academic year, semester, or summer.
Additional information Member institutions include South Dakota School of Mines and Technology, South Dakota State University, and Augustana College. Educational affiliates include Black Hills State University, the University of South Dakota, Dakota State University, Lower Brule Community College, Oglala Lakota College, Sinte Gleska University, and Lake Area Technical Institute.
Number awarded Varies each year. Approximately $70,000 is available for this program annually.
Deadline January of each year.

[461]
SOUTH TEXAS UNIT SCHOLARSHIPS

Herb Society of America-South Texas Unit
Attn: Education Committee Chair
P.O. Box 6515
Houston, TX 77265-6515
(713) 513-7808
Web: www.herbsociety-stu.org/Scholarship.htm

Purpose To provide financial assistance to Texas students majoring in agronomy, horticulture, botany, or a related field.

Eligibility This program is open to students who are studying agronomy, horticulture, botany, or a closely-related discipline at an accredited 4-year college or university. Applicants must be either a permanent resident of Texas or attending an accredited college or university in Texas. They must have completed at least 2 full years of college and be entering their junior or senior year. Selection is based on academic achievement, letters of recommendation, and a 2- to 3-paragraph statement on their short- and long-term career goals, including examples of special interests or projects in plants, herbs, gardening, etc.

Financial data The stipend is $1,000.
Duration 1 year.
Number awarded 1 each year.
Deadline March of each year.

[462]
SOUTHERN ASSOCIATION OF STEEL FABRICATORS SCHOLARSHIP

American Institute of Steel Construction
Attn: Director of University Relations
1 East Wacker Drive, Suite 700
Chicago, IL 60601-1802
(312) 670-5408 Fax: (312) 670-5403
E-mail: rosenberg@aisc.com
Web: www.aisc.org/scholarship&fellowship

Purpose To provide financial assistance to undergraduate engineering students from southern states who are interested in the structural field, especially structural steel.

Eligibility This program is open to full-time civil or architectural engineering students entering their third or fourth year at universities in Alabama, Arkansas, Florida, Georgia, Kentucky, Louisiana, Mississippi, and Tennessee. Preference is given to students who have selected a concentration in the structural field, with particular emphasis on structural steel. Along with their application, they must submit a 2-page essay on their overall career objective and an original sample structural steel analysis/design solution, with calculations. Selection is based on those submissions, academic performance, and a faculty recommendation. U.S. citizenship is required.

Financial data The stipend is $2,500.
Duration 1 year.
Additional information This program is funded by the Southern Association of Steel Fabricators.
Number awarded 1 each year.
Deadline April of each year.

[463]
SOUTHWEST ATHLETIC TRAINERS' ASSOCIATION UNDERGRADUATE SCHOLARSHIP

Southwest Athletic Trainers' Association
c/o Mike Pruitt, Scholarship Committee Chair
Trinity High School
500 North Industrial
Euless, TX 76039
(817) 571-0271, ext. 259 Fax: (817) 354-3330
Web: www.swata.com/scholarship/index.htm

Purpose To provide financial assistance to undergraduate student members of the Southwest Athletic Trainers Association (SWATA).

Eligibility This program is open to undergraduates at colleges and universities in Arkansas and Texas who are members of SWATA and the National Association of Athletic Trainers (NATA). Applicants must have worked as a student athletic trainer on the collegiate level for at least 1 year and have a GPA of 2.5 or higher. They may not be on a full athletic or academic scholarship and may not be a member of an intercollegiate sports team. Financial need is not considered in the selection process.

Financial data A stipend is awarded (amount not specified).

Duration 1 year.

Additional information SWATA serves as District 6 of NATA.

Number awarded Varies each year; recently, 18 of these scholarships were awarded.

Deadline February of each year.

[464]
SPIE SCHOLARSHIP PROGRAM

SPIE-The International Society for Optical Engineering
Attn: Scholarship Committee
1000 20th Street
P.O. Box 10
Bellingham, WA 98227-0010
(360) 676-3290 Toll-free: (888) 504-8171
Fax: (360) 647-1445 E-mail: scholarships@spie.org
Web: www.spie.org/info/scholarships

Purpose To provide financial assistance to entering or continuing undergraduate and graduate student members of SPIE-The International Society for Optical Engineering who are preparing for a career in optical science or engineering.

Eligibility This program is open to high school seniors planning to attend college, current undergraduate students, and current graduate students. Applicants must be society members majoring or planning to enroll full time and major in optical engineering, optical science, or optics at a college or university anywhere in the world. They must submit a 450-word essay that describes 1) their proposed research and/or course of study related to optics, photonics, imaging, or optoelectronics; 2) their career objectives; 3) how this scholarship would help them attain their objectives; and 4) what they have achieved and learned through their studies and activities. Financial need is not considered in the selection process.

Financial data Stipends typically provide support for tuition and related expenses, travel to technical meetings, and supplemental funding for research and teaching assistantships.

Duration 1 year.

Additional information The International Society for Optical Engineering was founded in 1955 as the Society of Photo-Optical Instrumentation Engineers (SPIE). This program includes the following special named scholarships: the D.J. Lovell Scholarship, sponsored by SPIE with contributions from Labsphere, Inc. and Laser Focus World; the William H. Price Scholarship in Optical Engineering, established in 1985 for a full-time graduate or undergraduate student in the field of optical design and engineering; the Laser Technology, Engineering and Applications Scholarship (formerly the F-MADE Scholarship), sponsored by the Forum for Military Applications of Directed Energy (F-MADE) in recognition of a student's scholarly achievement in laser technology, engineering, or applications; and the BACUS Photomask Scholarship, awarded to a full-time undergraduate or graduate student in the field of microlithography with an emphasis on optical tooling and/or semiconductor manufacturing technologies, sponsored by BACUS (SPIE's photomask international technical group).

Number awarded Varies each year. Recently, this program awarded 108 scholarships: the 4 named awards plus 104 others (including 70 in North America, 7 in Asia, 23 in Europe, and 4 in the South Pacific).

Deadline January of each year.

[465]
SPIRIT OF APOLLO SCHOLARSHIP

American Institute of Aeronautics and Astronautics-Houston Section
Attn: Douglas Schwaab, Scholarship Committee Chair
P.O. Box 57524
Webster, TX 77598
Web: www.aiaa-houston.org/scholarship

Purpose To provide financial assistance to students working on a degree in a field related to aerospace at colleges and universities in Texas.

Eligibility This program is open to students who have completed at least 1 academic year of full-time study at a college or university in Texas with a GPA of 3.0 or higher. Applicants must be majoring in a field of engineering, mathematics, or science that is relevant to the technical activities of the American Institute of Aeronautics and Astronautics (AIAA), including physical science, physics, or computer science. Along with their application, they must submit an essay of 500 to 1,000 words on their career objectives and the academic program required to achieve those objectives. U.S. citizenship or permanent resident status is required. Selection is based on personal and academic merit, as demonstrated by the essay, academic achievement, letters of recommendation, and extracurricular activities.

Financial data The stipend is $1,000.

Duration 1 year; recipients may reapply.

Number awarded 1 or more each year.

Deadline May of each year.

SCIENCES

[466]
SPORTY'S/CINCINNATI AVIONICS SCHOLARSHIP

Aircraft Electronics Association
Attn: AEA Educational Foundation
4217 South Hocker Drive
Independence, MO 64055-4723
(816) 373-6565   Fax: (816) 478-3100
E-mail: info@aea.net
Web: www.aea.net

Purpose To provide financial assistance to students who are interested in majoring in avionics in college.

Eligibility This program is open to high school seniors and currently-enrolled college students who are attending (or planning to attend) an accredited school in an avionics program. Applicants must submit an official transcript (cumulative GPA of 2.5 or higher), a statement about their career plans, a description of their involvement in school and community activities, and a 300-word essay on how the job requirements of aviation technicians will change with advancements in technology. Selection is based on merit.

Financial data The stipend is $2,000.

Duration 1 year.

Number awarded 1 each year.

Deadline February of each year.

[467]
SPS FUTURE TEACHER SCHOLARSHIP

Society of Physics Students
c/o American Institute of Physics
One Physics Ellipse
College Park, MD 20740-3843
(301) 209-3007   Fax: (301) 209-0839
E-mail: sps@aip.org
Web: www.spsnational.org

Purpose To provide financial assistance to members of the Society of Physics Students (SPS) interested in preparing for a career as a physics teacher.

Eligibility This program is open to full-time college juniors who are active members of the society. Applicants must be enrolled in a teacher education program with plans to prepare for a career in physics education. Selection is based on 1) high scholastic performance both in physics and overall studies, 2) potential for continued scholastic development in physics, 3) active participation in society programs, and 4) a statement of experiences and ambitions with regard to teaching physics.

Financial data The stipend is $2,000.

Duration 1 year.

Additional information This program is sponsored by the Sigma Pi Sigma Trust Fund and the American Institute of Physics.

Number awarded 1 each year.

Deadline February of each year.

[468]
STATE ASSOCIATION OF REAL PROPERTY AGENTS SCHOLARSHIP

International Right of Way Association
Attn: Right of Way International Education Foundation
19750 South Vermont Avenue, Suite 220
Torrance, CA 90502-1144
(310) 538-0233   Fax: (310) 538-1471
Web: www.irwaonline.org

Purpose To provide financial assistance to members of the International Right of Way Association (IRWA) and their families who are working on or planning to work on an undergraduate or graduate degree related to the work of the association.

Eligibility This program is open to IRWA members and their families (spouses, children, stepchildren, and grandchildren) who are enrolled or planning to enroll as a full-time undergraduate or graduate student. Applicants must be planning to study a field related to the right of way profession and/or public works administration (e.g., real estate, civil engineering, law, property management, business administration, public administration). They must have a GPA of 3.0 or higher. Along with their application, they must submit a 250-word essay on their plans and goals in the right of way and/or public works administration profession. Financial need is not considered in the selection process.

Financial data A stipend is awarded (amount not specified).

Duration 1 year.

Additional information This program was established in 1991 when the IRWA agreed to administer scholarship funds on behalf of the State Association of Real Property Agents (SARPA).

Number awarded 1 or 2 each year.

Deadline January of each year.

[469]
STATE WATER HEATERS SCHOLARSHIP

Plumbing-Heating-Cooling Contractors-National Association
Attn: PHCC Educational Foundation
180 South Washington Street
P.O. Box 6808
Falls Church, VA 22040
(703) 237-8100, ext. 221   Toll-free: (800) 533-7694
Fax: (703) 237-7442
E-mail: scholarships@naphcc.org
Web: www.foundation.phccweb.org

Purpose To provide financial assistance to entering or continuing undergraduate students interested in the plumbing, heating, and cooling industry.

Eligibility This program is open to 1) full-time undergraduate students (entering or continuing) who are majoring in a field related to plumbing, heating, and cooling (e.g., business management, construction management with a specialization in mechanical construction, mechanical engineering) at a 4-year college or university, and 2) students enrolled in an approved apprenticeship program or a full-time certificate or degree program at a 2-year technical college, community college, or trade school in business management, mechanical CAD design, construction management with a specialty in mechanical construction, or plumbing or HVACR installation, service, and repair. Students enrolled in an approved plumbing or HVAC apprenticeship program must be working full time for a licensed plumbing or HVAC contractor who is a member of the Plumbing-Heating-Cooling Contractors-National Association (PHCC). Applicants must submit a letter of recommendation from a member with 2 years' good standing in the PHCC; a copy of school transcripts; and a letter of recommendation from a school principal, counselor, or dean. U.S. or Canadian citizenship is required. Financial need is not considered in the selection process.

Financial data The stipend is $2,500 per year.

Duration 1 year; nonrenewable.

Additional information This program is sponsored by State Water Heaters.

Number awarded 1 each year.

Deadline May of each year.

[470]
STUDENT CORRUGATED PACKAGING DESIGN COMPETITION

Association of Independent Corrugated Converters
Attn: AICC Student Design Competition
113 South West Street, Third Floor
P.O. Box 25708
Alexandria, VA 22313
(703) 836-AICC   Toll-free: (877) 836-AICC
Fax: (703) 836-2795   E-mail: info@aiccbox.org
Web: www.aiccbox.org/student/Student_info.asp

Purpose To recognize and reward college students who submit outstanding corrugated packaging designs.

Eligibility This competition is open to undergraduate students enrolled in packaging courses at colleges, universities, and/or technical schools in Canada and the United States. Individual and team entries are accepted. Applicants construct, develop, and/or manufacture packaging designs using corrugated as the primary medium. Entries are accepted in 3 categories: design to a problem, open design, and corrugated as art. In the selection process, heavy emphasis is placed on a written essay describing the project. The first- and second-place winners in the categories of design to a problem and open design compete in a "Best of the Best" program in which they make a presentation about their entry as they might to a prospective customer.

Financial data In each of the categories, first place is $500, second $250, and third $100. The first-place winners in each category also receive all-expense paid trips to the sponsor's annual fall meeting and trade fair in September. In the "Best of the Best" program, the prize is $2,500, second $1,000, third $750, and fourth $500. The first-place winner's school receives a $5,000 grant.

Duration The competition is held annually.

Additional information The "Best of the Best" program is produced later in the fall and broadcast live to packaging schools throughout North America. The 4 participating student teams make their presentations from their home campuses. That portion of the competition is sponsored by the International Corrugated Packaging Foundation.

Number awarded 9 winners (3 in each category) are selected in the first level of competition; 4 additional prizes are awarded for the "Best of the Best" program.

Deadline May of each year.

[471]
STUDENT DESIGN COMPETITION IN ACOUSTICS

Robert Bradford Newman Student Award Fund
c/o Acoustical Society of America
2 Huntington Quadrangle, Suite 1NO1
Melville, NY 11747-4502
(516) 576-2360   Fax: (516) 576-2377
E-mail: asa@aip.org
Web: www.newmanfund.org

Purpose To recognize and reward undergraduate and graduate students who submit outstanding entries in an acoustics design competition.

Eligibility This competition is open to undergraduate and graduate students who enter as individuals or as members of teams of up to 3 students. Applicants must submit an acoustics design for a problem given by the competition. Selection is based on technical merit, design vision, adherence to the design prompt and program requirements, and effectiveness of the presentation.

Financial data The prize for the winning individual or team is $1,250. Commendation awards are $700.

Duration The competition is held annually.

Additional information This competition is sponsored by the Technical Committee for Architectural Acoustics of the Acoustical Society of America and the National Council of Acoustical Consultants. Information is also available from Bob Coffeen, University of Kansas, School of Architecture and Urban Design, 1465 Jayhawk Boulevard, Lawrence, KS 66045, (785) 864-4376, Fax: (913) 649-7063.

Number awarded 1 winner and 4 commendation awards are presented each year.

Deadline Students must register by April of each year.

[472]
STUDENT ESSAY COMPETITION IN HEALTHCARE MANAGEMENT

American College of Healthcare Executives
Attn: Associate Director, Division of Research and
  Development
One North Franklin Street, Suite 1700
Chicago, IL 60606-3529
(312) 424-9444   Fax: (312) 424-0023
E-mail: ache@ache.org
Web: www.ache.org

Purpose To recognize and reward undergraduate or graduate student members of the American College of Healthcare Executives (ACHE) who submit outstanding essays on health care administration.

Eligibility This competition is open to ACHE student associates or affiliates who are enrolled in an undergraduate or graduate program in health care management at an accredited college or university in the United States or Canada. Applicants must submit an essay, up to 15 pages in length, on a topic with a focus on such health management topics as strategic planning and policy; accountability of and/or relationships among board, medical staff, and executive management; financial management; human resources management; systems management; plant and facility management; comprehensive systems of services; quality assessment and assurance; professional, public, community, or interorganization relations; government relations or regulation; marketing; education; research; or law and ethics. Selection is based on significance of the subject to health care management, innovativeness in approach to the topic, thoroughness and precision in developing the subject, practical usefulness for guiding management action, and clarity and conciseness of expression.

Financial data The first-place winners in each division (undergraduate and graduate) receive $3,000 and their programs receive $1,000. The second-place winner receives $2,000 and third $1,000.

Duration The competition is held annually.

Additional information This program was established in 1989.

Number awarded 6 each year: 3 undergraduate and 3 graduate students.

Deadline December of each year.

[473]
STUDENT MANUFACTURING DESIGN COMPETITION

ASME International
Attn: Manufacturing Engineering Division
Three Park Avenue
New York, NY 10016-5990
(212) 591-7787   Toll-free: (800) THE-ASME
Fax: (212) 591-7671   E-mail: ElGhobashyN@asme.org
Web: divisions.asme.org

Purpose To recognize and reward outstanding manufacturing engineering designs by student members of the American Society of Mechanical Engineers (ASME).

Eligibility This competition is open to undergraduate and graduate student members of the society who submit projects that promote the art, science, and practice of manufacturing engineering. Technical areas include, but are not limited to, computer integrated manufacturing and robotics; machine tools, sensors, and controllers; manufacturing systems management and optimization; materials processing; and new areas of manufacturing engineering. Applicants must submit a report, from 1,500 to 3,000 words, that includes 1) a functional description of the concept, idea, model, or system; 2) design features and manufacturing engineering content and/or application; 3) the tools, equipment, and/or computer aided design procedures used and how they enhanced the design process; and 4) the concept's practicality and how it improves upon existing designs that do the same or similar tasks.

Financial data First prize is $1,000, second $750, and third $500.

Duration The competition is held annually.

Number awarded 3 each year.

Deadline May of each year.

[474]
STUDENT SAFETY ENGINEERING DESIGN CONTEST

ASME International
Attn: Safety Engineering and Risk Analysis Division
Three Park Avenue
New York, NY 10016-5990
(212) 591-7863   Toll-free: (800) THE-ASME
Fax: (212) 591-7671   E-mail: ulvilar@asme.org
Web: divisions.asme.org

Purpose To recognize and reward outstanding safety engineering design papers by undergraduate and graduate students.

Eligibility This competition is open to undergraduate and graduate students enrolled in an ABET-accredited mechanical engineering curriculum. Applicants must submit a senior design or other in-class project that describes an analysis, design, or engineering study that will prevent occupational injuries, illnesses, and deaths. Selection is based on background (20%), methodology (30%), feasibility (30%), and system safety (20%).

Financial data First prize is $2,000 plus a travel allowance of $400 to present the winning paper; the faculty advisor receives $500. Second prize is $500; the faculty advisor receives $200.

Duration The competition is held annually.

Additional information This program is jointly sponsored by the Safety Engineering and Risk Analysis Division of ASME (the professional organization for mechanical engineering) and the National Institute for Occupational Safety and Health (NIOSH). Additional funding is provided by FM Global, American Hazard Control Consultants, Inc., and several individuals.

Number awarded 2 each year.

Deadline May of each year.

[475]
SUSAN MISZKOWICZ MEMORIAL SCHOLARSHIP

Society of Women Engineers
230 East Ohio Street, Suite 400
Chicago, IL 60611-3265
(312) 596-5223   Toll-free: (877) SWE-INFO
Fax: (312) 644-8557
E-mail: scholarshipapplication@swe.org
Web: www.swe.org/scholarships

Purpose To provide financial assistance to undergraduate women majoring in computer science or engineering.

Eligibility This program is open to women who are entering their sophomore, junior, or senior year at a 4-year ABET-accredited college or university. Applicants must be majoring in computer science or engineering and have a GPA of 3.0 or higher. Along with their application, they must submit a 1-page essay on why they want to be an engineer or computer scientist, how they believe they will make a difference as an engineer or computer scientist, and what influenced them to study engineering or computer science. Selection is based on merit.

Financial data The stipend is $1,000.

Duration 1 year.

Additional information This program was established in 2002 to honor a member of the Society of Women Engineers who was killed in the New York World Trade Center on September 11, 2001.

Number awarded 1 each year.

Deadline January of each year.

[476]
SWE PAST PRESIDENTS SCHOLARSHIPS

Society of Women Engineers
230 East Ohio Street, Suite 400
Chicago, IL 60611-3265
(312) 596-5223   Toll-free: (877) SWE-INFO
Fax: (312) 644-8557
E-mail: scholarshipapplication@swe.org
Web: www.swe.org/scholarships

Purpose To provide financial assistance to women working on an undergraduate or graduate degree in engineering or computer science.

Eligibility This program is open to women who will be sophomores, juniors, seniors, or graduate students at ABET-accredited colleges and universities. Applicants must be U.S. citizens majoring in computer science or engineering and have a GPA of 3.0 or higher. Along with their application, they must submit a 1-page essay on why they want to be an engineer or computer scientist, how they believe they will make a difference as an engineer or computer scientist, and what influenced them to study engineering or computer science. Selection is based on merit.

Financial data The stipend is $1,500.

Duration 1 year.

Additional information This program was established in 1999 by an anonymous donor to honor the commitment and accomplishments of past presidents of the Society of Women Engineers (SWE).

Number awarded 2 each year.

Deadline January of each year.

[477]
TAGGED FOR GREATNESS SCHOLARSHIPS

Ohio Cattlemen's Association
Attn: Foundation
10600 U.S. Highway 42
Marysville, OH 43040
(614) 873-6736   Fax: (614) 873-6835
E-mail: beef@ohiobeef.org
Web: ohiocattle.org/scholarships.aspx

Purpose To provide financial assistance to high school seniors and college students in Ohio who are interested in studying agriculture.

Eligibility This program is open to Ohio residents who are high school seniors or college students. Applicants must be enrolled or planning to enroll in an agricultural program at a college or university. Along with their application, they must submit a brief statement on their involvement in the beef industry, ambitions, goals, and background. Selection is based on academic achievement and extracurricular activities.

Financial data The stipend is $1,000.

Duration 1 year.

Additional information This program is supported by the sale of Ohio's beef specialty license plates.

Number awarded 2 each year.

Deadline October of each year.

[478]
TAU BETA PI NATIONAL LAUREATE AWARDS

Tau Beta Pi
c/o University of Tennessee at Knoxville
508 Dougherty Engineering Building
1512 Middle Drive
P.O. Box 2697
Knoxville, TN 37901-2697
(865) 546-4578   Fax: (865) 546-4579
E-mail: Fellowships@tbp.org
Web: www.tbp.org

Purpose To recognize and reward undergraduate members of Tau Beta Pi, the engineering honor society, who demonstrate outstanding contributions in other areas of activity.

Eligibility This program is open to undergraduate members of the society who are nominated by their chapters. Nominees must have made outstanding contributions in helping to achieve the goal of the society: "to foster a spirit of liberal culture in engineering colleges." The areas of "other" activity for which they may be nominated include arts, athletics, diverse achievements, and service. Letters of nomination should include a half-page biographical sketch of the nominee prior to enrollment as an engineering student, a 3-page description of the contributions by the nominee to the fostering of liberal culture, a short description of Tau Beta Pi activities, an unofficial transcript, a personal resume, and 3 reference letters.

Financial data The award is $2,500.

Duration Awards are presented annually.

Additional information This program was established in 1984.

Number awarded Up to 5 each year.

Deadline March of each year.

[479]
TAU BETA PI UNDERGRADUATE SCHOLARSHIPS

Tau Beta Pi
c/o University of Tennessee at Knoxville
508 Dougherty Engineering Building
1512 Middle Drive
P.O. Box 2697
Knoxville, TN 37901-2697
(865) 546-4578   Fax: (865) 546-4579
E-mail: Fellowships@tbp.org
Web: www.tbp.org

Purpose To provide financial assistance to undergraduate members of Tau Beta Pi, the engineering honor society, who are entering their senior year.

Eligibility This program is open to members of the society who are entering their senior year of full-time undergraduate engineering study. Applicants must submit statements on 1) their plan or purpose for the next 3 years, and 2) how this scholarship will help them meet a financial need in attaining their college education that cannot be met through other sources of financial aid. Selection is based on academic standing, contribution to campus or community activities, and 2 letters of reference. Most of the scholarships are not need based, but some require demonstrated financial need.

Financial data The stipend is $2,000, payable in 2 increments (in September and January).

Duration 1 year.

Additional information This program, established in 1998, includes the following named scholarships: the R.H. Nagel Scholarship (awarded to the applicant judged most outstanding), the Charles R. Dodson Scholarship (preference given to members of Maryland Beta chapter), the Vincent A. Stabile Scholarship (established in 1999), the Leroy E. Record Scholarships (consideration also given to financial need), the Ruth M. and Cleveland L. Campbell Scholarship (consideration also given to community service and ethical standards), the Elsa and Peter Soderberg Scholarship (first awarded in 1998), the Tau Beta Pi Distinguished Alumnus Scholarship (established in 2002), the A.C. Scribner Scholarship (established in 2003), the Tau Beta Pi Mentor Scholarship (established in 2003), and the Albert H. Winkler Scholarship (established in 2004). Other scholarships are provided by the Alabama Power Foundation, Fluor, and General Motors. Information is also available from D. Stephen Pierre, Jr., Director of Fellowships, Alabama Power Company, 150 St. Joseph Street, P.O. Box 2247, Mobile, AL 36652-2247, (251) 694-2512, Fax: (251) 694-2310.

Number awarded Varies each year; recently, 69 of these scholarships were awarded. Of those, 50 were Leroy A. Record Scholarships, which include financial need as a selection criterion.

Deadline February of each year.

[480]
TERREY HAWTHORNE MEMORIAL SCHOLARSHIP

ASME International
Attn: Rail Transportation Division
Three Park Avenue
New York, NY 10016-5990
(212) 591-7797   Toll-free: (800) THE-ASME
Fax: (212) 591-7671   E-mail: manese@asme.org
Web: divisions.asme.org

Purpose To provide financial assistance to undergraduate mechanical engineering students who intend to enter the railway industry.

Eligibility This program is open to undergraduate students in mechanical engineering who are interested in a career in the railway industry and have a family connection to the industry. Applicants must submit 1) a statement of intent to pursue mechanical engineering in the railway industry as a career; 2) a statement of the importance of rail transportation in the overall field of transporting freight and passengers; 3) information on experiences in the railroad realm (i.e., work, model railroading, photography); 4) an abstract of any papers written related to the railroad industry; 5) a list of courses proposed for the upcoming term; 6) a transcript of previous college years; and 7) a letter of recommendation from a faculty advisor or department head.

They must plan to attend a college or university in North America (including Alaska, Canada, Hawaii, Mexico, and Puerto Rico). Financial need is not considered.

Financial data The award is $2,000 per year.

Duration 1 year.

Additional information Further information is also available from Samuel R. Williams, Manager of Division Affairs, 5759 Scotia Court, Dublin, OH 43016-3256, (614) 766-6970, E-mail: srwilliams@columbus.rr.com.

Number awarded 1 each year.

Deadline April of each year.

[481]
TEXAS INSTRUMENTS DEMANA-WAITS SCHOLARSHIP

National Council of Teachers of Mathematics
Attn: Mathematics Education Trust
1906 Association Drive
Reston, VA 20191-1502
(703) 620-9840, ext. 2112   Fax: (703) 476-2970
E-mail: exec@nctm.org
Web: www.nctm.org/about/met/demana-waits.htm

Purpose To provide financial assistance to undergraduate student members of the National Council of Teachers of Mathematics (NCTM) who are preparing for a career as a secondary school mathematics teacher.

Eligibility This program is open to full-time undergraduate students who are 1) student members of NCTM, 2) currently completing their sophomore year of college with a GPA of 3.0 or higher, 3) scheduled for full-time study at a 4-year or 5-year college or university in the next academic year, and 4) preparing for a career as a certified teacher of secondary school mathematics. Applicants must submit a proposal that includes official transcripts, a list of courses remaining to be completed in order to fulfill the requirements for teacher certification within a 3-year period, an itemized budget that includes how they plan to allocate funds from this scholarship for the third and fourth years of full-time study, a list of extracurricular or professional activities that demonstrate their commitment to becoming a secondary school mathematics teacher, letters of recommendation, and a 2-page essay on why they have chosen to prepare for a career as a secondary school mathematics teacher. Selection is based on academic achievement and commitment to a teaching career in secondary school mathematics.

Financial data The stipend is $5,000 per year. Funds must be used for tuition, fees, course materials, and other expenses directly related to the recipient's academic program of study. No more than 10% of the total (or $1,000) may be used for acquisition of equipment.

Duration 2 years (the junior and senior year of undergraduate study).

Additional information Texas Instruments sponsors these scholarships to recognize the contributions to mathematics education by professors Frank Demana and Bert K. Waits of the Ohio State University. Recipients are required to submit a transcript and a brief report at the end of each year of study.

Number awarded Up to 2 each year.

Deadline May of each year.

[482]
THOMAS G. NEUSOM SCHOLARSHIPS
Conference of Minority Transportation Officials
Attn: National Scholarship Program
818 18th Street, N.W., Suite 850
Washington, DC 20006
(202) 530-0551 Fax: (202) 530-0617
Web: www.comto.org/scholarship.htm

Purpose To provide financial assistance for college or graduate school to members of the Conference of Minority Transportation Officials (COMTO).

Eligibility This program is open to undergraduate and graduate students who have been members of COMTO for at least 1 year. Applicants must be working on a degree in a field related to transportation with a GPA of 2.5 or higher. Along with their application, they must submit a cover letter with a 500-word statement of career goals. Financial need is not considered in the selection process. U.S. citizenship is required.

Financial data The stipend is $5,500. Funds are paid directly to the recipient's college or university.

Duration 1 year.

Additional information COMTO was established in 1971 to promote, strengthen, and expand the roles of minorities in all aspects of transportation. Recipients are expected to attend the COMTO National Scholarship Luncheon.

Number awarded 2 each year.

Deadline April of each year.

[483]
THOMAS PRATTE MEMORIAL SCHOLARSHIPS
Surfrider Foundation
Attn: Pratte Scholarship
P.O. Box 6010
San Clemente, CA 92674-6010
(949) 492-8170 Fax: (949) 492-8142
E-mail: prattescholarship@surfrider.org
Web: www.surfrider.org

Purpose To provide financial assistance to members of the Surfrider Foundation working on an undergraduate or graduate degree in an environmental field.

Eligibility This program is open to members of the foundation working on an undergraduate, master's, or doctoral degree in a field consistent with the foundation's mission, including (but not limited to) oceanography, marine affairs, environmental sciences, public policy, community planning, or natural resources. Applicants must be enrolled at an accredited college or university in the United States or Puerto Rico as an upper-division or graduate student. Undergraduates must have a GPA of 3.4 or higher and graduate students 3.6 or higher. Along with their application, they must submit 1) a personal statement describing their career goals, volunteer activities, work, or summer plans as they pertain to the coastal environmental issues relevant to the foundation and its mission; and 2) a description of their current research and how it relates to the foundation's stated mission and environmental programs. Financial need is not considered in the selection process.

Financial data The stipend is $2,000 for an undergraduate, $3,000 for a master's degree student, and $5,000 for a doctoral student.

Duration 1 year.

Additional information This foundation, established in 1984 by a group of surfers, is a nonprofit environmental grassroots organization dedicated to the protection and preservation of the world's waves, oceans, and beaches. It currently has 50,000 members with 60 chapters in 22 states.

Number awarded 3 each year: 1 for a student at each academic level.

Deadline June of each year.

[484]
THROLSON AMERICAN BISON FOUNDATION SCHOLARSHIPS
National Bison Association
Attn: Throlson American Bison Foundation
8690 Wolff Court, Suite 200
Westminster, CO 80031
(303) 292-2833 Fax: (303) 292-2564
E-mail: info@bisoncentral.com
Web: www.bisoncentral.com

Purpose To provide financial assistance to upper-division and graduate students studying bison or fields related to the bison industry.

Eligibility This program is open to college juniors, college seniors, and graduate students in a recognized livestock, animal science, veterinary, agriculture, or human nutrition program in the United States or Canada. Applicants must be preparing for a career related to the bison or bison industry. Selection is based on essays on the following topics: how they may play a role in the growth of the bison industry in the next 15 years (30 points); community and professional organizations to which they belong and their involvement with them (10 points); their livestock, veterinary, biological, zoological, human nutrition, agribusiness, or agricultural work experience (10 points); their hobbies and leisure activities (5 points); their philosophy of bison in today's environment (10 points); what they believe to be the most critical issue affecting their field of study during the next 10 years (10 points); and their career goals and objectives (25 points).

Financial data The stipend is either $2,000 or $1,000.

Duration 1 year; nonrenewable.

Number awarded 3 each year: 1 at $2,000 and 2 at $1,000.

Deadline September of each year.

[485]
TMC/SAE DONALD D. DAWSON TECHNICAL SCHOLARSHIP
Society of Automotive Engineers
Attn: Scholarship Administrator
400 Commonwealth Drive
Warrendale, PA 15096-0001
(724) 772-4047 Fax: (724) 776-3049
E-mail: scholarships@sae.org
Web: students.sae.org

Purpose To provide financial support to students interested in working on a college degree in engineering.

Eligibility This program is open to U.S. citizens who intend to earn an ABET-accredited degree in engineering. Applicants must be 1) high school seniors with a GPA of

SCIENCES

3.25 or higher and minimum SAT scores of 600 in mathematics and 550 in critical reading or ACT scores of 27 or higher; 2) transfer students from 4-year colleges or universities with a GPA of 3.0 or higher; or 3) transfer students from postsecondary technical or vocational schools with a GPA of 3.5 or higher. Selection is based on school transcripts; evidence of some type of hands-on technical experience or activity (e.g., rebuilding engines, working on cars or trucks); SAT or ACT scores; school-related extracurricular activities; non-school related activities; academic honors, civic honors, and awards; and a 250-word essay on their goals, plans, experiences, and interests in mobility engineering. Financial need is not considered.

Financial data The stipend is $1,500 per year.

Duration 1 year; may be renewed up to 3 additional years if the recipient maintains a GPA of 3.0 or higher.

Additional information The Society of Automotive Engineers (SAE) and The Maintenance Council (TMC) of American Trucking Associations established this scholarship to honor the leadership of Donald D. Dawson. Candidates must include a $5 processing fee with their applications.

Number awarded 1 each year.

Deadline November of each year.

[486]
TOBIN SORENSON PHYSICAL EDUCATION SCHOLARSHIP

Pi Lambda Theta
Attn: Scholarships Committee
4101 East Third Street
P.O. Box 6626
Bloomington, IN 47407-6626
(812) 339-3411   Toll-free: (800) 487-3411
Fax: (812) 339-3462   E-mail: office@pilambda.org
Web: www.pilambda.org

Purpose To provide financial assistance to students preparing for careers as a teacher of physical education or a related field.

Eligibility This program is open to students preparing for careers at the K-12 level. Applicants must be interested in becoming a physical education teacher, adaptive physical education teacher, coach, recreational therapist, dance therapist, or similar professional teaching the knowledge and use of the human body. They must be sophomores or above and have a GPA of 3.5 or higher. Selection is based on academic achievement, potential for leadership, and extracurricular involvement in physical/sports education, recreation therapy, or similar activities (e.g., coaching, tutoring, volunteer work for appropriate organizations on or off campus).

Financial data The stipend is $1,000.

Duration 1 year.

Additional information This program was established in 1999. If the recipient is not already a member of Pi Lambda Theta (an international honor and professional association in education), a complimentary 1-year honorary membership is also awarded.

Number awarded 1 every other year.

Deadline February of each odd-numbered year.

[487]
TOCA PUBLISHERS SCHOLARSHIP PROGRAM

Turf and Ornamental Communicators Association
120 West Main Street, Suite 200
P.O. Box 156
New Prague, MN 56071
(952) 758-6340   Fax: (952) 758-5813
E-mail: tocaassociation@aol.com
Web: www.toca.org/scholar.html

Purpose To provide financial assistance to undergraduate students preparing for a career in green industry communications.

Eligibility This program is open to undergraduate students majoring or minoring in technical communications or in a green industry-related field (e.g., horticulture, plant sciences, botany, agronomy, plant pathology). Applicants must demonstrate an interest in using this course of study in the field of communications. They must have a GPA of 2.5 or higher overall and 3.0 or higher in their major field of study. Along with their application, they must submit 2 academic or professional references, a writing sample (a news article published or prepared for publication), a resume, their transcript, and an essay (500 words or less) that describes how they became interested in the turf and ornamental industry and their professional goals.

Financial data The stipend is $1,000. Funds are paid through the bursar's office at the recipient's college or university.

Duration 1 year.

Number awarded Up to 2 each year.

Deadline February of each year.

[488]
TRAILBLAZER SCHOLARSHIPS

Conference of Minority Transportation Officials
Attn: National Scholarship Program
818 18th Street, N.W., Suite 850
Washington, DC 20006
(202) 530-0551   Fax: (202) 530-0617
Web: www.comto.org/scholarship.htm

Purpose To provide financial assistance to undergraduate and graduate minority students working on a degree in a field related to transportation.

Eligibility This program is open to undergraduate and graduate students who are working on a degree in a field related to transportation with a GPA of 2.5 or higher. Along with their application, they must submit a cover letter with a 500-word statement of career goals. Financial need is not considered in the selection process. U.S. citizenship is required.

Financial data The stipend is $2,500. Funds are paid directly to the recipient's college or university.

Duration 1 year.

Additional information The Conference of Minority Transportation Officials (COMTO) was established in 1971 to promote, strengthen, and expand the roles of minorities in all aspects of transportation. Recipients are expected to attend the COMTO National Scholarship Luncheon.

Number awarded 2 each year.

Deadline April of each year.

[489]
TWEEDALE SCHOLARSHIPS
U.S. Navy
Attn: Chief of Naval Education and Training
Code N79A2
250 Dallas Street
Pensacola, FL 32508-5220
(850) 452-4941, ext. 29381
Toll-free: (800) NAV-ROTC, ext. 29381
Fax: (850) 452-2486
E-mail: PNSC_NROTC.scholarship@navy.mil
Web: www.nrotc.navy.mil/scholarships.cfm

Purpose To provide financial assistance to currently-enrolled college students who are interested in joining Navy ROTC and majoring in a technical field in college.

Eligibility This program is open to students who have completed at least 1 but not more than 4 academic terms with a cumulative GPA that places them above their peer mean or 3.0, whichever is higher, and a grade of "C" or better in all classes attempted. They must have a strong mathematics and science background in high school (with a grade of "B" or higher in calculus, if taken) and completed at least 1 academic term of college-level mathematics or science. They must be majoring in specified technical fields (recently, those were chemistry, computer science, engineering, mathematics, and physics). Students must be interviewed by the Professor of Naval Science (PNS) at their college or university and must comply with standards of leadership potential and military/physical fitness. They must submit a plan indicating that they will complete the introductory naval science course as soon as possible and be able to complete all naval science requirements and graduate on time with their class.

Financial data These scholarships provide payment of full tuition and required educational fees, as well as a specified amount for textbooks, supplies, and equipment. The program also provides a stipend for 10 months of the year that is $300 per month as a sophomore, $350 per month as a junior, and $400 per month as a senior.

Duration 2 or 3 years, until the recipient completes the bachelor's degree.

Additional information Applications must be made through the PNS at 1 of the 70 schools hosting the Navy ROTC program. Prior to final selection, applicants must attend, at Navy expense, a 6-week summer training course at the Naval Science Institute at Newport, Rhode Island. After completing the program, all participants are commissioned as ensigns in the Naval Reserve or second lieutenants in the Marine Corps Reserve with an 8-year service obligation, including 4 years of active duty.

Number awarded Approximately 140 each year: 2 at each college and university with a Navy ROTC unit.

Deadline March of each year.

[490]
TWEET COLEMAN AVIATION SCHOLARSHIP
American Association of University Women-Honolulu Branch
Attn: Scholarship Committee
1802 Keeaumoku Street
Honolulu, HI 96822
(808) 537-4702   Fax: (808) 537-4702
E-mail: aauwhnb@att.net

Purpose To provide financial assistance to women in Hawaii who are interested in a career in aviation.

Eligibility This program is open to women who are residents of Hawaii and either college graduates or attending an accredited college in the state. Applicants must be able to pass a First Class FAA medical examination. As part of their application, they must include a 2-page statement on "Why I Want to be a Pilot." Selection is based on the merit of the applicant and a personal interview.

Financial data The amount awarded varies.

Duration 1 year.

Additional information This scholarship was first awarded in 1990.

Number awarded Varies; at least 1 each year.

Deadline September of each year.

[491]
UNCF/MERCK UNDERGRADUATE SCIENCE RESEARCH SCHOLARSHIPS
United Negro College Fund
Attn: Merck Science Initiative
8260 Willow Oaks Corporate Drive, Suite 110
P.O. Box 10444
Fairfax, VA 22031-4511
(703) 205-3503   Fax: (703) 205-3574
E-mail: uncfmerck@uncf.org
Web: www.uncf.org/merck/programs/undergrd.htm

Purpose To provide financial assistance and summer work experience to African American undergraduates who are interested in preparing for a career in biomedical research.

Eligibility This program is open to African American students currently enrolled as full-time juniors and planning to graduate in the coming year. Applicants must be majoring in a life or physical science, have completed 2 semesters of organic chemistry, be interested in biomedical research, and have a GPA of 3.3 or higher. They must be interested in working at Merck as a summer intern. Candidates for professional (Pharm.D., D.V.M., D.D.S., etc.) and engineering degrees are ineligible. U.S. citizenship or permanent resident status is required. Selection is based on GPA, demonstrated interest in a scientific education and a career in scientific research, and interest in and ability to perform laboratory work.

Financial data The total award is $35,000, including up to $25,000 for tuition, fees, room, and board, and at least $5,000 per year for 2 summer internship stipends. In addition, the department of the award recipient may receive a grant of up to $10,000.

Duration 1 academic year plus internships of 10 to 12 weeks during the preceding and following summers.

Additional information This program, established in 1995, is funded by the Merck Company Foundation. Internships are performed at a Merck research facility in Rahway (New Jersey), West Point, (Pennsylvania), or Boston (Massachusetts).
Number awarded At least 15 each year.
Deadline December of each year.

[492]
UNDERGRADUATE SCHOLARSHIP PROGRAM OF THE ALABAMA SPACE GRANT CONSORTIUM

Alabama Space Grant Consortium
c/o University of Alabama in Huntsville
Materials Science Building, Room 205
Huntsville, AL 35899
(256) 824-6800 Fax: (256) 824-6061
E-mail: reasonj@uah.edu
Web: www.uah.edu/ASGC

Purpose To provide financial assistance to undergraduates who are studying space-related subjects at universities participating in the Alabama Space Grant Consortium (ASGC).
Eligibility This program is open to full-time students entering their junior or senior year at universities participating in the ASGC. Applicants must be studying in a field related to space, including the physical, natural, and biological sciences; engineering, education; economics; business; sociology; behavioral sciences; computer science; communications; law; international affairs; and public administration. They must be U.S. citizens and have a GPA of 3.0 or higher. Individuals from underrepresented groups (African Americans, Hispanic, American Indians, Pacific Islanders, Asian Americans, and women) are especially encouraged to apply. Interested students should submit a completed application with a career goal statement, personal references, a brief resume, and transcripts. Selection is based on 1) academic qualifications, 2) quality of the career goal statement, and 3) assessment of the applicant's motivation for a career in aerospace.
Financial data The stipend is $1,000 per year.
Duration 1 year; may be renewed 1 additional year.
Additional information The member universities are University of Alabama in Huntsville, Alabama A&M University, University of Alabama, University of Alabama at Birmingham, University of South Alabama, Tuskegee University, and Auburn University. Funding for this program is provided by NASA.
Number awarded Varies each year; recently, 32 of these scholarships were awarded.
Deadline February of each year.

[493]
UNDERGRADUATE STUDENTS IN TECHNICAL RESEARCH PROGRAM

National Society of Black Engineers
Attn: Programs Department
1454 Duke Street
Alexandria, VA 22314
(703) 549-2207, ext. 305 Fax: (703) 683-5312
E-mail: programs@nsbe.org
Web: www.nsbe.org/programs/ustr.php

Purpose To recognize and reward outstanding student members of the National Society of Black Engineers (NSBE) who present outstanding posters of technical research projects.
Eligibility This program is open to current paid-up undergraduate members of the society who present a poster at a regional conference. Posters may be based on a senior project, company sponsored research program, or independent study course, but they must reflect practical applications of engineering technology. Selection of winners is based on technical content of the displays, oral presentation skills, and a 10-minute question and answer session with judges. The 3 top winners from each region compete at the national level.
Financial data In the regional competitions, first prize is $200, second $100, and third $50. National awards are $1,000 for first, $500 for second, and $250 for third.
Duration The awards are presented annually.
Number awarded 18 each year: 3 in each of the 6 regions, of whom 3 are selected as national winners.
Deadline October of each year.

[494]
VERMONT SPACE GRANT UNDERGRADUATE SCHOLARSHIPS

Vermont Space Grant Consortium
c/o University of Vermont
College of Engineering and Mathematics
Votey Building, Room 209
12 Colchester Avenue
Burlington, VT 05405-0156
(802) 656-1429 Fax: (802) 656-1102
E-mail: zeno@cems.uvm.edu
Web: www.vtspacegrant.org/vtscholarship.htm

Purpose To provide financial assistance for undergraduate study in space-related fields to students in Vermont.
Eligibility This program is open to Vermont residents who are 1) enrolled in an undergraduate degree program at a Vermont institution of higher education with a GPA of 3.0 or higher or 2) seniors graduating from a high school in Vermont. Applicants must be planning to pursue a professional career that has direct relevance to the U.S. aerospace industry and the goal of the National Aeronautics and Space Administration (NASA) in such fields as astronomy, biology, engineering, mathematics, physics, and other basic sciences (including earth sciences and medicine). They must submit an essay, up to 3 pages in length, on their career plans and the relationship of those plans to areas of interest to NASA. U.S. citizenship is required. Selection is based on academic standing, letters of recommendation, and the essay. The Vermont Space Grant Consortium (VSGC) is a

component of the NASA Space Grant program, which encourages participation by women, underrepresented minorities, and persons with disabilities.

Financial data The stipend is $1,500 per year.

Duration 1 year; may be renewed upon reapplication.

Additional information This program is funded by NASA. Participating institutions are the College of Engineering and Mathematics at the University of Vermont, St. Michael's College, Norwich University, Vermont Technical College, the Vermont State Mathematics Coalition, and Burlington Aviation Technology School/Burlington Technical Center.

Number awarded Varies each year; recently, 8 of these scholarships were awarded.

Deadline April of each year.

[495] VIRGINIA COUNCIL OF TEACHERS OF MATHEMATICS SCHOLARSHIPS

Virginia Council of Teachers of Mathematics
c/o Edward A. Anderson, Jr., Scholarship Committee
Northern Virginia Community College, Manassas Campus
6901 Sudley Road
Manassas, VA 20109-2399
(703) 257-6552   E-mail: eanderson@nvcc.edu
Web: www.vctm.org/scholarship.htm

Purpose To provide financial assistance to Virginia residents who are preparing for a career as a mathematics teacher.

Eligibility This program is open to residents of Virginia who are enrolled full time in a college mathematics program and scheduled to graduate during the following year. Applicants must be planning to teach mathematics in Virginia at the elementary, middle school, high school, or college level. Students in a program leading to a degree as a mathematics lead teacher or mathematics specialist are also eligible. Along with their application, they must submit a 1-page statement indicating why they wish to be a mathematics teacher. Selection is based on potential for a successful career teaching mathematics, as indicated by that statement, recommendations of 2 faculty members, and academic records.

Financial data The stipend is $1,000.

Duration 1 year.

Number awarded 1 or 2 each year.

Deadline December of each year.

[496] VIRGINIA P. HENRY SCHOLARSHIP

Federated Garden Clubs of Maryland
Attn: Executive Secretary
1106A Providence Road
Baltimore, MD 21286-1790
(410) 296-6961   E-mail: fgcofmd@aol.com
Web: hometown.aol.com/fgcofmd/scholarships.html

Purpose To provide financial assistance to Maryland residents who are interested in working on an undergraduate degree in horticulture.

Eligibility This program is open to undergraduate students who are Maryland residents attending an accredited college or university anywhere in the United States. Applicants must be interested in working on a degree in horticultural studies. Selection is based on ability, worthiness, and determination.

Financial data Stipends range up to $1,000.

Duration 1 year.

Number awarded 1 or more each year.

Deadline April of each year.

[497] V.L. PETERSON SCHOLARSHIP

American Jersey Cattle Association
Attn: Dr. Cherie L. Bayer
6486 East Main Street
Reynoldsburg, OH 43068-2362
(614) 861-3636   Fax: (614) 861-8040
E-mail: cbayer@usjersey.com
Web: www.usjersey.com

Purpose To provide financial assistance for college to members of the American Jersey Cattle Association (AJCA) who have worked with Jersey cattle.

Eligibility This program is open to AJCA members who have significant and extensive experience in breeding, managing, and showing Jersey cattle. Applicants must have completed at least 1 year of college. Along with their application, they must describe their activities with Jersey cattle; summarize their extracurricular activities during high school and college; and describe their background, ambitions, and goals. They must have a GPA of 2.5 or higher. Financial need is not considered in the selection process.

Financial data The stipend is approximately $1,000.

Duration 1 year.

Number awarded 1 each year.

Deadline June of each year.

[498] W. DAVID SMITH, JR. STUDENT PAPER AWARD

American Institute of Chemical Engineers
Attn: Awards Administrator
Three Park Avenue
New York, NY 10016-5991
(212) 591-7107   Fax: (212) 591-8890
E-mail: awards@aiche.org
Web: www.aiche.org/About/Awards/Division.aspx

Purpose To recognize and reward outstanding student papers in chemical engineering computing and systems technology.

Eligibility Published works on the application of computing and systems technology to chemical engineering that were completed while the author was working on a graduate or undergraduate degree in chemical engineering may be submitted.

Financial data The award consists of a plaque and $1,500.

Duration This award is presented annually.

Additional information This award, first presented in 1983, was formerly known as the Ted Peterson Student

Paper Award. It is sponsored by E.I. duPont de Nemours and Company, Inc.
Number awarded 1 each year.
Deadline April of each year.

[499]
WAHPERD STUDENT SCHOLARSHIP AWARDS

Wisconsin Association for Health, Physical Education, Recreation, and Dance
Attn: Executive Director
University of Wisconsin at La Crosse
24 Mitchell Hall
1725 State Street
La Crosse, WI 54601-3788
(608) 785-8175   Toll-free: (800) 441-4568
E-mail: wahperd@uwlax.edu
Web: www.wahperd.org/scholarships.htm

Purpose To provide financial assistance to members of the Wisconsin Association for Health, Physical Education, Recreation and Dance (WAHPERD) who are working on a college degree.
Eligibility This program is open to WAHPERD members who have completed at least 2 years of study at a 4-year college or university with a major in physical education, health education, exercise fitness, recreation, athletic training, sports management, or dance. Applicants must have a GPA of 3.2 or higher, at least 2 years' of membership, and a record of professional involvement and leadership responsibility. They must submit a resume and 2 letters of recommendation. Financial need is not considered in the selection process.
Financial data The stipend is $1,000.
Duration 1 year.
Number awarded 4 each year.
Deadline March of each year.

[500]
WALTER J. CLORE SCHOLARSHIP

Washington Association of Wine Grape Growers
Attn: Washington Wine Industry Foundation
P.O. Box 716
Cashmere, WA 98815-0716
(509) 782-1108   Fax: (509) 782-1203
E-mail: info@wawgg.org
Web: www.wawgg.org/index.php?page_id=76

Purpose To provide financial assistance to residents of Washington who are interested in studying viticulture and/or enology in college.
Eligibility This program is open to students who are enrolled or planning to enroll in a college or university to study viticulture and/or enology. Preference is given to residents of Washington, although they may study in any state. Applicants must submit a 500-word essay on their career objective and why they want to receive this scholarship. Selection is based on academic merit, leadership abilities, and interest in the study of enology and/or viticulture; financial need is not considered.
Financial data Stipends range from $500 to $2,000.
Duration 1 year.

Additional information This program was established in 1997.
Number awarded 1 or more each year.
Deadline December of each year.

[501]
WALTER SAMUEL MCAFEE SCHOLARSHIP IN SPACE PHYSICS

National Society of Black Physicists
Attn: Scholarship Committee Chair
6704G Lee Highway
Arlington, VA 22205
(703) 536-4207   Fax: (703) 536-4203
E-mail: scholarship@nsbp.org
Web: www.nsbp.org

Purpose To provide financial assistance to African American students majoring in space physics in college.
Eligibility This program is open to African American students who are entering their junior or senior year of college and majoring in space physics. Applicants must submit an essay on their academic and career objectives, information on their participation in extracurricular activities, a description of any awards and honors they have received, and 3 letters of recommendation. Financial need is not considered.
Financial data The stipend is $1,000.
Duration 1 year; nonrenewable.
Additional information This program is offered in partnership with the American Astronomical Society.
Number awarded 1 each year.
Deadline November of each year.

[502]
WARNER N. PLUMMER SCHOLARSHIP

New Hampshire Land Surveyors Foundation
Attn: Scholarship Committee
77 Main Street
P.O. Box 689
Raymond, NH 03077-0689
(603) 895-4822   Toll-free: (800) 698-5447
Fax: (603) 895-0157   E-mail: info@nhlsa.org
Web: www.nhlsa.org/scholarship.htm

Purpose To provide financial assistance to residents of New Hampshire who are preparing for a career in land surveying.
Eligibility This program is open to New Hampshire residents enrolled in the second, third, or fourth year of a 4-year program in surveying or surveying engineering at a college or university in the United States or Canada. Applicants must have shown serious interest, capability, and outstanding accomplishments in surveying courses. They must be preparing for a career in land surveying. Along with their application, they must submit an essay about their professional aspirations, their goals in college and afterwards, and factors that make them particularly deserving of support. Financial need is not required.
Financial data The stipend is $2,000.
Duration 1 year.
Number awarded 1 each year.

Deadline October of each year.

[503]
WARREN/SANDERS/MCNAUGHTON OCEANOGRAPHIC SCHOLARSHIP

Woman's National Farm and Garden Association, Inc.
P.O. Box 1175
Midland, MI 48641-1175
Web: www.wnfga.org/code/scholarships.htm

Purpose To provide financial assistance to undergraduate and graduate students working on a degree in oceanography.

Eligibility This program is open to undergraduate and graduate students in oceanography and related fields. There is no formal application. Interested students must submit a letter with a statement of their objectives and interests, a resume with references, 2 letters of recommendation, academic transcripts, and a description of their planned program at an educational institution.

Financial data The stipend ranges from $1,000 to $1,500.

Duration 1 year.

Additional information Information is also available from Markie Phillips, 83 Webster Road, Weston, MA 02493. Students who accept the fellowships must agree to devote themselves to the study outlined in their application and to submit any proposed change in their plan to the committee for approval. They must send the committee at least 2 reports on their work, 1 at the end of the first semester and another upon completion of the year's work.

Number awarded 1 each year.

Deadline May of each year.

[504]
WASHINGTON NASA SPACE GRANT CONSORTIUM UNDERGRADUATE SCHOLARSHIPS

Washington NASA Space Grant Consortium
c/o University of Washington
Johnson Hall, Room 141
Box 351310
Seattle, WA 98195-1310
(206) 543-1943   Toll-free: (800) 659-1943
Fax: (206) 543-0179   E-mail: nasa@u.washington.edu
Web: www.waspacegrant.org/undergr.html

Purpose To provide financial assistance for college to students in Washington who wish to study science, engineering, or mathematics with an emphasis on space.

Eligibility This program is open to residents of Washington who are attending or planning to attend designated institutions that are members of the Washington NASA Space Grant Consortium. Applicants must be interested in majoring in space-related aspects of science, engineering, or mathematics. U.S. citizenship is required. The program values diversity and strongly encourages women and minorities to apply.

Financial data Stipends vary at participating institutions, but range from $1,000 to $5,000.

Duration 1 year; may be renewed.

Additional information This program is funded by the U.S. National Aeronautics and Space Administration (NASA). Members of the consortium that offer undergraduate scholarships are Northwest Indian College, Seattle Central Community College, University of Washington, and Washington State University.

Number awarded Varies each year.

Deadline Each participating institution sets its own deadline.

[505]
WASHINGTON STATE POTATO FOUNDATION SCHOLARSHIPS

Washington State Potato Foundation
P.O. Box 5051
Pasco, WA 99302
(509) 542-0595   Fax: (509) 271-0006
E-mail: kbalcom@potatoes.com
Web: www.potatoes.com/PotatoFoundation.cfm

Purpose To provide financial assistance for college to residents of Oregon and Washington who have a connection to potato growing.

Eligibility This program is open to residents of Oregon and Washington who 1) pay assessment to the Washington State Potato Commission; 2) are commercial growers, processors, packers, or shippers of potatoes; or 3) are employees or children of employees of commercial growers, processors, packers, or shippers of potatoes. Applicants must be working on or planning to work on a 2- or 4-year degree or technical certification at an institution of higher education; preference is given to those studying an agriculture-related field. Along with their application, they must submit a 500-word essay about their educational and career goals, how they plan to achieve those goals, how their field of study is related to the agricultural industry, the relevance in the current market, and how their talents can lend to its success. Financial need is not considered in the selection process.

Financial data Stipends range from $1,000 to $2,500.

Duration 1 year; recipients may reapply.

Number awarded Varies each year; recently, 28 of these scholarships were awarded.

Deadline February of each year.

[506]
WEC MINI BAJA CHALLENGE FOR WOMEN TEAM LEADERS

Society of Automotive Engineers
Attn: Award Program Staff
400 Commonwealth Drive
Warrendale, PA 15096-0001
(724) 772-4009   Fax: (724) 776-1830
E-mail: awards@sae.org
Web: www.sae.org/awards/wecminibaja.htm

Purpose To recognize and reward student teams with women leaders and predominantly women members who enter the Society of Automotive Engineers (SAE) Mini Baja Competition.

Eligibility The SAE Mini Baja is open to teams of student members of the society who design and build a prototype of a rugged, single seat, off-road recreational vehicle. For 3 competitions held in North America, all team members

must be 1) enrolled as degree-seeking undergraduate or graduate students (team members who have graduated during the 7-month period prior to the competition remain eligible to participate) and 2) SAE members. This award is presented to the team with a woman leader and/or predominantly women members who submit the outstanding project proposal prior to the deadline.
Financial data The award is $1,000. Funds may be used to help the winning team complete its vehicle and travel to the event.
Duration The award is presented annually.
Additional information This award is presented by the SAE Women Engineers Committee (WEC).
Number awarded 1 each year.
Deadline Proposals must be submitted by October of each year.

[507]
WERNER B. THIELE MEMORIAL SCHOLARSHIPS

Gravure Association of America
Attn: Gravure Education Foundation
1200-A Scottsville Road
Rochester, NY 14624
(315) 589-8879   Fax: (585) 436-7689
E-mail: lwshatch@gaa.org
Web: www.gaa.org/GEF/scholarships.htm

Purpose To provide financial assistance to upper-division students interested in a career in printing.
Eligibility This program is open to juniors and seniors who are enrolled full time in a field related to printing at a designated learning resource center supported by the Gravure Education Foundation (GEF) of the Gravure Association of America. Applicants must have a GPA of 3.0 or higher. Along with their application, they must submit a 300-word essay that demonstrates their interest in gravure technology. Financial need is not considered in the selection process.
Financial data The stipend is $1,250.
Duration 1 year.
Additional information GEF learning resource centers are located at the following universities: Rochester Institute of Technology, Western Michigan University, California Polytechnic State University at San Luis Obispo, Arizona State University, Clemson University, Murray State University, and the University of Wisconsin at Stout.
Number awarded 2 each year.
Deadline May of each year.

[508]
WEST MICHIGAN CHAPTER AWMA SCHOLARSHIPS

Air & Waste Management Association-West Michigan Chapter
c/o Loretta Campbell-Jones, Scholarship Chair
Access Business Group
7575 East Fulton Road, MC-26-2D
Ada, MI 49355
E-mail: loretta_campbell-jones@accessbusinessgroup.com
Web: www.wmawma.org

Purpose To provide financial assistance to upper-division and master's degree students in Michigan who are interested in preparing for a career in an environmental field.
Eligibility This program is open to 1) students currently enrolled at an accredited college or university in Michigan; and 2) members of the West Michigan Chapter of the Air & Waste Management Association (AWMA) and their children who are attending an accredited college or university in any state. Applicants must be entering their junior or senior year of undergraduate studies or enrolled in a master's degree program and preparing for a career in air pollution control, hazardous waste management, or other environmental area. Preferred courses of study include environmental engineering, physical or natural sciences, or natural resources. Selection is based on academic achievement (GPA of 3.0 or higher), an essay of 500 to 600 words on interests and objectives, and participation in extracurricular activities.
Financial data The stipend is $1,500.
Duration 1 year; recipients may reapply.
Number awarded 5 each year.
Deadline November of each year.

[509]
WESTERN FEDERATION OF PROFESSIONAL SURVEYORS SCHOLARSHIPS

Western Federation of Professional Surveyors
Attn: Executive Director
P.O. Box 2722
Santa Rosa, CA 95405
(707) 578-1130   Fax: (707) 578-4406
E-mail: admin@wfps.org
Web: www.wfps.org/files/scholarsh.html

Purpose To provide financial assistance to upper-division students majoring in surveying at colleges and universities in 13 designated western states.
Eligibility This program is open to students attending accredited private and public colleges that 1) offer a program leading to a 4-year bachelor's degree with a land surveying major, and 2) that are in the states of Alaska, Arizona, California, Colorado, Hawaii, Idaho, Montana, Nevada, New Mexico, Oregon, Utah, Washington, or Wyoming. Applicants must have completed at least 2 years of study. Community college students must be planning to transfer to an eligible 4-year school. Candidates must submit a 1-page essay on their educational goals, career goals, and why their qualifications justify their receiving this scholarship. Selection is based on the quality and neatness of the essay, academic achievement, professional qualifications, college activities, community activities, work experience, and letters of recommendation.

Financial data The stipend is $1,200.
Duration 1 year; recipients may reapply.
Additional information Information is also available from Paul A. Reid, Scholarship Committee, 1533 Pinion Drive, Cheyenne, WY 82001, E-mail: preidpls@bresnan.net.
Number awarded Varies each year; recently, 3 of these scholarships were awarded.
Deadline March of each year.

[510]
WILLARD B. SIMMONS SCHOLARSHIP
National Community Pharmacists Association
Attn: NCPA Foundation
100 Daingerfield Road
Alexandria, VA 22314-2888
(703) 683-8200   Toll-free: (800) 544-7447
Fax: (703) 683-3619   E-mail: info@ncpanet.org
Web: www.ncpanet.org.org

Purpose To provide financial assistance for full-time education in pharmacy to student members of the National Community Pharmacists Association (NCPA).
Eligibility All pharmacy students who are student members of the association and enrolled in an accredited U.S. school or college of pharmacy on a full-time basis are eligible. Applicants must submit a copy of their most recent transcript, 2 letters of recommendation, a resume or curriculum vitae, and a statement outlining their school and citizenship accomplishments and future career objectives in independent community pharmacy. Selection is based on leadership qualities and academic achievement.
Financial data The stipend is $2,000, paid directly to the recipient's school or college of pharmacy.
Duration 1 year; nonrenewable.
Additional information Until October 1996, the NCPA, the national association representing independent retail pharmacy, was known as NARD (the National Association of Retail Druggists).
Number awarded 1 each year.
Deadline February of each year.

[511]
WILLIAM A. RUSSELL SCHOLARSHIP FOR ADVANCED STUDIES
American Jersey Cattle Association
Attn: Dr. Cherie L. Bayer
6486 East Main Street
Reynoldsburg, OH 43068-2362
(614) 861-3636   Fax: (614) 861-8040
E-mail: cbayer@usjersey.com
Web: www.usjersey.com

Purpose To provide financial assistance to undergraduate and graduate student working on a degree related to the dairy industry.
Eligibility This program is open to undergraduate and graduate students who are working on a degree in large animal veterinary practice, dairy production, dairy manufacturing, or dairy product marketing. Applicants must be members of the American Jersey Cattle Association with significant and extensive experience in breeding, managing, and showing Jersey cattle. They must demonstrate substantial progress toward their intended degree and an intention to prepare for a career in agriculture. A GPA of 2.5 or higher is required. Financial need is not considered in the selection process.
Financial data The stipend is approximately $1,000.
Duration 1 year.
Number awarded 1 each year.
Deadline June of each year.

[512]
WILLIAM E. SCHWABE MEMORIAL SCHOLARSHIP
Association for Iron & Steel Technology
Attn: AIST Foundation
186 Thorn Hill Road
Warrendale, PA 15086-7528
(724) 776-6040, ext. 621   Fax: (724) 776-1880
E-mail: lwharrey@aist.org
Web: www.aist.org/foundation/scholarships.htm

Purpose To provide financial assistance for college to students interested in preparing for a career in the iron and steel or steel-related industries.
Eligibility This program is open to full-time students majoring in metallurgy, materials science, or engineering at accredited universities in North America. Applicants must have a GPA of 3.0 or higher and a demonstrated interest in the iron and steel industry. Along with their application, they must submit 3 letters of recommendation; a resume with work experience and extracurricular activities, noting any leadership positions; a current academic transcript; and a 2-page essay on their professional goals, explaining why they are interested in a career in the steel industry and how their skills could be applied to enhance the industry. Financial need is not considered in the selection process.
Financial data The stipend is $1,500.
Duration 1 year; recipients may reapply.
Additional information The AIST was formed in 2004 by the merger of the Iron and Steel Society (ISS) and the Association of Iron and Steel Engineers (AISE). This scholarship was established in 2005 by the Steel Manufacturers Association.
Number awarded 1 each year.
Deadline April of each year.

[513]
WILLIAM E. WEISEL SCHOLARSHIP AWARD
Society of Manufacturing Engineers
Attn: SME Education Foundation
One SME Drive
P.O. Box 930
Dearborn, MI 48121-0930
(313) 425-3300   Toll-free: (800) 733-4763, ext. 3300
Fax: (313) 425-3411   E-mail: foundation@sme.org
Web: www.sme.org

Purpose To provide financial assistance to students preparing for a career in robotics or automated systems.
Eligibility Applicants must be U.S. or Canadian citizens who are full-time students attending a regionally accredited school in engineering or technology and preparing for a career in robotics or automated systems used in manufac-

turing or robotics used in the medical field. They must have completed at least 30 units with a GPA of 3.5 or higher. Along with their application, they must submit a 300-word essay that covers their career and educational objectives, how this scholarship will help them attain those objectives, and why they want to enter this field. Financial need is not considered in the selection process.

Financial data This stipend is $2,000 per year; funds are paid directly to the recipient.

Duration 1 year; may be renewed.

Number awarded 1 each year.

Deadline January of each year.

[514]
WILLIAM J. FEINGOLD SCHOLARSHIP

American Society for Quality
Attn: Biomedical Division
600 North Plankinton Avenue
P.O. Box 3005
Milwaukee, WI 53201-3005
(414) 272-8575　　　　Toll-free: (800) 248-1946
Fax: (414) 272-1734　　　E-mail: cs@asqu.org
Web: www.asq.org/biomed/scholarship/index.html

Purpose To provide financial assistance to undergraduate and graduate students working on a degree in a field related to quality in the biomedical community.

Eligibility This program is open to students who have completed at least 2 years of study in a program that involves the use of quality principles, concepts, and technologies in the biomedical community. Applicants must have a GPA of 3.0 or higher. Along with their application, they must submit essays on 1) their career objectives and how they relate to quality issues within the biomedical community; and 2) why quality systems are important in the biomedical community. Graduate students are eligible, but preference is given to undergraduates. Priority is given to students who 1) are enrolled in a technical or scientific course of study; 2) have a demonstrated contribution or participation in activities related to quality in the biomedical community; and 3) have a higher GPA or more compelling essay.

Financial data The stipend is $5,000 per year.

Duration 1 year; may be renewed 1 additional year.

Additional information This program was approved in 2004. Information is also available from Hal Greenberg, 6 Coe Road, Framingham, MA 01701.

Number awarded 1 each year.

Deadline April of each year.

[515]
WILLIAM L. CULLISON SCHOLARSHIP

Technical Association of the Pulp and Paper Industry
Attn: TAPPI Foundation
15 Technology Parkway South
Norcross, GA 30092
(770) 209-7536　　　　Toll-free: (800) 332-8686
Fax: (770) 446-6947　　E-mail: vedmondson@tappi.org
Web: www.tappi.org

Purpose To provide financial assistance to college students who are interested in preparing for a career in the pulp and paper industry.

Eligibility This program is open to full-time students who have completed the first 2 years at a designated university with a pulp and paper program and have a GPA of 3.5 or better. Applicants must demonstrate outstanding leadership abilities and a significant interest in the pulp and paper industry. They must submit 50-word essays on the persons who have influenced them most deeply and why, what attracts them to a career in the pulp and paper industry, the extent to which they have participated in activities related to the pulp and paper industry, and why they think they are more likely to make a major contribution to the pulp and paper industry than other engineers or scientists. Financial need is not considered in the selection process.

Financial data The stipend is $4,000 per year.

Duration 1 year (the junior year); may be renewed for the senior year if the recipient maintains at least a 3.0 GPA and pursues courses in the pulp and paper curriculum.

Additional information This program was established in 1999. In the United States, the participating universities are Auburn University, Georgia Institute of Technology, Miami University of Ohio, Michigan State University, Mississippi State University, North Carolina State University, Oregon State University, Rutgers University, San Jose State University, the State University of New York, the University of Idaho, the University of Maine, the University of Minnesota, the University of New Hampshire, the University of Washington, the University of Wisconsin at Stevens Point, and Western Michigan University. Other participating universities are located in several foreign countries.

Number awarded 1 or 2 each year.

Deadline April of each year.

[516]
WILLIAM LOWELL PUTNAM COMPETITION

Mathematical Association of America
1529 18th Street, N.W.
Washington, DC 20036-1358
(202) 387-5200　　　　Toll-free: (800) 741-9415
Fax: (202) 265-2384　　E-mail: maahq@maa.org
Web: www.maa.org/Awards/putnam.html

Purpose To recognize and reward outstanding collegiate participants in a mathematics competition.

Eligibility This competition is open to students at colleges and universities in Canada and the United States. Entrants take a test containing mathematics problems designed to measure originality as well as technical competence. Institutions with at least 3 registered participants obtain a team ranking based on the scores of 3 designated individuals. Awards are presented to both individuals and teams.

Financial data In the individual competition, the 5 individuals with the highest scores receive $2,500 each, the next 10 receive $1,000 each, and the next 10 receive $250 each. In the team competition, the university of the first-place team receives $25,000 and each team member receives $1,000; the university of the second-place team receives $20,000 and each team member receives $800; the university of the third-place team receives $15,000 and each team member receives $600; the university of the fourth-

place team receives $10,000 and each team member receives $400; the university of the fifth-place team receives $5,000 and each team member receives $200.
Duration The competition is held annually.
Additional information This competition was first held in 1938.
Number awarded 25 individuals and 5 teams and their members win cash prizes each year.
Deadline October of each year.

[517]
WILLIAM RUCKER GREENWOOD SCHOLARSHIP

Association for Women Geoscientists
Attn: AWG Foundation
P.O. Box 30645
Lincoln, NE 68503-0645
E-mail: awgscholarship@yahoo.com
Web: www.awg.org/members/po_scholarships.html

Purpose To provide financial assistance to minority women working on an undergraduate or graduate degree in the geosciences in the Potomac Bay region.
Eligibility This program is open to minority women who are currently enrolled as full-time undergraduate or graduate geoscience majors in an accredited, degree-granting college or university in Delaware, the District of Columbia, Maryland, Virginia, or West Virginia. Selection is based on the applicant's 1) participation in geoscience or earth science educational activities, and 2) potential for leadership as a future geoscience professional.
Financial data The stipend is $1,000. The recipient also is granted a 1-year membership in the Association for Women Geoscientists (AWG).
Duration 1 year.
Additional information This program is sponsored by the AWG Potomac Area Chapter. Information is also available from Laurel M. Bybell, U.S. Geological Survey, 926 National Center, Reston, VA 20192.
Number awarded 1 each year.
Deadline April of each year.

[518]
WILLIAM W. BURGIN, JR. MD EDUCATION RECOGNITION AWARD

American Association for Respiratory Care
Attn: American Respiratory Care Foundation
9425 North MacArthur Boulevard, Suite 100
Irving, TX 75063-4706
(972) 243-2272   Fax: (972) 484-2720
E-mail: info@arcfoundation.org
Web: www.arcfoundation.org

Purpose To provide financial assistance to second-year college students interested in becoming respiratory therapists.
Eligibility This program is open to students who have completed 2 semesters in an accredited respiratory care bachelor's degree program. Applicants must be U.S. citizens with a GPA of 3.0 or higher. They must submit an original referenced paper on an aspect of respiratory care and a paper of at least 1,200 words describing how the award will assist them in reaching their objective of a baccalaureate degree and their ultimate goal of leadership in health care. Selection is based on academic performance.
Financial data The stipend is $2,500. The award also provides 1 night's lodging and registration for the international congress of the association.
Duration 1 year.
Additional information This program is sponsored by the National Board for Respiratory Care (NBRC) and its wholly owned subsidiary, Applied Measurement Professionals, Inc. (AMP).
Number awarded 1 each year.
Deadline June of each year.

[519]
WILLIE HOBBS MOORE-HARRY L. MORRISON-ARTHUR B.C. WALKER SCHOLARSHIPS

National Society of Black Physicists
Attn: Scholarship Committee Chair
6704G Lee Highway
Arlington, VA 22205
(703) 536-4207   Fax: (703) 536-4203
E-mail: scholarship@nsbp.org
Web: www.nsbp.org

Purpose To provide financial assistance to African American students majoring in physics in college.
Eligibility This program is open to African American students who are entering their junior or senior year of college and majoring in physics. Applicants must submit an essay on their academic and career objectives, information on their participation in extracurricular activities, a description of any awards and honors they have received, and 3 letters of recommendation. Financial need is not considered.
Financial data The stipend is $1,000.
Duration 1 year; nonrenewable.
Additional information This program was initiated in 2002 with support from *Black Enterprise Magazine*.
Number awarded 3 each year.
Deadline November of each year.

[520]
WIRE REINFORCEMENT INSTITUTE EDUCATION FOUNDATION SCHOLARSHIPS

Wire Reinforcement Institute Education Foundation
Attn: Scholarship Selection Committee
942 Main Street, Suite 300
Hartford, CT 06103
(860) 808-3000, ext. 356   Toll-free: (800) 552-4WRI
Fax: (860) 808-3009
E-mail: admin@wirereinforcementinstitute.org
Web: www.wirereinforcementinstitute.org

Purpose To provide financial assistance to undergraduate and graduate students working on a degree in civil or structural engineering.
Eligibility This program is open to high school seniors, high school graduates, undergraduates, and graduate students enrolled or planning to enroll full time at a 4-year college or university in the United States or Canada. Applicants must be planning to work on a degree in structural and/or civil engineering. Along with their application, they must

submit brief essays on 1) their anticipated career plans, and 2) a topic of their choice related to the field of structural and/or civil engineering and why they selected that as their course of undergraduate or graduate study. Financial need is not considered in the selection process.

Financial data Stipends range from $2,500 to $10,000. Funds are paid directly to the recipient's college or university.

Duration 1 year.

Number awarded Varies each year; recently, 3 of these scholarships were awarded.

Deadline April of each year.

[521]
WISCONSIN ASSOCIATION OF PROFESSIONAL AGRICULTURAL CONSULTANTS SCHOLARSHIPS

Wisconsin Association of Professional Agricultural Consultants
Attn: Executive Secretary
7310 Farmington Way
Madison, WI 53717
(608) 833-7989   Fax: (608) 833-1965
E-mail: wapac@itis.com
Web: www.wapac.info/Scholarships.htm

Purpose To provide financial assistance to college students in Wisconsin who are preparing for a career in production agriculture or applied research.

Eligibility This program is open to undergraduate students enrolled at colleges and universities in Wisconsin. Applicants must be preparing for a career in production agriculture or applied crop or livestock research. They must have been enrolled the previous summer in an internship that was production-relation. Selection is based on merit; financial need is not considered.

Financial data The stipend is $1,500.

Duration 1 year.

Number awarded 1 or more each year.

Deadline November of each year.

[522]
WOMAN OF DISTINCTION AWARD

Electronic Document Systems Foundation
Attn: EDSF Scholarship Awards
608 Silver Spur Road, Suite 280
Rolling Hills Estates, CA 90274-3616
(310) 265-5510   Fax: (310) 265-5588
E-mail: jmowlds@edsf.org
Web: www.edsf.org/scholarships.cfm

Purpose To provide financial assistance to women working on an undergraduate or graduate degree in a field related to the high volume transaction output (HVTO) industry.

Eligibility This program is open to female undergraduate and graduate students who are working on a degree in field related to the HVTO industry, including information technology, graphic arts, or business. Applicants must be enrolled full time at a technical school, trade school, community college, university, college, or graduate school in the United States with a GPA of 3.0 or higher. Along with their application, they must submit a statement of their career goals in the field of document communications, an essay on a topic related to their view of the future of the document management and production industry, a list of current professional and college extracurricular activities and achievements, college transcripts, samples of their creative work, and 2 letters of recommendation. Financial need is not considered.

Financial data The stipend is $5,000.

Duration 1 year.

Additional information This program is sponsored by COPI/OutputLinks.

Number awarded 1 each year.

Deadline May of each year.

[523]
WOMEN@MICROSOFT HOPPERS SCHOLARSHIP

Fargo-Moorhead Area Foundation
Attn: Gifts and Grants Specialist
502 First Avenue North, Suite 202
Fargo, ND 58102-4804
(701) 234-0756   E-mail: wendy@areafoundation.org
Web: www.areafoundation.org/page27556.cfm

Purpose To provide financial assistance to women who are interested in studying computer science at a college or university in Minnesota or the Dakotas.

Eligibility This program is open to women who are accepted or enrolled in a college or university in Minnesota, North Dakota, or South Dakota. Applicants must be undergraduates with a declared major in either computer science or a related computer science intensive discipline and a GPA of 3.0 or higher. Along with their application, they must submit essays, up to 500 words each, on 2 of the following topics: 1) What do you see as the computer industry's primary shortcomings? If you were a leader in the technical world today, in what direction would you guide technology and why? 2) Why have you chosen a degree in the discipline you are currently pursuing? 3) Describe a coding, class, or work project related to your field of study that you significantly contributed towards. Describe your contribution and what impact this project had on you or others. Along with the essays, selection is based on extracurricular activities, awards and honors, community service, work experience, letters of recommendation, and transcripts.

Financial data The stipend is $1,500.

Duration 1 year.

Additional information This program was established in 1990 as part of an effort to make Microsoft a great place for women. In addition to scholarships, other Hoppers committees deal with outreach, technical women, mentoring, program, career development, and diversity. The program is named for Grace Hopper, a computer science pioneer.

Number awarded 1 each year.

Deadline March of each year.

[524]
WOMEN'S NATIONAL AGRICULTURAL AVIATION ASSOCIATION SCHOLARSHIP ESSAY CONTEST

National Agricultural Aviation Association
Attn: Women of the NAAA
1005 E Street, S.E.
Washington, DC 20003-2947
(202) 546-5722　　　　　Fax: (202) 546-5726
E-mail: information@agaviation.org
Web: www.agaviation.org/scholarship.htm

Purpose To recognize and reward outstanding student essays on agricultural aviation.

Eligibility This competition is open to the children, grandchildren, sons-in-law, daughters-in-law, or spouses of any National Agricultural Aviation Association operator, pilot member, retired operator, or pilot who maintains an active membership in the association. The contest is also open to the children, grandchildren, sons-in-law, daughters-in-law, or spouses of an allied industry member. Entrants must be high school seniors, high school graduates, or college students. They may be of any age pursuing any area of education beyond high school. They are invited to submit an essay, up to 1,500 words, on a theme related to agricultural aviation that changes annually; recently, the topic was "Agricultural Aviation's Contribution to the World's Food Supply." A photograph of the entrant and a short biography should accompany the submission. Essays are judged on theme, development, clarity, and originality.

Financial data First prize is $2,000; second prize is $1,000.

Duration The competition is held annually.

Number awarded 2 each year.

Deadline August of each year.

[525]
YANMAR/SAE SCHOLARSHIP

Society of Automotive Engineers
Attn: Scholarship Administrator
400 Commonwealth Drive
Warrendale, PA 15096-0001
(724) 772-4047　　　　　Fax: (724) 776-3049
E-mail: scholarships@sae.org
Web: students.sae.org

Purpose To provide financial support to college seniors and graduate students majoring in engineering.

Eligibility Applicants must be entering their senior year of an undergraduate engineering program or enrolled in a graduate engineering or related science program at a college or university in Canada, Mexico, or the United States. They must be pursuing a course of study or research related to the conservation of energy in transportation, agriculture, construction, or power generation. Emphasis is placed on research or study related to the internal combustion engine. Canadian, Mexican, or U.S. citizenship is required. Selection is based on academic and leadership achievement related to engineering or science, scholastic performance and special study or honors in the field of the award, and a 1-page essay on their study or research related to the field of their award. Financial need is not considered.

Financial data The stipend is $1,000 per year.

Duration 2 years.

Additional information Funding for this program is provided by Yanmar Diesel American Corporation. Candidates must include a $5 processing fee with their application.

Number awarded 1 each year.

Deadline March of each year.

[526]
YOUNG DESIGN ENGINEER'S PROJECT COMPETITION

ASME International
Attn: Design Engineering Division
Three Park Avenue
New York, NY 10016-5990
(212) 591-7722　　　　Toll-free: (800) THE-ASME
Fax: (212) 591-7674　　E-mail: infocentral@asme.org
Web: divisions.asme.org/ded/educomm/YEDPC.html

Purpose To recognize and reward outstanding web-based presentations of an engineering design project by student members of ASME, the professional organization for mechanical engineering.

Eligibility This competition is open to senior students who are members of ASME. Applicants must submit a web site on an engineering design project that was completed while the author was an undergraduate. Selection is based on the solution to the design problem; the design process; effectiveness, ease, and clarity of the web site; and quality of written project summary.

Financial data The winner receives $1,000 and other finalists receive $500. All finalists also receive an additional $500 for travel support to present their papers at the ASME International Congress and Exposition.

Duration The competition is held annually.

Number awarded 4 each year: 1 winner and 3 other finalists.

Deadline June of each year.

[527]
50TH ANNIVERSARY–INSPIRATION FOR TOMORROW SCHOLARSHIP

Institute of Food Technologists
Attn: Scholarship Department
525 West Van Buren, Suite 1000
Chicago, IL 60607
(312) 782-8424　　　　　Fax: (312) 782-8348
E-mail: info@ift.org
Web: www.ift.org

Purpose To provide financial assistance to undergraduates interested in studying food science or food technology.

Eligibility This program is open to sophomores, juniors, and seniors in a food science or food technology program at an educational institution in the United States or Canada. Applicants must have an outstanding scholastic record and a well-rounded personality. Along with their application, they must submit an essay on their career aspirations; a list of awards, honors, and scholarships they have received; a list of extracurricular activities and/or hobbies; and a summary of their work experience. Financial need is not considered in the selection process.

Financial data The stipend is $2,000.

Duration 1 year; recipients may reapply if they are members of the Institute of Food Technologists.

Additional information Correspondence and completed applications must be submitted to the department head of the educational institution the applicant is attending.

Number awarded 1 each year.

Deadline January of each year.

Social Sciences

Described here are 246 merit and other no-need funding programs that 1) reward outstanding speeches, essays, organizational involvement, and other activities in the social sciences or 2) support college studies in a number of social science fields, including accounting, business administration, criminology, economics, education, geography, home economics, international relations, labor relations, political science, sales and marketing, sociology, social services, sports and recreation, and tourism. These programs are available to currently-enrolled and returning college students to fund studies on the undergraduate level in the United States. If you are looking for a particular program and don't find it here, be sure to check the Program Title Index to see if it is covered elsewhere in the directory.

SOCIAL SCIENCES

[528]
ACCESS INTELLIGENCE SCHOLARSHIP
Society of Satellite Professionals International
Attn: Scholarship Program
New York Information Technology Center
55 Broad Street, 14th Floor
New York, NY 10004
(212) 809-5199   Fax: (212) 825-0075
E-mail: sspi@sspi.org
Web: www.sspi.org

Purpose To provide financial assistance to student members of the Society of Satellite Professionals International (SSPI) who are interested in working on an undergraduate or graduate degree in the satellite field.

Eligibility This program is open to SSPI members who are high school seniors, college undergraduates, or graduate students interested in preparing for a career in satellite technologies, policies, or applications. Applicants must be interested in majoring in a satellite-related field that emphasizes the commercial and/or humanitarian aspects of new technologies and services. They may be from any country. The scholarships is presented to the applicant who best analyzes the entrepreneurial possibilities of new satellite services, technologies, or applications from a profit-driven or public service-oriented perspective. Financial need is not considered.

Financial data The stipend ranges from $2,000 to $5,000.

Duration 1 year.

Number awarded 1 each year.

Deadline Preliminary applications must be submitted by February of each year.

[529]
ACCOUNTEMPS/AICPA STUDENT SCHOLARSHIP
American Institute of Certified Public Accountants
Attn: Academic and Career Development Division
1211 Avenue of the Americas
New York, NY 10036-8775
(212) 596-6224   Fax: (212) 596-6292
E-mail: educat@aicpa.org
Web: www.aicpa.org

Purpose To provide financial assistance to student affiliate members of the American Institute of Certified Public Accountants (AICPA) who are working on an undergraduate or graduate degree in accounting, finance, or information systems.

Eligibility This program is open to full-time undergraduate and graduate students who are AICPA student affiliate members with a declared major in accounting, finance, or information systems. Applicants must have completed at least 30 semester hours, including at least 6 semesters in accounting, with a GPA of 3.0 or higher, and be a U.S. citizen. Students who will be transferring to a 4-year school must include an acceptance letter from that school. Selection is based on outstanding academic achievement, leadership, and future career interests.

Financial data The stipend is $2,500.

Duration 1 year.

Number awarded 2 each year.

Deadline March of each year.

[530]
AGATHA PRATOR SCHOLARSHIP
Delta Kappa Gamma Society International-Kappa State Organization
c/o Kathryn Dickinson
4338 Hempstead 2
Hope, AR 71801-8852
(870) 777-6618
Web: www.deltakappagamma.org

Purpose To provide financial assistance to residents of Arkansas who are enrolled in a pre-service teaching program.

Eligibility This program is open to residents of Arkansas (and Texarkana, Texas) who are enrolled as a student teacher, either as a senior or as an intern. The student's school must be NCATE-approved. Selection is based on academic record, leadership, and potential for future service to the field of education.

Financial data The stipend is $2,500.

Duration 1 semester.

Number awarded 1 each year.

Deadline March of each year for fall semester; November of each year for spring semester.

[531]
AITP OMAHA SCHOLARSHIP
Association of Information Technology Professionals-Omaha Chapter
Attn: Scholarship Committee
P.O. Box 583
Omaha, NE 68101
(402) 449-2180   E-mail: aitp@novia.net
Web: www.aitpomaha.org/scholarship/Default.htm

Purpose To provide financial assistance to high school seniors and college students who either reside in or will be studying in Nebraska or western Iowa and who plan to major in information systems.

Eligibility This program is open to 1) students who are enrolled or planning to enroll at a 4-year college or university, community college, or technical school in Nebraska or western Iowa and major in information systems or a related field, and 2) members of the Omaha or Lincoln chapters of the Association of Information Technology Professionals, their spouses, and their children who are interested in attending a college or university in any state and majoring in information systems. Applicants must include an essay of 250 to 500 words on 1) what motivated them to choose the field of information technology, the goals they have set, and how they plan to achieve those goals; or 2) a challenge facing professionals entering the field today and what they have done to prepare for that challenge. Selection is based on the essay, 2 letters of recommendation, academic achievement, job experience, participation in local community organizations, participation in high school and/or college extracurricular activities, and leadership and other awards received. Financial need is not considered.

Financial data The maximum stipend is $1,000.

Duration 1 year.

Number awarded Several each year.

Deadline April of each year.

[532]
A.J. (ANDY) SPIELMAN SCHOLARSHIPS
American Society of Travel Agents
Attn: ASTA Foundation
1101 King Street, Suite 200
Alexandria, VA 22314-2944
(703) 739-8721 Fax: (703) 684-8319
E-mail: scholarship@astahq.com
Web: www.astanet.com/education/scholarshipf.asp

Purpose To provide financial assistance to reentry students who are interested in preparing for a career in the travel/tourism industry.

Eligibility This program is open to students who are enrolled or preparing to enroll at a recognized proprietary travel school as reentry students. Applicants must have a GPA of 2.5 or higher, be citizens or permanent residents of the United States or Canada, and write a 500-word essay on "Why I Have Chosen the Travel Profession for My Re-Entry into the Work Force."

Financial data The stipend is $2,500.

Duration 1 year.

Additional information This scholarship was established in 1988 by the Central Atlantic Chapter of the American Society of Travel Agents (ASTA).

Number awarded Up to 2 each year.

Deadline August of each year.

[533]
AL SCHUMAN ECOLAB UNDERGRADUATE ENTREPRENEURIAL SCHOLARSHIPS
National Restaurant Association Educational
  Foundation
Attn: Scholarships and Mentoring Program
175 West Jackson Boulevard, Suite 1500
Chicago, IL 60604-2702
(312) 715-1010, ext. 744
Toll-free: (800) 765-2122, ext. 744
Fax: (312) 566-9733 E-mail: scholars@nraef.org
Web: www.nraef.org/scholarships/AlSchuman

Purpose To provide financial assistance to students entering or currently enrolled at selected universities who have demonstrated entrepreneurship relevant to the food service industry.

Eligibility This program is open to students entering their freshman, sophomore, or junior year at any of 10 designated universities. Applicants must be enrolled or planning to enroll full time in a restaurant and/or food service program and have a GPA of 3.0 or higher. Along with their application, they must submit an entrepreneurial project that they have completed. Selection is based on that project, presentation of the application, GPA, strength of letters of recommendation, and academic honors and achievements.

Financial data The stipend is $7,500 per year.

Duration 1 year.

Additional information The participating universities are California State Polytechnic University at Pomona, the Culinary Institute of America, Johnson and Wales University, Michigan State University, Pennsylvania State University, Purdue University, University of Denver, University of Houston, University of Nevada at Las Vegas, and University of Massachusetts at Amherst.

Number awarded 1 or more each year.

Deadline April of each year.

[534]
ALASKA AIRLINES SCHOLARSHIP
American Society of Travel Agents
Attn: ASTA Foundation
1101 King Street, Suite 200
Alexandria, VA 22314-2944
(703) 739-8721 Fax: (703) 684-8319
E-mail: scholarship@astahq.com
Web: www.astanet.com/education/scholarshipe.asp

Purpose To provide financial assistance to undergraduate students working on a degree in travel and tourism or closely-related fields.

Eligibility This program is open to college sophomores, juniors, or seniors enrolled at a 4-year college or university. Applicants must have a GPA of 2.5 or higher, be residents of the United States or Canada, and write a 500-word essay on why they are preparing for a career in the travel and tourism industry, including at least 2 career goals. Financial need is not considered in the selection process.

Financial data The stipend is $2,000.

Duration 1 year; may be renewed.

Additional information This scholarship was established in 1987.

Number awarded 1 each year.

Deadline August of each year.

[535]
ALLYN & BACON PSYCHOLOGY AWARDS
Psi Chi
825 Vine Street
P.O. Box 709
Chattanooga, TN 37401-0709
(423) 756-2044 Fax: (877) 774-2443
E-mail: awards@psichi.org
Web: www.psichi.org/awards/home.asp

Purpose To recognize and reward outstanding research conducted by undergraduate members of Psi Chi (an honor society in psychology).

Eligibility All undergraduate students who are members of the society are eligible to submit completed research papers (up to 12 pages long). The awards are presented to the best overall empirical studies.

Financial data First place is $1,000, second $650, and third $350.

Duration The prizes are awarded annually.

Additional information This program is sponsored by Allyn & Bacon Publishers.

Number awarded 3 each year.

Deadline April of each year.

SOCIAL SCIENCES

[536]
AMERICAN BUSINESS EDUCATORS SCHOLARSHIPS

Scholarship Administrative Services, Inc.
Attn: ABE Program
2000 Rock Street, Suite 3
Mountain View, CA 94043

Purpose To provide financial assistance to students interested in working on a bachelor's or master's degree in business education.

Eligibility This program is open to full-time students working on or planning to work on a bachelor's or master's degree in business education. Applicants must have a GPA of 3.0 or higher and be able to demonstrate a record of involvement in extracurricular and work activities related to business. Along with their application, they must submit a 1,000-word essay on their educational and career goals, why they believe business is essential to America, and how they plan to make an impact as a business teacher at the secondary level. Financial need is not considered in the selection process.

Financial data The stipend is $5,000 per year.

Duration 1 year; may be renewed 1 additional year if the recipient maintains full-time enrollment and a GPA of 3.0 or higher.

Additional information This program is sponsored by American Business Educators (ABE) and administered by Scholarship Administrative Services, Inc. ABE was established in 2004 to encourage more American students to consider a career as a business teacher at the secondary level. Requests for applications should be accompanied by a self-addressed stamped envelope, the student's e-mail address, and the source where they found the scholarship information.

Number awarded Up to 20 each year.

Deadline April of each year.

[537]
AMERICAN EXPRESS TRAVEL SCHOLARSHIP

American Society of Travel Agents
Attn: ASTA Foundation
1101 King Street, Suite 200
Alexandria, VA 22314-2944
(703) 739-8721   Fax: (703) 684-8319
E-mail: scholarship@astahq.com
Web: www.astanet.com/education/scholarshipf.asp

Purpose To provide financial assistance to students preparing for a career in the travel industry at a 2-year college, 4-year college or university, or proprietary travel school.

Eligibility This program is open to students who are enrolled or able to provide proof of acceptance at a proprietary travel school or a 2- or 4-year college in the United States or Canada that offers a travel and tourism program. Applicants must have a GPA of 2.5 or higher, be residents of the United States or Canada, and write a 500-word essay on their plans in travel and tourism and their view of the travel industry's future. Selection is based on academic record, work performance, potential, and plans for a career in the travel/tourism industry.

Financial data A stipend is awarded (amount not specified).

Duration 1 year.

Additional information This scholarship was established in 1989.

Number awarded 1 each year.

Deadline August of each year.

[538]
AMERICAN HUMANICS ACADEMIC AWARDS

American Humanics, Inc.
Attn: Academic Award Committee
1100 Walnut Street, Suite 1900
Kansas City, MO 64106
(816) 561-6415, ext. 113
Toll-free: (800) 343-6466, ext. 113
Fax: (816) 531-3527   E-mail: mturner@humanics.org
Web: www.humanics.org

Purpose To provide financial assistance to student members of American Humanics (AH) who are preparing for a career as a professional with nonprofit human services or youth agencies.

Eligibility This program is open to students who are enrolled at 1 of 75 designated colleges and universities that have an AH program to prepare undergraduates for careers with youth and human service agencies. Applicants must have completed 180 or more course work contact hours in nonprofit management with a GPA of 3.0 or higher. They must be active AH student members and involved in the AH student association on their campus. Along with their application, they must submit 1-page essays on 1) why AH should invest in them and their career preparation; 2) their biggest accomplishment or contribution to their AH program; and 3) their immediate plans upon completion of their requirements for AH certification. Financial need is not considered.

Financial data The stipend is $1,000 for full-time students or $500 for part-time students.

Duration 1 year; recipients may reapply.

Additional information For a list of the participating colleges and universities, contact the sponsor.

Number awarded Varies each year.

Deadline March of each year.

[539]
AMERICAN INDIAN FELLOWSHIP IN BUSINESS SCHOLARSHIP

National Center for American Indian Enterprise
    Development
Attn: Scholarship Committee
953 East Juanita Avenue
Mesa, AZ 85204
(480) 545-1298, ext. 243
Toll-free: (800) 4-NCAIED, ext. 243
Fax: (480) 545-4208   E-mail: events@ncaied.org
Web: www.ncaied.org/fundraising/scholar.html

Purpose To provide financial assistance to American Indian upper-division and graduate students working on a business degree.

Eligibility This program is open to American Indians who are currently enrolled full time in college at the upper-division or graduate school level and working on a business degree. Applicants must submit a letter on their reasons for pursuing higher education and their plans following completion of their degree. Selection is based on grades (30%), an essay on their community involvement (30%), an essay on personal challenges they have faced (25%), an essay on their paid or volunteer business experience (10%), and the quality of those essays (10%).

Financial data A stipend is awarded (amount not specified).

Duration 1 year.

Number awarded Up to 5 each year.

Deadline August of each year.

[540] AMERICAN SOCIETY OF FARM MANAGERS AND RURAL APPRAISERS AGRICULTURAL SCHOLARSHIP

California 4-H Foundation
Attn: Youth Development Program
University of California
Agriculture and Natural Resources
One Hopkins Road
Davis, CA 95616-8575
(530) 754-8518   Fax: (530) 757-8739
E-mail: fourhstateofc@ucdavis.edu
Web: www.ca4h.org/4hresource/ir

Purpose To provide financial assistance to students in California and Nevada who have belonged to 4-H and are interested in majoring in a field related to agribusiness or education at a college in California.

Eligibility This program is open to residents of California or Nevada who are or were (at the time of their high school graduation) enrolled in the California or Nevada 4-H Youth Development Program. Applicants must have a GPA of 3.0 or higher and be high school seniors, high school graduates, or currently-enrolled college students between 16 and 25 years of age. If they are already in college, they must be enrolled full time. They must be attending or planning to attend a California 4-year university or 2-year community college to work on a degree and prepare for a career in the field of rural appraising, agricultural education, agricultural management, or agricultural financial services. Selection is based on leadership and citizenship experiences, agriculture-related 4-H project work, and future plans in agriculture.

Financial data The stipend is $1,000 for students at 4-year universities or $250 for students at 2-year community colleges. Funds are sent directly to the recipient's school.

Duration 1 year.

Additional information These scholarships, first awarded in 2006, are supported by the California chapter of the American Society of Farm Managers and Rural Appraisers (ASFMRA).

Number awarded 3 each year: 2 at $1,000 for 4-year university students and 1 at $250 for community college students.

Deadline April of each year.

[541] AMERICAN STAR IN AGRIBUSINESS AWARD

National FFA Organization
Attn: Star Award Program
6060 FFA Drive
P.O. Box 68960
Indianapolis, IN 46268-0960
(317) 802-4255   Fax: (317) 802-5255
E-mail: star@ffa.org
Web: www.ffa.org

Purpose To recognize and reward members of FFA who participate in a Supervised Agricultural Experience (SAE) in agribusiness.

Eligibility This program is open to current members who have been working on an SAE and have completed the degree level of Greenhand, Chapter FFA Degree, and State FFA Degree. Applicants for the American FFA Degree must have been an active member for the past 3 years, have a record of satisfactory participation in chapter and state activities, have completed the equivalent of at least 3 years of secondary school instruction in an agricultural education program or have completed the program of agricultural education offered in the secondary school last attended, have graduated from high school at least 12 months prior to the national convention at which the award is to be granted with a GPA of 2.0 or better, and have operated and maintained an SAE in agribusiness in which they have earned and productively invested at least $7,500 or at least $1,150 in combination with at least 2,250 hours of work beyond class time. The outstanding recipients of the American FFA Degree are considered for these awards.

Financial data The first-place winner receives $2,000, a plaque, and a medal. Each runner-up receives $1,000 and a plaque.

Duration The competition is held annually.

Additional information Recently, approximately 1,900 members received the American FFA Degree and qualified for these awards. This program is sponsored by the National FFA Foundation, Pioneer Hi-Bred International, Inc. of Des Moines, Iowa, Case IH of Lake Forest, Illinois, and the Farm Credit System of Washington, D.C.

Number awarded 4 each year: 1 winner and 3 runners-up.

Deadline June of each year.

[542] ANA MULTICULTURAL EXCELLENCE SCHOLARSHIP

American Association of Advertising Agencies
Attn: AAAA Foundation
405 Lexington Avenue, 18th Floor
New York, NY 10174-1801
(212) 682-2500   Toll-free: (800) 676-9333
Fax: (212) 682-2028   E-mail: ameadows@aaaa.org
Web: www.aaaa.org

Purpose To provide financial assistance to multicultural students who are working on an undergraduate degree in advertising.

Eligibility This program is open to undergraduate students who are U.S. citizens of proven multicultural heritage and have at least 1 grandparent of multicultural heritage.

SOCIAL SCIENCES

Applicants must be participating in the Multicultural Advertising Intern Program (MAIP). They must be entering their senior year at an accredited college or university in the United States with a GPA of 3.0 or higher. Selection is based on academic ability.

Financial data The stipend is $2,000.

Duration 1 year.

Additional information This program was established by the Association of National Advertisers (ANA) in 2001. The American Association of Advertising Agencies (AAAA) assumed administration in 2003.

Number awarded 3 each year.

[543]
APPLEGATE/JACKSON/PARKS FUTURE TEACHER SCHOLARSHIP

National Institute for Labor Relations Research
Attn: Future Teacher Scholarships
5211 Port Royal Road, Suite 510
Springfield, VA 22151
(703) 321-9606   Fax: (703) 321-7342
E-mail: research@nilrr.org
Web: www.nilrr.org/scholarships.htm

Purpose To provide financial assistance to students majoring in education who oppose compulsory unionism in the education community.

Eligibility This program is open to undergraduate and graduate students majoring in education at institutions of higher learning in the United States. Applicants must demonstrate the potential to complete a degree program in education and receive a teaching license. Along with their application, they must submit an essay of approximately 500 words demonstrating an interest in and a knowledge of the right to work principle as it applies to educators. Selection is based on scholastic ability and a demonstrated interest in the work of the sponsoring organization to promote voluntary unionism.

Financial data The stipend is $1,000.

Duration 1 year.

Additional information This program was established in 1989 to honor Carol Applegate, Kay Jackson, and Dr. Anne Parks, 3 Michigan public school teachers who lost their jobs because they refused to pay union dues.

Number awarded 1 each year.

Deadline December of each year.

[544]
APPRAISAL INSTITUTE EDUCATION TRUST SCHOLARSHIP

Appraisal Institute
Attn: Appraisal Institute Education Trust
550 West Van Buren Street, Suite 1000
Chicago, IL 60607
(312) 335-4100   Fax: (312) 335-4400
E-mail: ocarreon@appraisalinstitute.org
Web: www.appraisalinstitute.org

Purpose To provide financial assistance to graduate and undergraduate students majoring in real estate or allied fields.

Eligibility This program is open to U.S. citizens who are graduate or undergraduate students majoring in real estate appraisal, land economics, real estate, or related fields. Applicants must submit a statement regarding their general activities and intellectual interests in college; college training; activities and employment outside of college; contemplated line of study for a degree; and career they expect to follow after graduation. Selection is based on academic excellence.

Financial data The stipend is $3,000 for graduate students or $2,000 for undergraduate students.

Duration 1 year.

Number awarded At least 1 each year.

Deadline March of each year.

[545]
ARC OF WASHINGTON TRUST FUND STIPEND AWARD PROGRAM

ARC of Washington Trust Fund
c/o Neal Lessenger, Secretary
P.O. Box 27028
Seattle, WA 98125-1428
(206) 363-2206   E-mail: arcwatrust@charter.net
Web: www.arcwa.org/student_grants.htm

Purpose To provide financial assistance to undergraduate and graduate students in northwestern states who have a career interest in work relating to mental retardation.

Eligibility This program is open to upper-division and graduate students in schools in Washington, Oregon, Alaska, and Idaho who have a demonstrated interest in the field of mental retardation or other developmental or intellectual disabilities. Applicants must submit a statement of interest in the field of mental retardation or closely-related field, academic and other qualifications, achievements, immediate and long-term goals, and letters of endorsement from at least 2 faculty sponsors. Financial need is not considered in the selection process.

Financial data The stipend is $5,000 per year, paid in 4 equal installments. Funds are sent to the recipient's school and must be used for tuition, books, and general living expenses.

Duration 1 year.

Number awarded Several each year.

Deadline February of each year.

[546]
ARIZONA CHAPTER GOLD SCHOLARSHIP

American Society of Travel Agents
Attn: ASTA Foundation
1101 King Street, Suite 200
Alexandria, VA 22314-2944
(703) 739-8721   Fax: (703) 684-8319
E-mail: scholarship@astahq.com
Web: www.astanet.com/education/scholarshipe.asp

Purpose To provide financial assistance to college students in Arizona interested in preparing for a career in the travel industry.

Eligibility This program is open to students enrolled as a sophomore, junior, or senior at a 4-year college or university in Arizona with a GPA of 2.5 or higher. Applicants must be U.S. citizens or permanent residents. Along with their application, they must submit a 500-word essay on their career plans in the travel industry and their interest in the business of travel and tourism. Financial need is not considered in the selection process.

Financial data The stipend is $3,000.

Duration 1 year.

Additional information This program was established in 1992.

Number awarded 1 each year.

Deadline August of each year.

[547]
ARKANSAS SOCIETY OF CERTIFIED PUBLIC ACCOUNTANTS STUDENT EDUCATION FUND SCHOLARSHIPS

Arkansas Society of Certified Public Accountants
Attn: Student Education Fund
11300 Executive Center Drive
Little Rock, AR 72211-4352
(501) 664-8739 Toll-free: (800) 482-8739 (within AR)
Fax: (501) 664-8320 E-mail: ascpa@arcpa.org
Web: www.arcpa.org/Student/Scholarships.htm

Purpose To provide financial assistance to students at colleges and universities in Arkansas who are majoring in accounting.

Eligibility This program is open to accounting majors at 4-year colleges and universities in Arkansas. Applicants must have completed at least 84 semester hours of course work (including 15 semester hours of accounting) with a GPA of 3.5 or higher in accounting classes. They must certify that they are pursuing the requirements to sit for the C.P.A. examination and intend to pursue the C.P.A. professional certification. Each accounting department at an Arkansas 4-year college or university offering an accounting degree may nominate 1 student per faculty member who is a regular member in good standing of the Arkansas Society of Certified Public Accountants. Selection is based on a 150-word statement on why they should be considered for this scholarship, academic achievement, and professional promise.

Financial data The stipend is $2,000 per year.

Duration 1 year.

Additional information Recipients are also awarded a 1-year student membership in the Arkansas Society of Certified Public Accountants.

Number awarded Varies each year.

Deadline January of each year.

[548]
ARNOLD SADLER MEMORIAL SCHOLARSHIP

American Council of the Blind
Attn: Coordinator, Scholarship Program
1155 15th Street, N.W., Suite 1004
Washington, DC 20005
(202) 467-5081 Toll-free: (800) 424-8666
Fax: (202) 467-5085 E-mail: info@acb.org
Web: www.acb.org

Purpose To provide financial assistance to undergraduate or graduate students who are blind and are interested in studying in a field of service to persons with disabilities.

Eligibility This program is open to students in rehabilitation, education, law, or other fields of service to persons with disabilities. Applicants must be legally blind and U.S. citizens. In addition to letters of recommendation and copies of academic transcripts, applications must include an autobiographical sketch. A cumulative GPA of 3.3 or higher is generally required. Selection is based on demonstrated academic record, involvement in extracurricular and civic activities, and academic objectives. The severity of the applicant's visual impairment and his/her study methods are also taken into account.

Financial data The stipend is $2,000. In addition, the winner receives a Kurzweil-1000 Reading System.

Duration 1 year.

Additional information This scholarship is funded by the Arnold Sadler Memorial Scholarship Fund. Scholarship winners are expected to be present at the council's annual conference; the council will cover all reasonable expenses connected with convention attendance.

Number awarded 1 each year.

Deadline February of each year.

[549]
ART PFAFF SCHOLARSHIP PROGRAM

Missouri Middle School Association
c/o Jane Haskell, Executive Director
P.O. Box 487
Rolla, MO 65402-0487
(573) 364-9307 Fax: (573) 364-9307
E-mail: hasmmsa@fidnet.com
Web: www.mmsa-mo.org/pfaff_scholarship.html

Purpose To provide financial assistance to students in Missouri who are working on a degree to receive entry level certification to teach at the middle school level.

Eligibility This program is open to students currently enrolled in an education program that will qualify them for entry level middle school certification in Missouri. Applicants must be classified as a sophomore or higher by their college or university and have a cumulative GPA of 2.5 or higher. They must have made a commitment to be trained as a middle level teacher and to teach at that level after completing their degree. Along with their application, they must submit a brief autobiographical sketch and essays on why they have chosen to become a middle school teacher, how they think they can make a difference as a middle school teacher, the activities during high school and/or college in which they have been involved with middle school age children, what someone would expect to see if they came into their middle school classroom, why a middle school should be different from a typical junior high school, and how this scholarship will help them attain their career goals. Financial need is not considered.

Financial data The stipend is $1,000.

Duration 1 year.

Additional information Information is also available from Bob Stewart, 12836 Sycamore, Grandview, MO 64030, (816) 316-5600, E-mail: rstewart4@kc.rr.com.

Number awarded 1 or more each year.

Deadline February of each year.

SOCIAL SCIENCES

[550]
ASSOCIATION OF GOVERNMENT ACCOUNTANTS ACADEMIC MERIT SCHOLARSHIPS

Association of Government Accountants
Attn: National Awards Committee
2208 Mount Vernon Avenue
Alexandria, VA 22301-1314
(703) 684-6931   Toll-free: (800) AGA-7211, ext. 309
Fax: (703) 548-9367   E-mail: rortiz@agacgfm.org
Web: www.agacgfm.org/membership/awards

Purpose To provide financial assistance to members of the Association of Government Accountants (AGA) and their families who wish to work on a degree in financial management.

Eligibility This program is open to members of the association and their spouses, children, and grandchildren. Applicants may be pursuing or intending to pursue an undergraduate or graduate degree in a financial management discipline, including accounting, auditing, budgeting, economics, finance, electronic data processing, information resources management, or public administration. Along with their application, they must submit a 2-page essay on "Why I want a career in public financial management," high school or college transcripts, and a letter of recommendation from an AGA member. Financial need is not considered.

Financial data The annual stipends are $1,000 for full-time study or $500 for part-time study.

Duration 1 year; renewable.

Number awarded Up to 16 each year: 8 to high school seniors and graduates (6 for full-time study and 2 for part-time study) and 8 to undergraduate and graduate students (6 for full-time study and 2 for part-time study).

Deadline March of each year.

[551]
ATFRA SCHOLARSHIP

Boy Scouts of America
Attn: Learning for Life Division, S210
1325 West Walnut Hill Lane
P.O. Box 152079
Irving, TX 75015-2079
(972) 580-2418   Fax: (972) 580-2137
Web: www.learning-for-life.org

Purpose To provide financial assistance for college to Explorer Scouts who plan a career as law enforcement executives.

Eligibility This program is open to Explorer Scouts who are at least seniors in high school and active members of a Law Enforcement Explorer post registered with Boy Scouts of America. Applicants must be interested in a career in law enforcement. Selection is based on academic record, letters of recommendation, and a personal essay describing at least 3 personal attributes or skills that they believe are the most important for a law enforcement professional to develop and how their undergraduate studies will help them develop those attributes and skills.

Financial data The stipend is $1,000.

Duration 1 year; nonrenewable.

Additional information This program is sponsored by the Bureau of Alcohol, Tobacco, Firearms and Explosives Retiree's Association (ATFRA). Information is also available from the Bureau's Office of Law Enforcement, 650 Massachusetts Avenue, N.W., Room 8290, Washington, DC 20226.

Number awarded 1 or more every other year, depending on the availability of funds.

Deadline March of even-numbered years.

[552]
ATTORNEY-CPA FOUNDATION UNDERGRADUATE ESSAY CONTEST

American Association of Attorney-Certified Public Accountants Foundation
Attn: Executive Director
3921 Old Lee Highway, Suite 71A
Fairfax, VA 22030
(703) 352-8064   Toll-free: (888) ATTY-CPA
Fax: (703) 352-8073
E-mail: aaacpa@attorney-cpa.com
Web: www.attorney-cpa.com

Purpose To recognize and reward outstanding undergraduate student essays on a topic related to accounting.

Eligibility Undergraduate accounting students are invited to enter this essay contest. The topic of the essay changes annually but always deals with the law and accounting; recently, students were asked to compare and contrast client privileges with respect to communications with an attorney and with a C.P.A. under federal law, in their state, and in 1 of the following states: New York, Florida, California, or Texas. The essay should be no more than 20 pages, including footnotes or endnotes.

Financial data The grand prize is $2,500, runner-up prize is $1,500, third prize is $500, fourth prize is $500, and regional prizes are $250.

Duration The competition is held annually.

Number awarded 8 each year: 1 grand prize, 1 runner-up, 1 third prize, 1 fourth prize, and 4 regional prizes.

Deadline June of each year.

[553]
AVIS SCHOLARSHIP

American Society of Travel Agents
Attn: ASTA Foundation
1101 King Street, Suite 200
Alexandria, VA 22314-2944
(703) 739-8721   Fax: (703) 684-8319
E-mail: scholarship@astahq.com
Web: www.astanet.com/education/scholarshiph.asp

Purpose To provide financial assistance to travel industry professionals who have returned to college or graduate school.

Eligibility This program is open to travel industry professionals who have at least 2 years of full-time experience in the travel industry (e.g., tour operator, travel agency, hotel, airlines, car rental) or an undergraduate degree in travel and tourism. Applicants must be currently employed in the travel industry and enrolled in at least 2 courses per semester in an accredited undergraduate or graduate program in business or equivalent degree program at an accredited 4-year college or university. They must have earned a GPA of 3.0 or higher during their previous academic term. Selection is

based on an essay of 500 to 750 words on how their degree program relates to their future career in the travel industry.
Financial data The stipend is $2,000.
Duration 1 year; may be renewed up to 2 additional years.
Additional information This award was established in 1987.
Number awarded 1 each year.
Deadline August of each year.

[554] AWORLDCONNECTED.ORG ESSAY CONTEST
A World Connected
c/o Institute for Humane Studies
George Mason University
3301 North Fairfax Drive, Suite 440
Arlington, VA 22201
(703) 993-4880 Toll-free: (800) 697-8799
Fax: (703) 993-4890
E-mail: info@aworldconnected.org
Web: www.aworldconnected.org

Purpose To recognize and reward undergraduate and graduate students and other young people who submit outstanding essays on a theme related to globalization.
Eligibility This competition is open to 1) full-time undergraduate and graduate students of any age, and 2) other people 25 years of age and younger. Entrants may be from any country and any academic discipline. High school students are not eligible. Applicants must submit an essay, from 600 to 2,500 words in length, on a topic that changes annually. Recently, entrants were invited to write on global education, poverty, and entrepreneurship. Selection is based on the essays' clarity, rigor, and eloquence.
Financial data First prize is $2,000, second $1,250, third $750, and honorable mentions $250.
Duration The competition is held annually.
Additional information This competition was first held in 2003.
Number awarded 7 each year: 3 prize winners and 4 honorable mentions.
Deadline May of each year.

[555] B. JUNE WEST RECRUITMENT GRANT
Delta Kappa Gamma Society International-Theta State Organization
c/o Pat Graff, Committee on Professional Affairs Chair
8101 Krim N.E.
Albuquerque, NM 87109-5223
E-mail: pgraff@aol.com
Web: www.deltakappagamma.org/NM

Purpose To provide financial assistance to women in New Mexico who are interested in preparing for a career as a teacher.
Eligibility This program is open to women residents of New Mexico who are 1) graduating high school seniors planning to go into education; 2) college students majoring in education; or 3) teachers needing educational assistance. Applicants must submit a list of activities in which they are involved, 3 letters of recommendation, a list of achievements and awards, and a statement of their educational goal and how this grant would be of assistance to them. Financial need is not considered in the selection process.
Financial data A stipend is awarded (amount not specified).
Duration 1 year.
Number awarded 1 or more each year.
Deadline February of each year.

[556] BARBARA ALICE MOWER MEMORIAL SCHOLARSHIP
Barbara Alice Mower Memorial Scholarship Committee
c/o Nancy A. Mower
1536 Kamole Street
Honolulu, HI 96821-1424
(808) 373-2901

Purpose To provide financial assistance to female residents of Hawaii who are interested in women's studies and are attending college on the undergraduate or graduate level in the United States or abroad.
Eligibility This program is open to female residents of Hawaii who are at least juniors in college, are interested in and committed to women's studies, and have worked or studied in the field. Selection is based on interest in studying about and commitment to helping women, previous work and/or study in that area, previous academic performance, character, personality, and future plans to help women (particularly women in Hawaii).
Financial data The stipend ranges from $1,000 to $3,500.
Duration 1 year; may be renewed.
Additional information Recipients may use the scholarship at universities in Hawaii, on the mainland, or in foreign countries. They must focus on women's studies or topics that relate to women in school.
Number awarded 1 or more each year.
Deadline April of each year.

[557] BARBARA JORDAN MEMORIAL SCHOLARSHIP
Association of Texas Professional Educators
Attn: Scholarships
305 East Huntland Drive, Suite 300
Austin, TX 78752-3792
(512) 467-0071 Toll-free: (800) 777-ATPE
Fax: (512) 467-2203 E-mail: atpe@atpe.org
Web: www.atpe.org/Awards/bjordaninfo.htm

Purpose To provide financial assistance to undergraduate and graduate students enrolled in educator preparation programs at predominantly ethnic minority institutions in Texas.
Eligibility This program is open to juniors, seniors, and graduate students enrolled in educator preparation programs at predominantly ethnic minority institutions in Texas. Applicants must submit a 2-page essay on their personal philosophy toward education, why they want to become an educator, who influenced them the most in making their career decision, and why they are applying for the scholarship. Financial need is not considered in the selection process.

Financial data The stipend is $1,500 per year.

Duration 1 year.

Additional information The qualifying institutions are Huston-Tillotson College, Jarvis Christian College, Our Lady of the Lake University, Paul Quinn College, Prairie View A&M University, St. Mary's University of San Antonio, Sul Ross State University, Sul Ross State University Rio Grande College, Texas A&M International University, Texas A&M University at Kingsville, Texas Southern University, University of Houston, University of Houston-Downtown, University of Texas at Brownsville and Texas Southmost College, University of Texas at El Paso, University of Texas at San Antonio, University of Texas-Pan American, University of the Incarnate Word, and Wiley College.

Number awarded Up to 6 each year.

Deadline May of each year.

[558]
BETTY RENDEL SCHOLARSHIPS

National Federation of Republican Women
Attn: Scholarships and Internships
124 North Alfred Street
Alexandria, VA 22314-3011
(703) 548-9688   Fax: (703) 548-9836
E-mail: mail@nfrw.org
Web: www.nfrw.org/programs/scholarships.htm

Purpose To provide financial assistance to undergraduate Republican women who are majoring in political science, government, or economics.

Eligibility This program is open to women who have completed at least 2 years of college. Applicants must be majoring in political science, government, or economics. Along with their application, they must submit 3 letters of recommendation, an official transcript, a 1-page essay on why they should be considered for the scholarship, and a 1-page essay on career goals. Optionally, a photograph may be supplied. Applications must be submitted to the Republican federation president in the applicant's state. Each president chooses 1 application from her state to submit for scholarship consideration. Financial need is not a factor in the selection process. U.S. citizenship is required.

Financial data The stipend is $1,000.

Duration 1 year; nonrenewable.

Additional information This program was established in 1995.

Number awarded 3 each year.

Deadline Applications must be submitted to the state federation president by May of each year.

[559]
BILL KANE UNDERGRADUATE SCHOLARSHIP

American Association for Health Education
Attn: Scholarship Committee
1900 Association Drive
Reston, VA 20191-1599
(703) 476-3437   Toll-free: (800) 213-7193, ext. 437
Fax: (703) 476-6638   E-mail: aahe@aahperd.org
Web: www.aahperd.org/aahe/heawards/AAHE.html

Purpose To provide financial assistance to undergraduates who are currently enrolled in a health education program.

Eligibility This program is open to undergraduate students who are enrolled full time in a health education program at a 4-year college or university. Applicants must have a GPA of 3.25 or higher as a sophomore, junior, or senior. Along with their application, they must submit an essay of 400 to 500 words on what they hope to accomplish as a health educator (during training and in the future) and the attributes and aspirations they bring to the field of health education. Selection is based on evidence of leadership potential, academic talent, and activity in health education profession-related activities or organizations at the college, university, and/or community level.

Financial data The stipend is $1,000 plus a 1-year complimentary student membership in the association.

Duration 1 year; nonrenewable.

Additional information This program was formerly known as the American Association for Health Education Undergraduate Scholarship.

Number awarded 1 each year.

Deadline November of each year.

[560]
BROWN FOUNDATION ACADEMIC SCHOLARSHIPS

Brown Foundation for Educational Equity, Excellence and Research
Attn: Scholarship Committee
1515 S.E. Monroe
P.O. Box 4862
Topeka, KS 66604
(785) 235-3939   Fax: (785) 235-1001
E-mail: brownfound@juno.com
Web: brownvboard.org

Purpose To provide financial assistance to currently-enrolled college juniors of color who are interested in preparing for a teaching career.

Eligibility This program is open to members of minority groups entering their junior year of college in preparation for a teaching career. Applicants must be enrolled at least half time at an institution of higher education with an accredited program in education and have GPA of 3.0 or higher. Along with their application, they must submit brief essays on 1) their involvement in school, religious, community, and/or other activities; 2) why they aspire to a career in education, their goals, and the level at which they plan to teach; and 3) the impact *Brown v. the Board of Education* has had on the field of education. Selection is based on the essays; GPA; school, community, and leisure activities; career plans and goals in education; and recommendations.

Financial data The stipend is $1,000 per year.

Duration 2 years (junior and senior years).

Additional information The first Brown Foundation Scholarships were awarded in 1989.

Number awarded Varies each year; recently, 3 of these scholarships were awarded.

Deadline March of each year.

[561]
BUSINESS ACHIEVEMENT AWARDS

Golden Key International Honour Society
621 North Avenue N.E., Suite C-100
Atlanta, GA 30308
(404) 377-2400   Toll-free: (800) 377-2401
Fax: (678) 420-6757
E-mail: scholarships@goldenkey.org
Web: www.goldenkey.org

Purpose To recognize and reward members of the Golden Key International Honour Society who submit outstanding papers on topics related to the field of business.

Eligibility This program is open to undergraduate, graduate, and postgraduate members of the society who submit a paper or report, up to 10 pages in length, on a topic related to business. Applicants must also submit 1) an essay, up to 2 pages in length, describing the assignment for writing the paper, the greatest challenge in writing the paper, the lessons learned from completing the assignment, and what they would change if they could redo the paper; 2) a letter of recommendation; and 3) academic transcripts. Selection of the winners is based on academic achievement and the quality of the paper.

Financial data The winner receives a $1,000 scholarship, second place a $750 scholarship, and third place a $500 scholarship.

Duration These awards are presented annually.

Additional information This program began in 2001.

Number awarded 3 each year.

Deadline February of each year.

[562]
CALIFORNIA HOTEL & LODGING ASSOCIATION GENERAL SCHOLARSHIPS

California Hotel & Lodging Association
Attn: CH&LA Educational Foundation
414 29th Street
Sacramento, CA 95816-3211
(916) 444-5780   Fax: (916) 444-5848
E-mail: Kathy@calodging.com
Web: www.calodging.com

Purpose To provide financial assistance to residents of California who are interested in attending college to prepare for a career in the lodging industry.

Eligibility This program is open to residents of California who graduated from high school with a GPA of 2.7 or higher and are currently enrolled or planning to enroll at an accredited college or university. California residents who are not high school graduates but who have lodging work experience are also eligible. Preference is given to students attending schools in California. Applicants must be preparing for a career in the lodging industry. Students working on a culinary degree are not eligible, although they may be considered if they are interested in hotel-related food and beverage operations. Selection is based on merit and submission of financial information is optional.

Financial data Stipends range from $500 to $1,500 per year.

Duration 1 year; may be renewed.

Number awarded Several each year.

Deadline April of each year.

[563]
CALIFORNIA STATE FAIR INTERNATIONAL STUDIES SCHOLARSHIPS

California State Fair
Attn: Friends of the Fair Scholarship Program
1600 Exposition Boulevard
P.O. Box 15649
Sacramento, CA 95852
(916) 274-5969   E-mail: entryoffice@calexpo.com
Web: www.bigfun.org

Purpose To provide financial assistance to residents of California working on an undergraduate or graduate degree in international studies at a college or university in the state.

Eligibility This program is open to residents of California who are enrolled as undergraduate or graduate students at a college or university in the state. Applicants must be studying or majoring in international studies. They must have a GPA of 3.0 or higher. Along with their application, they must submit a 500-word essay on a topic that changes annually; recently, students were invited to write on the effect of China's growing involvement with agriculture on California's economy. Selection is based on personal commitment, goals established for their chosen field, leadership potential, and civic accomplishments.

Financial data Stipends are $1,500 or $500.

Duration 1 year.

Additional information The Friends of the Fair Scholarship Program was established in 1993.

Number awarded 2 each year: 1 at $1,500 and 1 at $500.

Deadline March of each year.

[564]
CARTOGRAPHY AND GEOGRAPHIC INFORMATION SOCIETY SCHOLARSHIP AWARD

American Congress on Surveying and Mapping
Attn: Scholarships
6 Montgomery Village Avenue, Suite 403
Gaithersburg, MD 20879
(240) 632-9716, ext. 113   Fax: (240) 632-1321
E-mail: pat.canfield@acsm.net
Web: www.acsm.net/scholar.html

Purpose To provide financial assistance for undergraduate or graduate study in cartography or geographic information science to members of the American Congress on Surveying and Mapping (ACSM).

Eligibility This program is open to ACSM members who are enrolled full time in a 4-year or graduate degree program in cartography, GIS, or other mapping sciences. Applicants must submit a statement describing their educational program, future plans for study or research, and why the award is merited. Selection is based on that statement (30%), academic record (30%), letters of recommendation (20%), and professional activities (20%).

Financial data The stipend is $1,000.

Duration 1 year.

Additional information This award is funded by the Cartography and Geographic Information Society (CaGIS) and administered by ACSM.

Number awarded 1 each year.

Deadline January of each year.

[565]
CASE STUDY COMPETITION IN CORPORATE COMMUNICATIONS

Institute for Public Relations Research and Education
c/o University of Florida
2096 Weimer Hall
P.O. Box 118400
Gainesville, FL 32611-8400
(352) 392-0280　　　　　　　Fax: (352) 846-1122
E-mail: iprceo@jou.ufl.edu
Web: www.instituteforpr.com

Purpose To recognize and reward undergraduate and graduate students in business, communications, or journalism who win a competition in public relations.

Eligibility This competition is open to undergraduate and graduate students enrolled at accredited schools of business, communications, or journalism. Students may participate as sole authors or members of a case-writing team (not to exceed 4 people). Each student author or case-writing team must be sponsored by a faculty member. Applicants must submit a case study on a topic within the field of corporate communication or public relations, including but not limited to crisis or issues management, government relations, integrated marketing communications, internal or employee communications, investor relations, measuring communications impact, interactive or Internet public relations, or reputation management. Cases should clearly describe a business problem, not the solutions to the problem. They must be accompanied by a teaching note and a PowerPoint presentation. Selection is based on the relevance, purpose, and timeliness of the entry (15 points); significance of the business problem and the critical issues identified on the entry (15 points); balance, fairness, and absence of bias in the entry (15 points); factual and accurate nature of the entry (15 points); entry's style, tone, and quality of expression (15 points); quality of the teaching note (15 points); and quality of the PowerPoint presentation (10 points). Separate competitions are held for business schools and for communications and journalism schools.

Financial data The prizes for submissions from business schools and from communications and journalism schools are $2,500 for first, $1,500 for second, and $800 for third. The faculty advisor for the first-place winners receive $650, for the second-place winners $350, and for the third-place winners $200. The grand prize is $5,000 for the student(s) and $1,500 for the faculty advisor.

Duration The competition is held annually.

Additional information This competition is sponsored by the Arthur W. Page Society, 317 Madison Avenue, Suite 2320, New York, NY 10017, (212) 400-7959, Fax: (212) 922-9198, E-mail: admin@awpagesociety.com. A non-refundable entry fee of $25 is required.

Number awarded 6 winners are selected each year (3 from business schools and 3 from communications and journalism schools). From those, 1 is selected as the grand prize winner.

Deadline Entries must be submitted by January of each year.

[566]
CCIM INSTITUTE EDUCATION FOUNDATION UNDERGRADUATE UNIVERSITY SCHOLARSHIPS

CCIM Institute
Attn: Education Foundation
717 Princess Street
Alexandria, VA 22314
(703) 683-5295　　　　　　Toll-free: (877) CCIM-EF1
Fax: (703) 683-0018
E-mail: EdFoundation@ccim.com
Web: www.ccimeducationfoundation.org

Purpose To provide financial assistance to upper-division students working on a degree in real estate.

Eligibility This program is open to juniors and seniors attending 1 of 23 participating universities (contact the sponsor for a list) who are nominated by their university. Applicants must be preparing for a career in commercial investment real estate or an allied industry. They must have a GPA of 3.0 or higher in their major and practical experience in the field (through an internship or a job). Along with their application, they must submit a statement of 150 to 300 words explaining why they are studying and planning a career in real estate (or a related field) and what CCIM means to them. Selection is based on academic record, commitment to real estate or allied industry career, honors and awards, extracurricular activities, history of employment, and personal and professional references.

Financial data The stipend is $1,000.

Duration 1 year.

Additional information This program started in 1988. The CCIM Institute was formerly the Commercial Investment Real Estate Institute.

Number awarded Varies each year; recently, 17 of these scholarships were awarded.

Deadline Students must submit their applications to their university by August of each year. Universities must forward their nominations to a CCIM Institute chapter by October of each year.

[567]
CHUCK PEACOCK MEMORIAL SCHOLARSHIP

Aircraft Electronics Association
Attn: AEA Educational Foundation
4217 South Hocker Drive
Independence, MO 64055-4723
(816) 373-6565　　　　　　　Fax: (816) 478-3100
E-mail: info@aea.net
Web: www.aea.net

Purpose To provide financial assistance to students interested in preparing for a career in aviation management.

Eligibility This program is open to high school seniors and currently-enrolled college students who are attending (or planning to attend) an accredited postsecondary institution in an aviation management program. Applicants must submit an official transcript (cumulative GPA of 2.5 or higher), a statement about their career plans, a description of their involvement in school and community activities, and a 300-word essay on how the job requirements of aviation technicians will change with advancements in technology. Selection is based on merit.

Financial data The stipend is $1,000.

Duration 1 year.
Number awarded 1 each year.
Deadline February of each year.

[568]
CLAMPITT PAPER/HENRY PHILLIPS MEMORIAL SCHOLARSHIP

Printing and Imaging Association of MidAmerica
Attn: Dodie Royals
8828 North Stemmons, Suite 505
Dallas, TX 75247
(214) 630-8871, ext. 205   Toll-free: (800) 788-2040
E-mail: dodier@piamidam.org
Web: www.piamidam.org/scholar.php

Purpose To provide financial assistance to residents of Oklahoma and Texas who are attending college to prepare for a career in the printing industry.
Eligibility This program is open to students enrolled in an educational institution that offers a 2- or 4-year degree in printing technology or management. Applicants must be residents of Oklahoma or Texas. They should be attending a school in those states, but they may go elsewhere if they can demonstrate the appropriate aptitude and industry interest. Along with their application, they must submit a 1-page statement outlining their career goals and a letter of endorsement from their faculty sponsor that reinforces their stated intention to prepare for a career in the printing industry. Selection is based on interest in the industry, activities, and GPA; financial need is not considered.
Financial data The stipend is $1,000.
Duration 1 year.
Number awarded 1 or more each year.
Deadline February of each year.

[569]
CLAUDE E. POPE SCHOLARSHIP

Mortgage Bankers Association of the Carolinas, Inc.
5821 Fairview Road, Suite 217
P.O. Box 11721
Charlotte, NC 28220-1721
(704) 552-2860   Fax: (704) 552-7071
E-mail: info@mbac.org
Web: www.mbac.org

Purpose To provide financial assistance to upper-division students who are preparing for a career in mortgage banking at colleges and universities in the Carolinas.
Eligibility This program is open to rising juniors at 4-year accredited colleges and universities in North Carolina or South Carolina who are working on a degree related to mortgage banking or mortgage financing (e.g., real estate, banking, economics). Applicants must be residents of North Carolina or South Carolina, although they may attend school in either state. They must have a GPA of 3.0 or higher. Financial need is not considered in the selection process.
Financial data The stipend is $2,500 per year.
Duration 2 years.
Additional information This award was established in 1972.
Number awarded 2 each year.
Deadline April of each year.

[570]
CNF PROFESSIONAL GROWTH SCHOLARSHIPS

School Nutrition Association
Attn: Child Nutrition Foundation Scholarship Committee
700 South Washington Street, Suite 300
Alexandria, VA 22314-4287
(703) 739-3900   Toll-free: (800) 877-8822
Fax: (703) 739-3915   E-mail: cnf@schoolnutrition.org
Web: www.schoolnutrition.org/Index.aspx?ID=1043

Purpose To provide financial assistance to members of the School Nutrition Association (SNA) who are interested in additional undergraduate or graduate study.
Eligibility This program is open to active SNA members who meet all 4 of the following criteria: 1) plan to work on an undergraduate or graduate degree at a college or vocational/technical institution that has a program designed to improve school food service (e.g., nutrition, food service management, business administration); 2) have a history of employment in school food service and at least 1 year's SNA membership; 3) have a satisfactory academic record; and 4) express a desire to make school food service a career. Applicants must submit a 1-page personal essay (up to 500 words) stating their reason for selecting school food service as a profession; what they expect to gain from continuing their education; and their long-term professional goals/plans. Selection is based on the essay (35 points), letters of recommendation (20 points), SNA state and local chapter activity participation (15 points), organization and neatness (10 points), program of study (15 points), and GPA (5 points).
Financial data Stipends up to $1,000 are available.
Duration 1 year; may be renewed up to 3 additional years.
Additional information The SNA was formerly the American School Food Service Administration.
Number awarded Varies each year; recently, 21 of these scholarships were awarded.
Deadline April of each year.

[571]
COLORADO YOUNG FARMERS SCHOLARSHIPS

Colorado Young Farmers Educational Association
c/o Northeastern Junior College
100 College Drive
Sterling, CO 80751
(970) 521-6690   Fax: (970) 521-6801
E-mail: info@coloradoyoungfarmer.com
Web: www.coloradoyoungfarmer.com

Purpose To provide financial assistance to entering or continuing undergraduate students in Colorado interested in preparing for a career teaching agricultural education.
Eligibility This program is open to Colorado residents who are 1) freshmen and sophomores majoring in agriculture, and 2) juniors and seniors majoring in agricultural education and working toward teacher certification. Applicants must be enrolled full time at a community college, university, or college in Colorado. Selection is based on scholar-

ship, activities, and interest in agriculture and teaching agricultural education.
Financial data Stipends are $500 for freshmen and sophomores, $750 for juniors, or $1,250 for seniors.
Duration 1 year.
Additional information This program, which began in 1992, is supported by Case IH.
Number awarded 5 each year: 2 to entering freshmen and 1 each to a sophomore, junior, and senior.
Deadline March of each year.

[572]
COMMUNITY SERVICE SCHOLARSHIPS
Association of Government Accountants
Attn: National Awards Committee
2208 Mount Vernon Avenue
Alexandria, VA 22301-1314
(703) 684-6931   Toll-free: (800) AGA-7211, ext. 309
Fax: (703) 548-9367   E-mail: rortiz@agacgfm.org
Web: www.agacgfm.org/membership/awards

Purpose To provide financial assistance to high school seniors and undergraduate and graduate students who are interested in majoring in financial management and are involved in community service.
Eligibility This program is open to graduating high school seniors, high school graduates, college and university undergraduates, and graduate students. Applicants must be working on or planning to work on a degree in a financial management discipline, including accounting, auditing, budgeting, economics, finance, electronic data processing, information resources management, or public administration. They must have a GPA of 2.5 or higher and be actively involved in community service projects. Along with their application, they must submit a 2-page essay on "My community service accomplishments," high school or college transcripts, and a reference letter from a community service organization. Selection is based on community service involvement and accomplishments; financial need is not considered.
Financial data The annual stipend is $1,000.
Duration 1 year; renewable.
Number awarded 2 each year: 1 to a high school senior or graduate and 1 to an undergraduate or graduate student.
Deadline March of each year.

[573]
COMTO NJ SCHOLARSHIPS
Conference of Minority Transportation Officials-New Jersey Chapter
Attn: Scholarship Committee
P.O. Box 22968
Newark, NJ 07101
E-mail: comtonj@mail.comtonj.org
Web: www.comtonj.org/scholarshipInfo.asp

Purpose To provide financial assistance to entering or enrolled college students from New Jersey interested in working on a degree in a field related to transportation.
Eligibility This program is open to students entering or attending colleges and universities in New Jersey to major in a field related to transportation (e.g., environmental disciplines, public service, safety, transportation, urban planning). Applicants must have a GPA of 3.0 or higher. Along with their application, they must submit a 500-word essay on why they chose a career in transportation. Selection is based on the essay, academic achievement, extracurricular and community activities, and letters of recommendation.
Financial data Stipends are $1,000 or $500.
Duration 1 year.
Additional information The sponsor is the New Jersey chapter of the Conference of Minority Transportation Officials (COMTO). The national organization was founded in 1971 to promote, strengthen, and expand the roles of minorities in all aspects of transportation. This program includes the Lewis R. Rosser Scholarship, the Paul Smith Scholarship, and the Garrett Morgan Scholarship. Recipients must attend the COMTO NJ Scholarship Gala to accept the award.
Number awarded 4 each year: 1 at $1,000 and 3 at $500.
Deadline April of each year.

[574]
CONNECTICUT HOSPITALITY EDUCATIONAL FOUNDATION SCHOLARSHIPS
Connecticut Hospitality Educational Foundation
Attn: Scholarships
100 Roscommon Drive, Suite 320
Middletown, CT 06457
(860) 635-7775   Toll-free: (800) 382-5619 (within CT)
Fax: (860) 635-6400   E-mail: jim@cthef.org
Web: www.cthef.org

Purpose To provide financial assistance to Connecticut residents interested in preparing for a career in the tourism, lodging, or food service industries.
Eligibility This program is open to residents of Connecticut who are 1) graduating high school seniors, 2) high school graduates who have not yet enrolled in college, 3) undergraduates at a 2- or 4-year college or university, or 4) first-year master's students. Applicants must be attending or planning to attend an institution in Connecticut and enroll in a tourism or hospitality degree program. Along with their application, they must submit a personal letter of intent explaining how the scholarship will help them achieve their academic goals. Selection is based on academic and personal achievement as well as a demonstrated interest in the food service, lodging, or tourism industries.
Financial data The stipend is $1,000.
Duration 1 year.
Additional information The Connecticut Hospitality Education Foundation was established in 2001 as a partnership of the Connecticut Restaurant Association and the Connecticut Lodging Association.
Number awarded 6 each year.
Deadline August of each year.

[575]
CONSTRUCTMYFUTURE.COM SCHOLARSHIPS
ConstructMyFuture.com
111 East Wisconsin Avenue, Suite 1000
Milwaukee, WI 53202
(414) 272-0943　　　Toll-free: (866) AEM-0442
Fax: (414) 272-1170　　　E-mail: nhallada@aem.org
Web: www.constructmyfuture.com

Purpose To provide financial assistance for college to students who are interested in preparing for a career in the construction industry.

Eligibility This program is open to 1) graduating high school seniors; 2) students currently enrolled in a postsecondary educational institution; and 3) workers currently employed in the construction industry. Applicants must be interested in 1) entering or continuing in a college program to prepare for a career in the construction industry; or 2) purchasing tools for use in a construction industry job. Along with their application, they must submit a 1,000-word essay on their interest in the construction industry, their educational goals, and any other information such as specialized hobbies, skills, rewards, or achievements they wish to share. Selection is based on current and past involvement in the construction field; financial need is not considered.

Financial data The stipend is $1,000.

Duration 1 year; nonrenewable.

Number awarded 3 each year.

Deadline February of each year.

[576]
DAN WHITWORTH MEMORIAL SCHOLARSHIP
Texas Amateur Athletic Federation
P.O. Box 1789
Georgetown, TX 78627-1789
(512) 863-9400　　　Fax: (512) 869-2393
E-mail: marklord@cox-internet.com
Web: www.taaf.com/pages/schlorship.asp

Purpose To provide financial assistance to entering or continuing undergraduate and graduate students at institutions in Texas who are interested in preparing for a career in the parks and recreation profession.

Eligibility This program is open to residents of Texas who are enrolled or planning to enroll full time at a college or university in an accredited bachelor's, master's, or doctoral degree program for sports sciences or another major relating to the field of parks and recreation. Preference is given to students attending a Texas college or university. Graduating high school seniors must have a class rank in the top quarter, a GPA of 2.5 or higher, an SAT score of 850 or higher, or an ACT score of 21 or higher. Students already enrolled in college or graduate school must have a GPA of 2.5 or higher. In addition to grades and test scores, selection is based on honors and awards from, and participation in, activities, endeavors, volunteerism, and work related to athletics and/or the field of parks and recreation. Financial need is not considered.

Financial data A stipend is awarded (amount not specified).

Duration 1 year.

Number awarded 1 or more each year.

Deadline April of each year.

[577]
DAVID HOODS MEMORIAL SCHOLARSHIP
Electronic Document Systems Foundation
Attn: EDSF Scholarship Awards
608 Silver Spur Road, Suite 280
Rolling Hills Estates, CA 90274-3616
(310) 265-5510　　　Fax: (310) 265-5588
E-mail: jmowlds@edsf.org
Web: www.edsf.org/scholarships.cfm

Purpose To provide financial assistance to upper-division and graduate students interested in working with electronic documents as a career.

Eligibility This program is open to full-time juniors, seniors, and graduate students who demonstrate a strong interest in working with electronic documents as a career (including graphic communications, document management, document content, and/or document distribution). Special consideration is given to students interested in marketing and public relations. Applicants must submit a statement of their career goals in the field of document communications, an essay on a topic related to their view of the future of the document management and production industry, a list of current professional and college extracurricular activities and achievements, college transcripts (GPA of 3.0 or higher), samples of their creative work, and 2 letters of recommendation. Financial need is not considered.

Financial data The stipend is $2,000.

Duration 1 year.

Additional information This program was established in 1999.

Number awarded 1 each year.

Deadline May of each year.

[578]
DCBMBAA CHAPTER UNDERGRADUATE SCHOLARSHIP PROGRAM
National Black MBA Association-Washington, DC Chapter
P.O. Box 14042
Washington, DC 20044
(202) 628-0138　　　E-mail: outreach@dcbmbaa.org
Web: www.dcbmbaa.org/scholarships.htm

Purpose To provide financial assistance to minority students from the Washington, D.C. area who are working on an undergraduate degree in business or management.

Eligibility This program is open to minority students who are enrolled full time in an undergraduate business or management program and working on a bachelor's degree. Applicants must currently reside in Washington, D.C., Maryland, or Virginia, either permanently or as a student. Along with their application, they must submit a 2-page essay on a topic that changes annually; recently, students were asked to write on the unique actions that businessmen and women can perform to give back to their community. Selection is based on the essay, transcripts, and a list of extracurricular activities and awards. Financial need is not considered.

Financial data The stipend is $1,000.

Duration 1 year.
Additional information This program began in 2000.
Number awarded 1 each year.
Deadline May of each year.

[579]
DEFENSE OF ACADEMIC FREEDOM AWARD

National Council for the Social Studies
Attn: Recognition Programs Assistant
8555 16th Street, Suite 500
Silver Spring, MD 20910-2844
(301) 588-1800, ext. 106 Fax: (202) 966-2061
E-mail: excellence@ncss.org
Web: www.socialstudies.org

Purpose To recognize and reward individuals who contributed significantly to the preservation of academic freedom in the area of social studies education.

Eligibility Teachers, administrators, professionals in other areas of education, parents, and students are eligible to be nominated for the award or may nominate themselves. Nominees must have 1) engaged in or be currently engaged in activities that support academic freedom in the face of personal challenge or promote awareness of and support for academic freedom; 2) personal involvement in a particular controversy, the use of controversial issues or materials, defense of the presentation of divergent materials and views, and/or the preparation of materials involving controversy and divergent views; and 3) personal involvement in activities that highlight issues surrounding censorship and academic freedom through writings, speeches, or other advocacy. The defense or advocacy of academic freedom must have been related to the teaching of social studies.

Financial data The amount awarded is $1,500.
Duration This award is presented annually.
Additional information This award is co-sponsored by the National Council for the Social Studies and SIRS Mandarin.
Number awarded 1 each year.
Deadline March of each year.

[580]
DELOITTE NATIONAL STUDENT CASE STUDY SEMINAR

Deloitte Foundation
Attn: Academic Development and University Relations
10 Westport Road
Wilton, CT 06897-0820
(203) 761-3248 Fax: (203) 563-2324
Web: www.deloitte.com

Purpose To recognize and reward accounting students who participate in an accounting competition.

Eligibility This program is open to accounting students at universities in the United States. The sponsoring firm's Accounting Research Department develops case studies of accounting problems. Teams of students from participating universities present their cases and solutions to a panel of active and retired partners of the firm who play the role of senior management or the audit committee of a client company. The panel members raise questions and issues for response and discussion, and then rank the teams based on their presentations and ability to identify and resolve the relevant accounting issues.

Financial data Each participant on the winning team receives a $1,000 scholarship and those on the second-place team receive $500. Other participating student finalists receive $250.

Duration The competition is held annually.
Additional information This competition, held at the Deloitte Development Center in Scottsdale, Arizona, was first conducted in 1996.
Number awarded Varies each year; recently, 6 teams participated in the competition finals.

[581]
DELTA NU ALPHA FOUNDATION SCHOLARSHIPS

Delta Nu Alpha
Attn: Foundation
1451 Hill Pike, Suite 158
Nashville, TN 37210
(615) 360-6863 Fax: (615) 360-1891
E-mail: carolh24@msn.com
Web: www.deltanualpha.org/educatio.htm

Purpose To provide financial assistance to undergraduate students working on a degree in the fields of transportation, logistics, or supply chain management.

Eligibility This program is open to students working on an associate or bachelor's degree in the fields of transportation, logistics, or supply chain management. Applicants must submit essay on their career interests and objectives; any special school projects, papers, and/or internships related to their major field of study; and how this award will help them, including why they feel they should be considered for this scholarship. Selection is based on scholastic achievement, career goals, related transportation and logistics interests, and letters of recommendation.

Financial data Stipends range from $1,000 to $2,000.
Duration 1 year.
Additional information Information is also available from Tom Bock, DNA Foundation Scholarship Chair, 4123 Apple Blossom Road, Lutz, FL 33558, (813) 288-2640, ext. 101, E-mail: tbock@oilpursys.com. Delta Nu Alpha is an association of professionals in logistics and transportation.
Number awarded 1 or more each year.
Deadline April of each year.

[582]
DIRECT MARKETING SCHOLARSHIP

New England Direct Marketing Association
Attn: NEDMA Foundation
193 Haverhill Street
North Reading, MA 01864
(978) 664-3877 Fax: (978) 664-2835
E-mail: nedmafdn@comcast.net
Web: www.nedma.com/foundation.html

Purpose To provide financial assistance and work experience to upper-division students in New England who are preparing for a career in direct marketing.

Eligibility This program is open to students who have completed their sophomore or junior year at a college or university in New England. Applicants must be majoring in marketing, advertising, communications, journalism, or other field designed to prepare them for a career in direct marketing. Along with their application, they must submit essays covering why they are applying for this scholarship, what courses in their major have interested them the most and why, the extracurricular activities in which they have participated, their employment or internship experiences (especially those related to marketing, advertising, or journalism), their special interest in the field, how they believe this scholarship will affect their short- and long-term goals, and what direct marketing means to them. Financial need is not considered in the selection process.

Financial data The award includes a stipend of $3,000 to be applied to college tuition, attendance at a nationally sponsored seminar on the basics of direct marketing, a paid summer internship at a New England firm that represents a segment of the direct marketing industry, and attendance at the annual conference of the New England Direct Marketing Association (NEDMA).

Duration 1 year.

Number awarded 1 each year.

Deadline February of each year.

[583]
DONALD W. FOGARTY INTERNATIONAL STUDENT PAPER COMPETITION

American Production & Inventory Control Society
Attn: Educational & Research Foundation
5301 Shawnee Road
Alexandria, VA 22312-2317
(703) 354-8851, ext. 2202
Toll-free: (800) 444-2742, ext. 2202
Fax: (703) 354-8794   E-mail: foundation@apicshq.org
Web: www.apics.org

Purpose To recognize and reward outstanding undergraduate and graduate student papers on resource management.

Eligibility This competition is open to undergraduate and graduate students who submit papers on a topic related to resource management, including inventory management, logistics, manufacturing processes, master planning, just-in-time, material and capacity requirements planning, production activity control, systems and technologies, and supply chain management. Papers must be the original work of 1 or more authors and normally between 10 and 20 pages; they may have been developed as part of a regular class assignment, but theses and dissertations are not acceptable. Papers are first submitted to local chapters, then forwarded to regional competitions, from which the winning entries are submitted to an international level. Selection is based on relevance of the topic to resource management, timeliness, understanding of topic and depth of coverage, accuracy of material, organization and clarity of the presentation, and originality of treatment.

Financial data At the regional level, first prize is $250, second $150, and third $100. At the international level, first prize is $1,000, second $500, and third $250.

Number awarded 6 prizes are awarded at the international level each year: 3 for undergraduates and 3 for graduate students.

Deadline May for the chapter competitions, June for the regional level, and July for the international contest.

[584]
DREW YOUNG AWARD

Dallas Human Resource Management Association, Inc.
Attn: Student Chair
4100 Spring Valley Road, Suite 300
Dallas, TX 75244
(214) 631-8775   Fax: (214) 631-4533
E-mail: info@dallashr.org
Web: www.dallashr.org

Purpose To provide financial assistance to members of the Society for Human Resource Management (SHRM) who are working on an undergraduate or graduate degree in the field of human resource management.

Eligibility This program is open to undergraduate and graduate student members of SHRM who are preparing for a career in the field of human resource management. Undergraduates must have completed at least 2 years of full-time study with a GPA of 3.0 or higher. Graduate students must be enrolled full time and have a GPA of 3.0 or higher. Students must be nominated by their SHRM chapter. Along with their application, they must submit a 100-word essay detailing their participation in their SHRM chapter and why they should be chosen to receive this scholarship. Selection is based on that essay, scholastic average and standing, participation in SHRM chapter affairs and programs, and participation in school programs.

Financial data The stipend is $2,000.

Duration 1 year.

Additional information The sponsor is the local affiliate of SHRM.

Number awarded 1 each year.

Deadline August of each year.

[585]
D.W. SIMPSON & COMPANY ACTUARIAL SCIENCE SCHOLARSHIP

D.W. Simpson & Company
1800 West Larchmont Avenue
Chicago, IL 60613
(312) 867-2300   Toll-free: (800) 837-8338
Fax: (312) 951-8386
E-mail: scholarship@dwsimpson.com
Web: www.actuaryjobs.com/scholar.html

Purpose To provide financial assistance to college seniors majoring in actuarial science.

Eligibility This program is open to students who are entering their senior year of undergraduate study in actuarial science. Applicants must have a GPA of 3.0 or higher overall and 3.2 or higher in their major, have passed at least 1 actuarial examination, and be eligible to work in the United States. Along with their application, they must submit 1) a list of internships, scholarships, honors, and extracurricular activities; and 2) an essay on their long-term career goals. Financial need is not considered in the selection process.

Financial data The stipend is $1,000 per semester.

Duration 1 semester; nonrenewable.

Number awarded 2 each year (1 per semester).

Deadline April of each year for the fall scholarship; October of each year for the spring scholarship.

[586]
EARL G. GRAVES SCHOLARSHIP

National Association for the Advancement of Colored People
Attn: Education Department
4805 Mt. Hope Drive
Baltimore, MD 21215-3297
(410) 580-5760   Toll-free: (877) NAACP-98
E-mail: youth@naacpnet.org
Web: www.naacp.org

Purpose To provide financial assistance to upper-division and graduate students majoring in business.

Eligibility This program is open to full-time juniors, seniors, and graduate students working on a degree in business. Applicants must be currently in good academic standing, making satisfactory progress toward an undergraduate or graduate degree, and in the top 20% of their class. Along with their application, they must submit a 1-page essay on their interest in their major and a career, their life's ambition, what they hope to accomplish in their lifetime, and what position they hope to attain. Financial need is not considered in the selection process.

Financial data The stipend is $5,000 per year.

Duration 1 year.

Additional information Information is also available from the United Negro College Fund, Scholarships and Grants Administration, 8260 Willow Oaks Corporate Drive, Fairfax, VA 22031, (703) 205-3400.

Number awarded Varies each year; recently, 20 of these scholarships were awarded.

Deadline March of each year.

[587]
EDDIE G. COLE MEMORIAL SCHOLARSHIPS

California State Fair
Attn: Friends of the Fair Scholarship Program
1600 Exposition Boulevard
P.O. Box 15649
Sacramento, CA 95852
(916) 274-5969   E-mail: entryoffice@calexpo.com
Web: www.bigfun.org

Purpose To provide financial assistance for college to residents of California who are interested in majoring in designated fields or preparing for a career in the Fair industry.

Eligibility This program is open to residents of California currently working on an undergraduate degree at a college or university in the state. Applicants must be 1) majoring in physical education, agriculture, or equine studies; or 2) preparing for a career in the Fair industry. They must have a GPA of 3.0 or higher. Along with their application, they must submit a 2-page essay on why they are pursuing their desired career and life goals. Selection is based on personal commitment, goals established for their chosen field, leadership potential, and civic accomplishments.

Financial data Stipends are $1,000 or $250.

Duration 1 year.

Additional information The Friends of the Fair Scholarship Program was established in 1993.

Number awarded 2 each year: 1 at $1,000 and 1 at $250.

Deadline March of each year.

[588]
EDSF BOARD OF DIRECTORS SCHOLARSHIPS

Electronic Document Systems Foundation
Attn: EDSF Scholarship Awards
608 Silver Spur Road, Suite 280
Rolling Hills Estates, CA 90274-3616
(310) 265-5510   Fax: (310) 265-5588
E-mail: jmowlds@edsf.org
Web: www.edsf.org/scholarships.cfm

Purpose To provide financial assistance to college juniors, seniors, and graduate students interested in working with electronic documents as a career.

Eligibility This program is open to juniors, seniors, and graduate students who are committed to preparing for a career in document management and communications marketplace, including computer science and engineering, graphic and media communications, e-commerce, imaging science, printing, web authoring, electronic publishing, telecommunications, and business (e.g., sales, marketing). Applicants must be enrolled full time at a college, university, or graduate school in the United States with a GPA of 3.0 or higher. Along with their application, they must submit a statement of their career goals in the field of document communications, an essay on a topic related to their view of the future of the document management and production industry, a list of current professional and college extracurricular activities and achievements, college transcripts, samples of their creative work, and 2 letters of recommendation. Financial need is not considered.

Financial data The stipend ranges from $1,000 to $2,000.

Duration 1 year.

Number awarded Varies each year. Recently, 28 of these scholarships were awarded: 10 at $2,000, 1 at $1,500, and 17 at $1,000.

Deadline May of each year.

[589]
EDSF BOARD OF DIRECTORS TECHNICAL AND COMMUNITY COLLEGE SCHOLARSHIP

Electronic Document Systems Foundation
Attn: EDSF Scholarship Awards
608 Silver Spur Road, Suite 280
Rolling Hills Estates, CA 90274-3616
(310) 265-5510   Fax: (310) 265-5588
E-mail: jmowlds@edsf.org
Web: www.edsf.org/scholarships.cfm

Purpose To provide financial assistance to students in technical schools and community colleges who are interested in working with electronic documents as a career.

Eligibility This program is open to first- and second-year students at technical and trade schools and community colleges. Applicants must be working on a degree in the field of electronic document communication, including graphic communication, computer science, and multimedia, and have a GPA of 3.0 or higher. Along with their application,

they must submit a 1-page essay on 1 of the following topics: 1) a definition of their career goals in the field of document management and communications; 2) a recent technological change and how it has or will affect the document communication industry; or 3) a definition of the document communication industry. Selection is based on the essay, extracurricular activities and achievements, high school transcripts, samples of creative work, and 2 letters of recommendation. Financial need is not considered.
Financial data The stipend is $1,000.
Duration 1 year.
Number awarded 5 each year.
Deadline May of each year.

[590]
EDUCATION ACHIEVEMENT AWARDS
Golden Key International Honour Society
621 North Avenue N.E., Suite C-100
Atlanta, GA 30308
(404) 377-2400 Toll-free: (800) 377-2401
Fax: (678) 420-6757
E-mail: scholarships@goldenkey.org
Web: www.goldenkey.org

Purpose To recognize and reward undergraduate and graduate members of the Golden Key International Honour Society who submit outstanding papers on topics related to the field of education.
Eligibility This program is open to undergraduate, graduate, and postgraduate members of the society who submit a paper or report, up to 10 pages in length, on a topic related to education. Applicants must also submit 1) an essay, up to 2 pages in length, describing the assignment for writing the paper, the greatest challenge in writing the paper, the lessons learned from completing the assignment, and what they would change if they could redo the paper; 2) a letter of recommendation; and 3) academic transcripts. Selection of the winners is based on academic achievement and the quality of the paper.
Financial data The winner receives a $1,000 scholarship, second place a $750 scholarship, and third place a $500 scholarship.
Duration These awards are presented annually.
Additional information This program began in 2001.
Number awarded 3 each year.
Deadline February of each year.

[591]
EDUCATIONAL FOUNDATION COLLEGE/UNIVERSITY SCHOLARSHIPS
Colorado Society of Certified Public Accountants
Attn: CSCPA Educational Foundation
7979 East Tufts Avenue, Suite 1000
Denver, CO 80237-2845
(303) 773-2877 Toll-free: (800) 523-9082 (within CO)
Fax: (303) 773-6344 E-mail: gmantz@cocpa.org
Web: www.cocpa.org

Purpose To provide financial assistance to upper-division and graduate students in Colorado who are studying accounting.
Eligibility This program is open to upper-division and graduate students at colleges and universities in Colorado who have completed at least 8 semester hours of accounting courses (including at least 1 intermediate accounting class). Applicants must have a GPA, both overall and in accounting, of at least 3.0. Financial need is not considered in the selection process.
Financial data The stipend is $2,500. Funds are paid directly to the recipient's school to be used for books, C.P.A. review materials, tuition, fees, and dormitory room and board.
Duration 1 year; recipients may reapply.
Number awarded 1 or more each year.
Deadline June of each year for fall semester or quarter; November of each year for winter quarter or spring semester.

[592]
ERNEST F. HOLLINGS UNDERGRADUATE SCHOLARSHIP PROGRAM
National Oceanic and Atmospheric Administration
Attn: Office of Education
1315 East-West Highway
SSMC3, Room 10703
Silver Spring, MD 20910
(301) 713-9437 Fax: (301) 713-9465
E-mail: StudentScholarshipPrograms@noaa.gov
Web: www.oesd.noaa.gov/Hollings_info.html

Purpose To provide financial assistance and summer research experience to upper-division students who are working on a degree in a field of interest to the National Oceanic and Atmospheric Administration (NOAA).
Eligibility This program is open to full-time students entering their junior year at an accredited college or university in the United States or its territories. Applicants must be majoring in a discipline related to oceanic and atmospheric science, research, technology, and education, and supportive of the purposes of NOAA's programs and mission, including, but not limited to biological, life, and agricultural sciences; computer and information sciences; mathematics; engineering; physical sciences; behavioral and social sciences; or teacher education. They must have a GPA of 3.0 or higher. As part of their program, they must be interested in participating in summer research and development activities at NOAA headquarters (Silver Spring, Maryland) or field centers. U.S. citizenship is required.
Financial data This program provides a stipend of $8,000 per academic year and $650 per week during the internship, a housing subsidy and limited travel reimbursement for round-trip transportation to the internship site, and travel expenses to the scholarship program conference at the completion of the internship.
Duration 2 academic years plus 10 weeks during the intervening summer.
Additional information This program was established in 2005.
Number awarded Approximately 100 each year.
Deadline February of each year.

SOCIAL SCIENCES

[593]
ESTHER MAYO SHERARD SCHOLARSHIP
American Health Information Management Association
Attn: Foundation of Research and Education
233 North Michigan Avenue, Suite 2150
Chicago, IL 60601-5806
(312) 233-1131   Fax: (312) 233-1431
E-mail: fore@ahima.org
Web: www.ahima.org/fore/student/programs.asp

Purpose To provide financial assistance to African American members of the American Health Information Management Association (AHIMA) who are interested in working on an undergraduate or graduate degree in health information administration or technology.

Eligibility This program is open to AHIMA members who are African Americans enrolled in a health information administration or health information technology program accredited by the Commission on Accreditation of Allied Health Education Programs. Applicants must be working on an undergraduate or graduate degree on at least a half-time basis and have a GPA of 3.0 or higher. U.S. citizenship is required. Selection is based (in order of importance) on GPA and academic achievement, volunteer and work experience, commitment to the health information management profession, suitability to the health information management profession, quality and suitability of references provided, and clarity of application.

Financial data The stipend ranges from $1,000 to $5,000.

Duration 1 year; nonrenewable.

Additional information This program was established in 2000 by the Esther Mayo Sherard Foundation.

Number awarded 1 each year.

Deadline April of each year.

[594]
FEDERAL PLANNING DIVISION ANNUAL STUDENT SCHOLARSHIP
American Planning Association
Attn: Federal Planning Division
122 South Michigan Avenue, Suite 1600
Chicago, IL 60603-6107
(312) 431-9100   Fax: (312) 431-9985
E-mail: fpd-info@list.planning.org
Web: www.FedPlan.org

Purpose To provide financial assistance to undergraduate and graduate students preparing for a career in planning, especially as it relates to activities of the federal government.

Eligibility This program is open to juniors, seniors, and graduate students at U.S. and Canadian accredited colleges and universities. Applicants must be preparing for a career in public service, especially at the federal level, as a planner. They must have a GPA of 3.0 or higher. Along with their application, they must submit an essay that addresses the federal government's role in managing its lands and resources in the best interests of the United States. Selection is based primarily on the essay, which is judged on clarity of message, freshness of idea, and potential for implementation.

Financial data Stipends range from $500 to $2,500.

Duration 1 year.

Additional information This program began in 2004. Information is also available from Justin Hollander, U.S. General Services Administration, 26 Federal Plaza, Room 1609, New York, NY 10278, (212) 264-1622.

Number awarded 1 or more each year.

Deadline November of each year.

[595]
FLORENCE TURNER KARLIN SCHOLARSHIP
Lincoln Community Foundation
215 Centennial Mall South, Suite 100
Lincoln, NE 68508
(402) 474-2345   Fax: (402) 476-8532
E-mail: lcf@lcf.org
Web: www.lcf.org

Purpose To provide financial assistance to upper-division and graduate students majoring in education in Nebraska.

Eligibility This program is open to graduates of Nebraska high schools working on an undergraduate or graduate degree in education at a college or university in the state. Applicants must have completed at least their sophomore year and have a GPA of 3.0 or higher. Along with their application, undergraduates must submit essays on their plans for teaching after college and where they plan to teach and why; graduate students must explain why they are working on a graduate degree in education. Financial need is not considered in the selection process.

Financial data Stipends provided by the foundation generally range from $500 to $2,000. Funds may be used only for college credit courses, not for workshops, seminars, or similar types of training opportunities.

Duration 1 year; recipients may reapply.

Number awarded 1 each year.

Deadline March of each year for undergraduates; May of each year for graduate students.

[596]
FLORIDA BANKERS EDUCATIONAL FOUNDATION GRANTS
Florida Bankers Association
Attn: Florida Bankers Educational Foundation
1001 Thomasville Road, Suite 201
P.O. Box 1360
Tallahassee, FL 32302-1360
(850) 224-2265, ext. 139   Fax: (850) 224-2423
E-mail: lnewton@flbankers.net
Web: www.floridabankers.com

Purpose To provide financial assistance to upper-division and graduate students who are interested in preparing for a career in Florida banking.

Eligibility This program is open to college juniors, seniors, and graduate students who have at least 5 years of full-time experience working in Florida banking. Applicants must be Florida residents, registered at 1 of 27 participating colleges or universities in the state, and taking banking-related classes. They must have a GPA of 2.5 or higher. Along with their application, they must submit 2 letters of recommendation from their place of employment: 1 from the bank president or other high-level employee and 1 from an immediate supervisor. Selection is based on interest in Florida banking, scholastic achievement, aptitude, ability, leadership, and character.

Financial data The amount of assistance is based on the number of semester hours the student has remaining until graduation. The maximum award is $1,500 per year for the freshman and sophomore years, $2,000 per year for the junior and senior years, and $5,000 as a graduate student.

Duration Up to 4 years as an undergraduate and another 2 years as a graduate student.

Additional information Recipients must maintain a 2.5 GPA and take at least 12 credit hours per calendar year.

Number awarded Several each year.

Deadline February, May, August, or November of each year.

[597]
FORD MOTOR COMPANY BUSINESS AND LEADERSHIP SCHOLARSHIP

Golden Key International Honour Society
621 North Avenue N.E., Suite C-100
Atlanta, GA 30308
(404) 377-2400   Toll-free: (800) 377-2401
Fax: (678) 420-6757
E-mail: scholarships@goldenkey.org
Web: www.goldenkey.org

Purpose To provide financial assistance to members of the Golden Key International Honour Society who are working on an undergraduate or graduate degree in business.

Eligibility This program is open to members of the society who are either undergraduates or recent graduates (within the past 3 years) in business. Applicants must submit 1) a personal resume that includes a list of extracurricular activities, involvement in Golden Key, work history, and special circumstances; 2) a 1,000-word essay that states why they are applying for the scholarship, how they have demonstrated leadership on their campus, and how the society's commitment to academic excellence will be furthered by their studies; 3) academic transcripts; 4) at least 3 letters of recommendation; and 5) either a paper they have prepared or some other piece of work related to the field of business. Selection is based on academic achievement, leadership achievement, involvement in their local chapter, and extracurricular activities.

Financial data The stipend is $10,000.

Duration 1 year; nonrenewable.

Additional information This program is sponsored by Ford Motor Company.

Number awarded 1 each year.

Deadline February of each year.

[598]
FORE UNDERGRADUATE MERIT SCHOLARSHIPS

American Health Information Management Association
Attn: Foundation of Research and Education
233 North Michigan Avenue, Suite 2150
Chicago, IL 60601-5806
(312) 233-1131   Fax: (312) 233-1431
E-mail: fore@ahima.org
Web: www.ahima.org/fore/student/programs.asp

Purpose To provide financial assistance to members of the American Health Information Management Association (AHIMA) who are interested in working on an undergraduate degree in health information administration or technology.

Eligibility This program is open to AHIMA members who are enrolled in a health information administration or health information technology program accredited by the Commission on Accreditation of Allied Health Education Programs. Applicants must be working on a degree on at least a half-time basis and have a GPA of 3.0 or higher. U.S. citizenship is required. Selection is based (in order of importance) on GPA and academic achievement, volunteer and work experience, commitment to the health information management profession, suitability to the health information management profession, quality and suitability of references provided, and clarity of application.

Financial data Stipends range from $1,000 to $5,000.

Duration 1 year; nonrenewable.

Additional information This program includes the following named scholarships (not all of which may be offered each year): the David A. Cohen Scholarship (established in 2004), the Jimmy Gamble Memorial Scholarship (established in 2001 and sponsored by 3M Health Information Systems), the Sanfra L. Key Memorial Scholarship (established in 2003 and sponsored by Healthcare Contract Resources), the Lucretia Spears Scholarship (established in 1998), the Julia LeBlond Memorial Undergraduate Scholarships (sponsored by Ingenix Companies), the Rita Finnegan Memorial Scholarship (established in 2001 and sponsored by MC Strategies, Inc.), the Annie Blaylock Memorial Scholarship (established in 2002), the Connie Marshall Memorial Scholarship (established in 2004 and sponsored by MedQuist Inc.), the Bright Future Scholarship (sponsored by previous Merit Scholarship recipients).

Number awarded Varies each year; recently, 65 of these scholarships were awarded.

Deadline April of each year.

[599]
FOUNDATION OR RESEARCH AND EDUCATION DIVERSITY SCHOLARSHIPS

American Health Information Management Association
Attn: Foundation of Research and Education
233 North Michigan Avenue, Suite 2150
Chicago, IL 60601-5806
(312) 233-1131   Fax: (312) 233-1431
E-mail: fore@ahima.org
Web: www.ahima.org/fore/student/programs.asp

Purpose To provide financial assistance to minority members of the American Health Information Management Association (AHIMA) who are interested in working on an undergraduate or graduate degree in health information administration or technology.

Eligibility This program is open to AHIMA members who are enrolled in a health information administration or health information technology program accredited by the Commission on Accreditation of Allied Health Education Programs. Applicants must be minorities, be working on an undergraduate or graduate degree on at least a half-time basis, and have a GPA of 3.0 or higher. U.S. citizenship is required. Selection is based (in order of importance) on GPA and academic achievement, volunteer and work experience, commitment to the health information management profession, suitability to the health information management profession, quality and suitability of references provided, and clarity of application.

Financial data Stipends range from $1,000 to $5,000.
Duration 1 year; nonrenewable.
Number awarded Varies each year. Recently, 9 of these scholarships were awarded.
Deadline April of each year.

[600]
FRANCES A. MAYS SCHOLARSHIP AWARD

Virginia Association for Health, Physical Education,
  Recreation, and Dance
c/o Jack Schiltz, Executive Director
817 West Franklin Street
P.O. Box 842020
Richmond, VA 23284-2020
(804) 828-1948   Toll-free: (800) 918-9899
Fax: (804) 828-1946   E-mail: info@vahperd.org
Web: www.vahperd.org

Purpose To provide financial assistance to college seniors majoring in health, physical education, recreation, or dance in Virginia.

Eligibility This program is open to students who have been working full time for 3 years on a degree in health, physical education, recreation, or dance at a college or university in Virginia. Candidates must be nominated by their school and be members of the Virginia Association of Health, Physical Education, Recreation, and Dance (VAHPERD) and the American Association for Health, Physical Education, Recreation, and Dance (AAHPERD). Selection is based on academic achievement, leadership in campus life activities, service to college or university, awards and honors, and service to the community.

Financial data A stipend is awarded (amount not specified).
Duration 1 year.
Number awarded 1 each year.
Deadline September of each year.

[601]
FRANK L. GREATHOUSE GOVERNMENT ACCOUNTING SCHOLARSHIP

Government Finance Officers Association
Attn: Scholarship Committee
203 North LaSalle Street, Suite 2700
Chicago, IL 60601-1210
(312) 977-9700   Fax: (312) 977-4806
Web: www.gfoa.org/services/scholarships.shtml

Purpose To provide financial assistance to undergraduate and graduate students who are preparing for a career in public accounting.

Eligibility This program is open to 1) undergraduates who are completing at least their junior year of college, and 2) graduate students. Applicants must be enrolled full time in an accounting program and preparing for a career in state and local government finance. They must be citizens or permanent residents of the United States or Canada and able to provide a letter of recommendation from their academic advisor or the chair of their accounting program. Along with their application, they must submit a statement of proposed career plan in state and local government finance and, if applicable, a plan of graduate study. Selection is based on that statement, strength of past course work and present plan of study, letters of recommendation, and undergraduate and graduate GPA. Financial need is not considered.

Financial data The stipend is $3,500.
Duration 1 year.
Number awarded 1 each year.
Deadline February of each year.

[602]
FRED WIESNER EDUCATIONAL EXCELLENCE SCHOLARSHIP

Association of Texas Professional Educators
Attn: Scholarships
305 East Huntland Drive, Suite 300
Austin, TX 78752-3792
(512) 467-0071   Toll-free: (800) 777-ATPE
Fax: (512) 467-2203   E-mail: atpe@atpe.org
Web: www.atpe.org/Awards/fwiesnerinfo.htm

Purpose To provide financial assistance to undergraduate and graduate students enrolled in educator preparation programs at institutions in Texas.

Eligibility This program is open to juniors, seniors, and graduate students enrolled in educator preparation programs at colleges and universities in Texas. Applicants must submit a 2-page essay on their personal philosophy toward education, why they want to become an educator, who influenced them the most in making their career decision, and why they are applying for the scholarship. Financial need is not considered in the selection process.

Financial data The stipend is $1,500 per year.
Duration 1 year.
Number awarded 4 each year: 3 to undergraduates and 1 to a graduate student.
Deadline May of each year.

[603]
FTE UNDERGRADUATE MAJOR IN TECHNOLOGY EDUCATION SCHOLARSHIP

International Technology Education Association
Attn: Foundation for Technology Education
1914 Association Drive, Suite 201
Reston, VA 20191-1539
(703) 860-2100   Fax: (703) 860-0353
E-mail: itea@iteaconnect.org
Web: www.iteaconnect.org/l3d.html

Purpose To provide financial support to undergraduate members of the International Technology Education Association (ITEA) who are majoring in technology education teacher preparation.

Eligibility Applicants must be members of the association (membership may be enclosed with the scholarship application), in college but not yet seniors, majoring in technology education teacher preparation with a GPA of 2.5 or higher, and enrolled full time. Selection is based on interest in teaching, academic ability, and faculty recommendations.

Financial data The stipend is $1,000. Funds are provided directly to the recipient.

Duration 1 year.

Number awarded 1 each year.

Deadline November of each year.

[604]
FUTURE ENTREPRENEUR OF THE YEAR AWARD

National Association for the Self-Employed
P.O. Box 612067
DFW Airport
Dallas, TX 75261-2067
Toll-free: (800) 232-NASE   Fax: (800) 551-4446
Web: www.nase.org

Purpose To provide financial assistance to high school seniors and college undergraduates interested in studying entrepreneurship.

Eligibility This program is open to high school seniors and college undergraduates who demonstrate leadership, academic excellence, ingenuity, and entrepreneurial spirit. Applicants must be interested in a program that stresses the philosophy of entrepreneurship rather than a specific field of study.

Financial data The stipend is $12,000 for the first year and $4,000 for each subsequent year.

Duration 1 year; may be renewed up to 3 additional years.

Number awarded 1 each year.

Deadline April of each year.

[605]
G.A. MAVON MEMORIAL SCHOLARSHIP

Professional Independent Insurance Agents of Illinois
Attn: College Scholarship Program
4360 Wabash Avenue
Springfield, IL 62711-7009
(217) 793-6660   Toll-free: (800) 628-6436
Fax: (217) 793-6744   E-mail: info@piiai.org
Web: www.piiai.org/youngagents/scholarship.htm

Purpose To provide financial assistance to upper-division students from Illinois who are majoring in business and have an interest in insurance.

Eligibility This program is open to residents of Illinois who are full-time juniors or seniors in college. Applicants must be enrolled in a business degree program with an interest in insurance. They must have a letter of recommendation from a current or retired member of the Professional Independent Insurance Agents of Illinois. Along with their application, they must submit an essay (500 words or less) on the contribution the insurance industry makes to society. Financial need is not considered in the selection process.

Financial data The stipend is $2,000, payable in 2 equal installments. Funds are paid directly to the recipient's school.

Duration 1 year.

Number awarded 1 each year.

Deadline June of each year.

[606]
GENE SWACKHAMER AG ECONOMICS/AG BUSINESS GRANT

Alpha Gamma Rho Fraternity
Attn: Educational Foundation of AGR
10101 North Ambassador Drive
Kansas City, MO 64153-1395
(816) 891-9200   Fax: (816) 891-9401
E-mail: agr@AlphaGammaRho.org
Web: www.agrs.org

Purpose To provide financial assistance to members of Alpha Gamma Rho Fraternity (a national agricultural fraternity) who are majoring in agribusiness in college.

Eligibility This program is open to undergraduate members of the fraternity who are majoring in agricultural economics, agribusiness, resource management, or a closely-related field of study. Applicants must submit 3 essays on their involvement in the fraternity. Brothers living in the chapter house (where applicable) are given priority in the selection process. Financial need is not considered.

Financial data The stipend is $1,000.

Duration 1 year.

Number awarded 1 each year.

Deadline April of each year.

SOCIAL SCIENCES

[607]
GENERAL ELECTRIC FUND/LEAGUE OF UNITED LATIN AMERICAN CITIZENS SCHOLARSHIPS

League of United Latin American Citizens
Attn: LULAC National Education Service Centers
2000 L Street, N.W., Suite 610
Washington, DC 20036
(202) 835-9646 Fax: (202) 835-9685
E-mail: scholarships@lnesc.org
Web: www.lnesc.org

Purpose To provide financial assistance to minority students who are studying engineering or business in college.

Eligibility Eligible to apply are minority students who will be enrolled as college sophomores pursuing full-time studies in a program leading to a baccalaureate degree in engineering or business at colleges or universities in the United States approved by the League of United Latin American Citizens (LULAC) and General Electric. They must have a GPA of 3.25 or higher and be U.S. citizens or legal residents. Selection is based on academic performance, likelihood of preparing for a career in business or engineering, performance in business or engineering subjects, writing ability, extracurricular activities, and community involvement.

Financial data The stipends are $5,000 per year. The funds are to be used to pay for tuition, required fees, room and board, and required educational materials and books. The funds are sent directly to the college or university and deposited in the scholarship recipient's name.

Duration 1 year; may be renewed if the recipient maintains a GPA of 3.0 or higher.

Additional information Funding for this program is provided by the General Electric Fund. All requests for applications or information must include a self-addressed stamped envelope.

Number awarded Varies each year; recently, 6 of these scholarships were awarded.

Deadline July of each year.

[608]
GEORGE A. NIELSEN PUBLIC INVESTOR SCHOLARSHIP

Government Finance Officers Association
Attn: Scholarship Committee
203 North LaSalle Street, Suite 2700
Chicago, IL 60601-1210
(312) 977-9700 Fax: (312) 977-4806
Web: www.gfoa.org/services/scholarships.shtml

Purpose To provide financial assistance to public employees who are undergraduate and graduate students and have research or career interests in the investment of public funds.

Eligibility This program is open to employees (for at least 1 year) of a local government or other public entity who are enrolled or planning to enroll in an undergraduate or graduate program in public administration, finance, business administration, or a related field. Applicants must be citizens or permanent residents of the United States or Canada and able to provide a letter of recommendation from their employer. They must have a research or career interest in the efficient and productive investment of public funds. Financial need is not considered in the selection process.

Financial data The stipend is $5,000 or $2,500.

Duration 1 year.

Additional information Funds for this program are provided by George A. Nielsen LLP.

Number awarded Each year, either 1 scholarship at $5,000 or 2 at $2,500 are awarded.

Deadline February of each year.

[609]
GEORGE AND DONNA NIGH PUBLIC SERVICE SCHOLARSHIP

Oklahoma State Regents for Higher Education
Attn: Director of Scholarship and Grant Programs
655 Research Parkway, Suite 200
P.O. Box 108850
Oklahoma City, OK 73101-8850
(405) 225-9239 Toll-free: (800) 858-1840
Fax: (405) 225-9230 E-mail: studentinfo@osrhe.edu
Web: www.okhighered.org

Purpose To provide financial assistance for college to residents in Oklahoma who are interested in a career in public service.

Eligibility This program is open to residents of Oklahoma who are enrolled full time in an undergraduate program at a public or private college or university in the state. Applicants must be enrolled in a degree program leading to a career in public service (as determined by the institution). Selection is based on academic achievement, including GPA, class rank, national awards, scholastic achievement, honors, teachers' recommendations, and participation in extracurricular activities. Each participating college or university may nominate 1 student each year.

Financial data The stipend is $1,000 per year.

Duration 1 year; nonrenewable.

Additional information This program, established in 1999, operates in conjunction with the George and Donna Nigh Institute, Downtown College Consortium, 120 North Robinson, Suite 500 C, Oklahoma City, OK 73102, (405) 319-3085, E-mail: mbigger@okc.cc.ok.us. Scholarship recipients participate in seminars on public service offered by the Institute.

Number awarded Varies each year.

[610]
GEORGE D. MILLER SCHOLARSHIP

National Fire Protection Association
Attn: Fire Safety Educational Memorial Fund Committee
1 Batterymarch Park
Quincy, MA 02169-7471
(617) 984-7244 Fax: (617) 984-7222
E-mail: cellis@nfpa.org
Web: www.nfpa.org

Purpose To provide financial assistance to undergraduate and graduate students enrolled in fire service or public administration programs.

Eligibility Colleges and universities in the United States and Canada are invited to nominate up to 2 undergraduate or graduate students enrolled in a fire service or public administration program. Nominees must exhibit scholastic achievement, leadership qualities, concern for others (volunteerism), and intent to prepare for a career in fire service or public administration.

Financial data The stipend is at least $5,000.

Duration 1 year.

Additional information This fund was established in 2001.

Number awarded 1 each year.

Deadline March of each year.

[611]
GEORGE LEBER SCHOLARSHIP

American Hellenic Educational Progressive Association
Attn: AHEPA Educational Foundation
1909 Q Street, N.W., Suite 500
Washington, DC 20009
(202) 232-6300   Fax: (202) 232-2140
E-mail: ahepa@ahepa.org
Web: www.ahepa.org

Purpose To provide financial assistance for college to students with a connection to the American Hellenic Educational Progressive Association (AHEPA), particularly those interested in majoring in political science or history.

Eligibility This program is open to 1) members in good standing of the Order of Ahepa, Daughters of Penelope, Sons of Pericles, or Maids of Athena, and 2) the children of Order of Ahepa or Daughters of Penelope members in good standing. Applicants must be currently enrolled or planning to enroll in a college or university in the following fall. They may major in any area, but preference is given to upper-division students majoring in political science, history, or international relations. Along with their application, they must submit a 500-word biographical essay and their most recent college transcripts. Selection is based on academic achievement; extracurricular, personal, and volunteer activities; athletic achievements; and work experience. Financial need is not considered.

Financial data The annual stipend ranges from $500 to $2,000.

Duration 1 year.

Additional information A processing fee of $20 must accompany each application.

Number awarded Varies each year; recently, 2 of these scholarships were awarded.

Deadline March of each year.

[612]
GLOBAL AUTOMOTIVE AFTERMARKET SYMPOSIUM SCHOLARSHIPS

Global Automotive Aftermarket Symposium
c/o Motor & Equipment Manufacturers Association
10 Laboratory Drive
P.O. Box 13966
Research Triangle Park, NC 27709-3966
(919) 549-4800   Fax: (919) 549-4824
E-mail: jdowd@mema.org
Web: www.automotivescholarships.com

Purpose To provide financial assistance for college to students interested in preparing for a career in the automotive aftermarket.

Eligibility This program is open to graduating high school seniors and to students who graduated from high school within the past 2 years. Applicants must be enrolled full time in a college-level program or an automotive technician program in the United States or Canada accredited by the National Automotive Technician Education Foundation (NATEF). They must submit a 250-word essay on why they believe they deserve to receive this scholarship. Preference is given to applicants who are 1) planning to become technicians in automotive, collision, heavy duty, or agricultural fields; 2) preparing for a career in the automotive aftermarket; and 3) children of families employed in the automotive aftermarket. Financial need is not considered in the selection process.

Financial data The stipend is $1,000 per year. Recipients who graduate from their program and show proof of employment in the automotive aftermarket for at least 12 months are awarded a further matching grant.

Duration 1 year.

Additional information Funding for this program, established in 1996, is provided by automotive aftermarket associations that donate the proceeds from the annual Global Automotive Aftermarket Symposium (GAAS). The sponsoring associations are the Automotive Parts Rebuilders Association (APRA), the Automotive Aftermarket Industry Association (AAIA), the Alliance of State Automotive Aftermarket Associations (ASAAA), the Automotive Warehouse Distributors Association (AWDA), the Automotive Industries Association of Canada (AIA Canada), the Motor & Equipment Manufacturers Association (MEMA), the Specialty Equipment Market Association (SEMA), and the Tire Industry Association.

Number awarded Varies each year; recently, 145 of these scholarships were awarded.

Deadline April of each year.

[613]
GOODMAN & COMPANY ANNUAL SCHOLARSHIP

Virginia Society of Certified Public Accountants
Attn: Educational Foundation
4309 Cox Road
P.O. Box 4620
Glen Allen, VA 23058-4620
(804) 270-5344   Toll-free: (800) 733-8272
Fax: (804) 273-1741   E-mail: foundation@vscpa.com
Web: www.vscpa.com

Purpose To provide financial assistance to upper-division students enrolled in an accounting program in Virginia.

Eligibility This program is open to juniors and seniors currently enrolled in a Virginia college or university undergraduate accounting program. Applicants must be U.S. citizens, be intending to take the C.P.A. examination, and have a GPA of 3.0 or higher. Along with their application, they must submit a 500-word essay describing a situation in which they 1) demonstrated the ability to influence, inspire, and motivate an individual or group of individuals to achieve desired results; 2) were confronted with an ethical dilemma and how they dealt with the issue; and/or 3) demonstrated effective problem solving through their decision-making

skills, personal insight, judgment, and creativity. Selection is based on the essay, their most recent transcript, a current resume, and a faculty letter of recommendation.
Financial data The stipend is $2,500.
Duration 1 year.
Additional information This program is sponsored by Goodman & Company.
Number awarded 1 each year.
Deadline April of each year.

[614]
HAINES MEMORIAL SCHOLARSHIP
South Dakota Board of Regents
Attn: Scholarship Committee
306 East Capitol Avenue, Suite 200
Pierre, SD 57501-2545
(605) 773-3455   Fax: (605) 773-2422
E-mail: info@ris.sdbor.edu
Web: www.sdbor.edu

Purpose To provide financial assistance to students at public universities in South Dakota who are enrolled in a teacher education program.
Eligibility This program is open to sophomores, juniors, and seniors at public universities in South Dakota. Applicants must have a GPA of 2.5 or higher and a declared major in a teacher education program. They must submit a statement that describes their personal philosophy and their philosophy of education.
Financial data The stipend is $2,150; funds are allocated to the institution for distribution to the student.
Duration 1 year; nonrenewable.
Number awarded 1 each year.
Deadline February of each year.

[615]
HAROLD AND MARIA RANSBURG AMERICAN PATRIOT SCHOLARSHIPS
Association for Intelligence Officers
Attn: Scholarships Committee
6723 Whittier Avenue, Suite 303A
McLean, VA 22101-4533
(703) 790-0320   Fax: (703) 991-1278
E-mail: afio@afio.com
Web: www.afio.com

Purpose To provide financial assistance to undergraduate and graduate students who have a career interest in intelligence and national security.
Eligibility This program is open to undergraduates who have completed their first or second year of study and graduate students who apply in their senior undergraduate year or first graduate year. Applicants must share the sponsor's educational mission on behalf of "national security, patriotism, and loyalty to the constitution." Along with their application, undergraduates must submit a 1-page book review on the subject of intelligence and national security. Graduate students must submit a dissertation or thesis proposal. Selection is based on merit, character, estimated future potential, background, and relevance of their studies to the full spectrum of national security interests and career ambitions.

Financial data Stipends range from $1,500 to $3,000.
Duration 1 year.
Number awarded Several each year.
Deadline August of each year.

[616]
HARRIET IRSAY SCHOLARSHIP GRANT
American Institute of Polish Culture, Inc.
Attn: Scholarship Committee
1440 79th Street Causeway, Suite 117
Miami, FL 33141
(305) 864-2349   Fax: (305) 865-5150
E-mail: info@ampolinstitute.org
Web: www.ampolinstitute.org.ic.pl

Purpose To provide financial assistance to Polish American and other students interested in working on an undergraduate or graduate degree in selected fields.
Eligibility This program is open to students working full time on an undergraduate or graduate degree in the following fields: communications, education, film, history, international relations, journalism, liberal arts, Polish studies, and public relations. Also eligible are graduate students in business programs whose thesis is directly related to Poland and to graduate students in all majors whose thesis is on a Polish subject. U.S. citizenship or permanent resident status is required. Preference is given to applicants of Polish heritage. Along with their application, they must submit an essay of 200 to 400 words on why they should receive the scholarship, an article (up to 700 words) on any subject about Poland, transcripts, a detailed resume, and 3 letters of recommendation. Selection is based on merit.
Financial data The stipend is $1,000.
Duration 1 year.
Additional information There is a $10 processing fee.
Number awarded 10 to 15 each year.
Deadline May of each year.

[617]
HARRY A. APPLEGATE SCHOLARSHIP AWARD
DECA
1908 Association Drive
Reston, VA 20191-1594
(703) 860-5000   Fax: (703) 860-4013
E-mail: decainc@aol.com
Web: www.deca.org/scholarships_index.html

Purpose To provide financial assistance to DECA members interested in working on a college degree in marketing, entrepreneurship, or management.
Eligibility This program is open to DECA members in either the high school or Delta Epsilon Chi (collegiate) division. Applicants must intend to work full time on a 2- or 4-year degree in marketing, entrepreneurship, or management. Complete applications are to be submitted to the state advisor. Each state is told the number of applications it may forward to the national organization. Selection is based on DECA involvement, leadership ability, community service, and grades. The program is merit based.
Financial data The stipend is $1,000. Funds are paid directly to the recipient's college or university.
Duration 1 year.

Number awarded Varies each year; recently, 20 of these scholarships were awarded.
Deadline Each state sets its own deadline, usually in January.

[618]
HEALTHCARE INFORMATION MANAGEMENT SYSTEMS SCHOLARSHIPS

Healthcare Information and Management Systems Society
Attn: HIMSS Foundation Scholarship Program Coordinator
230 East Ohio Street, Suite 500
Chicago, IL 60611-3270
(312) 664-HIMSS   Fax: (312) 664-6143
E-mail: foundation@himss.org
Web: www.himss.org/ASP/scholarship_hims.asp

Purpose To provide financial assistance to upper-division and graduate student members of the Healthcare Information and Management Systems Society (HIMSS) who are interested in the field of health care information and management systems.

Eligibility This program is open to student members of the society, although an application for membership, including dues, may accompany the scholarship application. Applicants must be upper-division or graduate students enrolled in an accredited program designed to prepare them for a career in health care information or management systems, which may include industrial engineering, health care informatics, operations research, computer science and information systems, mathematics, and quantitative programs in business administration and hospital administration. Selection is based on academic achievement and demonstration of leadership potential, including communication skills and participation in society activity.

Financial data The stipend is $5,000. The award also includes an all-expense paid trip to the annual HIMSS conference and exhibition.

Duration 1 year.

Additional information This program was established in 1986 for undergraduate and master's degree students. The first Ph.D. scholarship was awarded in 2002.

Number awarded 3 each year: 1 to an undergraduate student, 1 to a master's degree student, and 1 to a Ph.D. candidate.

Deadline October of each year.

[619]
HEIDELBERG USA SCHOLARSHIP

Electronic Document Systems Foundation
Attn: EDSF Scholarship Awards
608 Silver Spur Road, Suite 280
Rolling Hills Estates, CA 90274-3616
(310) 265-5510   Fax: (310) 265-5588
E-mail: jmowlds@edsf.org
Web: www.edsf.org/scholarships.cfm

Purpose To provide financial assistance to college juniors, seniors, and graduate students working on a degree in the field of document/graphic communication.

Eligibility This program is open to juniors, seniors, and graduate students who are working on a degree in the field of document/graphic communication, including such document-related technologies as graphic communications, document management, document content and/or distribution, or multimedia. Applicants must be enrolled full time at a college, university, or graduate school in the United States with a GPA of 3.0 or higher. Along with their application, they must submit a statement of their career goals in the field of document communications, an essay on a topic related to their view of the future of the document management and production industry, a list of current professional and college extracurricular activities and achievements, college transcripts, samples of their creative work, and 2 letters of recommendation. industry. Financial need is not considered.

Financial data The stipend is $2,000.

Duration 1 year.

Additional information This program is sponsored by Heidelberg USA.

Number awarded 1 each year.

Deadline May of each year.

[620]
HELP DESK SCHOLARSHIP CONTEST

Thomson Course Technology
c/o Suelaine Frongello
25 Thomson Place
Boston, MA 02210
(617) 757-7900
E-mail: Suelaine.Frongello@course.com
Web: www.course.com/helpdesk/scholarship.cfm

Purpose To recognize and reward, with scholarships, college students who submit outstanding essays related to help desk courses.

Eligibility This competition is open to U.S. citizens who are enrolled in a public or private college, university, or career school. Applicants must be enrolled in a help desk course at the time of entry. They must submit an essay on 1 of the following topics: 1) describe a help desk internship that you've recently held and how it will help you land a job in the help desk industry; or 2) identify the ways in which you can contribute to the help desk field. Selection is based on the thoughtfulness of the essay.

Financial data The award is $1,000, paid directly to the college or university as a credit toward tuition.

Duration The competition is held annually.

Additional information This competition was first held in 2001.

Number awarded 1 each year.

Deadline May of each year.

SOCIAL SCIENCES

[621]
HERMAN LERDAL SCHOLARSHIP
South Dakota Bankers Association
Attn: Foundation
109 West Missouri Avenue
P.O. Box 1081
Pierre, SD 57501-1081
(605) 224-1653   Fax: (605) 224-7835
Web: www.sdba.com

Purpose To provide financial assistance to students at South Dakota colleges or universities who are preparing for a career in banking or finance.

Eligibility This program is open to juniors at colleges or universities in South Dakota who are working on a business-related degree in preparation for a career in banking or finance. Applicants must have at least a 3.0 GPA. Along with their application, they must submit a statement on their career interests, a description of their special talents and leadership abilities, a statement on obstacles they have overcome, and 3 letters of recommendation. Financial need is not considered in the selection process.

Financial data The stipend is $1,000.

Duration 1 year.

Number awarded 1 each year.

Deadline March of each year.

[622]
HHSMA SCHOLARSHIPS
Hawai'i Hospitality Sales and Marketing Association
Attn: Newton Wong, Scholarship Chair
P.O. Box 89619
Honolulu, HI 96830
(808) 921-5570   E-mail: nwong@radissonwaikiki.com
Web: www.hhsma.org

Purpose To provide financial assistance to residents of Hawaii who are interested in attending college to prepare for a career in the travel or hospitality industry.

Eligibility This program is open to residents of Hawaii who are graduating high school seniors, recent graduates, or current undergraduates. Applicants must be majoring or planning to major in a field related to the hospitality and travel industry. They must have a GPA of 2.75 or higher. Along with their application, they must submit a 1-page essay on why they have chosen the hospitality/travel industry as their major field of study, their long-term goals in the industry, and how they plan to accomplish those goals. Selection is based on the essay, GPA, a resume, and community involvement.

Financial data The stipend is $1,000.

Duration 1 year.

Additional information Information is also available from Wes Duke, Brigham Young University Hawaii, Administration Building 1980, 55-220 Kulanui Street, Laie, HI 96762, (808) 293-3530. E-mail: scholarship@byuh.edu.

Number awarded Varies each year; recently, 6 of these scholarships were awarded.

Deadline October of each year.

[623]
HOLLAND AMERICA LINE-WESTOURS, INC. SCHOLARSHIPS
American Society of Travel Agents
Attn: ASTA Foundation
1101 King Street, Suite 200
Alexandria, VA 22314-2944
(703) 739-8721   Fax: (703) 684-8319
E-mail: scholarship@astahq.com
Web: www.astanet.com/education/scholarshipf.asp

Purpose To provide financial assistance to undergraduate students interested in preparing for a career in the travel/tourism industry.

Eligibility This program is open to undergraduates who are enrolled in travel and tourism courses at 2- or 4-year colleges or universities or recognized proprietary travel schools in the United States or Canada. Applicants must have a GPA of 2.5 or higher, be residents of the United States or Canada, and write a 500-word essay on the future of the cruise industry. Financial need is not considered in the selection process.

Financial data The stipend is $3,000.

Duration 1 year; may be renewed.

Additional information This program was established in 1984.

Number awarded 2 each year.

Deadline August of each year.

[624]
HRA-NCA ACADEMIC SCHOLARSHIPS
Human Resource Association of the National Capital Area
Attn: Chair, College Relations
P.O. Box 2153
Springfield, VA 22152
(703) 451-0222   Toll-free: (855) 5-HRA-NCA
Fax: (703) 912-4202   E-mail: info@hra-nca.org
Web: hra-nca.org/studentservices.asp

Purpose To provide financial assistance to students working on an undergraduate or graduate degree in human resources at colleges and universities in the Washington, D.C. metropolitan area.

Eligibility This program is open to undergraduate and graduate students working on a degree in human resources or a related field at a college or university in the Washington, D.C. metropolitan area. Applicants must have completed at least half of their degree program and have at least a full semester remaining. Selection is based on academic performance and commitment to human resources as demonstrated by participation in a student chapter of the Society for Human Resource Management (SHRM), an internship, or relevant work experience or community service.

Financial data The stipend is $1,500.

Duration 1 year.

Additional information The Human Resource Association of the National Capital Area (HRA-NCA) is the local affiliate of SHRM.

Number awarded 2 each year.

Deadline April of each year.

[625]
HSMAI SCHOLARSHIPS

Hospitality Sales and Marketing Association
   International
Attn: HSMAI Foundation
8201 Greensboro Drive, Suite 300
McLean, VA 22102
(703) 610-9024 Fax: (703) 610-9005
E-mail: info@hsmai.org
Web: www.hsmai.org/Resources/scholarships.cfm

Purpose To provide financial assistance to undergraduate and graduate students in accredited schools of hospitality management.

Eligibility This program is open to full-time students who are currently enrolled in hospitality management or a related field, have hospitality work experience, are interested in a career in hospitality sales and marketing, and have good academic standing. Applications are accepted from 2 categories of students: 1) baccalaureate and graduate degree candidates, and 2) associate degree candidates. Along with their application, they must submit 3 essays: their interest in the hospitality industry and their career goals, the personal characteristics that will enable them to succeed in reaching those goals, and a situation in which they faced a challenge or were in a leadership role and how they dealt with the situation. Selection is based on the essays, industry-related work experience, GPA, extracurricular involvement, 2 letters of recommendation, and presentation of the application.

Financial data The stipend is $2,000 for baccalaureate/graduate degree students or $500 for associate degree students.

Duration 1 year.

Number awarded 4 each year: 2 at $2,000 and 2 at $500.

Deadline May of each year.

[626]
HUMANE STUDIES FELLOWSHIPS

Institute for Humane Studies at George Mason
   University
3301 North Fairfax Drive, Suite 440
Arlington, VA 22201-4432
(703) 993-4880 Toll-free: (800) 697-8799
Fax: (703) 993-4890 E-mail: ihs@gmu.edu
Web: www.TheIHS.org

Purpose To provide financial assistance to undergraduate and graduate students in the United States or abroad who intend to pursue "intellectual careers" and have demonstrated an interest in classical liberal principles.

Eligibility This program is open to students who will be full-time college juniors, seniors, or graduate students planning academic or other intellectual careers, including law, public policy, and journalism. Applicants must have a clearly demonstrated interest in the classical liberal/libertarian tradition of individual rights and market economics. Applications from students outside the United States or studying abroad receive equal consideration. Selection is based on academic or professional performance, relevance of work to the advancement of a free society, and potential for success.

Financial data The maximum stipend is $12,000.

Duration 1 year; may be renewed upon reapplication.

Additional information As defined by the sponsor, the core principles of the classical liberal/libertarian tradition include the recognition of individual rights and the dignity and worth of each individual; protection of these rights through the institutions of private property, contract, the rule of law, and freely evolved intermediary institutions; voluntarism in all human relations, including the unhampered market mechanism in economic affairs; and the goals of free trade, free migration, and peace. This program began in 1983 as Claude R. Lambe Fellowships. The application fee is $25.

Number awarded Approximately 110 each year.

Deadline December of each year.

[627]
HVTO STEWARDSHIP AWARD

Electronic Document Systems Foundation
Attn: EDSF Scholarship Awards
608 Silver Spur Road, Suite 280
Rolling Hills Estates, CA 90274-3616
(310) 265-5510 Fax: (310) 265-5588
E-mail: jmowlds@edsf.org
Web: www.edsf.org/scholarships.cfm

Purpose To provide financial assistance to students working on an undergraduate or graduate degree in a field related to the high volume transaction output (HVTO) industry.

Eligibility This program is open to undergraduate and graduate students who are working on a degree in field related to the HVTO industry, including information technology, graphic arts, or business. Applicants must be enrolled full time at a technical school, trade school, community college, university, college, or graduate school in the United States with a GPA of 3.0 or higher. They must be able to demonstrate leadership and contribution to volunteer and community activities. Along with their application, they must submit a statement of their career goals in the field of document communications, an essay on a topic related to their view of the future of the document management and production industry, a list of current professional and college extracurricular activities and achievements, college transcripts, samples of their creative work, and 2 letters of recommendation. Financial need is not considered.

Financial data The stipend is $1,000.

Duration 1 year.

Additional information This program is sponsored by COPI/OutputLinks.

Number awarded 1 each year.

Deadline May of each year.

SOCIAL SCIENCES

[628]
IAHPERD SCHOLARSHIPS

Illinois Association for Health, Physical Education, Recreation and Dance
Attn: Executive Secretary
1713 South West Street
Jacksonville, IL 62650
(217) 245-6413 Fax: (217) 245-5261
E-mail: iahperd@iahperd.org
Web: www.iahperd.org

Purpose To provide financial assistance to upper-division students in Illinois who are majoring in health, physical education, recreation, or dance.

Eligibility This program is open to juniors and seniors at colleges and universities in Illinois who are majoring in health, physical education, recreation, or dance. Applicants must submit a personal letter explaining why they chose to go into their field and where they see themselves professionally in 5 years. Selection is based on that letter, involvement in professional organizations, involvement in extracurricular activities, involvement in community organizations, transcripts, and 2 letters of recommendation.

Financial data Stipends are $1,000 or $750.

Duration 1 year.

Number awarded 6 each year: 1 at $1,000 and 5 at $750.

Deadline April of each year.

[629]
IDAHO SOCIETY OF CERTIFIED PUBLIC ACCOUNTANTS SCHOLARSHIPS

Idaho Society of Certified Public Accountants
Attn: Executive Director
250 Bobwhite Court, Suite 240
Boise, ID 83706
(208) 344-6261 Fax: (208) 344-8984
Web: www.idcpa.org

Purpose To provide financial assistance to students majoring in accounting at colleges and universities in Idaho.

Eligibility This program is open to residents of Idaho enrolled full time as a junior or senior at a college or university in the state. Applicants must be majoring in accounting and have a GPA of 2.75 or higher. Along with their application, they must submit brief essays on their career goals and objectives; some of the jobs they have held; extracurricular activities, honors, awards, and offices held; community service achievements; what sparked their interest in working on a degree in accounting and what excites them about the profession; why they should be awarded this scholarship. Financial need is not considered in the selection process.

Financial data The stipend is $1,000.

Duration 1 year.

Number awarded 1 or more each year.

Deadline March of each year.

[630]
IDDBA SCHOLARSHIP

International Dairy-Deli-Bakery Association
Attn: Scholarship Committee
636 Science Drive
P.O. Box 5528
Madison, WI 53705-0528
(608) 310-5000 Fax: (608) 238-6330
E-mail: iddba@iddba.org
Web: www.iddba.org/scholars.htm

Purpose To provide financial assistance to high school seniors, undergraduates, or graduate students employed in a supermarket dairy, deli, or bakery department who are interested in majoring in a food-related field.

Eligibility This program is open to high school seniors, college students, vocational/technical students, and graduate students. Applicants must be currently employed in a supermarket dairy, deli, or bakery department or be employed by a company that services those departments (e.g., food manufacturers, brokers, or wholesalers). They must be majoring in a food-related field, e.g., culinary arts, baking/pastry arts, food science, business, or marketing. Their employer must be a member of the International Dairy-Deli-Bakery Association (IDDBA). While a GPA of 2.5 or higher is required, this may be waived for first-time applicants. Selection is based on academic achievement, work experience, and a statement of career goals and/or how their degree will be beneficial to their job. Financial need is not considered.

Financial data Stipends range from $250 to $1,000. Funds are paid jointly to the recipient and the recipient's school. If the award exceeds tuition fees, the excess may be used for other educational expenses.

Duration 1 year; recipients may reapply.

Number awarded Varies each year; a total of $75,000 is available for this program annually.

Deadline Applications must be submitted prior to the end of March, June, September, or December of each year.

[631]
IFMA FOUNDATION SCHOLARSHIPS

International Facility Management Association
Attn: IFMA Foundation
1 East Greenway Plaza, Suite 1100
Houston, TX 77046
(713) 623-4362 Fax: (713) 623-6124
E-mail: foundation@ifmafoundation.org
Web: www.ifmafoundation.org

Purpose To provide financial assistance to undergraduate and graduate students working on a degree in facility management.

Eligibility This program is open to students enrolled full time at an accredited 4-year college or university in an undergraduate or graduate program in facility management or a related field. Undergraduates must have completed at least 2 years of study and have a GPA of 3.0 or higher. Graduate students must have a GPA of 3.5 or higher. Applicants may not be currently employed full time in facility management. Selection is based on a letter of intent, resume, achievement, accomplishments, involvement, and faculty appraisals; financial need is not considered.

Financial data Stipends range from $1,000 to $5,000.

Duration 1 year.

Additional information The IFMA Foundation was established in 1990. Its programs include the following named awards: the Barbara Pryor Scholarship, the Doug Underwood Scholarship, the George Graves Scholarship, and the Lee Forrest Scholarship.

Number awarded Varies each year. Recently, 15 of these scholarships were awarded: 1 at $5,000, 4 at $3,000, 1 at $2,500, 1 at $1,500, and 8 at $1,000. Since the foundation was established, it has awarded 123 scholarships worth $230,000.

[632] IMA MEMORIAL EDUCATION FUND SCHOLARSHIPS

Institute of Management Accountants
Attn: Committee on Students
10 Paragon Drive
Montvale, NJ 07645-1718
(201) 573-9000   Toll-free: (800) 638-4427, ext. 1543
Fax: (201) 474-1600   E-mail: students@imanet.org
Web: www.imanet.org

Purpose To provide financial assistance to student members of the Institute of Management Accountants (IMA) who are interested in preparing for a career in a field related to management accounting.

Eligibility This program is open to undergraduate and graduate student IMA members who have a GPA of 2.8 or higher. Applicants must be preparing for a career in management accounting, financial management, or information technology. They must submit a 2-page statement on their reasons for applying for the scholarship, reasons that they deserve the award, specific contributions to the IMA, ideas on how they will promote awareness and increase membership and certification within IMA, and their career goals and objectives. Selection is based on that statement, academic merit, IMA participation, the quality of the presentation, a resume, and letters of recommendation.

Financial data Stipends range from $1,000 to $2,500 per year.

Duration 1 year.

Additional information Up to 30 finalists in each category (including the scholarship winners) receive a scholarship to take 5 parts of the Certified Management Accountant (CMA) and/or Certified in Financial Management (CFM) examination within a year of graduation.

Number awarded Varies each year; recently, 10 of these scholarships were awarded.

Deadline February of each year.

[633] INSTITUTE OF MANAGEMENT ACCOUNTANTS NATIONAL STUDENT VIDEO CASE COMPETITION

Institute of Management Accountants
Attn: Committee on Students
10 Paragon Drive
Montvale, NJ 07645-1718
(201) 573-9000   Toll-free: (800) 638-4427, ext. 294
Fax: (201) 474-1600   E-mail: students@imanet.org
Web: www.imanet.org

Purpose To recognize and reward students who respond to a published case in management accounting with a video presentation.

Eligibility Each year, a case in management accounting is distributed to student chapters of the Institute of Management Accountants (IMA), Beta Alpha Psi chapters, IMA academic mentors, and IMA chapter presidents; it is also published in *Strategic Finance*. Each college and university in the country may select a team or teams of 3 to 5 students. No more than half of the team may be master's degree candidates; doctoral degree candidates are not eligible. The team prepares a video, up to 15 minutes in length, presenting a solution to the case. Each team member is required to be an equal part of the presentation. Selection is based on content, style of presentation, and response to the case requirements. Judges select 4 videos as finalists, and those team members are invited to the final competition at the IMA Annual Conference & Expo. The 4 finalist teams present their video solutions and respond to additional questions on which they are judged.

Financial data The winning team receives $5,000 and each runner-up team receives $3,000.

Duration The competition is held annually.

Number awarded 1 winner and 3 runners-up are selected each year.

Deadline January of each year.

[634] INTERNATIONAL PUBLIC MANAGEMENT ASSOCIATION FOR HUMAN RESOURCES SCHOLARSHIP

International Public Management Association for Human Resources
Attn: Fellowship Committee
1617 Duke Street
Alexandria, VA 22314
(703) 549-7100   Fax: (703) 684-0948
Web: www.ipma-hr.org

Purpose To provide financial assistance to children of members of the International Public Management Association for Human Resources (IPMA-HR), especially those interested in majoring in human resources or public administration.

Eligibility This program is open to students who are enrolled or planning to enroll at an accredited college or university. At least 1 parent or legal guardian must have been an IPMA-HR member for at least the previous 3 years. Preference is given to applicants in business administration or public administration with a human resources concentration. Applicants must submit a list of activities and awards, a statement of goals and objectives, high school and undergraduate transcripts, and (for entering freshmen) a copy of their college acceptance letter. Financial need is not considered in the selection process.

Financial data The stipend is $1,000 per year.

Duration 1 year.

Number awarded Up to 2 each year.

Deadline May of each year.

[635]
ISFA COLLEGE SCHOLARSHIPS

National Association of Insurance Women
Attn: Insurance Scholarship Foundation of America
P.O. Box 866
Hendersonville, NC 28793-0866
(828) 890-3328 Fax: (828) 891-2667
E-mail: foundation@inssfa.org
Web: www.inssfa.org

Purpose To provide financial assistance to college and graduate students working on a degree in insurance and risk management.

Eligibility This program is open to candidates for a bachelor's degree or higher with a major or minor in insurance, risk management, or actuarial science. Applicants must 1) be completing or have completed their second year of college; 2) have an overall GPA of 3.0 or higher; 3) have successfully completed at least 2 insurance, risk management, or actuarial science courses; and 4) not be receiving full reimbursement for the cost of tuition, books, or other educational expenses from their employer or any other outside source. Selection is based on academic record and honors, extracurricular and personal activities, work experience, 3 letters of recommendation, and a 500-word essay on career path and goals.

Financial data Stipends range from $500 to $2,500 per year; funds are paid jointly to the institution and to the student.

Duration 1 year.

Additional information Members of the National Association of Insurance Women established the Insurance Scholarship Foundation of America (ISFA) in 1993. It provides financial assistance to both men and women interested in careers in the insurance industry.

Number awarded Varies each year; recently, 10 of these scholarships were awarded.

Deadline February of each year.

[636]
ITS WASHINGTON/WTS SCHOLARSHIP

Women's Transportation Seminar-Puget Sound Chapter
c/o Kristin Overleese, Scholarship Chair
City of Shoreline, Capital Projects Manager
17544 Midvale Avenue North
Shoreline, WA 98133-4821
(206) 546-1700 Fax: (206) 546-2200
TDD: (206) 546-0457
Web: www.wtsinternational.org/puget_sound

Purpose To provide financial assistance to undergraduate and graduate students from Washington working on a degree related to intelligent transportation systems (ITS).

Eligibility This program is open to students who are residents of Washington, studying at a college in the state, or working as an intern in the state. Applicants must be currently enrolled in an undergraduate or graduate degree program related to the design, implementation, operation, and maintenance of ITS technologies. They must be majoring in transportation or a related field, including transportation engineering, systems engineering, electrical engineering, planning, finance, or logistics, and be taking courses in such ITS-related fields of study as computer science, electronics, and digital communications. In addition, they must have a GPA of 3.0 or higher and plans to prepare for a career in a transportation-related field. Minority candidates are encouraged to apply. Along with their application, they must submit a 500-word statement about their career goals after graduation, how those relate to ITS, and why they think they should receive this scholarship award. Selection is based on that statement, academic record, and transportation-related activities or job skills. Financial need is not considered.

Financial data The stipend is $1,500.

Duration 1 year.

Additional information This program is co-sponsored by ITS Washington.

Number awarded 1 each year.

Deadline October of each year.

[637]
JAMES A. TURNER, JR. MEMORIAL SCHOLARSHIP

American Welding Society
Attn: AWS Foundation, Inc.
550 N.W. LeJeune Road
Miami, FL 33126
(305) 445-6628 Toll-free: (800) 443-9353, ext. 461
Fax: (305) 443-7559 E-mail: found@aws.org
Web: www.aws.org

Purpose To provide financial assistance to college students interested in a management career related to welding.

Eligibility This program is open to full-time undergraduate students who are working on a 4-year bachelor's degree in business that will lead to a management career in welding store operations or a welding distributorship. Applicants must be U.S. citizens who are currently employed for at least 10 hours a week at a welding distributorship. Financial need is not required.

Financial data The stipend is $3,000.

Duration 1 year; recipients may reapply.

Number awarded 1 each year.

Deadline January of each year.

[638]
JANE M. KLAUSMAN WOMEN IN BUSINESS SCHOLARSHIPS

Zonta International
Attn: Foundation
557 West Randolph Street
Chicago, IL 60661-2202
(312) 930-5848　　　　　　Fax: (312) 930-0951
E-mail: Zontafdtn@Zonta.org
Web: www.zonta.org

Purpose To provide financial assistance to women working on an undergraduate degree in business.

Eligibility This program is open to women who are entering the third or fourth year of a business-related undergraduate degree program at a college or university anywhere in the world. Applicants first enter at the club level, and then advance to district and international levels. Along with their application, they must submit a 500-word essay that describes their academic and professional goals, the relevance on their program to the business field, and how this scholarship will assist them in reaching their goals. Selection is based on that essay, academic record, demonstrated intent to complete a program in business, achievement in business-related subjects, and 2 letters of recommendation.

Financial data Each winner at the U.S. district level receives a small scholarship; the international winners receive a $5,000 scholarship.

Duration 1 year.

Additional information This program was established in 1997.

Number awarded Several U.S. district winners and 6 international winners are selected each year.

Deadline Clubs set their own deadlines but must submit their winners to the district governor by May of each year.

[639]
JEAN C. OSAJDA FUND

Polish Roman Catholic Union of America
Attn: Education Fund Scholarship Program
984 North Milwaukee Avenue
Chicago, IL 60622-4101
(773) 782-2600　　　　Toll-free: (800) 772-8632
Fax: (773) 278-4595　　E-mail: info@prcua.org
Web: www.prcua.org

Purpose To provide financial assistance to undergraduate and graduate education students of Polish heritage.

Eligibility This program is open to students enrolled full time as sophomores, juniors, or seniors in an undergraduate program or full or part time as a graduate or professional school student. Applicants must be majoring in education. Selection is based on academic achievement, Polonia involvement, and community service.

Financial data A stipend is awarded (amount not specified). Funds are paid directly to the institution.

Duration 1 year.

Number awarded 1 or more each year.

Deadline May of each year.

[640]
JEWELL L. TAYLOR NATIONAL FELLOWSHIPS

American Association of Family and Consumer Sciences
Attn: Manager of Awards and Grants
400 North Columbus Street, Suite 202
Alexandria, VA 22314
(703) 706-4600　　Toll-free: (800) 424-8080, ext. 119
Fax: (703) 706-4663　　E-mail: staff@aafcs.org
Web: www.aafcs.org/programs/fellowships.html

Purpose To provide financial assistance to undergraduate and graduate students in the field of family and consumer sciences.

Eligibility Undergraduate and graduate students working on a degree in an area of family and consumer sciences are eligible to apply for this award if they are U.S. citizens or permanent residents and present clearly-defined plans for full-time graduate study. Selection is based on scholarship and special aptitudes for advanced study and research, educational and/or professional experiences, professional contributions to family and consumer sciences, and significance of the proposed research problem to the public well-being and the advancement of family and consumer sciences. Preference is given to applicants who have at least 1 year of work experience in family and consumer sciences, serving in such positions as a graduate/undergraduate assistant, trainee, or intern.

Financial data The stipend is $5,000.

Duration 1 year.

Additional information The application fee is $40. The association reserves the right to reconsider an award in the event the student receives a similar scholarship for the same academic year.

Number awarded Up to 20 each year: 1 for an undergraduate and up to 19 for graduate students.

Deadline January of each year.

[641]
JOE PERDUE SCHOLARSHIPS

Club Foundation
Attn: Scholarship Coordinator
1733 King Street
Alexandria, VA 22314-2720
(703) 739-9500　　　　　　Fax: (703) 739-0124
E-mail: schaverr@clubfoundation.org
Web: www.clubfoundation.org/stuscholar.html

Purpose To provide financial assistance for college to students planning a career in private club management.

Eligibility This program is open to students who are currently attending an accredited 4-year college or university and are actively preparing for a managerial career in the private club industry. Applicants must have completed their freshman year with a GPA of 2.5 or higher. Along with their application, they must submit an essay of 500 to 1,000 words on their career objectives and goals, the characteristics they possess that will allow them to succeed as a club manager, how their experiences with the Club Management Association of America (CMAA) shaped their perception of the association and the private club management industry, their specified interests within the private club management field, and why they feel the Club Foundation should select them as a scholarship recipient. Selection is based on academic record (20 points), extracurricular activities (15 points), the essay (20 points), and employment record (15 points).

Financial data The stipend is $2,500 per year. Funds are paid directly to the recipient's college or university.

Duration 1 year.

Additional information The Club Foundation was formerly the Club Management Institute Foundation. It is the nonprofit foundation affiliated with the CMAA.

Number awarded Varies each year; recently, 7 of these scholarships were awarded.

Deadline April of each year.

[642]
JOHN A. LOPIANO SCHOLARSHIP

Electronic Document Systems Foundation
Attn: EDSF Scholarship Awards
608 Silver Spur Road, Suite 280
Rolling Hills Estates, CA 90274-3616
(310) 265-5510   Fax: (310) 265-5588
E-mail: jmowlds@edsf.org
Web: www.edsf.org/scholarships.cfm

Purpose To provide financial assistance to college juniors, seniors, and graduate students interested in working with electronic documents as a career.

Eligibility This program is open to juniors, seniors, and graduate students who are committed to preparing for a career in document management and communications marketplace, including computer science and engineering, graphic and media communications, e-commerce, imaging science, printing, web authoring, electronic publishing, telecommunications, and business (e.g., sales, marketing). Applicants must be enrolled full time at a college, university, or graduate school in the United States with a GPA of 3.0 or higher. Along with their application, they must submit a statement of their career goals in the field of document communications, an essay on a topic related to their view of the future of the document management and production industry, a list of current professional and college extracurricular activities and achievements, college transcripts, samples of their creative work, and 2 letters of recommendation. Priority consideration is given to students who work in or whose family member has worked or currently works in a segment of the high volume transaction output (HVTO) industry. Financial need is not considered.

Financial data The stipend is $2,000.

Duration 1 year.

Additional information This program is sponsored by COPI/OutputLinks.

Number awarded 1 each year.

Deadline May of each year.

[643]
JOHN CHARLES WILSON SCHOLARSHIPS

International Association of Arson Investigators
Attn: Educational Foundation
12772 Boenker Road
St. Louis, MO 63044
(314) 739-4224   Fax: (314) 739-4219
E-mail: jimwhitaker@firearson.com
Web: www.firearson.com/ef/jwscholar/index.asp

Purpose To provide financial assistance to the members and dependents or nominees of members of the International Association of Arson Investigators (IAAI) who are interested in preparing for a career in fire and arson investigation.

Eligibility This program is open to association members and their immediate families who are enrolled or planning to enroll at an accredited 2- or 4-year college or university that offers course work in fire science, law enforcement, or fire and arson investigation. Also eligible are nonmembers who are recommended and sponsored by association members in good standing. Applicants must submit transcripts and an essay of 500 words or less providing background information and their future plans in police or fire sciences. Financial need is not considered.

Financial data Stipends are $1,000 or $500.

Duration 1 year.

Additional information These scholarships were first awarded in 1981.

Number awarded Varies each year. Recently, 7 of these scholarships were awarded: 1 at $1,000 and 6 at $500.

Deadline February of each year.

[644]
JOHN CULVER WOODDY SCHOLARSHIPS

Actuarial Foundation
Attn: Actuarial Education and Research Fund
  Committee
475 North Martingale Road, Suite 800
Schaumburg, IL 60173-2226
(847) 706-3565   Fax: (847) 706-3599
E-mail: scholarships@actfnd.org
Web: www.actuarialfoundation.org

Purpose To provide financial assistance to undergraduate students who are preparing for a career in actuarial science.

Eligibility Eligible to be nominated are undergraduate students who will have senior standing in the semester after receiving the scholarship. Applicants must rank in the top quartile of their class and have successfully completed 1 actuarial examination. Each university may nominate only 1 student. Preference is given to candidates who have demonstrated leadership potential by participating in extracurricular activities. Financial need is not considered in the selection process.

Financial data The stipend is $2,000 per academic year.

Duration 1 year.

Additional information This program was established in 1996.

Number awarded Varies each year; recently, 8 of these scholarships were awarded.

Deadline June of each year.

[645]
JOHN GEAGAN SCHOLARSHIP PROGRAM
Service Employees International Union
Attn: Education Department
1313 L Street, N.W.
Washington, DC 20005
(202) 898-3326 Toll-free: (800) 424-8592
Fax: (202) 898-3348 TDD: (202) 898-3481
Web: www.seiu.org/mbe/scholarships/geagan.cfm

Purpose To provide financial assistance to members and children of members of the Service Employees International Union (SEIU) who are interested in working on a college degree in labor studies.

Eligibility This program is open to members of an SEIU local or affiliated union and their children. applicants must be interested in attending a 2-year or 4-year institution, labor studies center, or certificate or online program to earn an associate or bachelor's degree in labor studies Preference is given to applicants who are not served by traditional educational institutions, typically adults who have been in the workforce and have decided to go, or return, to college. Along with their application, they must submit a personal statement of 500 words or less that describes what the labor movement has meant to them, how they have been active in their union, why they want to work on a degree in labor studies, the program in which they plan to enroll, and the role they see for themselves in building the labor movement. Selection is based on originality, clarity, and commitment to social and economic justice in the workplace.

Financial data The stipend is $2,500 per year.
Duration 2 years.
Additional information This program is administered by Scholarship Program Administrators, Inc., 1201 Eighth Avenue South, P.O. Box 23737, Nashville, TN 27202-3737, (615) 320-3149, Fax: (615) 320-3151, E-mail: info@spaprog.com. The recipient must agree to participate in some paid or course credit internships or work experiences in social change organizations during the years they receive this award.
Number awarded 1 or more each year.
Deadline February of each year.

[646]
JOHN KELLY LABOR STUDIES SCHOLARSHIP FUND
Office and Professional Employees International Union
Attn: Scholarship Fund
1660 L Street, N.W., Suite 801
Washington, DC 20036
(202) 393-4464 Fax: (202) 347-0649
Web: www.opeiu.org/benefits.html

Purpose To provide financial assistance to members of the Office and Professional Employees International Union (OPEIU) who wish to study labor relations on the undergraduate or graduate level.

Eligibility Applicants must be a member or an associate member of the union in good standing, unless a member leaves employment to study on a full-time basis, retires, becomes disabled, or is terminated by employer layoffs and plant closings. They must be enrolled in or accepted for enrollment in a program of graduate or undergraduate study in labor studies, industrial relations, social science, or a related field. All applicants must submit high school transcripts, college transcripts (if appropriate), an essay of 300 to 500 words on occupational goals, and a statement of intent to remain within the union for a period of 2 years. Only 1 award will be made to a family for a lifetime.

Financial data The stipend is $2,000.
Duration Up to 4 years.
Number awarded 10 each year (at least 1 per region).
Deadline March of each year.

[647]
JOURNALISM EDUCATION ASSOCIATION FUTURE TEACHER SCHOLARSHIP
Journalism Education Association
c/o Kansas State University
103 Kedzie Hall
Manhattan, KS 66506-1505
(785) 532-5532 Toll-free: (866) JEA-5JEA
Fax: (785) 532-5563 E-mail: jea@spub.ksu.edu
Web: www.jea.org/awards/futureteacheraward.html

Purpose To provide financial assistance to upper-division and master's degree students majoring in education who intend to teach journalism.

Eligibility This program is open to upper-division undergraduates and master's degree students in a college program designed to prepare them for teaching journalism at the secondary school level. Applicants must submit a 250-word essay explaining their desire to teach high school journalism, 2 letters of recommendation, and college transcripts. They must also provide information on the journalism courses they have completed, their high school journalism experience, and their experiences working with high school journalists since they graduated from high school.

Financial data The stipend is $1,000.
Duration 1 year.
Additional information This scholarship was first awarded in 2000.
Number awarded Up to 3 each year.
Deadline September of each year.

[648]
J.P. GUILFORD UNDERGRADUATE RESEARCH AWARDS
Psi Chi
825 Vine Street
P.O. Box 709
Chattanooga, TN 37401-0709
(423) 756-2044 Fax: (877) 774-2443
E-mail: awards@psichi.org
Web: www.psichi.org/awards/home.asp

Purpose To recognize and reward outstanding research papers written by undergraduate members of Psi Chi (an honor society in psychology).

Eligibility All undergraduate students who are members of the honor society are eligible to submit completed research papers (up to 12 pages long). For the purpose of

this award, "research" is broadly defined to be based on any methodology relevant to psychology, including experiments, correlational studies, historical studies, case histories, and evaluation studies.
Financial data First place is $1,000, second $650, and third $350.
Duration The prizes are awarded annually.
Number awarded 3 each year.
Deadline April of each year.

[649]
JUDITH CARY MEMORIAL SCHOLARSHIP
P. Buckley Moss Society
20 Stoneridge Drive, Suite 102
Waynesboro, VA 22980
(540) 943-5678   Fax: (540) 949-8408
E-mail: society@mosssociety.org
Web: www.mosssociety.org

Purpose To provide financial assistance to students working on a bachelor's or master's degree in special education.
Eligibility Eligible to be nominated for this scholarship are students who have completed at least 2 years of undergraduate study and are working on a bachelor's or master's degree in special education. Nominations may be submitted by society members only. The nomination packet must include proof of acceptance into a specific program to teach special needs students, 2 letters of recommendation, a short essay on school and community work activities and achievements, and an essay of 250 to 500 words on their career goals, teaching philosophies, reasons for choosing this career, and ways in which they plan to make a difference in the lives of special needs students. Financial need is not considered in the selection process.
Financial data The stipend is $1,000. Funds are paid to the recipient's college or university.
Duration 1 year.
Additional information This program was established in 1999.
Number awarded 2 each year.
Deadline March of each year.

[650]
JUNE P. GALLOWAY SCHOLARSHIP
North Carolina Alliance for Athletics, Health, Physical Education, Recreation and Dance
Attn: Executive Director
P.O. Box 27751
Raleigh, NC 27611
Toll-free: (888) 840-6500   Fax: (919) 833-7700
E-mail: ncaahperd@ncaahperd.org
Web: www.ncaahperd.org/awards/scholarships.htm

Purpose To provide financial assistance for college to members of the North Carolina Alliance for Athletics, Health, Physical Education, Recreation and Dance (NCAAHPERD).
Eligibility This program is open to rising seniors majoring in health, physical education, recreation, and/or dance who are members of NCAAHPERD. Applicants must have a GPA of 2.0 or higher for all college work and 3.0 or higher for their major. Selection is based two-thirds on academic achievement and one-third on leadership and contributions to the profession. Financial need is not considered.
Financial data The stipend is $1,000 per year.
Duration 1 year.
Number awarded 1 each year.
Deadline June of each year.

[651]
KEITH PAYNE MEMORIAL SCHOLARSHIP
Professional Independent Insurance Agents of Illinois
Attn: College Scholarship Program
4360 Wabash Avenue
Springfield, IL 62711-7009
(217) 793-6660   Toll-free: (800) 628-6436
Fax: (217) 793-6744   E-mail: info@piiai.org
Web: www.piiai.org/youngagents/scholarship.htm

Purpose To provide financial assistance to upper-division students from Illinois who are majoring in business and have an interest in insurance.
Eligibility This program is open to residents of Illinois who are full-time juniors or seniors in college. Applicants must be enrolled in a business degree program with an interest in insurance. They must have a letter of recommendation from a current or retired member of the Professional Independent Insurance Agents of Illinois. Along with their application, they must submit an essay (500 words or less) on the contribution the insurance industry makes to society. Financial need is not considered in the selection process.
Financial data The stipend is $1,000, payable in 2 equal installments. Funds are paid directly to the recipient's school.
Duration 1 year.
Number awarded 1 each year.
Deadline June of each year.

[652]
KEMPER SCHOLARS GRANT PROGRAM
James S. Kemper Foundation
20 North Wacker Drive, Suite 1823
Chicago, IL 60606
(312) 332-3114   E-mail: dmattison@jskemper.org
Web: www.jskemper.org/kemper_scholar_pgm.htm

Purpose To provide financial assistance and work experience to freshmen at selected colleges and universities who are interested in preparing for a career in business and/or administration.
Eligibility This program is open to students enrolled as freshmen at 1 of 15 participating colleges and universities. Applicants must be interested in preparing for a career in administration and/or business and must have a record of academic achievement, extracurricular activity, community service, and leadership ability. They must be willing to participate in community service by engaging in campus activities, exploring their vocational calling outside the classroom, and participating in a full-time summer work program with a nonprofit organization in Chicago.
Financial data All scholars receive a stipend of at least $3,000 per year (regardless of financial need). Scholars who demonstrate financial need may receive up to $8,000 per year. During the summer between their sophomore and

junior years, scholars receive a stipend of $6,000 for their work at a nonprofit organization in Chicago. During the summer between their junior and senior years, scholars work on an independent project, for which they receive a stipend of $2,000 to $6,000, depending on the expenses associated with the project.

Duration 3 years, as long as the scholar maintains a GPA of 3.0 or higher each academic term.

Additional information The 15 participating schools are Agnes Scott College (Decatur, Georgia), Beloit College (Beloit, Wisconsin), Knox College (Galesburg, Illinois), Lake Forest College (Lake Forest, Illinois), LaSalle University (Philadelphia, Pennsylvania), Millikin University (Decatur, Illinois), Pitzer College (Claremont, California), Southwestern University (Georgetown, Texas), University of the Incarnate Word (San Antonio, Texas), Ursinus College (Collegeville, Pennsylvania), Valparaiso University (Valparaiso, Indiana), Xavier University of Louisiana (New Orleans, Louisiana), Washington and Lee University (Lexington, Virginia), Wake Forest University (Winston-Salem, North Carolina), and Willamette University (Salem, Oregon). Summer assignments are at major nonprofit organizations in Chicago.

Number awarded Varies each year; recently, 19 of these grants were awarded.

Deadline Deadlines vary at each institution.

[653]
KENTUCKY SOCIETY OF CERTIFIED PUBLIC ACCOUNTANTS COLLEGE SCHOLARSHIPS

Kentucky Society of Certified Public Accountants
Attn: Educational Foundation
1735 Alliant Avenue
Louisville, KY 40299-6326
(502) 266-5272 Toll-free: (800) 292-1754 (within KY)
Fax: (502) 261-9512 E-mail: cpa2be@kycpa.org
Web: www.cpa2be.org

Purpose To provide financial assistance to undergraduate and graduate students in Kentucky who are interested in majoring in accounting.

Eligibility This program is open to students who are currently enrolled as a sophomore, junior, senior, or graduate student at a Kentucky college or university. Applicants must have an overall GPA of at least 2.75 and an accounting GPA of at least 3.0. They must have completed the "principles of accounting" course and must be currently enrolled in or have completed intermediate accounting. Along with their application, they must submit a 1-page essay on their career goals, reasons for choosing accounting, how they are financing their education, and why their should receive this scholarship. At least 1 scholarship is reserved for a student member of the Kentucky Society of Certified Public Accountants (KSCPA). Financial need is not considered in the selection process.

Financial data The stipend is $1,000.

Duration 1 year.

Additional information This program was established in 1988. Winners are presented at the society's spring awards banquet.

Number awarded Several each year, including at least 1 for a KSCPA student member.

Deadline January of each year.

[654]
L. GORDON BITTLE MEMORIAL SCHOLARSHIPS

California Teachers Association
Attn: Human Rights Department
1705 Murchison Drive
P.O. Box 921
Burlingame, CA 94011-0921
(650) 697-1400 Fax: (650) 552-5001
E-mail: scholarships@cta.org
Web: www.cta.org

Purpose To provide financial assistance to active student members of the Student California Teachers Association (SCTA) who are interested in preparing for a teaching career.

Eligibility This program is open to active student members of the association who are interested in working on a teaching credential. Applicants may be undergraduate, credential, or graduate students. Members of the California Teachers Association (CTA) currently working in public schools are not eligible. High school seniors must have a GPA of 3.5 or higher. College course work should reflect high academic achievement. Along with their application, they must submit a 200-word statement that describes their personal attributes, unique qualities, and future goals; the statement should include an explanation of any special circumstances related to medical, physical, or psychological condition that may have affected their grades. Selection is based on that statement (30%), school and community activities (20%), the first letter of recommendation (25%), and the second letter of recommendation (25%).

Financial data The stipend is $2,000.

Duration 1 year; nonrenewable.

Number awarded 3 each year.

Deadline January of each year.

[655]
LAMACCHIA FAMILY SCHOLARSHIP

Tourism Cares for Tomorrow
Attn: Program Manager
585 Washington Street
Canton, MA 02021
(781) 821-5990 Fax: (781) 821-8949
E-mail: info@tourismcares.org
Web: www.tourismcares.org

Purpose To provide financial assistance to college students in Wisconsin who are majoring in tourism.

Eligibility This program is open to full-time students enrolled at a 4-year college or university in Wisconsin. Applicants must be entering their junior or senior year, have at least a 3.0 GPA, and be majoring in a travel or tourism-related field (e.g., hotel management, restaurant management, tourism).

Financial data The stipend is $1,000 per year.

Duration 1 year.

Additional information This program was established in 2005.

Number awarded 1 each year.

Deadline March of each year.

[656]
LARS NAERLAND SCHOLARSHIP
Nordmanns-Forbundet
Pacific Northwest Chapter
c/o Bernice Chouery
6738 19th Avenue N.W.
Seattle, WA 98117
E-mail: bchouery@hotmail.com

Purpose To provide financial assistance to college students in the Pacific Northwest who are interested in studying about Norway or in Norway.

Eligibility This program is open to part-time and full-time college students who have demonstrated an interest in studying subjects that would strengthen the ties between the people of Norway and the people of the United States. Applicants should be members of the Nordmanns-Forbundet or be of Norwegian descent. Special attention is paid to applicants whose project or course of study will take them to Norway or will help to foster the social, cultural, and economic ties between the Pacific Northwest and Norway. Applicants must submit 3 letters of recommendation, a copy of their high school or college transcript, and an essay explaining why they are applying for the scholarship. Financial need is not considered in the selection process.

Financial data The stipend is generally $1,000.

Duration 1 year.

Additional information Information is also available from the Scholarship Committee, 3925 151st Avenue, S.E., Bellevue, WA 98006-1712.

Number awarded At least 1 each year.

Deadline February of each year.

[657]
LAW ENFORCEMENT CAREER SCHOLARSHIP PROGRAM
Association of Former Agents of the United States Secret Service, Inc.
Attn: Executive Director
525 S.W. Fifth Street, Suite A
Des Moines, IA 50309-4501
(515) 282-8192   Fax: (515) 282-9117
Web: www.oldstar.org

Purpose To provide financial assistance to students working on an undergraduate or graduate degree in law enforcement or police science.

Eligibility This program is open to undergraduate students who have completed at least 1 year of study in law enforcement or police administration. Students working toward an advanced degree are also eligible if their graduate study is in law enforcement or police administration. Applications may be submitted by more than 1 member of the same family, but no more than 1 scholarship will be granted to any 1 family. Past recipients are not eligible for a second award. Financial need is not considered in the selection process.

Financial data The stipend is $1,000.

Duration 1 year; may not reapply.

Additional information This program includes the following named scholarships: the J. Clifford Dietrich Scholarship, the John Hays Hanly Memorial Scholarship, and the Julie Y. Cross Scholarship.

Number awarded At least 3 each year.

Deadline April of each year.

[658]
LCPA EDUCATION FOUNDATION SCHOLARSHIP PROGRAM
Society of Louisiana Certified Public Accountants
Attn: LCPA Education Foundation
2400 Veterans Boulevard, Suite 500
Kenner, LA 70062-4739
(504) 464-1040   Toll-free: (800) 288-5272
Fax: (504) 469-7930
Web: www.lcpa.org/LCPAScholarships.html

Purpose To provide financial assistance to currently-enrolled college students in Louisiana who are interested in becoming certified public accountants.

Eligibility This program is open to Louisiana residents who are currently enrolled full time in an accounting program at a 4-year college or university in Louisiana. Applicants must have completed at least 4 semesters by the fall of the academic year in which the application is filed and have a GPA of 2.5 or higher. Along with their application, they must submit a 2-page essay on their perception of the C.P.A.'s role on the job and in the community, including how they plan to contribute to the profession and to the community.

Financial data Stipends range from $1,000 to nearly $3,000.

Duration 1 year.

Additional information The sponsor offers a number of named scholarships, including The Alex Postlethwaite Scholarship ($1,000) and the Christopher ÚKitÛ Smith Scholarship ($2,700). Individual chapters of the society also offer scholarships. The Baton Rouge Chapter awards $1,000 scholarships to students at in-town colleges and universities. Central Louisiana Chapter awards approximately $500 to students at Louisiana College, Northwestern State University, and Louisiana State University at Alexandria. Lafayette Chapter gives $1,000 to a student at the University of Southwestern Louisiana. Lake Charles Chapter contributes $1,000 to student scholarships at McNeese State. Northeast Chapter grants scholarships between $250 and $1,000 to students at Northeastern Louisiana University, Louisiana Tech, and Grambling State. Northshore Chapter gives a $1,000 scholarship to 2 students at Southeastern University. Shreveport Chapter offers 2 or 3 scholarships (approximately $1,500) to local students. South Central Chapter awards a $250 scholarship to a student at Nicholls State University.

Number awarded Several each year.

[659]
LEAP SCHOLARSHIPS
Missouri Society of Certified Public Accountants
Attn: LEAP Program
275 North Lindbergh Boulevard, Suite 10
P.O. Box 419042
St. Louis, MO 63141-9042
(314) 997-7966   Toll-free: (800) 264-7966 (within MO)
Fax: (314) 997-2592   E-mail: scholarships@mocpa.org
Web: www.mocpa.org/leap/index.html

Purpose To provide financial assistance to residents of Missouri who are majoring in accounting at colleges and universities in the state.

Eligibility This program is open to residents of Missouri who are majoring in accounting as a full-time student at a college or university in the state. Applicants must submit a 500-word essay on how the C.P.A. credential will enhance their career path. Selection is based on the essay, academic achievement, and demonstrated leadership potential. Financial need is not considered. The highest-ranked applicant is awarded the Dan Breimeier Memorial Scholarship.

Financial data The stipend is $1,000 per year. The recipient of the Dan Breimeier Memorial Scholarship is awarded an additional $1,000.

Duration 1 year.

Additional information These scholarships are offered through the sponsor's Lead and Enhance the Accounting Profession (LEAP) program, established in 2001. The Dan Breimeier Memorial Scholarship was first awarded in 2006.

Number awarded Varies each year.

Deadline January of each year.

[660]
LEGAL ASSISTANTS SECTION SCHOLARSHIPS
State Bar of Michigan
Attn: Legal Assistants Section
306 Townsend Street
Lansing, MI 48133-2083
Toll-free: (800) 968-1442   Fax: (517) 482-6248
Web: www.michbar.org

Purpose To provide financial assistance to Michigan residents who are enrolled or planning to enroll in a legal assistant program in the state.

Eligibility This program is open to residents of Michigan who are high school seniors planning to enroll or students currently enrolled in a legal assistant degree/certificate program at a college or university in the state. Applicants must have a GPA of 2.0 or higher (or at least 70%). Along with their application, they must submit 2 letters of recommendation, transcripts, a 1-page autobiographical statement, and an essay of 250 to 1,000 words on their career goals and desires. Selection is based on scholastic or legal career achievements, future career goals, and leadership ability; financial need is not considered.

Financial data Stipends range from $250 to $1,000.

Duration 1 year; nonrenewable.

Additional information Information is also available from Heather A. Hill, Scholarship Chair, c/o O'Reilly Rancilio P.C., 12900 Hall Road, Suite 350, Sterling Heights, MI 48313-1151, (586) 997-6493, Fax: (586) 726-1560, E-mail: hhill@orlaw.com.

Number awarded At least 2 each year.

Deadline June of each year.

[661]
LEONARD R. BRICE UNDERGRADUATE LEADERSHIP AWARD
Society for Human Resource Management
Attn: Student Programs
1800 Duke Street
Alexandria, VA 22314-3499
(703) 535-6084   Toll-free: (800) 283-SHRM
Fax: (703) 739-0399   TDD: (703) 548-6999
E-mail: SHRMStudent@shrm.org
Web: www.shrm.org/students/ags_published

Purpose To recognize and reward outstanding leadership skills by undergraduate student members of the Society for Human Resource Management (SHRM).

Eligibility This program is open to full-time undergraduate students who have completed their sophomore year, have maintained a GPA of 2.0 or higher, and are national student members of the society. Selection is based on the leadership ability demonstrated in an SHRM student chapter, commitment to the human resources profession, scholastic average and standing, and additional leadership activities (such as service to a campus organization and/or a community or charitable organization).

Financial data The award includes a $1,000 honorarium, a commemorative plaque, and complimentary registration to the society's annual conference and exposition.

Duration The award is offered annually.

Number awarded 1 each year.

Deadline February of each year.

[662]
L.L. WATERS SCHOLARSHIP PROGRAM
American Society of Transportation and Logistics, Inc.
Attn: Scholarship Judging Panel
1700 North Moore Street, Suite 1900
Arlington, VA 22209-1904
(703) 524-5011   Fax: (703) 524-5017
E-mail: astl@nitl.org
Web: www.astl.org/scholar.htm

Purpose To provide financial assistance to advanced undergraduate and graduate students in the field of transportation.

Eligibility This program is open to undergraduate students in their junior year at fully-accredited 4-year colleges or universities who are majoring in transportation, logistics, or physical distribution. Students in graduate school in the same areas are also eligible. Applicants must submit a letter explaining why they have chosen transportation, logistics, or physical distribution as their field of study and describing their professional objectives. Recipients are selected without regard to race, color, religion, sex, or national origin. Selection is based on scholastic performance and potential as well as commitment to a professional career in the field. Financial need is not considered.

Financial data The stipend is $2,000.

Duration 1 year; recipients may apply again but not in consecutive years.

SOCIAL SCIENCES

Number awarded 1 or more each year.
Deadline September of each year.

[663]
LOUISE MORITZ MOLITORIS LEADERSHIP AWARD

Women's Transportation Seminar
Attn: National Headquarters
1701 K Street, N.W., Suite 800
Washington, DC 20006
(202) 955-5085 Fax: (202) 955-5088
E-mail: wts@wtsinternational.org
Web: www.wtsinternational.org

Purpose To provide financial assistance to undergraduate women interested in a career in transportation.
Eligibility This program is open to women who are working on an undergraduate degree in transportation or a transportation-related field (e.g., transportation engineering, planning, finance, or logistics). Applicants must have a GPA of 3.0 or higher. Along with their application, they must submit a 500-word statement about their career goals after graduation and why they think they should receive the scholarship award; their statement should specifically address the issue of leadership. Applications must be submitted first to a local chapter; the chapters forward selected applications for consideration on the national level. Minority candidates are encouraged to apply. Selection is based on transportation involvement and goals, job skills, academic record, and leadership potential; financial need is not considered.
Financial data The stipend is $3,000.
Duration 1 year.
Additional information Local chapters may also award additional funding to winners for their area.
Number awarded 1 each year.
Deadline Applications must be submitted by November to a local WTS chapter.

[664]
MAJOR JAMES W. LOVELL SCHOLARSHIPS

100th Infantry Battalion Veterans Club
Attn: Scholarship Committee
520 Kamoku Street
Honolulu, HI 96826
(808) 732-5216 E-mail: daisyy@hgea.net
Web: emedia.leeward.hawaii.edu/mnakano

Purpose To provide financial assistance to high school seniors and college students who major in education and exemplify the sponsor's motto of "Continuing Service."
Eligibility This program is open to high school seniors planning to attend an institution of higher learning and full-time undergraduate students at community colleges, vocational/trade schools, 4-year colleges, and universities. Applicants must have a GPA of 2.5 or higher and be able to demonstrate civic responsibility and community service. They must be majoring or planning to major in education. Along with their application, they must submit a 4-page essay that explains how lifelong learning (including academic success, experiential learning, intellectual growth, social and economic growth, leadership skills, and civic responsibility) is important for citizens and their state and country. Selection is based on that essay and the applicant's demonstration that he or she can effectively promote the legacy of the 100th Infantry Battalion and its motto of "Continuing Service." Financial need is not considered.
Financial data The stipend is $1,000.
Duration 1 year; nonrenewable.
Number awarded 2 each year.
Deadline April of each year.

[665]
MARC LAWSON CRIMINAL JUSTICE SCHOLARSHIP

National Association of Government Employees
Attn: Kevin Doyle
159 Burgin Parkway
Quincy, MA 02169
(617) 376-7214 Toll-free: (866) 412-7762
E-mail: kdoyle@nage.org
Web: www.nage.org/schol.shtml

Purpose To provide financial assistance to members and their families of the National Association of Government Employees (NAGE) and affiliated organizations who are working on an undergraduate degree in criminal justice.
Eligibility This program is open to active members and the spouses, children, grandchildren, nieces, nephews, dependents, and significant others of members of NAGE, the International Brotherhood of Police Officers (IBPO), the International Brotherhood of Correctional Officers (IBCO), or the International Association of EMTs and Paramedics (IAEP). Family of members killed in the line of duty are also eligible. Applicants must be attending or planning to attend an accredited college, university, or community college to work full time on a degree in criminal justice. Along with their application, they must submit 1) a statement of 200 words or less describing what the labor movement has meant to them and their family; and 2) a statement of 500 words or less describing their education and career goals in criminal justice. Selection is based on originality, clarity, and commitment to excellence in criminal justice.
Financial data The stipend is $1,000.
Duration 1 year.
Additional information This program began in 2006.
Number awarded 1 each year.
Deadline August of each year.

[666]
MARYLAND ASSOCIATION FOR HEALTH, PHYSICAL EDUCATION, RECREATION AND DANCE UNDERGRADUATE SCHOLARSHIPS

Maryland Association for Health, Physical Education, Recreation and Dance
Attn: Office Coordinator
828 Dulaney Valley Road, Suite 8
Towson, MD 21204
(410) 583-1370 Fax: (410) 583-1374
E-mail: mewilliams@mahperd.org
Web: www.mahperd.org/hs_scholarships.htm

Purpose To provide financial assistance to upper-division students in Maryland who are preparing for a career as a teacher of health, physical education, recreation, or dance.

Eligibility This program is open to students completing their sophomore or junior year at a college or university in Maryland and enrolled full time in a teacher preparation program in dance, health, physical education, or recreation. Applicants must have a GPA of 3.0 or higher in their major and 2.5 or higher overall. They should be able to demonstrate leadership qualities in the community and extracurricular participation, especially those that may have an impact on the future career in teaching. Along with their application, they must submit a letter describing their plans for a career, community activities, awards, and other recognitions. Financial need is not considered in the selection process.

Financial data The stipend is $1,000.

Duration 1 year.

Number awarded 1 or more each year.

Deadline August of each year.

[667]
MAUD BERGGREN SCHOLARSHIP
Nordmanns-Forbundet
Pacific Northwest Chapter
c/o Bernice Chouery
6738 19th Avenue N.W.
Seattle, WA 98117
E-mail: bchouery@hotmail.com

Purpose To provide financial assistance to college students in the Pacific Northwest who are interested in studying about Norway or in Norway.

Eligibility This program is open to part-time and full-time college students who have demonstrated an interest in studying subjects that would strengthen the ties between the people of Norway and the people of the United States. Applicants should be members of the Nordmanns-Forbundet or be of Norwegian descent. Special attention is paid to applicants whose project or course of study will take them to Norway or will help to foster the social, cultural, and economic ties between the Pacific Northwest and Norway. Applicants must submit 3 letters of recommendation, a copy of their high school or college transcript, and an essay explaining why they are applying for the scholarship. Financial need is not considered in the selection process.

Financial data The stipend is generally $1,000.

Duration 1 year.

Additional information Information is also available from the Scholarship Committee, 3925 151st Avenue, S.E., Bellevue, WA 98006-1712.

Number awarded At least 1 each year.

Deadline March of each year.

[668]
METRO NEW YORK CHAPTER UNDERGRADUATE SCHOLARSHIP AWARD
National Black MBA Association-New York Chapter
Attn: Scholarship Committee
P.O. Box 8138
New York, NY 10116
(917) 723-4906   E-mail: scholarship@nyblackmba.org
Web: www.nyblackmba.org/scholarship.html

Purpose To provide financial assistance to minority students from New York interested in majoring in business or management.

Eligibility This program is open to minority students who are residents of New York and either high school seniors or full-time undergraduate students working on a bachelor's degree in business or management. Applicants must submit a 2-page essay on a topic that changes annually but recently was "What are the major benefits that a large corporation seeks by expanding its business internationally?" Special consideration is given to applicants who have participated in the sponsor's Leaders of Tomorrow program. Financial need is not considered in the selection process.

Financial data A stipend is awarded (amount not specified).

Duration 1 year.

Number awarded Varies each year; recently, 2 of these scholarships were awarded.

Deadline November of each year.

[669]
MINNESOTA BUSINESS EDUCATORS AWARD FOR BUSINESS EDUCATION TEACHING MAJORS
Minnesota Business Educators, Inc.
c/o Kathryn Larson, MBEI Awards Chair
Owatonna High School
333 East School Street
Owatonna, MN 55060
(507) 444-8800
E-mail: klarson1@owatonna.k12.mn.us
Web: www.mbei-online.org

Purpose To provide financial assistance for college to members of Minnesota Business Educators, Inc. (MBEI) who are enrolled in a business teaching licensure program at a Minnesota college or university.

Eligibility This program is open to student members of MBEI enrolled as a major in a business teacher licensure program at a Minnesota college or university. Applicants must submit a letter indicating why they merit this award, a 2-page resume, 2 letters of recommendation, and a transcript.

Financial data A stipend is awarded (amount not specified).

Duration 1 year.

Additional information This award was first presented in 1989.

Number awarded 1 each year.

Deadline February of each year.

SOCIAL SCIENCES

[670]
MINNESOTA CHAPTER WTS SCHOLARSHIPS
Women's Transportation Seminar-Minnesota Chapter
c/o Jessica Overmohle, Director
URS Corporation
700 Third Street South
Minneapolis, MN 55415-1199
(612) 373-6404 Fax: (612) 370-1378
E-mail: Jessica_Overmohle@URSCorp.com
Web: www.wtsinternational.org

Purpose To provide financial assistance to women working on an undergraduate or graduate degree in a transportation-related field at colleges and universities in Minnesota.

Eligibility This program is open to women currently enrolled in an undergraduate or graduate degree program at a college or university in Minnesota. Applicants must be preparing for a career in transportation or a transportation-related field and be majoring in such fields as transportation engineering, planning, finance, or logistics. They must have a GPA of 3.0 or higher. Along with their application, they must submit a 750-word statement on their career goals after graduation and why they think they should receive this award. Selection is based on transportation goals, academic record, and transportation-related activities or job skills.

Financial data The stipend is $2,000.

Duration 1 year.

Additional information Winners are also nominated for scholarships offered by the national organization of the Women's Transportation Seminar.

Number awarded 2 each year: 1 undergraduate and 1 graduate student.

Deadline November of each year.

[671]
MINORITIES IN GOVERNMENT FINANCE SCHOLARSHIP
Government Finance Officers Association
Attn: Scholarship Committee
203 North LaSalle Street, Suite 2700
Chicago, IL 60601-1210
(312) 977-9700 Fax: (312) 977-4806
Web: www.gfoa.org/services/scholarships.shtml

Purpose To provide financial assistance to minority upper-division and graduate students who are preparing for a career in state and local government finance.

Eligibility This program is open to upper-division and graduate students who are preparing for a career in public finance with a major in public administration, accounting, finance, political science, economics, or business administration (with a specific focus on government or nonprofit management). Applicants must be members of a minority group, citizens or permanent residents of the United States or Canada, and able to provide a letter of recommendation from a representative of their school. Selection is based on career plans, academic record, plan of study, letters of recommendation, and GPA. Financial need is not considered.

Financial data The stipend is $5,000.

Duration 1 year.

Number awarded 1 or more each year.

Deadline February of each year.

[672]
MISSOURI SOIL AND WATER CONSERVATION SOCIETY SCHOLARSHIPS
Soil and Water Conservation Society-Missouri Show-Me Chapter
c/o Natural Resources Conservation Service
Parkade Center, Suite 250
601 Business Loop 70 West
Columbia, MO 65203-2546
(573) 876-0912
Web: swcs.missouri.edu

Purpose To provide financial assistance to entering or continuing undergraduate students at Missouri colleges and universities interested in preparing for a career in natural resources conservation.

Eligibility This program is open to residents of Missouri who are graduating high school seniors or full-time undergraduates at an accredited college or university. Applicants must be majoring or planning to major in a natural resource conservation or resource-related field, including soil science, land use planning, fisheries, forestry, wildlife management, agricultural engineering, hydrology, rural sociology, agronomy, agricultural economics, agricultural education, water management, or a related environmental field. They must submit 2 letters of recommendation; an essay on a topic that changes annually; a list of positions of leadership in such organizations as the Soil and Water Conservation Society, 4-H, FFA, and student groups; publishing and speaking activities in which they participated; and their most recent high school, college, or university transcript. Financial need is not considered in the selection process.

Financial data First place is $2,000 and second place is $1,000. Payment is made directly to the college or university.

Duration 1 year.

Additional information These scholarships were formerly known as the Betty Broemmelsiek Memorial Conservation Scholarships. Information is also available from Beverly Maltsberger, Buchanan County Extension Center, 4125 Mitchell Avenue, P.O. Box 7077, St. Joseph, MO 64507-7077, (816) 279-1691, E-mail: maltsbergerb@missouri.edu.

Number awarded 2 each year.

Deadline November of each year.

[673]
MISSOURI TRAVEL COUNCIL SCHOLARSHIP
Missouri Travel Council
204 East High Street
Jefferson City, MO 65101-3287
(573) 636-2814 Fax: (573) 636-5783
E-mail: info@missouritravel.com
Web: www.missouritravel.com/scholarship.htm

Purpose To provide financial assistance to Missouri residents preparing for a hospitality-related career at a college or university in the state.

Eligibility This program is open to residents of Missouri currently enrolled as a sophomore, junior, or senior at an accredited college or university in the state. Applicants must be working on a degree related to hospitality, (e.g., hotel and restaurant management, parks and recreation). They must have a GPA of 3.0 or higher. Along with their application, they must submit a statement on their goals and future career plans and why they are preparing for a career in the hospitality/tourism field. Selection is based on the essay (20%), community involvement (20%), academic activities and achievement (30%), hospitality-related experience (30%), and letters of recommendation (10%).

Financial data The stipend is $1,000. Funds are paid directly to the recipient's institution.

Duration 1 year.

Number awarded 2 each year.

Deadline February of each year.

[674]
MOEFACS SCHOLARSHIPS
Missouri Educators of Family and Consumer Sciences
c/o Cynthia Arendt
Department of Elementary and Secondary Education
Family and Consumer Sciences Education
P.O. Box 480
Jefferson City, MO 65102-0480
(573) 751-7965   Fax: (573) 526-4261
E-mail: debbit.pohl@dese.mo.us
Web: dese.mo.gov/divcareered/facs_moefacs.htm

Purpose To provide financial assistance to high school seniors and current college students who plan to earn an education degree in family and consumer sciences at a Missouri college or university.

Eligibility This program is open to 1) graduating high school seniors, and 2) college students who have completed at least 60 credit hours. Applicants must have a GPA of 3.0 or higher and be planning to earn an education degree in family and consumer sciences at a Missouri college or university. They must submit (as an essay, video, pamphlet, etc.) an explanation of why they want to become a teacher in the field of family and consumer sciences. Financial need is not considered in the selection process.

Financial data The stipend is $1,000 per year.

Duration 1 year.

Additional information Information is also available from Renee Meents, President, Route 1, Box 655, Greenfield, MO 65661.

Number awarded 2 each year: 1 to a graduating high school senior and 1 to a current college student.

Deadline February of each year.

[675]
MORRIS K. UDALL SCHOLARSHIPS
Morris K. Udall Foundation
130 South Scott Avenue
Tucson, AZ 85701-1922
(520) 670-5529   Fax: (520) 670-5530
Web: www.udall.gov/scholarship

Purpose To provide financial assistance to 1) college sophomores and juniors who intend to prepare for a career in environmental public policy and 2) Native American and Alaska Native students who intend to prepare for a career in health care or tribal public policy.

Eligibility Each 2-year and 4-year college and university in the United States and its possessions may nominate up to 6 sophomores or juniors for either or both categories of this program: 1) students who intend to prepare for a career in environmental public policy, and 2) Native American and Alaska Native students who intend to prepare for a career in health care or tribal public policy. For the first category, the program seeks future leaders across a wide spectrum of environmental fields, such as policy, engineering, science, education, urban planning and renewal, business, health, justice, and economics. For the second category, the program seeks future Native American and Alaska Native leaders in public and community health care, tribal government, and public policy affecting Native American communities, including land and resource management, economic development, and education. Nominees must be U.S. citizens, nationals, or permanent residents with a GPA of 3.0 or higher. Along with their application, they must submit an 800-word essay discussing a significant public speech, legislative act, or public policy statement by former Congressman Morris K. Udall and its impact on their field of study, interests, and career goals. Selection is based on demonstrated commitment to 1) environmental issues through substantial commitment to and participation in 1 or more of the following: campus activities, research, community service, or public service; or 2) tribal public policy or Native American health through substantial contributions to and participation in 1 or more of the following: campus activities, tribal involvement, community or public service, or research; a course of study and proposed career likely to lead to positions where the nominee can make significant contributions to the shaping of environmental, tribal public policy, or Native American health care issues; and leadership, character, desire to make a difference, and general well-roundedness.

Financial data The maximum stipend for scholarship winners is $5,000 per year. Funds are to be used for tuition, fees, books, and room and board. Honorable mention stipends are $350.

Duration 1 year; recipients nominated as sophomores may be renominated in their junior year.

Number awarded Approximately 80 scholarships and 50 honorable mentions are awarded each year.

Deadline Faculty representatives must submit their nominations by early March of each year.

[676]
NAIW AWARD OF EXCELLENCE
National Association of Insurance Women
Attn: Insurance Scholarship Foundation of America
P.O. Box 866
Hendersonville, NC 28793-0866
(828) 890-3328   Fax: (828) 891-2667
E-mail: foundation@inssfa.org
Web: www.inssfa.org

Purpose To provide financial assistance to college and graduate students working on a degree in insurance and risk management.

Eligibility This program is open to candidates for a bachelor's degree or higher with a major in insurance, risk management, or actuarial science. Applicants must 1) be completing or have completed their third year of college; 2) have an overall GPA of 3.75 or higher; 3) have successfully completed at least 2 insurance, risk management, or actuarial science courses; 4) not be receiving full reimbursement for the cost of tuition, books, or other educational expenses from their employer or any other outside source; and 5) be a student member of the National Association of Insurance Women (NAIW). Selection is based on academic record and honors, extracurricular and personal activities, work experience, 3 letters of recommendation, and a 500-word essay on career path and goals. This award is presented at the discretion of the foundation to an applicant who demonstrates the qualities necessary to excel in the industry.

Financial data The award is $1,000; funds are paid jointly to the institution and to the student.

Duration 1 year.

Additional information Members of the National Association of Insurance Women established the Insurance Scholarship Foundation of America in 1993. It provides financial assistance to both men and women interested in careers in the insurance industry.

Number awarded Generally, 1 each year.

Deadline February of each year.

[677]
NANCY CURRY SCHOLARSHIP

School Nutrition Association
Attn: Child Nutrition Foundation Scholarship Committee
700 South Washington Street, Suite 300
Alexandria, VA 22314-4287
(703) 739-3900   Toll-free: (800) 877-8722
Fax: (703) 739-3915   E-mail: cnf@schoolnutrition.org
Web: www.schoolnutrition.org/Index.aspx?ID=1043

Purpose To provide assistance to members (or children of members) of the School Nutrition Association (SNA) who are interested in studying school food service management on the undergraduate or graduate school level.

Eligibility This program is open to high school, undergraduate, and graduate students who meet all 4 of the following criteria: 1) plan to attend a college or vocational/technical institution that has a program designed to improve school food service (e.g., nutrition, food service management, business administration); 2) be an active SNA member or the child of an active member with a history of employment in school food service; 3) have a GPA of 3.0 or higher; and 4) express a desire to make school food service a career. Applicants must submit a 1-page personal essay stating their reason for selecting school food service as a profession; what they expect to gain from continuing their education; and their long-term professional goals/plans. Selection is based on the essay (35 points), letters of recommendation (20 points), SNA state and local chapter activity participation (15 points), organization and neatness (10 points), program of study (15 points), and GPA (5 points).

Financial data A stipend is awarded (amount not specified).

Duration 1 year.

Additional information The SNA was formerly the American School Food Service Administration. This program is sponsored by Handgards Inc.

Number awarded 1 each year.

Deadline April of each year.

[678]
NAOMI BERBER MEMORIAL SCHOLARSHIP

Print and Graphics Scholarship Foundation
Attn: Scholarship Competition
200 Deer Run Road
Sewickley, PA 15143-2600
(412) 259-1740   Toll-free: (800) 910-GATF
Fax: (412) 741-2311   E-mail: pgsf@piagatf.org
Web: www.gain.net

Purpose To provide financial assistance for college to women who want to prepare for a career in the printing or publishing industry.

Eligibility This program is open to females who are high school seniors or already in college. They must be interested in preparing for a career in publishing or printing while in college. This is a merit-based program; financial need is not considered.

Financial data The stipend ranges from $1,000 to $1,500, depending upon the funds available each year.

Duration 1 year; may be renewed for up to 3 additional years.

Additional information This program is named for Naomi Berber, the first woman elected to the Graphic Arts Technical Foundation Society of Fellows. Recipients must attend school on a full-time basis.

Number awarded 1 or more each year.

Deadline February of each year for high school seniors; March of each year for students already in college.

[679]
NATHAN TAYLOR DODSON SCHOLARSHIP

North Carolina Alliance for Athletics, Health, Physical
   Education, Recreation and Dance
Attn: Executive Director
P.O. Box 27751
Raleigh, NC 27611
Toll-free: (888) 840-6500   Fax: (919) 833-7700
E-mail: ncaahperd@ncaahperd.org
Web: www.ncaahperd.org/awards/scholarships.htm

Purpose To provide financial assistance for college to members of the North Carolina Alliance for Athletics, Health, Physical Education, Recreation and Dance (NCAAHPERD).

Eligibility This program is open to rising seniors majoring in health, physical education, recreation, and/or dance who are members of NCAAHPERD. Applicants must have a GPA of 2.0 or higher for all college work and 3.0 or higher for their major. Selection is based two-thirds on academic achievement and one-third on leadership and contributions to the profession. Financial need is not considered.

Financial data The stipend is $1,000 per year.

Duration 1 year.

Number awarded 1 each year.

Deadline June of each year.

[680]
NATIONAL ASSOCIATION OF INSURANCE WOMEN COLLEGE SCHOLARSHIP

National Association of Insurance Women
Attn: Insurance Scholarship Foundation of America
P.O. Box 866
Hendersonville, NC 28793-0866
(828) 890-3328   Fax: (828) 891-2667
E-mail: foundation@inssfa.org
Web: www.inssfa.org

Purpose To provide financial assistance to college and graduate students working on a degree in insurance and risk management.

Eligibility This program is open to candidates for a bachelor's degree or higher with a major in insurance, risk management, or actuarial science. Applicants must 1) be completing or have completed their third year of college; 2) have an overall GPA of 3.75 or higher; 3) have successfully completed at least 2 insurance, risk management, or actuarial science courses; 4) not be receiving full reimbursement for the cost of tuition, books, or other educational expenses from their employer or any other outside source; and 5) be a student member of the National Association of Insurance Women (NAIW). Selection is based on academic record and honors, extracurricular and personal activities, work experience, 3 letters of recommendation, and a 500-word essay on career path and goals.

Financial data Stipends range from $2,500 to $5,000 per year; funds are paid jointly to the institution and to the student.

Duration 1 year.

Additional information Members of the National Association of Insurance Women established the Insurance Scholarship Foundation of America in 1993. It provides financial assistance to both men and women interested in careers in the insurance industry.

Number awarded Varies each year; recently, 2 of these scholarships were awarded.

Deadline February of each year.

[681]
NATIONAL BLACK MBA ASSOCIATION UNDERGRADUATE SCHOLARSHIP PROGRAM

National Black MBA Association
180 North Michigan Avenue, Suite 1400
Chicago, IL 60601
(312) 236-BMBA, ext. 8086   Fax: (312) 236-0390
E-mail: Scholarship@nbmbaa.org
Web: www.nbmbaa.org/scholarship.cfm

Purpose To provide financial assistance to African American students interested in working on an undergraduate business degree.

Eligibility This program is open to African American students who wish to work on an undergraduate degree in a field related to business. Applicants must submit a completed application, high school or undergraduate transcripts, and an essay on a topic that changes annually. Selection is based on GPA, extracurricular activities, and quality of the essay.

Financial data The stipend is $1,000.

Duration 1 year.

Additional information This program is funded by the national office of the National Black MBA Association (NBMBAA), which develops the application and selects the essay topics. It is administered by local chapters, which select the winners. Applications must be submitted to local chapters; for the name and address of a contact person at each chapter, write to the association. Recipients must attend college on a full-time basis.

Number awarded Each year, each NBMBAA chapter selects 1 recipient. Currently, there are 39 chapters in the United States.

Deadline Each chapter determines its deadline date; most are in the spring.

[682]
NATIONAL FFA SCHOLARSHIPS FOR UNDERGRADUATES IN THE SOCIAL SCIENCES

National FFA Organization
Attn: Scholarship Office
6060 FFA Drive
P.O. Box 68960
Indianapolis, IN 46268-0960
(317) 802-4321   Fax: (317) 802-5321
E-mail: scholarships@ffa.org
Web: www.ffa.org/programs/scholarships/index.html

Purpose To provide financial assistance to FFA members who wish to study agribusiness and related fields in college.

Eligibility This program is open to current and former members of the organization who are working or planning to work full time on a degree in fields related to business and the social sciences; this includes: agribusiness, agricultural economics, agricultural education, agricultural finance, and agricultural marketing. For most of the scholarships, applicants must be high school seniors; others are open to students currently enrolled in college. The program includes a large number of designated scholarships that specify the locations where the members must live, the schools they must attend, the fields of study they must pursue, or other requirements. Some consider family income in the selection process, but most do not. Selection is based on academic achievement (10 points for GPA, 10 points for SAT or ACT score, 10 points for class rank), leadership in FFA activities (30 points), leadership in community activities (10 points), and participation in the Supervised Agricultural Experience (SAE) program (30 points). U.S. citizenship is required.

Financial data Stipends vary, but most are at least $1,000.

Duration 1 year or more.

Additional information Funding for these scholarships is provided by many different corporate sponsors.

Number awarded Varies; generally, a total of approximately 1,000 scholarships are awarded annually by the association.

Deadline February of each year.

SOCIAL SCIENCES

[683]
NATIONAL RESTAURANT ASSOCIATION ACADEMIC SCHOLARSHIPS FOR UNDERGRADUATE STUDENTS

National Restaurant Association Educational Foundation
Attn: Scholarships and Mentoring Program
175 West Jackson Boulevard, Suite 1500
Chicago, IL 60604-2702
(312) 715-1010, ext. 744
Toll-free: (800) 765-2122, ext. 744
Fax: (312) 566-9733   E-mail: scholars@nraef.org
Web: www.nraef.org/scholarships/undergraduate

Purpose To provide financial assistance to undergraduate students who are interested in preparing for a career in the hospitality industry.

Eligibility This program is open to full-time college students who have completed at least 1 term of a certificate, associate, or bachelor's degree program in food service or hospitality with a GPA of 2.75 or higher. Applicants must have 750 hours of work experience in the restaurant and hospitality industry. Along with their application, they must submit essays on 1) how their education will help them achieve their career objectives and future goals, and 2) a challenging situation or experience related to the restaurant and food service industry that demonstrates their ability to overcome adversity. Selection is based on the essays, presentation of the application, GPA, industry-related work experience, and letters of recommendation.

Financial data The stipend is $2,000 per year.

Duration 1 year.

Number awarded Approximately 200 each year.

Deadline April or November of each year.

[684]
NATIONAL TOUR ASSOCIATION SCHOLARSHIP

Tourism Cares for Tomorrow
Attn: Program Manager
585 Washington Street
Canton, MA 02021
(781) 821-5990   Fax: (781) 821-8949
E-mail: info@tourismcares.org
Web: www.tourismcares.org

Purpose To provide financial assistance to upper-division students who are majoring in tourism.

Eligibility This program is open to students entering their junior or senior year at an accredited 4-year college or university in the United States or Canada. Applicants must be working on a degree in a travel and tourism-related program and have a GPA of 3.0 or higher. Along with their application, they must submit a 2-page essay on why they have chosen to prepare for a career in the hospitality and tourism industry. Financial need is not considered in the selection process.

Financial data The stipend is $2,500.

Duration 1 year.

Additional information This program is sponsored by the National Tour Association (NTA).

Number awarded 1 each year.

Deadline March of each year.

[685]
NAVAJO NATION TEACHER EDUCATION PROGRAM

Navajo Nation
Navajo Nation Scholarship and Financial Assistance
Attn: Navajo Nation Teacher Education Program
P.O. Box 4380
Window Rock, AZ 86515-4380
(928) 871-7453   Toll-free: (800) 243-2956
Fax: (928) 871-6443
E-mail: onnsfacentral@navajo.org
Web: www.onnsfa.org/nntep.asp

Purpose To provide financial assistance to members of the Navajo Nation who wish to prepare for a career as a bilingual or bicultural teacher.

Eligibility This program is open to enrolled members of the Navajo Nation who are enrolled in or planning to enroll in an undergraduate teacher education program, a post-baccalaureate program for teacher licensure, or a master's degree program in education. Applicants must complete an emphasis in either Navajo Language or Navajo Culture, taken concurrently each semester with teacher education courses. They may be specializing in elementary education, early childhood education, bilingual multicultural education, special education, educational leadership, school counseling, curriculum and instruction, library science, or science and mathematics secondary education. Students working on a second master's degree are not eligible. Financial need is not considered in the selection process.

Financial data Recipients are reimbursed for each course they complete at the rate of $250 per course for lower-division undergraduate courses or $500 for upper-division and graduate courses.

Duration 1 semester; may be renewed for undergraduate courses completed with a grade of "C" or better and for graduate courses completed with a grade of "B" or better.

Number awarded Varies each year; recently, 250 undergraduates and 225 graduate students were participating in the program.

Deadline June of each year for fall term; November of each year for winter or spring terms; April of each year for summer session.

[686]
NDPRB UNDERGRADUATE SCHOLARSHIP PROGRAM

National Dairy Promotion and Research Board
c/o Dairy Management Inc.
10255 West Higgins Road, Suite 900
Rosemont, IL 60018-5616
(847) 803-2000   Fax: (847) 803-2077
E-mail: marykateg@rosedmi.com
Web: www.dairycheckoff.com

Purpose To provide financial assistance to undergraduate students in fields related to the dairy industry.

Eligibility This program is open to sophomores, juniors, and seniors enrolled in college and university programs that emphasize dairy. Eligible majors include agricultural education, business, communications and/or public relations, economics, food science, journalism, marketing, and nutrition. Fields related to production (e.g., animal science) are not eligible. Selection is based on academic performance; interest in a career in dairy; involvement in extracurricular activities, especially those relating to dairy; and evidence of leadership ability, initiative, character, and integrity. The applicant who is judged most outstanding is awarded the James H. Loper Jr. Memorial Scholarship.

Financial data Stipends are $2,500 or $1,500.

Duration 1 year; may be renewed.

Additional information Dairy Management Inc. manages this program on behalf of the National Dairy Promotion and Research Board (NDPRB).

Number awarded 20 each year: the James H. Loper Jr. Memorial Scholarship at $2,500 and 19 other scholarships at $1,500.

Deadline May of each year.

[687]
NDTA ACADEMIC SCHOLARSHIP PROGRAM A

National Defense Transportation Association
Attn: Forum, Education and Professional Development Committee
50 South Pickett Street, Suite 220
Alexandria, VA 22304-7296
(703) 751-5011   Fax: (703) 823-8761
E-mail: info@ndtahq.com
Web: www.ndtahq.com/scholarships.htm

Purpose To provide financial assistance to college students who are members or dependents of members of the National Defense Transportation Association (NDTA) and are majoring in transportation.

Eligibility This program is open to NDTA members and dependents of members who have satisfactorily completed 45 semester hours of work at a regionally accredited college or university. Applicants must be majoring in transportation, physical distribution, logistics, or a combination of those. They must 1) provide college transcripts; 2) attach a listing of academic and other honors and awards received, extracurricular activities, and work experiences; 3) identify the courses in transportation, physical distribution, or logistics that they plan to incorporate into their degree program; and 4) submit a 300- to 500-word statement outlining their career goals and methods of attaining those goals, indicating why they should be awarded the scholarship. Financial need is not considered in the selection process.

Financial data A stipend is awarded (amount not specified).

Duration 1 year; may be renewed.

Number awarded 1 or more each year.

Deadline April of each year.

[688]
NEBRASKA BANKERS EDUCATIONAL FOUNDATION SCHOLARSHIPS

Nebraska Bankers Association
Attn: Educational Foundation
233 South 13th Street, Suite 700
P.O. Box 80008
Lincoln, NE 68501-0008
(402) 474-1555   Fax: (402) 474-2148
E-mail: karen.miller@nebankers.org
Web: www.nebankers.org/public/consumer.html

Purpose To provide financial assistance to Nebraska residents working on a degree in business at a college or university in the state.

Eligibility This program is open to residents of Nebraska who are enrolled as juniors or seniors at a college or university in the state (except for the University of Nebraska). Applicants must be working on a bachelor of science in business administration with an emphasis on finance, accounting, or economics and have a GPA of 3.0 or higher. Along with their application, they must submit an essay of 100 to 200 words on how the banking industry has impacted their community or the role they expect the banking industry to play in their future. Financial need is not considered in the selection process.

Financial data The stipend is $1,000.

Duration 1 year.

Number awarded 8 each year (including 4 designated as William B. Brandt Memorial Scholarships).

Deadline January of each year.

[689]
NEBRASKA SOCIETY OF CERTIFIED PUBLIC ACCOUNTANTS SCHOLARSHIPS

Nebraska Society of Certified Public Accountants
Attn: Foundation
635 South 14th Street, Suite 330
Lincoln, NE 68508
(402) 476-8482   Toll-free: (800) 642-6178
Fax: (402) 476-8731   E-mail: society@nescpa.org
Web: www.nescpa.org/scholarships.php

Purpose To provide financial assistance to upper-division accounting students at colleges and universities in Nebraska.

Eligibility This program is open to students who are majoring in accounting and have completed their junior year at a Nebraska college or university. Applicants must have the interest and capabilities of becoming a successful C.P.A., be planning to pursue their career in Nebraska, and be planning to take the C.P.A. examination. They must be nominated by accounting faculty members. Institutions having fifth-year accounting (150-hour) programs may also nominate up to 2 students for scholarships specifically designated for such students. Selection is based on scholarship, leadership, and character; the highest scholastic average is not necessarily required.

Financial data Stipends range from $750 to $2,500. Scholarships for fifth-year students are at least $1,500.

Duration March of each year.

Additional information This program includes the following named awards: the Arnold L. Magnuson Scholarship, the James R. Greisch Scholarship, the Delmar A. Lienemann, Sr. Scholarship, the Nancy J. Stara Scholarship, and the Irving R. Dana III Scholarship. Scholarships for fifth-year students include the Aureus Financial Scholarship (funded by Aureus Financial of Lincoln and Omaha) and the J. Edmunds Miller Scholarship.

Number awarded Varies each year; recently, 50 of these scholarships (including 16 fifth-year scholarships) were awarded.

Deadline March of each year.

[690]
NEEBC SCHOLARSHIP PROGRAM

New England Employee Benefits Council
440 Totten Pond Road
Waltham, MA 02451
(781) 684-8700   Fax: (781) 684-9200
E-mail: info@neebc.org
Web: www.neebc.org/scholar/scholar.html

Purpose To provide financial assistance to residents and students in the New England states who are working on an undergraduate or graduate degree in a field related to employee benefits.

Eligibility This program is open to full-time undergraduate and graduate students who are residents of New England or enrolled at a college in the region. Applicants must be interested in preparing for a career in such areas as the actuarial sciences; ERISA and legal aspects of employee benefits; pension design and planning; work and family issues; or corporate employee benefits, design, analysis, and management. Along with their application, they must submit an essay (up to 500 words) describing why they are interested in entering the employee benefits field and what careers within the field are of interest to them and why. Selection is based on 1) study, activities, and goals related to employee benefits; 2) school and community activities; 3) work experience; and 4) academic performance and potential.

Financial data The stipend is $5,000 per year.

Duration 1 year; may be renewed up to 3 additional years or until completion of a degree.

Number awarded 1 or more each year.

Deadline March of each year.

[691]
NEHRA FUTURE STARS IN HR SCHOLARSHIPS

Northeast Human Resources Association
Attn: Scholarship Awards
One Washington Street, Suite 101
Wellesley, MA 02481
(781) 235-2900   Fax: (781) 237-8745
E-mail: info@nehra.com
Web: www.nehra.com/about/scholarships.cfm

Purpose To provide financial assistance to undergraduate and graduate students at colleges and universities in New England who are preparing for a career in human resources.

Eligibility This program is open to full-time undergraduate and graduate students at accredited colleges and universities in New England. Applicants must have completed at least 1 course related to human resources and have a GPA of 3.0 or higher. Along with their application, they must submit 2 essays: 1) why they are interested in becoming a human resources professional; and 2) what qualities they believe are critical to the success of a human resources professional, which of those they currently possess, and how they intend to acquire the others. Selection is based on interest in becoming a human resources professional, academic success, leadership skills, and participation in non-academic activities. Applicants who are judged most outstanding receive the John D. Erdlen Scholarship Award and the Yahoo! Hotjobs Scholarship.

Financial data Stipends are $5,000, $3,000, or $2,500 per year.

Duration 1 year; may be renewed.

Additional information The sponsor is an affiliate of the Society for Human Resource Management (SHRM).

Number awarded 3 each year: 1 at $5,000 (the Yahoo! Hotjobs Scholarship), 1 at $3,000 (the John D. Erdlen Scholarship Award), and 1 at $2,500.

Deadline March of each year.

[692]
NETWORK OF EXECUTIVE WOMEN SCHOLARSHIP

Network of Executive Women
Attn: Scholarship Program
Accenture/Avanade
161 North Clark Street, 37th Floor
Chicago, IL 60601
(312) 373-5683   Fax: (312) 726-4704
E-mail: ngranger@newonline.org
Web: www.newonline.org/scholarships.cfm

Purpose To provide financial assistance to upper-division and graduate student women preparing for a career in the consumer products and retail industry.

Eligibility This program is open to women enrolled full time as juniors, seniors, or graduate students in a retail, food, or consumer packaged goods related program at a U.S. college or university. Applicants must have a GPA of 3.0 or higher. Along with their application, they must submit a 1-page essay explaining why they merit this scholarship and outlining their food, retail, and consumer packaged goods industry interests. Selection is based on that essay, a current resume, a transcript, and 2 letters of recommendation; financial need is not considered.

Financial data A stipend is awarded.

Duration 1 year.

Number awarded 1 or more each year.

Deadline February of each year.

[693]
NEW HORIZONS KATHY LETARTE SCHOLARSHIP

Tourism Cares for Tomorrow
Attn: Program Manager
585 Washington Street
Canton, MA 02021
(781) 821-5990   Fax: (781) 821-8949
E-mail: info@tourismcares.org
Web: www.tourismcares.org

Purpose To provide financial assistance to upper-division students from Michigan who are majoring in tourism.

Eligibility This program is open to residents of Michigan entering their junior year at an accredited 4-year college or university in the United States or Canada. Applicants must be working on a degree in a travel and tourism-related program and have a GPA of 3.0 or higher. Along with their application, they must submit a 2-page essay on niche marketing, with an emphasis of student markets. Financial need is not considered in the selection process.

Financial data The stipend is $1,000.

Duration 1 year.

Additional information This program was established in 2000.

Number awarded 1 each year.

Deadline March of each year.

[694]
NEW JERSEY SOCIETY OF CERTIFIED PUBLIC ACCOUNTANTS COLLEGE SCHOLARSHIP PROGRAM

New Jersey Society of Certified Public Accountants
Attn: Student Programs Coordinator
425 Eagle Rock Avenue, Suite 100
Roseland, NJ 07068-1723
(973) 226-4494, ext. 209   Fax: (973) 226-7425
E-mail: njscpa@njscpa.org
Web: www.njscpa.org

Purpose To provide financial assistance to upper-division and graduate students in New Jersey who are preparing for a career as a certified public accountant.

Eligibility This program is open to residents of New Jersey who are attending a college or university in the state. Applicants must be 1) juniors who are majoring or concentrating in accounting; or 2) graduate students entering an accounting-related program. Students may apply directly or be nominated by the accounting department chair at their college. Selection is based on academic achievement (GPA of 3.0 or higher).

Financial data The stipend is $3,000.

Duration 1 year. Each student may receive only 1 undergraduate and 1 graduate scholarship during their academic career.

Number awarded Varies each year; recently, 53 of these scholarships were awarded.

Deadline January of each year.

[695]
NEW YORK BEEF PRODUCERS' ASSOCIATION SCHOLARSHIP

New York Beef Producers' Association
Attn: Executive Secretary
3 Second Street
Camden, NY 13316
(315) 245-3386   E-mail: nybpa1@twcny.rr.com
Web: www.tjbailey.com/nybpa/youthprograms.htm

Purpose To provide financial assistance to college students from New York who are preparing for a career in the cattle industry.

Eligibility This program is open to residents of New York who are currently enrolled in an accredited 2-year or 4-year agricultural college. Applicants must be majoring in a field of study related to agriculture (e.g., animal and/or crop science, business, economics, communications, agricultural engineering) and planning a career related to the beef industry. Along with their application, they must submit an essay that covers the following: 1) their experience and interest in the beef industry; 2) their involvement in agricultural-related activities, including organizations (community, school, 4-H), events, awards, and leadership positions; 3) their future intentions and career plans as they relate to the beef industry; and 4) how they view the future of the beef industry. Selection is based primarily on involvement in the beef industry and future plans. Financial need is not considered.

Financial data The stipend is $1,000.

Duration 1 year.

Number awarded 1 each year.

Deadline December of each year.

[696]
NFIB YOUNG ENTREPRENEUR PLAN FOR THE FUTURE COMPETITION

National Federation of Independent Business
Attn: NFIB Young Entrepreneur Foundation
1201 F Street, N.W., Suite 200
Washington, DC 20004
(202) 314-2062   Toll-free: (800) NFIB-NOW
E-mail: chantel.bartlett@nfib.org
Web: www.nfib.com

Purpose To recognize and reward high school and college entrepreneurs who submit outstanding business plans.

Eligibility This competition is open to entrepreneurs currently enrolled in high school or college. Applicants must submit a business plan, up to 20 pages in length, that includes an executive summary, company background, business concept and identity, market analysis, products and services, competition (existing and potential), operations, financial planning, and market opportunity. Selection is based on the plan's innovation and creativity in the business concept; market analysis, sales, and marketing strategy; competitive analysis; operational procedures for production and distribution; management and human resource background; financial highlights; clarity portrayed as a concise and well-written plan; and market opportunity demonstrating demand and interest.

Financial data Prizes are $7,500 for first, $5,000 for second, and $2,500 for third; those funds may be used as seed money for the implementation of the business plan. In addition, college scholarships of $1,000 are awarded.

Duration The competition is held annually.

Additional information This competition, which began in 2006, is sponsored by BizFilings of Madison, Wisconsin.

Number awarded 3 prizes and 10 scholarships (2 in each region of the NFIB) are awarded each year.

Deadline May of each year.

[697]
NIB GRANT M. MACK MEMORIAL SCHOLARSHIP

American Council of the Blind
Attn: Coordinator, Scholarship Program
1155 15th Street, N.W., Suite 1004
Washington, DC 20005
(202) 467-5081   Toll-free: (800) 424-8666
Fax: (202) 467-5085   E-mail: info@acb.org
Web: www.acb.org

Purpose To provide financial assistance to students who are blind and working on an undergraduate or graduate degree in business or management.

Eligibility All legally blind persons who are majoring in business or management (undergraduate or graduate) and are U.S. citizens or resident aliens are eligible to apply. In addition to letters of recommendation and copies of academic transcripts, applications must include an autobiographical sketch. A cumulative GPA of 3.3 or higher is generally required. Selection is based on demonstrated academic record, involvement in extracurricular and civic activities, and academic objectives. The severity of the applicant's visual impairment and his/her study methods are also taken into account.

Financial data The stipend is $2,000. In addition, the winner receives a Kurzweil-1000 Reading System.

Duration 1 year.

Additional information This scholarship is sponsored by National Industries for the Blind (NIB) in honor of a dedicated leader of the American Council of the Blind. Scholarship winners are expected to be present at the council's annual conference; the council will cover all reasonable expenses connected with convention attendance.

Number awarded 1 each year.

Deadline February of each year.

[698]
NOLAN MOORE MEMORIAL EDUCATION FOUNDATION SCHOLARSHIP

Printing and Imaging Association of MidAmerica
Attn: Dodie Royals
8828 North Stemmons, Suite 505
Dallas, TX 75247
(214) 630-8871, ext. 205   Toll-free: (800) 788-2040
E-mail: dodier@piamidam.org
Web: www.piamidam.org/scholar.php

Purpose To provide financial assistance to residents of designated states who are attending college to prepare for a career in the graphic arts industry.

Eligibility This program is open to students enrolled or planning to enroll in an educational institution that offers a 2- or 4-year degree in printing technology, printing management, or related field. Applicants must be residents of Kansas, Missouri, Oklahoma, or Texas. They should be attending a school in those states, but they may go elsewhere if they can demonstrate the appropriate aptitude and industry interest. Along with their application, they must submit a 1-page statement outlining their career goals and a letter of endorsement from their faculty sponsor that reinforces their stated intention to prepare for a career in the graphic arts industry. Selection is based on interest in the industry and GPA; financial need is not considered.

Financial data The stipend is $2,500.

Duration 1 year; may be enrolled if the recipient remains enrolled full time with a GPA of 2.5 or higher.

Number awarded 1 or more each year.

Deadline February of each year.

[699]
NORTH CAROLINA CPA FOUNDATION OUTSTANDING MINORITY ACCOUNTING STUDENT SCHOLARSHIPS

North Carolina Association of Certified Public Accountants
Attn: North Carolina CPA Foundation, Inc.
3100 Gateway Centre Boulevard
P.O. Box 80188
Raleigh, NC 27623-0188
(919) 469-1040, ext. 133   Toll-free: (800) 722-2836
Fax: (919) 469-3959   E-mail: vpironio@ncacpa.org
Web: www.ncacpa.org

Purpose To provide financial assistance to minority undergraduate and graduate students majoring in accounting at colleges and universities in North Carolina.

Eligibility This program is open to North Carolina residents who have completed at least 36 semester hours, including at least 4 accounting courses, at a college or university in the state. Applicants must be members of a minority group, defined as Black, Native American/Alaskan Native, Asian or Pacific Islander, or Hispanic. They must be enrolled full time in an academic program leading to a degree in accounting or its equivalent and have a GPA of 3.0 or higher. Along with their application, they must submit a 1,000-word essay on 1) the importance of minority C.P.A.s in society today, or 2) how minority C.P.A.s can have a positive impact on increasing the financial literacy of North Carolina citizens. Selection is based on GPA (30%), extracurricular activities (20%), essay content (25%), and essay grammar (25%).

Financial data Stipends are $3,000 or $1,500.

Duration 1 year; may be renewed up to 2 additional years.

Number awarded 3 each year: 1 at $3,000 and 2 at $1,500.

Deadline September of each year.

[700]
NORTH CAROLINA CPA FOUNDATION SCHOLARSHIPS

North Carolina Association of Certified Public Accountants
Attn: North Carolina CPA Foundation, Inc.
3100 Gateway Centre Boulevard
P.O. Box 80188
Raleigh, NC 27623-0188
(919) 469-1040, ext. 133   Toll-free: (800) 722-2836
Fax: (919) 469-3959   E-mail: vpironio@ncacpa.org
Web: www.ncacpa.org

Purpose To provide financial assistance to students majoring in accounting at colleges and universities in North Carolina.

Eligibility This program is open to North Carolina residents majoring in accounting at a college or university in the state. Applicants must have completed at least 36 semester hours, including at least 1 college or university-level accounting course, and have a GPA of 3.0 or higher. They must be sponsored by an accounting faculty member. Along with their application, they must submit a 1,000-word essay on the role C.P.A.s play in society and whether that role should change, given the events of the past few years. Selection is based on GPA (20%), extracurricular activities (20%), essay content (30%), and essay grammar (30%).

Financial data Stipends range from $1,000 to $5,000.

Duration 1 year; may be renewed up to 2 additional years.

Number awarded Varies each year. Recently, 19 of these scholarships were awarded: 1 at $5,000, 1 at $4,000, 1 at $3,000, 1 at $2,000, and 15 at $1,000.

Deadline February of each year.

[701]
NORTH CAROLINA TEACHER ASSISTANT SCHOLARSHIP FUND

North Carolina State Education Assistance Authority
Attn: Teacher Assistant Scholarship Fund
P.O. Box 13663
Research Triangle Park, NC 27709-3663
(919) 549-8614, ext. 313
Toll-free: (800) 700-1775, ext. 313
Fax: (919) 248-4687   E-mail: ralbritton@ncseaa.edu
Web: www.ncseaa.edu/TAS.htm

Purpose To provide financial assistance to public school teacher assistants in North Carolina who are interested in working on a college degree to become a teacher.

Eligibility This program is open to teacher assistants employed full time in North Carolina public schools. Applicants must be enrolled in at least 6 semester hours pursuing teacher licensure at an accredited 2-year or 4-year college in North Carolina with a teacher education program. They must have a GPA of 3.0 or higher and remain employed as a teacher assistant while attending college part time.

Financial data Students at 4-year institutions receive $1,200 per term, up to an annual maximum of $3,600. Students at 2-year institutions receive $600 per term, up to an annual maximum of $1,800. The maximum amount that a student can receive over time through this program is $25,200.

Duration 1 year; may be renewed if the recipient completes at least 12 semester hours with a GPA of 2.8 or higher.

Number awarded Varies each year; recently, a total of 222 students were receiving $524,900 in support through this program.

Deadline March of each year.

[702]
NTA STATE AND PROVINCIAL SCHOLARSHIP

Tourism Cares for Tomorrow
Attn: Program Manager
585 Washington Street
Canton, MA 02021
(781) 821-5990   Fax: (781) 821-8949
E-mail: info@tourismcares.org
Web: www.tourismcares.org

Purpose To provide financial assistance to upper-division students who are majoring in tourism.

Eligibility This program is open to students entering their junior or senior year at an accredited 4-year college or university in the United States or Canada. Applicants must be working on a degree in a travel and tourism-related program and have a GPA of 3.0 or higher. Along with their application, they must submit a 2-page essay on why they have chosen to prepare for a career in the hospitality and tourism industry. Financial need is not considered in the selection process.

Financial data The stipend is $1,000.

Duration 1 year.

Additional information This program is sponsored by the National Tour Association (NTA).

Number awarded 1 each year.

Deadline March of each year.

[703]
OHIO SOCIETY OF CPAS COLLEGE SCHOLARSHIP PROGRAM

Ohio Society of CPAs
535 Metro Place
P.O. Box 1810
Dublin, OH 43017-7810
(614) 764-2727   Toll-free: (800) 686-2727, ext. 344
Fax: (614) 764-5880   E-mail: oscpa@ohio-cpa.com
Web: www.ohioscpa.com

Purpose To provide financial assistance to undergraduate and graduate students at Ohio colleges and universities who are majoring in accounting.

Eligibility This program is open to undergraduate and graduate students majoring in accounting at Ohio colleges and universities who are student affiliate members of the Ohio Society of CPAs. Applicants must have a GPA of 3.0 or higher overall and in accounting and have completed intermediate financial accounting or a comparable course with a grade of 3.0 or higher. Along with their application, they must submit official transcripts; a current resume describing work experience, honors, awards, involvement in clubs and organizations, and community involvement; and a letter describing why they should be awarded a scholarship. Based on that information, winners are selected for each region of the Ohio Society of CPAs. Regional winners are then invited to interviews on scholarship day at the offices of the society. The student who demonstrates the best knowledge of the issues facing the accounting profession receives an additional scholarship.

Financial data Regional winners receive $1,000 scholarships. The winner who demonstrates the best knowledge of the issues facing the accounting profession during the interviews receives an additional $3,000.

Duration The awards are presented annually.

Number awarded 11 regional winners are selected each year; 1 of them is selected to receive the additional scholarship.

Deadline November of each year.

[704]
OKLAHOMA 4-H ENTREPRENEURSHIP SCHOLARSHIP

Oklahoma 4-H
c/o Oklahoma State University
Oklahoma Cooperative Extension Service
205 4-H Youth Development Building
Stillwater, OK 74078-6063
(405) 744-5390   Fax: (405) 744-6522
Web: oklahoma4h.okstate.edu

Purpose To provide financial assistance for college to high school seniors in Oklahoma who have participated in 4-H entrepreneurship activities.

Eligibility This program is open to college students and seniors graduating from high schools in Oklahoma who have participated in 4-H entrepreneurship activities. Applicants must submit 3 pages of pictures or other supporting information on their entrepreneurship activities, 2 copies of the 4-H news information sheet, transcripts, and a letter of recommendation from their school advisor. Selection is based on educational plans (5 points), 4-H leadership and community service experiences (15 points), 4-H accomplishments (10 points), goals and objectives for their business enterprise (15 points), marketing (10 points), management (15 points), success of business (20 points), and future plans (10 points).

Financial data The stipend is $1,000.

Duration 1 year.

Number awarded 1 each year.

Deadline April of each year.

[705]
OLIVE W. GARVEY STUDENT FELLOWSHIPS

Independent Institute
Attn: Academic Affairs Director
100 Swan Way
Oakland, CA 94621-1428
(510) 632-1366, ext. 117   Fax: (510) 568-6040
E-mail: cclose@independent.org
Web: www.independent.org/students/garvey

Purpose To recognize and reward undergraduate and graduate students who submit outstanding essays on a topic related to personal liberty.

Eligibility This competition is open to undergraduate and graduate students from all nations who are younger than 35 years of age. Applicants must submit an essay, from 1,500 to 3,000 words in length, on a topic that changes but relates to the meaning of economic and personal liberty. Recently, students were invited to comment on a quotation from F.A. Hayek: "The great aim of the struggle for liberty has been equality before the law." Selection is based on clarity, rigor, and eloquence.

Financial data Prizes are $2,500 for first, $1,500 for second, and $1,000 for third.

Duration The competition, which began in 1974, is currently held biennially, in odd-numbered years.

Number awarded 3 every other year.

Deadline April of each odd-numbered year.

[706]
OSCPA EDUCATIONAL FOUNDATION COLLEGE SCHOLARSHIPS

Oregon Society of CPAs
Attn: OSCPA Educational Foundation
10206 S.W. Laurel Street
P.O. Box 4555
Beaverton, OR 97076-4555
(503) 641-7200   Toll-free: (800) 255-1470, ext. 29
Fax: (503) 626-2942   E-mail: oscpa@orcpa.org
Web: www.orcpa.org/scholarships.html

Purpose To provide financial assistance to currently-enrolled undergraduate and graduate students in Oregon who are working on a degree in accounting.

Eligibility This program is open to Oregon college and university students who are working full time on an undergraduate or master's degree in accounting. Applicants must have a GPA of 3.2 or higher in accounting/business classes and overall. Along with their application, they must submit 3 letters of recommendation and a recent transcript. Selection is based on scholastic ability and interest in the accounting profession.

Financial data For graduate students and undergraduates enrolled in or transferring to 4-year colleges and universities, stipends range from $1,000 to $3,000. For students enrolled in community colleges, the stipend is $500.

Duration 1 year.

Number awarded Varies each year.

Deadline February of each year.

[707]
PAT ROBERTS INTELLIGENCE SCHOLARS PROGRAM FOR GLOBAL NETWORK ANALYSTS

National Security Agency
Attn: Office of Recruitment and Staffing (Roberts)
9800 Savage Road, Suite 6779
P.O. Box 1661, Suite 6779
Fort Meade, MD 20755-6779
(410) 854-4725   Toll-free: (866) 672-4473
Web: www.nsa.gov/careers/students_4.cfm

Purpose To provide financial assistance and work experience to college sophomores and juniors interested in preparing for a career with the National Security Agency (NSA) as a global network analyst.

Eligibility This program is open to college sophomores and juniors whose academic program includes 1 of the following areas of emphasis: 1) technical studies (computer science major with a minor in political science or international relations); 2) topical studies (terrorism, proliferation or related sciences, international banking and finance, or telecommunications and information systems networks); or 3) disciplines (technical intelligence analysis, information assurance, networks, and telecommunications). Applicants must be enrolled full time with a GPA of 3.0 or higher. Along with their application, they must submit a 1-page essay describing how the proposed program of study will improve their ability to analyze information and to think and write critically. U.S. citizenship and eligibility to obtain a high-level security clearance are required.

Financial data The stipend is $25,000 per year. During the summer after application, students participate in a Global Network Analysis internship. After graduation, they have an employment obligation to NSA equal to 1.5 times the length of educational support provided.

Duration 1 year; may be renewed 1 additional year. The summer internship program is for 12 weeks.

Additional information After graduation, participants enter NSA's Global Network Analysis Internship Program as a full-time employee.

Number awarded Varies each year.

Deadline October of each year.

[708]
PAT ROBERTS INTELLIGENCE SCHOLARS PROGRAM FOR INTELLIGENCE ANALYSTS

National Security Agency
Attn: Office of Recruitment and Staffing (Roberts)
9800 Savage Road, Suite 6779
P.O. Box 1661, Suite 6779
Fort Meade, MD 20755-6779
(410) 854-4725   Toll-free: (866) 672-4473
Web: www.nsa.gov/careers/students_4.cfm

Purpose To provide financial assistance to college juniors interested in preparing for a career with the National Security Agency (NSA) as an intelligence analyst.

Eligibility This program is open to college juniors whose academic program includes 1 of the following areas of emphasis: 1) regional studies (Middle East or south, east, or central Asia); 2) topical studies (terrorism, proliferation or related sciences, international banking and finance, or telecommunications and information systems networks); or 3) disciplines (intelligence analysis, philosophy, or international relations; familiarity with foreign languages, particularly Arabic, Chinese, Dari, Farsi, Hindi, Korean, Pashto, Urdu, or a central Asian language is desirable; highly qualified applicants studying social network analysis, library science, or geographic information systems may also be considered). Applicants must be enrolled full time with a GPA of 3.0 or higher. Along with their application, they must submit a 1-page essay describing how the proposed program of study will improve their ability to analyze information and to think and write critically. U.S. citizenship and eligibility to obtain a high-level security clearance are required.

Financial data The stipend is $25,000 per year. After graduation, recipients have an employment obligation to NSA equal to 1.5 times the length of educational support provided.

Duration 1 year (the senior year of college).

Additional information After graduation, participants enter NSA's Intelligence Analysis Development Program as a full-time employee.

Number awarded Varies each year.

Deadline October of each year.

[709]
PENNSYLVANIA AFL-CIO SCHOLARSHIP ESSAY CONTEST

Pennsylvania AFL-CIO
Attn: Director of Education
231 State Street, Seventh Floor
Harrisburg, PA 17101-1110
(717) 231-2843   Toll-free: (800) 242-2770
Fax: (717) 238-8541
Web: www.paaflcio.org

Purpose To recognize and reward high school and college students in Pennsylvania who submit outstanding essays on a labor topic.

Eligibility This program is open to 1) graduating high school seniors at high schools in Pennsylvania; 2) students currently enrolled in accredited postsecondary school programs in the state; and 3) affiliated union members attending an accredited institution. Applicants must submit essays on topics that change annually but relate to labor unions. Recently, high school students were to write a descriptive essay on the life of a union member (parent, sibling, grandparent, etc.) and why union membership is important to them. College students were to write on the effects of the global economy on working families. Union members were to write on the recent presidential election and its import on working families. In each competition, all essays must be 1,500 words in length and include 3 references, of which at least 1 must be a labor organization.

Financial data First prize is $2,000, second $1,000, and third $500.

Duration The competition is held annually.

Number awarded 9 each year: 3 in each of the 3 categories.

Deadline January of each year.

[710]
PETER K. NEW STUDENT PRIZE COMPETITION

Society for Applied Anthropology
P.O. Box 2436
Oklahoma City, OK 73101-2436
(405) 843-5113   Fax: (405) 843-8553
E-mail: info@sfaa.net
Web: www.sfaa.net/pknew/pknew.html

Purpose To recognize and reward the best student research papers in applied social, health, or behavioral sciences.

Eligibility This competition is open to currently-enrolled undergraduate and graduate students in the applied social, health, and behavioral sciences. Applicants must not have already earned a doctoral degree (e.g., a person with an M.D. degree who is now registered as a student in a Ph.D. program is not eligible). Eligible students are invited to submit a manuscript that reports on research which, in large measure, has not been previously published. Research should be in the domain of health care or human services (broadly defined). The competition is limited to manuscripts that have a single author; multiple-authored papers are not eligible. The paper should be double spaced and must be less than 45 pages in length, including footnotes, tables, and appendices. Selection is based on originality, research design/method, clarity of analysis and presentation, and contribution to the social or behavioral sciences.

Financial data The winner receives $1,000 plus a $350 travel allowance to partially offset the cost of transportation and lodging at the society's annual meeting.

Duration The competition is held annually.

Additional information The winning paper is published in the society's journal, *Human Organization*. Applicants who transmit their manuscripts by fax must pay a fee for duplication. Manuscripts may not be submitted electronically. The winner must attend the society's annual meeting to present the paper.

Number awarded 2 each year.

Deadline December of each year.

[711]
PHI CHI THETA SCHOLARSHIPS

Phi Chi Theta
Attn: Foundation
1508 East Beltline Road, Suite 104
Carrollton, TX 75006
(972) 245-7202   E-mail: PCTEdScholarship@aol.com
Web: www.phichitheta.org

Purpose To provide financial assistance to members of Phi Chi Theta (an honorary society for women in business-related fields) who are working on a degree in business administration or economics.

Eligibility This program is open to members who have completed at least 1 semester or 2 quarters of full-time study in business administration or economics. Applicants must be enrolled at an approved college or university in the United States in a bachelor's, master's, or doctoral degree program. Along with their application, they must submit an essay on where they see themselves in 3 and 5 years and a statement of career goals and philosophy. Selection is based on the essay and statement, Phi Chi Theta achievements and contributions; scholastic achievement; school and community achievements and activities; a faculty letter of recommendation; and a Phi Chi Theta member letter of recommendation.

Financial data The stipend is $1,000 or $500.

Duration 1 year.

Additional information Phi Chi Theta is a national honorary society for women in business administration and economics. Information is also available from Mary Ellen Lewis, 1886 South Poplar Street, Denver, CO 80224-2272, (303) 757-2535. This program includes the following named awards: the Anna E. Hall Memorial Scholarship (established in 1989), the Helen D. Snow Memorial Scholarship, the Irene Meyer Memorial Scholarship, the Lester F. Richardson Memorial Scholarship (established in 2005), and the Naomi L. Satterfield Scholarship (established in 2001).

Number awarded Varies each year. Recently, 4 of these scholarships were awarded: 1 at $1,000 and 3 at $500.

Deadline April of each year.

[712]
PHI DELTA KAPPA INTERNATIONAL SCHOLARSHIP GRANTS FOR PROSPECTIVE EDUCATORS

Phi Delta Kappa International
Attn: Scholarship Programs
408 North Union Street
P.O. Box 789
Bloomington, IN 47402-0789
(812) 339-1156   Toll-free: (800) 766-1156
Fax: (812) 339-0018   E-mail: scholarships@pdkintl.org
Web: www.pdkintl.org/awards/pros_ed.htm

Purpose To provide financial assistance to high school seniors and undergraduate members of Phi Delta Kappa (PDK) who are interested in becoming teachers.

Eligibility This program is open to graduating high school seniors and current college undergraduates who are PDK members. Applicants must be interested in preparing for a teaching career. They must submit a 500-word essay on a topic related to education that changes annually; recently, they were invited to explain why they have selected education as their career choice, the skills and attributes that will make them a successful educator, and how they plan to use their education degree to make a difference in the lives of their students. Selection is based on the essay, academic standing, letters of recommendation, and leadership activities; financial need is not considered.

Financial data Stipends range from $200 to $2,000. Funds are paid directly to the recipient's college or university to be applied to the cost of tuition and fees.

Duration 1 year; some of the scholarships may be renewed up to 3 additional years.

Additional information This program contains a number of named scholarships that are offered as funding permits. Those include the Edna Wilhelmina Snell Nichols Scholarship, the Wilmer Bugher Endowed Scholarship, the Meissner Family Fund Scholarship, the Charlie Q. Coffman Endowed Scholarship, the Sara J. Ingrassia Memorial Scholarship, the R. Gerald Melton Scholarship, the Edward J. Milliken Scholarship, and the Edith Renee Hill Memorial Scholarship.

Number awarded Varies each year. Recently, 49 of these scholarships were awarded: 1 at $2,000, 1 at $1,500, 1 at $1,250, 26 at $1,000, 1 at $800, 1 at $750, 2 at $600, 11 at $500, and 5 at $200.

Deadline January of each year.

[713]
PHI UPSILON SCHOLARSHIPS

Phi Upsilon Omicron
Attn: Educational Foundation
P.O. Box 329
Fairmont, WV 26555-0329
(304) 368-0612   E-mail: rickards@mountain.net
Web: phiu.unl.edu/webdoc3.htm

Purpose To provide financial assistance to undergraduate student members of Phi Upsilon Omicron, a national honor society in family and consumer sciences.

Eligibility This program is open to members of the society who are working on a bachelor's degree in family and consumer sciences or a related area. Selection is based on scholastic record, participation in society and other collegiate activities, a statement of professional aims and goals, professional services, and recommendations.
Financial data The stipend is $1,000.
Duration 1 year.
Additional information There are a number of named scholarships, including the Parnitzke/Clarke Scholarship, the Geraldine Clewell Scholarship, the Nell Bryant Robinson Scholarship, and the Treva C. Kintner Scholarship.
Number awarded 1 each year.
Deadline January of each year.

[714]
PICPA STUDENT WRITING COMPETITION
Pennsylvania Institute of Certified Public Accountants
Attn: Careers in Accounting Team
1650 Arch Street, 17th Floor
Philadelphia, PA 19103-2099
(215) 496-9272   Toll-free: (888) CPA-2001 (within PA)
Fax: (215) 496-9212   E-mail: schools@picpa.org
Web: www.cpazone.org/events/swc/index.asp

Purpose To recognize and reward outstanding essays written by students in Pennsylvania on an accounting topic that changes annually.
Eligibility This competition is open to 1) accounting and business majors at Pennsylvania colleges and universities, and 2) Pennsylvania residents who attend college out-of-state. Candidates are invited to submit an essay on an issue (changes annually) that affects the accounting profession. Recently, the topic was: "Assessing the Impact of Frequent Financial Information Restatements." Essays should be from 1,000 to 1,500 words in length and include a 50- to 75-word abstract. Selection is based on content, method of presentation, and writing style.
Financial data First place is $2,000, second $1,200, and third $800. The top 3 schools receive, respectively, $1,000, $600, and $400.
Duration The competition is held annually.
Additional information The first-place manuscript is published in the fall issue of the *Pennsylvania CPA Journal*.
Number awarded 3 each year.
Deadline April of each year.

[715]
PSSC LEGACY FUND SCHOLARSHIP
Society of Satellite Professionals International
Attn: Scholarship Program
New York Information Technology Center
55 Broad Street, 14th Floor
New York, NY 10004
(212) 809-5199   Fax: (212) 825-0075
E-mail: sspi@sspi.org
Web: www.sspi.org

Purpose To provide financial assistance to student members of the Society of Satellite Professionals International (SSPI) who are interested in working on an undergraduate or graduate degree in international satellite applications and/or distance education.
Eligibility This program is open to SSPI members who are high school seniors, college undergraduates, or graduate students interested in preparing for a career in satellite technologies, policies, or applications. Applicants must be interested in majoring in international satellite applications and/or distance education. They may be from any country. Selection is based on academic and leadership achievement; commitment to pursue educational and career opportunities in the satellite industry or a field making direct use of satellite technology; potential for significant contribution to that industry; and a scientific, engineering, research, business or creative submission. Financial need is not considered.
Financial data The stipend is $2,500.
Duration 1 year.
Number awarded 1 each year.
Deadline Preliminary applications must be submitted by February of each year.

[716]
PUBLIC SERVICE SCHOLARSHIPS
Public Employees Roundtable
P.O. Box 75248
Washington, DC 20013-5248
(202) 927-4926   Fax: (202) 927-4920
E-mail: info@theroundtable.org
Web: www.theroundtable.org/23/pssp.html

Purpose To provide financial assistance to undergraduate and graduate students preparing for a career in government service.
Eligibility This program is open to full-time undergraduates and graduate students who are preparing for a career in government service at the local, state, or federal level. Applicants must have completed at least 1 year of college with a GPA of 3.5 or higher. Selection is based on merit. Preference is given to students with prior public service or volunteer experience.
Financial data The stipend is $1,000 (or $500 for part-time graduate students).
Duration 1 year; nonrenewable.
Additional information This program began in 1986. Requests for applications must be accompanied by a self-addressed stamped envelope.
Number awarded 8 to 10 each year.
Deadline May of each year.

[717]
REDI-TAG CORPORATION SCHOLARSHIP
American Health Information Management Association
Attn: Foundation of Research and Education
233 North Michigan Avenue, Suite 2150
Chicago, IL 60601-5806
(312) 233-1131   Fax: (312) 233-1431
E-mail: fore@ahima.org
Web: www.ahima.org/fore/student/programs.asp

Purpose To provide financial assistance to members of the American Health Information Management Association (AHIMA) who are single parents interested in working on an undergraduate or graduate degree in health information administration or technology.

Eligibility This program is open to AHIMA members who are single parents enrolled in a health information administration or health information technology program accredited by the Commission on Accreditation of Allied Health Education Programs. Applicants must be working on an undergraduate or graduate degree on at least a half-time basis and have a GPA of 3.0 or higher. U.S. citizenship is required. Selection is based (in order of importance) on GPA and academic achievement, volunteer and work experience, commitment to the health information management profession, suitability to the health information management profession, quality and suitability of references provided, and clarity of application.

Financial data The stipend ranges from $1,000 to $5,000.

Duration 1 year; nonrenewable.

Additional information Funding for this program is provided by the Redi-Tag Corporation.

Number awarded 1 each year.

Deadline April of each year.

[718] RENE CAMPBELL MEMORIAL SCHOLARSHIP

Tourism Cares for Tomorrow
Attn: Program Manager
585 Washington Street
Canton, MA 02021
(781) 821-5990   Fax: (781) 821-8949
E-mail: info@tourismcares.org
Web: www.tourismcares.org

Purpose To provide financial assistance to upper-division students from North Carolina who are majoring in tourism.

Eligibility This program is open to residents of North Carolina entering their junior or senior year at an accredited 4-year college or university in the United States or Canada. Applicants must be working on a degree in a travel and tourism-related program and have a GPA of 3.0 or higher. Along with their application, they must submit a resume, a letter of recommendation, and a copy of their transcript. Financial need is not considered in the selection process.

Financial data The stipend is $1,000.

Duration 1 year.

Number awarded 1 each year.

Deadline March of each year.

[719] RICHARD B. COMBS HOSPITALITY SCHOLARSHIP

Connecticut Commission on Culture and Tourism
Attn: Tourism Division
505 Hudson Street, Second Floor
Hartford, CT 06106
(860) 270-8089   Fax: (860) 270-8077
E-mail: joyce.fredericks@po.state.ct.us
Web: www.tourism.state.ct.us/tourism.asp

Purpose To provide financial assistance to high school, undergraduate, and graduate students from Connecticut who are interested in preparing for a career in the hospitality industry.

Eligibility This program is open to residents of Connecticut who are high school seniors, high school graduates who have not yet enrolled in college, or enrolled undergraduate or graduate students at an accredited college or university. Applicants must be preparing for a career in the hospitality industry. Along with their application, they must submit an essay on a topic about hospitality as it relates to Connecticut tourism, 2 letters of recommendation, a current transcript, a personal letter of intent explaining how this scholarship will help them to achieve their academic goals, and a personal resume. Selection is based on personal achievement and demonstrated interest in the hospitality industry.

Financial data The stipend is $1,000.

Duration 1 year.

Number awarded 1 each year.

Deadline September of each year.

[720] RICHARD G. MUNSELL MEMORIAL SCHOLARSHIP

California Planning Roundtable
c/o M. Thomas Jacobson, President
Sonoma State University
Department of Environmental Studies and Planning
Rohnert Park, CA 94928
(707) 664-3145   Fax: (707) 664-4202
E-mail: tom.jacobson@sonoma.edu
Web: www.cproundtable.org

Purpose To recognize and reward outstanding essays on urban planning by undergraduate and graduate students in planning at universities in California.

Eligibility This program is open to full-time undergraduate and graduate students in planning or urban studies at universities in California. Applicants must submit an essay of 1,500 to 2,000 words on a topic that changes every year but relates to planning.

Financial data The award is a $1,000 scholarship.

Duration The awards are presented annually.

Additional information The winning essays may be published in *California Planner* and/or posted on the California Planning Roundtable's web site.

Number awarded 2 each year: 1 to an undergraduate and 1 to a graduate student.

[721] RICHARD P. COVERT, PH.D., FHIMSS SCHOLARSHIP

Healthcare Information and Management Systems Society
Attn: HIMSS Foundation Scholarship Program Coordinator
230 East Ohio Street, Suite 500
Chicago, IL 60611-3270
(312) 664-HIMSS   Fax: (312) 664-6143
E-mail: foundation@himss.org
Web: www.himss.org/ASP/scholarship_ms.asp

Purpose To provide financial assistance to student members of the Healthcare Information and Management Systems Society (HIMSS) who are working on an undergraduate or graduate degree in management engineering.

Eligibility This program is open to student members of the society, although an application for membership, including dues, may accompany the scholarship application. Applicants must be upper-division or graduate students working on a degree in management engineering. Selection is based on academic achievement and demonstration of leadership potential, including communication skills and participation in society activity.
Financial data The stipend is $5,000. The award includes an all-expense paid trip to the annual HIMSS conference and exhibition.
Duration 1 year.
Additional information This program was established in 2004.
Number awarded 1 each year.
Deadline October of each year.

[722]
RICHARD PODLESAK MEMORIAL SCHOLARSHIP
Association of Certified Fraud Examiners-Heartland Chapter
Attn: Scholarships Program Coordinator
P.O. Box 460726
Papillion, NE 68046
(402) 563-5936   Fax: (402) 563-5380
E-mail: President@HeartlandCFE.com
Web: www.heartlandcfe.com

Purpose To provide financial assistance to undergraduate and graduate students in Iowa, Nebraska, and South Dakota who are majoring in fields related to detecting, deterring, and preventing fraud.
Eligibility This program is open to full-time undergraduates and part-time graduate students at colleges and universities in Iowa, Nebraska, and South Dakota. Applicants must be majoring in accounting, business, criminal justice, or other fields related to detecting, deterring, and preventing fraud and white-collar crime. Along with their application, they must submit a brief essay on why they desire to receive the scholarship and how fraud awareness will enhance their professional career. Selection is based on the essay, academic achievement, letters of recommendation, and an interview.
Financial data Stipends range from $500 to $1,000.
Duration 1 year.
Number awarded 1 or more each year.
Deadline November of each year.

[723]
RITA LOWE COLLEGE SCHOLARSHIPS
Washington State Mathematics Council
c/o Pat Reistroffer, Scholarship Chair
146 Scenic View Drive
Longview, WA 98632
(360) 636-5125   E-mail: preistrof@aol.com
Web: www.wsmc.net/ritalowe

Purpose To provide financial assistance to students majoring in mathematics education at colleges and universities in Washington.
Eligibility This program is open to students currently attending a college or university in Washington and majoring in mathematics education. Applicants must be preparing for teaching certification in order to become a professional educator teaching mathematics at the elementary or secondary level. They must submit a transcript (from the ninth grade to the date of application), a 300-word statement on their experience with and interest in mathematics, and 2 letters of recommendation. Selection is based on academic achievement, demonstrated intent to become a mathematics educator, character, academic potential, and leadership potential.
Financial data The stipend is $1,000 per year.
Duration 1 year.
Number awarded 2 each year.
Deadline April of each year.

[724]
RITCHIE-JENNINGS MEMORIAL SCHOLARSHIPS PROGRAM
Association of Certified Fraud Examiners
Attn: Scholarship Program
The Gregor Building
716 West Avenue
Austin, TX 78701-2727
(512) 478-9070   Toll-free: (800) 245-3321
Fax: (512) 478-9297   E-mail: scholarships@ACFE.com
Web: www.acfe.com/Membership/rjennings.asp

Purpose To provide financial assistance to undergraduate and graduate students working on an accounting or criminal justice degree.
Eligibility This program is open to students working full time on an undergraduate or graduate degree in accounting or criminal justice at a 4-year college or university in any country. Applicants must submit an essay of 250 to 500 words on why they deserve the award and how fraud awareness will affect their professional career development. Selection is based on the essay, academic achievement, and 3 letters of recommendation (including at least 1 from a certified fraud examiner for students in Canada and the United States or 1 from a major professor for students from outside North America).
Financial data The stipend is $1,000. Funds are paid directly to the student's university.
Duration 1 year.
Additional information This program was established in 1995 and given its current name in 1998.
Number awarded 30 each year.
Deadline April of each year.

SOCIAL SCIENCES

[725]
RMEL FOUNDATION SCHOLARSHIPS
Rocky Mountain Electrical League
Attn: RMEL Foundation
2170 South Parker Road, Suite 225
Denver, CO 80231
(303) 695-0089   Fax: (303) 695-0704
E-mail: edblum@rmel.org
Web: www.rmel.org

Purpose To provide financial assistance to students sponsored by a member of the Rocky Mountain Electrical League (RMEL) who wish to study selected fields in college in order to prepare for a career in the electric energy industry.

Eligibility This program is open to high school seniors, high school graduates, and college undergraduates who have an RMEL-member company as a sponsor. Applicants must be working on or planning to work on 1) an electric industry position certificate or associate degree, or 2) a full-time undergraduate degree. Their field of study must be engineering; business; information systems; plant, line, or distribution technology; line worker; or other program related to a career in the electric energy industry. U.S. citizenship is required. Selection is based on goals and aspirations in the electric energy industry, motivation to succeed, service to community and school, and academic ability.

Financial data The stipend is $1,000.

Duration 1 year.

Additional information The RMEL serves 17 states: Arizona, Colorado, Idaho, Iowa, Kansas, Minnesota, Missouri, Montana, Nebraska, Nevada, New Mexico, North Dakota, Oklahoma, South Dakota, Texas, Utah, and Wyoming.

Number awarded Varies each year; recently, 5 of these scholarships were awarded.

Deadline March of each year.

[726]
ROB BRANHAM SCHOLARSHIP
Advertising Club of Connecticut
95 West Street
Rocky Hill, CT 06067
(860) 721-7400   Fax: (860) 721-7406
E-mail: adclubct@snet.net
Web: www.adclubct.com/scholarship

Purpose To provide financial assistance to residents of Connecticut interested in attending college to study fields related to advertising.

Eligibility This program is open to Connecticut residents entering or attending an accredited university or technical/trade school. Applicants must be interested in studying advertising, marketing, broadcast media, or print production. Along with their application, they must submit a 500-word essay on their interest in advertising, marketing, broadcast media, and/or print production; the occupation they propose to pursue after graduating; their long-term goals; and how they plan to achieve those. They must be sponsored by a member of the Advertising Club of Connecticut. Selection is based on the essay, academic achievement, volunteer activities, work experience, and honors and scholarships. Financial need is not considered.

Financial data The stipend is $1,000.

Duration 1 year.

Number awarded Varies each year; recently, 2 of these scholarships were awarded.

Deadline March of each year.

[727]
ROBERT J. DORAN SCHOLARSHIP
International Association of Arson Investigators
Attn: Educational Foundation
12772 Boenker Road
St. Louis, MO 63044
(314) 739-4224   Fax: (314) 739-4219
E-mail: jimwhitaker@firearson.com
Web: www.firearson.com/ef/jwscholar/index.asp

Purpose To provide financial assistance to the members and dependents or nominees of members of the International Association of Arson Investigators (IAAI) who are interested in preparing for a career in fire and arson investigation.

Eligibility This program is open to association members and their immediate families who are enrolled or planning to enroll at an accredited 2- or 4-year college or university that offers course work in fire science, law enforcement, or fire and arson investigation. Also eligible are nonmembers who are recommended and sponsored by association members in good standing. Applicants must submit transcripts and an essay of 500 words or less providing background information and their future plans in police or fire sciences. Financial need is not considered.

Financial data The stipend is $1,000.

Duration 1 year.

Additional information This scholarship was first awarded in 2006.

Number awarded 1 each year.

Deadline February of each year.

[728]
ROSA L. PARKS SCHOLARSHIPS
Conference of Minority Transportation Officials
Attn: National Scholarship Program
818 18th Street, N.W., Suite 850
Washington, DC 20006
(202) 530-0551   Fax: (202) 530-0617
Web: www.comto.org/scholarship.htm

Purpose To provide financial assistance for college to children of members of the Conference of Minority Transportation Officials (COMTO) and to other students working on a bachelor's or master's degree in transportation.

Eligibility This program is open to 1) college-bound high school seniors whose parent has been a COMTO member for at least 1 year; 2) undergraduates who have completed at least 60 semester credit hours in a transportation discipline; and 3) students working on a master's degree in transportation who have completed at least 15 credits. Applicants must have a GPA of 3.0 or higher. Along with their application, they must submit a cover letter with a 500-word statement of career goals. Financial need is not considered in the selection process. U.S. citizenship is required.

Financial data The stipend is $4,500. Funds are paid directly to the recipient's college or university.
Duration 1 year.
Additional information COMTO was established in 1971 to promote, strengthen, and expand the roles of minorities in all aspects of transportation. Recipients are expected to attend the COMTO National Scholarship Luncheon.
Number awarded 2 each year.
Deadline April of each year.

[729]
ROY & HARRIET ROBINSON SCHOLARSHIP

Professional Independent Insurance Agents of Illinois
Attn: College Scholarship Program
4360 Wabash Avenue
Springfield, IL 62711-7009
(217) 793-6660   Toll-free: (800) 628-6436
Fax: (217) 793-6744   E-mail: info@piiai.org
Web: www.piiai.org/youngagents/scholarship.htm

Purpose To provide financial assistance to upper-division students from Illinois who are majoring in business and have an interest in insurance.
Eligibility This program is open to residents of Illinois who are full-time juniors or seniors in college. Applicants must be enrolled in a business degree program and have an interest in insurance. They must have a letter of recommendation from a current or retired member of the Professional Independent Insurance Agents of Illinois. Along with their application, they must submit an essay (500 words or less) on the contribution the insurance industry makes to society. Financial need is not considered in the selection process.
Financial data The stipend is $1,000, payable in 2 equal installments. Funds are paid directly to the recipient's school.
Duration 1 year.
Number awarded 1 each year.
Deadline June of each year.

[730]
RUDOLPH DILLMAN MEMORIAL SCHOLARSHIP

American Foundation for the Blind
Attn: Scholarship Committee
11 Penn Plaza, Suite 300
New York, NY 10001
(212) 502-7661   Toll-free: (800) AFB-LINE
Fax: (212) 502-7771   TDD: (212) 502-7662
E-mail: afbinfo@afb.net
Web: www.afb.org/scholarships.asp

Purpose To provide financial assistance to legally blind undergraduate or graduate students studying in the field of rehabilitation and/or education of visually impaired and blind persons.
Eligibility Applicants must be able to submit evidence of legal blindness, U.S. citizenship, and acceptance in an accredited undergraduate or graduate training program within the broad field of rehabilitation and/or education of blind and visually impaired persons. Along with their application, they must submit an essay that includes the field of study they are pursuing and why they have chosen it; their educational and personal goals; their work experience; any extracurricular activities with which they have been involved, including those in school, religious organizations, and the community; and how they intend to use scholarship monies that may be awarded.
Financial data The stipend is $2,500 per year.
Duration 1 academic year; previous recipients may not reapply.
Number awarded 4 each year: 3 without consideration of financial need and 1 to an applicant who can submit evidence of financial need.
Deadline April of each year.

[731]
RUTH ABERNATHY UNDERGRADUATE PRESIDENTIAL SCHOLARSHIP

American Alliance for Health, Physical Education, Recreation and Dance
Attn: Presidential Scholarships
1900 Association Drive
Reston, VA 20191-1598
(703) 476-3400   Toll-free: (800) 213-7193
E-mail: dcallis@aahperd.org
Web: www.aahperd.org

Purpose To provide financial assistance to undergraduate student members of the American Alliance for Health, Physical Education, Recreation and Dance (AAHPERD).
Eligibility This program is open to AAHPERD members who are juniors or seniors at a baccalaureate-granting college or university. Applicants must be majoring in health, physical education, recreation, or dance and have a GPA of 3.5 or higher. They must submit a statement of their professional goals. Selection is based on academic proficiency; evidence of leadership; school, community, and professional activity and service; and character attributes.
Financial data The stipend is $1,000.
Duration 1 year; nonrenewable.
Additional information This program, established in 1995, was formerly designated the National Presidential Undergraduate Scholarships of AAHPERD.
Number awarded 3 each year.
Deadline October of each year.

[732]
SAKAE TAKAHASHI SCHOLARSHIP

100th Infantry Battalion Veterans Club
Attn: Scholarship Committee
520 Kamoku Street
Honolulu, HI 96826
(808) 732-5216   E-mail: daisyy@hgea.net
Web: emedia.leeward.hawaii.edu/mnakano

Purpose To provide financial assistance to high school seniors and college students who major in business, political science, or law and exemplify the sponsor's motto of "Continuing Service."
Eligibility This program is open to high school seniors planning to attend an institution of higher learning and full-time undergraduate students at community colleges, vocational/trade schools, 4-year colleges, and universities. Applicants must have a GPA of 2.5 or higher and be able

to demonstrate civic responsibility and community service. They must be majoring or planning to major in business, political science, or law. Along with their application, they must submit a 4-page essay on the characteristics of positive leaders and the ways in which they are an extraordinary leader. Selection is based on that essay and the applicant's demonstration that he or she can effectively promote the legacy of the 100th Infantry Battalion and its motto of "Continuing Service." Financial need is not considered.

Financial data The stipend is $1,000.
Duration 1 year; nonrenewable.
Number awarded 1 each year.
Deadline April of each year.

[733]
SCHOLARSHIPS IN MATHEMATICS EDUCATION

Illinois Council of Teachers of Mathematics
c/o Sue Pippen, ICTM Scholarship
24807 Winterberry Lane
Plainfield, IL 60585
E-mail: bsrich@ilstu.edu
Web: www.ictm.org/scholarship.html

Purpose To provide financial assistance to undergraduate students in Illinois who are interested in preparing for a career as a mathematics teacher.

Eligibility This program is open to juniors and seniors at accredited colleges and universities in Illinois. Applicants must have a GPA of 3.0 or higher and a mathematics education major, a mathematics major with an education minor, or an education major with an official mathematics concentration. Along with their application, they must submit an essay of 200 to 300 words on why they wish to teach mathematics and what they see as their contribution to the profession. Selection is based on the essay, a lesson plan, transcripts from all colleges attended, and letters of recommendation from 2 mathematics teachers (high school or college).

Financial data The stipend is $1,500.
Duration 1 year.
Additional information This program began in 1989. Requests for applications must be accompanied by a self-addressed stamped envelope.
Number awarded 2 to 5 each year.
Deadline March of each year.

[734]
SCHWAN'S FOOD SERVICE SCHOLARSHIPS

School Nutrition Association
Attn: Child Nutrition Foundation Scholarship Committee
700 South Washington Street, Suite 300
Alexandria, VA 22314-4287
(703) 739-3900   Toll-free: (800) 877-8822
Fax: (703) 739-3915   E-mail: cnf@schoolnutrition.org
Web: www.schoolnutrition.org/Index.aspx?ID=1043

Purpose To provide assistance to members (or children of members) of the School Nutrition Association (SNA) who are interested in studying school food service management on the undergraduate or graduate school level.

Eligibility This program is open to undergraduate and graduate students who meet all 4 of the following criteria: 1) plan to attend a college or vocational/technical institution that has a program designed to improve school food service (e.g., nutrition, food service management, business administration); 2) be an active SNA member or the child of an active member planning to study in a school food service-related field; 3) have a satisfactory academic record; and 4) express a desire to make school food service a career. Applicants must submit a 1-page personal essay (up to 500 words) stating the reason for selecting school food service as a profession; what they expect to gain from continuing their education; and their long-term professional goals/plans. Selection is based on the essay (35 points), letters of recommendation (20 points), SNA state and local chapter activity participation (15 points), organization and neatness (10 points), program of study (15 points), and GPA (5 points).

Financial data The stipend ranges up to $1,000.
Duration 1 year; may be renewed up to 3 additional years.
Additional information The SNA was formerly the American School Food Service Administration. This program, established in 1983, is sponsored by Schwan's Food Service.
Number awarded Varies each year; recently, 53 of these scholarships were awarded.
Deadline April of each year.

[735]
SHARON D. BANKS MEMORIAL UNDERGRADUATE SCHOLARSHIP

Women's Transportation Seminar
Attn: National Headquarters
1701 K Street, N.W., Suite 800
Washington, DC 20006
(202) 955-5085   Fax: (202) 955-5088
E-mail: wts@wtsinternational.org
Web: www.wtsinternational.org

Purpose To provide financial assistance to undergraduate women interested in a career in transportation.

Eligibility This program is open to women who are working on an undergraduate degree in transportation or a transportation-related field (e.g., transportation engineering, planning, finance, or logistics). Applicants must have a GPA of 3.0 or higher and be interested in a career in transportation. Along with their application, they must submit a 500-word statement about their career goals after graduation and why they think they should receive the scholarship award. Applications must be submitted first to a local chapter; the chapters forward selected applications for consideration on the national level. Minority candidates are encouraged to apply. Selection is based on transportation involvement and goals, job skills, and academic record; financial need is not considered.

Financial data The stipend is $3,000.
Duration 1 year.
Additional information This program was established in 1992. Local chapters may also award additional funding to winners for their area.
Number awarded 1 each year.
Deadline Applications must be submitted by November to a local WTS chapter.

[736]
SHERYL A. HORAK LAW ENFORCEMENT EXPLORER MEMORIAL SCHOLARSHIP

Boy Scouts of America
Attn: Learning for Life Division, S210
1325 West Walnut Hill Lane
P.O. Box 152079
Irving, TX 75015-2079
(972) 580-2418   Fax: (972) 580-2137
Web: www.learning-for-life.org

Purpose To provide financial assistance for college to Explorer Scouts who plan a career as a law enforcement executive.

Eligibility This program is open to Explorer Scouts who are at least seniors in high school. Selection is based on academic record, leadership ability, extracurricular activities, and a personal statement on "Why I want to pursue a career in law enforcement." Applicants must be active members of a Law Enforcement Explorer post registered with Boy Scouts of America.

Financial data The stipend is $1,000.

Duration 1 year; nonrenewable.

Additional information This program was established in 1987.

Number awarded Varies each year, depending on the availability of funds.

Deadline March of each year.

[737]
SHRM FOUNDATION UNDERGRADUATE SCHOLARSHIPS

Society for Human Resource Management
Attn: Foundation Administrator
1800 Duke Street
Alexandria, VA 22314-3499
(703) 535-6020   Toll-free: (800) 283-SHRM
Fax: (703) 535-6490   TDD: (703) 548-6999
E-mail: speyton@shrm.org
Web: www.shrm.org/students/ags_published

Purpose To provide financial assistance for college to undergraduate student members of the Society for Human Resource Management (SHRM).

Eligibility This program is open to undergraduate student members of the society. Applicants must have completed at least 55 semester hours of course work in a human relations major or human relations emphasis area (including at least 1 human relations management course) and have an overall GPA of 3.0 or higher.

Financial data The stipend is $2,500.

Duration 1 year.

Number awarded 2 each year.

Deadline October of each year.

[738]
SIGMA IOTA EPSILON UNDERGRADUATE SCHOLARSHIPS

Sigma Iota Epsilon
c/o Colorado State University
Management Department
324 Rockwell Hall
Fort Collins, CO 80523-1275
(970) 491-7200   Fax: (970) 491-3522
E-mail: brenda.ogden@colostate.edu
Web: www.sienational.com/scholarships.htm

Purpose To provide financial assistance to undergraduate student members of Sigma Iota Epsilon (SIE), the national honorary and professional management fraternity.

Eligibility This program is open to active undergraduate student members. Applicants must submit a brief description of their career objectives. Selection is based on scholastic, fraternity, and other extracurricular achievements.

Financial data Stipends are $1,000 or $500.

Number awarded Each year, 5 scholarships for $1,000 are awarded; the number of $500 awards varies each year, but has been 2 in recent years.

Deadline May of each year.

[739]
SODEXHO PAN ASIAN NETWORK GROUP SCHOLARSHIP

US Pan Asian American Chamber of Commerce
Attn: Scholarship Coordinator
1329 18th Street, N.W.
Washington, DC 20036
(202) 296-5221   Fax: (202) 296-5225
E-mail: administrator@uspaacc.com
Web: www.uspaacc.com/sodexho

Purpose To provide financial assistance and work experience to Asian American college students interested in preparing for a career in the hospitality industry.

Eligibility This program is open to college sophomores and juniors of Asian heritage who are U.S. citizens or permanent residents. Applicants must be enrolled full time at an accredited 4-year college or university in the United States and working on a degree in business management, preferably food service management, hotel restaurant institution management, facilities management, or similar program leading to a bachelor's degree. They must be willing to commit to a paid internship with Sodexho during the summer. Along with their application, they must submit a 500-word essay on how they plan to use their special talents to achieve their professional goals. Selection is based on academic excellence (GPA of 3.0 or higher), leadership in extracurricular activities, and community service involvement.

Financial data The stipend is $5,000. Funds are paid directly to the recipient's college or university. An additional stipend is paid for the internship.

Duration 1 academic year for the scholarship; 8 weeks for the internship.

Additional information This program, established in 2005, is sponsored by Sodexho USA and its Pan Asian Network Group (PANG). Funding is not provided for correspon-

SOCIAL SCIENCES

dence courses, Internet courses, or study in a country other than the United States.
Number awarded 1 each year.
Deadline February of each year.

[740]
SOUTH CAROLINA ASSOCIATION OF CPA'S SCHOLARSHIP PROGRAM

South Carolina Association of Certified Public Accountants
Attn: Educational Fund, Inc.
570 Chris Drive
West Columbia, SC 29169
(803) 791-4181 Toll-free: (888) 557-4814 (within SC)
Fax: (803) 791-4196
Web: www.scacpa.org

Purpose To provide financial assistance to upper-division and graduate students majoring in accounting in South Carolina.
Eligibility This program is open to South Carolina residents who are majoring in accounting at a college or university in the state. Applicants must be juniors, seniors, or graduate students with a GPA of 3.25 or higher overall and 3.5 or higher in accounting. They must submit their college transcripts, a listing of awards and other scholarships, 2 letters of reference, a resume, a 250-word essay on their personal career goals, and certification of their accounting major. Financial need is not considered in the selection process.
Financial data Stipends range from $500 to $2,000. Funds are paid to the recipient's school.
Duration 1 year.
Number awarded Varies each year.
Deadline June of each year.

[741]
SOUTH CAROLINA SPACE GRANT CONSORTIUM PRE-SERVICE TEACHER SCHOLARSHIPS

South Carolina Space Grant Consortium
c/o College of Charleston
Department of Geology and Environmental Sciences
66 George Street
Charleston, SC 29424
(843) 953-5463 Fax: (843) 953-5446
E-mail: scozzarot@cofc.edu
Web: www.cofc.edu/~scsgrant/scholar/overview.html

Purpose To provide financial assistance to upper-division and graduate students in South Carolina who are preparing for a career as a science and mathematics teacher.
Eligibility This program is open to juniors, seniors, and graduate students at member institutions of the South Carolina Space Grant Consortium. Applicants must be working on a teaching certificate in science, mathematics, or engineering. Their areas of interest may include, but are not limited to, the basic sciences, astronomy, science education, planetary science, environmental studies, or engineering. U.S. citizenship is required. Selection is based on academic qualifications of the applicant; 2 letters of recommendation; a description of past activities, current interests, and future plans concerning a space science or aerospace-related field; a sample lesson plan using curriculum materials available from the U.S. National Aeronautics and Space Administration (NASA); and faculty sponsorship. Women, minorities, and persons with disabilities are encouraged to apply.
Financial data The stipend is $2,000. Funds may be used for such expenses as 1) partial payment of tuition; 2) travel and registration for attending science and mathematics education workshops or conferences for the purpose of professional development; 3) purchase of supplies for student teaching activities; or 4) other supportive activities that lead to successful professional development and graduation as an educator in South Carolina.
Duration 1 year.
Additional information Members of the consortium are Benedict College, The Citadel, College of Charleston, Clemson University, Coastal Carolina University, Furman University, University of South Carolina, Wofford College, South Carolina State University, The Medical University of South Carolina, and University of the Virgin Islands. This program is funded by NASA.
Number awarded Varies each year.
Deadline January of each year.

[742]
SOUTH DAKOTA EXCELLENCE IN ACCOUNTING SCHOLARSHIPS

South Dakota CPA Society
Attn: Executive Director
1000 North West Avenue, Suite 100
P.O. Box 1798
Sioux Falls, SD 57101-1798
(605) 334-3848 Fax: (605) 334-8595
E-mail: lcoome@iw.net
Web: www.sdcpa.org

Purpose To provide financial assistance to college seniors and fifth-year students in South Dakota who are majoring in accounting.
Eligibility This program is open to accounting majors in South Dakota who have completed at least 90 credit hours with a demonstrated excellence in academics, leadership potential, and an interest in the profession of pubic accountancy. Applicants must submit information on their extracurricular activities, civic activities, awards, job experience, and career goals and objectives. Financial need is not considered in the selection process.
Financial data The stipend ranges from $500 to $1,000.
Duration 1 year; recipients may reapply.
Number awarded Varies each year; recently, 10 accounting students received $7,000 in these scholarships.
Deadline April of each year.

[743]
SOUTHERN CALIFORNIA CHAPTER/PLEASANT HAWAIIAN HOLIDAYS SCHOLARSHIP

American Society of Travel Agents
Attn: ASTA Foundation
1101 King Street, Suite 200
Alexandria, VA 22314-2944
(703) 739-8721   Fax: (703) 684-8319
E-mail: scholarship@astahq.com
Web: www.astanet.com/education/scholarshipe.asp

Purpose To provide financial assistance to college students interested in preparing for a career in the travel industry.

Eligibility Applicants must be U.S. citizens, have a GPA of 2.5 or higher, be attending a 4-year college or university either in southern California (Los Angeles, Kern, Riverside, San Bernardino, San Luis Obispo, Santa Barbara, and Ventura counties) or anywhere in the United States, and be working on a travel and tourism degree. They must submit a 500-word essay on "My goals in the travel industry." Financial need is not considered in the selection process.

Financial data The stipend is $2,500.

Duration 1 year.

Additional information This award was established in 1991.

Number awarded 2 each year: 1 for a student attending school in the southern California chapter area and 1 for a student attending school anywhere in the United States.

Deadline August of each year.

[744]
SPS FUTURE TEACHER SCHOLARSHIP

Society of Physics Students
c/o American Institute of Physics
One Physics Ellipse
College Park, MD 20740-3843
(301) 209-3007   Fax: (301) 209-0839
E-mail: sps@aip.org
Web: www.spsnational.org

Purpose To provide financial assistance to members of the Society of Physics Students (SPS) interested in preparing for a career as a physics teacher.

Eligibility This program is open to full-time college juniors who are active members of the society. Applicants must be enrolled in a teacher education program with plans to prepare for a career in physics education. Selection is based on 1) high scholastic performance both in physics and overall studies, 2) potential for continued scholastic development in physics, 3) active participation in society programs, and 4) a statement of experiences and ambitions with regard to teaching physics.

Financial data The stipend is $2,000.

Duration 1 year.

Additional information This program is sponsored by the Sigma Pi Sigma Trust Fund and the American Institute of Physics.

Number awarded 1 each year.

Deadline February of each year.

[745]
STATE ASSOCIATION OF REAL PROPERTY AGENTS SCHOLARSHIP

International Right of Way Association
Attn: Right of Way International Education Foundation
19750 South Vermont Avenue, Suite 220
Torrance, CA 90502-1144
(310) 538-0233   Fax: (310) 538-1471
Web: www.irwaonline.org

Purpose To provide financial assistance to members of the International Right of Way Association (IRWA) and their families who are working on or planning to work on an undergraduate or graduate degree related to the work of the association.

Eligibility This program is open to IRWA members and their families (spouses, children, stepchildren, and grandchildren) who are enrolled or planning to enroll as a full-time undergraduate or graduate student. Applicants must be planning to study a field related to the right of way profession and/or public works administration (e.g., real estate, civil engineering, law, property management, business administration, public administration). They must have a GPA of 3.0 or higher. Along with their application, they must submit a 250-word essay on their plans and goals in the right of way and/or public works administration profession. Financial need is not considered in the selection process.

Financial data A stipend is awarded (amount not specified).

Duration 1 year.

Additional information This program was established in 1991 when the IRWA agreed to administer scholarship funds on behalf of the State Association of Real Property Agents (SARPA).

Number awarded 1 or 2 each year.

Deadline January of each year.

[746]
STEWART ESTOPINAL CCIM MEMORIAL SCHOLARSHIP

CCIM Institute
Attn: Education Foundation
717 Princess Street
Alexandria, VA 22314
(703) 683-5295   Toll-free: (877) CCIM-EF1
Fax: (703) 683-0018
E-mail: EdFoundation@ccim.com
Web: www.ccimeducationfoundation.org

Purpose To provide financial assistance to upper-division and graduate students working on a degree in real estate who are the children of a Certified Commercial Investment Member (CCIM).

Eligibility This program is open to children of CCIMs who are enrolled as college juniors, seniors, or graduate students. Applicants must be preparing for a career in real estate or a related field. They must have a GPA of 3.0 or higher in their major and practical experience in the field (through an internship or a job). Along with their application, they must submit a statement of 150 to 300 words explaining why they are studying and planning a career in real estate (or a related field) and what CCIM means to them. Selection is based on academic record, commitment to real

estate or allied industry career, honors and awards, extracurricular activities, history of employment, and personal and professional references.
Financial data The stipend is $1,000.
Duration 1 year.
Additional information This program started in 2001. The CCIM Institute was formerly the Commercial Investment Real Estate Institute.
Number awarded 1 each year.
Deadline December of each year.

[747]
STUART CAMERON AND MARGARET MCLEOD MEMORIAL SCHOLARSHIP
Institute of Management Accountants
Attn: Committee on Students
10 Paragon Drive
Montvale, NJ 07645-1718
(201) 573-9000   Toll-free: (800) 638-4427, ext. 1543
Fax: (201) 474-1600   E-mail: students@imanet.org
Web: www.imanet.org

Purpose To provide financial assistance to undergraduate or graduate student members of the Institute of Management Accountants (IMA) who are interested in preparing for a career in management accounting or financial management.
Eligibility This program is open to undergraduate and graduate student IMA members who have a GPA of 2.8 or higher. Applicants must be preparing for a career in management accounting, financial management, or information technology. They must submit a 2-page statement on their reasons for applying for the scholarship, reasons that they deserve the award, specific contributions to IMA, ideas on how they will promote awareness and increase membership and certification within IMA, and their career goals and objectives. Selection is based on that statement, academic merit, IMA participation, quality of the presentation, their resume, and letters of recommendation.
Financial data The stipend is $5,000.
Duration 1 year.
Additional information The recipient is required to participate in the parent chapter, at the council level, or at the national level.
Number awarded 1 each year.
Deadline February of each year.

[748]
STUDENT ESSAY COMPETITION IN HEALTHCARE MANAGEMENT
American College of Healthcare Executives
Attn: Associate Director, Division of Research and Development
One North Franklin Street, Suite 1700
Chicago, IL 60606-3529
(312) 424-9444   Fax: (312) 424-0023
E-mail: ache@ache.org
Web: www.ache.org

Purpose To recognize and reward undergraduate or graduate student members of the American College of Healthcare Executives (ACHE) who submit outstanding essays on health care administration.
Eligibility This competition is open to ACHE student associates or affiliates who are enrolled in an undergraduate or graduate program in health care management at an accredited college or university in the United States or Canada. Applicants must submit an essay, up to 15 pages in length, on a topic with a focus on such health management topics as strategic planning and policy; accountability of and/or relationships among board, medical staff, and executive management; financial management; human resources management; systems management; plant and facility management; comprehensive systems of services; quality assessment and assurance; professional, public, community, or interorganization relations; government relations or regulation; marketing; education; research; or law and ethics. Selection is based on significance of the subject to health care management, innovativeness in approach to the topic, thoroughness and precision in developing the subject, practical usefulness for guiding management action, and clarity and conciseness of expression.
Financial data The first-place winners in each division (undergraduate and graduate) receive $3,000 and their programs receive $1,000. The second-place winner receives $2,000 and third $1,000.
Duration The competition is held annually.
Additional information This program was established in 1989.
Number awarded 6 each year: 3 undergraduate and 3 graduate students.
Deadline December of each year.

[749]
THOMAS PRATTE MEMORIAL SCHOLARSHIPS
Surfrider Foundation
Attn: Pratte Scholarship
P.O. Box 6010
San Clemente, CA 92674-6010
(949) 492-8170   Fax: (949) 492-8142
E-mail: prattescholarship@surfrider.org
Web: www.surfrider.org

Purpose To provide financial assistance to members of the Surfrider Foundation working on an undergraduate or graduate degree in an environmental field.
Eligibility This program is open to members of the foundation working on an undergraduate, master's, or doctoral degree in a field consistent with the foundation's mission, including (but not limited to) oceanography, marine affairs, environmental sciences, public policy, community planning, or natural resources. Applicants must be enrolled at an accredited college or university in the United States or Puerto Rico as an upper-division or graduate student. Undergraduates must have a GPA of 3.4 or higher and graduate students 3.6 or higher. Along with their application, they must submit 1) a personal statement describing their career goals, volunteer activities, work, or summer plans as they pertain to the coastal environmental issues relevant to the foundation and its mission; and 2) a description of their current research and how it relates to the foundation's stated mission and environmental programs. Financial need is not considered in the selection process.

Financial data The stipend is $2,000 for an undergraduate, $3,000 for a master's degree student, and $5,000 for a doctoral student.
Duration 1 year.
Additional information This foundation, established in 1984 by a group of surfers, is a nonprofit environmental grassroots organization dedicated to the protection and preservation of the world's waves, oceans, and beaches. It currently has 50,000 members with 60 chapters in 22 states.
Number awarded 3 each year: 1 for a student at each academic level.
Deadline June of each year.

[750]
TIM SMITH MEMORIAL SCHOLARSHIP
Colorado Fiscal Managers Association
c/o Roger Cusworth, Scholarship Selection Committee
VPBF - Controller - Operations
University of Colorado
Boulder, CO 80309-0436
(303) 492-9714   E-mail: roger.cusworth@cusys.edu
Web: www.state.co.us/cfma/Scholarship/scholar.htm

Purpose To provide financial assistance to Colorado students majoring in accounting, finance, or related fields.
Eligibility This program is open to residents of Colorado entering their sophomore, junior, or senior year at an accredited state-supported higher education institution in the state. Applicants must be enrolled in a degree program with a declared major in accounting, finance, or other financial management study. Selection is based on academic achievement, involvement in extracurricular organizations and/or activities, work experience, and community involvement.
Financial data The stipend is $1,500.
Duration 1 year.
Additional information This scholarship was first awarded in 1992.
Number awarded 4 each year.
Deadline June of each year.

[751]
TOBIN SORENSON PHYSICAL EDUCATION SCHOLARSHIP
Pi Lambda Theta
Attn: Scholarships Committee
4101 East Third Street
P.O. Box 6626
Bloomington, IN 47407-6626
(812) 339-3411   Toll-free: (800) 487-3411
Fax: (812) 339-3462   E-mail: office@pilambda.org
Web: www.pilambda.org

Purpose To provide financial assistance to students preparing for careers as a teacher of physical education or a related field.
Eligibility This program is open to students preparing for careers at the K-12 level. Applicants must be interested in becoming a physical education teacher, adaptive physical education teacher, coach, recreational therapist, dance therapist, or similar professional teaching the knowledge and use of the human body. They must be sophomores or above and have a GPA of 3.5 or higher. Selection is based on academic achievement, potential for leadership, and extracurricular involvement in physical/sports education, recreation therapy, or similar activities (e.g., coaching, tutoring, volunteer work for appropriate organizations on or off campus).
Financial data The stipend is $1,000.
Duration 1 year.
Additional information This program was established in 1999. If the recipient is not already a member of Pi Lambda Theta (an international honor and professional association in education), a complimentary 1-year honorary membership is also awarded.
Number awarded 1 every other year.
Deadline February of each odd-numbered year.

[752]
TOMMY RAMEY SCHOLARSHIP
Tommy Ramey Foundation
Attn: Scholarship Committee
1052 Highland Colony Parkway, Suite 125
Ridgeland, MS 39157
E-mail: admin@tommyrameyscholarship.org
Web: www.tommyrameyscholarship.org

Purpose To provide financial assistance to college students who reside in Mississippi and are majoring in either 1) marketing or a related field or 2) culinary arts or a related field.
Eligibility This program is open to Mississippi residents who are full-time students at an accredited postsecondary institution, have at least a 2.5 GPA, and are enrolled in either 1) marketing or a related field (business, advertising, communications, public relations, journalism, graphic design) or 2) culinary arts or a related field (travel or tourism, hotel or restaurant management, food production). Applicants must submit a list of student activities and a 500-word essay on either "My favorite TV commercial" (marketing students) or "My favorite meal" (culinary students). Selection is based more on personal merit than on academic record; financial need is not required.
Financial data The stipend is either $5,000 or $2,500.
Duration 1 year.
Number awarded Up to 4 each year: either 1 at $5,000 or 2 at $2,500 for marketing students and either 1 at $5,000 or 2 at $2,500 for culinary students.
Deadline October of each year.

[753]
TRI STATE SURVEYING AND PHOTOGRAMMETRY KRIS M. KUNZE MEMORIAL SCHOLARSHIP
American Congress on Surveying and Mapping
Attn: Scholarships
6 Montgomery Village Avenue, Suite 403
Gaithersburg, MD 20879
(240) 632-9716, ext. 113   Fax: (240) 632-1321
E-mail: pat.canfield@acsm.net
Web: www.acsm.net/scholar.html

Purpose To provide financial assistance to members of

the American Congress on Surveying and Mapping (ACSM) who are interested in additional study in business.

Eligibility This program is open to ACSM members enrolled at a 2-year or 4-year college or university. First priority is given to licensed Professional Land Surveyors or Certified Protogrammetrists taking college-level courses in business administration or business management. Second priority is certified land survey interns taking college-level courses in business administration or business management. Third priority is full-time students enrolled in a degree program in surveying and mapping but taking a program of study that includes business administration or business management. Along with their application, they must submit a statement describing their educational program, future plans for study or research, and why the award is merited. Selection is based on that statement (30%), academic record (30%), letters of recommendation (20%), and professional activities (20%).

Financial data The stipend is $1,000.
Duration 1 year.
Number awarded 1 each year.
Deadline October of each year.

[754]
UNITED STATES TOUR OPERATORS ASSOCIATION SCHOLARSHIP

Tourism Cares for Tomorrow
Attn: Program Manager
585 Washington Street
Canton, MA 02021
(781) 821-5990   Fax: (781) 821-8949
E-mail: info@tourismcares.org
Web: www.tourismcares.org

Purpose To provide financial assistance to upper-division students who are majoring in tourism.

Eligibility This program is open to students entering their junior or senior year at an accredited 4-year college or university in the United States or Canada. Applicants must be working on a degree in a travel and tourism-related program and have a GPA of 3.0 or higher. Along with their application, they must submit a 2-page essay on why they have chosen to prepare for a career in the hospitality and tourism industry. Financial need is not considered in the selection process.

Financial data The stipend is $2,500.
Duration 1 year.
Additional information This program is sponsored by the United States Tour Operators Association.
Number awarded 1 each year.
Deadline March of each year.

[755]
VIRGINIA CHILD CARE PROVIDER SCHOLARSHIP

Virginia Department of Social Services
c/o Northern Virginia Community College
6901 Sudley Road
Manassas, VA 20109
(703) 257-6579   Toll-free: (866) 636-1608
E-mail: childcare.scholarship@nvcc.edu
Web: www.dss.virginia.gov/family/cc/scholarship.html

Purpose To provide financial assistance to Virginia residents who are interested in working on a degree or certificate in preschool education.

Eligibility This program is open to current and future child care providers. Applicants must 1) already be providing child care in a program located in Virginia, 2) live in Virginia but be employed in a child care program outside of the state, or 3) live in Virginia and be planning to become employed in child care. Scholarships are not available to individuals who are or plan to become teachers or teachers' aides in the public or private school system for mandatory instructional programs serving school-age children and special education programs serving preschool children. Scholarships are available, however, to public or private school personnel who are employed in preschool programs, before-school child care programs, or after-school child care programs (e.g., Head Start, Virginia Preschool Initiatives). Scholarship are awarded on a first-come, first-served basis.

Financial data The scholarship award pays the tuition and technology fee for each qualifying course, up to a lifetime maximum of $1,707.60. Funds are paid to the recipient's school. These funds may not be used to pay for books.

Duration 2 courses per semester, up to a total of 8 courses.

Additional information Recipients may work on the following degrees: career studies certificate in early childhood education; career studies certificate in school age child care education; career studies certificate in child care management; advanced career studies certificate in early childhood education; associate degree in early childhood education; or bachelor's degree in early childhood education. This program is provided by the Virginia Department of Social Services but administered by Northern Virginia Community College. Recipients must attend school in Virginia.

Number awarded Varies each year.

Deadline January of each year for the spring semester; May of each year for the summer semester; August of each year for the fall semester.

[756]
VIRGINIA COUNCIL OF TEACHERS OF MATHEMATICS SCHOLARSHIPS

Virginia Council of Teachers of Mathematics
c/o Edward A. Anderson, Jr., Scholarship Committee
Northern Virginia Community College, Manassas Campus
6901 Sudley Road
Manassas, VA 20109-2399
(703) 257-6552   E-mail: eanderson@nvcc.edu
Web: www.vctm.org/scholarship.htm

Purpose To provide financial assistance to Virginia residents who are preparing for a career as a mathematics teacher.

Eligibility This program is open to residents of Virginia who are enrolled full time in a college mathematics program and scheduled to graduate during the following year. Applicants must be planning to teach mathematics in Virginia at the elementary, middle school, high school, or college level. Students in a program leading to a degree as a mathematics lead teacher or mathematics specialist are also eligible. Along with their application, they must submit a 1-page statement indicating why they wish to be a mathematics teacher. Selection is based on potential for a successful career teaching mathematics, as indicated by that statement, recommendations of 2 faculty members, and academic records.

Financial data The stipend is $1,000.
Duration 1 year.
Number awarded 1 or 2 each year.
Deadline December of each year.

[757]
VIRGINIA SOCIETY FOR HEALTHCARE HUMAN RESOURCES ADMINISTRATION SCHOLARSHIP

Virginia Society for Healthcare Human Resources Administration
c/o Dee Borgoyn
Shenandoah Valley Westminster-Canterbury
300 Westminster-Canterbury Drive
Winchester, VA 22603
(540) 665-5924   Fax: (540) 665-5921
E-mail: info@vashhra.org
Web: www.vashhra.org

Purpose To provide financial assistance to undergraduate and graduate students in Virginia working on a degree in human relations and interested in a career in a health care setting.

Eligibility This program is open to residents of Virginia currently enrolled in an accredited college or university in the state and working on an undergraduate or graduate degree in human resources administration or a related field. Applicants must be at least a second-semester sophomore when the application is submitted and have a demonstrated interest in working in a health care setting. Selection is based on a 1-page statement outlining the applicant's life and work experiences that support an interest in human relations, specifically in a health care setting; official transcripts; and 2 letters of recommendation from faculty members.

Financial data The stipend is $1,000.
Duration 1 year.
Number awarded 1 each year.
Deadline August of each year.

[758]
VIRGINIA SOCIETY OF CERTIFIED PUBLIC ACCOUNTANTS EDUCATIONAL FOUNDATION UNDERGRADUATE SCHOLARSHIP

Virginia Society of Certified Public Accountants
Attn: Educational Foundation
4309 Cox Road
P.O. Box 4620
Glen Allen, VA 23058-4620
(804) 270-5344   Toll-free: (800) 733-8272
Fax: (804) 273-1741   E-mail: foundation@vscpa.com
Web: www.vscpa.com

Purpose To provide financial assistance to students enrolled in an undergraduate accounting program in Virginia.

Eligibility Applicants must be currently enrolled in a Virginia college or university undergraduate accounting program. They must be U.S. citizens, be majoring in accounting, have completed at least 3 hours of accounting, be currently registered for 3 more credit hours of accounting, and have a GPA of 3.0 or higher. Along with their application, they must submit a 500-word essay describing a situation in which they 1) demonstrated the ability to influence, inspire, and motivate an individual or group of individuals to achieve desired results; 2) were confronted with an ethical dilemma and how they dealt with the issue; and/or 3) demonstrated effective problem solving through their decision-making skills, personal insight, judgment, and creativity. Selection is based on the essay, their most recent transcript, a current resume, and a faculty letter of recommendation.

Financial data The stipend is generally $1,500.
Duration 1 year.
Number awarded Varies each year; recently, 8 of these scholarships were awarded.
Deadline April of each year.

[759]
VIRGINIA TUITION ASSISTANCE FOR EARLY CHILDHOOD SPECIAL EDUCATORS SPEECH-LANGUAGE PATHOLOGISTS, AND PARAPROFESSIONALS

Virginia Department of Education
Attn: Division of Teacher Education and Licensure
P.O. Box 2120
Richmond, VA 23218-2120
(804) 225-2096   Toll-free: (800) 292-3820
Fax: (804) 786-6759
E-mail: pat.burgess@doe.virginia.gov
Web: www.pen.k12.va.us

Purpose To provide financial assistance for additional study to early childhood special educators in Virginia.

Eligibility This program is open to Virginia residents who are 1) special educators holding a 3-year nonrenewable or 5-year renewable license with an early childhood special education endorsement; 2) licensed teachers seeking an early childhood special education endorsement; 3) certain speech-language pathologists; and 4) full-time special education paraprofessionals assisting students with disabilities ages birth to 5. Teachers must be enrolled in graduate-level courses meeting competencies in the early childhood endorsement area. Eligible speech and language pathologists are those for whom preschoolers with disabilities make up at least 50% of their caseloads and who are enrolled in graduate-level course work directly related to the area in which they are providing services or in early childhood special education. Eligible paraprofessionals are those who are employed full time in an early childhood special education program and are enrolled in undergraduate or graduate-level course work related to the early childhood special education area. Assistance is awarded on a first-come, first-served basis.

Financial data Tuition assistance is provided at the rate of $600 per course for up to 3 courses per year.

Duration 1 year; may be renewed.

Number awarded Varies each year.

Deadline August of each year.

[760]
VSCPA EDUCATIONAL FOUNDATION MINORITY UNDERGRADUATE SCHOLARSHIP

Virginia Society of Certified Public Accountants
Attn: Educational Foundation
4309 Cox Road
P.O. Box 4620
Glen Allen, VA 23058-4620
(804) 270-5344   Toll-free: (800) 733-8272
Fax: (804) 273-1741   E-mail: foundation@vscpa.com
Web: www.vscpa.com

Purpose To provide financial assistance to minority students enrolled in an undergraduate accounting program in Virginia.

Eligibility Applicants must be minority students (African Americans, Hispanic Americans, Native American Indians, or Asian Pacific Americans) currently enrolled in a Virginia college or university undergraduate accounting program. They must be U.S. citizens, be majoring in accounting, have completed at least 3 hours of accounting, be currently registered for 3 more credit hours of accounting and have a GPA of 3.0 or higher. Along with their application, they must submit a 500-word essay describing a situation in which they 1) demonstrated the ability to influence, inspire, and motivate an individual or group of individuals to achieve desired results; 2) were confronted with an ethical dilemma and how they dealt with the issue; and/or 3) demonstrated effective problem solving through their decision-making skills, personal insight, judgment, and creativity. Selection is based on the essay, their most recent transcript, a current resume, and a faculty letter of recommendation.

Financial data The stipend is generally $1,500.

Duration 1 year.

Number awarded Varies each year; recently, 4 of these scholarships were awarded.

Deadline April of each year.

[761]
VSI SCHOLARSHIP PROGRAM

Virginia Sheriffs' Institute
701 East Franklin Street, Suite 706
Richmond, VA 23219
(804) 225-7152   Fax: (804) 225-7162
E-mail: vsavsi@virginiasheriffs.org
Web: www.virginiasheriffs.org

Purpose To provide financial assistance to Virginia residents who are majoring or planning to major in law enforcement or criminal justice in college.

Eligibility This program is open to Virginia residents who live in areas where the sheriffs are members of the Virginia Sheriffs' Institute and authorized the Institute to conduct a direct mail special appeal to raise funds for the scholarship program. Applicants must be attending or planning to attend a college or university in Virginia and major in law enforcement or criminal justice. Along with their application, they must submit a short essay on their proposed course of college study, how they reached that decision, what they expect to gain from college, and their personal goals and ambitions. Financial need is not considered in the selection process.

Financial data A stipend is awarded (amount not specified). Checks are made payable directly to the recipient's educational institution.

Duration 1 year; may be renewed.

Number awarded Varies each year.

Deadline April of each year.

[762]
WAHPERD STUDENT SCHOLARSHIP AWARDS

Wisconsin Association for Health, Physical Education, Recreation, and Dance
Attn: Executive Director
University of Wisconsin at La Crosse
24 Mitchell Hall
1725 State Street
La Crosse, WI 54601-3788
(608) 785-8175   Toll-free: (800) 441-4568
E-mail: wahperd@uwlax.edu
Web: www.wahperd.org/scholarships.htm

Purpose To provide financial assistance to members of the Wisconsin Association for Health, Physical Education, Recreation and Dance (WAHPERD) who are working on a college degree.

Eligibility This program is open to WAHPERD members who have completed at least 2 years of study at a 4-year college or university with a major in physical education, health education, exercise fitness, recreation, athletic training, sports management, or dance. Applicants must have a GPA of 3.2 or higher, at least 2 years' of membership, and a record of professional involvement and leadership responsibility. They must submit a resume and 2 letters of recommendation. Financial need is not considered in the selection process.

Financial data The stipend is $1,000.

Duration 1 year.

Number awarded 4 each year.

Deadline March of each year.

[763]
WALLACE S. AND WILMA K. LAUGHLIN FOUNDATION TRUST SCHOLARSHIPS

Nebraska Funeral Directors Association
Attn: Laughlin Trust Committee
201 North Eighth Street, Suite 400
P.O. Box 83313
Lincoln, NE 68501-3313
(402) 423-8900 Fax: (402) 476-6547
E-mail: nefda@assocoffice.net
Web: www.nefda.org/careers

Purpose To provide financial assistance to residents of Nebraska who are interested in preparing for a career in mortuary science.

Eligibility This program is open to residents of Nebraska who are graduates of a high school in the state and have met the pre-mortuary academic requirements set by the state prior to entering a mortuary science college. Students planning to attend a 1-year course of study must apply prior to entering an accredited mortuary school. Students planning a 4-year course of study must apply prior to entering the third year of study. Applicants must be recommended by a member of the Nebraska Funeral Directors Association. Interviews are required. Financial need is not considered in the selection process.

Financial data Stipends are at least $1,000 per year. Funds are paid directly to the recipient's school.

Duration 1 year.

Additional information Recipients must return to Nebraska after graduation from mortuary school.

Number awarded Varies, depending upon the funds available.

Deadline June of each year.

[764]
WALTER SCHOENKNECHT TOURISM AND TRAVEL SCHOLARSHIP

Connecticut Commission on Culture and Tourism
Attn: Tourism Division
505 Hudson Street, Second Floor
Hartford, CT 06106
(860) 270-8089 Fax: (860) 270-8077
E-mail: joyce.fredericks@po.state.ct.us
Web: www.tourism.state.ct.us/tourism.asp

Purpose To provide financial assistance to high school, undergraduate, and graduate students from Connecticut who are preparing for a career in the tourism industry.

Eligibility This program is open to residents of Connecticut who are high school seniors, high school graduates who have not yet enrolled in college, or enrolled undergraduate or graduate students at an accredited college or university. Applicants must be preparing for a career in the tourism industry. Along with their application, they must submit an essay on a topic about tourism as it relates to Connecticut, 2 letters of recommendation, a current transcript, a personal letter of intent explaining how this scholarship will help them to achieve their academic goals, and a personal resume. Selection is based on personal achievement and demonstrated interest in the tourism industry.

Financial data The stipend is $1,000.

Duration 1 year.

Number awarded 1 each year.

Deadline September of each year.

[765]
WASHINGTON SOCIETY OF CPAS SCHOLARSHIPS FOR ACCOUNTING MAJORS

Washington Society of Certified Public Accountants
Attn: Scholarship Committee
902 140th Avenue N.E.
Bellevue, WA 98005-3480
(425) 644-4800 Toll-free: (800) 272-8273 (within WA)
Fax: (425) 562-8853
E-mail: memberservices@wscpa.org
Web: www.wscpa.org

Purpose To provide financial assistance to undergraduate students in Washington who are majoring in accounting.

Eligibility This program is open to accounting majors in Washington who have completed their sophomore year at an accredited 4-year institution or 2 terms at a 2-year institution. Preference is given to residents of Washington. Applicants must be U.S. citizens or have applied for citizenship and have a GPA of 3.0 or higher. Along with their application, they must submit essays on 1) what sparked their interest in working on a degree in accounting and what excites them about the profession; 2) their career goals; 3) their involvement in an extracurricular activity, organization, or community service experience and how it affected their life; and 4) why they should be awarded a scholarship. Selection is based on the essays, academic achievement, campus and/or community activities, work history, 2 letters of recommendation, and probability of success in obtaining a C.P.A. license. Financial need is not considered.

Financial data The stipend is $1,000 per year. Funds may be used to pay for tuition only.

Duration 1 year; nonrenewable.

Number awarded 10 each year.

Deadline April of each year.

[766]
WILLIAM E. GREGORY SCHOLARSHIP

Imperial Polk Advertising Federation
Attn: Scholarship Program
P.O. Box 24201
Lakeland, FL 33802-4201
(863) 858-3736 Fax: (863) 858-3736
Web: www.polkadfed.com

Purpose To provide financial assistance to undergraduate students majoring in fields related to advertising at Florida colleges.

Eligibility This program is open to full-time undergraduate students at universities, colleges, and technical schools in Florida. Applicants must be working on a degree in advertising, communications, graphic design, or marketing. They must have a GPA of 3.0 or higher. Along with their application, they must submit 1) a 500-word essay describing their future professional and educational goals; and 2) a project they have recently completed for a class or internship. Financial need is not considered in the selection process.

Financial data A total of $2,000 is available for this program each year.

Duration 1 year; nonrenewable.
Additional information Information is also available from Samantha Hocker, Scholarship Chair, (863) 701-7789, E-mail: shocker@keisercollege.edu.
Number awarded 1 or more each year.
Deadline November of each year.

[767]
WISCONSIN PROFESSIONAL POLICE ASSOCIATION SCHOLARSHIP PROGRAM

Wisconsin Professional Police Association
Attn: Scholarship Committee
340 Coyier Lane
Madison, WI 53713
(608) 273-3840   Fax: (608) 273-3904
E-mail: bahr@wppa.com
Web: www.wppa.com

Purpose To provide financial assistance to residents of Wisconsin and the upper peninsula of Michigan who are entering or attending a program in law enforcement.
Eligibility This program is open to residents of Wisconsin and the upper peninsula of Michigan who are enrolled or planning to enroll in a 2-year or 4-year program in police science, criminal justice, or a related field of law enforcement. Applicants must submit a 200-word essay on why they have chosen a career in law enforcement, including any special projects relating to their interest in the field. Financial need is not considered in the selection process.
Financial data Stipends range from $500 to $1,000; funds are sent directly to the recipient.
Duration 1 year.
Number awarded Approximately 10 each year.
Deadline January of each year.

[768]
WISCONSIN RESTAURANT ASSOCIATION EDUCATION FOUNDATION SCHOLARSHIP IN FOODSERVICE

Wisconsin Restaurant Association
Attn: Education Foundation
2801 Fish Hatchery Road
Madison, WI 53713-3120
(608) 270-9950   Toll-free: (800) 589-3211
Fax: (608) 270-9960
Web: www.wirestaurant.org

Purpose To provide financial assistance to Wisconsin residents interested in preparing for a career in the food service industry.
Eligibility This program is open to residents of Wisconsin who are currently working for a food service employer in the state. Applicants must be either 1) enrolled or planning to enroll in a food service program or a culinary apprenticeship program at a technical college in Wisconsin as a full-time student, or 2) enrolled or planning to enroll in a food service program at a 4-year college or university anywhere in the United States as a full-time student. Students who are already in a technical college or a 4-year institution must submit a current transcript of grades. New students and entering freshmen must provide an acceptance letter from the college or university that includes the intended program. All applicants must submit high school transcripts, a letter of nomination from their employer, and a letter of nomination from an instructor. They must also submit essays on their thoughts on 3 topics: the major challenges in the food service industry today, how they would meet those challenges, and why they want a career in food service. Another set of required essays relate to their future goals, how they intend to reach them, and why they are deserving of this scholarship. Selection is based on their thought essays (15 points), goals and aspirations essays (6 points), academic record and achievements (4 points), and food service employment and experience (5 points).
Financial data Stipends are either $1,500 or $750.
Duration 1 year.
Number awarded Varies each year; recently, 22 of these scholarships with a total value of $32,000 were awarded.
Deadline March of each year.

[769]
WOMAN OF DISTINCTION AWARD

Electronic Document Systems Foundation
Attn: EDSF Scholarship Awards
608 Silver Spur Road, Suite 280
Rolling Hills Estates, CA 90274-3616
(310) 265-5510   Fax: (310) 265-5588
E-mail: jmowlds@edsf.org
Web: www.edsf.org/scholarships.cfm

Purpose To provide financial assistance to women working on an undergraduate or graduate degree in a field related to the high volume transaction output (HVTO) industry.
Eligibility This program is open to female undergraduate and graduate students who are working on a degree in field related to the HVTO industry, including information technology, graphic arts, or business. Applicants must be enrolled full time at a technical school, trade school, community college, university, college, or graduate school in the United States with a GPA of 3.0 or higher. Along with their application, they must submit a statement of their career goals in the field of document communications, an essay on a topic related to their view of the future of the document management and production industry, a list of current professional and college extracurricular activities and achievements, college transcripts, samples of their creative work, and 2 letters of recommendation. Financial need is not considered.
Financial data The stipend is $5,000.
Duration 1 year.
Additional information This program is sponsored by COPI/OutputLinks.
Number awarded 1 each year.
Deadline May of each year.

[770]
WOMEN IN FEDERAL LAW ENFORCEMENT SCHOLARSHIP

Women in Federal Law Enforcement
Attn: Scholarship Coordinator
2200 Wilson Boulevard, Suite 102
PMB 204
Arlington, VA 22201-3324
(703) 548-9211   Toll-free: (866) 399-4353
Fax: (410) 451-7373   E-mail: WIFLE@comcast.net
Web: www.wifle.com/scholarshipprogram.htm

Purpose To provide financial assistance for college or graduate school to women interested in preparing for a career in law enforcement.

Eligibility This program is open to women who are enrolled full time at an accredited 4-year college or university (or at a community college with the intention of transferring to a 4-year school). Applicants must be preparing for a career in law enforcement (including special agents, forensic scientists, intelligence analysts, fingerprint and firearms examiners, bomb technicians, public information specialists, computer specialists, attorneys, and other related fields). They must have completed at least 1 year of college and have a GPA of 3.0 or higher. Students in graduate and postgraduate programs are also eligible, but those working on an associate degree are not. Along with their application, they must submit a 500-word essay describing a community project in which they have been involved and the results or impact to the community. Selection is based on academic potential, achievement, and commitment to serving communities in the field of law enforcement.

Financial data Stipends range from $500 to $2,000.

Duration 1 year; may be renewed.

Additional information Information is also available from the WIFLE Scholarship Fund, P.O. Box 1480, Edgewater, MD 21037-7480.

Number awarded Several each year.

Deadline April of each year.

[771]
WOMEN'S BUSINESS ALLIANCE SCHOLARSHIP PROGRAM

Choice Hotels International
Attn: Foundation
10750 Columbia Pike
Silver Spring, MD 20901
(301) 592-6258
Web: www.choicehotels.com

Purpose To provide financial assistance to women interested in preparing for a career in the hospitality industry.

Eligibility This program is open to female high school seniors, undergraduates, and graduate students. Applicants must be U.S. citizens or permanent residents interested in preparing for a career in the hospitality industry. They must submit an essay of 500 words or less on their experience or interest in the hospitality industry and how it relates to their career goals, including any community service experience that has impacted their career goals or their interest in the industry. Financial need is not considered in the selection process.

Financial data The stipend is $2,000.

Duration 1 year; recipients may reapply.

Number awarded 2 or more each year.

Deadline January or July of each year.

[772]
YELLOW RIBBON SCHOLARSHIP

Tourism Cares for Tomorrow
Attn: Program Manager
585 Washington Street
Canton, MA 02021
(781) 821-5990   Fax: (781) 821-8949
E-mail: info@tourismcares.org
Web: www.tourismcares.org

Purpose To provide financial assistance for college to students with disabilities who are planning a career in the travel and tourism industry.

Eligibility This program is open to students with a physical or sensory disability (verified by an accredited physician) who are entering or attending an accredited 2- or 4-year college or university in the United States or Canada. Applicants must be working on or planning to work on a degree in a field related to travel and tourism. High school seniors must have a GPA of 3.0 or higher; college students must have at least a 2.5. Along with their application, they must submit a 2-page essay on how they intend to use their education in making a career in travel and tourism.

Financial data The stipend is $3,500.

Duration 1 year.

Additional information This program was established in 1993.

Number awarded 1 each year.

Deadline March of each year.

[773]
YOUNG ENTREPRENEUR OF THE YEAR AWARDS

National Foundation for Teaching Entrepreneurship
Attn: Student/Alumni Awards Committee
120 Wall Street, 29th Floor
New York, NY 10005
(212) 232-3333   Toll-free: (800) 367-6383, ext. 336
Fax: (212) 232-2244   E-mail: nfte@nfte.com
Web: www.nfte.com/alumni

Purpose To recognize and reward students and alumni who have participated in programs of the National Foundation for Teaching Entrepreneurship (NFTE) and have started or plan to start their own business.

Eligibility This program is open to students and alumni of the NFTE entrepreneurship program offered in high schools throughout the country. Applicants may enter in either of 2 categories: business plan (for plans for businesses not yet established) and operational business (for revenue-generating businesses). They must submit information describing their proposed or operating business, including a complete business plan. Selection is based on application presentation (neatness, legibility, visual appeal, and completeness); business viability (including profit potential and, for the operating business category, current revenue); social responsibility (knowledge of the community and how the business contributes to its well-being); and entrepreneurial spirit (use of innovative and/or creative business methods).

Financial data Awards are $750 for the business plan category or $1,000 for the operational business category. Funds may be used for a business or college education. Awardees also receive a commemorative plaque and an all-expense paid trip to New York City to receive the award.

Duration The awards are presented annually.

Additional information These awards were first offered in 1994.

Number awarded Varies each year; recently, 10 business plan and 15 operational business awards were granted.

Deadline January of each year.

Humanities

Described here are 241 merit and other no-need funding programs that 1) reward outstanding artistic and creative work or 2) support college studies in the humanities, including architecture, art, creative writing, design, history, journalism, languages, literature, music, and religion. These programs are available to currently-enrolled and returning college students to fund studies on the undergraduate level in the United States. If you are looking for a particular program and don't find it here, be sure to check the Program Title Index to see if it is covered elsewhere in the directory.

HUMANITIES

[774]
ABE VORON SCHOLARSHIP
Broadcast Education Association
Attn: Scholarships
1771 N Street, N.W.
Washington, DC 20036-2891
(202) 429-3935 Toll-free: (888) 380-7222
E-mail: beainfo@beaweb.org
Web: www.beaweb.org/scholarships.html

Purpose To provide financial assistance to upper-division and graduate students who are interested in preparing for a career in radio broadcasting.

Eligibility This program is open to juniors, seniors, and graduate students enrolled full time at a college or university where at least 1 department is an institutional member of the Broadcast Education Association. Applicants must be studying for a career in radio. Selection is based on evidence that the applicant possesses integrity, superior academic ability, potential to be an outstanding electronic media professional, and a sense of personal and professional responsibility.

Financial data The stipend is $5,000.

Duration 1 year; may not be renewed.

Additional information Information is also available from Peter B. Orlik, Central Michigan University, 344 Moore Hall, Mt. Pleasant, MI 48859, (989) 774-7279.

Number awarded 1 each year.

Deadline October of each year.

[775]
ACADEMY OF TELEVISION ARTS & SCIENCES COLLEGE TELEVISION AWARDS
Academy of Television Arts & Sciences Foundation
Attn: Education Department
5220 Lankershim Boulevard
North Hollywood, CA 91601-3109
(818) 754-2830 Fax: (818) 761-ATAS
E-mail: collegeawards@emmys.org
Web: www.emmys.tv/foundation/collegetvawards.php

Purpose To recognize and reward outstanding college student videos.

Eligibility Eligible to be submitted are videos produced by full-time undergraduate and graduate students for course credit during the preceding 15 months. U.S. citizenship is not required, but all applicants must be enrolled at colleges and universities in the United States. All entries must be submitted on Beta, Beta SP, VHS, or DVD. Competitions are held in the following categories: 1) comedy; 2) drama; 3) music programs; 4) documentary; 5) newscasts; 6) magazine shows; 7) traditional animation; 8) nontraditional or computer-generated animation; and 9) children's programs. The maximum length is 1 hour (30 minutes for newscasts, magazine shows, comedy, and children's programs entries).

Financial data The awards per category are: first place, $2,000; second place, $1,000; and third place, $500. In addition, each of the first- and second-place winners receive Eastman Product Grants ($2,000 of Kodak film stock for the first-place winner and $1,000 of film stock for the second-place winner). The Seymour Bricker College Award of $4,000 is also presented to the first-place College Award winner from any category whose work best represents a humanitarian concern.

Duration The competition is held annually.

Additional information Excerpts from the winning films and videos are screened at the awards ceremony, known as the College Awards Gala. They are also screened at the academy's "Festival of Winners," the day after the Awards Gala.

Number awarded 23 each year: 1 first-place winner, 1 second-place winner, and 1 third-place winner in each category except music programs and children's programs (1 award only in each of those 2 categories).

Deadline December of each year.

[776]
ACP CARTOONING AWARDS
Associated Collegiate Press
Attn: ACP Contest
2221 University Avenue S.E., Suite 121
Minneapolis, MN 55414
(612) 625-8335 Fax: (612) 626-0720
E-mail: info@studentpress.org
Web: www.studentpress.org/acp/contests.html

Purpose To recognize and reward outstanding work by student cartoonists at college newspapers that are members of the Associated Collegiate Press (ACT).

Eligibility This competition is open to students on the staff of an ACP member publication. Entries are accepted in 2 categories: editorial (limited to 2 entries per person or per publication) and comic panels/strips (limited to 1 entry per person or 2 entries per publication). Cartoons must have been published in an ACP member publication during the preceding calendar year.

Financial data A total of $1,000 in prizes is available for this competition.

Duration The competition is held annually.

Additional information This competition is sponsored by Universal Press Syndicate.

Number awarded Varies each year.

Deadline June of each year.

[777]
ACP REPORTER OF THE YEAR AWARDS
Associated Collegiate Press
Attn: ACP Contest
2221 University Avenue S.E., Suite 121
Minneapolis, MN 55414
(612) 625-8335 Fax: (612) 626-0720
E-mail: info@studentpress.org
Web: www.studentpress.org/acp/contests.html

Purpose To recognize and reward outstanding reporting by journalism students at college newspapers that are members of the Associated Collegiate Press (ACT).

Eligibility This competition is open to reporters enrolled as full-time students and working on the staff of an ACP member publication. Applicants must submit copies of their 3 best single news or feature stories published during the preceding academic year. Stories must be the work of 1 reporter, although 1 of the 3 may have been published under a shared byline. The stories may be of any length.

Only 1 student from each newspaper may enter the contest. Reporters compete in separate categories for 2-year colleges and 4-year colleges and universities.
Financial data For each category, first prize is $1,000, second $500, and third $250.
Duration The competition is held annually.
Additional information The competition for 4-year colleges and universities is co-sponsored by MCT Campus.
Number awarded 6 each year: 3 in each category.
Deadline June of each year.

[778]
ACSA/AISC STUDENT DESIGN COMPETITION
Association of Collegiate Schools of Architecture
Attn: Project Manager
1735 New York Avenue, N.W.
Washington, DC 20006
(202) 785-2324, ext. 8   Fax: (202) 628-0448
E-mail: competitions@acsa-arch.org
Web: www.acsa-arch.org/competitions/home.aspx

Purpose To recognize and reward architecture and design students who submit outstanding entries in a design competition that utilizes steel as a building material.
Eligibility This competition is open to architecture students in their third year or higher, including graduate students, at colleges and universities in the United States, Canada, and Mexico that are members of the Association of Collegiate Schools of Architecture (ACSA). Participants are invited to submit a design that addresses the specific criteria outlined in the competition program. Specifications change each year but involve the use of steel in design and construction. The competition currently includes 2 categories: 1 for the design of a Museum of Steel in Pittsburgh and 1 for an open competition. Presentations must include a site plan showing the relationship of surrounding development, landscaping, and circulation patterns; floor plans; elevations and sections sufficient to show site context and major program elements; large-scale drawings, either orthographic or 3-dimensional, illustrating the use of structural steel; and a 3-dimensional representation in the form of an axonometric, perspective, or model photographs. Submissions must be sponsored by a faculty member and are to be principally the product of design studio work. Both individual and team entries are eligible. Selection is based on creative use of structural steel in the design solution; successful response of the design to its surrounding context; and successful response to such basic architectural concepts as human activity needs, structural integrity, and coherence of architectural vocabulary.
Financial data In each category, first prize is $2,500 for the student and $1,000 for the faculty sponsor, second prize is $1,500 for the student and $750 for the faculty sponsor, and third prize is $750 for the student and $500 for the faculty sponsor.
Duration The competition is held annually.
Additional information This competition, first held in 2000, is sponsored by the American Institute of Steel Construction (AISC).
Number awarded 6 student prizes (3 in each category) are awarded each year.

Deadline Faculty who wish to enroll their studio classes must register by February of each year. Entries must be submitted by May.

[779]
AGO/QUIMBY REGIONAL COMPETITIONS FOR YOUNG ORGANISTS
American Guild of Organists
475 Riverside Drive, Suite 1260
New York, NY 10115
(212) 870-2310   Fax: (212) 870-2163
E-mail: competitions@agohq.org
Web: www.agohq.org/competitions/index.html

Purpose To recognize and reward outstanding student organists.
Eligibility Eligible to compete are student organists 23 years of age or younger. Competitions are held in each of the 9 regions of the American Guild of Organists (AGO); contestants may enter the region either where they reside or where they attend school. The repertoire consists of 4 pieces: 1) a prelude and fugue by Bach; 2) a hymn chosen from a designated list; 3) a work by a composer born between 1800 and 1880; and 4) a work composed after 1930. The total performance time may not exceed 40 minutes. Students first compete in their local chapter; winners advance to the regional competitions.
Financial data Each region awards a cash prize of $1,000 to the first-place winner and $500 to the second-place winner.
Duration The competition is held biennially, in odd-numbered years.
Additional information This competition is supported by Quimby Pipe Organs, Inc. A $25 registration fee is charged.
Number awarded 18 each year: a first and second prize in each of the AGO regions.
Deadline Competitors must register with their chapter by mid-January of each odd-numbered year.

[780]
AIKO SUSANNA TASHIRO HIRATSUKA MEMORIAL SCHOLARSHIP
Japanese American Citizens League
Attn: National Scholarship Awards
1765 Sutter Street
San Francisco, CA 94115
(415) 921-5225   Fax: (415) 931-4671
E-mail: jacl@jacl.org
Web: www.jacl.org/leadership_development_5.php

Purpose To provide financial assistance for undergraduate education in the performing arts to student members of the Japanese American Citizens League (JACL).
Eligibility This program is open to JACL members who are enrolled in undergraduate study in the performing arts. Applicants should provide a recording of themselves performing, along with published critical reviews and/or evaluations by their instructor. Along with their application, they must submit a 2-page essay on what American society can learn from the Japanese American experience. Selection is based on academic history, JACL involvement, extracurric-

ular activities, scholastic honors, and a letter of recommendation. Professional artists are not eligible.
Financial data The stipend depends on the availability of funds but usually ranges from $1,000 to $5,000.
Duration 1 year; nonrenewable.
Additional information Applications must be submitted to the JACL National Scholarship Program, c/o San Diego JACL Chapter, 1031 25th Street, San Diego, CA 92102.
Number awarded 1 each year.
Deadline March of each year.

[781]
ALEXANDER M. TANGER SCHOLARSHIP
Broadcast Education Association
Attn: Scholarships
1771 N Street, N.W.
Washington, DC 20036-2891
(202) 429-3935　　　　Toll-free: (888) 380-7222
E-mail: beainfo@beaweb.org
Web: www.beaweb.org/scholarships.html

Purpose To provide financial assistance to upper-division and graduate students who are interested in preparing for a career in broadcasting.
Eligibility This program is open to juniors, seniors, and graduate students enrolled full time at a college or university where at least 1 department is an institutional member of the Broadcast Education Association. Applicants may be studying any area of broadcasting. Selection is based on evidence that the applicant possesses high integrity, superior academic ability, potential to be an outstanding electronic media professional, and a sense of personal and professional responsibility.
Financial data The stipend is $5,000.
Duration 1 year; may not be renewed.
Additional information Information is also available from Peter B. Orlik, Central Michigan University, 344 Moore Hall, Mt. Pleasant, MI 48859, (989) 774-7279.
Number awarded 1 each year.
Deadline October of each year.

[782]
ALPHA CORRINE MAYFIELD SCHOLARSHIP
National Federation of Music Clubs
1336 North Delaware Street
Indianapolis, IN 46202-2481
(317) 638-4003　　　　Fax: (317) 638-0503
E-mail: info@nfmc-music.org
Web: www.nfmc-music.org

Purpose To recognize and reward outstanding young opera singers who are members of the National Federation of Music Clubs (NFMC).
Eligibility Entrants must be opera singers, senior members of the federation, U.S. citizens, and between 20 and 35 years of age.
Financial data The award is $2,000.
Duration The competition is held biennially, in odd-numbered years.
Additional information Applications and further information are available from Frances Brown, 855 Cherokee Road N.E., Gainesville, GA 30501; information on all federation scholarships and awards is available from Chair, Competitions and Awards Board, Dr. George R. Keck, 421 Cherry Street, Arkadelphia, AR 71923-5116, E-mail: keckg@obu.edu. There is a $10 entry fee.
Number awarded 1 every other year.
Deadline January of odd-numbered years.

[783]
AMERICAN INDIAN ARTS COUNCIL SCHOLARSHIP PROGRAM
American Indian Arts Council, Inc.
Attn: Scholarship Committee
725 Preston Forest Shopping Center, Suite B
Dallas, TX 75230
(214) 891-9640　　　　Fax: (214) 891-0221
E-mail: aiac@flash.net

Purpose To provide financial assistance to American Indian undergraduates or graduate students planning a career in the arts or arts administration.
Eligibility This program is open to American Indian undergraduate and graduate students who are preparing for a career in fine arts, visual and performing arts, communication arts, creative writing, or arts administration or management. Applicants must be currently enrolled in and attending a fully-accredited college or university. They must provide official tribal documentation verifying American Indian heritage and have a GPA of 2.5 or higher. Applicants majoring in the visual or performing arts (including writing) must submit slides, photographs, videotapes, audio tapes, or other examples of their work. Letters of recommendation are required. Awards are based on either merit or merit and financial need. If the applicants wish to be considered for a need-based award, a letter from their financial aid office is required to verify financial need.
Financial data Stipends range from $250 to $1,000 per semester.
Duration 1 semester; may be renewed if the recipient maintains a GPA of 2.5 or higher.
Additional information This program was established in 1993.
Number awarded Varies each year.
Deadline September of each year for the fall semester; February of each year for the spring semester.

[784]
ANDREW E. NUQUIST AWARD
University of Vermont
Attn: Center for Research on Vermont
Nolin House
589 Main Street
Burlington, VT 05401-3439
(802) 656-4389　　　　Fax: (802) 656-8518
E-mail: crv@uvm.edu
Web: www.uvm.edu/~crvt

Purpose To recognize and reward undergraduate students who submit outstanding papers on Vermont topics.
Eligibility This program is open to all college and university undergraduate students. Candidates must submit a paper (of any length) that represents a culminating study.

The paper may have taken more than a year to complete and may result from an internship with government agencies or other nonacademic groups. The topic must relate in some way to a Vermont theme. Submissions must include a letter of recommendation from a nominating faculty member. Selection is based on the creativity, analysis, and quality of presentation as well as evidence of comprehensive and systematic research.
Financial data A cash prize is awarded.
Duration The competition is held annually.
Additional information This program began in 1982. Award-winning projects become a permanent part of the University of Vermont's Special Collections Department at Bailey/Howe Library.
Number awarded 1 each year.
Deadline February of each year.

[785]
ANDREW M. ECONOMOS SCHOLARSHIP
Broadcast Education Association
Attn: Scholarships
1771 N Street, N.W.
Washington, DC 20036-2891
(202) 429-3935   Toll-free: (888) 380-7222
E-mail: beainfo@beaweb.org
Web: www.beaweb.org/scholarships.html

Purpose To provide financial assistance to upper-division and graduate students who are interested in preparing for a career in radio broadcasting.
Eligibility This program is open to juniors, seniors, and graduate students enrolled full time at a college or university where at least 1 department is an institutional member of the Broadcast Education Association (BEA). Applicants must be interested in preparing for a career in radio. Selection is based on evidence that the applicant possesses high integrity, superior academic ability, potential to be an outstanding electronic media professional, and a sense of personal and professional responsibility.
Financial data The stipend is $3,500.
Duration 1 year; may not be renewed.
Additional information Information is also available from Peter B. Orlik, Central Michigan University, 344 Moore Hall, Mt. Pleasant, MI 48859, (989) 774-7279. This program is sponsored by the RCS Charitable Foundation and administered by the BEA.
Number awarded 1 each year.
Deadline October of each year.

[786]
ANGELUS AWARDS
Angelus Student Film Festival
c/o Family Theater Productions
7201 Sunset Boulevard
Hollywood, CA 90046
(323) 874-6633   Toll-free: (800) 874-0999
E-mail: info@angelus.org
Web: www.angelus.org

Purpose To recognize and reward outstanding student films on themes that "honor the fundamental dignity of the human person."
Eligibility This program is open to undergraduate and graduate film and video students. Applicants must submit films that reflect such values as redemption, spirituality, dignity, tolerance, equality, diversity, hope, and the triumph of the human spirit. Acceptable genres include live action (drama, comedy, and narrative), animation, and documentary. Entries must 1) be in English, have English subtitles, or be dubbed in English; 2) be under 90 minutes in length; 3) have been completed during the previous 2 years while the filmmaker was a student at a recognized educational institute; and 4) be submitted on 1/2 or 3/4 inch VHS (NTSC) for jury screening. Prizes include the Grand Prize (designated the Excellence in Filmmaking Award in Honor of Fr. Patrick Peyton, CSC) for the live action film documentary, or animation that best reflects the sponsor's theme through story, direction, and technical excellence; Priddy Brothers Entertainment Triumph Award for the live action film whose theme best reflects the triumph of the human spirit; the Fuji-Film Audience Impact Award for the live action film whose compelling story, imagery, content, and technical excellence delivers strong emotional audience impact; the Mole-Richardson Award for Production Design for the live-action film with outstanding production design; the Outstanding Documentary Award; the Angelus Award for Outstanding Animation; and the Act One Award for Outstanding Screenplay.
Financial data The Excellence in Filmmaking Award in Honor of Fr. Patrick Peyton, CSC is $10,000; the Priddy Brothers Entertainment Triumph Award is $5,000; the Fuji-Film Audience Impact Award is $2,500; the Mole-Richardson Award for Production Design is $2,500; the Outstanding Documentary Award is $3,000; the Angelus Award for Outstanding Animation is $2,000; and the Act One Award for Outstanding Screenplay is $1,500.
Duration The festival is held annually.
Additional information A $45 fee must accompany each entry.
Number awarded Varies each year.
Deadline June of each year.

[787]
ARTHUR POISTER SCHOLARSHIP COMPETITION IN ORGAN PLAYING
American Guild of Organists-Syracuse Chapter
c/o Will Headlee
1650 James Street
Syracuse, NY 13203-2816
(315) 471-8451   E-mail: Wheadlee@aol.com
Web: home.twcny.rr.com/agosyracuse

Purpose To recognize and reward young organists.
Eligibility This competition is open to organists younger than 30 years of age.
Financial data First prize is $2,500 and second is $1,000.
Duration The competition is held annually.
Additional information The entry fee is $35.
Number awarded 2 prizes are awarded each year.
Deadline February of each year.

[788]
ARTHUR WYNNE JR. MEMORIAL AWARD
Public Relations Student Society of America
Attn: Vice President of Member Services
33 Maiden Lane, 11th Floor
New York, NY 10038-5150
(212) 460-1474 Fax: (212) 995-0757
E-mail: prssa@prsa.org
Web: www.prssa.org

Purpose To recognize and reward members of the Public Relations Student Society of America (PRSSA) who develop an outstanding public relations program for a hypothetical product launch.

Eligibility This program is open to members of the society who are enrolled full time as a junior or senior majoring or minoring in public relations, journalism, communications, or marketing. Applicants must submit, as individuals or teams, a general public relations program for a product launch, utilizing MediaContacts and other software developed by BurrellesLuce. Entries must include clearly stated objectives for product launch and publicity/promotional campaign, key messaging points for target launch, description of target media for product launch and a list of key media contacts developed using MediaContacts, overview of promotional plan, and description of how they will monitor and evaluate their news coverage. Selection is based on clarity of objectives, consistency and appropriateness of messaging points, accuracy of media list and inclusion of proper media outlets, overall creativity and originality, clarity of monitoring instructions, and specific details regarding the evaluation of the coverage.

Financial data The award is $1,000.
Duration The award is presented annually.
Additional information This award, first presented in 2005, is sponsored by BurrellesLuce.
Number awarded 1 each year.
Deadline October of each year.

[789]
ASCAP FOUNDATION YOUNG JAZZ COMPOSER AWARDS
American Society of Composers, Authors and Publishers
Attn: ASCAP Foundation
ASCAP Building
One Lincoln Plaza
New York, NY 10023
(212) 621-6219 Fax: (212) 621-6236
E-mail: ascapfoundation@ascap.com
Web: www.ascapfoundation.org/awards.html

Purpose To recognize and reward outstanding jazz compositions.

Eligibility This competition is open to U.S. citizens and permanent residents who are younger than 30 years of age. Applicants may be students in grades K-12, college undergraduates, graduate students, or recipients of a D.M.A. degree. They must submit completely original jazz compositions that have not previously earned awards or prizes in major national competitions. Arrangements are not eligible. Entries include a completed application form; the notated score of 1 composition; a cassette or CD of the composition; and biographical information that includes prior music studies, background, and experience.

Financial data Winners share $25,000 in prizes.
Duration The prizes are presented annually.
Additional information This program, established in 2002, is currently supported by the Gibson Foundation.
Number awarded Varies each year; recently, 24 composers shared these awards.
Deadline November of each year.

[790]
ASEI UNDERGRADUATE SCHOLARSHIPS
American Society of Engineers of Indian Origin
c/o Ramu Ramamurthy, Scholarship Committee Chair
47790 Pavillon Road
Canton, MI 48188
(248) 226-6895 Fax: (248) 226-7166
E-mail: awards@aseimichigan.org.
Web: www.aseisocal.org/scholarships.html

Purpose To provide financial assistance to undergraduate students of Indian origin (from India) who are majoring in architecture, engineering, or related areas.

Eligibility This program is open to undergraduate students of Indian origin (by birth, ancestry, or relation). They must be enrolled full time at an accredited college or university in the United States and majoring in engineering, architecture, computer science, or allied science with a GPA of 3.2 or higher. They must be members of the American Society of Engineers of Indian Origin (ASEI) Selection is based on demonstrated ability, academic achievement (including GPA, honors, and awards), career objectives, faculty recommendations, involvement in science fair and campus activities, and industrial exposure (including part-time work and internships).

Financial data Stipends range from $500 to $1,000.
Duration 1 year.
Number awarded Several each year.
Deadline July of each year.

[791]
ASSOCIATION FOR WOMEN IN SPORTS MEDIA SCHOLARSHIP/INTERNSHIP PROGRAM
Association for Women in Sports Media
c/o Rachel Cohen, Scholarship Coordinator
Dallas Morning News
P.O. Box 655237
Dallas, TX 75265
(979) 450-0146 E-mail: rcohen@dallasnews.com
Web: www.awsmonline.org/scholarship.htm

Purpose To provide financial assistance and work experience to women undergraduate and graduate students who are interested in preparing for a career in sportswriting.

Eligibility This program is open to women who are enrolled in college or graduate school full time and plan to prepare for a career in sportswriting, sports copy editing, sports broadcasting, or sports public relations. Applicants must submit a 1-page essay describing their most memorable experience in sports or sports media, a 1-page resume highlighting their journalism experience, 2 letters of recommendation, up to 5 samples of their work, and a $15 application fee.

Financial data Awardees receive a paid summer internship, a $1,000 scholarship for the next year of college or graduate school, $300 toward travel expenses to attend the annual convention of the Association for Women in Sports Media, waived convention fees, and free lodging at the host hotel. Copy editing interns receive an additional $1,000 scholarship from the Associated Press Sports Editors.

Duration 1 year; nonrenewable.

Additional information Organizations that have hosted interns in the past include *Arizona Republic, Cleveland Plain Dealer, Colorado Springs Gazette, Detroit News,* ESPN, *Fort Worth Star-Telegram, Miami Herald, Newark Star-Ledger, Newsday,* Nike, *Sports Illustrated, St. Petersburg Times,* United States Olympic Committee, and USA Track & Field.

Number awarded Varies each year.

Deadline October of each year.

[792]
ASTA NATIONAL SOLO COMPETITION–SENIOR DIVISION

American String Teachers Association
Attn: Competitions
4153 Chain Bridge Road
Fairfax, VA 22030
(703) 279-2113   Fax: (703) 279-2114
E-mail: asta@astaweb.com
Web: www.astaweb.com/competitions.htm

Purpose To reward outstanding performers on stringed instruments.

Eligibility Eligible to compete are students between 19 and 25 years of age who have graduated from high school. Competitions are held for violin, viola, cello, double bass, classical guitar, and harp. Candidates must be members of the American String Teachers Association (ASTA) or current students of ASTA members. They first enter their state competitions; they may enter either in their state of residency or the state in which they are studying. The state chairs then submit tapes of the winners in their state to the national chair. Musicians who live in states that do not have a state competition may submit tapes directly to the national chair. The repertoire must consist of a required work and a work of the competitor's choice; tapes of performances should run from 17 to 20 minutes. Based on those tapes, finalists are invited to the national competition where the winners are selected.

Financial data Prizes vary each year; recently, they were $7,000 for first place, $4,000 for second, $2,000 for third, and $1,000 for fourth.

Duration The competition is held biennially, in odd-numbered years.

Additional information The entry fee is $75.

Number awarded 4 each odd-numbered year.

Deadline Each state sets the date of its competition, but all state competitions must be completed by mid-November of even-numbered years so the winning tapes reach the national chair by the end of that month. The national competition is in March.

[793]
ATLANTA PRESS CLUB JOURNALISM SCHOLARSHIP AWARD

Atlanta Press Club, Inc.
34 Broad Street, 18th Floor
Atlanta, GA 30303
(404) 57-PRESS   Fax: (404) 223-3706
E-mail: info@atlpressclub.org
Web: www.atlpressclub.org

Purpose To provide financial assistance to college students majoring in journalism at a Georgia college or university.

Eligibility This program is open to residents of Georgia currently majoring in journalism at a college or university in the state at the sophomore or junior level. Applicants must submit an essay of 250 to 500 words describing their career aspirations and why they want a career in journalism. Print applicants must also submit 4 to 6 newspaper or magazine clips. Television applicants must also submit 3 to 6 packaged stories of a newscast they have done. Radio applicants must also submit a 4-minute newscast. Selection is based on skill, achievement, and commitment to journalism. Financial need is not considered in the selection process. A personal interview may be required.

Financial data The stipend is $1,500.

Duration 1 year; nonrenewable.

Additional information The broadcast awards are sponsored by WXIA-TV, Channel 11 and WAGA-TV, Fox 5 (this must go to an outstanding student from the Atlanta University complex).

Number awarded 4 each year: 2 to print journalism students and 2 to broadcast journalism students.

Deadline February of each year.

[794]
ATLAS SHRUGGED ESSAY CONTEST

Ayn Rand Institute
Attn: Essay Contests
2121 Alton Parkway, Suite 250
Irvine, CA 92606-4926
(949) 222-6550   Fax: (949) 222-6558
E-mail: essay@aynrand.org
Web: www.aynrand.org

Purpose To recognize and reward outstanding essays written by college students on Ayn Rand's novel, *Atlas Shrugged.*

Eligibility Entrants must be enrolled full time in an undergraduate degree program. They must submit a typewritten essay on questions selected each year from Ayn Rand's novel, *Atlas Shrugged.* The essay must be between 1,000 and 1,200 words. Selection is based on style and content. Judges look for writing that is clear, articulate, and logically organized. To win, an essay must demonstrate an outstanding grasp of the philosophic meaning of the novel.

Financial data First prize is $5,000; second prizes are $1,000; third prizes are $400, finalist prizes are $100, and semifinalist prizes are $50.

Duration The competition is held annually.

Additional information This competition began in the academic year 1998-99.

Number awarded 49 each year: 1 first prize, 3 second prizes, 5 third prizes, 20 finalist prizes, and 20 semifinalist prizes.
Deadline September of each year.

[795]
AUDREY TANZER SCHOLARSHIP

American Women in Radio and Television-New York City Chapter
Attn: Scholarship
152 Madison Avenue, Suite 801
New York, NY 10016
(212) 481-3038   Fax: (212) 481-3071
E-mail: mgmtoffice@aol.com
Web: www.awrtnyc.org/tanzer.html

Purpose To provide financial assistance to students majoring in broadcast communications at colleges and universities in the New York tri-state area.
Eligibility This program is open to students majoring in broadcast communications at colleges and universities in New York City, New Jersey, and Connecticut. Applicants must have a GPA of 3.0 or higher. Along with their application, they must submit a 300-word essay on their career goals. Financial need is not considered in the selection process.
Financial data The stipend is $1,000.
Duration 1 year.
Additional information This program was established in 2004.
Number awarded 1 each year.
Deadline April of each year.

[796]
AWARD TO HONOR EXCELLENCE IN NEWSPAPER ADVERTISING (ATHENA)

Newspaper Association of America
Attn: ATHENA Awards
1921 Gallows Road, Suite 600
Vienna, VA 22182-3900
(703) 902-1656   Fax: (703) 902-1935
E-mail: jake.kelderman@naa.org
Web: www.athenaawards.com

Purpose To recognize and reward outstanding creative advertisements in the newspaper industry.
Eligibility Entries must be published in a newspaper for the first time during the preceding calendar year. They may be submitted by agencies, clients, printing companies, and/or newspapers. Nominations may be made in any of 10 categories: automotive, beverage, business products and services, entertainment, financial, health care products and services, leisure and travel, media, public service, and student ads.
Financial data The grand prize is $100,000; the student ad prize is $5,000. Gold, silver, and bronze medals are also awarded.
Duration The competition is held annually.
Additional information This program was revived in 1997 after a prolonged hiatus.

Number awarded Varies each year; recently, 50 prizes were awarded, including 1 grand prize, 1 student prize, 9 gold awards, 13 silver awards, and 26 bronze awards (of which 7 were in the student division).
Deadline April of each year.

[797]
AWIC-DC SCHOLARSHIP

Association for Women in Communications-Washington DC Area Chapter
Attn: Frappa Stout, Vice President of Student Affairs
USA Weekend
7950 Jones Branch Drive
McLean, VA 22108-0001
Toll-free: (800) 487-2956   Fax: (703) 854-2122
E-mail: fstout@usaweekend.com
Web: www.awcdc.net/scholar_app.shtml

Purpose To provide financial assistance to women who are working on undergraduate degrees in a communications-related field at universities in the Washington, D.C. area.
Eligibility This program is open to female sophomores and juniors attending a Washington, D.C. area university or college studying advertising, communications, graphic arts, journalism, marketing, public relations, or a related field. Applicants must have an overall GPA of 3.0 or higher and work experience in communications or a related field. They must be active in extracurricular activities, including family obligations, volunteer work, clubs, and organizations, and their involvement must show versatility and commitment. Along with their application, they must submit a 500-word essay on how their present communications-related activities will contribute to the achievement of their career goals. Selection is based on that essay, at least 2 letters of recommendation, academic achievement, and communications activities; financial need is not considered.
Financial data The stipend is $1,000.
Duration 1 year.
Number awarded 1 each year.
Deadline March of each year.

[798]
B. PHINIZY SPALDING AND HUBERT B. OWENS SCHOLARSHIPS

Georgia Trust
Attn: Scholarship Committee
1516 Peachtree Street, N.W.
Atlanta, GA 30309
(404) 881-9980   Fax: (404) 875-2205
E-mail: info@georgiatrust.org
Web: www.georgiatrust.org

Purpose To provide financial assistance to Georgia residents working on a degree in a field related to historical preservation at a college or university in the state.
Eligibility This program is open to Georgia residents currently enrolled full time in their first year of college in the state. Applicants must be majoring in historic preservation or such related fields as archaeology, architecture, history, or planning. U.S. citizenship is required. Selection is based

on academic achievement and past and planned involvement with preservation-related fields.
Financial data The stipend is $1,000.
Duration 1 year.
Additional information Recipients are encouraged to plan to stay and work in Georgia following graduation.
Number awarded 2 each year.
Deadline January of each year.

[799]
BARNUM FESTIVAL FOUNDATION/JENNY LIND COMPETITION FOR SOPRANOS
Barnum Festival Foundation
Attn: Director
1070 Main Street
Bridgeport, CT 06604
(203) 367-8495   Toll-free: (866) 867-8495
E-mail: office@barnumfestival.com
Web: www.barnumfestival.com

Purpose To recognize and reward (with scholarships and a concert trip to Sweden) outstanding young female singers who have not yet reached professional status.
Eligibility Applicants must be sopranos between the ages of 20 and 30 who have not yet attained professional status and who are residents and citizens of the United States. Past finalists may reapply, but former first-place winners and mezzo-sopranos are not eligible. The preliminary audition for 16 contestants chosen on the basis of audio tapes is held at the Barnum Festival in Bridgeport, Connecticut every April. From this audition, 6 finalists are chosen. Final selection of the winner is based on technique, musicianship, diction, interpretation, and stage presence.
Financial data The winner of the competition is presented with a $2,000 scholarship award to further her musical education at a recognized voice training school, academy, or college or with a recognized voice teacher or coach. She is featured in a concert in June with the Swedish Jenny Lind at a locale in Connecticut and is sent to Sweden with her Swedish counterpart to perform in concerts for 2 weeks in July and August. The runner-up receives a $500 scholarship.
Duration The competition is held annually.
Additional information The winner of this competition serves as the American Jenny Lind, a 21st-century counterpart of the Swedish Nightingale brought to the United States for a successful concert tour in 1850 by P.T. Barnum. There is a $35 application fee.
Number awarded 2 each year: 1 winner and 1 runner-up.
Deadline March of each year.

[800]
BEA 2-YEAR/COMMUNITY COLLEGE AWARD
Broadcast Education Association
Attn: Scholarships
1771 N Street, N.W.
Washington, DC 20036-2891
(202) 429-3935   Toll-free: (888) 380-7222
E-mail: beainfo@beaweb.org
Web: www.beaweb.org/scholarships.html

Purpose To provide financial assistance to current or former community college students who are interested in preparing for a career in broadcasting.
Eligibility This program is open to students who are either 1) enrolled full time at a community college, or 2) graduates of a community college enrolled full time at a 4-year college or university. Their current or former community college must be an institutional member of the Broadcast Education Association. Applicants must be studying for a career in broadcasting. Selection is based on evidence that the applicant possesses high integrity, superior academic ability, potential to be an outstanding electronic media professional, and a sense of personal and professional responsibility.
Financial data The stipend is $1,500.
Duration 1 year; may not be renewed.
Additional information Information is also available from Peter B. Orlik, Central Michigan University, 344 Moore Hall, Mt. Pleasant, MI 48859, (989) 774-7279.
Number awarded 2 each year.
Deadline October of each year.

[801]
BENJAMIN C. BLACKBURN SCHOLARSHIP
Friends of the Frelinghuysen Arboretum
Attn: Scholarship Committee
53 East Hanover Avenue
P.O. Box 1295
Morristown, NJ 07962-1295
(973) 326-7603   Fax: (973) 644-9627
TDD: (800) 852-7899
Web: www.arboretumfriends.org/blackburn.html

Purpose To provide financial assistance to residents of New Jersey who are working on an undergraduate or graduate degree in horticulture, landscape architecture, or related fields.
Eligibility This program is open to New Jersey residents who are working on an undergraduate or graduate degree in 1 of the following: horticulture, botany, landscape architecture, or a related field. Undergraduates must have completed at least 24 college credits with a GPA of 3.0 or higher. Applicants must submit brief essays on their short-term goals, work experience related to their career goals, involvement in community activities, and long-term career goals. Selection is based on those essays, college transcripts, 2 letters of recommendation from professors, and 2 letters of recommendation from people in their community. Financial need is not considered in the selection process.
Financial data The stipend is $5,000. Funds are sent directly to the recipient's institution.
Duration 1 year.

HUMANITIES

Number awarded 1 each year.
Deadline April of each year.

[802]
BERTHA MACDONALD SCHOLARSHIP

St. Andrew's Society of New Hampshire
c/o Mrs. Tammy Melcher
37 Norton Road
Kittery, ME 03904
E-mail: sasocietynh@comcast.net
Web: www.standrewsocietynh.org

Purpose To provide financial assistance for study and training to students (of any age) of the Scottish performing arts.
Eligibility Students of the Scottish performing arts (music, dancing, piping, fiddling, clarsach, drumming, and song) are eligible to apply. Preference is given to applicants from New Hampshire and northern New England. All applicants must have at least 2 years of experience in their specialty. They must be seeking additional training (school, workshop, lessons). A recommendation from their current teacher is required (no application without this letter will be considered); the letter should address the applicant's skill level, progress made this year, commitment, demonstrated proficiency, and anticipated development. Selection is based on the applicant's objectives, commitment, demonstrated proficiency, anticipated development, and future goals.
Financial data The amount of the stipend varies, depending upon the scope of training requested. Grants are sent directly to the recipient's school and must be returned if the student does not attend.
Duration 1 year.
Additional information Academic and arts/crafts scholarships are not provided.
Deadline March of each year.

[803]
BETSY PLANK/PRSSA SCHOLARSHIPS

Public Relations Student Society of America
Attn: Vice President of Member Services
33 Maiden Lane, 11th Floor
New York, NY 10038-5150
(212) 460-1474   Fax: (212) 995-0757
E-mail: prssa@prsa.org
Web: www.prssa.org

Purpose To provide financial assistance for college to members of the Public Relations Student Society of America (PRSSA).
Eligibility This program is open to members of the society who are currently enrolled as juniors or seniors in a program of public relations studies and preparing for a career in public relations. Applicants must be nominated by their PRSSA chapter. They must submit a statement (up to 300 words) expressing their commitment to public relations and its ethical practice. Selection is based on academic achievement in public relations and overall studies, demonstrated leadership, practical experience (e.g., internships, other jobs, work with student firm), and commitment to public relations (particularly as expressed in their statement). Financial need is not considered.
Financial data The highest-ranked applicant receives a scholarship of $2,000, second $1,500, and third $750. An additional scholarship may be awarded if there are qualifying applicants and sufficient funds.
Duration 1 year.
Additional information This program was established in 1988.
Number awarded 3 or 4 each year.
Deadline May of each year.

[804]
BODIE MCDOWELL SCHOLARSHIP AWARDS

Outdoor Writers Association of America
121 Hickory Street, Suite 1
Missoula, MT 59801
(406) 728-7434   Toll-free: (800) 692-2477
Fax: (406) 728-7445
Web: www.owaa.org/scholarships.htm

Purpose To provide financial assistance for college or graduate school to students interested in a career in outdoor writing.
Eligibility This program is open to undergraduates entering their junior or senior year of study and graduate students. Applicants must be majoring in a field related to outdoor communications, including print, photography, film, art, or broadcasting. Selection is based on 1) career goals in outdoor communications, 2) examples of work, and 3) letters of recommendation; academic achievement is also considered but is not among the top 3 selection criteria.
Financial data Stipends range from $1,000 to $4,000 per year.
Number awarded Varies each year. Recently, 6 of these scholarships were awarded: 3 to graduate students and 3 to undergraduates.
Deadline February of each year.

[805]
BUSINESS REPORTING INTERN PROGRAM FOR MINORITY COLLEGE SOPHOMORES AND JUNIORS

Dow Jones Newspaper Fund
P.O. Box 300
Princeton, NJ 08543-0300
(609) 452-2820   Fax: (609) 520-5804
E-mail: newsfund@wsj.dowjones.com
Web: DJNewspaperFund.dowjones.com

Purpose To provide work experience and financial assistance to minority college students who are interested in careers in journalism.
Eligibility This program is open to college sophomores and juniors who are U.S. citizens interested in careers in journalism and participating in a summer internship at a daily newspaper as a business reporter. Applicants must be members of a minority group (African American, Hispanic, Asian American, Pacific Islander, American Indian, or Alaskan Native) enrolled as full-time students. They must submit a resume, 3 to 5 recently-published clips, a list of courses

with grades, and a 500-word essay on why they want to spend the summer writing business news.

Financial data Interns receive a salary of at least $350 per week during the summer and a $1,000 scholarship at the successful completion of the program.

Duration 10 weeks for the summer internship; 1 year for the scholarship.

Additional information Interns attend a 1-week training seminar and then work as business reporters on a daily newspaper. Recently, the seminar was held at New York University.

Number awarded Up to 12 each year.

Deadline October of each year.

[806]
CALIFORNIA RESTAURANT ASSOCIATION EDUCATIONAL FOUNDATION SCHOLARSHIPS FOR UNDERGRADUATE STUDENTS

California Restaurant Association
Attn: Educational Foundation
1011 10th Street
Sacramento, CA 95814
(916) 447-5793   Toll-free: (800) 765-4842, ext. 2728
Fax: (916) 447-6182   E-mail: warmour@calrest.org
Web: www.calrest.org/edfoundation/scholarships.asp

Purpose To provide financial assistance to California residents enrolled in a postsecondary culinary program.

Eligibility This program is open to residents of California who are currently enrolled full time in a college or university (may be in any state) in a culinary program. Applicants must have completed at least 1 academic term with a GPA of 2.75 or higher. They must be U.S. citizens or permanent residents who have been employed at least 750 hours in a hospitality-related field. Along with their application, they must submit essays on 1) how their education will help them achieve their career objectives and future goals, and 2) a challenging situation or experience related to the restaurant and food service industry that demonstrates their ability to overcome adversity. Selection is based on the essays, presentation of the application, GPA, industry-related work experience, and letters of recommendation.

Financial data The stipend is $2,000 per year.

Duration 1 year; recipients may reapply.

Number awarded Varies each year.

Deadline April of each year.

[807]
CALIFORNIA STATE FAIR ARTS SCHOLARSHIPS

California State Fair
Attn: Friends of the Fair Scholarship Program
1600 Exposition Boulevard
P.O. Box 15649
Sacramento, CA 95852
(916) 274-5969   E-mail: entryoffice@calexpo.com
Web: www.bigfun.org

Purpose To provide financial assistance to residents of California who are studying the arts in college.

Eligibility This program is open to residents of California currently working on an undergraduate degree at a college or university in the state. Applicants must be studying the arts (e.g., visual arts, dance, music, film). They must have a GPA of 3.0 or higher. Along with their application, they must submit a 2-page essay on why they are pursuing their desired career and life goals. Selection is based on personal commitment, goals established for their chosen field, leadership potential, and civic accomplishments.

Financial data Stipends are $1,000 or $500.

Duration 1 year.

Additional information The Friends of the Fair Scholarship Program was established in 1993.

Number awarded 2 each year: 1 at $1,000 and 1 at $500.

Deadline March of each year.

[808]
CALIFORNIA STATE FAIR CULINARY COOKING AND HOSPITALITY MANAGEMENT SCHOLARSHIPS

California State Fair
Attn: Friends of the Fair Scholarship Program
1600 Exposition Boulevard
P.O. Box 15649
Sacramento, CA 95852
(916) 274-5969   E-mail: entryoffice@calexpo.com
Web: www.bigfun.org

Purpose To provide financial assistance to residents of California who are studying culinary cooking or hospitality management.

Eligibility This program is open to residents of California currently working on an associate degree at a culinary specialty school in the state. Applicants must be enrolled in a culinary cooking or hospitality management program. They must have a GPA of 3.0 or higher. Along with their application, they must submit a 2-page essay on why they are pursuing their desired career and life goals. Selection is based on personal commitment, goals established for their chosen field, leadership potential, and civic accomplishments. field, and civic accomplishments.

Financial data Stipends are $1,000 or $500.

Duration 1 year.

Additional information The Friends of the Fair Scholarship Program was established in 1993.

Number awarded 2 each year: 1 at $1,000 and 1 at $500.

Deadline March of each year.

[809]
CARMEL MUSIC SOCIETY COMPETITION

Carmel Music Society
Attn: Chair, Competition Committee
P.O. Box 22783
Carmel, CA 93922
(831) 625-9938   Fax: (831) 625-6823
E-mail: carmelmusic@sbcglobal.net
Web: www.carmelmusic.org

Purpose To recognize and reward outstanding young musicians in California, Oregon, and Washington.

Eligibility Eligible are residents or full-time students in California, Oregon, and Washington and persons born in those states. Applicants must be between 18 and 30 years of age. The competition cycles around 3 rotating formats, covering instrumentalists, vocalists, and pianists in successive years. Applicants must submit an audition (on tape or CD) of 20 to 25 minutes representing at least 3 musical style periods. Finalists are invited to an audition in Carmel at which they perform the same program as submitted on the tape or CD. Performers currently under professional management and previous Carmel Music Society award winners are not eligible.

Financial data The grand prize is $4,000 and the opportunity to appear the following year on the Carmel Music Society's subscription series; other prizes are $1,500 for second place, $1,000 for third place, and $500 for runners-up.

Duration The competition is held annually.

Additional information The competition cycle is: instrumental in 2008, vocal in 2009, and piano in 2010. A nonrefundable fee of $40 must accompany each application.

Number awarded 1 grand prize, 1 second prize, 1 third prize, and 5 runners-up prizes are awarded each year.

Deadline February of each year.

[810]
CAROLE SIMPSON SCHOLARSHIP

Radio and Television News Directors Foundation
1600 K Street, N.W., Suite 700
Washington, DC 20006-2838
(202) 467-5218   Fax: (202) 223-4007
E-mail: irvingw@rtndf.org
Web: www.rtndf.org

Purpose To provide financial assistance to outstanding undergraduate students, especially minorities, who are interested in preparing for a career in electronic journalism.

Eligibility Eligible are sophomore or more advanced undergraduate students enrolled in an electronic journalism sequence at an accredited or nationally-recognized college or university. Applicants must submit 1 to 3 examples of reporting or producing skills on audio or video cassette tapes (no more than 15 minutes total), a description of their role on each story and a list of who worked on each story and what they did, a statement explaining why they are seeking a career in broadcast or cable journalism, and a letter of endorsement from a faculty sponsor that verifies the applicant has at least 1 year of school remaining. Preference is given to undergraduate students of color.

Financial data The stipend is $2,000, paid in semiannual installments of $1,000 each.

Duration 1 year.

Additional information The Radio and Television News Directors Foundation (RTNDF) also provides an all-expense paid trip to the Radio-Television News Directors Association (RTNDA) annual international conference. It defines electronic journalism to include radio, television, cable, and online news. Previous winners of any RTNDF scholarship or internship are not eligible.

Number awarded 1 each year.

Deadline April of each year.

[811]
CAROLINA FILM AND VIDEO FESTIVAL AWARDS

Carolina Film and Video Festival
c/o University of North Carolina
211 Brown Building
P.O. Box 26170
Greensboro, NC 27402
(336) 334-4197   Fax: (336) 334-5039
E-mail: cfvf@uncg.edu
Web: www.uncg.edu/bcn/cfvf

Purpose To recognize and reward outstanding independent film and video productions.

Eligibility This competition is open to students and nonstudents producing films and videotapes. Categories include narrative, documentary, and experimental/animation. Entries must be accompanied by a film synopsis of 25 words or less. Screenplays are also accepted for a scriptwriting competition. All works must be submitted in VHS format for pre-screening. Final submissions are accepted in 16mm, Beta, SVHS (NTSC), and VHS (NTSC).

Financial data A total of $2,500 is awarded each year.

Duration The competition is held annually, in March.

Additional information Early entry fees are $5 for high school students, $20 for college students, or $30 for independents. Standard entry fees are $10 for high school students, $30 for college students, or $40 for independents.

Deadline September of each year for early entry; October of each year for standard entry.

[812]
CASE STUDY COMPETITION IN CORPORATE COMMUNICATIONS

Institute for Public Relations Research and Education
c/o University of Florida
2096 Weimer Hall
P.O. Box 118400
Gainesville, FL 32611-8400
(352) 392-0280   Fax: (352) 846-1122
E-mail: iprceo@jou.ufl.edu
Web: www.instituteforpr.com

Purpose To recognize and reward undergraduate and graduate students in business, communications, or journalism who win a competition in public relations.

Eligibility This competition is open to undergraduate and graduate students enrolled at accredited schools of business, communications, or journalism. Students may participate as sole authors or members of a case-writing team (not to exceed 4 people). Each student author or case-writing team must be sponsored by a faculty member. Applicants must submit a case study on a topic within the field of corporate communication or public relations, including but not limited to crisis or issues management, government relations, integrated marketing communications, internal or employee communications, investor relations, measuring communications impact, interactive or Internet public relations, or reputation management. Cases should clearly describe a business problem, not the solutions to the problem. They must be accompanied by a teaching note and a PowerPoint presentation. Selection is based on the relevance, purpose, and timeliness of the entry (15 points); significance of the business problem and the critical issues identified on the entry (15 points); balance, fairness, and absence of bias in the entry (15 points); factual and accurate nature of the entry (15 points); entry's style, tone, and quality of expression (15 points); quality of the teaching note (15 points); and quality of the PowerPoint presentation (10 points). Separate competitions are held for business schools and for communications and journalism schools.

Financial data The prizes for submissions from business schools and from communications and journalism schools are $2,500 for first, $1,500 for second, and $800 for third. The faculty advisor for the first-place winners receive $650, for the second-place winners $350, and for the third-place winners $200. The grand prize is $5,000 for the student(s) and $1,500 for the faculty advisor.

Duration The competition is held annually.

Additional information This competition is sponsored by the Arthur W. Page Society, 317 Madison Avenue, Suite 2320, New York, NY 10017, (212) 400-7959, Fax: (212) 922-9198, E-mail: admin@awpagesociety.com. A non-refundable entry fee of $25 is required.

Number awarded 6 winners are selected each year (3 from business schools and 3 from communications and journalism schools). From those, 1 is selected as the grand prize winner.

Deadline Entries must be submitted by January of each year.

[813]
CHARLES D. MAYO STUDENT SCHOLARSHIP

International Furnishings and Design Association
Attn: IFDA Educational Foundation
191 Clarksville Road
Princeton Junction, NJ 08550
(609) 799-3423   Fax: (609) 799-7032
E-mail: info@ifda.com
Web: www.ifdaef.org/scholarships.html

Purpose To provide financial assistance to undergraduate students working on a degree in interior design.

Eligibility This program is open to full-time undergraduate students majoring in interior design or a related field. Applicants must submit an essay of 300 to 500 words on their future plans and goals and why they believe they deserve the scholarship. Selection is based on the essay; the applicant's achievements, awards, and accomplishments; and a letter of recommendation from a professor or instructor. Financial need is not considered.

Financial data The stipend is $1,000.

Duration 1 year.

Additional information This program was established in 1998. Information is also available from Joan Long, Director of Grants, 5522 Estates Drive, Oakland, CA 94618, E-mail: jlongdesigns@yahoo.com.

Number awarded At least 1 each year.

Deadline March of each year.

[814]
CHARLES M. SCHULZ AWARD FOR COLLEGE CARTOONISTS

Scripps Howard Foundation
Attn: Vice President, Programs
312 Walnut Street, 28th Floor
P.O. Box 5380
Cincinnati, OH 45201
(513) 977-3035   Toll-free: (800) 888-3000, ext. 3030
Fax: (513) 977-3800   E-mail: porters@scripps.com
Web: foundation.scripps.com

Purpose To recognize and reward outstanding college cartoonists.

Eligibility Any student cartoonist at a college newspaper or magazine in the United States or its territories may enter this competition. Work must have been completed during the calendar year of the contest. Cartoons may be panels, strips, and/or editorial cartoons. Entries must include a 250-word statement by the cartoonist outlining his or her goals in cartooning.

Financial data The prize is $10,000 and a trophy.

Duration The competition is held annually.

Additional information This award was first presented in 1980.

Number awarded 1 each year.

Deadline January of each year.

[815]
CHARLOTTE HOYT BAGNALL SCHOLARSHIP FOR CHURCH MUSICIANS

First Church of Christ
Attn: Charlotte Hoyt Bagnall Scholarship Committee
17 Beaverbrook Road
West Simsbury, CT 06092
(860) 658-7405   Fax: (860) 408-9229
E-mail: CHBScholarship@1stchurchsimsbury.org
Web: www.chbscholarship.com

Purpose To provide financial assistance to high school and college students interested in studying religious music.

Eligibility This program is open to musicians interested in improving their ability to support religious worship services by studying religious music and liturgy. Applicants must be interested in a program of organ lessons; high school, college, or graduate level studies related to organ or religious music; or participation in organ festivals, seminars, or music camps. Competitions are limited to high school musicians in even-numbered years and to musicians of all ages who have completed their junior year in high school in odd-numbered years. Along with their application, they must submit essays on their 1) goals and aspirations, including what they want to achieve in their ministry of music; and 2) course of study, including the course of study for which they want to use the scholarship and how it will help them achieve their goals and aspirations. Up to 6 finalists are selected and invited to an interview that includes a demonstration of keyboard skills on the organ and/or piano. The winner is the finalist whose goals are consistent with the beliefs of the religious organization they serve or plan to serve, plan of study is consistent with the goals, and keyboard skills are adequate to achieve the goals.

Financial data The stipend is $1,500 for the winner and lesser amounts for special award recipients.
Duration 1 year.
Additional information This program was established in 1995.
Number awarded Varies each year; recently, 1 winner and 2 special award recipients were selected.
Deadline December of each year.

[816]
CHIPS QUINN SCHOLARS PROGRAM
Freedom Forum
Attn: Chips Quinn Scholars Program
1101 Wilson Boulevard
Arlington, VA 22209
(703) 284-3934   Fax: (703) 284-3543
E-mail: kcatone@freedomforum.org
Web: www.chipsquinn.org

Purpose To provide work experience, career mentoring, and scholarship support to minority college students and recent graduates who are majoring in journalism.
Eligibility This program is open to students of color who are college juniors, seniors, or recent graduates with journalism majors or career goals in newspapers. Candidates must be nominated or endorsed by journalism faculty, campus media advisers, editors of newspapers, or leaders of minority journalism associations. Along with their application, they must submit a resume, transcripts, 2 letters of recommendation, and an essay of 200 to 500 words on why they want to be a Chips Quinn Scholar. Reporters must also submit 6 samples of published articles they have written; photographers must submit 6 samples of their work on a CD. Applicants must have a car and be available to work as a full-time intern during the spring or summer. U.S. citizenship or permanent resident status is required. Campus newspaper experience is strongly encouraged.
Financial data Students chosen for this program receive a travel stipend to attend a workshop at the Freedom Forum in Arlington, Virginia prior to reporting for their internship. Upon completion of the internship, they receive a $1,600 scholarship.
Duration Internships are for 10 to 12 weeks; the scholarship is for 1 year.
Additional information This program was established in 1991 in memory of the late John D. Quinn Jr., managing editor of the *Poughkeepsie Journal.* Funding is provided by the Freedom Forum, formerly the Gannett Foundation. After graduating from college and obtaining employment with a newspaper, alumni of this program are eligible to apply for fellowship support to attend professional journalism development activities.
Number awarded Approximately 70 each year. Since the program began, 1,020 scholars have been selected.
Deadline October of each year.

[817]
CLAMPITT PAPER/HENRY PHILLIPS MEMORIAL SCHOLARSHIP
Printing and Imaging Association of MidAmerica
Attn: Dodie Royals
8828 North Stemmons, Suite 505
Dallas, TX 75247
(214) 630-8871, ext. 205   Toll-free: (800) 788-2040
E-mail: dodier@piamidam.org
Web: www.piamidam.org/scholar.php

Purpose To provide financial assistance to residents of Oklahoma and Texas who are attending college to prepare for a career in the printing industry.
Eligibility This program is open to students enrolled in an educational institution that offers a 2- or 4-year degree in printing technology or management. Applicants must be residents of Oklahoma or Texas. They should be attending a school in those states, but they may go elsewhere if they can demonstrate the appropriate aptitude and industry interest. Along with their application, they must submit a 1-page statement outlining their career goals and a letter of endorsement from their faculty sponsor that reinforces their stated intention to prepare for a career in the printing industry. Selection is based on interest in the industry, activities, and GPA; financial need is not considered.
Financial data The stipend is $1,000.
Duration 1 year.
Number awarded 1 or more each year.
Deadline February of each year.

[818]
CLEVELAND ADVERTISING ASSOCIATION EDUCATION FOUNDATION SCHOLARSHIPS
Cleveland Advertising Association
Attn: Education Foundation
20325 Center Ridge Road, Suite 670
Cleveland, OH 44116
(440) 673-0020   Fax: (440) 673-0025
E-mail: adassoc@clevead.com
Web: www.clevead.com/education/scholarships.php

Purpose To provide financial assistance to undergraduate students who are residents of Ohio majoring in a field related to advertising at a college or university in the state.
Eligibility This program is open to residents of Ohio who are full-time seniors, juniors, or second-semester sophomores at colleges and universities in the state. Applicants must be majoring in advertising or a related communications or marketing field and have a GPA of 3.0 or higher. They must submit transcripts, 2 letters of recommendation, and an essay describing their career goals. Financial need is not considered in the selection process. Some of the scholarships are set aside for U.S. citizens of African, Asian, Hispanic, Native American, or Pacific Island descent.
Financial data Stipends range from $1,000 to $3,000.
Duration 1 year.
Additional information This program includes the following named scholarships: the Arras Group Minority Scholarship, the Wyse Advertising Scholarship, the Thomas Brennan Memorial Scholarship, the Hitchcock Fleming Scholarship, the Innis Maggiore Scholarship, the Marcus Thomas Scholarship, the Laurie Mitchell and Company Scholarship,

the Stern Advertising Scholarship, the Huntington National Bank Scholarship, the Rob Spademan Scholarship, and the Plain Dealer/Jerry Hoegner Scholarship.

Number awarded Varies each year. Recently, this program awarded 10 scholarships: 1 at $3,000, 2 at $2,500, 1 at $2,000, 5 at $1,500, and 1 at $1,000.

Deadline October of each year.

[819]
COATING AND GRAPHIC ARTS DIVISION SCHOLARSHIPS

Technical Association of the Pulp and Paper Industry
Attn: TAPPI Foundation
15 Technology Parkway South
Norcross, GA 30092
(770) 209-7536   Toll-free: (800) 332-8686
Fax: (770) 446-6947   E-mail: vedmondson@tappi.org
Web: www.tappi.org

Purpose To provide financial assistance to student members of the Technical Association of the Pulp and Paper Industry (TAPPI) who are interested in preparing for a career in the paper industry, with a focus on coating and graphic arts.

Eligibility This program is open to TAPPI student members who are enrolled full time in a program related to the coated paper and paperboard or the graphic arts industries. Applicants must be juniors or higher with a GPA of 3.0 or higher; graduate students are also eligible if they have not advanced to doctoral candidacy. Selection is based on demonstrated interest in a career in the coating and graphic arts industry; financial need is not considered.

Financial data The stipend is $1,000.

Duration 1 year.

Additional information This program includes the Robert W. Hagemeyer Scholarship.

Number awarded Up to 4 each year.

Deadline January of each year.

[820]
COLLEGE PHOTOGRAPHER OF THE YEAR

National Press Photographers Foundation
c/o University of Missouri at Columbia
Attn: CPOY Director
109 Lee Hills Hall
Columbia, MO 65211
(573) 882-4442   Fax: (573) 884-4999
E-mail: info@cpoy.org
Web: www.cpoy.org

Purpose To recognize and reward the outstanding photographic work of college students.

Eligibility Students currently working on an undergraduate or graduate degree are eligible to submit work completed during the previous academic year. Single picture categories are: 1) spot news; 2) general news; 3) feature; 4) sports action; 5) sports feature; 6) portrait; 7) pictorial; 8) illustration; and 9) personal vision. Multiple picture categories are: 10) domestic picture story; 11) international picture story; 12) sports portfolio; 13) documentary; 14) portfolio; 15) individual online or multimedia photo story or essay; and 16) team online or multimedia photo story or essay. Professional photographers who have worked 2 years or more are not eligible.

Financial data In the portfolio competition, the first-place winner receives a Nikon Digital SLR System, a 14-week internship at National Geographic Magazine, the Colonel William J. Lookadoo Award of $1,000, a Canon camera, and a plaque; second-place winner receives the Milton Freier Award of $500, a Nikon Digital SLR camera, and a full fellowship to Poynter Institute's Winning Photojournalism Seminar; third-place winner receives a Nikon Digital SLR camera and a plaque; the online/multimedia category winner receives a full participant fellowship to the Multimedia Reporting Seminar at Poynter Institute; the documentary category winner receives a tuition scholarship to the Missouri Photo Workshop; each of the other individual category winners receive certificates.

Duration The competition is held annually, in the fall.

Additional information The competition is sponsored by the National Press Photographers Foundation, Missouri Photo Workshop, Nikon Camera, National Geographic Magazine, Poynter Institute for Media Studies, Kappa Alpha Mu, and the University of Missouri's School of Journalism. The entry fee is $25 per photographer.

Deadline October of each year.

[821]
COLORADO BROADCASTERS ASSOCIATION COLLEGE SCHOLARSHIPS

Colorado Broadcasters Association
Attn: Education Committee
2042 Boreas Pass Road
P.O. Box 2369
Breckenridge, CO 80424
(970) 547-1388   Fax: (970) 547-1384
E-mail: cobroadcasters@earthlink.net
Web: www.e-cba.org/education.asp

Purpose To provide financial assistance to Colorado residents who are working on an undergraduate degree related to broadcasting at a college or university in the state.

Eligibility This program is open to residents of Colorado who are enrolled in an accredited college or university in the state that offers undergraduate degree programs in broadcast journalism, production or management, communications, speech, telecommunications, new media, or some other aspect of professional media education that explicitly prepares students for careers in broadcasting. Students must be nominated by their department, each of which may nominate up to 3 candidates but must identify a faculty or staff member who will be a liaison to the sponsoring organization. Applicants must submit a resume, their school transcript and any other relevant academic records, a statement of their educational and professional goals and their qualifications for the scholarship, and a letter of recommendation from a faculty member.

Financial data The stipend is $2,000.

Duration 1 year.

Number awarded 3 each year.

Deadline February of each year.

HUMANITIES

[822]
COLORADO BROADCASTERS ASSOCIATION VOCATIONAL SCHOOL SCHOLARSHIP

Colorado Broadcasters Association
Attn: Education Committee
2042 Boreas Pass Road
P.O. Box 2369
Breckenridge, CO 80424
(970) 547-1388   Fax: (970) 547-1384
E-mail: cobroadcasters@earthlink.net
Web: www.e-cba.org/education.asp

Purpose To provide financial assistance to Colorado residents who are enrolled in a vocational broadcast program.

Eligibility This program is open to residents of Colorado who are enrolled in an accredited professional training school offering programs in broadcasting or some other aspect of professional media education that explicitly prepares students for careers in broadcasting. Students must be nominated by their school, each of which may nominate up to 3 candidates but must identify a faculty or staff member who will be a liaison to the sponsoring organization. Applicants must submit a resume, their school transcript and any other relevant academic records, a statement of their educational and professional goals and their qualifications for the scholarship, and a letter of recommendation from a faculty member.

Financial data The stipend is $1,000.

Duration 1 year.

Number awarded 1 each year.

Deadline February of each year.

[823]
CONCRETE THINKING FOR A SUSTAINABLE WORLD STUDENT DESIGN COMPETITION

Association of Collegiate Schools of Architecture
Attn: Project Manager
1735 New York Avenue, N.W.
Washington, DC 20006
(202) 785-2324, ext. 8   Fax: (202) 628-0448
E-mail: competitions@acsa-arch.org
Web: www.acsa-arch.org/competitions/home.aspx

Purpose To recognize and reward architecture and design students who submit outstanding entries in a design competition that utilizes Portland cement-based materials to achieve sustainable design objectives.

Eligibility This competition is open to architecture students in their third year or higher, including graduate students, at colleges and universities in the United States, Canada, and Mexico that are members of the Association of Collegiate Schools of Architecture (ACSA). Participants are invited to submit a design that addresses the specific criteria outlined in the competition program. Specifications change each year but involve the use of Portland cement in design and construction. The competition currently includes 2 categories: the component category in which students design a single construction component or methodology using Portland cement-based products, and the structure category in which students create a comprehensive building design incorporating Portland cement-based products. Submissions must be sponsored by a faculty member and are to be principally the product of design studio work. Both individual and team entries are eligible. Selection is based on skill in integrating Portland cement-based materials to achieve sustainable development objectives; originality of design innovation; response to such basic architectural concepts as human activity needs, climatic considerations, structural integrity, site planning, creative insight, and coherence of architectural vocabulary; integration of concrete's multiple benefits to address such sustainable design issues as land use, air and water quality, energy, resource use and reuse, durability, and disaster resistance; and clear and comprehensive design.

Financial data In each category, the winning student individuals or teams receive $1,700 and the faculty sponsors receive $800. Each winning school receives a complete package of pcaStructurePoint software.

Duration The competition is held annually.

Additional information This competition, first held in 2006, is sponsored by the Portland Cement Association.

Number awarded 4 student prizes (2 in each category) are awarded each year.

Deadline Faculty who wish to enroll their studio classes must register by February of each year. Entries must be submitted by June.

[824]
COPY EDITING SCHOLARSHIPS

American Copy Editors Society
Attn: Carol DeMasters, ACES Administrator
38309 Genesee Lake Road
Oconomowoc, WI 53066
E-mail: carolafj@execpc.com
Web: www.copydesk.org/scholarships.htm

Purpose To provide financial assistance to undergraduate and graduate students interested in becoming copy editors.

Eligibility This program is open to college juniors, seniors, and graduate students who are interested in a career as a copy editor. Graduating students who will take full-time jobs or internships as copy editors are also eligible. Applicants must submit 1) a list of course work relevant to copy editing they have completed; 2) information on their copy editing experience, including work on student and professional newspapers; 3) an essay, up to 750 words, on what they think makes a good copy editor and why they want to prepare for that career; 4) 2 letters of recommendation; 5) 5 to 10 headlines they have written; and 6) a copy of a story they have edited, including an explanation of the changes they have made and the circumstances under which it was edited. Selection is based on commitment to copy editing as a career, work experience in copy editing, and abilities in copy editing. Financial need is not considered. The highest ranked applicant receives the Merv Aubespin Scholarship.

Financial data Stipends are $2,500 (for the Merv Aubespin Scholarship) or $1,000.

Duration 1 year.

Number awarded 4 or 5 each year.

Deadline October of each year.

[825] CRAZY HORSE MEMORIAL JOURNALISM SCHOLARSHIP

South Dakota Newspaper Association
527 Main Avenue, Suite 202
P.O. Box 8100
Brookings, SD 57006-8100
Toll-free: (800) 658-3697   Fax: (605) 692-6388
E-mail: sdna@sdna.com
Web: www.sdna.com

Purpose To provide financial assistance to Native American students interested in preparing for a career in journalism.

Eligibility This program is open to Native American students enrolled or planning to enroll at a college or university. Applicants must be interested in preparing for a journalism career, although they are not required to major in journalism in college. Along with their application, they must submit a 500-word essay explaining their interest in journalism and 2 letters of reference.

Financial data The stipend is $2,000.

Duration 1 year.

Additional information This program is sponsored by the Crazy Horse Memorial Foundation.

Number awarded 1 each year.

Deadline March of each year.

[826] CTASLA STUDENT SCHOLARSHIP

American Society of Landscape Architects-Connecticut Chapter
Attn: Scholarship Committee
87 Willow Street
New Haven, CT 06511
Toll-free: (800) 878-1474
E-mail: executivedirector@ctasla.org
Web: www.ctasla.org/scholarship.htm

Purpose To provide financial assistance to residents of Connecticut interested in working on a college degree in landscape architecture.

Eligibility This program is open to Connecticut residents entering or enrolled in an accredited environmental education program at a college or university. Applicants must submit a brief statement explaining why they desire this financial aid and why they have chosen landscape architecture as their field of study.

Financial data The stipend is $2,500.

Duration 1 year.

Number awarded 1 or 2 each year.

Deadline March of each year.

[827] CULINARY TRUST SCHOLARSHIPS

International Association of Culinary Professionals Foundation
Attn: Culinary Trust Scholarship Program
304 West Liberty Street, Suite 201
Louisville, KY 40202
(502) 581-9786, ext. 264   Toll-free: (800) 928-4227
Fax: (502) 589-3602   E-mail: tgribbins@hqtrs.com
Web: www.iacpfoundation.org/html/scholarships.html

Purpose To provide financial assistance to culinary professionals and students interested in pursuing additional training in the United States or abroad in the culinary arts.

Eligibility This program is open to 1) culinary professionals who have at least 2 years of food service experience (paid, volunteer, or a combination of both); and 2) students who have a GPA of 3.0 or higher. Applicants must submit 2 letters of recommendation and a 2-page essay on their educational and career goals and how they plan to achieve them. They may be from any country. Selection is based on merit, food service work experience, culinary goals and skills, and references.

Financial data Stipends range from $1,500 to $5,000.

Duration 1 year.

Additional information This program includes a number of named scholarships that vary each year, many of them for specified culinary arts schools. Recently, support was available at L'Academie de Cuisine (Gaithersburg, Maryland), the Art Institute of New York City, the Institute of Culinary Education (New York, New York), Le Cordon Bleu Adelaide, Le Cordon Bleu London, Le Cordon Bleu Mexico, Le Cordon Bleu Paris, Le Cordon Bleu Sydney, New England Culinary Institute (Montpelier, Vermont), the French Culinary Institute (New York, New York), the Culinary Institute of America at Greystone (St. Helena, California), and the CIA at The Rudd Center (Napa, California). Other scholarships included the Cuisinart Scholarship for students of any nationality at any accredited culinary school, the Charlie Trotter Culinary Education Foundation Scholarship for residents of Illinois, the Julia Child Endowment Fund Scholarship for independent study in France, and the Julia Child Fund at the Boston Foundation Scholarship for research, writing, or teaching in France. There is a $25 application fee.

Number awarded Varies each year.

Deadline December of each year.

[828] C2C/CITDA STUDENT COMPETITION

American Association of Textile Chemists and Colorists
Attn: Technical Center
1 Davis Drive
P.O. Box 12215
Research Triangle Park, NC 27709-2215
(919) 549-8141   Fax: (919) 549-8933
E-mail: holmes@aatcc.org
Web: www.aatcc.org

Purpose To recognize and reward undergraduate and graduate students who submit outstanding textile designs in a national competition.

Eligibility This competition is open to undergraduate and graduate students who work as individual or in teams of up to 4 members. Applicants are invited to submit textile designs in 2 main categories: interior design (recently restricted to table lines) and apparel design (recently restricted to rainwear). Within each category, they may enter sub-categories of print design or product design. Students may enter only 1 sub-category. Entries must be submitted digitally in files less than 50 megabytes with resolution no less than 300 dpi. Selection is based on color, texture, visual appeal, pleasure, aesthetics, reproducibility, and how those aspects relate to functionality.

Financial data In each category, first prize is $1,000 and second prize is $500. Winners also receive complimentary student registration for the sponsor's international conference and exhibition.

Duration The competition is held annually.

Additional information This competition was first held in 1994 by the Computer Integrated Textile Design Association (CITDA). In 2005, CITDA transitioned its assets, including its student scholarship competition, to the American Association of Textile Chemists and Colorists (AATCC). The competition currently operates as part of AATCC's Concept 2 Consumer (C2C) interest group. The entry fee is $25, but that is waived for AATCC student members.

Number awarded 8 each year: 1 first prize and 1 second prize in each of the 4 sub-categories.

Deadline November of each year.

[829]
DANCE SOCIETY OF AMERICA SCHOLARSHIPS

Scholarship Administrative Services, Inc.
Attn: DSA Program
457 Ives Terrace
Sunnyvale, CA 94087

Purpose To provide financial assistance to students preparing for a career as a dancer at a college, university, or other institution.

Eligibility This program is open to students enrolled or planning to enrolled in a dance program at a college, university, or other recognized school of dance. Applicants must have a record of successful participation in dance competitions at the youth and high school level. They must submit a letter of recommendation from a dance instructor with whom they previously studied and a 500-word essay on what inspired them to become a dancer. Financial need is not considered in the selection process.

Financial data The stipend is $5,000 per year.

Duration 1 year; nonrenewable.

Additional information This program is sponsored by the Dance Society of America (DSA) and administered by Scholarship Administrative Services, Inc. DSA was established in 2005 to encourage more American students to consider a career as a dancer. Requests for applications should be accompanied by a self-addressed stamped envelope, the student's e-mail address, and the source where they found the scholarship information.

Number awarded Up to 20 each year.

Deadline April of each year.

[830]
DANIEL J. EDELMAN AWARD

Public Relations Student Society of America
Attn: Vice President of Member Services
33 Maiden Lane, 11th Floor
New York, NY 10038-5150
(212) 460-1474 Fax: (212) 995-0757
E-mail: prssa@prsa.org
Web: www.prssa.org

Purpose To provide financial assistance for college to members of the Public Relations Student Society of America.

Eligibility This program is open to members of the society who are currently enrolled in a full-time program of study at an accredited 4-year college or university. Applicants must submit 2 letters of recommendation and 10 samples of their individual public relations work. Selection is based on leadership, achievements and activities in public relations, and recommendations from faculty members and/or industry professionals. Financial need is not considered.

Financial data The winner receives a cash award of $1,500, of which $1,000 is paid upon winning the award and $500 at the start of a 3-month paid internship at an Edelman Worldwide office in the United States. The runner-up receives $500 and an opportunity to interview at an Edelman U.S. office for a full-time position.

Duration 1 year.

Additional information This program was established by Edelman in 1990. Information is also available from Edelman Worldwide, Attn: Ana Vazquez, 200 East Randolph Drive, 63rd Floor, Chicago, IL 60601, (312) 240-3000.

Number awarded 1 winner and 1 runner-up are selected each year.

Deadline December of each year.

[831]
DAVID HOODS MEMORIAL SCHOLARSHIP

Electronic Document Systems Foundation
Attn: EDSF Scholarship Awards
608 Silver Spur Road, Suite 280
Rolling Hills Estates, CA 90274-3616
(310) 265-5510 Fax: (310) 265-5588
E-mail: jmowlds@edsf.org
Web: www.edsf.org/scholarships.cfm

Purpose To provide financial assistance to upper-division and graduate students interested in working with electronic documents as a career.

Eligibility This program is open to full-time juniors, seniors, and graduate students who demonstrate a strong interest in working with electronic documents as a career (including graphic communications, document management, document content, and/or document distribution). Special consideration is given to students interested in marketing and public relations. Applicants must submit a statement of their career goals in the field of document communications, an essay on a topic related to their view of the future of the document management and production industry, a list of current professional and college extracurricular activities and achievements, college transcripts (GPA of 3.0 or higher), samples of their creative work, and 2 letters of recommendation. Financial need is not considered.

Financial data The stipend is $2,000.
Duration 1 year.
Additional information This program was established in 1999.
Number awarded 1 each year.
Deadline May of each year.

[832]
DAVID L. STASHOWER VISIONARY SCHOLARSHIPS

Liggett-Stashower, Inc.
Attn: Scholarship Award Committee
1228 Euclid Avenue
Cleveland, OH 44115
(216) 373-8278   Toll-free: (800) 877-4573
Fax: (216) 861-1284   E-mail: bstolarski@liggett.com
Web: www.liggett.com

Purpose To provide financial assistance to students at colleges and universities in Ohio who are majoring in fields related to communications.
Eligibility This program is open to students entering their senior year at colleges and universities in Ohio. Applicants must be majoring in advertising, graphic design, public relations, or communications. Selection is based on academic achievement, faculty recommendations, and documentation of work (portfolio, writing samples, or other form of communication the applicant considers appropriate). Financial need is not considered.
Financial data The stipend is $2,000 per year.
Duration 1 year; nonrenewable.
Additional information This scholarship was first offered in 1998.
Number awarded 2 each year.
Deadline April of each year.

[833]
DAVID S. BARR AWARDS

Newspaper Guild-CWA
501 Third Street, N.W., Suite 250
Washington, DC 20001-2797
(202) 434-7177   Fax: (202) 434-1472
E-mail: guild@cwa-union.org
Web: www.newsguild.org

Purpose To recognize and reward student journalists whose work has helped promote social justice.
Eligibility This program is open to high school students (including those enrolled in vocational, technical, or special education programs) and college students (including those in community colleges and in graduate programs). Applicants must submit work published or broadcast during the preceding calendar year; entries should help to right a wrong, correct an injustice, or promote justice and fairness.
Financial data The award is $1,500 for college students or $500 for high school students.
Duration The awards are presented annually.
Number awarded 2 each year.
Deadline January of each year.

[834]
DAVID W. MILLER AWARD FOR STUDENT JOURNALISTS

Chronicle of Higher Education
Attn: Deputy Managing Editor
1255 23rd Street, N.W.
Washington, DC 20037
E-mail: milleraward@chronicle.com   (202) 466-1000
Web: chronicle.com/help/milleraward.htm

Purpose To recognize and reward college journalists who submit outstanding samples of their published work.
Eligibility This competition is open to undergraduate students in any country. Applicants are invited to submit up to 3 samples of their published work (in English), accompanied by a 1-page letter describing the articles and why they were chosen for submission. Entries must have appeared in a campus publication during the previous academic year. Each piece should be journalistic, using expository, explanatory, narrative, or other techniques to report evenhandedly on a topic of intellectual interest. Opinion essays, personal columns, scholarly or research papers, and articles that present the author's own research findings are ineligible.
Financial data The award is $2,000.
Duration The award is presented annually.
Additional information This program was established in 2003.
Number awarded 1 each year.
Deadline June of each year.

[835]
DENDEL SCHOLARSHIPS

Handweavers Guild of America, Inc.
Attn: Scholarship Committee
1255 Buford Highway, Suite 211
Suwanee, GA 30024
(678) 730-0010   Fax: (678) 730-0836
E-mail: hga@weavespindye.org
Web: www.weavespindye.org

Purpose To provide financial assistance to undergraduate and graduate students working on a degree in the field of fiber arts.
Eligibility This program is open to undergraduate and graduate students enrolled in accredited colleges and universities in the United States, its possessions, and Canada. Applicants must be working on a degree in the field of fiber arts, including training for research, textile history, and conservation. Along with their application, they must submit 1) a 50-word essay on their study goals and how those fit into their future plans, and 2) 5 to 16 slides of their work. Selection is based on artistic and technical merit; financial need is not considered.
Financial data A stipend is awarded (amount not specified). Recipients may use the funds for tuition, materials (e.g., film for photographs), or travel.
Duration Funds must be spent within 1 year.
Number awarded Varies; more than $4,000 is available for this program each year.
Deadline March of each year.

[836]
DES MOINES SYMPHONY ALLIANCE COLLEGE/EMERGING PROFESSIONAL DIVISION YOUNG ARTIST COMPETITION

Des Moines Symphony Alliance
221 Walnut Street
Des Moines, IA 50309
(515) 280-4000 Fax: (515) 280-4005
E-mail: info@dmsymphony.org
Web: www.dmsymphony.org

Purpose To recognize and reward outstanding college-age student musicians in Iowa.

Eligibility Eligible to compete are 1) currently-enrolled full- and part-time undergraduate and graduate students; and 2) recent college graduates. Applicants must be younger than 25 years of age and either residents of Iowa or students at an Iowa college or university. Competitions are held in 3 categories: 1) piano; 2) violin, viola, cello, and bass; 3) brass, woodwinds, harp, and percussion. Each contestant must play an entire standard concerto accompanied by piano and a solo or concert piece in a contrasting style to the concerto; all selections must be performed from memory. They must submit cassette tapes; finalists are invited to an audition. The total performance time is 20 minutes.

Financial data First prize in each category is $1,000 and second prize is $750. The Grand Prize winner also receives a full tuition plus room and board scholarship to the summer Aspen Music School and may be invited to perform with the Des Moines Symphony.

Duration The competition is held annually.

Additional information A non-refundable fee of $30 must accompany the application and tape.

Number awarded 6 each year: a first and second prize in each of the 3 categories.

Deadline December of each year.

[837]
DIRECT MARKETING SCHOLARSHIP

New England Direct Marketing Association
Attn: NEDMA Foundation
193 Haverhill Street
North Reading, MA 01864
(978) 664-3877 Fax: (978) 664-2835
E-mail: nedmafdn@comcast.net
Web: www.nedma.com/foundation.html

Purpose To provide financial assistance and work experience to upper-division students in New England who are preparing for a career in direct marketing.

Eligibility This program is open to students who have completed their sophomore or junior year at a college or university in New England. Applicants must be majoring in marketing, advertising, communications, journalism, or other field designed to prepare them for a career in direct marketing. Along with their application, they must submit essays covering why they are applying for this scholarship, what courses in their major have interested them the most and why, the extracurricular activities in which they have participated, their employment or internship experiences (especially those related to marketing, advertising, or journalism), their special interest in the field, how they believe this scholarship will affect their short- and long-term goals, and what direct marketing means to them. Financial need is not considered in the selection process.

Financial data The award includes a stipend of $3,000 to be applied to college tuition, attendance at a nationally sponsored seminar on the basics of direct marketing, a paid summer internship at a New England firm that represents a segment of the direct marketing industry, and attendance at the annual conference of the New England Direct Marketing Association (NEDMA).

Duration 1 year.

Number awarded 1 each year.

Deadline February of each year.

[838]
DORE SCHARY AWARDS

Anti-Defamation League
Attn: Dore Schary Awards
823 United Nations Plaza
New York, NY 10017
(212) 885-7804 Fax: (212) 885-5855
E-mail: asquires@adl.org
Web: www.adl.org/doreschary_awards

Purpose To recognize and reward outstanding film and video productions on human rights topics by students and young filmmakers.

Eligibility This competition is open to 1) university and graduate students majoring in film and/or television, and 2) amateur and professional filmmakers 30 years of age or younger. Applicants must submit productions that were completed during the 2 preceding calendar years and deal with such themes as prejudice, discrimination, hatred, bigotry, racism, anti-Semitism, or any theme that supports diversity. Entries may include, but are not limited to, narrative, documentary, experimental, and animated productions. All phases of production (except actors in dramatic films, who may be professionals) must be completed by the filmmaker. Productions based on previously published works of fiction are not eligible. All entries should be submitted in DVD, mini DVD, BETA, or VHS format. Selection is based on subject matter, imagination and creativity, and technical excellence.

Financial data The prizes are $2,000 for first and $1,000 for second. Winners are flown to Los Angeles for the awards ceremony.

Duration The competition is held annually.

Additional information This program was established in 1982.

Number awarded 2 each year.

Deadline May of each year.

[839]
DR. AUREL ZAJTA SCHOLARSHIP
Electronic Document Systems Foundation
Attn: EDSF Scholarship Awards
608 Silver Spur Road, Suite 280
Rolling Hills Estates, CA 90274-3616
(310) 265-5510   Fax: (310) 265-5588
E-mail: jmowlds@edsf.org
Web: www.edsf.org/scholarships.cfm

Purpose To provide financial assistance to undergraduate and graduate students working on a degree in mathematics-based studies related to the graphic arts.

Eligibility This program is open to undergraduate and graduate students who are working on a degree in mathematics-based studies related to the graphic arts, font, print, or Internet-related studies. Applicants must be enrolled full time at a technical school, trade school, community college, university, college, or graduate school in the United States with a GPA of 3.0 or higher. Along with their application, they must submit a statement of their career goals in the field of document communications, an essay on a topic related to their view of the future of the document management and production industry, a list of current professional and college extracurricular activities and achievements, college transcripts, samples of their creative work, and 2 letters of recommendation. Financial need is not considered.

Financial data The stipend is $1,000.

Duration 1 year.

Additional information This program is sponsored by COPI/OutputLinks.

Number awarded 1 each year.

Deadline May of each year.

[840]
E. LANIER (LANNY) FINCH SCHOLARSHIP
Georgia Association of Broadcasters, Inc.
Attn: Scholarship Foundation
8010 Roswell Road, Suite 150
Atlanta, GA 30350
(770) 395-7200   Toll-free: (877) 395-7200 (within GA)
Fax: (770) 395-7235
Web: www.gab.org

Purpose To provide financial assistance to students in Georgia interested in preparing for a career in broadcasting.

Eligibility This program is open to residents of Georgia who are rising juniors or seniors studying for a career in broadcasting at a college, professional school, or university in the state. Applicants must submit brief essays on the specific area of broadcasting that interests them most and why, what they think is the broadcaster's primary responsibility, and the most important facts that the judges should know about them. Selection is based on academic records, extracurricular activities, community involvement, and leadership potential.

Financial data The stipend is $1,500. Funds are paid directly to the recipient's institution.

Duration 1 year.

Number awarded 4 each year: 1 in each designated region in the state.

Deadline March of each year.

[841]
E. NELSON JAMES SCHOLARSHIPS
Sigma Tau Delta
c/o William C. Johnson, Executive Director
Northern Illinois University
Department of English
DeKalb, IL 60115-2863
(815) 753-1612   E-mail: sigmatd@niu.edu
Web: www.english.org/scholarships.shtml

Purpose To provide financial assistance to undergraduate student members of Sigma Tau Delta (the international English honor society).

Eligibility Eligible to be nominated are members of the society who are currently enrolled as college juniors. Each chapter may nominate 3 active juniors for this scholarship. Candidates are required to provide proof of registration in at least 50% of a full load of courses as part of an English degree program. Selection is based on academic record, chapter service, awards, professional goals, an application essay (up to 400 words on a topic that changes annually), and 2 letters of recommendation.

Financial data The stipend is $2,500 for winners or $750 for runners-up.

Duration 1 year.

Additional information Information is also available from the Scholarship Committee Chair, Dr. Sidney Watson, Oklahoma Baptist University, 500 West University, OBU Box 61238, Shawnee, OK 74804.

Number awarded 4 each year: 3 winners and 1 runner-up.

Deadline October of each year.

[842]
ED BRADLEY SCHOLARSHIP
Radio and Television News Directors Foundation
1600 K Street, N.W., Suite 700
Washington, DC 20006-2838
(202) 467-5218   Fax: (202) 223-4007
E-mail: irvingw@rtndf.org
Web: www.rtndf.org

Purpose To provide financial assistance to outstanding undergraduate students, especially minorities, who are preparing for a career in electronic journalism.

Eligibility Eligible are sophomore or more advanced undergraduate students enrolled in an electronic journalism sequence at an accredited or nationally-recognized college or university. Applicants must submit 1 to 3 examples of reporting or producing skills on audio or video cassette tapes (no more than 15 minutes total), a statement explaining why they are interested in a career in broadcast or cable journalism, and a letter of endorsement from a faculty sponsor that verifies the applicant has at least 1 year of school remaining. Preference is given to undergraduate students of color.

Financial data The stipend is $10,000, paid in semiannual installments of $5,000 each.

Duration 1 year.

Additional information The Radio and Television News Directors Foundation (RTNDF) also provides an all-expense paid trip to the Radio-Television News Directors Association (RTNDA) annual international conference. It defines elec-

tronic journalism to include radio, television, cable, and online news. Previous winners of any RTNDF scholarship or internship are not eligible.
Number awarded 1 each year.
Deadline April of each year.

[843]
EDSF BOARD OF DIRECTORS SCHOLARSHIPS
Electronic Document Systems Foundation
Attn: EDSF Scholarship Awards
608 Silver Spur Road, Suite 280
Rolling Hills Estates, CA 90274-3616
(310) 265-5510   Fax: (310) 265-5588
E-mail: jmowlds@edsf.org
Web: www.edsf.org/scholarships.cfm

Purpose To provide financial assistance to college juniors, seniors, and graduate students interested in working with electronic documents as a career.
Eligibility This program is open to juniors, seniors, and graduate students who are committed to preparing for a career in document management and communications marketplace, including computer science and engineering, graphic and media communications, e-commerce, imaging science, printing, web authoring, electronic publishing, telecommunications, and business (e.g., sales, marketing). Applicants must be enrolled full time at a college, university, or graduate school in the United States with a GPA of 3.0 or higher. Along with their application, they must submit a statement of their career goals in the field of document communications, an essay on a topic related to their view of the future of the document management and production industry, a list of current professional and college extracurricular activities and achievements, college transcripts, samples of their creative work, and 2 letters of recommendation. Financial need is not considered.
Financial data The stipend ranges from $1,000 to $2,000.
Duration 1 year.
Number awarded Varies each year. Recently, 28 of these scholarships were awarded: 10 at $2,000, 1 at $1,500, and 17 at $1,000.
Deadline May of each year.

[844]
EDSF BOARD OF DIRECTORS TECHNICAL AND COMMUNITY COLLEGE SCHOLARSHIP
Electronic Document Systems Foundation
Attn: EDSF Scholarship Awards
608 Silver Spur Road, Suite 280
Rolling Hills Estates, CA 90274-3616
(310) 265-5510   Fax: (310) 265-5588
E-mail: jmowlds@edsf.org
Web: www.edsf.org/scholarships.cfm

Purpose To provide financial assistance to students in technical schools and community colleges who are interested in working with electronic documents as a career.
Eligibility This program is open to first- and second-year students at technical and trade schools and community colleges. Applicants must be working on a degree in the field of electronic document communication, including graphic communication, computer science, and multimedia, and have a GPA of 3.0 or higher. Along with their application, they must submit a 1-page essay on 1 of the following topics: 1) a definition of their career goals in the field of document management and communications; 2) a recent technological change and how it has or will affect the document communication industry; or 3) a definition of the document communication industry. Selection is based on the essay, extracurricular activities and achievements, high school transcripts, samples of creative work, and 2 letters of recommendation. Financial need is not considered.
Financial data The stipend is $1,000.
Duration 1 year.
Number awarded 5 each year.
Deadline May of each year.

[845]
EDWARD G. GILLOOLY JOURNALISM SCHOLARSHIP
National Association of Government Employees
Attn: Kevin Doyle
159 Burgin Parkway
Quincy, MA 02169
(617) 376-7214   Toll-free: (866) 412-7762
E-mail: kdoyle@nage.org
Web: www.nage.org/schol.shtml

Purpose To provide financial assistance to members of the National Association of Government Employees (NAGE) and their families who are working on an undergraduate degree in journalism.
Eligibility This program is open to NAGE members and their spouses, children, grandchildren, nieces, nephews, dependents, and significant others. Applicants must be attending or planning to attend an accredited college, university, or community college to work full time on a degree in journalism. Along with their application, they must submit 1) a statement of 200 words or less describing what the labor movement has meant to them and their family; and 2) a statement of 500 words or less describing their education and career goals in journalism. Selection is based on originality, clarity, and commitment to excellence in journalism.
Financial data The stipend is $1,000.
Duration 1 year.
Additional information This program began in 2006.
Number awarded 1 each year.
Deadline August of each year.

[846]
EVANGELICAL PRESS ASSOCIATION SCHOLARSHIPS
Evangelical Press Association
Attn: Scholarships
P.O. Box 28129
Crystal, MN 55428
(763) 535-4793   Fax: (763) 535-4794
E-mail: director@epassoc.org
Web: www.epassoc.org/scholarships.html

Purpose To provide financial assistance to upper-division and graduate students interested in preparing for a career in Christian journalism.

Eligibility This program is open to entering juniors, seniors, and graduate students who have at least 1 year of full-time study remaining. Applicants must be majoring or minoring in journalism or communications, preferably with an interest in the field of Christian journalism. They must be enrolled at an accredited Christian or secular college or university in the United States or Canada with a GPA of 3.0 or higher. Along with their application, they must submit a biographical sketch that includes their birth date, hometown, family, and something about the factors that shaped their interest in Christian journalism; a copy of their academic record; references from their pastor and from an instructor; samples of published writing from church or school publications; and an original essay (from 500 to 700 words) on the state of journalism today.

Financial data Stipends range from $500 to $2,000.

Duration 1 year.

Additional information This program includes the Mel Larson Memorial Scholarship.

Number awarded Varies each year: recently, 3 of these scholarships were awarded.

Deadline March of each year.

[847]
EVERT CLARK/SETH PAYNE AWARD FOR YOUNG SCIENCE JOURNALISTS

National Press Foundation
1211 Connecticut Avenue, N.W., Suite 310
Washington, DC 20036
(202) 663-7280   Fax: (202) 530-2855
E-mail: npf@nationalpress.org
Web: www.nationalpress.org

Purpose To recognize and reward young science writers and reporters.

Eligibility The award is limited to non-technical print journalism only. Articles published in newspapers (including college newspapers), magazines, and newsletters are eligible. Both freelancers and staff writers may enter. Books, as well as articles in technical journals and trade association publications, are not considered. Since the prize is managed by *Business Week* staffers, stories in that magazine will not be accepted. Science writing is broadly defined. It includes, but is not limited to, writing in the biological, physical, environmental, computer, and space sciences, along with technology, mathematics, medicine, health, and science policy. Entries are judged on the basis of accuracy, clarity, insightfulness, fairness, resourcefulness, and timeliness. Applicants must be 30 years of age or younger. They may submit a single article or series, up to 4 individual pieces. Applications may be submitted by the author or on the author's behalf.

Financial data The winner receives $1,000 and expenses to attend the annual meeting of the American Association for the Advancement of Science.

Duration The award is presented annually.

Additional information This award was first presented in 1989. It is given by the Evert Clark Fund and the National Association of Science Writers, in conjunction with the National Press Foundation, which administers the endowment.

Number awarded 1 each year.

Deadline December of each year.

[848]
FFTA SCHOLARSHIP COMPETITION

Flexographic Technical Association
Attn: Foundation of Flexographic Technical Association
900 Marconi Avenue
Ronkonkoma, NY 11779-7212
(631) 737-6020   Fax: (631) 737-6813
E-mail: education@flexography.org
Web: www.flexography.org

Purpose To provide financial assistance for college to students interested in a career in flexography.

Eligibility This program is open to 1) high school seniors enrolled in a Flexo in High School program and planning to attend a postsecondary school; and 2) students currently enrolled at a college offering a course of study in flexography. Applicants must demonstrate interest in a career in flexography, exhibit exemplary performance in their studies (particularly in the area of graphic arts), and have an overall GPA of 3.0 or higher. Along with their application, they must submit a 1-page essay providing personal information about themselves (including special circumstances, interests, and activities); career and/or educational goals and how those relate to the flexo industry; employment and internship experience; and reasons why they feel they should be selected for this scholarship. Financial need is not considered.

Financial data Stipends are $2,000 per year.

Duration 1 year; may be renewed.

Number awarded Varies each year; recently, 14 of these scholarships were awarded.

Deadline March of each year.

[849]
FLINT GROUP TECHNICAL WRITING AWARDS

Gravure Association of America
Attn: Gravure Education Foundation
1200-A Scottsville Road
Rochester, NY 14624
(315) 589-8879   Fax: (585) 436-7689
E-mail: lwshatch@gaa.org
Web: www.gaa.org

Purpose To recognize and reward undergraduate and graduate students who submit outstanding technical research papers on gravure technology.

Eligibility This competition is open to full-time undergraduate and graduate students who submit technical research papers, approximately 10 pages in length, that address an aspect of gravure technology. Selection is based on the relevancy of the topic to gravure, the depth and comprehensiveness of the research, the organization of material, and the clarity of presentation.

Financial data Prizes are $1,500 for the graduate student winner, $1,000 for the undergraduate first-place winner, and $500 for the undergraduate second-place winner.

Duration The competition is held annually.

Additional information This program is supported by Flint Ink.

Number awarded 3 each year.

HUMANITIES

Deadline February of each year.

[850]
FORREST BASSFORD STUDENT AWARD
Livestock Publications Council
910 Currie Street
Fort Worth, TX 76107
(817) 336-1130   Fax: (817) 232-4820
E-mail: dianej@flash.net
Web: www.livestockpublications.com/awards.htm

Purpose To provide financial assistance to students majoring in agricultural communications or related fields.

Eligibility This program is open to college juniors and seniors majoring in agricultural journalism, agricultural communications, or agricultural public relations. Applicants must have at least 1 semester of school remaining at the time they receive the award. Along with their application, they must submit a 200-word essay on the future of agricultural communications and how they fit in that career. Selection is based on that essay, a transcript of college work completed and a list of courses in progress, scholarships and awards received, club and other organization memberships, extracurricular activities, employment record, a 1-page press release announcing that they have won this award, and 3 samples of communications work.

Financial data The winner receives a $1,500 scholarship, plus a $500 travel scholarship (to attend the council's annual meeting). The runners-up receive $500 travel scholarships to attend the meeting.

Duration 1 year.

Additional information The funds for this program are provided by the Livestock Publications Council and the Chicago Mercantile Exchange. Information is also available from Angie Stump Denton, *Hereford World*, 1039 Vista Road, Blue Rapids, KS 66411, (785) 363-7263.

Number awarded 1 winner and 3 runners-up are selected each year.

Deadline February of each year.

[851]
FPREF SCHOLARSHIPS
Florida Public Relations Association
Attn: Florida Public Relations Education Foundation
40 Sarasota Center Boulevard, Suite 107
Sarasota, FL 34240
(941) 365-2135   Fax: (941) 906-1556
E-mail: state@fpra.org
Web: www.fpra.org/student_scholarships.asp

Purpose To provide financial assistance to upper-division students majoring in public relations at colleges and universities in Florida.

Eligibility This program is open to students enrolled in a public relations major or emphasis track at 4-year colleges and universities in Florida. Applicants must be juniors or seniors with a GPA of 3.0 or higher. They must be members of the Florida Public Relations Association (FPRA) or an FPRA student chapter. Along with their application, they must submit a 2-page essay on "The Future of Public Relations and the Role I Plan to Play In It." Selection is based on the essay, transcripts, and a resume; financial need is not considered.

Financial data The stipend is $1,500.

Duration 1 year.

Number awarded 2 each year.

Deadline February of each year.

[852]
FRANCES A. MAYS SCHOLARSHIP AWARD
Virginia Association for Health, Physical Education, Recreation, and Dance
c/o Jack Schiltz, Executive Director
817 West Franklin Street
P.O. Box 842020
Richmond, VA 23284-2020
(804) 828-1948   Toll-free: (800) 918-9899
Fax: (804) 828-1946   E-mail: info@vahperd.org
Web: www.vahperd.org

Purpose To provide financial assistance to college seniors majoring in health, physical education, recreation, or dance in Virginia.

Eligibility This program is open to students who have been working full time for 3 years on a degree in health, physical education, recreation, or dance at a college or university in Virginia. Candidates must be nominated by their school and be members of the Virginia Association of Health, Physical Education, Recreation, and Dance (VAHPERD) and the American Association for Health, Physical Education, Recreation, and Dance (AAHPERD). Selection is based on academic achievement, leadership in campus life activities, service to college or university, awards and honors, and service to the community.

Financial data A stipend is awarded (amount not specified).

Duration 1 year.

Number awarded 1 each year.

Deadline September of each year.

[853]
FREEDOM FORUM–NCAA SPORTS JOURNALISM SCHOLARSHIPS
National Collegiate Athletic Association
Attn: Leadership Advisory Board
700 West Washington Avenue
P.O. Box 6222
Indianapolis, IN 46206-6222
(317) 917-6477   Fax: (317) 917-6888
Web: www.ncaa.org

Purpose To provide financial assistance to upper-division students interested in preparing for a career in sports journalism.

Eligibility Applicants must be college juniors who are planning a career in sports journalism and are either majoring in journalism or have experience in campus sports journalism. Along with their application, they must submit their official college transcript, 3 examples of sports journalism work, a letter of recommendation from a journalism professor, and (if they have had a professional internship) a letter of recommendation from their employer. They must also include a statement, 200 to 500 words in length, on assigned topics that change annually. Financial need is not considered.

Financial data The stipend is $3,000.

Duration The award is to be used in the recipient's senior year as a full-time student.

Additional information This program is supported by a grant from the Freedom Forum to the National Collegiate Athletic Association (NCAA) Foundation.

Number awarded 8 each year: 1 in each of the geographical districts of the NCAA.

Deadline December of each year.

[854]
FREEDOM FROM RELIGION FOUNDATION COLLEGE ESSAY CONTEST

Freedom from Religion Foundation
P.O. Box 750
Madison, WI 53701
(608) 256-8900   Toll-free: (608) 256-1116
E-mail: dbarker@ffrf.org
Web: www.ffrf.org/essay/college.php

Purpose To recognize and reward outstanding college student essays on the separation of church and state.

Eligibility Any currently-enrolled college student may write an essay on topics that change annually but involve rejecting religion; recent topics were "Why I am an Atheist or Agnostic," "Growing Up a Freethinker," or "Rejecting Religion." Students may write about their own experiences in rejecting religion in a religious society or use a philosophical or historical approach. Essays should be 4 to 5 typed double-spaced pages, accompanied by a paragraph biography identifying the student's college or university, year in school, major, and interests.

Financial data First prize is $2,000, second $1,000, and third $500.

Duration The competition is held annually.

Additional information First prize was previously designated as the Saul Jakel Memorial Award, but after 1996 it was redesignated the Phyllis Stevenson Grams Memorial Award. This contest has been held since 1979. Applicants must send a self-addressed stamped envelope to receive additional information.

Number awarded 3 each year.

Deadline June of each year.

[855]
FRIENDS-IN-ART SCHOLARSHIP

Friends-in-Art
c/o Harvey Miller
402 East French Broad Street
Brevard, NC 28712-3410
(828) 862-3412   E-mail: hhmiller@citcom.net

Purpose To provide financial assistance to blind students who are majoring or planning to major in fields related to the arts.

Eligibility This program is open to blind and visually impaired high school seniors and college students who are majoring or planning to major in music, art, drama, or creative writing. Required submissions are a recording of 2 contrasting pieces for music students; 10 slides of their work for art students; a recording of 1 dramatic and 1 comic scene for drama students; and a varied selection of their writing for creative writing students. Selection is based on achievement, talent, and excellence in the arts.

Financial data The stipend is $1,000.

Duration 1 year.

Additional information This program began in 1999.

Number awarded 1 each year.

Deadline April of each year.

[856]
GEF CORPORATE LEADERSHIP SCHOLARSHIPS

Gravure Association of America
Attn: Gravure Education Foundation
1200-A Scottsville Road
Rochester, NY 14624
(315) 589-8879   Fax: (585) 436-7689
E-mail: lwshatch@gaa.org
Web: www.gaa.org/GEF/scholarships.htm

Purpose To provide financial assistance to undergraduate and graduate students who are interested in a career in printing.

Eligibility This program is open to sophomores, juniors, seniors, and graduate students who are enrolled full time with a major in printing, graphic arts, or graphic communications. Applicants must be attending a designated learning resource center or an educational partner program supported by the Gravure Education Foundation (GEF) of the Gravure Association of America. They must have a GPA of 3.0 or higher. Along with their application, they must submit a 300-word essay on "How I Can Contribute My Leadership Skills to the Print Communications Industry." Selection is based on the essay, academic success, and leadership development efforts through clubs or associations, sports, community participation, or volunteer activity. Financial need is not considered.

Financial data The stipend is $1,500.

Duration 1 year.

Additional information GEF learning resource centers are located at the following universities: Rochester Institute of Technology, Western Michigan University, California Polytechnic State University at San Luis Obispo, Arizona State University, Clemson University, Murray State University, and the University of Wisconsin at Stout. GEF educational partner programs are at Central Missouri State University and Pittsburg State University of Kansas. This program is supported by the following corporate sponsors: The Cerutti Group, Johnson Polymer, Resinall Corporation, Shamrock Technologies, Stora Enso North America, and IMC America.

Number awarded 6 each year.

Deadline May of each year.

[857]
GEORGE B. BRYAN AWARD
University of Vermont
Attn: Center for Research on Vermont
Nolin House
589 Main Street
Burlington, VT 05401-3439
(802) 656-4389   Fax: (802) 656-8518
E-mail: crv@uvm.edu
Web: www.uvm.edu/~crvt

Purpose To recognize and reward undergraduate students who submit outstanding papers on Vermont topics.
Eligibility This program is open to all college and university undergraduate students. Candidates must submit a paper, from 15 to 25 pages in length, that was completed for a 1-semester course during the preceding calendar year. The topic of the paper must relate in some way to a Vermont theme. Submissions must include a letter of recommendation from a nominating faculty member. Selection is based on the creativity, analysis, and quality of presentation.
Financial data A cash prize is awarded.
Duration The competition is held annually.
Additional information This program began in 1997. Award-winning projects become a permanent part of the University of Vermont's Special Collections Department at Bailey/Howe Library.
Number awarded 1 each year.
Deadline February of each year.

[858]
GEORGE LEBER SCHOLARSHIP
American Hellenic Educational Progressive Association
Attn: AHEPA Educational Foundation
1909 Q Street, N.W., Suite 500
Washington, DC 20009
(202) 232-6300   Fax: (202) 232-2140
E-mail: ahepa@ahepa.org
Web: www.ahepa.org

Purpose To provide financial assistance for college to students with a connection to the American Hellenic Educational Progressive Association (AHEPA), particularly those interested in majoring in political science or history.
Eligibility This program is open to 1) members in good standing of the Order of Ahepa, Daughters of Penelope, Sons of Pericles, or Maids of Athena, and 2) the children of Order of Ahepa or Daughters of Penelope members in good standing. Applicants must be currently enrolled or planning to enroll in a college or university in the following fall. They may major in any area, but preference is given to upper-division students majoring in political science, history, or international relations. Along with their application, they must submit a 500-word biographical essay and their most recent college transcripts. Selection is based on academic achievement; extracurricular, personal, and volunteer activities; athletic achievements; and work experience. Financial need is not considered.
Financial data The annual stipend ranges from $500 to $2,000.
Duration 1 year.
Additional information A processing fee of $20 must accompany each application.
Number awarded Varies each year; recently, 2 of these scholarships were awarded.
Deadline March of each year.

[859]
GLADYS C. ANDERSON MEMORIAL SCHOLARSHIP
American Foundation for the Blind
Attn: Scholarship Committee
11 Penn Plaza, Suite 300
New York, NY 10001
(212) 502-7661   Toll-free: (800) AFB-LINE
Fax: (212) 502-7771   TDD: (212) 502-7662
E-mail: afbinfo@afb.net
Web: www.afb.org/scholarships.asp

Purpose To provide financial assistance to legally blind high school, undergraduate, or graduate women who are interested in studying religious or classical music.
Eligibility This program is open to legally blind women who are U.S. citizens and have been accepted in an accredited undergraduate or graduate program in religious or classical music. Along with their application, they must submit an essay that includes the field of study they are pursuing and why they have chosen it; their educational and personal goals; their work experience; any extracurricular activities with which they have been involved, including those in school, religious organizations, and the community; and how they intend to use scholarship monies that may be awarded. They must also submit a sample performance tape (a voice or instrumental selection).
Financial data The stipend is $1,000.
Duration 1 academic year.
Number awarded 1 each year.
Deadline April of each year.

[860]
GLENN MILLER SCHOLARSHIP COMPETITION
Glenn Miller Birthplace Society
Attn: Scholarship Program
107 East Main Street
P.O. Box 61
Clarinda, IA 51632
(712) 542-2461   Fax: (712) 542-2461
E-mail: gmbs@heartland.net
Web: www.glennmiller.org/scholar.htm

Purpose To recognize and reward, with college scholarships, present and prospective college music majors.
Eligibility Eligible to apply are 1) graduating high school seniors planning to major in music in college and 2) freshmen music majors at an accredited college, university, or school of music. Both instrumentalists and vocalists may compete. Those who entered as high school seniors and did not win first place are eligible to enter again as college freshmen. Each entrant must submit an audition tape, from which 10 instrumentalist finalists and 10 vocalist finalists are selected. Finalists audition in person. They must perform a composition of concert quality, up to 5 minutes in length, sight read selections chosen by the judges, and perform technical exercises. They must also submit a statement that they intend to make music performance or teaching a cen-

tral part of their future life. Selection is based on talent in any field of applied music; the competition is not intended to select Glenn Miller look-alikes or sound-alikes.

Financial data Awards are $3,000 for first place, $2,000 for second, or $1,000 for third. The funds are to be used for any school-related expense.

Duration The competition is held annually, in June.

Additional information Finalists compete in auditions at the Glenn Miller Festival stage show, in Clarinda, Iowa. The scholarship for the first-place vocalist is designated the GMBS-Ray Eberle Vocal Scholarship; the scholarship for the second-place vocalist is designated the GMBS-Ralph Brewster Vocal Scholarship; the scholarship for the third-place vocalist is designated the GMBS-Jack Pullan Memorial Vocal Scholarship. Applicants selected as finalists on the basis of their audition tapes are responsible for their own transportation expenses to go to Clarinda to perform at the auditions.

Number awarded 6 each year: 3 for instrumentalists and 3 for vocalists.

Deadline March of each year.

[861]
GOLDEN KEY LITERARY ACHIEVEMENT AWARDS

Golden Key International Honour Society
621 North Avenue N.E., Suite C-100
Atlanta, GA 30308
(404) 377-2400   Toll-free: (800) 377-2401
Fax: (678) 420-6757
E-mail: scholarships@goldenkey.org
Web: www.goldenkey.org

Purpose To recognize and reward literary achievements by members of the Golden Key International Honour Society.

Eligibility This competition is open to undergraduate, graduate, and postgraduate members of the Golden Key International Honour Society. Applicants may compete in the following 4 categories: fiction, nonfiction, poetry, or news writing. All entries must be original and limited to 1,500 words. Only 1 composition per member is accepted. Selection is based on the quality of the submitted writing.

Financial data The winners receive $1,000 awards and publication of their work in CONCEPTS.

Duration The competition is held annually.

Number awarded 4 each year: 1 in each category.

Deadline March of each year.

[862]
GRAVURE CATALOG AND INSERT COUNCIL SCHOLARSHIP

Gravure Association of America
Attn: Gravure Education Foundation
1200-A Scottsville Road
Rochester, NY 14624
(315) 589-8879   Fax: (585) 436-7689
E-mail: lwshatch@gaa.org
Web: www.gaa.org/GEF/scholarships.htm

Purpose To provide financial assistance to upper-division students interested in a career in printing.

Eligibility This program is open to juniors or seniors who are enrolled full time in a field related to printing at a designated learning resource center supported by the Gravure Education Foundation (GEF) of the Gravure Association of America. Applicants must have a GPA of 3.0 or higher. Along with their application, they must submit a 300-word essay that demonstrates their interest in gravure technology and the print communications industry. Financial need is not considered in the selection process.

Financial data The stipend is $1,000.

Duration 1 year.

Additional information GEF learning resource centers are located at the following universities: Rochester Institute of Technology, Western Michigan University, California Polytechnic State University at San Luis Obispo, Arizona State University, Clemson University, Murray State University, and the University of Wisconsin at Stout. The Gravure Catalog and Insert Council is an organization headed by end-users of gravure printing.

Number awarded 1 each year.

Deadline May of each year.

[863]
HALLMARK GRAPHIC ARTS SCHOLARSHIP

Gravure Association of America
Attn: Gravure Education Foundation
1200-A Scottsville Road
Rochester, NY 14624
(315) 589-8879   Fax: (585) 436-7689
E-mail: lwshatch@gaa.org
Web: www.gaa.org/GEF/scholarships.htm

Purpose To provide financial assistance to upper-division students interested in a career in printing.

Eligibility This program is open to juniors and seniors who are enrolled full time in a field related to printing at a designated learning resource center supported by the Gravure Education Foundation (GEF) of the Gravure Association of America. Applicants must have a GPA of 3.0 or higher. Along with their application, they must submit a 300-word essay on "Why I am Interested in a Career in Graphic Arts." Selection is based on the essay, academic success, and leadership development efforts through clubs or associations, sports, community participation, or volunteer activity. Financial need is not considered.

Financial data The stipend is $1,500.

Duration 1 year.

Additional information GEF learning resource centers are located at the following universities: Rochester Institute of Technology, Western Michigan University, California Polytechnic State University at San Luis Obispo, Arizona State University, Clemson University, Murray State University, and the University of Wisconsin at Stout. This program is supported by Hallmark Cards, Inc.

Number awarded 1 each year.

Deadline May of each year.

[864]
HAMPTONS INTERNATIONAL FILM FESTIVAL STUDENT AWARDS

Hamptons International Film Festival
3 Newtown Mews
East Hampton, NY 11937
(631) 324-4600   Fax: (631) 324-5116
E-mail: info@hamptonsfilmfest.org
Web: www.hamptonsfilmfest.org/about/awards.php

Purpose To recognize and reward outstanding student films and videos entered in the Hamptons International Film Festival.

Eligibility This festival accepts works produced by undergraduate and graduate students that have been completed within the past year. Entries may be in 16mm, 35mm, video (Beta SP), or DVD format. Works may not have been released theatrically or shown on television prior to the festival.

Financial data The prizes are $1,000.

Duration The festival is held annually.

Additional information These awards are sponsored by Ray-Ban.

Number awarded 8 student works are honored each year.

Deadline June of each year.

[865]
HAROLD E. FELLOWS SCHOLARSHIPS

Broadcast Education Association
Attn: Scholarships
1771 N Street, N.W.
Washington, DC 20036-2891
(202) 429-3935   Toll-free: (888) 380-7222
E-mail: beainfo@beaweb.org
Web: www.beaweb.org/scholarships.html

Purpose To provide financial assistance to upper-division and graduate students who are interested in preparing for a career in broadcasting.

Eligibility This program is open to juniors, seniors, and graduate students enrolled full time at a college or university where at least 1 department is an institutional member of the Broadcast Education Association (BEA). Applicants may be studying in any area of broadcasting. They must have worked (or their parent must have worked) as an employee or paid intern at a station that is a member of the National Association of Broadcasters (NAB). Selection is based on evidence that the applicant possesses high integrity, superior academic ability, potential to be an outstanding electronic media professional, and a sense of personal and professional responsibility.

Financial data The stipend is $1,250.

Duration 1 year; may not be renewed.

Additional information Information is also available from Peter B. Orlik, Central Michigan University, 344 Moore Hall, Mt. Pleasant, MI 48859, (989) 774-7279. This program is sponsored by the NAB and administered by the BEA.

Number awarded 4 each year.

Deadline October of each year.

[866]
HARRIET IRSAY SCHOLARSHIP GRANT

American Institute of Polish Culture, Inc.
Attn: Scholarship Committee
1440 79th Street Causeway, Suite 117
Miami, FL 33141
(305) 864-2349   Fax: (305) 865-5150
E-mail: info@ampolinstitute.org
Web: www.ampolinstitute.org.ic.pl

Purpose To provide financial assistance to Polish American and other students interested in working on an undergraduate or graduate degree in selected fields.

Eligibility This program is open to students working full time on an undergraduate or graduate degree in the following fields: communications, education, film, history, international relations, journalism, liberal arts, Polish studies, and public relations. Also eligible are graduate students in business programs whose thesis is directly related to Poland and to graduate students in all majors whose thesis is on a Polish subject. U.S. citizenship or permanent resident status is required. Preference is given to applicants of Polish heritage. Along with their application, they must submit an essay of 200 to 400 words on why they should receive the scholarship, an article (up to 700 words) on any subject about Poland, transcripts, a detailed resume, and 3 letters of recommendation. Selection is based on merit.

Financial data The stipend is $1,000.

Duration 1 year.

Additional information There is a $10 processing fee.

Number awarded 10 to 15 each year.

Deadline May of each year.

[867]
HARRY BARFIELD KBA SCHOLARSHIP PROGRAM

Kentucky Broadcasters Association
101 Enterprise Drive
Frankfort, KY 40601
(502) 848-0426   Toll-free: (888) THE-KBA1
Fax: (502) 848-5710   E-mail: kba@mis.net
Web: www.kba.org/Scholarship.htm

Purpose To provide financial assistance to currently-enrolled college students in Kentucky who are majoring in broadcasting.

Eligibility This program is open to Kentucky residents who are currently enrolled in college in the state (preferably but not limited to second-semester sophomore status) and majoring in broadcasting or telecommunications. Applicants must submit a college transcript, a 500-word autobiographical sketch including career goals, a list of extracurricular activities and scholarships, and 1 recommendation from a faculty member. Financial need is not required, but it is the deciding factor if merit qualifications are equal.

Financial data The stipend is $1,000 per year.

Duration 1 year; may be renewed for 1 additional year if the recipient maintains a GPA of 3.0 or higher.

Additional information Information on this program, which began in 1993, is also available from the KBA Scholarship Chair, Carl Nathe, University of Kentucky, Mathews Building, Room 104, Lexington, KY 40506-0047, (859) 257-1754, Fax: (859) 257-2635, E-mail: cnath1@email.uky.edu.

Number awarded 1 or more each year.
Deadline May of each year.

[868]
HAWAIIAN HOMES COMMISSION CAREER AND TECHNICAL EDUCATION SCHOLARSHIP

Hawai'i Community Foundation
Attn: Scholarship Department
1164 Bishop Street, Suite 800
Honolulu, HI 96813
(808) 566-5570   Toll-free: (888) 731-3863
Fax: (808) 521-6286
E-mail: scholarships@hcf-hawaii.org
Web: www.hawaiicommunityfoundation.org

Purpose To provide financial assistance to residents of Hawaii who are interested in enrolling in a vocational training program in the state.

Eligibility This program is open to residents of Hawaii who are native Hawaiian (50% or more Hawaiian ancestry) or a homestead lessee (at least 25% Hawaiian ancestry). Applicants must be attending or planning to attend a vocational college or institution that is part of the University of Hawaii community college system. Programs include culinary arts, auto repair, diesel mechanics, cosmetology, computer graphics, and assistive medical technology. Applicants must submit a personal statement explaining their personal background and interests, the vocational program they plan to pursue, their career goals, and anything else that demonstrates their worthiness to receive this scholarship. Financial need is not considered in the selection process.

Financial data The stipend is $500 per semester. Funds are mailed directly to the financial aid office at the recipient's institution.

Duration 1 semester; may be renewed for up to 3 additional semesters.

Additional information This program, which began in 2006, is sponsored by the state Department of Hawaiian Home Lands.

Number awarded Varies each year.

Deadline June of each year for fall and spring semester scholarships; September of each year for spring semester scholarships.

[869]
HEARST JOURNALISM AWARDS PROGRAM BROADCAST NEWS COMPETITIONS

William Randolph Hearst Foundation
90 New Montgomery Street, Suite 1212
San Francisco, CA 94105-4504
(415) 543-6033, ext. 308   Fax: (415) 348-0887
E-mail: journalism@hearstfdn.org
Web: www.hearstfdn.org/hearst_journalism

Purpose To recognize and reward outstanding college student broadcast news journalists.

Eligibility Eligible are full-time undergraduate students majoring in journalism at 1 of the 105 accredited colleges and universities that are members of the Association of Schools of Journalism and Mass Communication (ASJMC). For each of the 2 semifinal competitions, each student submits either an audio tape or a videotape originating with and produced by the undergraduate student with primary responsibility for the entry. Entries must have been "published" in the sense of having been made available to an anonymous audience of substantial size. The first competition of each year is for "features;" entries must be soft news: non-deadline reporting of personalities, events, or issues. They may be based on, but not limited to, public affairs, business, investigations, science, sports, or weather. The second competition of each year is for "news;" entries must be hard news, including enterprise reporting. They may be based on, but not limited to, public affairs reporting, business reporting, investigative reporting, sports reporting, or weather reporting, as long as they have a hard news focus. All entries must have been produced since September of the previous year and must consist of at least 2 reports. Broadcast news tapes are judged on the basis of writing quality, understandability, clarity, depth, focus, editing, knowledge of subject, and broadcast skills. The 10 audio tapes and 10 videotapes selected by the judges as the best in the semifinals are then entered in the finals. The finalists submit new and different tapes, up to 10 minutes in length with a minimum of 3 reports, of which only 1 may have been submitted previously. The reports must include at least 1 news story and 1 feature. Judges select the top 5 audio tapes and the top 5 videotapes, and those 10 finalists go to San Francisco for an on-the-spot news assignment to rank the winners. Radio and television entries are judged separately.

Financial data In each of the 2 semifinal competitions for both radio and television, the first-place winner receives a $2,000 scholarship, second place $1,500, third place $1,000, fourth place $750, fifth place $600, and sixth through tenth places $500 each; identical grants are awarded to the journalism schools attended by the winning students. For the finals competitions for both radio and television, additional scholarships are awarded of $5,000 to the first-place winner, $4,000 to the second, $3,000 to the third, and $1,500 to each of the other 2 finalists; in addition, the students who make the best use of radio for news coverage and the best use of television for news coverage each receive another scholarship of $1,000. Scholarship funds are paid to the college or university and credited to the recipients' educational costs (tuition, matriculation and other fees, and room and board provided by or approved by the college or university). Schools receive points for their students who place in the top 20 places in the semifinals and in the finals; the school with the most points receives an additional cash prize of $10,000, second wins $5,000, and third wins $2,500. The total amount awarded in scholarships and grants in this and the writing and photojournalism competitions is nearly $500,000 per year.

Duration The competition is held annually.

Additional information This program began in 1960. It is conducted by the William Randolph Hearst Foundation under the auspices of the ASJMC. If scholarship funds are awarded after a competing student has graduated, the college or university may credit funds retroactively.

Number awarded 20 semifinal (10 for radio and 10 for television) and 10 final (5 for radio and 5 for television) winners are chosen each year. In addition, 1 scholarship is awarded each year for best use of radio 1 for best use of television.

Deadline The deadline for the first competition is in November of each year and for the second competition in early February of each year. Additional entries by finalists must be submitted by the end of March of each year. The competition among the top 10 finalists takes place in San Francisco in June.

[870]
HEARST JOURNALISM AWARDS PROGRAM PHOTOJOURNALISM COMPETITIONS

William Randolph Hearst Foundation
90 New Montgomery Street, Suite 1212
San Francisco, CA 94105-4504
(415) 543-6033, ext. 308   Fax: (415) 348-0887
E-mail: photos@hearstfdn.org
Web: www.hearstfdn.org/hearst_journalism

Purpose To recognize and reward outstanding college student photojournalists.

Eligibility Eligible are full-time undergraduate students majoring in journalism at 1 of the 105 accredited colleges and universities that are members of the Association of Schools of Journalism and Mass Communication (ASJMC). For each of the 3 semifinal competitions, each student submits photographs in 35mm slide form. For the first competition of each year, the categories are portrait/personality and feature; entries consist of 2 photographs in each of those 2 categories. For the second competition of each year, the categories are sports and news; entries consist of 2 photographs in each of those 2 categories. For the third competition of each year, the category is picture story/series; each entry must include 1 picture story/series, with up to 15 images. All photographs must have been taken since September of the previous year and may be in color or black and white. Photography is judged on the basis of quality, versatility, consistency, human interest, news value, and originality. The judges select the top 10 entrants in each of the 3 competitions; of those 10, the 4 top scoring entrants qualify for the photojournalism finals. Those 12 finalists must submit a portfolio consisting of prints of the slides previously judged, plus 2 additional photographs (published or unpublished) from each of the other categories in the overall contest; complete portfolios must thus consist of 2 pictures each in news, features, sports, portrait/personality, plus a picture story/series. Based on those portfolios, judges select the top 6 finalists to go to San Francisco for on-the-spot assignments to rank the winners.

Financial data In each of the 3 semifinal competitions, the first-place winner receives a $2,000 scholarship, second place $1,500, third place $1,000, fourth place $750, fifth place $600, and sixth through tenth places $500 each; identical grants are awarded to the journalism schools attended by the winning students. For the finals competition, additional scholarships are awarded of $5,000 to the first-place winner, $4,000 to the second, $3,000 to the third; and $1,500 to each of the other 3 finalists. In addition, the photographers who submit the best single photo and the best picture story each receive another scholarship of $1,000. Scholarship funds are paid to the college or university and credited to the recipients' educational costs (tuition, matriculation and other fees, and room and board provided by or approved by the college or university). Schools receive points for their students who place in the top 20 places in the semifinals and in the finals; the school with the most points receives an additional cash prize of $10,000, second wins $5,000, and third wins $2,500. The total amount awarded in scholarships and grants in this and the writing and broadcast news competitions is nearly $500,000 per year.

Duration The competition is held annually.

Additional information This program began in 1960. It is conducted by the William Randolph Hearst Foundation under the auspices of the ASJMC. If scholarship funds are awarded after a competing student has graduated, the college or university may credit funds retroactively.

Number awarded 30 semifinal and 6 final winners are chosen each year, and 2 additional scholarships are awarded each year for the best single photo and best picture story.

Deadline The deadline for the first competition is in early November of each year, for the second competition in late January of each year, and for the third competition in early March of each year. Additional entries by finalists must be submitted by late May of each year. The competition among the top 6 finalists takes place in San Francisco in June.

[871]
HEARST JOURNALISM AWARDS PROGRAM WRITING COMPETITIONS

William Randolph Hearst Foundation
90 New Montgomery Street, Suite 1212
San Francisco, CA 94105-4504
(415) 543-6033, ext 308   Fax: (415) 348-0887
E-mail: journalism@hearstfdn.org
Web: www.hearstfdn.org/hearst_journalism

Purpose To recognize and reward outstanding college student journalists.

Eligibility Eligible are full-time undergraduate students majoring in journalism at 1 of the 105 accredited colleges or universities that are members of the Association of Schools of Journalism and Mass Communication (ASJMC). Each entry consists of a single article written by the student with primary responsibility for the work and published in a campus or professional publication. Each month, a separate competition is held; October: feature writing—a background, color, or mood article as opposed to a conventional news story or personality profile; November: editorials or signed columns of opinion—must be well researched and express a clear and cogent viewpoint; December: in-depth writing—must illustrate the student's ability to handle a complex subject clearly, precisely, and with sufficient background; January: sports writing—relevant to an event or issue, not to a sports personality; February: personality profile—a personality sketch of someone; and March: spot news writing—articles written about a breaking news event and against a deadline. The 6 monthly winners and the 2 finalists who place highest in their top 2 scores in the monthly competitions qualify for the national writing championship held in San Francisco in June; at that time, competition assignments consist of an on-the-spot assignment and a news story and personality profile from a press interview of a prominent individual in the San Francisco area. Writing is judged on the basis of knowledge of subject, understandability, clarity, color, reporting in depth, and construction. Additional awards are presented for article of the year and best reporting technique.

Financial data In each of the 6 competitions, the first-place winner receives a $2,000 scholarship, second place $1,500, third place $1,000, fourth place $750, fifth place $600, and sixth through tenth places $500; identical grants are awarded to the journalism schools attended by the students. For the finalists whose articles are judged best in the national writing championship, additional scholarships of $5,000 are awarded to the first-place winner, $4,000 to the second place, $3,000 to third place, and $1,500 each to the other 5 finalists. The additional awards for article of the year and best reporting technique are each $1,000. Scholarship awards are paid to the college or university and credited to the recipients' educational costs (tuition, matriculation and other fees, and room and board provided by or approved by the college or university). Schools receive points for each of their students who place in the top 20 places in each monthly competition; the school with the most points receives an additional cash prize of $10,000, second wins $5,000, and third wins $2,500. The total amount awarded in scholarships and grants in this and the photojournalism and broadcast news competitions is nearly $500,000 per year.

Duration The competition is held annually.

Additional information This program began in 1960. It is conducted by the William Randolph Hearst Foundation under the auspices of the ASJMC. If scholarship funds are awarded after a competing student has graduated, the college or university may credit funds retroactively.

Number awarded Each year, 60 scholarships are awarded to the monthly winners, and an additional 8 are presented to the national finalists.

Deadline Articles for the monthly competitions must be submitted by the end of the respective month of each year. The championship is held in June of each year.

[872]
HEIDELBERG USA SCHOLARSHIP

Electronic Document Systems Foundation
Attn: EDSF Scholarship Awards
608 Silver Spur Road, Suite 280
Rolling Hills Estates, CA 90274-3616
(310) 265-5510   Fax: (310) 265-5588
E-mail: jmowlds@edsf.org
Web: www.edsf.org/scholarships.cfm

Purpose To provide financial assistance to college juniors, seniors, and graduate students working on a degree in the field of document/graphic communication.

Eligibility This program is open to juniors, seniors, and graduate students who are working on a degree in the field of document/graphic communication, including such document-related technologies as graphic communications, document management, document content and/or distribution, or multimedia. Applicants must be enrolled full time at a college, university, or graduate school in the United States with a GPA of 3.0 or higher. Along with their application, they must submit a statement of their career goals in the field of document communications, an essay on a topic related to their view of the future of the document management and production industry, a list of current professional and college extracurricular activities and achievements, college transcripts, samples of their creative work, and 2 letters of recommendation. industry. Financial need is not considered.

Financial data The stipend is $2,000.

Duration 1 year.

Additional information This program is sponsored by Heidelberg USA.

Number awarded 1 each year.

Deadline May of each year.

[873]
HELEN J. SIOUSSAT/FAY WELLS SCHOLARSHIPS

Broadcast Education Association
Attn: Scholarships
1771 N Street, N.W.
Washington, DC 20036-2891
(202) 429-3935   Toll-free: (888) 380-7222
E-mail: beainfo@beaweb.org
Web: www.beaweb.org/scholarships.html

Purpose To provide financial assistance to upper-division and graduate students who are interested in preparing for a career in broadcasting.

Eligibility This program is open to juniors, seniors, and graduate students enrolled full time at a college or university where at least 1 department is an institutional member of the Broadcast Education Association. Applicants may be studying in any area of broadcasting. Selection is based on evidence that the applicant possesses high integrity, superior academic ability, potential to be an outstanding electronic media professional, and a sense of personal and professional responsibility.

Financial data The stipend is $1,250.

Duration 1 year; may not be renewed.

Additional information Information is also available from Peter B. Orlik, Central Michigan University, 344 Moore Hall, Mt. Pleasant, MI 48859, (989) 774-7279.

Number awarded 2 each year.

Deadline October of each year.

[874]
HENRY AND CHIYO KUWAHARA CREATIVE ARTS AWARD

Japanese American Citizens League
Attn: National Scholarship Awards
1765 Sutter Street
San Francisco, CA 94115
(415) 921-5225   Fax: (415) 931-4671
E-mail: jacl@jacl.org
Web: www.jacl.org/leadership_development_5.php

Purpose To provide financial assistance to student members of the Japanese American Citizens League (JACL) interested in working on an undergraduate or graduate degree in the creative arts.

Eligibility This program is open to JACL members who are interested in working on an undergraduate or graduate degree in the creative arts. Professional artists are not eligible. Applicants must submit a detailed proposal on the nature of their project, including a time-plan, anticipated date of completion, and itemized budget. They must also submit a 2-page essay on what American society can learn from the Japanese American experience. Selection is based on academic history, JACL involvement, extracurricular activities, scholastic honors, and a letter of recommendation. Preference is given to students who are interested in creative projects that reflect the Japanese American experience and culture.

Financial data The stipend depends on the availability of funds but usually ranges from $1,000 to $5,000.

Duration 1 year; nonrenewable.

Additional information Applications must be submitted to the JACL National Scholarship Program, c/o San Diego JACL Chapter, 1031 25th Street, San Diego, CA 92102.

Number awarded At least 1 each year.

Deadline March of each year.

[875]
HENRY REGNERY ENDOWED SCHOLARSHIPS

Sigma Tau Delta
c/o William C. Johnson, Executive Director
Northern Illinois University
Department of English
DeKalb, IL 60115-2863
(815) 753-1612   E-mail: sigmatd@niu.edu
Web: www.english.org/scholarships.shtml

Purpose To provide financial assistance to undergraduate and graduate student members of Sigma Tau Delta (the international English honor society).

Eligibility Eligible to be nominated are members of the society who are upper-division or graduate school students. Each chapter may nominate 3 active members for this scholarship. Nominees must provide proof of registration in at least 50% of a full load of courses as part of an English degree program. They must submit a paper (from 2,000 to 3,000 words), originally prepared for a course, with the endorsement from the course professor. Selection is based on academic record, chapter service, awards, professional goals, an application essay (up to 400 words on a topic that changes annually), the sample paper, and 2 letters of recommendation.

Financial data The stipend is $2,500 for winners or $500 for runners-up.

Duration 1 year.

Additional information This program was established in 1992. Information is also available from the Scholarship Committee Chair, Dr. Sidney Watson, Oklahoma Baptist University, 500 West University, OBU Box 61238, Shawnee, OK 74804, E-mail: sidneywatson@okbu.edu. Recipients must attend school on at least a half-time basis.

Number awarded 2 each year: 1 winner and 1 runner-up.

Deadline October of each year.

[876]
HGA SCHOLARSHIPS

Handweavers Guild of America, Inc.
Attn: Scholarship Committee
1255 Buford Highway, Suite 211
Suwanee, GA 30024
(678) 730-0010   Fax: (678) 730-0836
E-mail: hga@weavespindye.org
Web: www.weavespindye.org

Purpose To provide financial assistance to undergraduate and graduate students working on a degree in the field of fiber arts.

Eligibility This program is open to undergraduate and graduate students enrolled in accredited colleges and universities in the United States, its possessions, and Canada. Applicants must be working on a degree in the field of fiber arts, including training for research, textile history, and conservation. Along with their application, they must submit 1) a 50-word essay on their study goals and how those fit into their future plans, and 2) 5 to 16 slides of their work. Selection is based on artistic and technical merit; financial need is not considered.

Financial data A stipend is awarded (amount not specified). Use of funds is restricted to tuition.

Duration Funds must be spent within 1 year.

Number awarded Varies; more than $4,000 is available for this program each year.

Deadline March of each year.

[877]
HIGH PLAINS JOURNAL/KJLA SCHOLARSHIP

Kansas Livestock Association
Attn: Kansas Livestock Foundation
6031 S.W. 37th Street
Topeka, KS 66614-5129
(785) 273-5115   Fax: (785) 273-3399
E-mail: kla@kla.org
Web: www.kla.org/scholarapp.htm

Purpose To provide financial assistance to upper-division students majoring in agricultural communications at universities in Kansas.

Eligibility This program is open to juniors and seniors at Kansas universities who are majoring in agricultural communications. Selection is based on academic achievement (20 points), personal livestock enterprises (25 points), Kansas Junior Livestock Association and other industry organization activities and leadership (30 points), school activities and honors (30 points), other activities and leadership (25 points), work experience (25 points), significant honors or recognition (25 points), and career plans (20 points).

Financial data The stipend is $1,000. Funds are paid directly to the recipient in 2 equal installments at the beginning of each semester, upon proof of enrollment.

Duration 1 year.

Additional information This program is sponsored by the Kansas Junior Livestock Association (KJLA) in conjunction with the *High Plains Journal*.

Number awarded 1 each year.

Deadline May of each year.

[878]
HOME BUILDERS ASSOCIATION OF ILLINOIS STUDENT OF THE YEAR SCHOLARSHIPS
Home Builders Association of Illinois
112 West Edwards Street
Springfield, IL 62704
(217) 753-3963 TDD: (800) 255-6047
Fax: (217) 753-3811
Web: www.hbai.org/Student/index.asp

Purpose To recognize and reward, with funds for continuing education, students in Illinois who are preparing for a career in the building industry.

Eligibility This program is open to students enrolled in a building trades or architecture program at a high school, university, community college, or technical school in Illinois. Students must be nominated by a local affiliate of the Home Builders Association of Illinois. They must have a "C+" average or higher. Selection is based on academics, involvement with the building industry, leadership and extracurricular activities, community involvement, and awards and honors.

Financial data Awards are $2,000 for first place, $1,500 for second place, and $1,000 for third place. Funds are paid to the student's school to be used for continuing education. If the recipients do not remain in school, they may use the award for certified graduate builder or remodeler courses offered through the home builders association.

Duration Awards are offered annually.

Number awarded 3 each year.

[879]
HUMANE STUDIES FELLOWSHIPS
Institute for Humane Studies at George Mason University
3301 North Fairfax Drive, Suite 440
Arlington, VA 22201-4432
(703) 993-4880 Toll-free: (800) 697-8799
Fax: (703) 993-4890 E-mail: ihs@gmu.edu
Web: www.TheIHS.org

Purpose To provide financial assistance to undergraduate and graduate students in the United States or abroad who intend to pursue "intellectual careers" and have demonstrated an interest in classical liberal principles.

Eligibility This program is open to students who will be full-time college juniors, seniors, or graduate students planning academic or other intellectual careers, including law, public policy, and journalism. Applicants must have a clearly demonstrated interest in the classical liberal/libertarian tradition of individual rights and market economics. Applications from students outside the United States or studying abroad receive equal consideration. Selection is based on academic or professional performance, relevance of work to the advancement of a free society, and potential for success.

Financial data The maximum stipend is $12,000.

Duration 1 year; may be renewed upon reapplication.

Additional information As defined by the sponsor, the core principles of the classical liberal/libertarian tradition include the recognition of individual rights and the dignity and worth of each individual; protection of these rights through the institutions of private property, contract, the rule of law, and freely evolved intermediary institutions; voluntarism in all human relations, including the unhampered market mechanism in economic affairs; and the goals of free trade, free migration, and peace. This program began in 1983 as Claude R. Lambe Fellowships. The application fee is $25.

Number awarded Approximately 110 each year.

Deadline December of each year.

[880]
IAHPERD SCHOLARSHIPS
Illinois Association for Health, Physical Education, Recreation and Dance
Attn: Executive Secretary
1713 South West Street
Jacksonville, IL 62650
(217) 245-6413 Fax: (217) 245-5261
E-mail: iahperd@iahperd.org
Web: www.iahperd.org

Purpose To provide financial assistance to upper-division students in Illinois who are majoring in health, physical education, recreation, or dance.

Eligibility This program is open to juniors and seniors at colleges and universities in Illinois who are majoring in health, physical education, recreation, or dance. Applicants must submit a personal letter explaining why they chose to go into their field and where they see themselves professionally in 5 years. Selection is based on that letter, involvement in professional organizations, involvement in extracurricular activities, involvement in community organizations, transcripts, and 2 letters of recommendation.

Financial data Stipends are $1,000 or $750.

Duration 1 year.

Number awarded 6 each year: 1 at $1,000 and 5 at $750.

Deadline April of each year.

[881]
IDDBA SCHOLARSHIP
International Dairy-Deli-Bakery Association
Attn: Scholarship Committee
636 Science Drive
P.O. Box 5528
Madison, WI 53705-0528
(608) 310-5000 Fax: (608) 238-6330
E-mail: iddba@iddba.org
Web: www.iddba.org/scholars.htm

Purpose To provide financial assistance to high school seniors, undergraduates, or graduate students employed in a supermarket dairy, deli, or bakery department who are interested in majoring in a food-related field.

Eligibility This program is open to high school seniors, college students, vocational/technical students, and graduate students. Applicants must be currently employed in a supermarket dairy, deli, or bakery department or be employed by a company that services those departments (e.g., food manufacturers, brokers, or wholesalers). They must be majoring in a food-related field, e.g., culinary arts, baking/pastry arts, food science, business, or marketing. Their employer must be a member of the International Dairy-Deli-Bakery Association (IDDBA). While a GPA of 2.5 or higher is required, this may be waived for first-time applicants. Selection is based on academic achievement, work experience, and a statement of career goals and/or how their degree will be beneficial to their job. Financial need is not considered.

Financial data Stipends range from $250 to $1,000. Funds are paid jointly to the recipient and the recipient's school. If the award exceeds tuition fees, the excess may be used for other educational expenses.

Duration 1 year; recipients may reapply.

Number awarded Varies each year; a total of $75,000 is available for this program annually.

Deadline Applications must be submitted prior to the end of March, June, September, or December of each year.

[882]
IFDA EDUCATIONAL FOUNDATION STUDENT SCHOLARSHIP

International Furnishings and Design Association
Attn: IFDA Educational Foundation
191 Clarksville Road
Princeton Junction, NJ 08550
(609) 799-3423   Fax: (609) 799-7032
E-mail: info@ifda.com
Web: www.ifdaef.org/scholarships.html

Purpose To provide financial assistance to undergraduate student members of the International Furnishings and Design Association (IFDA).

Eligibility This program is open to association members who are full-time undergraduate students majoring in interior design or a related field. Applicants must submit an essay of 300 to 500 words on their future plans and goals and why they believe they deserve the scholarship. Selection is based on the essay; the applicant's achievements, awards, and accomplishments; and a letter of recommendation from a professor or instructor. Financial need is not considered.

Financial data The stipend is $3,000.

Duration 1 year.

Additional information Information is also available from Joan Long, Director of Grants, 5522 Estates Drive, Oakland, CA 94618, E-mail: jlongdesigns@yahoo.com.

Number awarded At least 1 each year.

Deadline March of each year.

[883]
IHA STUDENT DESIGN COMPETITION

International Housewares Association
Attn: Design Programs Coordinator
6400 Shafer Court, Suite 650
Rosemont, IL 60018
(847) 692-0136   Fax: (847) 292-4211
E-mail: vmatranga@nhma.com
Web: www.housewares.org

Purpose To recognize and reward outstanding young designers of housewares products.

Eligibility Students participating in this competition must be juniors, seniors, or graduate students at an IDSA-affiliated school. They are invited to design a housewares product in any of the following categories: household and personal care small electric appliances; tabletop, serving products, and accessories; cook and bakeware; kitchenware; outdoor products and accessories; bath, laundry, closet; cleaning products; furniture; decorative accessories; and juvenile and pet products. Students may submit more than 1 entry, but they may not be awarded more than 1 prize. Selection is based on design research, design, ergonomics, and skills and communication.

Financial data First place is $2,500, second place is $1,700, and third place is $1,000. Winners also receive transportation and lodging for the International Housewares Show.

Duration The competition is held annually.

Number awarded 6 each year: 1 first place, 2 second places, and 3 third places.

Deadline November of each year.

[884]
IMA HOGG YOUNG ARTIST COMPETITION

Houston Symphony
Attn: Director of Education and Community Relations
Jones Hall
615 Louisiana Street, Suite 102
Houston, TX 77002-2798
(713) 238-1449   Fax: (713) 224-0453
E-mail: e&o@houstonsymphony.org
Web: www.houstonsymphony.org

Purpose To recognize and reward outstanding young musicians.

Eligibility This competition is open to citizens of the United States, Mexico, and Canada and to foreign students currently enrolled in a U.S. college, university, or conservatory. Applicants must be between 16 and 25 years of age. They must submit a cassette recording of a required solo work for their instrument as well as additional non-concerto solo works of their choice, representing a style and period different from the required work. The competition is open to the following orchestral instruments: piano, violin, viola, cello, bass, flute, oboe, clarinet, bassoon, horn, trumpet, trombone, tuba, harp, and marimba. Semifinalists are selected on the basis of the tapes and invited to Houston for further competition, where they perform the required solo work and either a required concerto or 1 of several optional concertos. The finals consist of the concerto not performed in the semifinals.

Financial data The first-prize winner receives the Grace Woodson Memorial Award of $5,000 and a performance with the Houston Symphony; the second-prize winner receives the Houston Symphony League Jerry Priest Award of $2,500 and a performance with the Houston Symphony; the third-prize winner receives the Selma Neumann Memorial Award with a cash prize of $1,000; the fourth prize is $300.

Additional information Housing accommodations at no cost are provided for semifinalists and their accompanists. A non-refundable application fee of $30 must accompany the preliminary audition tapes.

Number awarded 4 cash prizes are awarded each year.

Deadline Preliminary audition tapes must be received by February of each year.

[885]
INDIANA BROADCASTERS ASSOCIATION COLLEGE SCHOLARSHIPS

Indiana Broadcasters Association
Attn: Scholarship Administrator
3003 East 98th Street, Suite 161
Indianapolis, IN 46280
(317) 573-0119   Toll-free: (800) 342-6276 (within IN)
Fax: (317) 573-0895   E-mail: INDBA@aol.com
Web: www.indianabroadcasters.org

Purpose To provide financial assistance to college students in Indiana who are interested in preparing for a career in a field related to broadcasting.

Eligibility This program is open to residents of Indiana who are attending a college or university in the state that is a member of the Indiana Broadcasters Association (IBA) or has a radio/TV facility on campus. Applicants must be majoring in broadcasting, electronic media, telecommunications, or broadcast journalism and have a GPA of 3.0 or higher. They must be actively participating on a college broadcast facility or working for a commercial broadcast facility while attending college. Along with their application, they must submit an essay on why they have chosen the broadcasting field as a career. Financial need is not considered in the selection process.

Financial data The stipend is $2,000.

Duration 1 year.

Additional information These scholarships were first offered in 1995.

Number awarded Varies each year: recently, 6 of these scholarships were awarded.

Deadline March of each year.

[886]
INDIANA PROFESSIONAL CHAPTER OF SPJ DIVERSITY IN JOURNALISM SCHOLARSHIP

Society of Professional Journalists-Indiana Professional Chapter
P.O. Box 441765
Indianapolis, IN 46244-1765
(317) 925-2702   Fax: (317) 925-6624
E-mail: indyprospj@gmail.com
Web: indyprospj.iupui.edu

Purpose To recognize and reward, with college scholarships, minority high school students in Indiana who are preparing for a career in journalism.

Eligibility This competition is open to minority students at high schools in Indiana who plan to major in journalism at a college or university in the state. Minorities are defined as U.S. citizens who are African American, Hispanic, Asian American, Native American, or Pacific Islander. Applicants must attend a workshop at which they cover a speech by a professional journalist. They have an hour to write a concise print or broadcast news article about the speech.

Financial data The award is $2,500.

Duration The competition is held annually.

Additional information This competition is sponsored by the Indiana Professional chapter of the Society of Professional Journalists, the Indianapolis Association of Black Journalists, and the Indiana High School Press Association. Funding is provided by the Lilly Endowment.

Number awarded At least 2 each year.

Deadline October of each year.

[887]
INTEGRITY GRAPHICS COMMUNICATIONS SCHOLARSHIP AWARDS

Integrity Graphics, Inc.
Attn: Scholarship Contest
1010 Day Hill Road
P.O. Box 458
Windsor, CT 06095-0458
(860) 688-5200
Toll-free: (800) 343-1248 (within CT and MA)
Fax: (860) 285-8414
Web: www.integrity-usa.com

Purpose To recognize and reward high school seniors and college students in New England and New York who demonstrate outstanding work in digital photography, graphic arts, or website design.

Eligibility This competition is open to 1) current high school seniors who will be attending a college, university, or trade school in New England or New York in the following fall, and 2) students currently enrolled part time or full time at a college, university, or trade school in the New England states or New York. Applicants must be majoring in graphic arts or photography. They must submit samples of their work in 3 categories: graphic arts, digital photography, or website design. Graphic arts applicants must document the process through which they created their submission; selection is based on creativity and the printability of the item. Digital photography applicants must document the process in which the photograph was taken and any modifications made to the shot; selection is based on creativity and the printability of the item. Website design applicants must submit at least 3 pages for each site design and describe the design considerations incorporated in the website; selection is based on creativity, originality, usability, and the ability to implement the design in HTML.

Financial data The awards are $2,000. Funds are to be used to pay for educational costs.

Duration The competition is held annually.

Additional information This competition began in 2001.

Number awarded 3 each year: 1 in each category.

Deadline June of each year.

[888]
INTERNATIONAL ASSOCIATION OF LIGHTING DESIGNERS SCHOLARSHIPS

International Association of Lighting Designers
Attn: Education Trust Fund
The Merchandise Mart, Suite 9-104
200 World Trade Center
Chicago, IL 60654
(312) 527-3677   Fax: (312) 527-3680
Web: www.iald.org/educational_trust_scholarship.php

Purpose To provide financial assistance to students pursuing a program in architectural lighting design.

Eligibility This program is open to students who are pursuing architectural lighting design as a course of study. Applicants must submit 1) a 2-page resume; 2) an official

transcript; 3) 2 letters of reference; 4) up to 10 images of their artwork that show their design ability; and 5) a personal statement, up to 2 pages, on their experience with lighting, why they want to study lighting, or why they should receive this scholarship. Selection is based on those submissions; financial need is not considered.
Financial data Stipends range from $1,000 to $5,000.
Duration 1 year.
Number awarded Varies each year. Recently, 7 of these scholarships were awarded: 1 at $5,000, 1 at $3,000, 4 at $2,000, and 1 at $1,000.
Deadline February of each year.

[889]
INTERNATIONAL COMMUNICATIONS INDUSTRIES FOUNDATION AV SCHOLARSHIPS
InfoComm International
International Communications Industries Foundation
11242 Waples Mill Road, Suite 200
Fairfax, VA 22030
(703) 273-7200   Toll-free: (800) 659-7469
Fax: (703) 278-8082   E-mail: dwilbert@infocomm.org
Web: www.infocomm.org/Foundation/Scholarships

Purpose To provide financial assistance to high school seniors and college students who are interested in preparing for a career in the audiovisual (AV) industry.
Eligibility This program is open to high school seniors and students already enrolled in college. Applicants must have a GPA of 2.75 or higher and be majoring or planning to major in audiovisual subjects, including audio, visual, electronics, telecommunications, technical aspects of the theater, data networking, software development, or information technology. Students in other programs, such as journalism, may be eligible if they can demonstrate a relationship to career goals in the AV industry. Along with their application, they must submit essays on why they are applying for this scholarship, why they are interested in the audiovisual industry, and their professional plans following graduation. Minority and women candidates are especially encouraged to apply. Selection is based on the essays, presentation of the application, GPA, work experience, and letters of recommendation.
Financial data The stipend is $1,200.
Duration 1 year.
Additional information InfoComm International, formerly the International Communications Industries Association, established the International Communications Industries Foundation (ICIF) to manage its charitable and educational activities.
Number awarded Varies each year; recently, 29 of these scholarships were awarded.
Deadline April of each year.

[890]
IRENE RYAN ACTING SCHOLARSHIPS
John F. Kennedy Center for the Performing Arts
Education Department
Attn: Kennedy Center American College Theater Festival
2700 F Street, N.W.
Washington, DC 20566
(202) 416-8857   Fax: (202) 416-8802
E-mail: skshaffer@kennedy-center.org
Web: kennedy-center.org/education/actf/actfira.html

Purpose To recognize and reward outstanding college actors.
Eligibility Eligible are students enrolled in an accredited junior or senior college in the United States or in countries contiguous to the continental United States. Participants must appear as actors in plays produced by their college and entered in 1 of the 8 regional festivals of the Kennedy Center American College Theater Festival (KCACTF). Undergraduate students must be carrying at least 6 semester hours, graduate students must be enrolled in at least 3 semester hours, and continuing part-time students must be enrolled in a regular degree or certificate program. From each of the regional festivals, 2 winners and their acting partners are invited to the national festival at the John F. Kennedy Center for the Performing Arts in Washington, D.C. to participate in an "Evening of Scenes." Scholarships are awarded to outstanding student performers at each regional festival and from the "Evening of Scenes."
Financial data Regional winners receive $500 scholarships and payment of expenses (transportation, lodging, and per diem) to attend the national festival. National winners receive $2,500 scholarships; the best partner receives the Kingsley Colton Award. All scholarship funds are paid directly to the institutions designated by the recipients and may be used for any field of study.
Duration The competition is held annually.
Additional information These awards have been presented since 1972 by the Irene Ryan Foundation of Encino, California. The national finalists are also eligible to receive 1) a fellowship (initiated in 1992) to participate in the National Stage Combat Workshop conducted by the Society of American Fight Directors; 2) a Classical Acting Award of Excellence (initiated in 1995) of $2,500 to attend a major professional acting training program; 3) the Mark Twain Comedy Acting Awards (initiated in 1999 and supported by Comedy Central, Inc.) of $2,500 for first place and $2,000 for second place for comic acting; 4) the Dell'Arte Fellowship (initiated in 2001) to participate in the 1-month Dell'Arte Mad River Festival in northern California; 5) the Margolis Method Summer Intensive Acting Fellowship (initiated in 2001) to participate in a 7-day program at the Margolis Brown Theater Company in Minneapolis, Minnesota; 6) the Sundance Theatre Laboratory Acting Fellowship (initiated in 2001) to participate in a 3-week workshop in Sundance, Utah; and 7) the TVI Actors Studio Career Enrichment Awards (introduced in 2003) to provide 9 full-tuition scholarships for the TVI Summer Professional Acting Training Program in Los Angeles. Actors of color are eligible to receive an apprenticeship to participate in an 11-week workshop at the Williamstown Theatre Festival in the Berkshire Hills of northwest Massachusetts. Students from all ethnic backgrounds are eligible for the $3,000 Dell'Arte/KCACTF Diver-

sity scholarship to attend the professional actor training program in Blue Lake, California, but preference is given to students who assist in the goal of the Dell'Arte International School of Physical Theatre to have a more diverse student body. The sponsoring college or university must pay a registration fee of $250 for each production.
Number awarded The number of regional winners varies each year; at the national festival "Evening of Scenes," 2 performers receive scholarships. Several other awards are also presented.
Deadline The regional festivals are held in January and February of each year; the national festival is held in April of each year. Application deadlines are set within each region.

[891]
IRIS CHANG MEMORIAL ESSAY CONTEST
Global Alliance for Preserving the History of WWII in Asia
Attn: Iris Chang Memorial Fund
P.O. Box 641324
San Jose, CA 95164-1324
E-mail: Iris-Chang-Memorial-Fund@global-alliance.net
Web: www.global-alliance.net

Purpose To recognize and reward authors of outstanding essays on the history of World War II in Asia.
Eligibility This competition is open to anyone interested in submitting an essay, up to 2,500 words, in English. The topic of the essay changes each year but relates to the history of World War II in Asia; recently, authors were invited to write on how Iris Chang's book, *The Rape of Nanking: the Forgotten Holocaust of WWII*, has affected their life and thinking.
Financial data First prize is $1,000, second $500, third $250, and honorable mention $50.
Duration The competition is held annually.
Number awarded 3 prizes and several honorable mentions are awarded each year.
Deadline July of each year.

[892]
J. NEEL REID PRIZE
Georgia Trust
Attn: Scholarship Committee
1516 Peachtree Street, N.W.
Atlanta, GA 30309
(404) 881-9980   Fax: (404) 875-2205
E-mail: info@georgiatrust.org
Web: www.georgiatrust.org

Purpose To recognize and reward architecture students and architects, especially those with a connection to Georgia, who are interested in a study travel program in the United States or abroad.
Eligibility This program is open to architecture students, architect interns, and recently registered architects who are interested in a study travel program. The focus of the study travel should involve historic architecture (built prior to Neel Reid's death in 1926), historic preservation of classic architecture, or new construction that is classic and context-related. Applicants are encouraged to propose an independent study, but participation in an existing program is acceptable. Priority is given to applicants with a connection to Georgia (a resident of the state, a student in a Georgia academic institution, or an employee of a Georgia firm). The travel may be to any location in the world.
Financial data The prize is $3,500.
Duration The study travel should be completed within a year and a half of the announcement of the winner.
Number awarded 1 each year.
Deadline February of each year.

[893]
JAMES H. PATREMOS MEMORIAL SCHOLARSHIP
Phi Mu Alpha Sinfonia Fraternity of America
Attn: Sinfonia Educational Foundation
10600 Old State Road
Evansville, IN 47711-1399
(812) 867-2433   Toll-free: (800) 473-2649, ext. 110
Fax: (812) 867-0633   E-mail: sef@sinfonia.org
Web: www.sinfoniafoundation.org

Purpose To provide financial assistance to collegiate members of Phi Mu Alpha Sinfonia fraternity (an organization of male students in music).
Eligibility This program is open to college students who have been members in good standing for at least 2 semesters. Applicants must submit an essay of 1 to 2 pages on how a Sinfonian takes an active role in the building of better men in society. Selection is based on integrity, ethics, initiative, and overall devotion to the object of the fraternity.
Financial data The stipend is $1,000.
Duration 1 year.
Number awarded 1 each year.
Deadline January of each year.

[894]
JAMES J. WYCHOR SCHOLARSHIPS
Minnesota Broadcasters Association
Attn: Scholarship Program
3033 Excelsior Boulevard, Suite 301
Minneapolis, MN 55416
(612) 926-8123   Toll-free: (800) 245-5838
Fax: (612) 926-9761
E-mail: meischen@minnesotabroadcasters.com
Web: www.minnesotabroadcasters.com

Purpose To provide financial assistance to Minnesota residents interested in studying broadcasting in college.
Eligibility This program is open to residents of Minnesota who are accepted or enrolled at an accredited postsecondary institution offering a broadcast-related curriculum. Applicants must have a high school or college GPA of 2.5 or higher and must submit a 200-word essay on why they wish to prepare for a career in broadcasting or electronic media. Employment in the broadcasting industry is not required, but students who are employed must include a letter from their general manager describing the duties they have performed as a radio or television station employee and evaluating their potential for success in the industry. Financial need is not considered in the selection process.

Some of the scholarships are awarded only to minority and women candidates.

Financial data The stipend is $1,500.

Duration 1 year; recipients who are college seniors may reapply for an additional 1-year renewal.

Number awarded 10 each year, distributed as follows: 3 within the 7-county metro area, 5 allocated geographically throughout the state (northeast, northwest, central, southeast, southwest), and 2 reserved specifically for women and minority applicants.

Deadline May of each year.

[895]
JAMES L. GOLDEN OUTSTANDING STUDENT ESSAY IN RHETORIC AWARD

National Communication Association
Attn: Executive Assistant
1765 N Street, N.W.
Washington, DC 20036-2802
(202) 464-4622   Fax: (202) 464-4600
E-mail: shendon@natcom.org
Web: www.natcom.org/nca/Template2.asp?bid=5336

Purpose To recognize and reward undergraduate and graduate students who submit outstanding essays on the history, theory, or criticism of rhetoric.

Eligibility This competition is open to 1) undergraduates, and 2) graduate students who have not yet completed a master's degree. Applicants must submit an essay, up to 20 pages in length, on the history, theory, or criticism of rhetoric. Selection is based on contribution to the understanding of rhetorical process and outcomes, excellence of conception and grounding, weight of argument, strength of evidence, and eloquence of expression.

Financial data The winner receives a cash prize of $1,000, an award certificate, and travel support to present the essay at the annual convention of the National Communication Association.

Duration The award is granted annually.

Number awarded 1 each year.

Deadline May of each year.

[896]
JEAN KENNEDY SMITH PLAYWRITING AWARD

John F. Kennedy Center for the Performing Arts
Education Department
Attn: Kennedy Center American College Theater
    Festival
2700 F Street, N.W.
Washington, DC 20566
(202) 416-8857   Fax: (202) 416-8802
E-mail: skshaffer@kennedy-center.org
Web: kennedy-center.org/education/actf/actfjks.html

Purpose To recognize and reward the student authors of plays on the theme of disability.

Eligibility Students at any accredited junior or senior college in the United States or in countries contiguous to the continental United States are eligible to compete, provided their college agrees to participate in the Kennedy Center American College Theater Festival (KCACTF). Undergraduate students must be carrying at least 6 semester hours, graduate students must be enrolled in at least 3 semester hours, and continuing part-time students must be enrolled in a regular degree or certificate program. This award is presented to the best student-written script that explores the human experience of living with a disability.

Financial data The winning playwright receives a cash award of $2,500, active membership in the Dramatists Guild, Inc., and a fellowship providing transportation, housing, and per diem to attend a prestigious playwriting program.

Duration The award is presented annually.

Additional information This award, first presented in 1999, is part of the Michael Kanin Playwriting Awards Program. The Dramatists Guild, Inc. and Very Special Arts participate in the selection of the winning script. The sponsoring college or university must pay a registration fee of $250 for each production.

Number awarded 1 each year.

Deadline November of each year.

[897]
JEAN SIBELIUS MEMORIAL FUND

Finlandia Foundation-New York Metropolitan Chapter
Attn: Scholarships
P.O. Box 165, Bowling Green Station
New York, NY 10274-0165
E-mail: scholarships@finlandiafoundationny.org
Web: www.finlandiafoundationny.org

Purpose To provide financial assistance to students interested in studying or conducting research on the Finnish arts in Finland or the United States.

Eligibility This program is open to students at colleges and universities in the United States who are interested in studying or conducting research on the Finnish arts in Finland or the United States. Applicants must submit information on their language proficiency, work experience, memberships (academic, professional, and social), fellowships and scholarships, awards, publications, exhibitions, performances, and future goals and ambitions. Financial need is not considered in the selection process.

Financial data Stipends range from $500 to $5,000 per year.

Duration 1 year.

Additional information Information is also available from Leena Toivonen, (718) 680-1716, E-mail: leenat@hotmail.com.

Number awarded 1 or more each year.

Deadline February of each year.

[898]
JOANNE ROBINSON MEMORIAL SCHOLARSHIP

JoAnne Robinson Memorial Scholarship Fund
WEWS
3001 Euclid Avenue
Cleveland, OH 44115
(216) 431-5555

Purpose To provide financial assistance to African American undergraduates who are majoring in broadcast journalism.

Eligibility This program is open to full-time college students who are African American and majoring in broadcast journalism. Applicants must exemplify the following characteristics: hard working, detail oriented, outstanding communication and interpersonal skills, and dedication to excellence (personally and professionally). Along with their application, they must submit a statement on their personal background, goals, values, and characteristics that make them worthy of this scholarship. Financial need is not considered in the selection process.

Financial data The stipend is $1,000. Funds may be used for tuition, books, and other educational expenses.

Duration 1 year; nonrenewable.

Additional information This scholarship is administered by the Scripps Howard Foundation, which forwards the stipend to the recipient's institution.

Number awarded 1 each year.

Deadline February of each year.

[899]
JOEL POLSKY ACADEMIC ACHIEVEMENT AWARD

American Society of Interior Designers
Attn: Department of Education
608 Massachusetts Avenue, N.E.
Washington, DC 20002-6006
(202) 546-3480   Fax: (202) 546-3240
E-mail: education@asid.org
Web: www.asid.org

Purpose To recognize and reward outstanding interior design research or thesis projects by graduate or undergraduate students.

Eligibility The competition is open to all undergraduate and graduate interior design students. Research papers, master's theses, or doctoral dissertations should address such interior design topics as educational research, behavioral science, business practice, design process, theory, or other technical subjects. Submissions are judged on actual content, breadth of material, comprehensive coverage of topic, innovative subject matter, bibliography, and references.

Financial data The award is $1,000.

Duration 1 year.

Number awarded 1 each year.

Deadline March of each year.

[900]
JOHN CAUBLE SHORT PLAY AWARD

John F. Kennedy Center for the Performing Arts
Education Department
Attn: Kennedy Center American College Theater Festival
2700 F Street, N.W.
Washington, DC 20566
(202) 416-8857   Fax: (202) 416-8802
E-mail: skshaffer@kennedy-center.org
Web: kennedy-center.org.education/actf/actfspa.html

Purpose To recognize and reward outstanding undergraduate and graduate student playwrights.

Eligibility Students at any accredited junior or senior college in the United States or in countries contiguous to the continental United States are eligible to compete, provided their college agrees to participate in the Kennedy Center American College Theater Festival (KCACTF). Undergraduate students must be carrying at least 6 semester hours, graduate students must be enrolled in at least 3 semester hours, and continuing part-time students must be enrolled in a regular degree or certificate program. For the Short Play Awards Program, students must submit a play of 1 act without intermission that, within itself, does not constitute a full evening of theater. The plays selected as the best by the judges are considered for presentation at the national festival and their playwrights receive these awards.

Financial data The prize is $1,000. Other benefits for the recipients of these awards include appropriate membership in the Dramatists Guild and publication by Samuel French, Inc.

Duration The competition is held annually.

Additional information This award, first presented in 1988, is part of the Michael Kanin Playwriting Awards Program. The sponsoring college or university must pay a registration fee of $250 for each production.

Number awarded 1 or more each year.

Deadline The final script must be submitted by November of each year.

[901]
JOHN SCHWARTZ SCHOLARSHIP

American Institute of Wine & Food-Pacific Northwest Chapter
c/o Ken Rudee, Scholarship Chair
Barnes & Watson Fine Teas
P.O. Box 24061
Seattle, WA 98124
(206) 625-9435
E-mail: Krudee@barnesandwatson.com
Web: www.aiwf.org/pnw/scholarships.html

Purpose To provide financial assistance to students in Washington state working on a degree in the culinary arts.

Eligibility This program is open to Washington residents who have been enrolled for at least 2 quarters in a culinary arts program in the state. Applicants must submit an essay that explains why they think they qualify for a scholarship, including their 2-year and 5-year professional goals. Selection is based on merit, including the essay, a resume, 2 letters of reference, and GPA (must be at least 3.0).

Financial data The stipend is $1,000.

Duration 1 year.

Additional information The recipient is given a 1-year membership in the American Institute of Wine & Food. Recipients must prepare an article for publication in the Pacific Northwest newsletter 6 months into their school year discussing their program and success.

Number awarded 1 each year.

[902]
JOSEPHINE DE KARMAN FELLOWSHIPS

Josephine de Kármán Fellowship Trust
Attn: Judy McClain, Secretary
P.O. Box 3389
San Dimas, CA 91773
(909) 592-0607 E-mail: info@dekarman.org
Web: www.dekarman.org

Purpose To provide financial assistance to outstanding college seniors or students in their last year of a Ph.D. program.

Eligibility This program is open to students in any discipline who will be entering their senior undergraduate year or their terminal year of a Ph.D. program in the fall of the next academic year. Postdoctoral students are not eligible. Foreign students may apply if they are already enrolled in a university in the United States. Applicants must be able to demonstrate exceptional ability and seriousness of purpose. Special consideration is given to applicants in the humanities and to those who have completed their qualifying examinations for the doctoral degree.

Financial data The stipend is $16,000 per year for graduate students or $8,000 per year for undergraduates. Funds are paid in 2 installments to the recipient's school. No funds may be used for travel.

Duration 1 year; may not be renewed or postponed.

Additional information This fund was established in 1954 by Dr. Theodore von Kármán, renowned aeronautics expert and director of the Guggenheim Aeronautical Laboratory at the California Institute of Technology. Study must be carried out in the United States.

Number awarded At least 10 each year.

Deadline January of each year.

[903]
JULIUS & ESTHER STULBERG INTERNATIONAL STRING COMPETITION

Julius & Esther Stulberg Competition, Inc.
359 South Kalamazoo Mall, Suite 14
Kalamazoo, MI 49007
(269) 343-2776 Fax: (269) 343-2797
E-mail: Stulbergcomp@yahoo.com
Web: www.stulberg.org

Purpose To recognize and reward outstanding young string musicians.

Eligibility This competition is open to string players 19 years of age or younger who are studying violin, viola, cello, or double bass. Applicants must submit a CD of a performance from the standard solo repertoire (up to 20 minutes in length). The CD must include required selections by Bach for the applicant to be considered for the Bach Award. On the basis of the tapes, judges select 12 finalists to come to Kalamazoo to compete.

Financial data First place is the Stulberg Burdick-Thorne Gold Medal of $5,000 and a solo performance award. Second place is $4,000 and a solo recital at the Fontana Chamber Arts Summer Festival. Third place is $3,000 and a performance with the Kalamazoo Junior Symphony Society. The Bach Award is $500. Funds are to be used for the musical training and education of the winners.

Duration The competition is held annually, in March.

Additional information This competition was organized in 1975 as a memorial to Julius Stulberg, director of the Kalamazoo Junior Symphony for 31 years and professor of music at Western Michigan University for 27 years. The application fee is $75.

Number awarded 4 cash prizes are awarded each year.

Deadline December of each year.

[904]
JUNE P. GALLOWAY SCHOLARSHIP

North Carolina Alliance for Athletics, Health, Physical Education, Recreation and Dance
Attn: Executive Director
P.O. Box 27751
Raleigh, NC 27611
Toll-free: (888) 840-6500 Fax: (919) 833-7700
E-mail: ncaahperd@ncaahperd.org
Web: www.ncaahperd.org/awards/scholarships.htm

Purpose To provide financial assistance for college to members of the North Carolina Alliance for Athletics, Health, Physical Education, Recreation and Dance (NCAAHPERD).

Eligibility This program is open to rising seniors majoring in health, physical education, recreation, and/or dance who are members of NCAAHPERD. Applicants must have a GPA of 2.0 or higher for all college work and 3.0 or higher for their major. Selection is based two-thirds on academic achievement and one-third on leadership and contributions to the profession. Financial need is not considered.

Financial data The stipend is $1,000 per year.

Duration 1 year.

Number awarded 1 each year.

Deadline June of each year.

[905]
KCACTF MUSICAL THEATER AWARD

John F. Kennedy Center for the Performing Arts
Education Department
Attn: Kennedy Center American College Theater Festival
2700 F Street, N.W.
Washington, DC 20566
(202) 416-8857 Fax: (202) 416-8802
E-mail: skshaffer@kennedy-center.org
Web: kennedy-center.org/education/actf/actfmta.html

Purpose To recognize and reward outstanding musical playwrights in college.

Eligibility This program is open to teams (consisting of composers, lyricists, and authors) that submit original and copyrighted musical plays (including a completed manuscript of the book, the score of the music, the lyrics, and a cassette recording of the score). At least 50% of the team must be students at colleges in the United States, Canada, or Mexico who have agreed to participate in the Kennedy Center American College Theater Festival (KCACTF). Undergraduate students must be carrying a minimum of 6 semester hours, graduate students must be enrolled in at least 3 semester hours, and continuing part-time students must be enrolled in a regular degree or certificate program.

Financial data Prizes of $1,000 each are awarded to the composer(s) for the music, lyricist(s) for the lyrics, and

author(s) for the book. In addition, the sponsoring college or university that produced the winning musical receives $1,000.
Duration The competition is held annually.
Additional information This award, first presented in 1982, is part of the Michael Kanin Playwriting Awards Program. The sponsoring college or university must pay a registration fee of $250 for each production.
Number awarded 3 awards to individuals and 1 to a college or university are made for the winning musical each year.
Deadline The manuscript and the score must be submitted by November of each year.

[906]
KEN KASHIWAHARA SCHOLARSHIP
Radio and Television News Directors Foundation
1600 K Street, N.W., Suite 700
Washington, DC 20006-2838
(202) 467-5218   Fax: (202) 223-4007
E-mail: irvingw@rtndf.org
Web: www.rtndf.org

Purpose To provide financial assistance to outstanding undergraduate students, especially minorities, who are interested in preparing for a career in electronic journalism.
Eligibility Eligible are sophomore or more advanced undergraduate students enrolled in an electronic journalism sequence at an accredited or nationally-recognized college or university. Applicants must submit 1 to 3 examples of reporting or producing skills on audio or video cassette tapes (no more than 15 minutes total), a description of their role on each story and a list of who worked on each story and what they did, a statement explaining why they are seeking a career in broadcast or cable journalism, and a letter of endorsement from a faculty sponsor that verifies the applicant has at least 1 year of school remaining. Preference is given to undergraduate students of color.
Financial data The stipend is $2,500, paid in semiannual installments of $1,250 each.
Duration 1 year.
Additional information The Radio and Television News Directors Foundation (RTNDF) also provides an all-expense paid trip to the Radio-Television News Directors Association (RTNDA) annual international conference. It defines electronic journalism to include radio, television, cable, and online news. Previous winners of any RTNDF scholarship or internship are not eligible.
Number awarded 1 each year.
Deadline April of each year.

[907]
KENNEDY CENTER AMERICAN COLLEGE THEATER FESTIVAL TEN-MINUTE PLAY FESTIVAL AWARD
John F. Kennedy Center for the Performing Arts
Education Department
Attn: Kennedy Center American College Theater Festival
2700 F Street, N.W.
Washington, DC 20566
(202) 416-8857   Fax: (202) 416-8802
E-mail: skshaffer@kennedy-center.org
Web: kennedy-center.org/education/actf/actften.html

Purpose To recognize and reward outstanding 10-minute plays by student playwrights.
Eligibility Students at any accredited junior or senior college in the United States or in a country contiguous to the continental United States are eligible to compete in a regional 10-minute play festival. Undergraduate students must be carrying at least 6 semester hours, graduate students must be enrolled in at least 3 semester hours, and continuing part-time students must be enrolled in a regular degree or certificate program. The 8 regional winners are then entered in the national competition.
Financial data The national prize is $1,000. Dramatic Publishing Company publishes each of the 8 regional winners' plays.
Duration The competition is held annually.
Additional information This award, first presented in 2000, is part of the Michael Kanin Playwriting Awards Program. Colleges and universities that have at least 1 participating or associate entry in the Kennedy Center American College Theater Festival (KCACTF) may enter this festival at no additional charge. Regional submissions from schools with no entries in the KCACTF must pay a $20 entry fee per submission to this festival.
Number awarded 1 each year.
Deadline November of each year.

[908]
LATINA/LATINO PLAYWRITING AWARD
John F. Kennedy Center for the Performing Arts
Education Department
Attn: Kennedy Center American College Theater Festival
2700 F Street, N.W.
Washington, DC 20566
(202) 416-8857   Fax: (202) 416-8802
E-mail: skshaffer@kennedy-center.org
Web: kennedy-center.org/education/actf/actfsitv.html

Purpose To recognize and reward outstanding plays by Latino student playwrights.
Eligibility Latino students at any accredited junior or senior college in the United States are eligible to compete, provided their college agrees to participate in the Kennedy Center American College Theater Festival (KCACTF). Undergraduate students must be carrying at least 6 semester hours, graduate students must be enrolled in at least 3 semester hours, and continuing part-time students must be enrolled in a regular degree or certificate program. This

award is presented to the best student-written play by a Latino.

Financial data The prize is $2,500. The winner also receives an internship to a prestigious playwriting retreat program. Dramatic Publishing Company presents the winning playwright with an offer of a contract to publish, license, and market the winning play. A grant of $500 is made to the theater department of the college or university producing the award-winning play.

Duration The award is presented annually.

Additional information This award, first presented in 2000, is part of the Michael Kanin Playwriting Awards Program. The sponsoring college or university must pay a registration fee of $250 for each production.

Number awarded 1 each year.

Deadline November of each year.

[909] LAWRENCE G. FOSTER AWARD FOR EXCELLENCE IN PUBLIC RELATIONS

Public Relations Student Society of America
Attn: Vice President of Member Services
33 Maiden Lane, 11th Floor
New York, NY 10038-5150
(212) 460-1474   Fax: (212) 995-0757
E-mail: prssa@prsa.org
Web: www.prssa.org

Purpose To recognize and reward members of the Public Relations Student Society of America (PRSSA) who write outstanding essays on excellence in public relations.

Eligibility This program is open to members of the society who are currently enrolled in an undergraduate program of study at an accredited college or university. Applicants must submit an essay of 1,000 to 1,200 words describing their conception of excellence in public relations and how they plan to achieve excellence in their own careers. They should address the ethical and work standards that they believe will be required of them as public relations professionals and describe how they personally will aspire to excellence in those areas. Students should also list those leadership qualities they believe are most important in public relations, and why.

Financial data The prize is $1,500.

Duration The competition is held annually.

Number awarded 1 each year.

Deadline May of each year.

[910] LAWRENCE R. CAMPBELL RESEARCH AWARD

Association for Education in Journalism and Mass Communication
Attn: Scholastic Journalism Division
234 Outlet Pointe Boulevard, Suite A
Columbia, SC 29210-5667
(803) 798-0271   Fax: (803) 772-3509
E-mail: aejmc@aejmc.org
Web: www.aejmc.org

Purpose To recognize and reward outstanding student papers on scholastic journalism.

Eligibility Undergraduate and graduate students are invited to submit papers that involve any area of mass communication research that can be applied to secondary school journalism.

Financial data A plaque and a cash award are presented.

Duration The competition is held annually.

Additional information These awards were first presented in 1985.

Number awarded 1 each year.

Deadline March of each year.

[911] LEADING EDGE STUDENT DESIGN COMPETITION

New Buildings Institute
Attn: Program Manager
142 East Jewett Boulevard
P.O. Box 2349
White Salmon, WA 98672
(509) 493-4468, ext. 12   Fax: (509) 493-4078
E-mail: pat@newbuildings.org
Web: www.leadingedgecompetition.org

Purpose To recognize and reward undergraduate and graduate students who submit outstanding energy-efficient entries in a design competition.

Eligibility This competition is open to undergraduate and graduate students enrolled in architecture, engineering, drafting, or environmental design programs at 2-year colleges, 4- or 5-year colleges or programs, graduate programs, and technical schools. The first category is for students in their third, fourth, or fifth year of undergraduate study and all graduate and post-baccalaureate students; the second category is for students in the first or second year of their undergraduate design education. Entries may be submitted by individuals or teams. Participants are invited to submit designs for a problem at an actual site. Complete information is provided on site history, demographics, climate, utilities, site description, and special requirements. Each design must satisfy the sociological and environmental concerns of the community while also addressing advanced energy efficiency and sustainable building design issues.

Financial data In each category, first prize is $3,000 and second prize is $2,000. If winning entries are submitted by teams of students, the prizes must be divided equally among them. The schools of the winning teams receive $1,500 for first prize and $1,000 for second prize.

Duration The competition is held annually.

Additional information This competition was first held in 1992.

Number awarded 4 cash prizes are awarded each year: 2 in each category.

Deadline Registration must be completed by March of each year. Completed entries are due in June.

[912]
LEONARD M. PERRYMAN COMMUNICATIONS SCHOLARSHIP FOR ETHNIC MINORITY STUDENTS

United Methodist Communications
Attn: Communications Resourcing Team
810 12th Avenue South
P.O. Box 320
Nashville, TN 37202-0320
(615) 742-5481   Toll-free: (888) CRT-4UMC
Fax: (615) 742-5485
E-mail: scholarships@umcom.org
Web: crt.umc.org/interior.asp?ptid=44&mid=10270

Purpose To provide financial assistance to minority United Methodist college students who are interested in careers in religious communications.

Eligibility This program is open to United Methodist ethnic minority students enrolled in accredited institutions of higher education as juniors or seniors. Applicants must be interested in preparing for a career in religious communications. For the purposes of this program, "communications" is meant to cover audiovisual, electronic, and print journalism. Selection is based on Christian commitment and involvement in the life of the United Methodist church, academic achievement, journalistic experience, clarity of purpose, and professional potential as a religious journalist.

Financial data The stipend is $2,500 per year.
Duration 1 year.
Additional information The scholarship may be used at any accredited institution of higher education.
Number awarded 1 each year.
Deadline March of each year.

[913]
LINDA SIMMONS EDUCATIONAL SCHOLARSHIP

Alaska Broadcasters Association
700 West 41st Street
P.O. Box 102424
Anchorage, AK 99510
(907) 258-2424   Fax: (907) 258-2414
E-mail: akba@gci.net
Web: www.alaskabroadcasters.org

Purpose To provide financial assistance to residents of Alaska who are attending college to prepare for a career in broadcasting.

Eligibility This program is open to Alaska residents who are working on an undergraduate degree or certified course of study at an accredited junior or community college, professional trade school, college, or university in any state. They must be majoring in public relations, journalism, advertising, radio, and/or television broadcasting; if there are no candidates with those majors, students whose main interest is in a communication profession but whose major is another field are considered. Applicants must submit a resume that covers employment, school and community extracurricular activities, awards, and honors; 3 letters of reference; and a short essay on personal goals. Financial need is not considered.

Financial data The stipend is $2,000. Funds are paid directly to the student's institution.
Duration 1 year.
Number awarded 1 each year.
Deadline March of each year.

[914]
LORD ACTON ESSAY COMPETITION

Acton Institute for the Study of Religion and Liberty
161 Ottawa N.W., Suite 301
Grand Rapids, MI 49503
(616) 454-3080   Fax: (616) 454-9454
E-mail: awards@acton.org
Web: www.acton.org/programs/students/essay

Purpose To recognize and reward seminarians and students at all levels who submit outstanding essays on the themes of religion and liberty.

Eligibility This competition is open to seminarians, undergraduates, graduate students, and postgraduates studying religion, theology, philosophy, or related fields, regardless of religious affiliation or denomination. Applicants must submit a 4- to 6-page essay focusing on a topic that changes annually but relates to themes of religion and freedom. Applications from those outside the United States and those studying abroad receive equal consideration. Selection is based on the integration of economic, theological, and political thought in response to the annual topic.

Financial data First place is $2,000, second $1,000, and third $500.
Duration The competition is held annually.
Additional information This competition was first held in 1992. The 3 prize winners and 2 honorable mentions are published on the sponsor's web site.
Number awarded 3 cash prizes are awarded each year.
Deadline November of each year.

[915]
LORRAINE HANSBERRY PLAYWRITING AWARD

John F. Kennedy Center for the Performing Arts
Education Department
Attn: Kennedy Center American College Theater
    Festival
2700 F Street, N.W.
Washington, DC 20566
(202) 416-8857   Fax: (202) 416-8802
E-mail: skshaffer@kennedy-center.org
Web: kennedy-center.org/education/actf/actflha.html

Purpose To recognize and reward student authors of plays on the African American experience in America.

Eligibility Students at any accredited junior or senior college in the United States or in countries contiguous to the continental United States are eligible to compete, provided their college agrees to participate in the Kennedy Center American College Theater Festival (KCACTF). Undergraduate students must be carrying at least 6 semester hours, graduate students must be enrolled in at least 3 semester hours, and continuing part-time students must be enrolled in a regular degree or certificate program. These awards are presented to the best student-written plays on the subject of the African American experience.

Financial data The first-place award is $2,500 and the second-place award is $1,000. The first-place winner also receives publication of the play by Dramatic Publishing

Company. In addition to the student awards, grants of $750 and $500 are made to the theater departments of the colleges or universities producing the first- and second-place plays.

Duration The awards are presented annually.

Additional information This program is supported by the Kennedy Center and Dramatic Publishing Company. It honors the first African American playwright to win the New York Drama Critics Award who died in 1965 at the age of 34. First presented in 1977, it is part of the Michael Kanin Playwriting Awards Program. The sponsoring college or university must pay a registration fee of $250 for each production.

Number awarded 2 students and 2 sponsoring institutions receive awards each year.

Deadline November of each year.

[916]
LOU AND CAROLE PRATO SPORTS REPORTING SCHOLARSHIP

Radio and Television News Directors Foundation
1600 K Street, N.W., Suite 700
Washington, DC 20006-2838
(202) 467-5218　　　　　　　Fax: (202) 223-4007
E-mail: irvingw@rtndf.org
Web: www.rtndf.org

Purpose To provide financial assistance for undergraduate education to students whose career objective is radio or television sports reporting.

Eligibility This program is open to sophomores, juniors, and seniors who are enrolled full time in electronic journalism in a college or university where such a major is offered. Applicants must submit 1 to 3 examples of reporting or producing skills on audio or video cassette tapes (no more than 15 minutes total), a description of their role on each story and a list of who worked on each story and what they did, a statement explaining why they are seeking a career in broadcast or cable journalism, and a letter of endorsement from a faculty sponsor certifying that the candidate has at least 1 year of school remaining. They must be planning a career as a sports reporter in television or radio.

Financial data The stipend is $1,000.

Duration 1 year.

Additional information The Radio and Television News Directors Foundation (RTNDF) also provides an all-expense paid trip to the Radio-Television News Directors Association (RTNDA) annual international conference. This program was established in 2001. Previous winners of any RTNDF scholarship or internship are not eligible.

Number awarded 1 each year.

Deadline April of each year.

[917]
LYNN FREEMAN OLSON COMPOSITION AWARD

National Federation of Music Clubs
1336 North Delaware Street
Indianapolis, IN 46202-2481
(317) 638-4003　　　　　　　Fax: (317) 638-0503
E-mail: info@nfmc-music.org
Web: www.nfmc-music.org

Purpose To recognize and reward outstanding young composers who are members of the National Federation of Music Clubs.

Eligibility This competition is open to keyboard composers in the advanced division (high school graduate through 25 years of age), the high school division (grades 10-12), or the intermediate division (grades 7 through 9). Applicants may be citizens of any country, but they must be members of either the junior or student division of the federation. They may not previously have published any works for the purpose of general public use or sales. Compositions must be written within the skill levels of early elementary through intermediate levels of piano study.

Financial data The award is $1,500 for the advanced division, $1,000 for the high school division, or $500 for the intermediate division. Funds must be used for further music study.

Additional information Further information on this award is also available from James Schnars, 28 Evonaire Circle, Belleair FL 33756-1602; information on all federation scholarships and awards is available from Chair, Competitions and Awards Board, Dr. George R. Keck, 421 Cherry Street, Arkadelphia, AR 71923-5116, E-mail: keckg@obu.edu.

Number awarded 3 every other year: 1 in each of the divisions.

Deadline February of odd-numbered years.

[918]
M. JOSEPHINE O'NEAL ARTS AWARD

Delta Kappa Gamma Society International-Lambda State Organization
c/o Betty W. Carbol
920 Buena Road
Lake Forest, IL 60045-2927
Web: www.deltakappagamma.org/IL

Purpose To provide financial assistance to women residents of Illinois who are studying an arts-related field in college.

Eligibility This program is open to women residents of Illinois who are in or approaching junior standing at an accredited college or university or in the sophomore year at an accredited community college. Applicants must be majoring in 1 or more areas of the arts, including music, visual arts, dance, theater, and the literary arts. Along with their application, they must submit 1) evidence of the quality and extent of accomplishment in the arts, such as programs of performances, catalogs, articles from the media, published reviews of their work, listings of awards and prizes, or other recognition; 2) samples of their work on 35mm slides, videotapes, or audio tapes; 3) college transcripts; 4) letters of recommendation; and 5) a personal essay on their family, personal interests, awards, achievements, goals (short- and long-term), and philosophy. Selection is based on the essay, letters of recommendation, academic background, and evidence from all sources of potential for contribution to society.

Financial data The stipend ranges up to $6,000.

Duration 1 year.

Additional information The sponsor is an honorary society of women educators.

Number awarded 1 each year.

Deadline January of each year.

[919] MARC A. KLEIN PLAYWRITING AWARD

Case Western Reserve University
Attn: Department of Theater and Dance
Eldred Hall
Cleveland, OH 44106-7077
(216) 368-4868
Web: www.case.edu/artsci/thtr

Purpose To recognize and reward outstanding college playwrights.

Eligibility Any student currently enrolled in an advanced theater program at a U.S. college or university may submit an original, previously unpublished or unproduced full-length play to enter this competition. Musicals and children's plays are not accepted. Manuscripts must be endorsed by a teacher of drama, a member of a theater department, or a recognized critic, director, or playwright.

Financial data The award is $1,000: $500 upon announcement and $500 during the rehearsal period in order to help pay travel costs and living expenses while in residence for the world premier production of the play.

Duration The competition is held annually.

Additional information The award includes full mainstage production of the play while the playwright is in residence at Case Western Reserve University.

Number awarded 1 each year.

Deadline November of each year.

[920] MARK TWAIN COMEDY PLAYWRITING AWARD

John F. Kennedy Center for the Performing Arts
Education Department
Attn: Kennedy Center American College Theater Festival
2700 F Street, N.W.
Washington, DC 20566
(202) 416-8857   Fax: (202) 416-8802
E-mail: skshaffer@kennedy-center.org
Web: kennedy-center.org

Purpose To recognize and reward the student authors of comedy plays.

Eligibility Students at any accredited junior or senior college in the United States or in countries contiguous to the continental United States are eligible to compete, provided their college agrees to participate in the Kennedy Center American College Theater Festival (KCACTF). Undergraduate students must be carrying at least 6 semester hours, graduate students must be enrolled in at least 3 semester hours, and continuing part-time students must be enrolled in a regular degree or certificate program. This award is presented to the best student-written full length comedy play.

Financial data A first-place award of $2,500 and a second-place award of $1,500 are presented to student authors. Dramatic Publishing Company presents the winning playwright with an offer of a contract to publish, license, and market the winning play. In addition to the student awards, grants of $750 and $500 are made to the theater departments of the colleges or universities producing the first- and second-place plays.

Duration The award is presented annually.

Additional information This award, first presented in 2000, is supported by Comedy Central, Inc. the cable television company. It is part of the Michael Kanin Playwriting Program. The sponsoring college or university must pay a registration fee of $250 for each production.

Number awarded 2 student winners and 2 sponsoring institutions each year.

Deadline November of each year.

[921] MARY GRAHAM LASLEY SCHOLARSHIP COMPETITION

Symphony Orchestra League of Alexandria
2121 Eisenhower Avenue, Suite 608
Alexandria, VA 22314
(703) 548-0885   Fax: (703) 548-0985
E-mail: alex@alexsym.org
Web: www.alexsym.org/lasley.shtml

Purpose To recognize and reward outstanding student musicians who study or reside in the Washington, D.C. area.

Eligibility Eligible are 1) full-time undergraduate and graduate students currently studying music at a college, university, or conservatory in Virginia, Maryland, or the District of Columbia or 2) residents of those 3 areas who are currently studying elsewhere. Previous competitors (except past winners) are also eligible. Contestants may be no more than 26 years of age at the time of the competition. Solos must be performed from memory on strings, winds, piano, or percussion.

Financial data First prize is $1,500, second $1,000, and third $750.

Duration The competition is held annually.

Additional information This competition is sponsored by the Alexandria Symphony Orchestra and the Symphony Orchestra League of Alexandria. Information is also available from William E. Clayton, Scholarship Competition Chair, (703) 548-0958, E-mail: tbclayton@verizon.net. Applications must be accompanied by a $25 nonrefundable entry fee.

Number awarded 3 each year.

Deadline January of each year.

[922]
MCDERMOTT FELLOWSHIP FOR TRAVELING STUDIES IN ARCHITECTURE

Dallas Architectural Foundation
1444 Oak Lawn Avenue, Suite 600
Dallas, TX 75207
(214) 742-DAIA   Fax: (214) 742-3253
E-mail: info@aiadallas.org
Web: www.dallasaia.org

Purpose To provide financial assistance for travel to advanced architecture students and recent graduates from Texas.

Eligibility This program is open to residents Texas who either 1) are enrolled in the fourth, fifth, or sixth year of an architectural program at a college or university, or 2) graduated from an architectural program in the last 3 years. Applicants must be interested in a travel program for additional study in architecture. They must be proposing to research, develop, and disseminate knowledge of the built environment. Along with their application, they must submit a 350-word essay describing the objectives, methodology, and itinerary of their proposed study program and how and why it can benefit the architectural community. U.S. citizenship is required.

Financial data The stipend is $2,000.

Duration Funds must be used within 1 year. The award is not renewable.

Number awarded 1 each year.

Deadline March of each year.

[923]
METROPOLITAN OPERA NATIONAL COUNCIL AUDITIONS

Metropolitan Opera
Attn: National Council Auditions
Lincoln Center
New York, NY 10023
(212) 870-4515   Fax: (212) 870-7606
E-mail: ncouncil@metopera.org
Web: www.metoperafamily.org

Purpose To recognize and reward singers who have the potential to appear in the Metropolitan Opera.

Eligibility This competition is open to singers between 20 and 30 years of age who have a voice with operatic potential (exceptional quality, range, projection, charisma, communication, and natural beauty) as well as musical training and background. They must be able to sing correctly in more than 1 language and show artistic aptitude. Applicants should be citizens of the United States or Canada; foreign applicants must show proof of a 1-year residency or full-time enrollment at a university or conservatory in the United States or Canada. Singers must present 5 arias of their choice and of no more than 8 minutes' duration, in contrasting languages and styles. The competition begins at the district level, with winners advancing to regional auditions. The winners from each of the 15 regions represent their region at the national semifinals in New York and then 10 of those singers are selected as national finalists. At the National Grand Finals concert, which is held exactly 1 week later, the 10 National Grand Finalists perform 2 arias each on the stage of the Metropolitan Opera accompanied by the MET Orchestra in a nationally-broadcast concert. The national winners are selected at that concert.

Financial data At the regional level, each first-place winner receives the $800 Mrs. Edgar Tobin Award, each second-place winner receives $600, and each third-place winner receives $400; some regions award additional prizes or encouragement awards. At the national level, each winner receives $15,000, each finalist receives $5,000, and each semifinalist receives $1,500. Educational grants up to $5,000 are available to national finalists and winners.

Duration The competition is held annually.

Additional information Applicants enter in the district in which they are currently living, attending school, or have a professional singing contract. For further information on districts or regions nationwide, write or call the Metropolitan Opera. A nonrefundable fee of $30 must accompany each application.

Number awarded The country is divided into 15 regions, in each of which 3 prizes are awarded. The 15 regional winners are national semifinalists, from whom 10 national finalists are selected. From those finalists, up to 5 national winners are chosen.

Deadline Deadlines are chosen by local districts and regions; most of them are in early to late fall of each year. District auditions usually occur from October through February, with the winners advancing to the regional auditions, usually between October and February. The national competition in New York usually takes place in late March or early April.

[924]
MINNESOTA PRO CHAPTER OF THE SOCIETY OF PROFESSIONAL JOURNALISTS SCHOLARSHIP

Society of Professional Journalists-Minnesota
   Professional Chapter
c/o Yvonne Klinnert
Stillwater Courier
1815 Northwestern Avenue
Stillwater, MN 55082
E-mail: minnesota.spj@gmail.com
Web: www.mnspj.org/category/scholarships

Purpose To provide financial assistance to undergraduate students from Minnesota interested in preparing for a career in journalism.

Eligibility This program is open to undergraduate students who are enrolled in a postsecondary institution in Minnesota or graduates of high schools in the state who are enrolled in a postsecondary institution in any state. Applicants must be preparing for a career in journalism. Preference is given to members of the Society of Professional Journalists (SPJ). Along with their application, they must submit a resume, college transcript, 2 letters of recommendation, a 500-word essay on why they have chosen journalism as a career, and samples of their work (up to 2 clippings or articles for print journalism, 2 printed screen shots for web journalism, 2 radio or TV samples for broadcast journalism, or up to 5 photographs for photojournalism). Financial need is not considered in the selection process.

Financial data The stipend is $2,000.

Duration 1 year.

Number awarded 1 each year.
Deadline February of each year.

[925]
MOE FONER SCHOLARSHIP PROGRAM FOR VISUAL AND PERFORMING ARTS
Service Employees International Union
Attn: Education Department
1313 L Street, N.W.
Washington, DC 20005
(202) 898-3326 Toll-free: (800) 424-8592
Fax: (202) 898-3348 TDD: (202) 898-3481
Web: www.seiu.org/mbe/scholarships/moefoner.cfm

Purpose To provide financial assistance to members and children of members of the Service Employees International Union (SEIU) who are interested in studying the visual or performing arts in college.

Eligibility This program is open to members of an SEIU local or affiliated union and their children. Applicants must be working on or planning to work on a degree or training program in the visual or performing arts at a 2-year or 4-year college or university, community college, technical or trade school, or an alternate course of study or training in an arts-related field. Along with their application, they must submit a 200-word essay describing what the labor movement has meant to them and their family; a 200-word essay describing their educational and career goals in the visual or performing arts (including how they plan to use this education to improve the lives of working families and work for economic and social justice); a high school transcript; and either 1) an essay of 500 words or less identifying a workplace issue and how they would use visual and performing arts to reflect the stories and struggles of working people, or 2) 6 copies of their creative work, showing how they would interpret the theme of working people and their struggles through the visual or performing arts. Selection is based on originality, clarity, and commitment to social and economic justice in the workplace.

Financial data The stipend is $5,000.
Duration 1 year; nonrenewable.
Additional information This program is administered by Scholarship Program Administrators, Inc., 1201 Eighth Avenue South, P.O. Box 23737, Nashville, TN 27202-3737, (615) 320-3149, Fax: (615) 320-3151, E-mail: info@spaprog.com.
Number awarded 1 each year.
Deadline February of each year.

[926]
MORTON GOULD YOUNG COMPOSER AWARDS
American Society of Composers, Authors and Publishers
Attn: ASCAP Foundation
ASCAP Building
One Lincoln Plaza
New York, NY 10023
(212) 621-6320 Fax: (212) 621-6236
E-mail: ascapfoundation@ascap.com
Web: www.ascapfoundation.org/awards.html

Purpose To recognize and reward outstanding young American composers.

Eligibility Applicants must be U.S. citizens, permanent residents, or enrolled students with proper visas who are younger than 30 years of age, including students in grades K-12, undergraduates, graduate students, and recipients of a D.M.A. degree. Original music of any style is considered. However, works that have earned awards or prizes in other national competitions are ineligible, as are arrangements. To compete, each applicant must submit a completed application form, 1 reproduction of a manuscript or score, biographical information, a list of compositions to date, and 2 professional recommendations. Only 1 composition per composer may be submitted. A cassette tape or CD of the composition may be included. So that music materials may be returned, each entry must be accompanied by a self-addressed envelope with sufficient postage.

Financial data The winners share cash awards of more than $30,000.
Duration The award is presented annually.
Additional information Morton Gould was president of the American Society of Composers, Authors and Publishers. This program was established in 1979. The awards include the Leo Kaplan Award.
Number awarded Varies each year; recently, 29 students received these awards.
Deadline February of each year.

[927]
MUSIC THERAPY SCHOLARSHIP
Sigma Alpha Iota Philanthropies, Inc.
One Tunnel Road
Asheville, NC 28805
(828) 251-0606 Fax: (828) 251-0644
E-mail: philonline@sai-national.org
Web: www.sai-national.org/phil/philsch1.html

Purpose To provide financial assistance to members of Sigma Alpha Iota (an organization of women musicians) who are interested in working on an undergraduate or graduate degree in music therapy.

Eligibility Members of the organization may apply for these scholarships if they wish to study music therapy at the undergraduate or graduate level. Applicants must submit an essay that includes their personal definition of music therapy, their career plans and professional goals as a music therapist, and why they feel they are deserving of this scholarship. Selection is based on music therapy skills, musicianship, fraternity service, community service, leadership, self-reliance, and dedication to the field of music therapy as a career.

Financial data The stipend is $1,000.
Duration 1 year.
Additional information There is a $25 nonrefundable application fee.
Number awarded 1 each year.
Deadline March of each year.

[928]
NAOMI BERBER MEMORIAL SCHOLARSHIP
Print and Graphics Scholarship Foundation
Attn: Scholarship Competition
200 Deer Run Road
Sewickley, PA 15143-2600
(412) 259-1740 Toll-free: (800) 910-GATF
Fax: (412) 741-2311 E-mail: pgsf@piagatf.org
Web: www.gain.net

Purpose To provide financial assistance for college to women who want to prepare for a career in the printing or publishing industry.

Eligibility This program is open to females who are high school seniors or already in college. They must be interested in preparing for a career in publishing or printing while in college. This is a merit-based program; financial need is not considered.

Financial data The stipend ranges from $1,000 to $1,500, depending upon the funds available each year.

Duration 1 year; may be renewed for up to 3 additional years.

Additional information This program is named for Naomi Berber, the first woman elected to the Graphic Arts Technical Foundation Society of Fellows. Recipients must attend school on a full-time basis.

Number awarded 1 or more each year.

Deadline February of each year for high school seniors; March of each year for students already in college.

[929]
NATHAN TAYLOR DODSON SCHOLARSHIP
North Carolina Alliance for Athletics, Health, Physical Education, Recreation and Dance
Attn: Executive Director
P.O. Box 27751
Raleigh, NC 27611
Toll-free: (888) 840-6500 Fax: (919) 833-7700
E-mail: ncaahperd@ncaahperd.org
Web: www.ncaahperd.org/awards/scholarships.htm

Purpose To provide financial assistance for college to members of the North Carolina Alliance for Athletics, Health, Physical Education, Recreation and Dance (NCAAHPERD).

Eligibility This program is open to rising seniors majoring in health, physical education, recreation, and/or dance who are members of NCAAHPERD. Applicants must have a GPA of 2.0 or higher for all college work and 3.0 or higher for their major. Selection is based two-thirds on academic achievement and one-third on leadership and contributions to the profession. Financial need is not considered.

Financial data The stipend is $1,000 per year.

Duration 1 year.

Number awarded 1 each year.

Deadline June of each year.

[930]
NATION INSTITUTE/I.F. STONE AWARD FOR STUDENT JOURNALISM
Nation Institute
33 Irving Place
New York, NY 10003
(212) 209-5448
Web: www.nationinstitute.org/awards

Purpose To recognize and reward outstanding college journalists.

Eligibility Undergraduate students majoring in journalism at any college or university in the United States may enter this competition. Entrants may submit up to 3 articles, preferably published in student publications during the preceding year; unpublished articles will also be considered unless they were written as assignments for regular course work. Articles may be submitted by the writers themselves or nominated by editors of student publications or faculty members.

Financial data The prize is $1,000.

Duration The competition is held annually.

Additional information The winning article will be published in a fall issue of The Nation.

Number awarded 1 each year.

Deadline June of each year.

[931]
NATIONAL AD 2 STUDENT CREATIVE COMPETITION
National Ad 2
c/o Jocelyn Lee, Treasurer
Starr Seigle Advertising
1001 Bishop Street, ASB Tower, 19th Floor
Honolulu, HI 96813
(808) 544-3032 Fax: (808) 523-7443
E-mail: treasurer@ad2.org
Web: www.ad2.org/education/education.htm

Purpose To recognize and reward students who enter an advertising competition.

Eligibility This competition is open to students enrolled full or part time in an accredited U.S. college, university, or commercial art school. Applicants must be majoring in advertising or a closely-related field (e.g., art, communication, journalism, marketing, or public relations). They must submit a complete advertisement in 1 of the following categories: sales promotion, collateral material, direct marketing, newspaper, interactive media, editorial design, radio, television, campaigns, or elements of advertising. The work must be the student's own individual effort and developed specifically for this competition or submitted from previous projects or competitions. Work developed for paying clients is not accepted. Entries must be submitted through a local Ad 2 Club.

Financial data The grand-prize winner receives $1,000, plus complimentary registration and travel vouchers for the sponsor's national conference.

Duration The competition is held annually.

Additional information National Ad 2 is a division of the American Advertising Federation (AAF) for members under 32 years of age. The entry fee is set by local clubs but recommended to be $20.

Number awarded 1 each year.
Deadline March of each year.

[932]
NATIONAL ASSOCIATION OF NEGRO MUSICIANS SCHOLARSHIP CONTEST

National Association of Negro Musicians, Inc.
Attn: National Scholarship Chair
11551 South Laflin Street
P.O. Box 43053
Chicago, IL 60643
(773) 568-3818   Fax: (773) 785-5388
E-mail: nanm@nanm.org
Web: www.nanm.org/Scholarship_competition.htm

Purpose To recognize and reward (with scholarships for additional study) young musicians who are sponsored by a branch of the National Association of Negro Musicians.

Eligibility This competition is open to musicians between 18 and 30 years of age. Contestants must be sponsored by a branch in good standing, although they do not need to be a member of a local branch or the national organization. Ineligible people include former first-place winners of this competition; full-time public school teachers and college faculty (although graduate students holding teaching assistantships are still eligible if they receive less than 50% of their employment from that appointment); vocalists who have contracts as full-time solo performers in operatic, oratorio, or other types of professional singing organizations; instrumentalists with contractual full-time orchestral or ensemble jobs; and professional performers under management. Local branches nominate competitors for regional competitions. Regional winners advance to the national competition. Selection is based on musical accuracy (20 points), intonation (20 points), interpretation (20 points), tone quality (20 points), technical proficiency (10 points), and stage presence (10 points). The category of the competition rotates on a 5-year schedule as follows: 2008: organ; 2009: winds; 2010: piano; 2011: voice; 2012: strings.

Financial data In the national competition, first place in $1,500, second $1,000, third $750, fourth $500, and fifth $250. All funds are paid directly to the winner's teacher/coach or institution.

Duration The competition is held annually.

Additional information The National Association of Negro Musicians was founded in 1919. Students must submit a $5 fee to enter a local branch competition. The branch must submit a $10 fee to enter the student in the regional competition. The region must submit a $15 fee to enter the student in the national competition.

Number awarded 5 each year.

[933]
NATIONAL CHOPIN PIANO COMPETITION

Chopin Foundation of the United States, Inc.
Attn: Executive Director
1440 79th Street Causeway, Suite 117
Miami, FL 33141
(305) 868-0624   Fax: (305) 865-5150
E-mail: info@chopin.org
Web: www.chopin.org/competition.html

Purpose To recognize and reward young American pianists for their outstanding performances of Chopin's works.

Eligibility This competition is open to U.S. citizens (native born or naturalized) who are between the ages of 17 and 26. Most entrants are currently enrolled in college. In the competition, they must play preselected works of Chopin.

Financial data Prizes vary in each competition. Recently, first prize was $18,000, a debut recital at the Carnegie/Weill Recital Hall in New York, a concert recital at the Smithsonian in Washington, and 20 concerts arranged by the foundation; second prize was $12,000; third prize was $8,000; and fourth prize was $5,000. Special awards in the amount of $1,000 were also awarded for best performance of a polonaise, best performance of a mazurka, and best performance of a concerto. After each of these competitions, the 4 top winners go to Warsaw, Poland (all expenses paid) to compete in the International Chopin Piano Competition.

Duration The competition is held every 5 years (2010, 2015, etc.).

Additional information The first competition took place in 1975. The application fee is $75.

Number awarded 4 prizes and 3 special awards and presented at each competition.

Deadline November of the year prior to the competition.

[934]
NATIONAL FFA SCHOLARSHIPS FOR UNDERGRADUATES IN THE HUMANITIES

National FFA Organization
Attn: Scholarship Office
6060 FFA Drive
P.O. Box 68960
Indianapolis, IN 46268-0960
(317) 802-4321   Fax: (317) 802-5321
E-mail: scholarships@ffa.org
Web: www.ffa.org/programs/scholarships/index.html

Purpose To provide financial assistance to FFA members who wish to study agricultural journalism and related fields in college.

Eligibility This program is open to current and former members of the organization who are working or planning to work full time on a degree in fields related to agricultural journalism and communications, floriculture, and landscape design. For most of the scholarships, applicants must be high school seniors; others are open to students currently enrolled in college. The program includes a large number of designated scholarships that specify the locations where the members must live, the schools they must attend, the fields of study they must pursue, or other requirements. Some consider family income in the selection process, but most do not. Selection is based on academic achievement (10 points for GPA, 10 points for SAT or ACT score, 10 points for class rank), leadership in FFA activities (30 points), leadership in community activities (10 points), and participation in the Supervised Agricultural Experience (SAE) program (30 points). U.S. citizenship is required.

Financial data Stipends vary, but most are at least $1,000.

Duration 1 year or more.

Additional information Funding for these scholarships is provided by many different corporate sponsors.

Number awarded Varies; generally, a total of approximately 1,000 scholarships are awarded annually by the association.

Deadline February of each year.

[935]
NATIONAL MAKE IT YOURSELF WITH WOOL CONTEST

American Sheep Industry Women
c/o Marie Lehfeldt
P.O. Box 175
Lavina, MT 59046
(406) 636-2036   Fax: (406) 636-2731
E-mail: levi@midrivers.com
Web: www.sheepusa.org

Purpose To encourage the use of wool by offering scholarship awards to students who sew, knit, or crochet fashionable wool garments.

Eligibility The junior division is open to all persons between 13 and 16 years of age, and the senior division is for 17 through 24 years of age; most states also have a preteen division for competitors 12 years of age and younger and an adult division for persons over 24 years of age. Competitors enter machine or hand-knitted, woven, or crocheted garments, or garments containing any part that has been knitted or crocheted; all entries must be made from loomed, knitted, or felted fabric or yarn with a minimum of 60% wool and no more than 40% synthetic fiber. All entrants must select, construct, and model the garment themselves. The garments in the junior, senior, and adult divisions may be 2-piece outfits (coat, jacket, blouse/shirt, vest or sweater with dress, skirt, pants, or shorts), ensembles (3 or more garments worn together at a time), or 1-piece garments (dresses, outerwear jackets, coats, capes, or jumpers). Preteens may enter a dress, jumper, skirt, pants, shorts, vest, sweater, blouse/shirt, or jacket. Selection is based on appropriateness of the garment to the contestant's lifestyle, coordination of fabric/yarn with garment style and design, contestant's presentation, creativity, and construction quality. Contestants must participate in the state where they live or attend school. State winners in the junior and senior divisions advance to the national competition. Scholarships are awarded to national junior and senior division winners.

Financial data Scholarships awarded at the national level are $2,000 or $1,000, to be used for tuition, books, and fees; funds are paid directly to registrars of approved accredited colleges.

Duration The competition is held annually.

Additional information The $1,000 scholarships at the national level are sponsored by the Mohair Council of America, American Wool Council, and Pendleton Woolen Mills.

The entry fee is $10 in the junior, senior, and adult divisions or $5 in the preteen division.

Number awarded 6 national scholarships are awarded each year: 2 at $2,000 (1 for the junior winner and 1 for the senior winner) and 4 at $1,000 (2 from the Mohair Council of America for the junior and senior winners of complete garments made of mohair, the Pendleton Woolen Mills award for the junior winner, and the American Wool Council Fashion/Apparel Design Award).

Deadline November of each year.

[936]
NATIONAL OPERA ASSOCIATION SCHOLARSHIP DIVISION AWARDS

National Opera Association
Attn: Executive Secretary
P.O. Box 60869
Canyon, TX 79016-0869
(806) 651-2857   Fax: (806) 651-2958
E-mail: rhansen@mail.wtamu.edu
Web: www.noa.org

Purpose To provide financial assistance for continuing education to opera students.

Eligibility This program is open to opera students between the ages of 18 and 24 who are currently enrolled in an undergraduate or graduate program or equivalent. Their teacher or coach must be a member of the National Opera Association. Applicants must submit a cassette tape or CD with 2 arias, and judges select the finalists on the basis of those recordings. Finalists are then invited to auditions where they present 4 arias in contrasting styles and periods, in 3 languages (including 1 originally in English). The singer chooses the first selection, after which the judges request 1 or more selections.

Financial data Prizes range from $500 to $2,000; funds are paid directly to the winner's school, voice teacher, or vocal coach for further study. In addition, the first-place winner receives a scholarship for summer study at the American Institute of Musical Studies (AIMS) Graz Experience in Austria.

Duration The competition is held annually.

Additional information This program includes the Nick Vrenios Memorial Award and the Constance Eberhardt Memorial Awards. Contestants must pay a $20 nonrefundable entry fee.

Number awarded 1 or more each year.

Deadline October of each year.

[937]
NATIONAL SOCIETY OF NEWSPAPER COLUMNISTS SCHOLARSHIP CONTEST

National Society of Newspaper Columnists
P.O. Box 156885
San Francisco, CA 94115-6885
Toll-free: (866) 440-NSNC   Fax: (866) 635-5759
Web: www.columnists.com

Purpose To recognize and reward, with college scholarships, undergraduate journalism students who write outstanding columns.

Eligibility This competition is open to undergraduates who write bylined general interest or editorial page columns for their college newspapers. It is not open to columnists writing on sports, arts, health, or other specialized topics. Candidates must submit 3 columns published during a 12-month period prior to the deadline. Columns published online are eligible if they also appeared in print editions.

Financial data First prize is a $1,000 scholarship; second prize is a $500 scholarship.

Duration The prize is presented annually.

Additional information Information is also available from Russell Frank, Pennsylvania State University, (814) 863-6415, E-mail: rbf5@psu.edu.

Number awarded 1 each year.

Deadline February of each year.

[938] NATIONAL STUDENT ADVERTISING COMPETITION

American Advertising Federation
Attn: Education Services Program
1101 Vermont Avenue, Suite 500
Washington, DC 20005
(202) 898-0089   Toll-free: (800) 999-2231
Fax: (202) 898-0159   E-mail: Education@aaf.org
Web: www.aaf.org/college/nsac.html

Purpose To recognize and reward student members of the American Advertising Federation (AAF) who participate in an advertising competition.

Eligibility This competition is open to teams of undergraduate students who are members of their AAF college chapter. Each team may consist of up to 5 students. Teams develop advertising campaigns for actual nonprofit or for-profit organizations; recently, the client was the Coca-Cola Company. Competitions are first held in the 15 AAF districts. Winners of those competitions, along with a "wild card" team that is judged the best from the second-place winners, advance to the national competition.

Financial data The first-place team wins a $3,500 prize, second $2,500, third $2,000, fourth $1,000, and other finalists $500.

Duration The competition is held annually.

Additional information This competition was first held in 1973.

Number awarded 16 teams win prizes each year.

Deadline Teams must indicated their intent to enter the competition by March of each year.

[939] NATIONAL STUDENT PLAYWRITING AWARD

John F. Kennedy Center for the Performing Arts
Education Department
Attn: Kennedy Center American College Theater Festival
2700 F Street, N.W.
Washington, DC 20566
(202) 416-8857   Fax: (202) 416-8802
E-mail: skshaffer@kennedy-center.org
Web: kennedy-center.org/education/actf/actfnsp.html

Purpose To recognize and reward outstanding undergraduate and graduate school playwrights.

Eligibility Students at any accredited junior or senior college in the United States or in countries contiguous to the continental United States are eligible to compete, provided their college agrees to participate in the Kennedy Center American College Theater Festival (KCACTF). Undergraduate students must be carrying at least 6 semester hours, graduate students must be enrolled in at least 3 semester hours, and continuing part-time students must be enrolled in a regular degree or certificate program. For the Michael Kanin Playwriting Awards Program, students must submit either 1 major work or 2 or more shorter works based on a single theme or encompassed within a unifying framework; all entries must provide a full evening of theater. The work must be written while the student was enrolled, and the production must be presented during that period or within 2 years after enrollment ends. The play selected as the best by the judges is presented at the national festival and its playwright receives this award.

Financial data The winning playwright receives 1) production of the play at the Kennedy Center as part of the KCATF national festival, with expenses paid for the production and the playwright; 2) a cash prize of $2,500; 3) the Dramatists Guild Award of active membership in the Guild; 4) the Samuel French Award of publication of the play by Samuel French, Inc.; and 5) an all-expense paid fellowship to participate in the Sundance Theater Laboratory in Sundance, Utah. The Association for Theatre in Higher Education (ATHE) presents a cash award of up to $1,000 to the theater department of the school producing the national wining script and $100 to the schools producing the winning plays at each of the 8 KCATF regional festivals.

Duration The competition is held annually.

Additional information This award was first presented in 1974. The sponsoring college or university must pay a registration fee of $250 for each production.

Number awarded 1 each year.

Deadline The final draft of the script must be submitted by November of each year.

[940]
NATIONAL TRUMPET COMPETITION AWARDS

National Trumpet Competition
c/o Executive Director
3500 North Third Street
Arlington, VA 22201
E-mail: denny@nationaltrumpetcomp.org
Web: www.nationaltrumpetcomp.org

Purpose To recognize and reward outstanding student trumpet players.

Eligibility This program is open to trumpet players who are interested in competing in the following divisions: the Stu's Music Shop Middle School Division (for students between 11 and 14 years of age); the Stephen & Bonnie Simon High School division (for students between 15 and 18 years of age); the Vincent Bach College Division (for full-time undergraduates up to 23 years of age); the Blackburn Trumpets Masters Division (for students up to 28 years of age); the Dillon Music Jazz Division (for students up to 28 years of age); the Southern Ohio Music Company Trumpet Ensemble Division (for ensembles of 4 to 8 students up to 28 years of age); the NTC Endowment Historical Trumpet Division (including the Shore Award for up to 18 years of age, the Fantini Award for students from 19 to 28 years of age, the Reiche Award for musicians 29 years of age and older, and the ensemble award for ensembles of 3 applicants of any age); or the NTC Endowment Pro-Am Division (for musicians 29 years of age and older). Entrants submit tapes of their performances; times and repertoire vary according to division. Based on those tapes, semifinalists are selected and invited to the competitions at George Mason University in March.

Financial data A total of $30,000 in cash awards and prizes is presented each year.

Duration The competition is held annually.

Additional information This competition began in 1992, at George Mason University. It is the largest competitive event for young trumpet players in the world. Sponsors include Stu's Music Shop of Westminster, Maryland; Southern Ohio Music Company of Cincinnati, Ohio; Rayburn Musical Instrument Company of Boston, Massachusetts; Vincent Bach of Elkhart, Indiana; Yamaha; Interlochen Arts Camp; International Trumpet Guild (ITG); GR Technologies Family; and Maller Baroque Brass Instruments. Recently, the following named awards were presented: in the Stu's Music Shop Middle School Division, first prize was the Bach Award for Artistic Excellence, second prize was the Tom Crown Mutes Young Artist Award, and third prize was the Najoom Music Products Award; in the Stephen & Bonnie Simon High School Division, first prize was an Interlochen full tuition scholarship, second prize was the Bach Award for Young Artists, and third prize was the Anthony L. Pasquarelli Award; in the Vincent Bach College Division, first prize was a TrumpeTech Bb or C trumpet, second prize was the Bob and Gloria Murray Memorial Award, third prize was the Ron Taylor Group Award for Artistic Merit, fourth prize was the Anthony L. Pasquarelli Award, fifth prize was the Christian Anderson TrumCor Mutes Award, and sixth prize was the Zaja Musical Products Award; in the Blackburn Trumpets Masters Division, first prize was the ITG Award for Artistic Excellence, second prize was the Dr. Joe Utley Award for Artistry, third prize was the Ron Taylor Group Award for Artistic Merit, and fourth prize was the NTC Young Artist Endowment Award; in the Dillon Music Jazz Division, first prize was the GR Technologies Family Award, second prize was the Stu's Music Shop Award, and third prize was the Frank Scimonelli Award; in the Southern Ohio Music Company Trumpet Ensemble Division, first prize was the ITG Award, second prize was the Maller Baroque Instrument Award, and third prize was the Southern Ohio Music Company Award; in the Historical Trumpet Division, the Shore Award was $500, the Fantini Award was $400, the Reiche Award was a Naumann Baroque Trumpet valued at more than $2,000, and the ensemble award was $300; in the pro-am division, first prize was the Shilke Award for Artistry and second prize was the Stu's Music Shop Award. Entrants who need an NTC accompanist must pay a $90 fee. Application fees are $60 for the middle school division; $65 for the high school division; $70 for the college, master's, jazz, historic trumpets, and pro-am divisions; and $40 per player in the trumpet ensemble division.

Number awarded Varies each year.

Deadline December of each year.

[941]
NEW MEXICO BROADCASTERS ASSOCIATION SCHOLARSHIPS

New Mexico Broadcasters Association
Attn: Scholarship Program
8014 Menaul Boulevard, N.E.
Albuquerque, NM 87110
(505) 881-4444   Toll-free: (800) 622-2414
Fax: (505) 881-5353
Web: www.newmexicobroadcasters.org

Purpose To provide financial assistance to undergraduate students in New Mexico who are preparing for a career in the broadcast industry.

Eligibility This program is open to residents of New Mexico who are entering their sophomore, junior, or senior year at an accredited college, vocational institution, or university in the state. Applicants must be preparing for a career in the broadcast industry, including news, announcing, sales, accounting, management, engineering, traffic and billing, promotion, community affairs, programming, production, or other aspects of the industry. They must submit brief statements on their work experience at a broadcast facility and why they want to prepare for a career in the field. Race, gender, age, and financial need are not considered in the selection process. Nontraditional and reentry students are encouraged to apply.

Financial data The maximum stipend is $2,500 per year. Funds are sent directly to the student to help pay the cost of tuition, books, supplies and fees.

Duration 1 year.

Additional information Recipients must secure an internship with a New Mexico broadcast facility.

Number awarded Up to 10 each year.

Deadline May of each year.

[942]
NEW YORK BEEF PRODUCERS' ASSOCIATION SCHOLARSHIP

New York Beef Producers' Association
Attn: Executive Secretary
3 Second Street
Camden, NY 13316
(315) 245-3386   E-mail: nybpa1@twcny.rr.com
Web: www.tjbailey.com/nybpa/youthprograms.htm

Purpose To provide financial assistance to college students from New York who are preparing for a career in the cattle industry.

Eligibility This program is open to residents of New York who are currently enrolled in an accredited 2-year or 4-year agricultural college. Applicants must be majoring in a field of study related to agriculture (e.g., animal and/or crop science, business, economics, communications, agricultural engineering) and planning a career related to the beef industry. Along with their application, they must submit an essay that covers the following: 1) their experience and interest in the beef industry; 2) their involvement in agricultural-related activities, including organizations (community, school, 4-H), events, awards, and leadership positions; 3) their future intentions and career plans as they relate to the beef industry; and 4) how they view the future of the beef industry. Selection is based primarily on involvement in the beef industry and future plans. Financial need is not considered.

Financial data The stipend is $1,000.

Duration 1 year.

Number awarded 1 each year.

Deadline December of each year.

[943]
NEWSPAPER COPY EDITING PROGRAM FOR COLLEGE JUNIORS, SENIORS AND GRADUATE STUDENTS

Dow Jones Newspaper Fund
P.O. Box 300
Princeton, NJ 08543-0300
(609) 452-2820   Fax: (609) 520-5804
E-mail: newsfund@wsj.dowjones.com
Web: DJNewspaperFund.dowjones.com

Purpose To provide financial assistance and work experience to undergraduate and graduate students interested in preparing for a career in journalism.

Eligibility College juniors, college seniors, and graduate students are eligible to apply for the internship if they are full-time students interested in a career in journalism. Along with their application, they must submit a resume, a list of courses with grades, and a 500-word essay. Interns returning to undergraduate or graduate studies receive a scholarship. U.S. citizenship or permanent resident status is required. College professors and instructors and former full-time professional journalists are ineligible.

Financial data Interns receive a salary of at least $350 per week during the summer and a $1,000 scholarship at the successful completion of the program.

Duration 10 weeks for the summer internship; 1 year for the scholarship.

Additional information Interns attend a 2-week editing residency and then work as copy editors on a daily newspaper. Residencies have been held at Temple University, University of Central Florida, University of Missouri at Columbia, San Jose State University, Pennsylvania State University, University of North Carolina at Chapel Hill, and University of Texas at Austin.

Number awarded Up to 100 each year.

Deadline October of each year.

[944]
NFMC BIENNIAL STUDENT AUDITION AWARDS

National Federation of Music Clubs
1336 North Delaware Street
Indianapolis, IN 46202-2481
(317) 638-4003   Fax: (317) 638-0503
E-mail: info@nfmc-music.org
Web: www.nfmc-music.org

Purpose To recognize and reward outstanding young musicians who are members of the National Federation of Music Clubs (NFMC).

Eligibility Instrumentalists must be between 16 and 26 years of age; vocalists must be between 18 and 26. All applicants must be U.S. citizens and either student or junior division members of the federation. Competition categories include: women's voice, men's voice, piano, organ, harp, classical guitar, violin, viola, cello, double bass, orchestral woodwinds, orchestral brass, and percussion. Awards are presented at the national level after auditions at the state and district levels.

Financial data The winner in each category is awarded $1,500.

Duration The competition is held biennially, in odd-numbered years.

Additional information Applications and further information on these awards are available from Mrs. Robert Carroll, 17583 North 1090 East Road, Pontiac, IL 61764-9801; information on all federation scholarships and awards is available from Chair, Competitions and Awards Board, Dr. George R. Keck, 421 Cherry Street, Arkadelphia, AR 71923-5116. Students who enter this competition are also automatically considered for the following awards: the Annie Lou Ellis Piano Award, the Dr. Barbara Irish Violin Award, the Dr. Barbara M. Irish Award, the Hazel Heffner Becchina Award, the Irene S. Muir Award, the Janice Clarkson Cleworth Award, the Josef Kaspar Awards, the Josephine Trott Strings Award, the Lawrence Foster Violoncello Award, the Louise L. Henderson Violoncello Award, the Louise Oberne Strings Awards, the Marie Morrisey Keith Awards, the Ruby Simmonds Vought Organ Award, the Thor Johnson Strings Awards, the Lucille Heimrich Awards, and the Virginia Peace Mackey-Althouse Voice Award. The entry fee is $30 for each category.

Deadline January of odd-numbered years.

[945]
NOLAN MOORE MEMORIAL EDUCATION FOUNDATION SCHOLARSHIP

Printing and Imaging Association of MidAmerica
Attn: Dodie Royals
8828 North Stemmons, Suite 505
Dallas, TX 75247
(214) 630-8871, ext. 205   Toll-free: (800) 788-2040
E-mail: dodier@piamidam.org
Web: www.piamidam.org/scholar.php

Purpose To provide financial assistance to residents of designated states who are attending college to prepare for a career in the graphic arts industry.

Eligibility This program is open to students enrolled or planning to enroll in an educational institution that offers a 2- or 4-year degree in printing technology, printing management, or related field. Applicants must be residents of Kansas, Missouri, Oklahoma, or Texas. They should be attending a school in those states, but they may go elsewhere if they can demonstrate the appropriate aptitude and industry interest. Along with their application, they must submit a 1-page statement outlining their career goals and a letter of endorsement from their faculty sponsor that reinforces their stated intention to prepare for a career in the graphic arts industry. Selection is based on interest in the industry and GPA; financial need is not considered.

Financial data The stipend is $2,500.

Duration 1 year; may be enrolled if the recipient remains enrolled full time with a GPA of 2.5 or higher.

Number awarded 1 or more each year.

Deadline February of each year.

[946]
OHIO NEWSPAPERS FOUNDATION UNIVERSITY JOURNALISM SCHOLARSHIP

Ohio Newspapers Foundation
1335 Dublin Road, Suite 216-B
Columbus, OH 43215-7038
(614) 486-6677   Fax: (614) 486-4940
E-mail: kpouliot@ohionews.org
Web: www.ohionews.org/scholarships.html

Purpose To provide financial assistance to students majoring in journalism at a college or university in Ohio.

Eligibility This program is open to sophomores, juniors, and seniors at Ohio colleges and universities who are majoring in journalism and have a GPA of 2.5 or higher. Applicants must demonstrate the ability to write clearly in an autobiography of 750 to 1,000 words that describes their academic and career interests, awards, extracurricular activities, and journalism-related activities. Priority is given to students planning careers in newspaper or print journalism.

Financial data The stipend is $1,500.

Duration 1 year.

Number awarded 1 each year.

Deadline March of each year.

[947]
OKLAHOMA NEWSPAPER FOUNDATION SCHOLARSHIPS

Oklahoma Press Association
Attn: Oklahoma Newspaper Foundation
3601 North Lincoln Boulevard
Oklahoma City, OK 73105
(405) 499-0020   Fax: (405) 499-0048
Web: www.okpress.com

Purpose To provide financial assistance to upper-division journalism students at Oklahoma colleges and universities.

Eligibility This program is open to full-time students entering their junior or senior year at a college or university in Okalahoma. Applicants must be majoring in journalism or an equivalent field (e.g., advertising, communications, public relations); preference is given to students demonstrating a career commitment to newspaper journalism. Along with their application, they must submit a statement on their career goals within the journalism industry, how they plan to achieve those goals, and what they expect to be doing professionally 5 and 10 years after graduation. Financial need is not considered in the selection process.

Financial data The stipend is $1,500.

Duration 1 year.

Number awarded 3 each year.

Deadline February of each year.

[948]
ONLINE EDITING PROGRAM FOR COLLEGE JUNIORS, SENIORS AND GRADUATE STUDENTS

Dow Jones Newspaper Fund
P.O. Box 300
Princeton, NJ 08543-0300
(609) 452-2820   Fax: (609) 520-5804
E-mail: newsfund@wsj.dowjones.com
Web: DJNewspaperFund.dowjones.com

Purpose To provide financial assistance and work experience to undergraduate and graduate students interested in preparing for a career in online journalism.

Eligibility College juniors, college seniors, and graduate students are eligible to apply for the internship if they are full-time students interested in a career in online journalism. Along with their application, they must submit a resume, a list of courses with grades, and a 500-word essay. Interns returning to undergraduate or graduate studies receive a scholarship. U.S. citizenship or permanent resident status is required. College professors and instructors and former full-time professional journalists are ineligible.

Financial data Interns receive a salary of at least $350 per week during the summer and a $1,000 scholarship at the successful completion of the program.

Duration 10 weeks for the summer internship; 1 year for the scholarship.

Additional information This program was established in 2006 with support from Yahoo! News. Interns attend a 2-week training program and then work as editors for media companies with news web sites. Recently, the training program was held at Western Kentucky University in Bowling Green.

Number awarded 12 each year.

Deadline October of each year.

[949]
OREGON ASSOCIATION OF BROADCASTERS SCHOLARSHIPS

Oregon Association of Broadcasters
Attn: OAB Foundation Scholarship Committee
7150 S.W. Hampton Street, Suite 240
Portland, OR 97223-8366
(503) 443-2299 Fax: (503) 443-2488
E-mail: theoab@theoab.org
Web: www.theoab.org/eduopps_foundation.htm

Purpose To provide financial assistance to students in Oregon who are interested in majoring in broadcast-related fields in college.

Eligibility This program is open to Oregon residents who are enrolled or accepted for enrollment at a 2- or 4-year public or private college or university in the state. Applicants must be planning to enroll or be currently enrolled in a full-time undergraduate course of study, majoring in broadcast journalism, production, management, or another broadcast-related field. They must be graduating high school seniors, first- or second-year students in a 2-year program, or sophomores, juniors, or seniors in a 4-year program. Along with their application, they must submit an essay that explains their reasons for choosing a broadcast major and includes any broadcast activities in which they have participated, their first job preference after college, their 10-year goals, any other scholarships they have received, and any academic honors they have received. Financial need is not considered in the selection process.

Financial data Stipends range from $1,000 to $2,500.
Duration 1 year.
Number awarded 6 each year: 2 to graduating high school seniors and 4 to students currently enrolled in 2- or 4-year college broadcast programs. Recently, scholarships included 1 at $2,500, 1 at $1,500, and 4 at $1,000.
Deadline February of each year.

[950]
OVERSEAS PRESS CLUB FOUNDATION SCHOLARSHIPS

Overseas Press Club
Attn: Director, Overseas Press Club Foundation
40 West 45th Street
New York, NY 10036
(212) 626-9220 Fax: (212) 626-9210
E-mail: foundation@opcofamerica.org
Web: www.opcofamerica.org

Purpose To provide financial assistance to undergraduate and graduate students who are preparing for a career as a foreign correspondent.

Eligibility This program is open to undergraduate and graduate students who are studying in the United States and are interested in working as a foreign correspondent after graduation. Applicants are invited to submit an essay (up to 500 words) on an area of the world or an international topic that is in keeping with their interest. Also, they should attach a 1-page autobiographical letter that addresses such questions as how they developed their interest in that particular part of the world or issue, how they would use a scholarship to further their journalistic ambitions, and how they think journalists can deepen American interest in international affairs.

Financial data The stipend is $2,000.
Duration 1 year.
Additional information This program began in 1992.
Number awarded 12 each year.
Deadline November of each year.

[951]
PARTNERSHIP FOR EXCELLENCE UNDERGRADUATE FELLOWS PROGRAM

The Fund for Theological Education, Inc.
Attn: Partnership for Excellence
825 Houston Mill Road, Suite 250
Atlanta, GA 30329
(404) 727-1450 Fax: (404) 727-1490
E-mail: fte@thefund.org
Web: www.thefund.org

Purpose To provide financial assistance to undergraduate students who are considering the ministry as a career.

Eligibility This program is open to rising juniors and seniors in accredited undergraduate programs at North American colleges and universities. Applicants must be considering ministry as a career. They must demonstrate a GPA of 3.0 or higher, a love of God and church, imagination, creativity, compassion, a capacity for critical thinking, leadership skills, personal integrity, spiritual depth, dedication to a faith tradition, and an ability to understand and to serve the needs of others. U.S. or Canadian citizenship is required.

Financial data The stipend is $1,500 per year; travel expenses for participation in the summer conference and a mentoring stipend of $500 are also provided.
Duration 1 year.
Additional information Fellows are invited to attend a summer conference that offers lectures, student panels, and an opportunity to meet with some of the leading American scholars and theological educators. This program started in 1999.
Number awarded Up to 70 each year.
Deadline February of each year.

[952]
PAT ROBERTS INTELLIGENCE SCHOLARS PROGRAM FOR INTELLIGENCE ANALYSTS

National Security Agency
Attn: Office of Recruitment and Staffing (Roberts)
9800 Savage Road, Suite 6779
P.O. Box 1661, Suite 6779
Fort Meade, MD 20755-6779
(410) 854-4725 Toll-free: (866) 672-4473
Web: www.nsa.gov/careers/students_4.cfm

Purpose To provide financial assistance to college juniors interested in preparing for a career with the National Security Agency (NSA) as an intelligence analyst.

Eligibility This program is open to college juniors whose academic program includes 1 of the following areas of emphasis: 1) regional studies (Middle East or south, east, or central Asia); 2) topical studies (terrorism, proliferation or related sciences, international banking and finance, or telecommunications and information systems networks); or 3) disciplines (intelligence analysis, philosophy, or international relations; familiarity with foreign languages, particularly Arabic, Chinese, Dari, Farsi, Hindi, Korean, Pashto, Urdu, or a central Asian language is desirable; highly qualified applicants studying social network analysis, library science, or geographic information systems may also be considered). Applicants must be enrolled full time with a GPA of 3.0 or higher. Along with their application, they must submit a 1-page essay describing how the proposed program of study will improve their ability to analyze information and to think and write critically. U.S. citizenship and eligibility to obtain a high-level security clearance are required.

Financial data The stipend is $25,000 per year. After graduation, recipients have an employment obligation to NSA equal to 1.5 times the length of educational support provided.

Duration 1 year (the senior year of college).

Additional information After graduation, participants enter NSA's Intelligence Analysis Development Program as a full-time employee.

Number awarded Varies each year.

Deadline October of each year.

[953]
PAULA VOGEL AWARD IN PLAYWRITING

John F. Kennedy Center for the Performing Arts
Education Department
Attn: Kennedy Center American College Theater Festival
2700 F Street, N.W.
Washington, DC 20566
(202) 416-8857   Fax: (202) 416-8802
E-mail: skshaffer@kennedy-center.org
Web: kennedy-center.org

Purpose To recognize and reward the student authors of plays that relate to tolerance of diversity.

Eligibility Students at any accredited junior or senior college in the United States or in countries contiguous to the continental United States are eligible to compete, provided their college agrees to participate in the Kennedy Center American College Theater Festival (KCACTF). Undergraduate students must be carrying at least 6 semester hours, graduate students must be enrolled in at least 3 semester hours, and continuing part-time students must be enrolled in a regular degree or certificate program. This award is presented to the best student-written script that celebrates diversity and encourages tolerance while exploring issues of disempowered voices not traditionally considered mainstream.

Financial data The winning playwright receives a cash award of $2,500 and a fellowship to attend the New Play Development Laboratory; the producing department receives a grant of $500. The second-place playwright receives a cash award of $1,000 and the producing department receives a grant of $250.

Duration The award is presented annually.

Additional information This award, first presented in 2003, is part of the Michael Kanin Playwriting Awards Program. The sponsoring college or university must pay a registration fee of $250 for each production.

Number awarded 1 each year.

Deadline November of each year.

[954]
PAYNE STUDENT AWARD FOR ETHICS IN JOURNALISM

University of Oregon
Attn: School of Journalism and Communication
1275 University of Oregon
Eugene, OR 97403-1275
(541) 346-3738   Toll-free: (888) 644-7989
Fax: (541) 346-0682
E-mail: payneawards@jcomm.uoregon.edu
Web: jcomm.uoregon.edu/departments/payneawards

Purpose To recognize and reward student journalists whose work has encouraged public trust in the media.

Eligibility This program is open to student journalists enrolled in a 2- or 4-year college where the nominated work is published. Nominations are accepted from journalists, news organizations, and the public. Entries must have been published in a regularly distributed medium (a student or professional newspaper, magazine, broadcast, or cablecast news program or an edited Internet publication) during the previous calendar year. The award honors a student journalist "who reports with insight and clarity in the face of political or economic pressures."

Financial data The award is $1,000.

Duration The award is presented annually.

Additional information This award was first presented in 1999.

Number awarded 1 each year.

Deadline February of each year.

[955]
PCI STUDENT ARCHITECTURAL DESIGN COMPETITION

Precast/Prestressed Concrete Institute
Attn: Director of Education
209 West Jackson Boulevard
Chicago, IL 60604-9773
(312) 786-0300   Fax: (312) 786-0353
E-mail: pjohal@pci.org
Web: www.pci.org

Purpose To recognize and reward architecture students and interns who submit outstanding entries in a design competition utilizing precast and prestressed concrete.

Eligibility This competition is open to 3 categories of entrants: 1) students in architecture or architecture-related programs who submit designs for a designated site-specific project; 2) students in architecture or architecture-related programs who select a site and incorporate information regarding the site and its impact on the submitted design into the submitted material; and 3) interns who are college graduates in the Intern Development Program (IDP) and are not yet licensed architects. Applicants submit drawings of projects (either site-specific or non-site-specific) that make

100% utilization of precast and prestressed concrete. Selection is based on such design criteria as ability to design creatively and integrate technically architectural and structural total precast concrete systems; utilization of the many forms of precast concrete in building design and site development; elegant and expressive use of precast concrete as a material; response to specific architectural concepts of the program; landscape architecture, lighting, coherence of architectural vocabulary, etc.; level of attention paid to preserving and enhancing the surrounding environment; effectiveness of the solution in meeting the stated goals of the program; and ability to integrate functional aspects of the challenge in an appropriate manner.

Financial data Up to $25,000 in prizes is awarded to winning students and their schools and to IDP interns and their supervisors and design firms.

Duration The competition is held annually.

Additional information This competition was first held in 2002.

Number awarded 18 each year: a first, second, and third prize to the student and their advisor/supervisor in each of the 3 categories.

Deadline April of each year.

[956]
PENNSYLVANIA PUBLIC RELATIONS SOCIETY SCHOLARSHIPS

Pennsylvania Public Relations Society
Attn: Student Development Committee
359 Martingale Drive
Camp Hill, PA 17011
(717) 728-2545   E-mail: TRHolder1@comcast.net
Web: www.pprs-hbg.org

Purpose To provide financial assistance to upper-division students from Pennsylvania who are majoring in a communications-related field at a college or university in the state.

Eligibility This program is open to full-time students entering their junior or senior year at a college or university in Pennsylvania with a GPA of 2.75 or higher. Applicants must be residents of Pennsylvania majoring in a communications-related field of study (e.g., public relations, mass communications, journalism). Along with their application, they must submit a 300-word essay on why they are interested in a career in the communications field and their career goals and aspirations. Selection is based on that essay, grades, and participation in extracurricular activities related to the communications field. Financial need is not considered.

Financial data The stipend is $1,000.

Duration 1 year; recipients may reapply.

Number awarded 1 each year.

Deadline March of each year.

[957]
PHI ALPHA THETA/WESTERN FRONT ASSOCIATION UNDERGRADUATE ESSAY PRIZE

Phi Alpha Theta
c/o University of South Florida
SOC 107
4202 East Fowler Avenue
Tampa, FL 33620-8100
(813) 974-8212   Toll-free: (800) 394-8195
Fax: (813) 974-8215
E-mail: phialpha@phialphatheta.org
Web: www.phialphatheta.org/awards2.htm

Purpose To recognize and reward outstanding papers by undergraduate members of Phi Alpha Theta (the national honor society in history) on the American experience during World War I.

Eligibility This program is open to undergraduate student members of the society. They are invited to submit an essay (from 12 to 15 pages) on the American experience during World War I. The entry may cover almost any aspect of the American involvement in the World War I era from 1912 to 1924. Papers must present evidence of the use of primary sources.

Financial data The prize is $1,000.

Duration The competition is held annually.

Additional information This program is sponsored by the Western Front Association.

Number awarded 1 each year.

Deadline December of each year.

[958]
PHILO T. FARNSWORTH SCHOLARSHIP

Broadcast Education Association
Attn: Scholarships
1771 N Street, N.W.
Washington, DC 20036-2891
(202) 429-3935   Toll-free: (888) 380-7222
E-mail: beainfo@beaweb.org
Web: www.beaweb.org/scholarships.html

Purpose To provide financial assistance to upper-division and graduate students who are interested in preparing for a career in broadcasting.

Eligibility This program is open to juniors, seniors, and graduate students enrolled full time at a college or university where at least 1 department is an institutional member of the Broadcast Education Association (BEA). Applicants may be studying in any area of broadcasting. Selection is based on evidence that the applicant possesses high integrity, superior academic ability, potential to be an outstanding electronic media professional, and a sense of personal and professional responsibility.

Financial data The stipend is $1,500.

Duration 1 year; may not be renewed.

Additional information Information is also available from Peter B. Orlik, Central Michigan University, 344 Moore Hall, Mt. Pleasant, MI 48859, (989) 774-7279, E-mail: orlik1pb@cmich.edu.

Number awarded 1 each year.

Deadline October of each year.

[959]
PIEF GENERAL SCHOLARSHIPS

Printing Industries Association, Inc. serving Northern Kentucky and Ohio
Attn: Printing Industries Education Funds, Inc.
88 Dorcester Square
P.O. Box 819
Westerville, OH 43086-0819
(614) 794-2300   Toll-free: (888) 576-1971
Fax: (614) 794-2049   E-mail: pianko@pianko.org
Web: www.pianko.org/pief

Purpose To provide financial assistance to residents of Kentucky and Ohio who are interested in preparing for a career in the graphic communications industry.

Eligibility This program is open to residents of Kentucky and Ohio who are high school seniors or graduates or college freshmen, sophomores, or juniors with a GPA of 2.5 or higher. Applicants must 1) be enrolled at a 2-year or 4-year college in northern Kentucky or Ohio with an accredited graphic communications program, or 2) be a professional working in an Ohio or northern Kentucky graphic communications company seeking to increase their industry knowledge. They must be preparing for a career in the graphic communications industry, preferably in Ohio or northern Kentucky. Financial need is not considered in the selection process.

Financial data The stipend is generally $1,000.

Duration 1 year; may be renewed provided the recipient maintains a GPA of 2.5 or higher.

Additional information This program includes the following named scholarships: the Carl Zellers Scholarship, the Graphic Arts Council of Cleveland Scholarship, the William L. Stickney Endowed Scholarship, and the Hopkins Printing Endowed Scholarship.

Number awarded Varies each year; recently 22 of these scholarships were awarded.

Deadline February of each year.

[960]
PRINT AND GRAPHICS SCHOLARSHIP FOUNDATION SCHOLARSHIPS

Print and Graphics Scholarship Foundation
Attn: Scholarship Competition
200 Deer Run Road
Sewickley, PA 15143-2600
(412) 259-1740   Toll-free: (800) 910-GATF
Fax: (412) 741-2311   E-mail: pgsf@gatf.org
Web: www.gain.net/employment/scholarships.html

Purpose To provide financial assistance to college students interested in preparing for a career in the graphic communications industries.

Eligibility This program is open to high school seniors, high school graduates who have not yet started college, and currently-enrolled college students. Applicants must be interested in a career in the graphic communications industry and be willing to attend school on a full-time basis (scholarships are not awarded for part-time study). To apply, high school students must 1) take the SAT or ACT and indicate that their test scores are to be sent to the Graphic Arts Technical Foundation and 2) fill out the foundation's application form. Current college students are requested to submit transcripts and a letter of recommendation from their major area advisor. College freshmen also need to submit a high school transcript. Semifinalists are interviewed. Selection is based on academic records and honors, extracurricular activities, and letters of recommendation.

Financial data Stipends range from $1,000 to $1,500 per year. Funds are paid directly to the college selected by the award winner; the college will be authorized to draw upon the award to pay for tuition and other fees.

Duration 1 year; may be renewed for up to 3 additional years if the recipient maintains a GPA of 3.0 or higher and full-time enrollment.

Number awarded Approximately 300 per year.

Deadline February of each year for high school seniors; March of each year for students already in college.

[961]
PROFESSOR SIDNEY GROSS MEMORIAL AWARD

Public Relations Student Society of America
Attn: Director of Education
33 Maiden Lane, 11th Floor
New York, NY 10038-5150
(212) 460-1474   Fax: (212) 995-0757
E-mail: prssa@prsa.org
Web: www.prssa.org

Purpose To recognize and reward members of the Public Relations Student Society of America (PRSSA) who write outstanding essays on ethical principles.

Eligibility This program is open to members of the society who are currently enrolled in a full-time program of study at an accredited 4-year college or university. Applicants are presented with a hypothetical scenario of a situation they might encounter as a public relations professional. They must submit a 1-page essay on their response to the situation. Selection is based on their essay's demonstrated understanding of ethical principals in public relations.

Financial data The prize is $1,000.

Duration The competition is held annually.

Number awarded 1 each year.

Deadline May of each year.

[962]
RADIO AND TELEVISION NEWS DIRECTORS FOUNDATION PRESIDENTS' SCHOLARSHIPS

Radio and Television News Directors Foundation
1600 K Street, N.W., Suite 700
Washington, DC 20006-2838
(202) 467-5218   Fax: (202) 223-4007
E-mail: irvingw@rtndf.org
Web: www.rtndf.org

Purpose To provide financial assistance to undergraduate students whose career objective is radio or television news.

Eligibility This program is open to sophomores, juniors, and seniors who are enrolled full time in electronic journalism in a college or university where such a major is offered. Applicants must submit 1 to 3 examples of reporting or producing skills on audio or video cassette tapes (no more than

15 minutes total), a description of their role on each story and a list of who worked on each story and what they did, a statement explaining why they are seeking a career in broadcast or cable journalism, and a letter of endorsement from a faculty sponsor certifying that the candidate has at least 1 year of school remaining.

Financial data This scholarship is $2,500.

Duration 1 year.

Additional information The Radio and Television News Directors Foundation (RTNDF) also provides an all-expense paid trip to the Radio-Television News Directors Association (RTNDA) annual international conference. It defines electronic journalism to include radio, television, cable, and online news. It includes the following named scholarships: the Jim Byron Undergraduate Scholarship, the Ben Chatfield Undergraduate Scholarship, the Richard Cheverton Undergraduate Scholarship, the Bruce Dennis Undergraduate Scholarship, the John Hogan Undergraduate Scholarship, the Theodore Koop Undergraduate Scholarship, the James McCulla Undergraduate Scholarship, the Bruce Palmer Undergraduate Scholarship, and the John Salisbury Undergraduate Scholarship. Previous winners of any RTNDF scholarship or internship are not eligible.

Number awarded 2 each year.

Deadline April of each year.

[963] RADIO-TELEVISION JOURNALISM DIVISION PRIZES

Association for Education in Journalism and Mass Communication
Attn: Radio-Television Journalism Division
234 Outlet Pointe Boulevard, Suite A
Columbia, SC 29210-5667
(803) 798-0271   Fax: (803) 772-3509
E-mail: aejmc@aejmc.org
Web: www.aejmc.org

Purpose To recognize and reward outstanding student and faculty papers on broadcast journalism.

Eligibility Faculty members and students are invited to submit research papers on an aspect of broadcast journalism or electronic communication with a journalism emphasis. A variety of methodological approaches are welcome. Papers are to be no more than 25 pages in length and must have been written during the past year.

Financial data Cash prizes are awarded.

Duration The competition is held annually.

Additional information Information is also available from Kim Piper-Aiken, Michigan State University, School of Journalism, 355 Communication Arts Building, East Lansing, MI 48824-1212, (517) 353-6405, E-mail: piperaik@msu.edu.

Number awarded 2 each year: 1 to a student and 1 to a faculty member.

Deadline March of each year.

[964] RAY WILKINSON COMMUNICATIONS SCHOLARSHIP

North Carolina 4-H Development Fund
c/o North Carolina State University
Department of 4-H Youth Development
202 Ricks Hall
P.O. Box 7606
Raleigh, NC 27695-7606
(919) 515-8486   Fax: (919) 515-7812
Web: www.nc4h.org

Purpose To provide financial assistance to students in North Carolina who are members of 4-H and interested in majoring in communications in college.

Eligibility This program is open to 4-H members who are graduating from high schools in North Carolina. Applicants must be planning to major in communications at a college or university in the state. If no entering freshman is eligible, the award may be given to a continuing upperclassman. Selection is based on accomplishments in 4-H (50%), academic achievement as indicated by GPA and class rank (25%), and aptitude for college as indicated by grades and SAT or ACT scores (25%).

Financial data The stipend is $1,000 per year.

Duration 1 year.

Number awarded 1 each year.

Deadline January of each year.

[965] RHODA D. HOOD MEMORIAL SCHOLARSHIP

Northwest Baptist Convention
Attn: Woman's Missionary Union
3200 N.E. 109th Avenue
Vancouver, WA 98682
(360) 882-2100   Fax: (360) 882-2295
Web: www.nwbaptist.org

Purpose To provide financial assistance for college or seminary to women from the Northwest who are preparing for a career in vocational ministry, preferably with a Southern Baptist Convention church.

Eligibility This program is open to women who have been active members of a church affiliated with the Northwest Baptist Convention and a member of the Woman's Missionary Union within their church. Special consideration is given to children of ministers from the Northwest. Applicants must be attending or planning to attend an accredited college, university, or Southern Baptist seminary with the intention of serving in a vocational ministry position through a church or denomination; priority is given to applicants going into a mission vocation affiliated with the Southern Baptist Convention. Along with their application, they must submit 1) a written account of their conversion experience and their call to vocational ministry; and 2) a written endorsement from their church.

Financial data A stipend is awarded (amount not specified).

Duration 1 year; may be renewed if the recipient maintains a GPA of 2.5 or higher.

Number awarded 1 or more each year.

Deadline May of each year for fall term; October of each year for spring term.

[966]
RHYTHM & HUES STUDIOS COMPUTER GRAPHICS SCHOLARSHIPS

Rhythm & Hues Studios
Attn: Scholarship
5404 Jandy Place
Los Angeles, CA 90066
(310) 448-7500   Fax: (310) 448-7600
E-mail: scholarship@rhythm.com
Web: www.rhythm.com

Purpose To provide financial assistance to undergraduate and graduate students interested in a career in computer modeling, computer character animation, or digital cinematography (color and lighting).

Eligibility This program is open to all students enrolled full time in an accredited undergraduate or graduate degree program within 6 months prior to the deadline. Students may apply for scholarships in 1 of 3 categories: computer modeling, computer character animation, and digital cinematography. Entries must be submitted on an individual basis only; group projects submitted by the group are not acceptable. Multiple entries by a single student are permitted. Only noncommercial work is eligible; professional work created at a production studio during an internship is not acceptable. In the computer modeling category, students must submit still frames from a minimum of 4 different angles of a fully-rendered 3-D digital model or environment; these entries may be submitted on slides or videotape. Entries in this category are judged on concept, design, and execution of the models only; animation content is not important, although attention to lighting may enhance a model's appearance. In the computer character animation category, students must submit a wireframe or rendered sequence of animated, 3-D character(s) that lasts at least 30 seconds. Entries may be submitted on videotape, but not on Beta tapes, CD-ROMs, web sites, or floppy disks. Entries in this category are judged on quality and clarity of animation and storytelling only; modeling and lighting content are not important, although attention to sound may enhance the animation. In the digital cinematography (color and lighting) category, students must submit still frames from a minimum of 4 different angles of a fully-rendered digital environment or objects, or a full-rendered sequence of a camera move through a 3-D digital environment or around 3-D digital objects. Integration of 3-D digital objects or environments with live action is acceptable. Entries may only be submitted on slides or videotape; no Beta tapes, CD-ROMs, web sites, or floppy disks will be accepted. Entries in this category are judged on artistic effectiveness and expression of the color and lighting only; animation content is not important, although attention to modeling may enhance the effectiveness of the lighting.

Financial data In each of the 3 categories, student stipends are $1,000; a $4,000 matching grant is given to each winner's academic department.

Duration The stipends are presented annually.

Number awarded 5 each year: 1 in the computer modeling category, 1 in the computer character animation category, and 3 in the digital cinematography category.

Deadline May of each year.

[967]
R.L. GILLETTE SCHOLARSHIPS

American Foundation for the Blind
Attn: Scholarship Committee
11 Penn Plaza, Suite 300
New York, NY 10001
(212) 502-7661   Toll-free: (800) AFB-LINE
Fax: (212) 502-7771   TDD: (212) 502-7662
E-mail: afbinfo@afb.net
Web: www.afb.org/scholarships.asp

Purpose To provide financial assistance to legally blind undergraduate women who are studying literature or music.

Eligibility This program is open to women who are legally blind, U.S. citizens, and enrolled in a 4-year baccalaureate degree program in literature or music. Along with their application, they must submit an essay that includes the field of study they are pursuing and why they have chosen it; their educational and personal goals; their work experience; any extracurricular activities with which they have been involved, including those in school, religious organizations, and the community; and how they intend to use scholarship monies that may be awarded. They must also submit a sample performance tape (not to exceed 30 minutes) or a creative writing sample.

Financial data The stipend is $1,000.

Duration 1 academic year.

Number awarded 2 each year.

Deadline April of each year.

[968]
ROB BRANHAM SCHOLARSHIP

Advertising Club of Connecticut
95 West Street
Rocky Hill, CT 06067
(860) 721-7400   Fax: (860) 721-7406
E-mail: adclubct@snet.net
Web: www.adclubct.com/scholarship

Purpose To provide financial assistance to residents of Connecticut interested in attending college to study fields related to advertising.

Eligibility This program is open to Connecticut residents entering or attending an accredited university or technical/trade school. Applicants must be interested in studying advertising, marketing, broadcast media, or print production. Along with their application, they must submit a 500-word essay on their interest in advertising, marketing, broadcast media, and/or print production; the occupation they propose to pursue after graduating; their long-term goals; and how they plan to achieve those. They must be sponsored by a member of the Advertising Club of Connecticut. Selection is based on the essay, academic achievement, volunteer activities, work experience, and honors and scholarships. Financial need is not considered.

Financial data The stipend is $1,000.

Duration 1 year.

Number awarded Varies each year; recently, 2 of these scholarships were awarded.

Deadline March of each year.

[969]
ROLLING STONE COLLEGE JOURNALISM COMPETITION

Rolling Stone
Attn: College Journalism Competition
1290 Avenue of the Americas, Second Floor
New York, NY 10104-0298
(212) 484-1636   E-mail: kerry.smith@rollingstone.com
Web: www.rollingstone.com/journalismcontest

Purpose To recognize and reward outstanding articles published in college newspapers or magazines on popular entertainment or other subjects.

Eligibility Entries may be submitted in 3 categories: entertainment reporting (reporting on popular music, film, or television, including artist profiles and interviews), feature writing (stylishly-written narratives and profiles that illuminate issues and trends), or essays and criticism (commentary, including expressions of opinion and humor, on any subject). All entries must have been published in a student newspaper or magazine during the previous year; the author must have been an undergraduate or graduate student (full or part time) at the time the item was published. Students may enter in more than 1 category, but they are limited to 1 entry per category. Tear sheets (from the original newspaper or magazine) must be provided. The submissions are judged by the editors of Rolling Stone.

Financial data The prize is $2,500.

Duration The competition is held annually.

Additional information This competition started in 1976.

Number awarded 3 each year: 1 in each of the categories.

Deadline June of each year.

[970]
RUTH ABERNATHY UNDERGRADUATE PRESIDENTIAL SCHOLARSHIP

American Alliance for Health, Physical Education,
    Recreation and Dance
Attn: Presidential Scholarships
1900 Association Drive
Reston, VA 20191-1598
(703) 476-3400   Toll-free: (800) 213-7193
E-mail: dcallis@aahperd.org
Web: www.aahperd.org

Purpose To provide financial assistance to undergraduate student members of the American Alliance for Health, Physical Education, Recreation and Dance (AAHPERD).

Eligibility This program is open to AAHPERD members who are juniors or seniors at a baccalaureate-granting college or university. Applicants must be majoring in health, physical education, recreation, or dance and have a GPA of 3.5 or higher. They must submit a statement of their professional goals. Selection is based on academic proficiency; evidence of leadership; school, community, and professional activity and service; and character attributes.

Financial data The stipend is $1,000.

Duration 1 year; nonrenewable.

Additional information This program, established in 1995, was formerly designated the National Presidential Undergraduate Scholarships of AAHPERD.

Number awarded 3 each year.

Deadline October of each year.

[971]
RUTH CLARK SCHOLARSHIP

International Furnishings and Design Association
Attn: IFDA Educational Foundation
191 Clarksville Road
Princeton Junction, NJ 08550
(609) 799-3423   Fax: (609) 799-7032
E-mail: info@ifda.com
Web: www.ifdaef.org/scholarships.html

Purpose To provide financial assistance to undergraduate students pursuing degrees in residential furniture design.

Eligibility This program is open to full-time undergraduate students enrolled in a design program at an accredited college or design school with a focus on residential upholstered and/or wood furniture design. Applicants must have completed at least 1 semester of postsecondary education. Along with their application, they must submit 1) a 200-word essay on their future plans and goals and why they believe they deserve the scholarship; 2) at least 5 examples of their original designs; 3) a short description of each illustration; 4) an official college transcript; and 5) a letter of recommendation from a professor or instructor. Financial need is not considered.

Financial data The stipend is $1,500.

Duration 1 year.

Additional information Information is also available from Joan Long, Director of Grants, 5522 Estates Drive, Oakland, CA 94618, E-mail: jlongdesigns@yahoo.com.

Number awarded 1 each year.

Deadline March of each year.

[972]
RUTH LILLY POETRY FELLOWSHIPS

Poetry Magazine
Attn: Poetry Foundation
1030 North Clark Street
Chicago, IL 60610-5412
(312) 787-7070   Fax: (312) 787-6650
E-mail: mail@poetryfoundation.org
Web: www.poetryfoundation.org

Purpose To provide financial assistance to undergraduate and graduate students who are studying poetry.

Eligibility This program is open to undergraduate and graduate students in creative writing or English who have not yet received a master's or doctoral degree. Program directors and department chairs at colleges and universities in the United States are invited to nominate 1 student-poet from their program. Candidates must be younger than 31 years of age and may not have published a book of poems. Nominations must be accompanied by samples of the candidate's poetry.

Financial data The stipend is $15,000 per year.

Duration 1 year.

Additional information This program began in 1989.

Number awarded 2 each year.

Deadline April of each year.

[973]
SALLY HEET MEMORIAL SCHOLARSHIP
Public Relations Society of America-Puget Sound Chapter
c/o Diane Beins
1006 Industry Drive
Seattle, WA 98188-4801
(206) 623-8632
E-mail: prsascholarship@asi-seattle.net
Web: www.prsapugetsound.org/heet.html

Purpose To provide financial assistance to upper-division students in Washington who are interested in preparing for a career in public relations.

Eligibility This program is open to U.S. citizens who are entering their junior or senior year of full-time study at colleges and universities in Washington. Applicants must be preparing for a career in public relations. They must be able to demonstrate aptitude in public relations and related courses, activities, and/or internships. Along with their application, they must submit a description of their career goals and the skills that are most important to a public relations career (20 points in the selection process); a description of their activities in communications in class, on campus, in the community, or during internships, including 3 samples of their work (30 points); a statement on the value of public relations to an organization (10 points); a certified transcript (20 points); and 2 or more letters of recommendation (20 points).

Financial data The stipend is $2,500.

Duration 1 year.

Additional information This program was established in 1986.

Number awarded 1 each year.

Deadline April of each year.

[974]
SAMUEL ROBINSON AWARD
Presbyterian Church (USA)
Attn: Office of Financial Aid for Studies
100 Witherspoon Street, Room M-052
Louisville, KY 40202-1396
(502) 569-5745   Toll-free: (888) 728-7228, ext. 5745
Fax: (502) 569-8766   E-mail: KSmith@ctr.pcusa.org
Web: www.pcusa.org

Purpose To recognize and reward students in Presbyterian colleges who write essays on religious topics.

Eligibility Eligible are juniors and seniors enrolled full time in 1 of the 65 colleges related to the Presbyterian Church (USA). Applicants must successfully recite the answers to the Westminster Shorter Catechism and write a 2,000-word original essay on an assigned topic related to the Shorter Catechism.

Financial data Awards range from $200 to $1,000.

Duration 1 year; nonrenewable.

Number awarded 1 each year.

Deadline March of each year.

[975]
SCHOLARSHIP IN BOOK PRODUCTION AND PUBLISHING
Bookbuilders West
Attn: Scholarships
1032 Irving Street, Number 602
San Francisco, CA 94122-2200
(415) 402-2373   E-mail: scholarship@bookbuilders.org
Web: www.bookbuilders.org/Gen-scholarship.html

Purpose To recognize and reward outstanding sample book projects created by students in the western states.

Eligibility Applicants must be currently enrolled at a college, university, or technical school in the western states (Alaska, Arizona, California, Colorado, Hawaii, Idaho, Montana, Nevada, New Mexico, Oregon, Utah, Washington, and Wyoming). They must intend to prepare for a career in the field of book production or publishing, have at least a 2.0 GPA, and submit a sample book project (which usually comes from a course assignment). In addition to identifying and describing the subject book, the project submission should include the following items: a brief summary of the concept of the book selected for design and production; a definition of the design objective for the cover, interior, and any special features (e.g., slipcase); written design specifications for the cover, title page, table of contents, sample chapter opening, and interior text pages; a dummy that includes sample pages for the items listed above; and (optionally) a hand binding of the sample pages, slipcases, and other packaging. The project is judged in terms of creativity, meeting defined design objectives, and presentation of material.

Financial data The stipend is $1,000.

Duration 1 year.

Number awarded 1 or more each year.

Deadline May of each year.

[976]
SCHOLARSHIPS IN TECHNICAL COMMUNICATION
Society for Technical Communication
901 North Stuart Street, Suite 904
Arlington, VA 22203-1822
(703) 522-4114   Fax: (703) 522-2075
E-mail: stc@stc.org
Web: www.stc.org/scholarshipInfo01_national.asp

Purpose To provide financial assistance to undergraduate and graduate students who are preparing for a career in some area of technical communications.

Eligibility This program is open to 1) full-time undergraduate students working on a bachelor's degree in technical communications who have completed at least 1 year of college and 2) full-time graduate students working on a master's or doctoral degree in technical communications. Applicants must be studying communication of information about technical subjects; other majors, such as general journalism, electronic communication engineering, computer programming, entertainment, and creative writing are not eligible. Selection is based on academic record, experience with technical communication, and potential for contributing to the profession.

Financial data The stipend is $1,500; funds are paid to the school for the benefit of the recipient.
Duration 1 year.
Number awarded 4 each year: 2 to undergraduate students and 2 to graduate students.
Deadline February of each year.

[977]
SCRIPPS HOWARD TOP TEN SCHOLARSHIP PROGRAM

Scripps Howard Foundation
Attn: Vice President, Programs
312 Walnut Street, 28th Floor
P.O. Box 5380
Cincinnati, OH 45201
(513) 977-3035   Toll-free: (800) 888-3000, ext. 3030
Fax: (513) 977-3800   E-mail: porters@scripps.com
Web: foundation.scripps.com

Purpose To provide financial assistance to college juniors and seniors interested in a career in journalism.
Eligibility This program is open to full-time students entering their junior or senior year with a major in journalism. They must be nominated by the college or university they attend. Selection is based on academic achievement and a demonstrated interest in a career in journalism. Nominees also must submit a personal essay emphasizing their long-term goals.
Financial data The stipend is $10,000.
Duration 1 year; nonrenewable.
Additional information This program began in 1999.
Number awarded 10 each year.
Deadline May of each year.

[978]
SHIRLEY WILKINS VALENTIN VIOLIN AWARD

National Federation of Music Clubs
1336 North Delaware Street
Indianapolis, IN 46202-2481
(317) 638-4003   Fax: (317) 638-0503
E-mail: info@nfmc-music.org
Web: www.nfmc-music.org

Purpose To recognize and reward outstanding young violinists who are members of the National Federation of Music Clubs.
Eligibility Entrants must be between 18 and 25 years of age and student members of the federation. They must submit an audio or CD of a violin performance.
Financial data The prize is $1,000.
Duration The competition is held annually.
Additional information Applications and further information are available from Betty Hall, 4137 Whitfield, Fort Worth, TX 79109, E-mail: bettyhall@mymailstation.com; information on all federation scholarships and awards is available from Chair, Competitions and Awards Board, Dr. George R. Keck, 421 Cherry Street, Arkadelphia, AR 71923-5116, E-mail: keckg@obu.edu.
Number awarded 1 each year.
Deadline March of each year.

[979]
SHORT FILM AND VIDEO COMPETITION

USA Film Festival
6116 North Central Expressway, Suite 105
Dallas, TX 75206
(214) 821-6300   Fax: (214) 821-6364
E-mail: usafilmfestival@aol.com
Web: www.usafilmfestival.com

Purpose To recognize and reward outstanding short films and videos submitted by student, nonprofessional, or professional filmmakers.
Eligibility Entries up to 60 minutes in length may be submitted by professional, nonprofessional, or student film/videomakers in 16mm or 35mm film, Beta SP, Digi Beta, DVD, or conventional VHS videocassettes. The 4 submission categories are fiction (for narrative works, dramatized events, and adaptations of literary or dramatic works), non-fiction (for documentaries or portraits of actual persons or events), animation (of graphics or 3-dimensional objects), and experimental (for works that explore personal experience of film and video forms in innovative ways). The Family Award is presented to the work that best represents a standard of excellence for audiences of all ages. The G. William Jones Texas Award is presented to a work by a Texas resident. The Student Award is presented to the outstanding work by a student in any category. Special Jury Awards are presented to outstanding entries in any category.
Financial data The first-prize winner in each category receives $1,000. In addition, the Family Award is $500, the G. William Jones Texas Award is $500, the Student Award is $500, and the Special Jury Awards are $250.
Duration The competition is held annually, in April.
Additional information There is an entry fee of $40 for early submissions prior to the end of January, or $50 for regular submissions.
Number awarded Each year, 4 first-place awards, 3 other awards, and 4 Special Jury Awards are presented.
Deadline February of each year for regular submissions.

[980]
SIGMA ALPHA IOTA SCHOLARSHIPS FOR UNDERGRADUATE PERFORMANCE

Sigma Alpha Iota Philanthropies, Inc.
One Tunnel Road
Asheville, NC 28805
(828) 251-0606   Fax: (828) 251-0644
E-mail: philonline@sai-national.org
Web: www.sai-national.org/phil/philsch3.html

Purpose To recognize and reward outstanding performances in vocal and instrumental categories by undergraduate members of Sigma Alpha Iota (an organization of women musicians).
Eligibility Undergraduate student members of the organization may enter this competition if they are vocalists or instrumentalists. Entrants must be younger than 25 years of age. Selection is based on taped auditions in 4 categories: voice, keyboard and percussion, strings, and winds and brass.
Financial data The stipend is $1,500.
Duration The competition is held triennially.

HUMANITIES

Additional information This program consists of the following named awards: the Blanche Z. Hoffman Memorial Award for Voice, the Mary Ann Starring Memorial Award for Piano, the Dorothy E. Morris Memorial Award for Strings or Harp, and the Mary Ann Starring Memorial Award for Woodwinds or Brass. There is a $25 nonrefundable application fee.
Number awarded 4 every 3 years: 1 in each of the 4 categories.
Deadline March of the year of the awards (2009, 2012, etc.).

[981]
SIGMA TAU DELTA SCHOLARS AWARD

Sigma Tau Delta
c/o William C. Johnson, Executive Director
Northern Illinois University
Department of English
DeKalb, IL 60115-2863
(815) 753-1612 E-mail: sigmatd@niu.edu
Web: www.english.org/scholarships.shtml

Purpose To provide financial assistance to undergraduate or graduate student members of Sigma Tau Delta (the international English honor society).
Eligibility Eligible to be nominated are members of the society who are currently enrolled in college or graduate school. Each chapter may nominate 3 active members for this scholarship. Candidates are required to provide proof of registration in at least 50% of a full load of courses as part of an English degree program. Along with their application, they must submit a paper, from 2,000 to 3,000 words in length, that was originally submitted for a junior, senior, or graduate class. Selection is based on that paper, academic record, chapter service, awards, professional goals, an application essay (up to 400 words on a topic that changes annually), and 2 letters of recommendation.
Financial data The stipend is $3,000.
Duration 1 year.
Additional information Information is also available from the Scholarship Committee Chair, Dr. Sidney Watson, Oklahoma Baptist University, 500 West University, OBU Box 61238, Shawnee, OK 74804.
Number awarded 1 each year.
Deadline October of each year.

[982]
SINFONIA EDUCATIONAL FOUNDATION SCHOLARSHIPS

Phi Mu Alpha Sinfonia Fraternity of America
Attn: Sinfonia Educational Foundation
10600 Old State Road
Evansville, IN 47711-1399
(812) 867-2433 Toll-free: (800) 473-2649, ext. 110
Fax: (812) 867-0633 E-mail: sef@sinfonia.org
Web: www.sinfoniafoundation.org

Purpose To provide financial assistance to collegiate members of Phi Mu Alpha Sinfonia fraternity (an organization of male students in music).
Eligibility This program is open to college students who have been members in good standing for at least 2 semesters. Applicants must submit an essay of 1 to 2 pages on how the work of the fraternity is integral in creating a philanthropic culture that benefits the common good of society. Selection is based on integrity, ethics, initiative, and overall devotion to the object of the fraternity.
Financial data The stipend is $5,000 or $2,500.
Duration 1 year.
Number awarded 2 each year: 1 at $5,000 and 1 at $2,500.
Deadline January of each year.

[983]
SONS OF ITALY ITALIAN LANGUAGE SCHOLARSHIP

Order Sons of Italy in America
Attn: Sons of Italy Foundation
219 E Street, N.E.
Washington, DC 20002
(202) 547-2900 Fax: (202) 546-8168
E-mail: scholarships@osia.org
Web: www.osia.org/public/scholarships/grants.asp

Purpose To provide financial assistance to upper-division students majoring in Italian.
Eligibility This program is open to U.S. citizens of Italian descent who are enrolled as full-time undergraduate juniors or seniors at an accredited 4-year college or university. Applicants must be majoring in the Italian language. They must submit an essay of 750 to 1,000 words in Italian on why learning Italian is important in today's world and how they plan to use their degree in Italian language in their career. Financial need is not considered in the selection process.
Financial data Stipends range from $5,000 to $25,000.
Duration 1 year; nonrenewable.
Additional information Applications must be accompanied by a $30 processing fee.
Number awarded 1 each year.
Deadline February of each year.

[984]
SPHINX COMPETITION AWARDS

Sphinx Organization
Attn: Artistic Director
400 Renaissance Center, Suite 2550
Detroit, MI 48243
(313) 877-9100 Fax: (313) 877-0164
E-mail: info@sphinxmusic.org
Web: www.sphinxmusic.org

Purpose To recognize and reward outstanding junior high, high school, and college-age Black and Latino string instrumentalists.
Eligibility This competition is open to Black and Latino instrumentalists in 2 divisions: junior, for participants who are younger than 18 years of age, and senior, for participants who are at least 18 but younger than 27 years of age. All entrants must be current U.S. residents who can compete in the instrumental categories of violin, viola, cello, and double bass. Along with their applications, they must submit a preliminary audition tape that includes all of the required preliminary repertoire for their instrument category.

Based on those tapes, qualifiers are invited to participate in the semifinals and finals competitions, held at sites in Detroit and Ann Arbor, Michigan.

Financial data In the senior division, the first-place winner receives a $10,000 cash prize, solo appearances with major orchestras, and a performance with the Sphinx Symphony; the second-place winner receives a $5,000 cash prize and a performance with the Sphinx Symphony; the third-place winner receives a $3,500 cash prize and a performance with the Sphinx Symphony. In the junior division, the first-place winner receives a $5,000 cash prize and 2 performances with the Sphinx Symphony; the second-place winner receives a $3,500 cash prize and a performance with the Sphinx Symphony; the third-place winner receives a $2,000 cash prize and a performance with the Sphinx Symphony. All semifinalists receive scholarships to attend a summer program at Aspen, Blossom, BU Tanglewood, Chautauqua, Eastern Music Festival, ENCORE, Greenwood Music Festival, Interlochen, Meadowmount, National Symphony Summer Institute, National Orchestral Institute, Youth Orchestra of the Americas, Sewanee, or Walnut Hill School. They also receive modest stipends to augment their instrumental studies from the Music Assistance Fund (MAF) of the American Symphony Orchestra League.

Duration The competition is held annually.

Additional information The sponsoring organization was incorporated in 1996 to hold this competition, first conducted in 1998. The Sphinx Symphony is an all African American and Latino orchestra that performs at Orchestra Hall in Detroit. The MAF program was established by the New York Philharmonic in 1965 and transferred to the American Symphony Orchestra League in 1994. In 2002, it partnered with the Sphinx Organization to provide scholarships to all 18 semifinalists. Additional support for MAF is provided by the Brown Foundation, Inc. of Houston, Texas. Major support for the Sphinx Competition Awards is provided by JPMorganChase. Applications must be accompanied by a $35 fee. That fee may be waived if demonstrable need is shown.

Number awarded 18 semifinalists (from both divisions and all instrumental categories) are selected each year. Of those, 3 junior and 3 senior competitors win cash prizes.

Deadline November of each year.

[985]
SPORTS COPY EDITING PROGRAM FOR COLLEGE JUNIORS, SENIORS AND GRADUATE STUDENTS

Dow Jones Newspaper Fund
P.O. Box 300
Princeton, NJ 08543-0300
(609) 452-2820   Fax: (609) 520-5804
E-mail: newsfund@wsj.dowjones.com
Web: DJNewspaperFund.dowjones.com

Purpose To provide financial assistance and work experience to undergraduate and graduate students interested in preparing for a career in sports reporting.

Eligibility College juniors, college seniors, and graduate students are eligible to apply for the internship if they are full-time students interested in a career in sports journalism. Along with their application, they must submit a resume, a list of courses with grades, and a 500-word essay. Interns returning to undergraduate or graduate studies receive a scholarship. U.S. citizenship or permanent resident status is required. College professors and instructors and former full-time professional journalists are ineligible.

Financial data Interns receive a salary of at least $350 per week during the summer and a $1,000 scholarship at the successful completion of the program.

Duration 10 weeks for the summer internship; 1 year for the scholarship.

Additional information Interns attend a 2-week editing residency and then work as sports copy editors on a daily newspaper. Recently, the residency was held at the University of Nebraska.

Number awarded Varies each year.

Deadline October of each year.

[986]
STEPHEN D. PISINSKI MEMORIAL SCHOLARSHIP

Public Relations Student Society of America
Attn: Vice President of Member Services
33 Maiden Lane, 11th Floor
New York, NY 10038-5150
(212) 460-1474   Fax: (212) 995-0757
E-mail: prssa@prsa.org
Web: www.prssa.org

Purpose To provide financial assistance to upper-division members of the Public Relations Student Society of America (PRSSA).

Eligibility This program is open to members of the society who are majoring in journalism, communications, or public relations. Applicants must be juniors or seniors with a GPA of 3.3 or higher. They must submit a resume that includes academic honors, special projects, activities, and/or work experience; an official transcript; an essay, up to 1,000 words, on their career goals; 2 writing samples; and 2 letters of recommendation. Financial need is not considered in the selection process.

Financial data The stipend is $1,500.

Duration 1 year.

Additional information This program was established in 2002.

Number awarded 1 each year.

Deadline May of each year.

[987]
STUDENT ACADEMY AWARDS

Academy of Motion Picture Arts and Sciences
Attn: Academy Foundation
8949 Wilshire Boulevard
Beverly Hills, CA 90211-1972
(310) 247-3000, ext. 131   Fax: (310) 859-9619
E-mail: rmiller@oscars.org
Web: www.oscars.org/saa/index.html

Purpose To recognize and reward college filmmakers with no previous professional experience.

Eligibility This program is open to student filmmakers who are enrolled in degree-granting programs at accredited colleges and universities as full-time students and have no previous professional experience. Applicants must submit films that they have completed within the past year as part of a teacher-student relationship within the curricular structure of their institution. There are 4 award categories: alternative, animation, narrative, and documentary. Entries must be submitted in DVD-R format and be no longer than 60 minutes. Selection is based on resourcefulness, originality, entertainment, and production quality, without regard to cost of production or subject matter.

Financial data Gold, silver, and bronze awards in each category are $5,000, $3,000, and $2,000, respectively.

Duration The awards are presented annually.

Additional information These awards were first presented in 1973. The academy reserves the right to disqualify from competition any film in which professional camera persons, directors, writers, or editors have exercised undue influence.

Number awarded Up to 12 awards may be presented each year: 3 in each of the 4 categories.

Deadline March of each year.

[988]
STUDENT CORRUGATED PACKAGING DESIGN COMPETITION

Association of Independent Corrugated Converters
Attn: AICC Student Design Competition
113 South West Street, Third Floor
P.O. Box 25708
Alexandria, VA 22313
(703) 836-AICC   Toll-free: (877) 836-AICC
Fax: (703) 836-2795   E-mail: info@aiccbox.org
Web: www.aiccbox.org/student/Student_info.asp

Purpose To recognize and reward college students who submit outstanding corrugated packaging designs.

Eligibility This competition is open to undergraduate students enrolled in packaging courses at colleges, universities, and/or technical schools in Canada and the United States. Individual and team entries are accepted. Applicants construct, develop, and/or manufacture packaging designs using corrugated as the primary medium. Entries are accepted in 3 categories: design to a problem, open design, and corrugated as art. In the selection process, heavy emphasis is placed on a written essay describing the project. The first- and second-place winners in the categories of design to a problem and open design compete in a "Best of the Best" program in which they make a presentation about their entry as they might to a prospective customer.

Financial data In each of the categories, first place is $500, second $250, and third $100. The first-place winners in each category also receive all-expense paid trips to the sponsor's annual fall meeting and trade fair in September. In the "Best of the Best" program, the prize is $2,500, second $1,000, third $750, and fourth $500. The first-place winner's school receives a $5,000 grant.

Duration The competition is held annually.

Additional information The "Best of the Best" program is produced later in the fall and broadcast live to packaging schools throughout North America. The 4 participating student teams make their presentations from their home campuses. That portion of the competition is sponsored by the International Corrugated Packaging Foundation.

Number awarded 9 winners (3 in each category) are selected in the first level of competition; 4 additional prizes are awarded for the "Best of the Best" program.

Deadline May of each year.

[989]
STUDENT DESIGN COMPETITION IN ACOUSTICS

Robert Bradford Newman Student Award Fund
c/o Acoustical Society of America
2 Huntington Quadrangle, Suite 1NO1
Melville, NY 11747-4502
(516) 576-2360   Fax: (516) 576-2377
E-mail: asa@aip.org
Web: www.newmanfund.org

Purpose To recognize and reward undergraduate and graduate students who submit outstanding entries in an acoustics design competition.

Eligibility This competition is open to undergraduate and graduate students who enter as individuals or as members of teams of up to 3 students. Applicants must submit an acoustics design for a problem given by the competition. Selection is based on technical merit, design vision, adherence to the design prompt and program requirements, and effectiveness of the presentation.

Financial data The prize for the winning individual or team is $1,250. Commendation awards are $700.

Duration The competition is held annually.

Additional information This competition is sponsored by the Technical Committee for Architectural Acoustics of the Acoustical Society of America and the National Council of Acoustical Consultants. Information is also available from Bob Coffeen, University of Kansas, School of Architecture and Urban Design, 1465 Jayhawk Boulevard, Lawrence, KS 66045, (785) 864-4376, Fax: (913) 649-7063.

Number awarded 1 winner and 4 commendation awards are presented each year.

Deadline Students must register by April of each year.

[990]
SUSAN G. MORAN SCHOLARSHIPS

Society for Technical Communication-Central Ohio Chapter
c/o Kathleen Stohrer, Education Chair
Battelle
505 King Avenue
Columbus, OH 43201
(614) 424-3507   E-mail: stohrer@battelle.org
Web: www.centralohiostc.org/scholarship.html

Purpose To provide financial assistance to students from Ohio who are working on an undergraduate degree in technical communication.

Eligibility This program is open to students working on a bachelor's or associate degree in a technical communication program, including (but not limited to) such courses as introductory and advanced technical communication, introductory and advanced technical editing, online documentation, technical presentations, document design and delivery methods, proofreading, style and mechanics for writers, desktop publishing, report writing, public relations writing, design, or engineering graphics. Applicants must be residents of Ohio or attending an Ohio institution. Along with their application, they must submit a 1- to 3-page description of their career goals and significant achievements to date, a transcript, 2 letters of recommendation, and a set of instructions on how to explain to space aliens how to brush their teeth. Financial need is not considered in the selection process.

Financial data The stipend is $1,000.
Duration 1 year.
Additional information This program was established in 1997.
Number awarded 2 each year.
Deadline April of each year.

[991]
TEXAS CHORAL DIRECTORS ASSOCIATION STUDENT SCHOLARSHIPS

Texas Choral Directors Association
Attn: Executive Director
7900 Centre Park Drive, Suite A
Austin, TX 78754
(512) 474-2801   Fax: (512) 474-7873
E-mail: tcda@ensemble.org
Web: www.ensemble.org/tcda/scholarship.htm

Purpose To provide financial assistance to upper-division and graduate students in Texas who are working on a degree in choral music or church music.

Eligibility Eligible to apply for this scholarship are undergraduates who have completed at least 60 hours and graduate students. Applicants must be enrolled at a Texas college or university, have at least a 3.0 GPA, and be enrolled in a program of study that will lead to a degree in elementary or secondary choral music or church music. Selection is based on musical contributions and accomplishments, potential for success in the choral music profession, and personal qualifications.

Financial data The stipend is $1,000.
Duration 1 year.
Additional information This program includes the TCDA/Gandy Ink Student Scholarship, the TCDA/Carroll Barnes Student Scholarship, and the TCDA/Past Presidents Student Scholarship.
Number awarded 5 each year.
Deadline March of each year.

[992]
THEATRE FOR YOUTH PLAYWRITING AWARD

John F. Kennedy Center for the Performing Arts
Education Department
Attn: Kennedy Center American College Theater Festival
2700 F Street, N.W.
Washington, DC 20566
(202) 416-8857   Fax: (202) 416-8802
E-mail: skshaffer@kennedy-center.org
Web: kennedy-center.org

Purpose To recognize and reward the student authors of plays on themes that appeal to young people.

Eligibility Students at an accredited junior or senior college in the United States or in countries contiguous to the continental United States are eligible to compete, provided their college agrees to participate in the Kennedy Center American College Theater Festival (KCACTF). Undergraduate students must be carrying at least 6 semester hours, graduate students must be enrolled in at least 3 semester hours, and continuing part-time students must be enrolled in a regular degree or certificate program. These awards are presented to the best student-written plays based on a theme appealing to young people from kindergarten through grade 12. Special consideration is given to scripts that emphasize the growth of the central character.

Financial data The prize is $1,000. The winner also receives a $1,250 fellowship to attend the Bonderman IUPUI National Youth Theatre Playwriting Development Workshop and Symposium in Indianapolis (in odd-numbered years) or the Kennedy Center's New Visions/New Voices development laboratory (in even-numbered years).

Duration The award is presented annually.
Additional information This award, first presented in 1997, is supported by the Children's Theatre Foundation of America. It is part of the Michael Kanin Playwriting Awards Program. The sponsoring college or university must pay a registration fee of $250 for each production.
Number awarded 1 each year.
Deadline November of each year.

[993]
THOMAS R. KEATING FEATURE WRITING COMPETITION

Indianapolis Press Club Foundation Inc.
Attn: Scholarship Committee
P.O. Box 501100
Indianapolis, IN 46250
(317) 237-6222   E-mail: info@indypressfoundation.org
Web: www.indypressfoundation.org/52/61.html

Purpose To recognize and reward journalism students in Indiana who submit outstanding entries in a writing competition.

Eligibility This competition is open to students enrolled at colleges and universities in Indiana. Applicants first submit 3 samples of their writing. from which finalists are selected. They are invited to a newsroom in the state where they are given approximately 5 hours to develop a feature story under deadline pressure. Stories are judged the day of the competition and prizes are awarded at a banquet that evening.

Financial data Prizes vary; recently, the first-place winner received $2,750, second $800, and third $500. A special prize for the best entry by a student from Marion County was $250.

Duration The competition is held annually.
Additional information This program was established in 1987.
Number awarded 4 each year.
Deadline Initial entries must be submitted in October of each year.

[994]
TOCA PUBLISHERS SCHOLARSHIP PROGRAM
Turf and Ornamental Communicators Association
120 West Main Street, Suite 200
P.O. Box 156
New Prague, MN 56071
(952) 758-6340   Fax: (952) 758-5813
E-mail: tocaassociation@aol.com
Web: www.toca.org/scholar.html

Purpose To provide financial assistance to undergraduate students preparing for a career in green industry communications.

Eligibility This program is open to undergraduate students majoring or minoring in technical communications or in a green industry-related field (e.g., horticulture, plant sciences, botany, agronomy, plant pathology). Applicants must demonstrate an interest in using this course of study in the field of communications. They must have a GPA of 2.5 or higher overall and 3.0 or higher in their major field of study. Along with their application, they must submit 2 academic or professional references, a writing sample (a news article published or prepared for publication), a resume, their transcript, and an essay (500 words or less) that describes how they became interested in the turf and ornamental industry and their professional goals.

Financial data The stipend is $1,000. Funds are paid through the bursar's office at the recipient's college or university.

Duration 1 year.

Number awarded Up to 2 each year.

Deadline February of each year.

[995]
TOMMY RAMEY SCHOLARSHIP
Tommy Ramey Foundation
Attn: Scholarship Committee
1052 Highland Colony Parkway, Suite 125
Ridgeland, MS 39157
E-mail: admin@tommyrameyscholarship.org
Web: www.tommyrameyscholarship.org

Purpose To provide financial assistance to college students who reside in Mississippi and are majoring in either 1) marketing or a related field or 2) culinary arts or a related field.

Eligibility This program is open to Mississippi residents who are full-time students at an accredited postsecondary institution, have at least a 2.5 GPA, and are enrolled in either 1) marketing or a related field (business, advertising, communications, public relations, journalism, graphic design) or 2) culinary arts or a related field (travel or tourism, hotel or restaurant management, food production). Applicants must submit a list of student activities and a 500-word essay on either "My favorite TV commercial" (marketing students) or "My favorite meal" (culinary students). Selection is based more on personal merit than on academic record; financial need is not required.

Financial data The stipend is either $5,000 or $2,500.

Duration 1 year.

Number awarded Up to 4 each year: either 1 at $5,000 or 2 at $2,500 for marketing students and either 1 at $5,000 or 2 at $2,500 for culinary students.

Deadline October of each year.

[996]
TOWN OF WILLISTON HISTORICAL SOCIETY SCHOLARSHIP
Vermont Student Assistance Corporation
Attn: Scholarship Programs
10 East Allen Street
P.O. Box 2000
Winooski, VT 05404-2601
(802) 654-3798   Toll-free: (888) 253-4819
Fax: (802) 654-3765   TDD: (802) 654-3766
TDD: (800) 281-3341 (within VT)
E-mail: info@vsac.org
Web: www.vsac.org

Purpose To provide financial assistance to residents of Vermont who are working on an undergraduate degree in history.

Eligibility This program is open to residents of Vermont enrolled at an accredited postsecondary school. Applicants must be working on a 4-year degree in history. Selection is based on required essays.

Financial data The stipend is $1,000.

Duration 1 year; nonrenewable.

Additional information The Town of Williston Historical Society established this scholarship in 2002.

Number awarded 1 each year.

Deadline May of each year.

[997]
VICTOR HERBERT ASCAP YOUNG COMPOSER AWARDS
National Federation of Music Clubs
1336 North Delaware Street
Indianapolis, IN 46202-2481
(317) 638-4003   Fax: (317) 638-0503
E-mail: info@nfmc-music.org
Web: www.nfmc-music.org

Purpose To recognize and reward outstanding young composers who are members of the National Federation of Music Clubs.

Eligibility Entrants must be between 18 and 26 years of age, U.S. citizens, and student members of the federation. Awards are presented in 4 categories of student compositions: 1) sonata or comparable work for solo wind or string instrument with piano or for any combination of 3 to 5 instruments (including piano), at least 8 minutes in length; 2) choral work, either unaccompanied or with an accompaniment of piano, organ, or a group of up to 10 wind or string instruments, in English, at least 4 minutes in length; 3) piano solo, either a sonata or theme and variations, at least 5 minutes in length; and 4) vocal solo, with piano, organ, or orchestral accompaniment, text in English, at least 4 minutes in length.

Financial data In each category, first prize is $1,000, second $500, and third $500. Special recognition awards of $50 are also presented.

Duration The competition is held annually.

Additional information Applications and further information are available from Wilmot Irish, 600 Warren Road,

Apartment 3-2A, Ithaca, NY 14850; information on all federation scholarships and awards is available from Chair, Competitions and Awards Board, Dr. George R. Keck, 421 Cherry Street, Arkadelphia, AR 71923-5116, E-mail: keckg@obu.edu. The entry fee is $5 per manuscript.

Number awarded 12 prizes (3 in each category) and 2 special recognition awards each year.

Deadline February of each year.

[998]
VIDEO CONTEST FOR COLLEGE STUDENTS
The Christophers
Attn: Youth Department Coordinator
12 East 48th Street
New York, NY 10017
(212) 759-4050   Fax: (212) 838-5073
E-mail: youth-coordinator@christophers.org
Web: www.christophers.org/contests.html

Purpose To recognize and reward videos produced by college students that best illustrate the motto of The Christophers, "It's better to light one candle than to curse the darkness."

Eligibility Currently-enrolled college students are invited to submit films or videos on the theme: "One Person Can Make a Difference." They may use any style or format to express this theme in 5 minutes or less. Entries may be created using film or video, but they must be submitted on 3/4 inch or VHS cassette. Selection is based on content (the ability to capture the theme), artistic and technical proficiency, and adherence to all contest rules.

Financial data First prize is $3,000, second prize is $2,000, third prize is $1,000, and honorable mention is $100.

Additional information The Christophers, a nonprofit organization, use the mass media to share 2 basic ideas: "There's nobody like you" and "you can make a difference." All entries are returned after the winners are announced. The winning entries are aired nationwide on the Christopher Closeup television series. The competition began in 1987. Winners agree to the use of their work in any Christopher production: broadcast, nonbroadcast, and/or promotional activities related to this contest.

Number awarded 8 each year: 1 each for first, second, and third place plus 5 honorable mentions.

Deadline June of each year.

[999]
VIRGINIA ALLISON ACCOMPANYING AWARD
National Federation of Music Clubs
1336 North Delaware Street
Indianapolis, IN 46202-2481
(317) 638-4003   Fax: (317) 638-0503
E-mail: info@nfmc-music.org
Web: www.nfmc-music.org

Purpose To recognize and reward outstanding young musicians who are members of the National Federation of Music Clubs (NFMC).

Eligibility Applicants must be majoring in vocal or instrumental accompanying. They must be between 18 and 25 years of age, U.S. citizens, and student members of the federation. Selection is based on a cassette tape, from 15 to 20 minutes in length, The tape must include, for vocal accompanying, some early Italian selections, German lied, French chanson, and at least 1 American composition, and, for instrumental accompanying, 1 selection for each period of music, including at least 1 American composition.

Financial data The award is $2,000.

Additional information Information on this award is also available from Anita Blackmon, 1101 South Ricky Road, Kennett, MO 63857, (573) 888-3998, E-mail: ablackmon@angelfire.com; information on all federation scholarships and awards is available from Chair, Competitions and Awards Board, Dr. George R. Keck, 421 Cherry Street, Arkadelphia, AR 71923-5116. There is a $30 entry fee.

Number awarded 1 every other year.

Deadline February of odd-numbered years.

[1000]
VIRGINIA MUSEUM OF FINE ARTS UNDERGRADUATE FELLOWSHIPS
Virginia Museum of Fine Arts
Attn: Education and Outreach Division
200 North Boulevard
Richmond, VA 23220-4007
(804) 204-2661   Fax: (804) 204-2675
E-mail: lee.schultz@vmfa.museum
Web: www.vmfa.museum/LearnMoreArtists.html

Purpose To offer financial support to residents of Virginia who are interested in working on an undergraduate degree in the arts.

Eligibility This program is open to 1) legal residents of Virginia and 2) undergraduate students who have been registered in-state students for at least 1 year before the application deadline. Applicants must be enrolled or planning to enroll full time at an accredited college, university, or school of the arts. They should submit a completed application form; 10 35mm slides representing recent works or 3 videos (VHS), research papers, or published articles; their most recent transcript; and references from 2 art professionals. Only noncommercial, noninstructional projects over which the applicant had control and primary creative responsibility will be considered. Applications are accepted for work or study in the following artistic fields: crafts, drawing, painting, film/video, mixed media, printmaking, photography, or sculpture. Applicants may apply in only 1 of these categories. Awards are not offered for commercial design, theater/performing arts, or architecture. Awards are made to those applicants with the highest artistic merit.

Financial data The stipend is $4,000 or $2,000.

Duration 1 year.

Additional information This program was established in 1940.

Number awarded Varies each year. Recently, 16 of these fellowships were awarded: 12 at $4,000 and 4 at $2,000.

Deadline February of each year.

HUMANITIES

[1001]
W. ELDRIDGE AND EMILY LOWE SCHOLARSHIP
Phi Mu Alpha Sinfonia Fraternity of America
Attn: Sinfonia Educational Foundation
10600 Old State Road
Evansville, IN 47711-1399
(812) 867-2433   Toll-free: (800) 473-2649, ext. 110
Fax: (812) 867-0633   E-mail: sef@sinfonia.org
Web: www.sinfoniafoundation.org

Purpose To provide financial assistance to collegiate members of Phi Mu Alpha Sinfonia fraternity (an organization of male students in music).

Eligibility This program is open to college students who have been members in good standing for at least 2 semesters. Applicants must submit an essay of 1 to 2 pages on a Sinfonian's role in the advancement of music in America beyond his academic institution. Selection is based on integrity, ethics, initiative, and overall devotion to the object of the fraternity.

Financial data The stipend is $1,000.

Duration 1 year.

Number awarded 1 each year.

Deadline January of each year.

[1002]
WAHPERD STUDENT SCHOLARSHIP AWARDS
Wisconsin Association for Health, Physical Education, Recreation, and Dance
Attn: Executive Director
University of Wisconsin at La Crosse
24 Mitchell Hall
1725 State Street
La Crosse, WI 54601-3788
(608) 785-8175   Toll-free: (800) 441-4568
E-mail: wahperd@uwlax.edu
Web: www.wahperd.org/scholarships.htm

Purpose To provide financial assistance to members of the Wisconsin Association for Health, Physical Education, Recreation and Dance (WAHPERD) who are working on a college degree.

Eligibility This program is open to WAHPERD members who have completed at least 2 years of study at a 4-year college or university with a major in physical education, health education, exercise fitness, recreation, athletic training, sports management, or dance. Applicants must have a GPA of 3.2 or higher, at least 2 years' of membership, and a record of professional involvement and leadership responsibility. They must submit a resume and 2 letters of recommendation. Financial need is not considered in the selection process.

Financial data The stipend is $1,000.

Duration 1 year.

Number awarded 4 each year.

Deadline March of each year.

[1003]
WALTER S. PATTERSON SCHOLARSHIPS
Broadcast Education Association
Attn: Scholarships
1771 N Street, N.W.
Washington, DC 20036-2891
(202) 429-3935   Toll-free: (888) 380-7222
E-mail: beainfo@beaweb.org
Web: www.beaweb.org/scholarships.html

Purpose To provide financial assistance to upper-division and graduate students who are interested in preparing for a career in radio.

Eligibility This program is open to juniors, seniors, and graduate students enrolled full time at a college or university where at least 1 department is an institutional member of the Broadcast Education Association (BEA). Applicants must be studying for a career in radio. Selection is based on evidence that the applicant possesses high integrity, superior academic ability, potential to be an outstanding electronic media professional, and a sense of personal and professional responsibility.

Financial data The stipend is $1,250.

Duration 1 year; may not be renewed.

Additional information Information is also available from Peter B. Orlik, Central Michigan University, 344 Moore Hall, Mt. Pleasant, MI 48859, (989) 774-7279. This program is sponsored by the National Association of Broadcasters of Washington, D.C. and administered by the BEA.

Number awarded 2 each year.

Deadline October of each year.

[1004]
WALTER W. RISTOW PRIZE
Washington Map Society
c/o John Docktor
3100 North Highway A1A PHA 1
Fort Pierce, FL 34949-8831
E-mail: washmap@earthlink.net
Web: home.earthlink.net/~docktor/ristow.htm

Purpose To recognize and reward outstanding student papers on cartographic history and map librarianship.

Eligibility This competition is open to all full- and part-time undergraduate students, graduate students, and first-year postdoctorates. Applicants must submit research papers or bibliographic studies that relate to cartographic history and/or map librarianship. In the case of undergraduate and graduate students, the entries must have been completed in fulfillment of requirements for course work. A short edition of a longer paper is permitted, but the text may not exceed 7,500 words. All entries must be in English. Papers must be fully documented, in a style of the author's choice. Entries are judged on the importance of the research, the quality of the research, and the quality of writing.

Financial data The prize is $1,000 and membership in the society.

Duration The prize is offered annually.

Additional information This prize was first awarded in 1994. The winning manuscript is published in the society's journal, *The Portolan*. Information is also available from

Robert G. Rhodes, 2733 Carter Farm Court, Alexandria, VA 22306, E-mail: rgrhodes@starpower.net.
Number awarded 1 each year.
Deadline May of each year.

[1005]
WAMSO YOUNG ARTIST COMPETITION AWARDS AND SCHOLARSHIPS

WAMSO-Minnesota Orchestra Volunteer Association
Orchestra Hall
1111 Nicollet Mall
Minneapolis, MN 55403-2477
(612) 371-5654　　　　　Fax: (612) 371-7176
E-mail: wamso@mnorch.org
Web: www.wamso.org/yac.html

Purpose To recognize and reward outstanding young musicians from the Midwest and selected areas in Canada who perform in the Women's Association of the Minnesota Orchestra (WAMSO) competition.

Eligibility Contestants must be performers of instruments that have permanent chairs in the Minnesota Orchestra and be legal residents of or students in Illinois, Indiana, Iowa, Kansas, Michigan, Minnesota, Missouri, Nebraska, North Dakota, South Dakota, Wisconsin, Manitoba, or Ontario. They must be 26 years of age or younger. The repertoire for audition tapes is at their discretion but must include a concerto and 2 solo works representing contrasting styles and periods. Based on those tapes, 16 contestants advance to the semifinals held in January at Macalester College in St. Paul. The finals are held in Orchestra Hall.

Financial data The first-prize winner receives the WAMSO Young Artist Award of $5,000, the WAMSO Achievement Award of $2,250, a performance with the Minnesota Orchestra, a taped performance on WQXR, New York, and (at the discretion of the Minnesota Orchestra music director) the Grant Prize of $1,000. The second-prize winner receives the WAMSO Award of $4,000 and a taped performance on WQXR, New York. The third-prize winner receives the WAMSO Award of $2,000. Other awards include the Elaine Louise Lagerstrom Memorial Award of $1,000 for violin, the Mathilda Heck Award of $1,000 for woodwind, the Twin Cities Musicians Union AFM Award of $1,000, the Mary Winston Smail Memorial Award of $500 for piano, and the Vincent R. Bastien Memorial Award of $500 for cello. Summer program scholarships are awarded to Aspen Music School, Madeline Island Music Camp, and Interlochen Center for the Arts.

Duration The competition is held annually.

Additional information This competition was first held in 1956. There is a $75 application fee.

Number awarded A large number of awards and scholarships are offered annually.

Deadline Applications must be submitted by September of each year and tapes by October of each year.

[1006]
WASHINGTON FASHION GROUP INTERNATIONAL SCHOLARSHIP

Fashion Group International of Washington
Attn: Scholarship Co-Chairs
Congressional Quarterly, Inc.
1255 22nd Street, N.W., Suite 700
Washington, DC 20037
E-mail: esheldon@cq.com

Purpose To provide financial assistance for college or graduate school to residents of Maryland, Virginia, and Washington, D. C. interested in preparing for a career in fashion or a fashion-related field.

Eligibility This program is open to residents of Washington, D.C. and all cities and counties in Maryland and Virginia. Applicants must be graduating high school seniors or current undergraduate or graduate students enrolled in a fashion or fashion-related degree program (commercial arts, textiles and clothing design, interior design, journalism, merchandising, or photography). They must submit a 200-word personal statement on their career goals and motivation for entering a fashion-related career. Selection is based on that statement, academic achievement, creative ability, related work activity (paid or unpaid), extracurricular activities and awards, and 3 letters of reference. Finalists are interviewed and asked to submit a portfolio of their work.

Financial data The maximum stipend is $5,000.

Duration 1 year; nonrenewable.

Number awarded 1 or more each year.

Deadline February of each year.

[1007]
WENDELL IRISH VIOLA AWARDS

National Federation of Music Clubs
1336 North Delaware Street
Indianapolis, IN 46202-2481
(317) 638-4003　　　　　Fax: (317) 638-0503
E-mail: info@nfmc-music.org
Web: www.nfmc-music.org

Purpose To recognize and reward outstanding young violists who are members of the National Federation of Music Clubs (NFMC).

Eligibility Eligible to compete are violists between 12 and 19 years of age. Applicants must be members of the junior division of the federation and U.S. citizens. They must present at least 2 pieces selected from contrasting style periods.

Financial data The award is $1,000.

Additional information Information on these awards is also available from Dr. George Keck, 421 Cherry Street, Arkadelphia, AR 71923, E-mail: keckg@obu.edu.

Number awarded 4 each year: 1 in each NFMC region.

Deadline January of each year.

HUMANITIES

[1008]
WERNER B. THIELE MEMORIAL SCHOLARSHIPS

Gravure Association of America
Attn: Gravure Education Foundation
1200-A Scottsville Road
Rochester, NY 14624
(315) 589-8879 Fax: (585) 436-7689
E-mail: lwshatch@gaa.org
Web: www.gaa.org/GEF/scholarships.htm

Purpose To provide financial assistance to upper-division students interested in a career in printing.

Eligibility This program is open to juniors and seniors who are enrolled full time in a field related to printing at a designated learning resource center supported by the Gravure Education Foundation (GEF) of the Gravure Association of America. Applicants must have a GPA of 3.0 or higher. Along with their application, they must submit a 300-word essay that demonstrates their interest in gravure technology. Financial need is not considered in the selection process.

Financial data The stipend is $1,250.

Duration 1 year.

Additional information GEF learning resource centers are located at the following universities: Rochester Institute of Technology, Western Michigan University, California Polytechnic State University at San Luis Obispo, Arizona State University, Clemson University, Murray State University, and the University of Wisconsin at Stout.

Number awarded 2 each year.

Deadline May of each year.

[1009]
WILLIAM B. RUGGLES RIGHT TO WORK SCHOLARSHIP

National Institute for Labor Relations Research
Attn: Scholarship Selection Committee
5211 Port Royal Road, Suite 510
Springfield, VA 22151
(703) 321-9606 Fax: (703) 321-7342
E-mail: research@nilrr.org
Web: www.nilrr.org/scholarships.htm

Purpose To provide financial assistance for the undergraduate or graduate education of journalism students who are knowledgeable about the Right to Work principle.

Eligibility This program is open to undergraduate and graduate students majoring in journalism at institutions of higher learning in the United States. Applicants must demonstrate the potential to complete the educational requirements of the degree program in journalism. Along with their application, they must submit an essay of approximately 500 words demonstrating an understanding of the principles of voluntary unionism and the economic and social problems of compulsory unionism. Selection is based on scholastic ability and a demonstrated interest in the work of the sponsoring organization to promote voluntary unionism.

Financial data The stipend is $2,000.

Duration 1 year.

Additional information This scholarship was established in 1974 to honor the Texas journalist who coined the phrase "Right to Work." The sponsor considers only the first 150 applications received.

Number awarded 1 each year.

Deadline December of each year.

[1010]
WILLIAM E. GREGORY SCHOLARSHIP

Imperial Polk Advertising Federation
Attn: Scholarship Program
P.O. Box 24201
Lakeland, FL 33802-4201
(863) 858-3736 Fax: (863) 858-3736
Web: www.polkadfed.com

Purpose To provide financial assistance to undergraduate students majoring in fields related to advertising at Florida colleges.

Eligibility This program is open to full-time undergraduate students at universities, colleges, and technical schools in Florida. Applicants must be working on a degree in advertising, communications, graphic design, or marketing. They must have a GPA of 3.0 or higher. Along with their application, they must submit 1) a 500-word essay describing their future professional and educational goals; and 2) a project they have recently completed for a class or internship. Financial need is not considered in the selection process.

Financial data A total of $2,000 is available for this program each year.

Duration 1 year; nonrenewable.

Additional information Information is also available from Samantha Hocker, Scholarship Chair, (863) 701-7789, E-mail: shocker@keisercollege.edu.

Number awarded 1 or more each year.

Deadline November of each year.

[1011]
WISCONSIN BROADCASTERS ASSOCIATION FOUNDATION COLLEGE/UNIVERSITY STUDENT SCHOLARSHIP PROGRAM

Wisconsin Broadcasters Association
Attn: WBA Foundation
44 East Mifflin Street, Suite 900
Madison, WI 53703-2800
(608) 255-2600 Fax: (608) 256-3986
E-mail: contact@wi-broadcasters.org
Web: www.wi-broadcasters.org

Purpose To provide financial assistance to students at Wisconsin colleges and universities who are preparing for a career in broadcasting.

Eligibility This program is open to upper-division students majoring in broadcasting, communication, or a related field at a 4-year public or private college or university in Wisconsin. Applicants must be planning a career in radio or television broadcasting. Along with their application, they must submit an official transcript, 2 letters of recommendation, and an essay forecasting what the broadcasting industry will be like in 5 years and how they will contribute to radio or television during that time. Finalists may be asked to participate in a personal interview.

Financial data The stipend is $2,000.

Duration 1 year; nonrenewable.

Number awarded 4 each year.
Deadline October of each year.

[1012]
WTVR NEWS 6 NETWORK SCHOLARSHIP
WTVR News 6
Attn: Black Advisory Council Scholarship Committee
P.O. Box 11064
Richmond, VA 23230
(804) 254-3616
Web: www.wtvr.com

Purpose To provide financial assistance to upper-division and graduate students in Virginia who are African Americans and preparing for a career in broadcasting.

Eligibility Applicants must be in their junior or senior year of college or entering graduate school in Virginia. They must be African Americans and working on a degree in communications, broadcasting or related fields. Along with their application, they must submit a 50-word statement on their reasons for choosing a career in broadcasting. Selection is based on academic achievement, career interest and intent, and personal accomplishments.

Financial data Stipends range from $1,000 to $7,500.
Duration 1 year.
Additional information This is also known as the Black Advisory Council (BAC) Scholarship.
Number awarded Varies each year.
Deadline April of each year.

[1013]
XERNONA CLAYTON BRADY SCHOLARSHIP
Atlanta Association of Black Journalists
P.O. Box 54128
Atlanta, GA 30308
(770) 593-5837   E-mail: scholarship.aabj.org
Web: www.aabj.org

Purpose To provide financial assistance to African Americans from any state majoring in communication-related fields at Georgia colleges or universities.

Eligibility This program is open to African Americans enrolled in Georgia colleges and universities who are working full time on a degree in mass communications or journalism. Applicants must have a GPA of 3.0 or higher and be U.S. citizens or permanent residents. Along with their application, they must submit an essay of 500 words or less on a topic that changes annually; recently, applicants were invited to discuss how African American journalists can impact the quality of life in their community. Selection is based on the essay, transcripts, 2 letters of recommendation, and samples of published work.

Financial data The grand prize scholarship is $5,000; the first runner-up receives $3,000 and the second runner-up receives $2,000.
Duration 1 year.
Additional information Information is also available from Greg Morrison, (404) 678-4164.
Number awarded 3 each year.
Deadline April of each year.

[1014]
YOUNG FILM COMPOSERS COMPETITION
Turner Classic Movies
Attn: Young Film Composers Competition
1050 Techwood Drive, N.W.
Atlanta, GA 30318
(404) 885-5535   E-mail: tcm@turner.com
Web: www.turnerclassicmovies-yfcc/com

Purpose To recognize and reward outstanding student and entry-level composers of music for movies.

Eligibility This competition is open to students and other residents of the United States, United Kingdom, and Canada (except Québec) who are between 18 and 35 years of age, have Internet access, and are not under exclusive contracts with a publisher. During the 2 months prior to the deadline, candidates must log on to the web site of the sponsor, select 1 video clip of a silent film (from 4 choices, each 60 seconds long), and compose an original musical work appropriate for scoring the selected video clip. That demo must then be submitted to the sponsor online. Semifinalists are selected on the basis of the score's originality, creativity, quality, and appropriateness to the video clip. They are notified of their selection as semifinalists and must then submit a copy of their professional resume, a copy of their original score for the demo they submitted, and answers to 5 essay questions.

Financial data The grand prize winner receives a cash award of $10,000, a trip to Los Angeles, and the opportunity to score a silent film for showing on Turner Classic Movies. The other winners receive musical equipment.

Duration The competition is held annually.

Additional information This competition, first held in 2000, is jointly sponsored by Turner Classic Movies, Guitar Center, Film Music Publications, Inc., and Todd A-O. During the 7-day visit to Los Angeles, the grand prize winner is mentored through the process of scoring a silent film by a team of music and film industry professionals and has the opportunity to have his/her music recorded and married to the silent film for exhibition on the sponsor's network and/or web site.

Number awarded 1 cash prize is awarded each year. A total of 4 other winners receive other prizes.
Deadline March of each year.

Any Subject Area

Described here are 309 merit and other no-need funding programs that can be used to support study in any subject area (although the programs may be restricted in other ways). These programs are available to currently-enrolled and returning college students to fund studies on the undergraduate level in the United States. If you are looking for a particular program and don't find it here, be sure to check the Program Title Index to see if it is covered elsewhere in the directory.

ANY SUBJECT AREA

[1015]
A. PATRICK CHARNON SCHOLARSHIP
Center for Education Solutions
P.O. Box 208
San Francisco, CA 94104-0208
(925) 934-7304
E-mail: scholarship@cesresources.org
Web: www.cesresources.org/charnon.html

Purpose To provide financial assistance to entering or continuing undergraduate students who demonstrate a commitment to their community.

Eligibility Applicants must be admitted or enrolled in a full-time undergraduate program of study at an accredited 4-year college or university. They must demonstrate dedication and commitment to their communities. Along with their application, they must submit a 2- to 4-page essay on how community service experiences have shaped their lives and how they will use their college education to build communities in a manner consistent with values of compassion, tolerance, generosity, and respect. The selection committee looks for candidates whose values reflect the goals of the program and who have demonstrated their commitments to those values by their actions.

Financial data The stipend is $1,500 per year.

Duration 1 year; may be renewed up to 3 additional years.

Additional information This program was established in 1995.

Number awarded 1 each year.

Deadline March of each year.

[1016]
AFRICAN AMERICAN UNIVERSITY SCHOLARSHIPS OF THE CALIFORNIA STATE FAIR
California State Fair
Attn: Friends of the Fair Scholarship Program
1600 Exposition Boulevard
P.O. Box 15649
Sacramento, CA 95852
(916) 274-5969   E-mail: entryoffice@calexpo.com
Web: www.bigfun.org

Purpose To provide financial assistance to African American residents of California who plan to attend a 4-year college or university in the state.

Eligibility This program is open to African Americans who are currently enrolled in a high school or community college in California. Applicants must be planning to attend a 4-year college or university in the state in the following fall. They must have a GPA of 3.0 or higher. Along with their application, they must submit a 2-page essay on a topic that changes annually; recently, students were invited to present their opinion on who is California's current African American superhero and why. Selection is based on personal commitment, goals established for their chosen field, leadership potential, and civic accomplishments.

Financial data Stipends are $1,000 or $250.

Duration 1 year.

Additional information The Friends of the Fair Scholarship Program was established in 1993. This program is sponsored by Phillips Enterprise and a private individual.

Number awarded 2 each year: 1 at $1,000 and 1 at $250.

Deadline March of each year.

[1017]
AGRON SEAL SCHOLARSHIP
Naval Special Warfare Foundation
Attn: Scholarship Committee
P.O. Box 5965
Virginia Beach, VA 23471
(757) 363-7490   Fax: (757) 363-7491
E-mail: info@nswfoundation.org
Web: www.nswfoundation.org

Purpose To provide financial assistance for college to Navy personnel serving on active duty in the SEALS and their families.

Eligibility This program is open to active-duty SEALs, their current spouses, and immediate children. Applicants must be high school seniors or current college students working on or planning to work on an associate or bachelor's degree. Selection is based on academic merit, extracurricular and community activities, and contributions made within the SEAL community.

Financial data The stipend is $1,000 per year.

Duration Up to 4 years, provided the recipient maintains a GPA of 3.2 or higher.

Number awarded 1 each year.

Deadline March of each year.

[1018]
AHEPA DISTRICT SCHOLARSHIP AWARDS
American Hellenic Educational Progressive Association
Attn: AHEPA Educational Foundation
1909 Q Street, N.W., Suite 500
Washington, DC 20009
(202) 232-6300   Fax: (202) 232-2140
E-mail: ahepa@ahepa.org
Web: www.ahepa.org

Purpose To provide financial assistance for college to students who apply through district foundations or committees of the American Hellenic Educational Progressive Association (AHEPA).

Eligibility This program is open to students who are enrolled or planning to enroll in a college or university. Recipients are selected by AHEPA districts that qualify to receive funding from the national foundation. Districts establish their own requirements, but they may follow procedures similar to those of the national organization: applicants must be members in good standing of the Order of Ahepa, Daughters of Penelope, Sons of Pericles, or Maids of Athena, or the children of Order of Ahepa or Daughters of Penelope members in good standing. High school seniors must submit their most recent official transcript as well as SAT or ACT scores; college freshmen and sophomores must submit high school transcripts, SAT or ACT scores, and their most recent college transcript; college juniors and seniors must submit their most recent college transcript. Along with their application, they must also submit a 500-word biographical essay. Selection is based on academic achievement; extracurricular, personal, and volunteer activities; athletic achievements; and work experience. Financial need is not considered.

Financial data The stipend is $1,000 per year.

Duration 1 year.

Additional information This program includes the following named scholarships: the Sam Nakos Scholarship, the Nicholas Kounaris Scholarship, the P.A. Margaronis Scholarship, the Carlos T. Touris Scholarship, and the William P. Thomas Scholarship. Applications for this scholarship must be submitted to the AHEPA local district scholarship committee chair, who selects the recipients.

Number awarded Varies each year; recently, 20 of these scholarships were awarded.

Deadline Recommendation forms must be submitted to the national office by June of each year.

[1019]
AIR FORCE ENHANCED ROTC HISPANIC SERVING INSTITUTION SCHOLARSHIP PROGRAM

U.S. Air Force
Attn: Headquarters AFROTC/RRUC
551 East Maxwell Boulevard
Maxwell AFB, AL 36112-5917
(334) 953-2091   Toll-free: (866) 423-7682
Fax: (334) 953-6167
Web: www.afrotc.com

Purpose To provide financial assistance to students at designated Hispanic Serving Institutions (HSIs) who are willing to join Air Force ROTC in college and serve as Air Force officers following completion of their bachelor's degree.

Eligibility This program is open to U.S. citizens who are at least 17 years of age and currently enrolled at 1 of 8 designated HSIs that have an Air Force ROTC unit on campus. Applicants do not need to be Hispanic as long as they are enrolled at the university and have a cumulative GPA of 2.5 or higher. At the time of commissioning, they may be no more than 31 years of age. They must be able to pass the Air Force Officer Qualifying Test (AFOQT) and the Air Force ROTC Physical Fitness Test. Currently, the program is accepting applications from students with any major.

Financial data Awards are type 2 AFROTC scholarships that provide for payment of tuition and fees, to a maximum of $15,000 per year, plus an annual book allowance of $600. Recipients are also awarded a tax-free subsistence allowance for 10 months of each year that is $300 per month during the sophomore year, $350 during the junior year, and $400 during the senior year.

Duration Up to 3 and a half years (beginning as early as the spring semester of the freshman year).

Additional information The designated universities are California State University at Fresno, California State University at San Bernardino, New Mexico State University, the University of Miami, the University of New Mexico, the University of Puerto Rico at Rio Piedras, the University of Puerto Rico at Mayaguez, and the University of Texas at San Antonio. While scholarship recipients can major in any subject, they must complete 4 years of aerospace studies courses. They must also attend a 4-week summer training camp at an Air Force base, usually between their sophomore and junior years; 2-year scholarship awardees attend in the summer after their junior year. Current military personnel are eligible for early release from active duty in order to enter the Air Force ROTC program. Following completion of their bachelor's degree, scholarship recipients earn a commission as a second lieutenant in the Air Force and serve at least 4 years.

Number awarded Up to 120 each year: 15 at each of the participating AFROTC units.

Deadline Applications may be submitted at any time.

[1020]
AIR FORCE ENHANCED ROTC HISTORICALLY BLACK COLLEGES AND UNIVERSITIES SCHOLARSHIP PROGRAM

U.S. Air Force
Attn: Headquarters AFROTC/RRUC
551 East Maxwell Boulevard
Maxwell AFB, AL 36112-5917
(334) 953-2091   Toll-free: (866) 423-7682
Fax: (334) 953-6167
Web: www.afrotc.com

Purpose To provide financial assistance to students at designated Historically Black Colleges and Universities (HBCUs) who are willing to join Air Force ROTC and serve as Air Force officers following completion of their bachelor's degree.

Eligibility This program is open to U.S. citizens at least 17 years of age who are currently enrolled as freshmen at 1 of the 8 HBCUs that has an Air Force ROTC unit on campus. Applicants do not need to be African American as long as they are attending an HBCU and have a cumulative GPA of 2.5 or higher. At the time of commissioning, they may be no more than 31 years of age. They must be able to pass the Air Force Officer Qualifying Test (AFOQT) and the Air Force ROTC Physical Fitness Test. Currently, the program is accepting applications from students with any major.

Financial data Awards are type 2 AFROTC scholarships that provide for payment of tuition and fees, to a maximum of $15,000 per year, plus an annual book allowance of $600. Recipients are also awarded a tax-free subsistence allowance for 10 months of each year that is $300 per month during the sophomore year, $350 during the junior year, and $400 during the senior year.

Duration Up to 3 and a half years (beginning as early as the spring semester of the freshman year).

Additional information The participating HBCUs are Tuskegee University (Tuskegee, Alabama), Alabama State University (Montgomery, Alabama), Howard University (Washington, D.C.), Grambling State University (Grambling, Louisiana), North Carolina A&T State University (Greensboro, North Carolina), Fayetteville State University (Fayetteville, North Carolina), Tennessee State University (Nashville, Tennessee), and Jackson State University (Jackson, Mississippi). While scholarship recipients can major in any subject, they must complete 4 years of aerospace studies courses at 1 of the HBCUs that have an Air Force ROTC unit on campus. Recipients must also attend a 4-week summer training camp at an Air Force base, usually between their sophomore and junior years; 2-year scholarship awardees attend in the summer after their junior year. Current military personnel are eligible for early release from active duty in order to enter the Air Force ROTC program. Following completion of their bachelor's degree, scholarship recipients earn a commission as a second lieutenant in the Air Force and serve at least 4 years.

Number awarded Up to 120 each year: 15 at each of the participating AFROTC units.

Deadline Applications may be submitted at any time.

[1021]
AIR FORCE REGULAR ROTC HISPANIC SERVING INSTITUTION SCHOLARSHIP PROGRAM

U.S. Air Force
Attn: Headquarters AFROTC/RRUC
551 East Maxwell Boulevard
Maxwell AFB, AL 36112-5917
(334) 953-2091   Toll-free: (866) 423-7682
Fax: (334) 953-6167
Web: www.afrotc.com

Purpose To provide financial assistance to students at Hispanic Serving Institutions (HSIs) who are willing to join Air Force ROTC in college and serve as Air Force officers following completion of their bachelor's degree.

Eligibility This program is open to U.S. citizens at least 17 years of age who are currently enrolled at 1 of the 42 HSIs that has an Air Force ROTC unit on campus or that has a cross-enrollment agreement with another school that hosts a unit. Applicants do not need to be Hispanic as long as they are attending an HSI and have a cumulative GPA of 2.5 or higher. At the time of commissioning, they may be no more than 31 years of age. They must be able to pass the Air Force Officer Qualifying Test (AFOQT) and the Air Force ROTC Physical Fitness Test. Currently, the program is accepting applications from students with any major.

Financial data Awards are type 2 AFROTC scholarships that provide for payment of tuition and fees, to a maximum of $15,000 per year, plus an annual book allowance of $600. Recipients are also awarded a tax-free subsistence allowance for 10 months of each year that is $300 per month during the sophomore year, $350 during the junior year, and $400 during the senior year.

Duration 2 to 3 years, beginning during the current term.

Additional information While scholarship recipients can major in any subject, they must complete 4 years of aerospace studies courses. They must also attend a 4-week summer training camp at an Air Force base, usually between their sophomore and junior years; 2-year scholarship awardees attend in the summer after their junior year. Current military personnel are eligible for early release from active duty in order to enter the Air Force ROTC program. Following completion of their bachelor's degree, scholarship recipients earn a commission as a second lieutenant in the Air Force and serve at least 4 years.

Number awarded Varies each year. AFROTC units at every HSI may nominate an unlimited number of cadets to receive these scholarships.

Deadline Applications may be submitted at any time.

[1022]
AIR FORCE REGULAR ROTC HISTORICALLY BLACK COLLEGES AND UNIVERSITIES SCHOLARSHIP PROGRAM

U.S. Air Force
Attn: Headquarters AFROTC/RRUC
551 East Maxwell Boulevard
Maxwell AFB, AL 36112-5917
(334) 953-2091   Toll-free: (866) 423-7682
Fax: (334) 953-6167
Web: www.afrotc.com

Purpose To provide financial assistance to students at Historically Black Colleges and Universities (HBCUs) who are willing to serve as Air Force officers following completion of their bachelor's degree.

Eligibility This program is open to U.S. citizens at least 17 years of age who are currently enrolled at 1 of the 48 HBCUs that has an Air Force ROTC unit on campus or that has a cross-enrollment agreement with another school that hosts a unit. Applicants do not need to be African American as long as they are attending an HBCU and have a cumulative GPA of 2.5 or higher. At the time of commissioning, they may be no more than 31 years of age. They must be able to pass the Air Force Officer Qualifying Test (AFOQT) and the Air Force ROTC Physical Fitness Test. Currently, the program is accepting applications from students with any major.

Financial data Awards are type 2 AFROTC scholarships that provide for payment of tuition and fees, to a maximum of $15,000 per year, plus an annual book allowance of $600. Recipients are also awarded a tax-free subsistence allowance for 10 months of each year that is $300 per month during the sophomore year, $350 during the junior year, and $400 during the senior year.

Duration 2 to 3 years, beginning during the current term.

Additional information While scholarship recipients can major in any subject, they must complete 4 years of aerospace studies courses at 1 of the HBCUs that have an Air Force ROTC unit on campus. Recipients must also attend a 4-week summer training camp at an Air Force base, usually between their sophomore and junior years; 2-year scholarship awardees attend in the summer after their junior year. Current military personnel are eligible for early release from active duty in order to enter the Air Force ROTC program. Following completion of their bachelor's degree, scholarship recipients earn a commission as a second lieutenant in the Air Force and serve at least 4 years.

Number awarded Varies each year. AFROTC units at every HBCU may nominate an unlimited number of cadets to receive these scholarships.

Deadline Applications may be submitted at any time.

[1023]
AIR FORCE ROTC GENERAL MILITARY COURSE INCENTIVE

U.S. Air Force
Attn: Headquarters AFROTC/RRUC
551 East Maxwell Boulevard
Maxwell AFB, AL 36112-5917
(334) 953-2091   Toll-free: (866) 423-7682
Fax: (334) 953-6167
Web: www.afrotc.com/overview/programs.php

Purpose To provide financial assistance to college sophomores interested in joining Air Force ROTC and serving as Air Force officers following completion of their bachelor's degree.

Eligibility This program is open to U.S. citizens who are entering the spring semester of their sophomore year in the general military course at a college or university with an Air Force ROTC unit on campus or a college with a cross-enrollment agreement with such a school. Applicants must be full-time students, have a GPA of 2.0 or higher both cumulatively and during the prior term, be enrolled in both the Aerospace Studies 200 class and the Leadership Laboratory, pass the Air Force Officer Qualifying Test, meet Air Force physical fitness and weight requirements, and be able to be commissioned before they become 31 years of age. They must agree to serve for at least 4 years as active-duty Air Force officers following graduation from college.

Financial data Selected cadets receive up to $1,500 for tuition and a stipend of $250 per month.

Duration 1 semester (the spring semester of junior year); nonrenewable.

Additional information Upon successful completion of their sophomore year, recipients of these scholarships may upgrade to the Professional Officer Course Incentive. They also remain eligible to apply for other AFROTC in-college scholarship programs.

[1024]
AIR FORCE ROTC PROFESSIONAL OFFICER CORPS INCENTIVE

U.S. Air Force
Attn: Headquarters AFROTC/RRUC
551 East Maxwell Boulevard
Maxwell AFB, AL 36112-5917
(334) 953-2091   Toll-free: (866) 423-7682
Fax: (334) 953-6167
Web: www.afrotc.com/overview/programs.php

Purpose To provide financial assistance for undergraduate and graduate education to individuals who have completed 2 years of college and who are willing to join Air Force ROTC and serve as Air Force officers following completion of their degree.

Eligibility Applicants must be U.S. citizens who have completed 2 years of the general military course at a college or university with an Air Force ROTC unit on campus or a college with a cross-enrollment agreement with such a college. They must be full-time students, have a GPA of 2.0 or higher both cumulatively and for the prior term, be enrolled in both Aerospace Studies class and Leadership Laboratory, pass the Air Force Officer Qualifying Test, meet Air Force physical fitness and weight requirements, and be able to be commissioned before they become 31 years of age. They must agree to serve for at least 4 years as active-duty Air Force officers following graduation from college with either a bachelor's or graduate degree.

Financial data This scholarship provides $3,000 per year for tuition and a monthly subsistence allowance of $350 as a junior or $400 as a senior.

Duration Until completion of a graduate degree.

Additional information Scholarship recipients must complete 4 years of aerospace studies courses at 1 of the 144 colleges and universities that have an Air Force ROTC unit on campus; students may also attend other colleges that have cross-enrollment agreements with the institutions that have an Air Force ROTC unit on campus. Recipients must also attend a 4-week summer training camp at an Air Force base between their junior and senior year.

Number awarded Varies each year.

[1025]
AIR FORCE SERGEANTS ASSOCIATION SCHOLARSHIPS

Air Force Sergeants Association
Attn: Scholarship Coordinator
P.O. Box 50
Temple Hills, MD 20757
(301) 899-3500, ext. 237   Toll-free: (800) 638-0594
Fax: (301) 899-8136   E-mail: staff@amf.org
Web: www.afsahq.org/body_education01.htm

Purpose To provide financial assistance for undergraduate education to the dependent children of Air Force enlisted personnel.

Eligibility This program is open to the unmarried children (including stepchildren and legally adopted children) of active-duty, retired, or veteran members of the U.S. Air Force, Air National Guard, or Air Force Reserves. Applicants must be younger than 23 years of age and dependent upon the parent or guardian for more than half of their support. Their parent must be a member of the Air Force Sergeants Association or its auxiliary. Selection is based on academic ability (SAT score of 1100 or higher or ACT score of 24 or higher and GPA of 3.5 or higher), character, leadership, writing ability. and potential for success. Financial need is not a consideration.

Financial data Stipends range from $1,000 to $2,500 per year. Scholarships may be used for tuition, room and board, fees, books, supplies, and transportation.

Duration 1 year; may be renewed if the student maintains full-time enrollment.

Additional information This program began in 1968. Requests for applications must be accompanied by a stamped self-addressed envelope.

Number awarded Varies each year. Recently, 17 of these scholarships were awarded, including the Frank C. Fini, the Hardy B. Abbott, and the Claude Klobus Scholarships (each at $2,500), 3 at $2,000, 10 at $1,500, and 1 at $1,000. Since the program began, it has awarded 429 scholarships worth $568,600.

Deadline March of each year.

[1026]
AIR FORCE SERVICES CLUB MEMBERSHIP SCHOLARSHIP PROGRAM
Air Force Services Agency
Attn: HQ AFSVA/SVICO
10100 Reunion Place, Suite 501
San Antonio, TX 78216-4138
(210) 652-6312   Toll-free: (800) 443-4834
Fax: (210) 652-7041   E-mail: svi@agency.afsv.af.mil
Web: www-p.afsv.af.mil/Clubs/Scholarship.htm

Purpose To recognize and reward, with college scholarships, Air Force Club members and their families who submit outstanding essays.

Eligibility This program is open to Air Force Club members and their spouses, children, and stepchildren who have been accepted by or are enrolled at an accredited college or university. Grandchildren are eligible if they are a dependent of the club member. Applicants may be undergraduate or graduate students enrolled full or part time. They must submit an essay of up to 500 words on a topic that changes annually; a recent topic was "My Hero, and Why." Applicants must also include a 1-page summary of their long-term career and life goals and previous accomplishments, including civic, athletic, and academic awards.

Financial data Awards are scholarships of $6,000 for first place, $5,500 for second place, $4,500 for third place, $3,500 for fourth place, $3,000 for fifth place, and $2,500 for sixth place.

Duration The competition is held annually.

Additional information This competition, first held in 1997, is sponsored by Chase Bank and MasterCard.

Number awarded 6 each year.

Deadline Entries must be submitted to the member's base services commander or division chief by July of each year.

[1027]
AIR FORCE SPOUSE SCHOLARSHIPS
Air Force Association
Attn: Member Services
1501 Lee Highway
Arlington, VA 22209-1198
(703) 247-5800   Toll-free: (800) 727-3337
Fax: (703) 247-5853   E-mail: AFAStaff@afa.org
Web: www.afa.org/aef/aid/spouse.asp

Purpose To provide financial assistance for undergraduate or graduate study to spouses of Air Force members.

Eligibility This program is open to spouses of Air Force active duty, Air National Guard, or Air Force Reserve members. Spouses who are themselves military members or in ROTC are not eligible. Applicants must have a GPA of 3.5 or higher in college (or high school if entering college for the first time) and be able to provide proof of acceptance into an accredited undergraduate or graduate degree program. They must submit a 2-page essay on their academic and career goals, the motivation that led them to that decision, and how Air Force and other local community activities in which they are involved will enhance their goals. Selection is based on the essay and 2 letters of recommendation.

Financial data The stipend is $1,000 per year; funds are sent to the recipients' schools to be used for any reasonable cost related to working on a degree.

Duration 1 year; nonrenewable.

Additional information This program was established in 1995.

Number awarded 30 each year.

Deadline April of each year.

[1028]
AIRCRAFT ELECTRONICS ASSOCIATION MEMBERS SCHOLARSHIP PROGRAM
Aircraft Electronics Association
Attn: AEA Educational Foundation
4217 South Hocker Drive
Independence, MO 64055-4723
(816) 373-6565   Fax: (816) 478-3100
E-mail: info@aea.net
Web: www.aea.net

Purpose To provide financial assistance for college in the United States or abroad to members of the Aircraft Electronics Association (AEA) and their relatives.

Eligibility This program is open to high school seniors, high school graduates, and currently-enrolled college students who are either members or the children, grandchildren, or other dependents of members of the association. Applicants must be planning to work on a college degree in any field of study at an accredited U.S. postsecondary institution or international equivalent institution. Along with their application, they must submit a transcript of high school or college grades (GPA of 2.5 or higher), a letter of recommendation, and a 300-word essay on why they believe they have talent or ability related to their academic major and career goal. Financial need is not considered.

Financial data The stipend is $1,500; funds must be used for tuition.

Duration 1 year.

Additional information This program includes the following named scholarships: the Chuck Peacock Honorary Scholarship, the Gene Baker Memorial Scholarship, and the Jim Cook Honorary Scholarship.

Number awarded 2 each year.

Deadline February of each year.

[1029]
AIRMEN MEMORIAL FOUNDATION SCHOLARSHIP PROGRAM
Air Force Sergeants Association
Attn: Scholarship Coordinator
P.O. Box 50
Temple Hills, MD 20757
(301) 899-3500, ext. 237   Toll-free: (800) 638-0594
Fax: (301) 899-8136   E-mail: staff@amf.org
Web: www.afsahq.org/body_education01.htm

Purpose To provide financial assistance for college to the dependent children of enlisted Air Force personnel.

Eligibility This program is open to the unmarried children (including stepchildren and legally adopted children) of active-duty, retired, or veteran members of the U.S. Air Force, Air National Guard, or Air Force Reserves. Applicants

must be younger than 23 years of age and dependent upon the parent or guardian for more than half of their support. Selection is based on academic ability (SAT score of 1100 or higher or ACT score of 24 or higher and GPA of 3.5 or higher), character, leadership, writing ability. and potential for success. Financial need is not a consideration.
Financial data The stipend is $1,500 or $1,000; funds may be used for tuition, room and board, fees, books, supplies, and transportation.
Duration 1 year; may be renewed if the recipient maintains full-time enrollment.
Additional information The Air Force Sergeants Association administers this program on behalf of the Airmen Memorial Foundation. The highest ranked applicant receives the Sharon L. Piccoli Memorial Scholarship. This program began in 1987. Requests for applications must be accompanied by a stamped self-addressed envelope.
Number awarded 20 each year: the Sharon L. Piccoli Memorial Scholarship at $1,500 and 19 others at $1,000 each.
Deadline March of each year.

[1030]
ALABAMA G.I. DEPENDENTS' SCHOLARSHIP PROGRAM
Alabama Department of Veterans Affairs
770 Washington Avenue, Suite 530
P.O. Box 1509
Montgomery, AL 36102-1509
(334) 242-5077 Fax: (334) 242-5102
E-mail: willie.moore@va.state.al.us
Web: www.va.state.al.us/scholarship.htm

Purpose To provide educational benefits to the dependents of disabled, deceased, and other Alabama veterans.
Eligibility Eligible are spouses, children, stepchildren, and unremarried widow(er)s of veterans who served honorably for 90 days or more and 1) are currently rated as 20% or more service-connected disabled or were so rated at time of death; 2) were a former prisoner of war; 3) have been declared missing in action; 4) died as the result of a service-connected disability; or 5) died while on active military duty in the line of duty. The veteran must have been a permanent civilian resident of Alabama for at least 1 year prior to entering active military service; veterans who were not Alabama residents at the time of entering active military service may also qualify if they have a 100% disability and were permanent residents of Alabama for at least 5 years prior to filing the application for this program or prior to death, if deceased. Children and stepchildren must be under the age of 26, but spouses and unremarried widow(er)s may be of any age.
Financial data Eligible dependents may attend any state-supported Alabama institution of higher learning or enroll in a prescribed course of study at any Alabama state-supported trade school without payment of any tuition, book fees, or laboratory charges.
Duration This is an entitlement program for 4 years of full-time undergraduate or graduate study or part-time equivalent. Spouses and unremarried widow(er)s whose veteran spouse is rated between 20 and 90% disabled, or 100% disabled but not permanently so, may attend only 2 standard academic years.
Additional information Benefits for children, spouses, and unremarried widow(er)s are available in addition to federal government benefits. Assistance is not provided for noncredit courses, placement testing, GED preparation, continuing educational courses, pre-technical courses, or state board examinations.
Number awarded Varies each year.
Deadline Applications may be submitted at any time.

[1031]
ALASKA FREE TUITION FOR SPOUSES AND DEPENDENTS OF ARMED SERVICES MEMBERS
Department of Military and Veterans Affairs
Attn: Office of Veterans Affairs
P.O. Box 5800
Fort Richardson, AK 99505-5800
(907) 428-6016 Fax: (907) 428-6019
E-mail: jerry_beale@ak-prepared.com
Web: www.ak-prepared.com

Purpose To provide financial assistance for college to dependents and spouses in Alaska of service members who died or were declared prisoners of war or missing in action.
Eligibility Eligible for this benefit are the spouses and dependent children of Alaska residents who died in the line of duty, died of injuries sustained in the line of duty, or were listed by the Department of Defense as a prisoner of war or missing in action. Applicants must be in good standing at a state-supported educational institution in Alaska.
Financial data Those eligible may attend any state-supported educational institution in Alaska without payment of tuition or fees.
Duration 1 year; may be renewed.
Additional information Information is available from the financial aid office of state-supported universities in Alaska.
Number awarded Varies each year.

[1032]
ALBERTA E. CROWE STAR OF TOMORROW AWARD
United States Bowling Congress
Attn: SMART Program
5301 South 76th Street
Greendale, WI 53129-1192
(414) 423-3343 Toll-free: (800) 514-BOWL, ext. 3343
Fax: (414) 421-3014 E-mail: smart@bowl.com
Web: www.bowl.com/scholarships/main.aspx

Purpose To provide financial assistance for college to outstanding women bowlers.
Eligibility This program is open to women amateur bowlers who are current members in good standing of the United States Bowling Congress (USBC) or USBC Youth and competitors in events sanctioned by those organizations. Applicants must be high school or college students younger than 22 years of age, have a GPA of 2.5 or higher, and have a bowling average of 175 or greater. They may not have competed in a professional bowling tournament. Along with their application, they must submit an essay, up to 500 words, on how this scholarship will influence their bowling, aca-

demic, and personal goals. Selection is based on bowling performances on local, regional, state, and national levels; academic achievement; and extracurricular involvement.
Financial data The stipend is $1,500 per year.
Duration 1 year; may be renewed for 3 additional years.
Number awarded 1 each year.
Deadline September of each year.

[1033]
ALFRED H. NOLLE SCHOLARSHIPS
Alpha Chi
Attn: Executive Director
900 East Center Avenue
Harding University Box 12249
Searcy, AR 72149-0001
(501) 279-4443   Toll-free: (800) 477-4225
Fax: (501) 279-4589   E-mail: dorgan@harding.edu
Web: www.harding.edu/alphachi/nolle.htm

Purpose To provide financial assistance for college to members of Alpha Chi, a national honor scholarship society.
Eligibility Eligible to be nominated for these funds are full-time college juniors who have been initiated into Alpha Chi; they must have 1 full year of college left before graduation. Only 2 nominations may be submitted by each chapter. Included in the nomination package must be an academic paper or other appropriate work in the student's major field (e.g., painting, music score, film, slides, video, cassette tape recording, or other medium). Students must also submit a letter of application outlining their plans for study and detailing their extracurricular activities. Financial need is not considered.
Financial data The stipend is $1,500.
Duration 1 year.
Additional information Recipients must be enrolled in college full time during the scholarship year.
Number awarded 10 each year.
Deadline February of each year.

[1034]
ALL-INK COLLEGE SCHOLARSHIPS
All-Ink.com
P.O. Box 50868
Provo, UT 84606
(801) 794-0123   Toll-free: (888) 567-6511
Fax: (801) 794-0124
E-mail: Scholarship2006@all-ink.com
Web: www.all-ink.com/scholarship.aspx

Purpose To provide financial assistance for college or graduate school to students who submit a scholarship application online.
Eligibility This program is open to U.S. citizens and permanent residents who are enrolled or planning to enroll at an accredited college or university at any academic level from freshman through graduate student. Applicants must have a GPA of 2.5 or higher. They must submit, through an online process, an essay of 50 to 200 words on a person who has had the greatest impact on their life and another essay of the same length on what they hope to achieve in their personal and professional life after graduation. Applications are not accepted through the mail.

Financial data Stipends range up to $5,000.
Duration 1 year.
Number awarded Varies each year; recently 5 of these scholarships were awarded.
Deadline December of each year.

[1035]
ALPHA KAPPA ALPHA MERIT SCHOLARSHIPS
Alpha Kappa Alpha Sorority, Inc.
Attn: Educational Advancement Foundation
5656 South Stony Island Avenue
Chicago, IL 60637
(773) 947-0026   Toll-free: (800) 653-6528
Fax: (773) 947-0277   E-mail: akaeaf@aol.com
Web: www.akaeaf.org/scholarships.htm

Purpose To provide financial assistance to undergraduate and graduate students (especially African American women) who have excelled academically.
Eligibility This program is open to undergraduate and graduate students who have completed at least 1 year in an accredited degree-granting institution and are planning to continue their program of education. Applicants must have demonstrated exceptional academic achievement (GPA of 3.0 or higher) and present evidence of leadership through community service and involvement. Men and women of all ethnic groups are eligible for these scholarships, but the sponsor is a traditionally African American women's sorority.
Financial data The stipend is $1,000 per year.
Duration 1 year; nonrenewable.
Number awarded Varies each year. Recently, 27 of these scholarships were awarded: 20 to undergraduates and 7 to graduate students.
Deadline January of each year.

[1036]
AME CHURCH PREACHER'S KID SCHOLARSHIP
African Methodist Episcopal Church
Connectional Ministers' Spouses, Widows and
  Widowers
c/o Jennifer Green, Scholarship Committee Chair
2386 S.W. 102nd Avenue
Miramar, FL 33025-6509
E-mail: ConnMSWAWOPk@aol.com
Web: www.amemswwpk.org

Purpose To provide financial assistance for college to children of ministers in the African Methodist Episcopal (AME) Church.
Eligibility This program is open to dependent children under 21 years of age whose parent or legal guardian is an AME minister. Applicants must be a member of the AME Church, have a satisfactory score on the SAT or ACT, rank in the top 50% of their high school class, and have a cumulative GPA of 2.5 or higher. Along with their application, they must submit a 300-word essay on how the AME Church has made a difference in their life and what they will do to support their church. Their minister parent must be a member of the Connectional AME Ministers' Spouses, Widows and Widowers Organization.

Financial data The scholarship stipend is $2,500. Book awards are $250.
Duration 1 year.
Number awarded Varies each year. Recently, the program awarded 2 scholarships (1 for AME districts 1-13 and 1 for districts 14-20) and 4 book awards.
Deadline April of each year.

[1037]
AMERICAL DIVISION VETERANS ASSOCIATION SCHOLARSHIP

Americal Division Veterans Association
P.O. Box 1381
Boston, MA 02104
Web: www.americal.org/scholar.shtml

Purpose To provide financial assistance for college to the dependents of members of the Americal Division Veterans Association.
Eligibility This program is open to the children and grandchildren of members of the Americal Division Veterans Association and to the children of Americal Division veterans who were killed in action or died while on active duty with the Division. Applicants must submit an essay of 200 to 300 words on subjects pertaining to Americal Division history, national pride, loyalty to the nation, patriotism, or a related topic. Financial need is not considered in the selection process.
Financial data Stipends range from $250 to $3,000 per year.
Duration 1 year; recipients may reapply.
Additional information Information is also available from the Scholarship Foundation Chair, Bob Short, 3839 Old Savannah Drive, Kalamazoo, MI 49009, (269) 372-2192, E-mail: c146thinf@aol.com.
Number awarded Varies each year. Recently, 36 of these scholarships were available: 1 at $3,000, 1 at $2,500, 1 at $2,000, 2 at $1,500, 9 at $1,000, 21 at $500, and 1 at $250.
Deadline April of each year.

[1038]
AMERICAN DARTS ORGANIZATION MEMORIAL SCHOLARSHIPS

American Darts Organization
230 North Crescent Way, Suite K
Anaheim, CA 92801-6707
(714) 254-0212   Fax: (714) 254-0214
E-mail: ADOdarts1@aol.com
Web: www.adodarts.com

Purpose To provide financial aid for college to players in the American Darts Organization (ADO) Youth Playoff Program.
Eligibility This program is open to ADO members who are area or national winners in the Youth Playoff Program and under 21 years of age. Applicants must be enrolled or accepted at an accredited U.S. college as a full-time student with a GPA of 2.0 or higher. They must be U.S. citizens or have lived in the United States for at least 2 years.
Financial data Stipends are: $500 for quarter finalists in the National Championship; $750 for each semifinalist; $1,000 for each runner-up; and $1,500 for each National Champion. Any participant/winner who is eligible to compete in more than 1 area/national championship may repeat as a scholarship winner, up to $8,000 in prizes. Funds may be used for any legitimate college expense, including fees for parking stickers, library fees, student union fees, tuition, and books.
Duration The funds are awarded annually.
Number awarded 8 each year: 4 quarter finalists, 2 semifinalists, 1 runner-up, and 1 National Champion.

[1039]
AMERICAN POLICE HALL OF FAME EDUCATIONAL SCHOLARSHIP FUND

American Police Hall of Fame and Museum
Attn: Police Family Survivor's Fund
6350 Horizon Drive
Titusville, FL 32780
(321) 264-0911   Fax: (321) 264-0033
E-mail: policeinfo@aphf.org
Web: www.aphf.org/scholarships.html

Purpose To provide financial assistance for college to children of deceased law enforcement officers.
Eligibility Applicants must be the son or daughter of a law enforcement officer killed in the line of duty. They must be attending or planning to attend a private or public college or a vocational program. Financial need is not considered in the selection process.
Financial data The stipend is $1,500 per year.
Duration 1 year; may be renewed up to 3 additional years if funds permit.
Additional information This program was established in 1992.
Number awarded Varies each year, depending on the availability of funds.

[1040]
AMERICORPS NATIONAL CIVILIAN COMMUNITY CORPS

Corporation for National and Community Service
1201 New York Avenue, N.W.
Washington, DC 20525
(202) 606-5000, ext. 144   Toll-free: (800) 942-2677
Fax: (202) 565-2791   TTY: (202) 606-3472
TTY: (800) 833-3722
E-mail: questions@americorps.org
Web: www.americorps.org/about/programs/nccc.asp

Purpose To enable young Americans to receive experience and training by participating in a residential national service program while earning funds for higher education.
Eligibility Eligible are U.S. citizens or permanent residents between the ages of 18 and 24. Members work on a variety of projects, most involving improvement of the environment: construction, mapping, and improvement of rural and urban parks; restoration of streams and rivers; environmental education programs in schools and community centers. Other projects operate in the areas of education, public safety, homeland security, disaster relief, and other community needs. Selection is based on an application, personal references, and a telephone interview.

Financial data Corps members receive a living allowance of approximately $4,000, housing, meals, limited medical insurance, up to $400 per month for child care (if necessary), member uniforms, and an education award of $4,725 for future education costs or repayment of student loans.
Duration 10 months.
Additional information Participants in this program are housed in 1 of 5 campuses serving 5 regions of the country: Denver, Colorado for the central region; Charleston, South Carolina for the southeast region; Sacramento, California for the western region; Perry Point, Maryland for the northeast region; and Washington, D.C. for the capital region. Members with dependent children may choose a matching funds plan to assist with child care, but children must reside off-campus.
Number awarded Varies each year.
Deadline March of each year for the fall cycle; July of each year for the winter cycle.

[1041]
ANGIE M. HOUTZ MEMORIAL FUND SCHOLARSHIP

Angie M. Houtz Memorial Fund
P.O. Box 634
Olney, MD 20830-0634
E-mail: angiefund@yahoo.com
Web: www.angiemhoutzmemorialfund.com

Purpose To provide financial assistance to students enrolled at public colleges and universities in Maryland.
Eligibility This program is open to graduating high school seniors or current college students from any state who are attending or planning to attend a public 2-year or 4-year college or university in Maryland. Applicants must have a GPA of 3.0 or higher and a record of community volunteer activities beyond their high school graduation requirements. They must submit an essay or 250 to 500 words on an assigned topic, transcripts, and 3 letters of recommendation. Financial need is not considered in the selection process.
Financial data The stipend is $3,000.
Duration 1 year.
Additional information This program was established after September 11, 2001 to honor 1 of the victims of the events of that day.
Number awarded 1 each year.
Deadline April of each year.

[1042]
ANN PHIPPS MEMORIAL SCHOLARSHIPS

National Head Start Association
Attn: Scholarships and Awards
1651 Prince Street
Alexandria, VA 22314
(703) 739-0875, ext. 7506   Fax: (703) 739-0878
E-mail: satkinson@nhsa.org
Web: www.nhsa.org

Purpose To provide financial assistance for college to Head Start parents.
Eligibility This program is open to Head Start parents who are enrolled or planning to enroll at a 4-year college or university, 2-year community college, or vocational/technical school. Applicants must submit a 200-word statement on their personal goals. Selection is based on that statement (40 points), Head Start involvement and community contribution (30 points), letters of reference or recommendation (20 points), and completeness of information (10 points). Parents must submit their applications to their local program, which forwards 1 to the state association. Each state association forwards 2 applications to the regional association, which selects 2 for nomination to the national headquarters.
Financial data The stipend is $1,500.
Duration 1 year.
Additional information These scholarships were first awarded in 1979.
Number awarded 2 each year.
Deadline Regional associations must submit applications to national headquarters by December of each year.

[1043]
AOWCGWA SCHOLARSHIP PROGRAM

Army Officers' Wives' Club of the Greater Washington Area
c/o Sandy Oujiri, Scholarship Committee Chair
7753 Jewelweed Court
Springfield, VA 22152
E-mail: aowcgwascScholarship@fmthriftshop.org
Web: www.fmthriftshop.org/scholarshippage.html

Purpose To provide financial assistance for college to the children and spouses of U.S. Army personnel and veterans in the Washington, D.C. metropolitan area.
Eligibility This program is open to 1) high school seniors who are children of Army personnel, 2) college students under 22 years of age who are children of Army personnel; and 3) spouses of Army personnel. High school seniors and spouses must reside with their sponsor in the Washington metropolitan area; the sponsor of college students must reside in that area. Sponsors may be active-duty, retired, or deceased, and officer or enlisted. Applicants must submit a 500-word statement on their personal ambitions and goals; a list of extracurricular activities, honors, church activities, community service, and employment; an official transcript that includes (for high school seniors) their SAT or ACT scores; and a letter of recommendation. Students who plan to attend a service academy or receive another full scholarship are not eligible. Selection is based on scholastic merit and community involvement; financial need is not considered.
Financial data The stipend is at least $2,000.
Duration 1 year.
Additional information The Washington metropolitan area is defined to include the Virginia cities of Alexandria, Fairfax, Falls Church, Manassas, and Manassas Park; the Virginia counties of Arlington, Fairfax, Fauquier, Loudoun, Prince William, and Stafford; the Maryland counties of Calvert, Charles, Frederick, Montgomery, and Prince George's; and the District of Columbia. This program is supported in part by the First Command Educational Foundation.
Number awarded 1 or more each year.
Deadline March of each year.

[1044]
ARMY AVIATION ASSOCIATION OF AMERICA SCHOLARSHIPS

Army Aviation Association of America Scholarship Foundation
Attn: AAAA Scholarship Foundation
755 Main Street, Suite 4D
Monroe, CT 06468-2830
(203) 268-2450   Fax: (203) 268-5870
E-mail: aaaa@quad-a.org
Web: www.quad-a.org/scholarship.htm

Purpose To provide financial aid for undergraduate or graduate study to members of the Army Aviation Association of America (AAAA) and their relatives.

Eligibility This program is open to AAAA members and their spouses, unmarried siblings, unmarried children, and unmarried grandchildren. Applicants must be enrolled or accepted for enrollment as an undergraduate or graduate student at an accredited college or university. Graduate students must include a 250-word essay on their life experiences, work history, and aspirations. Some scholarships are specifically reserved for enlisted, warrant officer, company grade, and Department of the Army civilian members. Selection is based on academic merit and personal achievement.

Financial data Stipends range from $1,000 to $4,000.

Duration Scholarships may be for 1 year, 2 years, or 4 years.

Number awarded Varies each year; since the program began in 1963, the foundation has awarded more than $2.2 million to more than 1,300 qualified applicants.

Deadline April of each year.

[1045]
ARMY ROTC ADVANCED COURSE

U.S. Army
ROTC Cadet Command
Attn: ATCC-OP-I-S
55 Patch Road, Building 56
Fort Monroe, VA 23651-1052
(757) 727-4558   Toll-free: (800) USA-ROTC
E-mail: atccps@usaac.army.mil
Web: www.rotc.usaac.army.mil

Purpose To provide financial assistance to non-scholarship participants in the Army ROTC Program who have qualified for the Advanced Course.

Eligibility Non-scholarship cadets in the ROTC Program are eligible to apply for this program if they have qualified for the ROTC Advanced Course. The Advanced Course is usually taken during the final 2 years of college.

Financial data Participants receive a stipend of $350 per month during their junior year and $400 per month during their senior year, as well as pay for attending the 6-week advanced camp during the summer between the junior and senior years of college.

Duration 2 years.

Additional information Non-scholarship graduates may serve 3 years on active duty and 5 years in the Reserve Forces, or they may select or be selected to serve all 8 years on Reserve Forces Duty (RFD). If RFD is selected, graduates attend an Officer Basic Course and spend the remainder of their 8-year obligation in the Reserve Forces.

Number awarded Varies each year.

[1046]
ARMY ROTC COLLEGE SCHOLARSHIP PROGRAM

U.S. Army
ROTC Cadet Command
Attn: ATCC-OP-I-S
55 Patch Road, Building 56
Fort Monroe, VA 23651-1052
(757) 727-4558   Toll-free: (800) USA-ROTC
E-mail: atccps@usaac.army.mil
Web: www.rotc.usaac.army.mil

Purpose To provide financial assistance to students who are or will be enrolled in Army ROTC.

Eligibility This program is open to U.S. citizens at least 17 years of age who have already completed 1 or 2 years in a college or university with an Army ROTC unit on campus or in a college with a cross-enrollment agreement with a college with an Army ROTC unit on campus. Applicants must have 2 or 3 years remaining for their bachelor's degree (or 4 years of a 5-year bachelor's program) and must be able to complete that degree before their 31st birthday. They must have a GPA of 2.5 or higher in their previous college study and scores of at least 920 on the SAT or 19 on the ACT.

Financial data These scholarships provide financial assistance for college tuition and educational fees, up to an annual amount of $16,000. In addition, a flat rate of $510 is provided for the purchase of textbooks, classroom supplies, and equipment. Recipients are also awarded a stipend for up to 10 months of each year that is $300 per month during their sophomore year, $350 per month during their junior year, and $400 per month during their senior year.

Duration 2 or 3 years, until the recipient completes the bachelor's degree.

Additional information Applications must be made through professors of military science at 1 of the schools hosting the Army ROTC program. Preference is given to students who have already enrolled as non-scholarship students in military science classes at 1 of the more than 270 institutions with an Army ROTC unit on campus, at 1 of the 75 college extension centers, or at 1 of the more than 1,000 colleges with cross-enrollment or extension agreements with 1 of the colleges with an Army ROTC unit. Scholarship winners must serve in the military for 8 years. That service obligation may be fulfilled 1) by serving on active duty for 4 years followed by service in the Army National Guard (ARNG), the United States Army Reserve (USAR), or the Inactive Ready Reserve (IRR) for the remainder of the 8 years; or 2) by serving 8 years in an ARNG or USAR troop program unit that includes a 3- to 6-month active-duty period for initial training.

Number awarded Varies each year; a recent allocation provided for 700 4-year scholarships, 1,800 3-year scholarships, and 2,800 2-year scholarships.

Deadline December of each year.

[1047] ASIAN PACIFIC ISLANDER UNIVERSITY SCHOLARSHIPS OF THE CALIFORNIA STATE FAIR

California State Fair
Attn: Friends of the Fair Scholarship Program
1600 Exposition Boulevard
P.O. Box 15649
Sacramento, CA 95852
(916) 274-5969   E-mail: entryoffice@calexpo.com
Web: www.bigfun.org

Purpose To provide financial assistance to California residents of Asian Pacific Islander heritage who plan to attend a 4-year college or university in the state.

Eligibility This program is open to Asian Pacific Islanders who are currently enrolled in a high school or community college in California. Applicants must be planning to attend a 4-year college or university in the state in the following fall. They must have a GPA of 3.0 or higher. Along with their application, they must submit a 2-page statement on their Asian Pacific Islander background, community involvement, career goals, and desire to give back to their community. Selection is based on personal commitment, goals established for their chosen field, leadership potential, and civic accomplishments.

Financial data The stipend is $1,000 or $250.

Duration 1 year.

Additional information The Friends of the Fair Scholarship Program was established in 1993. This program is sponsored by Capital Foundation.

Number awarded 2 each year: 1 at $1,000 and 1 at $250.

Deadline March of each year.

[1048] ASSISTANCE FOR SURVIVING CHILDREN OF NAVAL PERSONNEL DECEASED AFTER RETIREMENT (CDR)

Navy-Marine Corps Relief Society
Attn: Education Division
875 North Randolph Street, Suite 225
Arlington, VA 22203-1977
(703) 696-4960   Fax: (703) 696-0144
E-mail: education@hq.nmcrs.org
Web: www.nmcrs.org/child-dec.html

Purpose To provide financial assistance for college to the children of Navy or Marine Corps personnel who died as a result of disabilities or length of service.

Eligibility Eligible for this assistance are the unmarried, dependent children, stepchildren, or legally adopted children under the age of 23 of members of the Navy or Marine Corps who died after retirement due to disability or length of service.

Financial data Grants up to $4,000 per year are available.

Additional information This program is limited to undergraduate studies and vocational training.

Number awarded Varies each year.

Deadline February of each year.

[1049] BETA SIGMA PSI EDUCATIONAL FOUNDATION AWARDS

Beta Sigma Psi Educational Foundation
2408 Lebanon Avenue
Belleville, IL 62221
(618) 235-0014   Fax: (618) 235-0051
E-mail: office@betasigmapsi.org
Web: www.betasigmapsi.org/ef.html

Purpose To provide financial assistance to members of Beta Sigma Psi, a Lutheran social fraternity.

Eligibility This program is open to fraternity brothers who are currently enrolled in college and are interested in applying for 1 of the following categories of scholarships: financial need, academic achievement, or campus involvement. The first category requires a clergy or church worker to complete part of the application; the other categories require a letter of reference.

Financial data The amounts of the awards depend on the availability of funds and the qualifications of the recipient; recently, stipends averaged $1,000.

Duration 1 year.

Additional information Information is also available from the Scholarship Chairman, Jake Allen, 5536 Lundsford Drive, Indianapolis, IN 46237, (317) 783-4148, E-mail: alle1lh@comcast.net.

Number awarded Varies each year; recently, 15 of these scholarships were awarded.

Deadline April of each year.

[1050] BETTY HANSEN NATIONAL SCHOLARSHIPS

Danish Sisterhood of America
Attn: Lizette Burtis, Scholarship Chair
3020 Santa Juanita Court
Santa Rosa, CA 95405-8219
(707) 539-1884   E-mail: lburtis@sbcglobal.net
Web: www.danishsisterhood.org/rschol.asp

Purpose To provide financial assistance for educational purposes in the United States or Denmark to members or relatives of members of the Danish Sisterhood of America.

Eligibility This program is open to members or the family of members of the sisterhood who are interested in attending an accredited 4-year college or university as a full-time undergraduate or graduate student. Members must have belonged to the sisterhood for at least 1 year. Selection is based on academic excellence (at least a 2.5 GPA). Upon written request, the scholarship may be used for study in Denmark.

Financial data The stipend is $1,000.

Duration 1 year; nonrenewable.

Number awarded Up to 8 each year.

Deadline February of each year.

[1051]
BILLY WELU SCHOLARSHIP

Professional Bowlers Association
Attn: Billy Welu Bowling Scholarship
719 Second Avenue, Suite 701
Seattle, WA 98104
(206) 332-9688   Fax: (206) 654-6030
Web: www.pba.com/corporate/scholarships.asp

Purpose To provide financial assistance to college students who are active bowlers.

Eligibility This program is open to currently-enrolled college students who compete in the sport of bowling. Applicants must submit a 500-word essay describing how the scholarship will positively affect their bowling, academic, and personal goals. They must have a GPA of 2.5 or higher. Financial need is not considered in the selection process.

Financial data The stipend is $1,000.

Duration 1 year.

Number awarded 1 each year.

Deadline May of each year.

[1052]
BOEING COMPANY SCHOLARSHIP

Independent Colleges of Washington
600 Stewart Street, Suite 600
Seattle, WA 98101
(206) 623-4494   Fax: (206) 625-9621
E-mail: info@icwashington.org
Web: www.icwashington.org

Purpose To provide financial assistance to students entering or enrolled at colleges and universities that are members of Independent Colleges of Washington (ICW).

Eligibility This program is open to students entering or enrolling at ICW-member colleges and universities. Applicants must submit a 1-page essay on how their education at an independent college will impact their role in the future of Washington. Selection is based on merit.

Financial data The stipend is $2,500.

Duration 1 year; nonrenewable.

Additional information The ICW-member institutions are Gonzaga University, Heritage College, Pacific Lutheran University, Saint Martin's College, Seattle Pacific University, Seattle University, University of Puget Sound, Walla Walla College, Whitman College, and Whitworth College. This program was established by the Boeing Company in 2006.

Number awarded 1 each year.

Deadline March of each year.

[1053]
BRUCE VAN ESS SCHOLARSHIP

International Union of Electronic, Electrical, Salaried, Machine, and Furniture Workers
Attn: IUE-CWA International Scholarship Program
501 Third Street, N.W., Suite 975
Washington, DC 20001
(202) 434-1417   Fax: (202) 434-1250
E-mail: bgray@iue-cwa.org
Web: www.iue-cwa.org/skills.html

Purpose To provide financial assistance for undergraduate education to children and grandchildren of members and employees of the International Union of Electronic, Electrical, Salaried, Machine, and Furniture Workers (IUE)-Communications Workers of America (CWA).

Eligibility This program is open to children and grandchildren of IUE-CWA members and employees. Applicants must be accepted for admission or already enrolled as full-time students at an accredited college, university, nursing school, or technical school offering college credit classes. Along with their application, they must submit an academic transcript (including rank in class, GPA, and SAT/ACT scores); a short statement of interests and civic activities; an essay (300 to 500 words) describing their career goals and aspirations, highlighting their relationship with the union and the labor movement, and explaining why they are deserving of a union scholarship. They must also have demonstrated a commitment to equality of opportunity for all, a concern for improving the quality of life for all people, an interest in service to the community, good character, leadership ability, and a desire to improve and move ahead.

Financial data The stipend is $2,500 per year.

Duration 1 year.

Number awarded 1 each year.

Deadline March of each year.

[1054]
CALGON TAKE ME AWAY TO COLLEGE SCHOLARSHIPS

Coty US LLC
One Park Avenue, Fifth Floor
New York, NY 10016
(212) 479-4300   Fax: (212) 479-4399
Web: www.takemeaway.com

Purpose To recognize and reward, with college scholarships, women who are graduating high school seniors or already enrolled in college and provide excellent answers to online essay questions.

Eligibility This competition is open to women residents of the United States who are 18 years of age or older. Applicants must be enrolled or planning to enroll as a full-time undergraduate student at a 4-year U.S. college or university and have a GPA of 3.0 or higher. They must submit online answers (up to 900 characters) to questions that change annually; recently, applicants were invited to write on 1) how stepping outside their comfort zone to try something new has taken them on an unexpected path and changed their life; and 2) a childhood event that they feel has most shaped who they are and what they believe in. Those short answers are judged on the basis of originality, quality of expression, and accordance with standard rules of English grammar, mechanics, and spelling. Financial need is not considered. The 35 finalists are then invited to submit a short essay on a specified topic, transcripts, a list of extracurricular activities, and other documents as part of an application packet to be provided. Scholarship America ranks the finalists on the basis of merit, exclusive of the essays. Maddenmedia selects the winner on the basis of that ranking and the essays.

Financial data First place is a $5,000 scholarship, second a $2,000 scholarship, third a $1,000 scholarship, and runners-up $500 scholarships.

Duration The competition is held annually.

Additional information This annual competition began in 1999. Information is also available from Scholarship America, One Scholarship Way, P.O. Box 297, St. Peter, MN 56082, (507) 931-1682, (800) 537-4180, Fax: (507) 931-9168, E-mail: smsinfo@csfa.org, and from Maddenmedia, 1650 East Fort Lowell Road, Suite 100, Tucson, AZ 85719.

Number awarded 9 each year: 1 first place, 1 second, 1 third, and 6 runners-up.

Deadline February of each year.

[1055]
CALIFORNIA FEE WAIVER PROGRAM FOR DEPENDENTS OF TOTALLY DISABLED VETERANS

California Department of Veterans Affairs
Attn: Division of Veterans Services
1227 O Street, Room 101
Sacramento, CA 95814
(916) 503-8397   Toll-free: (800) 952-LOAN (within CA)
Fax: (916) 653-2563   TDD: (800) 324-5966
E-mail: ruckergl@cdva.ca.gov
Web: www.cdva.ca.gov/service/feewaiver.asp

Purpose To provide financial assistance for college to dependents of disabled and other California veterans.

Eligibility Eligible for this program are spouses (including registered domestic partners), children, and unremarried widow(er)s of veterans who are currently totally service-connected disabled (or are being compensated for a service-connected disability at a rate of 100%) or who died of a service-connected cause or disability. The veteran parent must have served during a qualifying war period and must have been discharged or released from military service under honorable conditions. The child cannot be over 27 years of age (extended to 30 if the student was in the military); there are no age limitations for spouses or surviving spouses. This program does not have an income limit. Dependents in college are not eligible if they are qualified to receive educational benefits from the U.S. Department of Veterans Affairs. Applicants must be attending or planning to attend a community college, branch of the California State University system, or campus of the University of California.

Financial data Full-time college students receive a waiver of tuition and registration fees at any publicly-supported community or state college or university in California.

Duration Children of eligible veterans may receive postsecondary benefits until the needed training is completed or until the dependent reaches 27 years of age (extended to 30 if the dependent serves in the armed forces). Widow(er)s and spouses are limited to a maximum of 48 months' full-time training or the equivalent in part-time training.

Number awarded Varies each year.

[1056]
CALIFORNIA P.E.O. SCHOLARSHIPS

P.E.O. Foundation-California State Chapter
c/o Liz Wetzel
1887 Rim Rock Canyon Road
Laguna Beach, CA 92651
(949) 376-1568   E-mail: elwglw@cox.net

Purpose To provide financial assistance to undergraduate and graduate school women in California whose education has been interrupted.

Eligibility This program is open to female residents of California who have completed 4 years of high school (or the equivalent), are enrolled at or accepted by an accredited college, university, vocational school, or graduate school, and have an excellent academic record. Selection is based on financial need, character, academic ability, and school and community activities.

Financial data Stipends range from $200 to $4,000.

Duration 1 year; may be renewed for up to 3 additional years.

Additional information This program includes the following named scholarships: the Barbara Furse Mackey Scholarship (for women whose education has been interrupted); the Beverly Dye Anderson Scholarship (for the fields of teaching or health care); the Marjorie M. McDonald P.E.O. Scholarship (for women who are continuing their education after a long hiatus from school); the Ora Keck Scholarship (for women who are preparing for a career in music or the fine arts); the Phyllis J. Van Deventer Scholarship (for women who are preparing for a career in music performance or music education); the Stella May Nau Scholarship (for women who are interested in reentering the job market); the Linda Jones Memorial Fine Arts Scholarship (for women studying fine arts); the Polly Thompson Memorial Music Scholarship (for women studying music); the Ruby W. Henry Scholarship; the Jean W. Gratiot Scholarship; the Pearl Prime Scholarship; and the Helen D. Thompson Memorial Scholarship.

Number awarded Varies each year; recently, 18 of these scholarships were awarded.

Deadline February of each year.

[1057]
CAPITAL DISTRICT 3 SCHOLARSHIPS

American Hellenic Educational Progressive Association-District 03
c/o Nicholas Vamvakias, District Marshall
5102 Gainsborough Drive
Fairfax, VA 22032-2709
(703) 323-7153   E-mail: nickpvamvakias@aol.com
Web: www.district3ahepa.com/scholarship.html

Purpose To provide financial assistance to high school seniors and current college students whose parents are members of organizations affiliated with the American Hellenic Educational Progressive Association (AHEPA) in its District 3 (Maryland, North Carolina, Virginia, Washington, D.C., and West Virginia).

Eligibility This program is open to high school seniors and current full-time undergraduates who are residents of Maryland, North Carolina, Virginia, Washington, D.C., or West Virginia. Applicants must be the children (not nieces, nephews, grandchildren, or other relatives) of a member of the Order of Ahepa, the Daughters of Penelope, the Maids of Athena, or the Sons of Pericles. They must have a GPA of 2.5 or higher. Along with their application, they must submit an essay of 300 words or less on the value of a college education. For high school seniors and first-year college students, selection is based on the essay (30 points), SAT score (10 points), class standing (10 points), GPA (20 points), National Honor Society (10 points), and honors and extracurricular activities (20 points). For upper-division college students, selection is based on the essay (30 points), GPA (40 points), dean's list (10 points), honors and extracurricular activities (10 points), and part-time employment (10 points). Applicants may also request to have financial need considered.

Financial data A stipend is awarded (amount not specified).

Duration 1 year; recipients are eligible to receive a maximum of 2 undergraduate scholarships and 1 graduate scholarship.

Number awarded Varies each year.

Deadline March of each year.

[1058]
CAPTAIN CALIENDO COLLEGE ASSISTANCE FUND SCHOLARSHIP

U.S. Coast Guard Chief Petty Officers Association
Attn: CCCAF Scholarship Committee
5520-G Hempstead Way
Springfield, VA 22151-4009
(703) 941-0395   Fax: (703) 941-0397
E-mail: cgcpoa@aol.com
Web: www.uscgcpoa.org

Purpose To recognize and reward, with college scholarships, children of members or deceased members of the U.S. Coast Guard Chief Petty Officers Association (CPOA) or the Coast Guard Enlisted Association (CGEA) who submit outstanding essays.

Eligibility This competition is open to children of members or deceased members of the CPOA or CGEA who are attending or planning to attend a college, university, or vocational school. Applicants may not be older than 24 years of age (the age limit does not apply to disabled children). They must submit an essay, up to 500 words, on a topic that changes annually; a recent topic was "What impact does the Patriot Act make on you and your community?" The author of the essay judged most outstanding receives this scholarship.

Financial data The award is a $3,500 scholarship.

Duration The competition is held annually.

Number awarded 1 each year.

Deadline February of each year.

[1059]
CARPE DIEM SCHOLARSHIPS

Carpe Diem Foundation of Illinois
Attn: Executive Director
P.O. Box 3194
Chicago, IL 60690-3194
E-mail: glevine@carpediemfoundation.org
Web: www.carpediemfoundation.org

Purpose To provide financial assistance to entering or continuing undergraduate students, especially those whose families have demonstrated a commitment to public service.

Eligibility This program is open to high school seniors and college freshmen, sophomores, or juniors. High school seniors and college freshmen do not need to have declared a major, but they should have a vision for the future and be able to describe their role in pursuing their goals. Applicants must submit 1) a 200-word essay on their accomplishments during high school in which they take the greatest pride; 2) a 200-word essay on their family, especially with regard to service occupations and involvement in community organizations; and 3) a 500-word essay explaining why they have chosen their course of study. Music and art applicants must also submit samples of their work. Preference is given to students whose parents are or have been employed in public service positions, including education; local, state, or federal government; social service; public health (including medical providers); the administration of justice; and the fine arts. Selection is based on demonstrated leadership, community service, character, academics, and potential to improve the quality of human life. Applicants must be U.S. citizens, but they may be residents of any state.

Financial data Stipends range from $2,500 to $5,000 per year.

Duration 1 year; may be renewed for up to 3 additional years if the recipient maintains a GPA of "B+" or higher, full-time enrollment, and participation in activities that improve the quality of the academic and social life of their community.

Additional information This program was established in 2002. There is a $14.25 application fee.

Number awarded Varies each year; recently, 18 of these scholarships were awarded.

Deadline May of each year.

[1060]
CHINESE AMERICAN CITIZENS ALLIANCE FOUNDATION SCHOLARSHIPS

Chinese American Citizens Alliance
Attn: Scholarship Foundation
763 Yale Street
Los Angeles, CA 90012
(213) 628-6368
Web: www.cacanational.org/foundation-scholar.html

Purpose To provide financial assistance to Chinese American undergraduate students at colleges and universities in California.

Eligibility This program is open to students of Chinese descent who have completed the sophomore year at a college or university in California. Applicants must provide information on their volunteer work, accomplishments and honors received in college, organizational membership and offices held, previous scholarship awards, career plans, and how they will benefit from the scholarship. Financial need is not considered. Applicants must be available for an in-person interview in Los Angeles.

Financial data The stipend is $1,000.

Duration 1 year.

Additional information This program consists of the following named scholarships: the Yoke Quong Jung Memorial Scholarship, the Huan Lin Cheng Memorial Scholarship, the Y.C. Hong Memorial Scholarship, the Collin and Susan Lai Scholarship, the Julian and Eleanor Sue Scholarship, and the Robert and Edith Jung Scholarship.

Number awarded 6 each year.

Deadline June of each year.

[1061]
CHRISTINE O. GREGOIRE YOUTH/YOUNG ADULT AWARD

American Legacy Foundation
2030 M Street, N.W., Sixth Floor
Washington, DC 20036
(202) 454-5555   Fax: (202) 454-5999
E-mail: awards@americanlegacy.org
Web: www.americanlegacy.org/awards

Purpose To recognize and reward young people who contribute to the health of the public through use of tobacco documents.

Eligibility This competition is open to people under 24 years of age who use documents provided by the tobacco industry to further the goals of tobacco prevention and control. Nominees should have made a notable impact through innovative use of tobacco industry documents as applied to research, policy, or advocacy. Letters of nomination should be accompanied by 250-word statements on 1) the nominee's involvement with the tobacco control field; 2) what makes their use of tobacco industry documents unique and innovative for policy, advocacy, or research; 3) how their work has raised awareness or demonstrated leadership among their peer group; 4) any lessons that are applicable to other potential uses of documents in research, policy, or advocacy; and 5) how the challenges faced by the nominee relate to advancing or promoting the use of tobacco industry documents.

Financial data The award is $7,500.

Duration The award is presented annually.

Number awarded 1 each year.

Deadline July of each year.

[1062]
CHUCK HALL STAR OF TOMORROW AWARD

United States Bowling Congress
Attn: SMART Program
5301 South 76th Street
Greendale, WI 53129-1192
(414) 423-3343   Toll-free: (800) 514-BOWL, ext. 3343
Fax: (414) 421-3014   E-mail: smart@bowl.com
Web: www.bowl.com/scholarships/main.aspx

Purpose To provide financial assistance for college to outstanding male bowlers.

Eligibility This program is open to men amateur bowlers who are current members in good standing of the United States Bowling Congress (USBC) or USBC Youth and competitors in events sanctioned by those organizations. Applicants must be high school or college students younger than 22 years of age, have a GPA of 2.5 or higher, and have a bowling average of 175 or greater. They may not have competed in a professional bowling tournament. Along with their application, they must submit an essay, up to 500 words, on how bowling has influenced their life, academic, and personal goals. Selection is based on bowling performances on local, state, and national levels; academic achievement; and community involvement.

Financial data The stipend is $1,250 per year.

Duration 1 year; may be renewed up to 3 additional years.

Number awarded 1 each year.

Deadline November of each year.

[1063]
CIVIL AIR PATROL ACADEMIC SCHOLARSHIPS

Civil Air Patrol
Attn: Scholarship Committee
105 South Hansell Street
Maxwell Air Force Base, AL 36112-6332
(334) 953-5315   Toll-free: (877) 227-9142, ext. 324
Fax: (334) 953-5235   E-mail: keasterling@cap.gov
Web: level2.cap.gov/index.cfm?nodeID=5589

Purpose To provide financial assistance to Civil Air Patrol (CAP) members who are interested in working on a vocational, undergraduate, or graduate degree.

Eligibility This program is open to 1) CAP cadets who have received the Billy Mitchell Award and 2) CAP senior members who received the Billy Mitchell Award as a cadet or received the Senior Rating in Cadet Programs Specialty Track of the Senior Training Program. Applicants must be a high school graduate or have a GED certificate and must have been accepted at an accredited vocational/technical school, college, or university. They may be eligible for 4 types of scholarships: undergraduate (for students who have completed less than 60 credit hours), advanced undergraduate (for students who have completed at least 60 credit hours), graduate, or vocational/technical. Selection is based on academic achievement, CAP accomplishments and activities, and extracurricular or community service activities.

Financial data Stipends range from $250 to $1,000 per year.

Duration 1 year; may be renewed if the recipient maintains good academic standing as a full-time student.

Number awarded Varies each year. Recently, 93 of these scholarships were awarded: 3 at $1,000, 8 at $750, 22 at $500, and 60 at $250.

Deadline January of each year.

[1064]
CIVIL AIR PATROL USAA SCHOLARSHIPS
Civil Air Patrol
Attn: Scholarship Committee
105 South Hansell Street
Maxwell Air Force Base, AL 36112-6332
(334) 953-5315   Toll-free: (877) 227-9142, ext. 324
Fax: (334) 953-5235   E-mail: keasterling@cap.gov
Web: level2.cap.gov/index.cfm?nodeID=5589

Purpose To provide financial assistance to Civil Air Patrol (CAP) members who are interested in working on an undergraduate or graduate degree on a full-time basis.

Eligibility This program is open to 1) CAP cadets who have received the Billy Mitchell Award and 2) CAP senior members who received the Billy Mitchell Award as a cadet or received the Senior Rating in Cadet Programs Specialty Track of the Senior Training Program. Applicants must be a high school graduate or have a GED certificate and must have been accepted at a college or university. The top applicants for CAP scholarships at the undergraduate, graduate, or vocational school level are awarded these scholarships. Selection is based on academic achievement, CAP accomplishments and activities, and extracurricular or community service activities.

Financial data The stipend is $1,000.

Duration 1 year.

Additional information This program is sponsored by USAA Insurance Corporation.

Number awarded Varies each year; recently, 3 of these scholarships were awarded.

Deadline January of each year.

[1065]
CLARA E. LIVINGSTON CADET SCHOLARSHIP
Civil Air Patrol
Attn: Scholarship Committee
105 South Hansell Street
Maxwell Air Force Base, AL 36112-6332
(334) 953-5315   Toll-free: (877) 227-9142, ext. 324
Fax: (334) 953-5235   E-mail: keasterling@cap.gov
Web: level2.cap.gov/index.cfm?nodeID=5589

Purpose To provide financial assistance for college or other educational activities to Civil Air Patrol (CAP) members from Puerto Rico.

Eligibility This program is open to CAP cadets from Puerto Rico who have received the Billy Mitchell Award. Applicants must be a high school graduate or have a GED certificate. They must be seeking funding for a program of preparation and training for any field, including flying, the professions, academics, business, manual arts, or for travel that will expand their horizons. Selection is based on a transcript of high school credits, a transcript of college credits (if applicable), college entrance examination scores, and activities in CAP, high school, and college.

Financial data The stipend is $4,000.

Duration 1 year.

Number awarded 1 each year.

Deadline January of each year.

[1066]
CLIFTON SCHOLARSHIP FUND
Hawai'i Community Foundation
Attn: Scholarship Department
1164 Bishop Street, Suite 800
Honolulu, HI 96813
(808) 566-5570   Toll-free: (888) 731-3863
Fax: (808) 521-6286
E-mail: scholarships@hcf-hawaii.org
Web: www.hawaiicommunityfoundation.org

Purpose To provide financial assistance to residents of Hawaii who are interested in enrolling in a vocational training program in the state.

Eligibility This program is open to residents of Hawaii who are attending or planning to attend a vocational college or institution that is part of the University of Hawaii community college system. Programs include culinary arts, auto repair, diesel mechanics, cosmetology, computer graphics, and assistive medical technology. Applicants must submit a personal statement explaining their personal background and interests, the vocational program they plan to pursue, their career goals, and anything else that demonstrates their worthiness to receive this scholarship. Financial need is not considered in the selection process.

Financial data The stipend is $500 per semester. Funds are mailed directly to the financial aid office at the recipient's institution.

Duration 1 semester; may be renewed for up to 3 additional semesters.

Additional information This program began in 2006.

Number awarded Varies each year.

Deadline June of each year for fall and spring semester scholarships; September of each year for spring semester scholarships.

[1067]
COCA-COLA TWO-YEAR COLLEGE SCHOLARSHIPS
Coca-Cola Scholars Foundation, Inc.
P.O. Box 1615
Atlanta, GA 30301-1615
Toll-free: (800) 306-COKE   Fax: (404) 733-5439
E-mail: questions@coca-colascholars.org
Web: www.coca-colascholars.org

Purpose To provide financial assistance to students at 2-year colleges.

Eligibility This program is open to U.S. citizens and permanent residents who are nominated by the 2-year degree-granting institution they are attending. Applicants must have a GPA of 2.5 or higher and be able to document at least 100 hours of community service they have performed in the past 12 months. They must be planning to enroll in at least 2 courses during the next term. Selection is based on merit.

Financial data The stipend is $1,000.

Duration 1 year; nonrenewable.

Additional information This program was established in 2000 through a grant from the Joseph B. Whitehead Foundation.

Number awarded 400 each year.

Deadline May of each year.

ANY SUBJECT AREA

[1068] COHEAO SCHOLARSHIPS

Coalition of Higher Education Assistance Organizations
c/o Dean, Blakey, and Moskowitz
1101 Vermont Avenue, N.W., Suite 400
Washington, DC 20005-3586
(202) 289-3910 Fax: (202) 371-0197
Web: www.coheao.org/scholarship/scholarship.asp

Purpose To provide financial assistance to students at colleges and universities that are members of the Coalition of Higher Education Assistance Organizations (COHEAO).

Eligibility This program is open to students entering their sophomore, junior, or senior year at a member institution. Applicants must have a GPA of 3.75 or higher and be a U.S. citizen. Along with their application, they must submit a 300-word essay on their future plans and goals, and how this scholarship will benefit them. Financial need is not considered in the selection process.

Financial data The stipend is $1,000.

Duration 1 year.

Additional information This program was established in 1994. Information on this program is available only through the Internet, not the mail.

Number awarded Up to 8 each year.

Deadline March of each year.

[1069] COLIN HIGGINS FOUNDATION YOUTH COURAGE AWARDS

Colin Higgins Foundation
Attn: Youth Courage Awards
P.O. Box 29903
San Francisco, CA 94129-0903
(415) 561-6350 Fax: (415) 561-6401
E-mail: info@colinhiggins.org
Web: www.colinhiggins.org/courageawards/index.cfm

Purpose To recognize and reward young people who have shown courage in the face of adversity related to discrimination against members of the lesbian, gay, bisexual, transgender, and questioning (LGBTQ) communities.

Eligibility Eligible to be nominated for these awards are young people under 24 years of age who are 1) LGBTQ youth who have "bravely stood up to hostility and intolerance based on their sexual orientation and triumphed over bigotry;" or 2) allies who are working to end homophobia and discrimination against LGBTQ communities. Letters of nomination must include 350-word essays describing why the nominee represents the ideals of this award. Self-nominations are not accepted.

Financial data The award is a $10,000 grant.

Duration The awards are presented annually.

Additional information This award program was established in 2000.

Number awarded 2 or 3 each year.

Deadline March of each year.

[1070] COLORADO FEDERATION OF NARFE

Colorado Federation of NARFE Chapters
c/o Federal Employee Education and Assistance Fund
Attn: Scholarship Program
8441 West Bowles Avenue, Suite 200
Littleton, CO 80123-9501
(303) 933-7580 Toll-free: (800) 323-4140
Fax: (303) 933-7587 E-mail: admin@feea.org
Web: www.feea.org/schol_info/specialschols.html

Purpose To provide financial assistance for college or graduate school to children and grandchildren of federal employees in Colorado.

Eligibility This program is open to the college-bound children and grandchildren of federal employees who are graduating from high schools in Colorado. Membership in the National Active and Retired Federal Employees Association (NARFE) is not required. Applicants or their sponsoring federal employee must have at least 3 years of civilian federal service. Dependents must be full-time students; federal employees may be part-time students. Along with their application, they must submit a 2-page essay on a topic related to a career in public service with the federal government, a letter of recommendation, a transcript with a GPA of 3.0 or higher, and a copy of their federal "Notice of Personnel Action;" high school seniors must also submit a copy of their ACT, SAT, or other examination scores. Financial need is not considered in the selection process.

Financial data The stipend is $1,000 per year.

Duration 1 year; may be renewed.

Additional information This program is jointly administered with the Colorado Federation of Federal Employee Education and Assistance Fund (FEEA).

Number awarded 1 or more each year.

Deadline March of each year.

[1071] COMMONWEALTH "GOOD CITIZEN" SCHOLARSHIPS

Association of Independent Colleges and Universities of Pennsylvania
101 North Front Street
Harrisburg, PA 17101-1405
(717) 232-8649 Fax: (717) 233-8574
E-mail: info@aicup.org
Web: www.aicup.org

Purpose To provide financial assistance to students at member institutions of the Association of Independent Colleges and Universities of Pennsylvania (AICUP) who have demonstrated outstanding commitment to community service.

Eligibility This program is open to full-time undergraduate students at AICUP colleges and universities. Applicants must have shown an extraordinary commitment to community service and have demonstrated creativity in shaping their volunteer activities. As part of their application, they must submit a 2-page essay on their volunteer or extracurricular activities on and off campus, how those activities relate to their major, their career and academic goals after graduation, and how they will remain involved in their community after graduation. Selection is based on the extent of their volunteer and community service activities (30%), leadership activities and taking initiative (30%), evidence of commitment to community service (30%), and additional material, such as reference letters (10%). There is no minimum GPA requirement; grades are considered only in the event of a tie. Applications must be submitted to the financial aid office at the AICUP college or university that the student attends.

Financial data The stipend is $1,000.

Duration 1 year.

Additional information The AICUP includes 83 private colleges and universities in Pennsylvania. For a list of those institutions, contact AICUP.

Number awarded Varies each year; recently, 6 of these scholarships were awarded.

Deadline April of each year.

[1072]
CONNECTICUT NATIONAL GUARD FOUNDATION SCHOLARSHIPS

Connecticut National Guard Foundation, Inc.
Attn: Scholarship Committee
360 Broad Street
Hartford, CT 06105-3795
(860) 241-1550   Fax: (860) 293-2929
E-mail: scholarship.committee@ctngfoundation.org
Web: www.ctngfoundation.org/Scholarship.asp

Purpose To provide financial assistance for college to members of the Connecticut National Guard and their families.

Eligibility This program is open to members of the Connecticut Army National Guard and Organized Militia, their children, and their spouses. Applicants must be enrolled or planning to enroll in an accredited college degree or technical program. Along with their application, they must submit a letter of recommendation, list of extracurricular activities, high school or college transcripts, and a 200-word statement on their educational and future goals. Selection is based on achievement and citizenship.

Financial data The stipend is $1,500.

Duration 1 year.

Number awarded 3 each year.

Deadline April of each year.

[1073]
DANA CHRISTMAS SCHOLARSHIP FOR HEROISM

New Jersey Higher Education Student Assistance Authority
Attn: Financial Aid Services
4 Quakerbridge Plaza
P.O. Box 540
Trenton, NJ 08625-0540
(609) 588-2349   Toll-free: (800) 792-8670
Fax: (609) 588-3450   E-mail: gjoachim@hesaa.org
Web: www.hesaa.org

Purpose To provide financial assistance for college or graduate school to residents of New Jersey who have performed an act of heroism.

Eligibility This program is open to U.S. citizens and eligible noncitizens who are New Jersey residents and have performed an act of heroism when they were 21 years of age or younger. Both applications and nominations from others are required. Letters of nomination must be accompanied by a description of the act of heroism, including such additional documentation as newspaper articles. Nominees must be enrolled or planning to enroll as an undergraduate or graduate student at an institution eligible to participate in the federal Title IV student aid programs.

Financial data The stipend is $10,000.

Duration 1 year; nonrenewable.

Additional information This program was established in 2001 to honor Dana Christmas, the Seton Hall resident advisor whose heroism saved many lives during the dormitory fire on January 19, 2001. Recipients who are not yet of college age will have their funds held in escrow until they enroll in postsecondary education.

Number awarded 5 each year.

Deadline May of each year for students who received a Tuition Aid Grant in the preceding year; September of each year for new applicants for fall term; February of each year for new applicants for spring term only.

[1074]
DAUGHTERS OF PENELOPE CITRUS DISTRICT 2 SCHOLARSHIPS

Daughters of Penelope-District 2
c/o Sophie Caras
6511 Lake Clark Drive
Palm Beach, FL 33406
(561) 582-9619   E-mail: sophieh@adelphia.net
Web: www.ahepad2.org

Purpose To provide financial assistance for college or graduate school to women who are residents of Florida or the Bahamas and members of organizations affiliated with the American Hellenic Educational Progressive Association (AHEPA).

Eligibility This program is open to women who are residents of Citrus District 2 (Florida and the Bahamas) and high school seniors, undergraduates, or graduate students with a high school or college GPA of 3.0 or higher. Applicants must have been a member of the Maids of Athena for at least 2 years or have an immediate family member who has belonged to the Daughters of Penelope or Order of Ahepa for at least 2 years. They must submit a personal essay of 200 to 500 words to give the selection committee a sense of their goals and personal effort. Selection is based on merit.

Financial data A stipend is awarded (amount not specified).

Duration 1 year; may be renewed.

Additional information This program includes the Past District Governors/Julie P. Microutsicos Scholarship, awarded to the runner-up.

Number awarded 2 each year.

Deadline May of each year.

[1075]
DAUGHTERS OF PENELOPE UNDERGRADUATE SCHOLARSHIPS

Daughters of Penelope
Attn: Daughters of Penelope Foundation, Inc.
1909 Q Street, N.W., Suite 500
Washington, DC 20009-1007
(202) 234-9741   Fax: (202) 483-6983
E-mail: daughters@ahepa.org
Web: www.ahepa.org

Purpose To provide financial assistance for college to women of Greek descent.

Eligibility This program is open to women who have been members of the Daughters of Penelope or the Maids of Athena for at least 2 years, or whose parents or grandparents have been members of the Daughters of Penelope or the Order of Ahepa for at least 2 years. Applicants must be 1) high school seniors or recent high school graduates applying to a college, university, or accredited technical school, or 2) current undergraduates at the college level. They must have taken the SAT or ACT (or Canadian, Greek, or Cypriot equivalent) and must write an essay (in English) about their educational and vocational goals. Selection is based on academic merit only.

Financial data Stipends are $1,500 or $1,000 per year.

Duration 1 year; nonrenewable.

Additional information This program includes the following endowed awards: the Daughters of Penelope Past Grand Presidents' Memorial Scholarship, the Kottis Family Scholarship, the Mary M. Verges Scholarship, the Joanne V. Hologgitas, Ph.D. Scholarship, the Eos #1 Mother Lodge Chapter Scholarship, and the Paula J. Alexander Memorial Scholarship. Information is also available from Helen Santire, National Scholarship Chair, P.O. Box 19709, Houston, TX 77242-9709, (713) 468-6531.

Number awarded Varies each year. Recently, 9 of these scholarships were awarded: 1 at $1,500 and 8 at $1,000.

Deadline May of each year.

[1076]
DAVID M. IRWIN FRIEND OF HIGHER EDUCATION AWARD

Independent Colleges of Washington
600 Stewart Street, Suite 600
Seattle, WA 98101
(206) 623-4494   Fax: (206) 625-9621
E-mail: info@icwashington.org
Web: www.icwashington.org

Purpose To provide financial assistance to upper-division students enrolled at colleges and universities that are members of Independent Colleges of Washington (ICW).

Eligibility This program is open to students completing their sophomore or junior year at ICW-member colleges and universities. Applicants must submit a 1-page essay on how their education at this college will impact their career choice. Selection is based on leadership qualities. Students with a cumulative GPA between 2.5 and 3.0 are encouraged to apply.

Financial data The stipend is $1,000.

Duration 1 year; nonrenewable.

Additional information The ICW-member institutions are Gonzaga University, Heritage College, Pacific Lutheran University, Saint Martin's College, Seattle Pacific University, Seattle University, University of Puget Sound, Walla Walla College, Whitman College, and Whitworth College. This program was established in 1998.

Number awarded 1 each year.

Deadline March of each year.

[1077]
DEDICATED ARMY NATIONAL GUARD (DEDARNG) SCHOLARSHIPS

U.S. Army
ROTC Cadet Command
Attn: ATCC-OP-I-S
55 Patch Road, Building 56
Fort Monroe, VA 23651-1052
(757) 727-4558   Toll-free: (800) USA-ROTC
E-mail: atccps@usaac.army.mil
Web: www.rotc.usaac.army.mil

Purpose To provide financial assistance to college and graduate students who are interested in enrolling in Army ROTC and serve in the Army National Guard following graduation.

Eligibility This program is open to full-time students entering their junior year of college with a GPA of 2.5 or higher. Graduate students are also eligible if they have only 2 years remaining for completion of their graduate degree. Students who have been awarded an ROTC campus-based scholarship may apply to convert to this program during their freshman year. Applicants must meet all medical and moral character requirements for enrollment in Army ROTC. They must be willing to enroll in the Simultaneous Membership Program (SMP) of an ROTC unit on their campus; the SMP requires simultaneous membership in Army ROTC and the Army National Guard.

Financial data Participants receive reimbursement of tuition (up to $28,000 per year), a grant of $600 per year for books, plus an ROTC stipend for 10 months of the year at $350 per month during their junior year and $400 per month during their senior year. As a member of the Army National Guard, they also receive weekend drill pay at the pay grade of E-5 during their junior year or E-6 during their senior year.

Duration Normally 2 years. Students who convert to this program may be eligible for support up to 4 years.

Additional information After graduation, participants serve 3 to 6 months on active duty in the Officer Basic Course (OBC). Following completion of OBC, they are released from active duty and are obligated to serve 8 years in the Army National Guard.

Number awarded 594 each year (11 in each state or U.S. territory).

[1078]
DEPARTMENT OF HOMELAND SECURITY UNDERGRADUATE SCHOLARSHIPS

Oak Ridge Institute for Science and Education
Attn: Science and Engineering Education
P.O. Box 117
Oak Ridge, TN 37831-0117
(865) 576-8239　　　　　Fax: (865) 241-5219
E-mail: igrid.gregory@orau.gov
Web: www.orau.gov/orise.htm

Purpose To provide financial assistance and summer research experience to undergraduate students who are working on a degree in a field of interest to the Department of Homeland Security (DHS).

Eligibility This program is open to 1) full-time students who are in their second year of college as of the application deadline; and 2) part-time students who have completed at least 45 but no more than 60 semester hours as of the application deadline. Applicants must be majoring in the agricultural sciences, biological and life sciences, computer and information sciences, engineering, mathematics, physical sciences, psychology, social sciences, or selected humanities (religious studies, cultural studies, public policy, advocacy, communications, or science writing). They must have a GPA of 3.3 or higher. Along with their application, they must submit 2 statements on 1) their educational and professional goals, the kinds of research they are interested in conducting, specific questions that interest them, and how they became interested in them; and 2) how they think their interests, talents, and initiative would contribute to make the homeland safer and secure. Selection is based on those statements, academic record, references, and SAT or ACT scores, As part of their program, they must be interested in participating in summer research and development activities at a DHS-designated facility. U.S. citizenship is required.

Financial data This program provides a stipend of $1,000 per month during the academic year and $5,000 for the internship plus full payment of tuition and mandatory fees.

Duration 2 academic years plus 10 weeks during the intervening summer.

Additional information This program, established in 2003, is funded by DHS and administered by Oak Ridge Institute for Science and Education (ORISE). Recipients must enroll full time.

Number awarded Approximately 50 each year.

Deadline January of each year.

[1079]
DESCENDANTS OF THE SIGNERS OF THE DECLARATION OF INDEPENDENCE SCHOLARSHIPS

Descendants of the Signers of the Declaration of Independence
c/o Mrs. Leslie Pickett Sheehan, Scholarship Chair
P.O. Box 8223
Savannah, GA 31412
E-mail: Lsheehan302@comcast.net
Web: www.dsdi1776.com

Purpose To provide financial assistance for college or graduate school to members of the Society for Descendants of the Signers of the Declaration of Independence (DSDI).

Eligibility Eligible are high school seniors planning to attend a 4-year college or university in the United States on a full-time basis or current full-time undergraduate or graduate students. Membership in the society is required. Applications must include high school and college transcripts, 3 letters of recommendation, a list of extracurricular activities, and proof of direct lineal descent from a signer of the Declaration of Independence. Selection is based on merit.

Financial data Stipends generally average $1,500.

Duration 1 year; recipients may reapply.

Number awarded Varies each year; recently, 19 of these scholarships were awarded.

Deadline March of each year.

[1080]
DR. JOHN C. YAVIS SCHOLARSHIPS

American Hellenic Educational Progressive Association
Attn: AHEPA Educational Foundation
1909 Q Street, N.W., Suite 500
Washington, DC 20009
(202) 232-6300　　　　　Fax: (202) 232-2140
E-mail: ahepa@ahepa.org
Web: www.ahepa.org

Purpose To provide financial assistance to high school, undergraduate, and graduate students with a connection to the American Hellenic Educational Progressive Association (AHEPA).

Eligibility This program is open to 1) members in good standing of the Order of Ahepa, Daughters of Penelope, Sons of Pericles, or Maids of Athena, and 2) the children of Order of Ahepa or Daughters of Penelope members in good standing. Applicants must be currently enrolled or planning to enroll as undergraduate or graduate students. High school seniors must submit their most recent official transcript as well as SAT or ACT scores; college freshmen and sophomores must submit high school transcripts, SAT or ACT scores, and their most recent college transcript; college juniors and seniors must submit their most recent college transcript; graduate students must submit college transcripts, GRE or MCAT scores (if available), and their most recent graduate school transcript. Along with their application, they must also submit a 500-word biographical essay. Selection is based on academic achievement; extracurricular, personal, and volunteer activities; athletic achievements; and work experience. Financial need is not considered.

Financial data Stipends range from $500 to $2,000 per year.

Duration 1 year.

Additional information A processing fee of $20 must accompany each application.

Number awarded Varies each year; recently, 2 of these scholarships were awarded.

Deadline March of each year.

[1081]
DR. NICHOLAS S. DICAPRIO SCHOLARSHIP

American Council of the Blind
Attn: Coordinator, Scholarship Program
1155 15th Street, N.W., Suite 1004
Washington, DC 20005
(202) 467-5081   Toll-free: (800) 424-8666
Fax: (202) 467-5085   E-mail: info@acb.org
Web: www.acb.org

Purpose To provide financial assistance to outstanding blind undergraduates.

Eligibility Eligible to apply for this scholarship are legally blind U.S. citizens or resident aliens who are undergraduate students. In addition to letters of recommendation and copies of academic transcripts, applications must include an autobiographical sketch. A cumulative GPA of 3.3 or higher is generally required. Selection is based on demonstrated academic record, involvement in extracurricular and civic activities, and academic objectives. The severity of the applicant's visual impairment and his/her study methods are also taken into account.

Financial data The stipend is $2,500. In addition, the winner receives a Kurzweil-1000 Reading System.

Duration 1 year.

Additional information The scholarship winner is expected to be present at the council's annual national convention; the council will cover all reasonable costs connected with convention attendance.

Number awarded 1 each year.

Deadline February of each year.

[1082]
DR. RICHARD CHINN SCHOLARSHIP

American Atheists
P.O. Box 5733
Parsippany, NJ 07054-6733
(908) 276-7300   Fax: (908) 276-7402
E-mail: info@atheists.org
Web: www.atheists.org/family/temp/scholarship

Purpose To provide financial assistance for college to gay and lesbian students who identify themselves as atheists.

Eligibility This program is open to college-bound high school seniors and current college students. Applicants must be lesbian or gay, be atheists, and have a cumulative GPA of 2.5 or higher. Selection is based on activism, with special attention given to students who show activism in their schools (e.g., starting atheist/freethinker groups, fighting against violations of the separation of church and state in the school).

Financial data The stipend is $1,000.

Duration 1 year.

Additional information Information is also available from the American Atheists Scholarship Fund, 1308 Centennial Avenue, Suite 101, Piscataway, NJ 08854. The scholarship is also designated the American Atheists Gay/Lesbian College Scholarship (AAGLCS). The funding includes $500 donated by Dr. Richard Chinn and $500 in matching funds from American Atheists.

Number awarded 1 each year.

Deadline January of each year.

[1083]
DUMITRU GOLEA GOLDY-GEMU SCHOLARSHIPS

Romanian Orthodox Episcopate of America
Attn: Scholarship Committee
P.O. Box 309
Grass Lake, MI 49240-0309
(517) 522-3656   Fax: (517) 522-5907
E-mail: roeasolia@aol.com
Web: www.roea.org/schol/schol-goldy.htm

Purpose To provide financial assistance for college to students of Romanian origin.

Eligibility This program is open to students of Romanian origin who are citizens or permanent residents of the United States or Canada. Applicants may be 1) high school seniors who have completed a college preparatory course, have taken the SAT or ACT examination, have taken or arranged to take a College Entrance Board Examination (CEEB), and are in the upper third of their class; 2) undergraduate students enrolled full time at a 4-year college or university; or 3) students returning to college full time after an interruption in their education. Along with their application, they must submit a 300-word essay on how their Romanian heritage helps make them a better American/Canadian. Selection is based on the essay, academic achievement, extracurricular activities, honors received, community activities, and character; financial need is not considered.

Financial data The stipend is $1,500.

Duration 1 year; may be renewed up to 3 additional years.

Number awarded 1 or more each year.

Deadline May of each year.

[1084]
DWAA JUNIORS EDUCATIONAL AWARD

Dog Writers Association of America
c/o Pat Santi, Secretary
173 Union Road
Coatesville, PA 19320
(610) 384-2436   Fax: (610) 384-2471
E-mail: dwaa@dwaa.org
Web: www.dwaa.org

Purpose To recognize and reward college students who submit outstanding essays related to their experience with dogs.

Eligibility This competition is open to students between 18 and 22 years of age. Applicants must have a GPA of 3.0 or higher. They must submit 3 samples of dog-related writing that have been published (but not necessarily paid for). They are also expected to have experience with dogs, documented by letters of recommendation. Selection is based on grades (25%), dog experience (25%), and writing (50%).

Financial data Awards range from $500 to $1,000.

Duration The competition is held annually. Winners may enter in following years.

Additional information Information is also available from Deb Eldredge, 4753 Deans Highway, Vernon, NY 13476, E-mail: Debme@juno.com.

Number awarded 1 to 3 each year.
Deadline September of each year.

[1085]
EAGLES MEMORIAL FOUNDATION EDUCATIONAL GRANTS FOR MILITARY AND OTHER SERVICE PERSONNEL

Fraternal Order of Eagles
Attn: Eagles Memorial Foundation
4710 14th Street West
Bradenton, FL 34207
(941) 758-5456   Fax: (941) 758-4042
Web: www.foe.com

Purpose To provide financial assistance for college to the children of deceased members of the Fraternal Order of Eagles or its Ladies Auxiliary who died in action.

Eligibility Applicants must be the minor (under 25 years of age) unmarried children of a deceased parent who was a member of the Fraternal Order of Eagles or its Ladies Auxiliary at the time of death; the member must have died from injuries or diseases incurred or aggravated in the line of duty while serving 1) in the armed forces of the United States or Canada; 2) as volunteer law enforcement officers in the United States; 3) as volunteer fire fighters; or 4) as volunteer emergency medical service officers.

Financial data Stipends up to $6,000 per school year are provided. Funds must be used for tuition, fees, books, and course-related supplies. Room and board expenses are not covered.

Duration 1 year; may be renewed for up to 4 additional years, provided the recipient maintains a GPA of 2.0 or higher and remains an unmarried dependent.

Number awarded Varies each year.

[1086]
EDEN SERVICES CHARLES H. HOENS, JR. SCHOLARS PROGRAM

Autism Society of America
Attn: Awards and Scholarships
7910 Woodmont Avenue, Suite 300
Bethesda, MD 20814-3015
(301) 657-0881   Toll-free: (800) 3-AUTISM
Fax: (301) 657-0869   E-mail: info@autism-society.org
Web: www.autism-society.org

Purpose To provide financial assistance for college to high school seniors, high school graduates, and college students with autism.

Eligibility This program is open to high school seniors or graduates who have been accepted to or are already enrolled in an accredited postsecondary school (college, trade school, etc.) and who have autism. Applicants must submit 3 copies of 1) documentation of their status as an individual with autism; 2) secondary school transcripts; 3) documentation of acceptance into an accredited postsecondary educational or vocational program of study; 4) 2 letters of recommendation; and 5) a 500-word statement outlining their qualifications and proposed plan of study. A telephone interview may be required.

Financial data The stipend is $1,000.

Duration 1 year.

Additional information This program was formerly known as the Ann M. Martin Scholarship.

Number awarded 1 each year.

Deadline February of each year.

[1087]
EDUCATION IS POWER SCHOLARSHIPS

MedProRx, Inc.
Attn: Scholarship Coordinator
8392 Six Forks Road. Suite 201
Raleigh, NC 27615-3061
Toll-free: (888) 571-3100   Fax: (800) 582-9315
E-mail: educationispower@medprorx.com
Web: www.medprorx.com/scholarship.php

Purpose To provide financial assistance for college to people with bleeding disorders.

Eligibility This program is open to people living with hemophilia, von Willebrand Disease, or other bleeding disorders. Applicants must be entering or attending a community college, junior college, 4-year college or university, or vocational school. Along with their application, they may choose to submit a 100-word essay on 1 of the following: 1) their dreams and aspirations; 2) what they are most passionate about; 3) how living with a bleeding disorder has affected their life; or 4) if they had the power to change something in the world, what it would be. Selection is based on that optional essay, letters of recommendation, and community involvement and/or volunteer work.

Financial data Stipends range from $500 to $2,500.

Duration 1 year.

Number awarded At least 8 each year.

Deadline April of each year.

[1088]
EDWIN W. GASTON, JR. SCHOLARSHIPS

Alpha Chi
Attn: Executive Director
900 East Center Avenue
Harding University Box 12249
Searcy, AR 72149-0001
(501) 279-4443   Toll-free: (800) 477-4225
Fax: (501) 279-4589   E-mail: dorgan@harding.edu
Web: www.harding.edu/alphachi/nolle.htm

Purpose To provide financial assistance for college to members of Alpha Chi, a national honor scholarship society.

Eligibility Eligible to be nominated for these funds are full-time college juniors who have been initiated into Alpha Chi; they must have 1 full year of college left before graduation. Only 2 nominations may be submitted by each chapter. Included in the nomination package must be an academic paper or other appropriate work in the student's major field (e.g., painting, music score, film, slides, video, cassette tape recording, or other medium). Students must also submit a letter of application outlining their plans for study and detailing their extracurricular activities. Financial need is not considered.

Financial data The stipend is $2,500.

Duration 1 year.

Additional information Recipients must be enrolled in college full time during the scholarship year.

Number awarded 2 each year.
Deadline February of each year.

[1089]
EL CAMINO REAL DISTRICT 20 SCHOLARSHIPS

American Hellenic Educational Progressive Association-District 20
Attn: El Camino Real Scholarship Foundation
c/o Catherine Vackrinos, Secretary
5710 Sugar Pine Drive
Yorba Linda, CA 92886
(714) 572-6147   E-mail: c.vackrinos@worldnet.att.net
Web: www.ahepa20.org/scholarship

Purpose To provide financial assistance for college to members and families of members of organizations affiliated with the American Hellenic Educational Progressive Association (AHEPA) in its District 20 (Arizona, southern California, parts of Nevada, and parts of Utah).

Eligibility This program is open to residents of Arizona, southern California, parts of Nevada, and parts of Utah who are 1) members of the Sons of Pericles or Maids of Athena, or 2) children of members of the Order of Ahepa or Daughters of Penelope. Applicants must be high school seniors planning to enter college in the following fall or already enrolled in a college or university with at least 12 semester hours completed for an undergraduate degree. High school seniors must have a GPA of 3.5 or higher; college freshmen, sophomores, and juniors must have a GPA of 3.4 or higher. Along with their application, they must submit an essay of 500 words or less describing their career aspirations, honors classes or activities, extracurricular or community activities, and participation in AHEPA family or church-related activities. Financial need is not considered in the selection process.

Financial data A stipend is awarded (amount not specified).

Duration 1 year; may be renewed up to 3 additional years.

Additional information This foundation began awarding scholarships in 1963. It includes the following named scholarships: the George Brotsis Memorial Scholarship, the John Dratos Memorial Scholarship, the Lt. Col. William L. Kokenes, USMC (Ret) Scholarship, the James Panousis Memorial Scholarship, the Peter John Peterson Memorial Scholarship, the Sam Platis Memorial Scholarship, the Frank Rhodes Scholarship, and the Peter Stevens Memorial Scholarship.

Number awarded Varies each year; recently, 15 of these scholarships were awarded.

Deadline February of each year.

[1090]
EUNICE FIORITO MEMORIAL SCHOLARSHIP

American Council of the Blind
Attn: Coordinator, Scholarship Program
1155 15th Street, N.W., Suite 1004
Washington, DC 20005
(202) 467-5081   Toll-free: (800) 424-8666
Fax: (202) 467-5085   E-mail: info@acb.org
Web: www.acb.org

Purpose To provide financial assistance to outstanding blind undergraduates.

Eligibility This program is open to legally blind U.S. citizens or resident aliens who are undergraduate students. Applicants must be planning to enter the advocacy/disability field. In addition to letters of recommendation and copies of academic transcripts, they must include an autobiographical sketch. A cumulative GPA of 3.3 or higher is generally required. Preference is given to students with little or no vision. Selection is based on demonstrated academic record, involvement in extracurricular and civic activities, and academic objectives. The severity of the applicant's visual impairment and his/her study methods are also taken into account.

Financial data The stipend is $2,000. In addition, the winner receives a Kurzweil-1000 Reading System.

Duration 1 year.

Additional information The scholarship winner is expected to be present at the council's annual national convention; the council will cover all reasonable costs connected with convention attendance.

Number awarded 1 each year.

Deadline February of each year.

[1091]
EXEMPTION FROM TUITION FEES FOR DEPENDENTS OF KENTUCKY VETERANS

Kentucky Department of Veterans Affairs
Attn: Division of Field Operations
545 South Third Street, Room 123
Louisville, KY 40202
(502) 595-4447   Toll-free: (800) 928-4012 (within KY)
Fax: (502) 595-4448
Web: www.kdva.net/tuitionwaiver.htm

Purpose To provide financial assistance for undergraduate or graduate education to the children or unremarried widow(er)s of deceased Kentucky veterans.

Eligibility This program is open to the children, stepchildren, adopted children, and unremarried widow(er)s of veterans who were residents of Kentucky when they entered military service or joined the Kentucky National Guard. The qualifying veteran must have been killed in action during a wartime period or died as a result of a service-connected disability incurred during a wartime period. Applicants must be attending or planning to attend a state-supported college or university in Kentucky to work on an undergraduate or graduate degree.

Financial data Eligible dependents and survivors are exempt from tuition and matriculation fees at any state-supported institution of higher education in Kentucky.

Duration There are no age or time limits on the waiver.

Number awarded Varies each year.

[1092]
FAAMA-FEEA SCHOLARSHIP PROGRAM
Federal Aviation Administration Managers Association
c/o Federal Employee Education and Assistance Fund
Attn: Scholarship Program
8441 West Bowles Avenue, Suite 200
Littleton, CO 80123-9501
(303) 933-7580   Toll-free: (800) 323-4140
Fax: (303) 933-7587   E-mail: admin@feea.org
Web: www.feea.org/schol_info/specialschols.html

Purpose To provide financial assistance for college or graduate school to members of the Federal Aviation Administration Managers Association (FAAMA) and their dependents.

Eligibility This program is open to FAAMA members and their spouses and children entering or enrolled in an accredited 2- or 4-year postsecondary, graduate, or postgraduate program. Applicants or their sponsoring federal employee must have at least 3 years of civilian federal service. Dependents must be full-time students; federal employees may be part-time students. Along with their application, they must submit a 2-page essay on a topic related to a career in public service with the federal government, a letter of recommendation, a transcript with a GPA of 3.0 or higher, and a copy of their federal "Notice of Personnel Action;" high school seniors must also submit a copy of their ACT, SAT, or other examination scores. Financial need is not considered in the selection process.

Financial data The stipend is $1,000 per year.

Duration 1 year; may be renewed.

Additional information This program is jointly administered by FAAMA and the Federal Employee Education and Assistance Fund (FEEA). Information is also available directly from FAAMA, 4410 Massachusetts Avenue, N.W., Washington, DC 20016, (202) 741-9415.

Number awarded Varies each year; recently, 11 of these scholarships were awarded.

Deadline March of each year.

[1093]
FABRICATORS AND MANUFACTURERS ASSOCIATION FOUNDATION TRADE OR TECHNICAL SCHOOL SCHOLARSHIPS
Fabricators and Manufacturers Association
Attn: FMA Foundation
833 Featherstone Road
Rockford, IL 61107-6302
(815) 381-1338   Fax: (815) 484-7767
E-mail: foundation@fmanet.org
Web: www.fma-foundation.org/Scholarships.cfm

Purpose To provide financial assistance for trade or technical school to students with an affiliation to the Fabricators and Manufacturers Association, International (FMA) or the Tube and Pipe Association, International (TPA).

Eligibility This program is open to personal members of the FMA and TPA, children and dependents of personal members of the FMA and TPA, student members of the FMA and TPA, and employees of member companies of the FMA and TPA. Applicants must be planning to attend a trade or technical school to major in a program that may lead to a career in manufacturing. They must have a GPA of 2.5 or higher and be enrolled or planning to enroll full time. Along with their application, they must submit information on their educational and career objectives, employment experience, extracurricular activities, and the experience that has influenced or confirmed their decision to prepare for a career in manufacturing. Financial need is not considered in the selection process.

Financial data Stipends are $1,000 per year.

Duration 1 year.

Additional information Recipients are also offered a 3-day internship, worth $1,500, to the FMA exposition and conference. The internship includes travel, hotel, meals, technical educational sessions, and free admission.

Number awarded 1 or more each year.

Deadline Applications may be submitted at any time.

[1094]
FCRV SCHOLARSHIPS
Family Campers and RVers
c/o Herb and Marie Petersen
76 Gaymore Road
Port Jefferson Station, NY 11776
E-mail: petersen76@aol.com
Web: www.fcrv.org/programs/scholarship.php

Purpose To provide financial assistance for college to members of the Family Campers and RVers (FCRV) and their dependent children.

Eligibility Applicants must have been members of FCRV for at least 1 year or be their dependent children and have been accepted in a 2-year or 4-year accredited institution of higher learning. Applications are accepted from the United States and Canada, but those from other countries will be considered within the educational framework of that country. Students currently enrolled in college are given equal consideration with incoming freshmen; high school students or recent graduates should be in the upper 40% of their graduating class and students already in college should have a GPA of 2.7 or higher. Special consideration is given to students majoring in fields related to conservation, ecology, or outdoor activities, although applicants with any major are considered. Awards are based on maturity, leadership, related activities, and goals of the applicant as related to the objectives of FCRV.

Financial data Scholarships range from $500 to $2,000 per year.

Duration 1 year; may be renewed upon reapplication.

Additional information Family Campers and RVers was founded as the National Campers and Hikers Association, and these scholarships are awarded by the National Campers and Hikers Association Scholarship, Inc. (NCHA).

Deadline April of each year.

[1095]
FEDERAL EMPLOYEE EDUCATION AND ASSISTANCE FUND SCHOLARSHIPS

Federal Employee Education and Assistance Fund
Attn: Scholarship Program
8441 West Bowles Avenue, Suite 200
Littleton, CO 80123-9501
(303) 933-7580 Toll-free: (800) 323-4140
Fax: (303) 933-7587 E-mail: admin@feea.org
Web: www.feea.org/scholarships.html

Purpose To provide financial assistance for college or graduate school to civilian federal and postal employees and their families.

Eligibility This program is open to civilian federal and postal employees and their dependent children and spouses who are entering or enrolled in an accredited 2- or 4-year postsecondary, graduate, or postgraduate program. Applicants or their sponsoring federal employee must have at least 3 years of civilian federal service. Active-duty military members and their dependents are eligible only through a sponsoring civilian employee spouse. Military retirees and dependents are eligible if the retiree is a current civilian federal employee. Applicants who are dependents must be full-time students; applicants who are federal employees may be part-time students. Along with their application, they must submit a 2-page essay on a topic related to a career in public service with the federal government, a letter of recommendation, a transcript with a GPA of 3.0 or higher, and a copy of their federal "Notice of Personnel Action;" high school seniors must also submit a copy of their ACT, SAT, or other examination scores. Financial need is not considered in the selection process.

Financial data Stipends range from $500 to $2,500.

Duration 1 year; recipients may reapply.

Additional information Funding for these scholarships is provided by donations from federal and postal employees and by a contribution from the Blue Cross/Blue Shield Association. Requests for applications must be accompanied by a self-addressed stamped envelope.

Number awarded Approximately 500 each year.

Deadline March of each year.

[1096]
FEDERAL EMPLOYEE EDUCATION AND ASSISTANCE FUND-BLACKS IN GOVERNMENT SCHOLARSHIP PROGRAM

Blacks in Government
c/o Federal Employee Education and Assistance Fund
Attn: Scholarship Program
8441 West Bowles Avenue, Suite 200
Littleton, CO 80123-9501
(303) 933-7580 Toll-free: (800) 323-4140
Fax: (303) 933-7587 E-mail: admin@feea.org
Web: www.bignet.org/program/program/proplan.htm

Purpose To provide financial assistance for college or graduate school to members of Blacks in Government (BIG) and their dependents.

Eligibility This program is open to BIG members and their children, stepchildren, and grandchildren. Applicants or their sponsoring BIG member must have at least 3 years of federal, state, or local government employment and 2 years of membership in BIG. They must be entering or enrolled full time in an accredited 2- or 4-year postsecondary, graduate, or postgraduate program with a GPA of 3.0 or higher. Along with their application, they must submit a 2-page essay on a topic related to a career in public service with the government, a letter of recommendation, a transcript, a list of extracurricular and community service activities, and verification of government employment; high school seniors must also submit a copy of their ACT, SAT, or other examination scores. Financial need is not considered in the selection process.

Financial data The stipend is $1,000 per year.

Duration 1 year; may be renewed.

Additional information This program, established in 2007, is jointly administered by BIG and the Federal Employee Education and Assistance Fund (FEEA). Information is also available directly from BIG, 3005 Georgia Avenue N.W., Washington, DC 20001-5015, (202) 667-3280, Fax: (202) 667-3705, E-mail: BIG@bignet.org.

Number awarded 11 each year: 1 in each BIG region.

Deadline March of each year.

[1097]
FEEA-NTEU SCHOLARSHIPS

Federal Employee Education and Assistance Fund
Attn: Scholarship Program
8441 West Bowles Avenue, Suite 200
Littleton, CO 80123-9501
(303) 933-7580 Toll-free: (800) 323-4140
Fax: (303) 933-7587 E-mail: admin@feea.org
Web: www.feea.org/schol_info/feeanteuschol.html

Purpose To provide financial assistance for college or graduate school to civilian federal and postal employees and their families.

Eligibility This program is open to civilian federal and postal employees and their dependent children and spouses who are entering or enrolled in an accredited 2- or 4-year postsecondary, graduate, or postgraduate program. Applicants or their sponsoring federal employee must have at least 3 years of civilian federal service. Active-duty military members and their dependents are eligible only through a sponsoring civilian employee spouse. Military retirees and dependents are eligible if the retiree is a current civilian federal employee. Applicants who are dependents must be full-time students; applicants who are federal employees may be part-time students. Along with their application, they must submit a 2-page essay on a topic related to a career in public service with the federal government, a letter of recommendation, a transcript with a GPA of 3.0 or higher, and a copy of their federal "Notice of Personnel Action;" high school seniors must also submit a copy of their ACT, SAT, or other examination scores. Financial need is not considered in the selection process.

Financial data The stipend is $5,000.

Duration 1 year.

Additional information This program was established in 2006 when the National Treasury Employees Union (NTEU) donated unused administrative funds from a court case to the Federal Employee Education and Assistance (FEEA) Fund. Requests for applications must be accompanied by a self-addressed stamped envelope.

Number awarded At least 5 each year.
Deadline March of each year.

[1098]
FEEA/WORLD TRADE CENTER/PENTAGON FUND SCHOLARSHIPS
Federal Employee Education and Assistance Fund
Attn: Scholarship Program
8441 West Bowles Avenue, Suite 200
Littleton, CO 80123-9501
(303) 933-7580   Toll-free: (800) 323-4140
Fax: (303) 933-7587   E-mail: admin@feea.org
Web: www.feea.org/special_funds/wtcpentagon.html

Purpose To provide financial assistance for college or graduate school to children and spouses of civilian federal employees killed or injured in the Pentagon on September 11, 2001.
Eligibility This program is open to children who lost a civilian federal employee parent in the attack on the Pentagon on September 11, 2001. Children whose parent was critically injured are also eligible, as are victims' spouses who were already attending college on September 11. Spouses wishing to return to college are considered on a case-by-case basis.
Financial data Full college scholarships are available.
Number awarded All affected family members will be supported.

[1099]
FIRST LIEUTENANT MICHAEL L. LEWIS, JR. MEMORIAL FUND SCHOLARSHIP
American Legion Auxiliary
Attn: Department of New York
112 State Street, Suite 1310
Albany, NY 12207
(518) 463-1162   Toll-free: (800) 421-6348
Fax: (518) 449-5406
E-mail: alanyhdqtrs@worldnet.att.net
Web: www.deptny.org/Scholarships.htm

Purpose To provide financial assistance for college to members of the American Legion Auxiliary in New York.
Eligibility This program is open to 1) junior members of the New York Department of the American Legion Auxiliary who are high school seniors or graduates younger than 20 years of age; and 2) senior members who are continuing their education to further their studies or update their job skills. Applicants must submit a 200-word essay on "Why a college education is important to me," or "Why I want to continue my post high school education in a business or trade school." Selection is based on character (25%), Americanism (25%), leadership (25%), and scholarship (25%).
Financial data The stipend is $1,000.
Duration 1 year.
Number awarded 2 each year: 1 to a junior member and 1 to a senior member. If no senior members apply, both scholarships are awarded to junior members.
Deadline March of each year.

[1100]
FIRWOOD DISTRICT 22 SCHOLARSHIPS
American Hellenic Educational Progressive Association-District 22
Attn: Northwest AHEPA Family Educational Foundation
c/o St. Nicholas Greek Orthodox Church
1523 South Yakima Avenue
Tacoma, WA 98405-4460
(206) 243-5881   E-mail: xeniag13@aol.com
Web: www.ahepad22.org/d22_scholarships.htm

Purpose To provide financial assistance to undergraduate and graduate student members and families of members of organizations affiliated with the American Hellenic Educational Progressive Association (AHEPA) in its District 22 (Oregon and Washington).
Eligibility This program is open to District 22 (Oregon and Washington) members of the Order of Ahepa, the Daughters of Penelope, the Maids of Athena, or the Sons of Pericles who were inducted as members at least 1 year prior to applying for the scholarship. Children of members of the Order of Ahepa or Daughters of Penelope are also eligible. Applicants must be high school seniors, technical/vocational school students, undergraduates, or graduate students, Selection is based on academic achievement; school activities, honors, and awards; and AHEPA family, Greek community, and other civic activities. Financial need can also be considered, but only for students who complete a supplemental application.
Financial data A stipend is awarded (amount not specified).
Duration 1 year; recipients are eligible to receive a maximum of 2 undergraduate scholarships and 1 graduate scholarship.
Number awarded Varies each year.
Deadline April of each year.

[1101]
FLOYD QUALLS MEMORIAL SCHOLARSHIPS
American Council of the Blind
Attn: Coordinator, Scholarship Program
1155 15th Street, N.W., Suite 1004
Washington, DC 20005
(202) 467-5081   Toll-free: (800) 424-8666
Fax: (202) 467-5085   E-mail: info@acb.org
Web: www.acb.org

Purpose To provide financial assistance to undergraduate and graduate students who are blind.
Eligibility Students who are legally blind may apply for these scholarships. Recipients are selected in each of 4 categories: entering freshmen in academic programs, undergraduates (sophomores, juniors, and seniors) in academic programs, graduate students in academic programs, and vocational school students or students working on an associate's degree from a community college. In addition to letters of recommendation and copies of academic transcripts, applications must include an autobiographical sketch. A cumulative GPA of 3.3 or higher is generally required. Selection is based on demonstrated academic record, involvement in extracurricular and civic activities, and academic objectives. The severity of the applicant's

visual impairment and his/her study methods are also taken into account.

Financial data The stipend is $2,500. In addition, the winners receive a Kurzweil-1000 Reading System.

Duration 1 year.

Additional information Scholarship winners are expected to be present at the council's annual conference; the council will cover all reasonable expenses connected with convention attendance.

Number awarded Up to 8 each year: 2 in each of the 4 categories.

Deadline February of each year.

[1102]
FMA-FEEA SCHOLARSHIP PROGRAM

Federal Managers Association
c/o Federal Employee Education and Assistance Fund
Attn: Scholarship Program
8441 West Bowles Avenue, Suite 200
Littleton, CO 80123-9501
(303) 933-7580   Toll-free: (800) 323-4140
Fax: (303) 933-7587   E-mail: admin@feea.org
Web: www.feea.org/schol_info/specialschols.html

Purpose To provide financial assistance for college or graduate school to members of the Federal Managers Association (FMA) and their dependents.

Eligibility This program is open to FMA members (including retirees) and their spouses and children entering or enrolled in an accredited 2- or 4-year postsecondary, graduate, or postgraduate program. Applicants or their sponsoring federal employee must have at least 3 years of civilian federal service. Active-duty military members and their dependents are eligible only through a sponsoring civilian employee spouse. Military retirees and dependents are eligible if the retiree is a current civilian federal employee. Applicants who are dependents must be full-time students; applicants who are federal employees may be part-time students. Along with their application, they must submit a 2-page essay on a topic related to a career in public service with the federal government, a letter of recommendation, a transcript with a GPA of 3.0 or higher, and a copy of their federal "Notice of Personnel Action;" high school seniors must also submit a copy of their ACT, SAT, or other examination scores. Financial need is not considered in the selection process.

Financial data The stipend is $1,500 per year for the Frances Webb Scholarship or $1,000 per year for other scholarships.

Duration 1 year; may be renewed.

Additional information This program is jointly administered by FMA and the Federal Employee Education and Assistance Fund (FEEA). Information is also available directly from FMA, 1641 Prince Street, Alexandria, VA 22314-2818, (703) 683-8700, (703) 683-8707, E-mail: info@fedmanagers.org.

Number awarded 1 Frances Webb Scholarship and a varying number of other scholarships are awarded each year.

Deadline March of each year.

[1103]
FORD TRUCK SCHOLARSHIP PROGRAM

National FFA Organization
Attn: Scholarship Office
6060 FFA Drive
P.O. Box 68960
Indianapolis, IN 46268-0960
(317) 802-4321   Fax: (317) 802-5321
E-mail: scholarships@ffa.org
Web: www.ffa.org/programs/scholarships/index.html

Purpose To provide financial assistance to FFA members who are interested in working on a 2-year or 4-year college degree in any field.

Eligibility This program is open to members who are graduating high school seniors planning to enroll or students currently enrolled full time at an accredited 2- or 4-year college, university, or vocational/technical school. Applicants may be majoring in any field. They must visit a Ford Truck dealership and obtain a signature on the scholarship application. Selection is based on academic achievement (10 points for GPA, 10 points for SAT or ACT score, 10 points for class rank), leadership in FFA activities (30 points), leadership in community activities (10 points), and participation in the Supervised Agricultural Experience (SAE) program (30 points). U.S. citizenship is required.

Financial data The stipend is $1,000. Funds are paid directly to the recipient.

Duration 1 year; nonrenewable.

Additional information Funding for these scholarships is provided by the Ford Truck Division of the Ford Motor Company. This program began in 1998.

Number awarded Approximately 705 each year: approximately 700 on behalf of participating Ford Truck dealerships and 5 on a nationwide basis.

Deadline February of each year.

[1104]
GALLUP ORGANIZATION/CORNHUSKER STATE GAMES SCHOLARSHIP PROGRAM

Cornhusker State Games
Trabert Hall
2202 South 11th Street
P.O. Box 82411
Lincoln, NE 68501
(402) 471-2544 Toll-free: (800) 30-GAMES (within NE)
Fax: (402) 471-9712
E-mail: csg@cornhuskerstategames.com
Web: www.cornhuskerstategames.com

Purpose To provide financial assistance for college to athletes who participate in the Cornhusker State Games in Nebraska.

Eligibility This program is open to athletes who participate in the summer Cornhusker State Games. All residents of Nebraska are eligible to participate in the games if they have resided in Nebraska for at least 30 days prior to the competition and have amateur status in the sport in which they compete. High school athletes must abide by the rules of the Nebraska School Activities Association. College athletes must abide by national collegiate rules. Participants who are high school graduates (including members of the current graduating class) are eligible for these scholarships.

Selection is based on academic honors (15 points), athletic achievements (15 points), other activities (10 points), and an essay of 200 words or less in which they outline their educational objectives (20 points), career goals (20 points), and what this scholarship means to them (20 points).
Financial data The stipend is $1,000.
Duration 1 year.
Additional information These scholarships are sponsored by The Gallup Organization. Recipients must attend a postsecondary educational institution in Nebraska.
Number awarded 5 each year.
Deadline June of each year.

[1105]
GCSAA LEGACY AWARDS
Golf Course Superintendents Association of America
Attn: Environmental Institute for Golf
1421 Research Park Drive
Lawrence, KS 66049-3859
(785) 832-4424   Toll-free: (800) 472-7878, ext. 4424
Fax: (785) 832-3673   E-mail: ahoward@gcsaa.org
Web: www.gcsaa.org

Purpose To provide financial assistance for college to the offspring of members of the Golf Course Superintendents Association of America (GCSAA).
Eligibility This program is open to the children and grandchildren of GCSAA members who have been active in the association for 5 or more consecutive years or are retired or deceased. Applicants may be studying in a field unrelated to golf course management. They must be enrolled full time at an accredited institution of higher learning or, in the case of high school seniors, be accepted at such an institution for the next academic year. Selection is based on academic achievement, extracurricular and community involvement, leadership, outside employment, and an original 500-word essay on 1 of 8 assigned topics. Financial need is not considered.
Financial data The stipend is $1,500 per year.
Duration 1 year. Recipients may not reapply in the year after they receive the award, but they are eligible after a 1-year hiatus.
Additional information This program is sponsored by Syngenta Professional Products.
Number awarded Varies each year; recently, 20 of these scholarships were awarded.
Deadline April of each year.

[1106]
GEICO LIFE SCHOLARSHIPS
Golden Key International Honour Society
621 North Avenue N.E., Suite C-100
Atlanta, GA 30308
(404) 377-2400   Toll-free: (800) 377-2401
Fax: (678) 420-6757
E-mail: scholarships@goldenkey.org
Web: www.goldenkey.org

Purpose To provide financial assistance to members of the Golden Key International Honour Society who are working on an undergraduate degree while balancing other responsibilities.
Eligibility This program is open to undergraduate members of the society who have other commitments, such as family and/or career. Applicants must have completed at least 12 credit hours since their return to the university and must be working toward a baccalaureate degree. Along with the application, they must submit transcripts of all college work, a letter of recommendation from an employer or a professor, and an essay of up to 500 words describing their educational goals, their other commitments, and the obstacles they have overcome to achieve academic excellence. Selection is based on academic achievement, extracurricular activities, and family and/or career commitments.
Financial data The stipend is $1,000.
Duration 1 year.
Additional information This program is sponsored by GEICO Life Insurance.
Number awarded 10 each year.
Deadline March of each year.

[1107]
GENERAL MOTORS MINORITY DEALERS ASSOCIATION MINORITY SCHOLARSHIP PROGRAM
General Motors Minority Dealers Association
29433 Southfield Road, Suite 210
Southfield, MI 48076
(248) 552-9040   Toll-free: (888) 377-5233
Fax: (248) 552-9022
E-mail: scholarshipinfo@gmsac.com
Web: www.gmmda.org

Purpose To provide financial assistance for college to ethnic minority high school seniors and college students.
Eligibility This program is open to ethnic minority graduating high school seniors and current college students who are enrolled or planning to enroll full time at an accredited 2-year or 4-year college or university in the United States. Applicants must be U.S. citizens with a GPA of 3.0 or higher. Along with their application, they must submit a personal statement of 500 to 750 words explaining 1) how their school experiences, including academics, extracurricular activities, outside activities, and work experiences, are shaping their educational and career goals, and 2) why they should be considered for this scholarship. Selection is based on that statement, academic excellence, leadership and participation in school and community activities, work experience, education, and career aspirations.
Financial data The stipend is $2,500.
Duration 1 year.
Additional information This program began in 2004.
Number awarded Varies each year; recently, 18 of these scholarships were awarded.
Deadline November of each year.

ANY SUBJECT AREA

[1108]
GEORGE CHIRGOTIS SCHOLARSHIP
American Hellenic Educational Progressive Association
Attn: AHEPA Educational Foundation
1909 Q Street, N.W., Suite 500
Washington, DC 20009
(202) 232-6300 Fax: (202) 232-2140
E-mail: ahepa@ahepa.org
Web: www.ahepa.org

Purpose To provide financial assistance for college to students with a connection to the American Hellenic Educational Progressive Association (AHEPA).

Eligibility This program is open to 1) members in good standing of the Order of Ahepa, Daughters of Penelope, Sons of Pericles, or Maids of Athena, and 2) the children of Order of Ahepa or Daughters of Penelope members in good standing. Applicants must be currently enrolled or planning to enroll in a college or university. High school seniors must submit their most recent official transcript as well as SAT or ACT scores; college freshmen and sophomores must submit high school transcripts, SAT or ACT scores, and their most recent college transcript; college juniors and seniors must submit their most recent college transcript. Along with their application, they must also submit a 500-word biographical essay. Selection is based on academic achievement; extracurricular, personal, and volunteer activities; athletic achievements; and work experience. Financial need is not considered.

Financial data Stipends range from $500 to $2,000 per year.

Duration 1 year.

Additional information A processing fee of $20 must accompany each application.

Number awarded Varies each year; recently, 1 of these scholarships was awarded.

Deadline March of each year.

[1109]
GLAMOUR'S TOP TEN COLLEGE WOMEN COMPETITION
Glamour
4 Times Square
New York, NY 10036-6593
Toll-free: (800) 244-GLAM Fax: (212) 286-6922
E-mail: TTCW@glamour.com
Web: www.glamour.com

Purpose To recognize and reward outstanding college women.

Eligibility This competition is open to women enrolled full time in their junior year at accredited colleges and universities in the United States and Canada. Applications must be approved and signed by the appropriate members of the school's faculty and administration (i.e., faculty advisor, the director of public relations, the director of student activities, or the dean of students). There is no limit on the number of applicants from any 1 school. Applicants must write an essay (of 500 to 700 words) describing their most meaningful achievements and how those relate to their field of study and future goals. Selection is based on the essay, leadership experience, personal involvement in campus and community affairs, and academic excellence.

Financial data Each winner receives national recognition for herself and her college, a $2,000 cash prize, and a trip to New York City. Along with a photograph, a synopsis of the winner's accomplishments is featured in the October issue of *Glamour* magazine.

Duration The competition is held annually.

Additional information The first competition was held in 1990.

Number awarded 10 each year.

Deadline February of each year.

[1110]
GOLDEN KEY INTERNATIONAL STUDENT LEADER AWARDS
Golden Key International Honour Society
621 North Avenue N.E., Suite C-100
Atlanta, GA 30308
(404) 377-2400 Toll-free: (800) 377-2401
Fax: (678) 420-6757
E-mail: scholarships@goldenkey.org
Web: www.goldenkey.org

Purpose To recognize and reward members of the Golden Key International Honour Society who perform outstanding service to the society, campus, and community.

Eligibility This competition is open to active members of the society worldwide who are currently enrolled in an accredited undergraduate or graduate program. Applicants may apply for the international award, a regional award (for 10 regions within the United States, Canada, South Africa, or the Asia-Pacific region that covers Australia, New Zealand, and Malaysia), or both. Along with their application, they must submit a personal statement of up to 1,000 words explaining why they feel they should receive the award; a detailed list of Golden Key involvement and accomplishments; a list of extracurricular involvement in other organizations, honors and awards received, community service activities, and work experience; and a letter of recommendation from the Golden Key chapter advisor. Selection is based on leadership and involvement in Golden Key (50%), other extracurricular involvement (25%), and academic performance (25%).

Financial data The international award is $1,000; regional awards are $500.

Duration The awards are presented annually.

Number awarded 1 international and 13 regional awards are presented each year.

Deadline May of each year.

[1111]
GOODYEAR TIRE AND RUBBER COMPANY SCHOLARSHIPS

Brown Foundation for Educational Equity, Excellence and Research
Attn: Scholarship Committee
1515 S.E. Monroe
P.O. Box 4862
Topeka, KS 66604
(785) 235-3939   Fax: (785) 235-1001
E-mail: brownfound@juno.com
Web: brownvboard.org

Purpose To provide financial assistance to residents of Kansas who are high school seniors or currently-enrolled college students.

Eligibility This program is open to residents of Kansas who are graduating high school seniors or current college students. Applicants must be enrolled or planning to enroll at least half time at an institution of higher education in the state. They must have a GPA of 3.0 or higher. Along with their application, they must submit brief essays on 1) their involvement in school, religious, community, and/or other activities; and 2) the impact of *Brown v. the Board of Education* has had on their chosen field of study. Selection is based on the essays; GPA; school, community, and leisure activities; career plans and goals; and recommendations.

Financial data A stipend is awarded (amount not specified).

Duration 2 years.

Additional information This program, which began in 2006, is sponsored by the Goodyear Tire and Rubber Company of Topeka.

Number awarded 2 each year.

Deadline March of each year.

[1112]
GUARANTEED RESERVE FORCES DUTY (GRFD) SCHOLARSHIPS

U.S. Army
ROTC Cadet Command
Attn: ATCC-OP-I-S
55 Patch Road, Building 56
Fort Monroe, VA 23651-1052
(757) 727-4558   Toll-free: (800) USA-ROTC
E-mail: atccps@usaac.army.mil
Web: www.rotc.usaac.army.mil

Purpose To provide financial assistance to college and graduate students who are willing to enroll in Army ROTC and serve in a Reserve component of the Army following graduation.

Eligibility This program is open to full-time students entering their junior year of college with a GPA of 2.5 or higher. Graduate students are also eligible if they have only 2 years remaining for completion of their graduate degree. Applicants must meet all other medical and moral character requirements for enrollment in Army ROTC). They must be willing to enroll in the Simultaneous Membership Program (SMP) of an ROTC unit on their campus; the SMP requires simultaneous membership in Army ROTC and the Army National Guard or Army Reserve.

Financial data Participants receive reimbursement of tuition (up to $28,000 per year), a grant of $600 per year for books, plus an ROTC stipend for 10 months of the year at $350 per month during their junior year and $400 per month during their senior year. As a member of the Army National Guard or Army Reserve, they also receive weekend drill pay at the pay grade of E-5 during their junior year or E-6 during their senior year.

Duration 2 years.

Additional information After graduation, participants serve 3 to 6 months on active duty in the Officer Basic Course (OBC). Following completion of OBC, they are released from active duty and are obligated to serve 8 years in the Army National Guard or Army Reserve.

Number awarded 54 each year (1 in each state or U.S. territory).

[1113]
HALL/MCELWAIN MERIT SCHOLARSHIPS

Boy Scouts of America
Attn: National Eagle Scout Association
1325 West Walnut Hill Lane
P.O. Box 152079
Irving, TX 75015-2079
(972) 580-2431
Web: www.nesa.org/scholarships/index.html

Purpose To provide financial assistance for college to Eagle Scouts.

Eligibility This program is open to Eagle Scouts who are graduating high school seniors or currently-enrolled undergraduate students. Applicants must be able to demonstrate leadership ability in Scouting and a strong record of participation in activities outside of Scouting. Financial need is not considered.

Financial data The stipend is $1,000. Awards may be used only for tuition, room, board, and books.

Duration 1 year; nonrenewable.

Number awarded 72 each year: 18 in each region.

Deadline February of each year.

[1114]
HAZLEWOOD EXEMPTION FOR DEPENDENTS OF TEXAS VETERANS

Texas Higher Education Coordinating Board
Attn: Grants and Special Programs
1200 East Anderson Lane
P.O. Box 12788, Capitol Station
Austin, TX 78711-2788
(512) 427-6101   Toll-free: (800) 242-3062
Fax: (512) 427-6127
E-mail: grantinfo@thecb.state.tx.us
Web: www.collegefortexans.com

Purpose To exempt children of deceased veterans from payment of tuition at public universities in Texas.

Eligibility This program is open to the children of Texas servicemen who died in the line of duty or as a result of injury or illness directly related to service in the U.S. military or the National Guard. Applicants must have used up all federal educational benefits for which they are eligible. They must have resided in Texas for at least 12 months and be attending or planning to attend a public college or university in the state.

Financial data Eligible students are exempt from payment of tuition, dues, fees, and charges at state-supported colleges and universities in Texas.

Duration 1 year; may be renewed for a cumulative total of 150 credit hours.

Number awarded Varies each year; recently, 8 of these awards were granted.

[1115]
HAZLEWOOD EXEMPTION FOR TEXAS VETERANS

Texas Higher Education Coordinating Board
Attn: Grants and Special Programs
1200 East Anderson Lane
P.O. Box 12788, Capitol Station
Austin, TX 78711-2788
(512) 427-6101   Toll-free: (800) 242-3062
Fax: (512) 427-6127
E-mail: grantinfo@thecb.state.tx.us
Web: www.collegefortexans.com

Purpose To exempt Texas veterans from payment of tuition for undergraduate or graduate study at public universities in the state.

Eligibility This program is open to veterans who were legal residents of Texas at the time they entered the U.S. armed forces and served for at least 181 days of active military duty, excluding basic training. Applicants must have received an honorable discharge or separation or a general discharge under honorable conditions. They must be enrolled at a public college or university in Texas but have used up all other federal education benefits (e.g., Montgomery Bill, Pell Grants, federal SEOG grants).

Financial data Veterans who are eligible for this benefit are entitled to free tuition and fees at state-supported colleges and universities in Texas.

Duration Exemptions may be claimed up to a cumulative total of 150 credit hours, including undergraduate and graduate study.

Number awarded Varies each year; recently, 8,858 of these awards were granted.

[1116]
HEAR ME PROJECT HIV/AIDS STORY WRITING CONTEST

The Hear Me Project
375 Greenwich Street, Eighth Floor
New York, NY 10013
E-mail: contest@selectmedia.org
Web: www.hearmeproject.org

Purpose To recognize and reward high school and college students who submit outstanding stories about personal vulnerability to HIV/AIDS.

Eligibility This competition is open to all people between 14 and 22 years of age. Applicants must submit an essay, up to 5 pages in length, about personal vulnerability to HIV/AIDS. The essay may be fiction on nonfiction, but the characters in the story must be impacted by HIV/AIDS. Selection is based on originality, writing style, and aptness to subject.

Financial data The prize is $2,500.

Duration The competition is held annually.

Number awarded 1 each year.

Deadline November of each year.

[1117]
HEARTLAND SCHOLARSHIP PROGRAM

Oklahoma State Regents for Higher Education
Attn: Director of Scholarship and Grant Programs
655 Research Parkway, Suite 200
P.O. Box 108850
Oklahoma City, OK 73101-8850
(405) 225-9239   Toll-free: (800) 858-1840
Fax: (405) 225-9230   E-mail: studentinfo@osrhe.edu
Web: www.okhighered.org

Purpose To provide financial assistance for college to families of victims of the bombing of the Oklahoma City federal building.

Eligibility This program is open to dependent children of individuals killed in the April 19, 1995 bombing of the Alfred P. Murrah Federal Building in Oklahoma City, or surviving dependent children who were injured in the federal building daycare center. Applicants may attend accredited institutions of higher education in Oklahoma or outside the state.

Financial data Annual awards are $5,500 for students attending a comprehensive university, $4,000 for students attending a 4-year regional university, or $3,500 for students attending a 2-year college.

Duration Up to 5 years of undergraduate study.

Number awarded This is an entitlement program, open to all qualified individuals.

[1118]
HEATHER JOY MEMORIAL SCHOLARSHIP

Resource Center Scholarship Service
16362 Wilson Boulevard
Masaryktown, FL 34604-7335
(352) 796-0459
E-mail: info@resourcecenterscholarshipinfo.com
Web: www.resourcecenterscholarshipinfo.com

Purpose To provide financial assistance for college to students, regardless of their GPA or financial need.

Eligibility This program is open to students currently enrolled or planning to enroll in college. Along with their application, they must submit a 250-word essay on why they should be selected. GPA and financial need are not considered in the selection process.

Financial data The stipend is $1,000.

Duration 1 year.

Additional information The processing fee is $5.

Number awarded 2 each year: 1 in spring and 1 in fall.

Deadline April of each year for fall; October of each year for spring.

[1119]
HELEN ABBOTT INDIVIDUAL COMMUNITY SERVICE AWARDS

Arab American Institute Foundation
Attn: Executive Director
1600 K Street, N.W., Suite 601
Washington, DC 20006
(202) 429-9210   Fax: (202) 429-9214
E-mail: aaif@aaiusa.org
Web: www.aaiusa.org

Purpose To recognize and reward Arab American undergraduate students who can demonstrate a strong record of community service.

Eligibility This program is open to U.S. citizens and permanent residents of Arab descent who are currently enrolled as an undergraduate or about to enter such a program. Applicants must have a GPA of 3.0 or higher. Along with their application, they must submit 1) a resume that indicates a strong interest and commitment to community service; and 2) a 500-word essay on how their field of study is a springboard for a life of community service.

Financial data The award is $1,000.

Duration The awards are granted annually.

Number awarded 2 each year.

Deadline March of each year.

[1120]
HELM LEADERSHIP FELLOWS

Christian Church (Disciples of Christ)
Attn: Higher Education and Leadership Ministries
11477 Olde Cabin Road, Suite 310
St. Louis, MO 6314-7130
(314) 991-3000   Fax: (314) 991-2957
E-mail: helm@helmdisciples.org
Web: www.helmdisciples.org/aid/fellows.htm

Purpose To provide financial assistance for college to members of the Christian Church (Disciples of Christ) who are interested in taking a leadership role in the church.

Eligibility This program is open to high school seniors and transfers from community college who plan to be a full-time student at a 4-year college or university in the United States or Canada. Applicants must be a participating member of a congregation of the Christian Church (Disciples of Christ) who express a commitment to serve the church as a clergy or lay leader. Some preference is given to students attending colleges and universities related to the Christian Church (Disciples of Christ).

Financial data The stipend is $2,000 per year.

Duration 1 year; may be renewed up to 3 additional years, provided the recipient has a GPA of 2.5 or higher after the first semester of undergraduate work, 2.8 or higher after 3 semesters, and 3.0 or higher after 5 semesters.

Additional information This program began in 2001. Fellows must attend annual leadership conferences and hold summer internships at Disciples of Christ churches and the office of the Higher Education and Leadership Ministries (HELM). They also must agree to assist in the leadership of a ministry activity or program on or near their campus, under the mentorship of a campus minister or chaplain.

Number awarded Approximately 5 each year.

Deadline March of each year.

[1121]
HELPING HANDS BOOK SCHOLARSHIP PROGRAM

Helping Hands Foundation
Attn: Scholarship Director
4480-H South Cobb Drive
PMB 435
Smyrna, GA 30080
Fax: (770) 384-0376
E-mail: director@helpinghandsbookscholarship.com
Web: www.helpinghandsbookscholarship.com

Purpose To provide high school seniors, undergraduates, and graduate students with funds to purchase textbooks and other study materials.

Eligibility This program is open to students who are 16 years of age or older and who are planning to attend or are currently attending a 2-year or 4-year college, university, or vocational/technical institute. Applicants must be enrolled as a high school, college, or graduate student in the United States, Canada, or Mexico. Along with their application, they must submit a 500-word essay describing their educational plans as they relate to their career objectives and why they feel this scholarship will help them achieve those goals. Selection is based on academic record and career potential.

Financial data Stipends range from $100 to $1,000. Funds are intended to be used to purchase textbooks and study materials. Checks are sent directly to the recipient.

Duration These are 1-time nonrenewable awards.

Additional information There is a $5 application fee.

Number awarded Up to 50 each year.

Deadline July of each year for fall semester; December of each year for spring semester.

[1122]
HISTORICALLY BLACK COLLEGE SCHOLARSHIPS

U.S. Navy
Attn: Chief of Naval Education and Training
Code N79A2
250 Dallas Street
Pensacola, FL 32508-5220
(850) 452-4941, ext. 29381
Toll-free: (800) NAV-ROTC, ext. 29381
Fax: (850) 452-2486
E-mail: PNSC_NROTC.scholarship@navy.mil
Web: www.nrotc.navy.mil/scholarships.cfm

Purpose To provide financial assistance to students at specified Historically Black Colleges or Universities (HBCUs) who are interested in joining Navy ROTC.

Eligibility This program is open to students attending or planning to attend 1 of 7 specified HBCUs with a Navy ROTC unit on campus. Applicants must be nominated by the Professor of Naval Science at their institution and meet academic requirements set by each school. They must be U.S. citizens between 17 and 23 years of age who are willing to serve for 4 years as active-duty Navy officers following graduation from college. They must not have reached their 27th birthday by the time of college graduation and commissioning; applicants who have prior active-duty military service may be eligible for age adjustments for the amount of time equal to their prior service, up to a maximum of 36 months. The qualifying scores for the Navy option are 530 critical reading and 520 mathematics on the SAT or 22 on both English and mathematics on the ACT; for the Marine Corps option they are 1000 composite on the SAT or 22 composite on the ACT. Current enlisted and former military personnel are also eligible if they will complete the program by the age of 30.

Financial data These scholarships provide payment of full tuition and required educational fees, as well as a specified amount for textbooks, supplies, and equipment. The program also provides a stipend for 10 months of the year that is $250 per month as a freshman, $300 per month as a sophomore, $350 per month as a junior, and $400 per month as a senior.

Duration Up to 4 years.

Additional information Students may apply for either a Navy or Marine Corps option scholarship, but not for both. Recipients must complete 4 years of study in naval science classes as students at 1 of the following HBCUs: Florida A&M University, Hampton University, Morehouse College, Norfolk State University, Prairie View A&M University, Savannah State University, or Southern University and A&M College. After completing the program, all participants are commissioned as ensigns in the Naval Reserve or second lieutenants in the Marine Corps Reserve with an 8-year service obligation, including 4 years of active duty. Current military personnel who are accepted into this program are released from active duty and are not eligible for active-duty pay and allowances, medical benefits, or other active-duty entitlements.

Number awarded Varies each year.

Deadline January of each year.

[1123]
HISTORICALLY BLACK COLLEGES/UNIVERSITIES SCHOLARSHIP PROGRAM

U.S. Army
ROTC Cadet Command
Attn: ATCC-OP-I-S
55 Patch Road, Building 56
Fort Monroe, VA 23651-1052
(757) 727-4558   Toll-free: (800) USA-ROTC
E-mail: atccps@usaac.army.mil
Web: www.rotc.usaac.army.mil

Purpose To provide financial assistance to high school seniors or graduates who are interested in enrolling in Army ROTC at an Historically Black College or University (HBCU).

Eligibility Applicants for this program must 1) be U.S. citizens; 2) be at least 17 years of age by October of the year in which they are seeking a scholarship; 3) be able to complete a college degree and receive their commission before their 31st birthday; 4) score at least 920 on the SAT or 19 on the ACT; 5) have a high school GPA of 2.5 or higher; 6) meet medical and other regulatory requirements; and 7) be planning to attend 1 of 73 designated HBCUs that has an ROTC detachment or a cross-town agreement with a college or university that does. Current college or university students may apply if their school considers them beginning freshmen with 4 academic years remaining for a bachelor's degree.

Financial data This scholarship provides financial assistance of up to $20,000 per year for college tuition and educational fees or for room and board, whichever the student selects. In addition, a flat rate of $600 per year is provided for the purchase of textbooks, classroom supplies and equipment. Recipients are also awarded a stipend for up to 10 months of each year that is $250 per month during their freshman year; $300 per month during their sophomore year $350 per month during their junior year, and $400 per month during their senior year.

Duration 4 years.

Additional information Scholarship recipients participate in the Army ROTC program as part of their college curriculum by enrolling in 4 years of military science classes, pursuing an Army-approved academic discipline, and attending a 6-week summer camp between the junior and senior years. Following graduation, they receive a commission as a Regular Army, Army Reserve, or Army National Guard officer. Scholarship winners must serve in the military for 8 years. That service obligation may be fulfilled 1) by serving on active duty for 4 years followed by service in the Army National Guard (ARNG), the United States Army Reserve (USAR), or the Inactive Ready Reserve (IRR) for the remainder of the 8 years; or 2) by serving 8 years in an ARNG or USAR troop program unit that includes a 3- to 6-month active duty period for initial training.

Number awarded A limited number of these scholarships is offered each year.

Deadline November of each year.

[1124]
HO-CHUNK NATION ADULT VOCATIONAL TRAINING PROGRAM

Ho-Chunk Nation
Attn: Higher Education Division
P.O. Box 667
Black River Falls, WI 54615
(715) 284-4915   Toll-free: (800) 362-4476
Fax: (715) 284-1760   E-mail: highered@ho-chunk.com
Web: www.ho-chunknation.com

Purpose To provide financial assistance to enrolled members of the Ho-Chunk Nation who are interested in obtaining a postsecondary diploma/certificate (1-year program) or associate of arts degree (2-year program).

Eligibility Applicants must be enrolled members of the Ho-Chunk Nation and be planning to obtain either a diploma/certificate (1-year program) or an associate of arts degree (2-year program). They must intend to attend school on a full-time basis. Both need-based and non-need applicants are considered.

Financial data The tribal grants do not exceed $5,000 per academic year. Students who receive funding under this program are considered either need-based or non-need students. Students who show financial need receive 2 equal payments each academic term; one half of their term award is sent at the beginning of the term and the second half is sent in the middle of their term after verification that they are still enrolled on a full-time basis. Students who are determined to have "no financial need" (no-need students) may be considered for a grant to cover direct costs (tuition, fees, and books) only up to the maximum award amount, based upon the availability of funds.

Duration 1 year; may be renewed for a total of 6 semesters provided the recipient maintains a GPA of 2.0 or higher.
Deadline April of each year or 4 months before the start of the term.

[1125]
HONOLULU ALUMNAE PANHELLENIC ASSOCIATION COLLEGIATE SCHOLARSHIPS

Honolulu Alumnae Panhellenic Association
Attn: Scholarship and Recruitment Chair
P.O. Box 11962
Honolulu, HI 96828-0962
(808) 284-1290   E-mail: sdilbeck@netscape.net
Web: www.greekhawaii.com

Purpose To provide financial assistance to female college student from Hawaii who are members of a National Panhellenic Conference (NPC) sorority.
Eligibility This program is open to women who are initiated and active members of an NPC-affiliated sorority at a college or university where they are working on an undergraduate degree. Their permanent home address or college address must be in Hawaii. Along with their application, they must submit 1) a brief essay stating why they would like the scholarship, their plans, and the part they feel sorority membership has played in their lives; 2) a list of all school, sorority, and community activities and offices; and 3) letters of recommendation from a professor, sorority officer, and another person in the community. Financial need is not considered in the selection process.
Financial data A stipend is awarded (amount not specified).
Duration 1 year.
Number awarded 1 or more each year.
Deadline February of each year.

[1126]
HOWARD R. SWEARER STUDENT HUMANITARIAN AWARD

Campus Compact
c/o Brown University
339 Eddy Street
Box 1975
Providence, RI 02912
(401) 867-3950   Fax: (401) 867-3925
E-mail: campus@compact.org
Web: www.compact.org/awards/detail.php?id=15

Purpose To recognize and reward college students for outstanding public service.
Eligibility Only undergraduate students at Campus Compact-member institutions may be nominated (for a list of those colleges, write to the sponsor). Nominees should be able to demonstrate outstanding public service performed during the preceding 12 months. Of special interest to the sponsor is a student project that illustrates an innovative approach to a social, educational, environmental, health, economic, or legal issue within a community. The application should demonstrate the student's initiative and ability to translate ideas into practical results. Preference is given to nominees who have 1) connected service with academic study; 2) developed systems to ensure long-term support for the project; and 3) linked service to its larger social context through policy work and awareness raising.
Financial data The award is $1,500. Funds are to be used to support service programs of the recipients' design or choice; they cannot be used for personal or school expenses.
Duration The awards are granted annually.
Additional information Campus Compact, which operates at more than 1,000 colleges and universities, established this program in 1987.
Number awarded 5 each year.
Deadline February of each year.

[1127]
IAM SCHOLARSHIP COMPETITION

International Association of Machinists and Aerospace Workers
Attn: IAM Scholarship Program
9000 Machinists Place, Room 117
Upper Marlboro, MD 20772-2687
(301) 967-4500
Web: www.iamaw.org

Purpose To provide financial assistance for college to members and children of members of the International Association of Machinists and Aerospace Workers (IAM).
Eligibility This program is open to IAM members with 2 years of continuous good standing in the union in the United States or Canada, and their children, stepchildren, or legally adopted children. Members must be working in a company under contract with the IAM and expect to continue this work until entering school; they may be entering college as a freshman or some higher undergraduate level. Children of members must be graduating high school seniors; the qualifying parent must be living or must have died after the child entered high school. Scholarships are not available to applicants who do not intend to work without interruption for a bachelor's degree or a vocational/technical school certification, to members' children who are attending or have already attended college, to children of members on the payroll of the Grand Lodge, or to graduate students. Selection is based on grades, attitude toward study, personal references, available test scores, the opinion of counselors and teachers, and activities outside of school; for member applicants, weight also is given to participation in local lodge activities.
Financial data Awards to members are $2,000 per year. Awards to children attending college are $1,000 per year. Awards to children attending vocational/technical school are $2,000 per year.
Duration 1 year. For students in college, awards may be renewed up to 3 additional years or until completion of a bachelor's degree, whichever occurs first. For students in vocational/technical school, awards may be renewed 1 additional year or until certification, whichever occurs first.
Additional information This scholarship fund was established in 1960.
Number awarded Varies each year, depending on the availability of funds; recently, 3 members and 13 children received scholarships.
Deadline February of each year.

ANY SUBJECT AREA

[1128]
INTERNATIONAL PUBLIC MANAGEMENT ASSOCIATION FOR HUMAN RESOURCES SCHOLARSHIP

International Public Management Association for
   Human Resources
Attn: Fellowship Committee
1617 Duke Street
Alexandria, VA 22314
(703) 549-7100   Fax: (703) 684-0948
Web: www.ipma-hr.org

Purpose To provide financial assistance to children of members of the International Public Management Association for Human Resources (IPMA-HR), especially those interested in majoring in human resources or public administration.

Eligibility This program is open to students who are enrolled or planning to enroll at an accredited college or university. At least 1 parent or legal guardian must have been an IPMA-HR member for at least the previous 3 years. Preference is given to applicants in business administration or public administration with a human resources concentration. Applicants must submit a list of activities and awards, a statement of goals and objectives, high school and undergraduate transcripts, and (for entering freshmen) a copy of their college acceptance letter. Financial need is not considered in the selection process.

Financial data The stipend is $1,000 per year.

Duration 1 year.

Number awarded Up to 2 each year.

Deadline May of each year.

[1129]
IOWA UNITED METHODIST CHURCH SCHOLARSHIPS

Iowa United Methodist Foundation
2301 Rittenhouse Street
Des Moines, IA 50321
(515) 974-8927
Web: www.iumf.org/iums.asp

Purpose To provide financial assistance to members of United Methodist Church (UMC) congregations in Iowa who are interested in attending a UMC-affiliated college in the state.

Eligibility This program is open to members of UMC congregations in Iowa who are planning to attend a UMC-affiliated college in the state as a first-time student (including high school seniors and undergraduates transferring from other colleges). Applicants must be planning to work on a degree as a full-time student. Along with their application, they must submit a letter of nomination from the administrative board or council and a personal statement of their church involvement. Financial need is not considered in the selection process.

Financial data The stipend is $1,000.

Duration 1 year.

[1130]
IRMA AND KNUTE CARLSON AWARD

Vasa Order of America
Attn: Vice Grand Master
3236 Berkeley Avenue
Cleveland Heights, OH 44118-2055
(216) 371-5141   E-mail: rolf.bergman@sbcglobal.net
Web: www.vasaorder.com

Purpose To provide financial assistance for undergraduate or graduate study to members of the Vasa Order of America.

Eligibility Applicants must have been members of the organization for at least 1 year. They may be college juniors, seniors, or graduate students. Selection is based on a transcript, letters of recommendation from school and local Vasa lodge officials, and an essay of up to 1,000 words on a topic related to Vasa.

Financial data The stipend is $1,000.

Duration 1 year.

Additional information Vasa Order of America is a Swedish American fraternal organization incorporated in 1899. The organization also awards 2 similar scholarships to students from specific states: the Gladys A. and Russell M. Birtwistle Award and the L. Einar and Edith L. Nilsson Award.

Number awarded 1 each year.

Deadline February of each year.

[1131]
ISAAC ROTH NEWSCARRIER SCHOLARSHIPS

New Jersey Press Association
Attn: New Jersey Newspaper Foundation
840 Bear Tavern Road, Suite 305
West Trenton, NJ 08628-1019
(609) 406-0600, ext. 19   Fax: (609) 406-0300
E-mail: programs@njnf.org
Web: www.njpa.org/foundation/other.html

Purpose To provide financial assistance for college to newscarriers or the children of newscarriers in New Jersey.

Eligibility This program is open to carriers who have been employed by newspapers that are members of the New Jersey Press Association for at least 2 years. Applicants may be 1) adult carriers who are currently enrolled as full-time college students and plan to continue as full-time students in the fall; 2) youth carriers who are currently enrolled as full-time high school students and plan to attend college as full-time students in the fall; 3) children of adult carriers who are currently enrolled as full-time college students or high school students who plan to attend college as full-time students in the fall. High school students may apply as early as their freshmen year and then notify the sponsor when they have been accepted by the college they have chosen to attend. All applicants must submit an essay of 150 words on 1) how the content of their newspaper has improved their school work and enhanced the personal life of themselves and their family, and 2) why they like being a carrier. Selection is based on the essay, citizenship, scholastic achievement, and a route performance questionnaire completed by their employer.

Financial data The stipend is $2,000.

Duration 1 year.

Number awarded Up to 3 each year.
Deadline April of each year.

[1132]
JAMES B. CAREY SCHOLARSHIPS
International Union of Electronic, Electrical, Salaried, Machine, and Furniture Workers
Attn: IUE-CWA International Scholarship Program
501 Third Street, N.W., Suite 975
Washington, DC 20001
(202) 434-1417　　　　　　Fax: (202) 434-1250
E-mail: bgray@iue-cwa.org
Web: www.iue-cwa.org/skills.html

Purpose To provide financial assistance for undergraduate education to children and grandchildren of members and employees of the International Union of Electronic, Electrical, Salaried, Machine, and Furniture Workers (IUE)-Communications Workers of America (CWA).

Eligibility This program is open to children and grandchildren of IUE-CWA members and employees (including retired or deceased members or employees). Applicants must be accepted for admission or already enrolled as full-time students at an accredited college, university, nursing school, or technical school offering college credit classes. Along with their application, they must submit an academic transcript (including rank in class, GPA, and SAT/ACT scores); a short statement of interests and civic activities; an essay (300 to 500 words) describing their career goals and aspirations, highlighting their relationship with the union and the labor movement, and explaining why they are deserving of a union scholarship. They must also have demonstrated a commitment to equality of opportunity for all, a concern for improving the quality of life for all people, an interest in service to the community, good character, leadership ability, and a desire to improve and move ahead.

Financial data The stipend is $1,000 per year.
Duration 1 year.
Number awarded 9 each year: 8 divided among the 6 union districts and 1 at large.
Deadline March of each year.

[1133]
JEANNE E. BRAY MEMORIAL SCHOLARSHIP
National Rifle Association of America
Attn: Law Enforcement Activities Division
11250 Waples Mill Road
Fairfax, VA 22030-7400
(703) 267-1131　　　　E-mail: selkin@nrahq.org
Web: www.nrahq.org/law/lebenefits.asp

Purpose To provide financial assistance for college to children of law enforcement officers who are members of the National Rifle Association (NRA).

Eligibility This program is open to NRA members who are the dependent children of 1) currently serving full-time commissioned peace officers who are also NRA members; 2) deceased full-time commissioned peace officers who lost their lives in the performance of assigned peace officer duties and were current members of NRA at the time of their death; 3) retired full-time commissioned peace officers who are also NRA members; and 4) full-time commissioned peace officers, disabled and retired as a result of a line of duty incident, who are also current NRA members. Applicants must be U.S. citizens with a GPA of 3.0 or higher and scores of at least 950 on the SAT I or 25 on the ACT. Along with their application, they must submit an essay of 500 to 700 words in support of the rights secured by the second amendment to the constitution.

Financial data The stipend is $2,000 per year.
Duration Up to 4 years, provided the recipient maintains a GPA of 2.0 or higher.
Number awarded 1 or more each year.
Deadline November of each year.

[1134]
JESSE BROWN MEMORIAL YOUTH SCHOLARSHIP PROGRAM
Disabled American Veterans
Attn: National Service and Legislative Headquarters
807 Maine Avenue, S.W.
Washington, DC 20024
(202) 554-3501
Web: www.dav.org

Purpose To provide financial assistance to college students who demonstrate outstanding volunteer service to hospitalized disabled veterans.

Eligibility This program is open to students who are 21 years of age or younger and have volunteered at least 100 hours for the Department of Veterans Affairs Voluntary Service (VAVS) programs to assist disabled veterans. They may be attending an accredited college, university, community college, or vocational school. Nominations must be submitted by Chiefs of Voluntary Services at VA medical centers. Self-nominations are also accepted if the student includes a 750-word essay on what volunteering at a VA medical center means to them.

Financial data Stipends range up to $15,000.
Duration Funds must be used before the recipient's 25th birthday.
Additional information This program was established in 2000 as the DAV National Commander's Youth Volunteer Scholarships and given its current name in 2003.
Number awarded Varies each year; since the establishment of the program, 63 scholarships worth $413,000 have been awarded.
Deadline February of each year.

[1135]
JESSE JACKSON SCHOLARSHIP PROGRAM
Service Employees International Union
Attn: Education Department
1313 L Street, N.W.
Washington, DC 20005
(202) 898-3326　　　　　　Toll-free: (800) 424-8592
Fax: (202) 898-3348　　　　TDD: (202) 898-3481
Web: www.seiu.org

Purpose To provide financial assistance for college to members and children of members of the Service Employees International Union (SEIU) who share the vision of a "more just and humane society" held by the Rev. Jesse Jackson.

Eligibility This program is open to members of an SEIU local or affiliated union and their children. Applicants must be working on or planning to work on a degree at a 2-year community or junior college or 4-year college or university. Their record of work and aspirations for economic and social justice must "reflect the values and accomplishments of the Rev. Jesse Jackson." Along with their application, they must submit a personal statement of 500 words or less that describes what the labor movement has meant to them and their family; their social justice, labor, or political activism; goals for working for social and economic justice within an organization; and their plans to carry out this activism in their career after graduation. Selection is based on originality, clarity, and commitment to social and economic justice in the workplace.

Financial data The stipend is $5,000 per year.

Duration 1 year; may be renewed up to 3 additional years.

Additional information This program is administered by Scholarship Program Administrators, Inc., 1201 Eighth Avenue South, P.O. Box 23737, Nashville, TN 27202-3737, (615) 320-3149, Fax: (615) 320-3151, E-mail: info@spaprog.com. The recipient must agree to participate in some paid or course credit internships or work experiences in social change organizations during the years they receive this award.

Number awarded 1 each year.

Deadline February of each year.

[1136]
J.F. SCHIRMER SCHOLARSHIP
American Mensa Education and Research Foundation
1229 Corporate Drive West
Arlington, TX 76006-6103
(817) 607-0060   Toll-free: (800) 66-MENSA
Fax: (817) 649-5232
E-mail: info@mensafoundation.org
Web: www.mensafoundation.org

Purpose To provide financial assistance for undergraduate or graduate study to qualified students.

Eligibility Any student who is enrolled or will enroll in a degree program at an accredited American institution of postsecondary education is eligible to apply. Membership in Mensa is not required, but applicants must be U.S. citizens or permanent residents. There are no restrictions as to age, race, gender, level of postsecondary education, GPA, or financial need. Selection is based on a 550-word essay that describes the applicant's career, vocational, or academic goals.

Financial data The stipend is $1,000.

Duration 1 year; may be renewed for up to 3 additional years if the recipient remains in school and achieves satisfactory grades.

Additional information Applications are available only through participating Mensa local groups.

Number awarded 3 each year.

Deadline January of each year.

[1137]
JO ANNE J. TROW UNDERGRADUATE SCHOLARSHIPS
Alpha Lambda Delta
Attn: Executive Director
328 Orange Street
P.O. Box 4403
Macon, GA 31208-4403
Toll-free: (800) 9-ALPHA-1   Fax: (478) 744-9924
E-mail: ald@nationalald.org
Web: www.nationalald.org

Purpose To provide financial assistance for undergraduate study to members of Alpha Lambda Delta, a national society that honors academic excellence during a student's first year in college.

Eligibility This program is open to members who have a cumulative GPA of 3.5 or higher. Each chapter may submit 1 application (chapters initiating 150 to 299 members may submit 2 applicants and chapters initiating more than 300 members may submit 3 applicants). Each applicant must have been initiated during the previous calendar year. Along with their application, they must submit employment information for the last 2 years; a brief summary of their contributions to their campus chapter of Alpha Lambda Delta; a brief summary of significant campus activities, community activities, organizational memberships, and offices held; honors and recognitions received; career goals; and a 250-word essay on the value of Alpha Lambda Delta to their undergraduate education. Financial need is not considered in the selection process.

Financial data Stipends are $3,000 or $1,000.

Duration 1 year; nonrenewable.

Additional information This program began in 1988.

Number awarded 35 each year: 10 at $3,000 and 25 at $1,000.

Deadline March of each year.

[1138]
JOHN J. GUENTHER SCHOLARSHIP
Marine Corps Intelligence Association, Inc.
Attn: Marine Corps Intelligence Educational Foundation
P.O. Box 1028
Quantico, VA 22134-1028
Web: mcia-inc.org/mcief.htm

Purpose To provide financial assistance for college to members of the Marine Corps Intelligence Association (MCIA) and their dependent children.

Eligibility This program is open to current MCIA members, their dependent children, and their survivors. Applicants must be attending or planning to attend an accredited 4-year college or university as a full-time student. They must submit a 300-word essay on a risk that has led to a significant change in their personal or intellectual life, the most challenging obstacles they have had to overcome and what they learned from the experience, and where they envision themselves in 10 years. Selection is based on the essay, academic achievement, extracurricular activities, and work experience. Financial need is not considered.

Financial data The stipend is $1,500.

Duration 1 year.

Additional information Membership in the MCIA is open to Marine Corps intelligence personnel, including active duty, Reserve, and retired. Information is also available from John Carey, MCIA Scholarship Committee Chair, 15412 Silvan Glen Drive, Dumfries, VA 22025.
Number awarded At least 1 each year.
Deadline July of each year.

[1139]
JOHN N. STURDIVANT FAMILY SCHOLARSHIPS
American Federation of Government Employees
c/o Federal Employee Education and Assistance Fund
Attn: Scholarship Program
8441 West Bowles Avenue, Suite 200
Littleton, CO 80123-9501
(303) 933-7580   Toll-free: (800) 323-4140
Fax: (303) 933-7587   E-mail: admin@feea.org
Web: www.feea.org/schol_info/specialschols.html

Purpose To provide financial assistance for college or graduate school to members of the American Federation of Government Employees (AFGE) and their dependents.
Eligibility This program is open to AFGE members and their dependents entering or enrolled in an accredited 2- or 4-year postsecondary, graduate, or postgraduate program. Applicants or their sponsoring federal employee must have at least 3 years of civilian federal service. Active-duty military members and their dependents are eligible only through a sponsoring civilian employee spouse. Military retirees and dependents are eligible if the retiree is a current civilian federal employee. Applicants who are dependents must be full-time students; applicants who are federal employees may be part-time students. Along with their application, they must submit a 2-page essay on a topic related to a career in public service with the federal government, a letter of recommendation, a transcript with a GPA of 3.0 or higher, and a copy of their federal "Notice of Personnel Action;" high school seniors must also submit a copy of their ACT, SAT, or other examination scores. Financial need is not considered in the selection process.
Financial data The maximum stipend is $2,500 per year.
Duration 1 year; may be renewed.
Additional information As of 2007, this program was jointly administered by AFGE and the Federal Employee Education and Assistance Fund (FEEA). Information is also available directly from AFGE, 80 F Street, N.W., Washington, DC 20001, (202) 737-8700, E-mail: education@afge.org.
Number awarded 1 or more each year.
Deadline March of each year.

[1140]
JOSEPH AND RUBY SCHAFF/SCHAFF ANGUS RANCH SCHOLARSHIP
National Junior Angus Association
Attn: Director Junior Activities
3201 Frederick Avenue
St. Joseph, MO 64506
(816) 383-5100   Fax: (816) 233-9703
E-mail: info@njaa.info
Web: www.angusfoundation.org

Purpose To provide financial assistance to students who have been members of the National Junior Angus Association (NJAA) and are enrolled or planning to enroll in any field in college.
Eligibility Applicants must have been a member of the NJAA in the past and presently must be a junior, regular, or life member of the American Angus Association. They must be either a high school senior or already enrolled in college working full time on an undergraduate degree with a GPA of 2.0 or higher and younger than 25 years of age. All fields of study are eligible. Selection is based on involvement in Angus associations, other agriculture-related associations, school organizations, and church, civic, and community groups.
Financial data A stipend is awarded (amount not specified).
Duration 1 year; nonrenewable.
Additional information This program, established in 2006, is sponsored by the Angus Foundation.
Number awarded 1 each year.
Deadline April of each year.

[1141]
JOSEPH F. BRACONE MEMORIAL SCHOLARSHIP
Order Sons of Italy in America
Attn: Sons of Italy Foundation
219 E Street, N.E.
Washington, DC 20002
(202) 547-2900   Fax: (202) 546-8168
E-mail: scholarships@osia.org
Web: www.osia.org/public/scholarships/grants.asp

Purpose To provide financial assistance for college to students of Italian descent.
Eligibility Eligible are U.S. citizens of Italian descent who are enrolled at a 4-year college or university. Applicants may be majoring in any liberal arts field, but preference is given to those studying business, finance, or pre-law. Along with their application, they must submit essays, from 500 to 750 words in length, on the principal contribution of Italian Americans to the development of U.S. culture and society. These merit-based awards are presented to students who have demonstrated exceptional leadership qualities and distinguished scholastic abilities.
Financial data Stipends range from $5,000 to $25,000.
Duration 1 year; nonrenewable.
Additional information Applications must be accompanied by a $30 processing fee.
Number awarded 1 each year.
Deadline February of each year.

ANY SUBJECT AREA

[1142]
JOSEPH R. STONE SCHOLARSHIPS

American Society of Travel Agents
Attn: ASTA Foundation
1101 King Street, Suite 200
Alexandria, VA 22314-2944
(703) 739-8721 Fax: (703) 684-8319
E-mail: scholarship@astahq.com
Web: www.astanet.com/education/scholariship.asp

Purpose To provide financial assistance to undergraduate students whose parent is employed in the travel industry.

Eligibility This program is open to undergraduates who are enrolled at a 4-year postsecondary institution in the United States or Canada. At least 1 parent must be employed in the travel industry (hotel, car rental, airlines, travel agency, etc.). In addition, applicants must have a GPA of 2.5 or higher, be residents of the United States or Canada, and write a 500-word essay on their goals. Financial need is not considered in the selection process.

Financial data The stipend is $2,400.

Duration 1 year; may be renewed.

Additional information This scholarship was established in 1983.

Number awarded 3 each year.

Deadline August of each year.

[1143]
JOSEPHINE DE KARMAN FELLOWSHIPS

Josephine de Kármán Fellowship Trust
Attn: Judy McClain, Secretary
P.O. Box 3389
San Dimas, CA 91773
(909) 592-0607 E-mail: info@dekarman.org
Web: www.dekarman.org

Purpose To provide financial assistance to outstanding college seniors or students in their last year of a Ph.D. program.

Eligibility This program is open to students in any discipline who will be entering their senior undergraduate year or their terminal year of a Ph.D. program in the fall of the next academic year. Postdoctoral students are not eligible. Foreign students may apply if they are already enrolled in a university in the United States. Applicants must be able to demonstrate exceptional ability and seriousness of purpose. Special consideration is given to applicants in the humanities and to those who have completed their qualifying examinations for the doctoral degree.

Financial data The stipend is $16,000 per year for graduate students or $8,000 per year for undergraduates. Funds are paid in 2 installments to the recipient's school. No funds may be used for travel.

Duration 1 year; may not be renewed or postponed.

Additional information This fund was established in 1954 by Dr. Theodore von Kármán, renowned aeronautics expert and director of the Guggenheim Aeronautical Laboratory at the California Institute of Technology. Study must be carried out in the United States.

Number awarded At least 10 each year.

Deadline January of each year.

[1144]
JUNIOR GOLD CHAMPIONSHIPS

United States Bowling Congress
Attn: Junior Gold Program
5301 South 76th Street
Greendale, WI 53129-1192
(414) 423-3171 Toll-free: (800) 514-BOWL, ext. 3171
Fax: (414) 421-3014
E-mail: USBCjuniorgold@bowl.com
Web: www.bowl.com/bowl/yaba

Purpose To recognize and reward, with college scholarships, United States Bowling Congress (USBC) Junior Gold program members who achieve high scores in a national competition.

Eligibility This program is open to USBC members who qualify for the Junior Gold program by maintaining a bowling average score of 165 for girls or 175 for boys, based on at least 21 games. Competitions for Junior Gold members are held throughout the season at bowling centers and in bowling leagues in the United States. Each approved competition may enter its top 10% of scorers in the Junior Gold Championships, held annually at a site in the United States. In addition, USBC Junior Gold members who participate in the Pepsi USBC Youth Bowling Championship in the girls' and boys' 12 and over scratch categories and achieve high scores in state and zone competitions are eligible to advance to the national tournament of this program. They compete in separate divisions for boys and girls. Scholarships are awarded solely on the basis of bowling performance in the national tournament.

Financial data Scholarships depend on the availability of funding provided by sponsors. Recently, more than $50,000 in scholarships was awarded. Another $15,000 in scholarships was awarded to Junior Gold participants who qualified for the national tournament through the Pepsi competition. That includes $3,000 for first, $2,000 for second, $1,500 for third, and $1,000 for fourth for boys and girls.

Duration The competition is held annually.

Additional information This competition was first held in 1998. The sponsoring league or center must pay a fee of $150 for each participant who advances to the national tournament.

Number awarded Varies each year. Recently, a total of 1,458 spots were available at the national tournament and scholarships were provided to approximately 10% of the competitors. For bowlers from the Pepsi competition, 4 girls and 4 boys win scholarships.

Deadline Applications must by submitted by May of each year. The national finals are held in July.

[1145]
KANSAS EDUCATIONAL BENEFITS FOR DEPENDENTS OF POWS/KIAS/MIAS OF THE VIETNAM WAR

Kansas Commission on Veterans' Affairs
Jayhawk Towers
700 S.W. Jackson Street, Suite 701
Topeka, KS 66603-3150
(785) 296-3976   Fax: (785) 296-1462
E-mail: KVH007@ink.org
Web: www.kcva.org

Purpose To provide financial assistance for college to children of Kansas veterans who were prisoners of war or killed in Vietnam.
Eligibility Applicants for these benefits may be residents of any state as long as their veteran parent was a legal resident of Kansas upon entering military service and, while serving in Vietnam after January 1, 1960, either died of service-connected causes or was declared by the Secretary of Defense to be a prisoner of war or missing in action.
Financial data Eligible dependents receive free tuition and fees at any Kansas state-supported college, university, community college, or area vocational school.
Duration Up to 12 semesters.
Number awarded Varies each year.

[1146]
KATHERN F. GRUBER SCHOLARSHIPS

Blinded Veterans Association
477 H Street, N.W.
Washington, DC 20001-2694
(202) 371-8880   Toll-free: (800) 669-7079
Fax: (202) 371-8258   E-mail: bva@bva.org
Web: www.bva.org/services.html

Purpose To provide financial assistance for undergraduate or graduate study to spouses and children of blinded veterans.
Eligibility This program is open to dependent children and spouses of blinded veterans of the U.S. armed forces. The veteran need not be a member of the Blinded Veterans Association. The veteran's blindness may be either service connected or nonservice connected, but it must meet the following definition: central visual acuity of 20/200 or less in the better eye with corrective glasses, or central visual acuity of more than 20/200 if there is a field defect in which the peripheral field has contracted to such an extent that the widest diameter of visual field subtends an angular distance no greater than 20 degrees in the better eye. The applicant must have been accepted or be currently enrolled as a full-time student in an undergraduate or graduate program at an accredited institution of higher learning. Selection is based on high school and/or college transcripts, 3 letters of recommendation, and a 300-word essay on the applicant's career goals and aspirations.
Financial data The stipends are $2,000 or $1,000 and are intended to be used to cover the student's expenses, including tuition, other academic fees, books, dormitory fees, and cafeteria fees. Funds are paid directly to the recipient's school.
Duration 1 year; recipients may reapply.

Additional information Scholarships may be used for only 1 degree (vocational, bachelor's, or graduate) or non-graduate certificate (e.g., nursing, secretarial).
Number awarded 6 each year: 3 at $2,000 and 3 at $1,000.
Deadline April of each year.

[1147]
KENTUCKY DECEASED OR DISABLED LAW ENFORCEMENT OFFICER AND FIRE FIGHTER DEPENDENT TUITION WAIVER

Kentucky Fire Commission
Attn: Executive Director
300 North Main Street
Versailles, KY 40383
(859) 256-3478   Toll-free: (800) 782-6823
Fax: (859) 256-3125   E-mail: ronnie.day@kctcs.net
Web: www.kctcs.net/kyfirecommission

Purpose To provide financial assistance for college to the children and spouses of Kentucky police officers or fire fighters deceased or disabled in the line of duty.
Eligibility This program is open to spouses, widow(er)s, and children of Kentucky residents who became a law enforcement officer, fire fighter, or volunteer fire fighter and who 1) was killed while in active service or training for active service; 2) died as a result of a service-connected disability; or 3) became permanently and totally disabled as a result of active service or training for active service. Children must be younger than 23 years of age; spouses and widow(er)s may be of any age.
Financial data Recipients are entitled to a waiver of tuition at state-supported universities, community colleges, and technical training institutions in Kentucky.
Duration 1 year; may be renewed up to a maximum total of 36 months.
Number awarded Varies each year; all qualified applicants are entitled to this aid.

[1148]
KENTUCKY TURFGRASS COUNCIL LEGACY SCHOLARSHIP

Kentucky Turfgrass Council
c/o David Williams, Executive Secretary
University of Kentucky
Plant and Soil Science Department
N-222 Agriculture Science Center North
Lexington, KY 40546-0091
(859) 257-2715   Fax: (859) 323-1952
E-mail: dwilliam@uky.edu
Web: www.uky.edu

Purpose To provide financial assistance for college to children and grandchildren of members of the Kentucky Turfgrass Council (KTC).
Eligibility This program is open to high school seniors and currently-enrolled college students who are enrolled or planning to enroll full time at an accredited institution of higher learning. A parent or grandparent of the applicant must have been a KTC member for 5 or more consecutive years. Applicants must submit transcripts from high school or colleges attended and a 500-word essay on their future

goals and aspirations. Selection is based on academic achievement, extracurricular and community involvement, leadership, and outside employment. Financial need is not considered.

Financial data The stipend is $1,000.

Duration 1 year. Recipients are not eligible in the following year but they may reapply after a hiatus of 1 year.

Additional information Information is also available from Gary Duvardo, Scholarship Committee Chair, P.O. Box 323, Bardstown, KY 40004, E-mail: garyd67@hotmail.com.

Number awarded 1 each year.

Deadline October of each year.

[1149]
KENTUCKY VETERANS TUITION WAIVER PROGRAM

Kentucky Department of Veterans Affairs
Attn: Division of Field Operations
545 South Third Street, Room 123
Louisville, KY 40202
(502) 595-4447   Toll-free: (800) 928-4012 (within KY)
Fax: (502) 595-4448
Web: www.kdva.net/tuitionwaiver.htm

Purpose To provide financial assistance for college to the children, spouses, or unremarried widow(er)s of disabled or deceased Kentucky veterans.

Eligibility This program is open to the children, stepchildren, spouses, and unremarried widow(er)s of veterans who are residents of Kentucky (or were residents at the time of their death). The qualifying veteran must meet 1 of the following conditions: 1) died on active duty (regardless of wartime service); 2) died as a result of a service-connected disability (regardless of wartime service); 3) has a 100% service-connected disability; or 4) was a prisoner of war or declared missing in action. The military service may have been as a member of the U.S. armed forces, the Kentucky National Guard, or a Reserve component; service in the Guard or Reserves must have been on state active duty, active duty for training, inactive duty training, or active duty with the U.S. armed forces. Children of veterans must be under 23 years of age; no age limit applies to spouses or unremarried widow(er)s. All applicants must be attending or planning to attend a 2-year, 4-year, or vocational technical school operated and funded by the Kentucky Department of Education.

Financial data Eligible dependents and survivors are exempt from tuition and matriculation fees at any state-supported institution of higher education in Kentucky.

Duration Tuition is waived until the recipient completes 36 months of training, receives a college degree, or (in the case of children of veterans) reaches 23 years of age, whichever comes first. Spouses and unremarried widow(er)s are not subject to the age limitation.

Number awarded Varies each year.

[1150]
KEPPRA FAMILY EPILEPSY SCHOLARSHIP PROGRAM

UCB Pharma, Inc.
Keppra Scholarship Program
c/o S&R Communications Group
2511 Old Cornwallis Road, Suite 200
Durham, NC 27713
Toll-free: (888) 275-7928
E-mail: kepprascholarship@srcomgroup.com
Web: www.keppra.com

Purpose To provide financial assistance for college or graduate school to epilepsy patients and their family members and caregivers.

Eligibility This program is open to epilepsy patients and their family members and caregivers. Applicants must be working on or planning to work on an undergraduate or graduate degree at an institution of higher education in the United States. They must be able to demonstrate academic achievement, a record of participation in activities outside of school, and service as a role model. Along with their application, they must submit a 1-page essay explaining why they should be selected for the scholarship, how epilepsy has impacted their life either as a patient or as a family member or caregiver, and how they will benefit from the scholarship.

Financial data The stipend is $50,000.

Duration 1 year; nonrenewable.

Number awarded 30 each year: 20 to epilepsy patients and 10 to family members or caregivers.

Deadline May of each year.

[1151]
KEVIN CHILD SCHOLARSHIP

National Hemophilia Foundation
Attn: Department of Finance, Administration & MIS
116 West 32nd Street, 11th Floor
New York, NY 10001-3212
(212) 328-3700   Toll-free: (800) 42-HANDI, ext. 3700
Fax: (212) 328-3777   E-mail: info@hemophilia.org
Web: www.hemophilia.org

Purpose To provide financial assistance for college to students with hemophilia.

Eligibility This program is open to high school seniors entering their first year of undergraduate study as well as those currently enrolled in college. Applicants must have hemophilia or another bleeding disorder. Selection is based on academic performance, participation in school and community activities, and an essay on their occupational objectives and goals in life.

Financial data The stipend is $1,000.

Duration 1 year.

Additional information The program was established by the Child family after the death of 21-year old Kevin in 1989. Information is also available from Mary Child Smoot, (203) 968-2776, E-mail: Smooter@aol.com.

Number awarded 1 each year.

Deadline June of each year.

[1152]
LARRY STRICKLAND LEADERSHIP AWARD AND SCHOLARSHIP

Association of the United States Army
Attn: Strickland Memorial Scholarship Fund
2425 Wilson Boulevard
Arlington, VA 22201
(703) 841-4300, ext. 693
Toll-free: (800) 336-4570, ext. 693
E-mail: jspencer@ausa.org
Web: www.ausa.org

Purpose To recognize and reward, with funding for additional education, Army noncommissioned officers who demonstrate outstanding leadership.

Eligibility This award is presented to a noncommissioned officer who best exemplifies "the Army's vision and influences others in shaping future leaders." Candidates must also be interested in obtaining additional education.

Financial data The award consists of a plaque and $1,500 to assist in covering educational costs that Army tuition assistance does not pay, such as instructional fees, laboratory fees, and books.

Duration The award is presented annually.

Additional information This award was established in 2003 to honor SGM Larry L. Strickland, who was killed in the Pentagon on September 11, 2001.

Number awarded 1 each year.

[1153]
LEGISLATIVE INCENTIVE FOR FUTURE EXCELLENCE (LIFE) SCHOLARSHIP PROGRAM

South Carolina Commission on Higher Education
Attn: Director of Student Services
1333 Main Street, Suite 200
Columbia, SC 29201
(803) 737-2280 Toll-free: (877) 349-7183
Fax: (803) 737-2297 E-mail: srhyne@che.sc.gov
Web: www.che.sc.gov

Purpose To provide financial assistance for college to residents of South Carolina.

Eligibility This program is open to residents of South Carolina who graduate from high school or complete a homeschool program and attend an eligible South Carolina public or private college or university. As an entering freshman at a 4-year college or university, they must meet any 2 of the following requirements: 1) have earned a GPA of 3.0 or higher in high school; 2) score at least 1100 on the mathematics and critical reading sections of the SAT or 24 on the ACT; and/or 3) graduate in the top 30% of their high school class. Students entering a 2-year or technical institution must have a high school GPA of 3.0 or higher. Continuing college students must have completed an average of 30 credit hours for each academic year and maintained a GPA of 3.0 or higher. Students transferring must have completed 30 credit hours for a second-year transfer, 60 for a third-year transfer, or 90 for a fourth-year transfer; their cumulative GPA must be 3.0 or higher. U.S. citizenship or permanent resident status is required. Applicants may not have been convicted of any felonies or alcohol- or drug-related charges.

Financial data The stipend is $4,700 per year, plus a $300 book allowance, at 4-year colleges or universities. Students at public and private 2-year colleges receive a stipend of the cost of tuition at a regional campus of the University of South Carolina plus a $300 book allowance. Technical school students receive the cost of tuition plus a $300 book allowance. Funds may be applied only toward the cost of attendance at an eligible South Carolina institution.

Duration 1 year; may be renewed up to a total of 10 semesters for a 5-year program, 8 semesters for a 4-year program, 4 semesters for a 2-year program, or 2 semesters for a 1-year certificate or diploma program.

Additional information The South Carolina General Assembly established this program in 1998.

Number awarded Varies each year; recently, 28,390 of these scholarships, worth more than $127 million, were awarded.

[1154]
LIFE MEMBERS' SCHOLARSHIP

American Atheists
P.O. Box 5733
Parsippany, NJ 07054-6733
(908) 276-7300 Fax: (908) 276-7402
E-mail: info@atheists.org
Web: www.atheists.org/family/temp/scholarship

Purpose To provide financial assistance for college to students who identify themselves as atheists.

Eligibility This program is open to college-bound high school seniors and current college students. Applicants must be atheists and have a cumulative GPA of 2.5 or higher. Selection is based on activism, with special attention given to students who show activism in their schools (e.g., starting atheist/freethinker groups, fighting against violations of the separation of church and state in the school).

Financial data The stipend is $2,000.

Duration 1 year.

Additional information Information is also available from the American Atheists Scholarship Fund, 1308 Centennial Avenue, Suite 101, Piscataway, NJ 08854. The scholarship is also designated the American Atheists College Scholarship (AACS). The funding includes $1,000 donated by 5 life members of American Atheists and $1,000 in matching funds from the organization.

Number awarded 1 each year.

Deadline January of each year.

[1155]
LOUISIANA VETERANS STATE AID PROGRAM

Louisiana Department of Veterans Affairs
1885 Wooddale Boulevard, Room 1013
P.O. Box 94095, Capitol Station
Baton Rouge, LA 70804-9095
(225) 922-0500 Fax: (225) 922-0511
E-mail: dperkins@vetaffairs.com
Web: www.vetaffairs.com

Purpose To provide financial assistance for college to children and surviving spouses of certain disabled or deceased Louisiana veterans.

Eligibility Eligible under this program are children (between 16 and 25 years of age) of veterans who served during World War I, World War II, the Korean war, or the Vietnam conflict and either died or sustained a disability rated as 90% or more by the U.S. Department of Veterans Affairs. Deceased veterans must have resided in Louisiana for at least 12 months prior to entry into service. Living disabled veterans must have resided in Louisiana for at least 24 months prior to the child's admission into the program. Also eligible are surviving spouses (of any age) of veterans who had been residents of Louisiana for at least 1 year preceding entry into service and who died in war service in the line of duty or from an established wartime service-connected disability subsequently.

Financial data Eligible persons accepted as full-time students at Louisiana state-supported colleges, universities, trade schools, or vocational/technical schools will be admitted free and are exempt from payment of all tuition, laboratory, athletic, medical, and other special fees. Free registration does not cover books, supplies, room and board, or fees assessed by the student body on themselves (such as yearbooks and weekly papers).

Duration Tuition, fee exemption, and possible payment of cash subsistence allowance are provided for a maximum of 4 school years to be completed in not more than 5 years from date of original entry.

Additional information Attendance must be on a full-time basis. Surviving spouses must remain unmarried and must take advantage of the benefit within 10 years after eligibility is established.

Number awarded Varies each year.

Deadline Applications must be received no later than 3 months prior to the beginning of a semester.

[1156]
LTG AND MRS. JOSEPH M. HEISER SCHOLARSHIP

U.S. Army Ordnance Corps Association
Attn: Heiser Scholarship
P.O. Box 377
Aberdeen Proving Ground, MD 21005-0377
(410) 272-8540   Fax: (410) 272-8425
Web: www.usaoca.org/heiser.html

Purpose To provide financial assistance for college to students who submit, along with their application, an essay on the U.S. Army.

Eligibility This program is open to high school seniors and students already enrolled in college. Applicants must submit an essay of 1,000 to 1,500 words on a topic related to the history or heritage of the U.S. Army, a statement describing any circumstances that would impact their attending college, letters of recommendation, transcripts, and an essay of 300 to 500 words on their educational and career goals.

Financial data The stipend is $1,000.

Duration 1 year.

Number awarded Varies each year; recently, 4 of these scholarships were awarded.

Deadline June of each year.

[1157]
MAINE TUITION WAIVER PROGRAM FOR CHILDREN AND SPOUSES OF FIRE FIGHTERS, LAW ENFORCEMENT OFFICERS, AND EMERGENCY MEDICAL SERVICES PERSONNEL KILLED IN THE LINE OF DUTY

Finance Authority of Maine
Attn: Education Finance Programs
5 Community Drive
P.O. Box 949
Augusta, ME 04332-0949
(207) 623-3263   Toll-free: (800) 228-3734
Fax: (207) 623-0095   TTY: (207) 626-2717
E-mail: info@famemaine.com
Web: www.famemaine.com

Purpose To provide financial assistance for college to children and spouses of deceased law enforcement officers, fire fighters, and emergency medical services personnel in Maine.

Eligibility This program is open to children and spouses of fire fighters, law enforcement officers, and emergency medical services personnel who have been killed in the line of duty or died as a result of injuries received during the performance of their duties. Applicants must be enrolled in or accepted for enrollment in a branch of the University of Maine system, the Maine Community College System, or the Maine Maritime Academy.

Financial data Eligible students receive waivers of tuition and fees.

Duration 1 year; may be renewed up to 3 additional years.

[1158]
MAINE TUITION WAIVER PROGRAM FOR FOSTER CHILDREN UNDER THE CUSTODY OF THE DEPARTMENT OF HUMAN SERVICES

Finance Authority of Maine
Attn: Education Finance Programs
5 Community Drive
P.O. Box 949
Augusta, ME 04332-0949
(207) 623-3263   Toll-free: (800) 228-3734
Fax: (207) 623-0095   TTY: (207) 626-2717
E-mail: info@famemaine.com
Web: www.famemaine.com

Purpose To provide financial assistance for college to foster children in Maine.

Eligibility Applicants must have been foster children under the custody of the Maine Department of Human Services when they graduate from high school. They must be enrolled in or accepted for enrollment in a branch of the University of Maine system, the Maine Community College System, or the Maine Maritime Academy.

Financial data Eligible students receive waivers of tuition and fees.

Duration 1 year; may be renewed up to 3 additional years.

[1159]
MAINE VETERANS DEPENDENTS EDUCATIONAL BENEFITS

Bureau of Veterans' Services
117 State House Station
Augusta, ME 04333-0117
(207) 626-4464 Toll-free: (800) 345-0116 (within ME)
Fax: (207) 626-4471 E-mail: mainebvs@maine.gov
Web: www.mainebvs.org/benefits.htm

Purpose To provide financial assistance for undergraduate or graduate education to dependents of disabled and other Maine veterans.

Eligibility Applicants for these benefits must be children (high school seniors or graduates under 25 years of age), non-divorced spouses, or unremarried widow(er)s of veterans who meet 1 or more of the following requirements: 1) living and determined to have a total permanent disability resulting from a service-connected cause; 2) killed in action; 3) died from a service-connected disability; 4) died while totally and permanently disabled due to a service-connected disability but whose death was not related to the service-connected disability; or 5) a member of the armed forces on active duty who has been listed for more than 90 days as missing in action, captured, forcibly detained, or interned in the line of duty by a foreign government or power. The veteran parent must have been a resident of Maine at the time of entry into service or a resident of Maine for 5 years preceding application for these benefits. Children may be seeking no higher than a bachelor's degree. Spouses, widows, and widowers may work on an advanced degree if they already have a bachelor's degree at the time of enrollment into this program.

Financial data Recipients are entitled to free tuition at institutions of higher education supported by the state of Maine.

Duration Benefits extend for a maximum of 8 semesters. Recipients have 6 consecutive academic years to complete their education.

Additional information College preparatory schooling and correspondence courses do not qualify under this program.

Number awarded Varies each year.

[1160]
MAKE A STATEMENT SCHOLARSHIP CONTEST

Coty US LLC
One Park Avenue, Fifth Floor
New York, NY 10016
(212) 479-4300 Fax: (212) 479-4399
Web: www.exclamationbycoty.com/scholarship.html

Purpose To recognize and reward, with college scholarships, women who submit outstanding essays on how they are trying to make a difference in the world.

Eligibility This competition is open to women residents of the United States who are 18 years of age or older. Applicants must be enrolled or planning to enroll at a 2- or 4-year U.S. college, university, or vocational/technical school with a GPA of 3.0 or higher. They must submit an essay, up to 100 words, on what they would do or say if they had only 1 day to make a difference in the world and how they would accomplish it. Those essays are judged on the basis of originality, sincerity of expression, and grammar/mechanics. Financial need is not considered. The 35 finalists are then invited to complete a statement on a specified topic and submit transcripts, a list of extracurricular activities, and other documents as part of an application packet to be provided. Scholarship America ranks the finalists on the basis of past academic performance and future potential, leadership, participation in school and community activities, work experience, a statement of career and educational aspirations and goals, unusual personal or family circumstances, and an outside appraisal.

Financial data First place is a $3,000 scholarship, second a $2,000 scholarship, and third a $1,000 scholarship.

Duration The competition is held annually.

Additional information This annual competition began in 2006. Information is also available from Scholarship America, One Scholarship Way, P.O. Box 297, St. Peter, MN 56082, (507) 931-1682, (800) 537-4180, Fax: (507) 931-9168, E-mail: smsinfo@csfa.org, and from Madden Preprint Media, 1650 East Fort Lowell Road, Suite 100, Tucson, AZ 85719.

Number awarded 3 each year: 1 first place, 1 second, and 1 third.

Deadline April of each year.

[1161]
MARINE CORPS COUNTERINTELLIGENCE ASSOCIATION SCHOLARSHIPS

Marine Corps Counterintelligence Association
c/o Samuel L. Moyer
3125 Palmdale Drive
Oldsmar, FL 34677
E-mail: scholarship@mccia.org
Web: www.mccia.org

Purpose To provide financial assistance for college to dependents of members of the Marine Corps Counterintelligence Association (MCCIA).

Eligibility This program is open to children, grandchildren, and spouses of 1) current MCCIA members; 2) deceased Marines who were MCCIA members at the time of death; and 3) counterintelligence Marines who lost their lives in the line of duty (whether they were a member of MCCIA or not). Spouses of deceased Marines must also be MCCIA Auxiliary members. Applicants must be enrolled or planning to enroll as a full-time undergraduate student at an accredited college or university. Along with their application, they must submit a 1-page essay on a topic of their choice, letters of recommendation, SAT or ACT scores, transcripts, copies of awards and other honors, and evidence of acceptance at a college or university. Financial need is not considered.

Financial data Stipends are $1,000 or $500. Funds must be used to help pay for tuition, books, fees, and materials; they may not be used for personal or living expenses.

Duration 1 year; may be renewed up to 3 additional years (need not be consecutive).

Number awarded Varies each year; recently, 5 of these scholarships, at $1,000 each, were awarded.

Deadline June of each year.

[1162]
MARINE CORPS LEAGUE SCHOLARSHIPS
Marine Corps League
Attn: National Executive Director
P.O. Box 3070
Merrifield, VA 22116-3070
(703) 207-9588	Toll-free: (800) MCL-1775
Fax: (703) 207-0047	E-mail: mcl@mcleague.org
Web: www.mcleague.org

Purpose To provide college aid to students whose parents served in the Marines and to members of the Marine Corps League or Marine Corps League Auxiliary.

Eligibility The scholarships are awarded to qualified applicants in the following order of preference: 1) sons and daughters of Marines who lost their lives in the line of duty; 2) children and grandchildren of active Marine Corps Leaguers and/or Auxiliary members; and 3) members of the Marine Corps League and/or Marine Corps League Auxiliary who are honorably discharged and in need of rehabilitation training not provided by government programs. Applicants must be seeking further education and training as a full-time student and be recommended by the commandant of an active chartered detachment of the Marine Corps League or the president of an active chartered unit of the Auxiliary. Financial need is not considered in the selection process.

Financial data The stipend varies. Funds are paid directly to the recipient.

Duration 1 year; may be renewed up to 3 additional years (all renewals must complete an application and attach a transcript from the college or university).

Additional information Information is also available from the Marine Corps League Scholarship Committee, Vic Voltaggio, Chairman, 1049 Florian Way, Spring Hall, FL 34609-9021, (352) 683-8254, E-mail: reconvic@yahoo.com.

Number awarded Varies, depending upon the amount of funds available each year.

Deadline June of each year.

[1163]
MARLIN R. SCARBOROUGH MEMORIAL SCHOLARSHIP
South Dakota Board of Regents
Attn: Scholarship Committee
306 East Capitol Avenue, Suite 200
Pierre, SD 57501-2545
(605) 773-3455	Fax: (605) 773-2422
E-mail: info@ris.sdbor.edu
Web: www.sdbor.edu

Purpose To provide financial assistance to students at public universities in South Dakota who are entering their junior year.

Eligibility This program is open to students entering their junior year at public universities in South Dakota. Applicants must have a GPA of 3.5 or higher. They must be nominated by their university. Along with their application, they must submit an essay explaining their leadership and academic qualities, career plans, and educational interests.

Financial data The stipend is $1,500; funds are allocated to the institution for distribution to the student.

Duration 1 year; nonrenewable.

Number awarded 1 each year.

[1164]
MARSH SCHOLARSHIP
Eastern Surfing Association
P.O. Box 625
Virginia Beach, VA 23451
(757) 233-1790	Fax: (757) 233-1396
E-mail: info@surfesa.org
Web: www.surfesa.org/scholarships

Purpose To provide financial assistance for college to members of the Eastern Surfing Association.

Eligibility This program is open to current members in good standing. Applicants must submit an essay, up to 500 words, detailing their educational goals and how their choice of educational institutions will help them reach those goals. Selection is based on academic record and U.S. citizenship, not athletic ability.

Financial data Stipends range from $500 to $1,000.

Additional information This scholarship was established in 1981 in honor of Mike Marsh, who earned a law degree despite his battle against cancer. Information is also available from the ESA Marsh Scholarship Program, c/o Henningsen, 25 Old Post Road, Rye, NY 10580.

Number awarded Varies each year; a total of $8,000 is available for this program each year.

Deadline May of each year.

[1165]
MARTIN BARNES SCHOLARSHIPS
Martin Barnes Scholarship Fund
P.O. Box 448
Oxon Hill, MD 20750

Purpose To provide financial assistance for college to high school seniors and current undergraduates.

Eligibility Applicants may be high school seniors or currently-enrolled full-time undergraduate students. They must be U.S. citizens, have at least a 2.5 GPA, and have performed at least 100 hours of community service within the current academic year in the field of human outreach. Along with their application, they must submit a 250-word essay on an assigned topic related to their religious beliefs and moral judgments. Selection is based on leadership in school, civic, and other extracurricular activities; academic achievement; motivation to serve and succeed; and individual character.

Financial data The stipend is $1,500.

Duration 1 year.

Additional information This fund was established in 1997.

Number awarded 2 each year.

Deadline June of each year.

[1166]
MARY P. OENSLAGER SCHOLASTIC ACHIEVEMENT AWARDS

Recording for the Blind and Dyslexic
Attn: Strategic Communications Department
Anne T. Macdonald Center
20 Roszel Road
Princeton, NJ 08540
(609) 520-8044   Toll-free: (866) RFBD-585
E-mail: jhaggith@rfbd.org
Web: www.rfbd.org/applications_awards.htm

Purpose To recognize and reward the outstanding academic achievements of blind college seniors.

Eligibility To be eligible for this award, candidates must 1) be legally blind; 2) have received, or will receive, a bachelor's degree from a 4-year accredited college or university in the United States or its territories during the year the award is given; 3) have an overall academic average of 3.0 or higher; and 4) have been registered borrowers from Recording for the Blind and Dyslexic for at least 1 year and have borrowed at least 1 of its audiobooks during that time. Selection is based on evidence of leadership, enterprise, and service to others.

Financial data Top winners receive $6,000 each, Special Honors winners $3,000 each, and Honors winners $1,000 each.

Duration The awards are presented annually.

Additional information These awards are named for the founder of the program who established it in 1959 and endowed it with a gift of $1 million in 1990.

Number awarded 9 each year: 3 Top winners, 3 Special Honors winners, and 3 Honors winners.

Deadline February of each year.

[1167]
MENSA MEMBER AWARDS

American Mensa Education and Research Foundation
1229 Corporate Drive West
Arlington, TX 76006-6103
(817) 607-0060   Toll-free: (800) 66-MENSA
Fax: (817) 649-5232
E-mail: info@mensafoundation.org
Web: www.mensafoundation.org

Purpose To provide financial assistance for undergraduate or graduate study to members of American Mensa and their dependent children.

Eligibility This program is open to students who are enrolled or planning to enroll in a degree program at an accredited American institution of postsecondary education. Applicants must be current Mensa members or their dependent children. There are no restrictions as to age, race, gender, level of postsecondary education, GPA, or financial need. Selection is based on a 550-word essay that describes the applicant's career, vocational, or academic goals.

Financial data The stipend is $1,000.

Duration 1 year; nonrenewable.

Additional information Applications are only available through the advertising efforts of participating Mensa local groups. This program consists of the following named awards: the Tom and Elaine Ehrhorn Scholarship, the Verma Jeremiah Scholarship, the Pat Merk Scholarship, and the Scholarship in Memory of Jerry Salny.

Number awarded 4 each year.

Deadline January of each year.

[1168]
METROPOLITAN SOCIETY OF KARDAMYLIANS COLLEGE AWARDS

Metropolitan Society of Kardamylians, Inc.
7919 Third Avenue
Brooklyn, NY 11209
(718) 745-7414
Web: www.kardamyla.org/fsscholar.html

Purpose To provide financial assistance for college to members of the Metropolitan Society of Kardamylians.

Eligibility This program is open to members of the society who have been accepted as a full-time student at an accredited college or university in the United States for the current fall semester. Applicants who just graduated from high school and are entering college for the first time must have a PSAT/SAT score of 1200 or higher; applicants who have already completed some college study must have a GPA of 3.5 or higher. Students or their family members must have participated in at least 2 of the society's events during the year prior to the application deadline. All applicants who meet the eligibility requirements receive awards.

Financial data The stipend ranges from $250 to $1,000 per year.

Duration 1 year.

Additional information Membership in the society is based on ancestry in the Kardamyla area of Greece. This program includes the Captain Michael Frangos and Irene Frangos Memorial Scholarship Award. Recipients (or a parent) must be present to receive the award at the Kardamylitiko Glendi and Student Awards' night in the fall.

Number awarded 1 or more each year.

Deadline September of each year.

[1169]
MICHIGAN CHILDREN OF VETERANS TUITION GRANTS

Michigan Department of Treasury
Michigan Higher Education Assistance Authority
Attn: Office of Scholarships and Grants
P.O. Box 30462
Lansing, MI 48909-7962
(517) 373-0457   Toll-free: (888) 4-GRANTS
Fax: (517) 335-6851   E-mail: osg@michigan.gov
Web: www.michigan.gov/mistudentaid

Purpose To provide financial assistance for college to the children of Michigan veterans who are totally disabled or deceased as a result of service-connected causes.

Eligibility This program is open to children of Michigan veterans who are totally disabled as a result of wartime service, or died from service-connected conditions, or were killed in action, or are listed as missing in action. Applicants must be between 16 and 26 years of age and must have lived in Michigan at least 12 months prior to the date of application. They must be or plan to become a full-time undergraduate student at a public institution of higher edu-

cation in Michigan. U.S. citizenship or permanent resident status is required.
Financial data Recipients are exempt from payment of the first $2,800 per year of tuition or any other fee that takes the place of tuition.
Duration 1 year; may be renewed for up to 3 additional years if the recipient maintains full-time enrollment and a GPA of 2.25 or higher.
Additional information This program was formerly known as the Michigan Veterans Trust Fund Tuition Grants, administered by the Michigan Veterans Trust Fund within the Department of Military and Veterans Affairs. It was transferred to the Office of Scholarships and Grants in 2006.
Number awarded Varies each year.

[1170] MILITARY ORDER OF THE PURPLE HEART SCHOLARSHIP PROGRAM

Military Order of the Purple Heart
Attn: Scholarships
5413-B Backlick Road
Springfield, VA 22151-3960
(703) 642-5360 Fax: (703) 642-2054
E-mail: info@purpleheart.org
Web: www.purpleheart.org/scholar.html

Purpose To provide financial assistance for college or graduate school to spouses and children of members of the Military Order of the Purple Heart.
Eligibility This program is open to children (natural, step-, and adopted), grandchildren, great-grandchildren and spouses of veterans who are members in good standing of the order or who received the Purple Heart. Applicants must be U.S. citizens, graduating seniors or graduates of an accredited high school, enrolled or accepted for enrollment in a full-time program of study in a college, trade school, or graduate school with a GPA of 3.5 or higher. Selection is based on merit; financial need is not considered in the selection process.
Financial data The stipend is $1,750 per year.
Duration 1 year; may be renewed up to 3 additional years.
Number awarded Varies each year; recently, 28 of these scholarships were awarded.
Deadline March of each year.

[1171] MILITARY TUITION WAIVER DURING ASSIGNMENT AFTER TEXAS

Texas Higher Education Coordinating Board
Attn: Grants and Special Programs
1200 East Anderson Lane
P.O. Box 12788, Capitol Station
Austin, TX 78711-2788
(512) 427-6101 Toll-free: (800) 242-3062
Fax: (512) 427-6127
E-mail: grantinfo@thecb.state.tx.us
Web: www.collegefortexans.com

Purpose To provide educational assistance to the spouses and children of Texas military personnel assigned elsewhere.
Eligibility This program is open to the spouses and dependent children of members of the U.S. armed forces or commissioned officers of the Public Health Service who remain in Texas when the member is reassigned to duty outside of the state. The spouse or dependent child must reside continuously in Texas. Applicants must be attending or planning to attend a Texas public college or university.
Financial data Eligible students are entitled to pay tuition and fees at the resident rate at publicly-supported colleges and universities in Texas.
Duration The waiver remains in effect for the duration of the member's first assignment outside of Texas.
Additional information This program became effective in September, 2003.
Number awarded Varies each year.

[1172] MILTON WEINTRAUB SCHOLARSHIP FUND

Association of Theatrical Press Agents and Managers
1560 Broadway. Suite 700
New York, NY 10036-2501
(212) 719-3666 Toll-free: (800) 858-3667
Fax: (212) 302-1585 E-mail: info@atpam.com
Web: www.atpam.com/Events/Weintraub.htm

Purpose To provide financial assistance for college or graduate school to members and families of members of the Association of Theatrical Press Agents and Managers (ATPAM).
Eligibility This program is open to 1) association members in good standing working on a graduate or undergraduate degree, and 2) relatives of members (children, grandchildren, nieces, nephews, stepchildren, spouses, or domestic partners) interested in working on an undergraduate degree. First-time applicants must submit a transcript of their most recent grades and a 250-word essay on trade unionism; all applicants must submit a brief biography.
Financial data Stipends are $1,000 for members and their children, spouses, and domestic partners or $750 for nieces, nephews, and grandchildren.
Duration 1 year; may be renewed up to 3 additional years, provided the recipient maintains at least a "B+" average.
Additional information This fund was established in 1969 in memory of Milton Weintraub, secretary-treasurer of ATPAM from 1942 to 1968.
Number awarded Varies each year.
Deadline August of each year.

[1173] MINORITY COMMUNITY COLLEGE TRANSFER SCHOLARSHIPS

State University System of Florida
Attn: Office of Academic and Student Affairs
325 West Gaines Street, Suite 1501
Tallahassee, FL 32399-1950
(850) 245-0467 Fax: (850) 245-9667
Web: www.flbog.org/asa

Purpose To provide financial assistance to minority community college students in Florida who are interested in transferring to a school within the State University System of Florida (SUS).

Eligibility This program is open to minority community college students who complete A.A. or A.S. degrees from an accredited Florida community college between December and August of the current year. Applicants must have been admitted as degree-seeking junior-level students at an SUS institution. All recipients must have participated in, received a waiver for, or passed the College-Level Academic Skills Test program. In addition, male applicants must have complied with the Selective Service System registration requirements. Students may apply for need awards, merit/need awards, or merit awards. The minimum cumulative GPA on postsecondary credits is 2.0 for need-based applicants or 3.0 for merit/need and merit applicants.

Financial data A stipend is awarded (amount not specified); funds are paid in 2 equal installments.

Duration Up to 6 semesters, provided the need recipient maintains at least a 2.0 GPA and the need/merit or merit recipient maintains at least a 3.0 average.

Additional information This program is administered by the equal opportunity program at each of the 11 SUS 4-year institutions. Contact that office for further information.

Number awarded Several each year.

Deadline May of each year.

[1174] MISS AMERICA COMPETITION AWARDS

Miss America Pageant
Attn: Scholarship Department
Two Miss America Way, Suite 1000
Atlantic City, NJ 08401
(609) 345-7571, ext. 27   Toll-free: (800) 282-MISS
Fax: (609) 347-6079   E-mail: info@missamerica.org
Web: www.missamerica.org

Purpose To provide educational scholarships to participants in the Miss America Pageant on local, state, and national levels.

Eligibility To enter an official Miss America Preliminary Pageant, candidates must meet certain basic requirements and agree to abide by all the rules of the local, state, and national Miss America Pageants. Among the qualifications required are that the applicant be female, between the ages of 17 and 24, a resident of the town or state in which they first compete, in good health, of good moral character, and a citizen of the United States. A complete list of all eligibility requirements is available from each local and state pageant. In addition to the general scholarship awards, participants are also considered for a number of special awards: the Bernie Wayne Performing Arts Award is presented to the contestant with the highest talent score among those women with performing arts as a stated ambition; the Charles and Theresa Brown Scholarships are presented to Miss America, the 4 runners-up, Miss Alaska, Miss Hawaii, Miss Illinois, and Miss Ohio; and the Quality of Life Awards are presented to the 3 contestants who demonstrate the most outstanding commitment to enhancing the quality of life for others through volunteerism and community service.

Financial data More than $45 million in cash and tuition assistance is awarded annually at the local, state, and national Miss America Pageants. At the national level, a total of $455,000 is awarded: Miss America receives $30,000 in scholarship money, the first runner-up $20,000, second runner-up $15,000, third runner-up $10,000, fourth runner-up $8,000, finalists $7,000 each, and national contestants $3,000 each. Other awards include those for the preliminary talent winners at $2,000 each, the preliminary lifestyle and fitness in swimsuit winners at $1,000 each, and the non-finalist talent winners at $1,000 each. Of the special awards presented to national contestants, the Bernie Wayne Performing Arts Award is $2,500; the Charles and Theresa Brown Scholarships are $2,500 each; and the Quality of Life Awards are $3,000 for the winner, $3,000 for first runner-up, and $1,000 for second runner-up.

Duration The pageants are held every year.

Additional information The Miss America Pageant has been awarding scholarships since 1945. Scholarships are to be used for tuition, room, board, supplies, and other college expenses. Use of the scholarships must begin within 4 years from the date of the award (5 years if the recipient is Miss America) unless a reasonable extension is requested and granted. Training under the scholarship should be continuous and completed within 10 years from the date the scholarship is activated; otherwise, the balance of the scholarship may be canceled without further notice.

Number awarded At the national level, 52 contestants (1 from each state, the District of Columbia, and the Virgin Islands) share the awards.

Deadline Varies, depending upon the date of local pageants leading to the state and national finals.

[1175] MISS BLACK AMERICA

Miss Black America Pageant
P.O. Box 25668
Philadelphia, PA 19144
(215) 844-8872
Web: www.missblackamerica.com

Purpose To recognize and reward beautiful and talented Black American women.

Eligibility All African American women between 17 and 29 years of age, including married contestants and contestants with children, are eligible. Finalists who compete in the national pageant are selected after competitions on the local and state levels. The winner at the national pageant is chosen by a panel of judges on the basis of beauty, talent, and personality.

Financial data Miss Black America receives a cash award and an array of prizes.

Duration The competition is held annually.

Additional information This competition began in 1968. There is a $100 application fee and a $750 sponsorship fee.

Number awarded 1 each year.

Deadline December of each year.

[1176]
MISS INDIAN USA SCHOLARSHIP PROGRAM
American Indian Heritage Foundation
P.O. Box 6301
Falls Church, VA 22040
(703) 532-1921   E-mail: MissIndianUSA@indians.org
Web: www.indians.org

Purpose To recognize and reward the most beautiful and talented Indian women.

Eligibility American Indian women between the ages of 18 and 26 are eligible to enter this national contest if they are high school graduates and have never been married, cohabited with the opposite sex, been pregnant, or had children. U.S. citizenship is required. Selection is based on public appearance (20%), a traditional interview (15%), a contemporary interview (15%), beauty of spirit (15%), a cultural presentation (10%), scholastic achievement (10%), a platform question (10%), and a finalist question (5%).

Financial data Miss Indian USA receives an academic scholarship of $4,000 plus a cash grant of $6,500, a wardrobe allowance of $2,000, appearance fees of $3,000, a professional photo shoot worth $500, gifts worth more than $4,000, honoring gifts worth more than $2,000, promotional materials worth more than $2,000, and travel to Washington, D.C. with a value of approximately $2,000; the total value of the prize is more than $26,000. Members of her court receive scholarships of $2,000 for the first runner-up, $1,500 for the second runner-up, $1,000 for the third runner-up, and $500 for the fourth runner-up.

Duration This competition is held annually.

Additional information The program involves a weeklong competition in the Washington, D.C. metropolitan area that includes seminars, interviews, cultural presentations, and many public appearances. The application fee is $100 if submitted prior to mid-April or $200 if submitted later. In addition, a candidate fee of $750 is required.

Number awarded 1 winner and 4 runners-up are selected each year.

Deadline May of each year.

[1177]
MISS LATINA WORLD
Dawn Rochele Productions
6150 West El Dorado Parkway, Suite 160-120
McKinney, TX 75070
(206) 666-DAWN   E-mail: info@misslatina.com
Web: www.misslatina.com

Purpose To recognize and reward young Latina women who compete in a national beauty pageant.

Eligibility This program is open to women between 18 and 35 years of age who are at least 25% Hispanic. Applicants may be single, married, or divorced, and they may have children. They appear in a nationally-televised pageant where selection is based one third on an interview, one third on swimsuit appearances, and one third on evening gown appearances. Height and weight are not factors, but contestants should be proportionate. Pageant experience and fluency in Spanish are not required.

Financial data Each year, prizes include scholarships, gifts, a cruise to the Bahamas, a trip to Las Vegas, a modeling contract, and use of an apartment in Miami. The total value is more than $25,000.

Duration The pageant is held annually.

Number awarded 1 winner and 4 runners-up are selected each year.

[1178]
MISS TEEN USA
Miss Universe Organization
1370 Avenue of the Americas, 16th Floor
New York, NY 10019
(212) 373-4999   Fax: (212) 315-5378
E-mail: MissUPR@missuniverse.com
Web: www.missteenusa.com

Purpose To recognize and reward beautiful and talented women between 15 and 19 years of age in the United States.

Eligibility Some cities and all states have preliminary pageants. The winner of the city pageant goes on to compete in the state pageant for her home city. A delegate may also enter a state pageant without having won a city title. One delegate from each of the 50 states and the District of Columbia is selected to compete in the pageant. Participants must be between 15 and 19 years of age. They must never have been married or pregnant. Selection is based on beauty, intelligence, and ability to handle an interview.

Financial data Miss Teen USA receives cash and prizes worth more than $150,000. Recently, that included a $45,000 scholarship to the School for Film and Television, a Preciosa trophy worth $3,500, a crystal chandelier from Preciosa worth $5,000, a $2,500 pre-paid VISA BUXX card, a $2,000 cash prize and complimentary UV-Free Tanning for the year of her reign from Mystic Tan, a pearl tiara worth $12,000 from Mikimoto, a fashion footwear wardrobe from Nina Footwear, a swimwear wardrobe from Pink Sands Swim, a 5-day/4 night trip for 2 anywhere American Airlines flies in the continental United States or Caribbean, a pajama wardrobe by Jamatex worth $500, a 1-year salary, a luxury apartment while in New York City, a personal appearance wardrobe, a modeling portfolio, and other services and training. Other prizes included $3,000 for first runner-up, $2,000 for second runner-up, $1,000 for third and fourth runners-up, and $500 for semifinalists. In addition, the delegate selected by the television audience as Miss Photogenic and the delegate selected by her peers as Miss Congeniality each received $1,000 cash prizes and a commemorative Preciosa crystal trophy worth $3,500.

Duration The national pageant is held annually, usually at the end of the summer.

Additional information The competition began in 1983.

Number awarded 1 national winner each year.

Deadline June of each year.

[1179]
MISS USA

Miss Universe Organization
1370 Avenue of the Americas, 16th Floor
New York, NY 10019
(212) 373-4999   Fax: (212) 315-5378
E-mail: MissUPR@missuniverse.com
Web: www.missusa.com

Purpose To identify and reward the most beautiful women selected in a competition among women from each state.

Eligibility This program is open to women between 18 and 27 years of age who have never been married or pregnant. Entrants are first selected in state competitions, and then 51 women (1 from each state and the District of Columbia) compete in the Miss USA Pageant. Selection of the winner is based on interviews by pageant judges (on successes, talents, goals, and ambitions), a swimsuit competition (with swimsuit styles provided by the pageant), and an evening gown competition (with gowns chosen by the competitors). The Photogenic Award is presented to the delegate voted on and selected by the television audience, and the Congeniality Award is presented to the delegate selected by her sister delegates as the most charismatic and inspirational.

Financial data Miss USA receives cash and prizes that recently included a 2-year scholarship valued at $60,000 from The School for Film and Television, a pearl tiara worth $17,500 from Mikimoto, a cash prize of $3,000 and a shoe wardrobe from Steve Madden, a cash prize of $5,000 and a year supply of Covergirl cosmetics, a 1-year salary, a luxury apartment while in New York City, a personal appearance wardrobe from Tadashi Fashions, a modeling portfolio, and other services and training. Other prizes included $3,000 for first runner-up, $2,000 for second runner-up, $1,000 for third and fourth runners-up, and $500 for semifinalists. In addition, the delegate selected by the television audience as Miss Photogenic and the delegate selected by her peers as Miss Congeniality each received $1,000 cash prizes.

Duration The national pageant is held annually, in February or March.

Additional information This pageant began in 1952. Miss USA competes for additional prizes in the Miss Universe Pageant.

Number awarded 1 each year.

Deadline January of each year.

[1180]
MOAA BASE/POST SCHOLARSHIPS

Military Officers Association of America
Attn: Educational Assistance Program
201 North Washington Street
Alexandria, VA 22314-2539
(703) 549-2311   Toll-free: (800) 234-MOAA
E-mail: edassist@moaa.org
Web: www.moaa.org

Purpose To provide financial assistance for undergraduate education to dependents of active-duty military officers and enlisted personnel.

Eligibility This program is open to dependent children under 24 years of age of active-duty (including drilling Reserves and National Guard) officers and enlisted military personnel. Applicants are not required to be related to a member of the Military Officers Association of America (MOAA) and do not need to meet a minimum GPA requirement. Selection is based on a random drawing.

Financial data The stipend is $1,000 per year.

Duration 1 year.

Additional information The MOAA was formerly named The Retired Officers Association (TROA).

Number awarded 50 each year.

Deadline February of each year.

[1181]
MONTGOMERY GI BILL (ACTIVE DUTY)

Department of Veterans Affairs
810 Vermont Avenue, N.W.
Washington, DC 20420
(202) 418-4343   Toll-free: (888) GI-BILL1
Web: www.gibill.va.gov

Purpose To provide financial assistance for college, graduate school, and other types of postsecondary schools to new enlistees in any of the armed forces after they have completed their service obligation.

Eligibility This program is open to veterans who received an honorable discharge and have a high school diploma, a GED, or, in some cases, up to 12 hours of college credit. Applicants must also meet the requirements of 1 of the following categories: 1) entered active duty for the first time after June 30, 1985, had military pay reduced by $100 per month for the first 12 months, and continuously served for 3 years, or 2 years if that was original enlistment, or 2 years if they entered Selected Reserve within a year of leaving active duty and served 4 years (the 2 by 4 program); 2) entered active duty before January 1, 1977, had remaining entitlement under the Vietnam Era GI Bill on December 31, 1989, served at least 1 day between October 19, 1984 and June 30, 1985, and stayed on active duty through June 30, 1988 (or June 30, 1987 if they entered Selected Reserve within 1 year of leaving active duty and served 4 years; 3) on active duty on September 30, 1990 and separated involuntarily after February 2, 1991, involuntarily separated on or after November 30, 1993, or voluntarily separated under either the Voluntary Separation Incentive (VSI) or Special Separation Benefit (SSB) program, and before separation had military pay reduced by $1,200; or 4) on active duty on October 9, 1996, had money remaining in an account from the Veterans Educational Assistance Program (VEAP), elected MGIB by October 9, 1997, and paid $1,200. Certain National Guard servicemembers may also qualify under category 4 if they served on full-time active duty between July 1, 1985 and November 28, elected MGIB between October 9, 1996 and July 8, 1997, and paid $1,200. Following completion of their service obligation, participants may enroll in colleges or universities for associate, bachelor, or graduate degrees; in courses leading to a certificate or diploma from business, technical, or vocational schools; for apprenticeships or on-job training programs; in correspondence courses; in flight training; for preparatory courses necessary for admission to a college or graduate school; for licensing and certification tests approved for veterans; or in state-approved teacher certification programs. Veterans who wish to enroll in certain high-cost technology programs (life science, physical science, engineering, mathematics, engineering and science technology, computer specialties, and engineering, science, and computer management) may be eligible for an accelerated payment.

Financial data For veterans in categories 1, 3, and 4 who served on active duty for 3 years or more, the current monthly stipend for college or university work is $1,034 for full-time study, $775.50 for three-quarter time study, or $517 for half-time study, or $258.50 for quarter-time study or less; for apprenticeship and on-the-job training, the monthly stipend is $878.90 for the first 6 months, $672.10 for the second 6 months, and $465.30 for the remainder of the program. For enlistees whose initial active-duty obligation was less than 3 years, the current monthly stipend for college or university work is $840 for full-time study, $630 for three-quarter time study, $420 for half-time study, or $210 for quarter-time study or less; for apprenticeship and on-the-job training, the monthly stipend is $714 for the first 6 months, $546 for the second 6 months, and $378 for the remainder of the program. For veterans in category 2 with remaining eligibility, the current monthly stipend for institutional study full time is $1,222 for no dependents, $1,258 with 1 dependent, $1,289 with 2 dependents, and $16 for each additional dependent; for three-quarter time study, the monthly stipend is $917 for no dependents, $943.50 with 1 dependent, $967 with 2 dependents, and $12 for each additional dependent; for half-time study, the monthly stipend is $611 for no dependents, $629 with 1 dependent, $644.50 with 2 dependents and $8.50 for each additional dependent. For those veterans pursuing an apprenticeship or on-the-job training, the current monthly stipend for the first 6 months is $995.35 for no dependents, $1,009.38 with 1 dependent, $1,021.70 with 2 dependents, and $5.95 for each additional dependent; for the second 6 months, the current monthly stipend is $738.73 for no dependents, $749.78 with 1 dependent, $758.88 with 2 dependents, and $4.55 for each additional dependent; for the third 6 months, the current monthly stipend is $495.90 for no dependents, $503.78 with 1 dependent, $509.85 with 2 dependents, and $3.15 for each additional dependent; for the remainder of the training period, the current monthly stipend is $480.60 for no dependents, $488.03 with 1 dependent, $494.78 with 2 dependents, and $3.15 for each additional dependent. Other rates apply for less than half-time study, cooperative education, correspondence courses, and flight training. Veterans who qualify for the accelerated payment and whose entitlement does not cover 60% of tuition and fees receive an additional lump sum payment to make up the different between their entitlement and 60% of tuition and fees.

Duration 36 months; active-duty servicemembers must utilize the funds within 10 years of leaving the armed services; Reservists may draw on their funds while still serving.

Additional information Further information is available from local armed forces recruiters. This is the basic VA education program, referred to as Chapter 30.

Number awarded Varies each year.

[1182]
MONTGOMERY GI BILL (SELECTED RESERVE)

Department of Veterans Affairs
810 Vermont Avenue, N.W.
Washington, DC 20420
(202) 418-4343   Toll-free: (888) GI-BILL1
Web: www.gibill.va.gov

Purpose To provide financial assistance for college or graduate school to members of the Reserves or National Guard.

Eligibility Eligible to apply are members of the Reserve elements of the Army, Navy, Air Force, Marine Corps, and Coast Guard, as well as the Army National Guard and the Air National Guard. To be eligible, a Reservist must 1) have a 6-year obligation to serve in the Selected Reserves signed after June 30, 1985 (or, if an officer, to agree to serve 6 years in addition to the original obligation); 2) complete Initial Active Duty for Training (IADT); 3) meet the requirements for a high school diploma or equivalent certificate before completing IADT; and 4) remain in good standing in a drilling Selected Reserve unit. Reservists who enlisted after June 30, 1985 can receive benefits for undergraduate degrees, graduate training, or technical courses leading to certificates at colleges and universities. Reservists whose 6-year commitment began after September 30, 1990 may also use these benefits for a certificate or diploma from business, technical, or vocational schools; cooperative training; apprenticeship or on-the-job training; correspondence courses; independent study programs; tutorial assistance; remedial, deficiency, or refresher training; flight training; or state-approved alternative teacher certification programs.

Financial data The current monthly rate is $297 for full-time study, $222.75 for three-quarter time study, $148.50 for half-time study, or $74.25 for less than half-time study. For apprenticeship and on-the-job training, the monthly stipend is $252.45 for the first 6 months, $193.05 for the second 6 months, and $133.65 for the remainder of the program. Other rates apply for cooperative education, correspondence courses, and flight training.

Duration Up to 36 months for full-time study, 48 months for three-quarter study, 72 months for half-time study, or 144 months for less than half-time study.

Additional information This program is frequently referred to as Chapter 1606 (formerly Chapter 106). Reservists who are enrolled for three-quarter or full-time study are eligible to participate in the work-study program. The Department of Defense periodically offers "kickers" of additional benefits on behalf of individuals in critical military fields, as deemed necessary to encourage enlistment. Information on currently-available "kickers" is available from Reserve and National Guard recruiters. Benefits end 10 years from the date the Reservist became eligible for the program. The Department of Veterans Affairs (VA) may extend the 10-year period if the individual could not train because of a disability caused by Selected Reserve service. Certain individuals separated from the Selected Reserve due to downsizing of the military between October 1, 1991 and September 30, 1999 will also have the full 10 years to use their benefits.

Number awarded Varies each year.

Deadline Applications may be submitted at any time.

[1183] MONTGOMERY GI BILL TUITION ASSISTANCE TOP-UP

Department of Veterans Affairs
810 Vermont Avenue, N.W.
Washington, DC 20420
(202) 418-4343 Toll-free: (888) GI-BILL1
Web: www.gibill.va.gov

Purpose To supplement the tuition assistance provided by the military services to their members.

Eligibility This program is open to military personnel who have served at least 2 full years on active duty and are approved for tuition assistance by their military service. Applicants must be participating in the Montgomery GI Bill (MGIB) Active Duty program and be eligible for MGIB benefits. This assistance is available to service members whose military service does not pay 100% of tuition and fees.

Financial data This program pays the difference between what the military services pay for tuition assistance and the full amount of tuition and fees.

Duration Up to 36 months of payments are available.

Additional information This program was established in 2000.

Number awarded Varies each year.

[1184] MR. AND MRS. MOICHI OKAZAKI SCHOLARSHIP

100th Infantry Battalion Veterans Club
Attn: Scholarship Committee
520 Kamoku Street
Honolulu, HI 96826
(808) 732-5216 E-mail: daisyy@hgea.net
Web: emedia.leeward.hawaii.edu/mnakano

Purpose To provide financial assistance to high school seniors and college students from Hawaii who attend mainland institutions and exemplify the sponsor's motto of "Continuing Service."

Eligibility This program is open to high school seniors planning to attend an institution of higher learning on the mainland and full-time undergraduate students at mainland community colleges, vocational/trade schools, 4-year colleges, and universities. Applicants must have a GPA of 2.5 or higher and be able to demonstrate civic responsibility and community service. Along with their application, they must submit a 4-page essay on how their postsecondary education at an out-of-state school will benefit them, their community, and their state. Selection is based on that essay and the applicant's demonstration that he or she can effectively promote the legacy of the 100th Infantry Battalion and its motto of "Continuing Service." Financial need is not considered.

Financial data The stipend is $1,000.

Duration 1 year; nonrenewable.

Number awarded 1 each year.

Deadline April of each year.

[1185] MR. COLLEGIATE AFRICAN AMERICAN SCHOLARSHIP PROGRAM

Mr. Collegiate African American Scholarship Pageant
P.O. Box 841595
Houston, TX 77284-1595
(713) 927-6947 Toll-free: (888) 313-7431
E-mail: mrcollegiate@iwon.com

Purpose To recognize and reward, with college scholarships, outstanding African American men who participate in a pageant.

Eligibility This competition is open to African American men between 18 and 30 years of age attending 4-year colleges and universities. Applicants must be interested in participating in a pageant where they are judged on a personal and private interview (20%), platform expression (25%), talent (35%), evening wear (10%), and on-stage interview (10%).

Financial data The winner receives a $2,000 scholarship and $1,500 in prizes, including a $500 wardrobe allowance. The first runner-up receives a $1,200 scholarship and $300 in prizes. The second runner-up receives a $750 scholarship and $300 in prizes.

Duration The pageant is held annually.

Additional information This program was established in 1990. The pageant is held in Houston, Texas. Contestants must pay a $495 fee.

Number awarded 3 each year.

Deadline February of each year.

[1186] NACA REGIONAL COUNCIL STUDENT LEADER SCHOLARSHIPS

National Association for Campus Activities
Attn: NACA Foundation
13 Harbison Way
Columbia, SC 29212-3401
(803) 732-6222 Fax: (803) 749-1047
E-mail: scholarships@naca.org
Web: www.naca.org

Purpose To provide financial assistance to outstanding college student leaders.

Eligibility Eligible for this program are full-time undergraduate students who have made significant contributions to their campus communities, have played leadership roles in campus activities, and have demonstrated leadership skills and abilities. Financial need is not considered in the selection process.

Financial data The amounts of the awards vary each year; scholarships are to be used for educational expenses, including tuition, books, fees, or other related expenses.

Additional information This program was established in 1996.

Number awarded 7 each year: 1 in each of the association's regions.

Deadline April of each year.

[1187]
NANCIE RIDEOUT-ROBERTSON INTERNSHIP SCHOLARSHIP

American Water Ski Educational Foundation
Attn: Director
1251 Holy Cow Road
Polk City, FL 33868-8200
(863) 324-2472 Fax: (863) 324-3996
E-mail: info@waterskihalloffame.com
Web: www.waterskihalloffame.com

Purpose To provide financial assistance and work experience to upper-division and graduate students who are interested in water skiing.

Eligibility This program is open to upper-division and graduate students who are members of the United States Water Ski Association (USWSA) and the American Water Ski Educational Foundation (AWSEF). Applicants must have participated in the sport of water skiing as a skier, official, and/or volunteer worker and be able to demonstrate leadership potential. They must have a GPA of at least "B+" overall and an "A" average in their major field of study. Along with their application, they must submit 1) a 500-word personal statement on why they wish to be awarded this scholarship and serve as an intern at AWSEF; and 2) an internship proposal, covering their learning goals and how they want to apply the skills and knowledge related to their program of study in college or graduate school to their internship, the kinds of contributions they think they can make toward the goals of AWSEF, how they would allocate their time toward their internship activities, when they could complete their "onsite" requirement, and the kinds of skills and knowledge of people with whom they might like to work during their internship.

Financial data The stipend is $2,500.

Duration 1 year, including at least 4 weeks (during semester breaks, spring break, summer) at AWSEF headquarters in Polk City, Florida.

Additional information This program was established in 2004.

Number awarded 1 each year.

Deadline January of each year.

[1188]
NANCY REAGAN PATHFINDER SCHOLARSHIPS

National Federation of Republican Women
Attn: Scholarships and Internships
124 North Alfred Street
Alexandria, VA 22314-3011
(703) 548-9688 Fax: (703) 548-9836
E-mail: mail@nfrw.org
Web: www.nfrw.org/programs/scholarships.htm

Purpose To provide financial assistance for college or graduate school to Republican women.

Eligibility This program is open to women currently enrolled as college sophomores, juniors, seniors, or master's degree students. Recent high school graduates and first-year college women are not eligible. Applicants must submit 3 letters of recommendation, an official transcript, a 1-page essay on why they should be considered for the scholarship, and a 1-page essay on career goals. Optionally, a photograph may be supplied. Applications must be submitted to the Republican federation president in the applicant's state. Each president chooses 1 application from her state to submit for scholarship consideration. Financial need is not a factor in the selection process. U.S. citizenship is required.

Financial data The stipend is $2,500.

Duration 1 year; nonrenewable.

Additional information This program, established in 1985, is also known as the National Pathfinder Scholarship.

Number awarded 3 each year.

Deadline Applications must be submitted to the state federation president by May of each year.

[1189]
NATASHA MATSON FIFE SCHOLARSHIP

Kansas Women's Golf Association
c/o Phyllis Fast, Scholarship Chair
3006 S.E. Skylark Drive
Topeka, KS 66605
(785) 266-8033 E-mail: phast@networksplus.net
Web: www.kwga.org/scholarship.htm

Purpose To provide financial assistance for college to women in Kansas who have participated in activities of the Kansas Women's Golf Association (KWGA).

Eligibility This program is open to women in Kansas who are graduating or have graduated from a high school in the state. Applicants must have participated in at least 1 KWGA Junior Girls Championship or State Amateur Championship. They must be planning to attend an accredited collegiate institution in the following academic year. Eligibility is not limited to junior golfers. Along with their application, they must submit information on the number of years they have played golf; their handicap index; the KWGA amateur and junior championships and years in which they have participated; an essay of more than 100 words on why they play golf and the benefits they have gained from golf; their golf accomplishments; participation in other high school and/or community activities; a copy of their high school transcript (including name of school, year of graduation, and GPA); and 3 letters of recommendation.

Financial data A stipend is awarded (amount not specified). Funds are paid directly to the recipient's collegiate institution.

Duration 1 year; nonrenewable.

Number awarded 1 or more each year.

Deadline March of each year.

[1190]
NATHALIE A. PRICE MEMORIAL SCHOLARSHIP

Ocean State Women's Golf Association
P.O. Box 597
Portsmouth, RI 02871-0597
(401) 683-6301 E-mail: oswgari@aol.com
Web: www.oswga.org

Purpose To provide financial assistance for college to women in Rhode Island who have played golf.

Eligibility This program is open to women in Rhode Island who are graduating high school seniors or current college students. Applicants must have been active in golf, as a member of the Ocean State Women's Golf Association

(OSWGA), as a member of another association, or on their school golf team. Along with their application, they must submit a transcript, a list of their citizenship and community service activities, and letters of recommendation. Financial need is not considered.

Financial data A stipend is awarded (amount not specified).

Duration 1 year; may be renewed.

Additional information This scholarship was first awarded in 1996.

Number awarded Varies each year; recently, 8 of these scholarships were awarded.

Deadline June of each year.

[1191]
NATIONAL GUARD ASSOCIATION OF NEW JERSEY SCHOLARSHIP PROGRAM

National Guard Association of New Jersey
Attn: Scholarship Committee
101 Eggert Crossing Road
Lawrenceville, NJ 08648-2805
(609) 562-0222   Fax: (609) 562-0229
E-mail: dutko@njdmava.state.nj.us
Web: www.nganj.org

Purpose To provide financial assistance for college or graduate school to New Jersey National Guard members or their dependents.

Eligibility This program is open to active members of the New Jersey National Guard; the spouses, children, legal wards, and grandchildren of active members; and the children, legal wards, and grandchildren of retired (with at least 20 years of service) or deceased members. Applicants may be high school seniors or graduates entering college; students currently enrolled in college, business school, or trade school; or graduate students. Selection is based on civic and academic activities; offices, honors, awards, and special recognitions; and high school and/or college transcripts.

Financial data Stipends up to $1,000 are available.

Duration 1 year.

Number awarded Varies each year; recently, 10 of these scholarships were awarded.

Deadline March of each year.

[1192]
NATIONAL HUGUENOT SOCIETY SCHOLARSHIPS

National Huguenot Society
Attn: Executive Director
9033 Lyndale Avenue South, Suite 108
Bloomington, MN 55420-3535
(952) 885-9776
E-mail: scholarship@huguenot.netnation.com
Web: huguenot.netnation.com

Purpose To provide financial assistance for college or graduate school to members of the National Huguenot Society.

Eligibility This program is open to students at accredited colleges, universities, and graduate schools who have completed at least 2 years of college with a GPA of 3.0 or higher. Applicants must be a regular member of the National Huguenot Society, which requires that they 1) be at least 18 years of age; 2) adhere to the Huguenot principles of faith and liberty; 3) be a member of the Protestant faith; and 4) be lineally descended from a Huguenot who either emigrated from France to North America or another country between 1520 and 1787 or remained in France. Their program of study must have included at least 2 semesters of history, including a history of religion. Along with their application, they may submit a short statement on their scholastic achievements and goals and how a scholarship would be advantageous to them. Financial need is not considered in the selection process.

Financial data The stipend is $5,000.

Duration 1 year; nonrenewable.

Additional information Information is also available from Richard Dana Smith, Sr., Huguenot Scholarship Awards, 647 Brintons Bridge Road, West Chester, PA 19382.

Number awarded 1 each year.

[1193]
NATIONAL 4TH INFANTRY (IVY) DIVISION ASSOCIATION SCHOLARSHIP

National 4th Infantry (IVY) Division Association
c/o Alexander Cooker, Scholarship Administrator
78 North Dupont Road
Carneys Point, NJ 08069
(609) 299-4406   E-mail: alexcooker@aol.com
Web: www.4thinfantry.org

Purpose To provide financial assistance for college to members of the National 4th Infantry (IVY) Division Association and their families.

Eligibility This program is open to association members in good standing and all blood relatives of active association members in good standing. Recipients are chosen by lottery.

Financial data The stipend is $1,000.

Duration 1 year; may be renewed.

Additional information The trust fund from which these scholarships are awarded was created by the officers and enlisted men of the 4th Infantry Division as a living memorial to the men of the division who died in Vietnam. Originally, it was only open to children of members of the division who died in the line of duty while serving in Vietnam between August 1, 1966 and December 31, 1977. When all those eligible had completed college, it adopted its current requirements.

Number awarded 3 each year.

[1194]
NAVAL HELICOPTER ASSOCIATION UNDERGRADUATE SCHOLARSHIPS

Naval Helicopter Association
Attn: Scholarship Fund
P.O. Box 180578
Coronado, CA 92178-0578
(619) 435-7139   Fax: (619) 435-7354
E-mail: nhascholars@hotmail.com
Web: www.navalhelicopterassn.org

Purpose To provide financial assistance for full-time undergraduate study to students in the United States.

Eligibility This program is open to U.S. citizens, regardless of race, religion, age, or gender, who are seniors in high school or currently enrolled in or accepted at an accredited college or university in the United States in an undergraduate program. Selection is based on academic proficiency, scholastic achievements and awards, extracurricular activities, employment history, letters of recommendation, and a personal statement on educational plans and future goals.

Financial data Stipends are $3,000 or $1,500 per year.

Duration 1 year; may be renewed if the recipient maintains at least a 2.75 GPA.

Additional information This program includes the Sikorsky Scholarship (sponsored by Sikorsky Aircraft Corporation) and DPA's Thousand Points of Light Award (sponsored by D.P. Associates Inc. and L3 Communications). Recipients must enroll full time.

Number awarded 7 each year: 2 at $3,000 (the named scholarships) and 5 at $1,500.

Deadline November of each year.

[1195]
NAVAL SPECIAL WARFARE SCHOLARSHIPS FOR SPOUSES AND CHILDREN

Naval Special Warfare Foundation
Attn: Scholarship Committee
P.O. Box 5965
Virginia Beach, VA 23471
(757) 363-7490   Fax: (757) 363-7491
E-mail: info@nswfoundation.org
Web: www.nswfoundation.org

Purpose To provide financial assistance for college to dependents of military personnel serving on active duty in Naval Special Warfare (NSW) commands.

Eligibility This program is open to the dependent spouses and children of active-duty SEALs or Special Warfare Combatant crewmen (SWCC) and other active-duty military personnel serving in NSW commands. Family members of a SEAL or SWCC who died in service to the country are also eligible. Applicants must be entering or continuing in college with the goal of working on an associate or bachelor's degree. Selection is based on merit and academic potential, judged by scholastic achievement and a written essay.

Financial data A stipend is awarded (amount not specified).

Duration 1 year; may be renewed.

Number awarded 1 or more each year.

Deadline March of each year.

[1196]
NAVY COUNSELOR ASSOCIATION EDUCATIONAL SCHOLARSHIP FUND

Navy Counselor Association
Attn: National Headquarters
P.O. Box 15023
Norfolk, VA 23511-0023
Web: www.usnca.org/scholarships.htm

Purpose To provide financial assistance for college to the dependent children of members of the Navy Counselor Association (NCA).

Eligibility This program is open to the dependent children of active-duty, retired, and deceased NCA members. Applicants must be between 17 and 23 years of age and have proof of enrollment, acceptance, or certified intention to attend an accredited college, university, or vocational/technical school. Along with their application they must submit a 500-word essay on their educational and post-educational goals, and how those goals will benefit them and the community. Selection is based on the essay, academics, civic involvement, extracurricular activities, and goals.

Financial data Stipends are $2,500, $2,000, or $1,500.

Duration 1 year; may be renewed 1 additional year.

Additional information This scholarship is offered by the NCA with funds established from membership dues. More information on this program can also be obtained from the NCA at the parent's current duty station (or last duty station, if deceased).

Number awarded Varies each year. Recently, 3 of these scholarships were awarded: 1 at $2,500, 1 at $2,000, and 1 at $1,500.

Deadline April of each year.

[1197]
NAVY-MARINE CORPS ROTC COLLEGE PROGRAM

U.S. Navy
Attn: Chief of Naval Education and Training
Code N79A2
250 Dallas Street
Pensacola, FL 32508-5220
(850) 452-4941, ext. 29381
Toll-free: (800) NAV-ROTC, ext. 29381
Fax: (850) 452-2486
E-mail: PNSC_NROTC.scholarship@navy.mil
Web: www.nrotc.navy.mil

Purpose To provide financial assistance to lower-division students who are interested in joining Navy ROTC in college.

Eligibility Applicants must be U.S. citizens between the ages of 17 and 21 who are already enrolled as non-scholarship students in naval science courses at a college or university with a Navy ROTC program on campus. They must apply before the spring of their sophomore year. All applications must be submitted through the professors of naval science at the college or university attended.

Financial data Participants in this program receive free naval science textbooks, all required uniforms, and a stipend for 10 months of the year that is $250 per month as a freshman, $300 per month as a sophomore, $350 per month as a junior and $400 per month as a senior.

Duration 2 or 4 years.

Additional information Following acceptance into the program, participants attend the 6-week Naval Science Institute in Newport, Rhode Island (or in Quantico, Virginia for Marine-option students). After graduation from college, they are commissioned ensigns in the Naval Reserve or second lieutenants in the Marine Corps Reserve with an 8-year service obligation, including 3 years of active duty.

Deadline March of each year.

[1198]
NAVY-MARINE CORPS ROTC 2-YEAR SCHOLARSHIPS

U.S. Navy
Attn: Chief of Naval Education and Training
Code N79A2
250 Dallas Street
Pensacola, FL 32508-5220
(850) 452-4941, ext. 29381
Toll-free: (800) NAV-ROTC, ext. 29381
Fax: (850) 452-2486
E-mail: PNSC_NROTC.scholarship@navy.mil
Web: www.nrotc.navy.mil

Purpose To provide financial assistance to upper-division students who are interested in joining Navy ROTC in college.

Eligibility This program is open to students who have completed at least 2 years of college (or 3 years if enrolled in a 5-year program) with a GPA of 2.5 or higher overall and 2.0 or higher in calculus and physics. Preference is given to students at colleges with a Navy ROTC unit on campus or at colleges with a cross-enrollment agreement with a college with an NROTC unit. Applicants must be U.S. citizens between the ages of 17 and 21 who plan to pursue an approved course of study in college and complete their degree before they reach the age of 27. Former and current enlisted military personnel are also eligible if they will complete the program by the age of 30.

Financial data These scholarships provide payment of full tuition and required educational fees, as well as a specified amount for textbooks, supplies, and equipment. The program also provides a stipend for 10 months of the year that is $350 per month as a junior and $400 per month as a senior.

Duration 2 years, until the recipient completes the bachelor's degree.

Additional information Applications must be made through professors of naval science at 1 of the schools hosting the Navy ROTC program. Prior to final selection, applicants must attend, at Navy expense, a 6-week summer training course at the Naval Science Institute at Newport, Rhode Island. Recipients must also complete 4 years of study in naval science classes as students either at 1 of the 70 colleges with NROTC units or at 1 of the more than 100 institutions with cross-enrollment agreements (in which case they attend their home college for their regular academic courses but attend naval science classes at a nearby school with an NROTC unit). After completing the program, all participants are commissioned as ensigns in the Naval Reserve or second lieutenants in the Marine Corps Reserve with an 8-year service obligation, including 4 years of active duty.

Number awarded Approximately 800 each year.

Deadline March of each year.

[1199]
NCAIAW SCHOLARSHIP

North Carolina Alliance for Athletics, Health, Physical Education, Recreation and Dance
Attn: Executive Director
P.O. Box 27751
Raleigh, NC 27611
Toll-free: (888) 840-6500   Fax: (919) 833-7700
E-mail: ncaahperd@ncaahperd.org
Web: www.ncaahperd.org/awards/scholarships.htm

Purpose To provide financial assistance to women who are college seniors involved in sports at an institution that is a member of the former North Carolina Association of Intercollegiate Athletics for Women (NCAIAW).

Eligibility This program is open to women who have been a participant on 1 or more varsity athletic teams either as a player or in the support role of manager, trainer, etc. Applicants must be attending 1 of the following former NCAIAW colleges or universities in North Carolina: Appalachian State, Belmont Abbey, Bennett, Campbell, Davidson, Duke, East Carolina, Gardner-Webb, High Point, Mars Hill, Meredith, North Carolina A&T, North Carolina State, Pembroke State, Salem, University of North Carolina at Asheville, University of North Carolina at Chapel Hill, University of North Carolina at Charlotte, University of North Carolina at Wilmington, Wake Forest, or Western Carolina. They must be college seniors at the time of application, be able to demonstrate high standards of scholarship, and show evidence of leadership potential (as indicated by participation in school and community activities).

Financial data The stipend is $1,000. Funds are sent to the recipient's school.

Duration 1 year.

Additional information This scholarship was established in 1983.

Number awarded 1 each year.

Deadline June of each year.

[1200]
NCCE SCHOLARSHIPS

National Commission for Cooperative Education
360 Huntington Avenue, 384 CP
Boston, MA 02115-5096
(617) 373-3770   Fax: (617) 373-3463
E-mail: ncce@co-op.edu
Web: www.co-op.edu/scholarships.htm

Purpose To provide financial assistance to students participating or planning to participate in cooperative education projects at designated colleges and universities.

Eligibility This program is open to high school seniors and community college transfer students entering 1 of the 10 partner colleges and universities. Applicants must be planning to participate in college cooperative education. They must have a GPA of 3.5 or higher. Along with their application, they must submit a 1-page essay describing why they have chosen to enter a college cooperative education program. Applications are especially encouraged from minorities, women, and students interested in science, mathematics, engineering, and technology. Selection is based on merit; financial need is not considered.

Financial data The stipend is $5,000.

Duration 1 year.

Additional information The schools currently participating in this program are Antioch College (Yellow Springs, Ohio), Drexel University (Philadelphia, Pennsylvania), Johnson & Wales University (Providence, Rhode Island; Charleston, South Carolina; Norfolk, Virginia; North Miami, Florida; Denver, Colorado; and Charlotte, North Carolina), Kettering University (Flint, Michigan), C.W. Post Campus of Long Island University (Brookville, New York), Northeastern University (Boston, Massachusetts), Pace University (New York, New York; White Plains, New York; and Pleasantville, New York), Rochester Institute of Technology (Rochester, New York), University of Cincinnati (Cincinnati, Ohio), and University of Toledo (Toledo, Ohio). Applications must be sent directly to the college or university.

Number awarded 113 each year: 5 at Antioch, 15 at Drexel, 15 at Johnson & Wales, 15 at Kettering, 8 at C.W. Post Campus of LIU, 15 at Northeastern, 10 at Pace, 10 at Rochester Tech, 10 at Cincinnati, and 10 at Toledo.

Deadline February of each year for Antioch, Johnson & Wales, C.W. Post Campus of LIU, Northeastern, and Rochester Tech; March of each year for Drexel, Kettering, Pace, Cincinnati, and Toledo.

[1201]
NEBRASKA SPACE GRANT STATEWIDE SCHOLARSHIP COMPETITION

Nebraska Space Grant Consortium
c/o University of Nebraska at Omaha
Allwine Hall 422
6001 Dodge Street
Omaha, NE 68182-0406
(402) 554-3772
Toll-free: (800) 858-8648, ext. 4-3772 (within NE)
Fax: (402) 554-3781   E-mail: nasa@unomaha.edu
Web: nasa.unomaha.edu/Funding/funding.php

Purpose To provide financial assistance to undergraduate and graduate students at member institutions of the Nebraska Space Grant Consortium.

Eligibility This program is open to undergraduate and graduate students at schools that are members of the Nebraska Space Grant Consortium. Students in all academic disciplines are eligible. This program is sponsored by the U.S. National Aeronautics and Space Administration (NASA), which strongly encourages women, minorities, and students with disabilities to apply. U.S. citizenship is required. Financial need is not considered in the selection process.

Financial data A stipend is awarded (amount not specified).

Duration 1 year.

Additional information The following schools are members of the Nebraska Space Grant Consortium: University of Nebraska at Omaha, University of Nebraska at Lincoln, University of Nebraska at Kearney, University of Nebraska Medical Center, Creighton University, Western Nebraska Community College, Chadron State College, College of St. Mary, Metropolitan Community College, Grace University, Hastings College, Little Priest Tribal College, and Nebraska Indian Community College.

Number awarded At least 2 students from each institution are supported each year.

Deadline April of each year.

[1202]
NEBRASKA WAIVER OF TUITION FOR VETERANS' DEPENDENTS

Department of Veterans' Affairs
State Office Building
301 Centennial Mall South, Sixth Floor
P.O. Box 95083
Lincoln, NE 68509-5083
(402) 471-2458   Fax: (402) 471-2491
E-mail: dparker@notes.state.ne.us
Web: www.vets.state.ne.us

Purpose To provide financial assistance for college to dependents of deceased and disabled veterans and military personnel in Nebraska.

Eligibility Eligible are spouses, widow(er)s, and children who are residents of Nebraska and whose parent, stepparent, or spouse was a member of the U.S. armed forces and 1) died of a service-connected disability; 2) died subsequent to discharge as a result of injury or illness sustained while in service; 3) is permanently and totally disabled as a result of military service; or 4) is classified as missing in action or as a prisoner of war during armed hostilities after August 4, 1964. Applicants must be attending or planning to attend a branch of the University of Nebraska, a state college, or a community college in Nebraska.

Financial data Tuition is waived at public institutions in Nebraska.

Duration The waiver is valid for 1 degree, diploma, or certificate from a community college and 1 baccalaureate degree.

Additional information Applications may be submitted through 1 of the recognized veterans' organizations or any county service officer.

Number awarded Varies each year; recently, 302 of these grants were awarded.

[1203]
NEW JERSEY POW/MIA TUITION BENEFIT PROGRAM

New Jersey Department of Military and Veterans Affairs
Attn: Division of Veterans Programs
101 Eggert Crossing Road
P.O. Box 340
Trenton, NJ 08625-0340
(609) 530-7045   Toll-free: (800) 624-0508 (within NJ)
Fax: (609) 530-7075
Web: www.state.nj.us/military/veterans/programs.html

Purpose To provide financial assistance for college to the children of New Jersey military personnel reported as missing in action or prisoners of war during the southeast Asian conflict.

Eligibility Eligible to apply for this assistance are New Jersey residents attending or accepted at a New Jersey public or independent postsecondary institution whose parents were military service personnel officially declared prisoners of war or missing in action after January 1, 1960.

Financial data This program entitles recipients to full undergraduate tuition at any public or independent postsecondary educational institution in New Jersey.

Duration Assistance continues until completion of a bachelor's degree.

Number awarded Varies each year.

Deadline February of each year for the spring term and September for the fall and spring terms.

[1204]
NEW JERSEY SURVIVOR TUITION BENEFITS PROGRAM

New Jersey Higher Education Student Assistance Authority
Attn: Financial Aid Services
4 Quakerbridge Plaza
P.O. Box 540
Trenton, NJ 08625-0540
(609) 588-2349   Toll-free: (800) 792-8670
Fax: (609) 588-3450   E-mail: gjoachim@hesaa.org
Web: www.hesaa.org

Purpose To provide financial assistance to the spouses and children of New Jersey emergency service personnel or law enforcement officers killed in the performance of their duties.

Eligibility This program is open to surviving spouses, daughters, and sons of law enforcement officials and emergency service personnel killed on the job. Applicants must be residents of New Jersey attending or planning to attend a private or public undergraduate institution in the state. Surviving spouses must apply within 8 years of the date of death; children must apply within 8 years following high school graduation.

Financial data Grants pay the actual cost of tuition up to the highest tuition charged at a New Jersey public institution of higher education.

Duration 1 year; may be renewed for up to 7 additional years as long as the recipient attends a New Jersey institution of higher education as an undergraduate student on at least a half-time basis.

Additional information This program, originally established in 1979, was formerly called the New Jersey Public Tuition Benefits Program.

Number awarded Varies each year.

Deadline September of each year for fall and spring term; February of each year for spring term only.

[1205]
NEW JERSEY WORLD TRADE CENTER SCHOLARSHIP FUND

New Jersey Higher Education Student Assistance Authority
Attn: Financial Aid Services
4 Quakerbridge Plaza
P.O. Box 540
Trenton, NJ 08625-0540
(609) 588-2349   Toll-free: (800) 792-8670
Fax: (609) 588-3450   E-mail: gjoachim@hesaa.org
Web: www.hesaa.org

Purpose To provide financial assistance for college to residents of New Jersey whose parent or spouse was killed in the terrorist attacks of September 11, 2001.

Eligibility This program is open to the dependent children and surviving spouses of New Jersey residents who were killed in the terrorist attacks against the United States on September 11, 2001, or who died as the result of injuries received in the attacks, or who are missing and officially presumed dead as a direct result of the attacks. Applicants must be attending or planning to attend a college or university (may be in any state) as a full-time undergraduate. Surviving spouses must apply within 8 years of the date of death; children must apply within 8 years following high school graduation.

Financial data The maximum stipend is $6,500 per year. Funds must be used for tuition, fees, room, and board.

Duration 1 year; may be renewed.

Number awarded Varies each year.

Deadline May of each year for students who received a Tuition Aid Grant in the preceding year; September of each year for new applicants for fall term; February of each year for new applicants for spring term only.

[1206]
NEW MEXICO COMPETITIVE SCHOLARSHIPS

New Mexico Higher Education Department
Attn: Financial Aid Director
1068 Cerrillos Road
P.O. Box 15910
Santa Fe, NM 87506-5910
(505) 476-6506   Toll-free: (800) 279-9777
Fax: (505) 476-6511
E-mail: ofelia.morales@state.nm.us
Web: hed.state.nm.us/collegefinance/competitive.asp

Purpose To provide financial assistance to residents of other states who wish to attend a college or university in New Mexico.

Eligibility Students who are not residents of New Mexico but who wish to attend public institutions of higher education in New Mexico may apply for these scholarships. Selection is based on high school GPA and ACT scores.

Financial data For recipients, the out-of-state portion of tuition is waived and a stipend of at least $100 is paid.

Additional information Information is available at the financial aid office of any New Mexico public postsecondary institution.

Number awarded Varies each year, depending on the availability of funds.

Deadline Deadlines are established by the participating institutions.

[1207]
NEW MEXICO LOTTERY SUCCESS SCHOLARSHIPS
New Mexico Higher Education Department
Attn: Financial Aid Director
1068 Cerrillos Road
P.O. Box 15910
Santa Fe, NM 87506-5910
(505) 476-6506   Toll-free: (800) 279-9777
Fax: (505) 476-6511
E-mail: ofelia.morales@state.nm.us
Web: hed.state.nm.us/collegefinance/lotto.asp

Purpose To provide financial assistance to college students in New Mexico with good academic records.

Eligibility This program is open to full-time students at New Mexico public colleges and universities who graduated from a public or private high school in New Mexico or obtained a New Mexico GED. Applicants who earn at least a 2.5 GPA during their first college semester are eligible to begin receiving the award for their second semester of full-time enrollment.

Financial data Scholarships are equal to 100% of tuition at the New Mexico public postsecondary institution where the student is enrolled.

Duration Up to 8 consecutive semesters.

Additional information Information is available at the financial aid office of any New Mexico public postsecondary institution. Funding for these scholarships is provided from state lottery proceeds. The program began in 1997.

Number awarded Varies each year, depending on the availability of funds.

Deadline Deadlines are established by the participating institutions.

[1208]
NEW MEXICO VIETNAM VETERANS SCHOLARSHIPS
New Mexico Department of Veterans' Services
P.O. Box 2324
Santa Fe, NM 87504-2324
(505) 827-6300   Toll-free: (866) 433-VETS
Fax: (505) 827-6372   E-mail: nmdvs@state.nm.us
Web: www.state.nm.us/veterans/scholarship.html

Purpose To provide financial assistance for undergraduate and graduate education to Vietnam veterans in New Mexico.

Eligibility This program is open to Vietnam veterans who have been residents of New Mexico for at least 10 years. Applicants must have been honorably discharged and have been awarded the Vietnam Service Medal or the Vietnam Campaign Medal. They must be planning to attend a state-supported college, university, or community college in New Mexico to work on an undergraduate or graduate degree.

Financial data The scholarships pay tuition, fees, and books at any postsecondary institution in New Mexico, up to $1,520 for tuition and fees and $500 for books.

Duration 1 year.

[1209]
NEW MEXICO 3 PERCENT SCHOLARSHIP PROGRAM
New Mexico Higher Education Department
Attn: Financial Aid Director
1068 Cerrillos Road
P.O. Box 15910
Santa Fe, NM 87506-5910
(505) 476-6506   Toll-free: (800) 279-9777
Fax: (505) 476-6511
E-mail: ofelia.morales@state.nm.us
Web: hed.state.nm.us/collegefinance/three.asp

Purpose To provide financial assistance for college or graduate school to residents of New Mexico.

Eligibility This assistance is available to residents of New Mexico enrolled or planning to enroll at a public institution of higher education in the state as an undergraduate or graduate student. Selection is based on moral character, satisfactory initiative, scholastic standing, personality, and additional criteria established by each participating college or university. At least a third of the scholarships are based on financial need.

Financial data The amount of assistance varies but covers at least tuition and some fees.

Duration 1 year; may be renewed.

Additional information Information is available at the financial aid office of any New Mexico public postsecondary institution.

Number awarded Varies each year.

Deadline Deadlines are established by the participating institutions.

[1210]
NEW YORK METROPOLITAN CHAPTER SCHOLARSHIP FUND
Finlandia Foundation-New York Metropolitan Chapter
Attn: Scholarships
P.O. Box 165, Bowling Green Station
New York, NY 10274-0165
E-mail: scholarships@finlandiafoundationny.org
Web: www.finlandiafoundationny.org

Purpose To provide financial assistance for study or research to students, especially those of Finnish heritage.

Eligibility This program is open to students at colleges and universities in the United States. Applicants must submit information on their language proficiency, work experience, memberships (academic, professional, and social), fellowships and scholarships, awards, publications, exhibitions, performances, and future goals and ambitions. Financial need is not considered in the selection process. Preference is given to applicants of Finnish heritage.

Financial data Stipends range from $500 to $5,000 per year.

Duration 1 year.

Additional information Information is also available from Leena Toivonen, (718) 680-1716, E-mail: leenat@hotmail.com.

Number awarded 1 or more each year.

Deadline February of each year.

[1211]
NEW YORK STATE WORLD TRADE CENTER MEMORIAL SCHOLARSHIPS

New York State Higher Education Services Corporation
Attn: Student Information
99 Washington Avenue
Albany, NY 12255
(518) 473-1574 Toll-free: (888) NYS-HESC
Fax: (518) 473-3749 TDD: (800) 445-5234
E-mail: webmail@hesc.com
Web: www.hesc.com

Purpose To provide financial assistance to undergraduates in New York who are relatives of people killed or severely and permanently disabled as a result of the terrorist attacks on September 11, 2001.

Eligibility This program is open to the children, spouses, and financial dependents of deceased or severely and permanently disabled victims of the September 11, 2001 terrorist attacks or the subsequent rescue and recovery operations. Applicants must be attending or accepted at an approved program of study as full-time undergraduates at a public college or university or private institution in New York. They are not required to be New York residents or U.S. citizens. New York residents who were enrolled as an undergraduate at a college or university outside the state as of September 11, 2001 are eligible for scholarship payment at that school.

Financial data At public colleges and universities, this program provides payment of actual tuition and mandatory educational fees; actual room and board charged to students living on campus or an allowance for room and board for commuter students; and allowances for books, supplies, and transportation. At private institutions, the award is equal to the amount charged at the State University of New York (SUNY) for 4-year tuition and average mandatory fees (or the student's actual tuition and fees, whichever is less) plus allowances for room, board, books, supplies, and transportation.

Duration This program is available for 4 years of full-time undergraduate study (or 5 years in an approved 5-year bachelor's degree program).

Number awarded Varies each year.

Deadline April of each year.

[1212]
NHCFAE-FEEA SCHOLARSHIP PROGRAM

National Hispanic Coalition of Federal Aviation Employees
c/o Federal Employee Education and Assistance Fund
Attn: Scholarship Program
8441 West Bowles Avenue, Suite 200
Littleton, CO 80123-9501
(303) 933-7580 Toll-free: (800) 323-4140
Fax: (303) 933-7587 E-mail: admin@feea.org
Web: www.feea.org/schol_info/specialschols.html

Purpose To provide financial assistance for college or graduate school to members of the National Hispanic Coalition of Federal Aviation Employees (NHCFAE) and their dependents.

Eligibility This program is open to NHCFAE members and their spouses and children entering or enrolled in an accredited 2- or 4-year postsecondary, graduate, or postgraduate program. Applicants or their sponsoring federal employee must have at least 3 years of civilian federal service. Dependents must be full-time students; federal employees may be part-time students. Along with their application, they must submit a 2-page essay on a topic related to a career in public service with the federal government, a letter of recommendation, a transcript with a GPA of 3.0 or higher, and a copy of their federal "Notice of Personnel Action;" high school seniors must also submit a copy of their ACT, SAT, or other examination scores. Financial need is not considered in the selection process.

Financial data The stipend is $1,000 per year.

Duration 1 year; may be renewed.

Additional information This program is jointly administered by NHCFAE and the Federal Employee Education and Assistance Fund (FEEA). Information is also available directly from NCHFAE, P.O. Box 23276, Washington, DC 20026-3276, E-mail: NHCFAE@nhcfae.org.

Number awarded Varies each year; recently, 11 of these scholarships were awarded.

Deadline March of each year.

[1213]
NICHOLAS C. VRATARIC SCHOLARSHIP AWARDS PROGRAM

Paper, Allied-Industrial, Chemical and Energy Workers International Union
Attn: Scholarship Coordinator
3340 Perimeter Hill Drive
P.O. Box 1475
Nashville, TN 37202
(615) 834-8590 Fax: (615) 834-7741
E-mail: debitay@isdn.net
Web: www.paceunion.org

Purpose To provide financial assistance for college to members of the Paper, Allied-Industrial, Chemical and Energy Workers (PACE) International Union.

Eligibility This program is open to members of the union who are currently enrolled in a program to further their education (in any subject field). Applicants must submit a 500-word essay on the history of their local. Selection is based on a random drawing.

Financial data The stipend is $1,000.

Duration 1 year.

Additional information PACE was formed in 1999 as a result of the merger of the United Paperworkers International Union and the Oil, Chemical and Atomic Workers International Union.

Number awarded 2 each year.

Deadline March of each year.

[1214]
NICK COST SCHOLARSHIPS

American Hellenic Educational Progressive Association
Attn: AHEPA Educational Foundation
1909 Q Street, N.W., Suite 500
Washington, DC 20009
(202) 232-6300   Fax: (202) 232-2140
E-mail: ahepa@ahepa.org
Web: www.ahepa.org

Purpose To provide financial assistance to undergraduate and graduate students with a connection to the American Hellenic Educational Progressive Association (AHEPA).

Eligibility This program is open to 1) members in good standing of the Order of Ahepa, Daughters of Penelope, Sons of Pericles, or Maids of Athena, and 2) the children of Order of Ahepa or Daughters of Penelope members in good standing. Applicants must be currently enrolled or planning to enroll as undergraduate or graduate students. High school seniors must submit their most recent official transcript as well as SAT or ACT scores; college freshmen and sophomores must submit high school transcripts, SAT or ACT scores, and their most recent college transcript; college juniors and seniors must submit their most recent college transcript; graduate students must submit college transcripts, GRE or MCAT scores (if available), and their most recent graduate school transcript. Along with their application, they must also submit a 500-word biographical essay. Selection is based on academic achievement; extracurricular, personal, and volunteer activities; athletic achievements; and work experience. Financial need is not considered.

Financial data Stipends range from $500 to $2,000 per year.

Duration 1 year.

Additional information A processing fee of $20 must accompany each application.

Number awarded Varies each year; recently, 2 of these scholarships were awarded.

Deadline March of each year.

[1215]
NITSOS SCHOLARSHIPS

Evrytanian Association of America
121 Greenwich Road, Suite 212
Charlotte, NC 28211
(704) 366-6571   Toll-free: (800) 307-4795
Fax: (704) 366-6571   E-mail: velouchi@bellsouth.net
Web: www.evrytanianassociation.org

Purpose To provide financial assistance for college to students of Evrytanian (Greek) origin.

Eligibility This program is open to students in the United States who are of Evrytanian (Greek) origin and whose family belongs to the Evrytanian Association of America. Applicants must submit official transcripts from their high schools and, if appropriate, colleges. Selection is based on academic excellence; financial need is not considered in the selection process.

Financial data The stipend is $2,200.

Duration 1 year.

Additional information This association was established in 1944 by immigrants from the prefecture (state) of Evrytania, in mountainous central Greece. One of the largest projects supported by the association is their scholarship program.

Number awarded 1 each year.

Deadline February of each year.

[1216]
NON COMMISSIONED OFFICERS ASSOCIATION SCHOLARSHIP FUND

Non Commissioned Officers Association of the United States of America
Attn: Scholarship Administrator
10635 IH 35 North
P.O. Box 33610
San Antonio, TX 78265-3610
(210) 653-6161   Toll-free: (800) 662-2620
E-mail: membsvc@ncoausa.org
Web: www.ncoausa.org

Purpose To provide financial assistance for college to spouses and children of members of the Non Commissioned Officers Association.

Eligibility This program is open to spouses and children (under 25 years of age) of members of the association. Children must submit 2 letters of recommendation from teachers, a personal recommendation from an adult who is not a relative, a handwritten autobiography, a certified transcript of high school or college grades, ACT or SAT scores, and a composition on Americanism. Spouses must submit a copy of their high school diploma or GED equivalent; a certified transcript of all college courses completed (if any); a certificate of completion for any other courses or training; a brief biographical background statement; and a letter of intent that includes a description of their proposed course of study for a degree, plans for completion of a degree, and a paragraph on "What a College Degree Means to Me." Financial need is not normally considered in the selection process and no applicant will be rejected because of a lack of need, but in some cases of extreme need it may be used as a factor. Each year, 2 special awards are presented: the Mary Barraco Scholarship to the student submitting the best essay on Americanism, and the William T. Green Scholarship to the student with the best high school academic record.

Financial data The scholarship stipend is $900 and the special awards are $1,000; funds are paid directly to the designated school to be used for the recipient's room and board, tuition, library fees, textbooks, and related instructional material.

Duration 1 year; may be renewed if the student maintains a GPA of 3.0 or higher and carries at least 15 hours.

Additional information Spouses who receive a grant must apply for membership in 1 of the NCOA membership categories (regular, associate, veteran, or auxiliary).

Number awarded 15 each year: 9 scholarships to children of members, 4 scholarships to spouses of members, and 2 special awards.

Deadline March of each year.

[1217]
NORMAN AND RUTH GOOD EDUCATIONAL ENDOWMENT AWARDS

Lincoln Community Foundation
215 Centennial Mall South, Suite 100
Lincoln, NE 68508
(402) 474-2345　　　　　　Fax: (402) 476-8532
E-mail: lcf@lcf.org
Web: www.lcf.org

Purpose To provide financial assistance to upper-division students attending private colleges in Nebraska.

Eligibility This program is open to juniors or seniors attending a private college in Nebraska. Applicants must have at least a 3.5 GPA and be working on a degree program, not special studies. Selection is based on academic achievement; financial need is not considered.

Financial data The amount awarded varies, up to one half of the recipient's educational expenses.

Duration 1 year; recipients may reapply.

Number awarded Varies each year; recently, 14 of these awards were presented.

Deadline April of each year.

[1218]
NORTH CAROLINA LEGISLATIVE TUITION GRANTS

North Carolina State Education Assistance Authority
Attn: Scholarship and Grant Services
10 T.W. Alexander Drive
P.O. Box 14103
Research Triangle Park, NC 27709-4103
(919) 549-8614　　　　　　Toll-free: (800) 700-1775
Fax: (919) 549-8481　　E-mail: information@ncseaa.edu
Web: www.ncseaa.edu

Purpose To provide financial assistance to students enrolled in private colleges in North Carolina.

Eligibility This program is open to North Carolina residents attending a legislatively-designated private college in the state on a full-time basis. Financial need is not considered in the selection process. Students of theology, divinity, religious education, or any other course of study designed primarily for career preparation in a religious vocation are not eligible.

Financial data The stipend is $1,800 per year. Funds are paid to the institution on behalf of the recipient.

Duration 1 year; may be renewed.

Additional information This program was established in 1975.

Number awarded Varies each year; recently, a total of 31.672 students were receiving $49,713,788 through this program.

[1219]
NORTH CAROLINA SCHOLARSHIPS FOR CHILDREN OF WAR VETERANS

Division of Veterans Affairs
Albemarle Building
325 North Salisbury Street, Suite 1065
Raleigh, NC 27603-5941
(919) 733-3851　　　　　　Fax: (919) 733-2834
E-mail: Charlie.Smith@ncmail.net
Web: www.doa.state.nc.us/vets/va.htm

Purpose To provide financial assistance for college to the children of disabled and other classes of North Carolina veterans.

Eligibility Eligible applicants come from 5 categories: Class I-A: the veteran parent died in wartime service or as a result of a service-connected condition incurred in wartime service; Class I-B: the veteran parent is rated by the U.S. Department of Veterans Affairs (VA) as 100% disabled as a result of wartime service and currently or at the time of death drawing compensation for such disability; Class II: the veteran parent is rated by the VA as much as 20% but less than 100% disabled due to wartime service, or was awarded a Purple Heart medal for wounds received, and currently or at the time of death drawing compensation for such disability; Class III: the veteran parent is currently or was at the time of death receiving a VA pension for total and permanent disability, or the veteran parent is deceased but does not qualify under any other provisions, or the veteran parent served in a combat zone or waters adjacent to a combat zone and received a campaign badge or medal but does not qualify under any other provisions; Class IV: the veteran parent was a prisoner of war or missing in action. For all classes, the veteran parent must have been a legal resident of North Carolina at the time of entrance into the armed forces or the child must have been born in North Carolina and lived in the state continuously since birth.

Financial data Students in Classes I-A, II, III, and IV receive $4,500 per academic year if they attend a private college or junior college; if attending a public postsecondary institution, they receive free tuition, a room allowance, a board allowance, and exemption from certain mandatory fees. Students in Class I-B receive $1,500 per academic year if they attend a private college or junior college; if attending a public postsecondary institution, they receive free tuition and exemption from certain mandatory fees.

Duration 4 academic years.

Number awarded An unlimited number of awards are made under Classes I-A, I-B, and IV. Classes II and III are limited to 100 awards each year in each class.

Deadline April of each year.

[1220]
NORTH DAKOTA EDUCATIONAL ASSISTANCE FOR DEPENDENTS OF VETERANS

Department of Veterans Affairs
1411 32nd Street South
P.O. Box 9003
Fargo, ND 58106-9003
(701) 239-7165 Toll-free: (866) 634-8387
Fax: (701) 239-7166
Web: www.state.nd.us/veterans/benefits/waiver.html

Purpose To provide financial assistance for college to the spouses, widow(er)s, and children of disabled and other North Dakota veterans and military personnel.

Eligibility This program is open to the spouses, widow(er)s, and dependent children of veterans who are totally disabled as a result of service-connected causes, or who were killed in action, or who have died as a result of wounds or service-connected disabilities, or who were identified as prisoners of war or missing in action. Veteran parents must have been born in and lived in North Dakota until entrance into the armed forces (or must have resided in the state for at least 6 months prior to entrance into military service) and must have served during wartime.

Financial data Eligible dependents receive free tuition and are exempt from fees at any state-supported institution of higher education, technical school, or vocational school in North Dakota.

Duration Up to 36 months or 8 academic semesters.

Number awarded Varies each year.

[1221]
NSSA NATIONAL SCHOLARSHIP PROGRAM

National Scholastic Surfing Association
10031 Dana Drive
P.O. Box 495
Huntington Beach, CA 92648
(714) 378-0899 Fax: (714) 964-5232
E-mail: jaragon@nssa.org
Web: www.nssa.org/special_programs.htm

Purpose To provide financial assistance for college to members of the National Scholastic Surfing Association (NSSA).

Eligibility This program is open to members in good standing of the association who are enrolled or planning to enroll as full-time college students. Applicants must have a GPA of 3.0 or higher. Selection is based on scholastic achievement, leadership, community and/or NSSA service, career goals, transcripts, and letters of recommendation.

Financial data Stipends range from $100 to $1,000.

Duration 1 year.

Number awarded Varies each year.

Deadline May of each year.

[1222]
OHIO LEGION SCHOLARSHIPS

American Legion
Attn: Department of Ohio
60 Big Run Road
P.O. Box 8007
Delaware, OH 43015
(740) 362-7478 Fax: (740) 362-1429
E-mail: ohlegion@iwaynet.net
Web: www.ohioamericanlegion.org/scholars.htm

Purpose To provide financial assistance for college to Ohio Legionnaires, their spouses, and their descendants.

Eligibility Eligible to apply for these scholarships are residents of Ohio who are Legionnaires, direct descendants of living or deceased Legionnaires, and surviving spouses or children of deceased U.S. military personnel who died on active duty or of injuries received on active duty. All applicants must be attending or planning to attend colleges, universities, or other approved postsecondary schools in Ohio. Selection is based on academic achievement as measured by course grades, scholastic test scores, difficulty of curriculum, participation in outside activities, and the judging committee's general impression.

Financial data Stipends are at least $2,000.

Duration 1 year.

Number awarded Varies each year; recently, 18 of these scholarships were awarded.

Deadline April of each year.

[1223]
OHIO SAFETY OFFICERS COLLEGE MEMORIAL FUND

Ohio Board of Regents
Attn: State Grants and Scholarships
57 East Main Street, Fourth Floor
P.O. Box 182452
Columbus, OH 43218-2452
(614) 466-7420 Toll-free: (888) 833-1133
Fax: (614) 752-5903
E-mail: bmetheney@regents.state.oh.us
Web: www.regents.state.oh.us

Purpose To provide financial assistance for the undergraduate education of children of Ohio peace officers and fire fighters killed in the line of duty.

Eligibility This program is open to Ohio residents whose parent or spouse was a peace officer, fire fighter, or other safety officer killed in the line of duty anywhere in the United States. Applicants must be interested in attending a participating Ohio college or university.

Financial data At Ohio public colleges and universities, the program provides full payment of tuition. At Ohio private colleges and universities, the stipend is equivalent to the average amounts paid to students attending public institutions, currently $3,990 per year.

Duration 1 year; may be renewed up to 3 additional years.

Additional information Eligible institutions are Ohio state-assisted colleges and universities and Ohio institutions approved by the Board of Regents. This program was established in 1980.

Number awarded Varies each year; recently, 54 students received benefits from this program.
Deadline Application deadlines are established by each participating college and university.

[1224]
OHIO WAR ORPHANS SCHOLARSHIP
Ohio Board of Regents
Attn: State Grants and Scholarships
57 East Main Street, Fourth Floor
P.O. Box 182452
Columbus, OH 43218-2452
(614) 466-7420   Toll-free: (888) 833-1133
Fax: (614) 752-5903
E-mail: bmetheney@regents.state.oh.us
Web: www.regents.state.oh.us/sgs/warorphans.htm

Purpose To provide financial assistance for college to the children of deceased or disabled Ohio veterans.
Eligibility To be eligible for these scholarships, students must be between 16 and 21 years of age at the time of application; must have been residents of Ohio for the past year or, if the parent was not a resident of Ohio at the time of enlistment, for the year immediately preceding application and any other 4 of the last 10 years; and must be enrolled for full-time undergraduate study at an eligible Ohio college or university. At least 1 parent must have been a member of the U.S. armed forces, including the organized Reserves and Ohio National Guard, for a period of 90 days or more (or discharged because of a disability incurred after less than 90 days of service) who served during World War I, World War II, the Korean Conflict, the Vietnam era, or the Persian Gulf War, and who, as a result of that service, either was killed or became at least 60% service-connected disabled. Also eligible are children of veterans who have a permanent and total non-service connected disability and are receiving disability benefits from the U.S. Department of Veterans Affairs. Children of veteran parents who served in the organized Reserves or Ohio National Guard are also eligible if the parent was killed or became permanently and totally disabled while at a scheduled training assembly (of any duration or length) or active duty for training, pursuant to bona fide orders issued by a competent authority.
Financial data At Ohio public colleges and universities, the program provides full payment of tuition. At Ohio private colleges and universities, the stipend is equivalent to the average amount paid to students attending public institutions, currently $4,710 per year.
Duration 1 year; may be renewed up to 4 additional years.
Additional information Eligible institutions are Ohio state-assisted colleges and universities and Ohio institutions approved by the Board of Regents. This program was established in 1957.
Number awarded Varies, depending upon the funds available. If sufficient funds are available, all eligible applicants are given a scholarship. Recently, 861 students received benefits from this program.
Deadline June of each year.

[1225]
OK SCHOLARSHIP FUND
Federal Employee Education and Assistance Fund
Attn: Scholarship Program
8441 West Bowles Avenue, Suite 200
Littleton, CO 80123-9501
(303) 933-7580   Toll-free: (800) 323-4140
Fax: (303) 933-7587   E-mail: admin@feea.org
Web: www.feea.org/special_funds/okc.html

Purpose To provide financial assistance to the children of federal employees killed in the bombing of the Alfred P. Murrah Federal Building in Oklahoma City.
Eligibility All children of federal employees killed in the bombing, including the pre-schoolers in the daycare center who survived, are entitled to this assistance.
Financial data Scholarships are intended to cover the costs of college; recently, awards averaged approximately $7,000 per year.
Duration Up to 4 years.
Number awarded Recently, 57 students received assistance from this program; by the time it ends in 2018, more than 200 children will have participated.

[1226]
ONE PUKA PUKA SCHOLARSHIP
100th Infantry Battalion Veterans Club
Attn: Scholarship Committee
520 Kamoku Street
Honolulu, HI 96826
(808) 732-5216   E-mail: daisyy@hgea.net
Web: emedia.leeward.hawaii.edu/mnakano

Purpose To provide financial assistance for college to family members of veterans who served in the 100th Infantry Battalion of World War II.
Eligibility This program is open to direct family members and descendants of 100th Infantry Battalion World War II veterans. Applicants must be high school seniors planning to attend an institution of higher learning or full-time undergraduate students at community colleges, vocational/trade schools, 4-year colleges, and universities. Along with their application, they must submit a 4-page essay that reviews the experience of Nisei men who fought in the racially-segregated 100th Infantry Battalion during World War II and asks, in the light of that experience and the meaning of democracy, if American troops should continue fighting in Iraq. Selection is based on that essay, academic achievement, extracurricular activities, and community service. Financial need is not considered.
Financial data The stipend is $2,000.
Duration 1 year; nonrenewable.
Number awarded 1 each year.
Deadline April of each year.

[1227]
ORDER OF OMEGA SCHOLARSHIPS

National Order of Omega
Attn: Scholarship Committee
300 East Border Street
Arlington, TX 76010
(817) 265-4074   Fax: (817) 459-3355
E-mail: scholarship@orderofomega.org
Web: www.orderofomega.org

Purpose To recognize and reward outstanding college seniors who are members of the Order of Omega.

Eligibility Each chapter of the Order of Omega may nominate only 1 member for consideration. Nominees must be college seniors who have displayed leadership and service to the chapter, the Greek system, and campus life. Along with their application, students must submit a brief statement of their plans following completion of their undergraduate degree and a sample of leadership advice they want to pass on to future leaders in the Greek community.

Financial data The stipends are $1,000, $750, $500, or $100. Since 1985, the sponsor has awarded $428,750 in undergraduate scholarships.

Duration 1 year; nonrenewable.

Additional information This program includes the SBC Scholarship (at $1,000), the Parker F. Enright Scholarships (at $750 each), the Patrick W. Halloran Scholarships (at $500 each), and the Dr. Kent L. Gardner Scholarships (at $100 each). The SBC Scholarship is sponsored by SBC Communications Inc.

Number awarded Varies each year. Recently, 140 of these scholarships were awarded: 1 at $1,000, 16 at $750, 62 at $500, and 61 at $100.

Deadline November of each year.

[1228]
OSCAR AND MILDRED LARSON AWARD

Vasa Order of America
Attn: Vice Grand Master
3236 Berkeley Avenue
Cleveland Heights, OH 44118-2055
(216) 371-5141   E-mail: rolf.bergman@sbcglobal.net
Web: www.vasaorder.com

Purpose To provide financial assistance for college or graduate school to students of Swedish heritage.

Eligibility Applicants must be Swedish born or of Swedish ancestry; residents of the United States, Canada, or Sweden; and enrolled or accepted as full-time undergraduate or graduate students in an accredited 4-year college or university in the United States. Membership in Vasa Order of America is not required. Selection is based on a grade transcript, letters of recommendation from school and local Vasa lodge officials, and an essay of up to 1,000 words on a topic related to Vasa.

Financial data The stipend is $3,000 per year.

Duration 1 year; may be renewed up to 3 additional years for a total award of $16,000.

Additional information Vasa Order of America is a Swedish American fraternal organization incorporated in 1899.

Number awarded 1 each year.

Deadline February of each year.

[1229]
OUIDA MUNDY HILL MEMORIAL FUND

Hawai'i Community Foundation
Attn: Scholarship Department
1164 Bishop Street, Suite 800
Honolulu, HI 96813
(808) 566-5570   Toll-free: (888) 731-3863
Fax: (808) 521-6286
E-mail: scholarships@hcf-hawaii.org
Web: www.hawaiicommunityfoundation.org

Purpose To provide financial assistance to residents of Hawaii who are interested in enrolling in a vocational training program in the state.

Eligibility This program is open to residents of Hawaii who are attending or planning to attend a vocational college or institution that is part of the University of Hawaii community college system. Programs include culinary arts, auto repair, diesel mechanics, cosmetology, computer graphics, and assistive medical technology. Applicants must submit a personal statement explaining their personal background and interests, the vocational program they plan to pursue, their career goals, and anything else that demonstrates their worthiness to receive this scholarship. Financial need is not considered in the selection process.

Financial data The stipend is $500 per semester. Funds are mailed directly to the financial aid office at the recipient's institution.

Duration 1 semester; may be renewed for up to 3 additional semesters.

Additional information This program began in 2006.

Number awarded Varies each year.

Deadline June of each year for fall and spring semester scholarships; September of each year for spring semester scholarships.

[1230]
OUTSTANDING SECONDARY CAREER AND TECHNICAL EDUCATION STUDENT AWARD

Vocational Foundation of Nebraska
P.O. Box 22607
Lincoln, NE 68542-2607
(402) 423-6786

Purpose To provide financial assistance to career and technical students in Nebraska.

Eligibility This program is open to students who are currently enrolled in career and technical education in Nebraska or have been enrolled within the past 12 months. Students must be nominated by a teacher who 1) describes how they have demonstrated a high level of competence in the program through classroom, work experience, laboratory training, related projects, or extracurricular activities, and 2) explains what distinguishes them from others in terms of capability, motivation, achievements, performances, and contributions. Nominees must also complete an application in which they describe how they will apply their career and technical education to their future plans and list projects or experiences that have seemed most interesting or important to them, school and community activities, and honors or awards.

Financial data The award is a $1,000 scholarship. Funds must be used for attendance at a Nebraska postsecondary institution.

Duration The award is presented annually.

Number awarded 1 each year.

Deadline Nominations must be submitted by March of each year.

[1231]
PAUL JENNINGS SCHOLARSHIP

International Union of Electronic, Electrical, Salaried, Machine, and Furniture Workers
Attn: IUE-CWA International Scholarship Program
501 Third Street, N.W., Suite 975
Washington, DC 20001
(202) 434-1417 Fax: (202) 434-1250
E-mail: bgray@iue-cwa.org
Web: www.iue-cwa.org/skills.html

Purpose To provide financial assistance for undergraduate education to the children and grandchildren of officials of the International Union of Electronic, Electrical, Salaried, Machine, and Furniture Workers (IUE)-Communications Workers of America (CWA).

Eligibility This program is open to children and grandchildren of IUE-CWA members who are now or have been union elected officials. Applicants must be accepted for admission or already enrolled as full-time students at an accredited college, university, nursing school, or technical school offering college credit courses. Families of full-time international union officers or employees are not eligible to apply. Along with their application, they must submit an academic transcript (including rank in class, GPA, and SAT/ACT scores); a short statement of interests and civic activities; an essay (300 to 500 words) describing their career goals and aspirations, highlighting their relationship with the union and the labor movement, and explaining why they are deserving of a union scholarship. They must also have demonstrated a commitment to equality of opportunity for all, a concern for improving the quality of life for all people, interest in service to the community, good character, leadership ability, and a desire to improve and move ahead.

Financial data The stipend is $3,000 per year.

Duration 1 year.

Number awarded 1 each year.

Deadline March of each year.

[1232]
PEPSI ICW SCHOLARSHIPS

Independent Colleges of Washington
600 Stewart Street, Suite 600
Seattle, WA 98101
(206) 623-4494 Fax: (206) 625-9621
E-mail: info@icwashington.org
Web: www.icwashington.org

Purpose To provide financial assistance to students enrolled at colleges and universities that are members of Independent Colleges of Washington (ICW).

Eligibility This program is open to students enrolled at ICW-member colleges and universities with a GPA of 3.0 or higher. Selection is based on academic merit (50%) and school and community involvement. No application is required; each ICW institution makes a selection from all of its students.

Financial data The stipend is $1,200.

Duration 1 year; nonrenewable.

Additional information The ICW-member institutions are Gonzaga University, Heritage College, Pacific Lutheran University, Saint Martin's College, Seattle Pacific University, Seattle University, University of Puget Sound, Walla Walla College, Whitman College, and Whitworth College. This program is sponsored by the Pepsi-Cola Company.

Number awarded 10 each year: 1 at each of the 10 ICW colleges and universities.

Deadline Each institution sets its own deadline.

[1233]
PEPSI USBC YOUTH BOWLING CHAMPIONSHIPS

United States Bowling Congress
Attn: Pepsi-Cola Youth Bowling Event Manager
5301 South 76th Street
Greendale, WI 53129-1192
(414) 423-3442 Toll-free: (800) 514-BOWL, ext. 3442
Fax: (414) 421-3014
E-mail: maureen.vicena@bowl.com
Web: www.bowl.com

Purpose To recognize and reward (with college scholarships) members of the United States Bowling Congress (USBC) who achieve high scores in an international competition.

Eligibility This competition is open to USBC members in the United States, Puerto Rico, U.S. military zones, and Canada. Applicants enter in 1 of 6 categories: 11 and under boys' handicap, 12 and above boys' handicap, 12 and above boys' scratch, 11 and under girls' handicap, 12 and above girls' handicap, and 12 and above girls' scratch. Based on their bowling scores in state and zone competitions, the top bowlers in the 12 and above boys' and girls' handicap categories advance to the international finals. Also advancing to the international finals are the state and zone winners in the 12 and above boys' and girls' scratch categories who are also USBC Junior Gold members (boys must have an average of 175 or above, girls must have an average of 165 or above). All selected finalists (more than 200 qualify each year), are then assigned to Division I or Division II for the international competition, held annually at a site in the United States; assignment is based on their adjusted score from year-end averages and state and zone competitions. Bowlers whose scores are in the top half are assigned to Division I and bowlers whose scores are in the bottom half are assigned to Division II. Scholarships are awarded solely on the basis of bowling performance in the international finals.

Financial data At the international finals, the top finishers in each division receive scholarships of $2,000, $1,500, $1,000, and $500, respectively.

Duration The competition is held annually.

ANY SUBJECT AREA

Additional information This competition is sponsored by the Pepsi-Cola Company and conducted by the USBC. More than $300,000 is scholarships is awarded at state and zone competitions for all 6 categories. USBC also awards a $400 stipend to each competitor at the international finals (Canadian athletes are not eligible for the stipend and competitors from U.S. military bases must pay for their own transportation to the United States); the stipend is intended to assist with the cost of travel, meals, and housing.

Number awarded Each year, 16 scholarships are awarded: 8 are set aside for girls (4 in each division) and 8 for boys (4 in each division).

Deadline Qualifying tournaments are held in bowling centers from October through February of each year. Center and section qualifying takes place in March and April. State and zone competitions take place through the end of May. The national finals are held in July.

[1234]
PFIZER EPILEPSY SCHOLARSHIP AWARD

Pfizer Inc.
c/o Eden Communications Group
515 Valley Street, Suite 200
Maplewood, NJ 07040
(973) 275-6518   Toll-free: (800) AWARD-PF
Fax: (973) 275-9792
E-mail: info@epilepsy-scholarship.com
Web: www.epilepsy-scholarship.com

Purpose To provide financial assistance for undergraduate or graduate study to individuals with epilepsy.

Eligibility Applicants must be under a physician's care for epilepsy (and taking prescribed medication) and must submit an application with 2 letters of recommendation (1 from the physician) and verification of academic status. They must be high school seniors entering college in the fall; college freshmen, sophomores, or juniors continuing in the fall; or college seniors planning to enter graduate school in the fall. Along with their application, they must submit a 250-word essay on something of direct personal importance to them as a person with epilepsy. Selection is based on demonstrated achievement in academic and extracurricular activities; financial need is not considered.

Financial data The stipend is $3,000.

Duration 1 year; nonrenewable.

Number awarded 25 each year.

Deadline February of each year.

[1235]
POLANKI COLLEGE ACHIEVEMENT AWARDS

Polanki, The Polish Women's Cultural Club of Milwaukee
Attn: College Achievement Awards
P.O. Box 341458
Milwaukee, WI 53234
(414) 858=9357   E-mail: polanki@polanki.org
Web: www.polanki.org/scholar-main.html

Purpose To recognize and reward upper-division and graduate students of Polish heritage in Wisconsin who demonstrate academic excellence.

Eligibility This program is open to college juniors, seniors, and graduate students who are Wisconsin residents or attending college in the state. Applicants must be of Polish heritage or non-Polish students of Polish language, history, society, or culture. They must have a GPA of 3.0 or higher and be able to demonstrate knowledge of Polish culture. Along with their application, they must submit 1) an essay of 250 to 300 words on an aspect of Polish culture that interests them and that they have explored through books, articles, and/or the Internet; and 2) a paragraph of 100 to 150 words describing their career plans and goals. U.S. citizenship or permanent residence is required.

Financial data Awards range from $500 to $1,000.

Duration The awards are presented annually.

Additional information This program includes the following named awards: the Janet Dziadulewicz Branden Memorial Award (for an outstanding student in Polish studies), the Copernicus Award (for an outstanding student in a field of science), the Stanley F. and Helen Balcerzak Award, the Evelyn Appleyard Memorial Award, the Arthur B. Gurda Memorial Award, and the Msgr. Alphonse S. Popek Memorial Award. Other awards are limited to students at Marquette University and the University of Wisconsin at Milwaukee.

Number awarded Varies each year; recently, 10 of these awards were presented. An additional 2 awards were presented jointly with Marquette University and 4 with the University of Wisconsin at Milwaukee.

Deadline February of each year.

[1236]
POWDER RIVER BASIN SECTION ANNUAL SCHOLARSHIP AWARDS

Society of Petroleum Engineers-Powder River Basin Section
P.O. Box 3977
Gillette, WY 82717-3977

Purpose To provide financial assistance to Wyoming students interested in preparing for a career in the oil and gas industry.

Eligibility This program is open to Wyoming students preparing for a career in the oil and gas industry. Applicants should be majoring in engineering (especially petroleum engineering and petroleum technology), although some of the scholarships may go to non-engineering students. They must be enrolled full time as entering freshmen, sophomores, juniors, or seniors in a 4-year program or freshmen or sophomores in a 2-year program and have a GPA of 2.75 or higher. Along with their application, they must submit a letter that covers their academic qualifications, primary career interests, extracurricular activities, and names of 2 references. Financial need is not considered in the selection process.

Financial data Stipends range from $250 to $1,000.

Duration 1 year.

Additional information Information is also available from Bob Christofferson, Citation Oil and Gas Corporation, 1016 East Lincoln, Gillette, WY 82716, (307) 682-4853.

Number awarded 5 to 15 each year.

Deadline March of each year.

[1237]
PRIDE COLLEGE SCHOLARSHIP PROGRAM

Dobson Communications Corporation
Attn: PRIDE Scholarship
14201 Wireless Way
Oklahoma City, OK 73134
(405) 529-8382   Toll-free: (800) 522-9404
E-mail: cdavis@dobson.net
Web: www.dobson.net/com_pride.html

Purpose To provide financial assistance to high school seniors and undergraduates residing in the 17 states served by Dobson Cellular Systems.

Eligibility This program is open to full-time college students (either current or entering) who have a GPA of 3.5 or higher and are customers of Dobson Cellular Systems or Cellular One from Dobson Cellular Systems. Applicants are required to submit a completed application form, transcripts of their most recent years of education, a wallet-sized professional photograph, and 200-word essays on each of the following topics: 1) what attributes or goals would they look for in future PRIDE recipients, 2) develop a question and an answer that could be asked in an interview of PRIDE applicants, 3) what word best describes them, 4) if they could improve something in their community, what would that be, and 5) where do they see themselves in 10 years.

Financial data The stipend is $2,500.

Duration 1 year.

Additional information This program was established in 1996. PRIDE stands for Promoting Individual Development and Education. Dobson-owned companies include: Dobson Communications Corporation, McLoud Telephone Company, Dobson Telephone Company, Dobson Cellular Systems, and Logix Communications; for a list of states served by these companies, write to the sponsor.

Number awarded Approximately 100 each year.

Deadline December of each year.

[1238]
PRINCE KUHIO HAWAIIAN CIVIC CLUB SCHOLARSHIP

Prince Kuhio Hawaiian Civic Club
Attn: Scholarship Chair
P.O. Box 4728
Honolulu, HI 96812
E-mail: Caztwin@aol.com
Web: www.pkhcc.com/scholarship

Purpose To provide financial assistance for undergraduate or graduate studies to persons of Hawaiian descent.

Eligibility Applicants must be of Hawaiian descent (descendants of the aboriginal inhabitants of the Hawaiian Islands prior to 1778) who are high school seniors, recent graduates, or full-time undergraduate or graduate students. Graduating high school seniors and current undergraduate students must have a GPA of 2.5 or higher; graduate students must have at least a 3.3 GPA. Priority is given to members of the Prince Kuhio Hawaiian Civic Club in good standing, including directly-related family members. Special consideration is given to applicants majoring in Hawaiian studies, Hawaiian language, or journalism.

Financial data Stipends range from $500 to $1,000.

Duration 1 year.

Additional information Information is also available from Cyr Pakele, Kamehameha Schools, Haleakala Counseling Center, 210 Konia Circle, Honolulu, HI 96817, (808) 842-8934, (800) 842-IMUA, E-mail: cypakele@ksbe.edu.

Number awarded Varies each year.

Deadline March of each year.

[1239]
PROJECT RED FLAG ACADEMIC SCHOLARSHIP FOR WOMEN WITH BLEEDING DISORDERS

National Hemophilia Foundation
Attn: Department of Finance, Administration & MIS
116 West 32nd Street, 11th Floor
New York, NY 10001-3212
(212) 328-3700   Toll-free: (800) 42-HANDI, ext. 3700
Fax: (212) 328-3777   E-mail: info@hemophilia.org
Web: www.hemophilia.org

Purpose To provide financial assistance for college or graduate school to women who have a bleeding disorder.

Eligibility This program is open to women who are entering or already enrolled in an undergraduate or graduate program at a university, college, or accredited vocational school. Applicants must have von Willebrand disease, hemophilia or other clotting factor deficiency, or carrier status. Along with their application, they must submit a 250-word essay that describes their educational and future career plans, including how they intend to use their education to enhance the bleeding disorders community. Financial need is not considered in the selection process.

Financial data The stipend is $2,500.

Duration 1 year.

Additional information The program was established in 2005.

Number awarded 2 each year.

Deadline May of each year.

[1240]
R. PRESTON WOODRUFF, JR. SCHOLARSHIPS

Arkansas Student Loan Authority
101 East Capitol Avenue, Suite 401
Little Rock, AR 72201
Toll-free: (800) 443-6030
Web: www.asla.info

Purpose To provide financial assistance for college to residents of Arkansas or students attending a postsecondary institution in the state.

Eligibility This program is open to 1) residents of Arkansas, who may be attending a postsecondary institution in or out of the state, and 2) residents of other states attending a postsecondary institution in Arkansas. Postsecondary educational institutions include 2-year colleges, 4-year colleges and universities, and technical and trade schools. Applicants may enter online or by submitting a postcard with their name, address, telephone number, and name of their educational institution. Winners are selected at random.

Financial data The stipend is $1,000. Funds are mailed to the financial aid office at the designated school.

Duration 1 year; of the scholarships awarded each year, 1 may be renewed up to 3 additional years but the others are nonrenewable.
Number awarded 20 each year.
Deadline March of each year.

[1241]
REGIONAL UNIVERSITY BACCALAUREATE SCHOLARSHIP PROGRAM

Oklahoma State Regents for Higher Education
Attn: Director of Scholarship and Grant Programs
655 Research Parkway, Suite 200
P.O. Box 108850
Oklahoma City, OK 73101-8850
(405) 225-9239 Toll-free: (800) 858-1840
Fax: (405) 225-9230 E-mail: studentinfo@osrhe.edu
Web: www.okhighered.org

Purpose To provide financial assistance to Oklahoma residents who are attending designated publicly-supported regional universities in the state.
Eligibility This program is open to residents of Oklahoma who are attending 1 of 11 designated regional public institutions in the state and working on an undergraduate degree. Applicants must 1) be designated a National Merit Semifinalist or Commended Student, or 2) have an ACT score of at least 30 and have an exceptional GPA and class ranking as determined by the collegiate institution. Selection is based on academic promise.
Financial data The stipend is $3,000 per year. Awardees also receive a resident tuition waiver from the institution.
Duration Up to 4 years if the recipient maintains a cumulative GPA of 3.25 or higher and full-time enrollment.
Additional information Applicants apply through the financial aid office of the university. The participating regional universities are the University of Central Oklahoma, East Central University, Northeastern State University, Northwestern Oklahoma State University, Southeastern Oklahoma State University, Southwestern Oklahoma State University, Cameron University, Langston University, Rogers State University, Oklahoma Panhandle State University, and the University of Science and Arts of Oklahoma.
Number awarded Up to 165 each year: 15 at each of the 11 participating regional universities.

[1242]
RICHARD CECIL TODD AND CLAUDA PENNOCK TODD TRIPOD SCHOLARSHIP

Phi Sigma Pi
2119 Ambassador Circle
Lancaster, PA 17603
(717) 299-4710 Fax: (717) 390-3054
E-mail: pspoffice@phisigmapi.org
Web: www.phisigmapi.org/contribute/todd.html

Purpose To provide financial assistance for college or graduate school to members of Phi Sigma Pi Honor Society.
Eligibility This program is open to members of the society who are undergraduates working on a bachelor's degree or graduating seniors entering graduate school. Applicants must have a GPA of 3.0 or higher. Along with their application, they must submit a 1- to 3-page statement on how they have promoted scholarship, leadership, and fellowship within the fraternity, campus, and community since becoming a member of Phi Sigma Pi. Financial need is not considered in the selection process.
Financial data The stipend is $1,500.
Duration 1 year; nonrenewable.
Additional information This program was established in 1991.
Number awarded 1 or more each year.
Deadline April of each year.

[1243]
RICHARD V. BRADSHAW MEMORIAL SCHOLARSHIP

Connecticut Association of Purchasing Management, Inc.
Attn: Scholarship Committee
28 Sunset Hill Drive
Branford, CT 06405
(203) 488-2456 Fax: (203) 488-1891
E-mail: capminc@sbcglobal.net
Web: www.capminc.org/scholarships.htm

Purpose To provide financial assistance for college to children and grandchildren of members of the Connecticut Association of Purchasing Management (CAPM).
Eligibility This program is open to the children and grandchildren of CAPM members in good standing. Applicants must be high school seniors or currently attending college and 1) at least a sophomore; 2) completing the second year of a 2-year program; or 3) entering the junior or senior year of a 4- or 5-year undergraduate program. Along with their application, they must submit a 500-word autobiographical essay that includes why they are applying for the scholarship. Selection is based on academic achievement and supplementary activities.
Financial data A stipend is awarded (amount not specified).
Duration 1 year.
Additional information This program is administered by CAPM and funded by the Northeast Supply Management Group of the Institute for Supply Management.
Number awarded 1 or more each year.
Deadline February of each year.

[1244]
ROBERT L. LIVINGSTON SCHOLARSHIPS

International Union of Electronic, Electrical, Salaried, Machine, and Furniture Workers
Attn: IUE-CWA International Scholarship Program
501 Third Street, N.W., Suite 975
Washington, DC 20001
(202) 434-1417 Fax: (202) 434-1250
E-mail: bgray@iue-cwa.org
Web: www.iue-cwa.org/skills.html

Purpose To provide financial assistance for undergraduate education to children of members of the Automotive Conference Board of the International Union of Electronic, Electrical, Salaried, Machine, and Furniture Workers (IUE)-Communications Workers of America (CWA).

Eligibility This program is open to children of IUE-CWA Automotive Conference Board members. Applicants must be accepted for admission or already enrolled as full-time students at an accredited college, university, nursing school, or technical school offering college credit classes. Along with their application, they must submit a short statement of interests and goals, including career objectives, civic commitment and activities, and extracurricular activities. They must also have demonstrated a commitment to equality of opportunity for all, a concern for improving the quality of life for all people, an interest in service to the community, good character, leadership ability, and a desire to improve and move ahead.
Financial data The stipend is $1,500 per year.
Duration 1 year.
Number awarded 2 each year.
Deadline March of each year.

[1245]
ROSA L. PARKS SCHOLARSHIPS
Conference of Minority Transportation Officials
Attn: National Scholarship Program
818 18th Street, N.W., Suite 850
Washington, DC 20006
(202) 530-0551   Fax: (202) 530-0617
Web: www.comto.org/scholarship.htm

Purpose To provide financial assistance for college to children of members of the Conference of Minority Transportation Officials (COMTO) and to other students working on a bachelor's or master's degree in transportation.
Eligibility This program is open to 1) college-bound high school seniors whose parent has been a COMTO member for at least 1 year; 2) undergraduates who have completed at least 60 semester credit hours in a transportation discipline; and 3) students working on a master's degree in transportation who have completed at least 15 credits. Applicants must have a GPA of 3.0 or higher. Along with their application, they must submit a cover letter with a 500-word statement of career goals. Financial need is not considered in the selection process. U.S. citizenship is required.
Financial data The stipend is $4,500. Funds are paid directly to the recipient's college or university.
Duration 1 year.
Additional information COMTO was established in 1971 to promote, strengthen, and expand the roles of minorities in all aspects of transportation. Recipients are expected to attend the COMTO National Scholarship Luncheon.
Number awarded 2 each year.
Deadline April of each year.

[1246]
ROSS N. AND PATRICIA PANGERE FOUNDATION SCHOLARSHIPS
American Council of the Blind
Attn: Coordinator, Scholarship Program
1155 15th Street, N.W., Suite 1004
Washington, DC 20005
(202) 467-5081   Toll-free: (800) 424-8666
Fax: (202) 467-5085   E-mail: info@acb.org
Web: www.acb.org

Purpose To provide financial assistance for undergraduate or graduate study to outstanding blind students.
Eligibility Eligible to apply for this scholarship are legally blind U.S. citizens or resident aliens who are undergraduate or graduate students. In addition to letters of recommendation and copies of academic transcripts, applications must include an autobiographical sketch. A cumulative GPA of 3.3 or higher is generally required. Selection is based on demonstrated academic record, involvement in extracurricular and civic activities, and academic objectives. The severity of the applicant's visual impairment and his/her study methods are also taken into account.
Financial data A stipend is awarded (amount not specified). In addition, the winner receives a Kurzweil-1000 Reading System.
Duration 1 year.
Additional information The scholarship winner is expected to be present at the council's annual national convention; the council will cover all reasonable costs connected with convention attendance.
Number awarded 1 each year.
Deadline February of each year.

[1247]
SAL INGRASSIA SCHOLARSHIP
International Union of Electronic, Electrical, Salaried,
    Machine, and Furniture Workers
Attn: IUE-CWA International Scholarship Program
501 Third Street, N.W., Suite 975
Washington, DC 20001
(202) 434-1417   Fax: (202) 434-1250
E-mail: bgray@iue-cwa.org
Web: www.iue-cwa.org/skills.html

Purpose To provide financial assistance for undergraduate education to children and grandchildren of members and employees of the International Union of Electronic, Electrical, Salaried, Machine, and Furniture Workers (IUE)-Communications Workers of America (CWA).
Eligibility This program is open to children and grandchildren of IUE-CWA members and employees. Applicants must be accepted for admission or already enrolled as full-time students at an accredited college, university, nursing school, or technical school offering college credit classes. Along with their application, they must submit an academic transcript (including rank in class, GPA, and SAT/ACT scores); a short statement of interests and civic activities; an essay (300 to 500 words) describing their career goals and aspirations, highlighting their relationship with the union and the labor movement, and explaining why they are deserving of a union scholarship. They must also have demonstrated a commitment to equality of opportunity for all,

a concern for improving the quality of life for all people, an interest in service to the community, good character, leadership ability, and a desire to improve and move ahead.
Financial data The stipend is $2,500 per year.
Duration 1 year.
Number awarded 1 each year.
Deadline March of each year.

[1248]
SALLIE MAE 911 EDUCATION FUND SCHOLARSHIP PROGRAM
Sallie Mae 911 Education Fund
c/o The Community Foundation for the National Capital Region
1201 15th Street, N.W., Suite 420
Washington, DC 20005-2842
(202) 955-5890   Toll-free: (800) 441-4043
Fax: (202) 955-8084
Web: www.thesalliemaefund.org

Purpose To provide financial assistance for college to children of those killed or disabled in the terrorist attacks of September 11, 2001.
Eligibility This program is open to the children of the victims of the September 11, 2001 terrorist attacks, including children of people killed in airplanes or buildings as well as police, fire safety, or medical personnel killed or disabled as a result of the attacks. Applicants must be enrolled or planning to enroll full time as an undergraduate student at a public or private 2-year or 4-year college or university.
Financial data The stipend is $2,500 per year.
Duration 1 year; may be renewed up to 3 additional years.
Number awarded Varies each year.
Deadline May of each year.

[1249]
SAM DAKIS SCHOLARSHIP
American Hellenic Educational Progressive Association
Attn: AHEPA Educational Foundation
1909 Q Street, N.W., Suite 500
Washington, DC 20009
(202) 232-6300   Fax: (202) 232-2140
E-mail: ahepa@ahepa.org
Web: www.ahepa.org

Purpose To provide financial assistance for college to students with a connection to the American Hellenic Educational Progressive Association (AHEPA).
Eligibility This program is open to 1) members in good standing of the Order of Ahepa, Daughters of Penelope, Sons of Pericles, or Maids of Athena, and 2) the children of Order of Ahepa or Daughters of Penelope members in good standing. Applicants must be currently enrolled or planning to enroll in a college or university. High school seniors must submit their most recent official transcript as well as SAT or ACT scores; college freshmen and sophomores must submit high school transcripts, SAT or ACT scores, and their most recent college transcript; college juniors and seniors must submit their most recent college transcript. Along with their application, they must also submit a 500-word biographical essay. Selection is based on academic achievement; extracurricular, personal, and volunteer activities; athletic achievements; and work experience. Financial need is not considered.
Financial data Stipends range from $500 to $2,000 per year.
Duration 1 year.
Additional information A processing fee of $20 must accompany each application.
Number awarded Varies each year; recently, 1 of these scholarships was awarded.
Deadline March of each year.

[1250]
SCHOLARSHIPS FOR MILITARY CHILDREN
Defense Commissary Agency
Attn: SSP
1300 E Avenue
Fort Lee, VA 23801-1800
(804) 734-8134   Fax: (804) 734-8248
E-mail: info@militaryscholar.org
Web: www.militaryscholar.org

Purpose To provide financial assistance for college to the children of veterans and military personnel.
Eligibility This program is open to sons and daughters of U.S. military ID card holders, including active duty, retirees, Guard/Reserves and survivors of deceased members, who are enrolled or accepted for enrollment at a college or university. The eligibility of applicants, including survivors of deceased members, is based on the DoD ID Card Directive, which provides for eligibility up to 21 years of age, or 23 if still enrolled as a full-time student. Applicants must have a GPA of 3.0 or higher and write a short essay on "What Being a Military Dependent Means to Me." Selection is based on merit.
Financial data The stipend is $1,500.
Duration 1 year; recipients may reapply.
Additional information This program, established in 2001, is supported by the Fisher House Foundation. Recipients must enroll as a full-time undergraduate student.
Number awarded 1 scholarship is allocated for each of the commissaries worldwide operated by the Defense Commissary Agency (DeCA).
Deadline February of each year.

[1251]
SEATTLE JUNIOR CHAMBER OF COMMERCE SCHOLARSHIP PROGRAM
Seattle Junior Chamber of Commerce
Attn: Seattle Jaycees Scholarship Committee
109 West Mercer Street
Seattle, WA 98119
(206) 286-2014   Fax: (206) 286-4459
Web: www.seattlejaycees.org

Purpose To provide financial assistance to high school seniors and currently-enrolled undergraduate and graduate students interested in going to college in Washington.
Eligibility Applicants must be currently enrolled, accepted, or have an application pending at an institution of higher education (public or private) located in the state

of Washington. Past recipients may apply again, but they may not be awarded the scholarship more than twice. Non-residents may apply, provided they are or will be enrolled in an academic institution in the state. Selection is based on community service and/or extracurricular community involvement (80%), and the applicant's achievements and ability to reflect a balance of family, school, and professional areas (20%).

Financial data The stipend is $1,000 per year. Funds are paid directly to the recipient's institution and are to be used for tuition and fees.

Duration 1 year; recipients may reapply.

Additional information This program was established in 1988. Since then, more than $500,000 in scholarships has been awarded. There is a $5 processing fee.

Number awarded Varies each year; recently, 40 of these scholarships were presented: 20 to graduating high school seniors and 20 to students at other academic levels.

Deadline March of each year.

[1252]
SEIU 1-YEAR SCHOLARSHIPS

Service Employees International Union
Attn: Education Department
1313 L Street, N.W.
Washington, DC 20005
(202) 898-3326   Toll-free: (800) 424-8592
Fax: (202) 898-3348   TDD: (202) 898-3481
Web: www.seiu.org

Purpose To provide financial assistance for continuing education to members and children of members of the Service Employees International Union (SEIU).

Eligibility All members of SEIU in good standing for 3 continuous years or the children of those members are eligible. Applicants must be 1) returning to an accredited college or university as a sophomore, junior, or senior; or 2) attending an accredited community college, trade school, or technical school. As part of the application process, they must read the online essay "Uniting Our Strength to Win Big" and answer questions pertaining to the essay. Applicants who pass the test are eligible for a lottery drawing, from which winners are selected.

Financial data The stipend is $1,500.

Duration 1 year; may not be renewed.

Additional information This program is administered by Scholarship Program Administrators, Inc., 1201 Eighth Avenue South, P.O. Box 23737, Nashville, TN 27202-3737, (615) 320-3149, Fax: (615) 320-3151, E-mail: info@spaprog.com.

Number awarded 33 each year.

Deadline February of each year.

[1253]
SERTOMA COLLEGIATE CLUB SCHOLARSHIPS

Sertoma International
Attn: Director of Finance and Administration
1912 East Meyer Boulevard
Kansas City, MO 64132-1174
(816) 333-8300, ext. 214   Fax: (816) 333-4320
TTY: (816) 333-8300   E-mail: aellington@sertoma.org
Web: www.sertoma.org

Purpose To provide financial assistance for college to members of Sertoma Collegiate Club.

Eligibility This program is open to U.S. citizens who are active members of the organization. Applicants must be working full time on a bachelor's degree with a cumulative GPA of 3.2 or higher. Associate degrees, community colleges, and vocational programs do not qualify. Along with their application, they must submit a 1-page statement of purpose describing how this scholarship will help them achieve their goals. Selection is based on academic achievement and participation in both Sertoma Collegiate Club programs and non-Sertoma service activities.

Financial data The stipend is $1,000 per year.

Duration 1 year.

Additional information Sertoma, which stands for SERvice TO MAnkind, is a volunteer service organization with 25,000 members in 800 clubs across North America.

Number awarded 4 each year.

Deadline March of each year.

[1254]
SERTOMA SCHOLARSHIPS FOR HEARING-IMPAIRED STUDENTS

Sertoma International
Attn: Director of Finance and Administration
1912 East Meyer Boulevard
Kansas City, MO 64132-1174
(816) 333-8300, ext. 214   Fax: (816) 333-4320
TTY: (816) 333-8300   E-mail: aellington@sertoma.org
Web: www.sertoma.org

Purpose To provide financial assistance for college to hearing impaired students.

Eligibility This program is open to students who have a minimum 40dB bilateral hearing loss and are interested in working full time on a bachelor's degree at a 4-year college or university. Students working on a community college degree, associate degree, or vocational program degree are ineligible. Applicants must be able to document their hearing loss. They must be entering or continuing undergraduate studies in the United States. A GPA of at least 3.2 and U.S. citizenship are required. Selection is based on past academic performance, goals, a statement of purpose, and overall merit. Financial need is not considered.

Financial data The stipend is $1,000 per year.

Duration 1 year; may be renewed up to 4 times.

Additional information Sertoma, which stands for SERvice TO MAnkind, is a volunteer service organization with 25,000 members in 800 clubs across North America. Funding for this program is provided by Oticon, Inc. and the Sertoma Foundation. To request an application, students must send a self-addressed, stamped envelope.

Number awarded 20 each year.

Deadline April of each year.

[1255]
SGT FELIX DELGRECO JR. SCHOLARSHIP
Connecticut National Guard Foundation, Inc.
Attn: Scholarship Committee
360 Broad Street
Hartford, CT 06105-3795
(860) 241-1550   Fax: (860) 293-2929
E-mail: scholarship.committee@ctngfoundation.org
Web: www.ctngfoundation.org/Scholarship.asp

Purpose To provide financial assistance for college to children of members of the Connecticut Army National Guard.

Eligibility This program is open to children of members of the Connecticut Army National Guard who are enrolled or planning to enroll in an accredited college degree or technical program. Applicants must submit a letter of recommendation, list of extracurricular activities, high school or college transcripts, and a 200-word statement on their educational and future goals. Selection is based on achievement and citizenship.

Financial data The stipend is $2,500.

Duration 1 year.

Number awarded 1 each year.

Deadline April of each year.

[1256]
SHOPKO SCHOLARSHIPS
ShopKo Stores Inc.
700 Pilgrim Way
P.O. Box 19060
Green Bay, WI 54307-9060
(920) 497-2211
Web: www.shopko.com

Purpose To provide financial assistance for college to residents of states where ShopKo stores operate.

Eligibility This program is open to residents of California, Colorado, Idaho, Illinois, Iowa, Michigan, Minnesota, Montana, Nebraska, Nevada, Oregon, South Dakota, Utah, Washington, and Wisconsin. Applicants must be high school seniors or graduates who plan to enroll or students who are already enrolled in a full-time undergraduate course of study at an accredited 2-year or 4-year college, university, or vocational/technical school. Selection is based on academic record, potential to succeed, leadership and participation in school and community activities, honors, work experience, a statement of educational and career goals, and an outside appraisal. Financial need is not considered.

Financial data The stipend is $1,000 per year.

Duration 1 year; nonrenewable.

Additional information This program is managed by Scholarships Inc, P.O. Box 1873, Green Bay, WI 54305.

Number awarded 100 each year.

Deadline November of each year.

[1257]
SIKH COALITION DIVERSITY ESSAY COMPETITION
Sikh Coalition
396 Broadway, Suite 701
New York, NY 10013
(646) 613-8057   E-mail: essay@sikhcoalition.org
Web: www.sikhcoalition.org/essay.asp

Purpose To recognize and reward high school and college students who submit outstanding essays on topics related to diversity and faith.

Eligibility This competition is open to students at high schools and colleges in all countries. Applicants are invited to submit an essay on a topic that changes annually but relates to issues that confront our societies in the post-September 11 world. Recently, students were invited to argue for or against the proposition that racial, ethnic, or religious profiling makes the world more secure. Selection is based on originality, understanding of the issues involved, and relevance to the theme of the essay.

Financial data Prizes are $1,000 for first place, $500 for second, $250 for third, and $50 for honorable mention.

Duration The competition is held annually.

Additional information This competition was first held in 2004. A recent competition attracted 1,700 entries from 30 countries (most from the United States).

Number awarded 3 main prizes and a varying number (recently, 11) of honorable mentions are awarded each year.

Deadline February of each year.

[1258]
SIMULTANEOUS MEMBERSHIP PROGRAM (SMP)
U.S. Army
ROTC Cadet Command
Attn: ATCC-OP-I-S
55 Patch Road, Building 56
Fort Monroe, VA 23651-1052
(757) 727-4558   Toll-free: (800) USA-ROTC
E-mail: atccps@usaac.army.mil
Web: www.rotc.usaac.army.mil

Purpose To provide financial assistance to individuals who serve simultaneously in the Army National Guard or Army Reserve and the Army Reserve Officers' Training Corps (ROTC) while they are in college.

Eligibility Students who are members of the Army National Guard or the Army Reserve and Army ROTC at the same time are eligible for this assistance. Applicants must have completed basic training or the equivalent, have at least 4 years remaining on their current military obligation, be full-time students as college juniors, have a GPA of 2.0 or higher, and be U.S. citizens.

Financial data Advanced ROTC Simultaneous Membership Program (SMP) participants are paid at the rate of at least a Sergeant E-5 for their Guard or Reserve training assemblies (recently, $216 per month), plus an ROTC stipend for 10 months of the year at $350 per month during their junior year and $400 per month during their senior year.

Duration Up to 2 years.

Additional information Participants serve as officer trainees in their Guard or Reserve units and, under the close supervision of a commissioned officer, perform duties commensurate with those of a second lieutenant. Cadets who successfully complete the SMP program graduate with a commission as a second lieutenant. Once commissioned, they may continue to serve in their Guard or Reserve units, or they may apply for active duty in the U.S. Army.

Number awarded Varies each year.

[1259]
SMART PROGRAM SCHOLARSHIPS

United States Bowling Congress
Attn: SMART Program
5301 South 76th Street
Greendale, WI 53129-1192
(414) 423-3343   Toll-free: (800) 514-BOWL, ext. 3343
Fax: (414) 421-3014   E-mail: smart@bowl.com
Web: www.bowl.com/scholarships/main.aspx

Purpose To provide financial assistance for college and other educational activities to young bowlers.

Eligibility These awards are presented to bowlers at state and local levels throughout the United States and Canada. Some scholarships are presented to winners of bowling tournaments, but others require written applications. Some require demonstrations of financial need, but others are based on bowling and/or academic accomplishments. Some are limited to students, but others are open to bowlers at other levels. All scholarships must conform to standards of the Scholarship Management and Accounting Reports for Tenpins (SMART) program of the United States Bowling Congress (USBC).

Financial data The awards vary; recently, a total of $2,914,100 was awarded through this program. Some scholarships must be used at accredited colleges and universities for tuition, housing, and books. Other uses that are specified include: bowling camps and lessons; bowling coaching seminars; business, technical, or trade schools; continuing education classes; and educational camps in mathematics, science, art, or computers.

Additional information For a complete list of all scholarship opportunities, contact the sponsor.

Number awarded Varies each year; recently, more than 35,000 bowlers received scholarships.

[1260]
SONLIGHT SCHOLARSHIPS

Sonlight Curriculum, Ltd.
Attn: Scholarship Committee
8042 South Grant Way
Littleton, CO 80122-2705
(303) 730-6292   Fax: (303) 795-8668
E-mail: scholarship@sonlight.com
Web: www.sonlight.com/scholarships.html

Purpose To provide financial assistance for college to home-schooled students who have utilized Sonlight Core programs.

Eligibility This program is open to high school seniors and current college students who have been home schooled and used at least 3 Sonlight Core programs for at least 3 years. Applicants must submit 1) a 2-page personal essay on how their future plans and aspirations fit in with the purposes of God (including references to seeking God's Kingdom, asserting the crown rights of King Jesus, and how their future plans or purposes will help extend His Kingdom); 2) a 3-page project (e.g., review, digest, portfolio) on a mathematics, science, performing arts, or visual arts discipline of interest or concern to them; and 3) a 3-page argumentative essay on a topic of their choice. For some of the awards (which the sponsor designates as the "Green Criteria"), selection is based in the following order: creativity, mission-mindedness, or acts of kindness; spiritual-mindedness; heart for learning; academic performance; and activities and interests. For other awards (which the sponsor designates as the "Blue Criteria"), selection is based on the same criteria but in the following order: academic performance; spiritual-mindedness; heart for learning; creativity, mission-mindedness, or acts of kindness; leadership; and activities and interests. Students indicate on their applications the criteria by which they wish to be judged.

Financial data Stipends are $20,000 ($5,000 per year), $10,000 ($2,500 per year), or $4,000 ($1,000 per year).

Duration 4 years, provided the recipients maintain a GPA of 3.5 or higher and provide the sponsor with a copy of their college transcript.

Number awarded 8 each year: 1 at $5,000 per year, 2 at $2,500 per year, and 5 at $1,000 per year. The awards include 1 at $2,500 per year and 1 at $1,000 per year selected according to the "Green Criteria" and 1 at $5,000 per year, 1 at $2,500 per year, and 4 at $1,000 per year selected according to the "Blue Criteria."

Deadline December of each year.

[1261]
SONS AND DAUGHTERS SCHOLARSHIP PROGRAM

Society for Human Resource Management
Attn: Finance and Administration
1800 Duke Street
Alexandria, VA 22314-3499
(703) 548-3440   Toll-free: (800) 283-SHRM
Fax: (703) 535-6490   TDD: (703) 548-6999
E-mail: shrm@shrm.org
Web: www.shrm.org

Purpose To provide financial assistance for college to children of members of the Society for Human Resource Management (SHRM).

Eligibility This program is open to children of national members of SHRM who are high school seniors, high school graduates, or first-year college undergraduates enrolled or planning to enroll full time at an accredited 4-year college or university. Selection is based on academic achievement, leadership and participation in school and community activities, honors, work experience, a statement of educational and career goals, and recommendations.

Financial data The stipend is $1,500.

Duration 1 year; nonrenewable.

Number awarded 24 each year.

Deadline May of each year.

[1262]
SONS OF ITALY NATIONAL LEADERSHIP GRANTS

Order Sons of Italy in America
Attn: Sons of Italy Foundation
219 E Street, N.E.
Washington, DC 20002
(202) 547-2900   Fax: (202) 546-8168
E-mail: scholarships@osia.org
Web: www.osia.org/public/scholarships/grants.asp

Purpose To provide financial assistance to undergraduate and graduate students of Italian descent.

Eligibility Eligible are U.S. citizens of Italian descent who are enrolled as full-time students in an undergraduate or graduate program at an accredited 4-year college or university. Both high school seniors and students already enrolled in college are eligible for the undergraduate awards. Applications must be accompanied by essays, from 500 to 750 words in length, on the principal contribution of Italian Americans to the development of U.S. culture and society. These merit-based awards are presented to students who have demonstrated exceptional leadership qualities and distinguished scholastic abilities.

Financial data Stipends range from $5,000 to $25,000.

Duration 1 year; nonrenewable.

Additional information Applications must be accompanied by a $30 processing fee.

Number awarded Varies each year; recently, 8 of these awards were presented.

Deadline February of each year.

[1263]
SONS OF PERICLES UNDERGRADUATE SCHOLARSHIPS

American Hellenic Educational Progressive Association
Attn: AHEPA Educational Foundation
1909 Q Street, N.W., Suite 500
Washington, DC 20009
(202) 232-6300   Fax: (202) 232-2140
E-mail: ahepa@ahepa.org
Web: www.ahepa.org

Purpose To provide financial assistance to undergraduate students who are members of the Sons of Pericles.

Eligibility This program is open to current undergraduates who are members of the Sons of Pericles. Freshmen and sophomores must submit a complete high school transcript, SAT or ACT scores, and their most recent college transcript. Juniors and seniors must submit their most recent college transcript. Along with their application, they must also submit a 500-word biographical essay. Selection is based on academic achievement; extracurricular, personal, and volunteer activities; athletic achievements; and work experience. Financial need is not considered.

Financial data Stipends range from $500 to $2,000 per year.

Duration 1 year.

Additional information This program includes the George Kaloudis Memorial Scholarship and the John Katsimatides Memorial Scholarship. A processing fee of $20 must accompany each application.

Number awarded 1 each year.

Deadline March of each year.

[1264]
SONS OF UNION VETERANS OF THE CIVIL WAR SCHOLARSHIPS

Sons of Union Veterans of the Civil War
P.O. Box 1865
Harrisburg, PA 17105
(717) 232-7000   E-mail: suvcinc@aol.com
Web: www.suvcw.org/scholar.htm

Purpose To provide financial assistance for college to descendants of Union Civil War veterans.

Eligibility This program is open to both high school seniors and currently-enrolled 4-year college students. Applicants should 1) be a descendant of a Union Civil War veteran who was honorably discharged or who died while in service; 2) rank in the upper quarter of their high school graduating class (preferably in the upper tenth); 3) have a record of performance in school and community activities; 4) have an interest in and positive attitude toward college; 5) provide 3 letters of recommendation; and 6) submit an official grade transcript. Financial need is not considered in the selection process.

Financial data The stipend is $1,000. Funds are to be used for tuition and books. Checks are mailed directly to the recipient's school.

Duration 1 year.

Additional information Information is also available from John M. McNulty, 2501 Edgecomb Avenue, Glenside, PA 19038, (215) 884-3487, E-mail: jmm6@psu.edu. Recipients must attend a 4-year college or university.

Number awarded 2 each year.

Deadline March of each year.

[1265]
SOUTH CAROLINA ACCESS AND EQUITY UNDERGRADUATE SCHOLARS PROGRAM

South Carolina Commission on Higher Education
Attn: Director of Student Services
1333 Main Street, Suite 200
Columbia, SC 29201
(803) 737-2280   Toll-free: (877) 349-7183
Fax: (803) 737-2297   E-mail: srhyne@che.sc.gov
Web: www.che.sc.gov

Purpose To provide financial assistance to underrepresented students at public colleges or universities in South Carolina.

Eligibility Eligible to apply are residents of South Carolina who are members of a traditionally underrepresented group at the senior institution, regional campus of the University of South Carolina, or South Carolina technical college they are or will be attending. Full-time entering freshmen must have a high school GPA of at least 3.0; continuing full-time college students must have a cumulative GPA of at least 2.0; part-time students must have completed at least 12 hours of college work with a GPA of at least 2.0 and be at least 21 years old or have been out of school at least 2 years prior to reenrolling. Priority is given to full-time students. U.S. citizenship is required.

Financial data Stipends of up to $1,000 per year are provided, funding permitting.
Duration 1 year; may be renewed.
Number awarded Varies each year, but no more than 20% of the grant funds at each institution may be used for entering freshmen.

[1266]
SOUTH CAROLINA TUITION PROGRAM FOR CHILDREN OF CERTAIN WAR VETERANS

South Carolina Office of Veterans Affairs
1205 Pendleton Street, Suite 369
Columbia, SC 29201-3789
(803) 734-0200   Fax: (803) 734-0197
E-mail: va@oepp.sc.gov
Web: www.govoepp.state.sc.us/vetaff.htm

Purpose To provide free college tuition to the children of disabled and other South Carolina veterans.
Eligibility This program is open to the children of wartime veterans who were legal residents of South Carolina both at the time of entry into military or naval service and during service, or who have been residents of South Carolina for at least 1 year. Veteran parents must 1) be permanently and totally disabled as determined by the U.S. Department of Veterans Affairs; 2) have been a prisoner of war; 3) have been killed in action; 4) have died from other causes while in service; 5) have died of a disease or disability resulting from service; 6) be currently missing in action; 7) have received the Congressional Medal of Honor; 8) have received the Purple Heart Medal from wounds received in combat; or 9) now be deceased but qualified under categories 1 or 2 above. The veteran's child must be 26 years of age or younger and working on an undergraduate degree.
Financial data Children who qualify are eligible for free tuition at any South Carolina state-supported college, university, or postsecondary technical education institution. The waiver applies to tuition only. The costs of room and board, certain fees, and books are not covered.
Duration Students are eligible to receive this support as long as they are younger than 26 years of age and working on an undergraduate degree.
Number awarded Varies each year.

[1267]
SOUTH DAKOTA FREE TUITION FOR CHILDREN OF RESIDENTS WHO DIED DURING SERVICE IN THE ARMED FORCES

South Dakota Board of Regents
Attn: Scholarship Committee
306 East Capitol Avenue, Suite 200
Pierre, SD 57501-2545
(605) 773-3455   Fax: (605) 773-2422
E-mail: info@ris.sdbor.edu
Web: www.sdbor.edu

Purpose To provide free tuition at South Dakota public colleges and universities to children of military personnel who died while in service.
Eligibility This program is open to residents of South Dakota younger than 25 years of age. The applicant's parent must have been killed in action or died of other causes while on active duty and must have been a resident of South Dakota for at least 6 months immediately preceding entry into active service.
Financial data Eligible children are entitled to attend any South Dakota state-supported institution of higher education or state-supported technical or vocational school free of tuition and mandatory fees.
Duration 8 semesters or 12 quarters of either full- or part-time study.
Number awarded Varies each year.

[1268]
SOUTH DAKOTA FREE TUITION FOR DEPENDENTS OF PRISONERS OR MISSING IN ACTION

South Dakota Board of Regents
Attn: Scholarship Committee
306 East Capitol Avenue, Suite 200
Pierre, SD 57501-2545
(605) 773-3455   Fax: (605) 773-2422
E-mail: info@ris.sdbor.edu
Web: www.sdbor.edu

Purpose To provide free tuition at South Dakota public colleges and universities to dependents of prisoners of war (POWs) and persons missing in action (MIAs).
Eligibility This program is open to residents of South Dakota who are the spouses or children of POWs or of MIAs. Applicants may not be eligible for equal or greater benefits from any federal financial assistance program.
Financial data Eligible dependents are entitled to attend any South Dakota state-supported institution of higher education or state-supported technical or vocational school free of tuition and mandatory fees.
Duration 8 semesters or 12 quarters of either full- or part-time study.
Additional information Recipients must attend a state-supported school in South Dakota.
Number awarded Varies each year.

[1269]
SOUTH DAKOTA FREE TUITION FOR SURVIVORS OF DECEASED FIRE FIGHTERS, CERTIFIED LAW ENFORCEMENT OFFICERS, AND EMERGENCY MEDICAL TECHNICIANS

South Dakota Board of Regents
Attn: Scholarship Committee
306 East Capitol Avenue, Suite 200
Pierre, SD 57501-2545
(605) 773-3455   Fax: (605) 773-2422
E-mail: info@ris.sdbor.edu
Web: www.sdbor.edu

Purpose To provide free tuition at South Dakota public colleges and universities to children of deceased fire fighters, law enforcement officers, and emergency medical technicians.
Eligibility This program is open to residents of South Dakota who are the survivor of a fire fighter, certified law enforcement officer, or emergency medical technician who died as a direct result of injuries received in performance of official duties. Applicants must have been accepted for

enrollment at a state-supported institution of higher education or technical or vocational school.

Financial data Eligible survivors are entitled to attend any South Dakota state-supported institution of higher education or state-supported technical or vocational school free of tuition.

Duration Until completion of a bachelor's or vocational degree; the degree must be earned within 36 months or 8 semesters.

Number awarded Varies each year.

[1270]
SOUTH DAKOTA FREE TUITION FOR VETERANS AND OTHERS WHO PERFORMED WAR SERVICE

South Dakota Board of Regents
Attn: Scholarship Committee
306 East Capitol Avenue, Suite 200
Pierre, SD 57501-2545
(605) 773-3455   Fax: (605) 773-2422
E-mail: info@ris.sdbor.edu
Web: www.sdbor.edu

Purpose To provide free tuition at South Dakota public colleges and universities to certain veterans.

Eligibility This program is open to current residents of South Dakota who have been discharged from the military forces of the United States under honorable conditions. Applicants must meet 1 of the following criteria: 1) served on active duty at any time between August 2, 1990 and March 3, 1991; 2) received an Armed Forces Expeditionary Medal, Southwest Asia Service Medal, or other U.S. campaign or service medal for participation in combat operations against hostile forces outside the boundaries of the United States: or 3) have a service-connected disability rating of at least 10%. They may not be eligible for any other educational assistance from the U.S. government. Qualifying veterans must apply for this benefit within 20 years after the date proclaimed for the cassation of hostilities or within 6 years from and after the date of their discharge from military service, whichever is later.

Financial data Eligible veterans are entitled to attend any South Dakota state-supported institution of higher education or state-supported technical or vocational school free of tuition and mandatory fees.

Duration Eligible veterans are entitled to receive 1 month of free tuition for each month of qualifying service, from a minimum of 1 year to a maximum of 4 years.

Number awarded Varies each year.

[1271]
STANLEY O. MCNAUGHTON COMMUNITY SERVICE AWARD

Independent Colleges of Washington
600 Stewart Street, Suite 600
Seattle, WA 98101
(206) 623-4494   Fax: (206) 625-9621
E-mail: info@icwashington.org
Web: www.icwashington.org

Purpose To provide financial assistance to upper-division students enrolled at colleges and universities that are members of Independent Colleges of Washington (ICW).

Eligibility This program is open to students completing their sophomore or junior year at ICW-member colleges and universities. Applicants must submit a 1-page essay on their experience and views on volunteerism and community service. Selection is based on demonstrated commitment to volunteer community service both in high school and in college.

Financial data The stipend is $2,500.

Duration 1 year; nonrenewable.

Additional information The ICW-member institutions are Gonzaga University, Heritage College, Pacific Lutheran University, Saint Martin's College, Seattle Pacific University, Seattle University, University of Puget Sound, Walla Walla College, Whitman College, and Whitworth College.

Number awarded 1 each year.

Deadline March of each year.

[1272]
STANLEY W. MARION FUND

Polish Roman Catholic Union of America
Attn: Education Fund Scholarship Program
984 North Milwaukee Avenue
Chicago, IL 60622-4101
(773) 782-2600   Toll-free: (800) 772-8632
Fax: (773) 278-4595   E-mail: info@prcua.org
Web: www.prcua.org

Purpose To provide financial assistance to undergraduate and graduate students of Polish heritage.

Eligibility This program is open to students enrolled full time as sophomores, juniors, and seniors in an undergraduate program or full or part time as a graduate or professional school students. Selection is based on academic achievement, Polonia involvement, and community service.

Financial data A stipend is awarded (amount not specified). Funds are paid directly to the institution.

Duration 1 year.

Number awarded 1 or more each year.

Deadline May of each year.

[1273]
STUDENT AID FUND FOR NONREGISTRANTS

Mennonite Church USA
Executive Board
Attn: Student Aid Fund for Nonregistrants
P.O. Box 1245
Elkhart, IN 46515-1245
(574) 523-3041   E-mail: KathrynR@MennoniteUSA.org
Web: peace.mennolink.org/safnr.html

Purpose To provide financial assistance for college or graduate school to men who are ineligible to receive government grants and loans because they have declined to register with the U.S. Selective Service System for reasons of Christian conscience.

Eligibility Eligible to receive assistance from this fund are students who have declined to register with the U.S. Selective Service because of their Christian conscience. They must be either 1) attending a Mennonite Church USA college or seminary or 2) attending a congregation of Mennonite Church USA and enrolled in undergraduate or graduate studies in other-than-Mennonite institutions.

Financial data Aid is available in the form of both grants and loans. The amount of assistance is based on formulas that would have been used if the student were eligible for government aid. For loans, no interest is charged until 6 months following completion of undergraduate study; at that time (even if the recipient continues on to graduate school), the loan must be repaid with a fixed interest rate based upon the long-term 120% AFR monthly rate, set 90 days after the student graduates or discontinues school; the minimum payment is $50 per month and the total repayment period cannot exceed 10 years.

Additional information This fund was established in 1983 by the Mennonite Board of Congregational Ministries (MBCM) but is administered by the Mennonite Foundation. The home congregations of Mennonite nonregistrants are invited to contribute to the fund; students are expected to be an integral part of the communication process with their congregations.

Number awarded Varies each year. Recently, 4 students received grants worth $9,000 and 4 students received loans worth $17,250.

Deadline August of each year.

[1274]
SUPERCOLLEGE.COM STUDENT SCHOLARSHIPS

SuperCollege.com
Attn: Scholarship Application Request
4546 B10 El Camino Real, Number 281
Los Altos, CA 94022
(650) 618-2221
E-mail: supercollege@supercollege.com
Web: www.supercollege.com

Purpose To provide financial assistance for undergraduate or graduate study to U.S. citizens and permanent residents.

Eligibility This program is open to U.S. citizens and permanent residents who are high school students (grades 9-12), college undergraduates, or graduate students. Applicants must submit an essay, up to 1,000 words, on 1 of the following topics: 1) describe a person, place, or issue that is important to you; 2) tell us why you deserve to win this scholarship; or 3) if you could have 1 superpower, what would it be and why? They must also submit 5 20-word statements on their 5 most important academic or nonacademic achievements (e.g., projects, honors, awards, leadership positions, athletics, talents). Selection is based on the essays and academic and extracurricular achievement.

Financial data Stipends range from $500 to $2,500 per year. Funds must be used for tuition or tuition-related fees, textbooks, or room and board for undergraduate study at an accredited college or university in the United States.

Duration 1 year.

Number awarded 1 each year.

Deadline July of each year.

[1275]
SURVIVORS' AND DEPENDENTS' EDUCATIONAL ASSISTANCE PROGRAM

Department of Veterans Affairs
810 Vermont Avenue, N.W.
Washington, DC 20420
(202) 418-4343   Toll-free: (888) GI-BILL1
Web: www.gibill.va.gov

Purpose To provide financial assistance for undergraduate or graduate study to children and spouses of deceased and disabled veterans, MIAs, and POWs.

Eligibility Eligible for this assistance are spouses and children of 1) veterans who died or are permanently and totally disabled as the result of active service in the armed forces; 2) veterans who died from any cause while rated permanently and totally disabled from a service-connected disability; 3) servicemembers listed for more than 90 days as currently missing in action or captured in the line of duty by a hostile force; and 4) servicemembers listed for more than 90 days as presently detained or interned by a foreign government or power. Children must be between 18 and 26 years of age, although extensions may be granted. Spouses and children over 14 years of age with physical or mental disabilities are also eligible.

Financial data Monthly stipends from this program for study at an academic institution are $827 for full time, $621 for three-quarter time, or $413 for half-time. For farm cooperative work, the monthly stipends are $667 for full-time, $500 for three-quarter time, or $334 for half-time. For an apprenticeship or on-the-job training, the monthly stipend is $650 for the first 6 months, $507 for the second 6 months, $366 for the third 6 months, and $151 for the remainder of the program.

Duration Up to 45 months (or the equivalent in part-time training). Spouses must complete their training within 10 years of the date they are first found eligible.

Additional information Benefits may be used to work on associate, bachelor, or graduate degrees at colleges and universities, including independent study, cooperative training, and study abroad programs. Courses leading to a certificate or diploma from business, technical, or vocational schools may also be taken. Other eligible programs include apprenticeships, on-job training programs, farm cooperative courses, correspondence courses (for spouses only), secondary school programs (for recipients who are not high school graduates), tutorial assistance, remedial deficiency and refresher training, or work-study (for recipients who are enrolled at least three-quarter time). Eligible children who are handicapped by a physical or mental disability that prevents pursuit of an educational program may receive special restorative training that includes language retraining, lip reading, auditory training, Braille reading and writing, and similar programs. Eligible spouses and children over 14 years of age who are handicapped by a physical or mental disability that prevents pursuit of an educational program may receive specialized vocational training that includes specialized courses, alone or in combination with other courses, leading to a vocational objective that is suitable for the person and required by reason of physical or mental handicap. Ineligible courses include bartending or personality development courses; correspondence courses by dependent or surviving children; non-accredited independent study courses; any course given by radio; self-

improvement courses, such as reading, speaking, woodworking, basic seamanship, and English as a second language; audited courses; any course that is avocational or recreational in character; courses not leading to an educational, professional, or vocational objective; courses taken and successfully completed previously; courses taken by a federal government employee and paid for under the Government Employees' Training Act; and courses taken while in receipt of benefits for the same program from the Office of Workers' Compensation Programs.
Number awarded Varies each year.
Deadline Applications may be submitted at any time.

[1276]
TAILHOOK EDUCATIONAL FOUNDATION SCHOLARSHIPS
Tailhook Educational Foundation
9696 Businesspark Avenue
P.O. Box 26626
San Diego, CA 92196-0626
(858) 689-9223   Toll-free: (800) 269-8267
E-mail: thookassn@aol.com
Web: www.tailhook.org/Foundation.html

Purpose To provide financial assistance for college to personnel associated with naval aviation and their children.
Eligibility This program is open to 1) the children (natural, step, and adopted) of current or former U.S. Navy personnel who served as a naval aviator, naval flight officer, or designated naval air crewman, or 2) personnel and children of personnel who are serving or have served on board a U.S. Navy aircraft carrier as a member of the ship's company or assigned airwing. Applicants must be enrolled or accepted for enrollment at an accredited college or university. Selection is based on educational and extracurricular achievements, merit, and citizenship.
Financial data The stipend ranges from $2,000 to $3,000.
Duration 1 year.
Number awarded Varies each year; recently, 43 of these scholarships were awarded.
Deadline March of each year.

[1277]
TENNESSEE DEPENDENT CHILDREN SCHOLARSHIP
Tennessee Student Assistance Corporation
Parkway Towers
404 James Robertson Parkway, Suite 1950
Nashville, TN 37243-0820
(615) 741-1346   Toll-free: (800) 342-1663
Fax: (615) 741-6101   E-mail: tsac@mail.state.tn.us
Web: www.tnscholardollars.com

Purpose To provide financial assistance for college to the dependent children of disabled or deceased Tennessee law enforcement officers, fire fighters, or emergency medical service technicians.
Eligibility This program is open to Tennessee residents who are the dependent children of a Tennessee law enforcement officer, fire fighter, or emergency medical service technician who was killed or totally and permanently disabled in the line of duty. Applicants must be enrolled or accepted for enrollment as a full-time undergraduate student at a college or university in Tennessee.
Financial data The award covers tuition and fees, books, supplies, and room and board, minus any other financial aid for which the student is eligible.
Duration 1 year; may be renewed for up to 3 additional years or until completion of a program of study.
Additional information This program was established in 1990.
Number awarded Varies each year; recently, 19 students received $77,786 in support from this program.
Deadline July of each year.

[1278]
TEXAS AMATEUR ATHLETIC FEDERATION ATHLETE SCHOLARSHIPS
Texas Amateur Athletic Federation
P.O. Box 1789
Georgetown, TX 78627-1789
(512) 863-9400   Fax: (512) 869-2393
E-mail: marklord@cox-internet.com
Web: www.taaf.com/pages/schlorship.asp

Purpose To provide financial assistance to undergraduate and graduate students who have participated in activities of the Texas Amateur Athletic Federation (TAAF).
Eligibility This program is open to past and present Texas Amateur Athletic Federation (TAAF) athletes who have competed in 1 or more state level competitions or tournaments. Applicants must be enrolled or planning to enroll at a college or university, preferably in Texas, in an accredited bachelor's, master's, or doctoral degree program. They must have a GPA of 2.5 or higher. Selection is based on honors and awards from, and participation in, activities, endeavors, volunteerism, and work related to athletics and/or the field of parks and recreation. Financial need is not considered.
Financial data A stipend is awarded (amount not specified).
Duration 1 year.
Number awarded 1 or more each year.
Deadline April of each year.

[1279]
TEXAS CHILDREN OF DISABLED OR DECEASED FIREMEN, PEACE OFFICERS, GAME WARDENS, AND EMPLOYEES OF CORRECTIONAL INSTITUTIONS EXEMPTION PROGRAM
Texas Higher Education Coordinating Board
Attn: Grants and Special Programs
1200 East Anderson Lane
P.O. Box 12788, Capitol Station
Austin, TX 78711-2788
(512) 427-6101   Toll-free: (800) 242-3062
Fax: (512) 427-6127
E-mail: grantinfo@thecb.state.tx.us
Web: www.collegefortexans.com

Purpose To provide educational assistance to the children of disabled or deceased Texas fire fighters, peace officers, game wardens, and employees of correctional institutions.

Eligibility Eligible are children of Texas paid or volunteer fire fighters; paid municipal, county, or state peace officers; custodial employees of the Department of Corrections; or game wardens. The parent must have suffered an injury in the line of duty, resulting in disability or death. Applicants must be under 21 years of age.

Financial data Eligible students are exempted from the payment of all dues, fees, and tuition charges at publicly-supported colleges and universities in Texas.

Duration Support is provided for up to 120 semester credit hours of undergraduate study or until the recipient reaches 26 years of age, whichever comes first.

Number awarded Varies each year; recently, 116 students received support through this program.

[1280]
TEXAS CHILDREN OF U.S. MILITARY WHO ARE MISSING IN ACTION OR PRISONERS OF WAR EXEMPTION PROGRAM

Texas Higher Education Coordinating Board
Attn: Grants and Special Programs
1200 East Anderson Lane
P.O. Box 12788, Capitol Station
Austin, TX 78711-2788
(512) 427-6101   Toll-free: (800) 242-3062
Fax: (512) 427-6127
E-mail: grantinfo@thecb.state.tx.us
Web: www.collegefortexans.com

Purpose To provide educational assistance to the children of Texas military personnel declared prisoners of war or missing in action.

Eligibility Eligible are dependent children of Texas residents who are either prisoners of war or missing in action. Applicants must be under 21 years of age, or under 25 if they receive the majority of support from their parent(s).

Financial data Eligible students are exempted from the payment of all dues, fees, and tuition charges at publicly-supported colleges and universities in Texas.

Duration Up to 8 semesters.

Number awarded Varies each year; recently, 2 of these exemptions were granted.

[1281]
TEXAS EXEMPTION FOR PEACE OFFICERS DISABLED IN THE LINE OF DUTY

Texas Higher Education Coordinating Board
Attn: Grants and Special Programs
1200 East Anderson Lane
P.O. Box 12788, Capitol Station
Austin, TX 78711-2788
(512) 427-6101   Toll-free: (800) 242-3062
Fax: (512) 427-6127
E-mail: grantinfo@thecb.state.tx.us
Web: www.collegefortexans.com

Purpose To provide educational assistance to disabled Texas peace officers.

Eligibility This program is open to Texas residents permanently disabled as a result of an injury suffered as a peace officer who are unable to continue employment as a peace officer because of the disability. Applicants must be planning to attend a publicly-supported college or university in Texas as an undergraduate student.

Financial data Eligible students are exempted from the payment of all dues, fees, and tuition charges at publicly-supported colleges and universities in Texas.

Duration Up to 12 semesters.

Additional information For more information, students should contact the admission office at the institution they plan to attend.

Number awarded Varies each year; recently, 23 of these exemptions were awarded.

[1282]
TEXAS EXEMPTION FOR SURVIVING SPOUSES AND DEPENDENT CHILDREN OF CERTAIN DECEASED PUBLIC SERVANTS

Texas Higher Education Coordinating Board
Attn: Grants and Special Programs
1200 East Anderson Lane
P.O. Box 12788, Capitol Station
Austin, TX 78711-2788
(512) 427-6101   Toll-free: (800) 242-3062
Fax: (512) 427-6127
E-mail: grantinfo@thecb.state.tx.us
Web: www.collegefortexans.com

Purpose To provide educational assistance to the children and spouses of certain deceased Texas public employees.

Eligibility This program is open to residents of Texas whose parent or spouse was killed in the line of duty in certain public service positions after September 1, 2000. Eligible public service positions include peace officers, probation officers, parole officers, jailers, members of organized police reserve and auxiliary units, juvenile correctional employees, paid and volunteer fire fighters, and emergency medical service volunteers and paid personnel. Applicants must be enrolled or planning to enroll full time at a Texas public college or university.

Financial data Eligible students are exempted from the payment of all dues, fees, and tuition charges at publicly-supported colleges and universities in Texas. In addition, the institution provides them with an allowance for textbooks. If the student qualifies to live in the institution's housing, the institution must provide either free room and board or an equivalent room and board stipend.

Duration 1 year; may be renewed.

Number awarded Varies each year; recently, 65 students received support through this program.

[1283]
TEXAS WAIVERS OF NONRESIDENT TUITION FOR MILITARY PERSONNEL AND THEIR DEPENDENTS

Texas Higher Education Coordinating Board
Attn: Grants and Special Programs
1200 East Anderson Lane
P.O. Box 12788, Capitol Station
Austin, TX 78711-2788
(512) 427-6101   Toll-free: (800) 242-3062
Fax: (512) 427-6127
E-mail: grantinfo@thecb.state.tx.us
Web: www.collegefortexans.com

Purpose To exempt military personnel stationed in Texas and their dependents from the payment of nonresident tuition at public institutions of higher education in the state.

Eligibility Eligible for these waivers are members of the U.S. armed forces and commissioned officers of the Public Health Service from states other than Texas, their spouses, and dependent children. Applicants must be assigned to Texas and attending or planning to attend a public college or university in the state.

Financial data Although persons eligible under this program are classified as nonresidents, they are entitled to pay the resident tuition at Texas institutions of higher education, regardless of their length of residence in Texas.

Duration 1 year; may be renewed.

Number awarded Varies each year; recently, 10,333 students received these waivers.

[1284]
TEXAS WAIVERS OF NONRESIDENT TUITION FOR MILITARY SURVIVORS

Texas Higher Education Coordinating Board
Attn: Grants and Special Programs
1200 East Anderson Lane
P.O. Box 12788, Capitol Station
Austin, TX 78711-2788
(512) 427-6101   Toll-free: (800) 242-3062
Fax: (512) 427-6127
E-mail: grantinfo@thecb.state.tx.us
Web: www.collegefortexans.com

Purpose To provide a partial tuition exemption to the surviving spouses and dependent children of deceased military personnel who move to Texas following the service member's death.

Eligibility Eligible for these waivers are the surviving spouses and dependent children of members of the U.S. armed forces and commissioned officers of the Public Health Service who died while in service. Applicants must move to Texas within 60 days of the date of the death of the service member. They must be attending or planning to attend a public college or university in the state. Children are eligible even if the surviving parent does not accompany them to Texas.

Financial data Although persons eligible under this program are still classified as nonresidents, they are entitled to pay the resident tuition at Texas institutions of higher education on an immediate basis.

Duration 1 year.

Additional information This program became effective in 2003.

Number awarded Varies each year.

[1285]
TEXAS WAIVERS OF NONRESIDENT TUITION FOR VETERANS AND THEIR DEPENDENTS

Texas Higher Education Coordinating Board
Attn: Grants and Special Programs
1200 East Anderson Lane
P.O. Box 12788, Capitol Station
Austin, TX 78711-2788
(512) 427-6101   Toll-free: (800) 242-3062
Fax: (512) 427-6127
E-mail: grantinfo@thecb.state.tx.us
Web: www.collegefortexans.com

Purpose To exempt veterans who move to Texas and their dependents from the payment of nonresident tuition at public institutions of higher education in the state.

Eligibility Eligible for these waivers are former members of the U.S. armed forces and commissioned officers of the Public Health Service who are retired or have been honorably discharged, their spouses, and dependent children. Applicants must have moved to Texas upon separation from the service and be attending or planning to attend a public college or university in the state. They must have indicated their intent to become a Texas resident by registering to vote and doing 1 of the following: owning real property in Texas, registering an automobile in Texas, or executing a will indicating that they are a resident of the state.

Financial data Although persons eligible under this program are still classified as nonresidents, they are entitled to pay the resident tuition at Texas institutions of higher education on an immediate basis.

Duration 1 year.

Number awarded Varies each year.

[1286]
TEXTBOOKX.COM SCHOLARSHIP PROGRAM

Akademos, Inc.
Attn: TextbookX.com
25 Van Zant Street, Suite 1A-2
Norwalk, CT 06855-1727
(203) 866-0190   Fax: (203) 866-0199
Web: www.textbookx.com/scholarship

Purpose To recognize and reward undergraduate and graduate students who submit outstanding essays on a topic that changes annually.

Eligibility This competition is open to undergraduate and graduate students enrolled at an accredited college or university in the United States. Applicants must be legal residents of the United States or international students with valid visas. They must submit an essay, from 250 to 750 words in length, on a topic that changes each semester. Recently, the topic was "How, if at all, would American society change if the current legal right to abortion is either severely restricted or eliminated?" Essays must be the original work of the applicant and must reference a book that has influenced the response to the essay.

Financial data The grand prize is $2,000 and runner-up prizes are $250 gift certificates for the sponsor. Prizes are paid directly to the winners.
Duration The competition is held annually.
Additional information This competition began in 2002.
Number awarded 3 each semester: 1 grand prize and 2 runners-up.
Deadline April of each year for spring; October of each year for fall.

[1287]
TOTEM OCEAN TRAILER EXPRESS SCHOLARSHIPS

Independent Colleges of Washington
600 Stewart Street, Suite 600
Seattle, WA 98101
(206) 623-4494   Fax: (206) 625-9621
E-mail: info@icwashington.org
Web: www.icwashington.org

Purpose To provide financial assistance to residents of Alaska enrolled at colleges and universities that are members of Independent Colleges of Washington (ICW).
Eligibility This program is open to students enrolled at ICW-member colleges and universities who are residents of Alaska. Selection is based on academic merit. No application is required; each ICW institution makes a selection from all of its students.
Financial data The stipend is $1,000.
Duration 1 year; nonrenewable.
Additional information The ICW-member institutions are Gonzaga University, Heritage College, Pacific Lutheran University, Saint Martin's College, Seattle Pacific University, Seattle University, University of Puget Sound, Walla Walla College, Whitman College, and Whitworth College. This program is sponsored by Totem Ocean Trailer Express.
Number awarded 10 each year: 1 at each of the 10 ICW colleges and universities.
Deadline Each institution sets its own deadline.

[1288]
TREWA SCHOLARSHIPS

Texas Electric Cooperatives, Inc.
Attn: Vice President of Member Services
2550 South IH-35
Austin, TX 78704
(512) 454-0311   E-mail: twortham@texas-ec.org
Web: www.texas-ec.org

Purpose To provide financial assistance for college to members and children of members of the Texas Rural Electric Women's Association (TREWA).
Eligibility Eligible are current members of the association, their children, and their grandchildren. Applicants may be enrolled or planning to enroll in an accredited college, university, junior or community college, trade/technical school, or business school of their choice to work on a degree, certificate, diploma, or license. Grades received in high school are not the deciding factor in the selection process; leadership qualities, career focus, energy awareness, a 250-word essay on the applicant's plans and goals, and general knowledge of the rural electric problem are considered.
Financial data The stipend is $1,000. Funds are paid directly to the recipient's institution, half at the beginning of the first semester and half upon verification of completion of the first semester with passing grades.
Duration 1 year; nonrenewable.
Additional information This scholarship is sponsored by TREWA and administered by Texas Electric Cooperatives, Inc. Membership in TREWA is open to rural electric employees, directors, and co-op members. The organization is run by women, but men are also eligible to join.
Number awarded Varies each year; recently, 7 of these scholarships were awarded.
Deadline April of each year.

[1289]
TUITION WAIVER FOR DISABLED CHILDREN OF KENTUCKY VETERANS

Kentucky Department of Veterans Affairs
Attn: Division of Field Operations
545 South Third Street, Room 123
Louisville, KY 40202
(502) 595-4447   Toll-free: (800) 928-4012 (within KY)
Fax: (502) 595-4448
Web: www.kdva.net/tuitionwaiver.htm

Purpose To provide financial assistance for college to the children of Kentucky veterans who have a disability related to their parent's military service.
Eligibility This program is open to the children of veterans who have acquired a disability as a direct result of their parent's military service. The disability must have been designated by the U.S. Department of Veterans Affairs as compensable (currently defined as spina bifida). The veteran parent must 1) have served on active duty with the U.S. armed forces or in the National Guard or Reserve component on state active duty, active duty for training, or inactive duty training; and 2) be (or if deceased have been) a resident of Kentucky. Applicants must have been admitted to a state-supported university, college, or vocational training institute in Kentucky.
Financial data Eligible children are exempt from payment of tuition at state-supported institutions of higher education in Kentucky.
Duration There are no age or time limits on the waiver.
Number awarded Varies each year.

[1290]
UDT-SEAL SCHOLARSHIP

Naval Special Warfare Foundation
Attn: Scholarship Committee
P.O. Box 5965
Virginia Beach, VA 23471
(757) 363-7490   Fax: (757) 363-7491
E-mail: info@nswfoundation.org
Web: www.nswfoundation.org

Purpose To provide financial assistance for college to children of members of the UDT-SEAL Association.
Eligibility This program is open to children of members who are single, under 22 years of age, and a dependent of

a sponsoring member of the association. Sponsors must be serving or have served in the armed forces and the Naval Special Warfare Community, have been an association member for the last 4 consecutive years, and have paid their dues for the current year. Applicants may be high school seniors, high school graduates, or undergraduate students; preference is given to high school seniors. Along with their application, they must submit an essay, up to 2 pages in length, on a topic that changes annually; recently, the topic involved homeland security in the wake of the September 11 attacks on the World Trade Center and the Pentagon, and its relationship to personal freedoms guaranteed by the Constitution. Selection is based on the essay, academic achievement, and extracurricular activities.

Financial data A stipend is awarded (amount not specified).

Duration 1 year; may be renewed.

Additional information Membership in the association is open to all officers and enlisted personnel of the armed forces (active, retired, discharged, or separated) who have served with a Navy Combat Demolition Unit (NCDU), Underwater Demolition Team (UDT), or SEAL Team.

Number awarded 1 or more each year.

Deadline March of each year.

[1291]
UNDERGRADUATE AWARDS OF LIGHTHOUSE INTERNATIONAL

Lighthouse International
Attn: Scholarship Awards
111 East 59th Street
New York, NY 10022-1202
(212) 821-9428   Toll-free: (800) 829-0500
Fax: (212) 821-9703   TTY: (212) 821-9713
E-mail: kboyle@lighthouse.org
Web: www.lighthouse.org

Purpose To provide financial assistance to legally blind undergraduate students residing and attending school in designated eastern states.

Eligibility This program is open to blind and partially sighted U.S. citizens who are residents of Connecticut Delaware, Florida, Georgia, Maine, Maryland, Massachusetts, New Hampshire, New Jersey, New York, North Carolina, Pennsylvania, Rhode Island, South Carolina, Vermont, Virginia, Washington, D.C., or West Virginia. Applicants must be attending college (at any level) in those states They must submit a 500-word essay describing their academic achievements and career goals. Financial need is not considered in the selection process.

Financial data The stipend is $5,000.

Duration 1 year.

Number awarded 1 each year.

Deadline February of each year.

[1292]
UNITED PARCEL SERVICE FOUNDATION ICW SCHOLARSHIPS

Independent Colleges of Washington
600 Stewart Street, Suite 600
Seattle, WA 98101
(206) 623-4494   Fax: (206) 625-9621
E-mail: info@icwashington.org
Web: www.icwashington.org

Purpose To provide financial assistance to students enrolled at colleges and universities that are members of Independent Colleges of Washington (ICW).

Eligibility This program is open to students enrolled at ICW-member colleges and universities. Selection is based on merit as determined by the institution. No application is required; each ICW institution makes a selection from all of its students.

Financial data The stipend is $2,750.

Duration 1 year; nonrenewable.

Additional information The ICW-member institutions are Gonzaga University, Heritage College, Pacific Lutheran University, Saint Martin's College, Seattle Pacific University, Seattle University, University of Puget Sound, Walla Walla College, Whitman College, and Whitworth College. This program is sponsored by the UPS Foundation.

Number awarded 10 each year: 1 at each of the 10 ICW colleges and universities.

Deadline Each institution sets its own deadline.

[1293]
UNITED UNIVERSITY PROFESSIONS LABOR AND SOCIAL JUSTICE SCHOLARSHIP

United University Professions
Attn: Labor and Social Justice Scholarship Trust Fund
P.O. Box 15143
Albany, NY 12212-5143
(518) 640-6680   Toll-free: (800) 887-3863
Fax: (518) 640-6699   Fax: (866) 559-0516
E-mail: benefits@uupmail.org
Web: www.uupinfo.org/scholarships/scholarship.html

Purpose To provide financial assistance to undergraduate students currently enrolled in the State University of New York (SUNY) system who can demonstrate a commitment to social justice.

Eligibility This program is open to students currently enrolled full time at a state operated campus of SUNY. Those campuses include: Albany, Alfred, Binghamton, Brockport, Brooklyn HSC, Buffalo Center, Buffalo HSC, Buffalo State, Canton, Cobleskill, Cortland, Delhi, Empire State, Farmingdale, Fredonia, Geneseo, Morrisville, New Paltz, Old Westbury, Oneonta, Oswego, Plattsburgh, Potsdam, Purchase, Stony Brook, Stony Brook HSC, the Theatre Institute, Upstate Medical University, the Institute of Technology at Utica/Rome, the Maritime College at Fort Schuyler, the Environmental Science and Forestry campus, and the Optometry school. Applicants must have completed at least 16 semester credits with a GPA of 3.75 or higher. They must be able to demonstrate the qualities and values of the sponsoring organization: a dedication to the goals of the trade/labor union movements; integrity; a tireless quest for excellence in both academic and personal endeavors; and service to the community. Along with their application, they must submit a personal statement of 400 to 600 words discussing 1) their life experiences, goals, and commitment to social issues and traditional union values; and 2) how those traits make them uniquely qualified to receive a labor sponsored scholarship award. Financial need is not considered in the selection process.

Financial data The stipend is $2,000.
Duration 1 year; nonrenewable.
Number awarded 1 or more each year.
Deadline February of each year.

[1294]
UNIVERSITY WRITING SCHOLARSHIPS

Elder and Leemaur Publishers
115 Garfield Street, Number 5432
Sumas, WA 98295
(778) 549-7593
Web: www.elpublishers.com

Purpose To recognize and reward, with college scholarships, high school seniors and college undergraduates who submit essays on topics of academic interest.

Eligibility This competition is open to students enrolled in junior high school, senior high school, or college in Canada and the United States; there are no citizenship requirements. Applicants must submit an essay, up to 500 words in length, on topics related to 4 themes: challenging the experts, believing in greatness, authors of tomorrow, or voice of the future. Essays that rank in the top 1 to 2% of all submissions are selected for publication by the sponsor. Published essays are then considered for these awards.

Financial data Awards average $1,000. Funds must be used for payment of costs associated with winners' academic careers.
Duration Awards are presented quarterly.
Number awarded Varies each year; a total of $10,000 is available for awards each year.
Deadline February, June, September, or November of each year.

[1295]
USAF CHIEF OF STAFF SCHOLARSHIP

Civil Air Patrol
Attn: Scholarship Committee
105 South Hansell Street
Maxwell Air Force Base, AL 36112-6332
(334) 953-5315   Toll-free: (877) 227-9142, ext. 324
Fax: (334) 953-5235   E-mail: keasterling@cap.gov
Web: level2.cap.gov/index.cfm?nodeID=5356

Purpose To provide financial assistance for college to the Civil Air Patrol (CAP) Cadet of the Year.

Eligibility This scholarship is presented to the CAP Cadet of the Year. Candidates must be 1) CAP cadets who have received the Billy Mitchell Award or 2) CAP senior members who received the Billy Mitchell Award as a cadet or received the Senior Rating in Cadet Programs Specialty Track of the Senior Training Program. They must be a high school graduate or have a GED certificate and must have been accepted at a college or university. Selection is based on a transcript of high school credits, a transcript of college credits (if applicable), college entrance examination scores, and activities in CAP, high school, and college.

Financial data The stipend is $1,500. Funds are sent to the educational institution or training facility of the cadet's choice.
Duration 1 year.
Number awarded 1 each year.
Deadline January of each year.

[1296]
USBC YOUTH LEADERS OF THE YEAR AWARDS

United States Bowling Congress
Attn: SMART Program
5301 South 76th Street
Greendale, WI 53129-1192
(414) 423-3223   Toll-free: (800) 514-BOWL, ext. 3223
Fax: (414) 421-3014   E-mail: smart@bowl.com
Web: www.bowl.com/scholarships/main.aspx

Purpose To recognize and reward, with college scholarships, outstanding young bowlers.

Eligibility These awards are presented to participants in the Youth Leader program of the United States Bowling Congress (USBC) who are 18 years of age or older. Males and females are considered in separate competitions. Selection is based on exemplary Youth Leader activities and contributions to the sport of bowling.

Financial data The awards consist of $1,500 college scholarships.
Duration The awards are presented annually.
Additional information Awardees also serve for 2 years on the USBC Board of Directors.
Number awarded 2 each year: 1 for a female and 1 for a male.
Deadline Nominations must be submitted by January of each year.

[1297]
USO DESERT STORM EDUCATION FUND

USO World Headquarters
Attn: Scholarship Program
Washington Navy Yard, Building 198
901 M Street, S.E.
Washington, DC 20374
(202) 610-5700   Fax: (202) 610-5699
Web: www.desert-storm.com/soldiers/uso.html

Purpose To provide financial assistance for academic or vocational education to spouses and children of military personnel who died in the Persian Gulf War.

Eligibility This program is open to the spouses and children of armed service personnel killed, either through accidental causes or in combat, during Operations Desert Shield and Desert Storm. Department of Defense guidelines will be used to determine those service personnel who were taking part in either of these operations at the time of their deaths. This is an entitlement program; neither financial need nor academic achievement are factors in allocating support from the fund. All eligible candidates are contacted directly.

Financial data It is the purpose of the fund to provide as much financial support as possible to all eligible persons.

To this end, USO will distribute all of the fund to the eligible persons in equal amounts.
Number awarded All eligible survivors will receive funding.

[1298]
VASA ORDER OF AMERICA COLLEGE OR VOCATIONAL SCHOOL SCHOLARSHIPS

Vasa Order of America
Attn: Vice Grand Master
3236 Berkeley Avenue
Cleveland Heights, OH 44118-2055
(216) 371-5141   E-mail: rolf.bergman@sbcglobal.net
Web: www.vasaorder.com

Purpose To provide financial assistance for college or vocational education to members of the Vasa Order of America.

Eligibility Applicants must have been members of the organization for at least 1 year. They must be planning to continue their academic or vocational education on a full-time basis. Selection is based on a grade transcript, letters of recommendation from school and local Vasa lodge officials, and an essay of up to 1,000 words on a topic related to Vasa.

Financial data Stipends are $1,000.

Duration 1 year.

Additional information Vasa Order of America is a Swedish American fraternal organization incorporated in 1899.

Number awarded 10 each year.

Deadline February of each year.

[1299]
VETERANS OF THE VIETNAM WAR NATIONAL SCHOLARSHIP PROGRAM

Veterans of the Vietnam War, Inc.
Attn: Assistance in Education Program
805 South Township Boulevard
Pittston, PA 18640-3327
(570) 603-9740   Fax: (570) 603-9741
Web: www.vvnw.org

Purpose To provide financial assistance for college to members of Veterans of the Vietnam War (VVnW) and their families.

Eligibility This program is open to members of the VVnW in good standing for at least 1 year and their spouses, children, adopted children, foster children, and other immediate descendants. Applicants must be enrolled in or accepted to a program of postsecondary education. Selection is based on a random drawing; financial need, merit, and course of study are not considered.

Financial data The stipend is $1,000. Funds are paid directly to the recipient.

Duration 1 year.

Number awarded 1 or more each year, depending on the availability of funds.

Deadline October of each year.

[1300]
VII CORPS DESERT STORM VETERANS ASSOCIATION SCHOLARSHIP

VII Corps Desert Storm Veterans Association
Attn: Scholarship Committee
Army Historical Foundation
2425 Wilson Boulevard
Arlington, VA 22201
(703) 604-6565   E-mail: viicorpsdsva@aol.com
Web: www.desertstormvets.org

Purpose To provide financial assistance for college to students who served, or are the family members of individuals who served, with VII Corps in Operations Desert Shield, Desert Storm, or related activities.

Eligibility Applicants must have served, or be a family member of those who served, with VII Corps in Operations Desert Shield/Desert Storm, Provide Comfort, or 1 of the support base activities. Scholarships are limited to students entering or enrolled in accredited technical institutions (trade or specialty), 2-year colleges, and 4-year colleges or universities. Awards will not be made to individuals receiving military academy appointments or full 4-year scholarships. Letters of recommendation and a transcript are required. Selection is not based solely on academic standing; consideration is also given to extracurricular activities and other self-development skills and abilities obtained through on-the-job training or correspondence courses. Priority is given to survivors of VII Corps soldiers who died during Operations Desert Shield/Desert Storm or Provide Comfort, veterans who are also members of the VII Corps Desert Storm Veterans Association, and family members of veterans who are also members of the VII Corps Desert Storm Veterans Association.

Financial data The stipend is $5,000 per year. Funds are paid to the recipients upon proof of admission or registration at an accredited institution, college, or university.

Duration 1 year; recipients may reapply.

Additional information This program began in 1998.

Number awarded 3 each year.

Deadline January of each year.

[1301]
VIRGINIA TUITION ASSISTANCE GRANT PROGRAM

State Council of Higher Education for Virginia
Attn: Financial Aid Office
James Monroe Building
101 North 14th Street, Ninth Floor
Richmond, VA 23219-3659
(804) 225-2600   Toll-free: (877) 515-0138
Fax: (804) 225-2604   TDD: (804) 371-8017
E-mail: fainfo@schev.edu
Web: www.schev.edu

Purpose To provide financial assistance to undergraduate and graduate students attending private colleges or universities in Virginia.

Eligibility Undergraduate and graduate or professional students who are Virginia residents attending private colleges or universities in the state on a full-time basis in a degree program are eligible for this program. There is no

financial need requirement. Students pursuing religious training or theological education are not eligible.
Financial data The amount awarded varies, depending on annual appropriations and number of applicants; recently, the maximum award was $2,700 for undergraduates or $1,900 for graduate students.
Duration 1 year; may be renewed.
Additional information This program was established in 1972.
Number awarded Varies each year.
Deadline The deadline for priority consideration for fall semester is July of each year. Applicants submitted through the end of November are considered only if funds are available.

[1302]
VIRGINIA WAR ORPHANS EDUCATION PROGRAM

Virginia Department of Veterans' Affairs
270 Franklin Road, S.W., Room 503
Roanoke, VA 24011-2215
(540) 857-7104 Fax: (540) 857-7573
Web: www.dvs.virginia.gov/education_benefits.htm

Purpose To provide educational assistance to the children of disabled and other Virginia veterans or service personnel.
Eligibility This program is open to residents of Virginia who have at least 1 parent who served in the U.S. armed forces and is permanently and totally disabled due to an injury or disease incurred in a time of war or other period of armed conflict, has died as a result of war or other armed conflict, or is listed as a prisoner of war or missing in action. Applicants must be between 16 and 25 years of age and be accepted at a public secondary or postsecondary educational institution in Virginia. The veteran parent must have been a resident of Virginia at the time of entry into active military service or for at least 5 consecutive years immediately prior to the date of application or death. The surviving parent must have been a resident of Virginia for at least 5 years prior to marrying the deceased parent or for at least 5 years immediately prior to the date on which the application was submitted.
Financial data Eligible individuals receive free tuition and are exempted from any fees charged by state-supported schools in Virginia.
Duration Entitlement extends to a maximum of 48 months.
Additional information Individuals entitled to this benefit may use it to pursue any vocational, technical, undergraduate, or graduate program of instruction. Generally, programs listed in the academic catalogs of state-supported institutions are acceptable, provided they have a clearly defined educational objective (such as a certificate, diploma, or degree).
Number awarded Varies; generally more than 150 each year.

[1303]
VIRGINIA'S FUTURE LEADERS SCHOLARSHIP

Virginia Cable Telecommunications Association
Attn: Vice President of Public Affairs
1001 East Broad Street, Suite 210
Richmond, VA 23219
(804) 780-1776 Toll-free: (877) 861-5464
Fax: (804) 225-8036 E-mail: bdavis@vcta.com
Web: www.vcta.com

Purpose To provide financial assistance to residents of Virginia interested in working on an undergraduate degree.
Eligibility This program is open to Virginia residents who are attending or planning to attend a 2-year or 4-year college or university in Virginia. Applicants must submit a 500-word essay on either 1) a recent leadership experience they have had in an area of their life, their role in the situation, how they were effective, and what they learned; or 2) a situation in which they exhibited the ability to make a difference under difficult circumstances. Selection is based on the essay, academic transcripts, and extracurricular activities; financial need is not considered. U.S. citizenship is required.
Financial data A stipend is awarded (amount not specified).
Duration 1 year; nonrenewable.
Additional information This program, established in 2000, is sponsored by the Donald A. Perry Foundation and the Virginia cable industry.
Number awarded Varies; a total of $100,000 is available for this program each year.
Deadline April of each year.

[1304]
WAIVERS OF NONRESIDENT TUITION FOR DEPENDENTS OF MILITARY PERSONNEL MOVING TO TEXAS

Texas Higher Education Coordinating Board
Attn: Grants and Special Programs
1200 East Anderson Lane
P.O. Box 12788, Capitol Station
Austin, TX 78711-2788
(512) 427-6101 Toll-free: (800) 242-3062
Fax: (512) 427-6127
E-mail: grantinfo@thecb.state.tx.us
Web: www.collegefortexans.com

Purpose To exempt dependents of military personnel who move to Texas from the payment of nonresident tuition at public institutions of higher education in the state.
Eligibility Eligible for these waivers are the spouses and dependent children of members of the U.S. armed forces and commissioned officers of the Public Health Service who move to Texas while the service member remains assigned to another state. Applicants must be attending or planning to attend a public college or university in the state. They must indicate their intent to become a Texas resident. For dependent children to qualify, the spouse must also move to Texas.
Financial data Although persons eligible under this program are still classified as nonresidents, they are entitled to pay the resident tuition at Texas institutions of higher education on an immediate basis.
Duration 1 year.

Additional information This program became effective in September 2003.

Number awarded Varies each year.

[1305]
WAIVERS OF NONRESIDENT TUITION FOR DEPENDENTS OF MILITARY PERSONNEL WHO PREVIOUSLY LIVED IN TEXAS

Texas Higher Education Coordinating Board
Attn: Grants and Special Programs
1200 East Anderson Lane
P.O. Box 12788, Capitol Station
Austin, TX 78711-2788
(512) 427-6101   Toll-free: (800) 242-3062
Fax: (512) 427-6127
E-mail: grantinfo@thecb.state.tx.us
Web: www.collegefortexans.com

Purpose To provide a partial tuition exemption to the spouses and dependent children of military personnel who are Texas residents but are not assigned to duty in the state.

Eligibility Eligible for these waivers are the spouses and dependent children of members of the U.S. armed forces who are not assigned to duty in Texas but have previously resided in the state for at least 6 months. Service members must verify that they remain Texas residents by designating Texas as their place of legal residence for income tax purposes, registering to vote in the state, and doing 1 of the following: owning real property in Texas, registering an automobile in Texas, or executing a will indicating that they are a resident of the state. The spouse or dependent child must be attending or planning to attend a Texas public college or university.

Financial data Although persons eligible under this program are classified as nonresidents, they are entitled to pay the resident tuition at Texas institutions of higher education, regardless of their length of residence in Texas.

Duration 1 year.

Number awarded Varies each year.

[1306]
WARREN FENCL SCHOLARSHIPS

100th Infantry Battalion Veterans Club
Attn: Scholarship Committee
520 Kamoku Street
Honolulu, HI 96826
(808) 732-5216   E-mail: daisyy@hgea.net
Web: emedia.leeward.hawaii.edu/mnakano

Purpose To provide financial assistance to high school seniors and college students who exemplify the sponsor's motto of "Continuing Service."

Eligibility This program is open to high school seniors planning to attend an institution of higher learning and full-time undergraduate students at community colleges, vocational/trade schools, 4-year colleges, and universities. Applicants must have a GPA of 2.5 or higher and be able to demonstrate civic responsibility and community service. Along with their application, they must submit a 4-page essay that explains how valuing a diversity of different opinions, cultures, and lifestyles affects a nation that is challenged with resolving complex issues. Selection is based on that essay and the applicant's demonstration that he or she can effectively promote the legacy of the 100th Infantry Battalion and its motto of "Continuing Service." Financial need is not considered.

Financial data The stipend is $1,000.

Duration 1 year; nonrenewable.

Additional information This scholarship is named in honor of a World War II veteran of the 34th Infantry Division who fought alongside the Japanese American soldiers of the 100th Infantry Battalion and subsequently campaigned to correct the injustices committed against Japanese Americans during the war.

Number awarded 2 each year.

Deadline April of each year.

[1307]
WASHINGTON STATE POTATO FOUNDATION SCHOLARSHIPS

Washington State Potato Foundation
P.O. Box 5051
Pasco, WA 99302
(509) 542-0595   Fax: (509) 271-0006
E-mail: kbalcom@potatoes.com
Web: www.potatoes.com/PotatoFoundation.cfm

Purpose To provide financial assistance for college to residents of Oregon and Washington who have a connection to potato growing.

Eligibility This program is open to residents of Oregon and Washington who 1) pay assessment to the Washington State Potato Commission; 2) are commercial growers, processors, packers, or shippers of potatoes; or 3) are employees or children of employees of commercial growers, processors, packers, or shippers of potatoes. Applicants must be working on or planning to work on a 2- or 4-year degree or technical certification at an institution of higher education; preference is given to those studying an agriculture-related field. Along with their application, they must submit a 500-word essay about their educational and career goals, how they plan to achieve those goals, how their field of study is related to the agricultural industry, the relevance in the current market, and how their talents can lend to its success. Financial need is not considered in the selection process.

Financial data Stipends range from $1,000 to $2,500.

Duration 1 year; recipients may reapply.

Number awarded Varies each year; recently, 28 of these scholarships were awarded.

Deadline February of each year.

[1308]
WEST VIRGINIA GOLF ASSOCIATION FUND SCHOLARSHIPS

Greater Kanawha Valley Foundation
Attn: Scholarship Coordinator
1600 Huntington Square
900 Lee Street, East
P.O. Box 3041
Charleston, WV 25331-3041
(304) 346-3620   Fax: (304) 346-3640
E-mail: tgkvf@tgkvf.com
Web: www.tgkvf.com/scholar.html

Purpose To provide financial assistance for college to residents of West Virginia who have been involved in golf.

Eligibility This program is open to residents of West Virginia who are students at a college or university anywhere in the country. Applicants must 1) have played golf in West Virginia as an amateur for recreation or competition; or 2) have been or are presently employed in West Virginia as a caddie, grounds keeper, bag boy, or other golf-related job. Along with their application, they must include an essay explaining how the game of golf has made an impact on their life. They must have an ACT score of 20 or higher, be able to demonstrate good moral character, and have a GPA of 2.5 or higher. Selection is based on academic accomplishments, volunteer service, character, and level of exposure to the game of golf; skill level is not a major requirement.

Financial data The stipend is $1,000 per year.

Duration 1 year; may be renewed.

Additional information This program is sponsored by the West Virginia Golf Association, P.O. Box 850, Hurricane, WV 25526, (304) 757-3444, Fax: (304) 757-3479, E-mail: mail@wvga.org, Web site: www.wvga.org.

Number awarded Varies each year; recently, 2 of these scholarships were awarded.

Deadline February of each year.

[1309]
WEST VIRGINIA STATE WAR ORPHANS EDUCATIONAL PROGRAM

West Virginia Division of Veterans' Affairs
Charleston Human Resource Center
1321 Plaza East, Suite 101
Charleston, WV 25301-1400
(304) 558-3661   Toll-free: (888) 838-2332 (within WV)
Fax: (304) 558-3662   E-mail: wvdva@state.wv.us
Web: www.wvs.state.wv.us/va/state_fed.htm

Purpose To provide financial assistance for college to the children of deceased West Virginia veterans.

Eligibility Applicants must have been residents of West Virginia for at least 1 year, be between the ages of 16 and 23, and have a veteran parent who entered service as a resident of West Virginia, served during World War I, World War II, the Korean Conflict, the Vietnam Era from August 5, 1964 to May 7, 1975, or any other time of conflict declared by Congress, and died of injuries or disease as a result of that service.

Financial data High school students are eligible for a grant of $110 to $250 per semester. Students attending a state-supported college, university, or vocational school in West Virginia who are not receiving any aid from the U.S. Department of Veterans Affairs (VA) are entitled to a waiver of tuition and also to receive up to $500 per year for fees, board, room, books, supplies, and other expenses. Students attending a state-supported postsecondary institution who are getting VA assistance receive waiver of tuition and registration fees only. Students attending a private postsecondary school in West Virginia are only eligible for the monetary grant of $500 per year if they are not receiving any VA assistance.

Duration 1 year; may be renewed upon reapplication if the student maintains a cumulative GPA of at least 2.0.

Number awarded Varies each year.

Deadline July for the fall semester; November for the spring semester.

[1310]
WEST VIRGINIA STATE WAR ORPHANS EDUCATIONAL PROGRAM

West Virginia Division of Veterans' Affairs
Charleston Human Resource Center
1321 Plaza East, Suite 101
Charleston, WV 25301-1400
(304) 558-3661   Toll-free: (888) 838-2332 (within WV)
Fax: (304) 558-3662   E-mail: wvdva@state.wv.us
Web: www.wvs.state.wv.us/va/state_fed.htm

Purpose To provide financial assistance for college to the children of deceased West Virginia veterans.

Eligibility Applicants must have been residents of West Virginia for at least 1 year, be between the ages of 16 and 23, and have a veteran parent who entered service as a resident of West Virginia, served during World War I, World War II, the Korean Conflict, the Vietnam Era from August 5, 1964 to May 7, 1975, or any other time of conflict declared by Congress, and died of injuries or disease as a result of that service.

Financial data High school students are eligible for a grant of $110 to $250 per semester. Students attending a state-supported college, university, or vocational school in West Virginia who are not receiving any aid from the U.S. Department of Veterans Affairs (VA) are entitled to a waiver of tuition and also to receive up to $500 per year for fees, board, room, books, supplies, and other expenses. Students attending a state-supported postsecondary institution who are getting VA assistance receive waiver of tuition and registration fees only. Students attending a private postsecondary school in West Virginia are only eligible for the monetary grant of $500 per year if they are not receiving any VA assistance.

Duration 1 year; may be renewed upon reapplication if the student maintains a cumulative GPA of at least 2.0.

Number awarded Varies each year.

Deadline July for the fall semester; November for the spring semester.

ANY SUBJECT AREA

[1311]
WHO'S WHO CAP SCHOLARSHIP

Civil Air Patrol
Attn: Scholarship Committee
105 South Hansell Street
Maxwell Air Force Base, AL 36112-6332
(334) 953-5315 Toll-free: (877) 227-9142, ext. 324
Fax: (334) 953-5235 E-mail: keasterling@cap.gov
Web: level2.cap.gov/index.cfm?nodeID=5589

Purpose To provide financial assistance to Civil Air Patrol (CAP) members who are interested in working on an undergraduate degree on a full-time basis.

Eligibility This program is open to 1) CAP cadets who have received the Billy Mitchell Award and 2) CAP senior members who received the Billy Mitchell Award as a cadet or received the Senior Rating in Cadet Programs Specialty Track of the Senior Training Program. Applicants must be a high school graduate or have a GED certificate and must have been accepted at a college or university. The award is presented to 1 of the top applicants for CAP scholarships at the undergraduate or vocational school level. Selection is based on academic achievement, CAP accomplishments and of high school credits, a transcript of college credits (if applicable).

Financial data The stipend is $1,000.

Duration 1 year.

Additional information These awards are funded by the Educational Communications Scholarship Foundation of Educational Communications Inc., publisher of *Who's Who Among American High School Students.*

Number awarded 1 each year.

Deadline January of each year.

[1312]
WHO'S WHO SPORTS EDITION ALL-ACADEMIC BOWLING TEAM SCHOLARSHIPS

United States Bowling Congress
Attn: SMART Program
5301 South 76th Street
Greendale, WI 53129-1192
(414) 423-3223 Toll-free: (800) 514-BOWL, ext. 3223
Fax: (414) 421-3014 E-mail: smart@bowl.com
Web: www.bowl.com/scholarships/main.aspx

Purpose To provide financial assistance for college to members of the United States Bowling Congress (USBC) Youth who are also recognized in *Who's Who Among American High School Students-Sports Edition.*

Eligibility This program is open to USBC Youth members who are juniors or seniors in high school. Applicants must have a GPA of 2.5 or higher and not have competed in a professional bowling tournament. They must be listed in the current edition of *Who's Who Among American High School Students-Sports Edition.* Along with their application, they must submit an essay of 500 words on how their involvement in bowling has influenced their life, academic, and personal goals. Financial need is not considered in the selection process.

Financial data The stipend is $1,000.

Duration 1 year; nonrenewable.

Number awarded Up to 20 each year.

Deadline March of each year.

[1313]
WILLIAM R. STANITZ SCHOLARSHIP

Romanian Orthodox Episcopate of America
Attn: Scholarship Committee
P.O. Box 309
Grass Lake, MI 49240-0309
(517) 522-3656 Fax: (517) 522-5907
E-mail: roeasolia@aol.com
Web: www.roea.org/schol/schol-stanitz.htm

Purpose To provide financial assistance for college to active members of American Romanian Orthodox Youth (AROY).

Eligibility To qualify for this scholarship, applicants must be active AROY members, high school graduates, and currently enrolled or planning to enroll in college. The application packet submitted should include biographical history, educational background and grades, AROY and church activities, extracurricular interests and achievements, reasons why applying for the scholarship, photograph, and a letter of recommendation from a parish priest or AROY advisor regarding parish/AROY activities. Recipients are selected in a random drawing.

Financial data The stipend is $1,000.

Duration 1 year.

Additional information This fund was established in 1971.

Number awarded At least 2 each year.

Deadline June of each year.

[1314]
WILLIE RUDD SCHOLARSHIP

International Union of Electronic, Electrical, Salaried, Machine, and Furniture Workers
Attn: IUE-CWA International Scholarship Program
501 Third Street, N.W., Suite 975
Washington, DC 20001
(202) 434-1417 Fax: (202) 434-1250
E-mail: bgray@iue-cwa.org
Web: www.iue-cwa.org/skills.html

Purpose To provide financial assistance for undergraduate education to children and grandchildren of members and employees of the International Union of Electronic, Electrical, Salaried, Machine, and Furniture Workers (IUE)-Communications Workers of America (CWA).

Eligibility This program is open to children and grandchildren of IUE-CWA members and employees. Applicants must be accepted for admission or already enrolled as full-time students at an accredited college, university, nursing school, or technical school offering college credit classes. Along with their application, they must submit an academic transcript (including rank in class, GPA, and SAT/ACT scores); a short statement of interests and civic activities; an essay (300 to 500 words) describing their career goals and aspirations, highlighting their relationship with the union and the labor movement, and explaining why they are deserving of a union scholarship. They must also have demonstrated a commitment to equality of opportunity for all, a concern for improving the quality of life for all people, an interest in service to the community, good character, leadership ability, and a desire to improve and move ahead.

Financial data The stipend is $1,000 per year.

Duration 1 year.
Number awarded 1 each year.
Deadline March of each year.

[1315]
WISCONSIN G.I. BILL

Wisconsin Department of Veterans Affairs
30 West Mifflin Street
P.O. Box 7843
Madison, WI 53707-7843
(608) 266-1311   Toll-free: (800) WIS-VETS
Fax: (608) 267-0403
E-mail: wdvaweb@dva.state.wi.us
Web: dva.state.wi.us/Ben_education.asp

Purpose To provide financial assistance for college or graduate school to Wisconsin veterans and their dependents.

Eligibility This program is open to current residents of Wisconsin who 1) were residents of the state when they entered or reentered active duty in the U.S. armed forces, or 2) have moved to the state and have been residents for any consecutive 12-month period after entry or reentry into service. Applicants must have served on active duty for at least 2 continuous years or for at least 90 days during specified wartime periods. Also eligible are 1) qualifying children and unremarried surviving spouses of Wisconsin veterans who died in the line of duty; and 2) children and spouses of Wisconsin veterans who have a service-connected disability rated by the U.S. Department of Veterans Affairs as 30% or greater. Children must be between 18 and 26 years of age (regardless of the date of the veteran's death or initial disability rating), be a Wisconsin resident for tuition purposes, and register as a full-time student. Spouses remain eligible for 10 years following the date of the veteran's death or initial disability rating; they must be Wisconsin residents for tuition purposes but they may enroll full or part time. Students may attend any institution, center, or school within the University of Wisconsin (UW) System or the Wisconsin Technical College System (WCTS). There are no income limits, delimiting periods following military service during which the benefit must be used, or limits on the level of study (e.g., vocational, undergraduate, professional, or graduate).

Financial data Veterans who qualify as a Wisconsin resident for tuition purposes are eligible for a remission of 50% of tuition and fees at a UW or WCTS institution. Veterans who qualify as a Wisconsin veteran for purposes of this program but for other reasons fail to meet the definition of a Wisconsin resident for tuition purposes at the UW system are eligible for a remission of 100% of non-resident fees. Spouses and children of deceased or disabled veterans are entitled to a remission of 100% of tuition and fees at a UW or WCTS institution.

Duration Up to 8 semesters or 128 credits, whichever is greater.

Additional information This program was established in 2005 as a replacement for Wisconsin Tuition and Fee Reimbursement Grants.

Number awarded Varies each year.

Deadline Applications may be submitted at any time, but they should be received as early as possible prior to the intended date of enrollment.

[1316]
WOMEN'S BASKETBALL COACHES ASSOCIATION SCHOLARSHIP AWARDS

Women's Basketball Coaches Association
Attn: Manager of Awards
4646 Lawrenceville Highway
Lilburn, GA 30047-3620
(770) 279-8027, ext. 102   Fax: (770) 279-6290
E-mail: alowe@wbca.org
Web: www.wbca.org/WBCAScholarAward.asp

Purpose To provide financial assistance for undergraduate or graduate study to women's basketball players.

Eligibility This program is open to women's basketball players who are competing in any of the 4 intercollegiate divisions (NCAA Divisions I, II, and III, and NAIA). Applicants must be interested in completing an undergraduate degree or beginning work on an advanced degree. They must be nominated by a member of the Women's Basketball Coaches Association (WBCA). Selection is based on sportsmanship, commitment to excellence as a student-athlete, honesty, ethical behavior, courage, and dedication to purpose.

Financial data The stipend is $1,000 per year.

Duration 1 year.

Number awarded 2 each year.

[1317]
WOMEN'S GOLF ASSOCIATION OF MASSACHUSETTS JUNIOR SCHOLAR PROGRAM

Women's Golf Association of Massachusetts, Inc.
Attn: WGAM Junior Scholarship Fund, Inc.
William F. Connell Golf House & Museum
300 Arnold Palmer Boulevard
Norton, MA 02766
(774) 430-9010   Fax: (774) 430-9011
E-mail: info@wgam.org
Web: www.wgam.org/Junior/jrschol.htm

Purpose To provide financial assistance for college to women golfers from Massachusetts.

Eligibility This program is open to female golfers who have participated in the Women's Golf Association of Massachusetts (WGAM) junior golf program. Applicants must be attending or planning to attend a college or university. Selection is based on high school academic record and performance, leadership qualities, community and civic involvement, character, personality, and extent of participation in the WGAM junior golf program. Financial need may determine the size of the stipend, but it is not considered in the selection process. An interview is required.

Financial data A stipend is awarded (amount not specified).

Duration 1 year; may be renewed.

Additional information This program was established in 1985.

Number awarded Varies each year; recently, 8 of these scholarships were awarded.

Deadline May of each year.

[1318]
WOODLAWN FARMS ANGUS SCHOLARSHIP

National Junior Angus Association
Attn: Director Junior Activities
3201 Frederick Avenue
St. Joseph, MO 64506
(816) 383-5100 Fax: (816) 233-9703
E-mail: info@njaa.info
Web: www.angusfoundation.org

Purpose To provide financial assistance to students who have been members of the National Junior Angus Association (NJAA) and are enrolled or planning to enroll in any field in college.

Eligibility Applicants must have been a member of the NJAA in the past and presently must be a junior, regular, or life member of the American Angus Association. They must be either a high school senior or already enrolled in college working full time on an undergraduate degree with a GPA of 2.0 or higher and younger than 25 years of age. All fields of study are eligible. Selection is based on involvement in Angus associations, other agriculture-related associations, school organizations, and church, civic, and community groups.

Financial data A stipend is awarded (amount not specified).

Duration 1 year; nonrenewable.

Additional information This program, established in 2005, is sponsored by the Angus Foundation.

Number awarded 1 each year.

Deadline April of each year.

[1319]
WYOMING WAR ORPHANS SCHOLARSHIPS

Wyoming Veterans' Commission
Wyoming Army National Guard Armory
5905 CY Avenue, Room 101
Casper, WY 82604
(307) 265-7372 Toll-free: (800) 833-5987 (within WY)
Fax: (307) 265-7392 E-mail: wvac@bresnan.net
Web: uwadmnweb.uwyo.edu/sfa

Purpose To provide financial assistance for college to children of deceased, POW, or MIA Wyoming veterans.

Eligibility This program is open to children of veterans whose parent was a resident of Wyoming at the time of entering service and 1) died while in service during a period of war defined by law; 2) is listed officially as being a POW or MIA in the Korean or Vietnam conflicts; or 3) was honorably discharged from the military and subsequently died of an injury or disease incurred while in service and was a Wyoming resident at the time of death. Applicants must be attending or planning to attend the University of Wyoming or a community college in the state.

Financial data Qualifying veterans' children may be eligible for free resident tuition at the University of Wyoming or at any of the state's community colleges.

Duration Up to 10 semesters.

Additional information Applications may be obtained from the institution the applicant is attending or planning to attend.

Number awarded Varies each year.

Deadline Applications may be submitted at any time, but they should be received 2 or 3 weeks before the beginning of the semester.

[1320]
YANKEE DISTRICT 7 SCHOLARSHIPS

American Hellenic Educational Progressive Association-District 07
c/o Kip Kyprianou, Scholarship Committee Chair
5 Vista Drive
New Milford, CT 06776
(860) 350-6576 E-mail: KKyprianou@CompuAid.US
Web: www.ahepad7.org

Purpose To provide financial assistance to undergraduate student members and families of members of organizations affiliated with the American Hellenic Educational Progressive Association (AHEPA) in its District 7 (Connecticut and Rhode Island).

Eligibility This program is open to District 7 (Connecticut and Rhode Island) members of the Order of Ahepa, the Daughters of Penelope, the Maids of Athena, or the Sons of Pericles who were inducted as members at least 1 year prior to applying for the scholarship. Children of members of the Order of Ahepa or Daughters of Penelope are also eligible. Applicants must be attending or planning to attend a college or university. They must have a GPA of 2.5 or higher. Along with their application, they must submit an essay of 700 to 1,000 words on 1 of the following topics: 1) 2 of the greatest achievements of Greek civilization and their impact on western civilization; 2) the ethical considerations of stem cell research; or 3) the role of AHEPA in our society. They may also cite family hardship circumstances they wish to have considered.

Financial data A stipend is awarded (amount not specified).

Duration 1 year; recipients may reapply if they have not received 2 previous grants from this program.

Number awarded Varies each year.

Deadline April of each year.

[1321]
YOUNG AMERICAN AWARDS

Boy Scouts of America
Attn: Learning for Life Division, S210
1325 West Walnut Hill Lane
P.O. Box 152079
Irving, TX 75015-2079
(972) 580-2418 Fax: (972) 580-2137
Web: www.learning-for-life.org

Purpose To recognize and reward college and graduate students who demonstrate exceptional achievement and service.

Eligibility This program is open to students younger than 25 years of age who are currently enrolled in college or graduate school. Candidates must be nominated by a Boy Scout troop, Explorer post, Venturing crew, Learning for Life group, individual, or other community youth-serving organization that shares the same program objectives. Nominees must have 1) achieved exceptional excellence in 1 or more fields, such as art, athletics, business, community service,

education, government, humanities, literature, mathematics, music, religion, or science; 2) be involved in service in their community, state, or country that adds to the quality of life; and 3) have maintained an above-average GPA. They must submit high school and college transcripts (graduate students need to submit only college transcripts) and at least 3 letters of recommendation. Nominations must be submitted to a local Boy Scout council, but nominees are not required to be a participant in a council unit or program.
Financial data The award is $5,000. Local councils may also provide awards to their nominees.
Duration The awards are presented annually.
Additional information These awards were first presented in 1968.
Number awarded 5 each year.
Deadline Applications must be submitted to the local council office by November of each year.

[1322]
11TH ARMORED CAVALRY VETERANS OF VIETNAM AND CAMBODIA SCHOLARSHIP

11th Armored Cavalry Veterans of Vietnam and Cambodia
c/o Gene Johnson, Scholarship Committee Chair
3335 Casey Drive, Number 6-101
Las Vegas, NV 89120-1183
(702) 456-3218   E-mail: gene677@aol.com
Web: www.11thcavnam.com/scholar.html

Purpose To provide financial assistance to members of the 11th Armored Cavalry Veterans of Vietnam and Cambodia (ACVVC) and to their dependents.
Eligibility This program is open to 11th ACVVC members and to their dependents. In addition, dependents of deceased troopers who served with the 11th Armored Cavalry in Vietnam or Cambodia may apply (a copy of the father's obituary must be supplied). Affiliation with the cavalry must be documented. Applicants must submit brief essays on 1) the field of study they plan to enter and why; and 2) why they would be a worthy recipient of this scholarship. Selection is based on the essays and grades; financial need is no longer considered. Priority is given to children of members who were killed in action or died of wounds.
Financial data The stipend is $3,000; funds are paid directly to the recipient's school, in 2 equal installments.
Duration 1 year; nonrenewable.
Additional information Recipients must use the awarded money within 20 months of being notified.
Number awarded Varies each year; recently, 25 of these scholarships were awarded.
Deadline May of each year.

[1323]
4A-AT&T NATIONAL SCHOLARSHIP PROGRAM

Asian/Pacific American Association for Advancement at AT&T
c/o Suwathin Phiansunthon, Scholarship Committee
AT&T
200 South Laurel Avenue, Room A5-2D05
Middletown, NJ 07748
(732) 420-7339   E-mail: scholarship4A@list.att.com
Web: www.4a-att.org/National/scholarship.html

Purpose To provide financial assistance to full-time college juniors who have been involved in the Asian/Pacific American community.
Eligibility This program is open to full-time undergraduates who have completed at least 3 years of study at an accredited college or university in the United States. Applicants must be U.S. citizens or permanent residents. Along with their application, they must submit a list of extracurricular activities, information on achievements and awards, and a 350-word essay on the role of Asian Americans in American political life. After the initial screening process, the remaining eligible applicants are evaluated on their scholastic discipline, personal achievement, community involvement, and contributions to the Asian/Pacific American community.
Financial data The stipend is $1,000 per year.
Duration 1 year.
Number awarded 5 each year.
Deadline June of each year.

Indexes

Program Title Index •
Sponsoring Organization Index •
Residency Index •
Tenability Index •
Subject Index •
Calendar Index •

Program Title Index

If you know the name of a particular funding program and want to find out where it is covered in the directory, use the Program Title Index. Here, program titles are arranged alphabetically, word by word. To assist you in your search, every program is listed by all its known names or abbreviations. In addition, we've used an alphabetical code (within parentheses) to help you determine if the program falls within your general interest area: S = Sciences; SS = Social Sciences; H = Humanities; A = Any Subject Area. Here's how the code works: if a program is followed by (S) 41, the program is described in entry 41, in the Sciences section. If the same program title is followed by another entry number—for example, (A) 1001—the program is also described in entry 1001, in the Any Subject Area section. Remember: the numbers cited here refer to program entry numbers, not to page numbers in the book.

A. Patrick Charnon Scholarship, (A) 1015
A. Thomas Young Scholarship. See AIAA Foundation Undergraduate Scholarship Program, entry (S) 17
AACC International Foundation Undergraduate Scholarship Program, (S) 1
AACE International Competitive Scholarships, (S) 2
AAPA Veteran's Caucus Scholarships, (S) 3
AATCC Materials Design Competition, (S) 4
Abbott Individual Community Service Awards. See Helen Abbott Individual Community Service Awards, entry (A) 1119
Abbott Scholarship. See Air Force Sergeants Association Scholarships, entry (A) 1025
Abe Mittler Memorial Scholarship. See Quality Assurance Division Scholarships, entry (S) 401
Abe Voron Scholarship, (H) 774
Abernathy Undergraduate Presidential Scholarship. See Ruth Abernathy Undergraduate Presidential Scholarship, entries (S) 435, (SS) 731, (H) 970
A.C. Scribner Scholarship. See Tau Beta Pi Undergraduate Scholarships, entry (S) 479
Academy of Neonatal Nursing Scholarship Award, (S) 5
Academy of Television Arts & Sciences College Television Awards, (H) 775
Access Intelligence Scholarship, (S) 6, (SS) 528
Accountemps/AICPA Student Scholarship, (SS) 529
ACP Cartooning Awards, (H) 776
ACP Reporter of the Year Awards, (H) 777
ACSA/AISC Student Design Competition, (H) 778
ACSM Fellows Scholarship, (S) 7
Act One Award for Outstanding Screenplay. See Angelus Awards, entry (H) 786
Active International Scholarship for Business and Marketing. See Miss America Competition Awards, entry (A) 1174
Acton Essay Competition. See Lord Acton Essay Competition, entry (H) 914

ADC Communications and Foundation Scholarship, (S) 8
Adkins Memorial Scholarship. See Howard E. Adkins Memorial Scholarship, entry (S) 236
Adobe Systems Computer Science Corporate Scholarships. See National Society of Black Engineers Scholarship Program, entry (S) 343
Adobe Systems Computer Science Scholarships, (S) 9
AESF Undergraduate Scholarship Program, (S) 10
AFCEA Distance-Learning/On-Line Scholarships, (S) 11
African American Health Solutions Scholars Program, (S) 12
African American University Scholarships of the California State Fair, (A) 1016
African Methodist Episcopal Church Preacher's Kid Scholarship. See AME Church Preacher's Kid Scholarship, entry (A) 1036
Agatha Prator Scholarship, (SS) 530
AGCO Student Design Competition, (S) 13
AgLife for America Scholarships, (S) 14
AGO/Quimby Regional Competitions for Young Organists, (H) 779
Agriscience Student Program, (S) 15
Agron SEAL Scholarship, (A) 1017
AHEPA District Scholarship Awards, (A) 1018
AIAA Foundation Undergraduate Design Competitions, (S) 16
AIAA Foundation Undergraduate Scholarship Program, (S) 17
Aiko Susanna Tashiro Hiratsuka Memorial Scholarship, (H) 780
Air Force Enhanced ROTC Hispanic Serving Institution Scholarship Program, (A) 1019
Air Force Enhanced ROTC Historically Black Colleges and Universities Scholarship Program, (A) 1020
Air Force Regular ROTC Hispanic Serving Institution Scholarship Program, (A) 1021
Air Force Regular ROTC Historically Black Colleges and Universities Scholarship Program, (A) 1022
Air Force ROTC Biomedical Sciences Corps, (S) 18

S–Sciences   SS–Social Sciences   H–Humanities   A–Any Subject Area

Air Force ROTC Express Scholarships, (S) 19
Air Force ROTC General Military Course Incentive, (A) 1023
Air Force ROTC In–College Scholarship Program, (S) 20
Air Force ROTC Nursing Scholarships, (S) 21
Air Force ROTC Professional Officer Corps Incentive, (A) 1024
Air Force Sergeants Association Scholarships, (A) 1025
Air Force Services Club Membership Scholarship Program, (A) 1026
Air Force Spouse Scholarships, (A) 1027
Aircraft Electronics Association Members Scholarship Program, (A) 1028
Airmen Memorial Foundation Scholarship Program, (A) 1029
AISES IBM Scholarship, (S) 22
AITP Omaha Scholarship, (SS) 531
A.J. (Andy) Spielman Scholarships, (SS) 532
Al Piccetti NMA Memorial Scholarship. See NMA Undergraduate Scholarships, entry (S) 359
Al Qöyawayma Awards. See A.T. Anderson Memorial Scholarship Program, entry (S) 68
Al Schuman Ecolab Undergraduate Entrepreneurial Scholarships, (SS) 533
Alabama G.I. Dependents' Scholarship Program, (A) 1030
Alaska Airlines Scholarship, (SS) 534
Alaska Free Tuition for Spouses and Dependents of Armed Services Members, (A) 1031
Albert H. Winkler Scholarship. See Tau Beta Pi Undergraduate Scholarships, entry (S) 479
Alberta E. Crowe Star of Tomorrow Award, (A) 1032
Albuquerque Veterinary Association Scholarships, (S) 23
Alcoa Foundation Academic Scholarship, (S) 24
Alcohol, Tobacco, Firearms and Explosives Retiree's Association Scholarship. See ATFRA Scholarship, entry (SS) 551
Aldridge Scholarship. See AIAA Foundation Undergraduate Scholarship Program, entry (S) 17
Alex Postlethwaite Scholarship. See LCPA Education Foundation Scholarship Program, entry (SS) 658
Alexander M. Tanger Scholarship, (H) 781
Alexander Memorial Scholarship. See Daughters of Penelope Undergraduate Scholarships, entry (A) 1075
Alfred H. Nolle Scholarships, (A) 1033
Alfred Steele Engineering Scholarship, (S) 25
Alice Egan Multi-Year Mentoring Scholarship Program. See John and Alice Egan Multi-Year Mentoring Scholarship Program, entry (S) 264
Alice T. Schafer Mathematics Prize, (S) 26
All–Ink College Scholarships, (A) 1034
Allan MacCurrach Scholarship. See GCSAA Scholars Competition, entry (S) 204
Allan Murphy Endowed Memorial Scholarship. See Ethan and Allan Murphy Endowed Memorial Scholarship, entry (S) 170
Allen Memorial Scholarship. See SEG Scholarship Program, entry (S) 448
Allen W. Plumb Scholarship, (S) 27
Allhands Essay Competition. See James L. Allhands Essay Competition, entry (S) 255
Allison Accompanying Award. See Virginia Allison Accompanying Award, entry (H) 999
Allyn & Bacon Psychology Awards, (SS) 535
Alpha Corrine Mayfield Scholarship, (H) 782
Alpha Gamma Rho Excellence Scholarships, (S) 28
Alpha Kappa Alpha Merit Scholarships, (A) 1035

AME Church Preacher's Kid Scholarship, (A) 1036
Americal Division Veterans Association Scholarship, (A) 1037
American Academy of Physician Assistants Veteran's Caucus Scholarships. See AAPA Veteran's Caucus Scholarships, entry (S) 3
American Academy of Sanitarians Scholarships. See NEHA/AAS Scholarships, entry (S) 351
American Association for Health Education Undergraduate Scholarship. See Bill Kane Undergraduate Scholarship, entries (S) 79, (SS) 559
American Association of Occupational Health Nurses Foundation Academic Scholarship, (S) 29
American Association of Textile Chemists and Colorists Materials Design Competition. See AATCC Materials Design Competition, entry (S) 4
American Atheists College Scholarship (AACS). See Life Members' Scholarship, entry (A) 1154
American Atheists Gay/Lesbian College Scholarship (AAGLCS).. See Dr. Richard Chinn Scholarship, entry (A) 1082
American Business Educators Scholarships, (SS) 536
American Congress on Surveying and Mapping Fellows Scholarship. See ACSM Fellows Scholarship, entry (S) 7
American Council of Engineering Companies Scholarship Program, (S) 30
American Darts Organization Memorial Scholarships, (A) 1038
American Electroplaters and Surface Finishers Undergraduate Scholarship Program. See AESF Undergraduate Scholarship Program, entry (S) 10
American Express Travel Scholarship, (SS) 537
American Guild of Organists/Quimby Regional Competitions for Young Organists. See AGO/Quimby Regional Competitions for Young Organists, entry (H) 779
American Helicopter Society Student Design Competition, (S) 31
American Humanics Academic Awards, (SS) 538
American Indian Arts Council Scholarship Program, (H) 783
American Indian Fellowship in Business Scholarship, (SS) 539
American Institute of Aeronautics and Astronautics Foundation Undergraduate Design Competitions. See AIAA Foundation Undergraduate Design Competitions, entry (S) 16
American Institute of Aeronautics and Astronautics Foundation Undergraduate Scholarship Program. See AIAA Foundation Undergraduate Scholarship Program, entry (S) 17
American Meteorological Society Undergraduate Scholarships, (S) 32
American Meteorological Society 75th Anniversary Endowed Scholarship. See American Meteorological Society Undergraduate Scholarships, entry (S) 32
American Nuclear Society Undergraduate Scholarships. See ANS Undergraduate Scholarships, entry (S) 43
American Physical Society Scholarships for Minority Undergraduate Students Who Major in Physics. See APS Scholarships for Minority Undergraduate Students Who Major in Physics, entry (S) 45
American Police Hall of Fame Educational Scholarship Fund, (A) 1039
American Railway Engineering and Maintenance of Way Association Educational Foundation Undergraduate Scholarships. See AREMA Educational Foundation Undergraduate Scholarships, entry (S) 50

S–Sciences   SS–Social Sciences   H–Humanities   A–Any Subject Area

PROGRAM TITLE INDEX

American Society for Clinical Laboratory Science–Pennsylvania Memorial Undergraduate Scholarship. See ASCLS–PA Memorial Undergraduate Scholarship, entry (S) 56
American Society for Enology and Viticulture Scholarships, (S) 33
American Society for Horticultural Science Scholars Award. See ASHS Scholars Award, entry (S) 60
American Society of Civil Engineers/American Institute of Steel Construction Student Steel Bridge Competition. See ASCE/AISC Student Steel Bridge Competition, entry (S) 55
American Society of Composers, Authors and Publishers Foundation Young Jazz Composer Awards. See ASCAP Foundation Young Jazz Composer Awards, entry (H) 789
American Society of Engineers of Indian Origin Undergraduate Scholarships. See ASEI Undergraduate Scholarships, entries (S) 57, (H) 790
American Society of Farm Managers and Rural Appraisers Agricultural Scholarship, (S) 34, (SS) 540
American Society of Heating, Refrigerating and Air–Conditioning Engineers Student Design Project Competition. See ASHRAE Student Design Project Competition, entry (S) 58
American Society of Heating, Refrigerating and Air–Conditioning Engineers Undergraduate Senior Project Grants. See ASHRAE Undergraduate Senior Project Grants, entry (S) 59
American Society of Mechanical Engineers Foundation Scholarships. See ASME Foundation Scholarships, entry (S) 61
American Society of Mechanical Engineers Student Design Contest. See ASME Student Design Contest, entry (S) 62
American Standard Scholarships, (S) 35
American Star Farmer Award, (S) 36
American Star in Agribusiness Award, (SS) 541
American String Teachers Association National Solo Competition–Senior Division. See ASTA National Solo Competition–Senior Division, entry (H) 792
AmeriCorps National Civilian Community Corps, (A) 1040
Amgen Bachelor's Scholarships, (S) 37
AMS 75th Anniversary Endowed Scholarship. See American Meteorological Society Undergraduate Scholarships, entry (S) 32
ANA Multicultural Excellence Scholarship, (SS) 542
ANAC Student Diversity Mentorship Scholarship, (S) 38
Anderson Memorial Scholarship Program. See A.T. Anderson Memorial Scholarship Program, entry (S) 68
Anderson Memorial Scholarship. See Gladys C. Anderson Memorial Scholarship, entry (H) 859
Anderson Scholarship in Space Science. See Michael P. Anderson Scholarship in Space Science, entry (S) 318
Anderson Scholarship. See California P.E.O. Scholarships, entry (A) 1056
Anderson TrumCor Mutes Award. See National Trumpet Competition Awards, entry (H) 940
Andrea Long Memorial Scholarships. See AAPA Veteran's Caucus Scholarships, entry (S) 3
Andrew E. Nuquist Award, (H) 784
Andrew M. Economos Scholarship, (H) 785
Andrews Scholarship. See Miss America Competition Awards, entry (A) 1174
Andy Spielman Scholarships. See A.J. (Andy) Spielman Scholarships, entry (SS) 532

Angelo S. Bisesti Memorial Scholarship. See ANS Undergraduate Scholarships, entry (S) 43
Angelus Award for Outstanding Animation. See Angelus Awards, entry (H) 786
Angelus Awards, (H) 786
Angie M. Houtz Memorial Fund Scholarship, (A) 1041
Angus Foundation Scholarships, (S) 39
Anita Borg Scholarships, (S) 40
Ann M. Martin Scholarship. See Eden Services Charles H. Hoens, Jr. Scholars Program, entry (A) 1086
Ann Phipps Memorial Scholarships, (A) 1042
Anna E. Hall Memorial Scholarship. See Phi Chi Theta Scholarships, entry (SS) 711
Anne Maureen Whitney Barrow Memorial Scholarship, (S) 41
Annie Blaylock Memorial Scholarship. See FORE Undergraduate Merit Scholarships, entries (S) 186, (SS) 598
Annie Lou Ellis Piano Award. See NFMC Biennial Student Audition Awards, entry (H) 944
Annie's Environmental Studies Scholarships, (S) 42
ANS Undergraduate Scholarships, (S) 43
Anthony L. Pasquarelli Award. See National Trumpet Competition Awards, entry (H) 940
A.O. Smith Water Heaters Scholarship, (S) 44
AOWCGWA Scholarship Program, (A) 1043
Apker Award. See LeRoy Apker Award, entry (S) 292
Applegate Scholarship Award. See Harry A. Applegate Scholarship Award, entry (SS) 617
Applegate/Jackson/Parks Future Teacher Scholarship, (SS) 543
Appraisal Institute Education Trust Scholarship, (SS) 544
APS Scholarships for Minority Undergraduate Students Who Major in Physics, (S) 45
Aquatrols Essay Contest, (S) 46
ARC of Washington Trust Fund Stipend Award Program, (S) 47, (SS) 545
Arc Welding Awards—Division II, (S) 48
Arc Welding Awards—Division IV, (S) 49
AREMA Educational Foundation Undergraduate Scholarships, (S) 50
Arizona Chapter Gold Scholarship, (SS) 546
Arkansas Game and Fish Scholarship, (S) 51
Arkansas Society of Certified Public Accountants Student Education Fund Scholarships, (SS) 547
Armed Forces Communications and Electronics Association Distance–Learning/On–Line Scholarships. See AFCEA Distance–Learning/On–Line Scholarships, entry (S) 11
Army Aviation Association of America Scholarships, (A) 1044
Army Officers' Wives' Club of the Greater Washington Area Scholarship Program. See AOWCGWA Scholarship Program, entry (A) 1043
Army ROTC Advanced Course, (A) 1045
Army ROTC College Scholarship Program, (A) 1046
Arnold L. Magnuson Scholarship. See Nebraska Society of Certified Public Accountants Scholarships, entry (SS) 689
Arnold Sadler Memorial Scholarship, (S) 52, (SS) 548
Arras Group Minority Scholarship. See Cleveland Advertising Association Education Foundation Scholarships, entry (H) 818
Art Pfaff Scholarship Program, (SS) 549
Arthur B. Gurda Memorial Award. See Polanki College Achievement Awards, entry (A) 1235

S–Sciences   SS–Social Sciences   H–Humanities   A–Any Subject Area

Arthur B.C. Walker Scholarships. *See* Willie Hobbs Moore–Harry L. Morrison–Arthur B.C. Walker Scholarships, entry (S) 519

Arthur Memorial Turfgrass Scholarship. *See* Donnie Arthur Memorial Turfgrass Scholarship, entry (S) 139

Arthur Poister Scholarship Competition in Organ Playing, (H) 787

Arthur T. Schramm Memorial Scholarship, (S) 53

Arthur W. Pense Scholarship, (S) 54

Arthur Wynne Jr. Memorial Award, (H) 788

Arver Memorial Scholarship. *See* David Arver Memorial Scholarship, entry (S) 128

Arver Scholarship. *See* Dutch and Ginger Arver Scholarship, entry (S) 150

ArvinMeritor Suspension System Awards. *See* Formula SAE Competition Awards, entry (S) 187

ASCAP Foundation Young Jazz Composer Awards, (H) 789

ASCAP Young Composer Awards. *See* Victor Herbert ASCAP Young Composer Awards, entry (H) 997

ASCE/AISC Student Steel Bridge Competition, (S) 55

ASCLS–PA Memorial Undergraduate Scholarship, (S) 56

ASEI Undergraduate Scholarships, (S) 57, (H) 790

ASHRAE Student Design Project Competition, (S) 58

ASHRAE Undergraduate Senior Project Grants, (S) 59

ASHS Scholars Award, (S) 60

Asian Pacific Islander University Scholarships of the California State Fair, (A) 1047

ASME Foundation Scholarships, (S) 61

ASME Student Design Contest, (S) 62

Assistance for Surviving Children of Naval Personnel Deceased after Retirement (CDR), (A) 1048

Associated Collegiate Press Cartooning Awards. *See* ACP Cartooning Awards, entry (H) 776

Associated Collegiate Press Reporter of the Year Awards. *See* ACP Reporter of the Year Awards, entry (H) 777

Association for Iron & Steel Technology Scholarships, (S) 63

Association for the Advancement of Cost Engineering International Competitive Scholarships. *See* AACE International Competitive Scholarships, entry (S) 2

Association for Theater in Higher Education Award. *See* National Student Playwriting Award, entry (H) 939

Association for Women Geoscientists Minority Scholarship, (S) 64

Association for Women in Communications–District of Columbia Scholarship. *See* AWIC–DC Scholarship, entry (H) 797

Association for Women in Sports Media Scholarship/Internship Program, (H) 791

Association of Collegiate Schools of Architecture/American Institute of Steel Construction Student Design Competition. *See* ACSA/AISC Student Design Competition, entry (H) 778

Association of Cuban Engineers Scholarships, (S) 65

Association of Government Accountants Academic Merit Scholarships, (SS) 550

Association of Information Technology Professionals Omaha Scholarship. *See* AITP Omaha Scholarship, entry (SS) 531

Association of National Advertisers Multicultural Excellence Scholarship. *See* ANA Multicultural Excellence Scholarship, entry (SS) 542

Association of Nurses in AIDS Care Student Diversity Mentorship Scholarship. *See* ANAC Student Diversity Mentorship Scholarship, entry (S) 38

Association of Rehabilitation Nurses BSN Scholarship, (S) 66

Association of United Nurses Scholarships, (S) 67

ASTA National Solo Competition–Senior Division, (H) 792

A.T. Anderson Memorial Scholarship Program, (S) 68

ATFRA Scholarship, (SS) 551

Atlanta Falcons Undergraduate Scholarship Award. *See* Jerry Rhea/Atlanta Falcons Undergraduate Scholarship Award, entry (S) 259

Atlanta Press Club Journalism Scholarship Award, (H) 793

Atlas Shrugged Essay Contest, (H) 794

Attorney–CPA Foundation Undergraduate Essay Contest, (SS) 552

Aubespin Scholarship. *See* Copy Editing Scholarships, entry (H) 824

Auction Scholarship, (S) 69

Audrey Tanzer Scholarship, (H) 795

Aurel Zajta Scholarship. *See* Dr. Aurel Zajta Scholarship, entries (S) 143, (H) 839

Aureus Financial Scholarship. *See* Nebraska Society of Certified Public Accountants Scholarships, entry (SS) 689

Avis Scholarship, (SS) 553

Award To Honor Excellence in Newspaper Advertising (ATHENA), (H) 796

AWIC–DC Scholarship, (H) 797

aWorldConnected.org Essay Contest, (SS) 554

Ayer Aviation Scholarship. *See* Ernie Ayer Aviation Scholarship, entry (S) 168

B. June West Recruitment Grant, (SS) 555

B. Phinizy Spalding and Hubert B. Owens Scholarships, (H) 798

BAC Scholarship. *See* WTVR News 6 Network Scholarship, entry (H) 1012

Bach Award for Artistic Excellence. *See* National Trumpet Competition Awards, entry (H) 940

Bach Award for Young Artists. *See* National Trumpet Competition Awards, entry (H) 940

BACUS Photomask Scholarship. *See* SPIE Scholarship Program, entry (S) 464

Bagnall Scholarship for Church Musicians. *See* Charlotte Hoyt Bagnall Scholarship for Church Musicians, entry (H) 815

Bahethi Scholarship. *See* American Meteorological Society Undergraduate Scholarships, entry (S) 32

Baird Scholarship. *See* Ralph W. Baird Scholarship, entry (S) 404

Baker Memorial Scholarship. *See* Aircraft Electronics Association Members Scholarship Program, entry (A) 1028

Banks Memorial Undergraduate Scholarship. *See* Sharon D. Banks Memorial Undergraduate Scholarship, entries (S) 450, (SS) 735

Banks Scholarship in Astronomy. *See* Harvey Washington Banks Scholarship in Astronomy, entry (S) 227

Barbara Alice Mower Memorial Scholarship, (SS) 556

Barbara Furse Mackey Scholarship. *See* California P.E.O. Scholarships, entry (A) 1056

Barbara Irish Violin Award. *See* NFMC Biennial Student Audition Awards, entry (H) 944

Barbara Jordan Memorial Scholarship, (SS) 557

Barbara M. Irish Award. *See* NFMC Biennial Student Audition Awards, entry (H) 944

S–Sciences   **SS–Social Sciences**   **H–Humanities**   **A–Any Subject Area**

PROGRAM TITLE INDEX

Barbara McBride Scholarship, (S) 70
Barbara Pryor Scholarship. See IFMA Foundation Scholarships, entry (SS) 631
Barfield KBA Scholarship Program. See Harry Barfield KBA Scholarship Program, entry (H) 867
Barnes Scholarship. See Martin Barnes Scholarships, entry (A) 1165
Barnes Student Scholarship. See Texas Choral Directors Association Student Scholarships, entry (H) 991
Barnum Festival Foundation/Jenny Lind Competition for Sopranos, (H) 799
Barr Awards. See David S. Barr Awards, entry (H) 833
Barraco Scholarship. See Non Commissioned Officers Association Scholarship Fund, entry (A) 1216
Barrow Memorial Scholarship. See Anne Maureen Whitney Barrow Memorial Scholarship, entry (S) 41
Barry and Julia Smith Family Nurse Scholarship Program, (S) 71
Barry M. Goldwater Scholarships, (S) 72
Bassford Student Award. See Forrest Bassford Student Award, entries (S) 188, (H) 850
Bastien Memorial Award. See WAMSO Young Artist Competition Awards and Scholarships, entry (H) 1005
Baum Endowed Scholarship. See American Meteorological Society Undergraduate Scholarships, entry (S) 32
BEA 2-Year/Community College Award, (H) 800
Because Green Matters Scholarship Program, (S) 73
Becchina Award. See NFMC Biennial Student Audition Awards, entry (H) 944
Bechtel Foundation Scholarship, (S) 74
Ben Chatfield Undergraduate Scholarship. See Radio and Television News Directors Foundation Presidents' Scholarships, entry (H) 962
Ben Meadows Natural Resource Scholarships, (S) 75
Ben W. Fortson, Jr. Scholarship, (S) 76
Benjamin C. Blackburn Scholarship, (S) 77, (H) 801
Benjamin F. Fairless Scholarships. See Association for Iron & Steel Technology Scholarships, entry (S) 63
Benton Scholarship. See American Meteorological Society Undergraduate Scholarships, entry (S) 32
Berber Memorial Scholarship. See Naomi Berber Memorial Scholarship, entries (SS) 678, (H) 928
Berggren Scholarship. See Maud Berggren Scholarship, entry (SS) 667
Bernie Wayne Performing Arts Award. See Miss America Competition Awards, entry (A) 1174
Berntsen International Scholarship in Surveying, (S) 78
Bertha MacDonald Scholarship, (H) 802
Beta Sigma Psi Educational Foundation Awards, (A) 1049
Betsy Plank/PRSSA Scholarships, (H) 803
Betty Broemmelsiek Memorial Conservation Scholarships. See Missouri Soil and Water Conservation Society Scholarships, entries (S) 328, (SS) 672
Betty Hansen National Scholarships, (A) 1050
Betty Rendel Scholarships, (SS) 558
Beverly Dye Anderson Scholarship. See California P.E.O. Scholarships, entry (A) 1056
BFGoodrich Collegiate Inventors Program. See Collegiate Inventors Competition, entry (S) 114
Bianco Memorial Scholarship. See Quality Assurance Division Scholarships, entry (S) 401

Big Mama Andrews Scholarship. See Miss America Competition Awards, entry (A) 1174
Bill Haney, USA (Ret) Award for Leadership. See Hawaii Chapter AFCEA Scholarships, entry (S) 228
Bill Kane Undergraduate Scholarship, (S) 79, (SS) 559
Billy Welu Scholarship, (A) 1051
Birtwistle Award. See Irma and Knute Carlson Award, entry (A) 1130
Bisesti Memorial Scholarship. See ANS Undergraduate Scholarships, entry (S) 43
Bittle Memorial Scholarships. See L. Gordon Bittle Memorial Scholarships, entry (SS) 654
B.K. Krenzer Reentry Scholarship, (S) 80
Black Advisory Council Scholarship. See WTVR News 6 Network Scholarship, entry (H) 1012
Blackburn Scholarship. See Benjamin C. Blackburn Scholarship, entries (S) 77, (H) 801
Blaha Medical Grant. See M. Blaha Medical Grant, entry (S) 306
Blanche Z. Hoffman Memorial Award for Voice. See Sigma Alpha Iota Scholarships for Undergraduate Performance, entry (H) 980
Blaylock Memorial Scholarship. See FORE Undergraduate Merit Scholarships, entries (S) 186, (SS) 598
Bob and Gloria Murray Memorial Award. See National Trumpet Competition Awards, entry (H) 940
Bodie McDowell Scholarship Awards, (H) 804
Boeing Company Scholarship, (A) 1052
Borg Scholarships. See Anita Borg Scholarships, entry (S) 40
Born Memorial Scholarship. See SEG Scholarship Program, entry (S) 448
Boyd Scholarship. See Dr. William S. Boyd Scholarship, entry (S) 149
BP Exploration and Production Process Technology Scholarship, (S) 81
Bracone Memorial Scholarship. See Joseph F. Bracone Memorial Scholarship, entry (A) 1141
Bradford White Scholarships, (S) 82
Bradley Scholarship. See Ed Bradley Scholarship, entry (H) 842
Bradshaw Memorial Scholarship. See Richard V. Bradshaw Memorial Scholarship, entry (A) 1243
Brady Scholarship. See Xernona Clayton Brady Scholarship, entry (H) 1013
Brandt Memorial Scholarships. See Nebraska Bankers Educational Foundation Scholarships, entry (SS) 688
Branham Scholarship. See Rob Branham Scholarship, entries (SS) 726, (H) 968
Bray Memorial Scholarship. See Jeanne E. Bray Memorial Scholarship, entry (A) 1133
Breimeier Memorial Scholarship. See LEAP Scholarships, entry (SS) 659
Brennan Memorial Scholarship. See Cleveland Advertising Association Education Foundation Scholarships, entry (H) 818
Brennie Morgan Prize. See Frank and Brennie Morgan Prize, entry (S) 192
Brewster Vocal Scholarship. See Glenn Miller Scholarship Competition, entry (H) 860
Brian Jenneman Memorial Scholarship, (S) 83
Brice Undergraduate Leadership Award. See Leonard R. Brice Undergraduate Leadership Award, entry (SS) 661

S–Sciences   SS–Social Sciences   H–Humanities   A–Any Subject Area

Bricker College Award. *See* Academy of Television Arts & Sciences College Television Awards, entry (H) 775

Bright Future Scholarship. *See* FORE Undergraduate Merit Scholarships, entries (S) 186, (SS) 598

Broadcast Education Association 2-Year/Community College Award. *See* BEA 2-Year/Community College Award, entry (H) 800

Brocksbank Scholarship. *See* A.T. Anderson Memorial Scholarship Program, entry (S) 68

Broemmelsiek Memorial Conservation Scholarships. *See* Missouri Soil and Water Conservation Society Scholarships, entries (S) 328, (SS) 672

Brotsis Memorial Scholarship. *See* El Camino Real District 20 Scholarships, entry (A) 1089

Brown Foundation Academic Scholarships, (SS) 560

Brown Memorial Youth Scholarship Program. *See* Jesse Brown Memorial Youth Scholarship Program, entry (A) 1134

Brown Scholarships. *See* Miss America Competition Awards, entry (A) 1174

Bruce Dennis Undergraduate Scholarship. *See* Radio and Television News Directors Foundation Presidents' Scholarships, entry (H) 962

Bruce Palmer Undergraduate Scholarship. *See* Radio and Television News Directors Foundation Presidents' Scholarships, entry (H) 962

Bruce Van Ess Scholarship, (A) 1053

Bruel and Kjaer Quiet Car Cup. *See* Formula SAE Competition Awards, entry (S) 187

Bryan Award. *See* George B. Bryan Award, entry (H) 857

Bud Glover Memorial Scholarship, (S) 84

Bugher Endowed Scholarship. *See* Phi Delta Kappa International Scholarship Grants for Prospective Educators, entry (SS) 712

Burgin, Jr. MD Education Recognition Award. *See* William W. Burgin, Jr. MD Education Recognition Award, entry (S) 518

Burson Memorial Scholarship. *See* Dr. S. Bradley Burson Memorial Scholarship, entry (S) 148

Business Achievement Awards, (SS) 561

Business Reporting Intern Program for Minority College Sophomores and Juniors, (H) 805

Byron Undergraduate Scholarship. *See* Radio and Television News Directors Foundation Presidents' Scholarships, entry (H) 962

CA-ASA Scholarships, (S) 85

CAB/NJAA Scholarship, (S) 86

Cady McDonnell Memorial Scholarship, (S) 87

Calgon Take Me Away to College Scholarships, (A) 1054

Caliendo College Assistance Fund Scholarship. *See* Captain Caliendo College Assistance Fund Scholarship, entry (A) 1058

California Agricultural Irrigation Association Scholarship Program, (S) 88

California Association of Nurserymen Endowment for Research and Scholarship College Scholarships. *See* CANERS College Scholarships, entry (S) 93

California Farm Bureau Scholarships, (S) 89

California Fee Waiver Program for Dependents of Totally Disabled Veterans, (A) 1055

California Hotel & Lodging Association General Scholarships, (SS) 562

California Marine Sciences Scholarship, (S) 90

California P.E.O. Scholarships, (A) 1056

California Restaurant Association Educational Foundation Scholarships for Undergraduate Students, (H) 806

California State Fair Arts Scholarships, (H) 807

California State Fair Culinary Cooking and Hospitality Management Scholarships, (H) 808

California State Fair International Studies Scholarships, (SS) 563

California State Fair University Scholarships in Agriculture, (S) 91

California State Fair Viticulture/Enology Scholarships, (S) 92

Campbell Memorial Scholarship. *See* René Campbell Memorial Scholarship, entry (SS) 718

Campbell Research Award. *See* Lawrence R. Campbell Research Award, entry (H) 910

Campbell Scholarship. *See* Tau Beta Pi Undergraduate Scholarships, entry (S) 479

Campus Safety Health and Environmental Management Association Scholarship Award Program. *See* CSHEMA Scholarship Award Program, entry (S) 123

CANERS College Scholarships, (S) 93

Cannon Memorial Scholarship. *See* Kellie Cannon Memorial Scholarship, entry (S) 280

Capital District 3 Scholarships, (A) 1057

CAPT Jim Hickerson, USN (Ret) Award for Academic Achievement. *See* Hawaii Chapter AFCEA Scholarships, entry (S) 228

CAPT Ken Wiedking, USN (Ret) Award for Community Service. *See* Hawaii Chapter AFCEA Scholarships, entry (S) 228

Captain Caliendo College Assistance Fund Scholarship, (A) 1058

Captain Michael Frangos and Irene Frangos Memorial Scholarship Award. *See* Metropolitan Society of Kardamylians College Awards, entry (A) 1168

Carey Scholarships. *See* James B. Carey Scholarships, entry (A) 1132

Carl W. Kreitzberg Endowed Scholarship. *See* American Meteorological Society Undergraduate Scholarships, entry (S) 32

Carl Zellers Scholarship. *See* PIEF General Scholarships, entry (H) 959

Carlos T. Touris Scholarship. *See* AHEPA District Scholarship Awards, entry (A) 1018

Carlson Award. *See* Irma and Knute Carlson Award, entry (A) 1130

Carmel Music Society Competition, (H) 809

Carmen E. Turner Scholarships, (S) 94

Carol A. Ratza Memorial Scholarship, (S) 95

Carole Prato Sports Reporting Scholarship. *See* Lou and Carole Prato Sports Reporting Scholarship, entry (H) 916

Carole Simpson Scholarship, (H) 810

Carolina Film and Video Festival Awards, (H) 811

Carolyn S. Richardson Memorial Scholarship, (S) 96

Carpe Diem Scholarships, (A) 1059

Carroll Barnes Student Scholarship. *See* Texas Choral Directors Association Student Scholarships, entry (H) 991

Cartography and Geographic Information Society Scholarship Award, (S) 97, (SS) 564

PROGRAM TITLE INDEX

Cary Memorial Scholarship. See Judith Cary Memorial Scholarship, entry (SS) 649
Case Study Competition in Corporate Communications, (SS) 565, (H) 812
Caterpillar Scholars Award, (S) 98
Cauble Short Play Award. See John Cauble Short Play Award, entry (H) 900
CCIM Institute Education Foundation Undergraduate University Scholarships, (SS) 566
CDR Program. See Assistance for Surviving Children of Naval Personnel Deceased after Retirement (CDR), entry (A) 1048
Cedarcrest Farms Scholarship, (S) 99
Cen Cal California Diving & Aquatic Studies Scholarship. See California Marine Sciences Scholarship, entry (S) 90
Cen Cal Marine Science Scholarship. See California Marine Sciences Scholarship, entry (S) 90
Certified Angus Beef/National Junior Angus Association Scholarship. See CAB/NJAA Scholarship, entry (S) 86
Cessna/Raytheon Student Design/Build/Fly Competition, (S) 100
Chambers Statistical Software Award. See John M. Chambers Statistical Software Award, entry (S) 271
Chan–Padgett Special Forces Memorial Scholarship, (S) 101
Chang Memorial Essay Contest. See Iris Chang Memorial Essay Contest, entry (H) 891
Chapter 67 Scholarships. See Phoenix Chapter 67 Scholarships, entry (S) 390
Charles A. Dodson Scholarship. See Tau Beta Pi Undergraduate Scholarships, entry (S) 479
Charles and Theresa Brown Scholarships. See Miss America Competition Awards, entry (A) 1174
Charles D. Mayo Student Scholarship, (H) 813
Charles H. Hoens, Jr. Scholars Program. See Eden Services Charles H. Hoens, Jr. Scholars Program, entry (A) 1086
Charles M. Schulz Award for College Cartoonists, (H) 814
Charles R. Morris Student Research Award, (S) 102
Charles (Tommy) Thomas Memorial Scholarship, (S) 103
Charlie Q. Coffman Endowed Scholarship. See Phi Delta Kappa International Scholarship Grants for Prospective Educators, entry (SS) 712
Charlie Trotter Culinary Education Foundation Scholarship. See Culinary Trust Scholarships, entry (H) 827
Charline Hamilton Powell Scholarship, (S) 104
Charlotte Hoyt Bagnall Scholarship for Church Musicians, (H) 815
Charnon Scholarship. See A. Patrick Charnon Scholarship, entry (A) 1015
Chatfield Undergraduate Scholarship. See Radio and Television News Directors Foundation Presidents' Scholarships, entry (H) 962
Chem-E-Car Competition, (S) 105
Cheng Memorial Scholarship. See Chinese American Citizens Alliance Foundation Scholarships, entry (A) 1060
Chester Mendenhall Scholarship. See Heart of America Golf Course Superintendents Association Scholarships, entry (S) 231
Chet Mendenhall Award. See GCSAA Scholars Competition, entry (S) 204
Cheverton Undergraduate Scholarship. See Radio and Television News Directors Foundation Presidents' Scholarships, entry (H) 962
Chevron Corporation Scholarships, (S) 106

Chicago Mercantile Exchange Beef Industry Scholarship Program, (S) 107
Child Endowment Fund Scholarship. See Culinary Trust Scholarships, entry (H) 827
Child Fund at the Boston Foundation Scholarship. See Culinary Trust Scholarships, entry (H) 827
Child Nutrition Foundation Professional Growth Scholarships. See CNF Professional Growth Scholarships, entries (S) 111, (SS) 570
Child Scholarship. See Kevin Child Scholarship, entry (A) 1151
Chinese American Citizens Alliance Foundation Scholarships, (A) 1060
Chinn Scholarship. See Dr. Richard Chinn Scholarship, entry (A) 1082
Chips Quinn Scholars Program, (H) 816
Chirgotis Scholarship. See George Chirgotis Scholarship, entry (A) 1108
Chiyo Kuwahara Creative Arts Award. See Henry and Chiyo Kuwahara Creative Arts Award, entry (H) 874
Cho Scholarship. See KSEA Scholarships, entry (S) 286
Christen Distinguished Undergraduate Student Award. See Genevieve Christen Distinguished Undergraduate Student Award, entry (S) 212
Christian Anderson TrumCor Mutes Award. See National Trumpet Competition Awards, entry (H) 940
Christine O. Gregoire Youth/Young Adult Award, (A) 1061
Christmas Scholarship for Heroism. See Dana Christmas Scholarship for Heroism, entry (A) 1073
Christopher ÚKitÛ Smith Scholarship. See LCPA Education Foundation Scholarship Program, entry (SS) 658
Chuck Hall Star of Tomorrow Award, (A) 1062
Chuck Peacock Honorary Scholarship. See Aircraft Electronics Association Members Scholarship Program, entry (A) 1028
Chuck Peacock Memorial Scholarship, (S) 108, (SS) 567
Chunghi Hong Park Scholarship, (S) 109
CITDA Student Competition. See C2C/CITDA Student Competition, entry (H) 828
Civil Air Patrol Academic Scholarships, (A) 1063
Civil Air Patrol USAA Scholarships, (A) 1064
Civil Engineers of America Scholarships, (S) 110
Clampitt Paper/Henry Phillips Memorial Scholarship, (SS) 568, (H) 817
Clara E. Livingston Cadet Scholarship, (A) 1065
Clark Scholarship. See Ruth Clark Scholarship, entry (H) 971
Clark/Seth Payne Award for Young Science Journalists. See Evert Clark/Seth Payne Award for Young Science Journalists, entries (S) 171, (H) 847
Clarke Scholarship. See Phi Upsilon Scholarships, entry (SS) 713
Classical Acting Award of Excellence. See Irene Ryan Acting Scholarships, entry (H) 890
Clauda Pennock Todd Tripod Scholarship. See Richard Cecil Todd and Clauda Pennock Todd Tripod Scholarship, entry (A) 1242
Claude E. Pope Scholarship, (SS) 569
Claude Klobus Scholarship. See Air Force Sergeants Association Scholarships, entry (A) 1025
Claude R. Lambe Fellowships. See Humane Studies Fellowships, entries (SS) 626, (H) 879
Cleveland Advertising Association Education Foundation Scholarships, (H) 818

S–Sciences   SS–Social Sciences   H–Humanities   A–Any Subject Area

Cleveland L. Campbell Scholarship. *See* Tau Beta Pi Undergraduate Scholarships, entry (S) 479
Clewell Scholarship. *See* Phi Upsilon Scholarships, entry (SS) 713
Cleworth Award. *See* NFMC Biennial Student Audition Awards, entry (H) 944
Clifton Scholarship Fund, (A) 1066
Clore Scholarship. *See* Walter J. Clore Scholarship, entry (S) 500
Cluney Fund. *See* Johanna Drew Cluney Fund, entry (S) 262
CM Magazine Scholarship. *See* Gary B. Multanen/CM Magazine Scholarship, entry (S) 201
CNF Professional Growth Scholarships, (S) 111, (SS) 570
Coalition of Higher Education Assistance Organizations Scholarships. *See* COHEAO Scholarships, entry (A) 1068
Coating and Graphic Arts Division Scholarships, (S) 112, (H) 819
Cobb Memorial Scholarship. *See* J.C. and Rheba Cobb Memorial Scholarship, entry (S) 258
Coca-Cola Two-Year College Scholarships, (A) 1067
Coffman Endowed Scholarship. *See* Phi Delta Kappa International Scholarship Grants for Prospective Educators, entry (SS) 712
COHEAO Scholarships, (A) 1068
Cohen Scholarship. *See* FORE Undergraduate Merit Scholarships, entries (S) 186, (SS) 598
COL Bill Haney, USA (Ret) Award for Leadership. *See* Hawaii Chapter AFCEA Scholarships, entry (S) 228
Cole Memorial Scholarships. *See* Eddie G. Cole Memorial Scholarships, entries (S) 156, (SS) 587
Coleman Aviation Scholarship. *See* Tweet Coleman Aviation Scholarship, entry (S) 490
Colin Higgins Foundation Youth Courage Awards, (A) 1069
College Photographer of the Year, (H) 820
Collegiate Discussion Meet Awards, (S) 113
Collegiate Inventors Competition, (S) 114
Collin and Susan Lai Scholarship. *See* Chinese American Citizens Alliance Foundation Scholarships, entry (A) 1060
Colonel William J. Lookadoo Award. *See* College Photographer of the Year, entry (H) 820
Colorado Broadcasters Association College Scholarships, (H) 821
Colorado Broadcasters Association Vocational School Scholarship, (H) 822
Colorado Federation of NARFE, (A) 1070
Colorado Young Farmers Scholarships, (S) 115, (SS) 571
Colton Award. *See* Irene Ryan Acting Scholarships, entry (H) 890
Combs Hospitality Scholarship. *See* Richard B. Combs Hospitality Scholarship, entry (SS) 719
Committee 12-Rail Transit Undergraduate Scholarship, (S) 116
Commonwealth "Good Citizen" Scholarships, (A) 1071
Communications Scholarship for Ethnic Minority Students. *See* Leonard M. Perryman Communications Scholarship for Ethnic Minority Students, entry (H) 912
Community Service Scholarships, (SS) 572
Computer Integrated Textile Design Association Student Competition. *See* C2C/CITDA Student Competition, entry (H) 828
Computer Society International Design Competition, (S) 117
Computing Research Association Undergraduate Awards. *See* CRA Undergraduate Awards, entry (S) 121

COMTO NJ Scholarships, (S) 118, (SS) 573
Concept 2 Consumer/CITDA Student Competition. *See* C2C/CITDA Student Competition, entry (H) 828
Concrete Reinforcing Steel Institute Foundation Undergraduate Scholarship Program. *See* CRSI Foundation Undergraduate Scholarship Program, entry (S) 122
Concrete Thinking for a Sustainable World Student Design Competition, (H) 823
Connecticut American Society of Landscape Architects Student Scholarship. *See* CTASLA Student Scholarship, entry (H) 826
Connecticut Chapter Scholarship, (S) 119
Connecticut Hospitality Educational Foundation Scholarships, (SS) 574
Connecticut National Guard Foundation Scholarships, (A) 1072
Connie Marshall Memorial Scholarship. *See* FORE Undergraduate Merit Scholarships, entries (S) 186, (SS) 598
Constance Eberhart Memorial Awards. *See* National Opera Association Scholarship Division Awards, entry (H) 936
ConstructMyFuture.com Scholarships, (S) 120, (SS) 575
Cook Honorary Scholarship. *See* Aircraft Electronics Association Members Scholarship Program, entry (A) 1028
Copernicus Award. *See* Polanki College Achievement Awards, entry (A) 1235
Copy Editing Scholarships, (H) 824
Cornhusker State Games Scholarship Program. *See* Gallup Organization/Cornhusker State Games Scholarship Program, entry (A) 1104
Corporate-Sponsored Scholarships for Minority Undergraduate Students Who Major in Physics. *See* APS Scholarships for Minority Undergraduate Students Who Major in Physics, entry (S) 45
Cost Scholarships. *See* Nick Cost Scholarships, entry (A) 1214
Covert, Ph.D., FHIMSS Scholarship. *See* Richard P. Covert, Ph.D., FHIMSS Scholarship, entries (S) 411, (SS) 721
Cowles Youth Award. *See* Reuben R. Cowles Youth Award, entry (S) 408
CRA Undergraduate Awards, (S) 121
Craig Ivory Memorial Scholarships. *See* AAPA Veteran's Caucus Scholarships, entry (S) 3
Craig Memorial Scholarships. *See* Linda Craig Memorial Scholarships, entry (S) 295
Crazy Horse Memorial Journalism Scholarship, (H) 825
Cribbins Scholarship. *See* Joseph P. and Helen T. Cribbins Scholarship, entry (S) 274
Crippen Scholarship. *See* AIAA Foundation Undergraduate Scholarship Program, entry (S) 17
Cross Scholarship. *See* Law Enforcement Career Scholarship Program, entry (SS) 657
Crow Memorial Scholarship. *See* Loren W. Crow Memorial Scholarship, entry (S) 299
Crowe Star of Tomorrow Award. *See* Alberta E. Crowe Star of Tomorrow Award, entry (A) 1032
Crown Mutes Young Artist Award. *See* National Trumpet Competition Awards, entry (H) 940
CRSI Foundation Undergraduate Scholarship Program, (S) 122
CSHEMA Scholarship Award Program, (S) 123
CTASLA Student Scholarship, (H) 826
Cuisinart Scholarship. *See* Culinary Trust Scholarships, entry (H) 827
Culinary Trust Scholarships, (H) 827

S–Sciences   SS–Social Sciences   H–Humanities   A–Any Subject Area

PROGRAM TITLE INDEX

Cullison Scholarship. *See* William L. Cullison Scholarship, entry (S) 515
Cunningham Scholarship. *See* AREMA Educational Foundation Undergraduate Scholarships, entry (S) 50
Curry Scholarship. *See* Nancy Curry Scholarship, entries (S) 335, (SS) 677
C2C/CITDA Student Competition, (H) 828

Daedalian Academic Matching Scholarship Program, (S) 124
Daedalian Foundation Descendants' Scholarship Program, (S) 125
DaimlerChrysler Corporation Fund Scholarship, (S) 126
Dairy Management Inc. Milk Marketing Scholarships. *See* National Dairy Shrine/DMI Milk Marketing Scholarships, entry (S) 341
Dakis Scholarship. *See* Sam Dakis Scholarship, entry (A) 1249
Dan Breimeier Memorial Scholarship. *See* LEAP Scholarships, entry (SS) 659
Dan L. Meisinger, Sr. Memorial Learn to Fly Scholarship, (S) 127
Dan Whitworth Memorial Scholarship, (SS) 576
Dana Christmas Scholarship for Heroism, (A) 1073
Dana III Scholarship. *See* Nebraska Society of Certified Public Accountants Scholarships, entry (SS) 689
Dance Society of America Scholarships, (H) 829
Daniel J. Edelman Award, (H) 830
Daughters of Penelope Citrus District 2 Scholarships, (A) 1074
Daughters of Penelope Past Grand Presidents' Memorial Scholarship. *See* Daughters of Penelope Undergraduate Scholarships, entry (A) 1075
Daughters of Penelope Undergraduate Scholarships, (A) 1075
DAV National Commander's Youth Volunteer Scholarships. *See* Jesse Brown Memorial Youth Scholarship Program, entry (A) 1134
Dave Fearis Scholarship. *See* Heart of America Golf Course Superintendents Association Scholarships, entry (S) 231
David A. Cohen Scholarship. *See* FORE Undergraduate Merit Scholarships, entries (S) 186, (SS) 598
David Arver Memorial Scholarship, (S) 128
David Hoods Memorial Scholarship, (SS) 577, (H) 831
David J. Fitzmaurice Scholarship, (S) 129
David L. Stashower Visionary Scholarships, (H) 832
David M. Irwin Friend of Higher Education Award, (A) 1076
David Mann Scholarship, (S) 130
David S. Barr Awards, (H) 833
David W. Miller Award for Student Journalists, (H) 834
David Worthington Scholarship. *See* SEG Scholarship Program, entry (S) 448
Davis Memorial Scholarship. *See* Johnny Davis Memorial Scholarship, entry (S) 272
Dawson Technical Scholarship. *See* TMC/SAE Donald D. Dawson Technical Scholarship, entry (S) 485
DCBMBAA Chapter Undergraduate Scholarship Program, (SS) 578
de Kármán Fellowships. *See* Josephine de Kármán Fellowships, entries (H) 902, (A) 1143
Dean Memorial Legacy Scholarships, (S) 131
DeBenedetti Memorial Scholarship. *See* NMA Undergraduate Scholarships, entry (S) 359

Decommissioning, Decontamination and Reutilization Scholarship, (S) 132
DedARNG Scholarships. *See* Dedicated Army National Guard (DedARNG) Scholarships, entry (A) 1077
Dedicated Army National Guard (DedARNG) Scholarships, (A) 1077
DEED Technical Design Project, (S) 133
Defense of Academic Freedom Award, (SS) 579
Delgreco Jr. Scholarship. *See* SGT Felix Delgreco Jr. Scholarship, entry (A) 1255
Dell'Arte Fellowship. *See* Irene Ryan Acting Scholarships, entry (H) 890
Delmar A. Lienemann, Sr. Scholarship. *See* Nebraska Society of Certified Public Accountants Scholarships, entry (SS) 689
Deloitte National Student Case Study Seminar, (SS) 580
Delta Air Lines NSBE Scholarship. *See* National Society of Black Engineers Scholarship Program, entry (S) 343
Delta Faucet Company Scholarships, (S) 134
Delta Nu Alpha Foundation Scholarships, (SS) 581
Demana–Waits Scholarship. *See* Texas Instruments Demana–Waits Scholarship, entry (S) 481
Demonstration of Energy-Efficient Developments Technical Design Project. *See* DEED Technical Design Project, entry (S) 133
Dendel Scholarships, (H) 835
Dennis Undergraduate Scholarship. *See* Radio and Television News Directors Foundation Presidents' Scholarships, entry (H) 962
Department of Homeland Security Undergraduate Scholarships, (A) 1078
Des Moines Symphony Alliance College/Emerging Professional Division Young Artist Competition, (H) 836
Descendants of the Signers of the Declaration of Independence Scholarships, (A) 1079
Desert Storm Education Fund. *See* USO Desert Storm Education Fund, entry (A) 1297
Detroit Brazing and Soldering Division Scholarship. *See* Robert L. Peaslee–Detroit Brazing and Soldering Division Scholarship, entry (S) 422
Development Disabilities Scholastic Excellence Award for Lutheran Students in College, (S) 135
DiCaprio Scholarship. *See* Dr. Nicholas S. DiCaprio Scholarship, entry (A) 1081
Dick Spader Scholarships. *See* Angus Foundation Scholarships, entry (S) 39
Dietrich Memorial Scholarship. *See* ANS Undergraduate Scholarships, entry (S) 43
Dietrich Scholarship. *See* Law Enforcement Career Scholarship Program, entry (SS) 657
Digital Avionics Technical Committee Scholarships. *See* AIAA Foundation Undergraduate Scholarship Program, entry (S) 17
Dillman Memorial Scholarship. *See* Rudolph Dillman Memorial Scholarship, entries (S) 433, (SS) 730
Direct Marketing Scholarship, (SS) 582, (H) 837
DiSalvo Memorial Scholarship. *See* ANS Undergraduate Scholarships, entry (S) 43
District of Columbia Black MBA Association Chapter Undergraduate Scholarship Program. *See* DCBMBAA Chapter Undergraduate Scholarship Program, entry (SS) 578
Dixon Two-Year College Scholarship. *See* Peggy Dixon Two-Year College Scholarship, entry (S) 383

S–Sciences　　　　　SS–Social Sciences　　　　　H–Humanities　　　　　A–Any Subject Area

D.J. Lovell Scholarship. *See* SPIE Scholarship Program, entry (S) 464
DMI Milk Marketing Scholarships. *See* National Dairy Shrine/DMI Milk Marketing Scholarships, entry (S) 341
Dodson Scholarship. *See* Nathan Taylor Dodson Scholarship, entries (S) 337, (SS) 679, (H) 929
Dodson Scholarship. *See* Tau Beta Pi Undergraduate Scholarships, entry (S) 479
Dog Writers Association of America Juniors Educational Award. *See* DWAA Juniors Educational Award, entry (A) 1084
Dolores E. Fisher Award, (S) 136
Donald D. Dawson Technical Scholarship. *See* TMC/SAE Donald D. Dawson Technical Scholarship, entry (S) 485
Donald F. & Mildred Topp Othmer National Scholarship Awards, (S) 137
Donald G. Willems Scholarship, (S) 138
Donald R. Allen Memorial Scholarship. *See* SEG Scholarship Program, entry (S) 448
Donald W. Fogarty International Student Paper Competition, (SS) 583
Donna Jones Moritsugu Memorial Awards. *See* AAPA Veteran's Caucus Scholarships, entry (S) 3
Donna Nigh Public Service Scholarship. *See* George and Donna Nigh Public Service Scholarship, entry (SS) 609
Donnie Arthur Memorial Turfgrass Scholarship, (S) 139
Doran Scholarship. *See* Robert J. Doran Scholarship, entries (S) 421, (SS) 727
Dore Schary Awards, (H) 838
Dorothy E. Morris Memorial Award for Strings or Harp. *See* Sigma Alpha Iota Scholarships for Undergraduate Performance, entry (H) 980
Dorothy Lemke Howarth Scholarships, (S) 140
Dorothy Miller ASME Auxiliary Scholarships. *See* Frank and Dorothy Miller ASME Auxiliary Scholarships, entry (S) 193
Dorothy P. Morris Scholarship, (S) 141
Doug Underwood Scholarship. *See* IFMA Foundation Scholarships, entry (SS) 631
DPA's Thousand Points of Light Award. *See* Naval Helicopter Association Undergraduate Scholarships, entry (A) 1194
Dr. and Mrs. H.H. Nininger Meteorite Award, (S) 142
Dr. Aurel Zajta Scholarship, (S) 143, (H) 839
Dr. Barbara Irish Violin Award. *See* NFMC Biennial Student Audition Awards, entry (H) 944
Dr. Barbara M. Irish Award. *See* NFMC Biennial Student Audition Awards, entry (H) 944
Dr. Harold S. Wood Award for Excellence, (S) 144
Dr. Joe Utley Award for Artistry. *See* National Trumpet Competition Awards, entry (H) 940
Dr. John C. Yavis Scholarships, (A) 1080
Dr. Kent L. Gardner Scholarships. *See* Order of Omega Scholarships, entry (A) 1227
Dr. Lewis C. Hoffman Scholarship, (S) 145
Dr. Nicholas S. DiCaprio Scholarship, (A) 1081
Dr. Pedro Grau Undergraduate Scholarship. *See* American Meteorological Society Undergraduate Scholarships, entry (S) 32
Dr. Raymond K.J. Luomanen Fund, (S) 146
Dr. Richard Chinn Scholarship, (A) 1082
Dr. Robert W. Sims Memorial Scholarship, (S) 147
Dr. S. Bradley Burson Memorial Scholarship, (S) 148
Dr. William S. Boyd Scholarship, (S) 149
Dracup Memorial Scholarship. *See* Nettie Dracup Memorial Scholarship, entry (S) 352
Dracup Scholarship Award. *See* Joseph F. Dracup Scholarship Award, entry (S) 273
Dramatists Guild Award. *See* National Student Playwriting Award, entry (H) 939
Dratos Memorial Scholarship. *See* El Camino Real District 20 Scholarships, entry (A) 1089
Drew Young Award, (SS) 584
Duggan, Jr. Memorial Education Recognition Award. *See* Morton B. Duggan, Jr. Memorial Education Recognition Award, entry (S) 331
Dumitru Golea Goldy-Gemu Scholarships, (A) 1083
Dutch and Ginger Arver Scholarship, (S) 150
D.W. Simpson & Company Actuarial Science Scholarship, (SS) 585
DWAA Juniors Educational Award, (A) 1084
Dwyer Memorial Scholarship. *See* AAPA Veteran's Caucus Scholarships, entry (S) 3

E. Lanier (Lanny) Finch Scholarship, (H) 840
E. Nelson James Scholarships, (H) 841
E. Ted Sims, Jr. Memorial Scholarship, (S) 151
E. Wayne Kay Co-op Scholarship, (S) 152
E. Wayne Kay Community College Scholarships, (S) 153
E. Wayne Kay Scholarships, (S) 154
Eagles Memorial Foundation Educational Grants for Military and Other Service Personnel, (A) 1085
Earl G. Graves Scholarship, (SS) 586
Earl Walker Scholarship Award. *See* Myrtle and Earl Walker Scholarships, entry (S) 334
Eastman Product Grants. *See* Academy of Television Arts & Sciences College Television Awards, entry (H) 775
E.B. Miller Memorial Scholarship, (S) 155
Eberhart Memorial Awards. *See* National Opera Association Scholarship Division Awards, entry (H) 936
Eberle Vocal Scholarship. *See* Glenn Miller Scholarship Competition, entry (H) 860
E.C. "Pete" Aldridge Scholarship. *See* AIAA Foundation Undergraduate Scholarship Program, entry (S) 17
Ecolab Undergraduate Entrepreneurial Scholarships. *See* Al Schuman Ecolab Undergraduate Entrepreneurial Scholarships, entry (SS) 533
Economos Scholarship. *See* Andrew M. Economos Scholarship, entry (H) 785
Ed Bradley Scholarship, (H) 842
Eddie G. Cole Memorial Scholarships, (S) 156, (SS) 587
Edelman Award. *See* Daniel J. Edelman Award, entry (H) 830
Eden Services Charles H. Hoens, Jr. Scholars Program, (A) 1086
Edie Schmidt NMA Memorial Scholarship. *See* NMA Undergraduate Scholarships, entry (S) 359
Edith Jung Scholarship. *See* Chinese American Citizens Alliance Foundation Scholarships, entry (A) 1060
Edith L. Nilsson Award. *See* Irma and Knute Carlson Award, entry (A) 1130
Edith Renee Hill Memorial Scholarship. *See* Phi Delta Kappa International Scholarship Grants for Prospective Educators, entry (SS) 712

PROGRAM TITLE INDEX

Edna Wilhelmina Snell Nichols Scholarship. *See* Phi Delta Kappa International Scholarship Grants for Prospective Educators, entry (SS) 712
EDSF Board of Directors Scholarships, (SS) 588, (H) 843
EDSF Board of Directors Technical and Community College Scholarship, (SS) 589, (H) 844
Education Achievement Awards, (SS) 590
Education is Power Scholarships, (A) 1087
Educational Foundation College/University Scholarships, (SS) 591
Educational Partnership Program Undergraduate Scholarships, (S) 157
Edward G. Gillooly Journalism Scholarship, (H) 845
Edward J. Milliken Scholarship. *See* Phi Delta Kappa International Scholarship Grants for Prospective Educators, entry (SS) 712
Edwards Scholarship. *See* AAPA Veteran's Caucus Scholarships, entry (S) 3
Edwin W. Gaston, Jr. Scholarships, (A) 1088
Egan Multi-Year Mentoring Scholarship Program. *See* John and Alice Egan Multi-Year Mentoring Scholarship Program, entry (S) 264
Ehrhorn Scholarship. *See* Mensa Member Awards, entry (A) 1167
Eklund Educational Scholarship. *See* Sagebrush Circuit-Lew and JoAnn Eklund Educational Scholarship, entry (S) 439
El Camino Real District 20 Scholarships, (A) 1089
Elaine Ehrhorn Scholarship. *See* Mensa Member Awards, entry (A) 1167
Elaine Louise Lagerstrom Memorial Award. *See* WAMSO Young Artist Competition Awards and Scholarships, entry (H) 1005
Eleanor (Big Mama) Andrews Scholarship. *See* Miss America Competition Awards, entry (A) 1174
Eleanor Sue Scholarship. *See* Chinese American Citizens Alliance Foundation Scholarships, entry (A) 1060
Electronic Document Systems Foundation Board of Directors Scholarships. *See* EDSF Board of Directors Scholarships, entries (SS) 588, (H) 843
Electronic Document Systems Foundation Board of Directors Technical and Community College Scholarship. *See* EDSF Board of Directors Technical and Community College Scholarship, entries (SS) 589, (H) 844
Electronics for Imaging Scholarships, (S) 158
Eli Lilly and Company Corporate Scholarship. *See* National Society of Black Engineers Scholarship Program, entry (S) 343
Elizabeth Lowell Putnam Prize, (S) 159
Elizabeth McLean Memorial Scholarship, (S) 160
Ellen Ruckes Scholarship. *See* Paul and Ellen Ruckes Scholarship, entry (S) 379
Ellis Piano Award. *See* NFMC Biennial Student Audition Awards, entry (H) 944
Ellis Scholarship in Physics. *See* Robert A. Ellis Scholarship in Physics, entry (S) 415
Elmer S. Imes Scholarship in Physics, (S) 161
Elsa and Peter Soderberg Scholarship. *See* Tau Beta Pi Undergraduate Scholarships, entry (S) 479
Emily Lowe Scholarship. *See* W. Eldridge and Emily Lowe Scholarship, entry (H) 1001
Empire State Chapter Scholarship, (S) 162
Engineering Division Scholarships, (S) 163

Engineering in Medicine and Biology Society Student Design Competition Awards, (S) 164
Ennes Scholarship. *See* Harold E. Ennes Scholarship, entry (S) 225
Enright Scholarships. *See* Order of Omega Scholarships, entry (A) 1227
Environmental Educational Scholarship Program, (S) 165
Environmental Professionals' Organization of Connecticut Scholarship Fund. *See* EPOC Scholarship Fund, entry (S) 166
Environmental Sciences Division Scholarship. *See* Charles (Tommy) Thomas Memorial Scholarship, entry (S) 103
Eos #1 Mother Lodge Chapter Scholarship. *See* Daughters of Penelope Undergraduate Scholarships, entry (A) 1075
EPOC Scholarship Fund, (S) 166
Erdlen Scholarship Award. *See* NEHRA Future Stars in HR Scholarships, entry (SS) 691
Ernest F. Hollings Undergraduate Scholarship Program, (S) 167, (SS) 592
Ernie Ayer Aviation Scholarship, (S) 168
Esther Mayo Sherard Scholarship, (S) 169, (SS) 593
Esther Stulberg International String Competition. *See* Julius & Esther Stulberg International String Competition, entry (H) 903
Estopinal CCIM Memorial Scholarship. *See* Stewart Estopinal CCIM Memorial Scholarship, entry (SS) 746
Ethan and Allan Murphy Endowed Memorial Scholarship, (S) 170
Eugene C. Renzi Award for Academic Achievement. *See* Hawaii Chapter AFCEA Scholarships, entry (S) 228
Eunice Fiorito Memorial Scholarship, (A) 1090
Evangelical Press Association Scholarships, (H) 846
Evelyn Appleyard Memorial Award. *See* Polanki College Achievement Awards, entry (A) 1235
Evert Clark/Seth Payne Award for Young Science Journalists, (S) 171, (H) 847
Excel Geophysics Scholarship, (S) 172
Excellence in Filmmaking Award in Honor of Fr. Patrick Peyton, CSC. *See* Angelus Awards, entry (H) 786
Excellence in Sonography Award, (S) 173
Exemption from Tuition Fees for Dependents of Kentucky Veterans, (A) 1091
ExxonMobil Corporation NSBE Scholarships. *See* National Society of Black Engineers Scholarship Program, entry (S) 343

F. Maynard Lipe Scholarship Award, (S) 174
F-MADE Scholarship. *See* SPIE Scholarship Program, entry (S) 464
FAAMA-FEEA Scholarship Program, (A) 1092
Fabricators and Manufacturers Association Foundation College Scholarships, (S) 175
Fabricators and Manufacturers Association Foundation Trade or Technical School Scholarships, (A) 1093
Fairless Scholarships. *See* Association for Iron & Steel Technology Scholarships, entry (S) 63
Family Campers and RVers Scholarships. *See* FCRV Scholarships, entries (S) 177, (A) 1094
Fantini Award. *See* National Trumpet Competition Awards, entry (H) 940

S–Sciences   SS–Social Sciences   H–Humanities   A–Any Subject Area

Far West Athletic Trainers' Association Undergraduate Scholarships, (S) 176
Farnsworth Scholarship. See Philo T. Farnsworth Scholarship, entry (H) 958
Fay Wells Scholarships. See Helen J. Sioussat/Fay Wells Scholarships, entry (H) 873
FCRV Scholarships, (S) 177, (A) 1094
Fearis Scholarship. See Heart of America Golf Course Superintendents Association Scholarships, entry (S) 231
Federal Aviation Administration Managers Association–Federal Employee Education and Assistance Scholarship Program. See FAAMA–FEEA Scholarship Program, entry (A) 1092
Federal Employee Education and Assistance Fund Scholarships, (A) 1095
Federal Employee Education and Assistance Fund–Blacks in Government Scholarship Program, (A) 1096
Federal Employee Education and Assistance Fund–National Treasury Employees Union Scholarships. See FEEA–NTEU Scholarships, entry (A) 1097
Federal Employee Education and Assistance Fund/World Trade Center/Pentagon Fund Scholarships. See FEEA/World Trade Center/Pentagon Fund Scholarships, entry (A) 1098
Federal Land Bank Association of Hawaii Scholarship, (S) 178
Federal Managers Association–Federal Employee Education and Assistance Scholarship Program. See FMA–FEEA Scholarship Program, entry (A) 1102
Federal Planning Division Annual Student Scholarship, (SS) 594
FEEA–NTEU Scholarships, (A) 1097
FEEA/World Trade Center/Pentagon Fund Scholarships, (A) 1098
FEEA/World Trade Center/Pentagon Fund Scholarships. See FEEA/World Trade Center/Pentagon Fund Scholarships, entry (A) 1098
Feindt Scholarship. See Mary Feindt Scholarship, entry (S) 310
Feingold Scholarship. See William J. Feingold Scholarship, entry (S) 514
Felix Delgreco Jr. Scholarship. See SGT Felix Delgreco Jr. Scholarship, entry (A) 1255
Felix Memorial Scholarship. See Robert Felix Memorial Scholarship, entry (S) 420
Fellows Scholarships. See Harold E. Fellows Scholarships, entry (H) 865
FeMET scholarships. See Ferrous Metallurgy Education Today (FeMET) Scholarships, entry (S) 179
Fencl Scholarships. See Warren Fencl Scholarships, entry (A) 1306
Ferrous Metallurgy Education Today (FeMET) Scholarships, (S) 179
Festival of Trees Scholarship Fund, (S) 180
FFTA Scholarship Competition, (H) 848
Fields Scholarship. See Phillip M. Fields Scholarship, entry (S) 389
Fife Scholarship. See Natasha Matson Fife Scholarship, entry (A) 1189
Finch Scholarship. See E. Lanier (Lanny) Finch Scholarship, entry (H) 840
Fini Scholarship. See Air Force Sergeants Association Scholarships, entry (A) 1025
Finnegan Memorial Scholarship. See FORE Undergraduate Merit Scholarships, entries (S) 186, (SS) 598

Fiorito Memorial Scholarship. See Eunice Fiorito Memorial Scholarship, entry (A) 1090
First Lieutenant Michael L. Lewis, Jr. Memorial Fund Scholarship, (A) 1099
Firwood District 22 Scholarships, (A) 1100
Fisher Award. See Dolores E. Fisher Award, entry (S) 136
Fitzmaurice Scholarship. See David J. Fitzmaurice Scholarship, entry (S) 129
Fleming Scholarship. See Cleveland Advertising Association Education Foundation Scholarships, entry (H) 818
Fletcher Scholarship. See AIAA Foundation Undergraduate Scholarship Program, entry (S) 17
Flexible Packaging Industry Scholarship/Internship Program, (S) 181
Flint Group Technical Writing Awards, (S) 182, (H) 849
Florence Turner Karlin Scholarship, (SS) 595
Florida Bankers Educational Foundation Grants, (SS) 596
Florida Public Relations Education Foundation Scholarships. See FPREF Scholarships, entry (H) 851
Floyd Qualls Memorial Scholarships, (A) 1101
FMA–FEEA Scholarship Program, (A) 1102
Fogarty International Student Paper Competition. See Donald W. Fogarty International Student Paper Competition, entry (SS) 583
Foner Scholarship Program for Visual and Performing Arts. See Moe Foner Scholarship Program for Visual and Performing Arts, entry (H) 925
Food Engineering Scholarships Program, (S) 183
Ford Motor Company Business and Leadership Scholarship, (SS) 597
Ford Motor Company Engineering and Leadership Scholarship, (S) 184
Ford Motor Company SWE Scholarships, (S) 185
Ford Truck Scholarship Program, (A) 1103
FORE Diversity Scholarships. See Foundation or Research and Education Diversity Scholarships, entries (S) 190, (SS) 599
FORE Undergraduate Merit Scholarships, (S) 186, (SS) 598
Formula SAE Competition Awards, (S) 187
Forrest Bassford Student Award, (S) 188, (H) 850
Forrest Scholarship. See IFMA Foundation Scholarships, entry (SS) 631
Forrest Scholarship. See SEG Scholarship Program, entry (S) 448
Fortson, Jr. Scholarship. See Ben W. Fortson, Jr. Scholarship, entry (S) 76
Forum for Equal Opportunity Scholarship/Mary Feindt Scholarship. See Mary Feindt Scholarship, entry (S) 310
Forum for Military Applications of Directed Energy Scholarship. See SPIE Scholarship Program, entry (S) 464
Foster Award for Excellence in Public Relations. See Lawrence G. Foster Award for Excellence in Public Relations, entry (H) 909
Foster Violoncello Award. See NFMC Biennial Student Audition Awards, entry (H) 944
Foundation for Neonatal Research and Education Scholarships, (S) 189
Foundation for Technology Education Undergraduate Major in Technology Education Scholarship. See FTE Undergraduate Major in Technology Education Scholarship, entries (S) 195, (SS) 603

S–Sciences   SS–Social Sciences   H–Humanities   A–Any Subject Area

PROGRAM TITLE INDEX

Foundation of Flexographic Technical Association Scholarship Competition. *See* FFTA Scholarship Competition, entry (H) 848

Foundation of Research and Education Undergraduate Merit Scholarships. *See* FORE Undergraduate Merit Scholarships, entries (S) 186, (SS) 598

Foundation or Research and Education Diversity Scholarships, (S) 190, (SS) 599

FPREF Scholarships, (H) 851

Frances A. Mays Scholarship Award, (S) 191, (SS) 600, (H) 852

Frances Webb Scholarship. *See* FMA–FEEA Scholarship Program, entry (A) 1102

Frangos Memorial Scholarship Award. *See* Metropolitan Society of Kardamylians College Awards, entry (A) 1168

Frank and Brennie Morgan Prize, (S) 192

Frank and Dorothy Miller ASME Auxiliary Scholarships, (S) 193

Frank C. Fini Scholarship. *See* Air Force Sergeants Association Scholarships, entry (A) 1025

Frank DeBenedetti Memorial Scholarship. *See* NMA Undergraduate Scholarships, entry (S) 359

Frank L. Greathouse Government Accounting Scholarship, (SS) 601

Frank Rhodes Scholarship. *See* El Camino Real District 20 Scholarships, entry (A) 1089

Frank Scimonelli Award. *See* National Trumpet Competition Awards, entry (H) 940

Franke Family Foundation Scholarship. *See* AREMA Educational Foundation Undergraduate Scholarships, entry (S) 50

Fred Hilterman Scholarship. *See* SEG Scholarship Program, entry (S) 448

Fred Wiesner Educational Excellence Scholarship, (SS) 602

Frederick J. Heringer Honorary Award, (S) 194

Freedom Forum–NCAA Sports Journalism Scholarships, (H) 853

Freedom from Religion Foundation College Essay Contest, (H) 854

Freeman Scholarship. *See* AREMA Educational Foundation Undergraduate Scholarships, entry (S) 50

Freescale Semiconductor NSPE Scholarship. *See* National Society of Black Engineers Scholarship Program, entry (S) 343

Freier Award. *See* College Photographer of the Year, entry (H) 820

French Award. *See* National Student Playwriting Award, entry (H) 939

Friends–in–Art Scholarship, (H) 855

FTE Undergraduate Major in Technology Education Scholarship, (S) 195, (SS) 603

Fuels and Combustion Technologies Division Best Student Paper Award, (S) 196

Fuels and Combustion Technologies Division Scholarships, (S) 197

FujiFilm Audience Impact Award. *See* Angelus Awards, entry (H) 786

Fujimoto Memorial Scholarship. *See* Logan Nainoa Fujimoto Memorial Scholarship, entry (S) 298

Fulfilling the Legacy Scholarships, (S) 198

Fulfilling the Legacy Scholarships. *See* National Society of Black Engineers Scholarship Program, entry (S) 343

Future Entrepreneur of the Year Award, (SS) 604

Future Leaders of Manufacturing Scholarship, (S) 199

G. William Jones Texas Award. *See* Short Film and Video Competition, entry (H) 979

G.A. Mavon Memorial Scholarship, (SS) 605

Gail Wegdon Memorial Scholarship. *See* Far West Athletic Trainers' Association Undergraduate Scholarships, entry (S) 176

Galloway Scholarship. *See* June P. Galloway Scholarship, entries (S) 278, (SS) 650, (H) 904

Gallup Organization/Cornhusker State Games Scholarship Program, (A) 1104

Gamble Memorial Scholarship. *See* FORE Undergraduate Merit Scholarships, entries (S) 186, (SS) 598

Gandy Ink Student Scholarship. *See* Texas Choral Directors Association Student Scholarships, entry (H) 991

Garcia Rail Engineering Scholarship. *See* Michael and Gina Garcia Rail Engineering Scholarship, entry (S) 316

Garden Club of America Zone VI Fellowship in Urban Forestry. *See* GCA Zone VI Fellowship in Urban Forestry, entry (S) 203

Gardner Scholarships. *See* Order of Omega Scholarships, entry (A) 1227

GARMIN International Scholarship, (S) 200

Garrett Morgan Scholarship. *See* COMTO NJ Scholarships, entries (S) 118, (SS) 573

Gary B. Multanen/CM Magazine Scholarship, (S) 201

Gary Millay Memorial Scholarship. *See* Far West Athletic Trainers' Association Undergraduate Scholarships, entry (S) 176

Gaston, Jr. Scholarships. *See* Edwin W. Gaston, Jr. Scholarships, entry (A) 1088

Gaylor Memorial Scholarship. *See* Lowell Gaylor Memorial Scholarship, entry (S) 303

G.B. Gunlogson Student Environmental Design Competition, (S) 202

GCA Zone VI Fellowship in Urban Forestry, (S) 203

GCSAA Legacy Awards, (A) 1105

GCSAA Scholars Competition, (S) 204

GE Lloyd Trotter African American Forum Scholarship. *See* National Society of Black Engineers Scholarship Program, entry (S) 343

Geagan Scholarship Program. *See* John Geagan Scholarship Program, entry (SS) 645

GEF Corporate Leadership Scholarships, (S) 205, (H) 856

GEICO Life Scholarships, (A) 1106

Gene Baker Memorial Scholarship. *See* Aircraft Electronics Association Members Scholarship Program, entry (A) 1028

Gene Swackhamer Ag Economics/Ag Business Grant, (S) 206, (SS) 606

General Electric Fund/League of United Latin American Citizens Scholarships, (S) 207, (SS) 607

General Electric Women's Network Scholarships, (S) 208

General Motors Foundation Undergraduate Scholarships, (S) 209

General Motors Minority Dealers Association Minority Scholarship Program, (A) 1107

General Motors Minority Engineering and Science Scholarship Program, (S) 210

General Motors/League of United Latin American Citizens Scholarships, (S) 211

Genevieve Christen Distinguished Undergraduate Student Award, (S) 212

George A. Nielsen Public Investor Scholarship, (SS) 608

S–Sciences   **SS–Social Sciences**   **H–Humanities**   **A–Any Subject Area**

George and Donna Nigh Public Service Scholarship, (SS) 609
George B. Bryan Award, (H) 857
George Brotsis Memorial Scholarship. *See* El Camino Real District 20 Scholarships, entry (A) 1089
George Chirgotis Scholarship, (A) 1108
George D. Miller Scholarship, (S) 213, (SS) 610
George Graves Scholarship. *See* IFMA Foundation Scholarships, entry (SS) 631
George Kaloudis Memorial Scholarship. *See* Sons of Pericles Undergraduate Scholarships, entry (A) 1263
George Leber Scholarship, (SS) 611, (H) 858
George S. Benton Scholarship. *See* American Meteorological Society Undergraduate Scholarships, entry (S) 32
Georgia Space Grant Consortium Fellowships, (S) 214
Geraldine Clewell Scholarship. *See* Phi Upsilon Scholarships, entry (SS) 713
Geraldine Colby Zeiler Awards, (S) 215
Gilbreth Scholarship. *See* Lillian Moller Gilbreth Scholarship, entry (S) 294
Gillette Scholarships. *See* R.L. Gillette Scholarships, entry (H) 967
Gillooly Journalism Scholarship. *See* Edward G. Gillooly Journalism Scholarship, entry (H) 845
Gina Garcia Rail Engineering Scholarship. *See* Michael and Gina Garcia Rail Engineering Scholarship, entry (S) 316
Ginger Arver Scholarship. *See* Dutch and Ginger Arver Scholarship, entry (S) 150
Givaudan Flavor Corporation Scholarship, (S) 216
Gladys A. and Russell M. Birtwistle Award. *See* Irma and Knute Carlson Award, entry (A) 1130
Gladys C. Anderson Memorial Scholarship, (H) 859
Glamour's Top Ten College Women Competition, (A) 1109
Glenn Miller Scholarship Competition, (H) 860
Global Automotive Aftermarket Symposium Scholarships, (SS) 612
Gloria Murray Memorial Award. *See* National Trumpet Competition Awards, entry (H) 940
Glover Memorial Scholarship. *See* Bud Glover Memorial Scholarship, entry (S) 84
GMBS–Jack Pullan Memorial Vocal Scholarship. *See* Glenn Miller Scholarship Competition, entry (H) 860
GMBS–Ralph Brewster Vocal Scholarship. *See* Glenn Miller Scholarship Competition, entry (H) 860
GMBS–Ray Eberle Vocal Scholarship. *See* Glenn Miller Scholarship Competition, entry (H) 860
Golden Key Engineering/Technology Achievement Awards, (S) 217
Golden Key International Student Leader Awards, (A) 1110
Golden Key Literary Achievement Awards, (H) 861
Golden Outstanding Student Essay in Rhetoric Award. *See* James L. Golden Outstanding Student Essay in Rhetoric Award, entry (H) 895
Golden Torch Awards. *See* National Society of Black Engineers Scholarship Program, entry (S) 343
Goldman, Sachs Scholarships, (S) 218
Goldwater Scholarships. *See* Barry M. Goldwater Scholarships, entry (S) 72
Goldy–Gemu Scholarships. *See* Dumitru Golea Goldy–Gemu Scholarships, entry (A) 1083
Golf Course Superintendents Association of America Legacy Awards. *See* GCSAA Legacy Awards, entry (A) 1105

Golf Course Superintendents Association of America Scholars Competition. *See* GCSAA Scholars Competition, entry (S) 204
Golf Course Superintendents Association of America Student Essay Contest, (S) 219
Golf Course Superintendents Association of America Student Essay Contest. *See* Golf Course Superintendents Association of America Student Essay Contest, entry (S) 219
Good Educational Endowment Awards. *See* Norman and Ruth Good Educational Endowment Awards, entry (A) 1217
Goodman & Company Annual Scholarship, (SS) 613
Goodyear Tire and Rubber Company Scholarships, (A) 1111
Gould Young Composer Awards. *See* Morton Gould Young Composer Awards, entry (H) 926
Governor's Blue Ribbon Livestock Auction Scholarship, (S) 220
GR Technologies Family Award. *See* National Trumpet Competition Awards, entry (H) 940
Grace Woodson Memorial Award. *See* Ima Hogg Young Artist Competition, entry (H) 884
Grams Memorial Award. *See* Freedom from Religion Foundation College Essay Contest, entry (H) 854
Grant M. Mack Memorial Scholarships. *See* NIB Grant M. Mack Memorial Scholarship, entry (SS) 697
Graphic Arts Council of Cleveland Scholarship. *See* PIEF General Scholarships, entry (H) 959
Gratiot Scholarship. *See* California P.E.O. Scholarships, entry (A) 1056
Grau Undergraduate Scholarship. *See* American Meteorological Society Undergraduate Scholarships, entry (S) 32
Graves Scholarship. *See* Earl G. Graves Scholarship, entry (SS) 586
Graves Scholarship. *See* IFMA Foundation Scholarships, entry (SS) 631
Gravure Catalog and Insert Council Scholarship, (S) 221, (H) 862
Greathouse Government Accounting Scholarship. *See* Frank L. Greathouse Government Accounting Scholarship, entry (SS) 601
Green Cross Project Award. *See* AAPA Veteran's Caucus Scholarships, entry (S) 3
Green Scholarship. *See* Non Commissioned Officers Association Scholarship Fund, entry (A) 1216
Greenberg Scholarship. *See* Robert D. Greenberg Scholarship, entry (S) 417
Greenwood Scholarship. *See* William Rucker Greenwood Scholarship, entry (S) 517
Gregoire Youth/Young Adult Award. *See* Christine O. Gregoire Youth/Young Adult Award, entry (A) 1061
Gregory Scholarship. *See* William E. Gregory Scholarship, entries (SS) 766, (H) 1010
Greisch Scholarship. *See* Nebraska Society of Certified Public Accountants Scholarships, entry (SS) 689
GRFD Scholarships. *See* Guaranteed Reserve Forces Duty (GRFD) Scholarships, entry (A) 1112
Gross Memorial Award. *See* Professor Sidney Gross Memorial Award, entry (H) 961
Gruber Scholarships. *See* Kathern F. Gruber Scholarships, entry (A) 1146
Guaranteed Reserve Forces Duty (GRFD) Scholarships, (A) 1112

S–Sciences   **SS–Social Sciences**   **H–Humanities**   **A–Any Subject Area**

PROGRAM TITLE INDEX

Guenther Scholarship. *See* John J. Guenther Scholarship, entry (A) 1138
Guidant Foundation Scholarships, (S) 222
Guilford Undergraduate Research Award. *See* J.P. Guilford Undergraduate Research Awards, entry (SS) 648
Guiliano Mazzetti Scholarships, (S) 223
Guillemette Scholarship. *See* Pierre H. Guillemette Scholarship, entry (S) 391
Guillermo Salazar Rodriguez Scholarship. *See* American Meteorological Society Undergraduate Scholarships, entry (S) 32
Gunlogson Student Environmental Design Competition. *See* G.B. Gunlogson Student Environmental Design Competition, entry (S) 202
G.W. Hohmann Scholarships, (S) 224

Hagemeyer Scholarship. *See* American Meteorological Society Undergraduate Scholarships, entry (S) 32
Hagemeyer Scholarship. *See* Coating and Graphic Arts Division Scholarships, entries (S) 112, (H) 819
Haines Memorial Scholarship, (SS) 614
Haines Memorial Scholarship. *See* J.R. Haines Memorial Scholarship, entry (S) 275
Hall Memorial Scholarship. *See* Phi Chi Theta Scholarships, entry (SS) 711
Hall Star of Tomorrow Award. *See* Chuck Hall Star of Tomorrow Award, entry (A) 1062
Hall/McElwain Merit Scholarships, (A) 1113
Hallmark Graphic Arts Scholarship, (H) 863
Halloran Scholarships. *See* Order of Omega Scholarships, entry (A) 1227
Ham Scholarship. *See* KSEA Scholarships, entry (S) 286
Hamptons International Film Festival Student Awards, (H) 864
Handweavers Guild of America Scholarships. *See* HGA Scholarships, entry (H) 876
Haney, USA (Ret) Award for Leadership. *See* Hawaii Chapter AFCEA Scholarships, entry (S) 228
Hanks, Jr. Scholarship in Meteorology. *See* American Meteorological Society Undergraduate Scholarships, entry (S) 32
Hanly Memorial Scholarship. *See* Law Enforcement Career Scholarship Program, entry (SS) 657
Hansberry Playwriting Award. *See* Lorraine Hansberry Playwriting Award, entry (H) 915
Hansen National Scholarships. *See* Betty Hansen National Scholarships, entry (A) 1050
Hardy B. Abbott Scholarship. *See* Air Force Sergeants Association Scholarships, entry (A) 1025
Harold and Maria Ransburg American Patriot Scholarships, (SS) 615
Harold E. Ennes Scholarship, (S) 225
Harold E. Fellows Scholarships, (H) 865
Harold S. Wood Award for Excellence. *See* Dr. Harold S. Wood Award for Excellence, entry (S) 144
Harriet Irsay Scholarship Grant, (SS) 616, (H) 866
Harriet Robinson Scholarship. *See* Roy & Harriet Robinson Scholarship, entry (SS) 729
Harrison Scholarship. *See* SEG Scholarship Program, entry (S) 448
Harry A. Applegate Scholarship Award, (SS) 617

Harry Barfield KBA Scholarship Program, (H) 867
Harry L. Morrison–Arthur B.C. Walker Scholarships. *See* Willie Hobbs Moore–Harry L. Morrison–Arthur B.C. Walker Scholarships, entry (S) 519
Hartley Lord Scholarship, (S) 226
Harvey Washington Banks Scholarship in Astronomy, (S) 227
Hawaii Chapter AFCEA Scholarships, (S) 228
Hawai'i Hospitality Sales and Marketing Association Scholarships. *See* HHSMA Scholarships, entry (SS) 622
Hawaiian Homes Commission Career and Technical Education Scholarship, (S) 229, (H) 868
Hawthorne Memorial Scholarship. *See* Terrey Hawthorne Memorial Scholarship, entry (S) 480
Hazel Heffner Becchina Award. *See* NFMC Biennial Student Audition Awards, entry (H) 944
Hazlewood Exemption for Dependents of Texas Veterans, (A) 1114
Hazlewood Exemption for Texas Veterans, (A) 1115
Healthcare Information Management Systems Scholarships, (S) 230, (SS) 618
Hear Me Project HIV/AIDS Story Writing Contest, (A) 1116
Hearst Journalism Awards Program Broadcast News Competitions, (H) 869
Hearst Journalism Awards Program Photojournalism Competitions, (H) 870
Hearst Journalism Awards Program Writing Competitions, (H) 871
Heart of America Golf Course Superintendents Association Scholarships, (S) 231
Heartland Scholarship Program, (A) 1117
Heather Joy Memorial Scholarship, (A) 1118
Heck Prize. *See* WAMSO Young Artist Competition Awards and Scholarships, entry (H) 1005
Heet Memorial Scholarship. *See* Sally Heet Memorial Scholarship, entry (H) 973
Heidelberg USA Scholarship, (SS) 619, (H) 872
Heimrich Awards. *See* NFMC Biennial Student Audition Awards, entry (H) 944
Heiser Scholarship. *See* LTG and Mrs. Joseph M. Heiser Scholarship, entry (A) 1156
Helen Abbott Individual Community Service Awards, (A) 1119
Helen D. Snow Memorial Scholarship. *See* Phi Chi Theta Scholarships, entry (SS) 711
Helen D. Thompson Memorial Scholarship. *See* California P.E.O. Scholarships, entry (A) 1056
Helen Hagemeyer Scholarship. *See* American Meteorological Society Undergraduate Scholarships, entry (S) 32
Helen J. Sioussat/Fay Wells Scholarships, (H) 873
Helen T. Cribbins Scholarship. *See* Joseph P. and Helen T. Cribbins Scholarship, entry (S) 274
HELM Leadership Fellows, (A) 1120
Help Desk Scholarship Contest, (S) 232, (SS) 620
Helping Hands Book Scholarship Program, (A) 1121
Henderson Violoncello Award. *See* NFMC Biennial Student Audition Awards, entry (H) 944
Henry and Chiyo Kuwahara Creative Arts Award, (H) 874
Henry Phillips Memorial Scholarship. *See* Clampitt Paper/Henry Phillips Memorial Scholarship, entries (SS) 568, (H) 817
Henry Regnery Endowed Scholarships, (H) 875
Henry Salvatori Scholarship. *See* SEG Scholarship Program, entry (S) 448

S–Sciences   SS–Social Sciences   H–Humanities   A–Any Subject Area

Henry Scholarship. *See* California P.E.O. Scholarships, entry (A) 1056

Henry Scholarship. *See* Virginia P. Henry Scholarship, entry (S) 496

Herbert ASCAP Young Composer Awards. *See* Victor Herbert ASCAP Young Composer Awards, entry (H) 997

Herbert Memorial Undergraduate Scholarship. *See* Richard A. Herbert Memorial Undergraduate Scholarship, entry (S) 409

Heringer Honorary Award. *See* Frederick J. Heringer Honorary Award, entry (S) 194

Herman Lerdal Scholarship, (SS) 621

Hester Memorial Scholarship. *See* Foundation for Neonatal Research and Education Scholarships, entry (S) 189

Hewitt Scholarship. *See* SEG Scholarship Program, entry (S) 448

HGA Scholarships, (H) 876

H.H. Nininger Meteorite Award. *See* Dr. and Mrs. H.H. Nininger Meteorite Award, entry (S) 142

HHSMA Scholarships, (SS) 622

Hickerson, USN (Ret) Award for Academic Achievement. *See* Hawaii Chapter AFCEA Scholarships, entry (S) 228

Higgins Foundation Youth Courage Awards. *See* Colin Higgins Foundation Youth Courage Awards, entry (A) 1069

High Plains Journal/KJLA Scholarship, (H) 877

High Volume Transaction Output Stewardship Award. *See* HVTO Stewardship Award, entries (S) 238, (SS) 627

High Volume Transaction Output Woman of Distinction Award. *See* Woman of Distinction Award, entries (S) 522, (SS) 769

Higher Education and Leadership Ministries Leadership Fellows. *See* HELM Leadership Fellows, entry (A) 1120

Hill, Jr. Leadership Award. *See* A.T. Anderson Memorial Scholarship Program, entry (S) 68

Hill Memorial Fund. *See* Ouida Mundy Hill Memorial Fund, entry (A) 1229

Hill Memorial Scholarship. *See* Phi Delta Kappa International Scholarship Grants for Prospective Educators, entry (SS) 712

Hillquist Honorary SAE Scholarship. *See* Ralph K. Hillquist Honorary SAE Scholarship, entry (S) 403

Hilterman Scholarship. *See* SEG Scholarship Program, entry (S) 448

Hiratsuka Memorial Scholarship. *See* Aiko Susanna Tashiro Hiratsuka Memorial Scholarship, entry (H) 780

Historically Black College Scholarships, (A) 1122

Historically Black Colleges/Universities Scholarship Program, (A) 1123

Hitchcock Fleming Scholarship. *See* Cleveland Advertising Association Education Foundation Scholarships, entry (H) 818

Ho–Chunk Nation Adult Vocational Training Program, (A) 1124

Hoegner Scholarship. *See* Cleveland Advertising Association Education Foundation Scholarships, entry (H) 818

Hoens, Jr. Scholars Program. *See* Eden Services Charles H. Hoens, Jr. Scholars Program, entry (A) 1086

Hoffman Memorial Award for Voice. *See* Sigma Alpha Iota Scholarships for Undergraduate Performance, entry (H) 980

Hoffman Scholarship. *See* Dr. Lewis C. Hoffman Scholarship, entry (S) 145

Hogan Undergraduate Scholarship. *See* Radio and Television News Directors Foundation Presidents' Scholarships, entry (H) 962

Hogg Young Artist Competition. *See* Ima Hogg Young Artist Competition, entry (H) 884

Hohmann Scholarships. *See* G.W. Hohmann Scholarships, entry (S) 224

Holland America Line–Westours, Inc. Scholarships, (SS) 623

Hollings Undergraduate Scholarship Program. *See* Ernest F. Hollings Undergraduate Scholarship Program, entries (S) 167, (SS) 592

Hologgitas, Ph.D. Scholarship. *See* Daughters of Penelope Undergraduate Scholarships, entry (A) 1075

Home Builders Association of Illinois Student of the Year Scholarships, (S) 233, (H) 878

Honeywell Avionics Scholarship, (S) 234

Hong Memorial Scholarship. *See* Chinese American Citizens Alliance Foundation Scholarships, entry (A) 1060

Honolulu Alumnae Panhellenic Association Collegiate Scholarships, (A) 1125

Hood Memorial Scholarship. *See* Rhoda D. Hood Memorial Scholarship, entry (H) 965

Hoods Memorial Scholarship. *See* David Hoods Memorial Scholarship, entries (SS) 577, (H) 831

Hoosier Hampshire Swine Breeders Association Junior Scholarships, (S) 235

Hope Endowed Scholarship in Atmospheric Science. *See* American Meteorological Society Undergraduate Scholarships, entry (S) 32

Hopkins Printing Endowed Scholarship. *See* PIEF General Scholarships, entry (H) 959

Horak Law Enforcement Explorer Memorial Scholarship. *See* Sheryl A. Horak Law Enforcement Explorer Memorial Scholarship, entry (SS) 736

Hospitality Sales and Marketing Association International Scholarship. *See* HSMAI Scholarships, entry (SS) 625

Houston Symphony League Jerry Priest Award. *See* Ima Hogg Young Artist Competition, entry (H) 884

Houtz Memorial Fund Scholarship. *See* Angie M. Houtz Memorial Fund Scholarship, entry (A) 1041

Howard E. Adkins Memorial Scholarship, (S) 236

Howard H. Hanks, Jr. Scholarship in Meteorology. *See* American Meteorological Society Undergraduate Scholarships, entry (S) 32

Howard P. Wackman II Memorial Award, (S) 237

Howard R. Swearer Student Humanitarian Award, (A) 1126

Howard T. Orville Endowed Scholarship in Meteorology. *See* American Meteorological Society Undergraduate Scholarships, entry (S) 32

Howarth Scholarships. *See* Dorothy Lemke Howarth Scholarships, entry (S) 140

HRA–NCA Academic Scholarships, (SS) 624

HSMAI Scholarships, (SS) 625

Huan Lin Cheng Memorial Scholarship. *See* Chinese American Citizens Alliance Foundation Scholarships, entry (A) 1060

Hubert B. Owens Scholarships. *See* B. Phinizy Spalding and Hubert B. Owens Scholarships, entry (H) 798

Human Resource Association of the National Capital Area Academic Scholarships. *See* HRA–NCA Academic Scholarships, entry (SS) 624

Humane Studies Fellowships, (SS) 626, (H) 879

Huntington National Bank Scholarship. *See* Cleveland Advertising Association Education Foundation Scholarships, entry (H) 818

HVTO Stewardship Award, (S) 238, (SS) 627

PROGRAM TITLE INDEX

Hyundai Scholarships. See KSEA Scholarships, entry (S) 286

Iacobellis Scholarship. See AIAA Foundation Undergraduate Scholarship Program, entry (S) 17
IADR/Unilever Hatton Awards Competition, (S) 239
Iager Dairy Scholarship, (S) 240
IAHPERD Scholarships, (S) 241, (SS) 628, (H) 880
IAM Scholarship Competition, (A) 1127
IBM Corporation SWE Scholarships, (S) 242
Idaho Society of Certified Public Accountants Scholarships, (SS) 629
IDDBA Scholarship, (S) 243, (SS) 630, (H) 881
I.F. Stone Award for Student Journalism. See Nation Institute/I.F. Stone Award for Student Journalism, entry (H) 930
IFDA Educational Foundation Student Scholarship, (H) 882
IFMA Foundation Scholarships, (SS) 631
IHA Student Design Competition, (H) 883
Illinois Association for Health, Physical Education, Recreation and Dance Scholarships. See IAHPERD Scholarships, entries (S) 241, (SS) 628, (H) 880
Illinois Chapter ASHRAE Scholarship, (S) 244
Illinois Pork Donor–Advised Fund Scholarships, (S) 245
Illinois Pork Producers Association Scholarships. See Illinois Pork Donor–Advised Fund Scholarships, entry (S) 245
Illinois Tool Works Welding Companies Scholarship. See ITW Welding Companies Scholarship, entry (S) 252
Ima Hogg Young Artist Competition, (H) 884
IMA Memorial Education Fund Scholarships, (SS) 632
Imes Scholarship in Physics. See Elmer S. Imes Scholarship in Physics, entry (S) 161
INCE Student Paper Prize Competition, (S) 246
Indiana Broadcasters Association College Scholarships, (H) 885
Indiana Professional Chapter of SPJ Diversity in Journalism Scholarship, (H) 886
Ingrassia Memorial Scholarship. See Phi Delta Kappa International Scholarship Grants for Prospective Educators, entry (SS) 712
Ingrassia Scholarship. See Sal Ingrassia Scholarship, entry (A) 1247
Innis Maggiore Scholarship. See Cleveland Advertising Association Education Foundation Scholarships, entry (H) 818
Inspiration for Tomorrow Scholarship. See 50th Anniversary–Inspiration for Tomorrow Scholarship, entry (S) 527
Institute of Food Technologists College Scholarships, (S) 247
Institute of Food Technologists 50th Anniversary–Inspiration for Tomorrow Scholarship. See 50th Anniversary–Inspiration for Tomorrow Scholarship, entry (S) 527
Institute of Management Accountants Memorial Education Fund Scholarships. See IMA Memorial Education Fund Scholarships, entry (SS) 632
Institute of Management Accountants National Student Video Case Competition, (SS) 633
Institute of Noise Control Engineering Student Paper Prize Competition. See INCE Student Paper Prize Competition, entry (S) 246

Insurance Scholarship Foundation of America College Scholarship. See ISFA College Scholarships, entry (SS) 635
Integrity Graphics Communications Scholarship Awards, (H) 887
Intelligent Transportation Systems Washington/Women's Transportation Seminar Scholarship. See ITS Washington/WTS Scholarship, entries (S) 251, (SS) 636
International Association for Dental Research/Unilever Hatton Awards Competition. See IADR/Unilever Hatton Awards Competition, entry (S) 239
International Association of Lighting Designers Scholarships, (H) 888
International Association of Machinists and Aerospace Workers Scholarship Competition. See IAM Scholarship Competition, entry (A) 1127
International Communications Industries Foundation AV Scholarships, (S) 248, (H) 889
International Congress on Insect Neurochemistry and Neurophysiology Student Recognition Award in Insect Physiology, Biochemistry, Toxicology, and Molecular Biology, (S) 249
International Dairy–Deli–Bakery Association Scholarship. See IDDBA Scholarship, entries (S) 243, (SS) 630, (H) 881
International Facilities Management Association Foundation Scholarships. See IFMA Foundation Scholarships, entry (SS) 631
International Furnishings and Design Association Educational Foundation Student Scholarship. See IFDA Educational Foundation Student Scholarship, entry (H) 882
International Future Energy Challenge Student Competition, (S) 250
International Housewares Association Student Design Competition. See IHA Student Design Competition, entry (H) 883
International Public Management Association for Human Resources Scholarship, (SS) 634, (A) 1128
International Society for Optical Engineering Scholarship Program. See SPIE Scholarship Program, entry (S) 464
International Trumpet Guild Award for Artistic Excellence. See National Trumpet Competition Awards, entry (H) 940
Inyong Ham Scholarship. See KSEA Scholarships, entry (S) 286
Iowa United Methodist Church Scholarships, (A) 1129
IPPA Scholarships. See Illinois Pork Donor–Advised Fund Scholarships, entry (S) 245
Irene Frangos Memorial Scholarship Award. See Metropolitan Society of Kardamylians College Awards, entry (A) 1168
Irene Meyer Memorial Scholarship. See Phi Chi Theta Scholarships, entry (SS) 711
Irene Ryan Acting Scholarships, (H) 890
Irene S. Muir Award. See NFMC Biennial Student Audition Awards, entry (H) 944
Irene T. Powers Scholarship. See John J. and Irene T. Powers Scholarship, entry (S) 268
Iris Chang Memorial Essay Contest, (H) 891
Irish Award. See NFMC Biennial Student Audition Awards, entry (H) 944
Irish Viola Award. See Wendell Irish Viola Awards, entry (H) 1007
Irish Violin Award. See NFMC Biennial Student Audition Awards, entry (H) 944
Irma and Knute Carlson Award, (A) 1130

S–Sciences   SS–Social Sciences   H–Humanities   A–Any Subject Area

Irsay Scholarship Grant. *See* Harriet Irsay Scholarship Grant, entries (SS) 616, (H) 866
Irving R. Dana III Scholarship. *See* Nebraska Society of Certified Public Accountants Scholarships, entry (SS) 689
Irwin Friend of Higher Education Award. *See* David M. Irwin Friend of Higher Education Award, entry (A) 1076
Isaac Roth Newscarrier Scholarships, (A) 1131
ISFA College Scholarships, (SS) 635
ITG Award for Artistic Excellence. *See* National Trumpet Competition Awards, entry (H) 940
ITS Washington/WTS Scholarship, (S) 251, (SS) 636
ITW Welding Companies Scholarship, (S) 252
Ivory Memorial Scholarships. *See* AAPA Veteran's Caucus Scholarships, entry (S) 3

J. Clifford Dietrich Scholarship. *See* Law Enforcement Career Scholarship Program, entry (SS) 657
J. Edmunds Miller Scholarship. *See* Nebraska Society of Certified Public Accountants Scholarships, entry (SS) 689
J. Fielding Reed Scholarship, (S) 253
J. Neel Reid Prize, (H) 892
Jack Pullan Memorial Vocal Scholarship. *See* Glenn Miller Scholarship Competition, entry (H) 860
Jackson Memorial Scholarship. *See* Paul Jackson Memorial Scholarship, entry (S) 380
Jackson Scholarship Program. *See* Jesse Jackson Scholarship Program, entry (A) 1135
Jackson/Parks Future Teacher Scholarship. *See* Applegate/Jackson/Parks Future Teacher Scholarship, entry (SS) 543
Jakel Memorial Award. *See* Freedom from Religion Foundation College Essay Contest, entry (H) 854
James A. Turner, Jr. Memorial Scholarship, (SS) 637
James B. Carey Scholarships, (A) 1132
James F. Reville Scholarship, (S) 254
James H. Loper Jr. Memorial Scholarship. *See* NDPRB Undergraduate Scholarship Program, entries (S) 349, (SS) 686
James H. Patremos Memorial Scholarship, (H) 893
James J. Wychor Scholarships, (H) 894
James L. Allhands Essay Competition, (S) 255
James L. Golden Outstanding Student Essay in Rhetoric Award, (H) 895
James McCulla Undergraduate Scholarship. *See* Radio and Television News Directors Foundation Presidents' Scholarships, entry (H) 962
James Panousis Memorial Scholarship. *See* El Camino Real District 20 Scholarships, entry (A) 1089
James R. Greisch Scholarship. *See* Nebraska Society of Certified Public Accountants Scholarships, entry (SS) 689
James R. Vogt Radiochemistry Scholarship, (S) 256
James Scholarships. *See* E. Nelson James Scholarships, entry (H) 841
James W. Lovell Scholarships. *See* Major James W. Lovell Scholarships, entry (SS) 664
Jane M. Klausman Women in Business Scholarships, (SS) 638
Janet Dziadulewicz Branden Memorial Award. *See* Polanki College Achievement Awards, entry (A) 1235
Janice Clarkson Cleworth Award. *See* NFMC Biennial Student Audition Awards, entry (H) 944

Jay Woodward Scholarships, (S) 257
J.C. and Rheba Cobb Memorial Scholarship, (S) 258
Je Hyun Kim Scholarship. *See* KSEA Scholarships, entry (S) 286
Jean C. Osajda Fund, (SS) 639
Jean D. Franke Family Foundation Scholarship. *See* AREMA Educational Foundation Undergraduate Scholarships, entry (S) 50
Jean Kennedy Smith Playwriting Award, (H) 896
Jean Sibelius Memorial Fund, (H) 897
Jean W. Gratiot Scholarship. *See* California P.E.O. Scholarships, entry (A) 1056
Jeanne E. Bray Memorial Scholarship, (A) 1133
Jene and Marvin Hewitt Scholarship. *See* SEG Scholarship Program, entry (S) 448
Jenneman Memorial Scholarship. *See* Brian Jenneman Memorial Scholarship, entry (S) 83
Jennings Scholarship. *See* Paul Jennings Scholarship, entry (A) 1231
Jenny Lind Competition for Sopranos. *See* Barnum Festival Foundation/Jenny Lind Competition for Sopranos, entry (H) 799
Jeremiah Scholarship. *See* Mensa Member Awards, entry (A) 1167
Jerry Hoegner Scholarship. *See* Cleveland Advertising Association Education Foundation Scholarships, entry (H) 818
Jerry Lloyd Memorial Scholarship. *See* Far West Athletic Trainers' Association Undergraduate Scholarships, entry (S) 176
Jerry Priest Award. *See* Ima Hogg Young Artist Competition, entry (H) 884
Jerry Rhea/Atlanta Falcons Undergraduate Scholarship Award, (S) 259
Jesse Brown Memorial Youth Scholarship Program, (A) 1134
Jesse Jackson Scholarship Program, (A) 1135
Jessie and Sharon Edwards Scholarship. *See* AAPA Veteran's Caucus Scholarships, entry (S) 3
Jewell L. Taylor National Fellowships, (SS) 640
J.F. Schirmer Scholarship, (A) 1136
Jill S. Tietjen Scholarship, (S) 260
Jim and Ruth Harrison Scholarship. *See* SEG Scholarship Program, entry (S) 448
Jim Byron Undergraduate Scholarship. *See* Radio and Television News Directors Foundation Presidents' Scholarships, entry (H) 962
Jim Cook Honorary Scholarship. *See* Aircraft Electronics Association Members Scholarship Program, entry (A) 1028
Jim Hickerson, USN (Ret) Award for Academic Achievement. *See* Hawaii Chapter AFCEA Scholarships, entry (S) 228
Jimmy A. Young Memorial Education Recognition Award, (S) 261
Jimmy Gamble Memorial Scholarship. *See* FORE Undergraduate Merit Scholarships, entries (S) 186, (SS) 598
Jo Anne J. Trow Undergraduate Scholarships, (A) 1137
JoAnn Eklund Educational Scholarship. *See* Sagebrush Circuit–Lew and JoAnn Eklund Educational Scholarship, entry (S) 439
JoAnne Robinson Memorial Scholarship, (H) 898
Joanne V. Hologgitas, Ph.D. Scholarship. *See* Daughters of Penelope Undergraduate Scholarships, entry (A) 1075
Joe Perdue Scholarships, (SS) 641

S–Sciences   SS–Social Sciences   H–Humanities   A–Any Subject Area

PROGRAM TITLE INDEX

Joe Utley Award for Artistry. See National Trumpet Competition Awards, entry (H) 940
Joel Polsky Academic Achievement Award, (H) 899
Johanna Drew Cluney Fund, (S) 262
John A. Lopiano Scholarship, (S) 263, (SS) 642
John and Alice Egan Multi-Year Mentoring Scholarship Program, (S) 264
John and Anne Clifton Scholarship Fund. See Clifton Scholarship Fund, entry (A) 1066
John C. Bajus Scholarship, (S) 265
John C. Yavis Scholarships. See Dr. John C. Yavis Scholarships, entry (A) 1080
John Cauble Short Play Award, (H) 900
John Charles Wilson Scholarships, (S) 266, (SS) 643
John Culver Wooddy Scholarships, (SS) 644
John D. Erdlen Scholarship Award. See NEHRA Future Stars in HR Scholarships, entry (SS) 691
John Dratos Memorial Scholarship. See El Camino Real District 20 Scholarships, entry (A) 1089
John Geagan Scholarship Program, (SS) 645
John H. Wiechman Memorial Scholarship, (S) 267
John Hays Hanly Memorial Scholarship. See Law Enforcement Career Scholarship Program, entry (SS) 657
John Hogan Undergraduate Scholarship. See Radio and Television News Directors Foundation Presidents' Scholarships, entry (H) 962
John J. and Irene T. Powers Scholarship, (S) 268
John J. Cunningham Scholarship. See AREMA Educational Foundation Undergraduate Scholarships, entry (S) 50
John J. Guenther Scholarship, (A) 1138
John J. McKetta Undergraduate Scholarship, (S) 269
John Katsimatides Memorial Scholarship. See Sons of Pericles Undergraduate Scholarships, entry (A) 1263
John Kelly Labor Studies Scholarship Fund, (SS) 646
John L. and Sarah G. Merriam Scholarship, (S) 270
John M. Chambers Statistical Software Award, (S) 271
John M. Dwyer Memorial Scholarship. See AAPA Veteran's Caucus Scholarships, entry (S) 3
John N. Sturdivant Family Scholarships, (A) 1139
John R. Hope Endowed Scholarship in Atmospheric Science. See American Meteorological Society Undergraduate Scholarships, entry (S) 32
John R. Lamarsh Memorial Scholarship. See ANS Undergraduate Scholarships, entry (S) 43
John Salisbury Undergraduate Scholarship. See Radio and Television News Directors Foundation Presidents' Scholarships, entry (H) 962
John Schwartz Scholarship, (H) 901
Johnny Davis Memorial Scholarship, (S) 272
Johnson & Johnson NSBE Corporate Scholarship Program. See National Society of Black Engineers Scholarship Program, entry (S) 343
Johnson Strings Awards. See NFMC Biennial Student Audition Awards, entry (H) 944
Jones Memorial Fine Arts Scholarship. See California P.E.O. Scholarships, entry (A) 1056
Jones Texas Award. See Short Film and Video Competition, entry (H) 979
Jordan Memorial Scholarship. See Barbara Jordan Memorial Scholarship, entry (SS) 557
Josef Kaspar Awards. See NFMC Biennial Student Audition Awards, entry (H) 944

Joseph and Ruby Schaff/Schaff Angus Ranch Scholarship, (A) 1140
Joseph F. Bracone Memorial Scholarship, (A) 1141
Joseph F. Dracup Scholarship Award, (S) 273
Joseph M. Heiser Scholarship. See LTG and Mrs. Joseph M. Heiser Scholarship, entry (A) 1156
Joseph P. and Helen T. Cribbins Scholarship, (S) 274
Joseph R. Dietrich Memorial Scholarship. See ANS Undergraduate Scholarships, entry (S) 43
Joseph R. Stone Scholarships, (A) 1142
Josephine de Kármán Fellowships, (H) 902, (A) 1143
Josephine Trott Strings Award. See NFMC Biennial Student Audition Awards, entry (H) 944
Journalism Education Association Future Teacher Scholarship, (SS) 647
Joy Memorial Scholarship. See Heather Joy Memorial Scholarship, entry (A) 1118
J.P. Guilford Undergraduate Research Awards, (SS) 648
J.R. Haines Memorial Scholarship, (S) 275
Judith Cary Memorial Scholarship, (SS) 649
Judith Resnik Memorial Scholarship, (S) 276
Julia Child Endowment Fund Scholarship. See Culinary Trust Scholarships, entry (H) 827
Julia Child Fund at the Boston Foundation Scholarship. See Culinary Trust Scholarships, entry (H) 827
Julia LeBlond Memorial Undergraduate Scholarships. See FORE Undergraduate Merit Scholarships, entries (S) 186, (SS) 598
Julian and Eleanor Sue Scholarship. See Chinese American Citizens Alliance Foundation Scholarships, entry (A) 1060
Julie P. Microutsicos Scholarship.. See Daughters of Penelope Citrus District 2 Scholarships, entry (A) 1074
Julie Vande Velde Leadership Scholarship, (S) 277
Julie Y. Cross Scholarship. See Law Enforcement Career Scholarship Program, entry (SS) 657
Julius & Esther Stulberg International String Competition, (H) 903
June P. Galloway Scholarship, (S) 278, (SS) 650, (H) 904
Jung Memorial Scholarship. See Chinese American Citizens Alliance Foundation Scholarships, entry (A) 1060
Jung Scholarship. See Chinese American Citizens Alliance Foundation Scholarships, entry (A) 1060
Junior Gold Championships, (A) 1144

Kaloudis Memorial Scholarship. See Sons of Pericles Undergraduate Scholarships, entry (A) 1263
Kane Undergraduate Scholarship. See Bill Kane Undergraduate Scholarship, entries (S) 79, (SS) 559
Kanin Playwriting Awards Program. See National Student Playwriting Award, entry (H) 939
Kansas Educational Benefits for Dependents of POWs/KIAs/MIAs of the Vietnam War, (A) 1145
Kaplan Award. See Morton Gould Young Composer Awards, entry (H) 926
Karlin Scholarship. See Florence Turner Karlin Scholarship, entry (SS) 595
Kashiwahara Scholarship. See Ken Kashiwahara Scholarship, entry (A) 906
Kaspar Awards. See NFMC Biennial Student Audition Awards, entry (H) 944

S–Sciences   SS–Social Sciences   H–Humanities   A–Any Subject Area

Kathern F. Gruber Scholarships, (A) 1146
Kathryn D. Sullivan Science and Engineering Fellowship, (S) 279
Kathy LeTarte Scholarship. See New Horizons Kathy LeTarte Scholarship, entry (SS) 693
Katsimatides Memorial Scholarship. See Sons of Pericles Undergraduate Scholarships, entry (A) 1263
Kaufman Women's Scholarships. See Lucile B. Kaufman Women's Scholarships, entry (S) 304
Kay Co-op Scholarship Awards. See E. Wayne Kay Co-op Scholarship, entry (S) 152
Kay Community College Scholarships. See E. Wayne Kay Community College Scholarships, entry (S) 153
Kay Scholarships. See E. Wayne Kay Scholarships, entry (S) 154
KBA Scholarship Program. See Harry Barfield KBA Scholarship Program, entry (H) 867
KCACTF Musical Theater Award, (H) 905
Keating Feature Writing Competition. See Thomas R. Keating Feature Writing Competition, entry (H) 993
Keck Scholarship. See California P.E.O. Scholarships, entry (A) 1056
Keith Awards. See NFMC Biennial Student Audition Awards, entry (H) 944
Keith Payne Memorial Scholarship, (SS) 651
Kellie Cannon Memorial Scholarship, (S) 280
Kelly Labor Studies Scholarship Fund. See John Kelly Labor Studies Scholarship Fund, entry (SS) 646
Kemper Scholars Grant Program, (SS) 652
Ken Kashiwahara Scholarship, (H) 906
Ken Wiedking, USN (Ret) Award for Community Service. See Hawaii Chapter AFCEA Scholarships, entry (S) 228
Kennedy Center American College Theater Festival Musical Theater Award. See KCACTF Musical Theater Award, entry (H) 905
Kennedy Center American College Theater Festival Ten-Minute Play Festival Award, (H) 907
Kenneth Andrew Roe Scholarship, (S) 281
Kent L. Gardner Scholarships. See Order of Omega Scholarships, entry (A) 1227
Kentucky Broadcasters Association Scholarship Program. See Harry Barfield KBA Scholarship Program, entry (H) 867
Kentucky Deceased or Disabled Law Enforcement Officer and Fire Fighter Dependent Tuition Waiver, (A) 1147
Kentucky Horse Council Scholarships, (S) 282
Kentucky Society of Certified Public Accountants College Scholarships, (SS) 653
Kentucky Space Grant Consortium Undergraduate Scholarships, (S) 283
Kentucky Turfgrass Council Legacy Scholarship, (A) 1148
Kentucky Veterans Tuition Waiver Program, (A) 1149
Keppra Family Epilepsy Scholarship Program, (A) 1150
Kevin Child Scholarship, (A) 1151
Key Memorial Scholarship. See FORE Undergraduate Merit Scholarships, entries (S) 186, (SS) 598
Kidger Memorial Scholarship. See Michael Kidger Memorial Scholarship, entry (S) 317
Kim Scholarship. See KSEA Scholarships, entry (S) 286
Kingsley Colton Award. See Irene Ryan Acting Scholarships, entry (H) 890
Kintner Scholarship. See Phi Upsilon Scholarships, entry (SS) 713

Kirsten R. Lorentzen Award, (S) 284
Klausman Women in Business Scholarships. See Jane M. Klausman Women in Business Scholarships, entry (SS) 638
Klein Playwriting Award. See Marc A. Klein Playwriting Award, entry (H) 919
Klobus Scholarship. See Air Force Sergeants Association Scholarships, entry (A) 1025
Klucken Scholarship. See Ralph A. Klucken Scholarship, entry (S) 402
Klussendorf Association Scholarship, (S) 285
Knute Carlson Award. See Irma and Knute Carlson Award, entry (A) 1130
Kokenes, USMC (Ret) Scholarship. See El Camino Real District 20 Scholarships, entry (A) 1089
Koop Undergraduate Scholarship. See Radio and Television News Directors Foundation Presidents' Scholarships, entry (H) 962
Korean-American Scientists and Engineers Association Scholarships. See KSEA Scholarships, entry (S) 286
Korf Memorial Fund Scholarships. See Association for Iron & Steel Technology Scholarships, entry (S) 63
Kottis Family Scholarship. See Daughters of Penelope Undergraduate Scholarships, entry (A) 1075
Kounaris Scholarship. See AHEPA District Scholarship Awards, entry (A) 1018
Kreitzberg Endowed Scholarship. See American Meteorological Society Undergraduate Scholarships, entry (S) 32
Krenzer Reentry Scholarship. See B.K. Krenzer Reentry Scholarship, entry (S) 80
Kris M. Kunze Memorial Scholarship. See Tri State Surveying and Photogrammetry Kris M. Kunze Memorial Scholarship, entry (SS) 753
KSEA Scholarships, (S) 286
Kunze Memorial Scholarship. See Tri State Surveying and Photogrammetry Kris M. Kunze Memorial Scholarship, entry (SS) 753
Kuwahara Creative Arts Award. See Henry and Chiyo Kuwahara Creative Arts Award, entry (H) 874

L. Einar and Edith L. Nilsson Award. See Irma and Knute Carlson Award, entry (A) 1130
L. Gordon Bittle Memorial Scholarships, (SS) 654
L-3 Avionics Systems Scholarship, (S) 287
Lacy Memorial Scholarship. See ANS Undergraduate Scholarships, entry (S) 43
Lagerstrom Memorial Award. See WAMSO Young Artist Competition Awards and Scholarships, entry (H) 1005
Lai Scholarship. See Chinese American Citizens Alliance Foundation Scholarships, entry (A) 1060
LaMacchia Family Scholarship, (SS) 655
Lamarsh Memorial Scholarship. See ANS Undergraduate Scholarships, entry (S) 43
Lambe Fellowships. See Humane Studies Fellowships, entries (SS) 626, (H) 879
Landmark Graphics Scholarship. See SEG Scholarship Program, entry (S) 448
Landscape Educational Advancement Foundation Scholarships. See LEAF Scholarships, entry (S) 290
Lanny Finch Scholarship. See E. Lanier (Lanny) Finch Scholarship, entry (H) 840

S-Sciences   SS-Social Sciences   H-Humanities   A-Any Subject Area

PROGRAM TITLE INDEX

Larry Strickland Leadership Award and Scholarship, (A) 1152
Larry Wilson Scholarship for Environmental Studies, (S) 288
Lars Naerland Scholarship, (SS) 656
Larson Award. See Oscar and Mildred Larson Award, entry (A) 1228
Larson Memorial Scholarship. See Evangelical Press Association Scholarships, entry (H) 846
Laser Technology, Engineering and Applications Scholarship. See SPIE Scholarship Program, entry (S) 464
Lasley Scholarship Competition. See Mary Graham Lasley Scholarship Competition, entry (H) 921
Latina/Latino Playwriting Award, (H) 908
Laughlin Foundation Trust Scholarships. See Wallace S. and Wilma K. Laughlin Foundation Trust Scholarships, entry (SS) 763
Laurie Mitchell and Company Scholarship. See Cleveland Advertising Association Education Foundation Scholarships, entry (H) 818
Law Enforcement Career Scholarship Program, (SS) 657
Lawrence Foster Violoncello Award. See NFMC Biennial Student Audition Awards, entry (H) 944
Lawrence G. Foster Award for Excellence in Public Relations, (H) 909
Lawrence, MD Education Recognition Award. See Robert M. Lawrence, MD Education Recognition Award, entry (S) 423
Lawrence R. Campbell Research Award, (H) 910
Lawson Criminal Justice Scholarship. See Marc Lawson Criminal Justice Scholarship, entry (SS) 665
LCPA Education Foundation Scholarship Program, (SS) 658
Lead and Enhance the Accounting Profession Scholarships. See LEAP Scholarships, entry (SS) 659
Leading Edge Student Design Competition, (S) 289, (H) 911
LEAF Scholarships, (S) 290
LEAP Scholarships, (SS) 659
Leber Scholarship. See George Leber Scholarship, entries (SS) 611, (H) 858
LeBlond Memorial Undergraduate Scholarships. See FORE Undergraduate Merit Scholarships, entries (S) 186, (SS) 598
Lee Forrest Scholarship. See IFMA Foundation Scholarships, entry (SS) 631
Lee Tarbox Memorial Scholarship, (S) 291
Legal Assistants Section Scholarships, (SS) 660
Legislative Incentive for Future Excellence (LIFE) Scholarship Program, (A) 1153
Leo Kaplan Award. See Morton Gould Young Composer Awards, entry (H) 926
Leonard M. Perryman Communications Scholarship for Ethnic Minority Students, (H) 912
Leonard R. Brice Undergraduate Leadership Award, (SS) 661
Lerdal Scholarship. See Herman Lerdal Scholarship, entry (SS) 621
LeRoy Apker Award, (S) 292
Leroy E. Record Scholarships. See Tau Beta Pi Undergraduate Scholarships, entry (S) 479
Lester F. Richardson Memorial Scholarship. See Phi Chi Theta Scholarships, entry (SS) 711
LeTarte Scholarship. See New Horizons Kathy LeTarte Scholarship, entry (SS) 693
Lew and JoAnn Eklund Educational Scholarship. See Sagebrush Circuit–Lew and JoAnn Eklund Educational Scholarship, entry (S) 439

Lewis C. Hoffman Scholarship. See Dr. Lewis C. Hoffman Scholarship, entry (S) 145
Lewis, Jr. Memorial Fund Scholarship. See First Lieutenant Michael L. Lewis, Jr. Memorial Fund Scholarship, entry (A) 1099
Lewis R. Rosser Scholarship. See COMTO NJ Scholarships, entries (S) 118, (SS) 573
Liberty Leadership Fund Academic Scholarship, (S) 293
Lienemann, Sr. Scholarship. See Nebraska Society of Certified Public Accountants Scholarships, entry (SS) 689
Life Members' Scholarship, (A) 1154
Lillian Moller Gilbreth Scholarship, (S) 294
Lilly Poetry Fellowships. See Ruth Lilly Poetry Fellowships, entry (H) 972
Lincoln Memorial Scholarship. See Association for Iron & Steel Technology Scholarships, entry (S) 63
Lind Competition for Sopranos. See Barnum Festival Foundation/Jenny Lind Competition for Sopranos, entry (H) 799
Linda Craig Memorial Scholarships, (S) 295
Linda Jones Memorial Fine Arts Scholarship. See California P.E.O. Scholarships, entry (A) 1056
Linda Simmons Educational Scholarship, (H) 913
Liner Memorial Scholarship. See ANS Undergraduate Scholarships, entry (S) 43
Lipe Scholarship Award. See F. Maynard Lipe Scholarship Award, entry (S) 174
Liquid Propulsion Technical Committee Scholarship. See AIAA Foundation Undergraduate Scholarship Program, entry (S) 17
Livingston Cadet Scholarship. See Clara E. Livingston Cadet Scholarship, entry (A) 1065
Livingston Scholarships. See Robert L. Livingston Scholarships, entry (A) 1244
L.L. Waters Scholarship Program, (S) 296, (SS) 662
Lloyd Memorial Scholarship. See Far West Athletic Trainers' Association Undergraduate Scholarships, entry (S) 176
Lockheed Martin Aeronautics Company Scholarships, (S) 297
Lockheed Martin NSBE Corporate Scholarship Program. See National Society of Black Engineers Scholarship Program, entry (S) 343
Logan Nainoa Fujimoto Memorial Scholarship, (S) 298
Long Memorial Scholarships. See AAPA Veteran's Caucus Scholarships, entry (S) 3
Lookadoo Award. See College Photographer of the Year, entry (H) 820
Loper Memorial Jr. Scholarship. See NDPRB Undergraduate Scholarship Program, entries (S) 349, (SS) 686
Lopiano Scholarship. See John A. Lopiano Scholarship, entries (S) 263, (SS) 642
Lord Acton Essay Competition, (H) 914
Lord Scholarship. See Hartley Lord Scholarship, entry (S) 226
Loren W. Crow Memorial Scholarship, (S) 299
Lorentzen Award. See Kirsten R. Lorentzen Award, entry (S) 284
Lorraine Hansberry Playwriting Award, (H) 915
Lou and Carole Prato Sports Reporting Scholarship, (H) 916
Lou Wolf Memorial Scholarship, (S) 300
Louis J. Bianco Memorial Scholarship. See Quality Assurance Division Scholarships, entry (S) 401
Louise L. Henderson Violoncello Award. See NFMC Biennial Student Audition Awards, entry (H) 944

S–Sciences   SS–Social Sciences   H–Humanities   A–Any Subject Area

Louise Moritz Molitoris Leadership Award, (S) 301, (SS) 663
Louise Oberne Strings Awards. *See* NFMC Biennial Student Audition Awards, entry (H) 944
Louisiana Agricultural Consultants Association Scholarships, (S) 302
Louisiana Veterans State Aid Program, (A) 1155
Lovell Scholarship. *See* SPIE Scholarship Program, entry (S) 464
Lovell Scholarships. *See* Major James W. Lovell Scholarships, entry (SS) 664
Lowe College Scholarships. *See* Rita Lowe College Scholarships, entries (S) 412, (SS) 723
Lowe Scholarship. *See* W. Eldridge and Emily Lowe Scholarship, entry (H) 1001
Lowell Gaylor Memorial Scholarship, (S) 303
L.S. "Skip" Fletcher Scholarship. *See* AIAA Foundation Undergraduate Scholarship Program, entry (S) 17
Lt. Col. William L. Kokenes, USMC (Ret) Scholarship. *See* El Camino Real District 20 Scholarships, entry (A) 1089
LTG and Mrs. Joseph M. Heiser Scholarship, (A) 1156
LTG Thomas M. Rienzi, USA (Ret) Award for Academic Achievement. *See* Hawaii Chapter AFCEA Scholarships, entry (S) 228
Luciano Goicochea Award. *See* Association of Cuban Engineers Scholarships, entry (S) 65
Lucile B. Kaufman Women's Scholarships, (S) 304
Lucille Heimrich Awards. *See* NFMC Biennial Student Audition Awards, entry (H) 944
Lucretia Spears Scholarship. *See* FORE Undergraduate Merit Scholarships, entries (S) 186, (SS) 598
Luomanen Fund. *See* Dr. Raymond K.J. Luomanen Fund, entry (S) 146
Lydia I. Pickup Memorial Scholarship, (S) 305
Lynn Freeman Olson Composition Award, (H) 917

M. Blaha Medical Grant, (S) 306
M. Josephine O'Neal Arts Award, (H) 918
MacCurrach Scholarship. *See* GCSAA Scholars Competition, entry (S) 204
MacDonald Scholarship. *See* Bertha MacDonald Scholarship, entry (H) 802
Mack Memorial Scholarships. *See* NIB Grant M. Mack Memorial Scholarship, entry (SS) 697
Mackey Scholarship. *See* California P.E.O. Scholarships, entry (A) 1056
Mackey–Althouse Voice Award. *See* NFMC Biennial Student Audition Awards, entry (H) 944
Maggiore Scholarship. *See* Cleveland Advertising Association Education Foundation Scholarships, entry (H) 818
Magnuson Scholarship. *See* Nebraska Society of Certified Public Accountants Scholarships, entry (SS) 689
Maine Tuition Waiver Program for Children and Spouses of Fire Fighters, Law Enforcement Officers, and Emergency Medical Services Personnel Killed in the Line of Duty, (A) 1157
Maine Tuition Waiver Program for Foster Children Under the Custody of the Department of Human Services, (A) 1158
Maine Veterans Dependents Educational Benefits, (A) 1159

The Maintenance Council/Society of Automotive Engineers Donald D. Dawson Technical Scholarship. *See* TMC/SAE Donald D. Dawson Technical Scholarship, entry (S) 485
Maj Gen Rockly Triantafellu, USAF (Ret) Award for Academic. *See* Hawaii Chapter AFCEA Scholarships, entry (S) 228
Major James W. Lovell Scholarships, (SS) 664
Major Jessie and Sharon Edwards Scholarship. *See* AAPA Veteran's Caucus Scholarships, entry (S) 3
Make A Statement Scholarship Contest, (A) 1160
Maller Baroque Instrument Award. *See* National Trumpet Competition Awards, entry (H) 940
Mann Scholarship. *See* David Mann Scholarship, entry (S) 130
Marc A. Klein Playwriting Award, (H) 919
Marc Lawson Criminal Justice Scholarship, (SS) 665
Marcus Thomas Scholarship. *See* Cleveland Advertising Association Education Foundation Scholarships, entry (H) 818
Margaret McLeod Memorial Scholarship. *See* Stuart Cameron and Margaret McLeod Memorial Scholarship, entry (SS) 747
Margaronis Scholarship. *See* AHEPA District Scholarship Awards, entry (A) 1018
Maria Ransburg American Patriot Scholarships. *See* Harold and Maria Ransburg American Patriot Scholarships, entry (SS) 615
Marie Morrisey Keith Awards. *See* NFMC Biennial Student Audition Awards, entry (H) 944
Marine Corps Counterintelligence Association Scholarships, (A) 1161
Marine Corps League Scholarships, (A) 1162
Marine Technology Society Student Scholarships. *See* MTS Student Scholarships, entry (S) 332
Marion Fund. *See* Stanley W. Marion Fund, entry (A) 1272
Marjorie M. McDonald P.E.O. Scholarship. *See* California P.E.O. Scholarships, entry (A) 1056
Mark Twain Comedy Acting Awards. *See* Irene Ryan Acting Scholarships, entry (H) 890
Mark Twain Comedy Playwriting Award, (H) 920
Marliave Scholar Award, (S) 307
Marlin R. Scarborough Memorial Scholarship, (A) 1163
Marsh Scholarship, (A) 1164
Marshall Memorial Scholarship. *See* FORE Undergraduate Merit Scholarships, entries (S) 186, (SS) 598
Martin Barnes Scholarships, (A) 1165
Martin L. Stout Scholarship, (S) 308
Martin Scholarship. *See* Eden Services Charles H. Hoens, Jr. Scholars Program, entry (A) 1086
Martin Smilo Undergraduate Scholarship, (S) 309
Marvin Hewitt Scholarship. *See* SEG Scholarship Program, entry (S) 448
Mary Ann Starring Memorial Award for Piano. *See* Sigma Alpha Iota Scholarships for Undergraduate Performance, entry (H) 980
Mary Ann Starring Memorial Award for Woodwinds or Brass. *See* Sigma Alpha Iota Scholarships for Undergraduate Performance, entry (H) 980
Mary Barraco Scholarship. *See* Non Commissioned Officers Association Scholarship Fund, entry (A) 1216
Mary Feindt Scholarship, (S) 310
Mary Feindt Scholarship. *See* Mary Feindt Scholarship, entry (S) 310
Mary Graham Lasley Scholarship Competition, (H) 921

S–Sciences   SS–Social Sciences   H–Humanities   A–Any Subject Area

PROGRAM TITLE INDEX

Mary M. Verges Scholarship. *See* Daughters of Penelope Undergraduate Scholarships, entry (A) 1075
Mary P. Oenslager Scholastic Achievement Awards, (A) 1166
Mary V. Munger Memorial Scholarship, (S) 311
Mary Winston Smail Memorial Scholarship. *See* WAMSO Young Artist Competition Awards and Scholarships, entry (H) 1005
Maryland Association for Health, Physical Education, Recreation and Dance Undergraduate Scholarships, (SS) 666
Masonic–Range Science Scholarship, (S) 312
Mathilda Heck Prize. *See* WAMSO Young Artist Competition Awards and Scholarships, entry (H) 1005
Mathis Scholarship for Environmental Studies. *See* Randall Mathis Scholarship for Environmental Studies, entry (S) 405
Matthew Hester Memorial Scholarship. *See* Foundation for Neonatal Research and Education Scholarships, entry (S) 189
Maud Berggren Scholarship, (SS) 667
Mavon Memorial Scholarship. *See* G.A. Mavon Memorial Scholarship, entry (SS) 605
Mayfield Scholarship. *See* Alpha Corrine Mayfield Scholarship, entry (H) 782
Mayo Student Scholarship. *See* Charles D. Mayo Student Scholarship, entry (H) 813
Mays Scholarship Award. *See* Frances A. Mays Scholarship Award, entries (S) 191, (SS) 600, (H) 852
Mazzetti Scholarships. *See* Guiliano Mazzetti Scholarships, entry (S) 223
McAfee Scholarship in Space Physics. *See* Walter Samuel McAfee Scholarship in Space Physics, entry (S) 501
McBride Scholarship. *See* Barbara McBride Scholarship, entry (S) 70
McCormick and Company Endowment Scholarship, (S) 313
McCulla Undergraduate Scholarship. *See* Radio and Television News Directors Foundation Presidents' Scholarships, entry (H) 962
McDermott Fellowship for Traveling Studies in Architecture, (H) 922
McDonnell Memorial Scholarship. *See* Cady McDonnell Memorial Scholarship, entry (S) 87
McDowell Scholarship Awards. *See* Bodie McDowell Scholarship Awards, entry (H) 804
McKetta Undergraduate Scholarship. *See* John J. McKetta Undergraduate Scholarship, entry (S) 269
McLean Memorial Scholarship. *See* Elizabeth McLean Memorial Scholarship, entry (S) 160
McLeod Memorial Scholarship. *See* Stuart Cameron and Margaret McLeod Memorial Scholarship, entry (SS) 747
McNair Scholarship in Space and Optical Physics. *See* Ronald E. McNair Scholarship in Space and Optical Physics, entry (S) 430
McNaughton Community Service Award. *See* Stanley O. McNaughton Community Service Award, entry (A) 1271
Meadows Natural Resource Scholarships. *See* Ben Meadows Natural Resource Scholarships, entry (S) 75
Medtronic Emergency Response Systems Academic Scholarship, (S) 314
Meisinger, Sr. Memorial Learn to Fly Scholarship. *See* Dan L. Meisinger, Sr. Memorial Learn to Fly Scholarship, entry (S) 127

Meissner Family Fund Scholarship. *See* Phi Delta Kappa International Scholarship Grants for Prospective Educators, entry (SS) 712
Mel Larson Memorial Scholarship. *See* Evangelical Press Association Scholarships, entry (H) 846
Melton Scholarship. *See* Phi Delta Kappa International Scholarship Grants for Prospective Educators, entry (SS) 712
Mendenhall Award. *See* GCSAA Scholars Competition, entry (S) 204
Mendenhall Scholarship. *See* Heart of America Golf Course Superintendents Association Scholarships, entry (S) 231
Mensa Member Awards, (A) 1167
Merck Undergraduate Science Research Scholarships. *See* UNCF/Merck Undergraduate Science Research Scholarships, entry (S) 491
Meridith Thoms Memorial Scholarships, (S) 315
Merk Scholarship. *See* Mensa Member Awards, entry (A) 1167
Merriam Scholarship. *See* John L. and Sarah G. Merriam Scholarship, entry (S) 270
Merv Aubespin Scholarship. *See* Copy Editing Scholarships, entry (H) 824
Merwin Student Scholarship. *See* Richard E. Merwin Student Scholarship, entry (S) 410
Metro New York Chapter Undergraduate Scholarship Award, (SS) 668
Metropolitan Opera National Council Auditions, (H) 923
Metropolitan Society of Kardamylians College Awards, (A) 1168
Meyer Memorial Scholarship. *See* Phi Chi Theta Scholarships, entry (SS) 711
Michael and Gina Garcia Rail Engineering Scholarship, (S) 316
Michael Forrest Scholarship. *See* SEG Scholarship Program, entry (S) 448
Michael Frangos and Irene Frangos Memorial Scholarship Award. *See* Metropolitan Society of Kardamylians College Awards, entry (A) 1168
Michael Kanin Playwriting Awards Program. *See* National Student Playwriting Award, entry (H) 939
Michael Kidger Memorial Scholarship, (S) 317
Michael L. Lewis, Jr. Memorial Fund Scholarship. *See* First Lieutenant Michael L. Lewis, Jr. Memorial Fund Scholarship, entry (A) 1099
Michael P. Anderson Scholarship in Space Science, (S) 318
Michael W. and Jean D. Franke Family Foundation Scholarship. *See* AREMA Educational Foundation Undergraduate Scholarships, entry (S) 50
Michigan Children of Veterans Tuition Grants, (A) 1169
Michigan Veterans Trust Fund Tuition Grants. *See* Michigan Children of Veterans Tuition Grants, entry (A) 1169
Microsoft Corporation NSBE Scholarships. *See* National Society of Black Engineers Scholarship Program, entry (S) 343
Microsoft Corporation Scholarships, (S) 319
Microsoft National Scholarships, (S) 320
Microutsicos Scholarship.. *See* Daughters of Penelope Citrus District 2 Scholarships, entry (A) 1074
Mid–Continent Instrument Scholarship, (S) 321
Mike Shinn Distinguished Member of the Year Awards. *See* National Society of Black Engineers Scholarship Program, entry (S) 343

S–Sciences   SS–Social Sciences   H–Humanities   A–Any Subject Area

Mildred Larson Award. *See* Oscar and Mildred Larson Award, entry (A) 1228
Mildred Topp Othmer National Scholarship Awards. *See* Donald F. & Mildred Topp Othmer National Scholarship Awards, entry (S) 137
Military Officers Association of America Base/Post Scholarship. *See* MOAA Base/Post Scholarships, entry (A) 1180
Military Order of the Purple Heart Scholarship Program, (A) 1170
Military Tuition Waiver During Assignment After Texas, (A) 1171
Millay Memorial Scholarship. *See* Far West Athletic Trainers' Association Undergraduate Scholarships, entry (S) 176
Miller ASME Auxiliary Scholarships. *See* Frank and Dorothy Miller ASME Auxiliary Scholarships, entry (S) 193
Miller Award for Student Journalists. *See* David W. Miller Award for Student Journalists, entry (H) 834
Miller Memorial Scholarship. *See* E.B. Miller Memorial Scholarship, entry (S) 155
Miller Scholarship Competition. *See* Glenn Miller Scholarship Competition, entry (H) 860
Miller Scholarship. *See* George D. Miller Scholarship, entries (S) 213, (SS) 610
Miller Scholarship. *See* Nebraska Society of Certified Public Accountants Scholarships, entry (SS) 689
Milliken Scholarship. *See* Phi Delta Kappa International Scholarship Grants for Prospective Educators, entry (SS) 712
Milton Freier Award. *See* College Photographer of the Year, entry (H) 820
Milton Weintraub Scholarship Fund, (A) 1172
Mineral and Metallurgical Processing Division Scholarship, (S) 322
Minnesota Business Educators Award for Business Education Teaching Majors, (SS) 669
Minnesota Chapter WTS Scholarships, (S) 323, (SS) 670
Minnesota Pro Chapter of the Society of Professional Journalists Scholarship, (H) 924
Minorities in Government Finance Scholarship, (SS) 671
Minority Affairs Committee Award for Outstanding Scholastic Achievement, (S) 324
Minority Community College Transfer Scholarships, (A) 1173
Minority Scholarship Award in Physical Therapy, (S) 325
Miss America Competition Awards, (A) 1174
Miss Black America, (A) 1175
Miss Indian USA Scholarship Program, (A) 1176
Miss Latina World, (A) 1177
Miss Teen USA, (A) 1178
Miss USA, (A) 1179
Missouri Angus Auxiliary Ambassador Program, (S) 326
Missouri Angus Auxiliary Queen Program, (S) 327
Missouri Educators of Family and Consumer Sciences Scholarships. *See* MoEFACS Scholarships, entry (SS) 674
Missouri Soil and Water Conservation Society Scholarships, (S) 328, (SS) 672
Missouri Travel Council Scholarship, (SS) 673
Miszkowicz Memorial Scholarship. *See* Susan Miszkowicz Memorial Scholarship, entry (S) 475
Mittler Memorial Scholarship. *See* Quality Assurance Division Scholarships, entry (S) 401
MOAA Base/Post Scholarships, (A) 1180

Mobil Delvac Scholarship, (S) 329
Moe Foner Scholarship Program for Visual and Performing Arts, (H) 925
MoEFACS Scholarships, (SS) 674
Moichi Okazaki Scholarship. *See* Mr. and Mrs. Moichi Okazaki Scholarship, entry (A) 1184
Mole–Richardson Award for Production Design. *See* Angelus Awards, entry (H) 786
Molitoris Leadership Award. *See* Louise Moritz Molitoris Leadership Award, entries (S) 301, (SS) 663
Montgomery GI Bill (Active Duty), (A) 1181
Montgomery GI Bill (Selected Reserve), (A) 1182
Montgomery GI Bill Tuition Assistance Top–Up, (A) 1183
Moore Memorial Education Foundation Scholarship. *See* Nolan Moore Memorial Education Foundation Scholarship, entries (SS) 698, (H) 945
Moore–Harry L. Morrison–Arthur B.C. Walker Scholarships. *See* Willie Hobbs Moore–Harry L. Morrison–Arthur B.C. Walker Scholarships, entry (S) 519
Moran Scholarships. *See* Susan G. Moran Scholarships, entry (H) 990
Morgan Prize. *See* Frank and Brennie Morgan Prize, entry (S) 192
Morgan Scholarship. *See* COMTO NJ Scholarships, entries (S) 118, (SS) 573
Moritsugu Memorial Awards. *See* AAPA Veteran's Caucus Scholarships, entry (S) 3
Moritsugu Memorial Scholarship. *See* AAPA Veteran's Caucus Scholarships, entry (S) 3
Morris K. Udall Scholarships, (S) 330, (SS) 675
Morris Memorial Award for Strings or Harp. *See* Sigma Alpha Iota Scholarships for Undergraduate Performance, entry (H) 980
Morris Scholarship. *See* Dorothy P. Morris Scholarship, entry (S) 141
Morris Student Research Award. *See* Charles R. Morris Student Research Award, entry (S) 102
Morrison–Arthur B.C. Walker Scholarships. *See* Willie Hobbs Moore–Harry L. Morrison–Arthur B.C. Walker Scholarships, entry (S) 519
Morton B. Duggan, Jr. Memorial Education Recognition Award, (S) 331
Morton Gould Young Composer Awards, (H) 926
Mower Memorial Scholarship. *See* Barbara Alice Mower Memorial Scholarship, entry (SS) 556
Mr. and Mrs. Moichi Okazaki Scholarship, (A) 1184
Mr. Collegiate African American Scholarship Program, (A) 1185
Mrs. Edgar Tobin Award. *See* Metropolitan Opera National Council Auditions, entry (H) 923
Mrs. H.H. Nininger Meteorite Award. *See* Dr. and Mrs. H.H. Nininger Meteorite Award, entry (S) 142
Mrs. Joseph M. Heiser Scholarship. *See* LTG and Mrs. Joseph M. Heiser Scholarship, entry (A) 1156
Msgr. Alphonse S. Popek Memorial Award. *See* Polanki College Achievement Awards, entry (A) 1235
MTS Student Scholarships, (S) 332
Muir Award. *See* NFMC Biennial Student Audition Awards, entry (H) 944
Multanen/CM Magazine Scholarship. *See* Gary B. Multanen/CM Magazine Scholarship, entry (S) 201
Munger Memorial Scholarship. *See* Mary V. Munger Memorial Scholarship, entry (S) 311

S–Sciences   SS–Social Sciences   H–Humanities   A–Any Subject Area

PROGRAM TITLE INDEX 441

Munsell Memorial Scholarship. See Richard G. Munsell Memorial Scholarship, entry (SS) 720
Murphy Endowed Memorial Scholarship. See Ethan and Allan Murphy Endowed Memorial Scholarship, entry (S) 170
Murray Memorial Award. See National Trumpet Competition Awards, entry (H) 940
Music Therapy Scholarship, (S) 333, (H) 927
Myers Scholarship. See Rogers Family Scholarship, entry (S) 428
Myers Scholarship. See Russell W. Myers Scholarship, entry (S) 434
Myrtle and Earl Walker Scholarships, (S) 334

NACA Regional Council Student Leader Scholarships, (A) 1186
Naerland Scholarship. See Lars Naerland Scholarship, entry (SS) 656
Nagel Scholarship. See Tau Beta Pi Undergraduate Scholarships, entry (S) 479
NAIW Award of Excellence, (SS) 676
Najoom Music Products Award. See National Trumpet Competition Awards, entry (H) 940
Nakos Scholarship. See AHEPA District Scholarship Awards, entry (A) 1018
Nam Sook and Je Hyun Kim Scholarship. See KSEA Scholarships, entry (S) 286
Nancie Rideout–Robertson Internship Scholarship, (A) 1187
Nancy Curry Scholarship, (S) 335, (SS) 677
Nancy J. Stara Scholarship. See Nebraska Society of Certified Public Accountants Scholarships, entry (SS) 689
Nancy Reagan Pathfinder Scholarships, (A) 1188
Naomi Berber Memorial Scholarship, (SS) 678, (H) 928
Naomi L. Satterfield Scholarship. See Phi Chi Theta Scholarships, entry (SS) 711
NATA Undergraduate Scholarships, (S) 336
Natasha Matson Fife Scholarship, (A) 1189
Nathalie A. Price Memorial Scholarship, (A) 1190
Nathan Taylor Dodson Scholarship, (S) 337, (SS) 679, (H) 929
Nation Institute/I.F. Stone Award for Student Journalism, (H) 930
National Academy of Sports Medicine Scholarship, (S) 338
National Ad 2 Student Creative Competition, (H) 931
National Association for Campus Activities Regional Council Student Leader Scholarships. See NACA Regional Council Student Leader Scholarships, entry (A) 1186
National Association of Insurance Women Award of Excellence. See NAIW Award of Excellence, entry (SS) 676
National Association of Insurance Women College Scholarship, (SS) 680
National Association of Negro Musicians Scholarship Contest, (H) 932
National Athletic Trainers' Association Undergraduate Scholarships. See NATA Undergraduate Scholarships, entry (S) 336
National Aviation Explorer Scholarships, (S) 339
National Beef Ambassador Program, (S) 340
National Black MBA Association Undergraduate Scholarship Program, (SS) 681
National Chopin Piano Competition, (H) 933
National Civilian Community Corps. See AmeriCorps National Civilian Community Corps, entry (A) 1040

National Collegiate Athletic Association Sports Journalism Scholarships. See Freedom Forum–NCAA Sports Journalism Scholarships, entry (H) 853
National Commission for Cooperative Education Scholarships. See NCCE Scholarships, entries (S) 347, (A) 1200
National Community Pharmacists Association Foundation Presidential Scholarships. See NCPA Foundation Presidential Scholarships, entry (S) 348
National Dairy Promotion and Research Board Undergraduate Scholarship Program. See NDPRB Undergraduate Scholarship Program, entries (S) 349, (SS) 686
National Dairy Shrine/DMI Milk Marketing Scholarships, (S) 341
National Defense Transportation Association Academic Scholarship Program A. See NDTA Academic Scholarship Program A, entries (S) 350, (SS) 687
National Environmental Health Association/American Academy of Sanitarians Scholarships. See NEHA/AAS Scholarships, entry (S) 351
National Federation of Independent Business Young Entrepreneur Plan for the Future Competition. See NFIB Young Entrepreneur Plan for the Future Competition, entry (SS) 696
National Federation of Music Clubs Biennial Student Auditions Awards. See NFMC Biennial Student Audition Awards, entry (H) 944
National FFA Scholarships for Undergraduates in the Humanities, (H) 934
National FFA Scholarships for Undergraduates in the Sciences, (S) 342
National FFA Scholarships for Undergraduates in the Social Sciences, (SS) 682
National Guard Association of New Jersey Scholarship Program, (A) 1191
National Hispanic Coalition of Federal Aviation Employees–Federal Employee Education and Assistance Scholarship Program. See NHCFAE–FEEA Scholarship Program, entry (A) 1212
National Huguenot Society Scholarships, (A) 1192
National Industries for the Blind Grant M. Mack Memorial Scholarships. See NIB Grant M. Mack Memorial Scholarship, entry (SS) 697
National Junior Angus Association Scholarship. See CAB/NJAA Scholarship, entry (S) 86
National Make It Yourself with Wool Contest, (H) 935
National Meat Association Undergraduate Scholarships. See NMA Undergraduate Scholarships, entry (S) 359
National Opera Association Scholarship Division Awards, (H) 936
National Pathfinder Scholarship. See Nancy Reagan Pathfinder Scholarships, entry (A) 1188
National Presidential Undergraduate Scholarships of AAHPERD. See Ruth Abernathy Undergraduate Presidential Scholarship, entries (S) 435, (SS) 731, (H) 970
National Restaurant Association Academic Scholarships for Undergraduate Students, (SS) 683
National Scholastic Surfing Association National Scholarship Program. See NSSA National Scholarship Program, entry (A) 1221
National Society of Black Engineers Alumni Extension Technical Scholarships. See National Society of Black Engineers Scholarship Program, entry (S) 343

S–Sciences   SS–Social Sciences   H–Humanities   A–Any Subject Area

National Society of Black Engineers Fellows Scholarship Program. *See* National Society of Black Engineers Scholarship Program, entry (S) 343

National Society of Black Engineers Scholarship Program, (S) 343

National Society of Black Physicists Undergraduate Scholarship Award, (S) 344

National Society of Newspaper Columnists Scholarship Contest, (H) 937

National Society of Professional Surveyors Board of Governors Scholarship. *See* NSPS Board of Governors Scholarship, entry (S) 362

National Society of Professional Surveyors Forum for Equal Opportunity Scholarship/Mary Feindt Scholarship. *See* Mary Feindt Scholarship, entry (S) 310

National Society of Professional Surveyors Scholarships. *See* NSPS Scholarships, entry (S) 363

National Student Advertising Competition, (H) 938

National Student Playwriting Award, (H) 939

National Tour Association Scholarship, (SS) 684

National Tour Association State and Provincial Scholarship. *See* NTA State and Provincial Scholarship, entry (SS) 702

National Treasury Employees Union Scholarships. *See* FEEA–NTEU Scholarships, entry (A) 1097

National Trumpet Competition Awards, (H) 940

National Trumpet Competition Young Artist Endowment Award. *See* National Trumpet Competition Awards, entry (H) 940

National 4th Infantry (IVY) Division Association Scholarship, (A) 1193

Nau Scholarship. *See* California P.E.O. Scholarships, entry (A) 1056

Navajo Nation Teacher Education Program, (SS) 685

Naval Association of Physician Assistants Scholarship. *See* AAPA Veteran's Caucus Scholarships, entry (S) 3

Naval Helicopter Association Undergraduate Scholarships, (A) 1194

Naval Special Warfare Scholarships for Spouses and Children, (A) 1195

Navy College Assistance/Student Headstart (Navy–CASH) Program, (S) 345

Navy Counselor Association Educational Scholarship Fund, (A) 1196

Navy Nurse Candidate Program, (S) 346

Navy–Marine Corps ROTC College Program, (A) 1197

Navy–Marine Corps ROTC 2–Year Scholarships, (A) 1198

NCAA Sports Journalism Scholarships. *See* Freedom Forum–NCAA Sports Journalism Scholarships, entry (H) 853

NCAIAW Scholarship, (A) 1199

NCCE Scholarships, (S) 347, (A) 1200

NCPA Foundation Presidential Scholarships, (S) 348

NDPRB Undergraduate Scholarship Program, (S) 349, (SS) 686

NDTA Academic Scholarship Program A, (S) 350, (SS) 687

Nebraska Bankers Educational Foundation Scholarships, (SS) 688

Nebraska Society of Certified Public Accountants Scholarships, (SS) 689

Nebraska Space Grant Statewide Scholarship Competition, (A) 1201

Nebraska Waiver of Tuition for Veterans' Dependents, (A) 1202

NEEBC Scholarship Program, (SS) 690

NEHA/AAS Scholarships, (S) 351

NEHRA Future Stars in HR Scholarships, (SS) 691

Nell Bryant Robinson Scholarship. *See* Phi Upsilon Scholarships, entry (SS) 713

Nettie Dracup Memorial Scholarship, (S) 352

Network of Executive Women Scholarship, (SS) 692

Neumann Memorial Award. *See* Ima Hogg Young Artist Competition, entry (H) 884

Neuroscience Nursing Foundation Regular Scholarships, (S) 353

Neusom Scholarships. *See* Thomas G. Neusom Scholarships, entry (S) 482

NEV–ATA/Alert Scholarship. *See* Far West Athletic Trainers' Association Undergraduate Scholarships, entry (S) 176

Nevada Athletic Trainers Association/Alert Scholarship. *See* Far West Athletic Trainers' Association Undergraduate Scholarships, entry (S) 176

Nevada Space Grant Consortium Undergraduate Scholarship Program, (S) 354

New England Employee Benefits Council Scholarship Program. *See* NEEBC Scholarship Program, entry (SS) 690

New Hampshire Golf Course Superintendents Association Scholarship, (S) 355

New Horizons Kathy LeTarte Scholarship, (SS) 693

New Jersey POW/MIA Tuition Benefit Program, (A) 1203

New Jersey Public Tuition Benefits Program. *See* New Jersey Survivor Tuition Benefits Program, entry (A) 1204

New Jersey Society of Certified Public Accountants College Scholarship Program, (SS) 694

New Jersey Survivor Tuition Benefits Program, (A) 1204

New Jersey World Trade Center Scholarship Fund, (A) 1205

New Mexico Broadcasters Association Scholarships, (H) 941

New Mexico Competitive Scholarships, (A) 1206

New Mexico Lottery Success Scholarships, (A) 1207

New Mexico Professional Surveyors Scholarships, (S) 356

New Mexico Vietnam Veterans Scholarships, (A) 1208

New Mexico 3 Percent Scholarship Program, (A) 1209

New Student Prize Competition. *See* Peter K. New Student Prize Competition, entries (S) 385, (SS) 710

New York Beef Producers' Association Scholarship, (S) 357, (SS) 695, (H) 942

New York Metropolitan Chapter Scholarship Fund, (A) 1210

New York Section Scholarships, (S) 358

New York State World Trade Center Memorial Scholarships, (A) 1211

New York Water Environment Association Scholarships. *See* NYWEA Scholarships, entry (S) 365

Newspaper Copy Editing Program for College Juniors, Seniors and Graduate Students, (H) 943

Next Century of Flight Scholarships. *See* AIAA Foundation Undergraduate Scholarship Program, entry (S) 17

NFIB Young Entrepreneur Plan for the Future Competition, (SS) 696

NFMC Biennial Student Audition Awards, (H) 944

NHCFAE–FEEA Scholarship Program, (A) 1212

NIB Grant M. Mack Memorial Scholarship, (SS) 697

Nicholas C. Vrataric Scholarship Awards Program, (A) 1213

Nicholas Kounaris Scholarship. *See* AHEPA District Scholarship Awards, entry (A) 1018

Nicholas S. DiCaprio Scholarship. *See* Dr. Nicholas S. DiCaprio Scholarship, entry (A) 1081

Nichols Scholarship. *See* Phi Delta Kappa International Scholarship Grants for Prospective Educators, entry (SS) 712

S–Sciences   SS–Social Sciences   H–Humanities   A–Any Subject Area

PROGRAM TITLE INDEX

Nick Cost Scholarships, (A) 1214
Nick Vrenios Memorial Award. *See* National Opera Association Scholarship Division Awards, entry (H) 936
Nielsen Public Investor Scholarship. *See* George A. Nielsen Public Investor Scholarship, entry (SS) 608
Nigh Public Service Scholarship. *See* George and Donna Nigh Public Service Scholarship, entry (SS) 609
Nilsson Award. *See* Irma and Knute Carlson Award, entry (A) 1130
Nininger Meteorite Award. *See* Dr. and Mrs. H.H. Nininger Meteorite Award, entry (S) 142
Nitsos Scholarships, (A) 1215
NMA Undergraduate Scholarships, (S) 359
Noel Betancourt Award. *See* Association of Cuban Engineers Scholarships, entry (S) 65
Nolan Moore Memorial Education Foundation Scholarship, (SS) 698, (H) 945
Nolle Scholarships. *See* Alfred H. Nolle Scholarships, entry (A) 1033
Non Commissioned Officers Association Scholarship Fund, (A) 1216
Nonwovens Division Scholarship, (S) 360
Norman and Ruth Good Educational Endowment Awards, (A) 1217
North Carolina Association of Intercollegiate Athletics for Women Scholarship. *See* NCAIAW Scholarship, entry (A) 1199
North Carolina CPA Foundation Outstanding Minority Accounting Student Scholarships, (SS) 699
North Carolina CPA Foundation Scholarships, (SS) 700
North Carolina Legislative Tuition Grants, (A) 1218
North Carolina Scholarships for Children of War Veterans, (A) 1219
North Carolina Space Grant Consortium Undergraduate Scholarships, (S) 361
North Carolina Teacher Assistant Scholarship Fund, (SS) 701
North Dakota Educational Assistance for Dependents of Veterans, (A) 1220
Northeast Human Resources Association Future Stars in HR Scholarships. *See* NEHRA Future Stars in HR Scholarships, entry (SS) 691
Northrop Grumman NSBE Scholarships. *See* National Society of Black Engineers Scholarship Program, entry (S) 343
Nortrak–AREMA Presidents Scholarship. *See* AREMA Educational Foundation Undergraduate Scholarships, entry (S) 50
NSPS Board of Governors Scholarship, (S) 362
NSPS Scholarships, (S) 363
NSSA National Scholarship Program, (A) 1221
NTA State and Provincial Scholarship, (SS) 702
NTC Young Artist Endowment Award. *See* National Trumpet Competition Awards, entry (H) 940
NTEU Scholarships. *See* FEEA–NTEU Scholarships, entry (A) 1097
Nuclear Propulsion Officer Candidate (NUPOC) Program, (S) 364
NUPOC Program. *See* Nuclear Propulsion Officer Candidate (NUPOC) Program, entry (S) 364
Nuquist Award. *See* Andrew E. Nuquist Award, entry (H) 784
NYWEA Scholarships, (S) 365

Oberne Strings Awards. *See* NFMC Biennial Student Audition Awards, entry (H) 944
Oenslager Scholastic Achievement Awards. *See* Mary P. Oenslager Scholastic Achievement Awards, entry (A) 1166
Ohio Asphalt Scholarship Program, (S) 366
Ohio CattleWomen Scholarships, (S) 367
Ohio Legion Scholarships, (A) 1222
Ohio Newspapers Foundation University Journalism Scholarship, (H) 946
Ohio Safety Officers College Memorial Fund, (A) 1223
Ohio Society of CPAs College Scholarship Program, (SS) 703
Ohio War Orphans Scholarship, (A) 1224
OK Scholarship Fund, (A) 1225
Okazaki Scholarship. *See* Mr. and Mrs. Moichi Okazaki Scholarship, entry (A) 1184
Oklahoma Newspaper Foundation Scholarships, (H) 947
Oklahoma 4-H Entrepreneurship Scholarship, (SS) 704
Old Guard Prizes, (S) 368
Olive Lynn Salembier Scholarship, (S) 369
Olive W. Garvey Student Fellowships, (SS) 705
Oliver ASNT Scholarships. *See* Robert B. Oliver ASNT Scholarships, entry (S) 416
Olson Composition Award. *See* Lynn Freeman Olson Composition Award, entry (H) 917
Om and Saraswati (Sara) Bahethi Scholarship. *See* American Meteorological Society Undergraduate Scholarships, entry (S) 32
Oncology Nursing Certification Corporation Bachelor's Scholarships, (S) 370
One Puka Puka Scholarship, (A) 1226
O'Neal Arts Award. *See* M. Josephine O'Neal Arts Award, entry (H) 918
Online Editing Program for College Juniors, Seniors and Graduate Students, (H) 948
Ora Keck Scholarship. *See* California P.E.O. Scholarships, entry (A) 1056
Order of Omega Scholarships, (A) 1227
Order of St. Lazarus/Green Cross Project Award. *See* AAPA Veteran's Caucus Scholarships, entry (S) 3
Oregon Association of Broadcasters Scholarships, (H) 949
Oregon Society of Certified Public Accountants Educational Foundation College Scholarships. *See* OSCPA Educational Foundation College Scholarships, entry (SS) 706
Oregon Space Grant Undergraduate Scholarship Program, (S) 371
Orville Endowed Scholarship in Meteorology. *See* American Meteorological Society Undergraduate Scholarships, entry (S) 32
Osajda Fund. *See* Jean C. Osajda Fund, entry (SS) 639
Oscar and Mildred Larson Award, (A) 1228
OSCPA Educational Foundation College Scholarships, (SS) 706
Othmer National Scholarship Awards. *See* Donald F. & Mildred Topp Othmer National Scholarship Awards, entry (S) 137
Ouida Mundy Hill Memorial Fund, (A) 1229
Outstanding Documentary Award. *See* Angelus Awards, entry (H) 786
Outstanding Secondary Career and Technical Education Student Award, (A) 1230
Overseas Press Club Foundation Scholarships, (H) 950
Owens Scholarships. *See* B. Phinizy Spalding and Hubert B. Owens Scholarships, entry (H) 798

S–Sciences   SS–Social Sciences   H–Humanities   A–Any Subject Area

PROGRAM TITLE INDEX

P.A. Margaronis Scholarship. See AHEPA District Scholarship Awards, entry (A) 1018

Pacific Northwest Chapter ARPAS Scholarship, (S) 372

Palmer Undergraduate Scholarship. See Radio and Television News Directors Foundation Presidents' Scholarships, entry (H) 962

Pangere Foundation Scholarships. See Ross N. and Patricia Pangere Foundation Scholarships, entry (A) 1246

Panousis Memorial Scholarship. See El Camino Real District 20 Scholarships, entry (A) 1089

Paper and Board Division Scholarships, (S) 373

Park Scholarship. See Chunghi Hong Park Scholarship, entry (S) 109

Parker F. Enright Scholarships. See Order of Omega Scholarships, entry (A) 1227

Parks Future Teacher Scholarship. See Applegate/Jackson/Parks Future Teacher Scholarship, entry (SS) 543

Parks Scholarships. See Rosa L. Parks Scholarships, entries (S) 431, (SS) 728, (A) 1245

Parnitzke/Clarke Scholarship. See Phi Upsilon Scholarships, entry (SS) 713

Paros-Digiquartz Scholarship, (S) 374

Paros-Digiquartz Scholarship. See American Meteorological Society Undergraduate Scholarships, entry (S) 32

Partnership for Excellence Undergraduate Fellows Program, (H) 951

Pasquarelli Award. See National Trumpet Competition Awards, entry (H) 940

Past District Governors/Julie P. Microutsicos Scholarship.. See Daughters of Penelope Citrus District 2 Scholarships, entry (A) 1074

Past Presidents Scholarship, (S) 375

Pat Merk Scholarship. See Mensa Member Awards, entry (A) 1167

Pat Roberts Intelligence Scholars Program for Global Network Analysts, (S) 376, (SS) 707

Pat Roberts Intelligence Scholars Program for Intelligence Analysts, (S) 377, (SS) 708, (H) 952

Patremos Memorial Scholarship. See James H. Patremos Memorial Scholarship, entry (H) 893

Patricia Pangere Foundation Scholarships. See Ross N. and Patricia Pangere Foundation Scholarships, entry (A) 1246

Patrick W. Halloran Scholarships. See Order of Omega Scholarships, entry (A) 1227

Patterson Scholarships. See Walter S. Patterson Scholarships, entry (H) 1003

Paul A. Whelan Aviation Scholarship, (S) 378

Paul and Ellen Ruckes Scholarship, (S) 379

Paul Jackson Memorial Scholarship, (S) 380

Paul Jennings Scholarship, (A) 1231

Paul Smith Scholarship. See COMTO NJ Scholarships, entries (S) 118, (SS) 573

Paul W. Rodgers Scholarship, (S) 381

Paula J. Alexander Memorial Scholarship. See Daughters of Penelope Undergraduate Scholarships, entry (A) 1075

Paula Vogel Award in Playwriting, (H) 953

Payne Award for Young Science Journalists. See Evert Clark/Seth Payne Award for Young Science Journalists, entries (S) 171, (H) 847

Payne Memorial Scholarship. See Keith Payne Memorial Scholarship, entry (SS) 651

Payne Student Award for Ethics in Journalism, (H) 954

PCI Engineering Student Design "Big Beam" Competition, (S) 382

PCI Student Architectural Design Competition, (H) 955

Peacock Honorary Scholarship. See Aircraft Electronics Association Members Scholarship Program, entry (A) 1028

Peacock Memorial Scholarship. See Chuck Peacock Memorial Scholarship, entries (S) 108, (SS) 567

Pearl Prime Scholarship. See California P.E.O. Scholarships, entry (A) 1056

Pearson Scholarship. See Robert E. Pearson Scholarship, entry (S) 418

Peaslee-Detroit Brazing and Soldering Division Scholarship. See Robert L. Peaslee-Detroit Brazing and Soldering Division Scholarship, entry (S) 422

Pedro Grau Undergraduate Scholarship. See American Meteorological Society Undergraduate Scholarships, entry (S) 32

Peggy Dixon Two-Year College Scholarship, (S) 383

PEI Scholarship, (S) 384

Pennsylvania AFL-CIO Scholarship Essay Contest, (SS) 709

Pennsylvania Institute of Certified Public Accountants Student Writing Competition. See PICPA Student Writing Competition, entry (SS) 714

Pennsylvania Public Relations Society Scholarships, (H) 956

Pense Scholarship. See Arthur W. Pense Scholarship, entry (S) 54

Pepsi ICW Scholarships, (A) 1232

Pepsi USBC Youth Bowling Championships, (A) 1233

Perdue Scholarships. See Joe Perdue Scholarships, entry (SS) 641

Permian Basic Geophysical Society Scholarship. See SEG Scholarship Program, entry (S) 448

Perryman Communications Scholarship for Ethnic Minority Students. See Leonard M. Perryman Communications Scholarship for Ethnic Minority Students, entry (H) 912

Pete Aldridge Scholarship. See AIAA Foundation Undergraduate Scholarship Program, entry (S) 17

Peter John Peterson Memorial Scholarship. See El Camino Real District 20 Scholarships, entry (A) 1089

Peter K. New Student Prize Competition, (S) 385, (SS) 710

Peter Soderberg Scholarship. See Tau Beta Pi Undergraduate Scholarships, entry (S) 479

Peter Stevens Memorial Scholarship. See El Camino Real District 20 Scholarships, entry (A) 1089

Peterson Memorial Scholarship. See El Camino Real District 20 Scholarships, entry (A) 1089

Peterson Scholarship. See V.L. Peterson Scholarship, entry (S) 497

Peterson Student Paper Award. See W. David Smith, Jr. Student Paper Award, entry (S) 498

Petroleum Division College Scholarships, (S) 386

Pfaff Scholarship Program. See Art Pfaff Scholarship Program, entry (SS) 549

Pfizer Epilepsy Scholarship Award, (A) 1234

Pfizer Hatton Awards Competition, (S) 387

PHCC Educational Foundation Scholarship Program, (S) 388

Phi Alpha Theta/Western Front Association Undergraduate Essay Prize, (H) 957

Phi Chi Theta Scholarships, (SS) 711

Phi Delta Kappa International Scholarship Grants for Prospective Educators, (SS) 712

S–Sciences   SS–Social Sciences   H–Humanities   A–Any Subject Area

PROGRAM TITLE INDEX

Phi Upsilon Scholarships, (SS) 713
Phillip M. Fields Scholarship, (S) 389
Phillips Memorial Scholarship. See Clampitt Paper/Henry Phillips Memorial Scholarship, entries (SS) 568, (H) 817
Philo T. Farnsworth Scholarship, (H) 958
Phipps Memorial Scholarships. See Ann Phipps Memorial Scholarships, entry (A) 1042
Phoenix Chapter 67 Scholarships, (S) 390
Phyllis J. Van Deventer Scholarship. See California P.E.O. Scholarships, entry (A) 1056
Phyllis Stevenson Grams Memorial Award. See Freedom from Religion Foundation College Essay Contest, entry (H) 854
Piccetti NMA Memorial Scholarship. See NMA Undergraduate Scholarships, entry (S) 359
Piccoli Memorial Scholarship. See Airmen Memorial Foundation Scholarship Program, entry (A) 1029
Pickup Memorial Scholarship. See Lydia I. Pickup Memorial Scholarship, entry (S) 305
PICPA Student Writing Competition, (SS) 714
PIEF General Scholarships, (H) 959
Pierre H. Guillemette Scholarship, (S) 391
Pioneers of Flight Scholarship Program, (S) 392
Pisinski Memorial Scholarship. See Stephen D. Pisinski Memorial Scholarship, entry (H) 986
Plain Dealer/Jerry Hoegner Scholarship. See Cleveland Advertising Association Education Foundation Scholarships, entry (H) 818
Plank/PRSSA Scholarships. See Betsy Plank/PRSSA Scholarships, entry (H) 803
Plastics Pioneers Association Scholarships, (S) 393
Platis Memorial Scholarship. See El Camino Real District 20 Scholarships, entry (A) 1089
Pleasant Hawaiian Holidays Scholarship. See Southern California Chapter/Pleasant Hawaiian Holidays Scholarship, entry (SS) 743
Plumb Scholarship. See Allen W. Plumb Scholarship, entry (S) 27
Plumbing–Heating–Cooling Contractors Educational Foundation Scholarship Program. See PHCC Educational Foundation Scholarship Program, entry (S) 388
Plummer Scholarship. See Warner N. Plummer Scholarship, entry (S) 502
Podlesak Memorial Scholarship. See Richard Podlesak Memorial Scholarship, entry (SS) 722
Poister Scholarship Competition in Organ Playing. See Arthur Poister Scholarship Competition in Organ Playing, entry (H) 787
Polanki College Achievement Awards, (A) 1235
Polaris Intake Systems Design Award. See Formula SAE Competition Awards, entry (S) 187
Polingaysi Qöyawayma Award. See A.T. Anderson Memorial Scholarship Program, entry (S) 68
Polly Thompson Memorial Music Scholarship. See California P.E.O. Scholarships, entry (A) 1056
Polsky Academic Achievement Award. See Joel Polsky Academic Achievement Award, entry (H) 899
Pope Scholarship. See Claude E. Pope Scholarship, entry (SS) 569
Postlethwaite Scholarship. See LCPA Education Foundation Scholarship Program, entry (SS) 658
Powder River Basin Section Annual Scholarship Awards, (S) 394, (A) 1236
Powell Scholarship. See Charline Hamilton Powell Scholarship, entry (S) 104
Power Engineering Society Student Prize Paper Award in Honor of T. Burke Hayes, (S) 395
Power Systems Professional Scholarship, (S) 396
Powers Scholarship. See John J. and Irene T. Powers Scholarship, entry (S) 268
Prato Sports Reporting Scholarship. See Lou and Carole Prato Sports Reporting Scholarship, entry (H) 916
Praxair International Scholarship, (S) 397
Praxair NSBE Partnership Scholarship Program. See National Society of Black Engineers Scholarship Program, entry (S) 343
Precast/Prestressed Concrete Institute Engineering Student Design "Big Beam" Competition. See PCI Engineering Student Design "Big Beam" Competition, entry (S) 382
Precast/Prestressed Concrete Institute Student Architectural Design Competition. See PCI Student Architectural Design Competition, entry (H) 955
Pressman Scholarship, (S) 398
Pressure Vessels and Piping Division Student Paper Competition, (S) 399
Price Memorial Scholarship. See Nathalie A. Price Memorial Scholarship, entry (A) 1190
Price Scholarship in Optical Engineering. See SPIE Scholarship Program, entry (S) 464
Priddy Brothers Entertainment Triumph Award. See Angelus Awards, entry (H) 786
PRIDE College Scholarship Program, (A) 1237
Priest Award. See Ima Hogg Young Artist Competition, entry (H) 884
Prime Scholarship. See California P.E.O. Scholarships, entry (A) 1056
Prince Kuhio Hawaiian Civic Club Scholarship, (A) 1238
Print and Graphics Scholarship Foundation Scholarships, (H) 960
Printing Industries Education Funds General Scholarships. See PIEF General Scholarships, entry (H) 959
Professional Engineers in Industry Scholarship. See PEI Scholarship, entry (S) 384
Professor Sidney Gross Memorial Award, (H) 961
Project Red Flag Academic Scholarship for Women with Bleeding Disorders, (A) 1239
Promoting Individual Development Education College Scholarship. See PRIDE College Scholarship Program, entry (A) 1237
Pryor Scholarship. See IFMA Foundation Scholarships, entry (SS) 631
PSSC Legacy Fund Scholarship, (S) 400, (SS) 715
Public Service Scholarships, (SS) 716
Pullan Memorial Vocal Scholarship. See Glenn Miller Scholarship Competition, entry (H) 860
Putnam Competition. See William Lowell Putnam Competition, entry (S) 516
Putnam Prize. See Elizabeth Lowell Putnam Prize, entry (S) 159

Qöyawayma Awards. See A.T. Anderson Memorial Scholarship Program, entry (S) 68
Quality Assurance Division Scholarships, (S) 401

S–Sciences   SS–Social Sciences   H–Humanities   A–Any Subject Area

PROGRAM TITLE INDEX

Quality of Life Awards. *See* Miss America Competition Awards, entry (A) 1174
Qualls Memorial Scholarships. *See* Floyd Qualls Memorial Scholarships, entry (A) 1101
Quimby Regional Competitions for Young Organists. *See* AGO/Quimby Regional Competitions for Young Organists, entry (H) 779
Quinn Scholars Program. *See* Chips Quinn Scholars Program, entry (H) 816

R. Gerald Melton Scholarship. *See* Phi Delta Kappa International Scholarship Grants for Prospective Educators, entry (SS) 712
R. Preston Woodruff, Jr. Scholarships, (A) 1240
Radio and Television News Directors Foundation Presidents' Scholarships, (H) 962
Radio–Television Journalism Division Prizes, (H) 963
Ralph A. Klucken Scholarship, (S) 402
Ralph Brewster Vocal Scholarship. *See* Glenn Miller Scholarship Competition, entry (H) 860
Ralph K. Hillquist Honorary SAE Scholarship, (S) 403
Ralph W. Baird Scholarship, (S) 404
Ramey Scholarship. *See* Tommy Ramey Scholarship, entries (SS) 752, (H) 995
Randall Mathis Scholarship for Environmental Studies, (S) 405
Ransburg American Patriot Scholarships. *See* Harold and Maria Ransburg American Patriot Scholarships, entry (SS) 615
Ratza Memorial Scholarship. *See* Carol A. Ratza Memorial Scholarship, entry (S) 95
Ray Eberle Vocal Scholarship. *See* Glenn Miller Scholarship Competition, entry (H) 860
Ray Wilkinson Communications Scholarship, (H) 964
Raymond DiSalvo Memorial Scholarship. *See* ANS Undergraduate Scholarships, entry (S) 43
Raymond K.J. Luomanen Fund. *See* Dr. Raymond K.J. Luomanen Fund, entry (S) 146
Reagan Pathfinder Scholarship. *See* Nancy Reagan Pathfinder Scholarships, entry (A) 1188
Record Scholarships. *See* Tau Beta Pi Undergraduate Scholarships, entry (S) 479
Redi–Tag Corporation Scholarship, (S) 406, (SS) 717
Reed Scholarship. *See* J. Fielding Reed Scholarship, entry (S) 253
Regional University Baccalaureate Scholarship Program, (A) 1241
Regnery Endowed Scholarships. *See* Henry Regnery Endowed Scholarships, entry (H) 875
Reiche Award. *See* National Trumpet Competition Awards, entry (H) 940
Reid Prize. *See* J. Neel Reid Prize, entry (H) 892
Rendel Scholarships. *See* Betty Rendel Scholarships, entry (SS) 558
René Campbell Memorial Scholarship, (SS) 718
Renzi Award for Academic Achievement. *See* Hawaii Chapter AFCEA Scholarships, entry (S) 228
Resistance Welder Manufacturers' Association Scholarship, (S) 407
Resnik Memorial Scholarship. *See* Judith Resnik Memorial Scholarship, entry (S) 276

Reuben R. Cowles Youth Award, (S) 408
Reville Scholarship. *See* James F. Reville Scholarship, entry (S) 254
R.H. Nagel Scholarship. *See* Tau Beta Pi Undergraduate Scholarships, entry (S) 479
Rhea/Atlanta Falcons Undergraduate Scholarship Award. *See* Jerry Rhea/Atlanta Falcons Undergraduate Scholarship Award, entry (S) 259
Rheba Cobb Memorial Scholarship. *See* J.C. and Rheba Cobb Memorial Scholarship, entry (S) 258
Rhoda D. Hood Memorial Scholarship, (H) 965
Rhodes Scholarship. *See* El Camino Real District 20 Scholarships, entry (A) 1089
Rhythm & Hues Studios Computer Graphics Scholarships, (H) 966
Richard A. Herbert Memorial Undergraduate Scholarship, (S) 409
Richard and Helen Hagemeyer Scholarship. *See* American Meteorological Society Undergraduate Scholarships, entry (S) 32
Richard B. Combs Hospitality Scholarship, (SS) 719
Richard Cecil Todd and Clauda Pennock Todd Tripod Scholarship, (A) 1242
Richard Cheverton Undergraduate Scholarship. *See* Radio and Television News Directors Foundation Presidents' Scholarships, entry (H) 962
Richard Chinn Scholarship. *See* Dr. Richard Chinn Scholarship, entry (A) 1082
Richard "Dick" Spader Scholarships. *See* Angus Foundation Scholarships, entry (S) 39
Richard E. Merwin Student Scholarship, (S) 410
Richard G. Munsell Memorial Scholarship, (SS) 720
Richard P. Covert, Ph.D., FHIMSS Scholarship, (S) 411, (SS) 721
Richard Podlesak Memorial Scholarship, (SS) 722
Richard V. Bradshaw Memorial Scholarship, (A) 1243
Richardson Memorial Scholarship. *See* Carolyn S. Richardson Memorial Scholarship, entry (S) 96
Richardson Memorial Scholarship. *See* Phi Chi Theta Scholarships, entry (SS) 711
Rideout–Robertson Internship Scholarship. *See* Nancie Rideout–Robertson Internship Scholarship, entry (A) 1187
Rienzi, USA (Ret) Award for Academic Achievement. *See* Hawaii Chapter AFCEA Scholarships, entry (S) 228
Ristow Prize. *See* Walter W. Ristow Prize, entry (H) 1004
Rita Finnegan Memorial Scholarship. *See* FORE Undergraduate Merit Scholarships, entries (S) 186, (SS) 598
Rita Lowe College Scholarships, (S) 412, (SS) 723
Ritchie–Jennings Memorial Scholarships Program, (SS) 724
R.L. Gillette Scholarships, (H) 967
RMEL Foundation Scholarships, (S) 413, (SS) 725
RN Advancing Education Scholarship, (S) 414
Rob Branham Scholarship, (SS) 726, (H) 968
Rob Spademan Scholarship. *See* Cleveland Advertising Association Education Foundation Scholarships, entry (H) 818
Robert A. Ellis Scholarship in Physics, (S) 415
Robert and Edith Jung Scholarship. *See* Chinese American Citizens Alliance Foundation Scholarships, entry (A) 1060
Robert B. Oliver ASNT Scholarships, (S) 416

S–Sciences　　　　　SS–Social Sciences　　　　　H–Humanities　　　　　A–Any Subject Area

PROGRAM TITLE INDEX

Robert Bosch Corporation Engine Management System Awards. See Formula SAE Competition Awards, entry (S) 187
Robert D. Greenberg Scholarship, (S) 417
Robert E. Pearson Scholarship, (S) 418
Robert F. Sammataro Pressure Vessel Piping Division Scholarship, (S) 419
Robert Felix Memorial Scholarship, (S) 420
Robert G. Lacy Memorial Scholarship. See ANS Undergraduate Scholarships, entry (S) 43
Robert J. Doran Scholarship, (S) 421, (SS) 727
Robert L. Crippen Scholarship. See AIAA Foundation Undergraduate Scholarship Program, entry (S) 17
Robert L. Livingston Scholarships, (A) 1244
Robert L. Peaslee–Detroit Brazing and Soldering Division Scholarship, (S) 422
Robert M. Lawrence, MD Education Recognition Award, (S) 423
Robert T. Liner Memorial Scholarship. See ANS Undergraduate Scholarships, entry (S) 43
Robert W. Brocksbank Scholarship. See A.T. Anderson Memorial Scholarship Program, entry (S) 68
Robert W. Hagemeyer Scholarship. See Coating and Graphic Arts Division Scholarships, entries (S) 112, (H) 819
Robert W. Sims Memorial Scholarship. See Dr. Robert W. Sims Memorial Scholarship, entry (S) 147
Roberta Pierce Scofield Bachelor's Scholarships, (S) 424
Roberts Intelligence Scholars Program for Global Network Analysts. See Pat Roberts Intelligence Scholars Program for Global Network Analysts, entries (S) 376, (SS) 707
Roberts Intelligence Scholars Program for Intelligence Analysts. See Pat Roberts Intelligence Scholars Program for Intelligence Analysts, entries (S) 377, (SS) 708, (H) 952
Robinson Award. See Samuel Robinson Award, entry (H) 974
Robinson Memorial Scholarship. See JoAnne Robinson Memorial Scholarship, entry (H) 898
Robinson Scholarship. See Phi Upsilon Scholarships, entry (SS) 713
Robinson Scholarship. See Roy & Harriet Robinson Scholarship, entry (SS) 729
Rockefeller State Wildlife Scholarship, (S) 425
Rockly Triantafellu, USAF (Ret) Award for Academic Achievement. See Hawaii Chapter AFCEA Scholarships, entry (S) 228
Rockwell Automation Scholarships, (S) 426
Rocky Mountain Electrical League Foundation Scholarships. See RMEL Foundation Scholarships, entries (S) 413, (SS) 725
Rocky Mountain NASA Space Grant Consortium Undergraduate Scholarships, (S) 427
Rodgers Scholarship. See Paul W. Rodgers Scholarship, entry (S) 381
Rodriguez Scholarship. See American Meteorological Society Undergraduate Scholarships, entry (S) 32
Roe Scholarship. See Kenneth Andrew Roe Scholarship, entry (S) 281
Rogers Family Scholarship, (S) 428
Rohm and Haas Awards, (S) 429
Rolling Stone College Journalism Competition, (H) 969
Ron Taylor Group Award for Artistic Merit. See National Trumpet Competition Awards, entry (H) 940

Ronald E. Lincoln Memorial Scholarship. See Association for Iron & Steel Technology Scholarships, entry (S) 63
Ronald E. McNair Scholarship in Space and Optical Physics, (S) 430
Rosa L. Parks Scholarships, (S) 431, (SS) 728, (A) 1245
Ross N. and Patricia Pangere Foundation Scholarships, (A) 1246
Rosser Scholarship. See COMTO NJ Scholarships, entries (S) 118, (SS) 573
Roth Newscarrier Scholarships. See Isaac Roth Newscarrier Scholarships, entry (A) 1131
ROV Scholarships, (S) 432
Roy & Harriet Robinson Scholarship, (SS) 729
Ruby Schaff/Schaff Angus Ranch Scholarship. See Joseph and Ruby Schaff/Schaff Angus Ranch Scholarship, entry (A) 1140
Ruby Simmonds Vought Organ Award. See NFMC Biennial Student Audition Awards, entry (H) 944
Ruby W. Henry Scholarship. See California P.E.O. Scholarships, entry (A) 1056
Ruckes Scholarship. See Paul and Ellen Ruckes Scholarship, entry (S) 379
Rudd Scholarship. See Willie Rudd Scholarship, entry (A) 1314
Rudolph Dillman Memorial Scholarship, (S) 433, (SS) 730
Ruggles Right to Work Scholarship. See William B. Ruggles Right to Work Scholarship, entry (H) 1009
Rumie Cho Scholarship. See KSEA Scholarships, entry (S) 286
Russell M. Birtwistle Award. See Irma and Knute Carlson Award, entry (A) 1130
Russell Scholarship for Advanced Studies. See William A. Russell Scholarship for Advanced Studies, entry (S) 511
Russell W. Myers Scholarship, (S) 434
Ruth Abernathy Undergraduate Presidential Scholarship, (S) 435, (SS) 731, (H) 970
Ruth Clark Scholarship, (H) 971
Ruth Good Educational Endowment Awards. See Norman and Ruth Good Educational Endowment Awards, entry (A) 1217
Ruth Harrison Scholarship. See SEG Scholarship Program, entry (S) 448
Ruth Lilly Poetry Fellowships, (H) 972
Ruth M. and Cleveland L. Campbell Scholarship. See Tau Beta Pi Undergraduate Scholarships, entry (S) 479
Ryan Acting Scholarships. See Irene Ryan Acting Scholarships, entry (H) 890

S. Bradley Burson Memorial Scholarship. See Dr. S. Bradley Burson Memorial Scholarship, entry (S) 148
Sadler Memorial Scholarship. See Arnold Sadler Memorial Scholarship, entries (S) 52, (SS) 548
SAE Long Term Member Sponsored Scholarships, (S) 436
Safari Club International Upper–Level Two–Year Conservation Scholarships, (S) 437
SAFE Foundation Scholarships, (S) 438
Safer Athletic Field Environments Foundation Scholarships. See SAFE Foundation Scholarships, entry (S) 438
Sagebrush Circuit–Lew and JoAnn Eklund Educational Scholarship, (S) 439
Sakae Takahashi Scholarship, (SS) 732
Sal Ingrassia Scholarship, (A) 1247

S–Sciences   SS–Social Sciences   H–Humanities   A–Any Subject Area

PROGRAM TITLE INDEX

Salembier Scholarship. *See* Olive Lynn Salembier Scholarship, entry (S) 369
Salisbury Undergraduate Scholarship. *See* Radio and Television News Directors Foundation Presidents' Scholarships, entry (H) 962
Sallie Mae 911 Education Fund Scholarship Program, (A) 1248
Sally Heet Memorial Scholarship, (H) 973
Salvatori Scholarship. *See* SEG Scholarship Program, entry (S) 448
Sam Dakis Scholarship, (A) 1249
Sam F. Iacobellis Scholarship. *See* AIAA Foundation Undergraduate Scholarship Program, entry (S) 17
Sam Nakos Scholarship. *See* AHEPA District Scholarship Awards, entry (A) 1018
Sam Platis Memorial Scholarship. *See* El Camino Real District 20 Scholarships, entry (A) 1089
Sammataro Pressure Vessel Piping Division Scholarship. *See* Robert F. Sammataro Pressure Vessel Piping Division Scholarship, entry (S) 419
Samuel French Award. *See* National Student Playwriting Award, entry (H) 939
Samuel Robinson Award, (H) 974
Sanfra L. Key Memorial Scholarship. *See* FORE Undergraduate Merit Scholarships, entries (S) 186, (SS) 598
SAP America Scholarship Program, (S) 440
Sara J. Ingrassia Memorial Scholarship. *See* Phi Delta Kappa International Scholarship Grants for Prospective Educators, entry (SS) 712
Sarah G. Merriam Scholarship. *See* John L. and Sarah G. Merriam Scholarship, entry (S) 270
Saraswati (Sara) Bahethi Scholarship. *See* American Meteorological Society Undergraduate Scholarships, entry (S) 32
Satterfield Scholarship. *See* Phi Chi Theta Scholarships, entry (SS) 711
Saul Jakel Memorial Award. *See* Freedom from Religion Foundation College Essay Contest, entry (H) 854
SBC Scholarship. *See* Order of Omega Scholarships, entry (A) 1227
Scarborough Memorial Scholarship. *See* Marlin R. Scarborough Memorial Scholarship, entry (A) 1163
Schafer Mathematics Prize. *See* Alice T. Schafer Mathematics Prize, entry (S) 26
Schaff Angus Ranch Scholarship. *See* Joseph and Ruby Schaff/Schaff Angus Ranch Scholarship, entry (A) 1140
Schary Awards. *See* Dore Schary Awards, entry (H) 838
Schirmer Scholarship. *See* J.F. Schirmer Scholarship, entry (A) 1136
Schlumberger Scholarship. *See* SEG Scholarship Program, entry (S) 448
Schmidt NMA Memorial Scholarship. *See* NMA Undergraduate Scholarships, entry (S) 359
Schoenknecht Tourism and Travel Scholarship. *See* Walter Schoenknecht Tourism and Travel Scholarship, entry (SS) 764
Scholarship in Book Production and Publishing, (H) 975
Scholarship in Memory of Jerry Salny. *See* Mensa Member Awards, entry (A) 1167
Scholarship Management and Accounting Reports for Tenpins Program Scholarships. *See* SMART Program Scholarships, entry (A) 1259
Scholarships for Military Children, (A) 1250

Scholarships in Mathematics Education, (S) 441, (SS) 733
Scholarships in Technical Communication, (S) 442, (H) 976
Schonstedt Scholarship in Surveying, (S) 443
Schramm Memorial Scholarship. *See* Arthur T. Schramm Memorial Scholarship, entry (S) 53
Schulz Award for College Cartoonists. *See* Charles M. Schulz Award for College Cartoonists, entry (H) 814
Schuman Ecolab Undergraduate Entrepreneurial Scholarships. *See* Al Schuman Ecolab Undergraduate Entrepreneurial Scholarships, entry (SS) 533
Schwabe Memorial Scholarship. *See* William E. Schwabe Memorial Scholarship, entry (S) 512
Schwan's Food Service Scholarships, (S) 444, (SS) 734
Schwartz Scholarship. *See* John Schwartz Scholarship, entry (H) 901
Scimonelli Award. *See* National Trumpet Competition Awards, entry (H) 940
Scofield Bachelor's Scholarships. *See* Roberta Pierce Scofield Bachelor's Scholarships, entry (S) 424
Scott Tarbell Scholarships, (S) 445
Scotts Company Scholars Program, (S) 446
Scribner Scholarship. *See* Tau Beta Pi Undergraduate Scholarships, entry (S) 479
Scripps Howard Top Ten Scholarship Program, (H) 977
SeAh-Haiam Scholarship. *See* KSEA Scholarships, entry (S) 286
SEATA Memorial Undergraduate Scholarship, (S) 447
Seattle Junior Chamber of Commerce Scholarship Program, (A) 1251
Seaviews/Cen Cal Marine Science Scholarship. *See* California Marine Sciences Scholarship, entry (S) 90
SEG Scholarship Program, (S) 448
SEIU 1-Year Scholarships, (A) 1252
Selma Neumann Memorial Award. *See* Ima Hogg Young Artist Competition, entry (H) 884
Sertoma Collegiate Club Scholarships, (A) 1253
Sertoma Scholarships for Hearing-Impaired Students, (A) 1254
Service Employees International Union 1-Year Scholarships. *See* SEIU 1-Year Scholarships, entry (A) 1252
Seth Payne Award for Young Science Journalists. *See* Evert Clark/Seth Payne Award for Young Science Journalists, entries (S) 171, (H) 847
Seymour Bricker College Award. *See* Academy of Television Arts & Sciences College Television Awards, entry (H) 775
SGNA RN General Education Scholarship, (S) 449
SGT Felix Delgreco Jr. Scholarship, (A) 1255
Sharon D. Banks Memorial Undergraduate Scholarship, (S) 450, (SS) 735
Sharon Edwards Scholarship. *See* AAPA Veteran's Caucus Scholarships, entry (S) 3
Sharon L. Piccoli Memorial Scholarship. *See* Airmen Memorial Foundation Scholarship Program, entry (A) 1029
Shell Oil Company Process Technology Scholarship, (S) 451
Shell Oil International Scholarships, (S) 452
Sherard Scholarship. *See* Esther Mayo Sherard Scholarship, entries (S) 169, (SS) 593
Sheryl A. Horak Law Enforcement Explorer Memorial Scholarship, (SS) 736
Shilke Award for Artistry. *See* National Trumpet Competition Awards, entry (H) 940
Shirley Wilkins Valentin Violin Award, (H) 978

S—Sciences   SS—Social Sciences   H—Humanities   A—Any Subject Area

PROGRAM TITLE INDEX

Shoon Kyung Kim Scholarship. *See* KSEA Scholarships, entry (S) 286
ShopKo Scholarships, (A) 1256
Shore Award. *See* National Trumpet Competition Awards, entry (H) 940
Short Film and Video Competition, (H) 979
SHRM Foundation Undergraduate Scholarships, (SS) 737
Sibelius Memorial Fund. *See* Jean Sibelius Memorial Fund, entry (H) 897
Sidney Gross Memorial Award. *See* Professor Sidney Gross Memorial Award, entry (H) 961
Siegel Service Technology Scholarships, (S) 453
Sigma Alpha Iota Scholarships for Undergraduate Performance, (H) 980
Sigma Iota Epsilon Undergraduate Scholarships, (SS) 738
Sigma Tau Delta Scholars Award, (H) 981
Sikh Coalition Diversity Essay Competition, (A) 1257
Sikorsky Scholarship. *See* Naval Helicopter Association Undergraduate Scholarships, entry (A) 1194
Simmons Educational Scholarship. *See* Linda Simmons Educational Scholarship, entry (H) 913
Simmons Scholarship. *See* Willard B. Simmons Scholarship, entry (S) 510
Simpson & Company Actuarial Science Scholarship. *See* D.W. Simpson & Company Actuarial Science Scholarship, entry (SS) 585
Simpson Scholarship. *See* Carole Simpson Scholarship, entry (H) 810
Sims. Jr. Memorial Scholarship. *See* E. Ted Sims, Jr. Memorial Scholarship, entry (S) 151
Sims Memorial Scholarship. *See* Dr. Robert W. Sims Memorial Scholarship, entry (S) 147
Simultaneous Membership Program (SMP), (A) 1258
Sinfonia Educational Foundation Scholarships, (H) 982
Sioussat/Fay Wells Scholarships. *See* Helen J. Sioussat/Fay Wells Scholarships, entry (H) 873
Skip Fletcher Scholarship. *See* AIAA Foundation Undergraduate Scholarship Program, entry (S) 17
Smail Memorial Scholarship. *See* WAMSO Young Artist Competition Awards and Scholarships, entry (H) 1005
SMART Program Scholarships, (A) 1259
SME Education Foundation Family Scholarship, (S) 454
Smilo Undergraduate Scholarship. *See* Martin Smilo Undergraduate Scholarship, entry (S) 309
Smith, Jr. Graduate Student Paper Award. *See* W. David Smith, Jr. Student Paper Award, entry (S) 498
Smith Memorial Scholarship. *See* Tim Smith Memorial Scholarship, entry (SS) 750
Smith Playwriting Award. *See* Jean Kennedy Smith Playwriting Award, entry (H) 896
Smith Scholarship. *See* COMTO NJ Scholarships, entries (S) 118, (SS) 658
Smith Scholarship. *See* LCPA Education Foundation Scholarship Program, entry (SS) 573
Smith Water Heaters Scholarship. *See* A.O. Smith Water Heaters Scholarship, entry (S) 44
SMP. *See* Simultaneous Membership Program (SMP), entry (A) 1258
Snow Memorial Scholarship. *See* Phi Chi Theta Scholarships, entry (SS) 711

Society for Human Resource Management Foundation Undergraduate Scholarships. *See* SHRM Foundation Undergraduate Scholarships, entry (SS) 737
Society of Air Force Physician Assistants Scholarship. *See* AAPA Veteran's Caucus Scholarships, entry (S) 3
Society of Army Physician Assistants Scholarship. *See* AAPA Veteran's Caucus Scholarships, entry (S) 3
Society of Automotive Engineers Donald D. Dawson Technical Scholarship. *See* TMC/SAE Donald D. Dawson Technical Scholarship, entry (S) 485
Society of Automotive Engineers Long Term Member Sponsored Scholarships. *See* SAE Long Term Member Sponsored Scholarships, entry (S) 436
Society of Exploration Geophysicists Scholarship Program. *See* SEG Scholarship Program, entry (S) 448
Society of Flight Test Engineers Scholarships, (S) 455
Society of Gastroenterology Nurses and Associates RN Advancing Education Scholarship. *See* RN Advancing Education Scholarship, entry (S) 414
Society of Gastroenterology Nurses and Associates RN General Education Scholarship. *See* SGNA RN General Education Scholarship, entry (S) 449
Society of Manufacturing Engineers Directors' Scholarships, (S) 456
Society of Manufacturing Engineers Education Foundation Family Scholarship. *See* SME Education Foundation Family Scholarship, entry (S) 454
Society of Physics Students Future Teacher Scholarship. *See* SPS Future Teacher Scholarship, entries (S) 467, (SS) 744
Society of Physics Students Leadership Scholarships, (S) 457
Society of Physics Students Leadership Scholarships. *See* Society of Physics Students Leadership Scholarships, entry (S) 457
Society of Plastics Engineers' Composite Division Awards. *See* Formula SAE Competition Awards, entry (S) 187
Society of Women Engineers Past Presidents Scholarships. *See* SWE Past Presidents Scholarships, entry (S) 476
Soderberg Scholarship. *See* Tau Beta Pi Undergraduate Scholarships, entry (S) 479
Sodexho Pan Asian Network Group Scholarship, (SS) 739
Solid Waste Program Management Undergraduate Scholarship Program, (S) 458
Sonlight Scholarships, (A) 1260
Sons and Daughters Scholarship Program, (A) 1261
Sons of Italy Italian Language Scholarship, (H) 983
Sons of Italy National Leadership Grants, (A) 1262
Sons of Pericles Undergraduate Scholarships, (A) 1263
Sons of Union Veterans of the Civil War Scholarships, (A) 1264
Sophomore Scholarships, (S) 459
Sorenson Physical Education Scholarship. *See* Tobin Sorenson Physical Education Scholarship, entries (S) 486, (SS) 751
South Carolina Access and Equity Undergraduate Scholars Program, (A) 1265
South Carolina Association of CPA's Scholarship Program, (SS) 740
South Carolina Space Grant Consortium Pre–Service Teacher Scholarships, (SS) 741
South Carolina Tuition Program for Children of Certain War Veterans, (A) 1266
South Dakota Excellence in Accounting Scholarships, (SS) 742
South Dakota Free Tuition for Children of Residents Who Died During Service in the Armed Forces, (A) 1267

S–Sciences   SS–Social Sciences   H–Humanities   A–Any Subject Area

South Dakota Free Tuition for Dependents of Prisoners or Missing in Action, (A) 1268
South Dakota Free Tuition for Survivors of Deceased Fire Fighters, Certified Law Enforcement Officers, and Emergency Medical Technicians, (A) 1269
South Dakota Free Tuition for Veterans and Others Who Performed War Service, (A) 1270
South Dakota Space Grant Consortium Graduate Fellowships and Undergraduate Scholarships, (S) 460
South Texas Unit Scholarships, (S) 461
Southeast Athletic Trainers Association Memorial Undergraduate Scholarship. See SEATA Memorial Undergraduate Scholarship, entry (S) 447
Southern Association of Steel Fabricators Scholarship, (S) 462
Southern California Chapter/Pleasant Hawaiian Holidays Scholarship, (SS) 743
Southern Ohio Music Company Award for Artistry. See National Trumpet Competition Awards, entry (H) 940
Southern Ohio Music Company Award. See National Trumpet Competition Awards, entry (H) 940
Southwest Athletic Trainers' Association Undergraduate Scholarship, (S) 463
Space Transportation Technical Committee Scholarship. See AIAA Foundation Undergraduate Scholarship Program, entry (S) 17
Spademan Scholarship. See Cleveland Advertising Association Education Foundation Scholarships, entry (H) 818
Spader Scholarships. See Angus Foundation Scholarships, entry (S) 39
Spalding and Hubert B. Owens Scholarships. See B. Phinizy Spalding and Hubert B. Owens Scholarships, entry (H) 798
Spears Scholarship. See FORE Undergraduate Merit Scholarships, entries (S) 186, (SS) 598
Sphinx Competition Awards, (H) 984
Sphinx Competition. See Sphinx Competition Awards, entry (H) 984
SPIE Scholarship Program, (S) 464
Spielman Scholarships. See A.J. (Andy) Spielman Scholarships, entry (SS) 532
Spirit of Apollo Scholarship, (S) 465
Sports Copy Editing Program for College Juniors, Seniors and Graduate Students, (H) 985
Sporty's/Cincinnati Avionics Scholarship, (S) 466
SPS Future Teacher Scholarship, (S) 467, (SS) 744
SSGT Craig Ivory Memorial Scholarships. See AAPA Veteran's Caucus Scholarships, entry (S) 3
Stabile Scholarship. See Tau Beta Pi Undergraduate Scholarships, entry (S) 479
Stanitz Scholarship. See William R. Stanitz Scholarship, entry (A) 1313
Stanley F. and Helen Balcerzak Award. See Polanki College Achievement Awards, entry (A) 1235
Stanley O. McNaughton Community Service Award, (A) 1271
Stanley W. Marion Fund, (A) 1272
Star in Agricultural Agriscience. See American Star Farmer Award, entry (S) 36
Star in Agricultural Placement Award. See American Star Farmer Award, entry (S) 36
Stara Scholarship. See Nebraska Society of Certified Public Accountants Scholarships, entry (SS) 689
Starring Memorial Award for Piano. See Sigma Alpha Iota Scholarships for Undergraduate Performance, entry (H) 980
Starring Memorial Award for Woodwinds or Brass. See Sigma Alpha Iota Scholarships for Undergraduate Performance, entry (H) 980
Stashower Visionary Scholarship Award. See David L. Stashower Visionary Scholarships, entry (H) 832
State Association of Real Property Agents Scholarship, (S) 468, (SS) 745
State Water Heaters Scholarship, (S) 469
Steele Engineering Scholarship. See Alfred Steele Engineering Scholarship, entry (S) 25
Stella May Nau Scholarship. See California P.E.O. Scholarships, entry (A) 1056
Stephen D. Pisinski Memorial Scholarship, (H) 986
Stern Advertising Scholarship. See Cleveland Advertising Association Education Foundation Scholarships, entry (H) 818
Stevens Memorial Scholarship. See El Camino Real District 20 Scholarships, entry (A) 1089
Stewart Estopinal CCIM Memorial Scholarship, (SS) 746
Stickney Endowed Scholarship. See PIEF General Scholarships, entry (H) 959
Stone Award for Student Journalism. See Nation Institute/I.F. Stone Award for Student Journalism, entry (H) 930
Stone Scholarships. See Joseph R. Stone Scholarships, entry (A) 1142
Stout Scholarship. See Martin L. Stout Scholarship, entry (S) 308
Stuart Cameron and Margaret McLeod Memorial Scholarship, (SS) 747
Student Academy Awards, (H) 987
Student Aid Fund for Nonregistrants, (A) 1273
Student Corrugated Packaging Design Competition, (S) 470, (H) 988
Student Design Competition in Acoustics, (S) 471, (H) 989
Student Essay Competition in Healthcare Management, (S) 472, (SS) 748
Student Manufacturing Design Competition, (S) 473
Student Safety Engineering Design Contest, (S) 474
Stulberg Burdick–Thorne Gold Medal. See Julius & Esther Stulberg International String Competition, entry (H) 903
Stulberg International String Competition. See Julius & Esther Stulberg International String Competition, entry (H) 903
Sturdivant Family Scholarships. See John N. Sturdivant Family Scholarships, entry (A) 1139
Stu's Music Shop Award. See National Trumpet Competition Awards, entry (H) 940
Sue Scholarship. See Chinese American Citizens Alliance Foundation Scholarships, entry (A) 1060
Sullivan Science and Engineering Fellowship. See Kathryn D. Sullivan Science and Engineering Fellowship, entry (S) 279
Sundance Theatre Laboratory Acting Fellowship. See Irene Ryan Acting Scholarships, entry (H) 890
SuperCollege.com Student Scholarships, (A) 1274
Survivors' and Dependents' Educational Assistance Program, (A) 1275
Susan G. Moran Scholarships, (H) 990
Susan Lai Scholarship. See Chinese American Citizens Alliance Foundation Scholarships, entry (A) 1060
Susan Miszkowicz Memorial Scholarship, (S) 475
Swackhamer Ag Economics/Ag Business Grant. See Gene Swackhamer Ag Economics/Ag Business Grant, entries (S) 206, (SS) 606

S–Sciences   SS–Social Sciences   H–Humanities   A–Any Subject Area

PROGRAM TITLE INDEX

SWE Past Presidents Scholarships, (S) 476
Swearer Student Humanitarian Award. *See* Howard R. Swearer Student Humanitarian Award, entry (A) 1126

Tagged for Greatness Scholarships, (S) 477
Tailhook Educational Foundation Scholarships, (A) 1276
Takahashi Scholarship. *See* Sakae Takahashi Scholarship, entry (SS) 732
Tanger Scholarship. *See* Alexander M. Tanger Scholarship, entry (H) 781
Tanzer Scholarship. *See* Audrey Tanzer Scholarship, entry (H) 795
Tarbell Scholarships. *See* Scott Tarbell Scholarships, entry (S) 445
Tarbox Memorial Scholarship. *See* Lee Tarbox Memorial Scholarship, entry (S) 291
Tau Beta Pi Distinguished Alumnus Scholarship. *See* Tau Beta Pi Undergraduate Scholarships, entry (S) 479
Tau Beta Pi Mentor Scholarship. *See* Tau Beta Pi Undergraduate Scholarships, entry (S) 479
Tau Beta Pi National Laureate Awards, (S) 478
Tau Beta Pi Undergraduate Scholarships, (S) 479
Taylor Group Award for Artistic Merit. *See* National Trumpet Competition Awards, entry (H) 940
Taylor National Fellowships. *See* Jewell L. Taylor National Fellowships, entry (SS) 640
TCDA Past Presidents Student Scholarship. *See* Texas Choral Directors Association Student Scholarships, entry (H) 991
TCDA/Carroll Barnes Student Scholarship. *See* Texas Choral Directors Association Student Scholarships, entry (H) 991
TCDA/Gandy Ink Student Scholarship. *See* Texas Choral Directors Association Student Scholarships, entry (H) 991
Ted Born Memorial Scholarship. *See* SEG Scholarship Program, entry (S) 448
Ted Peterson Student Paper Award. *See* W. David Smith, Jr. Student Paper Award, entry (S) 498
Tennessee Dependent Children Scholarship, (A) 1277
Terrey Hawthorne Memorial Scholarship, (S) 480
Texas Amateur Athletic Federation Athlete Scholarships, (A) 1278
Texas Children of Disabled or Deceased Firemen, Peace Officers, Game Wardens, and Employees of Correctional Institutions Exemption Program, (A) 1279
Texas Children of U.S. Military Who Are Missing in Action or Prisoners of War Exemption Program, (A) 1280
Texas Choral Directors Association Past Presidents Student Scholarship. *See* Texas Choral Directors Association Student Scholarships, entry (H) 991
Texas Choral Directors Association Student Scholarships, (H) 991
Texas Choral Directors Association/Carroll Barnes Student Scholarship. *See* Texas Choral Directors Association Student Scholarships, entry (H) 991
Texas Choral Directors Association/Gandy Ink Student Scholarship. *See* Texas Choral Directors Association Student Scholarships, entry (H) 991
Texas Exemption for Peace Officers Disabled in the Line of Duty, (A) 1281
Texas Exemption for Surviving Spouses and Dependent Children of Certain Deceased Public Servants, (A) 1282

Texas Instruments Demana–Waits Scholarship, (S) 481
Texas Rural Electric Women's Association Scholarship. *See* TREWA Scholarships, entry (A) 1288
Texas Waivers of Nonresident Tuition for Military Personnel and Their Dependents, (A) 1283
Texas Waivers of Nonresident Tuition for Military Survivors, (A) 1284
Texas Waivers of Nonresident Tuition for Veterans and Their Dependents, (A) 1285
TextbookX.com Scholarship Program, (A) 1286
Theatre for Youth Playwriting Award, (H) 992
Theodore Koop Undergraduate Scholarship. *See* Radio and Television News Directors Foundation Presidents' Scholarships, entry (H) 962
Theresa Brown Scholarships. *See* Miss America Competition Awards, entry (A) 1174
Thiele Memorial Scholarships. *See* Werner B. Thiele Memorial Scholarships, entries (S) 507, (H) 1008
Thomas Brennan Memorial Scholarship. *See* Cleveland Advertising Association Education Foundation Scholarships, entry (H) 818
Thomas G. Neusom Scholarships, (S) 482
Thomas M. Rienzi, USA (Ret) Award for Academic Achievement. *See* Hawaii Chapter AFCEA Scholarships, entry (S) 228
Thomas Memorial Scholarship. *See* Charles (Tommy) Thomas Memorial Scholarship, entry (S) 103
Thomas Pratte Memorial Scholarships, (S) 483, (SS) 749
Thomas R. Keating Feature Writing Competition, (H) 993
Thomas Scholarship. *See* AHEPA District Scholarship Awards, entry (A) 1018
Thomas Scholarship. *See* Cleveland Advertising Association Education Foundation Scholarships, entry (H) 818
Thompson Memorial Music Scholarship. *See* California P.E.O. Scholarships, entry (A) 1056
Thompson Memorial Scholarship. *See* California P.E.O. Scholarships, entry (A) 1056
Thoms Memorial Scholarships. *See* Meridith Thoms Memorial Scholarships, entry (S) 315
Thor Johnson Strings Awards. *See* NFMC Biennial Student Audition Awards, entry (H) 944
Throlson American Bison Foundation Scholarships, (S) 484
Tietjen Scholarship. *See* Jill S. Tietjen Scholarship, entry (S) 260
Tim Smith Memorial Scholarship, (SS) 750
TMC/SAE Donald D. Dawson Technical Scholarship, (S) 485
Tobin Award. *See* Metropolitan Opera National Council Auditions, entry (H) 923
Tobin Sorenson Physical Education Scholarship, (S) 486, (SS) 751
TOCA Publishers Scholarship Program, (S) 487, (H) 994
Todd Tripod Scholarship. *See* Richard Cecil Todd and Clauda Pennock Todd Tripod Scholarship, entry (A) 1242
Tom and Elaine Ehrhorn Scholarship. *See* Mensa Member Awards, entry (A) 1167
Tom Crown Mutes Young Artist Award. *See* National Trumpet Competition Awards, entry (H) 940
Tommy Ramey Scholarship, (SS) 752, (H) 995
Tommy Thomas Memorial Scholarship. *See* Charles (Tommy) Thomas Memorial Scholarship, entry (S) 103
Totem Ocean Trailer Express Scholarships, (A) 1287

S–Sciences　　　　SS–Social Sciences　　　　H–Humanities　　　　A–Any Subject Area

Touris Scholarship. *See* AHEPA District Scholarship Awards, entry (A) 1018
Town of Williston Historical Society Scholarship, (H) 996
Trailblazer Scholarships, (S) 488
Treva C. Kintner Scholarship. *See* Phi Upsilon Scholarships, entry (SS) 713
TREWA Scholarships, (A) 1288
Tri State Surveying and Photogrammetry Kris M. Kunze Memorial Scholarship, (SS) 753
Triantafellu, USAF (Ret) Award for Academic Achievement. *See* Hawaii Chapter AFCEA Scholarships, entry (S) 228
Tripod Scholarship. *See* Richard Cecil Todd and Clauda Pennock Todd Tripod Scholarship, entry (A) 1242
Trott Strings Award. *See* NFMC Biennial Student Audition Awards, entry (H) 944
Trotter Culinary Education Foundation Scholarship. *See* Culinary Trust Scholarships, entry (H) 827
Trow Undergraduate Scholarships. *See* Jo Anne J. Trow Undergraduate Scholarships, entry (A) 1137
Tuition Waiver for Disabled Children of Kentucky Veterans, (A) 1289
Turf and Ornamental Communicators Association Publishers Scholarship Program. *See* TOCA Publishers Scholarship Program, entries (S) 487, (H) 994
Turner, Jr. Memorial Scholarship. *See* James A. Turner, Jr. Memorial Scholarship, entry (SS) 637
Turner Scholarships. *See* Carmen E. Turner Scholarships, entry (S) 94
TVI Actors Studio Career Enrichment Awards. *See* Irene Ryan Acting Scholarships, entry (H) 890
Twain Comedy Acting Awards. *See* Irene Ryan Acting Scholarships, entry (H) 890
Twain Comedy Playwriting Award. *See* Mark Twain Comedy Playwriting Award, entry (H) 920
Tweedale Scholarships, (S) 489
Tweet Coleman Aviation Scholarship, (S) 490
Twin Cities Musicians Union AFM Award. *See* WAMSO Young Artist Competition Awards and Scholarships, entry (H) 1005

Udall Scholarships. *See* Morris K. Udall Scholarships, entries (S) 330, (SS) 675
UDT-SEAL Scholarship, (A) 1290
UNCF/Merck Undergraduate Science Research Scholarships, (S) 491
Undergraduate Awards of Lighthouse International, (A) 1291
Undergraduate Scholarship Program of the Alabama Space Grant Consortium, (S) 492
Undergraduate Students in Technical Research Program, (S) 493
Underwood Scholarship. *See* IFMA Foundation Scholarships, entry (SS) 631
Unilever Hatton Awards Competition. *See* IADR/Unilever Hatton Awards Competition, entry (S) 239
United Parcel Service Foundation ICW Scholarships, (A) 1292
United States Bowling Congress Junior Gold Championships. *See* Junior Gold Championships, entry (A) 1144
United States Bowling Congress Youth Leaders of the Year Awards. *See* USBC Youth Leaders of the Year Awards, entry (A) 1296

United States Tour Operators Association Scholarship, (SS) 754
United University Professions Labor and Social Justice Scholarship, (A) 1293
University Writing Scholarships, (A) 1294
USA Film Festival Student Award. *See* Short Film and Video Competition, entry (H) 979
USAF Chief of Staff Scholarship, (A) 1295
USBC Youth Leaders of the Year Awards, (A) 1296
USO Desert Storm Education Fund, (A) 1297
Utley Award for Artistry. *See* National Trumpet Competition Awards, entry (H) 940

Valentin Violin Award. *See* Shirley Wilkins Valentin Violin Award, entry (H) 978
Van Deventer Scholarship. *See* California P.E.O. Scholarships, entry (A) 1056
Van Ess Scholarship. *See* Bruce Van Ess Scholarship, entry (A) 1053
Vande Velde Leadership Scholarship. *See* Julie Vande Velde Leadership Scholarship, entry (S) 277
Vasa Order of America College or Vocational School Scholarships, (A) 1298
Verges Scholarship. *See* Daughters of Penelope Undergraduate Scholarships, entry (A) 1075
Verma Jeremiah Scholarship. *See* Mensa Member Awards, entry (A) 1167
Vermont Space Grant Undergraduate Scholarships, (S) 494
Veterans of the Vietnam War National Scholarship Program, (A) 1299
Vicki Moritsugu Memorial Scholarship. *See* AAPA Veteran's Caucus Scholarships, entry (S) 3
Victor Herbert ASCAP Young Composer Awards, (H) 997
Video Contest for College Students, (H) 998
VII Corps Desert Storm Veterans Association Scholarship, (A) 1300
Vincent A. Stabile Scholarship. *See* Tau Beta Pi Undergraduate Scholarships, entry (S) 479
Vincent R. Bastien Memorial Award. *See* WAMSO Young Artist Competition Awards and Scholarships, entry (H) 1005
Virginia Allison Accompanying Award, (H) 999
Virginia Child Care Provider Scholarship, (SS) 755
Virginia Council of Teachers of Mathematics Scholarships, (S) 495, (SS) 756
Virginia Museum of Fine Arts Undergraduate Fellowships, (H) 1000
Virginia P. Henry Scholarship, (S) 496
Virginia Peace Mackey-Althouse Voice Award. *See* NFMC Biennial Student Audition Awards, entry (H) 944
Virginia Sheriffs' Institute Scholarship Program. *See* VSI Scholarship Program, entry (SS) 761
Virginia Society for Healthcare Human Resources Administration Scholarship, (SS) 757
Virginia Society of Certified Public Accountants Educational Foundation Undergraduate Scholarship, (SS) 758
Virginia Tuition Assistance for Early Childhood Special Educators Speech-Language Pathologists, and Paraprofessionals, (SS) 759
Virginia Tuition Assistance Grant Program, (A) 1301
Virginia War Orphans Education Program, (A) 1302

PROGRAM TITLE INDEX

Virginia's Future Leaders Scholarship, (A) 1303
V.L. Peterson Scholarship, (S) 497
Vogel Award in Playwriting. See Paula Vogel Award in Playwriting, entry (H) 953
Vogt Radiochemistry Scholarship. See James R. Vogt Radiochemistry Scholarship, entry (S) 256
Voron Scholarship. See Abe Voron Scholarship, entry (H) 774
Vought Organ Award. See NFMC Biennial Student Audition Awards, entry (H) 944
Vrataric Scholarship Awards Program. See Nicholas C. Vrataric Scholarship Awards Program, entry (A) 1213
Vrenios Memorial Award. See National Opera Association Scholarship Division Awards, entry (H) 936
VSCPA Educational Foundation Minority Undergraduate Scholarship, (SS) 760
VSI Scholarship Program, (SS) 761

W. David Smith, Jr. Student Paper Award, (S) 498
W. Eldridge and Emily Lowe Scholarship, (H) 1001
Wackman II Memorial Award. See Howard P. Wackman II Memorial Award, entry (S) 237
WAHPERD Student Scholarship Awards, (S) 499, (SS) 762, (H) 1002
Waivers of Nonresident Tuition for Dependents of Military Personnel Moving to Texas, (A) 1304
Waivers of Nonresident Tuition for Dependents of Military Personnel Who Previously Lived in Texas, (A) 1305
Walker Scholarship Award. See Myrtle and Earl Walker Scholarships, entry (S) 334
Walker Scholarships. See Willie Hobbs Moore–Harry L. Morrison–Arthur B.C. Walker Scholarships, entry (S) 519
Wallace S. and Wilma K. Laughlin Foundation Trust Scholarships, (SS) 763
Walter J. Clore Scholarship, (S) 500
Walter S. Patterson Scholarships, (H) 1003
Walter Samuel McAfee Scholarship in Space Physics, (S) 501
Walter Schoenknecht Tourism and Travel Scholarship, (SS) 764
Walter W. Ristow Prize, (H) 1004
WAMSO Young Artist Competition Awards and Scholarships, (H) 1005
Warner N. Plummer Scholarship, (S) 502
Warren Fencl Scholarships, (A) 1306
Warren/Sanders/McNaughton Oceanographic Scholarship, (S) 503
Washington Fashion Group International Scholarship, (H) 1006
Washington NASA Space Grant Consortium Undergraduate Scholarships, (S) 504
Washington Society of CPAs Scholarships for Accounting Majors, (SS) 765
Washington State Potato Foundation Scholarships, (S) 505, (A) 1307
Waters Scholarship Program. See L.L. Waters Scholarship Program, entries (S) 296, (SS) 662
Wayne Performing Arts Award. See Miss America Competition Awards, entry (A) 1174
Webb Scholarship. See FMA–FEEA Scholarship Program, entry (A) 1102
WEC Mini Baja Challenge for Women Team Leaders, (S) 506
Wegdon Memorial Scholarship. See Far West Athletic Trainers' Association Undergraduate Scholarships, entry (S) 176

Weintraub Scholarship Fund. See Milton Weintraub Scholarship Fund, entry (A) 1172
Weisel Scholarship Award. See William E. Weisel Scholarship Award, entry (S) 513
Wells Scholarships. See Helen J. Sioussat/Fay Wells Scholarships, entry (H) 873
Welu Scholarship. See Billy Welu Scholarship, entry (A) 1051
Wendell Irish Viola Awards, (H) 1007
Werner A. Baum Endowed Scholarship. See American Meteorological Society Undergraduate Scholarships, entry (S) 32
Werner B. Thiele Memorial Scholarships, (S) 507, (H) 1008
West Michigan Chapter AWMA Scholarships, (S) 508
West Recruitment Grant. See B. June West Recruitment Grant, entry (SS) 555
West Virginia Golf Association Fund Scholarships, (A) 1308
West Virginia State War Orphans Educational Program, (A) 1309–1310
Western Federation of Professional Surveyors Scholarships, (S) 509
WesternGeco Scholarship. See SEG Scholarship Program, entry (S) 448
WesternGeco/Henry Salvatori Scholarship. See SEG Scholarship Program, entry (S) 448
Whelan Aviation Scholarship. See Paul A. Whelan Aviation Scholarship, entry (S) 378
Whitworth Memorial Scholarship. See Dan Whitworth Memorial Scholarship, entry (SS) 576
Who's Who CAP Scholarship, (A) 1311
Who's Who Sports Edition All–Academic Bowling Team Scholarships, (A) 1312
Wiechman Memorial Scholarship. See John H. Wiechman Memorial Scholarship, entry (S) 267
Wiedking, USN (Ret) Award for Community Service. See Hawaii Chapter AFCEA Scholarships, entry (S) 228
Wiesner Educational Excellence Scholarship. See Fred Wiesner Educational Excellence Scholarship, entry (SS) 602
Wilkinson Communications Scholarship. See Ray Wilkinson Communications Scholarship, entry (H) 964
Willard B. Simmons Scholarship, (S) 510
Willems Scholarship. See Donald G. Willems Scholarship, entry (S) 138
William A. Russell Scholarship for Advanced Studies, (S) 511
William B. Brandt Memorial Scholarships. See Nebraska Bankers Educational Foundation Scholarships, entry (SS) 688
William B. Ruggles Right to Work Scholarship, (H) 1009
William E. Gregory Scholarship, (SS) 766, (H) 1010
William E. Schwabe Memorial Scholarship, (S) 512
William E. Weisel Scholarship Award, (S) 513
William H. Price Scholarship in Optical Engineering. See SPIE Scholarship Program, entry (S) 464
William J. Feingold Scholarship, (S) 514
William J. Lookadoo Award. See College Photographer of the Year, entry (H) 820
William L. Cullison Scholarship, (S) 515
William L. Kokenes, USMC (Ret) Scholarship. See El Camino Real District 20 Scholarships, entry (A) 1089
William L. Stickney Endowed Scholarship. See PIEF General Scholarships, entry (H) 959
William Lowell Putnam Competition, (S) 516

S–Sciences   SS–Social Sciences   H–Humanities   A–Any Subject Area

William P. Thomas Scholarship. *See* AHEPA District Scholarship Awards, entry (A) 1018
William R. Stanitz Scholarship, (A) 1313
William Rucker Greenwood Scholarship, (S) 517
William S. Boyd Scholarship. *See* Dr. William S. Boyd Scholarship, entry (S) 149
William T. Green Scholarship. *See* Non Commissioned Officers Association Scholarship Fund, entry (A) 1216
William W. Burgin, Jr. MD Education Recognition Award, (S) 518
Williamstown Theatre Festival Apprenticeship. *See* Irene Ryan Acting Scholarships, entry (H) 890
Willie Hobbs Moore–Harry L. Morrison–Arthur B.C. Walker Scholarships, (S) 519
Willie Rudd Scholarship, (A) 1314
Willy Korf Memorial Fund Scholarships. *See* Association for Iron & Steel Technology Scholarships, entry (S) 63
Wilma K. Laughlin Foundation Trust Scholarships. *See* Wallace S. and Wilma K. Laughlin Foundation Trust Scholarships, entry (SS) 763
Wilmer Bugher Endowed Scholarship. *See* Phi Delta Kappa International Scholarship Grants for Prospective Educators, entry (SS) 712
Wilson Scholarship for Environmental Studies. *See* Larry Wilson Scholarship for Environmental Studies, entry (S) 288
Wilson Scholarships. *See* John Charles Wilson Scholarships, entries (S) 266, (SS) 643
Winkler Scholarship. *See* Tau Beta Pi Undergraduate Scholarships, entry (S) 479
Wire Reinforcement Institute Education Foundation Scholarships, (S) 520
Wisconsin Association for Health, Physical Education, Recreation, and Dance Student Scholarship Awards. *See* WAHPERD Student Scholarship Awards, entries (S) 499, (SS) 762, (H) 1002
Wisconsin Association of Professional Agricultural Consultants Scholarships, (S) 521
Wisconsin Broadcasters Association Foundation College/University Student Scholarship Program, (H) 1011
Wisconsin G.I. Bill, (A) 1315
Wisconsin Professional Police Association Scholarship Program, (SS) 767
Wisconsin Restaurant Association Education Foundation Scholarship in Foodservice, (SS) 768
Wisconsin Tuition and Fee Reimbursement Grants. *See* Wisconsin G.I. Bill, entry (A) 1315
Wolf Memorial Scholarship. *See* Lou Wolf Memorial Scholarship, entry (S) 300
Woman of Distinction Award, (S) 522, (SS) 769
Women in Federal Law Enforcement Scholarship, (SS) 770
Women@Microsoft Hoppers Scholarship, (S) 523
Women's Association of the Minnesota Orchestra Young Artist Competition Awards and Scholarships. *See* WAMSO Young Artist Competition Awards and Scholarships, entry (H) 1005
Women's Basketball Coaches Association Scholarship Awards, (A) 1316
Women's Business Alliance Scholarship Program, (SS) 771
Women's Golf Association of Massachusetts Junior Scholar Program, (A) 1317
Women's National Agricultural Aviation Association Scholarship Essay Contest, (S) 524

Women's Transportation Seminar Minnesota Chapter Scholarships. *See* Minnesota Chapter WTS Scholarships, entries (S) 323, (SS) 670
Wood Award for Excellence. *See* Dr. Harold S. Wood Award for Excellence, entry (S) 144
Wooddy Scholarships. *See* John Culver Wooddy Scholarships, entry (SS) 644
Woodlawn Farms Angus Scholarship, (A) 1318
Woodruff, Jr. Scholarships. *See* R. Preston Woodruff, Jr. Scholarships, entry (A) 1240
Woodson Memorial Award. *See* Ima Hogg Young Artist Competition, entry (H) 884
Woodward Scholarships. *See* Jay Woodward Scholarships, entry (S) 257
World Trade Center/Pentagon Fund Scholarships. *See* FEEA/World Trade Center/Pentagon Fund Scholarships, entry (A) 1098
Worthington Scholarship. *See* SEG Scholarship Program, entry (S) 448
WTVR News 6 Network Scholarship, (H) 1012
Wychor Scholarships. *See* James J. Wychor Scholarships, entry (H) 894
Wynne Jr. Memorial Award. *See* Arthur Wynne Jr. Memorial Award, entry (H) 788
Wyoming War Orphans Scholarships, (A) 1319
Wyse Advertising Scholarship. *See* Cleveland Advertising Association Education Foundation Scholarships, entry (H) 818

Xernona Clayton Brady Scholarship, (H) 1013

Yahoo! Hotjobs Scholarship. *See* NEHRA Future Stars in HR Scholarships, entry (SS) 691
Yankee District 7 Scholarships, (A) 1320
Yanmar/SAE Scholarship, (S) 525
Yavis Scholarships. *See* Dr. John C. Yavis Scholarships, entry (A) 1080
Yazaki North America Cost Award. *See* Formula SAE Competition Awards, entry (S) 187
Yazaki North America Presentation Award. *See* Formula SAE Competition Awards, entry (S) 187
Y.C. Hong Memorial Scholarship. *See* Chinese American Citizens Alliance Foundation Scholarships, entry (A) 1060
Yellow Ribbon Scholarship, (SS) 772
Yohan and Rumie Cho Scholarship. *See* KSEA Scholarships, entry (S) 286
Yoke Quong Jung Memorial Scholarship. *See* Chinese American Citizens Alliance Foundation Scholarships, entry (A) 1060
Young American Awards, (A) 1321
Young Award. *See* Drew Young Award, entry (SS) 584
Young Design Engineer's Project Competition, (S) 526
Young Entrepreneur of the Year Awards, (SS) 773
Young Film Composers Competition, (H) 1014
Young Memorial Education Recognition Award. *See* Jimmy A. Young Memorial Education Recognition Award, entry (S) 261

S–Sciences   SS–Social Sciences   H–Humanities   A–Any Subject Area

PROGRAM TITLE INDEX

Young Scholarship. *See* AIAA Foundation Undergraduate Scholarship Program, entry (S) 17

Zaja Musical Products Award. *See* National Trumpet Competition Awards, entry (H) 940
Zajta Scholarship. *See* Dr. Aurel Zajta Scholarship, entries (S) 143, (H) 839
Zeiler Awards. *See* Geraldine Colby Zeiler Awards, entry (S) 215
Zellers Scholarship. *See* PIEF General Scholarships, entry (H) 959

11th Armored Cavalry Veterans of Vietnam and Cambodia Scholarship, (A) 1322
4A–AT&T National Scholarship Program, (A) 1323
50th Anniversary–Inspiration for Tomorrow Scholarship, (S) 527
ÛKitÛ Smith Scholarship. *See* LCPA Education Foundation Scholarship Program, entry (SS) 658

S–Sciences   SS–Social Sciences   H–Humanities   A–Any Subject Area

Sponsoring Organization Index

The Sponsoring Organization Index makes it easy to identify agencies that offer merit and other no–need college funding. In this index, sponsoring organizations are listed alphabetically, word by word. In addition, we've used an alphabetical code (within parentheses) to help you identify which programs sponsored by these organizations fall within your scope of interest: S = Sciences; SS = Social Sciences; H = Humanities; A = Any Subject Area. Here's how the code works: if an organization's name is followed by (S) 41, the program sponsored by that organization is described in entry 41, in the Sciences section. If that organization's name is followed by another entry number—for example, (A) 1001—the same or a different program sponsored by the organization is described in entry 1001, in the Any Subject Area section. Remember: the numbers cited here refer to program entry numbers, not to page numbers in the book.

AACC International, (S) 1
Abbott Laboratories, (S) 114
Academy of Motion Picture Arts and Sciences, (H) 987
Academy of Neonatal Nursing, (S) 5, 189
Academy of Television Arts & Sciences Foundation, (H) 775
Accountemps, (SS) 529
Acoustical Society of America, (S) 471, (H) 989
Acton Institute for the Study of Religion and Liberty, (H) 914
Actuarial Foundation, (SS) 644
ADC Foundation, (S) 8
Adobe Systems Incorporated, (S) 9, 343
Advertising Club of Connecticut, (SS) 726, (H) 968
African Methodist Episcopal Church, (A) 1036
AgLife for America, (S) 14
Agronomic Science Foundation, (S) 253
Agusta Corporation, (S) 31
Air Force Association, (A) 1027
Air Force Sergeants Association, (A) 1025, 1029
Air Line Pilots Association, (S) 339
Air & Waste Management Association. Connecticut Chapter, (S) 119
Air & Waste Management Association. West Michigan Chapter, (S) 508
Aircraft Electronics Association, (S) 84, 108, 128, 150, 200, 234, 272, 287, 291, 303, 321, 339, 466, (SS) 567, (A) 1028
Aircraft Owners and Pilots Association, (S) 339
Airmen Memorial Foundation, (A) 1029
Akademos, Inc., (A) 1286
Alabama Department of Veterans Affairs, (A) 1030
Alabama Golf Course Superintendents Association, (S) 139
Alabama Power Foundation, (S) 479
Alabama Space Grant Consortium, (S) 492
Alaska Broadcasters Association, (H) 913
Alaska. Office of Veterans Affairs, (A) 1031
Albuquerque Veterinary Association, Inc., (S) 23

Alcoa Foundation, (S) 24
Alexandria Symphony Orchestra, (H) 921
All–Ink.com, (A) 1034
Alliance of State Automotive Aftermarket Associations, (SS) 612
Allyn & Bacon Publishers, (SS) 535
Alpha Chi, (A) 1033, 1088
Alpha Gamma Rho Fraternity, (S) 28, 206, (SS) 606
Alpha Kappa Alpha Sorority, Inc., (A) 1035
Alpha Lambda Delta, (A) 1137
Americal Division Veterans Association, (A) 1037
American Academy of Oral and Maxillofacial Radiology, (S) 102
American Academy of Physician Assistants–Veterans Caucus, (S) 3, 101
American Advertising Federation, (H) 931, 938
American Airlines, (A) 1178
American Alliance for Health, Physical Education, Recreation and Dance, (S) 435, (SS) 731, (H) 970
American Angus Association, (S) 39, 86, (A) 1140, 1318
American Association for Dental Research, (S) 387
American Association for Geodetic Surveying, (S) 273
American Association for Health Education, (S) 79, (SS) 559
American Association for Respiratory Care, (S) 261, 331, 423, 518
American Association of Advertising Agencies, (SS) 542
American Association of Attorney–Certified Public Accountants Foundation, (SS) 552
American Association of Family and Consumer Sciences, (SS) 640
American Association of Neuroscience Nurses, (S) 353
American Association of Occupational Health Nurses, Inc., (S) 24, 29, 293, 314
American Association of Textile Chemists and Colorists, (S) 4, (H) 828

S–Sciences   SS–Social Sciences   H–Humanities   A–Any Subject Area

SPONSORING ORGANIZATION INDEX

American Association of University Women. Honolulu Branch, (S) 490
American Astronomical Society, (S) 227, 318, 430, 501
American Atheists, (A) 1082, 1154
American Business Educators, (SS) 536
American Ceramic Society, (S) 145
American College of Chiropractic Orthopedists, (S) 174
American College of Healthcare Executives, (S) 472, (SS) 748
American Composites Manufacturers Association, (S) 201
American Congress on Surveying and Mapping, (S) 7, 78, 87, 97, 273, 310, 352, 362–363, 443, (SS) 564, 753
American Copy Editors Society, (H) 824
American Council of Engineering Companies, (S) 30
American Council of the Blind, (S) 52, 148, 280, (SS) 548, 697, (A) 1081, 1090, 1101, 1246
American Dairy Science Association, (S) 212
American Darts Organization, (A) 1038
American Electroplaters and Surface Finishers Society, (S) 10
American Federation of Government Employees, (A) 1139
American Foundation for the Blind, (S) 379, 433, (SS) 730, (H) 859, 967
American Guild of Organists, (H) 779
American Guild of Organists. Syracuse Chapter, (H) 787
American Hazard Control Consultants, Inc., (S) 474
American Health Information Management Association, (S) 169, 186, 190, 406, (SS) 593, 598–599, 717
American Helicopter Society, (S) 31
American Hellenic Educational Progressive Association, (SS) 611, (H) 858, (A) 1018, 1080, 1108, 1214, 1249, 1263
American Hellenic Educational Progressive Association. District 03, (A) 1057
American Hellenic Educational Progressive Association. District 07, (A) 1320
American Hellenic Educational Progressive Association. District 20, (A) 1089
American Hellenic Educational Progressive Association. District 22, (A) 1100
American Humanics, Inc., (SS) 538
American Indian Arts Council, Inc., (H) 783
American Indian Heritage Foundation, (A) 1176
American Indian Science and Engineering Society, (S) 22, 68
American Institute of Aeronautics and Astronautics, (S) 16–17, 100
American Institute of Aeronautics and Astronautics. Houston Section, (S) 465
American Institute of Certified Public Accountants, (SS) 529
American Institute of Chemical Engineers, (S) 105, 137, 269, 324, 498
American Institute of Food and Wine. Connecticut Chapter, (H) 827
American Institute of Physics, (S) 383, 457, 467, (SS) 744
American Institute of Polish Culture, Inc., (SS) 616, (H) 866
American Institute of Steel Construction, (S) 55, 462, (H) 778
American Institute of Wine & Food. Pacific Northwest Chapter, (H) 901
American Iron and Steel Institute, (S) 55, 179
American Jersey Cattle Association, (S) 99, 380, 408, 497, 511
American Legacy Foundation, (A) 1061
American Legion. New York Auxiliary, (A) 1099
American Legion. Ohio Department, (A) 1222
American Mathematical Society, (S) 192

American Mensa Education and Research Foundation, (S) 130, (A) 1136, 1167
American Meteorological Society, (S) 32, 170, 299
American National CattleWomen, Inc., (S) 340
American Nuclear Society, (S) 43, 103, 132, 256
American Physical Society, (S) 45, 292
American Physical Therapy Association, (S) 325
American Planning Association, (SS) 594
American Police Hall of Fame and Museum, (A) 1039
American Production & Inventory Control Society, (SS) 583
American Public Power Association, (S) 133
American Railway Engineering and Maintenance of Way Association, (S) 50, 116, 316
American Registry of Professional Animal Scientists. Pacific Northwest Chapter, (S) 372
American Sheep Industry Women, (H) 935
American Society for Clinical Laboratory Science. Pennsylvania, (S) 56
American Society for Enology and Viticulture, (S) 33
American Society for Horticultural Science, (S) 60, 151
American Society for Nondestructive Testing, Inc., (S) 416
American Society for Quality, (S) 514
American Society of Agricultural and Biological Engineers, (S) 13, 202, 270
American Society of Agronomy, (S) 253
American Society of Agronomy. California Chapter, (S) 85
American Society of Civil Engineers, (S) 55
American Society of Composers, Authors and Publishers, (H) 789, 926
American Society of Cytopathology, (S) 215
American Society of Engineers of Indian Origin, (S) 57, (H) 790
American Society of Farm Managers and Rural Appraisers. California Chapter, (S) 34, (SS) 540
American Society of Heating, Refrigerating and Air-Conditioning Engineers, Inc., (S) 58–59
American Society of Heating, Refrigerating and Air-Conditioning Engineers, Inc. Illinois Chapter, (S) 244
American Society of Highway Engineers. Carolina Triangle Section, (S) 418
American Society of Interior Designers, (H) 899
American Society of Landscape Architects. Connecticut Chapter, (H) 826
American Society of Plumbing Engineers, (S) 25
American Society of Transportation and Logistics, Inc., (S) 296, (SS) 662
American Society of Travel Agents, (SS) 532, 534, 537, 546, 553, 623, 743, (A) 1142
American Standard Companies, (S) 35
American Statistical Association, (S) 271
American String Teachers Association, (H) 792
American Water Resources Association, (S) 409
American Water Ski Educational Foundation, (A) 1187
American Water Works Association. Montana Section, (S) 138
American Welding Society, (S) 236, 252, 397, 407, 422, (SS) 637
American Women in Radio and Television. New York City Chapter, (H) 795
American Wool Council, (H) 935
Amgen Inc., (S) 37
Angelus Student Film Festival, (H) 786
Angie M. Houtz Memorial Fund, (A) 1041
Angus Foundation, (S) 39, (A) 1140, 1318

S–Sciences　　　　SS–Social Sciences　　　　H–Humanities　　　　A–Any Subject Area

SPONSORING ORGANIZATION INDEX 459

Annie's Homegrown, Inc., (S) 42
Anthony J. Jannetti, Inc., (S) 189
Anti-Defamation League, (H) 838
A.O. Smith Water Heaters, (S) 44
Appaloosa Youth Foundation, Inc., (S) 439
Applied Measurement Professionals, Inc., (S) 423, 518
Appraisal Institute, (SS) 544
Aquatrols Corporation, (S) 46
Arab American Institute Foundation, (A) 1119
ARC of Washington Trust Fund, (S) 47, (SS) 545
Arizona State University. Center for Meteorite Studies, (S) 142
Arkansas Environmental Federation, (S) 288, 405
Arkansas Game and Fish Commission, (S) 51
Arkansas Society of Certified Public Accountants, (SS) 547
Arkansas Student Loan Authority, (A) 1240
Armed Forces Communications and Electronics Association, (S) 11
Armed Forces Communications and Electronics Association. Hawaii Chapter, (S) 228
Army Aviation Association of America Scholarship Foundation, (A) 1044
Army Officers' Wives' Club of the Greater Washington Area, (A) 1043
Arthur B. Klussendorf Memorial Association, (S) 285
Arthur W. Page Society, (SS) 565, (H) 812
ASME International, (S) 61–62, 193, 196–197, 281, 368, 399, 419, 458, 473–474, 480, 526
Associated Collegiate Press, (H) 776–777
Associated General Contractors of America, (S) 255
Associated Press Sports Editors, (H) 791
Association for Education in Journalism and Mass Communication, (H) 910, 963
Association for Intelligence Officers, (SS) 615
Association for Iron & Steel Technology, (S) 63, 179, 512
Association for the Advancement of Cost Engineering, (S) 2
Association for Theatre in Higher Education, (H) 939
Association for Women Geoscientists, (S) 64, 517
Association for Women in Communications. Washington DC Area Chapter, (H) 797
Association for Women in Mathematics, (S) 26
Association for Women in Science, (S) 284
Association for Women in Sports Media, (H) 791
Association of Certified Fraud Examiners, (SS) 724
Association of Certified Fraud Examiners. Heartland Chapter, (SS) 722
Association of Collegiate Schools of Architecture, (H) 778, 823
Association of Cuban Engineers, (S) 65
Association of Environmental and Engineering Geologists, (S) 307–308
Association of Former Agents of the United States Secret Service, Inc., (SS) 657
Association of Government Accountants, (SS) 550, 572
Association of Independent Colleges and Universities of Pennsylvania, (A) 1071
Association of Independent Corrugated Converters, (S) 470, (H) 988
Association of Information Technology Professionals. Omaha Chapter, (SS) 531
Association of National Advertisers, (SS) 542
Association of Nurses in AIDS Care, (S) 38
Association of Rehabilitation Nurses, (S) 66

Association of Schools of Journalism and Mass Communication, (H) 869–871
Association of Texas Professional Educators, (SS) 557, 602
Association of the United States Army, (S) 274, (A) 1152
Association of Theatrical Press Agents and Managers, (A) 1172
Association of United Nurses, (S) 67
Atlanta Association of Black Journalists, (H) 1013
Atlanta Press Club, Inc., (H) 793
Autism Society of America, (A) 1086
Automotive Aftermarket Industry Association, (SS) 612
Automotive Industries Association of Canada, (SS) 612
Automotive Parts Rebuilders Association, (SS) 612
Automotive Warehouse Distributors Association, (SS) 612
Ayn Rand Institute, (H) 794

Barbara Alice Mower Memorial Scholarship Committee, (SS) 556
Barnum Festival Foundation, (H) 799
Barry M. Goldwater Scholarship and Excellence in Education Foundation, (S) 72
Bechtel Foundation, (S) 74
Ben Meadows Company, (S) 75
Berntsen International, Inc., (S) 78
Beta Sigma Psi Educational Foundation, (A) 1049
Bethesda Lutheran Homes and Services, Inc., (S) 135
BizFilings, (SS) 696
Black Enterprise Magazine, (S) 519
Blacks in Government, (A) 1096
Blind Information Technology Specialist, Inc., (S) 280
Blinded Veterans Association, (A) 1146
Blue Cross/Blue Shield Association, (A) 1095
Boeing Company, (S) 62, (A) 1052
Bookbuilders West, (H) 975
Boy Scouts of America. Learning for Life Division, (S) 339, (SS) 551, 736, (A) 1321
Boy Scouts of America. National Eagle Scout Association, (A) 1113
BP Exploration and Production, Inc., (S) 81
Bradford White Corporation, (S) 82
Broadcast Education Association, (H) 774, 781, 785, 800, 865, 873, 958, 1003
Brown Foundation for Educational Equity, Excellence and Research, (SS) 560, (A) 1111
Brown Foundation, Inc., (H) 984
Bureau of Alcohol, Tobacco, Firearms and Explosives Retiree's Association, (SS) 551
Burlington Northern Santa Fe Foundation, (S) 50

Cactus and Pine Golf Course Superintendents Association, (S) 257
California Agricultural Irrigation Association, (S) 88
California Association of Nurseries and Garden Centers, (S) 93
California Department of Veterans Affairs, (A) 1055
California Environmental Health Association, (S) 309
California Farm Bureau Scholarship Foundation, (S) 89, 96, 194, 237, 267
California Hotel & Lodging Association, (SS) 562
California Landscape Contractors Association, (S) 290

S–Sciences   SS–Social Sciences   H–Humanities   A–Any Subject Area

SPONSORING ORGANIZATION INDEX

California Planning Roundtable, (SS) 720
California Restaurant Association, (H) 806
California State Fair, (S) 91–92, 156, (SS) 563, 587, (H) 807–808, (A) 1016, 1047
California Teachers Association, (SS) 654
California 4-H Foundation, (S) 34, 131, (SS) 540
Campus Compact, (A) 1126
Campus Safety Health and Environmental Management Association, (S) 123
Capital Foundation, (A) 1047
Carmel Music Society, (H) 809
Carolina Film and Video Festival, (H) 811
Carpe Diem Foundation of Illinois, (A) 1059
Cartography and Geographic Information Society, (S) 97, (SS) 564
Case IH, (S) 36, 115, (SS) 541, 571
Case Western Reserve University. Department of Theater and Dance, (H) 919
Caterpillar, Inc., (S) 98
Cattlemen's Beef Board, (S) 340
CCIM Institute, (SS) 566, 746
Center for Education Solutions, (A) 1015
Center for the Advancement of Process Technology, (S) 81, 451
Central California Council of Diving Clubs, (S) 90
Certified Angus Beef LLC, (S) 86
The Cerutti Group, (S) 205, (H) 856
Cessna Aircraft Company, (S) 100
Chase Bank, (A) 1026
Chevron Corporation, (S) 106
Chicago Mercantile Exchange, (S) 107, 188, (H) 850
Children's Theatre Foundation of America, (H) 992
Chinese American Citizens Alliance, (A) 1060
Chiropractic Association of Louisiana, (S) 149
Choice Hotels International, (SS) 771
Chopin Foundation of the United States, Inc., (H) 933
Christian Church (Disciples of Christ), (A) 1120
The Christophers, (H) 998
Chronicle of Higher Education, (H) 834
CH2M Hill, (S) 395
Civil Air Patrol, (A) 1063–1065, 1295, 1311
Civil Engineers of America, (S) 110
Cleveland Advertising Association, (H) 818
Club Foundation, (SS) 641
Coalition of Higher Education Assistance Organizations, (A) 1068
Coca-Cola Scholars Foundation, Inc., (A) 1067
Colin Higgins Foundation, (A) 1069
Colorado Broadcasters Association, (H) 821–822
Colorado Federation of NARFE Chapters, (A) 1070
Colorado Fiscal Managers Association, (SS) 750
Colorado Society of Certified Public Accountants, (SS) 591
Colorado Young Farmers Educational Association, (S) 115, (SS) 571
Comedy Central, Inc., (H) 890, 920
Community Foundation of Louisville, (S) 83
Computing Research Association, (S) 121
Concrete Reinforcing Steel Institute, (S) 122
Conference of Minority Transportation Officials, (S) 94, 431, 482, 488, (SS) 728, (A) 1245
Conference of Minority Transportation Officials. New Jersey Chapter, (S) 118, (SS) 573

Connecticut Association of Purchasing Management, Inc., (A) 1243
Connecticut Commission on Culture and Tourism, (SS) 719, 764
Connecticut Hospitality Educational Foundation, (SS) 574
Connecticut Lodging Association, (SS) 574
Connecticut National Guard Foundation, Inc., (A) 1072, 1255
Connecticut Restaurant Association, (SS) 574
ConstructMyFuture.com, (S) 120, (SS) 575
COPI/OutputLinks, (S) 143, 238, 263, 522, (SS) 627, 642, 769, (H) 839
Cornhusker State Games, (A) 1104
Coty US LLC, (A) 1054, 1160
Crazy Horse Memorial Foundation, (H) 825
Cumberland Valley Volunteer Firemen's Association, (S) 275

Daedalian Foundation, (S) 124–125, 264
DaimlerChrysler Corporation, (S) 126
Dairy Management Inc., (S) 341, 349, (SS) 686
Dallas Architectural Foundation, (H) 922
Dallas Human Resource Management Association, Inc., (SS) 584
Dance Society of America, (H) 829
Danish Sisterhood of America, (A) 1050
Daughters of Penelope, (A) 1075
Daughters of Penelope. District 2, (A) 1074
Dawn Rochele Productions, (A) 1177
DECA, (SS) 617
Dekker Foundation, (S) 269
Dell'Arte Mad River Festival, (H) 890
Deloitte Foundation, (SS) 580
Delta Air Lines, (S) 343
Delta Faucet Company, (S) 134
Delta Kappa Gamma Society International. Kappa State Organization, (SS) 530
Delta Kappa Gamma Society International. Lambda State Organization, (H) 918
Delta Kappa Gamma Society International. Theta State Organization, (SS) 555
Delta Nu Alpha, (SS) 581
Des Moines Symphony Alliance, (H) 836
Descendants of the Signers of the Declaration of Independence, (A) 1079
Disabled American Veterans, (A) 1134
Dobson Communications Corporation, (A) 1237
Dog Writers Association of America, (A) 1084
Donald A. Perry Foundation, (A) 1303
Donald F. & Mildred Topp Othmer Foundation, (S) 137
Dow Jones Newspaper Fund, (H) 805, 943, 948, 985
D.P. Associates Inc., (A) 1194
Dramatic Publishing Company, (H) 915
Dramatists Guild, Inc., (H) 896, 939
D.W. Simpson & Company, (SS) 585

Eastern Surfing Association, (A) 1164
Edelman Worldwide, Inc., (H) 830
Educational Communications Scholarship Foundation, (A) 1311
E.I. duPont de Nemours and Company, Inc., (S) 498

S–Sciences   SS–Social Sciences   H–Humanities   A–Any Subject Area

SPONSORING ORGANIZATION INDEX

Elder and Leemaur Publishers, (A) 1294
Electronic Document Systems Foundation, (S) 143, 238, 263, 522, (SS) 577, 588–589, 619, 627, 642, 769, (H) 831, 839, 843–844, 872
Electronics for Imaging, Inc., (S) 158
Eli Lilly and Company, (S) 343
Entomological Society of America, (S) 249
Environmental Professionals' Organization of Connecticut, (S) 166
Ernie Ayer Aviation Education Foundation, (S) 168
Eurocopter, (S) 31
European Power Electronics Association, (S) 250
Evangelical Press Association, (H) 846
Evrytanian Association of America, (A) 1215
Excel Geophysics, (S) 172
Experimental Aviation Association, (S) 339
ExxonMobil Corporation, (S) 329, 343
ExxonMobil Foundation, (S) 64

Fabricators and Manufacturers Association, (S) 175, (A) 1093
Family Campers and RVers, (S) 177, (A) 1094
Far West Athletic Trainers' Association, (S) 176
Fargo–Moorhead Area Foundation, (S) 523
Farm Credit Services of Hawaii, ACA, (S) 178
Farm Credit System, (S) 36, (SS) 541
Fashion Group International of Washington, (H) 1006
Federal Aviation Administration Managers Association, (A) 1092
Federal Employee Education and Assistance Fund, (A) 1070, 1092, 1095–1098, 1102, 1139, 1212, 1225
Federal Managers Association, (A) 1102
Federated Garden Clubs of Maryland, (S) 496
Film Music Publications, Inc., (H) 1014
Finlandia Foundation. New York Metropolitan Chapter, (S) 146, (H) 897, (A) 1210
First Church of Christ, (H) 815
First Command Educational Foundation, (A) 1043
Fisher House Foundation, (A) 1250
Flexible Packaging Association, (S) 181
Flexible Pavements of Ohio, (S) 366
Flexographic Technical Association, (H) 848
Flint Ink, (S) 182, (H) 849
Florida Association of Educational Data Systems, (S) 147
Florida Bankers Association, (SS) 596
Florida Public Relations Association, (H) 851
Fluor, (S) 479
FM Global, (S) 474
Food Processing Suppliers Association, (S) 183
Ford Motor Company, (S) 185, (A) 1103
Forum for Military Applications of Directed Energy, (S) 464
Fraternal Order of Eagles, (A) 1085
Freedom Forum, (H) 816, 853
Freedom from Religion Foundation, (H) 854
Freescale Semiconductor, (S) 343
Friends of the Frelinghuysen Arboretum, (S) 77, (H) 801
Friends–in–Art, (H) 855
The Fund for Theological Education, Inc., (H) 951

The Gallup Organization, (A) 1104
Garden Club of America, (S) 203
GE Fund, (S) 207, 343, (SS) 607
GE Healthcare, (S) 173
GEICO Insurance, (A) 1106
General Aviation Manufacturers Association, (S) 144, 339
General Electric Company. Women's Network, (S) 208
General Mills, Inc., (S) 105
General Motors Corporation, (S) 210–211, 479
General Motors Foundation, (S) 209
General Motors Minority Dealers Association, (A) 1107
George A. Nielsen LLP, (SS) 608
George and Donna Nigh Institute, (SS) 609
George Mason University. Department of Music, (H) 940
Georgia Association of Broadcasters, Inc., (H) 840
Georgia Space Grant Consortium, (S) 214
Georgia Trust, (H) 798, 892
Gibson Foundation, (H) 789
Givaudan Flavor Corporation, (S) 216
Glamour, (A) 1109
Glenn Miller Birthplace Society, (H) 860
Global Alliance for Preserving the History of WWII in Asia, (H) 891
Global Automotive Aftermarket Symposium, (SS) 612
Golden Key International Honour Society, (S) 184, 217, (SS) 561, 590, 597, (H) 861, (A) 1106, 1110
Goldman, Sachs & Company, (S) 218
Golf Course Superintendents Association of America, (S) 204, 219, 446, (A) 1105
Goodman & Company, (SS) 613
Goodyear Tire and Rubber Company, (A) 1111
Google Inc., (S) 40
Government Finance Officers Association, (SS) 601, 608, 671
GR Technologies Family, (H) 940
Gravure Association of America, (S) 182, 205, 221, 507, (H) 849, 856, 862–863, 1008
Great Lakes Commission, (S) 95
Greater Kanawha Valley Foundation, (A) 1308
Guidant Foundation, (S) 222
Guitar Center, (H) 1014

Hallmark Cards, Inc., (H) 863
Hamptons International Film Festival, (H) 864
Handgards Inc., (S) 335, (SS) 677
Handweavers Guild of America, Inc., (H) 835, 876
Hawai'i Community Foundation, (S) 229, 262, 298, (H) 868, (A) 1066, 1229
Hawaii. Department of Hawaiian Home Lands, (S) 229, (H) 868
Hawai'i Hospitality Sales and Marketing Association, (SS) 622
Healthcare Contract Resources, (S) 186, (SS) 598
Healthcare Information and Management Systems Society, (S) 230, 411, (SS) 618, 721
The Hear Me Project, (A) 1116
Heart of America Golf Course Superintendents Association, (S) 231
Heidelberg USA, (SS) 619, (H) 872
Helping Hands Foundation, (A) 1121
Hemophilia Health Services, (S) 445
Herb Society of America. South Texas Unit, (S) 461
High Plains Journal, (H) 877

S–Sciences   SS–Social Sciences   H–Humanities   A–Any Subject Area

SPONSORING ORGANIZATION INDEX

Ho–Chunk Nation, (A) 1124
Home Builders Association of Illinois, (S) 233, (H) 878
Honolulu Alumnae Panhellenic Association, (A) 1125
Hoosier Hampshire Swine Breeders Association, (S) 235
Hospitality Sales and Marketing Association International, (SS) 625
Houston Symphony, (H) 884
Human Resource Association of the National Capital Area, (SS) 624

IBM Corporation, (S) 22, 242
Idaho Society of Certified Public Accountants, (SS) 629
IEEE Computer Society, (S) 117, 410
Illinois Association for Health, Physical Education, Recreation and Dance, (S) 241, (SS) 628, (H) 880
Illinois Council of Teachers of Mathematics, (S) 441, (SS) 733
Illinois Pork Producers Association, (S) 245
Illinois Tool Works Welding Companies, (S) 252
IMC America, (S) 205, (H) 856
Imperial Polk Advertising Federation, (SS) 766, (H) 1010
Independent Colleges of Washington, (A) 1052, 1076, 1232, 1271, 1287, 1292
Independent Institute, (SS) 705
Indiana Broadcasters Association, (H) 885
Indiana High School Press Association, (H) 886
Indianapolis Association of Black Journalists, (H) 886
Indianapolis Press Club Foundation Inc., (H) 993
InfoComm International, (S) 248, (H) 889
Ingenix Companies, (S) 186, (SS) 598
Institute for Humane Studies at George Mason University, (SS) 626, (H) 879
Institute for Public Relations Research and Education, (SS) 565, (H) 812
Institute for Supply Management. Northeast Supply Management Group., (A) 1243
Institute of Electrical and Electronics Engineers. Engineering in Medicine and Biology Society, (S) 164
Institute of Electrical and Electronics Engineers. Industrial Electronics Society, (S) 250
Institute of Electrical and Electronics Engineers. Industry Applications Society, (S) 250
Institute of Electrical and Electronics Engineers. Power Electronics Society, (S) 250
Institute of Electrical and Electronics Engineers. Power Engineering Society, (S) 250, 395
Institute of Food Technologists, (S) 53, 216, 247, 268, 277, 313, 358, 375, 401, 459, 527
Institute of Management Accountants, (SS) 632–633, 747
Institute of Noise Control Engineering, (S) 246
Integrity Graphics, Inc., (H) 887
Interlochen Arts Camp, (H) 940
International Association for Dental Research, (S) 239
International Association for Great Lakes Research, (S) 381
International Association of Arson Investigators, (S) 266, 421, (SS) 643, 727
International Association of Culinary Professionals Foundation, (H) 827
International Association of Lighting Designers, (H) 888
International Association of Machinists and Aerospace Workers, (A) 1127

International Congress on Insect Neurochemistry and Neurophysiology, (S) 249
International Corrugated Packaging Foundation, (S) 470, (H) 988
International Dairy–Deli–Bakery Association, (S) 243, (SS) 630, (H) 881
International Facility Management Association, (SS) 631
International Furnishings and Design Association, (H) 813, 882, 971
International Housewares Association, (H) 883
International Petroleum Technology Institute, (S) 386
International Public Management Association for Human Resources, (SS) 634, (A) 1128
International Right of Way Association, (S) 468, (SS) 745
International Technology Education Association, (S) 195, (SS) 603
International Trumpet Guild, (H) 940
International Union of Electronic, Electrical, Salaried, Machine, and Furniture Workers, (S) 129, (A) 1053, 1132, 1231, 1244, 1247, 1314
Iowa United Methodist Foundation, (A) 1129
Irene Ryan Foundation, (H) 890
ITS Washington, (S) 251, (SS) 636

Jamatex, (A) 1178
James F. Lincoln Arc Welding Foundation, (S) 48–49, 55
James S. Kemper Foundation, (SS) 652
Japanese American Citizens League, (H) 780, 874
JoAnne Robinson Memorial Scholarship Fund, (H) 898
John F. Kennedy Center for the Performing Arts. American College Theater Festival, (H) 890, 896, 900, 905, 907–908, 915, 920, 939, 953, 992
Johnson & Johnson Medical, Inc., (S) 343
Johnson Polymer, (S) 205, (H) 856
Joseph B. Whitehead Foundation, (A) 1067
Josephine de Kármán Fellowship Trust, (H) 902, (A) 1143
Journalism Education Association, (SS) 647
JPMorganChase, (H) 984
Julius & Esther Stulberg Competition, Inc., (H) 903

Kansas Commission on Veterans' Affairs, (A) 1145
Kansas Junior Livestock Association, (H) 877
Kansas Livestock Association, (H) 877
Kansas Women's Golf Association, (A) 1189
Kappa Alpha Mu, (H) 820
Kentucky Broadcasters Association, (H) 867
Kentucky Department of Veterans Affairs, (A) 1091, 1149, 1289
Kentucky Fire Commission, (A) 1147
Kentucky Horse Council, (S) 282
Kentucky Society of Certified Public Accountants, (SS) 653
Kentucky Space Grant Consortium, (S) 283
Kentucky Turfgrass Council, (A) 1148
Kidger Optics Associates, (S) 317
Korean–American Scientists and Engineers Association, (S) 109, 286
Kurzweil Foundation, (S) 52, 148, 280, (SS) 548, 697, (A) 1081, 1090, 1101, 1246

S–Sciences   SS–Social Sciences   H–Humanities   A–Any Subject Area

SPONSORING ORGANIZATION INDEX

Labsphere, Inc., (S) 464
Laser Focus World, (S) 464
Lawrence Livermore National Laboratory, (S) 344
League of United Latin American Citizens, (S) 207, 211, (SS) 607
Liberty Leadership Fund, (S) 293
Liggett-Stashower, Inc., (H) 832
Lighthouse International, (A) 1291
Lilly Endowment, Inc., (H) 886
Lincoln Community Foundation, (SS) 595, (A) 1217
Livestock Publications Council, (S) 188, (H) 850
Lockheed Martin Aeronautics Company, (S) 297
Lockheed Martin Corporation, (S) 343
Louisiana Agricultural Consultants Association, (S) 302
Louisiana Department of Veterans Affairs, (A) 1155
Louisiana Office of Student Financial Assistance, (S) 425
L3 Communications, (A) 1194

Madden Preprint Media, (A) 1160
Maddenmedia, (A) 1054
Maine. Bureau of Veterans' Services, (A) 1159
Maine. Finance Authority, (A) 1157-1158
The Maintenance Council of American Trucking Associations, (S) 485
Maller Baroque Brass Instruments, (H) 940
Maple Lawn Farms, (S) 240
Margolis Brown Theater Company, (H) 890
Marine Corps Counterintelligence Association, (A) 1161
Marine Corps Intelligence Association, Inc., (A) 1138
Marine Corps League, (A) 1162
Marine Technology Society, (S) 265, 332, 374, 432
Martin Barnes Scholarship Fund, (A) 1165
Maryland Association for Health, Physical Education, Recreation and Dance, (SS) 666
MasterCard, (A) 1026
Mathematical Association of America, (S) 159, 192, 516
MC Strategies, Inc., (S) 186, (SS) 598
MCT Campus, (H) 777
MedProRx, Inc., (A) 1087
MedQuist Inc., (S) 186, (SS) 598
Medtronic Physio-Control Corporation, (S) 314
Mel Fisher Maritime Heritage Society and Museum, (S) 136
Mennonite Church USA, (A) 1273
Merck Company Foundation, (S) 491
Metropolitan Opera, (H) 923
Metropolitan Society of Kardamylians, Inc., (A) 1168
Michigan Department of Treasury, (A) 1169
Microsoft Corporation, (S) 117, 121, 319-320, 343
Mikimoto, (A) 1178-1179
Military Officers Association of America, (A) 1180
Military Order of the Purple Heart, (A) 1170
Minnesota Broadcasters Association, (H) 894
Minnesota Business Educators, Inc., (SS) 669
Minnesota Livestock Breeders' Association, (S) 69
Miss America Pageant, (A) 1174
Miss Black America Pageant, (A) 1175
Miss Universe Organization, (A) 1178-1179
Missouri Angus Association, (S) 326-327
Missouri Department of Natural Resources, (S) 165

Missouri Educators of Family and Consumer Sciences, (SS) 674
Missouri Middle School Association, (SS) 549
Missouri Photo Workshop, (H) 820
Missouri School of Journalism, (H) 820
Missouri Society of Certified Public Accountants, (SS) 659
Missouri Travel Council, (SS) 673
Mitsubishi Electric Research Lab, (S) 121
Mohair Council of America, (H) 935
Montana Office of Higher Education, (S) 453
Montana Water Environment Association, (S) 138
Morris K. Udall Foundation, (S) 330, (SS) 675
Morris Land Conservancy, (S) 428, 434
Mortgage Bankers Association of the Carolinas, Inc., (SS) 569
Motor & Equipment Manufacturers Association, (SS) 612
Mr. Collegiate African American Scholarship Pageant, (A) 1185
Mystic Tan, (A) 1178

NAC, Inc., (S) 464
Nation Institute, (H) 930
National Ad 2, (H) 931
National Agricultural Aviation Association, (S) 524
National Air Transportation Foundation, (S) 127, 392
National Association for Campus Activities, (A) 1186
National Association for the Advancement of Colored People, (SS) 586
National Association for the Self-Employed, (SS) 604
National Association of Broadcasters, (H) 865, 1003
National Association of Government Employees, (SS) 665, (H) 845
National Association of Insurance Women, (SS) 635, 676, 680
National Association of Negro Musicians, Inc., (H) 932
National Association of Science Writers, (S) 171, (H) 847
National Athletic Trainers' Association, (S) 336
National Bison Association, (S) 484
National Black MBA Association, (SS) 681
National Black MBA Association. New York Chapter, (SS) 668
National Black MBA Association. Washington, D.C. Chapter, (SS) 578
National Board for Respiratory Care, (S) 423, 518
National Campers and Hikers Association, (S) 177, (A) 1094
National Cattlemen's Foundation, (S) 107
National Center for American Indian Enterprise Development, (SS) 539
National Collegiate Athletic Association, (H) 853
National Commission for Cooperative Education, (S) 347, (A) 1200
National Communication Association, (H) 895
National Community Pharmacists Association, (S) 258, 348, 510
National Council for the Social Studies, (SS) 579
National Council of Acoustical Consultants, (S) 471, (H) 989
National Council of Teachers of Mathematics, (S) 481
National Dairy Promotion and Research Board, (S) 349, (SS) 686
National Dairy Shrine, (S) 240, 285, 341
National Defense Transportation Association, (S) 350, (SS) 687
National Environmental Health Association, (S) 351
National Federation of Independent Business, (SS) 696

S-Sciences   SS-Social Sciences   H-Humanities   A-Any Subject Area

National Federation of Music Clubs, (H) 782, 917, 944, 978, 997, 999, 1007
National Federation of Republican Women, (SS) 558, (A) 1188
National FFA Organization, (S) 15, 36, 342, (SS) 541, 682, (H) 934, (A) 1103
National Fire Protection Association, (S) 213, (SS) 610
National Foundation for Teaching Entrepreneurship, (SS) 773
National Geographic Society, (H) 820
National Guard Association of New Jersey, (A) 1191
National Head Start Association, (A) 1042
National Hemophilia Foundation, (A) 1151, 1239
National Hispanic Coalition of Federal Aviation Employees, (A) 1212
National Huguenot Society, (A) 1192
National Industries for the Blind, (SS) 697
National Institute for Labor Relations Research, (SS) 543, (H) 1009
National Intercollegiate Flying Association, (S) 144
National Inventors Hall of Fame, (S) 114
National Junior Angus Association, (S) 39, 86, (A) 1140, 1318
National Meat Association, (S) 359
National Opera Association, (H) 936
National Order of Omega, (A) 1227
National Organization for the Professional Advancement of Black Chemists and Chemical Engineers, (S) 429
National Press Foundation, (S) 171, (H) 847
National Press Photographers Foundation, (H) 820
National Restaurant Association Educational Foundation, (SS) 533, 683
National Rifle Association of America, (A) 1133
National Safety Council, (S) 123
National Scholastic Surfing Association, (A) 1221
National Society of Black Engineers, (S) 198, 343, 493
National Society of Black Physicists, (S) 161, 227, 318, 344, 415, 430, 501, 519
National Society of Newspaper Columnists, (H) 937
National Society of Professional Engineers, (S) 384
National Society of Professional Surveyors, (S) 310, 362–363
National Steel Bridge Alliance, (S) 55
National Strength and Conditioning Association, (S) 396
National Tour Association, (SS) 684, 702
National Treasury Employees Union, (A) 1097
National Trumpet Competition, (H) 940
National 4th Infantry (IVY) Division Association, (A) 1193
Navajo Nation, (SS) 685
Naval Helicopter Association, (A) 1194
Naval Special Warfare Foundation, (A) 1017, 1195, 1290
Navy Counselor Association, (A) 1196
Navy–Marine Corps Relief Society, (A) 1048
Nebraska Bankers Association, (SS) 688
Nebraska. Department of Veterans' Affairs, (A) 1202
Nebraska Funeral Directors Association, (SS) 763
Nebraska Society of Certified Public Accountants, (SS) 689
Nebraska Space Grant Consortium, (A) 1201
Network of Executive Women, (SS) 692
Nevada Space Grant Consortium, (S) 354
New Buildings Institute, (S) 289, (H) 911
New England Direct Marketing Association, (SS) 582, (H) 837
New England Employee Benefits Council, (SS) 690
New Hampshire Charitable Foundation, (S) 180
New Hampshire Department of Resources and Economic Development, (S) 180

New Hampshire Golf Course Superintendents Association, (S) 355
New Hampshire Land Surveyors Foundation, (S) 27, 502
New Jersey Department of Military and Veterans Affairs, (A) 1203
New Jersey Higher Education Student Assistance Authority, (A) 1073, 1204–1205
New Jersey Press Association, (A) 1131
New Jersey Society of Certified Public Accountants, (SS) 694
New Mexico Broadcasters Association, (H) 941
New Mexico Department of Veterans' Services, (A) 1208
New Mexico Higher Education Department, (A) 1206–1207, 1209
New Mexico Professional Surveyors, (S) 356
New York Beef Producers' Association, (S) 357, (SS) 695, (H) 942
New York State Higher Education Services Corporation, (A) 1211
New York Water Environment Association, (S) 365
Newspaper Association of America, (H) 796
Newspaper Guild–CWA, (H) 833
Nikon Camera, (H) 820
Nina Footwear, (A) 1178
Non Commissioned Officers Association of the United States of America, (A) 1216
Nordmanns–Forbundet. Pacific Northwest Chapter, (SS) 656, 667
North Carolina Alliance for Athletics, Health, Physical Education, Recreation and Dance, (S) 278, 337, (SS) 650, 679, (H) 904, 929, (A) 1199
North Carolina Association of Certified Public Accountants, (SS) 699–700
North Carolina. Division of Veterans Affairs, (A) 1219
North Carolina Space Grant Consortium, (S) 361
North Carolina State Education Assistance Authority, (SS) 701, (A) 1218
North Carolina 4–H Development Fund, (H) 964
North Dakota. Department of Veterans Affairs, (A) 1220
Northeast Human Resources Association, (SS) 691
Northrop Grumman Corporation, (S) 343
Northstar Engineering Consultants, Inc., (S) 288
Northwest Baptist Convention, (H) 965
Nucor Corporation, (S) 55
NYSARC, Inc., (S) 54, 254

Oak Ridge Institute for Science and Education, (A) 1078
Ocean State Women's Golf Association, (A) 1190
Office and Professional Employees International Union, (SS) 646
Ohio Board of Regents, (A) 1223–1224
Ohio Cattlemen's Association, (S) 367, 477
Ohio CattleWomen, (S) 367
Ohio Forestry Association, Inc., (S) 155
Ohio Newspapers Foundation, (H) 946
Ohio Society of CPAs, (SS) 703
Oklahoma Press Association, (H) 947
Oklahoma State Regents for Higher Education, (SS) 609, (A) 1117, 1241
Oklahoma 4–H, (SS) 704
Oncology Nursing Certification Corporation, (S) 370

S–Sciences   SS–Social Sciences   H–Humanities   A–Any Subject Area

SPONSORING ORGANIZATION INDEX

Oncology Nursing Society, (S) 37, 370, 424
Order Sons of Italy in America, (H) 983, (A) 1141, 1262
Oregon Association of Broadcasters, (H) 949
Oregon Society of CPAs, (SS) 706
Oregon Space Grant Consortium, (S) 371
Oticon, Inc., (A) 1254
Outdoor Writers Association of America, (H) 804
Overseas Press Club, (H) 950

P. Buckley Moss Society, (SS) 649
Pacers Foundation, Inc., (S) 295
Pacific Southwest Instruments, (S) 291
PacifiCare, (S) 12
Paper, Allied–Industrial, Chemical and Energy Workers International Union, (A) 1213
Pendleton Woolen Mills, (H) 935
Pennsylvania AFL–CIO, (SS) 709
Pennsylvania Institute of Certified Public Accountants, (SS) 714
Pennsylvania Public Relations Society, (H) 956
P.E.O. Foundation. California State Chapter, (A) 1056
Pepsi–Cola Company, (A) 1232–1233
Pfizer Consumer Healthcare Group, (S) 387
Pfizer Inc., (A) 1234
Phi Alpha Theta, (H) 957
Phi Chi Theta, (SS) 711
Phi Delta Kappa International, (SS) 712
Phi Mu Alpha Sinfonia Fraternity of America, (H) 893, 982, 1001
Phi Sigma Pi, (A) 1242
Phi Upsilon Omicron, (SS) 713
Phillips Enterprise, (A) 1016
Pi Lambda Theta, (S) 486, (SS) 751
Pink Sands Swim, (A) 1178
Pioneer Hi–Bred International, Inc., (S) 36, (SS) 541
Plastics Institute of America, (S) 393
Plastics Pioneers Association. Education Fund, (S) 393
Plumbing–Heating–Cooling Contractors–National Association, (S) 35, 44, 82, 134, 388, 469
Poetry Magazine, (H) 972
Polanki, The Polish Women's Cultural Club of Milwaukee, (A) 1235
Polish Roman Catholic Union of America, (SS) 639, (A) 1272
Portland Cement Association, (H) 823
Portsmouth Garden Club, (S) 180
Power Systems, Inc., (S) 396
Poynter Institute for Media Studies, (H) 820
Praxair, Inc., (S) 343, 397
Precast/Prestressed Concrete Institute, (S) 382, (H) 955
Preciosa, (A) 1178
Presbyterian Church (USA), (H) 974
Prince Kuhio Hawaiian Civic Club, (A) 1238
Print and Graphics Scholarship Foundation, (SS) 678, (H) 928, 960
Printing and Imaging Association of MidAmerica, (SS) 568, 698, (H) 817, 945
Printing Industries Association, Inc. serving Northern Kentucky and Ohio, (H) 959
Professional Bowlers Association, (A) 1051

Professional Independent Insurance Agents of Illinois, (SS) 605, 651, 729
Project EverGreen, (S) 73
Psi Chi, (SS) 535, 648
Public Employees Roundtable, (SS) 716
Public Relations Society of America. Puget Sound Chapter, (H) 973
Public Relations Student Society of America, (H) 788, 803, 830, 909, 961, 986

Quimby Pipe Organs, Inc., (H) 779

Radio and Television News Directors Foundation, (H) 810, 842, 906, 916, 962
Rayburn Musical Instrument Company, (H) 940
Raytheon Missile Systems, (S) 100
RCS Charitable Foundation, (H) 785
Recording for the Blind and Dyslexic, (A) 1166
Redi–Tag Corporation, (S) 406, (SS) 717
Resinall Corporation, (S) 205, (H) 856
Resource Center Scholarship Service, (S) 306, (A) 1118
Rhode Island Society of Professional Land Surveyors, (S) 391
Rhythm & Hues Studios, (H) 966
Robert Bradford Newman Student Award Fund, (S) 471, (H) 989
Rockwell Automation, Inc., (S) 426
Rocky Mountain Electrical League, (S) 413, (SS) 725
Rocky Mountain NASA Space Grant Consortium, (S) 427
Rohm and Haas Company, (S) 429
Rolling Stone, (H) 969
Romanian Orthodox Episcopate of America, (A) 1083, 1313

Safari Club International, (S) 437
Sallie Mae 911 Education Fund, (A) 1248
Samuel French, Inc., (H) 939
SAP America, Inc., (S) 440
SBC Communications Inc., (A) 1227
Scholarship Administrative Services, Inc., (S) 14, 67, 110, (SS) 536, (H) 829
Scholarship America, (S) 71, (A) 1054, 1160
Scholarship Program Administrators, Inc., (S) 445, (SS) 645, (H) 925, (A) 1135, 1252
Schonstedt Instrument Company, (S) 443
School Nutrition Association, (S) 111, 335, 444, (SS) 570, 677, 734
Schwan's Food Service, (S) 444, (SS) 734
Scotts Company, (S) 446
Scripps Howard Foundation, (H) 814, 898, 977
Seattle Junior Chamber of Commerce, (A) 1251
Senior Center at Lower Village, (S) 226
Sertoma International, (A) 1253–1254
Service Employees International Union, (SS) 645, (H) 925, (A) 1135, 1252
Shamrock Technologies, (S) 205, (H) 856
Shell Oil Company, (S) 451
Shell Oil International, (S) 452

S–Sciences   SS–Social Sciences   H–Humanities   A–Any Subject Area

ShopKo Stores Inc., (A) 1256
Sigma Alpha Iota Philanthropies, Inc., (S) 333, (H) 927, 980
Sigma Iota Epsilon, (SS) 738
Sigma Pi Sigma Trust Fund, (S) 383, 457, 467, (SS) 744
Sigma Tau Delta, (H) 841, 875, 981
Sikh Coalition, (A) 1257
Sikorsky Aircraft Corporation, (S) 31, (A) 1194
SIRS Mandarin, (SS) 579
Society for Applied Anthropology, (S) 385, (SS) 710
Society for Human Resource Management, (SS) 661, 737, (A) 1261
Society for Industrial and Applied Mathematics, (S) 192
Society for Mining, Metallurgy, and Exploration, Inc., (S) 322
Society for Range Management, (S) 312
Society for Technical Communication, (S) 442, (H) 976
Society for Technical Communication. Central Ohio Chapter, (H) 990
Society of American Fight Directors, (H) 890
Society of American Foresters, (S) 75
Society of Automotive Engineers, (S) 187, 403, 436, 453, 485, 506, 525
Society of Broadcast Engineers, (S) 225, 417
Society of Diagnostic Medical Sonography, (S) 173
Society of Exploration Geophysicists, (S) 70, 172, 224, 404, 448, 452
Society of Flight Test Engineers, (S) 455
Society of Gastroenterology Nurses and Associates, Inc., (S) 414, 449
Society of Louisiana Certified Public Accountants, (SS) 658
Society of Manufacturing Engineers, (S) 98, 152–154, 199, 223, 304, 334, 390, 454, 456, 513
Society of Motion Picture and Television Engineers, (S) 300
Society of Petroleum Engineers. Powder River Basin Section, (S) 394, (A) 1236
Society of Physics Students, (S) 383, 457, 467, (SS) 744
Society of Professional Journalists. Indiana Professional Chapter, (H) 886
Society of Professional Journalists. Minnesota Professional Chapter, (H) 924
Society of Satellite Professionals International, (S) 6, 400, (SS) 528, 715
Society of Women Engineers, (S) 8–9, 41, 74, 80, 106, 126, 140–141, 158, 160, 185, 208–209, 218, 222, 242, 260, 276, 294, 297, 305, 311, 315, 319, 369, 398, 426, 475–476
Sodexho USA, (SS) 739
Soil and Water Conservation Society. Empire State Chapter, (S) 162
Soil and Water Conservation Society. Missouri Show-Me Chapter, (S) 328, (SS) 672
Sonlight Curriculum, Ltd., (A) 1260
Sons of Union Veterans of the Civil War, (A) 1264
South Carolina Aquatic Plant Management Society, (S) 389
South Carolina Association of Certified Public Accountants, (SS) 740
South Carolina Commission on Higher Education, (A) 1153, 1265
South Carolina Office of Veterans Affairs, (A) 1266
South Carolina Sea Grant Consortium, (S) 279
South Carolina Space Grant Consortium, (S) 279, (SS) 741
South Dakota Bankers Association, (SS) 621
South Dakota Board of Regents, (SS) 614, (A) 1163, 1267–1270
South Dakota CPA Society, (SS) 742

South Dakota Newspaper Association, (H) 825
South Dakota Space Grant Consortium, (S) 460
Southeast Athletic Trainers Association, (S) 259, 338, 447
Southern Association of Steel Fabricators, (S) 462
Southern Ohio Music Company, (H) 940
Southwest Athletic Trainers' Association, (S) 463
Specialty Equipment Market Association, (SS) 612
Sphinx Organization, (H) 984
SPIE–The International Society for Optical Engineering, (S) 317, 464
Sports Turf Managers Association, (S) 438
St. Andrew's Society of New Hampshire, (H) 802
St. Vincent Sports Medicine Center, (S) 295
State Association of Real Property Agents, (S) 468, (SS) 745
State Bar of Michigan, (SS) 660
State University System of Florida, (A) 1173
State Water Heaters, (S) 469
Steve Madden Footwear, (A) 1179
Stora Enso North America, (S) 205, (H) 856
Stu's Music Shop, (H) 940
SuperCollege.com, (A) 1274
Surfrider Foundation, (S) 483, (SS) 749
Surveying and Mapping Society of Georgia, (S) 76
Symphony Orchestra League of Alexandria, (H) 921
Syngenta Professional Products, (A) 1105

Tadashi Fashions, (A) 1179
Tailhook Educational Foundation, (A) 1276
Tau Beta Pi, (S) 478–479
Tavis Smiley Foundation, (S) 12
Technical Association of the Pulp and Paper Industry, (S) 112, 163, 360, 373, 402, 515, (H) 819
Tennessee Student Assistance Corporation, (A) 1277
Tennessee 4-H Club Foundation, Inc., (S) 104
Texas Amateur Athletic Federation, (SS) 576, (A) 1278
Texas Choral Directors Association, (H) 991
Texas Electric Cooperatives, Inc., (A) 1288
Texas Farm Bureau, (S) 113
Texas Higher Education Coordinating Board, (A) 1114–1115, 1171, 1279–1285, 1304–1305
Texas Instruments, Inc., (S) 481
Texas Rural Electric Women's Association, (A) 1288
Thomson Course Technology, (S) 232, (SS) 620
Tire Industry Association, (SS) 612
Todd A-O, (H) 1014
Tom Joyner Foundation, (S) 12
Tommy Ramey Foundation, (SS) 752, (H) 995
Totem Ocean Trailer Express, (A) 1287
Tourism Cares for Tomorrow, (SS) 655, 684, 693, 702, 718, 754, 772
Town of Williston Historical Society, (H) 996
Tree Research and Education Endowment Fund, (S) 420
Turf and Ornamental Communicators Association, (S) 487, (H) 994
Turner Classic Movies, (H) 1014

UCB Pharma, Inc., (A) 1150
Unilever Corporation, (S) 239

S–Sciences SS–Social Sciences H–Humanities A–Any Subject Area

SPONSORING ORGANIZATION INDEX

United Methodist Church. Iowa Annual Conference, (A) 1129
United Methodist Communications, (H) 912
United Negro College Fund, (S) 491
United States Bowling Congress, (A) 1032, 1062, 1144, 1259, 1296, 1312
United States Patent and Trademark Office, (S) 114
United States Tour Operators Association, (SS) 754
United University Professions, (A) 1293
Universal Press Syndicate, (H) 776
University Aviation Association, (S) 378, 392
University of Oregon. School of Journalism and Communication., (H) 954
University of Vermont. Center for Research on Vermont, (H) 784, 857
UPS Foundation, (A) 1292
U.S. Air Force. Air Force Services Agency, (A) 1026
U.S. Air Force. Reserve Officers' Training Corps, (S) 18–21, (A) 1019–1024
U.S. Army Ordnance Corps Association, (A) 1156
U.S. Army. Reserve Officers' Training Corps, (A) 1045–1046, 1077, 1112, 1123, 1258
U.S. Centers for Disease Control and Prevention. National Institute for Occupational Safety and Health, (S) 474
U.S. Coast Guard Chief Petty Officers Association, (A) 1058
U.S. Corporation for National and Community Service, (A) 1040
U.S. Defense Commissary Agency, (A) 1250
U.S. Department of Commerce. National Oceanic and Atmospheric Administration, (S) 157, 167, 279, (SS) 592
U.S. Department of Energy. National Renewable Energy Laboratory, (S) 250
U.S. Department of Homeland Security, (A) 1078
U.S. Department of Veterans Affairs, (A) 1181–1183, 1275
U.S. National Aeronautics and Space Administration, (S) 214, 279, 283, 354, 361, 371, 427, 460, 492, 494, 504, (SS) 741, (A) 1201
U.S. National Security Agency, (S) 376–377, (SS) 707–708, (H) 952
U.S. Navy. Naval Medical Education and Training Command, (S) 346
U.S. Navy. Naval Personnel Command, (S) 345, 364
U.S. Navy. Reserve Officers' Training Corps, (S) 489, (A) 1122, 1197–1198
US Pan Asian American Chamber of Commerce, (SS) 739
USA Film Festival, (H) 979
USAA Insurance Corporation, (A) 1064
USO World Headquarters, (A) 1297

Vasa Order of America, (A) 1130, 1228, 1298
Vermont Space Grant Consortium, (S) 494
Vermont Student Assistance Corporation, (H) 996
Very Special Arts, (H) 896
Veterans of the Vietnam War, Inc., (A) 1299
VII Corps Desert Storm Veterans Association, (A) 1300
Vincent Bach, (H) 940
Virginia Association for Health, Physical Education, Recreation, and Dance, (S) 191, (SS) 600, (H) 852
Virginia Cable Telecommunications Association, (A) 1303
Virginia Council of Teachers of Mathematics, (S) 495, (SS) 756
Virginia Department of Education, (SS) 759
Virginia Department of Social Services, (SS) 755

Virginia Department of Veterans' Affairs, (A) 1302
Virginia Museum of Fine Arts, (H) 1000
Virginia Polytechnic Institute and State University. Department of Forestry, (S) 203
Virginia Sheriffs' Institute, (SS) 761
Virginia Society for Healthcare Human Resources Administration, (SS) 757
Virginia Society of Certified Public Accountants, (SS) 613, 758, 760
Virginia. State Council of Higher Education, (A) 1301
VistaCare Hospice Foundation, (S) 71
Vocational Foundation of Nebraska, (A) 1230

WAMSO–Minnesota Orchestra Volunteer Association, (H) 1005
Washington Association of Wine Grape Growers, (S) 500
Washington Map Society, (H) 1004
Washington NASA Space Grant Consortium, (S) 504
Washington Society of Certified Public Accountants, (SS) 765
Washington State Mathematics Council, (S) 412, (SS) 723
Washington State Potato Foundation, (S) 505, (A) 1307
West Virginia Division of Veterans' Affairs, (A) 1309–1310
West Virginia Golf Association, (A) 1308
Western Federation of Professional Surveyors, (S) 509
Western Front Association, (H) 957
William Morris Agency, (H) 939
William Randolph Hearst Foundation, (H) 869–871
Wire Reinforcement Institute Education Foundation, (S) 520
Wisconsin Association for Health, Physical Education, Recreation, and Dance, (S) 499, (SS) 762, (H) 1002
Wisconsin Association of Professional Agricultural Consultants, (S) 521
Wisconsin Broadcasters Association, (H) 1011
Wisconsin Department of Veterans Affairs, (A) 1315
Wisconsin Professional Police Association, (SS) 767
Wisconsin Restaurant Association, (SS) 768
Wisconsin State Fair, (S) 220
Woman's National Farm and Garden Association, Inc., (S) 503
Women in Aviation, International, (S) 339
Women in Federal Law Enforcement, (SS) 770
Women's Basketball Coaches Association, (A) 1316
Women's Golf Association of Massachusetts, Inc., (A) 1317
Women's Transportation Seminar, (S) 301, 450, (SS) 663, 735
Women's Transportation Seminar. Minnesota Chapter, (S) 323, (SS) 670
Women's Transportation Seminar. Puget Sound Chapter, (S) 251, (SS) 636
A World Connected, (SS) 554
WTVR News 6, (H) 1012
Wyoming Veterans' Commission, (A) 1319

Yahoo! News, (H) 948
Yamaha Corporation of America, (H) 940
Yanmar Diesel America Corporation, (S) 525
Young American Bowling Alliance, (A) 1233

Zonta International, (SS) 638

S–Sciences   SS–Social Sciences   H–Humanities   A–Any Subject Area

SPONSORING ORGANIZATION INDEX

100th Infantry Battalion Veterans Club, (SS) 664, 732, (A) 1184, 1226, 1306
11th Armored Cavalry Veterans of Vietnam and Cambodia, (A) 1322
3M Health Information Systems, (S) 186, (SS) 598

Residency Index

Some programs listed in this book are restricted to residents of a particular city, county, state, or region. Others are open to applicants wherever they may live. The Residency Index will help you pinpoint programs available only to residents in your area as well as programs that have no residency restrictions at all (these are listed under the term "United States"). To use this index, look up the geographic areas that apply to you (always check the listings under "United States"), jot down the entry numbers listed after the subject areas that interest you, and use those numbers to find the program descriptions in the directory. To help you in your search, we've provided some "see also" references in each index entry. Remember: the numbers cited here refer to program entry numbers, not to page numbers in the book.

Alabama: **Sciences,** 139, 451, 492; **Any Subject Area,** 1030. *See also* United States; names of specific cities and counties

Alaska: **Sciences,** 87; **Humanities,** 913; **Any Subject Area,** 1031, 1287. *See also* Northwestern states; United States; names of specific cities

Alexandria, Virginia: **Any Subject Area,** 1043. *See also* Virginia

Arizona: **Sciences,** 87, 257, 390, 413; **Social Sciences,** 546, 685, 725; **Any Subject Area,** 1089. *See also* United States; names of specific cities and counties

Arkansas: **Sciences,** 51, 288, 405; **Social Sciences,** 530; **Any Subject Area,** 1240. *See also* United States; names of specific cities and counties

Arlington, Virginia: **Any Subject Area,** 1043. *See also* Virginia

Australia: **Any Subject Area,** 1110. *See also* Foreign countries

Bahamas: **Any Subject Area,** 1074. *See also* Foreign countries

Britain. *See* United Kingdom

California: **Sciences,** 12, 34, 85, 87–93, 96, 131, 156, 194, 237, 267, 309, 451; **Social Sciences,** 540, 562–563, 587, 654, 720; **Humanities,** 806–809; **Any Subject Area,** 1016, 1047, 1055–1056, 1060, 1256. *See also* United States; names of specific cities and counties

California, southern: **Any Subject Area,** 1089. *See also* California

Calvert County, Maryland: **Any Subject Area,** 1043. *See also* Maryland

Canada: **Sciences,** 2, 33, 35, 37, 44, 50, 53, 62–63, 82, 95, 98, 116, 121, 133–134, 152–154, 159, 172–173, 177, 179, 183, 192, 199, 212–213, 216, 223, 247, 255, 268–270, 277, 285, 304, 313, 316, 320, 334, 358, 370, 375, 381, 388, 397, 401, 407, 422, 424, 454, 456, 458–459, 469–470, 472, 480, 484, 512–513, 516, 520, 525, 527; **Social Sciences,** 532, 534, 537, 594, 601, 608, 610, 612, 623, 671, 684, 702, 748, 754, 772; **Humanities,** 835, 846, 876, 884, 890, 896, 900, 905, 907, 915, 920, 923, 939–940, 951, 953, 988, 992, 1005, 1014; **Any Subject Area,** 1075, 1083, 1085, 1094, 1109–1110, 1120–1121, 1127, 1142, 1228, 1233, 1259, 1294. *See also* Foreign countries

Charles County, Maryland: **Any Subject Area,** 1043. *See also* Maryland

Colorado: **Sciences,** 87, 115, 413, 427; **Social Sciences,** 571, 591, 725, 750; **Humanities,** 821–822; **Any Subject Area,** 1070, 1256. *See also* United States; names of specific cities and counties

Connecticut: **Sciences,** 119, 166; **Social Sciences,** 574, 719, 726, 764; **Humanities,** 826, 968; **Any Subject Area,** 1072, 1243, 1255, 1291, 1320. *See also* New England states; United States; names of specific cities and counties

Cyprus: **Any Subject Area,** 1075. *See also* Foreign countries

Dallas County, Texas: **Humanities,** 922. *See also* Texas

Delaware: **Sciences,** 275; **Any Subject Area,** 1291. *See also* United States; names of specific cities and counties

Denton County, Texas: **Humanities,** 922. *See also* Texas

District of Columbia. *See* Washington, D.C.

Ellis County, Texas: **Humanities,** 922. *See also* Texas

Fairfax County, Virginia: **Any Subject Area,** 1043. *See also* Virginia

Fairfax, Virginia: **Any Subject Area,** 1043. *See also* Virginia

Falls Church, Virginia: **Any Subject Area,** 1043. *See also* Virginia

Fauquier County, Virginia: **Any Subject Area,** 1043. *See also* Virginia

Florida: **Sciences,** 147, 408; **Social Sciences,** 596, 766; **Humanities,** 1010; **Any Subject Area,** 1074, 1173, 1291. *See also* United States; names of specific cities and counties

Foreign countries: **Sciences,** 6, 17, 61–62, 164, 177, 239, 250, 300, 317, 386, 395, 400, 448, 464, 515; **Social Sciences,** 528, 554, 583, 626, 638, 705, 715, 724; **Humanities,** 827, 834, 879, 884, 891, 902, 914; **Any Subject Area,** 1094, 1143, 1250, 1257, 1286, 1294. *See also* names of specific continents; names of specific countries

Frederick County, Maryland: **Any Subject Area,** 1043. *See also* Maryland

Georgia: **Sciences,** 12, 76, 214, 331, 408; **Humanities,** 793, 798, 840, 892, 1013; **Any Subject Area,** 1291. *See also* United States; names of specific cities and counties

Great Britain. *See* United Kingdom

Greece: **Any Subject Area,** 1075. *See also* Foreign countries

Hawaii: **Sciences,** 87, 178, 228–229, 262, 298, 490; **Social Sciences,** 556, 622; **Humanities,** 868; **Any Subject Area,** 1066, 1125, 1184, 1229, 1238. *See also* United States; names of specific cities and counties

Henderson County, Texas: **Humanities,** 922. *See also* Texas

Hood County, Texas: **Humanities,** 922. *See also* Texas

Hunt County, Texas: **Humanities,** 922. *See also* Texas

Idaho: **Sciences,** 87, 413; **Social Sciences,** 629, 725; **Any Subject Area,** 1256. *See also* Northwestern states; United States; names of specific cities and counties

Illinois: **Sciences,** 95, 127, 233, 244–245; **Social Sciences,** 605, 651, 729; **Humanities,** 878, 918, 1005; **Any Subject Area,** 1256. *See also* United States; names of specific cities and counties

Indiana: **Sciences,** 95, 235, 295; **Humanities,** 885–886, 1005. *See also* United States; names of specific cities and counties

Iowa: **Sciences,** 413; **Social Sciences,** 725; **Humanities,** 836, 1005; **Any Subject Area,** 1129, 1256. *See also* United States; names of specific cities and counties

Iowa, western: **Social Sciences,** 531. *See also* Iowa

Johnson County, Texas: **Humanities,** 922. *See also* Texas

Kansas: **Sciences,** 127, 413; **Social Sciences,** 698, 725; **Humanities,** 945, 1005; **Any Subject Area,** 1111, 1189. *See also* United States; names of specific cities and counties

Kaufman County, Texas: **Humanities,** 922. *See also* Texas

Kentucky: **Sciences,** 236, 283; **Humanities,** 867, 959; **Any Subject Area,** 1091, 1147–1149, 1289. *See also* United States; names of specific cities and counties

Latin America. *See* Mexico

Loudoun County, Virginia: **Any Subject Area,** 1043. *See also* Virginia

Louisiana: **Sciences,** 149, 425, 451; **Social Sciences,** 658; **Any Subject Area,** 1155. *See also* United States; names of specific cities and parishes

Maine: **Any Subject Area,** 1157–1159, 1291. *See also* New England states; United States; names of specific cities and counties

Malaysia: **Any Subject Area,** 1110. *See also* Foreign countries

Manassas Park, Virginia: **Any Subject Area,** 1043. *See also* Virginia

Manassas, Virginia: **Any Subject Area,** 1043. *See also* Virginia

Maryland: **Sciences,** 12, 275, 496; **Social Sciences,** 578, 624, 666; **Humanities,** 921, 1006; **Any Subject Area,** 1057, 1291. *See also* United States; names of specific cities and counties

Massachusetts: **Any Subject Area,** 1291, 1317. *See also* New England states; United States; names of specific cities and counties

Mexico: **Sciences,** 33, 50, 62, 116, 179, 192, 212, 269, 316, 320, 458, 480, 525; **Humanities,** 884, 890, 896, 900, 905, 907, 915, 920, 939, 953, 992; **Any Subject Area,** 1121. *See also* Foreign countries

Michigan: **Sciences,** 95, 508; **Social Sciences,** 660, 693; **Humanities,** 1005; **Any Subject Area,** 1169, 1256. *See also* United States; names of specific cities and counties

Michigan, regional: **Social Sciences,** 767. *See also* Michigan

Minnesota: **Sciences,** 69, 95, 413; **Social Sciences,** 669, 725; **Humanities,** 894, 924, 1005; **Any Subject Area,** 1256. *See also* United States; names of specific cities and counties

Mississippi: **Social Sciences,** 752; **Humanities,** 995. *See also* United States; names of specific cities and counties

Missouri: **Sciences,** 127, 165, 326–328, 413; **Social Sciences,** 549, 659, 672–674, 698, 725; **Humanities,** 945, 1005. *See also* United States; names of specific cities and counties

Montana: **Sciences,** 87, 413, 453; **Social Sciences,** 725; **Any Subject Area,** 1256. *See also* United States; names of specific cities and counties

Montgomery County, Maryland: **Any Subject Area,** 1043. *See also* Maryland

Nebraska: **Sciences,** 413; **Social Sciences,** 531, 595, 688–689, 725, 763; **Humanities,** 1005; **Any Subject Area,** 1104, 1201–1202, 1217, 1230, 1256. *See also* United States; names of specific cities and counties

Nevada: **Sciences,** 34, 87, 354, 413; **Social Sciences,** 540, 725; **Any Subject Area,** 1089, 1256. *See also* United States; names of specific cities

RESIDENCY INDEX

New England states: **Social Sciences,** 582, 690–691; **Humanities,** 802, 837, 887. *See also* United States; names of specific states

New Hampshire: **Sciences,** 27, 355, 502; **Any Subject Area,** 1291. *See also* New England states; United States; names of specific cities and counties

New Hampshire, regional: **Sciences,** 180. *See also* New Hampshire

New Jersey: **Sciences,** 77, 118, 275, 428, 434; **Social Sciences,** 573, 694; **Humanities,** 801; **Any Subject Area,** 1073, 1131, 1191, 1203–1205, 1291. *See also* United States; names of specific cities and counties

New Mexico: **Sciences,** 23, 87, 413; **Social Sciences,** 555, 685, 725; **Humanities,** 941; **Any Subject Area,** 1207–1209. *See also* United States; names of specific cities and counties

New York: **Sciences,** 54, 95, 254, 275, 357, 365; **Social Sciences,** 695; **Humanities,** 887, 942; **Any Subject Area,** 1099, 1168, 1211, 1291, 1293. *See also* United States; names of specific cities and counties

New York County, New York. *See* New York, New York

New York, New York: **Social Sciences,** 668. *See also* New York

New Zealand: **Any Subject Area,** 1110. *See also* Foreign countries

North Carolina: **Sciences,** 275, 278, 337, 361, 408, 418; **Social Sciences,** 569, 650, 679, 699–701, 718; **Humanities,** 904, 929, 964; **Any Subject Area,** 1057, 1199, 1218–1219, 1291. *See also* United States; names of specific cities and counties

North Dakota: **Sciences,** 413; **Social Sciences,** 725; **Humanities,** 1005; **Any Subject Area,** 1220. *See also* United States; names of specific cities

Northwestern states: **Social Sciences,** 656, 667. *See also* United States; names of specific states

Ohio: **Sciences,** 95, 155, 367, 477; **Humanities,** 818, 959, 990; **Any Subject Area,** 1222–1224. *See also* United States; names of specific cities and counties

Oklahoma: **Sciences,** 413; **Social Sciences,** 568, 609, 698, 704, 725; **Humanities,** 817, 945; **Any Subject Area,** 1117, 1241. *See also* United States; names of specific cities and counties

Oklahoma City, Oklahoma: **Any Subject Area,** 1225. *See also* Oklahoma

Oregon: **Sciences,** 87, 371, 505; **Social Sciences,** 706; **Humanities,** 809, 949, 965; **Any Subject Area,** 1100, 1256, 1307. *See also* Northwestern states; United States; names of specific cities and counties

Pacific Northwest. *See* Northwestern states

Parker County, Texas: **Humanities,** 922. *See also* Texas

Pennsylvania: **Sciences,** 56, 95, 275; **Social Sciences,** 709, 714; **Humanities,** 956; **Any Subject Area,** 1291. *See also* United States; names of specific cities and counties

Prince George's County, Maryland: **Any Subject Area,** 1043. *See also* Maryland

Prince William County, Virginia: **Any Subject Area,** 1043. *See also* Virginia

Puerto Rico: **Sciences,** 65, 445, 458, 480, 483; **Social Sciences,** 749; **Any Subject Area,** 1065, 1233. *See also* United States

Rhode Island: **Sciences,** 391; **Any Subject Area,** 1190, 1291, 1320. *See also* New England states; United States; names of specific cities

Rockwall County, Texas: **Humanities,** 922. *See also* Texas

South Carolina: **Sciences,** 279, 331, 408; **Social Sciences,** 569, 740–741; **Any Subject Area,** 1153, 1265–1266, 1291. *See also* United States; names of specific cities and counties

South Dakota: **Sciences,** 413, 460; **Social Sciences,** 614, 725; **Humanities,** 1005; **Any Subject Area,** 1163, 1256, 1267–1270. *See also* United States; names of specific cities and counties

Stafford County, Virginia: **Any Subject Area,** 1043. *See also* Virginia

Sweden: **Any Subject Area,** 1228. *See also* Foreign countries

Tarrant County, Texas: **Humanities,** 922. *See also* Texas

Tennessee: **Sciences,** 104, 408; **Any Subject Area,** 1277. *See also* United States; names of specific cities and counties

Texas: **Sciences,** 12, 113, 413, 451, 461; **Social Sciences,** 557, 568, 576, 602, 698, 725; **Humanities,** 817, 922, 945, 979, 991; **Any Subject Area,** 1114–1115, 1171, 1278–1285, 1288, 1304–1305. *See also* United States; names of specific cities and counties

United Kingdom: **Humanities,** 1014. *See also* Foreign countries; names of specific countries

United States: **Sciences,** 1–11, 13–22, 24–26, 28–33, 35–50, 52–53, 55, 57–64, 66–68, 70–75, 78–84, 86, 94, 97–103, 105–112, 114, 116–117, 120–130, 132–138, 140–146, 148, 150–154, 157–164, 167–177, 179, 181–190, 192–193, 195–213, 215–219, 221–227, 230–232, 234, 236, 238–243, 246–250, 252–253, 255–256, 258–261, 263–266, 268–274, 276–277, 280–282, 284–287, 289–294, 296–297, 299–308, 310–325, 329–336, 338–353, 356, 358–360, 362–364, 366, 368–370, 372–389, 392–393, 395–404, 406–407, 409–411, 414–417, 419–424, 426, 429–433, 435–452, 454–459, 461–476, 478–489, 491, 493, 497–498, 501, 503, 506–507, 509–527; **Social Sciences,** 528–529, 532–539, 541–545, 547–548, 550–554, 558–561, 564–567, 570, 572, 575, 577–581, 583–586, 588–590, 592–594, 597–599, 601, 603–604, 606–608, 610–613, 615–621, 623, 625–628, 630–635, 637–649, 652–653, 657, 661–665, 670–671, 675–678, 680–687, 692, 696–697, 702–703, 705, 707–708, 710–717, 721–722, 724, 727–728, 730–739, 742–749, 751, 753–754, 758, 760, 765, 769–773; **Humanities,** 774–792, 794–797, 799–800, 802–805, 810–816, 819–820, 823–825, 827–835, 838–839, 841–851, 853–866, 869–877, 879–884, 888–891, 893, 895–900, 902–903, 905–912, 914–917, 919–921, 923, 925–928, 930–940, 943–944, 946–948,

950–955, 957–958, 960–963, 966–967, 969–972, 974–989, 992–994, 997–999, 1001, 1003–1004, 1007–1009, 1014; **Any Subject Area,** 1015, 1017–1029, 1032–1042, 1044–1046, 1048–1054, 1058–1059, 1061–1064, 1067–1069, 1071, 1075–1088, 1090, 1092–1098, 1101–1103, 1105–1110, 1112–1113, 1116, 1118–1124, 1126–1128, 1130, 1132–1146, 1150–1152, 1154, 1156, 1160–1162, 1164–1167, 1170, 1172, 1174–1183, 1185–1188, 1192–1198, 1200, 1206, 1210–1216, 1221, 1226–1228, 1231–1234, 1237–1239, 1242, 1244–1254, 1257–1264, 1271–1276, 1283, 1286, 1290, 1292, 1294–1300, 1306, 1311–1314, 1316, 1318, 1321–1323. *See also* names of specific cities, counties, states, and regions

Utah: **Sciences,** 87, 413, 427; **Social Sciences,** 725; **Any Subject Area,** 1089, 1256. *See also* United States; names of specific cities and counties

Vermont: **Sciences,** 494; **Humanities,** 784, 857, 996; **Any Subject Area,** 1291. *See also* New England states; United States; names of specific cities and counties

Virgin Islands: **Sciences,** 279; **Social Sciences,** 741. *See also* United States

Virginia: **Sciences,** 191, 275, 408, 495; **Social Sciences,** 578, 600, 624, 755–757, 759, 761; **Humanities,** 852, 921, 1000, 1006, 1012; **Any Subject Area,** 1057, 1291, 1301–1303. *See also* United States; names of specific cities and counties

Washington: **Sciences,** 87, 251, 412, 451, 500, 504–505; **Social Sciences,** 636, 723, 765; **Humanities,** 809, 901, 965, 973; **Any Subject Area,** 1100, 1251, 1256, 1307. *See also* Northwestern states; United States; names of specific cities and counties

Washington, D.C.: **Social Sciences,** 578, 624; **Humanities,** 921, 1006; **Any Subject Area,** 1043, 1057, 1291. *See also* United States

West Virginia: **Sciences,** 275; **Any Subject Area,** 1057, 1291, 1308–1310. *See also* United States; names of specific cities

Wisconsin: **Sciences,** 95, 220, 236, 499; **Social Sciences,** 655, 762, 767–768; **Humanities,** 1002, 1005, 1011; **Any Subject Area,** 1235, 1256, 1315. *See also* United States; names of specific cities and counties

Wyoming: **Sciences,** 87, 394, 413; **Social Sciences,** 725; **Any Subject Area,** 1236, 1319. *See also* United States; names of specific cities and counties

Tenability Index

Some programs listed in this book can be used only in specific cities, counties, states, or regions. Others may be used anywhere in the United States (or even abroad). The Tenability Index will help you locate funding that is restricted to a specific area as well as funding that has no tenability restrictions (these are listed under the term "United States"). To use this index, look up the geographic areas where you'd like to go (always check the listings under "United States"), jot down the entry numbers listed after the subject areas that interest you, and use those numbers to find the program descriptions in the directory. To help you in your search, we've provided some "see also" references in each index entry. Remember: the numbers cited here refer to program entry numbers, not to page numbers in the book.

Alabama: **Sciences,** 259, 338, 447, 462, 492; **Any Subject Area,** 1030. *See also* United States; names of specific cities and counties

Alaska: **Sciences,** 47, 509; **Social Sciences,** 545; **Humanities,** 975; **Any Subject Area,** 1031. *See also* Northwestern states; United States; names of specific cities

Albuquerque, New Mexico: **Any Subject Area,** 1019. *See also* New Mexico

Amherst, Massachusetts: **Social Sciences,** 533. *See also* Massachusetts

Arizona: **Sciences,** 257, 390, 509; **Social Sciences,** 546; **Humanities,** 975. *See also* United States; names of specific cities and counties

Arkansas: **Sciences,** 51, 288, 405, 462–463; **Social Sciences,** 530, 547; **Any Subject Area,** 1240. *See also* United States; names of specific cities and counties

Atlanta, Georgia: **Sciences,** 515; **Any Subject Area,** 1122. *See also* Georgia

Auburn, Alabama: **Sciences,** 515. *See also* Alabama

Austin, Texas: **Humanities,** 943. *See also* Texas

Australia: **Humanities,** 827; **Any Subject Area,** 1110. *See also* Foreign countries

Austria: **Humanities,** 936. *See also* Foreign countries

Bahamas: **Any Subject Area,** 1074. *See also* Foreign countries

Baton Rouge, Louisiana: **Any Subject Area,** 1122. *See also* Louisiana

Beloit, Wisconsin: **Social Sciences,** 652. *See also* Wisconsin

Berkeley, California: **Sciences,** 85. *See also* California

Big Rapids, Michigan: **Sciences,** 252. *See also* Michigan

Billings, Montana: **Sciences,** 453. *See also* Montana

Boston, Massachusetts: **Sciences,** 347, 491; **Any Subject Area,** 1200. *See also* Massachusetts

Bowling Green, Kentucky: **Humanities,** 948. *See also* Kentucky

Britain. *See* United Kingdom

Brookville, New York: **Sciences,** 347; **Any Subject Area,** 1200. *See also* New York

Butte, Montana: **Sciences,** 453. *See also* Montana

California: **Sciences,** 9, 12, 34, 88–93, 96, 156, 176, 194, 237, 267, 290, 309, 509; **Social Sciences,** 540, 562–563, 587, 654, 720; **Humanities,** 807–809, 890, 975; **Any Subject Area,** 1016, 1047, 1055–1056, 1060. *See also* United States; names of specific cities and counties

Canada: **Sciences,** 2, 33, 35, 37, 44, 50, 53, 62–63, 82, 95, 98, 116, 121, 133–134, 152–154, 159, 172–173, 177, 179, 183, 192, 199, 212–213, 216, 223, 247, 255, 268–270, 277, 285, 304, 313, 316, 320, 334, 358, 370, 375, 381, 388, 397, 401, 407, 422, 424, 454, 456, 458–459, 469–470, 472, 480, 484, 502, 512–513, 516, 520, 525, 527; **Social Sciences,** 532, 534, 537, 594, 601, 608, 610, 612, 623, 671, 684, 693, 702, 718, 748, 754, 772; **Humanities,** 835, 846, 876, 884, 890, 896, 905, 907, 915, 920, 923, 939–940, 951, 953, 988, 1005, 1014; **Any Subject Area,** 1075, 1083, 1085, 1094, 1109–1110, 1120–1121, 1127, 1142, 1233, 1259, 1294. *See also* Foreign countries

Chapel Hill, North Carolina: **Humanities,** 943. *See also* North Carolina

Charleston, South Carolina: **Sciences,** 347; **Any Subject Area,** 1040, 1200. *See also* South Carolina

Charlotte, North Carolina: **Sciences,** 347; **Any Subject Area,** 1200. *See also* North Carolina

Chicago, Illinois: **Social Sciences,** 652. *See also* Illinois

Chico, California: **Sciences,** 85. *See also* California

Cincinnati, Ohio: **Sciences,** 347; **Any Subject Area,** 1200. *See also* Ohio

Claremont, California: **Social Sciences,** 652. *See also* California

Clemson, South Carolina: **Sciences,** 205, 221, 507; **Humanities,** 856, 862–863, 1008. *See also* South Carolina

Cleveland, Ohio: **Humanities,** 919. *See also* Ohio
Collegeville, Pennsylvania: **Social Sciences,** 652. *See also* Pennsylvania
Colorado: **Sciences,** 115, 509; **Social Sciences,** 571, 591, 750; **Humanities,** 821–822, 975. *See also* United States; names of specific cities and counties
Columbia, Missouri: **Humanities,** 943. *See also* Missouri
Connecticut: **Social Sciences,** 574; **Humanities,** 795; **Any Subject Area,** 1291. *See also* New England states; United States; names of specific cities and counties
Coral Gables, Florida: **Any Subject Area,** 1019. *See also* Florida
Corvallis, Oregon: **Sciences,** 515. *See also* Oregon
Cyprus: **Any Subject Area,** 1075. *See also* Foreign countries

Davis, California: **Sciences,** 85. *See also* California
Decatur, Georgia: **Social Sciences,** 652. *See also* Georgia
Decatur, Illinois: **Social Sciences,** 652. *See also* Illinois
Delaware: **Sciences,** 517; **Any Subject Area,** 1291. *See also* Southeastern states; United States; names of specific cities and counties
Denmark: **Any Subject Area,** 1050. *See also* Foreign countries
Denver, Colorado: **Sciences,** 347, 427; **Social Sciences,** 533; **Any Subject Area,** 1040, 1200. *See also* Colorado
Detroit, Michigan: **Humanities,** 984. *See also* Michigan
District of Columbia. *See* Washington, D.C.
Durham, New Hampshire: **Sciences,** 515. *See also* New Hampshire

East Lansing, Michigan: **Sciences,** 515; **Social Sciences,** 533. *See also* Michigan
England: **Humanities,** 827. *See also* Foreign countries; United Kingdom

Fayetteville, North Carolina: **Any Subject Area,** 1020. *See also* North Carolina
Finland: **Sciences,** 146; **Humanities,** 897. *See also* Foreign countries
Flint, Michigan: **Sciences,** 347; **Any Subject Area,** 1200. *See also* Michigan
Florida: **Sciences,** 147, 259, 338, 447, 462; **Social Sciences,** 596, 766; **Humanities,** 851, 1010; **Any Subject Area,** 1173, 1291. *See also* Southeastern states; United States; names of specific cities and counties
Foreign countries: **Sciences,** 6, 61–62, 164, 177, 239, 250, 300, 317, 386, 395, 400, 448, 464, 515; **Social Sciences,** 528, 554, 556, 583, 626, 638, 705, 715, 724; **Humanities,** 834, 879, 891–892, 914; **Any Subject Area,** 1028, 1094, 1250, 1257, 1275. *See also* names of specific continents; names of specific countries
Fort Meade, Maryland: **Sciences,** 376; **Social Sciences,** 707. *See also* Maryland
France: **Humanities,** 827. *See also* Foreign countries
Fresno, California: **Sciences,** 85; **Any Subject Area,** 1019. *See also* California

Gaithersburg, Maryland: **Humanities,** 827. *See also* Maryland
Galesburg, Illinois: **Social Sciences,** 652. *See also* Illinois
Georgetown, Texas: **Social Sciences,** 652. *See also* Texas
Georgia: **Sciences,** 12, 214, 259, 331, 338, 447, 462; **Humanities,** 793, 798, 840, 892, 1013; **Any Subject Area,** 1291. *See also* Southeastern states; United States; names of specific cities and counties
Grambling, Louisiana: **Any Subject Area,** 1020. *See also* Louisiana
Great Britain. *See* United Kingdom
Great Falls, Montana: **Sciences,** 453. *See also* Montana
Greece: **Any Subject Area,** 1075. *See also* Foreign countries
Greensboro, North Carolina: **Any Subject Area,** 1020. *See also* North Carolina
Guam: **Sciences,** 176. *See also* United States

Hampton, Virginia: **Any Subject Area,** 1122. *See also* Virginia
Havre, Montana: **Sciences,** 453. *See also* Montana
Hawaii: **Sciences,** 176, 229, 262, 298, 490, 509; **Humanities,** 868, 975; **Any Subject Area,** 1066, 1125, 1229, 1238. *See also* United States; names of specific cities and counties
Helena, Montana: **Sciences,** 453. *See also* Montana
Houston, Texas: **Social Sciences,** 533. *See also* Texas
Hyde Park, New York: **Social Sciences,** 533. *See also* New York

Idaho: **Sciences,** 47, 372, 509; **Social Sciences,** 545, 629; **Humanities,** 975. *See also* Northwestern states; United States; names of specific cities and counties
Illinois: **Sciences,** 95, 128, 233, 241, 244, 441; **Social Sciences,** 628, 733; **Humanities,** 878, 880, 1005. *See also* United States; names of specific cities and counties
Indiana: **Sciences,** 95, 128, 295; **Humanities,** 885–886, 993, 1005. *See also* United States; names of specific cities and counties
Indianapolis, Indiana: **Humanities,** 992. *See also* Indiana
Iowa: **Sciences,** 128; **Social Sciences,** 722; **Humanities,** 836, 1005; **Any Subject Area,** 1129. *See also* United States; names of specific cities and counties
Iowa, western: **Social Sciences,** 531. *See also* Iowa

Jackson, Mississippi: **Any Subject Area,** 1020. *See also* Mississippi

Kalamazoo, Michigan: **Sciences,** 205, 221, 507, 515; **Humanities,** 856, 862–863, 1008. *See also* Michigan
Kansas: **Sciences,** 128, 231; **Social Sciences,** 698; **Humanities,** 877, 945, 1005; **Any Subject Area,** 1111, 1145. *See also* United States; names of specific cities and counties
Kentucky: **Sciences,** 236, 259, 282–283, 338, 447, 462; **Social Sciences,** 653; **Humanities,** 867; **Any Subject Area,** 1091, 1147, 1149, 1289. *See also* United States; names of specific cities and counties
Kentucky, northern: **Humanities,** 959. *See also* Kentucky

TENABILITY INDEX

Kern County, California: **Social Sciences,** 743. *See also* California

Lake Forest, Illinois: **Social Sciences,** 652. *See also* Illinois
Las Cruces, New Mexico: **Any Subject Area,** 1019. *See also* New Mexico
Las Vegas, Nevada: **Social Sciences,** 533. *See also* Nevada
Latin America. *See* Mexico
Lexington, Virginia: **Social Sciences,** 652. *See also* Virginia
Lincoln, Nebraska: **Humanities,** 985. *See also* Nebraska
Livermore, California: **Sciences,** 344. *See also* California
Los Angeles County, California: **Social Sciences,** 743. *See also* California
Louisiana: **Sciences,** 259, 302, 338, 425, 447, 462; **Social Sciences,** 658; **Any Subject Area,** 1155. *See also* United States; names of specific cities and parishes

Maine: **Any Subject Area,** 1157–1159, 1291. *See also* New England states; United States; names of specific cities and counties
Malaysia: **Any Subject Area,** 1110. *See also* Foreign countries
Maryland: **Sciences,** 12, 517; **Social Sciences,** 578, 624, 666; **Humanities,** 921; **Any Subject Area,** 1041, 1291. *See also* Southeastern states; United States; names of specific cities and counties
Massachusetts: **Humanities,** 890; **Any Subject Area,** 1291. *See also* New England states; United States; names of specific cities and counties
Mexico: **Sciences,** 33, 50, 62, 116, 179, 192, 212, 269, 316, 320, 458, 480, 525; **Humanities,** 827, 884, 890, 896, 905, 907, 915, 920, 939, 953; **Any Subject Area,** 1121. *See also* Foreign countries
Michigan: **Sciences,** 95, 128, 508; **Social Sciences,** 660; **Humanities,** 1005; **Any Subject Area,** 1169. *See also* United States; names of specific cities and counties
Minneapolis, Minnesota: **Sciences,** 515; **Humanities,** 890. *See also* Minnesota
Minnesota: **Sciences,** 95, 128, 323, 523; **Social Sciences,** 669–670; **Humanities,** 924, 1005. *See also* United States; names of specific cities and counties
Mississippi: **Sciences,** 259, 338, 447, 462; **Social Sciences,** 752; **Humanities,** 995. *See also* United States; names of specific cities and counties
Mississippi State, Mississippi: **Sciences,** 515. *See also* Mississippi
Missoula, Montana: **Sciences,** 453. *See also* Montana
Missouri: **Sciences,** 128, 165, 231; **Social Sciences,** 549, 659, 673–674, 698; **Humanities,** 945, 1005. *See also* United States; names of specific cities and counties
Montana: **Sciences,** 138, 509; **Humanities,** 975. *See also* United States; names of specific cities and counties
Montgomery, Alabama: **Any Subject Area,** 1020. *See also* Alabama
Montpelier, Vermont: **Humanities,** 827. *See also* Vermont
Moscow, Idaho: **Sciences,** 515. *See also* Idaho
Murray, Kentucky: **Sciences,** 205, 221, 507; **Humanities,** 856, 862–863, 1008. *See also* Kentucky

Napa, California: **Humanities,** 827. *See also* California
Nashville, Tennessee: **Any Subject Area,** 1020. *See also* Tennessee
Nebraska: **Sciences,** 128; **Social Sciences,** 531, 595, 688–689, 722; **Humanities,** 1005; **Any Subject Area,** 1104, 1201–1202, 1217, 1230. *See also* United States; names of specific cities and counties
Nevada: **Sciences,** 176, 354, 509; **Humanities,** 975. *See also* United States; names of specific cities
New Brunswick, New Jersey: **Sciences,** 515. *See also* New Jersey
New England states: **Social Sciences,** 582, 690–691; **Humanities,** 802, 837, 887. *See also* United States; names of specific states
New Hampshire: **Sciences,** 180; **Any Subject Area,** 1291. *See also* New England states; United States; names of specific cities and counties
New Jersey: **Sciences,** 118; **Social Sciences,** 573, 694; **Humanities,** 795; **Any Subject Area,** 1131, 1203–1204, 1291. *See also* United States; names of specific cities and counties
New Mexico: **Sciences,** 356, 509; **Social Sciences,** 555; **Humanities,** 941, 975; **Any Subject Area,** 1206–1209. *See also* United States; names of specific cities and counties
New Orleans, Louisiana: **Social Sciences,** 652. *See also* Louisiana
New York: **Sciences,** 54, 95, 162, 254, 515; **Humanities,** 887; **Any Subject Area,** 1211, 1291, 1293. *See also* United States; names of specific cities and counties
New York County, New York. *See* New York, New York
New York, New York: **Sciences,** 347; **Humanities,** 795, 805, 827, 923; **Any Subject Area,** 1200. *See also* New York
New Zealand: **Any Subject Area,** 1110. *See also* Foreign countries
Norfolk, Virginia: **Sciences,** 347; **Any Subject Area,** 1122, 1200. *See also* Virginia
North Carolina: **Sciences,** 278, 337, 361; **Social Sciences,** 569, 650, 679, 699–701; **Humanities,** 904, 929, 964; **Any Subject Area,** 1199, 1218–1219, 1291. *See also* Southeastern states; United States; names of specific cities and counties
North Dakota: **Sciences,** 128, 523; **Humanities,** 1005; **Any Subject Area,** 1220. *See also* United States; names of specific cities
North Miami, Florida: **Sciences,** 347; **Any Subject Area,** 1200. *See also* Florida
Northwestern states: **Social Sciences,** 656, 667. *See also* United States; names of specific states
Norway: **Social Sciences,** 656, 667. *See also* Foreign countries

Ohio: **Sciences,** 95, 366; **Social Sciences,** 703; **Humanities,** 818, 832, 946, 959, 990; **Any Subject Area,** 1222–1224. *See also* United States; names of specific cities and counties
Oklahoma: **Social Sciences,** 568, 609, 698, 704; **Humanities,** 817, 945, 947; **Any Subject Area,** 1117, 1241. *See also* United States; names of specific cities and counties
Oregon: **Sciences,** 47, 371–372, 509; **Social Sciences,** 545, 706; **Humanities,** 809, 949, 975. *See also* Northwestern states; United States; names of specific cities and counties
Orlando, Florida: **Humanities,** 943. *See also* Florida

Orono, Maine: **Sciences,** 515. *See also* Maine
Oxford, Ohio: **Sciences,** 515. *See also* Ohio

Pacific Northwest. *See* Northwestern states
Pennsylvania: **Sciences,** 56, 95; **Social Sciences,** 714; **Humanities,** 956; **Any Subject Area,** 1071, 1291. *See also* United States; names of specific cities and counties
Perry Point, Maryland: **Any Subject Area,** 1040. *See also* Maryland
Philadelphia, Pennsylvania: **Sciences,** 347; **Social Sciences,** 652; **Humanities,** 943; **Any Subject Area,** 1200. *See also* Pennsylvania
Pittsburg, Kansas: **Sciences,** 205; **Humanities,** 856. *See also* Kansas
Pleasantville, New York: **Sciences,** 347; **Any Subject Area,** 1200. *See also* New York
Poland: **Humanities,** 933. *See also* Foreign countries
Polk City, Florida: **Any Subject Area,** 1187. *See also* Florida
Pomona, California: **Sciences,** 85; **Social Sciences,** 533. *See also* California
Prairie View, Texas: **Any Subject Area,** 1122. *See also* Texas
Providence, Rhode Island: **Sciences,** 347; **Social Sciences,** 533; **Any Subject Area,** 1200. *See also* Rhode Island
Puerto Rico: **Sciences,** 445, 458, 480, 483; **Social Sciences,** 749; **Any Subject Area,** 1019, 1065, 1233. *See also* United States

Rahway, New Jersey: **Sciences,** 491. *See also* New Jersey
Raleigh, North Carolina: **Sciences,** 515. *See also* North Carolina
Rhode Island: **Any Subject Area,** 1291. *See also* New England states; United States; names of specific cities
Riverside, California: **Sciences,** 85. *See also* California
Riverside County, California: **Social Sciences,** 743. *See also* California
Rochester, New York: **Sciences,** 205, 221, 347, 507; **Humanities,** 856, 862–863, 1008; **Any Subject Area,** 1200. *See also* New York

Sacramento, California: **Any Subject Area,** 1040. *See also* California
Salem, Oregon: **Social Sciences,** 652. *See also* Oregon
San Antonio, Texas: **Social Sciences,** 652; **Any Subject Area,** 1019. *See also* Texas
San Bernardino, California: **Any Subject Area,** 1019. *See also* California
San Bernardino County, California: **Social Sciences,** 743. *See also* California
San Jose, California: **Sciences,** 515; **Humanities,** 943. *See also* California
San Luis Obispo, California: **Sciences,** 85, 205, 221, 507; **Humanities,** 856, 862–863, 1008. *See also* California
San Luis Obispo County, California: **Social Sciences,** 743. *See also* California
Santa Barbara County, California: **Social Sciences,** 743. *See also* California
Santa Cruz, California: **Sciences,** 85. *See also* California

Savannah, Georgia: **Any Subject Area,** 1122. *See also* Georgia
Seattle, Washington: **Sciences,** 515. *See also* Washington
Silver Spring, Maryland: **Sciences,** 167; **Social Sciences,** 592. *See also* Maryland
Singapore: **Humanities,** 827. *See also* Foreign countries
South Carolina: **Sciences,** 279, 331, 389; **Social Sciences,** 569, 740–741; **Any Subject Area,** 1153, 1265–1266, 1291. *See also* United States; names of specific cities and counties
South Dakota: **Sciences,** 128, 460, 523; **Social Sciences,** 614, 621, 722, 742; **Humanities,** 1005; **Any Subject Area,** 1163, 1267–1270. *See also* United States; names of specific cities and counties
Southeastern states: **Sciences,** 389. *See also* United States; names of specific states
St. Helena, California: **Humanities,** 827. *See also* California
Stevens Point, Wisconsin: **Sciences,** 515. *See also* Wisconsin
Stout, Wisconsin: **Sciences,** 205, 221, 507; **Humanities,** 856, 862–863, 1008. *See also* Wisconsin
Sundance, Utah: **Humanities,** 890, 920, 939. *See also* Utah
Sweden: **Humanities,** 799. *See also* Foreign countries

Tallahassee, Florida: **Any Subject Area,** 1122. *See also* Florida
Tempe, Arizona: **Sciences,** 205, 221, 507; **Humanities,** 856, 862–863, 1008. *See also* Arizona
Tennessee: **Sciences,** 259, 338, 447, 462; **Any Subject Area,** 1277. *See also* United States; names of specific cities and counties
Texas: **Sciences,** 12, 113, 461, 463, 465; **Social Sciences,** 557, 568, 576, 602, 698; **Humanities,** 817, 945, 991; **Any Subject Area,** 1114–1115, 1171, 1278–1285, 1288, 1304–1305. *See also* United States; names of specific cities and counties
Toledo, Ohio: **Sciences,** 347; **Any Subject Area,** 1200. *See also* Ohio
Tuskegee, Alabama: **Any Subject Area,** 1020. *See also* Alabama

United Kingdom: **Humanities,** 1014. *See also* Foreign countries; names of specific countries
United States: **Sciences,** 1–11, 13–33, 35–46, 48–50, 52–53, 55, 57–84, 86–87, 94, 97–112, 114, 116–117, 119–127, 129–137, 139–146, 148–155, 157–161, 163–164, 166–175, 177–179, 181–190, 192–193, 195–204, 206–213, 215–220, 222–228, 230, 232, 234–236, 238–240, 242–243, 245–250, 252–253, 255–258, 260–261, 263–266, 268–277, 280–281, 284–287, 289, 291–294, 296–297, 299–301, 303–308, 310–322, 324–336, 339–346, 348–353, 355, 357–360, 362–365, 367–370, 373–389, 391–393, 395–404, 406–411, 413–424, 426, 428–440, 442–446, 448–452, 454–459, 461, 464, 466–489, 491, 493, 495–498, 500–503, 505–506, 508, 510–514, 516, 518–520, 522, 524–527; **Social Sciences,** 528–529, 531–532, 534–539, 541–544, 548, 550–556, 558–562, 564–568, 570, 572, 575–577, 579–581, 583–586, 588–590, 592–594, 597–599, 601, 603–608, 610–612, 615–620, 622–623, 625–627, 630–635, 637–649, 651, 657, 661–665, 668, 671–672, 675–678, 680–687, 690, 692–693, 695–698, 702, 705, 707–719, 721, 724–732, 734–739,

743–749, 751, 753–754, 756, 763–764, 767–773; **Humanities,** 774–792, 794, 796, 799–806, 810–817, 819–820, 823–831, 833–836, 838–839, 841–850, 853–855, 857–861, 864–866, 869–876, 879, 881–884, 888–899, 902–903, 905–928, 930–940, 942–945, 948, 950–955, 957–958, 960–963, 965–972, 974, 976–989, 994, 997–999, 1001, 1003–1007, 1009, 1014; **Any Subject Area,** 1015, 1017–1018, 1021–1029, 1032–1039, 1042–1046, 1048–1051, 1053–1054, 1057–1059, 1061–1064, 1067–1070, 1072–1075, 1077–1090, 1092–1103, 1105–1110, 1112–1113, 1116–1121, 1123–1128, 1130–1144, 1146, 1148, 1150–1152, 1154, 1156, 1159–1162, 1164–1168, 1170, 1172, 1174–1198, 1205, 1210, 1212–1216, 1221, 1225–1228, 1231, 1233–1235, 1237–1240, 1242–1250, 1252–1264, 1272–1276, 1278, 1286, 1288, 1290, 1294–1300, 1306–1308, 1311–1314, 1316–1318, 1320–1323. *See also* names of specific cities, counties, states, and regions

University Park, Pennsylvania: **Social Sciences,** 533; **Humanities,** 943. *See also* Pennsylvania

Utah: **Sciences,** 427, 509; **Humanities,** 975. *See also* United States; names of specific cities and counties

Valparaiso, Indiana: **Social Sciences,** 652. *See also* Indiana

Ventura County, California: **Social Sciences,** 743. *See also* California

Vermont: **Sciences,** 494; **Humanities,** 784, 857, 996; **Any Subject Area,** 1291. *See also* New England states; United States; names of specific cities and counties

Virgin Islands: **Sciences,** 279; **Social Sciences,** 741. *See also* United States

Virginia: **Sciences,** 191, 517; **Social Sciences,** 578, 600, 613, 624, 755, 757–761; **Humanities,** 852, 921, 1000, 1012; **Any Subject Area,** 1291, 1301–1303. *See also* Southeastern states; United States; names of specific cities and counties

Warrensburg, Missouri: **Sciences,** 205; **Humanities,** 856. *See also* Missouri

Washington: **Sciences,** 47, 251, 372, 412, 504, 509; **Social Sciences,** 545, 636, 723, 765; **Humanities,** 809, 901, 973, 975; **Any Subject Area,** 1052, 1076, 1232, 1251, 1271, 1287, 1292. *See also* Northwestern states; United States; names of specific cities and counties

Washington, D.C.: **Sciences,** 517; **Social Sciences,** 578, 624; **Humanities,** 797, 900, 905, 915, 920–921, 939, 992; **Any Subject Area,** 1020, 1040, 1291. *See also* Southeastern states; United States

West Lafayette, Indiana: **Social Sciences,** 533. *See also* Indiana

West Point, Pennsylvania: **Sciences,** 491. *See also* Pennsylvania

West Virginia: **Sciences,** 517; **Any Subject Area,** 1291, 1309–1310. *See also* United States; names of specific cities

White Plains, New York: **Sciences,** 347; **Any Subject Area,** 1200. *See also* New York

Winston–Salem, North Carolina: **Social Sciences,** 652. *See also* North Carolina

Wisconsin: **Sciences,** 95, 128, 236, 499, 521; **Social Sciences,** 655, 762, 768; **Humanities,** 1002, 1005, 1011; **Any Subject Area,** 1235, 1315. *See also* United States; names of specific cities and counties

Wyoming: **Sciences,** 394, 509; **Humanities,** 975; **Any Subject Area,** 1236, 1319. *See also* United States; names of specific cities and counties

Yellow Springs, Ohio: **Sciences,** 347; **Any Subject Area,** 1200. *See also* Ohio

Subject Index

Use this index when you want to identify merit/no-need funding programs by subject. To help you pinpoint your search, we've also included hundreds of "see" and "see also" references. In addition to looking for terms that represent your specific subject interest, be sure to check the "General programs" entry; hundreds of programs are listed there that can be used to support study or other activities in *any* subject area (although the programs may be restricted in other ways). Remember: the numbers cited in this index refer to program entry numbers, not to page numbers in the book.

Accounting: 529, 547, 550, 552, 572, 580, 591, 601, 613, 629, 632–633, 653, 658–659, 671, 688–689, 694, 699–700, 703, 706, 714, 722, 724, 740, 742, 747, 750, 758, 760, 765, 941. *See also* Finance; General programs
Acoustical engineering. *See* Engineering, acoustical
Acoustics: 471, 989. *See also* General programs; Physics
Acquired Immunodeficiency Syndrome. *See* AIDS
Acting. *See* Performing arts
Actuarial sciences: 585, 605, 635, 644, 651, 676, 680, 690, 729. *See also* General programs; Statistics
Administration. *See* Business administration; Education, administration; Management; Nurses and nursing, administration; Personnel administration; Public administration
Adolescents: 538, 992. *See also* Child development; General programs
Advertising: 542, 582, 726, 752, 766, 796–797, 818, 832, 837, 913, 931, 938, 947, 968, 995, 1010. *See also* Communications; General programs; Marketing; Public relations
Aeronautical engineering. *See* Engineering, aeronautical
Aeronautics: 16–17, 100, 125, 465. *See also* Aviation; Engineering, aeronautical; General programs; Physical sciences
Aerospace engineering. *See* Engineering, aerospace
Aerospace sciences. *See* Space sciences
African American studies: 915. *See also* General programs
Aged and aging: 12, 226. *See also* General programs; Social sciences
Agribusiness: 34, 93, 206, 302, 357, 540–541, 606, 682, 695, 942. *See also* Agriculture and agricultural sciences; Business administration; General programs
Agricultural aviation: 524. *See also* Agriculture and agricultural sciences; Aviation; General programs
Agricultural communications: 86, 188, 341, 357, 487, 695, 850, 877, 934, 942, 994. *See also* Agriculture and agricultural sciences; Communications; General programs
Agricultural economics. *See* Economics, agricultural
Agricultural education. *See* Education, agricultural
Agricultural engineering. *See* Engineering, agricultural
Agricultural technology: 342. *See also* Agriculture and agricultural sciences; General programs; Technology

Agriculture and agricultural sciences: 14–15, 28, 34, 36, 69, 86, 88–89, 91, 96, 113, 115, 156, 162, 167, 178, 194, 235, 237, 267, 288, 302, 329, 341–342, 357, 367, 405, 420, 477, 484, 505, 521, 540, 571, 587, 592, 695, 934, 942, 1078, 1307. *See also* Biological sciences; General programs
Agrimarketing and sales. *See* Agribusiness
Agronomy: 73, 85, 219, 253, 302, 328, 461, 487, 672, 994. *See also* Agriculture and agricultural sciences; General programs
AIDS: 38. *See also* Disabilities; General programs; Medical sciences
Air conditioning engineering. *See* Engineering, refrigerating and air conditioning
Air conditioning industry. *See* Cooling industry
American history. *See* History, American
American Indian language. *See* Language, Native American
American Indian studies. *See* Native American studies
American literature. *See* Literature, American
Animal science: 69, 86, 285, 341–342, 357, 359, 372, 437, 484, 695, 942. *See also* General programs; Sciences; names of specific animal sciences
Animation: 775, 966. *See also* Cartoonists and cartoons; Filmmaking; General programs
Applied arts. *See* Arts and crafts
Aquatic sciences. *See* Oceanography
Arabic language. *See* Language, Arabic
Archaeology: 90, 798. *See also* General programs; History; Social sciences
Architectural engineering. *See* Engineering, architectural
Architecture: 20, 57–59, 233, 289, 382, 778, 790, 798, 823, 878, 892, 911, 922, 955. *See also* Fine arts; General programs
Arithmetic. *See* Mathematics
Art: 783, 804, 855, 874, 925, 931, 1000. *See also* General programs; Illustrators and illustrations; names of specific art forms
Art conservation: 201, 835, 876. *See also* Art; General programs
Arts and crafts: 1000. *See also* Art; General programs; names of specific crafts
Asian studies: 377, 708, 952. *See also* General programs; Humanities

479

Astronautics: 16–17, 100, 125, 465. *See also* General programs; Space sciences
Astronomy: 227, 741. *See also* General programs; Physical sciences
Athletic training: 176, 259, 336, 338, 396, 447, 463, 499, 762, 1002. *See also* Athletics; General programs
Athletics: 486, 576, 751, 791. *See also* Athletic training; Education, physical; General programs; Sports medicine; names of specific sports
Atmospheric sciences: 19, 32, 157, 167, 170, 299, 592. *See also* General programs; Physical sciences
Attorneys. *See* Law, general
Audiovisual materials and equipment: 248, 889. *See also* General programs; specific types of media
Automation. *See* Computer sciences; Information science; Technology
Automobile industry: 612. *See also* General programs
Automotive engineering. *See* Engineering, automotive
Automotive repair: 229, 262, 868, 1066, 1229. *See also* General programs
Automotive technology: 298, 453, 612. *See also* Engineering, automotive; General programs; Transportation
A.V. *See* Audiovisual materials and equipment
Aviation: 31, 84, 108, 124–125, 127–128, 144, 150, 168, 200, 234, 264, 272, 287, 291, 303, 321, 339, 378, 392, 466, 490, 567. *See also* General programs; Space sciences; Transportation

Ballet. *See* Dance
Banking: 376–377, 569, 596, 621, 707–708, 952. *See also* Finance; General programs
Barbering. *See* Hair design
Beef industry: 107, 326–327, 340, 357, 367, 477, 695, 942. *See also* General programs; Ranching
Behavioral sciences: 167, 385, 492, 592, 710. *See also* General programs; Social sciences; names of special behavioral sciences
Biochemistry: 249. *See also* Biological sciences; Chemistry; General programs
Biological sciences: 13, 90, 114, 148, 157, 165–167, 202, 249, 270, 302, 379, 487, 491–492, 592, 994, 1078. *See also* General programs; Sciences; names of specific biological sciences
Biomedical engineering. *See* Engineering, biomedical
Biomedical sciences: 514. *See also* Biological sciences; General programs; Medical sciences
Black American studies. *See* African American studies
Blindness. *See* Visual impairments
Botany: 73, 77, 253, 302, 389, 461, 487, 801, 994. *See also* Biological sciences; General programs
Broadcast engineering. *See* Engineering, broadcast
Broadcast journalism. *See* Journalism, broadcast
Broadcasting: 781, 791, 795, 800, 804, 821–822, 833, 840, 865, 867, 873, 885, 894, 913, 941, 949, 958, 1011–1012. *See also* Communications; Radio; Television
Building trades: 233, 878. *See also* General programs
Business administration: 2, 35, 44, 82, 111, 134, 207, 230, 238, 243, 263, 330, 335, 349, 388, 413, 440, 444, 468–469, 492, 522, 539, 553, 561, 565, 570, 578, 586, 588, 597, 605, 607–608, 616, 618, 621, 626–627, 630, 634, 637–638, 642, 651–652, 668, 671, 675, 677, 681, 686, 688, 697, 711, 722, 725, 729, 732, 734, 739, 745, 752–753, 769, 773, 812, 843, 866, 879, 881, 995, 1128, 1141. *See also* Entrepreneurship; General programs; Management
Business education. *See* Education, business
Business enterprises. *See* Entrepreneurship
Business reporting: 805. *See also* Broadcasting; Business administration; General programs; Journalism

Cable TV journalism. *See* Journalism, cable
Cancer: 37, 370, 424. *See also* Disabilities; General programs; Health and health care; Medical sciences
Cars. *See* Automobile industry; Engineering, automotive
Cartography: 76, 97, 157, 564, 1004. *See also* General programs; Geography
Cartoonists and cartoons: 776, 814. *See also* Art; General programs; Illustrators and illustrations
Cattle ranching. *See* Ranching
Cello. *See* Music, cello
Ceramic engineering. *See* Engineering, ceramic
Ceramics: 145. *See also* Arts and crafts; General programs
Chemical engineering. *See* Engineering, chemical
Chemistry: 1, 10, 20, 64, 114, 148, 157, 165–166, 256, 364, 393, 429. *See also* Engineering, chemical; General programs; Physical sciences
Child development: 685. *See also* Adolescents; General programs
Chinese language. *See* Language, Chinese
Chiropractic: 149, 174. *See also* General programs; Medical sciences
Choruses. *See* Voice
Church music. *See* Music, church
Cinema: 616, 807, 866. *See also* Filmmaking; General programs; Literature
City and regional planning: 118, 323, 330, 483, 573, 594, 670, 675, 720, 749, 798. *See also* General programs
Civil engineering. *See* Engineering, civil
Civil liberties: 705. *See also* General programs; Political science and politics
Classical music. *See* Music, classical
Clothing: 1006. *See also* Fashion design; General programs
Commerce. *See* Business administration
Communications: 251, 263, 349, 442, 492, 565, 577, 582, 588–589, 616, 619, 636, 642, 686, 752, 766, 788, 791, 795, 797, 804, 812, 818, 821, 831–832, 837, 843–844, 846, 866, 872, 895, 910, 912–913, 931, 947, 956, 959–960, 964, 976, 986, 990, 995, 1010–1013, 1078. *See also* General programs; Humanities
Communications, agricultural. *See* Agricultural communications
Community services. *See* Social services
Composers and compositions: 789, 905, 917, 926, 997, 1014. *See also* General programs; Music
Computer engineering. *See* Engineering, computer
Computer sciences: 2, 8–9, 11, 20, 22, 40, 57, 74, 80, 106, 114, 117, 121, 140–141, 147, 157–158, 167, 208, 214, 222, 228, 230, 242, 251, 260, 263, 280, 294, 305, 311, 315, 319–320, 369, 376, 379, 398, 410, 426, 440, 445, 455, 465, 475–476, 492, 498, 523, 588–589, 592, 618, 636, 642, 707, 770, 790, 843–844, 966, 1078. *See also* General programs; Information science; Libraries and librarianship; Mathematics; Technology
Computers. *See* Computer sciences
Conservation. *See* Art conservation; Environmental sciences
Construction. *See* Building trades

SUBJECT INDEX

Construction engineering. *See* Engineering, construction
Construction industry: 2, 35, 44, 82, 120, 122, 134, 255, 366, 388, 469, 575. *See also* Building trades; General programs
Consumer and family studies education. *See* Education, family and consumer studies
Cooking. *See* Culinary arts
Cooling industry: 35, 44, 82, 134, 388, 469. *See also* General programs
Cosmetology. *See* Hair design
Counselors and counseling, school: 685. *See also* General programs
Counter-intelligence service. *See* Intelligence service
Crafts. *See* Arts and crafts
Creative writing: 783, 855, 972. *See also* Fine arts; General programs
Criminal justice: 165, 266, 421, 551, 643, 657, 665, 722, 724, 727, 736, 761, 767, 770. *See also* General programs; Law, general
Culinary arts: 229, 243, 262, 630, 752, 768, 806, 808, 827, 868, 881, 901, 995, 1066, 1229. *See also* Food service industry; General programs

Dairy science: 99, 212, 240, 285, 341–342, 349, 372, 511, 686. *See also* Agriculture and agricultural sciences; General programs
Dance: 191, 241, 278, 337, 435, 486, 499, 600, 628, 650, 666, 679, 731, 751, 762, 807, 829, 852, 880, 904, 918, 929, 970, 1002. *See also* General programs; Performing arts
Dari language. *See* Language, Dari
Data entry. *See* Computer sciences
Dental hygiene: 102. *See also* Dentistry; General programs
Dentistry: 102, 239, 387. *See also* General programs; Health and health care; Medical sciences
Design: 4, 49, 813, 882–883, 971. *See also* Art; General programs
Developmental disabilities. *See* Disabilities, developmental
Dietetics. *See* Nutrition
Disabilities: 52, 548, 896. *See also* General programs; Rehabilitation; names of specific disabilities
Disabilities, developmental: 135, 254. *See also* Disabilities; General programs
Disabilities, visual. *See* Visual impairments
Disability law: 52, 548. *See also* General programs; Law, general
Discrimination, racial: 838. *See also* General programs
Discrimination, religious: 838. *See also* General programs; Religion and religious activities
Distance education: 400, 715. *See also* Education; General programs
Distance learning. *See* Distance education
Divinity. *See* Religion and religious activities
Documentaries. *See* Filmmaking
Drafting: 289, 911. *See also* General programs
Drama. *See* Plays

Early childhood education. *See* Education, preschool
Earth sciences: 64, 166, 284, 460, 517. *See also* General programs; Natural sciences; names of specific earth sciences
Ecology. *See* Environmental sciences

Economic development: 330, 675. *See also* Economics; General programs
Economic planning. *See* Economics
Economics: 330, 349, 492, 544, 550, 554, 558, 569, 572, 671, 675, 686, 688, 711, 914. *See also* General programs; Social sciences
Economics, agricultural: 206, 328, 341, 357, 606, 672, 682, 695, 942. *See also* Agriculture and agricultural sciences; Economics; General programs
Editors and editing: 990. *See also* General programs; Writers and writing
Education: 330, 437, 530, 543, 555, 557, 560, 579, 590, 595, 602, 614, 616, 639, 654, 664, 675, 701, 712, 866, 1056. *See also* General programs; specific types and levels of education
Education, administration: 685. *See also* Education; Management
Education, agricultural: 34, 115, 328, 341, 349, 540, 571, 672, 682, 686. *See also* Agriculture and agricultural sciences; Education; General programs
Education, bilingual: 685. *See also* Education; General programs
Education, business: 536, 669. *See also* Education; General programs
Education, elementary: 412, 486, 685, 723, 751. *See also* Education; General programs
Education, family and consumer studies: 674. *See also* Education; Family and consumer studies; General programs
Education, health: 79, 559. *See also* Education; General programs; Health and health care
Education, music: 860, 1056. *See also* Education; General programs; Music
Education, physical: 156, 191, 241, 278, 337, 396, 435, 486, 499, 587, 600, 628, 650, 666, 679, 731, 751, 762, 852, 880, 904, 929, 970, 1002. *See also* Athletics; Education; General programs
Education, preschool: 685, 755, 759. *See also* Education; General programs
Education, science and mathematics: 64, 167, 371, 412, 441, 467, 481, 492, 495, 592, 685, 723, 733, 741, 744, 756. *See also* Education; General programs; Sciences
Education, secondary: 412, 486, 536, 549, 647, 723, 751. *See also* Education; General programs
Education, special: 52, 433, 548, 649, 685, 730, 759. *See also* Disabilities; Education; General programs
Education, technology: 195, 603. *See also* Education; General programs; Technology
Electrical engineering. *See* Engineering, electrical
Electricity. *See* Utilities
Electronic journalism. *See* Journalism, broadcast
Electronics: 84, 128, 150, 200, 234, 248, 251, 272, 287, 291, 303, 321, 466, 636, 889. *See also* General programs; Physics
Elementary education. *See* Education, elementary
Emergency medical technician: 83. *See also* General programs; Health and health care
Eminent domain. *See* Real estate law
Employee benefits: 690. *See also* Employment; General programs
Employment: 1009. *See also* Employee benefits; General programs; Occupational therapy
Energy: 133, 250, 525. *See also* Environmental sciences; General programs; Natural resources

Engineering: 25, 30–31, 41, 49–50, 57, 63, 65, 68, 72, 80, 109, 114, 116, 119, 129, 140–141, 148, 157–158, 163, 167, 184, 198, 207–208, 210–211, 217, 228, 250, 260, 274, 279, 286, 289, 294, 305, 311, 315–316, 343, 347, 354, 360, 364, 369, 373, 379, 384, 398, 402, 404, 411, 413, 416, 427, 436, 440, 455, 458, 475–476, 478–479, 485, 493, 504, 512, 515, 525, 592, 607, 721, 725, 741, 790, 911, 1078, 1200. *See also* General programs; Physical sciences; names of specific types of engineering

Engineering, acoustical: 246. *See also* Acoustics; Engineering; General programs

Engineering, aeronautical: 19–20, 130, 276, 339, 465. *See also* Aeronautics; Engineering; General programs

Engineering, aerospace: 19–20, 197, 214, 276, 283, 361, 371, 378, 427, 460, 492, 494, 504, 741. *See also* Engineering; General programs; Space sciences

Engineering, agricultural: 2, 13, 165–166, 202, 270, 328, 342, 357, 672, 695, 942. *See also* Agriculture and agricultural sciences; Engineering; General programs

Engineering, architectural: 2, 20, 74, 122, 382, 462. *See also* Architecture; Engineering; General programs

Engineering, automotive: 185, 187, 209, 403, 506. *See also* Engineering; General programs

Engineering, biomedical: 164, 514. *See also* Engineering; General programs

Engineering, broadcast: 225, 300, 417, 941. *See also* Engineering; General programs; Radio; Television

Engineering, ceramic: 145. *See also* Engineering; General programs

Engineering, chemical: 2, 10–11, 22, 105–106, 137, 165–166, 197, 209–210, 222, 269, 288, 324, 405, 429, 498. *See also* Chemistry; Engineering; General programs

Engineering, civil: 2, 19–20, 55, 74, 106, 110, 122, 160, 165–166, 288, 366, 382, 405, 418, 462, 468, 520, 745. *See also* Engineering; General programs

Engineering, computer: 8, 11, 19–20, 22, 40, 106, 117, 121, 218, 222, 242, 263, 319–320, 410, 426, 588, 642, 843. *See also* Computer sciences; Engineering; General programs

Engineering, construction: 255, 366, 382. *See also* Engineering; General programs

Engineering, electrical: 2, 8, 11, 19–20, 22, 74, 126, 185, 209–210, 218, 222, 242, 251, 297, 320, 395, 410, 426, 636. *See also* Engineering; General programs

Engineering, environmental: 10, 19–20, 74, 165–166, 288, 330, 405, 508, 675. *See also* Engineering; Environmental sciences; General programs

Engineering, food: 183. *See also* Agriculture and agricultural sciences; Engineering; General programs

Engineering, geological: 307–308. *See also* Engineering; General programs; Geology

Engineering, heating: 58–59, 244. *See also* Engineering; General programs; Heating industry

Engineering, industrial: 2, 22, 185, 209–210, 222, 230, 390, 426, 618. *See also* Engineering; General programs

Engineering, manufacturing: 2, 98, 152–154, 175, 185, 199, 209–210, 222–223, 304, 334, 390, 454, 456, 473, 513. *See also* Engineering; General programs

Engineering, materials: 145, 209, 222. *See also* Engineering; General programs; Materials sciences

Engineering, mechanical: 2, 19–20, 22, 35, 44, 61–62, 74, 106, 126, 134, 165–166, 185, 193, 196–197, 209–210, 222, 281, 297, 368, 388, 399, 403, 419, 426, 469, 474, 480, 526. *See also* Engineering; General programs

Engineering, metallurgical: 10. *See also* Engineering; General programs; Metallurgy

Engineering, mining: 2, 322. *See also* Engineering; General programs; Mining industry

Engineering, nuclear: 43, 103, 132, 345. *See also* Engineering; General programs; Nuclear science

Engineering, ocean: 265, 332, 374, 432. *See also* Engineering; General programs; Oceanography

Engineering, optical: 317, 464. *See also* Engineering; General programs; Optics

Engineering, petroleum: 106, 386, 394, 1236. *See also* Engineering; General programs; Petroleum industry

Engineering, plastics: 201, 393. *See also* Engineering; General programs

Engineering, refrigerating and air conditioning: 58–59, 244. *See also* Cooling industry; Engineering; General programs

Engineering, structural: 382, 462, 520. *See also* Engineering; General programs

Engineering, surveying: 7, 78, 87, 273, 362–363, 443, 502. *See also* Engineering; General programs; Surveying

Engineering, systems: 11, 251, 636. *See also* Engineering; General programs

Engineering technology: 41, 50, 59, 61, 98, 116, 152–154, 193, 199, 223, 236, 252, 304, 316, 334, 382, 390, 397, 407, 419, 422, 454, 513. *See also* Engineering; General programs

Engineering, transportation: 251, 301, 323, 450, 636, 663, 670, 735. *See also* Engineering; General programs; Transportation

Engineering, welding: 236, 252, 397, 407, 422. *See also* Engineering; General programs; Welding

English language. *See* Language, English

English literature. *See* Literature, English

Enology and viticulture: 33, 92–93, 500. *See also* Agriculture and agricultural sciences; General programs

Entomology: 249, 302, 420. *See also* General programs

Entrepreneurship: 6, 528, 533, 604, 617, 696, 704, 773. *See also* Business administration; General programs

Environmental engineering. *See* Engineering, environmental

Environmental sciences: 42, 51, 75, 95, 103, 114, 118–119, 123, 132, 138, 157, 162, 165–166, 177, 202–203, 288, 309, 312, 328, 330, 342, 365, 381, 405, 425, 428, 434, 437, 460, 483, 508, 573, 672, 675, 741, 749, 826, 1094. *See also* General programs; Sciences

Equine science: 156, 282, 342, 439, 587. *See also* Agriculture and agricultural sciences; Animal science; General programs

Exercise science. *See* Athletic training

Eye doctors. *See* Optometry

Eye problems. *See* Visual impairments

Fabric. *See* Clothing

Family and consumer studies: 640, 713. *See also* General programs; Social sciences

Family and consumer studies education. *See* Education, family and consumer studies

Farming. *See* Agriculture and agricultural sciences

Farsi language. *See* Language, Farsi

Fashion design: 828, 1006. *See also* Design; General programs

Feminist movement. *See* Women's studies and programs

Fiber. *See* Textiles

Fiction: 794, 861, 918, 1116. *See also* General programs; Writers and writing

SUBJECT INDEX

Film as a literary art. See Cinema
Filmmaking: 775, 786, 804, 807, 811, 838, 864, 979, 987, 998, 1000. See also Audiovisual materials and equipment; General programs; Television
Finance: 34, 251, 301, 323, 376–377, 450, 529, 540, 550, 569, 572, 601, 608, 621, 632, 636, 663, 670–671, 682, 688, 707–708, 735, 747, 750, 952, 1141. See also Accounting; Banking; Economics; General programs
Fine arts: 783, 1000, 1056. See also General programs; Humanities; names of specific fine arts
Finnish studies: 897. See also General programs; Humanities
Fire science: 213, 266, 275, 421, 610, 643, 727. See also General programs; Sciences
Fishing industry: 51, 75, 288, 328, 405, 672. See also General programs
Flight science. See Aviation
Floriculture. See Horticulture
Flying. See Aviation
Food. See Culinary arts; Nutrition
Food science: 1, 53, 86, 216, 243, 247, 268, 277, 313, 342, 349, 358–359, 375, 401, 459, 527, 630, 686, 881. See also Food service industry; General programs; Nutrition
Food service industry: 111, 335, 444, 533, 570, 574, 641, 655, 673, 677, 683–684, 692–693, 702, 718–719, 734, 739, 752, 754, 768, 771–772, 806, 808, 995. See also General programs
Food technology. See Food science
Foreign affairs. See International affairs
Forensic science: 770. See also Criminal justice; General programs
Forestry management: 27, 75, 155, 203, 288, 328, 405, 425, 437, 672. See also General programs; Management
Funerals. See Mortuary science

Gardening. See Horticulture
Gender. See Women's studies and programs
General programs: 20, 39, 95, 104, 131, 177, 220, 229, 232, 235, 245, 262, 326–327, 340, 347, 355, 364, 367, 380, 408, 489, 497, 505, 524, 554, 556, 611, 615–616, 620, 634, 696, 709, 811, 825, 833, 854, 858, 866, 868, 891, 902, 974, 979, 998, 1015–1060, 1062–1077, 1079–1235, 1237–1244, 1246–1323
Genetics: 249. See also General programs; Medical sciences
Geography: 97, 157, 377, 564, 708, 952. See also General programs; Social sciences
Geological engineering. See Engineering, geological
Geology: 64, 165–166, 284, 288, 307–308, 405, 460, 517. See also General programs; Physical sciences
Geophysics: 64, 70, 172, 224, 284, 404, 448, 452. See also General programs; Meteorology; Oceanography; Physics
Geosciences. See Earth sciences
Geriatric nurses and nursing. See Nurses and nursing, geriatrics
Geriatrics. See Aged and aging
Gerontology. See Aged and aging
Golf course management. See Turfgrass science
Government. See Political science and politics; Public administration
Grade school. See Education, elementary
Graphic arts: 112, 143, 182, 205, 221, 229, 238, 262–263, 442, 507, 522, 577, 588–589, 619, 627, 642, 698, 726, 769, 819, 831, 839, 843–844, 848–849, 856, 862–863, 868, 872, 945, 960, 966, 968, 976, 1000, 1008, 1066, 1229. See also Art; General programs
Graphic design: 752, 766, 797, 832, 887, 959, 975, 990, 995, 1010. See also Design; General programs; Graphic arts

Hair design: 229, 262, 868, 1066, 1229. See also General programs
Handicapped. See Disabilities
Hawaiian language. See Language, Hawaiian
Hawaiian studies: 1238. See also General programs; Native American studies
Health and health care: 12, 24, 29, 123, 146, 169, 186, 190–191, 230, 241, 278, 288, 293, 314, 330, 337, 351, 385, 405–406, 435, 472, 499, 593, 598–600, 618, 628, 650, 666, 675, 679, 710, 717, 731, 748, 757, 762, 852, 880, 904, 929, 970, 1002, 1056. See also General programs; Medical sciences
Health education. See Education, health
Heating engineering. See Engineering, heating
Heating industry: 35, 44, 82, 134, 388, 469. See also Building trades; General programs
High schools. See Education, secondary
Hindi language. See Language, Hindi
Historical preservation: 798, 892. See also General programs; History
History: 611, 616, 798, 835, 858, 866, 876, 891, 996, 1004, 1192. See also Archaeology; General programs; Humanities; Social sciences; specific types of history
History, American: 957. See also General programs; History
History, Polish: 1235. See also General programs; Polish studies
Horses. See Equine science
Horticulture: 60, 73, 77, 93, 151, 180, 203, 290, 302, 342, 420, 428, 434, 461, 487, 496, 801, 934, 994. See also Agriculture and agricultural sciences; General programs; Landscape architecture; Sciences
Hospitality industry. See Hotel and motel industry
Hospitals. See Health and health care
Hotel and motel industry: 562, 574, 622, 625, 641, 655, 673, 684, 693, 702, 718–719, 739, 752, 754, 771–772, 808, 995. See also General programs
Human resources. See Personnel administration
Human services. See Social services
Humanities: 626, 879, 902, 1143. See also General programs; names of specific humanities
Hydrology: 32, 64, 166, 170, 299. See also Earth sciences; General programs

Illustrators and illustrations: 966. See also Art; General programs; Graphic arts
Industrial engineering. See Engineering, industrial
Industrial relations: 646, 737. See also General programs; Labor unions and members
Information science: 22, 147, 167, 169, 186, 190, 228, 230, 238, 248, 376–377, 406, 413, 522, 529, 531, 550, 572, 592–593, 598–599, 618, 627, 632, 707–708, 717, 725, 747, 769, 889, 952, 1078. See also Computer sciences; General programs; Libraries and librarianship
Insurance. See Actuarial sciences

SUBJECT INDEX

Intellectual freedom: 579. See also Civil liberties; General programs
Intelligence service: 615. See also General programs; International affairs
Interior design: 813, 828, 882, 899, 1006. See also Architecture; Design; General programs
International affairs: 376–377, 492, 563, 611, 616, 707–708, 858, 866, 950, 952. See also General programs; Political science and politics
International relations. See International affairs
Internet design and development: 143, 263, 588, 642, 839, 843, 887. See also General programs; Graphic arts; Technology
Internet journalism. See Journalism, online
Inventors and inventions: 114. See also Entrepreneurship; General programs; Technology
Iron and steel industry: 63, 179, 512. See also General programs; Metallurgy
Italian language. See Language, Italian

Jobs. See Employment
Journalism: 171, 188, 248, 349, 565, 616, 626, 647, 686, 752, 777, 788, 793, 797, 804–805, 812, 814, 816, 824–825, 833–834, 845–847, 850, 853, 861, 866, 871, 879, 886, 889, 910, 912–913, 924, 930–931, 937, 943, 946–947, 950, 954, 956, 969, 977, 986, 993, 995, 1006, 1009, 1013, 1238. See also Broadcasting; Communications; General programs; Writers and writing; names of specific types of journalism
Journalism, agriculture. See Agricultural communications
Journalism, broadcast: 726, 775, 793, 810, 821, 842, 869, 885–886, 894, 898, 906, 912, 916, 924, 941, 949, 954, 962–963, 968. See also Communications; General programs; Radio; Television
Journalism, business. See Business reporting
Journalism, cable: 810, 842, 906, 916, 954, 962. See also General programs; Journalism, broadcast
Journalism, medical. See Science reporting
Journalism, online: 810, 842, 906, 912, 924, 948, 954, 962. See also General programs; Journalism
Journalism, religion. See Religious reporting
Journalism, science. See Science reporting
Journalism, sports. See Sports reporting
Jurisprudence. See Law, general

Korean language. See Language, Korean

Labor unions and members: 645–646, 709. See also General programs; Industrial relations
Landscape architecture: 46, 77, 290, 420, 801, 826, 934. See also Botany; General programs; Horticulture
Language, Arabic: 377, 708, 952. See also General programs
Language, Chinese: 377, 708, 952. See also General programs
Language, Dari: 377, 708, 952. See also General programs
Language, English: 841, 875, 972, 981. See also General programs
Language, Farsi: 377, 708, 952. See also General programs
Language, Hawaiian: 1238. See also General programs
Language, Hindi: 377, 708, 952. See also General programs
Language, Italian: 983. See also General programs
Language, Korean: 377, 708, 952. See also General programs
Language, Native American: 685. See also General programs
Language, Pashto: 377, 708, 952. See also General programs
Language, Polish: 1235. See also General programs
Language, Urdu: 377, 708, 952. See also General programs
Law enforcement. See Criminal justice
Law, general: 492, 626, 732, 879, 1141. See also Criminal justice; General programs; Paralegal studies; Social sciences; names of legal specialties
Lawyers. See Law, general
Leadership: 1186. See also General programs; Management
Legal assistants. See Paralegal studies
Legal studies and services. See Law, general
Librarians. See Libraries and librarianship
Libraries and librarianship: 377, 708, 952, 1004. See also General programs; Information science; Social sciences
Libraries and librarianship, school: 685. See also General programs; Libraries and librarianship
Life insurance. See Actuarial sciences
Life sciences. See Biological sciences
Lighting: 888. See also Architecture; General programs
Literature: 918, 967. See also General programs; Humanities; Writers and writing; specific types of literature
Literature, American: 794. See also General programs; Literature
Literature, English: 841, 875, 972, 981. See also General programs; Literature
Logistics: 251, 296, 301, 323, 350, 450, 581, 583, 636, 662–663, 670, 687, 735. See also General programs; Transportation

Magazines. See Journalism; Literature
Management: 108, 169, 186, 190, 282, 406, 411, 472, 499, 550, 567–568, 572, 578, 583, 593, 598–599, 617, 631–633, 637, 641, 668, 681, 697–698, 717, 721, 738, 747–748, 753, 762, 783, 817, 941, 945, 1002. See also General programs; Social sciences
Management, nurses and nursing. See Nurses and nursing, administration
Manufacturing engineering. See Engineering, manufacturing
Maps and mapmaking. See Cartography
Marine sciences: 90, 136, 157, 265, 332, 374, 425, 432, 483, 749. See also General programs; Sciences; names of specific marine sciences
Marketing: 99, 243, 263, 341, 349, 511, 577, 582, 588, 617, 630, 642, 682, 686, 726, 752, 766, 788, 797, 818, 831, 837, 843, 881, 931, 968, 995, 1010. See also Advertising; General programs; Public relations; Sales
Marketing education. See Education, business
Mass communications. See Communications
Materials engineering. See Engineering, materials
Materials sciences: 10, 22, 63, 145, 179, 416, 429, 512. See also General programs; Physical sciences
Mathematics: 11, 20, 22, 26, 68, 72, 114, 143, 157, 159, 167, 192, 214, 230, 244, 320, 347, 354, 361, 364, 371, 412, 440–441, 445, 455, 460, 465, 481, 494–495, 504, 516, 592, 618, 723, 733, 756, 839, 1078, 1200. See also Computer sciences; General programs; Physical sciences; Statistics
Mechanical engineering. See Engineering, mechanical

SUBJECT INDEX

Media. *See* Broadcasting; Communications; names of specific media
Media specialists. *See* Libraries and librarianship; Libraries and librarianship, school
Medical journalism. *See* Science reporting
Medical sciences: 12, 68, 114, 146, 295, 306, 396, 427. *See also* General programs; Health and health care; Sciences; names of specific diseases; names of medical specialties
Medical technology: 12, 56, 173, 215, 229, 262, 868, 1066, 1229. *See also* General programs; Medical sciences; Technology
Mental retardation: 47, 254, 545. *See also* Disabilities, developmental; General programs; Medical sciences
Merchandising. *See* Sales
Metallurgical engineering. *See* Engineering, metallurgical
Metallurgy: 10, 63, 179, 322, 512. *See also* General programs; Sciences
Meteorology: 19–20, 32, 64, 157, 170, 299. *See also* Atmospheric sciences; General programs
Microcomputers. *See* Computer sciences
Microscopy. *See* Medical technology
Middle Eastern studies: 377, 708, 952. *See also* General programs; Humanities
Mining engineering. *See* Engineering, mining
Mining industry: 224. *See also* General programs
Missionary work. *See* Religion and religious activities
Mortuary science: 763. *See also* General programs
Motel industry. *See* Hotel and motel industry
Music: 779, 787, 807, 809, 836, 855, 860, 884, 893, 905, 918, 921, 932, 940, 944, 967, 980, 982, 991, 997, 999, 1001, 1005, 1056. *See also* Fine arts; General programs; Humanities; Performing arts
Music, cello: 1005. *See also* General programs; Music
Music, church: 815, 859, 991. *See also* General programs; Music; Performing arts; Religion and religious activities
Music, classical: 859. *See also* General programs; Music
Music education. *See* Education, music
Music, piano: 836, 933, 1005. *See also* General programs; Music
Music, strings: 792, 836, 903, 984. *See also* General programs; Music
Music therapy: 333, 927. *See also* General programs; Music
Music, viola: 1007. *See also* General programs; Music, strings
Music, violin: 978, 1005. *See also* General programs; Music, strings
Musicals: 905. *See also* Composers and compositions; General programs; Music

Native American language. *See* Language, Native American
Native American studies: 330, 675, 685. *See also* General programs
Natural resources: 68, 75, 162, 165–166, 180, 328, 330, 342, 428, 434, 437, 483, 508, 672, 675, 749. *See also* General programs; names of specific resources
Natural sciences: 72, 279, 492, 508. *See also* General programs; Sciences; names of specific sciences
Naval science: 489, 1122, 1197–1198. *See also* General programs
Neonatal and perinatal nurses and nursing. *See* Nurses and nursing, neonatal and perinatal
Neuroscience nurses and nursing. *See* Nurses and nursing, neuroscience

Newspapers. *See* Journalism
Nonfiction: 46, 136, 217, 219, 232, 255, 329, 385, 395, 399, 416, 474, 526, 535, 552, 554, 561, 583, 590, 620, 710, 714, 720, 834, 861, 891, 914, 918, 974, 1004, 1026, 1058, 1116, 1257, 1286, 1294. *See also* General programs; Writers and writing
Nonprofit sector: 538. *See also* General programs; Public administration
Norwegian studies: 656, 667. *See also* Humanities
Nuclear engineering. *See* Engineering, nuclear
Nuclear science: 43, 103, 132, 256. *See also* General programs; Physical sciences
Nurses and nursing, administration: 189. *See also* General programs; Management; Nurses and nursing, general
Nurses and nursing, general: 12, 21, 38, 67, 71, 346, 414, 449. *See also* General programs; Health and health care; Medical sciences; names of specific nursing specialties
Nurses and nursing, geriatrics: 226. *See also* Aged and aging; General programs; Nurses and nursing, general
Nurses and nursing, neonatal and perinatal: 5, 189. *See also* General programs; Nurses and nursing, general
Nurses and nursing, neuroscience: 353. *See also* General programs; Nurses and nursing, general
Nurses and nursing, occupational health: 24, 29, 293, 314. *See also* General programs; Nurses and nursing, general
Nurses and nursing, oncology: 37, 370, 424. *See also* General programs; Nurses and nursing, general
Nurses and nursing, rehabilitation: 66. *See also* General programs; Nurses and nursing, general; Rehabilitation
Nutrition: 111, 335, 341, 349, 444, 484, 570, 677, 686, 734. *See also* General programs; Medical sciences

Occupational health nurses and nursing. *See* Nurses and nursing, occupational health
Occupational therapy: 54. *See also* Employment; General programs
Ocean engineering. *See* Engineering, ocean
Oceanography: 32, 64, 90, 136, 167, 170, 299, 483, 503, 592, 749. *See also* General programs; Marine sciences
Oil industry. *See* Petroleum industry
Oncology. *See* Cancer
Oncology nurses and nursing. *See* Nurses and nursing, oncology
Online journalism. *See* Journalism, online
Opera. *See* Music; Voice
Operations research: 20, 230, 618. *See also* General programs; Mathematics; Sciences
Optical engineering. *See* Engineering, optical
Optics: 317, 430, 464. *See also* General programs; Physics
Optometry: 18. *See also* General programs; Medical sciences
Oratory: 340, 368, 895. *See also* General programs
Orthopedics: 174. *See also* General programs; Medical sciences

Packaging: 470, 960, 988. *See also* General programs
Packaging industry: 181. *See also* General programs
Painting: 1000. *See also* Art; General programs
Paper industry: 112, 163, 360, 373, 402, 515, 819. *See also* General programs

Paralegal studies: 660. *See also* General programs; Social sciences
Pashto language. *See* Language, Pashto
Pathology: 215. *See also* General programs; Medical sciences
Performing arts: 780, 783, 802, 807, 890, 925, 1174. *See also* General programs; Humanities; names of specific performing arts
Perinatal nurses and nursing. *See* Nurses and nursing, neonatal and perinatal
Personnel administration: 584, 624, 634, 661, 690–691, 737, 757, 1128. *See also* General programs; Management
Petroleum engineering. *See* Engineering, petroleum
Petroleum industry: 81, 394, 451, 1236. *See also* General programs
Pharmaceutical sciences: 12, 18, 258, 348, 510. *See also* General programs; Medical sciences
Philosophy: 914. *See also* General programs; Humanities
Photogrammetry: 157. *See also* Cartography; General programs; Photography
Photography: 804, 887, 1000, 1006. *See also* Fine arts; General programs
Photojournalism: 804, 816, 820, 870, 924. *See also* General programs; Journalism; Photography
Physical education. *See* Education, physical
Physical sciences: 68, 90, 142, 157, 167, 379, 465, 491–492, 508, 592, 1078. *See also* General programs; Sciences; names of specific physical sciences
Physical therapy: 18, 54, 295, 325, 396. *See also* Disabilities; General programs; Health and health care; Rehabilitation
Physician assistant: 3, 101. *See also* General programs; Health and health care; Medical sciences
Physics: 11, 20, 45, 114, 148, 157, 161, 284, 292, 320, 344, 364, 383, 403, 415, 430, 455, 457, 464–465, 467, 494, 501, 519, 744. *See also* General programs; Mathematics; Physical sciences
Physiology: 249. *See also* General programs; Medical sciences
Piano. *See* Music, piano
Plastics engineering. *See* Engineering, plastics
Plays: 855, 896, 900, 907–908, 915, 918–920, 939, 953, 992. *See also* General programs; Literature; Performing arts; Writers and writing
Plumbing industry: 35, 44, 82, 134, 388, 469. *See also* Building trades; General programs
Poetry: 861, 918, 972. *See also* General programs; Literature; Writers and writing
Poisons. *See* Toxicology
Police science. *See* Criminal justice
Polish history. *See* History, Polish
Polish language. *See* Language, Polish
Polish studies: 616, 866, 1235. *See also* General programs; Humanities
Political science and politics: 330, 376, 558, 611, 671, 675, 707, 732, 858, 914. *See also* General programs; Public administration; Social sciences
Pollution: 119, 508. *See also* Environmental sciences; General programs
Pomology: 93. *See also* General programs; Horticulture
Pork industry: 235. *See also* Agriculture and agricultural sciences; General programs
Posters. *See* Graphic arts
Poverty: 554. *See also* General programs; Social services
Preschool education. *See* Education, preschool
Preservation, historical. *See* Historical preservation
Presidents, U.S. *See* History, American
Press. *See* Journalism
Print journalism. *See* Journalism
Printing industry: 143, 182, 205, 221, 263, 507, 568, 588–589, 642, 678, 698, 817, 839, 843–844, 848–849, 856, 862–863, 928, 945, 1008. *See also* General programs
Prints. *See* Art; Graphic arts
Psychology: 12, 535, 648, 1078. *See also* Behavioral sciences; General programs; Social sciences
Public administration: 118, 213, 330, 468, 483, 492, 550, 572–573, 594, 601, 608–610, 626, 634, 652, 671, 675, 716, 745, 749, 879, 1078, 1128. *See also* General programs; Management; Political science and politics; Social sciences
Public affairs. *See* Public administration
Public health: 12, 309, 330, 351, 675. *See also* General programs; Health and health care
Public policy. *See* Public administration
Public relations: 51, 188, 349, 565, 577, 616, 686, 752, 788, 791, 797, 803, 812, 830–832, 850–851, 866, 909, 913, 931, 947, 956, 961, 973, 986, 995. *See also* General programs; Marketing
Public sector. *See* Public administration
Public service: 1126. *See also* General programs; Public administration; Social services
Public speaking. *See* Oratory
Public utilities. *See* Utilities
Publicity. *See* Public relations
Publishers and publishing: 678, 928, 960, 975, 990. *See also* General programs
Pulp and paper industry. *See* Paper industry

Race relations: 838. *See also* General programs
Racial discrimination. *See* Discrimination, racial
Racism. *See* Discrimination, racial
Radio: 774, 785, 840, 869, 913, 1003, 1011. *See also* Communications; General programs
Radiology: 102. *See also* General programs; Medical sciences
Ranching: 86, 312, 484. *See also* Agriculture and agricultural sciences; General programs
Real estate: 468, 544, 566, 569, 745–746. *See also* General programs
Real estate law: 468, 745. *See also* General programs; Law, general
Recreation: 75, 177, 191, 241, 278, 337, 428, 434–435, 437, 486, 499, 576, 600, 628, 650, 666, 673, 679, 731, 751, 762, 852, 880, 904, 929, 970, 1002, 1094. *See also* General programs; names of specific recreational activities
Reentry programs: 80, 369, 532, 1056, 1265. *See also* General programs
Refrigeration engineering. *See* Engineering, refrigerating and air conditioning
Refrigeration industry. *See* Cooling industry
Regional planning. *See* City and regional planning
Rehabilitation: 52, 66, 433, 548, 730. *See also* General programs; Health and health care; specific types of therapy
Religion and religious activities: 854, 914, 951, 965, 974, 998, 1078, 1192, 1273. *See also* General programs; Humanities
Religious reporting: 838, 846, 912. *See also* Broadcasting; General programs; Journalism; Religion and religious activities
Resource management: 51, 206, 606. *See also* Environmental sciences; General programs; Management

SUBJECT INDEX

Respiratory therapy: 261, 331, 423, 518. *See also* General programs; Health and health care
Restaurants. *See* Food service industry
Retailing. *See* Sales
Retardation. *See* Mental retardation
Risk management: 635, 676, 680. *See also* Actuarial sciences; Business administration; Finance; General programs
Robotics: 473, 513. *See also* General programs; Technology

Safety studies: 118, 123, 474, 573. *See also* Engineering; General programs
Sales: 263, 588, 642, 692, 843, 941, 1006. *See also* General programs; Marketing
School counselors. *See* Counselors and counseling, school
School libraries and librarians. *See* Libraries and librarianship, school
Schools. *See* Education
Science education. *See* Education, science and mathematics
Science reporting: 171, 487, 804, 847, 869, 994. *See also* Broadcasting; General programs; Journalism; Sciences; Writers and writing
Sciences: 68, 109, 114, 119, 163, 210, 244, 286, 309, 347, 354, 373, 402, 427, 504, 515, 741, 1200, 1235. *See also* General programs; names of specific sciences
Sculpture: 201, 1000. *See also* Fine arts; General programs
Secondary education. *See* Education, secondary
Secret service. *See* Intelligence service
Sewing: 935. *See also* Arts and crafts; General programs
Sight impairments. *See* Visual impairments
Singing. *See* Voice
Smoking. *See* Tobacco consumption
Social sciences: 167, 385, 579, 592, 626, 646, 710, 879, 1078. *See also* General programs; names of specific social sciences
Social services: 226, 385, 538, 710. *See also* General programs; Public service
Sociology: 328, 492, 672. *See also* General programs; Social sciences
Soils science: 85, 162, 166, 253, 270, 328, 420, 672. *See also* Agriculture and agricultural sciences; General programs; Horticulture
Songs. *See* Music
South Asian studies: 377, 708, 952. *See also* General programs; Humanities
Space sciences: 6, 17, 130, 214, 283–284, 318, 361, 371, 378, 400, 427, 430, 460, 465, 492, 494, 501, 504, 528, 715, 741, 1024. *See also* General programs; Physical sciences
Special education. *See* Education, special
Speech pathology: 759. *See also* General programs; Medical sciences
Speeches. *See* Oratory
Sports. *See* Athletics
Sports medicine: 295. *See also* General programs; Medical sciences
Sports reporting: 791, 853, 869, 916, 985. *See also* Broadcasting; General programs; Journalism; Writers and writing
Spying. *See* Intelligence service
Stage design. *See* Performing arts
Statistics: 271. *See also* General programs; Mathematics
Steel industry. *See* Iron and steel industry
Structural engineering. *See* Engineering, structural
Surveying: 2, 7, 27, 76, 78, 87, 273, 310, 352, 356, 362–363, 391, 443, 502, 509, 753. *See also* General programs
Surveying engineering. *See* Engineering, surveying
Swine industry. *See* Pork industry
Systems engineering. *See* Engineering, systems

Teaching. *See* Education
Technology: 49, 81, 114, 169, 186, 190, 217, 320, 347, 354, 361, 371, 393, 406, 427, 442, 451, 460, 593, 598–599, 717, 976, 990, 1200. *See also* Computer sciences; General programs; Sciences
Teenagers. *See* Adolescents
Telecommunications: 248, 263, 376–377, 588, 642, 707–708, 821, 843, 867, 885, 889, 952. *See also* Communications; General programs; Radio; Television
Television: 300, 775, 838, 840, 869, 913, 1011. *See also* Communications; Filmmaking; General programs
Textiles: 835, 876, 1006. *See also* Arts and crafts; General programs
Theater. *See* Performing arts; Plays
Theology. *See* Religion and religious activities
Tobacco consumption: 1061. *See also* General programs; Medical sciences
Tourism: 532, 534, 537, 546, 553, 574, 622–623, 655, 684, 693, 702, 718, 743, 752, 754, 764, 772, 995. *See also* General programs
Toxicology: 166, 249. *See also* General programs; Medical sciences
Trade unions. *See* Labor unions and members
Transportation: 94, 118, 251, 296, 301, 323, 350, 418, 431, 450, 480, 482, 488, 525, 573, 581, 636, 662–663, 670, 687, 728, 735, 1245. *See also* Automobile industry; Aviation; General programs; Space sciences
Transportation engineering. *See* Engineering, transportation
Travel and tourism. *See* Tourism
Turfgrass science: 46, 73, 139, 204, 219, 231, 257, 355, 438, 446, 487, 994. *See also* Biological sciences; General programs; Management
TV. *See* Television

Unions and unionization. *See* Industrial relations; Labor unions and members
Unrestricted programs. *See* General programs
Urban affairs: 720. *See also* City and regional planning; General programs
Urban planning. *See* City and regional planning
Urdu language. *See* Language, Urdu
Utilities: 133, 413, 725. *See also* Energy; General programs

Veterinary sciences: 23, 99, 114, 282, 484, 511. *See also* Animal science; General programs; Sciences
Video. *See* Filmmaking; Television
Viola. *See* Music, viola
Violin. *See* Music, violin
Visual arts: 783, 807, 918. *See also* General programs; Humanities; names of specific visual arts
Visual impairments: 433, 730. *See also* Disabilities; General programs; Health and health care

Viticulture. *See* Enology and viticulture
Voice: 782, 799, 809, 860, 918, 923, 932, 936, 944, 980, 991. *See also* General programs; Music; Performing arts

Water resources: 46, 73, 88, 138, 162, 166, 270, 328, 409, 672. *See also* Environmental sciences; General programs; Natural resources
Web design. *See* Internet design and development
Web journalism. *See* Journalism, online
Welding: 48–49, 236, 637. *See also* Building trades; General programs
Welding engineering. *See* Engineering, welding
Welfare. *See* Social services
Wildlife management: 51, 75, 165, 288, 328, 405, 425, 672. *See also* Environmental sciences; General programs
Wine making. *See* Enology and viticulture
Women's studies and programs: 556. *See also* General programs
Work. *See* Employment
World literature. *See* Literature
Writers and writing: 46, 48–49, 95, 102, 107, 136, 142, 171, 182, 192, 196, 217, 219, 232, 246, 255, 329, 385, 395, 399, 416, 429, 442, 472, 474, 498, 524, 526, 535, 552, 554, 561, 583, 590, 620, 648, 705, 709–710, 714, 720, 748, 784, 794, 811, 834, 847, 849, 854, 857, 861, 891, 895–896, 899–900, 905, 907–910, 914–915, 918–920, 930, 937, 939, 953, 957, 961, 963, 969, 974, 976, 992, 1004, 1026, 1054, 1058, 1078, 1084, 1116, 1160, 1257, 1286, 1294. *See also* General programs; Literature; specific types of writing

Youth. *See* Adolescents; Child development

Zoning, planning, and land use. *See* Real estate law

Calendar Index

Since most financial aid programs have specific deadline dates, some may have already closed by the time you begin to look for funding. You can use the Calendar Index to identify which programs are still open. To do that, look at the subject categories that interest you, think about when you'll be able to complete your application forms, go to the appropriate months, jot down the entry numbers listed there, and use those numbers to find the program descriptions in the directory. Keep in mind that the numbers cited here refer to program entry numbers, not to page numbers in the book. Note: not all sponsoring organizations supplied deadline information to us, so not all programs are listed in this index.

Sciences

January: 8–9, 17, 20, 37, 40, 43, 45, 53, 56, 70, 72, 74, 80, 97–98, 103, 106, 112, 126, 130, 132, 140–141, 152–154, 158, 160, 163, 172, 174, 185, 187, 198–199, 203, 208–209, 216, 218, 222–224, 236, 242, 247, 252, 254, 256, 260, 268, 276–277, 279, 284, 288, 294, 297, 302, 304–305, 308, 311–313, 315, 319–320, 334, 343, 351, 353, 358, 360, 365–366, 370–371, 373, 375, 390, 397–398, 401, 403–405, 422, 424, 426, 448, 452, 454, 456, 460, 464, 468, 475–476, 513, 527

February: 1, 3–4, 6, 31–33, 46–47, 52, 60, 84, 89, 96, 101, 108–109, 120, 128, 138, 144, 146–148, 150–151, 157, 167, 170, 176, 181–182, 184, 188, 194, 197, 200, 217, 234, 237, 258, 266–267, 271–272, 275, 280, 283, 286–287, 291, 295, 299, 303, 309, 321, 336, 342, 347–348, 381, 383, 400, 416, 421, 442, 446, 457, 459, 463, 466–467, 479, 486–487, 492, 505, 510

March: 16, 50, 61, 81, 91–93, 95, 113, 115–116, 123, 129, 135–136, 145, 156, 183, 193, 213, 219, 243, 253, 270, 281, 285, 289–290, 316–317, 330, 333, 339, 341, 354, 361, 382, 384, 393–394, 396, 413, 418–419, 428, 434, 436, 441, 451, 461, 478, 489, 499, 509, 523, 525

April: 5, 10, 14, 23, 28, 34, 39, 55, 63, 67, 71, 77, 86, 88, 90, 94, 104, 110–111, 118–119, 131, 155, 164, 166, 168–169, 175, 177–180, 186, 189–190, 206, 226, 241, 246, 248, 250, 265, 282, 307, 326–327, 332, 335, 350, 359, 374, 379, 386, 388–389, 406, 409, 412, 420, 431–433, 437, 444–445, 462, 471, 480, 482, 488, 494, 496, 498, 512, 514–515, 517, 520

May: 13, 35, 38, 41, 44, 48, 58, 64, 66, 73, 82, 114, 134, 137, 143, 165, 173, 202, 204–205, 210, 221, 232, 238, 245, 263, 269, 300, 324, 349, 369, 402, 410, 440, 453, 465, 469–470, 473–474, 481, 503, 507, 522

June: 18, 21, 36, 49, 51, 68, 75, 99, 102, 105, 122, 125, 149, 192, 201, 220, 225, 229, 235, 240, 243, 249, 257, 261–262, 274, 278, 292, 298, 306, 329, 331, 337, 380, 408, 417, 423, 427, 439, 455, 458, 483, 497, 511, 518, 526

July: 11–12, 15, 22, 57, 69, 83, 207, 211, 228, 264, 414, 425, 449

August: 25, 42, 340, 378, 524

September: 26, 191, 229, 239, 243, 262, 282, 296, 298, 372, 387, 395, 407, 438, 484, 490

October: 2, 7, 27, 78, 87, 100, 107, 121, 133, 139, 162, 196, 230, 251, 255, 273, 310, 322, 352, 355, 362, 376–377, 391, 399, 411, 435, 443, 477, 493, 502, 506, 516

November: 24, 29, 54, 59, 65, 79, 117, 127, 142, 161, 195, 227, 293, 301, 314, 318, 323, 325, 328, 344, 363, 415, 430, 450, 485, 501, 508, 519, 521

December: 30, 85, 171, 212, 231, 243–244, 259, 306, 338, 357, 367, 385, 392, 429, 447, 472, 491, 495, 500

Any time: 124

CALENDAR INDEX

Social Sciences

January: 547, 564–565, 617, 633, 637, 640, 653–654, 659, 688, 694, 709, 712–713, 741, 745, 755, 767, 771, 773
February: 528, 530, 545, 548–549, 555, 561, 567–568, 575, 582, 590, 592, 596–597, 601, 608, 614, 632, 635, 643, 645, 656, 661, 669, 671, 673–674, 676, 678, 680, 682, 692, 697–698, 700, 706, 715, 727, 739, 744, 747, 751
March: 529, 538, 544, 550–551, 560, 563, 571–572, 579, 586–587, 595, 610–611, 621, 629–630, 646, 649, 655, 667, 675, 678, 684, 689–691, 693, 701–702, 718, 725–726, 733, 736, 754, 762, 768, 772
April: 531, 533, 535–536, 540, 556, 562, 569–570, 573, 576, 581, 585, 593, 598–599, 604, 606, 612–613, 624, 628, 641, 648, 657, 664, 677, 683, 685, 687, 704–705, 711, 714, 717, 723–724, 728, 730, 732, 734, 742, 758, 760–761, 765, 770

May: 554, 557–558, 577–578, 583, 588–589, 595–596, 602, 616, 619–620, 625, 627, 634, 638–639, 642, 686, 696, 716, 738, 755, 769
June: 541, 552, 591, 605, 630, 644, 650–651, 660, 679, 685, 729, 740, 749–750, 763
July: 607, 771
August: 532, 534, 537, 539, 546, 553, 566, 574, 584, 596, 615, 623, 665–666, 743, 755, 757, 759
September: 600, 630, 647, 662, 699, 719, 764
October: 585, 618, 622, 636, 707–708, 721, 731, 737, 752–753
November: 559, 591, 594, 596, 603, 663, 668, 670, 672, 683, 685, 703, 722, 735, 766
December: 543, 626, 630, 695, 710, 746, 748, 756

Humanities

January: 779, 782, 798, 812, 814, 819, 833, 870–871, 893, 902, 918, 921, 944, 964, 982, 1001, 1007
February: 778, 783–784, 787, 793, 804, 809, 817, 821–823, 837, 849–851, 857, 869, 871, 884, 888, 892, 897–898, 917, 924–926, 928, 934, 937, 945, 947, 949, 951, 954, 959–960, 976, 979, 983, 994, 997, 999–1000, 1006
March: 780, 797, 799, 802, 807–808, 813, 825–826, 835, 840, 846, 848, 858, 860–861, 871, 874, 876, 881–882, 885, 899, 910–913, 922, 927–928, 931, 938, 946, 956, 960, 963, 968, 971, 974, 978, 980, 987, 991, 1002, 1014
April: 795–796, 801, 806, 810, 829, 832, 842, 855, 859, 870, 880, 889, 906, 916, 955, 962, 967, 972–973, 989–990, 1012–1013

May: 803, 831, 838–839, 843–844, 856, 862–863, 866–867, 872, 877, 894–895, 909, 941, 961, 965–966, 975, 977, 986, 988, 996, 1004, 1008
June: 776–777, 786, 834, 854, 864, 868, 881, 887, 904, 929–930, 969, 998
July: 790, 891
August: 845
September: 783, 794, 852, 868, 881, 1005
October: 774, 781, 785, 788, 791, 800, 805, 811, 816, 818, 820, 824, 841, 865, 871, 873, 875, 886, 936, 943, 948, 952, 958, 965, 970, 981, 985, 993, 995, 1003, 1011
November: 789, 828, 869, 871, 883, 896, 900, 905, 907–908, 914–915, 919–920, 933, 935, 939, 950, 953, 984, 992, 1010
December: 775, 815, 827, 830, 836, 847, 853, 871, 879, 881, 903, 940, 942, 957, 1009

Any Subject Area

January: 1035, 1063–1065, 1078, 1082, 1122, 1136, 1143, 1154, 1167, 1179, 1187, 1295–1296, 1300, 1311
February: 1028, 1033, 1048, 1050, 1054, 1056, 1058, 1073, 1081, 1086, 1088–1090, 1101, 1103, 1109, 1113, 1125–1127, 1129–1130, 1134–1135, 1141, 1163, 1166, 1180, 1185, 1200, 1203–1205, 1210, 1215, 1228, 1233–1235, 1243, 1246, 1250, 1252, 1257, 1262, 1291, 1293–1294, 1298, 1307–1308
March: 1015–1017, 1025, 1029, 1040, 1043, 1047, 1052–1053, 1057, 1068–1070, 1076, 1079–1080, 1092, 1095–1097, 1099, 1102, 1106, 1108, 1111, 1119–1120, 1132, 1137, 1139, 1170, 1189, 1191, 1195, 1197–1198, 1212–1214, 1216, 1230–1231, 1236, 1238, 1240, 1244, 1247, 1249, 1251, 1253, 1263–1264, 1271, 1276, 1290, 1312, 1314
April: 1027, 1036–1037, 1041, 1044, 1049, 1071–1072, 1087, 1094, 1100, 1105, 1118, 1124, 1131, 1140, 1146, 1160, 1184, 1186, 1196, 1201, 1211, 1217, 1219, 1222, 1226, 1242, 1245, 1254–1255, 1278, 1286, 1288, 1303, 1306, 1318, 1320

May: 1051, 1059, 1067, 1073–1075, 1083, 1110, 1128, 1144, 1150, 1164, 1173, 1176, 1188, 1205, 1221, 1239, 1248, 1261, 1272, 1317, 1322
June: 1018, 1060, 1066, 1104, 1151–1152, 1156, 1161–1162, 1165, 1178, 1190, 1199, 1224, 1229, 1294, 1313, 1323
July: 1026, 1040, 1061, 1121, 1138, 1274, 1277, 1301, 1309–1310
August: 1142, 1172, 1273
September: 1032, 1066, 1073, 1084, 1168, 1203–1205, 1229, 1294
October: 1118, 1148, 1286, 1299
November: 1062, 1107, 1116, 1123, 1133, 1194, 1227, 1256, 1294, 1301, 1309–1310, 1321
December: 1034, 1042, 1046, 1121, 1175, 1237, 1260
Any time: 1019–1022, 1030, 1093, 1182, 1275, 1315, 1319